DUE

ASSESSING STUDENTS WITH SPECIAL NEEDS

Fifth Edition

James A. McLoughlin
Cleveland State University

Rena B. Lewis
San Diego State University

Merrill
Prentice Hall

Upper Saddle River, New Jersey
Columbus, Ohio

Library of Congress Cataloging in Publication Data
McLoughlin, James A.
    Assessing students with special needs / James A. McLoughlin and Rena B. Lewis.—5th ed.
      p. cm.
    Rev. ed. of: Assessing special students. c1994.
    Includes bibliographical references and index.
    ISBN 0-13-085209-0
    1. Handicapped children—Education—United States. 2. Ability—Testing. 3. Educational
tests and measurements—United States. I. Lewis, Rena B. II. McLoughlin, James A.
Assessing special students. III. Title.
LC4031 .M42 2001
371.9—dc21

          00-028143
          CIP

Vice President and Publisher: Jeffery W. Johnston
Executive Editor: Ann Castel Davis
Editorial Assistant: Pat Grogg
Production Editor: Sheryl Glicker Langner
Project Editor: Kathy Davis, Carlisle Publishers Services
Design Coordinator: Diane C. Lorenzo
Cover Designer: Alan Bumpus
Cover art: Artville
Photo Coordinator: Nancy Harre Ritz
Production Manager: Laura Messerly
Electronic Text Management: Karen Bretz
Director of Marketing: Kevin Flanagan
Marketing Manager: Amy June
Marketing Services Manager: Krista Groshong

This book was set in Garamond by Carlisle Communications, Ltd. It was printed and bound by Von Hoffmann Press, Inc. The cover was printed by Von Hoffmann Press, Inc.

Photo Credits: Todd Yarrington, 1; Anne Vega, 3, 31, 143, 167, 331, 417, 460, 521, 550; Scott Cunningham, 53, 55, 329, 379; Barbara Schwartz 80, 109, 286; Silver Burdett Gin, 169; Edmark Corporation, 208; Robert Vega, 245; Anthony Magnacca, 505, 507.
Text Credits: BRIGANCE® is a registered trademark of Curriculum Associates, Inc.

10 9 8 7 6 5 4 3 2 1
ISBN: 0-13-085209-0

For our parents:
Kathleen and Peter McLoughlin
Margaret and Willard Bishopp

and our spouses:
Jo Ann McLoughlin
Jim Lewis

PREFACE

Assessment is at the center of all good teaching, and this book is designed to provide a clear, comprehensive guide to the assessment of students with mild disabilities. This book will give you an understanding of the assessment process as well as the practical skills needed to assess students with special needs successfully so that you can teach them well. To structure the process, we offer an assessment question model and we have developed the idea of the Individualized Assessment Plan (IAP). Our basis for the assessment questions and suggested procedures is a combination of best professional practices and legal mandates. This functional approach allows you sufficient flexibility to explore the areas and types of assessment in which you are particularly interested. In accordance with our belief that educators need useful information, we maintain a strong educational orientation toward assessment.

NEW TO THE FIFTH EDITION

This is the fifth edition of *Assessing Students with Special Needs,* and it reflects many changes in professional thought and practice in both special education and general education. Topics new to this edition include recent legislation (e.g., the Individuals with Disabilities Education Act Amendments), reform movements in general and special education, techniques for ongoing classroom assessment (e.g., functional assessment of behavior), test accommodations for students with disabilities, assessment for grading and report cards, evaluation of new areas of interest such as phonological processing, and the development of collaborative parent-professional partnerships in the assessment process.

The fifth edition is organized somewhat differently from previous editions, although the content covered is the same. The entire book has been thoroughly updated with current literature and coverage of pertinent issues, trends, and professional practices. Throughout we maintain our interest in the promotion of nonbiased assessment of culturally and linguistically diverse students. Chapter 14, in particular, focuses on strategies for the assessment of students who speak dialects of English and those who speak languages other than English.

Part One of the fifth edition, Introduction to Special Education Assessment, includes information on the purposes of assessment, laws and regulations governing assessment, the team approach to assessment, the organization of the assessment process using the assessment question model, and the steps in assessment. Part Two, Assessment Skills for Special Educators, contains chapters on selecting the tools for assessment, administration and scoring of standardized tests, and design and use of informal assessment techniques and procedures. A new chapter has also been introduced–Chapter 6, Classroom Assessment Techniques–and it describes a range of techniques for evaluating student progress in the classroom instructional program. These techniques include functional behavioral assessment, curriculum-based measurement, action research, and portfolio assessment. This chapter also discusses important issues in ongoing assessment such as managing student data, grading and report cards, and test accommodations.

Part Three of the fifth edition, Assessment of General Performance Areas, centers around the general performance areas most relevant to eligibility assessment: school performance, learning aptitude, specific learning abilities and strategies, and classroom behavior. Part Four, Assessment of Academic Areas, focuses on the assessment of academic skills: reading, mathematics, written language, and oral language and bilingual assessment. Part Five, Special Considerations, provides information on three important topics: parent and family involvement in assessment, assessment during the preschool years, and assessment for transition planning.

This edition also features new tests and assessment procedures, many of which are revised versions of measures described in earlier editions. More than 80 new published measures are included. Among the new instruments we discuss are:

- *Peabody Individual Achievement Test–Revised/Normative Update*
- *Hammill Multiability Achievement Test*
- *Wide Range Achievement Test–Revision 3*
- *BRIGANCE® Diagnostic Comprehensive Inventory of Basic Skills–Revised*
- *Batería Woodcock-Muñoz–Revisada*
- *Hammill Multiability Intelligence Test*
- *Test of Nonverbal Intelligence* (3rd ed.)
- *Scales of Independent Behavior–Revised*
- *Detroit Tests of Learning Aptitude* (4th ed.)
- *Developmental Test of Visual Perception* (2nd ed.)
- *Developmental Test of Visual-Motor Integration* (4th ed.)
- *Conners' Rating Scales–Revised*
- *Child Behavior Checklist*
- *The Instructional Environment Scale-II*
- *Comprehensive Test of Phonological Processing*
- *Test of Reading Comprehension* (3rd ed.)
- *Woodcock Reading Mastery Tests–Revised/Normative Update*
- *Monitoring Basic Skills Progress*
- *KeyMath Revised/Normative Update*
- *Stanford Diagnostic Mathematics Test* (4th ed.)
- *Test of Mathematical Abilities* (2nd ed.)
- *Mather-Woodcock Group Writing Tests*
- *Oral and Written Language Scales*
- *Test of Adolescent and Adult Language–3*
- *Test of Written Language–3*
- *Test of Written Spelling–4*
- *Test of Language Development–3, Primary* and *Intermediate*

- *Peabody Picture Vocabulary Test, Third Edition*
- *Comprehensive Receptive and Expressive Vocabulary Test*
- *Assessment, Evaluation, and Programming System for Infants and Children*
- *Hawaii Early Learning Profile*
- *BRIGANCE® Employability Skills Inventory*
- *Transition Planning Inventory*

FEATURES

Our goal in this book is to provide you with a foundation for understanding the assessment process and with the skills necessary for carrying out meaningful assessments. The chief strength of this text remains its balanced coverage of formal and informal assessment. Critiques of the strengths and weaknesses of formal tests and informal procedures help you to select the tools that will supply the information you need.

We have chosen to speak about popular assessment procedures as well as less well known, but distinctive, measures. Popular instruments are discussed in some depth, not necessarily because they are always the best techniques, but because they reflect current practice. On the other hand, information about less well known tests and techniques is provided to acquaint you with promising procedures. With this comprehensive coverage, you will find out not only what is currently being done (and how well) but also what needs to be changed and how to do that.

In addition, we provide the connection between gathering assessment information and using it to make decisions. There are regular reminders to consider assessment data in relation to the classroom setting and suggestions for making sense out of all the information gathered. This process is described in the context of a team approach to educational assessment but with particular emphasis on the role of the special education teacher.

To make our book a more practical classroom resource, we have included several useful case reports, sample test profiles, checklists, and illustrations. Also, information boxes throughout the chapters summarize the important characteristics of tests discussed in depth. We have tried to give you a feel for the procedures you will use in assessment and to critique and relate them to one another so that you can better understand how to use them. Each chapter begins with a brief topical outline of its contents and ends with a Study Guide containing factual review questions, applied activities, and discussion questions focusing on critical issues addressed in the chapter.

Companion Website

A companion website is available for both students and professors. Students can take self-quizzes and submit their responses online to the professor as well as view their scores and obtain page references in the text for answers to questions marked incorrect. Students also have access to chat rooms and bulletin boards for peer discussion. Instructors will have a Syllabus Builder™ which allows them to develop and customize a syllabus for their course. The address of the companion website for *Assessing Students with Special Needs* is:

www.prenhall.com/mcloughlin

Support Materials for Instructors

The instructor support package for the fifth edition includes an Instructor's Manual, Computerized Test Banks in both Macintosh and Windows formats, and the companion website described above.

Instructor's Manual

The Instructor's Manual, organized by chapter, contains a chapter overview, a detailed outline, glossary terms, a set of questions appropriate for class discussions, and suggested activities. Also within the manual are objective test questions (multiple-choice, true-false, and completion) as well as a set of instructional aids that could be used in teaching an assessment course to prospective special educators.

Computerized Test Bank

In addition to the printed test bank of questions found in the Instructor's Manual, the *Prentice Hall Custom Test* is available in either Macintosh® or Windows® format. This software is available upon request from your Prentice Hall sales representative.

AUTHORS AND CONTRIBUTORS FOR THE FIFTH EDITION

Revisions for the fifth edition were completed primarily by Rena B. Lewis, one of the co-authors of the first four editions. James M. McLoughlin was unable to participate in the revision, although his contributions to previous editions continue to add to the strength of this book.

Three contributors also participated in the development of the fifth edition, and we thank them for their willingness to share their perspectives and expertise. They are Eleanor W. Lynch, author of Chapter 15, Parent and Family Involvement; Laura J. Hall, author of Chapter 16, Early Childhood Assessment; and Jeanne B. Repetto, author of Chapter 17, Assessment for Transition Planning.

OUR THANKS

We would like to express our appreciation to the people who assisted in the preparation of this fifth edition. First of all, thanks go to the field reviewers for their feedback and suggestions: Jane Adams, Keys for Networking, Inc. (formerly at Washburn U., KS), Robert J. Evans, Marshall University (WV), Darcy Miller, Washington State University, Robert D. Morrow, University of the Pacific.

Second, we would like to thank the many publishers and agencies who answered our questions and gave us permission to reproduce their materials.

Third, we extend our appreciation to Debra Faris-Cole, who assisted in the revision of the Instructor's Manual and Test Bank that accompany this text.

Fourth, special thanks to Ann Castel Davis of Merrill/Prentice Hall, whose gentle but insistent prodding helped bring this revision into the world, and to Pat Grogg, her ever helpful assistant.

The Prentice Hall Companion Website: A Virtual Learning Environment

Technology is a constantly growing and changing aspect of our field that is creating a need for content and resources. To address this emerging need, Prentice Hall has developed an online learning environment for students and professors alike—Companion Websites—to support our textbooks.

In creating a Companion Website, our goal is to build on and enhance what the textbook already offers. For this reason, the content for each user-friendly website is organized by chapter and provides the professor and student with a variety of meaningful resources. Common features of a Companion Website include:

For the Professor—

Every Companion Website integrates **Syllabus Manager**™, an online syllabus creation and management utility.

- **Syllabus Manager**™ provides you, the instructor, with an easy, step-by-step process to create and revise syllabi, with direct links into Companion Website and other online content without having to learn HTML.
- Students may log on to your syllabus during any study session. All they need to know is the web address for the Companion Website and the password you've assigned to your syllabus.
- After you have created a syllabus using **Syllabus Manager**™, students may enter the syllabus for their course section from any point in the Companion Website.
- Class dates are highlighted in white and assignment due dates appear in blue. Clicking on a date, the student is shown the list of activities for the assignment. The activities for each assignment are linked directly to actual content, saving time for students.
- Adding assignments consists of clicking on the desired due date, then filling in the details of the assignment—name of the assignment, instructions, and whether or not it is a one-time or repeating assignment.
- In addition, links to other activities can be created easily. If the activity is online, a URL can be entered in the space provided, and it will be linked automatically in the final syllabus.
- Your completed syllabus is hosted on our servers, allowing convenient updates from any computer on the Internet. Changes you make to your syllabus are immediately available to your students at their next log on.

For the Student—

- **Chapter Objectives**–outline key concepts from the text
- **Interactive Self-quizzes**–complete with hints and automatic grading that provide immediate feedback for students
  After students submit their answers for the interactive self-quizzes, the Companion Website **Results Reporter** computes a percentage grade, provides a graphic representation of how many questions were answered correctly and incorrectly, and gives a question by question analysis of the quiz. Students are given the option to send their quiz to up to four email addresses (professor, teaching assistant, study partner, etc.).
- **Message Board**–serves as a virtual bulletin board to post—or respond to—questions or comments to/from a national audience
- **Net Searches**–offer links by key terms from each chapter to related Internet content
- **Web Destinations**–links to www sites that relate to chapter content

To take advantage of these and other resources, please visit the *Assessing Students with Special Needs* Companion Website at

www.prenhall.com/mcloughlin

CONTENTS

PART I

INTRODUCTION TO SPECIAL EDUCATION ASSESSMENT

CHAPTER 1

SPECIAL EDUCATION ASSESSMENT

- Definition of Assessment
- Historical Perspective
- Purposes
- Kinds of Assessment Procedures
- Students with Special Needs
- Team Approach
- Critical Issues
- The Assessment Question Model

Assessment is the process of gathering information for the purpose of making a decision. Everyone engages in assessment. As human beings, we are continuously gathering information, sifting and weighing that information, and making decisions based on our judgments and conclusions. When we wake up in the morning, we look outdoors to assess the weather. When we meet friends, loved ones, or acquaintances, we study their demeanor to assess their moods. Before we make a purchase, we weigh the merits of various products. Before we enter the voting booth, we investigate the worthiness of political candidates. And, as teachers, we assess our students.

Educational assessment is an integral part of the instructional process. Teachers observe their students as they enter the classroom, take their seats, and begin (or fail to begin) to work. Teachers ask questions and evaluate students' answers. They monitor students' behavior in the classroom and the other environments of the school.

Sometimes assessment is more structured and systematic. Teachers give quizzes and exams. They assign a written paper or project and evaluate the results. Teachers also take part in the school- or district-wide administration of standardized tests to evaluate students' progress in mastering the curriculum.

Although assessment is an important skill for all teachers, it is particularly important for special educators—teachers who serve students with disabilities. General education is designed to serve typical learners; special education, in contrast, is designed to meet the individual needs of students with school performance problems. The instructional plans for students with disabilities must be highly individualized, which means that special education teachers require precise information about their students' strengths and weaknesses and their areas of educational need. And that is where special education assessment comes in.

DEFINITION OF ASSESSMENT

Special education assessment is the assessment of students with disabilities. It can be defined as the systematic process of gathering educationally relevant information to make legal and instructional decisions about the provision of special services. There are many important aspects to this definition. First, assessment is an ongoing process; it is not a one-time event. Assessment takes place when students experience difficulty meeting the demands of the general education curriculum and are referred for consideration for special education services. Once students are found eligible for special education services, assessment continues in the special education classroom and other school environments where the special education teacher and others gather information related to the everyday concerns of instruction.

Second, special education assessment is systematic. In the early stages of the assessment process, an interdisciplinary team meets to plan strategies for the collection of useful information. Professionals such as special educators, psychologists, and speech-language clinicians work together to ensure that sufficient information is gathered to fully answer important questions. Classroom assessment of students with disabilities is also systematic. Teachers regularly monitor students' progress toward important instructional goals and, when necessary, modify instructional strategies.

Third, special education assessment focuses on the collection of educationally relevant information. School performance is a major concern, and teachers and other professionals evaluate students' progress in all pertinent areas of the school curriculum. In addition to academic achievement, professionals are interested in students' language, social, and behavioral skills. Students' learning abilities and strategies for learning are concerns, as are the characteristics of the learning environments in which students are asked to participate. All of these factors contribute to a better understanding of students' strengths and weaknesses and the types of support they may require to succeed in school.

Fourth, special education assessment is purposeful. Information is collected in order to make important decisions about schooling for students with special needs. Those decisions concern issues such as determining whether students meet legal criteria for special education services, selecting the most appropriate program and placement for students, setting instructional goals, choosing instructional methods and materials, and monitoring student progress and the effectiveness of instructional approaches.

Special education assessment extends beyond the school years because infants, preschoolers, and young adults with disabilities are served by special education. In the preschool years, assessment focuses on the development of infants and young children in important skill areas such as language, cognition, social-emotional behavior, and sensory and motor skills. In young adulthood, the concern is the successful transition of adolescents from the world of school into the world of work, higher education, careers, and other areas of adult life.

The term *assessment* is sometimes confused with two other terms: *testing* and *diagnosis*. Tests are one type of assessment technique and, as such, they are one of the many strategies used to gather information about students with special needs. Assessment is much broader; it is the entire data collection process and the decisions that result from that process. Testing is only one of the activities that take place in assessment, just as the use of textbooks or any other instructional tool is only one small part of the teaching process.

Diagnosis is a term borrowed from the medical profession. In a medical context, the cause of an illness or condition is identified or diagnosed so that appropriate treatment can be offered. The diagnosis typically results in a label such as "autism," and that label is linked to treatment. In contrast, educational assessment is not designed to establish causes, assign labels to students, or determine educational treatments based upon labels. When students are identified as having disabilities, that designation is given only to document eligibility for special services. Furthermore, special instructional programs are developed for individual students based upon their strengths and weaknesses in school learning, not upon labels for global syndromes or conditions. In other words, special educators would conclude from an assessment that a student has needs in the area of reading, rather than labeling the student as "dyslexic."

HISTORICAL PERSPECTIVE

Educational assessment practices for students with disabilities have been shaped by a variety of disciplines, forces, and trends. Assessment has evolved from the late 19th century to the beginning of the 21st. Changes in education, psychology, and medicine and in the beliefs that society holds regarding the educational process continue to influence how schools go about gathering assessment information to make decisions about the students they serve.

While the measurement of personality and other psychological factors was a topic of study in the late 1800s, the work of Alfred Binet and others led to the major development of assessment techniques in the early 1900s. Assessments were created to meet a variety of needs, including the screening of students in public schools and the evaluation of military personnel and potential employees. These early efforts became the prototypes for many current group and individual tests in psychology and education.

The controversy over the nature of intelligence has affected assessment practices used with students with disabilities. One debate centers on whether intelligence is one entity or is made up of a set of factors. Some tests attempt to address a variety of factors that comprise intelligence; these factors are then analyzed to identify individual strengths and weaknesses within the global set of abilities that make up intellectual performance.

Another cause for lively discussion has been the question of whether intelligence is changeable. Most professionals consider intelligence a product of the interaction between people and their environment and, therefore, subject to change. Educational assessment of students with disabilities now incorporates procedures that analyze the environment, as well as the person's abilities.

The field of medicine has had a profound effect on the development of educational assessment procedures. Many of the pioneers in special education were physicians who identified and described children with various types of disabilities and began the search for the causes and treatments of those disabilities. Some of these searches were successful, such as the development of vaccines to prevent diseases like polio. Others continue today in areas such as gene therapy and the use of sophisticated medical technologies to study brain functioning of persons with dyslexia and attention deficit hyperactivity disorders.

For many years, educators were hampered by the use of a medical model in the assessment of students with disabilities. Students were diagnosed with a condition (e.g., mental retardation or learning disabilities) and an educational treatment was prescribed based upon knowledge about that condition, rather than the characteristics of the individual student. In some cases, the condition was assumed to be permanent; in others (most notably, learning disabilities), educators sought to cure the disability by educational remediation. Considerable progress has been made toward the development of an assessment model that is more relevant to educational concerns. While identification of a specific disability is still part of current practice, the focus in assessment is the study of the individual student, his or her strengths and weaknesses, and the ways in which the instructional environment can be adapted to address the student's educational needs.

Other fields have also contributed to the assessment practices in special education. Tests of perception allow the study of how information is processed through vision, hearing, and other senses. Psychoeducational test batteries combine the analysis of psychological and educational factors. Applications of behavioral psychology have resulted in the use of several systems for behavioral observations of students in their school environments, including a special interest in the curriculum and the instructional tasks with

which students interact. Other forms of informal assessment, like interviewing, have been borrowed and adapted from fields such as anthropology and sociology.

With the end of World War II and the baby boom in the 1950s, services for students with disabilities grew tremendously, with a subsequent growth in assessment procedures, particularly tests. Tests designed for administration to individual students were developed in all academic areas—and in language, social skills, and vocational skills—with the help of commercial publishers. In addition, special educators and other professionals created informal procedures directly related to classroom needs. Criterion-referenced testing played a major role in linking assessment and instructional programming.

Unfortunately, many misuses and abuses of assessment procedures accompanied this growth. Invalid and unreliable measures were used, sometimes administered by untrained individuals. Some assessments were too narrow in nature; some discriminated on the basis of the student's language, cultural background, or gender. Results were used inappropriately, with students erroneously labeled "handicapped." The rights of students with disabilities and of their parents to due process under law were violated.

In 1975, the passage of PL 94-142, the Education for All Handicapped Children Act, exerted a strong, positive influence on the content and procedures used in the assessment of students with disabilities. The changes introduced in this federal law are maintained and extended in its most current version, PL 105-17, the Individuals with Disabilities Education Act (IDEA) Amendments of 1997. First and foremost, this law guarantees that students with disabilities shall receive a free, appropriate, public education in the least restrictive educational environment. In the area of assessment, the law mandates a set of due process procedures to protect students and their parents and detailed guidelines to correct past problems. Students with disabilities must be adequately assessed by a team and an Individualized Education Program (IEP) developed. In addition, state departments of education must comply with federal requirements to receive funding for special education programming.

The 1997 IDEA Amendments place special emphasis on assessment of students' involvement with and progress in the general education curriculum. These areas must be addressed in the development of IEPs as well as how students will participate in state and district assessments of school achievement. The IEP team must also consider a range of special factors including positive behavioral interventions and supports for students with behavioral problems, the language needs of students who are not proficient in English, and any requirements students might have for assistive technology devices and services.

Trends within the fields of education and special education have also influenced the development of assessment techniques and procedures. In the early years of special education, assessment focused solely on students and their deficits. That approach gave way to increased emphasis on the school curriculum and the specific instructional tasks with which students were experiencing difficulty. At present, the approach is more balanced. Both the student and the educational environment are of interest, particularly the ways in which interactions occur between individuals and school demands. In addition, influences from educational theories such as constructivism have contributed to special educators' perspectives on assessment. In the constructivist view, students construct their own knowledge by building upon the prior knowledge they bring with them to the learning situation (Cegelka, 1995).

One challenge that special education continues to face is the development of appropriate procedures to assess culturally and linguistically diverse students who are suspected of having a disability. Unsolved problems in this area have contributed to overrepresentation of some groups in special education programs and underrepresentation of others (Artiles & Trent, 1994; Patton, 1998). This issue is likely to persist as the population of the United States becomes more diverse in the next decades.

The movement to educate students with disabilities in more inclusive settings has created a greater need for both general and special education teachers to have tools to assess these students in multiple environments, including the general education classroom. Educators of students with disabilities are held accountable for ongoing evaluation of learning. They need to monitor student progress frequently, without the necessity of administering standardized tests. Such tests are too costly in terms of both time and money, and their results do not translate directly to classroom interventions. Instead, educators have turned to curriculum-based assessments, that is, procedures and techniques that evaluate student growth in relation to the current classroom curriculum. Curriculum-based approaches such as criterion-referenced assessment, curriculum-based measurement, and portfolio assessment produce results that assist in the development of instructional goals, objectives, and procedures.

Major educational reforms in the United States are making profound changes in the assessment and evaluation of all students, including those with disabilities. The standards movement, based upon the outcome-based evaluation model, has been adopted by virtually all states. Sets of academic standards have been developed and, in most states, student assessment is linked to these standards (American Federation of Teachers, 1996). In this evaluation model, results of standards-based assessments are used as the basis for judging student performance, deciding whether schools and teachers are functioning appropriately, and even forcing fundamental changes in teaching methods and the structure of schools. Increased emphasis on authentic assessment means that measures are more functional, holistic, and contextual in terms of real-life performance. They may incorporate observation of groups of students solving a problem together, followed by individual student activities and evaluation of portfolios of student work. In addition, the move toward the development of a national achievement test is placing greater pressure on schools to find legitimate ways to provide comparative data about the scholastic abilities of American students. In the midst of this national spirit of reform, the participation of students with disabilities in high-stakes testing across states and districts is a major concern. It is important to ensure that students with disabilities are not excluded while at the same time providing appropriate test accommodations and modifications to guarantee valid and reliable evaluation.

In summary, we can describe special educational assessment today in the following ways:

1. Special education assessment, like special education instruction, is individualized. It is tailored to the needs of each student with disabilities.
2. Assessment data are used to make decisions about the eligibility of students for special education services and about the types of services that are provided. Thus, decisions are both legal and instructional.
3. Assessment focuses on educationally relevant information so that an appropriate Individualized Education Program (IEP) can be developed, implemented, and monitored.
4. Assessment also focuses on the student's involvement with and progress in the general education curriculum.
5. The student is not the only subject of assessment. The learning environment is also evaluated as well as the student's interactions with classroom tasks.
6. A variety of procedures are used in assessment. Assessment is not limited to the administration of standardized tests.
7. Assessment is characterized by a team approach. Parents and educators, both special and general, are important members of that team.
8. Professionals strive for nonbiased assessment of all students, particularly those from culturally and linguistically diverse groups.
9. Assessment does not stop when instruction starts. Instructional programs are continuously monitored and evaluated.
10. Assessment procedures are available to determine the developmental needs of preschool children and the needs of older students for transition services.
11. New assessment tools continue to be developed in academic, language, and other skill areas.
12. Computer programs for test scoring and the reporting of test results are becoming increasingly common. Less common, but available in some subject areas, are computer-administered tests.

PURPOSES

Special education assessment has several purposes because it plays a role in each phase of programming for students with disabilities. From the first indication of a learning problem, special education teachers and others gather information to aid in decision making. In general, this information is used to document eligibility for special education services and/or adaptations of the general education curriculum and to plan and monitor the effectiveness of an Individualized Education Program (IEP). In particular, the five main purposes of special education assessment are identification, determination of eligibility, program planning, monitoring of student progress, and program evaluation.

Identification of students who may have disabilities is the first purpose of assessment. Two identification procedures are used: screening and prereferral strategies. Screening is a large-scale data collection activity used to quickly identify those students out of the entire school population who may be in need of further study. For example, most schools administer vision and hearing screening tests at regular intervals throughout the grades. When potential problems are detected, students are referred for a more in-depth evaluation.

Prereferral strategies, in contrast, are aimed at solving the school performance problems of individual students. Prereferral interventions begin when a general education teacher consults with others at the school site about a student experiencing difficulty in school. Information is gathered about the student's performance in areas of concern and about the instructional environment. In most cases, the prereferral team will develop a set of adaptations and modifications to try in an attempt to meet the student's academic and behavioral needs. These interventions are implemented and data are collected to determine their effectiveness. If the results suggest a persistent learning problem, the student may be referred for consideration for special education services.

Second, special education assessment is performed to determine whether a student meets eligibility criteria for special education services. Eligibility is based on two interrelated criteria: the student must have a school performance problem and that problem must be related to a disability. Each state develops its own eligibility requirements based upon federal laws, and individual districts may set additional guidelines for assessment. Eligibility assessment is much more thorough than assessment for screening or prereferral. Also, it is individualized; the assessment team determines what types of information it needs to gather for each individual student. Then students are assessed to determine their present levels of performance in areas related to the suspected disability. Typically, this involves investigation of the student's school skills, intellectual performance, hearing and vision, social and behavioral status, and language abilities. Information is also collected about the student's school history, current classroom performance, and the characteristics of the learning environment. Special attention is paid to the student's progress in the general education curriculum and the types of supports needed to maximize the student's probability of success in the general education classroom.

Third, educational assessment data are used to plan the IEP. After the student's educational needs are identified and prioritized, annual goals and short-term objectives are developed. The IEP team decides what types of special education and related services the student will receive and what kinds of supplementary aids and services will be needed to maintain the student within the general education classroom, if at all possible. The IEP indicates who will accomplish the goals and objectives, the settings in which services will take place, and the amount of time services will require. The plan also outlines how the student's progress will be monitored and how parents will be informed about their child's progress.

The fourth reason for assessment is to monitor the student's progress in the educational program. Information is gathered by teachers (and others, as appropriate) about the effects of instruction and other types of interventions. This type of assessment is usually performed at frequent intervals, perhaps weekly or even daily. A variety of procedures are used, although the most common are informal techniques such as observation of student behavior, review of student work, and direct measurement of performance in skill areas of interest. At this stage in the process, assessment and instruction blend together, with assessment data providing the information needed to guide instructional modifications.

The fifth purpose for special education assessment is program evaluation. Federal laws such as PL 105-17 require that the IEP of all students with disabilities be reviewed at least annually. School staff and parents examine the progress of the student and the results of the program over the previous year and decide if special education services should be continued as is, modified, or discontinued. In addition, the student's eligibility for special education services must be reviewed at least every 3 years. These types of program evaluation are designed to ensure that students with disabilities receive appropriate interventions and that those interventions continue only as long as they are required.

KINDS OF ASSESSMENT PROCEDURES

Many types of assessment procedures are available, and these types vary along several dimensions, including the amount of professional expertise required for their use. In general, special education assessment techniques can be divided into two major types: formal and informal strategies. Both are employed in all phases of assessment, although formal strategies are often considered more useful for gathering information for eligibility decisions and informal strategies are more useful for classroom instructional decisions.

Formal Strategies

Formal strategies are structured assessment procedures with specific guidelines for administration, scoring, and interpretation of results. The most common example is standardized tests, sometimes referred to as norm-referenced tests. These measures are designed to compare the performance of one individual to that of a normative group. Thus, their use is limited to students who are very similar to the group used in the development of the test. Norm-referenced tests may be designed for group or individual administration and are available for most academic subjects, intellectual performance, and other areas of learning. Directions for administration, scoring, and interpretation of these measures are usually very explicit. Because of this, professionals require training before they can be considered skilled in the use of a specific test. Test results are expressed in quantitative scores such as standard scores and percentile ranks, and the test manual provides information about the development of the test, the standardization sample, and test reliability and validity. Results of norm-referenced tests are used in a number of ways, including documentation of eligibility for special education and identification of general strengths and weaknesses in school learning.

Tests can be designed for administration to a group of individuals or to one person. Group procedures usually penalize students with disabilities. Such procedures are not recommended for this population because they may require students to read, follow directions independently, and work under timed conditions. Because students with disabilities often lack these skills, results of group tests tend to underestimate their abilities. However, group tests are the norm in general education because they are more efficient and require much less time to administer. When students with disabilities participate in such assessments, accommodations are often necessary.

The two types of group tests most frequently encountered in general education are achievement and aptitude tests. Students take academic achievement tests at regular intervals throughout the grades. These measures are used for screening, grouping, and evaluating student progress and for measuring school effectiveness. Aptitude tests are sometimes administered to students in the elementary grades. However, they are much more common in high school, where students take college entrance exams and other aptitude tests designed to predict future success. Like any group measure, group aptitude tests tend to underestimate the true skill levels of students with disabilities.

Tests that are individually administered are preferred in special education. The professional administering the test (usually called the examiner or tester) establishes rapport with the student and makes sure he or she understands the directions for the test tasks. Skills are measured separately so that it is possible to separate out a student's performance in reading from his or her skills or knowledge in other areas such as mathematics, science, or social studies. In many cases, students respond orally, so that poor writing skills are not penalized when writing is not the object of assessment. In addition, professionals can carefully observe students as they interact with test tasks to gain further insight into their strengths, weaknesses, and general work behaviors.

There are a number of individual measures available to measure both achievement and aptitude as well as other areas of concern. In the area of achievement, some individual tests survey several academic skills whereas others concentrate on one skill such as reading or mathematics. More global tests tend to assess basic skills (reading, mathematics, and spelling or writing) as well as content area subjects. Skill-specific tests concentrate on one skill area but probe several subskills; for example, a reading test might measure the ability to name letters, read sight words, decode unknown words, and comprehend passages. Individual aptitude measures, like achievement tests, tend to be divided into several subtests. The subtests measure specific aptitude areas such as reasoning and memory, and performances on the various subtests are combined to produce overall aptitude scores. In addition to aptitude and achievement measures, special educators often administer individual tests in other areas including adaptive behavior, specific learning abilities, social-emotional development, and oral language.

The Test Index at the back of this book lists each of the individual and group tests (and other published measures) discussed in this text. Inclusion of a test should not be considered an endorsement; some of the measures that we have described, although popular, do not meet recommended standards for technical adequacy. Test descriptions throughout this book include information about technical adequacy as well as the training required by examiners. In some cases, administration is limited to members of certain professional groups. For example, most states restrict the use of individual aptitude measures to licensed school psychologists.

Informal Strategies

Several types of informal procedures are used in educational assessments to determine current levels of performance, document student progress, and direct changes in the instructional program. A distinction is often made between the formal measures just described and these less formal techniques.

Informal procedures are usually less structured or are structured differently from standardized tests. Rather than administering a formal test, a teacher might observe a student with behavior problems, give the class a test on the spelling words studied that week, or assign mathematics homework. Like most informal measures, these are designed by the teacher rather than by a commercial publisher. Also, their purpose is to gather information directly related to instruction. There is an element of subjectivity in the design of informal measures as well as in their administration, scoring (if they are scored), and interpretation. In fact, interpretation is often quite difficult because of a lack of guidelines.

Although informal procedures lack the kinds of scores yielded by standardized tests, their results are relevant to instruction because they can be expressed in instructional terms. Informal assessment tools vary in how directly they measure student performance and instructional conditions. Some involve the student directly, whereas others rely on informants.

There are four major types of informal strategies: observation, curriculum-based assessments, techniques using informants, and approaches using a combination of techniques. Each type is discussed in detail in Chapter 4, the chapter on informal assessment.

Observation is the most direct informal assessment technique. In classroom observations, teachers watch as students engage in tasks related to instruction. In most cases, students are studied over time to discover patterns of behavior. The procedure can be used with any student (or group of students) for any purpose, but the most common is investigation of social and behavioral concerns. Requirements for training vary, depending upon how systematically the observations are conducted. The results usually are the number (or duration) of student behaviors; results are often graphed for easier interpretation. The quality of the observation depends upon factors such as how precisely the behavior to be observed is defined and the methods used to gather, record, and report data. Results can be used to help develop instructional goals or to direct systematic changes in the instructional program.

Curriculum-based assessments are typically designed by teachers to gather information about student progress in the classroom curriculum. There are a number of different types of curriculum-based assessment techniques: task analysis, work sample analysis, informal inventories, criterion-referenced tests, and others. For example, task analysis is used to determine the major components of a task and arrange those components into an appropriate instructional sequence. Work sample analysis, on the other hand, involves evaluation of a product developed by a student. The teacher examines the sample of student work to identify the areas in which the student is successful and the areas in which errors are most likely to occur. Those results, like the results of all curriculum-based assessments, can be directly translated into instructional plans.

Informal inventories are measures that sample students' skill or knowledge in some area of the curriculum. For example, at the end of a chapter or unit in social studies, the teacher might develop a test that covers many of the major points covered during instruction to gain an overview of students' mastery of the content. Criterion-referenced tests are somewhat different because their purpose is to compare students' performance to a specified level of mastery or achievement. For example, a classroom goal might be that all students will be able to write a complete sentence with appropriate capitalization and punctuation. To measure achievement of that goal, the teacher would ask students to write one or more sentences and then evaluate the students' responses using specific scoring criteria (e.g., to be considered complete, the sentence must contain both a subject and a verb). Although criterion-referenced tests tend to be time-consuming to design and administer, they do provide instructionally relevant information. While norm-referenced measures compare a student's performance to that of other students, criterion-referenced measures compare a student's performance to instructional goals. Results indicate whether or not goals are achieved.

Techniques using informants include checklists, rating scales, questionnaires, and interviews. An informant is someone who can provide valuable information about the student. Sometimes that person is the student himself or herself. Other typical informants are the student's parents, his or her peers, and teachers who have worked with the student in the past. Published checklists, rating scales, questionnaires, and interviews are available to aid in the assessment of several areas, including developmental history, adaptive behavior, current behavioral status, and progress through the curriculum.

Combination approaches are used in informal assessment when one type of measure is not sufficient to gather the type of information needed. One common example is portfolio assessment. In this approach, samples of student work are gathered to document changes in performance over time. This is considered a combination approach because any type of informal (or formal) measure can be included within the portfolio: student work samples in various formats (including written products, art work, photos, videos and audiotapes, and computer-based presentations), teacher-designed tests and inventories, observation results, interviews and questionnaires, and so on. Evaluators of the portfolio (including the student) typically look for changes between work done early in the year and later; it is also possible to evaluate the student's work using performance standards set by the district or state.

Because informal assessment strategies have a clear connection to the curriculum, the potential usefulness of the results they produce is high. However, it is important to point out that just because an assessment technique is informal does not mean that it is appropriate for all students with disabilities. Informal measures may contain barriers like those in group formal tests. For example, a classroom quiz might be timed or a

math assignment might require reading and writing skills. As is the case with formal measures, accommodations are often necessary.

STUDENTS WITH SPECIAL NEEDS

Special educational assessment involves students with disabilities. As defined by the 1997 IDEA Amendments, this includes children with:

> mental retardation, hearing impairments (including deafness), speech or language impairments, visual impairments (including blindness), serious emotional disturbance (hereinafter referred to as 'emotional disturbance'), orthopedic impairments, autism, traumatic brain injury, other health impairments, or specific learning disabilities . . . who, by reason thereof need special education and related services. (*Federal Register,* 1999, §300.7(a))

Students qualifying for these services are entitled to receive a free and appropriate education from special educators and other professionals.

The 1997 IDEA Amendments expanded the definition of "child with a disability" to include young children ages 3 through 9 who are "experiencing developmental delays . . . and who, by reason thereof, need special education and related services" (*Federal Register,* 1999, §300.7(b)). This allows young children to receive special services without the need to label them as having a specific disability. The law requires that delays be documented in one or more of these areas: physical, cognitive, communication, social or emotional, or adaptive development.

Another group of students benefiting from federal protections are those identified as having attention deficit hyperactivity disorders (ADHD). This disorder is described by Lerner, Lowenthal, and Lerner (1995) as a "condition characterized by developmentally inappropriate attention skills, impulsivity, and, in some cases, hyperactivity" (p. 4). The U.S. Department of Education ruled in 1991 that students with ADHD are eligible for services under Section 504 of the Rehabilitation Act of 1973. The 1997 IDEA Amendments added ADHD to the list of conditions covered under the "other health impairment" disability cate-

TABLE 1–1
Mild Disabilities

Mental Retardation	Significantly subaverage general intellectual functioning, existing concurrently with deficits in adaptive behavior and manifested during the developmental period, that adversely affects a child's educational performance. (*Federal Register,* 1999, §300.7(c)(6))
Emotional Disturbance	The term means a condition exhibiting one or more of the following characteristics over a long period of time and to a marked degree that adversely affects a child's educational performance: (A) An inability to learn that cannot be explained by intellectual, sensory, or health factors. (B) An inability to build or maintain satisfactory interpersonal relationships with peers and teachers. (C) Inappropriate types of behavior or feelings under normal circumstances. (D) A general pervasive mood of unhappiness or depression. (E) A tendency to develop physical symptoms or fears associated with personal or school problems. The term includes schizophrenia. The term does not apply to children who are socially maladjusted, unless it is determined that they have an emotional disturbance. (*Federal Register,* 1999, §300.7(c)(4))
Specific Learning Disabilities	A disorder in one or more of the basic psychological processes involved in understanding or in using language, spoken or written, that may manifest itself in an imperfect ability to listen, think, speak, read, write, spell, or do mathematical calculations, including conditions such as perceptual disabilities, brain injury, minimal brain dysfunction, dyslexia, and developmental aphasia. . . . The term does not include learning problems that are primarily the result of visual, hearing, or motor disabilities, of mental retardation, of emotional disturbance, or of environmental, cultural, or economic disadvantage. (*Federal Register,* 1999, §300.7(c)(10))

gory. According to the federal definition, other health impairment "means having limited strength, vitality or alertness, *including a heightened alertness to environmental stimuli,* that results in limited alertness with respect to the educational environment" (*Federal Register,* 1999, §300.7(c)(9), emphasis added). This limitation may be due to a variety of health problems including both attention deficit disorder and attention deficit hyperactivity disorder.

This book focuses on educational assessment of students with mild disabilities. Mild disabilities include mental retardation, emotional disturbance, and learning disabilities. As Table 1–1 indicates, federal laws recognize the need for special education services for students with disabilities in these areas. These students comprise the largest group of all students with disabilities, approximately 7% of the total school-age population and about 70% of the population of those identified as disabled (U.S. Department of Education, 1998). Because their disabilities are mild, these students are often members of general education classrooms and receive special education services on a part-time basis.

From an educational perspective, students with mild disabilities share many common psychological, academic, and social-behavioral problems that require assessment. Students with attention deficit hyperactivity disorder also share these characteristics. The educational assessment strategies described in this book apply to these types of students. Many of the procedures are also useful for students with other types of disabilities; however, educational assessment for students with severe disabilities and those with sensory and physical disabilities requires special considerations beyond the scope of this text.

This book is primarily concerned with school-aged students with classroom-related learning problems. However, procedures for the assessment of preschool children and their families are described in Chapter 16 and those for the assessment of adolescents and young adults in transition programs in Chapter 17.

TEAM APPROACH

Important educational decisions about students with disabilities are made by teams, rather than by a single individual. The team approach brings together individuals from different perspectives who contribute their expertise to the decision-making process. The team may be composed of the student's parents and professionals representing general education, special education, psychology, speech and language disorders, medicine, and other areas as needed. Each team member gathers data about the student and interprets it from his or her perspective, sharing it with others on the team. The team then analyzes all contributions, including those of the student's parents, in an attempt to make the most appropriate decision.

The team approach is not new to special education, although it has gained impetus in recent years. Federal laws such as the Individuals with Disabilities Education Act and its amendments explicitly require that teams rather than individuals make the following decisions:

1. Evaluation of the eligibility of students for special education and related services;
2. Formulation of Individualized Education Programs (IEPs);
3. Evaluation and modification of IEPs; and
4. Periodic review of the need for special education and related services.

The membership of educational decision-making teams varies. Different purposes require different numbers of team members and the representation of different disciplines. For example, the team that assesses a student for eligibility for special services is likely to have more members than the team responsible for formulating the IEP for the same student. The needs of the student also influence team membership. A student with several severe disabilities is likely to require a larger team representing more disciplines than a student with a mild disability.

Many individuals participate in educational teams. These participants make important contributions to assessment and to planning and monitoring the instructional program. The special educator plays a significant role in combining the input of all team members into a unified profile of the student's needs.

School Personnel

General and special education teachers who are involved directly with the student on a day-to-day basis are necessary team members. Teachers are able to provide information on all aspects of student development, especially academic performance and social and emotional status.

General education teachers contribute valuable information about students' social skills in dealing with their peers. They are also the major source of information about the instructional programs and procedures used in their classroom and have first-hand knowledge about the student's response to those programs and procedures. Their assessment procedures often consist of group-administered achievement tests, informal tests and inventories, classroom observations, and portfolios. Consequently, they can describe how well the student with a disability is progressing in the general education curriculum, compared to other students in the classroom. These types of information are particularly useful in determining the kinds of adaptations and accommodations the student will need to succeed in the regular classroom environment.

Special educators offer information about student performance from a somewhat different perspective. Their assessment procedures are generally more individualized; they gather formal and informal data not only about academic skills but also about performance in areas such as language and behavior. This information, when added to that of general educators, helps the team to make decisions about the types of services needed by students with disabilities.

Special education teachers are often members of school-based teams that collaborate with and provide consultation to classroom teachers.

In this role, special educators may perform classroom observations and work with the team to develop possible strategies to address learning and behavioral problems in the general education environment. When students are referred for consideration for special education services, special educators play a major role in the assessment process, serving as important members of the team with responsibility for gathering information about the student's current levels of performance in a number of areas.

School administrators on educational decision-making teams may include building principals, directors of special education, or other supervisory personnel. Building principals or vice principals are often included to enlist their cooperation in the education of students with disabilities at the school site and to encourage their support of special education and inclusion programs. Special education administrators and other supervisory personnel are able to share their knowledge of the special education programming options available in the school district or division.

Parents and Students

The intent of federal special education laws is encouragement of the meaningful participation of parents of students with disabilities and the students themselves, when appropriate, in the educational decision-making process. Parents and other family members have much to contribute to the team. They are knowledgeable about their child's behavior and have acted as the child's teacher as part of their caregiving role.

Like educators, parents provide information on many aspects of the student's current performance. However, parents and other family members have a somewhat different perspective because their observations take place in the home, neighborhood, and community. Another important contribution of parents is information about their student's past educational experiences, health history, and progress through the stages of development. Parents can complete questionnaires about their children or be interviewed by school personnel. They can be observed at home while interacting with their child or they can be asked to gather informal observational data about their child in the home environment. When parents become full participants in the team process, they contribute to better educational decisions and are more likely to support their child's instructional program.

Students themselves are also members of some educational teams, particularly in the higher grades. Students can contribute information about all aspects of school performance as well as their feelings, attitudes, goals, and aspirations for the future. Students assist in the data collection process in many ways. In addition to participating in assessment procedures such as formal tests and informal inventories, they may answer interview questions, complete rating scales, or answer questions on a questionnaire.

School Support Personnel

Psychologists, speech-language pathologists, and assistive technology specialists often support general and special educators, and they are frequently members of educational decision-making teams. During assessment, school psychologists gather data to help determine whether students are eligible for special education programs. In this role, the school psychologist is usually the professional responsible for administering and interpreting results of formal tests to determine general intelligence level.

Assessment reports prepared by the psychologist address concerns about the student's level of general ability, the status of specific skills involved in learning, and emotional and behavioral status. When combined with results of academic reports from teachers, psychological reports allow the team to compare a student's actual classroom performance with expected levels of achievement. In planning the educational program, psychologists can assist in establishing reasonable goals and provide information about the student's specific learning abilities.

Speech-language pathologists are involved in the assessment and instruction of students with speech and language disorders. They are responsible for evaluating the communication skills of students, referring students to other specialists as needed, providing direct instructional services, and consulting with other professionals working with those students.

The assessment procedures used by speech-language professionals are both formal and informal; they frequently solicit input from educators about a student's classroom speech and language performance. Special educators may screen students for speech and language problems, then refer students with suspected problems to speech-language pathologists for more in-depth evaluation. Furthermore, knowledge of the communicative status of a student helps the team understand academic and behavioral problems with speech or language components. In planning the IEP, speech-language pathologists specify goals for the student and indicate how others can support those goals. For some students with disabilities, speech-language instruction is the only special service received; for others, it is one of several services.

Assistive technology (AT) specialists are relatively new members of educational teams. Their role involves the use of assistive technology to increase the student's ability to participate in the educational program. The 1997 IDEA Amendments specifically require that the IEP team "consider whether the child requires assistive technology devices and services" (*Federal Register*, 1999, §300.346(a)(2)(v)). The AT specialist assists by evaluating the current functioning levels of the student and the ways in which devices such as adapted computers, communication devices, and aids for students with visual and hearing impairments might improve current performance.

Medical Personnel

Medical information about the student is obtained from the student's physician, the school nurse, and other medical specialists. This information may include results of vision and hearing screenings, the student's health history, as well as his or her current physical status.

All students should be screened for possible visual and hearing impairments. This screening is generally carried out by the school nurse (or the school health aide), who then refers students with possible problems to appropriate specialists. The results of screening and any subsequent evaluations are reported to the team by the school nurse. Of particular interest to the team is how vision and hearing problems affect assessment performance and subsequent programming.

The school nurse or physician may also report information about any relevant health problems, conditions, or diseases. Pediatricians, neurologists, psychiatrists, and other physicians may be involved. Also of interest is whether the student is currently receiving any medical treatment, such as drug therapy. All medical information should be reported so the educational implications are clear. Data from the assessment of classroom performance and other areas of functioning must be considered by the team in light of any medical problems.

Social Workers and Counselors

Social workers and school counselors provide information about the social and emotional status of the student. In the schools, social workers assist by preparing a social or developmental history of the student, conducting group and individual counseling with the child and his or her family, working with problems in a student's living situation that affect adjustment in school, and mobilizing school and community resources.

The assessment procedures used by social workers include interviews and home visits. Data gathered regarding a student's background and home environment can help the team interpret other assessment data. Social workers may also assist team members, particularly parents, in identifying goals and strategies for action at home and in the community.

Counselors also help in the area of emotional development. Counseling services, according to federal special education laws, may be provided by a variety of professionals such as social workers, psychologists, school counselors, and vocational rehabilitation counselors. Counselors use both formal and informal procedures to gather information about the emotional and social development of the student, and sometimes that of other family members. Counselors can add important information to the student profile. For instance, data from counseling may indicate the need for specific goals or shape decisions about placement or instructional strategies.

Transition Specialists

Current federal laws require that the IEPs for older students contain a description of the transition services needed by the students and, when appropriate, the ways in which schools will link with other agencies to facilitate the transition to adult life. Professionals who contribute to assessment and instruction in this area include vocational rehabilitation counselors, special education teachers at the secondary level who provide instruction in areas related to transition, and persons with special training in the assessment, instruction, and coordination skills needed for the provision of transition services.

Specifically, the 1997 IDEA Amendments require that the IEP includes:

- for each student with a disability beginning at age 14 (or younger, if determined appropriate by the IEP team) and updated annually, a statement of the transition service needs of the student under the applicable components of the student's IEP that focuses on the student's courses of study (such as participation in advanced-placement courses or a vocational education program);
- for each student beginning at age 16 (or younger, if determined appropriate by the IEP team), a statement of needed transition services for the student, including, if appropriate, a statement of the interagency responsibilities or any needed linkages. (*Federal Register,* 1999, §300.347(b))

While transition specialists focus on this area in assessment, other team members such as teachers, parents, and students themselves can also contribute valuable information.

Motor Skills Specialists

Information about the motor development of the student may be obtained from adaptive physical education teachers, physical therapists, and occupational therapists. In addition, the school nurse or a physician, such as an orthopedic surgeon, may also provide information about motor skills.

The adaptive physical education teacher is involved with the instruction of students who require special physical education programs, and he or she can provide information about the student's current motor abilities. Teachers, psychologists, and others may also have input about the student's gross and fine motor skills. In some cases, motor skill problems may be related to other kinds of difficulties, such as poor handwriting. Adaptive physical education teachers specify goals for the student and assist team members in programming for motor needs.

Physical and occupational therapists also contribute information. Some authors distinguish between physical therapists, who are concerned with gross motor development, and occupational therapists, who work with fine motor development. Both kinds of therapists use specialized assessment procedures; their data may be supplemented by results of interviews or experiences of other team members.

Teachers can report on classroom demands for motor skills and their observations of the student's strengths and weaknesses. Parents may also have useful data. The IEP contains goals related to motor development if necessary and allows the therapists to suggest strategies that are useful in the development of better motor coordination or realistic transition goals.

Other Personnel

Occasionally, team members other than those just described are needed to present important information about the student. Tutors or paraprofessional aides who work closely with the student may provide insight based on their experiences. Members of the community, such as employers or work supervisors, may be able to give the team a better understanding of realistic vocational goals and needed transition services. Other family members, such as grandparents, can sometimes supplement input from the parents and student.

Purpose of the Team Approach

The purpose of the team approach is to assemble all the information necessary for educational decision making through members' combined skills, knowledge, experience, and expertise. Teams are viewed as being more objective than individuals because multiple viewpoints are represented. Teams differ in size depending on the types of decisions under consideration. However, as a general rule, teams should be kept as small as possible so

TABLE 1–2

Primary Sources of Information about Student Functioning

TEAM MEMBER	TYPE OF INFORMATION						
	Health	Social and Emotional Status	General Ability	School Performance	Communicative Status	Motor Skills	Transition Factors
Educators		*		*	*		*
Parents	*	*			*	*	*
Students		*		*			*
Psychologists		*	*	*			
Speech-Language Pathologists					*		
Medical Personnel	*					*	
Counselors and Social Workers		*					*
Transition Specialists							*
Motor Skills Specialists						*	*

that parents feel comfortable making contributions. In some cases, such as some IEP teams, only the parents and educators may participate. In others, there is a need for wider representation because several different types of information are required.

Federal laws require that team decisions take into consideration several areas of student functioning, if those areas are pertinent to the educational needs of a specific student. Table 1-2 lists several possible areas of concern and the team members who are the primary sources of information for each area. Although certain team members take major responsibility for assessment in certain areas, any team member may provide additional information.

This book is written from the perspective of one member of the team, the special educator. Although many of the assessment procedures described here can be used by other professionals, the special educator is the team member who focuses on the needs of students with disabilities. Having the dual responsibilities of assessment and instruction, the special educator is in a unique position to maintain an educational focus in the special education assessment process.

CRITICAL ISSUES

Many issues face the field of educational assessment of students with disabilities. And many areas of assessment are subject to criticism. These controversies are discussed throughout the text, but a brief overview is provided here.

In the mid-1970s and early 1980s, early research on the implementation of PL 94-142 resulted in criticism of the assessment team process. Observations of some teams during their deliberations indicated lack of structure and purpose as well as considerable subjectivity (Ysseldyke, Algozzine, Regan, & McCue, 1981; Ysseldyke et al., 1983). All members of the team did not participate equally; most influential were those who were responsible for the collection of assessment data (Ysseldyke, Algozzine, & Epps, 1983). A particular concern was that parents were not active participants. Full compliance with due process procedures did not always occur, and there was evidence of role confusion and professional competition (Yoshida, 1984). In addition, the clinical judgment of assessment specialists was criticized (Davis & Shepard, 1983).

Another early concern related to the tests and other measures selected for use in assessment. There appeared to be little agreement among professionals in terms of choices of assessment devices and procedures (Ysseldyke et al., 1980), and tests intended for one purpose were used for others. The technical quality of many of the early test instruments, particularly those purporting to measure psychological processing abilities in students with possible learning disabilities, was heavily criticized. Also at issue was the lack of expertise demonstrated by some examiners in administering, scoring, and interpreting tests (McLoughlin, 1985).

Charges of discriminatory practices in assessment of students with disabilities remain an issue today (Macmillan & Reschly, 1998). Although federal special education laws require that assessment be nonbiased, that ideal is not always realized. This is due, at least in part, to the difficulty of developing measures that are fair to students from all cultural and linguistic groups. It is also due to the challenges presented by the growing diversity of students in the United States. In many cases, professionals have not acquired the cultural competence needed to conduct nonbiased assessments of their students. Also, in many schools, professionals who are skilled in assessment are not proficient in the languages spoken by the students being assessed. For these reasons, efforts to promote nonbiased assessment of culturally and linguistically diverse students must continue.

Another current issue relates to the relevance of assessment data to the instructional planning process. Norm-referenced tests have long been criticized for their lack of relevance to instruction, and informal measures, such as curriculum-based assessments, have been promoted as more appropriate (Tucker, 1985). Although both types of measures have their place in special education assessment, there is need to increase emphasis on the collection of data that will aid teachers to make the types of decisions necessary to plan, implement, and monitor instruction. One step toward that goal is the requirement of the 1997 IDEA Amendments that the IEP focus on the general education curriculum and the student's involvement with and progress in that curriculum.

No aspect of educational assessment escapes criticism, and each one merits considerable attention. As each facet of the assessment process is described in this text, these issues and others are considered in more detail. We hope the approaches and strategies we describe will help special educators and other professionals address each of these issues.

THE ASSESSMENT QUESTION MODEL

One way of improving practice in special education is to develop a systematic structure for the assessment process. The key to such a structure is identifying the questions that need to be answered in assessment in order to make important educational decisions. These assessment questions then guide the choice of assessment procedures and form a framework for the interpretation of results.

The special education assessment process consists of five major phases:

1. During identification, data are gathered to describe the possible learning problem of the student and to attempt to resolve that problem within the general education classroom.
2. Once a student has been formally referred, the student's eligibility for special education is studied by collecting information about school performance and whether it is related to a disability.
3. If the student is found eligible for special education, an in-depth assessment is performed to identify critical strengths and weaknesses in school skills and other important areas.
4. An IEP is developed that includes the priority goals for an intervention program.
5. The instructional program is implemented, the student's progress is carefully monitored, and the success of the program is evaluated on a regular basis.

Figure 1–1 presents the assessment question model recommended in this book. In this model, the phases of assessment are conceptualized as a series of assessment questions. The five main assessment questions incorporated in this model are: (a) Is there a school performance problem? (b) Is it related to a disability? (c) What are the student's educational needs? (d) What types of services are required to meet those needs? and (e) How effective is the educational program? The sections that follow describe these main questions as well as the others that make up the assessment process.

Is There a School Performance Problem?

In this phase of assessment, students with possible school problems are identified. Identification may occur through routine screening procedures or through teacher referral. The student's general

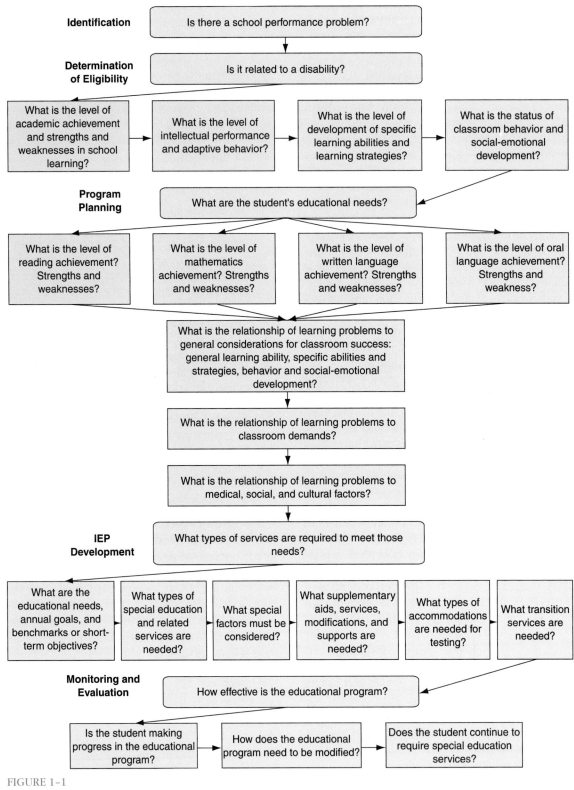

FIGURE 1-1
The Assessment Question Model

education teacher may bring the student to the attention of a school-based team in an attempt to find solutions for the student's learning problems. Several types of assessment data can be collected, including school history data (e.g., past grades and results of tests of achievement); information from parents about family background and the student's medical, developmental, and educational history; current grades and classroom work samples; and reports of current teachers about the types of instructional approaches used and their success.

Classroom assessment procedures can also be used to determine whether a learning problem exists. Systematic behavioral observations may identify a pattern of events affecting the student's achievement. Teachers may see a pattern of difficulty when they systematically analyze classroom activities and subsequent student responses. The general education curriculum itself serves as the framework for assessment, as the student's proficiency in component skills and performance at different levels are examined.

Based on this information, teachers may make instructional and environmental modifications and note an immediate change in the student's school performance. In this way, any student with temporary or situational learning problems will be identified, and further concern and assessment can be avoided. Students who do not respond to these efforts and whose learning difficulties are clearly documented are then referred for in-depth assessment. The outcome of the questioning is the identification of general problem areas, an assessment of their approximate severity, and a clear indication of the need for further assessment.

Is the School Performance Problem Related to a Disability?

After a student has been formally referred for consideration for special education services, an assessment team forms to determine the student's eligibility. Students with learning problems qualify for special education only if they meet the criteria for a disability as set forth in federal, state, and local guidelines. Although these criteria differ somewhat from one location to another, there

are two major requirements that must be met: the student has a school performance problem and that problem is related to a disability. According to federal special education laws, the disability must have an adverse effect on school performance. The presence of a disability alone, without an accompanying school problem, is not sufficient. Likewise, students with school performance problems that are not related to disabilities are not eligible for special education.

Information is collected in several areas in order to investigate school functioning and possible disabilities. These areas include academic achievement, general aptitude for learning (assessed through measures of intellectual performance and adaptive behavior), specific learning abilities and learning strategies, and classroom behavior and social-emotional development. The data collected are then weighed against eligibility standards.

As discussed earlier, students with all types of disabilities show school performance problems. These problems are documented with referral information, results of academic achievement tests, and data concerning the student's ability to conform to classroom behavioral requirements. All students are also assessed to determine general aptitude for learning. In the case of most mild disabilities, students show average or above average intellectual performance. However, in mental retardation, intellectual performance as well as adaptive behavior skills are below average. A learning disability is documented by poor performance in one or more specific learning abilities or learning strategies. Students identified as being emotionally disturbed must meet criteria related to classroom behavior, interpersonal relationships, and social-emotional development. To gather the information necessary to make these types of decisions, four assessment questions are asked.

What Is the Level of Academic Achievement; What Are the Strengths and Weaknesses in School Learning? The information needed here is an individualized assessment of the student's current level of school achievement. Although there is already strong indication of possible learning problems, formal and informal procedures are now used to describe the student's strengths and weaknesses. Norm-referenced achievement tests, administered individually, indicate the student's overall achievement level in relationship to other students of the same age or in the same grade. These results help to determine whether a serious problem exists. Informal procedures, such as interviews, classroom observations, and analysis of student work samples, help to describe the student's current skill levels. An academic assessment should identify global areas of need for further assessment and indicate the more severe problem areas.

What Are the Levels of Intellectual Functioning and Adaptive Behavior?

These two areas are assessed to determine general aptitude for learning. Intellectual functioning involves a composite of skills related to thinking, problem solving, and general academic aptitude. Adaptive behavior involves the ability to exist in and cope with environments other than the school classroom. Included are self-help, communication, and social and interpersonal skills. Normative data are needed in each area. The team must determine how students perform in comparison with their peers and whether that performance falls within average ranges. This information must be related to academic and other performance data before final judgments are made.

Norm-referenced tests, administered individually, provide information about intellectual performance. Both formal and informal procedures are appropriate for assessing adaptive behavior skills. Parents, teachers, and others familiar with the student may be interviewed or asked to complete adaptive behavior rating scales. School and home observations and examination of cultural practices contribute to a clearer understanding of the student's mastery of functional skills. Results of these assessments indicate whether students are markedly different from peers in global cognitive skills and adaptive behavior. This information is useful in making decisions about the presence of mild disabilities and in designing the IEP.

What Is the Level of Development of Specific Learning Abilities and Strategies?

Specific learning abilities are generally considered to underlie academic skills and other areas of development. Examples are specific abilities such as attention, perception, and memory. Learning strategies, in contrast, relate to the ways in which students use their learning abilities in the completion of school tasks. Students with learning disabilities often experience difficulty not only in one or more specific abilities but also in strategies for learning.

There are several formal procedures for the evaluation of specific learning abilities. These include both norm-referenced tests and standardized rating forms for teachers. Several formal tests assess a range of learning abilities; others concentrate on one specific ability, such as visual perception. Learning strategies are typically studied with informal measures and procedures. Examples are observations, checklists and rating scales, and interviews of teachers and students themselves. Results of these assessments are used to determine whether students have significant problems in specific learning abilities or strategies. This information may shed light on problems the student is encountering in academic and behavioral areas; it is also necessary for documentation of the disability of learning disabilities.

What Is the Status of Classroom Behavior and Social-Emotional Development?

To answer this question, the team assesses the student's classroom behavior, including conduct problems, interactions with teachers and peers, and the influences of the physical and instructional environments on the student's ability to meet expectations. Of interest is whether the student currently has the necessary social and behavioral skills to engage in learning activities in a general education classroom setting.

Both formal and informal procedures are used in the assessment of behavioral status. For example, results of norm-referenced rating scales completed by parents, teachers, and others are used to identify which behaviors at school and in other environments are considered inappropriate for the student's age, grade, and gender. Systematic behavioral observations are used to study specific behaviors; particular attention is paid to the conditions under which the problem behavior occurs and the consequences of the behavior. Other procedures include sociograms, analyzing interactions between the student and the teacher, and examining any relationships between behavior and medical and psychological considerations. Results of these assessments identify problems in the area of behavior and contribute to decisions about whether the student meets criteria for disabilities such as emotional disturbance. In addition, information about specific behavioral problems is useful for planning intervention programs.

What Are the Student's Educational Needs?

Once it has been established that the student is likely to meet the criteria for special education services, questions about educational needs should be considered. Four major assessment questions are asked, each relating to one of these basic school skills: reading, mathematics, written language, and oral language. Students with disabilities frequently have difficulties in these areas, and their problems with skill acquisition impede the learning of other school subjects such as science and history.

The needed information in each skill area is the same: (a) an indication of current level of performance and whether achievement is below average compared to other students; (b) specific strengths and weaknesses; and (c) the relationship of skills in one area to skills in other areas, such as the influence of reading upon mathematics. Both formal and informal devices and procedures are needed to gather this information.

What Is the Level of Reading Achievement; What Are the Strengths and Weaknesses?   Three main areas of concern in assessment of reading achievement are the student's ability to recognize or decode words, to comprehend what is read, and to use reading as a tool to learn new material. Formal tests provide information about the student's overall level of reading performance in relation to peers; these tests also help pinpoint skill areas that are possible strengths or potential weaknesses for the student. These skill areas are then studied in more detail using informal procedures such as criterion-referenced tests, informal reading inventories, teacher-made checklists, and analyses of reading errors and reading materials.

What Is the Level of Mathematics Achievement; What Are the Strengths and Weaknesses?   In mathematics, the areas of concern in the assessment of educational needs are computation, problem solving, and application skills. Like reading, both formal and informal techniques are used. For example, assessment may begin with a diagnostic mathematics test. Informal procedures such as classroom observations and analyses of student work samples are then used to gather additional information about areas of need.

What Is the Level of Written Language Development; What Are the Strengths and Weaknesses?   Spelling, handwriting, and composition skills are the major concerns in the study of written language. Assessment often begins with a broad-based test of writing skills that includes collection of a student writing sample. Rating scales may be used to evaluate handwriting, formal tests to evaluate spelling skills, and informal procedures to gain more information about the student's ability to write connected text. As with other academic skills, both formal and informal procedures contribute to the team's understanding of the student's educational needs.

What Is the Level of Oral Language Development; What Are the Strengths and Weaknesses?   The major areas to be assessed here relate to the student's ability to understand and express the four dimensions of oral language: phonology, syntax, semantics, and pragmatics. These dimensions are concerned with the sound system of language, language rules, the meaningful aspects of language, and the use of language for communication. Also of interest with students who speak languages other than English is their proficiency in English and in the other language spoken. Again, both formal and informal measures are used in the assessment of educational needs. In many cases, assessment duties in oral language are shared with speech-language pathologists and bilingual educators.

The outcome of the assessment of educational needs is a clear statement about the student's levels of performance, strengths, and weaknesses in each important area. When reviewing results, it is important to examine how task demands influence performance. For example, a student might do well in written computation but have difficulty with mental computation. The learning strategies of the student become more apparent when performance varies based upon the characteristics of the task.

It is also important to ask how problems in one area might influence performance in another area. For example, poor oral reading skills might be related to poor spelling skills. Relationships such as this may suggest a common underlying factor and lead to a plan for an instructional intervention.

The next step is to consider the results of academic assessments in relation to three important areas: general considerations for classroom success; the demands imposed by the classroom learning environment; and medical, social, and cultural factors.

What Is the Relationship of Learning Problems to General Considerations for Classroom Success?
General considerations for classroom success include the factors considered in the determination of a disability: general aptitude for learning, specific learning abilities and strategies, and classroom behavior and social-emotional development. The relationship between these factors and the student's educational needs provides a clearer picture of the student's performance, thereby facilitating the program planning process.

General learning aptitude, assessed with measures of intellectual performance and adaptive behavior, is compared to school achievement. With some disabilities (e.g., learning disabilities), the pattern is underachievement. That is, actual school performance falls below that expected given the student's general aptitude. In mental retardation, the pattern is different. Low levels of academic performance correlate with below-average performance on measures of intellectual performance and adaptive behavior.

Problems with specific learning abilities or learning strategies may be related to academic problems. Difficulty acquiring and using information can interfere with the development of reading, mathematics, and other subjects. For example, poor memory or difficulty in discriminating sounds may interfere with the student's ability to learn the sounds of letters. There might also

be relationships between task characteristics and the learning strategies the student uses to complete those tasks. For example, students with poor strategies for identifying the main ideas when reading may experience failure when asked to learn new information from content area textbooks.

Behavioral issues also play a role in academic achievement, as do the characteristics of the learning environment. Classroom conduct problems can interfere with all types of learning, and interventions for students with these difficulties may focus on different skills than intervention for students whose problems are primarily academic. For example, for students who have skills but do not complete assignments, instruction might focus first on work completion, rather than on acquisition of new skills. Environmental factors also affect school learning. For example, students who have difficulty paying attention may require special seating arrangements so that the teacher can help them focus on important aspects of instruction.

What Is the Relationship of Learning Problems to Classroom Demands?
Academic performance and disability characteristics also need to be considered in the context of classroom demands: the physical environment of the classroom and the tasks, methods, and materials used in instruction. Task analysis is a useful technique to determine what aspects of a learning task are creating difficulty for the student. If the student lacks prerequisite skills, these can become part of instruction. Sometimes it is also necessary to modify the task itself; for example, allowing students to answer questions orally rather than in writing may dramatically improve their performance on a science test.

The classroom learning environment can be studied through observations, interviews, and analysis of instructional materials. Possible assessment questions are:

1. What are the features of instructional materials? What prerequisite skills are required? What objectives do the materials address? Is the pace of instruction appropriate? Is the format clear? Do these materials match the learning needs of the student?

2. What instructional procedures are used by the teacher? Does the teacher use modeling, prompting, and reinforcement? Are the methods of instruction appropriate for the needs of the student?

3. Are the physical surroundings (lighting, heating, work space, noise level) conducive to learning? Will the physical environment facilitate the student's learning rather than impede it?

These types of information help prevent mismatches between the needs of the student and the classroom learning environment. Poor student performance in one or more skill areas may be directly related to inappropriate classroom conditions. If this is the case, then the problem lies with the environment, not with the student. Environmental modifications become a priority, and these data can guide the changes.

What Is the Relationship of Learning Problems to Medical, Social, and Cultural Factors? Medical, social, and cultural factors may affect student performance. Medical correlates to learning include general health status, vision, hearing, and motor development. Important social factors may include characteristics of the family constellation (e.g., the number and age of siblings in the home), the value the family places on schooling, emphasis on literacy at home, and provisions for doing homework. Other social background data include ages of playmates or friends and favorite pastimes. Cultural correlates include linguistic differences, forms of communication, and cultural perceptions of the value of school learning.

Much of this information is gathered when parents and others are interviewed and/or if they complete developmental and social histories. Home visits, observations in the neighborhood and on the playground, sociograms, and other informal techniques are used. Team input is imperative in this assessment area, as are consultations with physicians, social workers, and others who have worked or are familiar with the student. Copies of medical records and other information should be reviewed when necessary.

These factors may provide explanations for the learning problem. Inappropriate action can sometimes be avoided if these dimensions are considered; however, more typically, additional aspects of a student's learning problem are discovered. For example, although poor vision may partially explain a reading disability, both corrective lenses and an instructional program in reading may be necessary. Or if mental retardation is suspected because a student performs poorly on measures of intellectual performance and adaptive behavior, all assessment results must be reinterpreted if a severe hearing loss is discovered.

Noting interrelationships helps to integrate the information collected by the various members of the assessment team. By putting the results of the assessment in context, the team can make better decisions when planning the instructional program. A problem in academic achievement may be considered less extreme if the student's general ability to learn is low, if he or she is inattentive in class, if the tasks in the classroom have an inappropriate response requirement, or if the student has a hearing loss. Noting interrelationships produces a clearer understanding of the student's educational needs.

What Types of Services Are Required to Meet Those Needs?

The team of concerned professionals and the student's parents (as well as the student in some cases) is now ready to develop an educational plan. For students with disabilities, there are several areas to consider. Requirements for the IEP, spelled out in federal laws such as the 1997 IDEA Amendments, form the basis for several assessment questions.

What Are the Educational Needs, Annual Goals, and Benchmarks or Short-Term Objectives? The first step in development of the plan is description of the student's most pressing educational needs, identification of priority goals, and specification of benchmarks or objectives leading to those goals. First, the student's current levels of performance in all important areas are described. Second, the team determines which problems identified in the assessment process constitute the most important educational needs. To do this, it is necessary to consider the student's age and grade in school, the concerns and priorities of the parents and those of the student, and the family's culture and value system. For example, if a high school junior is concerned about preparing for a career, instruction in basic phonics skills may not be considered as important as learning to read job-related vocabulary words.

Next, the team sets annual goals for the student. These goals shape the direction of the student's program and become the guidelines for evaluation of its effectiveness. Benchmarks or short-term objectives are then identified for each goal. These objectives represent the intermediate steps the student must complete to reach the goals; as such they guide teachers and others responsible for the implementation of the program.

What Special Factors Must Be Considered? The 1997 IDEA Amendments added a new requirement for IEP teams. In developing the educational plan, the team must consider several special factors when identifying goals and making decisions about services. These factors are:

- The needs of students with behavioral problems, including the need for positive behavioral interventions;
- The language needs of students with limited proficiency in English;
- The need for instruction in Braille for students who are blind or visually impaired;
- The communication needs of all students, including those who are deaf or hard of hearing; and
- The need for assistive technology devices and services for all students.

These factors focus on important dimensions, although it is unlikely that all will apply to any one individual.

What Types of Special Education and Related Services Are Needed? The next step involves making decisions about the special education and related services needed to implement the educational program. A range of special education services is available, depending upon the severity of the student's needs. These services include full-time placement in a special classroom, part-time services outside the general education classroom from a resource or itinerant teacher, and instruction provided in the general education classrooms by special education personnel. The

last two options are the most common because the majority of students with disabilities spend at least part of the school day in the general education environment.

Related services are other types of services required by the student in order to benefit from special education. Included in this category are speech-language pathology and audiology services, physical and occupational therapy, social work services, and counseling.

What Types of Supplementary Aids, Services, Modifications, and Supports Are Needed? Another new requirement of federal special education law is specification in the IEP of the ways in which the educational environment must be modified to support the participation of the student with disabilities. The intent of the law is to make the educational environment, including the general education classroom, more accessible to students with disabilities. The 1997 IDEA Amendments define supplementary aids and services as "aids, services, and other supports that are provided in regular education classes or other education-related settings to enable children with disabilities to be educated with nondisabled children to the maximum extent appropriate" (*Federal Register,* 1999, §300.28).

Thus, the team must consider how best to include the student in the general education program and develop strategies to make that inclusion successful. Examples of some of the types of supports that might be provided are consultation to the general education teacher, special learning materials, in-class instruction delivered by special education personnel, and modification of assignments or tests by the classroom teacher.

What Types of Accommodations Are Needed for Testing? The 1997 IDEA Amendments require that students with disabilities participate in state or district assessments of academic achievement administered to general education students. In developing the IEP, the team decides what types of modifications are needed, if any, in the administration of these tests. The team can also determine that these assessments are not appropriate for a particular student; in that case, an alternative assessment procedure must be described.

What Transition Services Are Needed? Transition services are "a coordinated set of activities for a student with a disability that is designed within an outcome-oriented process, that promotes movement from school to post-school activities" (*Federal Register,* 1999, §300.29(a)(1)). Beginning at age 14, the IEP team must describe the transition needs of the student as they relate to his or her course of study in school. Beginning at age 16, or earlier if appropriate, the team must specify the transition services required by the student, including the coordination of services with other agencies. The types of services to be provided may include "instruction; related services; community experiences; the development of employment and other post-school adult living objectives; and, if appropriate, acquisition of daily living skills and functional vocational evaluation" (*Federal Register,* 1999, §300.29(a)(3)).

How Effective Is the Educational Program?

Once the IEP is implemented, its evaluation begins. The question here concerns the effectiveness of the educational program. Teachers and others responsible for implementation collect data as they provide services. At periodic intervals, parents receive progress reports, and each year the IEP is reviewed. Every few years, the student's need for special education services is reconsidered. All of these actions require assessment information and all are directed toward one goal: modification of the program, if necessary. Three assessment questions relate to the evaluation process.

Is the Student Making Adequate Progress in the Educational Program? Assessment of the student's progress begins when instruction begins. Teachers observe the student during instruction, analyze the responses the student makes, and evaluate performance on classroom learning tasks, assignments, and tests. These data are col-

lected to gauge the effectiveness of instructional strategies. If the student is not progressing at the expected rate, the instructional approach must be modified.

The IEP for each student contains not only annual goals but also a plan for measuring progress toward those goals. The assessment procedures outlined in that plan may be limited to the curriculum-based measures most often used by teachers or may include other more formal measures. In any event, teachers must inform parents of their child's progress on a regular basis. The 1997 IDEA Amendments require that parents receive progress reports at least as often as report cards are issued for general education students.

How Does the Educational Program Need to Be Modified? At least once a year, the IEP team must evaluate the educational plan and modify it as needed. Prior to the meeting, assessment information is collected in order to describe the student's current level of performance in each annual goal area. The team reviews the student's progress and discusses the effectiveness of the instructional program. Then a decision is made about whether the program should continue and, if so, how it should be modified. Typical modifications are a revised set of annual goals and objectives and changes in the types of services and supports provided.

Does the Student Continue to Require Special Education Services? Every 3 years, or more often if necessary, the student's eligibility for special education services must be reevaluated. This process may require the collection of assessment data about the student's disability, if the team believes such information is necessary. The purpose of this evaluation is to ensure that special education services are not provided when they are no longer needed—and that students who continue to require assistance from special education will receive that assistance.

REVIEW QUESTIONS

1. Define *special education assessment.*
2. In special education assessment, information is gathered about students with _____ .
3. Assessment is an on-going process, not a one-time event. (True or False)
4. The term *assessment* means the same as the term *testing.* (True or False)
5. Name the five main purposes of special education assessment.
6. Indicate whether each of the following is a *formal* or *informal* assessment strategy:
   a. Observation of students interacting during recess
   b. Teacher-made quiz or test
   c. Norm-referenced test of intellectual performance
   d. Interview of student's parents
   e. Group test of academic achievement
   f. Task analysis of classroom task
7. Students with disabilities tend to show better performance on group tests than on individual tests. (True or False)
8. Match the disability in Column A with the description in Column B.

Column A	*Column B*
a. Emotional disturbance	_____ A disorder in one or more of the basic psychological processes
b. Specific learning disability	_____ Subaverage general intellectual functioning
c. Mental retardation	_____ Impulsivity, poor attention skills
d. Attention deficit hyperactivity disorder	_____ Deficits in adaptive behavior
	_____ An inability to build or maintain satisfactory interpersonal relationships with peers and teachers
	_____ Imperfect ability to listen, think, speak, read, write, spell, or do mathematical calculations

9. The team approach is recommended in federal special education laws but is not required. (True or False)
10. Match the team member in Column A with the type of information he or she contributes to assessment in Column B.

Column A	*Column B*
a. Parent	_____ Vision and hearing
b. Adaptive physical education teacher	_____ Academic performance
c. School psychologist	_____ Motor skills
d. Speech-language pathologist	_____ Developmental and health histories
e. Educator	_____ Current intellectual performance
f. School nurse	_____ Oral language skills

11. The Assessment Question Model provides a systematic structure for assessment. (True or False)

12. Match the assessment question or questions in Column A with the assessment team's task in Column B.

<table>
<tr><td>Column A</td><td>Column B</td></tr>
<tr><td>a. Is there a school performance problem?</td><td>_____ Choosing annual goals and benchmarks or short-term objectives</td></tr>
<tr><td>b. Is it related to a disability?</td><td>_____ Deciding if the student is eligible for special education services</td></tr>
<tr><td>c. What are the student's educational needs?</td><td rowspan="2">_____ Considering special factors such as the need for assistive technology devices and services and the language needs of students with limited proficiency in English</td></tr>
<tr><td>d. What types of services are required to meet those needs?</td></tr>
<tr><td>e. How effective is the educational program?</td><td>_____ Determining if the student is making progress toward the annual goals</td></tr>
<tr><td></td><td>_____ Assessing the student's current intellectual performance</td></tr>
<tr><td></td><td>_____ Examining the relationship of learning problems to classroom demands</td></tr>
<tr><td></td><td>_____ Selecting the types of special education services to provide to the student</td></tr>
<tr><td></td><td>_____ Describing the student's strengths and weaknesses in reading, mathematics, written language, and other school skills</td></tr>
</table>

13. IEP teams must describe the transition needs of students beginning at what age?
14. Name two types of supplementary aids, services, or supports that might be provided in general education classes to assist students with disabilities.
15. At minimum, the student's eligibility for special education services must be evaluated every 5 years. (True or False)

ACTIVITIES

1. Interview three members of assessment teams. Choose professionals who represent at least two different perspectives (e.g., general education, special education, speech-language pathology). Ask each to define the term *assessment* and to explain the purposes of the assessment process. How are their answers similar? Different?
2. Assume you are a classroom teacher with a student who has a learning or behavior problem. You're going to be meeting with a team of other educators at your school to discuss possible interventions for the student. What types of assessment information will you collect to share with the team?
3. Visit the website for The Council for Exceptional Children (CEC), the major professional organization for special educators. Its address is http://www.cec.sped.org. Find out the name of the CEC division for professionals interested in special education assessment. What services does that division provide?

DISCUSSION QUESTIONS

1. Why is there a need for different types of assessment procedures? What problems would arise if only formal tests or informal measures were available?
2. Assessment teams include professionals who represent different perspectives. What possible conflicts could occur? How can differences be reconciled?
3. The 1997 IDEA Amendments require that teams take into consideration the student's involvement with and progress in the general education curriculum. What are the implications of this requirement for general education teachers? Are these teachers likely to become more involved in planning programs for students with disabilities?
4. Although federal special education laws require that assessment procedures be nonbiased, that is not always the case. What are some of the reasons for this and what can be done to improve current practices?

CHAPTER 2

THE ASSESSMENT PROCESS

- Types of Decisions
- Steps in the Assessment Process
- Identification and Referral
- Determination of Eligibility
- Program Planning
- Program Implementation and Evaluation

Special education assessment is a systematic process, one that proceeds in a logical sequence in order to gather the information needed to make important decisions about students' educational programs. The types and number of assessment procedures vary at different stages in that process because the reasons for gathering data are different. This chapter describes the entire assessment process, beginning with identification of possible learning problems and ending with the evaluation of special education services. First, however, it is useful to describe the types of decisions that educational teams must make and the ways in which these decisions influence the collection of assessment data.

TYPES OF DECISIONS

Special education assessment provides the information needed to make two types of decisions: legal decisions and instructional decisions. These decisions differ in several important ways.

Legal Decisions

The determination of eligibility for special services and the reevaluation of eligibility are essentially legal decisions. These decisions concern who will receive special education services. Their purpose is to determine whether individual students meet legal requirements for one or more disabilities in order to allow allocation of special education funds, resources, and personnel.

Federal special education laws such as the 1997 IDEA Amendments specify two major eligibility criteria: The student must be determined to have a disability, and that disability must have an adverse effect on the student's educational performance. These criteria guide the assessment process by indicating the essential information needed. Each disability is also defined by federal laws and state regulations. However, federal definitions tend to be general descriptions of conditions, as can be seen in Table 1–1 in Chapter 1. State guidelines may provide more specificity, al-

though they usually do not mandate particular assessment procedures. In most cases, these decisions are left to the professional judgment of team members. Considerable expertise is needed to put legal definitions into operation.

Legal decisions about mild disabilities require the contributions of several team members including parents, general and special educators, school psychologists, speech-language pathologists, and school nurses. Other professionals—such as physicians, adaptive physical education teachers, school social workers, and assistive technology specialists—participate when necessary.

In making decisions about the existence of mild disabilities, most states require assessment information about three areas of functioning: (a) general intellectual performance, (b) educational performance, and (c) performance related to specific disabilities. Table 2–1 compares the general criteria for the various mild disabilities in these three areas. Note that the term *behavioral disorder* is used instead of *emotional disturbance,* a legal term not favored by educators.

General intellectual performance is a concern in all mild disabilities. It is assessed by individual tests of intelligence and, in cases in which retardation is suspected, measures of adaptive behavior. Retardation is indicated when performance falls within the below average range. In other mild disabilities, the opposite is true. Intellectual performance must be at least average.

Educational performance is also a concern for all mild disabilities. In mental retardation, the pattern is typically poor performance in most or all areas. In contrast, other mild disabilities require low or below average performance in only one area. However, it is not uncommon for older students with learning disabilities, behavioral disorders, and attention deficit hyperactivity disorders to show poor performance in several school skills.

In all mild disabilities, the assessment team compares the student's expected and actual performance to determine whether a discrepancy is apparent. Expected performance is estimated by considering the student's age, grade, and intellectual functioning level. In retardation, students

TABLE 2-1

Comparison of Eligibility Criteria for Mild Disabilities

	MILD RETARDATION	LEARNING DISABILITY	BEHAVIORAL DISORDER	ATTENTION DEFICIT HYPERACTIVITY DISORDER
General Intellectual Functioning	Below average	Average or above	Average or above	Average or above
Educational Performance	Below average in most areas	Low or below average in at least one area	Low or below average in at least one area	Low or below average in at least one area
Index of Disability	Low or below average in adaptive behavior and most other areas	Low or below average in at least one specific learning ability or learning strategy	Low or below average in at least one area of behavior	Low or below average in attention, activity level, or both

show poor school performance in relation to age and grade; however, results of measures of intellectual performance and adaptive behavior are usually consistent with school achievement levels. In the other mild disabilities, a discrepancy does exist. Predictors of school performance suggest that students will show average achievement, but their actual school skills fall below this level.

The third major area of concern, the index of disability, differs across the four mild disabilities. Retardation is a comprehensive disability affecting school skills, adaptive behavior, and most other areas of functioning. Learning disabilities are indicated when students have deficits in one or more specific learning abilities or learning strategies, despite adequate general intellectual performance. Both behavioral disorders and attention deficit hyperactivity disorders require evidence of specific types of behavioral problems. Like learning disabilities, these disabilities occur despite adequate intellectual performance.

Eligibility decisions rely heavily on results of norm-referenced measures such as standardized tests. These instruments provide information that allows the team to compare a student's performance with that of other students. For example, results of academic achievement measures may indicate that

the student's school performance is sufficiently different from that of age or grade peers to warrant considering it to be a problem. Salvia and Ysseldyke (1991) maintain that, "when appropriately administered, scored, and interpreted, norm-referenced devices can serve to protect children from haphazard and capricious decision-making" (p. 613). Guidelines for interpreting standardized test results for eligibility decisions are presented in Chapter 4.

Informal assessment procedures also play a role in legal decisions. Checklists, interviews, rating scales, observations, portfolios, criterion-referenced tests, and other informal measures are used to confirm results of norm-referenced tests and to provide information not available from standardized measures. The team approach to making legal decisions helps to ensure that all important areas of functioning are considered and that the assessment procedures selected are the most appropriate for the task at hand.

Instructional Decisions

Planning, monitoring, and evaluating the student's special education program require instructional decisions. In fact, once a student has been found eligible for special education services, the majority of decisions to be made are instructional rather than legal. The major concerns are the content of the student's curriculum (i.e., what to teach), the instructional methods used to implement the curriculum (i.e., how to teach), and the overall effectiveness of the instructional program.

The first step is preparation of an Individualized Education Program, or IEP, for the student. Results of the eligibility assessment are reviewed and additional information is gathered as needed. The student's current levels of performance in important skill areas then serve as a basis for identifying annual goals and short-term objectives, selecting appropriate services and curricular modifications for the student, and planning strategies for the evaluation of the individualized program.

Once the IEP is implemented, the teacher and other professionals responsible for delivering educational services continue to make instructional decisions. These decisions are an integral part of the teaching process; data collection is ongoing and instructional decisions are made on a regular and frequent basis. Instruction takes place, the teacher gathers data on the student's response to instruction, and modifications are made based on the student's progress. This cycle is repeated continuously as the teacher monitors the effects of the intervention.

More formal evaluations of the instructional effort also take place. Several times during the school year, the teacher communicates with the student's parents about progress toward the annual goals specified in the IEP. This typically occurs when report cards are prepared for all students in the school. At least once each year, the entire IEP is reviewed by the student's parents and teachers. Progress toward the student's goals is reported, the effectiveness of the educational program is discussed, and a new plan is developed for the coming year.

Instructional decisions require specific information about the student's performance in relation to the classroom program. Because of this, informal assessment strategies are more useful than formal measures. Although standardized test results may help the assessment team identify areas of strength and weakness for the IEP, these measures are not designed for frequent assessment of

progress toward specific instructional goals. Informal techniques such as observation, informal inventories, portfolios, criterion-referenced tests, and the like are more appropriate.

STEPS IN THE ASSESSMENT PROCESS

Table 2–2 presents the steps in the assessment process. There are four main phases in assessment, beginning with the identification of students with possible special education needs. Each phase is made up of several steps, and the overall sequence parallels the purposes of assessment, the types of educational decisions to be made, and the assessment questions introduced in Chapter 1.

Two major factors influence the steps in assessment: special education laws and regulations at the national, state, and local levels and professional beliefs about preferred assessment practices. PL 94-142 and IDEA guarantee free, appropriate, public education to all students with disabilities. This guarantee requires that all students with possible

TABLE 2–2
Steps in Educational Assessment

Identification and Referral
- Screening and teacher identification of students with school problems
- Prereferral intervention strategies
- Referral and notification of parents

Determination of Eligibility
- Design of the Individualized Assessment Plan
- Parental permission for assessment
- Administration, scoring, and interpretation of assessment procedures
- Reporting results
- Decisions about eligibility

Program Planning
- Design of the Individualized Education Program (IEP)
- Parental agreement to the IEP

Program Implementation and Evaluation
- Implementation of the IEP
- Ongoing monitoring of student progress
- Annual review of the IEP
- Periodic reevaluation of eligibility

disabilities be identified and, if appropriate, assessed. Accompanying this guarantee are strict guidelines for the ways in which assessments must be carried out. Students and their parents are protected by legal requirements for due process, procedural safeguards, nondiscriminatory assessment, placement in the least restrictive educational environment, confidentiality of information, and development and regular monitoring of the IEP. States must conform to these regulations to receive federal aid for special education services.

Due process procedures are designed to safeguard the rights of students with disabilities and their parents. Due process has been described as "a procedure which seeks to insure the fairness of educational decisions and the accountability of both the professionals and parents making these decisions" (Turnbull, Strickland, & Brantley, 1982, p. 10). Due process provides protection to the consumers of the assessment process—for example, by requiring that parents give their consent before their child is assessed.

Although laws and regulations provide the general structure for assessment, specific procedures must be developed at the state and local levels. For example, there is considerable variation among states in the terminology used to identify the different disabilities; within states, there are differences in the forms that local districts develop to document referrals, parental consent for assessment, and IEPs. This flexibility allows professionals to consider local needs and act upon their beliefs about preferred practices in assessment.

IDENTIFICATION AND REFERRAL

The first phase in the assessment process is the identification of students with possible disabilities. This phase involves the largest number of students. However, identification does not necessarily result in referral for special education assessment. In some cases, students are referred for consideration for other types of services, such as bilingual education. In others, school problems are resolved through classroom interventions during the prereferral stage. When problems persist despite such efforts, students may be referred for assessment to determine their eligibility for special education.

Screening and Teacher Identification

According to federal special education laws, state education agencies are responsible for "child find," that is, the identification, location, and evaluation of all students with disabilities. States use several types of child find strategies, including mass media information campaigns, in an attempt to make the general public more aware of the needs of individuals with disabilities. These campaigns stress the signs and symptoms of disabilities as well as the availability of services within the state or a particular region.

School districts and other educational agencies also participate in child find activities. Screening procedures are used to gather information about large groups of students to identify those in need of more in-depth assessment. Teachers and other staff members are alerted to signs of various disabilities as well as the prereferral and referral processes. Teachers may be asked to complete checklists or rating forms for each of their students to help identify those with potential problems. School records may be examined to locate students with poor report card grades or low performance on group achievement tests.

Anyone within the community may identify a child with a possible disability. In the preschool years, parents often bring their child to the attention of education professionals. Once the child has entered the elementary grades, it is typically the general education teacher who first notices a potential problem. This is particularly true for mild disabilities because these disabilities often first become apparent when students are unable to meet classroom academic and behavioral expectations. When teachers identify students with problems in school, the first step is not referral. Instead, prereferral strategies are used in an attempt to ameliorate the problem.

Prereferral Strategies

General education teachers are expected to make modifications in a student's instructional program before beginning formal procedures for referring that student for special education assessment. The purpose of this prereferral intervention stage is twofold. First, many students who experience minor or transitory learning and behavior problems can be helped to succeed by relatively simple adaptations of the standard curriculum, instructional procedures, or of the behavior management program within the general education classroom. Also, there may be resources within the school, in addition to special education, that can assist the student; examples are peer tutoring programs and bilingual education. Second, when prereferral strategies are not effective in improving the student's performance, the information gathered during this stage provides direction for the special education team in its decisions about eligibility, intervention strategies, and placement options.

In many schools, the prereferral intervention stage is coordinated by a team of professionals (e.g., a child study or student assistance team) that includes general educators as well as special educators. A teacher with a student who is experiencing difficulty in school may ask the team for assistance in identifying strategies for modifying the classroom learning environment to improve the student's chances for success. As the checklist in Figure 2–1 illustrates, prereferral strategies can take many forms: conferences with students and parents, review of school records and results of medical screenings, changes in instruction, introduction of learning aids, and modifications of the classroom behavior management system. Checklists such as this are used to document the adaptations made in general education so that their effectiveness can be evaluated.

When prereferral interventions do not bring about desired changes, one option open to the team is referral for special education assessment. The referral may be instituted by the team or the student's classroom teacher. Referrals can also be made by others interested in the student's welfare: parents, tutors, physicians, or even the student himself or herself. However, general education teachers remain the most common source of special education referrals.

Referral and Parental Notification

Referrals are initiated when the parent, teacher, or another professional completes a referral form such as the one shown in Figure 2–2. Although forms differ from district to district, most require the person making the referral to describe the student's problem, tell how long the problem has been occurring, and discuss the types of classroom modifications that have been introduced in an attempt to solve the problem.

Once a student is formally referred for special education assessment, a chain of events is set in motion. School districts usually have an individual or team that receives referrals from schools in the district or, in the case of new students, from other agencies or individuals. A team forms and processes the referral by alerting the student's parents and by gathering all available data.

Federal special education law requires that parents be informed of any referral in writing. They must also be informed whenever any testing for possible special education program changes will take place. Parents have the right to participate in the assessment and in subsequent decisions about their child's program. They must give their permission for assessment and should receive an explanation of the results and any proposed action. They can ask for an independent evaluation, inspect all school records, and request a due process hearing whenever they disagree with a proposed action, such as placement in special education.

Students with disabilities have the right to be represented in assessment and other matters. When no parent or guardian can be identified, when their whereabouts are unknown, or when the student is a ward of the state, the state or local education agency can assign a surrogate parent. The person chosen must be qualified to serve the best interests of the child. He or she represents the student in all the matters mentioned here and cannot be employed by the school district.

DETERMINATION OF ELIGIBILITY

The eligibility determination stage of assessment begins with a careful planning process. Parents are informed of the assessment plan and their participation in team deliberations is encour-

---

Prereferral Intervention Checklist

Name _____ Age _____ Date _____
Teacher _____ Grade _____

1. Area(s) of Concern
    _____ academic   _____ language   _____ gross motor   _____ hearing
    _____ behavior   _____ speech   _____ fine motor
    _____ emotional   _____ physical   _____ vision

2. What kinds of strategies have been employed to resolve this problem?
    A. Records Review and Conference
    _____ student conference(s)   _____ review of educational records
    _____ parent conference(s)   _____ vision   _____ medical   _____ hearing

    B. Environmental Modifications
    _____ class seating arrangement   _____ group change   _____ other
    _____ individual seating   _____ teacher change
    _____ schedule modification   _____ teacher position in class

    C. Instructional
    _____ modifications in methods used with group or class
    _____ modifications in learning aids used with group or class
    _____ individual methods with regular materials
    _____ individual learning aids with regular materials
    _____ individual methods and materials different from group or class

    D. Management
    _____ modification in classroom management system
    _____ use of systematic group management techniques
    _____ use of individual behavior management techniques

3. What methods are currently employed to address the concern?_____
    _____
    _____
    _____
    _____

4. Where does this student stand in relationship to others in class, group or grade regarding
    systemwide tests, class average behavior, completion of work, etc.?

Student Behavior	Class or Group or Grade Behavior

FIGURE 2–1
Prereferral Intervention Checklist

aged. When the assessment procedures have been carried out, results are reported, and team members, including the student's parents, make legal decisions about eligibility for special education services.

Design of the Individualized Assessment Plan

Assessment of students with suspected disabilities must be systematic. To ensure this, a plan of

---

Prereferral Intervention Checklist

5. Is the concern generally associated with a particular time, subject, or person?

6. In what areas, under what conditions, does this student do best?

7. Assistance Requested (observation, materials, ideas, etc.):

_____
_____
_____
_____
_____
_____

Assistance Provided:

Dates	Nature of Assistance	Individuals Responsible	Outcome

FIGURE 2-1

Prereferral Intervention Checklist—*Continued*
Note: From Developing and Implementing Individualized Education Programs (3rd ed.) (pp. 66–67) by B. B. Strickland and A. P. Turnbull, 1990, New York: Merrill. Copyright 1990 by Merrill Publishing Company. Reprinted by permission.

action should be developed by the professionals responsible for the assessment. In this text, we call that plan an Individualized Assessment Plan, or IAP. Although it is not a legal requirement, the IAP serves to individualize the assessment process so that each student's unique needs are addressed. Standard sets of assessment procedures, administered by some districts to all students referred for special education assessment, are neither appropriate nor useful.

An IAP describes the steps in assessment and the procedures used in each step (Figure 2–3).

Referral for Special Education Services

Directions: Teachers or other individuals referring a student for special education services should complete all sections of this form. The completed form should be sent to the principal's office for processing. Complete and specific information will assist the assessment and IEP teams in determining the student's eligibility for special education and specific educational needs. Use behavioral descriptions whenever possible.

Teacher_____ Grade/Class_____ Report Date_____
Student_____ Age_____ Birth Date_____

1. What is the student's problem? How does it affect his or her ability to participate in classroom activities?

2. How frequently does the problem occur? (For example, once a week? Six times a week?)

3. What changes have occurred in the behavior during this school year?

4. What changes in classroom activities, assignment, procedures, and so on, have you made to try to solve the problem? What are the results of these changes?

5. What are the student's major strengths and talents?

6. What special interests, hobbies, or skills does the student have?

FIGURE 2-2

Referral for Special Education Services
Note: From *Teaching Special Students in General Education Classrooms* 5/e by Lewis/Doorlag, © 1999. Reprinted by permission of Prentice-Hall, Inc., Upper Saddle River, NJ.

This plan must address the reason the student was referred for assessment, focus on areas relevant to education, and provide information needed for decisions concerning instructional design, placement, and other aspects of the educational program. The three main concerns are (a) the student's skills and abilities, (b) the general education curriculum and the tasks with which the student is having difficulty, and (c) the classroom learning environment. In addition, the IAP may also consider physical, social, and behavioral characteristics as they relate to the student's educational needs. For example, a student

may have a severe reading disability due in part to a vision disorder.

The assessment question model described in Chapter 1 can be used to develop the IAP. The questions are arranged in sequential order and each major question is followed by a set of more detailed questions. Use of this model to organize the IAP can prevent the loss of precious time, energy, and resources. A vague, general question such as "What is the student's learning problem?" usually leads to an unfocused assessment with ambiguous results. More precise questions help to ensure that useful data will be gathered. For

Individualized Assessment Plan

Name _____ School _____

Birthdate _____ Age _____ Grade _____

Assessment Coordinator _____ Date of IAP _____

Reason for Referral: _____

_____

Assessment Questions	Assessment Procedures	Person(s) Responsible	Date/Time

For parental use: This assessment plan has been explained to me. I understand the need for assessing my child and the procedures to be used. I give my approval.

_____
Parent's Signature

_____
Date

FIGURE 2–3
Individualized Assessment Plan

example, the question "What is the level of mathematics achievement and what are the student's strengths and weaknesses in mathematics?" provides direction and suggests the choice of certain assessment procedures and the exclusion of others. In this case, assessment would likely begin with a standardized test of mathematics skills, followed as needed by informal measures of the skill areas in which problems were identified.

IAPs include formal and/or informal assessment procedures, depending upon the questions under consideration. The questions may address any area relevant to education; examples are academic skills (e.g., reading), social-emotional concerns (self-concept), and the physical environment of the classroom (seating arrangement). The choice of assessment procedures is often influenced by the types of information needed to answer the assessment question. For example, norm-referenced tests provide information to answer questions about level of proficiency, but they do not describe specific skill deficits. A parent interview, rather than a formal test, would be used to gather data about a student's family history and medical background. Other criteria for the selection of appropriate assessment procedures are described in Chapter 3.

Federal special education laws make several specific provisions for evaluation. Before a student receives special education services, a team of qualified professionals must assess the student to determine eligibility. This team is made up of the same individuals as those who serve on the IEP team. According to regulations for the 1997 IDEA Amendments, teams must include:

- The student's parents;
- A general education teacher if the student is or may be participating in general education;
- A special education teacher;
- A representative of the educational agency who can provide or supervise special education services and who is knowledgeable about the general curriculum and resources available within the agency;
- An individual able to interpret assessment results and their educational implications (this individual may be one of the professionals just listed);
- Others, as needed, with special expertise or knowledge about the student; and
- If appropriate, the student.

The law makes clear that one of the major purposes of the evaluation is to gather information for program planning. As Turnbull and Cilley (1999) observe, "Evaluation is the basis for determining not only whether the student has a disability but also, if that is the case, what the school must do about the disability (namely, develop and carry out an appropriate education through the IEP and provide services in the least restrictive environment of the general curriculum)" (p. 20). The 1997 IDEA Amendments also place new emphasis on the general education curriculum. In development of the educational program, the team must describe how the disability affects the student's involvement with and progress in the general curriculum.

In designing the IAP, the evaluation team should follow these principles:

1. Focus assessment on the education of the student; consider noneducational factors only as they contribute to the understanding of the educational problem.
2. Plan the assessment by asking important assessment questions, then select procedures that will gather the information needed to answer those questions.
3. Choose assessment procedures of the highest quality.
4. Coordinate the efforts of team members. Avoid duplication and take advantage of the expertise of persons with different perspectives.
5. Begin assessment in each area of interest by surveying general performance; continue assessment with more in-depth procedures only if a problem is identified.
6. Consider not only the student but also the learning tasks and the instructional environment.
7. Compare findings from different procedures to confirm the accuracy of assessment results. Be sure to include information about the student's current classroom performance in this comparison.

Decisions about eligibility for special education and program planning are important decisions. These principles help to ensure that students are assessed accurately, fully, and fairly so that useful information is available for decision making.

IAPs can be used to structure assessments other than the initial evaluation of eligibility. As described later in this chapter, educators and others have many occasions to assess the student's progress and evaluate the special education program's effectiveness.

Parental Permission for Assessment

Once an assessment plan has been developed, the student's parents must give their permission before the assessment can take place. Federal special education laws require that parents be notified in writing. The notice must be given a reasonable time before the school proposes to do the assessment, and it must include information about procedural safeguards, a clear explanation of the reasons for the assessment, and a description of each of the assessment procedures to be used.

There are additional legal requirements. The request for permission for assessment and all related communications must be clearly written in understandable language. When necessary, the notice must be translated into the parents' native language or other mode of communication (e.g., Braille), unless this is not feasible. If the parents do not use a written language for communication, the notice must be translated orally. The educational agency must document that these procedures have been followed. The goal is to ensure that, when parents agree to the assessment, the consent they give is an informed consent.

Administration, Scoring, and Interpretation of Assessment Procedures

Guidelines for administration, scoring, and interpretation of formal assessment procedures such as norm-referenced tests are discussed in detail in Chapter 4. These guidelines are supplemented by the specific directions that appear in the manuals that accompany published tests. Chapter 5 describes similar procedures for informal assessment procedures such as observations, interviews, and inventories. Although manuals are not available for most informal measures, principles of good practice guide professionals in their use of these assessment tools.

Like other aspects of the assessment process, special education laws govern the selection and use of assessment procedures. For example, assessment devices must be technically sound, and standardized tests must be administered by trained professionals who follow the directions provided by the test producer. A more complete discussion of these legal requirements appears in Chapter 3.

Reporting Results

When students are assessed for possible special education services, results must be reported to parents, whether or not the student is ultimately found to be eligible for services. The results are presented at a meeting of the evaluation team, and parents are to serve as members of this team. Parents must be clearly told if the student has a disability and is eligible for special education services. If so, the components of an Individualized Education Program (IEP) are developed.

Federal special education laws also specify that parents must be informed of their right to have access to all school records concerning their child's identification, assessment, and placement in special education. Frequently, parents wish to examine the records to better understand the school's basis for concern. A school system must respond promptly to such a request, in no more than 45 days.

If the parents have any questions about information in the records, the school system must also supply an explanation. If the parents feel statements in the records are inaccurate or misleading, or violate the child's rights to privacy, they can ask the school system to amend them. The school system must then respond within a reasonable amount of time. If the school refuses the parents' request, it must inform the parents and advise them of their right to a hearing.

Furthermore, these records are maintained by strict regulations of confidentiality. Parents must be informed of the procedures to store, disclose to another person, retain, or destroy any records concerning the child. Parents must give their permission before information concerning their child is given to anyone not authorized within the school system. Persons other than the parents and authorized school personnel who examine the records must list their name, the date, and their intent.

When the school system no longer needs the information for educational purposes, it must inform the parents. At their request, the records must be destroyed. Otherwise, only a limited set of information, such as the student's name, address, and grades, is retained.

By law, the school system must provide information about where parents can obtain an independent educational evaluation, if requested. The parents have the right to such as evaluation at public expense if they disagree with the school system's evaluation and the school system does not or cannot substantiate its own evaluation. If parents initiate an evaluation, the results must be considered by the school system in making any decision about special education services and may be presented at any hearing on the matter.

Decisions About Eligibility

Decisions about eligibility are usually made at the team meeting when results are reported. These legal decisions are based upon the eligibility criteria in federal laws and regulations as well as state and district policies. According to federal guidelines, the team must decide whether the student has a disability and, if so, if that disability adversely affects school performance. The disability must be one covered by federal law. Also, students with school performance problems due to limited proficiency in English or lack of instruction in reading or math are not considered disabled.

The school must provide parents with a copy of the assessment report and documentation of the eligibility decision. The next step, if the student is determined to be eligible for special education, is development of an individualized plan for the student's educational program.

PROGRAM PLANNING

The team now turns its attention to instructional matters and meets to develop the educational plan for the student. Once the student's parents have agreed to the proposed plan, the student's special education program can begin.

Design of the Individualized Education Program (IEP)

The IEP meeting must take place within 30 days of the determination that the student has a disability and is in need of special education services. The IEP must be developed before the student begins to receive special services and must be implemented without any undue delay after the meeting. Furthermore, a similar meeting must be held at least annually to reexamine the appropriateness of the IEP and revise it, if necessary.

The IEP team is composed of the same members as the assessment team. Thus, the team includes the student's parents and the professionals who will provide services to the student, such as special education teachers, general education teachers, and others as needed. Other required team members include a representative of the educational agency who has knowledge about special education, the general curriculum, and school resources (often the school principal or vice principal), and a person who is knowledgeable about the interpretation of assessment results (often the special education teacher or school psychologist). Students themselves may serve as members of the IEP team, when appropriate.

Schools must take steps to encourage parents to attend IEP meetings and participate in the development of their child's IEP. Requirements include:

1. Parents must be notified early enough in advance of the meeting that they have an opportunity to attend.
2. Parents must be informed of the purpose of the meeting, its time and location, and the persons who will attend.
3. Meetings must be scheduled at a mutually agreed-upon time and place.
4. When parents cannot attend, the school must use other means of communication to ensure parental participation (e.g., individual and conference telephone calls).
5. An IEP meeting may be held without the student's parents if the parents choose not to attend. In this case, the school must keep detailed records of all attempts to communicate with the parents and any responses.
6. At the meeting, every effort must be made to ensure that parents understand the proceedings. This may involve the use of interpreters

TABLE 2–3
IEP Requirements

---

§300.347 Content of the IEP
(a) *General.* The IEP for each child with a disability must include—
    (1) A statement of the child's present levels of educational performance, including—
        (i) How the child's disability affects the child's involvement and progress in the general curriculum (i.e., the same curriculum as for nondisabled children); or
        (ii) For preschool children, as appropriate, how the disability affects the child's participation in appropriate activities;
    (2) A statement of measurable annual goals, including benchmarks or short-term objectives, related to—
        (i) Meeting the child's needs that result from the child's disability to enable the child to be involved in and progress in the general curriculum (i.e., the same curriculum as for nondisabled children), or for preschool children, as appropriate, to participate in appropriate activities; and
        (ii) Meeting each of the child's other educational needs that result from the child's disability;
    (3) A statement of the special education and related services and supplementary aids and services to be provided to the child, or on behalf of the child, and a statement of the program modifications or supports for school personnel that will be provided for the child—
        (i) To advance appropriately toward attaining the annual goals;
        (ii) To be involved and progress in the general curriculum in accordance with paragraph (a)(1) of this section and to participate in extracurricular and other nonacademic activities; and
        (iii) To be educated and participate with other children with disabilities and nondisabled children in the activities described in this section;
    (4) An explanation of the extent, if any, to which the child will not participate with nondisabled children in the regular class and in the activities described in paragraph (a)(3) of this section;
    (5) (i) A statement of any individual modifications in the administration of State or district-wide assessments of student achievement that are needed in order for the child to participate in the assessment; and
        (ii) If the IEP Team determines that the child will not participate in a particular State or district-wide assessment of student achievement (or part of an assessment), a statement of—
            (A) Why that assessment is not appropriate for the child; and
            (B) How the child will be assessed;
    (6) The projected date for the beginning of the services and modifications described in paragraph (a)(3) of this section, and the anticipated frequency, location, and duration of those services and modifications; and
    (7) A statement of—
        (i) How the child's progress toward the annual goals described in paragraph (a)(2) of this section will be measured; and

---

for parents who are deaf or those who speak languages other than English.

7. Parents must receive a copy of their child's IEP at no cost.

Professionals and parents make decisions about the student's educational program based on the data gathered in the assessment. Many types of assessment data are needed to develop the components of the IEP. In fact, the full array of educational assessment procedures described in Chapter 1 may be used to make these instructional decisions.

Specific guidelines govern the content of the IEP. According to current federal laws, the IEP must contain information about:

a. The student's present levels of educational performance;

b. Annual goals and short-term objectives (also called benchmarks);

c. Needed special education and related services, supplementary aids and services, and program modifications and supports;

d. The extent to which the student will not participate with nondisabled students in the general education classroom and other school activities;

e. Procedures for the student's participation in state- or district-wide assessments of student achievement;

(ii) How the child's parents will be regularly informed (through such means as periodic report cards), at least as often as parents are informed of their nondisabled children's progress, of—
    (A) Their child's progress toward the annual goals; and
    (B) The extent to which that progress is sufficient to enable the child to achieve the goals by the end of the year.

(b) *Transition services.* The IEP must include—

(1) For each student with a disability beginning at age 14 (or younger, if determined appropriate by the IEP Team), and updated annually, a statement of the transition services needs of the student under the applicable components of the student's IEP that focuses on the student's courses of study (such as participation in advanced-placement courses or a vocational education program); and

(2) For each student beginning at age 16 (or younger, if determined appropriate by the IEP Team), a statement of needed transition services for the student, including, if appropriate, a statement of the interagency responsibilities or any needed linkages.

§300.346

(a) (2) *Consideration of special factors.* The IEP Team also shall—

(i) In the case of a child whose behavior impedes his or her learning or that of others, consider, if appropriate, strategies, including positive behavioral interventions, strategies, and supports to address that behavior;

(ii) In the case of a child with limited English proficiency, consider the language needs of the child as those needs relate to the child's IEP;

(iii) In the case of a child who is blind or visually impaired, provide for instruction in Braille and the use of Braille unless the IEP Team determines, after an evaluation of the child's reading and writing skills, needs, and appropriate reading and writing media (including an evaluation of the child's future needs for instruction in Braille or the use of Braille), that instruction in Braille or the use of Braille is not appropriate for the child;

(iv) Consider the communication needs of the child, and in the case of a child who is deaf or hard of hearing, consider the child's language and communication needs, opportunities for direct communications with peers and professional personnel in the child's language and communication mode, academic level, and full range of needs, including opportunities for direct instruction in the child's language and communication mode; and

(v) Consider whether the child requires assistive technology devices and services.

Note: From *Federal Register,* 1999 (Mar. 12), Washington, DC: U.S. Government Printing Office.

f. Strategies for measuring progress toward annual goals and informing parents of that progress;
g. For older students, transition services; and
h. When appropriate, special factors such as behavioral needs, language needs, instruction in Braille, communication needs, and assistive technology devices and services.

Table 2–3 presents excerpts from the 1997 IDEA Amendments regulations that address the content of the IEP.

Although the components of the IEP are mandated by federal laws, the IEP form itself is not. The form is developed by individual school districts or other educational agencies, causing some variation from one locale to another. See Figure 2–4 for one example of how federal IEP requirements have been translated into a workable form.

It is important to recognize that several components of the IEP focus on the general education curriculum and the student's access to and participation in that curriculum. In describing the student's present levels of educational performance, the team must address the effects of the disability on the student's ability to participate in the general curriculum. The team must develop annual goals and benchmarks (short-term objectives) related to involvement and progress in the

Orchard County Public Schools
Individualized Education Program (IEP)

Student Information

Name _____ Birthdate _____
Male ☐   Female ☐   Age _____ Grade _____ Ethnicity _____
Social Security Number _____ - _____ - _____   LEP   Yes ☐   No ☐
Home Language _____ Interpreter Required   Yes ☐   No ☐
Address _____
School of Residence _____
School of Attendance _____
Rationale for placement, if other than student's school of residence:

_____

Parent/Guardian Information

Name _____
Address _____
Home phone _____ Work phone _____
Interpreter Required   Yes ☐   No ☐

Assessment Information

Present Levels of Performance (include how disability affects involvement and progress in general curriculum)

_____
_____
_____
_____
_____

Modifications needed in State- and district-wide assessments _____
_____
_____

Why needed _____
_____

IEP Information

Date of Next IEP _____ Date of 3-year Review _____
Primary Disability Category _____
Primary Placement _____
P.E. Type _____
Transportation _____

Special Education & Related Services; Supplementary Aids & Services; Program Modifications	Start Date	Duration	Frequency	Location

FIGURE 2–4
Sample IEP Form

Extent to which student will not participate with nondisabled students in regular class _____

Explanation _____

Annual Goals, Short-term Objectives/Benchmarks, Progress Measures _____

Parents/guardians will be informed of student's progress via _____

As appropriate, the following factors were considered in the development of this IEP:
- ☐ for students whose behavior impedes learning, positive behavioral interventions, strategies and supports
- ☐ for students with limited English proficiency, language needs
- ☐ for students who are blind or visually impaired, instruction in and use of Braille and appropriate reading and writing media
- ☐ communication needs of the student
- ☐ for students who are deaf or hard of hearing, language and communication needs
- ☐ assistive technology devices and services

Transition Services
- ☐ Transition service needs included in this IEP
- ☐ Transition service needs described in attached Individualized Transition Plan
- ☐ Student has been informed of his or her rights

Signatures

My due process rights have been explained to me.
- ☐ I consent to the IEP.
- ☐ I consent to portions of the IEP as described on the attached form.
- ☐ I do not consent to the IEP.

Parent/Guardian's Signature	Date
Student's Signature	Date
Signature of Administrator/Designee	Date
Signature of General Education Teacher	Date
Signature of Special Education Teacher/Specialist	Date
Signature/Title of Additional Participant	Date
Signature/Title of Additional Participant	Date
Signature of Interpreter	Date

Developed by Tamarah M. Ashton PhD., Assistant Director of the Enhancing Writing Skills Project LITT, San Diego State University.

Note: From *Teaching Special Students in General Education Classrooms* (5th ed.) (pp. 49–51) by R. B. Lewis and D. H. Doorlag, 1999, Upper Saddle River, NJ: Merrill/Prentice-Hall. Copyright 1999 by Prentice-Hall, Inc. Reprinted by permission.

general curriculum. The team can specify several types of services for the student, if these are needed. These services include not only special education and related services, but also services and supports in the general education classroom. In addition, the team must describe how the student will participate in the State- or district-wide assessments of achievement (or, if participation is not considered appropriate, the alternative assessment procedures). The IEP must identify strategies for measuring the student's progress toward annual goals and specify a schedule for notifying parents of that progress; that schedule must be at least as frequent as the report card schedule for students without disabilities. Finally, the IEP team must explain any placement that constitutes a removal from the general education classroom. Although current federal laws do not require that students with disabilities remain in the general education classroom at all times, the IEP team must justify any removal to another educational setting or any action that curtails students' ability to participate in extracurricular activities or other nonacademic school activities.

Placement of students with disabilities is governed by the principle of Least Restrictive Environment (LRE). Regulations for the 1997 IDEA Amendments define LRE in this way:

> (b) Each public agency shall ensure—
> (1) That to the maximum extent appropriate, children with disabilities . . . are educated with children who are nondisabled; and
> (2) That special classes, separate schooling or other removal of children with disabilities from the regular educational environment occurs only if the nature or severity of the disability is such that education in regular classes with the use of supplementary aids and services cannot be achieved satisfactorily. (*Federal Register,* 1999, §300.550)

These regulations also require that local educational agencies maintain a continuum of alternative placements for students with disabilities. This continuum must include services provided in conjunction with regular class placement (e.g., resource rooms and itinerant instruction) as well as separate placements such as special classes, special schools, home instruction, and instruction in hospitals and institutions. Although these requirements appear somewhat contradictory,

they are not. In fact, they underscore one of the most important assumptions underlying the provision of special education services: All decisions about students with disabilities, including decisions about placement, must be made on an individual basis. Thus, the IEP team considers the needs of an individual student in order to design an educational program tailored to that student's unique needs.

Parental Agreement to the IEP

After parents and professionals work together to design the student's educational program, the parents must give their consent before the IEP can be implemented. Parents must approve the provisions of the IEP, including the educational services to be provided to the student. As with other important decisions, parents must give informed consent. This means that the IEP must be explained to parents in clear, understandable language with written or oral translations, as needed. The school must document that this and all other due process procedures have been followed.

Sometimes the parents and the school do not agree on one or more aspects of the IEP, such as the amount of support to be provided or the placement recommended for the student. In such cases, there are several options available to both parties in the dispute. The first is voluntary mediation. In mediation, the parents and the educational agency meet with an impartial mediator in an attempt to resolve the dispute. If the conflict is resolved, a written mediation agreement must result.

If mediation does not end in an agreement or if either party does not choose to participate, the next option is an impartial due process hearing. At such hearings, parents have the right to be advised by legal counsel and by persons knowledgeable about students with disabilities. The educational agency must inform the parents of free or low-cost legal services and other relevant services, if available in the area. An impartial hearing officer presides over the deliberations; that officer may not be an employee of the state or local educational agency. At the hearing, both parties have the right to present evidence, confront and cross-examine witnesses, and call their own witnesses. Both parties must disclose evaluations and recommendations they plan to present at least 5 days prior to the hearing. A record of the hearing, the finding of facts, and the decision must be provided to parents at no cost.

Decisions made in impartial due process hearings are final, unless the parents and/or the school wish to appeal to the state educational agency. The decision made by the state is final, unless either party wishes to take civil action. Civil actions can be brought in a state or U.S. district court.

Federal special education laws set up timelines for conducting both the impartial due process hearing and the state-level review so that decisions are made in an expeditious manner. In most cases, the student remains in the current educational placement during this period, unless the parents and the school system agree to an alternative placement. However, there are special procedures for placement in alternative educational settings for students charged with serious offenses such as use of illegal drugs or carrying a weapon to school.

PROGRAM IMPLEMENTATION AND EVALUATION

Once the student's parents have given their consent, the IEP can be implemented. The student's progress in the program is monitored and, at least once each year, the IEP is reviewed and revised. Also, at least every 3 years, the student's eligibility for special education is reconsidered. The purpose of these evaluation strategies is to determine whether the student's educational program is effective and, if it is not, to modify the program so that it more adequately meets the student's needs.

IEP Implementation and Ongoing Monitoring of Progress

The IEP must be implemented as soon as possible after it has been designed by the team and approved by the student's parents. All persons with responsibility for delivering services must have access to the IEP and be informed of their specific responsibilities in its implementation. This includes general education teachers involved in the student's education as well as special education teachers and others such as counselors and

speech-language pathologists. In particular, professionals must be made aware of the supports, accommodations, and modifications to be provided to the student.

The IEP sets forth the annual goals for the educational program, and these goals and their accompanying objectives become the framework for evaluation of the student's progress. The IEP must specify how the team will assess progress toward annual goals and how that progress will be reported to parents. Several types of assessment procedures are used to gather the data needed to monitor progress but, in most cases, informal assessment strategies are preferred. For example, observations, analysis of work samples, criterion-referenced tests, and informal inventories provide information about student performance and help professionals determine whether changes should be made in the instructional program.

In addition, the IEP describes the student's participation in state- or district-wide assessments of student achievement. There are three possible options. First, the student can participate in the assessments under conditions identical to those for typical students. Second, modifications may be made in administration procedures. For example, the student may be given extra time to complete a test or be allowed to type, rather than handwrite, essays. Third, if the IEP team determines that participation in such assessments is not appropriate for the student, the team must explain why and describe how the student will be assessed to monitor his or her progress in the general curriculum.

Annual Review of the IEP

At minimum, the IEP must be reviewed on an annual basis. In this review, the team evaluates the student's progress toward the annual goals. Both formal and informal assessment procedures may be used to gather data for this review. Norm-referenced tests may be administered to determine whether the student's performance has improved in relation to the performance of age or grade peers. Teachers and other team members may report results of classroom observations, portfolio assessments, criterion-referenced testing, and interviews with students and parents.

These data are used to decide whether the educational program described in the IEP should be continued, modified, or discontinued. If the annual goals have been achieved and no further special education needs are apparent, the student may be dismissed from special education. However, if all goals have not been fully accomplished or if additional goals are necessary, the IEP is revised and the student continues to receive special education services.

Schools must provide the special education and other services listed on the IEP and make a good-faith effort to assist students to meet their annual goals and objectives. However, schools and teachers may not be held accountable if students fail to meet those goals. When students do not achieve as expected, parents have the right to ask that the IEP be revised. For example, parents might request a change in the types of services provided to their child or an increase in the amount of services.

Periodic Reevaluation of Eligibility

A review of each student's eligibility for special education must be held every 3 years, or more often if requested by the student's parent or teacher. The purpose of this review is to determine whether the student continues to require special education services. As with the initial eligibility decision, a team meets to plan the data-collection process. Existing information about the student is reviewed, an assessment plan is prepared, and parents are asked for their consent before the assessment is conducted. In some cases, the team may decide that no additional information is needed to make the eligibility decision. If so, the team notifies the parents of its determination that further assessment is not necessary. If the parents agree with this decision, the student's eligibility is reviewed using existing information. If the parents disagree, they have the right to request that an assessment take place.

STUDY GUIDE

REVIEW QUESTIONS

1. Special education assessment provides information for two types of decisions: _____ decisions and _____ decisions.
2. Informal assessment procedures are preferred for _____ decisions and formal procedures for _____ decisions.
3. Place these steps in the assessment process in order. Write *1* before the step that occurs first, *2* before the step that occurs second, and so on.
   _____ Parental permission for assessment
   _____ Eligibility decisions
   _____ Screening
   _____ Annual review of the IEP
   _____ Referral
   _____ Design of the IEP
   _____ Design of the IAP
   _____ Prereferral interventions
   _____ Reevaluation of eligibility
   _____ Parental approval of the IEP
4. IAP stands for _____ _____ _____.
5. The three areas of functioning that are assessed when mild disabilities are suspected are general intellectual performance, _____ performance, and index of the _____.

6. Decide whether each of the following statements about the rights of parents is true or false.

_____ Parents must be notified in writing when their child has been referred for special education assessment.

_____ Parents must give their consent for special education assessment.

_____ Parents can examine only those portions of their child's school records that are not confidential.

_____ Parents who disagree with a decision of the school can request an impartial due process hearing.

_____ Parents must be informed of the results of eligibility decisions.

_____ Parents must obtain a judge's order before they can obtain an independent educational evaluation of their child.

7. _____ _____ procedures are designed to safeguard the rights of students with disabilities and their parents.

8. If a student's parents are not available, a surrogate parent can be appointed to represent the student's interests. (True or False)

9. Give three examples of prereferral intervention strategies.

10. According to federal law, only formal assessment procedures can be listed on the IAP. (True or False)

11. Districts have the right to bar students with disabilities from participation in state- or district-wide assessments of student achievement. (True or False)

12. The IEP team contains the same members as the team responsible for eligibility assessment. (True or False)

13. Match the IEP requirement in Column A with the examples in Column B.

Column A	*Column B*
a. Present levels of educational performance	_____ Jon will receive assistance from the resource teacher in reading for 30 minutes 3 days a week.
b. Annual goals and benchmarks	_____ Portfolio assessment of student work samples and teacher observation
c. Special education and related services	_____ Yvonne is achieving at grade level in all subjects except mathematics.
d. Supplementary aids, services, modifications, and supports	_____ Rose will write a complete sentence beginning with a capital letter and ending with appropriate punctuation.
e. Strategies for measuring progress	_____ Louie has significant problems in spelling and written expression.
	_____ Increase oral reading skills to the grade 3 level.
	_____ Dirk will use books on tape for 7th grade English.

14. According to the Least Restrictive Environment principle, students with disabilities should be educated with nondisabled students

a. at all times.

b. when clearly feasible.

c. to the maximum extent appropriate.

d. when parents give their permission.

15. When parents and the school disagree over one or more aspects of the IEP, the first step is
   a. an impartial due process hearing.
   b. mediation.
   c. a state-level review.
   d. civil action in a state or U.S. district court.

ACTIVITIES

1. Interview a special education teacher, school psychologist, or other professional about the assessment process in his or her school or district. What procedures are followed in prereferral, referral, assessment planning, and determination of eligibility? How could the process be improved?
2. Examine the IEP form used in a local district. Does it contain all of the components required by federal law?
3. Contact a school and ask for a copy of the notice given to parents advising them of their rights related to special education. Are all important rights included? Is the notice written clearly in language understandable to persons who are not special educators? Identify those portions of the notice that you feel are most in need of revision and rewrite them.

DISCUSSION QUESTIONS

1. Describe the differences between legal and instructional decisions. Discuss how these differences influence the choice of assessment procedures.
2. Tell why it is just as important to develop an Individualized Assessment Plan as it is to develop an Individualized Education Program. Explain the role of individualization in special education in your response.
3. Why is the prereferral intervention stage an important step in the assessment process? What potential problems does the inclusion of this stage prevent?
4. Federal laws accord parents equal status with professionals in decision making about the education of students with disabilities. What efforts must schools make to ensure that parents participate in their child's special education? What important contributions can parents make?

PART II

ASSESSMENT SKILLS
FOR SPECIAL EDUCATORS

CHAPTER 3

SELECTION OF ASSESSMENT TOOLS

- Criteria for the Selection of Assessment Tools
- Evaluating Technical Quality
- Test Scores and Other Assessment Results
- Promoting Nonbiased Assessment

Assessment is an information-gathering activity. Its purpose is to provide answers to important educational questions, whether these concern identification and placement, instructional planning, or monitoring of student progress and program effectiveness. The assessment process begins with careful planning, and one of the most critical preparatory steps is selection of appropriate tools.

The tools selected for assessment influence the success of the data-gathering process. Inaccurate measures produce useless and potentially harmful information; tools that are inappropriate, even if their results are accurate, fail to provide the type of information necessary to assist educational decision making.

The appropriateness of an assessment tool depends upon the context in which it will be used. Although poor-quality measures that yield inaccurate results are never appropriate, most tools provide information useful for some purposes, for some students, in some situations. In judging the worth of a measure or strategy, the professional first assures its technical adequacy and then determines its value for the particular assessment task.

Criticism of special education assessment practices in the 1960s and early 1970s centered on the inappropriate use of assessment tools, specifically the misuse of standardized intelligence tests with culturally and linguistically diverse students. Leaders such as Lloyd Dunn (1968) charged that special classes for students with mental retardation contained disproportionate numbers of children from minority groups. Researchers such as Jane Mercer (1973) attributed this overrepresentation to reliance on a single test score, the IQ, for placement decisions. The appropriateness of standard intelligence measures for diverse students was challenged in the courts. *Diana v. State Board of Education* (1970) questioned the use of English language IQ tests with children whose home language was Spanish. *Larry P. v. Riles* (1972, 1979, 1984) sought to establish the discriminatory nature of dominant culture intelligence measures for African American students.

Although some controversies surrounding testing continue, assessment practices today are much improved. One major impetus for this change was the enactment of federal and state laws setting forth specific guidelines for special education assessment and placement.

CRITERIA FOR THE SELECTION OF ASSESSMENT TOOLS

One purpose of the landmark special education law, the Education for All Handicapped Children Act of 1975, was the establishment of a set of procedures to guard against inappropriate assessment and placement practices. This law provided safeguards to prevent recurrence of past abuses. These safeguards are preserved and strengthened in the current federal statute, PL 105-17, the Individuals with Disabilities Education Act (IDEA) Amendments of 1997, as Table 3–1 illustrates. Appropriate assessment procedures are mandated by federal laws and regulations and the state laws resulting from them. However, actual practice may fall short of intended goals.

Legal Guidelines for Assessment

The regulations for PL 105-17 provide specific guidelines for the evaluation and placement of students with disabilities in special education programs. This law focuses on the use of assessment information for legal decisions, that is, decisions about identification and determination of eligibility for special education services. This type of information has implications for long-range instructional decisions such as those associated with design of the Individualized Education Program (IEP). However, no attempt is made to regulate classroom assessment and the day-to-day instructional decisions practitioners face.

PL 105-17 includes several guidelines for the selection of assessment tools and the conduct of the assessment process. They are described in the following sections.

TABLE 3–1

Legal Safeguards Against Assessment Abuses

PAST ABUSES	SAFEGUARDS
Students evaluated for special education without notice to parents or parental consent	Parents must be given written notice prior to evaluation; parents must give consent before evaluation. [§300.503, §300.505]
Culturally biased tests used in evaluation	Tests must be selected and administered so that they are not discriminatory on a racial or cultural basis. [§300.532]
Non-English-speaking students assessed in English	Tests must be provided and administered in the child's native language or other mode of communication, unless clearly not feasible. [§300.532]
Tests administered by untrained or poorly trained personnel	Trained and knowledgeable personnel must administer standardized tests according to test instructions. [§300.532]
Poor quality assessment instruments used for evaluation	Assessment instruments must be technically sound; tests must have been validated for the specific purpose for which they are used. [§300.532]
Tests used that penalized students with disabilities	Tests for children with impaired sensory, manual, or speaking skills must accurately reflect the child's ability, not the impaired skills (unless those skills are the subject of assessment). [§300.532]
Placement in services for students with mental retardation based solely on IQ scores	No one procedure may be used as the sole criterion for determination of a disability or of the educational program; tests selected for use in evaluation must include not merely those that yield a single general intelligence quotient. [§300.532]
Placement decisions made without a complete evaluation of the student	Individuals must be assessed in all areas related to the suspected disability (e.g., health, vision, hearing, social and emotional status, general intelligence, academic performance, communicative status, motor abilities); information must be considered from several sources (e.g., aptitude and achievement tests, parent input, teacher recommendations, physical condition, social or cultural background, adaptive behavior). [§300.532, §300.535]
Assessment focused only on the disability, not the educational program	Assessment must provide information directly relevant to the child's educational needs and the child's involvement and progress in the general curriculum. [§300.532]

The numbers in brackets refer to sections of the *Final Regulations* for PL 105-17, the Individuals with Disabilities Education Act (IDEA) Amendments of 1997 (*Federal Register,* 1999).

Note: From "Assessing Retarded Development" by R. B. Lewis, in *Mental Retardation* (p. 36) by P. T. Cegelka and H. J. Prehm (Eds.), 1982, New York: Merrill/Macmillan. Copyright 1982 by Macmillan Publishing Company. Adapted by permission.

Assessment is Nondiscriminatory. Federal special education law expressly forbids three types of discrimination. First, assessment tools must be free of racial and cultural bias. Tests and other procedures must be selected on this basis, and care must be taken to prevent the intrusion of bias into test administration. Second, if a student's native language is not English, every effort must be made to provide assessment tools in the student's language. This mandate extends not only to individuals who speak languages other than English, but also to those whose mode of communication is not spoken language. For example, students with hearing impairments who communicate through sign language should be assessed in sign language. However, according to PL 105-17, because appropriate assessment tools are not available in all languages, assessment may proceed if testing in the native language is clearly not feasible. Third, assessment tools must not discriminate on the basis of disability. Unless the purpose of assessment is to study the disability, tests and other procedures should bypass the student's problem. Specifically, the law states that tests must be chosen so that sensory, motor, and speaking impairments do not interfere with the assessment of other skills and abilities. For instance, if the purpose of assessment is to study spelling achievement, the student with impaired motor skills should not be required to write his or her answers.

Assessment Focuses on Educational Needs. The major purpose of assessment is to determine educational needs. Although the presence of a disability must be established to support eligibility for special education services, simply identifying a student as having a learning disability or being mentally retarded is insufficient. Attention must also be directed to the specific educational needs resulting from the disability. In addition, assessment must focus on the student's ability to participate in the general curriculum and the progress he or she has made in that curriculum.

Assessment is Comprehensive. All important areas of student performance must be studied. Although intelligence tests may be used, they must be accompanied by other measures that assess educational needs. The results of a single measure must never be the sole basis for placement in special education. The assessment must be so comprehensive that no important area of performance is neglected. Health, vision, hearing, social and emotional status, general intelligence, academic performance, communicative status, and motor abilities may be considered, if these are areas of potential need for the student under assessment. Several sources must be consulted for information about the student. These include results of formal and informal assessments carried out by special educators and other professionals, input from parents, and classroom teachers' observations and recommendations.

Assessment Tools are Technically Adequate and Administered by Trained Professionals. Assessment devices must be good measurement tools that have been validated for the specific purpose for which they will be used. They must display adequate technical quality to ensure accurate results. If the goal is study of reading achievement, the instrument chosen must be a valid measure of reading achievement. Assessment must also be conducted by trained professionals. The administration, scoring, and interpretation rules specified in the measure's manual must be scrupulously followed.

Rights of Students with Disabilities and Their Parents are Protected during Assessment. Throughout the assessment process, safeguards protect the rights of individuals with disabilities and their parents or guardians. As Chapter 2 discussed, parents must be notified when a student is referred for assessment; they must receive information about their rights; and they must give informed consent before assessment begins. No student may be placed in special education without a comprehensive assessment that includes evaluation of his or her educational needs. The student's progress in special education must be evaluated at least annually, and a complete reevaluation conducted at least every 3 years. Parents may review school records that concern their child's identification, assessment, and placement in special education; they also have the right to an explanation of the assessment results. In addition, parents participate as members of the IEP team and assist in the development of their child's educational program.

Professional Guidelines

There are several sources of guidance in the selection of assessment tools in addition to legal requirements. An important resource is *Standards for Educational and Psychological Testing* (1985), prepared by a joint committee of the American Educational Research Association, the American Psychological Association, and the National Council on Measurement in Education. This guide for test users and producers contains standards for tests, manuals, and reports; it also includes standards for reports of research on reliability and validity and standards for the use of tests.

Test catalogues, websites of test publishers, test manuals, and other information provided by producers of assessment tools may also aid in the selection process. Test catalogues and publishers' websites provide an overview of available instruments, particularly newer ones, and often include brief descriptions of each measure. However, the more detailed information needed for selection decisions can be found in test manuals. Manuals should discuss important characteristics of the instrument, including purpose, the procedures used for development, and data on psychometric quality. Not all manuals are complete, and few seek to emphasize the weak points of the measure, so the buyer must beware.

The Mental Measurements Yearbook series offers assistance in the evaluation of specific measures. Issued every few years, these references contain reviews of commercially available psychological, educational, and vocational tests. The most recent edition, the *Thirteenth Mental Measurements Yearbook* (Impara & Plake, 1998), includes information on more than 300 tests. The companion series, *Tests in Print,* serves as an index to the yearbooks. Another resource is *Tests* (Maddox, 1997). The fourth edition of this guide contains descriptions of approximately 2,000 tests used commonly in psychology, education, and business. Information about tests and other procedures is also available at the website of the ERIC Clearinghouse on Assessment and Evaluation (www.ericae.net).

Professional journals are the best source for research relating to assessment and for critical reviews of newly developed assessment tools. *Diagnostique,* published by the Council for Educational Diagnostic Services of the Council for Exceptional Children (CEC), focuses on special education assessment. Other journals that often contain articles about assessment tools and their use in special education are *Exceptional Children, Journal of Special Education,* and *Reme-*

dial and Special Education, as well as those journals that address specific disabilities (e.g., *Journal of Learning Disabilities, Behavioral Disorders,* and *Training in Mental Retardation and Developmental Disabilities).*

Evaluation Criteria

Whether an assessment team is faced with choosing the tools to gather information for an eligibility decision or a classroom teacher is searching for a measure to evaluate academic progress, the task is the same: selection of the most accurate, effective, and efficient means of data collection. The tools for assessment must be the most appropriate available. The questions that follow provide a structure for the evaluation of assessment tools.

Does the Tool Fit the Purpose of Assessment? A technically excellent assessment device is useless if it does not provide the particular information needed to answer an assessment question. Because the type of tool needed is related to the purpose of the assessment, the ways in which assessment information will be used must be clear. If the goal is to answer questions about a student's standing in relation to his or her peers, then norm-referenced measures are appropriate. If questions concern classroom behaviors, observational strategies are indicated; for questions about mastery of specific academic skills, the most valuable information sources may be criterion-referenced tests, informal inventories, classroom quizzes, and teacher checklists.

The form in which assessment results appear is also important. Sometimes comparative scores such as percentile ranks or standard scores are necessary; for other purposes, a simple frequency count of the number of times a student performs a particular behavior will suffice.

Other considerations are the content and scope of the measure: the specific achievement, aptitude, or attitude areas that are assessed. If the goal is study of a student's reading abilities, a test of mathematics skills is obviously inappropriate. Less apparent is the choice between a global achievement test designed to screen for problems in reading and other academic subjects and a diagnostic reading test that assesses decoding, structural analysis, comprehension, and vocabulary skills. Before it is possible to select the most appropriate tool, the purpose of the assessment must be clearly understood.

Is the Tool Appropriate for the Student?   The assessment instrument or strategy must fit the student's needs and abilities. If norm-referenced measures are used, the student's characteristics must be consistent with those of the norm group with which the test was standardized. The age or grade of the student is also important, because test norms are generally arranged by chronological age or grade in school. For instance, if a 5-year-old is administered a test normed with 6- to 12-year-olds, it is impossible to convert his or her responses to norm-referenced test scores.

With any type of measure, the assessment tasks must be compatible with the skills of the student. No student should be asked to attempt tasks clearly beyond his or her current functioning level. In addition to the content and difficulty level of the assessment task, other important skill considerations are:

- *Presentation mode,* or the method by which the test task is presented to the student. Is the student required to listen, read, look at figures or pictures, attend to a demonstration?
- *Response mode,* or the method by which the student must answer the question or perform the specified task. Must the student speak, make a check or darken a square, write words or sentences, point to the correct response?
- *Group versus individual administration,* or whether the student takes part in assessment as one of a group or as the only participant.
- *Time factors* such as the length of the assessment, particularly as it relates to the student's attention span, and whether the student is required to respond under timed conditions.

Tools should capitalize on the student's strengths rather than penalize weaknesses. Individual measures are more appropriate for students with difficulty maintaining attention during group testing. Students who write poorly should be assessed with measures that allow oral responses, unless the purpose of assessment is the study of writing skills. The assessment device should not discriminate against the student on the basis of race, culture, language, gender, or disability.

Is the Tool Appropriate for the Tester?   The assessment device must match the skills of the professional using it. No tool should be selected unless adequately trained personnel are available to take responsibility for administration of the measure, scoring of student responses, and interpretation of results. In untrained hands, even the best instrument can produce erroneous information.

Is the Tool Technically Adequate?   Before confidence can be placed in the results of an assessment tool, its quality must be demonstrated. The techniques used to construct the measure must be sound, it must produce reliable data, and it must show validity. Information on the measurement characteristics of norm-referenced standardized measures is generally presented in the test manual or a technical supplement. The same types of information may be available for less formal measures such as rating scales, criterion-referenced tests, checklists, and inventories. However, in many cases, the technical quality of informal instruments remains unknown. Although some technical considerations may not be relevant for certain types of informal measures (for example, standardization procedures in the case of unstandardized instruments), an assessment tool's reliability and validity and the methods used in its construction are always important.

Is the Tool an Efficient Data-Collection Mechanism? An efficient device produces the needed information with minimum expenditure of time and effort. Administration, preparation by the tester, scoring of assessment results, and interpretation of data are all factors to consider. Ease of use also influences efficiency; more difficult procedures typically take longer and introduce greater possibility of error. Measures are considered effective and efficient when their results are worth the time and effort of both student and professional.

If no available measure is appropriate for a particular assessment task, several options remain open. Two or more existing measures can be combined to produce a tool sufficiently comprehensive to collect the needed information. Or an instrument or data-collection strategy can be modified to fit the purposes of assessment and the characteristics of the student. However, when adaptations are made in procedures for standardized tests, test norms can no longer be used. Such measures should be considered informal and their results interpreted cautiously. Another alternative is to construct a new assessment tool that satisfies the demands of the situation. This solution is not simple and should be reserved for cases in which modification of available measures is clearly unacceptable. Devising a new assessment tool is time-consuming, and unless technical adequacy of the new device can be demonstrated, its quality remains unknown.

In many assessment situations, a professional or team puts together an assessment battery—a collection of tools designed to answer several assessment questions. For instance, in determining whether a student is eligible for special education, the team may pose a series of questions that necessitate the use of many types of assessment strategies. In selecting the measures for an assessment battery, these principles should be followed:

1. The assessment battery must be comprehensive and complete, but unnecessary duplication should be avoided.
2. An attempt should be made to select measures that include a variety of different activities.
3. In selecting the tools for an initial assessment, measures to substantiate the reasons for referral should be included.
4. In general, results of group measures should be used only as screening information.
5. If two procedures appear equally appropriate, the more efficient one should be selected.
6. If possible, only measures with known technical adequacy should be included in the battery.

EVALUATING TECHNICAL QUALITY

Technical quality refers to the adequacy of an assessment tool as a measurement device. Four major characteristics of an instrument are considered in the evaluation of technical quality: reliability, validity, measurement error, and, for norm-referenced and criterion-referenced measures, the reference group or standard against which a student's performance is compared. Before describing procedures for evaluating these characteristics, we will introduce some terminology used in the study of measurement.

Measurement Terminology

Everyone is familiar with common units of measurement—inches, centimeters, miles, pounds, pints, liters, and degrees. Each represents a scale for quantifying some physical property such as distance, weight, or temperature. Educational assessment is less precise because it deals with human, rather than physical, properties; the goal is the quantification of psychological dimensions such as aptitude, attitude, and achievement.

There are four types of measurement scales: nominal, ordinal, interval, and ratio scales.

Nominal

A nominal scale is divided into categories. For example, the students in a classroom could be categorized on the basis of hair color and sorted into blondes, brunettes, and redheads. In nominal measurement, no values are assigned to categories; categories are simply different from one another. Because of this, it is impossible to add, subtract, multiply, or divide this type of information. This restricts the ways in which nominal scales can be statistically analyzed.

Ordinal

Persons or other subjects of study are placed in sequence in an ordinal scale. In the classroom, the teacher might rank students according to their artistic ability: Maria, the class artist, is ranked first; then Henry, a skilled cartoonist; then Susette, a fair painter; and so forth. Ordinal scales only place individuals in position relative to one another; no assumption can be made about the distance between individuals. From the teacher's ranking of the class, we know Maria is more artistic than either Henry or Susette, but we do not know how much more. Maria may be just a little more proficient than Henry, or she may be six times more talented. Like nominal data, ordinal data cannot be arithmetically manipulated.

Interval

With interval scales, there are equal intervals between the units of measurement, and the scale begins at an arbitrary starting point. A quiz, for example, would yield interval data; John might earn a score of 10, Sally 8, Rose 6, and Harvey 5. Individuals can be ordered according to their scores; in addition, the distance between scores can be discussed. The distance between John's score of 10 and Sally's score of 8 is the same as the distance between Sally's score of 8 and Rose's score of 6. However, interval scales do not begin with a true zero; if a student earns a score of zero on a classroom quiz, it does not mean that he or she has zero information about the subject assessed. Thus, it is impossible to multiply or divide interval data; one cannot say that John's score of 10 represents two times as much knowledge as Harvey's score of 5. Despite this, most common statistical techniques are appropriate for interval data. Many psychological variables measured in educational assessment are arranged on interval scales.

Ratio

A ratio scale begins with a true zero and has equal intervals between units of measurement. These scales are considered the most sophisticated. They allow all arithmetic operations including multiplication and division, and any type of statistical procedure can be used. Unfortunately, few variables of interest in educational assessment are arranged on ratio scales; those that are include physical properties such as height and weight and also some physiological measures.

Descriptive statistics assist in summarizing information from all types of scales. Measures of central tendency describe a set or distribution of data with one index that represents the entire set. For example, instead of listing the exam scores of all 35 members of a class, the class mode, median, or mean can be computed. The *mode* is the most common value among a set of values, the score that occurs most frequently. The *median* is the middle score in a set of scores; one-half of the

scores are higher than the median score and one-half are lower. The *mean* is the arithmetic average of the scores and is computed by adding all scores together and dividing by the number of scores. If data are nominal, the only measure of central tendency that can be used is the mode. With ordinal data, the median is appropriate, as is the mode. Interval data allow the calculation of all three measures. For most interval data, the mean is the most accurate descriptor of central tendency. However, the median is a better choice if the distribution contains extreme scores.

Measures of variability are another type of descriptive statistic. Their purpose is description of the spread or dispersion of a distribution. Sets of scores, even those with identical means and medians, can differ in variability. One set might have scores clustering around the mean (e.g., 59, 60, 61) whereas another might have scattered scores (e.g., 40, 60, 80). The *range* can be used to describe scatter; it is the distance between the highest and lowest scores in the distribution. With interval data, a better estimate of variability is *standard deviation.* The standard deviation takes each score's relationship to the mean into account; the higher the standard deviation, the more variability within a set of scores. The computational formula for standard deviation (σ) is

$$\sigma = \sqrt{\frac{\sum X^2 - \dfrac{(\sum X)^2}{N}}{N}}$$

where $\sum$ signifies the addition operation, X the test scores, and N the number of cases. To determine $\sum X^2$, each score is squared; then the squares are added. To determine $(\sum X)^2$, the scores are first added; then the total sum is squared.

A third type of descriptive statistic is measures of *correlation.* These express the degree of relationship between two sets of scores. If two measures are highly correlated, the scores from one measure can be used to predict performance on the other. Several measures of correlation are available, but the most common is the Pearson product-moment correlation coefficient. The Pearson *r,* as it is often called, is appropriate for interval data. Correlation coefficients range in value from -1.00 to $+1.00$. A coefficient of 0 indicates no relationship between two sets of scores. A coefficient of +1.00 indicates a perfect positive correlation; individuals with the highest scores in the first set of scores also achieved the highest scores in the second set. A perfect negative correlation is represented by a coefficient of −1.00; in this case, the persons with the highest scores in the first data set obtained the lowest scores in the second.

Correlational techniques are frequently used to analyze the technical adequacy of assessment tools, particularly in the study of reliability and validity. Because of this, professionals should be able to interpret correlational data. The direction of a correlation coefficient refers to whether it is positive or negative; magnitude is the size of the coefficient. However, a correlation coefficient of .73 does not mean 73% of a perfect relationship between sets of scores. To determine the usefulness of the correlation coefficient, the coefficient of determination is computed; this is simply the square of the correlation coefficient. Thus, if the Pearson r is either −.70 or +.70, the coefficient of determination is 49% (.70 × .70 = .49 or 49%). This percentage indicates the degree to which one set of scores can be used to predict the other. As Ary, Jacobs, and Razavieh (1990) explain, "If we find a correlation of +.80 between achievement and intelligence, 64 percent of the variance in achievement is associated with variance in intelligence test scores" (p. 153).

Test Norms and Other Standards of Comparison

Some types of assessment tools compare an individual's performance with an outside reference or standard. With norm-referenced tests, the standard is the performance of a norm group, and with criterion-referenced tests, the standard is a curricular goal. For a tool to be appropriate for assessment, its standard of comparison must fit the purpose of assessment and the needs and characteristics of the student.

A norm group serves as the outside reference for norm-referenced tests. The test is administered to a large number of individuals selected to represent the types of persons with whom the test will be used. For instance, for a measure of beginning reading skills, the norm group might be a representative sample of first and second graders. Test norms are then derived from the performance of persons in the norm group. If results are to have meaning for a particular student, the norm group must be an appropriate standard against which to evaluate the student's performance. Factors to consider in determining the appropriateness of test norms are

1. *Age, grade, and gender of norm group members*. These characteristics must match the characteristics of the student. Many of the psychological variables of interest in educational assessment differ by gender and across age groups and grade levels. Thus, it is incorrect to administer a test to a student beyond the age or grade of the norms and then use the closest age or grade group to estimate results. Likewise, if the variable to be measured is related to gender, a test normed only with males is not appropriate for female students.

2. *Method of selection*. Norm groups are samples intended to represent some population of interest. Because randomly selected samples are most likely to approximate the characteristics of a population, norm groups obtained through this method are preferable. Samples selected only because of their accessibility to the test producer are unsatisfactory.

3. *Representativeness of the norm group*. A representative sample includes members from all important segments of the population. If the goal were to construct a national norm group representative of American schoolchildren, it would be unsuitable to select only 6-year-olds or only females. Important population characteristics in test construction are age, gender, geographic region (e.g., the Eastern Seaboard, the South, the Midwest), location of residence (rural, urban, suburban), ethnicity, and some index of socioeconomic status. Variables pertinent to school populations are grade, school placement (general versus special education), type of disability, and language or languages spoken.

4. *Size of the norm group*. Generally, larger samples produce more accurate results. If the norm group is divided into age or grade levels

for which separate norms are provided, the size of these subgroups should also be considered.

5. *Recency of test norms.* Test norms should reflect current standards of student performance. Norms established with first graders in 1980 may be a poor index for evaluating the first graders of 2000. Both test norms and test content should be periodically updated for subject areas that change over time.

It has been suggested that the norm groups of all tests used for special education purposes should include individuals identified as disabled (Fuchs, Fuchs, Benowitz, & Barringer, 1987). This makes sense if the purpose of assessment is to compare a student's performance to that of the total school population, including both students with and without disabilities. However, because in eligibility decisions it is necessary to determine whether achievement problems exist, the appropriate standard of comparison is the performance of students placed in general education classrooms. Norm groups drawn from general education classrooms will likely include students with mild disabilities, and test manuals should describe the characteristics of these students as fully as possible.

Criterion-referenced tests and other informal devices also provide a standard against which student performance can be compared. These measures determine whether students have mastered specific skills; they compare a student's performance to the desired curricular goal rather than to the performance of other students. Again, the appropriateness of the standard must be evaluated. Just as norm groups may not approximate the characteristics of a student, the content of a published criterion-referenced measure may not represent the student's current skill repertoire or the curriculum taught in the student's classroom. Even if a measure has been developed for curriculum-based assessment in a specific district, it may not reflect current instruction in all schools and classrooms within that district.

The manual accompanying the measure is the best source of information about test norms and other standards of comparison. Test producers are expected to provide a complete manual that describes the purpose of the measure, the method of its construction, characteristics of the norm group or other standard, and results of reliability and validity studies. However, not all manuals include these components.

Reliability

Reliability refers to consistency. In everyday language, a reliable person is one who can be counted on. A reliable assessment tool produces consistent results. For example, if a reliable test were to be administered several times to the same individual, the person's scores would remain stable and would not randomly fluctuate. Reliability, as defined by Anastasi (1988), is "the consistency of scores obtained by the same persons when reexamined with the same test on different occasions, or with different sets of equivalent items, or under other variable examining conditions" (p. 109).

Correlational techniques are the most usual methods for studying reliability. Although there are no set rules for determining if a correlation coefficient is of adequate magnitude, it appears logical to set .80 as a minimum. If two sets of scores are related at this level, the coefficient of determination is 64%, meaning that approximately two-thirds of the variance in the first set of scores is associated with the variance in the second. Explanation of this proportion of the variance should be regarded as a minimum standard. Salvia and Ysseldyke (1998) recommend a minimum level of .60 for group data used for administrative purposes, .80 for individual data that influence screening decisions, and .90 for individual data considered for important decisions such as placement in special education. Gay (1996) maintains that, "for achievement and aptitude tests, there is generally no good reason for selecting a test whose reliability is not at least .90" (p. 151).

There are several types of reliability. *Test-retest reliability* refers to the consistency of a measure from one administration to another. This is typically studied with some segment of the norm group; the measure is administered once during norming and then again to the same group of individuals after a brief period, perhaps a few weeks. *Equivalent-forms reliability* is of interest when there is more than one form of the same measure and these forms are designed to be used interchangeably. To determine if different forms of the same measure produce consistent results, all forms are administered to the same group and results are correlated.

Split-half reliability concerns a measure's internal consistency and is studied with one form of a measure and one group. After administration, the measure is divided in half (for instance, into odd-numbered and even-numbered items), and the scores from each half are correlated. The Kuder-Richardson procedures provide another approach to the study of internal consistency. Instead of splitting an instrument in half and comparing one half to the other, these methods consider the equivalence of all items and produce an estimate of inter-item consistency.

The last major type of reliability is *scorer reliability,* also called *interrater* or *interobserver reliability.* This type is concerned with the consistency among persons who evaluate the performance of the individual being assessed; it is most important when scoring standards are subject to interpretation. If two different professionals rate a student's responses to test items, their ratings should be consistent.

Perhaps the most typical assessment situation in which scorer reliability is a factor is in the use of observational techniques. When two observers collect data on the same student, they must ensure consistency. To calculate interobserver reliability, observation records are compared to determine the number of times observers agreed and disagreed on their ratings of behavior. The percentage of agreement is then computed with the following formula:

$$\frac{\%\ of}{agreement} = \frac{Number\ of\ agreements}{Number\ of\ agreements + Number\ of\ disagreements} \times 100$$

The minimum acceptable rate of agreement between observers is 80% (Cooper, Heron, & Heward, 1987; Sulzer-Azaroff & Mayer, 1977).

Validity

Validity refers to whether an assessment tool actually measures what it purports to measure. If a test claims to assess skill in driving a car but includes only multiple-choice questions on the parts of an engine, it is clearly invalid. Also, measurement tools can be valid for one purpose but not for another. For example, a test may be a valid method of screening for academic difficulties but not for differentiating among types of reading problems. According to the legal guidelines for assessment in federal law, assessment tools used with students with disabilities must be validated for the specific purpose for which they are used. Thus, studies of a measure's validity should include individuals with disabilities as subjects if that measure is to be used for special education purposes (Fuchs et al., 1987).

Validity is related to reliability. No measure can be considered valid if it produces inconsistent results. Valid instruments are reliable instruments, although a measure can lack validity and still be reliable. Validity is concerned with the content of the measure and whether that content enables the measure to perform its intended function.

Content validity is defined as "the extent to which the sample of items on a test are representative of some defined universe, or domain of content" (Ary et al., 1990, p. 257). Content validity, an important consideration in the evaluation of any measure, is particularly critical with criterion-referenced tests, inventories, and other informal instruments that compare student performance to curricular standards. Determination of a measure's content validity is a matter of judgment rather than statistical analysis. Factors to consider are:

- What content area does the measure claim to assess? What are the boundaries of that area?
- Does the measure attempt to assess the entire universe of content, or does it include only a sampling from that universe?
- If the measure assesses only a portion of the content universe, is the sample a representative one? Is it complete? Are all important elements included?
- What types of tasks are used to assess content? Are these appropriate for the skill or knowledge being assessed?

The content validity of an assessment tool must be evaluated in relation to the assessment task.

Even if an instrument does an adequate job of measuring the content area, it may be inappropriate for a particular student or the specific question guiding the assessment.

Another type of validity is *criterion-related validity*. The instrument is validated in terms of some outside criterion. For example, a new test of academic achievement might be validated against an existing achievement test, school grades, or teacher ratings of academic performance. This assumes, of course, that the criterion chosen is itself a valid measure of the content area.

There are two types of criterion-related validity: predictive and concurrent. *Predictive validity* refers to a measure's ability to predict future performance. It is studied by administering the measure in question to a group of individuals and then, sometime in the future, administering the criterion measure to the same group. For example, the predictive validity of a school readiness test could be established by administering it at the start of kindergarten, then correlating its results with teacher ratings of academic performance at the end of first grade. *Concurrent validity* is concerned with a measure's relationship to some current criterion. It is studied by administering both the measure in question and the criterion measure to the same group at the same time. For example, the concurrent validity of a new algebra test could be established by correlating its results with student grades in algebra.

The correlation coefficients resulting from the study of criterion-related validity are examined to determine their direction and magnitude. As a general rule, the greater the magnitude of a positive correlation between a measure and its criterion, the more support for that measure's validity. Unlike the study of reliability, there are no set rules for judging whether a validity coefficient is of adequate magnitude. At minimum, however, the correlation should be statistically significant (Anastasi, 1988). That is, there should be reason to believe that the relationship between the two measures is not simply due to chance. Information about statistical significance should be provided in the test's manual or technical report; statistical significance cannot be determined by inspecting the correlation coefficient's magnitude.

In evaluating criterion-related validity, the appropriateness of the criterion measure must be considered. If a test of reading skills is under study, another reading test should be selected as the criterion, not a test of general aptitude. The criterion should address and be a valid measure of the content of interest. According to Ary et al. (1990), appropriate criterion measures are relevant to the content area, reliable, and free from bias.

A third type of validity is *construct validity,* or the degree to which an instrument measures the theoretical construct it intends to measure. Many assessment devices claim to measure constructs such as intelligence, visual perception, and auditory processing. Theoretical constructs are not directly observable; they must be inferred from observed behaviors. The construct validity of a measure can be studied with correlational techniques. For example, if a new test of construct X is found to relate to an established measure of construct $X,$ the validity of the new test is supported. Other methods of determining construct validity include factor analysis, investigation of age differentiation for measures of developmental constructs, and validation by experimental intervention (Anastasi, 1988).

Measurement Error

Error intrudes into any measurement system, and assessment is no exception. If a test, even the most reliable and valid one, were to be administered twice to the same student by the same examiner, the scores obtained would likely differ—even if testing conditions were identical, the test was administered and scored correctly each time, and the student had not acquired new skills from one administration to the next. Test scores and other assessment results are observed scores made up of two parts—a hypothetical true score and an error component. The less error in an observed score, the more precise the measurement tool.

Although measurement error is inevitable, it can be quantified by a statistic called the *standard error of measurement.* The standard error of measurement can be determined if the standard deviation and reliability of the measure are known. Most manuals for norm-referenced tests provide information on standard error, or it can be calculated with the formula

$$SE_m = \sigma \sqrt{1 - r}$$

in which SE_m represents standard error of measurement, σ the standard deviation, and r reliability.

Measurement error is related to both the variability of scores and reliability. As variability increases, so does error. However, as reliability increases, error decreases. Thus, to reduce measurement error, professionals should select instruments with low variability and high reliability.

The standard error of measurement is an indicator of the technical quality of an assessment tool and assists with interpretation of results. As explained in the next chapter, standard error is used to construct confidence intervals around observed scores. This allows a student's performance to be reported as a range of scores where it is highly probable the true score lies, rather than as a single score known to include both the true score and error.

TEST SCORES AND OTHER ASSESSMENT RESULTS

Another consideration in the selection of assessment tools is the type of results needed to answer the assessment questions. Assessment data must be in a form that allows their use in educational decisions. With informal measures, comparing a student's performance to curricular goals or classroom behavioral expectations can produce very simple data such as the number of skills mastered or the number of inappropriate behaviors observed. Sometimes, that is the type of information needed. At other times, the more sophisticated results of norm-referenced tests are necessary to answer the assessment questions.

Results of Informal Measures

Most informal assessment results are straightforward, easy to understand, and descriptive in nature. Frequency counts are a typical example; they simply report the number of occurrences of a behavior. For example, findings from informal inventories are often expressed as the number of questions, problems, or items answered correctly. Frequency data are easily converted to percentages. If a student answers 8 out of 10 items correctly on a classroom quiz, the percentage correct is 80. Informal assessments also yield duration data. Duration refers to time elapsed; if a student begins work on an assignment at 9:00 a.m. and completes it at 9:25 a.m., the duration of this activity is 25 minutes.

Frequency counts and percentages are interval data that can be manipulated by addition or subtraction. A student's performance can be compared by examining the difference between the number or percentage correct on each occasion. For example, a student may answer 20 out of 45 questions correctly at the beginning of September but improve to 35 out of 45 correct by the end of October; this represents an increase of 15 questions. Duration data are ratio data; time scales have true zeros and may be added, subtracted, multiplied, or divided. Thus, it is correct to say duration has doubled if a student increases the time spent on homework each evening from 30 minutes to 1 hour.

Some informal measures produce nominal data. Criterion-referenced tests, for example, may yield categorical findings. The student's performance on many criterion-referenced measures is classified as either demonstrating or failing to demonstrate skill mastery; no other descriptive information is provided. Checklists also produce a form of categorical data. If a teacher checks all items that describe a student's typical classroom behavior, in effect each item is classified as either representative or not representative of the student's typical behavior.

Other informal assessments provide ordinal data. Rating scales list a set of descriptions in some logical order: "The spelling performance of this student is (a) below grade level, (b) at grade level, (c) above grade level." The task is to select the most appropriate description. Rating instruments are considered ordinal scales unless they are Likert-type. Likert-type scales appear to be divided into equal intervals. For instance, a student may be asked to express degree of agreement with the statement "My favorite school

TABLE 3–2
Results Available from Informal Measures

TYPE OF MEASURE	TYPICAL RESULTS	TYPE OF DATA
Criterion-referenced test	Pass/fail; the skill is mastered or not mastered	Nominal
Classroom quiz	Number or percentage correct	Interval
Inventory	Number or percentage correct	Interval
	Age or grade rating	Ordinal
Observation	Number of occurrences of a behavior	Interval
	Duration of a behavior	Ratio
Checklist	Yes/no; the description is appropriate or inappropriate	Nominal
Rating scale	Verbal description (e.g., "usually punctual")	Ordinal
	A numerical rating with Likert-type scales	Interval
Work sample analysis	Number or percentage correct and/or incorrect	Interval
Interview or questionnaire	Verbal description, if questions open-ended; otherwise, results similar to those of checklists and rating scales	Varies

subject is science" by selecting one of the following options:

1	2	3	4	5
Strongly Disagree	Disagree	Neutral	Agree	Strongly Agree

Likert-type scales are generally assumed to produce interval data.

Some informal measures are described as age-referenced or grade-referenced. For example, a developmental checklist that presents skills in the order in which they are usually acquired may provide age standards for each skill. Or an informal inventory may be referenced to the subject matter of specific grade levels; it may include first grade spelling words, second grade spelling words, and so forth. Such measures usually are not norm-referenced. If age or grade standards are derived from some source other than the performance of a norm group, the way in which these standards were determined must be carefully evaluated.

Age and grade ratings are ordinal data. Such scales place skills, traits, or other characteristics into some order; however, distances between points on these scales do not represent equal intervals. As with nominal scales, data from ordinal scales cannot be treated arithmetically.

Table 3–2 presents several informal assessment tools, their typical results, and the type of data they produce. This information can assist in selecting the most appropriate informal measure for an assessment purpose. If the assessment question demands numerical information, a measure yielding interval or ratio data is needed. Examples of numerical questions are "How many sight words can Sue Ellen read?" and "How much time does John take to complete his biology assignment?" Nominal scales are indicated if the assessment question is concerned with classification. Examples of categorical questions are "Has Yvonne mastered basic number facts?" and "Can Erin type 40 words per minute with no errors?" Ordinal scales fill the gap between numerical and categorical data; they provide descriptive information and answer questions about relative standing. Examples are "Is Louis considered to be one of the more industrious students in his class?" and "How would Joan's handwriting be characterized: neat and legible, messy but still legible, or illegible?"

Norm-Referenced Test Scores

The results of norm-referenced tests take many forms: age and grade equivalents, percentile ranks, stanines, standard scores, and so forth. The raw score is common to all norm-referenced measures. Raw scores are similar to scores on classroom quizzes. They are not related to the performance of a norm group, and they are used only to obtain other scores. In most cases, raw scores are an index of the number of test items answered correctly. They must be converted to derived scores before a student's test performance can be compared to a norm group.

Age and Grade Equivalents

Many norm-referenced measures provide age and/or grade equivalents. These derived scores express test performance in terms of the familiar units of chronological age or grade in school. For example, a student may receive an age score of 7 years, 6 months on a test of spoken language or a grade score of 4.5 on a reading achievement test. Of all norm-referenced scores, age and grade equivalents appear to be the easiest to understand and interpret, but they are quite complicated and are therefore subject to misinterpretation.

Age and grade scores are derived from the performance of the norm group. For example, if the third graders in the norm group earn an average raw score of 20, a grade equivalent of 3 is assigned to raw score 20. Anyone who achieves a raw score of 20 on this test will earn a grade equivalent of 3. Decimal grade equivalents (e.g., 3.1, 3.2, 3.3, and so forth) are usually derived by interpolation of data already available, rather than by testing separate groups of students or the same group at successive intervals. Also, the range of grade equivalents in test norms may exceed the range of grades of individuals within the norm group. For example, if a test was normed with only fourth, fifth, and sixth graders, its grade equivalent scores may extend below fourth grade and above sixth grade. If the average performance of grade 6 students is a raw score of 40, a grade equivalent of 9.5 may be assigned to a raw score of 48. Such scores are obtained by extrapolation; the known scores of sixth graders within the norm group are extended to produce estimates of how students in higher grades would have performed, had they taken the test.

Age and grade equivalents are ordinal data. Although an equal-interval time scale underlies chronological age and grade in school, there is not a one-to-one correspondence between time and skill mastery. The gain in achievement from grade 1.0 to grade 1.5 in reading is much greater than the gain from grade 10.0 to grade 10.5; the intervals do not represent equal units of measurement.

The deceptive simplicity of age and grade equivalents leads to their misinterpretation. Thus, professionals should select norm-referenced measures that offer other types of derived scores, either in addition to or instead of age and grade equivalents. This viewpoint is supported by the International Reading Association (1981) in *Resolution on Misuse of Grade Equivalents*. This resolution calls upon test publishers to eliminate grade equivalents and urges practitioners to stop using grade equivalents to report test performance. According to the International Reading Association:

> One of the most serious misuses of tests is the reliance on a grade equivalent as an indicator of absolute performance, when a grade equivalent should be interpreted as an indicator of a test-taker's performance in relation to the performance of other test-takers used to norm the test.

Percentile Ranks

Another type of derived score is the percentile rank. The percentile rank for a particular raw score indicates the percentage of individuals within the norm group who achieved this raw score or a lower one. If a raw score of 40 corresponds to a percentile rank of 62, this means that 62% of the norm group earned raw scores of 40 or less. A student whose raw score converts to the 62nd percentile can be said to perform at a level equal to or greater than that of 62% of the norm group and at a level lower than that of the remaining 38% of the norm group.

Usually, tests provide separate tables of percentile rank norms for different age or grade levels. One table may list norms for students age 6-0 to 6-11, another for students age 7-0 to 7-11, and so forth. This allows more precise description of student performance. For example, it may be possible to say that a 12-year-old performed at the 75th percentile when compared with age 12 students in the norm group.

Percentile ranks are relatively easy to understand as long as they are not confused with percentages. A percentile rank refers to a percentage of persons; percentage correct refers to a percentage of test items. A student may answer only 50% of the items on a test correctly but perform at the 99th percentile for his or her age. Percentile rank data indicate relative position within the norm group. Salvia and Ysseldyke (1998) prefer percentile ranks to other derived scores because "percentiles tell us nothing more than what any norm-referenced derived score can tell us—namely an individual's relative standing in a group" (p. 116).

Standard Scores

Standard scores are available on many norm-referenced measures. These derived scores transform raw scores to a new scale with a set mean and standard deviation. Standard scores are useful for comparing the performance of the same individual on two different measures, as long as the raw score distributions of the measures are similar. They also provide a standard scale for reporting norms for various age or grade groups within the total standardization sample.

Standard score distributions can be constructed using any mean or standard deviation; the values are arbitrary. The z score is one type of standard score, and its distribution has a mean of 0 and a standard deviation of 1. Many norm-referenced tests set the mean of the standard score distribution at 100 and the standard deviation at 15. On these tests, if a student's raw score converts to a standard score of 100, the student performed at the mean. A standard score of 115 indicates performance one standard deviation above the mean, and a standard score of 85 indicates performance one standard deviation below the mean.

The values selected for the mean and standard deviation of standard score distributions vary from measure to measure and sometimes among different parts of the same measure. For example, measures that provide two sets of standard scores—one for overall test performance and the other for performance on individual subtests—may use two separate score distributions to differentiate the scores. An example is the *Wechsler Intelligence Scale for Children–Third Edition*. Its total test scores, called IQ scores, have a mean of 100 and a standard deviation of 15. In contrast, the standard scores for the individual subtests, called scaled scores, have a mean of 10 and a standard deviation of 3. The term *scaled score* is frequently used to refer to subtest standard scores.

Separate standard score norms may be provided by age or grade. However, whatever the distribution for a particular standard score, the same scale is used for all students taking the test. A standard score mean of 100 is used to indicate average performance, whatever the student's age or grade. Thus, a 6-year-old would earn a standard score of 100 if his or her raw score equaled the mean of the 6-year-old segment of the norm group, and a 12-year-old would earn a standard score of 100 if his or her raw score equaled the mean of the 12-year-old segment of the norm group.

Comparison of standard scores from one test to another makes sense only if the raw score distributions of the two measures are similar. One way to ensure similarity is to select measures with raw score distributions that are normal or have been normalized by the test producer. As Figure 3–1 shows, most scores in a normal distribution are found in the middle and fewer at the ex-

FIGURE 3–1
Normal Distribution

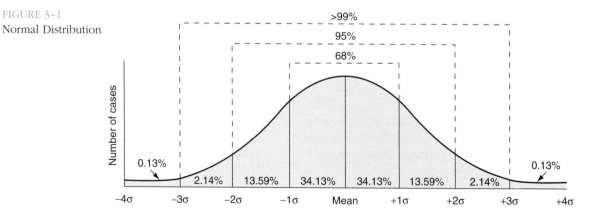

tremes. When a distribution is normal, it is possible to determine the exact percentage of cases that fall within any portion of the curve. The majority of cases fall in the center portion; 68% of the scores of a normally distributed measure occur in the range from one standard deviation below the mean to one standard deviation above—that is, from −1 to +1 standard deviations. Approximately 14% of the scores fall between −1 and −2 standard deviations, with the same percentage found between +1 and +2 standard deviations; thus, the range from −2 to +2 standard deviations includes approximately 95% of the cases. When the range is extended to include from −3 to +3 standard deviations, it accounts for more than 99% of the cases.

Standard scores based on normal distributions have special characteristics. They allow a student's performance to be related to the mean and standard deviation of the norm group, and they can be directly converted into percentile ranks. Figure 3–2 presents this relationship. If a student scores one standard deviation above the mean on a measure that is normally distributed, the percentile rank of that score is 84. A score equal to the mean earns a percentile rank of 50, and if a score lies one standard deviation below the mean, its percentile rank is 16. Thus, test performance can be described in relation to the mean and to a percentage of the norm group. With a measure in which the mean is 100, the standard deviation is 15, and scores are normally distributed, a standard score of 70 indicates performance that is (a) two standard deviations below the mean of the norm group and (b) equal to or greater than the performance of 2% of the norm group. Because they provide these two types of information, normalized standard scores

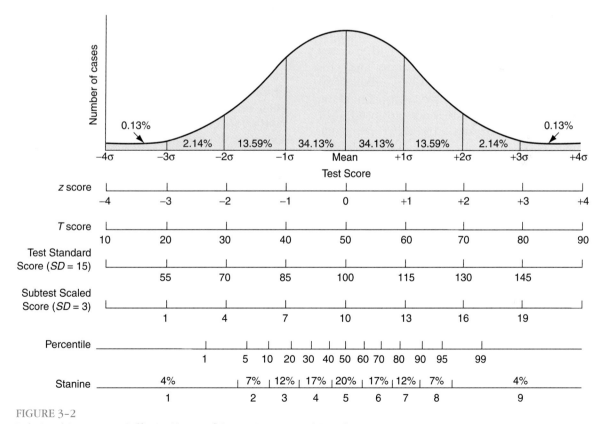

FIGURE 3-2

Relationships among Different Types of Scores in a Normal Distribution are particularly useful in the interpretation of norm-referenced test results.

Stanines

Stanines are another type of derived score. The stanine distribution is divided into nine segments, or standard nines, each of which is .5 standard deviation in width. Figure 3–2 illustrates the relationship among stanines, percentile ranks, and other standard scores. It also lists the percentage of cases expected to fall within each stanine if raw scores are normally distributed. Because stanines represent a range of performance rather than a specific score, the data they provide are less precise than those from standard scores.

It is apparent that norm-referenced measures offer a variety of different scores, and the types available from a particular measure should be considered as part of the selection process. In general, if the purpose of assessment is to compare a student's performance to that of a norm group, the most informative type of score is the normalized standard score. However, the same information can be obtained from a measure that is not normally distributed if it provides both standard scores and percentile ranks. Whenever possible, tests that offer only age or grade equivalents should be avoided. If age or grade scores are used, they should be accompanied by either percentile ranks or standard scores, or both.

PROMOTING NONBIASED ASSESSMENT

The potential for bias is not limited to the selection, administration, and interpretation of assessment devices (Oakland, 1980; Winzer & Mazurek, 1998). Bias can enter at any point in the special education process: prior to assessment in referral, screening, and the selection of assessment tools; during assessment in the utilization of data-collection strategies and in relation to student and examiner characteristics; and after assessment in placement, program planning, and reevaluation. Nevertheless, a major concern in the prevention of bias is the selection of appropriate assessment tools.

Issues in Assessment of Culturally and Linguistically Diverse Students

Much of the controversy surrounding special education in the past was due to the inappropriate use of standardized tests with students from diverse ethnic, cultural, and linguistic groups. Laosa (1977) summarizes one major objection to standardized testing for these students:

> Standardized tests are biased and unfair to persons from cultural and sociocultural minorities since most tests reflect largely white, middle-class values and attitudes and they do not reflect the experiences and the linguistic, cognitive, and other cultural styles and values of minority group persons. (p. 10)

This is a validity concern. With students who do not speak English, it is obvious that an achievement test written in English is an invalid measure of academic performance. Although cultural differences are sometimes less clear, it is equally discriminatory to assess students from diverse cultures with measures that are based upon the values, beliefs, and cultural heritage of the dominant American culture.

The problems associated with assessment of diverse students have stimulated a number of proposed solutions, although no solution has been accepted universally. Several of the proposals for reducing bias in assessment are described in the paragraphs that follow.

Translation of Measures into Languages other than English

For the assessment of students whose primary language is not English, it is recommended that tests and test directions be translated into the student's home language. Many of the standardized tests commonly used in special education assessment have been translated into Spanish. Several approaches have been used, including backward translation (i.e., translating from English into Spanish and then back again to English to discover significant discrepancies).

However, translating a measure from one language to another does not eliminate the possibility of bias. The translation must preserve not only the literal and cultural meanings of the original, but also the difficulty level of each test item. The measure must also be renormed with an appropriate standardization sample. If a Spanish-language version of a test is intended for use in the United States, norming it with a sample of students from Mexico City is very likely inappropriate. A related concern is regional differences. The Spanish spoken by students in Los Angeles may vary from that of New York or Miami.

Use of Interpreters

Another strategy for the assessment of students who speak languages other than English is the use of interpreters. The professional conducting the assessment can act as an interpreter, or another professional or even a member of the community could be asked to assist. This practice is not recommended. Spontaneous translations of test instructions and items are likely to include inaccuracies and, like any departure from the test's standardization conditions, they make the use of test norms impossible. Nonetheless, tests and other assessment tools are not available in all languages, and it is sometimes necessary to rely on interpreters.

Culture-Fair Tests

One of the methods proposed to combat cultural bias is the development of culture-free and culture-fair measures. These measures attempt to minimize factors that may depress the performance of diverse students such as high verbal demands, timed tasks, and emphasis on school learning. One of the first efforts to produce such measures was Cattell's *Culture Fair Intelligence Tests* (Cattell, 1950; Cattell & Cattell, 1960, 1963, 1977). The *Leiter International Performance Scale* (Leiter, 1948) and other nonverbal measures of intelligence are also considered by some to be culture-fair tests.

Results of attempts to produce culture-fair tests have been disappointing (Winzer & Mazurek, 1998). In fact, culture-fair measures may be just as discriminatory as the culturally biased verbal tests they were designed to replace. Even nonverbal measures require some degree of verbal mediation as the student thinks about the

test questions and how to respond. According to Gonzales (1982), a culturally fair measure must meet the following criteria:

1. The same predictions can be made from the results across cultures or given populations.
2. Language and reading are kept to a minimum.
3. Adequate representation of the target population is in the norming.
4. Subjects should not be penalized by time factors.
5. Target populations must have the opportunity to learn the material.
6. Item content must be familiar to all groups. (p. 385)

Culture-Specific Measures

Another strategy is the development of measures that relate directly to specific cultures. An early example is the *Black Intelligence Test of Cultural Homogeneity* (Williams, 1972). This 100-item, multiple-choice test was designed to assess knowledge of the black experience. According to Samuda (1975), "When applied to white subjects, the test becomes a measure of their sensitivity and responsiveness to the black culture" (p. 145). Although culture-specific measures can promote understanding of diverse cultures, they may not solve bias problems. Culture-specific measures are often not transportable from one region of the country to another. In addition, their predictive validity may be less than adequate (Duffey, Salvia, Tucker, & Ysseldyke, 1982).

Separate Norms

An alternative to culture-specific measures is the construction of separate norms for diverse students and dominant culture students. However, this practice would further encourage separation of these two groups (Alley & Foster, 1978). Gonzales (1982) recommends that separate local norms be established for diverse students only when their cultural and linguistic characteristics are significantly different from those of the dominant culture, as with some groups of Native American students. Valenzuela and Cervantes (1998) disagree. They do not support the use of local norms for any groups "if the result of the renormed tests will be used for the diagnosis of disability, a statement of achievement potential, or for placement purposes" (pp. 180–181).

Pluralistic Assessment

Another proposed solution is to include a broad range of skills in assessment to provide a pluralistic perspective that accounts for the strengths and preferences of various cultures. An early example is Mercer's assessment system, the *System of Multicultural Pluralistic Assessment (SOMPA)* (Mercer & Lewis, 1977b), which is described in Chapter 8. In the SOMPA, traditional assessment procedures are supplemented with sociocultural data so that a student's performance can be viewed within the perspective of his or her own culture. Although the *SOMPA* successfully reduced the number of students from diverse groups identified as mentally retarded (Gonzales, 1982), professionals were concerned about its ability to accurately predict such a student's likelihood of success in a dominant culture school (Oakland, 1979). Winzer and Mazurek (1998) conclude that "pluralistic assessment remains controversial" (p. 207), despite the development of newer measures.

Modification of Test Administration Procedures

Test administration procedures can be altered in an attempt to improve student performance. For example, students could be allowed unlimited time to perform tasks that usually have strict time limits. When administration procedures are altered, however, norm-referenced tests become informal procedures. Such modifications prevent the use of the test's norms and invalidate the comparative power of standardized tests. It may be useful to administer a test under standard conditions and then repeat administration with modified procedures.

A related strategy is to train students in test-taking skills (Duffey et al., 1982). If students are unfamiliar with testing procedures or certain assessment tasks, lack of preparation may hinder their performance. For example, many group tests require students to write responses on separate answer sheets. Preparing students by providing practice activities may help make them less anxious about testing and increase their ability to cope with test tasks.

Dynamic Assessment

In this approach, originally described by Feuerstein and his colleagues (1979), tests are administered using a test-teach-retest format. The examiner presents a test task, observes the student interacting with the task, and then coaches the student in an attempt to improve performance. The purpose is study of the student's learning ability, not his or her current intellectual performance. Feuerstein's measure, the *Learning Potential Assessment Device,* is described in Chapter 8. Like other approaches in which standard administration procedures are modified, results must be considered informal because test norms cannot be used. However, as Winzer and Mazurek (1998) point out, "the observations and results obtained during the assessment may lead directly to instructional suggestions because these techniques have been shown, in the assessment, to enhance the learning efficiency of a child" (p. 208).

Replacement of Standardized Tests with Informal Procedures

A more controversial proposal is to replace standardized measures with informal procedures such as criterion-referenced tests. Criterion-referenced tests evaluate a student's performance without reference to the performance of other students. Furthermore, criterion-referenced tests provide direction for instruction based upon the individual student's needs.

The fact that an assessment tool is informal, however, does not mean that it is nondiscriminatory. Criterion-referenced tests and other informal tools can be subjective (Laosa, 1977), and their results can be interpreted in a biased manner. In addition, replacement of standardized testing with informal assessment would be expensive in terms of time, personnel, and resources (Duffey et al., 1982).

Moratorium on Standardized Testing

The most controversial alternative is the abolition of standardized testing. In the 1970s, the Association of Black Psychologists and the National Education Association called for a moratorium on psychological testing, and other groups have made similar recommendations (Oakland & Laosa, 1977). In California, the *Larry P. v. Riles* court case (1972, 1979, 1984) resulted in a complete prohibition against the use of individual IQ tests with African American students for any special education purpose whatsoever. That ban was lifted in 1992 for students with disabilities other than mental retardation.

However, a total ban on standardized testing could have adverse consequences for culturally and linguistically diverse students who have special needs (Gonzales, 1982). Special education assessment would take more time, thereby delaying the provision of needed services. Also, professionals would be forced to rely on informal procedures that are open to charges of subjectivity and technical inadequacy. In addition, professionals would continue to remain susceptible to influence by irrelevant student traits such as gender, race, and socioeconomic status. According to Duffey and others (1982), the real bias comes in the use of assessment data, not from the instruments themselves. Standardized tests cannot prevent this type of bias, but carefully selected tests can provide professionals with objective information about a student's standing relative to other students.

Guidelines for the Selection of Nondiscriminatory Assessment Tools

By law, assessment devices and procedures must be nondiscriminatory. One difficulty in implementing this requirement is the lack of agreement about what constitutes nondiscriminatory assessment. Alley and Foster (1978) describe a nondiscriminatory measure as "one which results in similar performance distributions across cultural groups" (p. 3). Under this definition, all groups would need to perform equally well on a measure, with similar means and similar variability. However, the relative performance of groups is only one criterion (Lambert, 1981). Other concerns are the instrument's predictive validity, factor analytic structure, and the variance in item scores.

Another major impediment to nondiscriminatory assessment is the scarcity of appropriate assessment tools for diverse populations. There is little agreement about which norm-referenced tests are nondiscriminatory; few measures are available in languages other than English, and most of these are in Spanish.

However, the potential for bias can be minimized if assessment tools are carefully evaluated and selected. With norm-referenced measures, it is important to determine if the norm group is representative of the race, culture, and gender of the student. It is also necessary to consider how many of the individuals in the norm group have characteristics similar to those of the student. Although a norm group may accurately represent the general population by including the proper proportion of individuals from diverse groups, the total number of such individuals may be very small. Some tests avoid this difficulty by using several norm groups of approximately equal size; separate norms are offered by gender, ethnic group, or some other population variable.

Another step in evaluation is the review of test items for cultural bias. If items demand an experiential background inconsistent with that of the student, the student will probably perform poorly. There are many examples of test items that illustrate cultural bias. Williams (1974), as cited by Alley and Foster (1978), suggests that culture influences how a person responds to the test question "When is Washington's birthday?" If the person thinks of George Washington, the answer is February 22; if he or she thinks of Booker T., the answer is April 5. Another example is the following:

> The mountain boy who names the seasons of the year as "deer season, trout season, and bear season;" the desert child who responds "hot, rainy, and chilly;" the teenage Vietnamese refugee who answers "football, basketball, and baseball"—are these students less correct than their middle class American counterparts who reply "summer, fall, winter, and spring"? (Lynch & Lewis, 1987, p. 403)

Because norm-referenced tests have been the most criticized, they are associated with the issue of nonbiased assessment. Professionals today are aware of the ways these tests can be misused, so they attempt to select nondiscriminatory

Guide for the Evaluation of Assessment Tools

Name of measure _____

Author(s) _____ Date _____

Publisher _____ Cost _____

DESCRIPTION OF THE MEASURE

1. Purpose(s) of the measure, as stated in the manual
2. Type of measure (e.g., norm-referenced test, inventory, checklist)
3. Content area(s) assessed (description of each area and, if applicable, a list of subtests)
4. Student requirements
   a. Language
   b. Presentation mode
   c. Response mode
   d. Group or individual administration
   e. Time factors
5. Tester requirements
   a. Necessary training
   b. Administration time and other time requirements
   c. Ease of use
6. Test norms or other standards
   a. Type of reference (e.g., norm group or curricular goals)
   b. If applicable, characteristics of norm group
      (1) Age, grade, gender
      (2) Method of selection
      (3) Representativeness
      (4) Size
      (5) Recency of norms
   c. If applicable, description of curricular standards
      (1) Content domain
      (2) Representativeness of item pool
      (3) Completeness of item pool
      (4) Appropriateness of tasks
7. Reliability
   a. Test-retest reliability
   b. Equivalent-form reliability
   c. Internal consistency
   d. Scorer reliability
8. Validity
   a. Content validity
   b. Criterion-related validity (predictive and/or concurrent)
   c. Construct validity
9. Results
   a. Types of scores or other results
   b. Standard error of measurement
10. Other comments

CONSIDERATIONS IN NONBIASED ASSESSMENT

1. Is the norm group or other standard of comparison appropriate for the student in terms of race, ethnicity, culture, and gender?
2. Are test items free from cultural bias?
3. Is the language of the measure appropriate for the student?
4. Does the measure bypass the limitations imposed by the disability?

CONCLUSIONS

1. Does the tool fit the purpose of assessment?
2. Is the tool appropriate for the student?
3. Is the tool appropriate for the tester?
4. Is the tool technically adequate?
5. Is the tool an efficient data-collection mechanism?

FIGURE 3–3

Guide for the Evaluation of Assessment Tools

measures. However, other types of assessment tools can also be biased. The informal nature of an instrument or strategy is no guarantee that it is nondiscriminatory. Bailey and Harbin (1980) point out that "many of the discriminatory aspects of norm referenced measures, such as wording or content, can be found in criterion referenced measures as well" (p. 593).

Identifying appropriate assessment tools for students whose communication mode is not English poses special problems. No difficulties arise if the student speaks only one language, if technically adequate tools are available in that language, and if a professional who is fluent in the language has the assessment expertise necessary for the use of these tools. Unfortunately, this is seldom the case.

A final consideration is the disability of the student. Unless the purpose of assessment is exploration of that disability, the tools for assessment should minimize its effects. If a student's academic disability is in the skill area of reading, measures in which the tester presents questions orally or through demonstration are most appropriate. Other characteristics sometimes associated with disabilities are short attention span, impulsivity, poor self-concept, and expectation for failure. These factors should be considered in selecting assessment procedures.

The evaluation guide in Figure 3–3 can be used to review and critique norm-referenced tests and other assessment tools. It summarizes the important factors in selecting measures that produce nonbiased, accurate, and useful results.

STUDY GUIDE

REVIEW QUESTIONS

1. Tell whether each of the following statements about the selection of tools for assessment is true or false.
   _____ If the assessment procedure is appropriate for the age, grade, and ability level of the student, then its technical quality is not a consideration.
   _____ Trained professionals must be available to administer, score, and interpret the assessment.
   _____ Assessment devices must be selected and administered so they are not racially or culturally discriminatory.
   _____ The regulations for PL 105-17 provide a recommended list of tests and other procedures for use in special education assessment.
2. Assessment must be nondiscriminatory and must focus on the student's _____ needs.
3. Several descriptive statistics can be used to summarize information. Which would be the best statistic to report the central tendency of a set of test scores expressed as percentages?
   a. mode
   b. standard deviation
   c. mean
   d. range
4. Which of the following descriptive statistics describes the relationship between two sets of scores?
   a. median
   b. correlation coefficient
   c. standard deviation
   d. percentile rank
5. With norm-referenced tests, one factor that should be considered in evaluation is the appropriateness of the norm group. List three aspects of the norm group that should be examined.

6. Reliability and validity also influence technical adequacy. Which of these statements about test quality is true?
   a. Reliability refers to consistency.
   b. Validity refers to whether a test measures what it purports to measure.
   c. Correlational techniques are the most usual way of studying reliability.
   d. Valid tests are reliable, although a test may be reliable without being valid.
   e. All of these statements are true.

7. Match the terms in Column A with the best explanation in Column B.

Column A	*Column B*
a. Test-retest reliability	___ The test items appear to assess the skill areas the test is designed to measure.
b. Predictive validity	___ Current test results are related to future results on a criterion measure.
c. Alternate-form reliability	___ Results of a test given today will be related to results of the same test given next week.
d. Content validity	___ The results from one form of the test are related to the results from a second form.
e. Concurrent validity	___ Current test results are related to current results on a criterion measure.

8. The statistic used to quantify the measurement error present in a test score is called the _____ .

9. Tests and informal procedures produce many different types of results. Determine if these statements about assessment results are true or false.
   _____ Results of informal measures such as inventories are often expressed as frequency counts (for example, the number of items the student answers correctly).
   _____ Age and grade equivalents are useful scores because they are easy to understand and are rarely misinterpreted.
   _____ Percentile ranks are comparative scores that allow the student's performance to be contrasted with the performance of age or grade peers in the norm group.
   _____ When standard scores are based on a normal distribution, they are easily converted into percentile ranks, stanines, and other types of standard scores.

10. Fill in the blanks using these words: "high," "low." To decrease measurement error, assessment devices should have _____ reliability and _____ variability.

11. What type of data do Likert-type scales produce?
    a. nominal
    b. ordinal
    c. interval
    d. ratio

12. What type of data are age equivalent and grade equivalent scores?
    a. nominal
    b. ordinal
    c. interval
    d. ratio

13. A student performed at the 85th percentile on an achievement test. This means that the student's raw score equalled or exceeded the raw scores of _____ percent of the norm group.

14. Many suggestions have been made for reducing the potential for bias in assessment. Which of the following statements are true?
    _____ Translating a measure from one language to another eliminates bias due to language.

_____ Culture-fair tests eliminate concerns about bias due to culture.

_____ Pluralistic assessment systems are used widely in schools to avoid bias due to sociocultural factors.

_____ Most experts recommend that local norms be developed for culturally and linguistically diverse students.

15. When administration procedures are altered for standardized tests, test norms cannot be used and tests become _____ procedures.

ACTIVITIES

1. Visit the website of a test publisher such as American Guidance Service (www.agsnet.com), Pro-Ed (www.proedinc.com), Psychological Corporation (www.hbtpc.com), or Riverside Publishing (www.riverpub.com). What types of information are provided about tests? Is the norm group described? Are reliability, validity, and other aspects of technical adequacy addressed?
2. Figure 3–3 is a guide for the evaluation of assessment tools. Use this guide to critique a norm-referenced test or an informal assessment device.
3. One concern in the selection of assessment tools is the types of tasks that students are expected to perform. Analyze the assessment tasks on one of the academic achievement tests often used in special education. Consider presentation mode, response mode, group versus individual administration, and time factors.
4. Locate a review of a new test or assessment procedure in a professional journal such as *Diagnostique* or *Remedial and Special Education*. Read the review and write a brief summary of its major points.

DISCUSSION QUESTIONS

1. One major impetus for the passage of federal special education laws was concern over misuse of standardized tests with culturally and linguistically diverse students. Using Table 3–1 as a guide, discuss several inappropriate assessment practices of the past and explain the current legal safeguards to prevent the recurrence of these practices.
2. On norm-referenced tests, the standard of comparison against which a student's performance is evaluated is the performance of age or grade peers in the norm group. Explain the standard of comparison for informal assessment tools such as classroom quizzes, inventories, and criterion-referenced tests.
3. When professionals select a tool for assessment, they consider not only the technical quality of the measurement device but also the particular purpose for which it will be used. Tell why a technically poor measure is never an appropriate assessment tool. Then give an example of a situation in which a technically adequate measure is inappropriate because it does not fit the purpose of the assessment.
4. Grade equivalents are available on many tests, although there are many criticisms of this type of score. Describe the advantages and disadvantages of grade scores, giving your opinion on the International Reading Association's recommendation that grade equivalents be eliminated from standardized tests.
5. Discuss several potential sources of bias in the assessment process, including the selection of inappropriate procedures. Identify five ways in which bias can be introduced into assessment, and discuss how each can be prevented.

CHAPTER 4

STANDARDIZED TESTS

- Preparation for Testing
- Test Administration
- Observation of Test Behavior
- Scoring the Test
- Interpreting Test Results
- Computers as Tools for Assessment
- Modification of Testing Procedures
- Avoiding Bias in Testing

Tests are the best-known type of assessment measures. They are part of the school experience from the early grades to the college classroom. No one passes through the educational system without taking a weekly quiz, a test at the end of a unit, or a final exam. Tests range from informal measures devised by teachers for classroom use to very structured instruments known as norm-referenced standardized tests. These formal tests are also a regular feature of education, whether they are achievement tests administered at intervals throughout the grades, aptitude measures used for college admission, or individual tests used in special education.

In standardized testing, test tasks are presented under standard conditions so the student's performance can be contrasted to the performance of a norm group. The resulting data are comparative; the student's level of functioning is described in relation to typical or average performance. This type of information is necessary in screening and in determining eligibility; the goal is selection of students whose performance is so divergent from that of others that special attention is warranted. Results also help professionals to plan instruction by identifying curriculum areas in which students fail to perform as well as their peers and, in evaluation, to document changes in performance relative to age and grade level expectations.

Norm-referenced tests must be administered and scored in strict accordance with the standard conditions described in the test manual. If the conditions under which the test was normed are not duplicated, then the student's performance cannot be compared to the performance of the norm group. At the same time, the tester must ensure the full and active participation of the student. Because tests elicit only a sample of behavior, test performance must be an accurate representation of the student's capabilities. These concerns are as old as the history of standardized testing. Terman and Merrill pointed out in 1937:

> Three requirements must be satisfied: (1) the standard procedures must be followed; (2) the child's best efforts must be enlisted by the establishment and maintenance of adequate rapport; and (3) the responses must be correctly scored. It can hardly be said that any one of the three is more important than the others, for all are absolutely essential. (p. 52)

PREPARATION FOR TESTING

Testing does not begin immediately after an appropriate measure has been selected. The tester (that is, the professional responsible for test administration) must first ensure that he or she is adequately prepared to administer and score the test. Then, the testing environment is readied, and the student is carefully introduced to the testing experience.

Preparation of the Tester

Most standardized tests are designed for use by trained testers—professionals who have mastered the skills of test administration and scoring. Preparation programs for professionals such as special educators typically include training in assessment, with supervised practice in the use of standardized measures. As Anastasi and Urbina (1997) note:

> For individual testing, supervised training in the administration of the particular test is usually essential. Depending upon the nature of the test and the type of persons to be examined, such training may require from a few demonstration and practice sessions to over a year of instruction. (p. 14)

Tests differ in the amount of training needed to guarantee valid administration. Some measures, such as individual intelligence tests, require extensive preparation; in many states, school psychologists are the only school personnel licensed to administer them. Other tests, such as the achievement tests used by special educators, presume that the tester is knowledgeable about and trained in standardized testing procedures but holds no special license or certification. For example, some manuals say that the test can be administered by persons properly prepared by training and/or self-study.

It is the professional responsibility of the tester to administer only those tests he or she is trained for or, after extensive study, similar tests.

Measures administered by untrained testers produce highly questionable results that must be considered invalid. Incorrect administration may also render a test invalid for future use with a student if, for example, an inexperienced tester reveals the correct answers. Practice is necessary but not sufficient in learning new tests; the tester must receive feedback on the accuracy of his or her performance. No new test should be considered learned until the tester's administration and scoring skills have been checked by a qualified professional; it is too easy to make mistakes and allow them to become habits.

Preparation of the Testing Environment

The testing environment consists of the room where the test is administered, the seating arrangements, the testing equipment, and the participants. This environment can influence test performance. Think, for example, of trying to concentrate on an important examination in a stifling hot or noisy room. The tester should make every effort to create a comfortable testing environment.

The testing room should be just large enough to accommodate the testing procedures. Unless gross motor tasks such as running are part of the test, an office-sized room provides sufficient space. Large rooms such as classrooms are not recommended because they often contain distractions. The room's lighting, temperature, and ventilation should be adequate. Light from windows should not shine in the eyes of tester or student. Nonglare lighting is best, particularly when test materials are printed on shiny pages. Test administration should not be attempted in rooms with inadequate lighting, extremes of temperature, or poor ventilation.

The testing room should be in a quiet location, away from the playground, gymnasium, cafeteria, and music room. A constant noise source, such as an air conditioner, is permissible as long as it does not interfere with communication between the tester and student. The room should be free of visual distractions such as colorful bulletin boards, posters, and other attention-drawing stimuli; windows with interesting views should be curtained or masked. The goal is to make the test the most interesting aspect of the room.

The room should be secured so people cannot walk in and interrupt. The tester can post a notice on the door stating that testing is in progress; persons who use the room can be informed it will be occupied. Despite these precautions, interruptions such as a fire drill or other emergency may occur.

It is often impossible to find an ideal testing room, particularly with the time and space constraints in most public schools. Fortunately, valid tests can be given in less than ideal conditions as long as the tester is sensitive to the behavior of the student. The student is observed carefully, and if noises or other environmental factors appear to interfere with concentration, testing is immediately discontinued. The testing environment checklist in Figure 4–1 can assist the tester in evaluating the adequacy of the room and other important factors.

Testing should not be attempted if seating arrangements are inadequate: if the student or tester must stand, if chairs are so low or high as to affect vision, if no work surface is available, or if the work surface is very small or not level. Ideal seats are comfortable, straight-backed chairs. Chairs should be of correct size, so that the student's feet comfortably touch the floor; chairs should not swivel. Chairs with attached desks or work surfaces are unsuitable. They offer too little space for test materials, do not allow the tester to sit close to the student, and, if slanted, permit test materials to slide onto the floor.

A table is the most appropriate work surface. The tester and student should be able to sit and write comfortably at the table. Rectangular or square tables are preferred; the surface should be large enough to hold necessary materials, yet narrow enough for the tester to reach across to the student's side. Many standardized tests are designed so the tester can sit across the table from the student; this arrangement facilitates the observation of student behavior and discourages the student from attempting to view the test manual and score sheet. Other tests require that students sit across the corner of the table from the tester.

The tester should gather all materials needed for administration (the examiner's manual, pencils and paper, and so forth) and place these in

Testing Environment Checklist

The Room	Optimal	Adequate	Poor
Size	☐	☐	☐
Lighting	☐	☐	☐
Temperature/ventilation	☐	☐	☐
Noise level	☐	☐	☐
Freedom from distractions	☐	☐	☐
Freedom from interruptions	☐	☐	☐

Seating			
Chairs	☐	☐	☐
Table	☐	☐	☐
Arrangement	☐	☐	☐

Equipment	Available	Not Applicable	Not Available
Test materials	☐	☐	☐
Writing implements	☐	☐	☐
Timing device	☐	☐	☐

	Optimal	Adequate	Poor
Arrangement	☐	☐	☐

Participants	Present
Student	☐
Tester	☐
Other(s)	☐
Explain:_____	

Summary
☐ The testing environment was adequate for administration of a valid test.
☐ The testing environment was not adequate for administration of a valid test because

_____

_____

FIGURE 4-1
Testing Environment Checklist

the testing room before the start of the test. If the tester discovers a vital piece of equipment missing once administration has begun, testing should be discontinued at a logical breaking point (such as between subtests), and the missing item obtained.

Most tests include stimulus material to be shown to the student, an examiner's manual for the tester, and score sheets or student record booklets. Other equipment may be furnished as part of the test kit, or the tester may need to obtain materials from the classroom. Generally, testers provide writing implements for themselves and the student. Several sharpened pencils of the size and type used by the student in the classroom should be available; these may have erasers if not prohibited by the test manual. The tester will also

need several pencils with erasers. Some tests require precise timing of student responses. If timing must be accurate to the second, appropriate devices include a stopwatch, a digital watch with output in seconds, or a clock or watch with a second hand; if minutes must be timed, a wristwatch or clock will suffice. Timing devices should be silent so they do not distract the student.

When the materials are arranged, the test kit is placed near the tester, on either the floor or a separate chair. Materials are then transferred to the table as needed. All distracting materials should be removed from the student's view and reach. No extraneous items such as books or toys should clutter the table.

There should be no one in the testing room but the tester and the student. However, a parent may need to accompany a young child into the room to help acclimate the child to the new environment. Parents or others should leave the room before test administration begins; observation is best done through a one-way glass, if available. If for some reason parents must remain, they should be observers out of the child's view, not participants. Unless specifically allowed by the test manual, parents or others should not administer test items.

Preparation of the Student

Scheduling the test at an optimal time, seeing to the student's physical needs, and preparing the student psychologically are critical components in testing. If these factors are neglected by an insensitive tester, the student's attitude may be affected, and it may become impossible to elicit optimal performance.

Schools are busy places. Schedules for classes, lunch, buses, and special events such as assemblies must be considered when setting up a time and place for testing. Usually the tester coordinates scheduling with the classroom teacher. Most teachers, concerned about schoolwork missed during testing, prefer that the student leave the classroom during his or her best subject or during the subjects with which he or she experiences difficulty.

Students' preferences must also be considered. Test performance will likely be affected if students are removed from the classroom during a favorite activity; their attention may be on recess, art, or whatever they are missing, rather than on the testing situation. Many students work more efficiently at certain times of the day, such as the early morning or midafternoon. The classroom teacher should be consulted to determine when the student is most alert, and, if possible, the test should be scheduled for that time.

Because tests are usually scheduled well in advance, the tester must check the student's physical and emotional status on the day of the test. If the student is ill, the test should be postponed. A toothache, cold, or other physical ailment can depress performance; pain may distract the student, a cold could impair hearing, and even an over-the-counter medication can interfere with normal

functioning. Emotional well-being also affects test performance. If the student is upset (for example, by the death of a pet), testing should be delayed. If the tester learns after testing that the student was under physical or mental stress, test results should be considered invalid or, at minimum, interpreted with great caution.

Before beginning the test, the tester should attend to the physical needs of the student. Students are best able to focus attention on test tasks if they are not distracted by pressing physiological needs, such as hunger and thirst. Students should visit the drinking fountain and restroom before the test and during breaks. Some students, particularly younger children, will not ask to go to the restroom, even when they are in dire need of a toilet break. In addition, the tester must make sure that students are wearing eyeglasses, hearing aids, or other required prosthetic devices. If the student is receiving medication, the tester should find out if it has been administered that day and, if so, the medication's possible effects upon test performance.

Preparing a student psychologically for testing is called *establishing rapport*. This procedure is explained by Anastasi and Urbina (1997) as "the examiner's efforts to arouse the test takers' interest in the test, elicit their cooperation, and encourage them to respond in a manner appropriate to the objectives of the test" (p. 15). To establish a good working relationship with the student, the tester should follow these steps:

1. *Introduction of the tester to the student.* The introduction should be friendly and unhurried and should convey the tester's pleasure at meeting the student. The tester gives his or her name and some indication of profession. For example, the tester might say, "My name is Ms. Geller and I'm a teacher who visits this school twice a week."

2. *Elicitation of general information from the student.* The tester engages the student in conversation by asking for his or her full name, age, grade, and favorite school subjects. This allows the student a chance to relax and provides the tester with some indication of the student's manner of expression and knowledge of personal information.

TABLE 4–1
Pretest Information for Students

Before test administration begins, each of the following factors should be explained by the tester in language appropriate to the student's age and ability level.

Length of the Test
Tell the student approximately how long the test will take either in terms of hours and minutes or classroom activities ("You'll be back in Ms. Lloyd's room before lunchtime").

Test Activities
Briefly describe the types of activities involved: listening, looking at pictures, talking, reading, writing, doing math, and so forth. If several different activities are required, let the student know that test tasks will change.

Test Difficulty
If appropriate, inform the student that there will be both easy and difficult items. Let the student know that he or she is not expected to answer every question correctly because some were designed for older age groups.

Confirmation of Responses
Advise the student that he or she will not be told if answers are right or wrong. The tester cannot give information about response accuracy.

Timed Tests
If parts of the test are timed, tell the student so he or she will know that speed is important. If a stopwatch will be used for timing, show it to the student and demonstrate its use.

3. *Explanation of the purpose of testing.* The meeting should be presented as an occasion for work ("We're going to do some work together") rather than play ("Today, we're going to play some games"). If students believe the test is merely a game, they may not put forth their best effort. However, the word "test" should be avoided because students may associate testing with past failures.

4. *Description of test activities.* The tester should explain exactly what will happen during the test situation. This will prepare the student and may relieve some anxiety. Some tests provide instructions describing test activities for the tester to read to the student. Table 4–1 explains important points to cover during pretest preparation.

5. *Encouragement of student questions.* Students should be provided the opportunity to ask questions about the test. The tester determines if the student understands what will occur and also gauges the student's readiness to begin. Discussion continues until the student becomes comfortable, or if the student is obviously upset and ill at ease, testing is postponed.

TEST ADMINISTRATION

The goal in administration of standardized tests is to obtain the best possible sample of student behavior under standard conditions. Strict adherence to the test manual's guidelines for administration and scoring is an absolute necessity. The manual usually provides instructions and test items to be read to the student. These words often appear in color or bold print and must be read verbatim. The tester may tell the student that he or she must "read some directions." The tester should not attempt to recite information from memory, and test items and directions may not be paraphrased, unless specifically allowed by the manual. However, they should be read in a natural tone of voice. The test manual also specifies the order of administration, if there are several parts or subtests within the test. Often, the subtests must be given in a set order that the tester may not vary. The manual informs the tester if it is permissible to delete some subtests and, if so, which ones.

Testing requires strict conformance to administration rules, together with the establishment of a dynamic working relationship between student and tester. Achieving this balance is particularly difficult for educators because of the differences between testing and teaching. The teacher automatically praises, prompts, and provides information; the tester can do none of these, yet must maintain an atmosphere of encouragement to promote the student's best efforts. As early as 1905, Binet and Simon observed:

> An inexperienced examiner has no idea of the influence of words; he talks too much, he aids his subject, he puts him on the track, unconscious of the help he is thus giving. He plays the part of pedagogue, when he should remain psychologist. (as quoted by Kessen, 1965, p. 199)

Because each test is different, it is always necessary to refer to the manual for specific administration rules. However, standardized measures have many commonalities, making it possible to provide a set of general guidelines, as shown in Table 4–2.

Recording Student Responses

The tester is often responsible for keeping a record of student responses. As the student replies to each question, the tester writes down the answer on the score sheet or record booklet. Once the test record form has been filled in, it is known as the *test protocol*. The protocol serves as the minutes of the testing situation. Because this record is used to evaluate and score the student's responses, it must be both accurate and complete. Recording student responses takes skill, and several rules should be followed.

Concealment of the Test Protocol

The test protocol is hidden from student view. Students should not be allowed to look at it unless, of course, it is necessary for test administration. A protocol may contain correct answers to the questions, and should students see them, test results would be invalidated. The protocol also contains the tester's record and evaluation of the student's responses. Seeing how answers were scored would provide students information about response accuracy; knowing they made several

errors might upset some students and affect test performance.

Hiding the protocol may take some manipulation of test materials, because several objects must be managed by the tester at the same time (manual, protocol, stimulus materials for the student, writing implements, and perhaps a stopwatch). The method used to conceal the protocol depends upon the specific materials involved and the tester's preference. Some testers place the protocol behind a propped-up test manual; others keep it on a clipboard that rests on the edge of the table. Each tester should find his or her most comfortable method.

Verbatim Recording of Student Responses

The tester keeps an exact record of student responses for scoring purposes and to assist in interpretation of results. It is often of interest to examine not only which test items were missed by the student but also what responses he or she gave to these items. For example, knowing what types of errors a student made on a reading test may be just as valuable as knowing the score, particularly when planning instructional strategies. The specific information noted by the tester in verbatim recording depends upon the nature of the test task. The tester may make a prose record of student comments or simply write the number of the picture selected by the student from four options. The conventional notation for recording an "I don't know" response is *DK,* and for indicating the student did not answer, *NR* (no response).

Accurate Scoring During Administration

Some tests require that the tester make an on-the-spot decision whether the student's response is correct. Each response must be carefully but quickly evaluated; otherwise, the student will lose interest. The response is scored and then recorded. Recording systems vary across measures. On some tests, correct responses are denoted by a 1 and incorrect responses by a 0; on others, + indicates a correct answer and − an incorrect answer. Testers must observe the recording conventions of the particular test so that other professionals can interpret the protocol. If

TABLE 4-2
General Guidelines for Test Administration

Test administration is a skill, and testers must learn how to react to typical student comments and questions. The following general guidelines apply to the majority of standardized tests.

Student Requests for Repetition of Test Items
Students often ask the tester to repeat a question. This is usually permissible as long as the item is repeated verbatim and in its entirety. However, repetition of memory items that measure the student's ability to recall information is not allowed.

Asking Students to Repeat Responses
Sometimes the tester must ask the student to repeat a response. Perhaps the tester did not hear what the student said, or the student's speech is difficult to understand. However, the tester should make every effort to see or hear the student's first answer. The student may refuse to repeat a response or, thinking that the request for repetition means the first response was unsatisfactory, answer differently.

Student Modification of Responses
When students give one response, then change their minds and give a different one, the tester should accept the last response, even if the modification comes after the tester has moved to another item. However, some tests specify that only the first response may be accepted for scoring.

Confirming and Correcting Student Responses
The tester may not in any way—verbal or nonverbal—inform a student whether a response is correct. Correct responses may not be confirmed; wrong responses may not be corrected. This rule is critical for professionals who both teach and test, because their first inclination is to reinforce correct answers.

Reinforcing Student Work Behavior
Although testers cannot praise students for their performance on specific test items, good work behavior can and should be rewarded. Appropriate comments are, "You're working hard" and, "I like the way you're trying to answer every question." Students should be praised between test items or subtests to ensure that reinforcement is not linked to specific responses.

Encouraging Students to Respond
When students fail to respond to a test item, the tester can encourage them to give an answer. Students sometimes say nothing when presented with a difficult item, or they may comment, "I don't know" or "I can't do that one." The tester should repeat the item and say, "Give it a try" or "You can take a guess." The aim is to encourage the student to attempt all test items.

Questioning Students
Questioning is permitted on many tests. If, in the judgment of the tester, the response given by the student is neither correct nor incorrect, the tester repeats the student's answer in a questioning tone and says, "Tell me more about that." This prompts the student to explain so that the response can be scored. However, clearly wrong answers should not be questioned.

Coaching
Coaching differs from encouragement and questioning in that it helps a student arrive at an answer. The tester must *never* coach the student. Coaching invalidates the student's response; test norms are based on the assumption that students will respond without examiner assistance. Testers must be very careful to avoid coaching.

Administration of Timed Items
Some tests include timed items; the student must reply within a certain period to receive credit. In general, the time period begins when the tester finishes presentation of the item. A watch or clock should be used to time student performance.

a different system is used for some reason, the tester should write a key for that system on the protocol.

Use of Mechanical Recording Devices

Unless allowed by the manual, no mechanical recording equipment, such as tape recorders or video cameras, should be introduced into the testing environment. Many novice testers tape-record a session and then later review the tape to check their scoring of student responses or even to enter student responses on the protocol. This is a bad practice for several reasons. Mechanical devices are typically not part of the standard conditions for test administration, and recording equipment may distract the student. Even if recording is unobtrusive, tapes should not be trusted as the sole source of results. Breakdowns do occur; and if a tape were to fail, the only recourse would be readministration of the test. Although taping practice sessions can assist in learning a new test, testers should acquire the skills of recording student responses during test administration. Few practicing professionals have the leisure to review tapes of each testing session.

Administering Test Items

Before beginning the test, the tester and student should complete the identification section of the test form. Most forms provide space for the name of the student, the tester's name, the date of testing, and pertinent student data, such as age, gender, grade, and teacher. If appropriate, the student can fill in a portion of the form. Recording this information is a necessary step in testing; a form with only the student's first name is virtually useless. At minimum, a protocol should contain the student's full name, the date of testing, and the tester's name.

Some tests are designed so that each item is administered to each student; students begin with the first item and continue until the last is completed. More typically, standardized tests cover a wide range of difficulty, and students attempt only that portion of the test appropriate to their skill level. For example, no student could complete all items in measures for use with grades 1 through 12. Some items would likely be too easy and others too hard, and the time required for test administration would be prohibitive. Test items are arranged in order of difficulty, and whereas one student might receive items 10 to 30, another might attempt items 50 to 95. Demonstration items may be provided for administration at the start of the test or subtest. Demonstration items are activities similar to but usually easier than test tasks. They acquaint students with the type of items to follow and, if necessary, allow the tester to teach the student how to perform test tasks. The rules of teaching, not testing, apply to the presentation of demonstration items. The tester can and should coach the student, reinforce correct answers, and correct wrong ones. If the tester cannot elicit correct responses to these items, testing should be discontinued. Demonstration items are never included in the student's score.

Most test manuals tell how to locate the appropriate point within the test to begin presentation of items. For some students, the very first item is the suggested starting place; for others, it would be unrealistic to begin at the easiest item. Because guidelines differ across measures, the test manual must always be consulted. For example, a test manual might recommend beginning at item 1 for children aged 5 and at item 30 for children aged 6.

After selecting a starting point, the tester presents items to the student in an attempt to locate items of appropriate difficulty. The basal, or range of successful performance, is determined. Testing then continues to establish the ceiling, or the level at which the student is no longer successful.

The *basal* is the point in the test at which it can be assumed that the student would receive full credit for all easier items. To establish a basal, the tester administers items until the student has correctly completed some specified number of items. The student is then given credit for passing earlier, easier items, even though these were not administered. The basal allows the tester to skip items that would be too easy for the student, thereby saving time. The student, having answered several questions correctly, begins the test with a feeling of success.

Tests vary as to the number of items required to establish a basal. On some, the student must correctly answer three consecutively numbered items; for example, a basal would be established by correct responses for items 9, 10, and 11. On other measures, the student must correctly answer five or even eight consecutively numbered items for the tester to assume success on all easier items.

Determining the basal is not always easy. The tester begins administration at the suggested starting point and proceeds through the test items. If a 10-year-old is to be tested and the manual recommends beginning with item 20 for students ages 10 to 12, the tester begins with item 20. As shown in the following example, the student answers the question correctly, and the tester writes a + in the space next to the item number. The student also answers items 21 and 22 correctly. Because the basal requirement is three consecutive correct responses, a basal is established. The tester will continue administration with item 23.

BASAL: 3 consecutive correct responses

	18.	_____	
	19.	_____	
(10)	20.	___+___	First item administered
	21.	___+___	Second item administered
	22.	___+___	Third item administered

In this example, the starting point designated by the manual was appropriate for the student. Items were not too difficult and the student quickly achieved three consecutive correct responses. This is not always the case. Sometimes the first or second item administered to the student is answered incorrectly. When this happens, the tester has to present items out of order to establish the basal. Generally, when a student makes an error during the search for the basal, the tester immediately begins to proceed backward through the test. Table 4–3 explains this procedure.

Suggested starting points can also be too low. For example, the student may begin with item 5 and answer the next 15 questions correctly. At the start of a test, if there is indication that items are too easy for the student, the tester may move forward to more difficult items. Testers should take care, however, not to present very difficult items before students have achieved some success. It is far worse to discourage students than to use extra administration time presenting easy items.

Once the basal is determined, testing continues until a ceiling is reached. The *ceiling* is defined as the point at which it can be assumed that the student would receive no credit for all more difficult test items. The ceiling is established by a specified number of incorrect responses; the test ends when the ceiling is determined. Like basals, tests differ in the number of items required for the ceiling. Some measures specify three incorrect responses on consecutively numbered items; others require 5, 8, or even 10 consecutive errors. A ceiling can also be defined in terms of a range of items; for example, the ceiling might be five errors within seven consecutive responses.

Ceilings are established the same way as basals, except the tester seeks a series of incorrect responses. In the following example, the ceiling is three consecutive incorrect responses. The suggested starting item for third graders is item 3. The tester therefore began at item 3; a basal was achieved when the third grader answered items 3, 4, and 5 correctly. The student then missed items 6, 7, and 8, establishing a ceiling.

BASAL: 3 consecutive correct responses
CEILING: 3 consecutive incorrect responses

	1.	_____
	2.	_____
(3)	3.	___+___
	4.	___+___
	5.	___+___
	6.	___−___
	7.	___−___
	8.	___−___

Students often achieve a basal and then answer several questions correctly before missing any. When they encounter items that are difficult for them, they may answer some correctly and others incorrectly before reaching the ceiling. The following example depicts this type of response pattern. The tenth grade student began the test at the recommended starting point, item 15. The student answered several items correctly and did not make an error until item 19. Item 20

TABLE 4–3
Establishing the Basal

Sometimes the tester begins a test at exactly the right starting point, and the basal is easily achieved as the student correctly answers the first several questions. It is just as usual, however, for the student to miss one of the first items presented. When this occurs, the tester must present earlier, easier items.

Presume that a sixth grader was given a test in which the basal is four consecutive correct responses. The recommended starting point for sixth grade students is item 11, and the tester began there. The student answered the first item correctly but missed item 12. Here is what the protocol looked like at this point.

BASAL: 4 consecutive correct responses

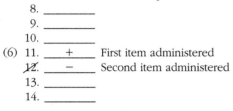

```
        8. _____
        9. _____
       10. _____
 (6)   11. ____+_____   First item administered
       12. ____–_____   Second item administered
       13. _____
       14. _____
```

The basal cannot be established without four consecutive correct responses. The tester proceeds backward until a basal of four consecutively numbered correct items is established. As shown in the following example, after the student missed item 12, the tester administered item 10, then item 9, then item 8. When the student answered these correctly, there was a basal. Testing will continue with item 13.

BASAL: 4 consecutive correct responses

```
        8. ____+_____   Fifth item administered
        9. ____+_____   Fourth item administered
       10. ____+_____   Third item administered
 (6)   11. ____+_____   First item administered
       12. ____–_____   Second item administered; when missed, tester moved to item 10
       13. _____
       14. _____
```

In this example, the tester moved backward item by item until a basal was achieved. However, some tests require that the tester skip back several items or move back to a previous page. The tester should check each manual for specific instructions.

was correct, 21 incorrect, and 22 correct; a ceiling was established with errors on items 23, 24, and 25.

BASAL: 3 consecutive correct responses
CEILING: 3 consecutive incorrect responses

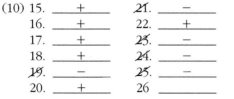

```
(10)  15. ____+_____    21. ____–_____
      16. ____+_____    22. ____+_____
      17. ____+_____    23. ____–_____
      18. ____+_____    24. ____–_____
      19. ____–_____    25. ____–_____
      20. ____+_____    26 _____
```

The test manual is the best source for information about suggested starting points and basal and ceiling rules. Some test forms also provide this information. Although they are no substitute for studying the manual, these brief notations on the test record serve as reminders during test administration.

Ending the Test and Retesting

The testing session should include periodic breaks to ward off fatigue. The length of the session and the endurance of the participants determine how often these breaks should occur. With elementary students, a short rest break should be given at least every half hour; more frequent breaks may be necessary with pre-school children. Secondary grade students and adults can usually work from 45 minutes to an hour before needing a rest period. Breaks should occur at a logical stopping point in administration, such as at the end of a test or subtest. During the break, students should be encouraged to stand up, move about, and visit the restroom and drinking fountain.

Testing ends when all scheduled activities are completed, the time allotted is exhausted, or the student is no longer able to work efficiently due to fatigue or loss of concentration. At the end of the session, the tester should thank the student for his or her cooperation and explain what will happen next. This might be further testing on another day, a meeting of the student and tester to go over results, or testing with another professional. The tester answers any questions the student may have and then accompanies the student back to the classroom. The tester should review the session as soon as possible and attempt to evaluate the quality of his or her relationship with the student and the adequacy of the administration process.

It may be necessary to readminister a test at some later date. Readministration of achievement measures to assess progress is routine; students may be given a reading test at the beginning of the school year and then again at the end to measure their growth. Sometimes, however, retesting must occur after only a brief interval. For example, the tester may need to readminister the test within a period of days or weeks, if the original administration was invalidated due to tester error or a student health problem.

Retesting can take place immediately if the test has multiple forms. For instance, if the results of form A were invalid for some reason, form B could be administered the next day. To determine the equivalency of alternate forms of a test, the tester should check the manual's description of equivalent-form reliability.

For measures with only one form, readministration should be delayed as long as possible, preferably for 2 to 4 weeks. If this is impossible, results of the second administration should be interpreted cautiously because a practice effect is likely. The test manual may provide information on how scores are affected by practice in a test-retest situation.

OBSERVATION OF TEST BEHAVIOR

Skilled testers handle the mechanics of test administration automatically so they can concentrate on observing the student's behavior during testing. How students act in the testing situation—what they do and say, how they approach a task, and what their general work methods are—is important in interpreting results. The student who is eager, attentive, and anxious to perform well during testing is quite different from one who is withdrawn and uncooperative. Such behavioral descriptions assist in interpretation of results and provide a beginning for planning instructional strategies.

Observation is a process of collecting data on student behavior. In the observation of test behavior, the tester records information about the student's words and actions. Observational data are objective, precise descriptions of how students behave, and they easily communicate what occurred during testing. Statements such as "John left his seat 13 times during the first 10 minutes of testing" provide useful assessment information. Judgments or opinions such as "Janice was shy and retiring" or "Darren was easily distracted" do not, unless substantiated by observational data. The specific techniques used in observation of student behavior are explained in Chapter 5. One of the first things the tester should observe is the student's approach to the testing situation. How does the student act when presented with directions and the first few tasks? Is he or she able to adjust quickly to the demands of this new working environment? The tester should be alert for both verbal and nonverbal clues. Students may comment, "I don't wanna stay here," "I like writing with pencils," or "I'm ready to work." They may also express themselves by actions, such as failure to establish eye contact. Also of interest is how students begin the first test task. Some start working immediately, whereas others appear to have difficulty focusing their attention on a new activity.

The tester should also observe the student's style of responding: the response mode selected,

TABLE 4-4
Observation of Response Style

Response Mode

Which response mode—verbal or nonverbal—does the student favor? If a question can be answered either by pointing to a response or by saying it, which mode does the student select? With questions requiring a yes or no response, does the student speak or gesture? Some students accompany even written responses with talk; others speak only when absolutely necessary.

Latency

Latency is the delay between presentation of the test task and the beginning of a response. Students may begin to answer as soon as or even before the tester finishes introducing the tasks; others may delay a few seconds. Some students wait for as long as a minute but then respond correctly. Very short or very long response latencies are noteworthy, particularly in relation to classroom performance.

Length

The length of an answer is not necessarily an indication of its accuracy; depending upon the content of the response and the scoring standards of the test, a brief response may earn as many points as a lengthy one. Verbal responses of students may be characterized by brevity or length. Such patterns should be noted by the tester.

Organization

Although the organization of a response may not be germane to scoring, it is important. A response may be logical and well organized; an equally correct one may be rambling and poorly ordered. How students organize answers provides information about their ability to structure, order, and clearly present their thoughts.

Method of Expressing Inability to Respond

The tester should watch for the student's method of responding when he or she does not know the answer to a question. Some will simply say, "I don't know." Others will say they don't know but will then attempt to explain their inability to answer ("That's fifth grade stuff and I haven't had it yet") or will substitute something they do know ("I can't spell *dog* but I can do *cat:* c-a-t"). Students who express ignorance before the tester has finished the question or who routinely respond to certain types of questions with "I can't do that" should be encouraged to attempt the item. With students who say nothing when they do not know an answer, the tester should wait a reasonable length of time and then encourage the student to at least take a guess. It is important to consider the student's typical response latency so as not to confuse a long delay before answering with an inability to respond.

Idiosyncratic Responses

Occasionally students will give responses that appear to have no relationship to the question. The tester should repeat the question to make sure the student understood what was asked, then ask the student to explain the answer. This is done by repeating the student's answer in a questioning tone and saying, "Tell me what you mean."

the latency between question and answer, the length of the response, and so forth. Table 4–4 describes several important dimensions of response style.

Another major concern is the general work style of the student. The following factors should be considered in observation:

1. *Activity level.* The tester should note obvious signs of activity (standing up, walking around the testing room), as well as more subtle behaviors. Students can be very active without ever leaving their seats. They can squirm around, tap their fingers, and jiggle their legs up and down. High activity levels can distract the student from the test tasks, thereby lowering test performance.

2. *Attention to task.* Some students are able to sustain attention to test tasks for several minutes or for the entire administration period; others appear to become distracted after a very short time. The tester can quantify inattention by counting the number of student remarks unrelated to test activities or the

number of times the student looks away from test materials. When the student's attention is away from the task 25% or more of the time, the tester should consider taking a break or ending the session.

3. *Perseverance.* When presented with an activity, is the student able to persevere until the task is finished? Or does the student give up after a brief attempt? The tester can collect data by timing how long the student works on a particular task.

4. *Need for reassurance.* Many students, anxious about their performance, query the tester about the accuracy of their responses. Even though it has been explained at the beginning of the test that the tester cannot tell them if their answers are right or wrong, students often end a response with the question, "Is that right?" The tester should reiterate that it is against the rules to let them know. An attempt should be made to reassure such students with positive comments such as, "You're working hard." The tester should begin to collect observational data if students persist with this concern.

Comments made during testing may provide information about student attitudes and feelings. Students may talk about how they perceive their abilities ("I'm dumb in school" or "I can do puzzles real good") or their performance on various test tasks ("I can read pretty well now" or "I'm lousy at spelling"). They may also comment about the test by asking, "Can I do more of these?" or "Are we almost done?" Testers should listen when students talk, answer when appropriate, and record any statements that may be useful in interpreting results.

Testers should also be alert to any warning signs of disabilities. The student's speech should be considered in terms of its intelligibility, articulation, pitch, and volume. Loud or unclear speech may be an indication of hearing problems, as are frequent requests for repetition of test items. Symptoms of vision problems include bringing reading materials close to the face, having red and watery eyes, and rubbing the eyes. If any aspect of the student's test behavior suggests possible speech, hearing, vision, physical, or emotional problems, the tester should refer the student to the appropriate professional for further assessment. If some severe difficulty is confirmed, test results will probably be invalid.

As observational data are collected during testing, they should be recorded. Testers should not trust their memories, particularly their recall of student comments. Some test forms provide space for notations about behaviors; others include checklists for use in rating the student's behavior. However, because space is limited on most forms, experienced testers often bring along extra paper to record observational data and student comments.

SCORING THE TEST

The standard conditions that form the basis of norm-referenced tests also apply to conversion of student responses into test scores. Scoring is a critical step that transforms the student's test responses into comparative data. Accuracy is imperative; every count and calculation must be correct. The amount of time and number of computations required for scoring differ with each test. Some are scored quickly with few calculations, whereas others may take as long or longer to score than to administer.

Tests should be scored as soon as possible after administration. At this time, the tester should also review the observational data, because these may aid in the interpretation of numerical scores. Many experienced testers score the test right after it is given and again later to recheck their accuracy.

Sometimes in scoring, it is necessary to know the student's exact chronological age—the number of years and months since birth. Calculation of the student's actual age at the time of testing requires both the student's birth date and the date of testing. Table 4–5 explains the computational procedure. Chronological age (CA) is generally written as two numbers separated by a hyphen. For instance, CA 6-3 refers to 6 years, 3 months. The hyphen cannot be replaced with a decimal point. CA 10.6 is not the same as CA 10-6. CA 10.6 is 10 years and 6/10 of a year, an older age than 10 1/2; CA 10-6 is 10 years, 6 months, equal to 10 1/2 years.

TABLE 4-5
Calculating Chronological Age

To determine the student's exact age at the time of testing, subtract the birth date from the test date. The year, month, and day of testing are written first, then the same information for the student's date of birth.

To subtract, the tester begins with the right-hand column and first subtracts days, then months, and finally years.

Year	Month	Day	
2000	11	29	Date of testing
−1988	8	11	Date of birth
12	3	18	Chronological age

If borrowing is required, convert 1 year into 12 months and 1 month into 30 days. In the following example, it was necessary to borrow 1 month (from 6 months) to convert 4 days to 34 days.

Year	Month	Day	
	5	34	
2001	6̸	4̸	Date of testing
−1987	3	31	Date of birth
14	2	3	Chronological age

In the next example, both years and months were converted before subtracting. First, 2 months were reduced to 1, and 8 days were increased to 38; then 2000 years were reduced to 1999 and 1 month increased to 13.

Year	Month	Day	
	13		
1999	1̸	38	
2̶0̶0̶0̶	2̸	8̸	Date of testing
−1990	10	28	Date of birth
9	3	10	Chronological age

Chronological age is generally reported in terms of years and months, but not days. However, the number of days is considered. The convention is to add 1 month if the number of days is greater than 15; if days equal 15 or less, the number of months is not changed. Thus,

8 years, 4 months, 9 days = 8 - 4
10 years, 6 months, 20 days = 10 - 7

Computing Raw Scores

Raw scores, the first to be computed by the tester, describe the number of points earned by a student on a test or subtest. The first step is to determine which test items were answered correctly. This is often done during administration. The tester then assigns point values to each correct response. On many tests, each item is simply worth 1 point; on others, a student can earn 0, 1, 2, or 3 points depending upon response accuracy. Items within a test can vary in point value. For example, easier items may be worth 1 point; more difficult items, 2 points; and the most difficult, 3 points. The test manual provides scoring guidelines with information on item point values.

The raw score is computed by adding the total number of points earned by the student to the total number of points assumed to be earned. Credit is given for the items below the basal that, although not administered, were assumed to be answered correctly. If items below the basal take on a range of possible points, the student is credited with the highest number; for instance, if correct responses receive either 1, 2, or 3 points, it is assumed the student would have earned a score of 3, had the item actually been administered.

Table 4–6 presents an example of raw score computation. The test began at item 3, and a basal was achieved when the student correctly answered items 3, 4, and 5. Incorrect responses

TABLE 4-6
Computing Raw Scores

Steps in Computing the Raw Score
Step 1: Rate each response correct or incorrect.
Step 2: Assign point values to each response.
Step 3: Calculate number of points earned (in the example below, 4).
Step 4: Calculate number of points assumed earned (2).
Step 5: Add the number of points earned and the number of points assumed earned (4 + 2 = 6).

Example of Raw Score Computation
BASAL: 3 consecutive correct responses
CEILING: 3 consecutive incorrect responses
Each item is worth 1 point.

1.	_____
2.	_____
3.	___+___
4.	___+___
5.	___+___
6.	___−___
7.	___+___
8.	___−___
9.	___−___
10.	___−___
RAW SCORE	6

on items 8, 9, and 10 established the ceiling. Because each item is worth 1 point, the student earned a total of 4 points by correctly answering questions 3, 4, 5, and 7. Credit must also be given for items 1 and 2, the items below the basal assumed to be correct. When the number of points earned (4) is added to the number of points assumed to be earned (2), a total raw score of 6 is obtained.

Converting Raw Scores to Derived Scores

Raw scores must be converted to other scores for a student's performance to be contrasted with that of the norm group. Depending on the test, several types of derived scores may be available: age equivalents, grade equivalents, percentile ranks, standard scores, and others.

Test manuals provide tables for converting raw scores into other scores. The student's raw score is computed, the correct norms table is located, and the derived score is read from the table. Table 4–7 presents sample test norms for students

age 9-0 to 9-6. The tester finds the student's raw score in the first column, then reads across to determine age equivalent, grade equivalent, percentile rank, and standard score. For example, a raw score of 5 for someone age 9-3 would be equivalent to a percentile rank of 35 and a standard score of 94. When no scores are listed for a particular raw score, the student's performance is considered either above or below norms. On the sample norms table, a raw score of 1 would be below norms, and a raw score of 12 above norms.

Sometimes the tester must consult more than one table to obtain all needed scores. For instance, one table may be used to convert raw scores to percentile ranks, and a second to convert percentile ranks to standard scores. Tests also differ in how tables are arranged; raw scores can be listed across the top of the table, down the left-hand side, or even down the middle. Testers should be careful to select appropriate tables for the age or grade of the student and to read each table accurately. Some testers find it helpful to use a ruler or index card to help keep their place.

TABLE 4–7
Sample Norms Table

AGE 9-0 TO 9-6				
Raw Score	Age Equivalent	Grade Equivalent	Percentile Rank	Standard Score
1	—	—	—	—
2	6-0	1.0	5	75
3	6-9	1.7	15	84
4	7-5	2.4	20	87
5	8-2	2.9	35	94
6	9-0	3.5	50	100
7	9-5	3.8	55	102
8	9-11	4.4	60	104
9	10-5	4.8	75	110
10	11-0	5.5	85	116
11	12-1	6.2	90	119
12	—	—	—	—

Many test protocols include graphs or profiles for plotting the student's derived scores. This visual representation may assist in interpreting and explaining test results to students and parents. Test manuals provide instructions for plotting the profile; as with all aspects of scoring, accuracy should be a prime concern.

INTERPRETING TEST RESULTS

Results of standardized tests are used to make educational decisions. Tests are administered and scored and their results interpreted to determine how students perform in relation to age or grade peers. Interpretation of results involves a number of considerations. These include determining the relationship of test behavior to test scores, weighing which test scores provide the most valuable information, allowing for measurement error when reporting results, and evaluating test performance in relation to norm-referenced criteria.

Test Behavior

During test administration, the tester observes the student's behavior. Observational data are then evaluated in relation to the student's scores. Some important questions the tester should consider in interpreting test behavior are:

1. Did the student show *consistent* test behavior? Or did behavior change from task to task or from early in the testing session to later?
2. What types of behaviors were exhibited during tests or subtests that assessed the student's *strengths,* that is, the areas in which the student earned the highest scores?
3. What types of behaviors were exhibited during tests or subtests that assessed the student's *weaknesses?*
4. Was the student's test behavior *representative* of usual classroom behavior? Of behavior in the home?

These factors influence test performance. For example, a student may attend well to the tasks presented at the start of assessment, whether those tasks represent strengths or weaknesses. However, he or she may soon lose interest in testing and respond quickly and carelessly. Or a student may refuse to attempt all tasks relating to a certain skill, such as reading or mathematics. Test behaviors should be described in detail when reporting results.

Choice of Test Scores

A standardized test may offer several types of scores—age and grade equivalents, percentile ranks, standard scores, and so forth. In interpreting test results, it is necessary to choose the scores that will be most useful for quantifying the student's performance and for reporting results to parents and professionals.

As Chapter 3 explained, age and grade equivalents appear to be the simplest scores to interpret but are, in fact, quite complicated. Their use is not recommended for this and other reasons. One major limitation is that they do not provide information about whether a student's performance is within average limits. If a 7-year-old earns a score of age 6 on a measure, this does not indicate the student's standing in relation to others of the same age. The performance of the student could be quite average for 7-year-olds or could fall below the average range of functioning for this age group. If a student in grade 4.3 earns an achievement score of grade 3.9, is the difference significant enough to suggest an achievement problem? Age and grade scores are not useful for answering such questions.

Age and grade scores only appear to provide precise information about a student's instructional or developmental level. If a student earns a grade score of 7.3, this means only that he or she earned a raw score roughly equivalent to that of the seventh grade students in the norm group, if there were seventh grade students in the norm group and the score is not the result of extrapolation. Grade scores do not describe the student's current instructional level. They are not even indicative of which test questions were answered correctly. Two students can earn the same age or grade score but not answer any of the same questions correctly. Anastasi and Urbina (1997) sum up this problem in the interpretation of age and grade scores:

> If a fourth-grade child obtains a grade equivalent of 6.9 in arithmetic, it does *not* mean that she mastered the arithmetic processes taught in the sixth grade. She undoubtedly obtained her score largely by superior performance in fourth-grade arithmetic. It certainly could not be assumed that she has the prerequisites for seventh-grade arithmetic. (p. 56)

Unfortunately, sometimes age and grade equivalents are the only available scores from a particular test. In this situation, they should be reported, but findings should be worded carefully to prevent misinterpretation.

Grade Equivalents

Jorge earned a grade equivalent score of 6.3 on Test X. This may mean that Jorge's raw score on this test was equal to the average raw score of grade 6.3 students in the test's norm group. However, because it is likely the decimal grade equivalents on Test X were derived from the scores earned by grade 6 students, it is more accurate to say that Jorge's raw score approximated the average raw score earned by grade 6 students in the test's norm group.

Age equivalent scores are reported in a similar fashion.

Percentile rank scores are preferable to age and grade equivalents because they are comparative scores. They are straightforward indicators of an individual's standing within a group and are easily interpreted. Percentile rank scores are reported by referring to that portion of the norm group against which the student is being compared.

Percentile Ranks

Harvey, aged 10-3, scored at the 32nd percentile on Text X when compared with age peers. This means that Harvey's performance on this test was equal to or better than that of 32% of the 10-year-old students in Test X's norm group.

Standard scores have many advantages. They are comparative, and when based upon a normal or normalized distribution of raw scores, they can be directly translated into percentile ranks. Also, because standard scores have a uniform mean and standard deviation, they can be compared from one subtest to the next and from one test administration to another.

In addition, standard scores provide information about whether a student's performance is within average limits. They describe the relationship of a student's score to the average score of the comparison group within the norming sample. For example, if standard scores on a particular test are distributed with a mean of 100 and a standard deviation of 15, a standard score of 70 indicates performance two standard deviations below the mean performance of the comparison group for students of any grade or age. That comparison group would be the grade 8 students within the norm group if an eighth grader's performance is being evaluated; if a first grader is under study, the comparison group would be the first graders within the norm group.

Standard Scores

Chau, a seventh grader, received a standard score of 115 on Test X when compared with grade peers. Because the mean standard score on this test is 100 and the standard deviation is 15, Chau's score indicates performance one standard deviation above the mean of seventh grade students in Test X's norm group.

Percentile ranks can be reported along with the student's standard scores.

Measurement Error

Test scores, like any other measurement, always contain some element of error. Even if a test is administered and scored in strict adherence to standardization conditions, the scores will be observed scores, consisting of the student's hypothetical true score plus an error component. Fortunately, with standardized tests, the standard error of measurement can be used to estimate the amount of error likely to occur within scores. As Chapter 3 explained, the standard error of measurement is based upon the test's reliability and standard deviation. Tests with poor reliability and large standard deviations produce large standard errors. The smaller the standard error of measurement, the more accurate the results. In most cases, standard errors are reported in the test manual. If not, they can be calculated by means of the formula provided in Chapter 3. The standard error of measurement is used to construct confidence intervals around observed scores. With confidence intervals, a student's performance is reported as a range of scores in which it is highly likely that the true score will fall, rather than as a single score known to include both the true score and error. Sattler (1988) recommends reporting scores in this way:

> The student obtained a score of 100 ± 4. The chances that the range of scores from 96 to 104 includes the student's true score are about 68 out of 100.

The procedure for constructing confidence intervals is quite straightforward. After an observed score has been obtained and the standard error of measurement for that score is known, a decision is made about the degree of confidence desired. The tester may be satisfied with 68% confidence that the student's true score will fall within the range of scores to be constructed. Or a higher degree of confidence may be called for, such as 90%, 95%, or even 99%. The standard error of measurement is then multiplied by a factor related to the level of confidence. The factors, the z scores associated with the confidence levels, are:

Confidence Level Desired	Factor by Which Standard Error Is Multiplied
68%	1.00
85%	1.44
90%	1.64
95%	1.96
99%	2.58

The product of the standard error times the factor is added to the student's observed score to determine the upper limit of the range. The product is then subtracted from the student's observed score to determine the lower limit.

For example, a student's observed score is 100, and the standard error of measurement for that score is 5. If the desired confidence level is 68%, the standard error (5) will be multiplied by the factor (1) to equal 5. The upper limit of the confidence interval becomes 105 (100 + 5), and the lower limit 95 (100 − 5). The student's score is reported as 100 ± 5, with a probability of 68% that the student's true score lies within that range.

If a more conservative estimate is needed, the confidence level could be set at 95%. In this case, the standard error (5) would be multiplied by 1.96 to equal 10. The confidence interval would then extend from 90 to 110, increasing the chances that this range would include the student's true score to 95 out of 100. When the level of confidence is increased, the width of the confidence interval also increases. In the previous example, increasing the confidence level from 68% to 95% changed the range of scores within the confidence interval from 95–105 to 90–110. The magnitude of the standard error of measurement also affects the width of the confidence interval. Consider these examples:

Example 1

Observed score	100
Standard error of measurement	5
Confidence level	68%
Confidence interval	95 to 105

Example 2

Observed score	100
Standard error of measurement	20
Confidence level	68%
Confidence interval	80 to 120

In these examples, the student's observed score and the level of confidence remain the same. When the standard error is 5, the confidence interval is 95 to 105. However, when the standard error increases to 20, the confidence interval becomes much larger. Tests with small standard errors of measurement allow more precision in the estimation of true scores.

Criteria for Evaluating Test Performance

Norm-referenced tests compare one student's performance against the performance of counterparts in the norm group. Standard score ranges should be used for this purpose.

Many standardized measures provide guidelines for test interpretation. These systems often are based upon a set of standard score ranges, each of which is given a descriptive label. For example, the manual for the *Wechsler Intelligence Scale for Children-Third Edition* (Wechsler, 1991) uses these labels to describe its standard score (IQ) ranges: "average" (the range from IQ 90 to 109), "low average" (80 to 89), "borderline" (70 to 79), "intellectually deficient" (69 and below). However, this system is not used consistently

from test to test. Some measures use different labels to describe student performance, and on others, the ranges into which standard scores are divided are defined in a different way.

Although there is no universally accepted system for describing ranges of performance, judicious use of standard score ranges can facilitate the interpretation of test results. In this book, we describe ranges of standard scores in terms of their distance from the test mean. Score ranges are defined in standard deviation units—within one standard deviation of the mean, between one and two standard deviations below the mean, and so forth. Ranges of performance are also defined in relation to the percentage of population each includes.

Thus, the *average range of performance* is the standard score range within one standard deviation from the mean. On a test with standard scores distributed with a mean of 100 and a standard deviation of 15, this range extends from standard score 85 to standard score 115. If the test is normally distributed, that range encompasses 68% of the norm group.

The *low average range of performance* is the standard score range between one and two standard deviations below the mean. It extends from standard score 70 to standard score 84 and includes approximately 14% of the population. Similarly, the *high average range of performance* is defined as the standard score range between one and two standard deviations above the mean. It includes standard scores 116 to 130 and represents approximately 14% of the population.

At the extreme ends of the distribution are the *below average range of performance* and the *above average range of performance*. Each represents approximately 2% of the population. The below average range encompasses standard scores 69 and below, and the above average range encompasses standard scores 131 and above. Figure 4–2 shows the ranges of performance in relation to the normal distribution.

Labels such as "average" and "low average" are arbitrary, although in this system they are tied to percentages of the population. Deciding that a score indicates below average performance by a standard such as "2 years below grade level" is even more arbitrary and is fraught with measurement

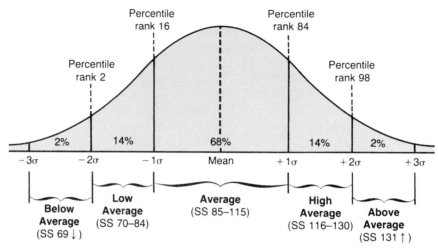

FIGURE 4-2
Test Interpretation Using Standard Score Ranges

difficulties. When linked with percentile ranks, standard score ranges fulfill the purpose of norm-referenced testing and compare the student's performance with that of his or her peers.

In reporting the results of standardized tests, keep in mind several factors. First, standard scores are preferred over other types of scores. Second, report scores as confidence intervals rather than as single scores, noting the level of confidence associated with the interval. Third, describe scores in relation to their range of performance, such as average, low average, and so on. Following these recommendations, a standard score of 79 on a test with a standard score mean of 100, a standard deviation of 15, and a standard error of measurement of 3 would be reported in the following way:

Standard Scores Expressed in Confidence Intervals

Priscilla, a fifth grader, earned a standard score of 79 ± 3 on Test X when compared with grade peers. The chances that the range of scores from 76 to 82 includes Priscilla's true score are about 68 out of 100. A score within this range indicates low average performance in comparison to the fifth grade students in Test X's norm group.

COMPUTERS AS TOOLS FOR ASSESSMENT

In the past decade, the number of computers in American schools has increased dramatically, and today most teachers have access to computers. Computers store, sort, and retrieve large amounts of information quickly, and this capability can expedite many aspects of the assessment process. As the following paragraphs discuss, computers can aid in the administration of tests, test scoring, interpretation of results, and report writing.

Test Administration

Just as computers can deliver instruction to students, they can also administer some types of tests. In this application of computer technology to assessment, the student sits down at a computer, reads the on-screen instructions, and types in answers to questions. The computer program then evaluates the student's responses, calculates test scores, and prepares a written report for the teacher.

At present, computer-assisted testing is rarely used with children and adolescents with disabilities. One major reason for this is that test administration by computer may depress student performance. Students with mild disabilities, as a group, have difficulty reading, writing, controlling their behavior, and focusing their attention on task. Using computers for test administration could exacerbate these difficulties. Although reading and keyboarding demands are concerns, the major drawback is the inability of the computer to monitor the student's behavior, provide motivation and encouragement, observe the student's interaction with the task, and direct the student's attention back to the task as necessary. Individual administration of standardized tests by a trained examiner remains the preferred practice for students with disabilities, at least at present.

Few standardized measures have been designed for (or converted to) computer administration, and most of those available are adult measures (e.g., career counseling tools and adult personality tests). However, development efforts continue, and computer-based measures of academic skills are becoming more common. Some are informal measures designed to help teachers track students' progress through the curriculum. Others are more formal tests of academic achievement. In some cases, these new devices use "computerized-adaptive testing." That is, not all test items are presented to all students; items are selected based upon the student's performance.

As more computer-based tests and other procedures become available for use in special education, professionals will need to learn how to evaluate, select, and interpret the results of these instruments, taking into account the ways in which the introduction of a computer alters the testing situation. The American Psychological Association (1986), in *Guidelines for Computer-Based Tests and Interpretations,* sets forth several recommendations for professionals who use computers for test administration. These include the following:

- Influences on test scores due to computer administration that are irrelevant to the purposes of assessment should be eliminated or taken into account in the interpretation of scores.
- The environment in which the testing terminal is located should be quiet, comfortable, and free from distractions.
- Test items presented on the display screen should be legible and free from noticeable glare.

- Test performance should be monitored, and assistance to the test taker should be provided, as is needed and appropriate. If technically feasible, the proctor should be signalled automatically when irregularities occur.
- Test takers should be trained on proper use of the computer equipment, and procedures should be established to eliminate any possible effect on test scores due to the test taker's lack of familiarity with the equipment.
- Reasonable accommodations must be made for individuals who may be at an unfair disadvantage in a computer testing situation. In cases where a disadvantage cannot be fully accommodated, scores obtained must be interpreted with appropriate caution. (pp. 10–12)

The last recommendation is of particular importance with lower-performing students. No test, computerized or teacher-administered, should discriminate against the student on the basis of disability. If a student has poor reading skills, knowledge of general science should not be assessed by forcing that student to read questions from the computer screen or from a printed page.

Test Scoring

At present, the most common—and most useful—application of computers to assessment is computation of test scores. Test scoring by computer is not a new application. Publishers of group-administered measures such as the achievement tests used in general education have long provided computer scoring services to schools. A more recent development is the use of computers by teachers at the school site for test scoring. Within the past decade, several programs have been developed for scoring the individual tests commonly used in special education. These programs represent an excellent use of computer technology; they decrease the probability of computation errors in scoring and speed up the scoring process, freeing the professional for other, more meaningful duties.

Most test-scoring programs for individual tests require that the professional administer the test and compute the raw scores for each subtest. Identifying information such as the student's name is entered into the program along with raw scores, and there may be choices to make about the types of scores to be calculated. It usually takes only a minute or two to enter the necessary data, and then only a few seconds for the computations. This is a substantial time savings—for some tests it takes 15 or even 30 minutes to compute derived scores by hand.

Test-scoring programs are available for many of the individual measures used in special education. This software is typically developed by the publisher of the test, although in some cases, publishers may certify as accurate a program developed by another agency. Publishers tend to develop scoring programs for selected tests—those that are most popular and difficult and/or time-consuming to score. Prices of scoring programs vary, but most are in the $100 to $300 range.

Test Interpretation and Reporting

Most scoring programs allow teachers to store student data for later use and to view score reports on the screen before printing them. The type of information included in the report varies from program to program, although all provide the basic information found on hand-scored protocols: identification information about the student and derived scores. Other common options are profiles of test results, score comparisons, and narrative explanations of results.

Scoring programs often go beyond simple reporting of scores and begin to contribute to the interpretation of test results. For example, the report may contain descriptions of each of the subtests on the test, a report of the student's scores, and comparison of the student's performance to that of the norm group. The report might also include analyses of any discrepancies in the student's performance on various subtests (e.g., reading versus math), analysis of any discrepancies between results on this measure and those on other measures (e.g., aptitude versus achievement), and profiles or graphs of the student's scores. In some cases, reports may even offer instructional recommendations based upon test performance.

When evaluating a computer program for test interpretation, it is extremely important to understand the decision-making rules the program uses to arrive at its conclusions. For example, one program might identify skill areas as weaknesses when standard scores fall below 85 whereas another program uses standard score 70 as the cutoff. Clearly, the interpretations resulting from these two programs are not comparable. Computer-generated test interpretations are best used as an aid to decision making, not as a substitute for the deliberations of the assessment team. Fortunately, most scoring programs allow testers to select the type of results they wish to print, so that interpretative reports can be omitted in favor of score reports.

MODIFICATION OF TESTING PROCEDURES

In many cases, test manuals dictate the exact words the tester is to use in presenting tasks to students, how the student may respond, and the ways the tester may respond to the student. If specified procedures are not followed, norm-referenced scores become meaningless because the norms assume administration under standard conditions. However, professionals sometimes believe that test results do not adequately reflect the student's capabilities. Certain administration requirements may, in fact, depress a student's performance. For example, a student may be able to complete a test task successfully but not within the required time limits. On most timed tests, students receive no credit for a late, albeit correct, response.

It *is* possible to modify administration procedures for standardized tests, although tests should be given under standard conditions before attempting any modification. In this way, the student's performance under both standard and altered conditions can be studied.

Results of tests administered under altered conditions must be interpreted with great caution. An example is allowing a fourth grade student to use a calculator for a computation test normed with students who were provided only with paper and pencil. With the aid of the calculator, the student's test score may improve; he or she may achieve a score indicating average performance for a fourth grader. However, it is no longer possible to compare the student's performance to that of students in the norm group. If the norm group had been supplied with calculators, perhaps the performance of the student in question would fall within the low average or below average range. There is simply no way to determine this. However, despite the necessity for caution in interpretation, results from tests given under altered conditions can provide useful information about the student's capabilities to perform test tasks. Results may also suggest ways to alter instructional strategies and requirements to increase chances for classroom success.

Before modifying administration procedures, the professional should consider the possible problems that may arise if the test is to be used again in the future with the same student. If the student somehow learns the questions and responses and is able to recall those responses, the test can no longer be used to compare the student's performance with the performance of others.

Sattler (1988) discusses the modification of administration procedures and calls this practice "testing of limits":

> There may be times when you want to go beyond the standard test procedures in order to gain additional information about the child's abilities. The information from testing-of-limits procedures can occasionally be helpful, especially in clinical or psychoeducational settings. (p. 111)

Administration conditions can be modified in several ways to determine if students are able to improve their performance. Methods include the following:

1. *Instructions* to the student may be paraphrased into simpler language.
2. The tester can provide a *demonstration* of how test tasks are to be performed.
3. *Time limits* for the completion of tasks can be extended or removed.
4. The *presentation mode* for tasks may be changed. For example, the tester could read items aloud to the student rather than requiring the student to read them.
5. The *response mode* required of the student may be changed. For example, instead of writing the answers, the student could respond orally.
6. The student may be allowed to use *aids* such as paper and pencil or a calculator.
7. The tester may provide the student with *prompts*. For example, the first step in the test task could be performed by the tester. Or the tester could question the student about his or her problem-solving method and then suggest an alternate approach.
8. The tester may give *feedback* to the student. This could include confirmation of correct responses or even correction of incorrect responses.
9. *Positive reinforcement* could be offered for correct responses and other appropriate work behaviors.
10. The *physical location* of the test may be changed. The test could be administered on the floor rather than at a table, or in a playroom rather than a testing room.
11. The *tester* may be changed. Someone with whom the student is comfortable, such as a parent or classroom teacher, could administer the test.

Valenzuela and Cervantes (1998) add these suggestions for culturally and linguistically diverse students:

- Substitution of dialectally/culturally appropriate vocabulary.
- Deletion/modification of culturally inappropriate items.
- Modification of scoring criteria (correct/incorrect), according to examiner's knowledge of student's culture/dialect/language . . .
- Translation. (pp. 181–182)

When administration procedures are altered, the modification must be described in a report of test results. Regulations for PL 105-17 require:

> If an assessment is not conducted under standard conditions, a description of the extent to which it varied from standard conditions (e.g., the qualifications of the person administering the test, or the method of test administration) must be included in the test report. (*Federal Register,* 1999, §300.532(c)(2))

Results obtained under nonstandard conditions should be reported as alternate scores. Although interpretation of these scores is difficult, successful performance with modified tasks may provide clues to ways for improving student functioning. For example, praising a student for each completed test item may increase the number of questions he or she is willing to attempt. Or spelling may improve when the student is allowed to spell orally rather than write the words.

Although these results are not determined in accordance with the rules of standardized testing, they may help identify specific problems in learning and suggest remedies for these problems.

AVOIDING BIAS IN TESTING

The potential for bias in assessment does not end with careful selection of assessment instruments. Even if standardized tests are deemed the most appropriate tools, discrimination remains a possibility during test administration and scoring and in the critical step of test interpretation.

Bias can be introduced into test administration in a number of ways. One important consideration is the professional preparation of the tester. Testing skill is absolutely essential for nonbiased assessment. Placing a standardized test in the hands of an untrained examiner is as poor a practice as the selection of a technically inadequate measure.

Professionals should also have knowledge about the types of students they assess, particularly individuals from cultures different from their own. Information about variations in age, gender, cultural group, and disability and the potential impact of these factors upon test performance is essential.

Tester attitudes are another important factor. If the tester holds strong beliefs about certain groups, he or she may fail to see students as individuals. For example, the belief that girls do not excel in mathematics may influence how diligently the tester attempts to elicit a female student's optimal performance on a math test. Tester attitudes affect expectations, which in turn affect test administration and scoring practices.

The working relationship between the student and tester is critical. Testers may need to take special care in building rapport with students of races, cultures, or experiential backgrounds different from their own. The tester may represent an unfamiliar culture to such students, requiring extra effort to help them feel at ease in the testing situation. Recommendations for the assessment of students from diverse groups include the following:

> Make every effort to enlist the child's motivation and interest by helping him or her feel as com-

fortable as possible in the assessment situation. You should take as much time as needed to ensure the child's cooperation. If at all possible, the clinician should be someone who is familiar to the child. (Sattler, 1988, p. 590)

It has been suggested that culturally and linguistically diverse students be tested only by examiners from the same group. Alley and Foster (1978) consider the matching of tester and student on race a simplistic approach to nonbiased assessment: It overlooks the impact of socioeconomic differences within cultures, the need for empathy on the examiner's part, and the issue of tester competence. Winzer and Mazurek (1998) point out evidence of a relationship between rapport with the examiner and academic performance for some African American students. These authors conclude that testers familiar to the student and those perceived as warm, friendly, and trustworthy are most likely to elicit optimal performance.

Selection of the tester becomes an important issue when the student's primary mode of communication is not English. Testers must be chosen carefully for students who speak a language other than English and for students who are deaf and communicate using sign language. In best practice, the tester will be able to communicate directly with the student using the student's communication mode. However, this is not always possible, particularly for students who speak one of the less common languages. When an interpreter must be used to translate the tester's questions to the student and the student's answers to the tester, standardized tests cannot be used for comparative purposes. At best, they provide informal information that must be evaluated with great care.

The potential for bias is also present during the interpretation of test results. Professionals can have a positive influence on this portion of the assessment process by using appropriate procedures for the interpretation of test scores, by understanding the limitations of standardized testing, by examining the attitudes they hold toward students from diverse cultures, and by becoming more familiar with the languages and cultures of the students they assess. To assist professionals in the identification of possible sources of bias during test interpretation, Turnbull, Strickland, and Brantley (1982) have prepared the checklist shown in Figure 4–3.

Checklist for Minimizing Bias During Interpretation of Results

Name _____   School _____

Examiner _____   Date _____

Examine Child's Score   *A check (√) indicates potential bias*

_____ Look for characteristics of the child which might bias or influence the results, such as:
     _____ language spoken in the home
     _____ age, health, nutrition
     _____ disabilities
     _____ mode of communication
     _____ sensory and performance modalities

_____ Look for characteristics of the tests and techniques which might bias or influence the results, such as:
     _____ purpose
     _____ communication modalities (a) child-test (b) child-examiner
     _____ norms
     _____ reliability and validity
     _____ type of measure
     _____ relevance of items
     _____ scoring criteria
     _____ type of scores

_____ Look for characteristics of the examiner which might bias or influence the results, such as:
     _____ appropriate training
     _____ communication mode and language
     _____ previous experience
     _____ attitudes
     _____ skills
     _____ knowledge

_____ Look for conditions within the assessment situation which might bias the performance
     _____ time of day
     _____ distractions
     _____ testing materials
     _____ inappropriate use of cues
     _____ length of session
     _____ comfort and accessibility of materials
     _____ order of assessment activities

_____ Look for conditions between the examiner and child which might bias the performance
     _____ rapport
     _____ attending behavior
     _____ initial success or failure
     _____ maintaining responding behavior
     _____ communication
     _____ dress and/or mannerisms

_____ Try to determine if the child's performance is representative and/or approximates his/her potential

_____ Compare the results of multiple measures

FIGURE 4–3

Checklist for Minimizing Bias During Interpretation of Results

Note: From *Developing and Implementing Individualized Education Programs* (2nd ed.) (p. 86) by A. P. Turnbull, B. B. Strickland, and J. C. Brantley (developed in conjunction with G. Harbin), 1982, New York: Merrill/Macmillan. Copyright 1982 by Macmillan Publishing Company. Adapted by permission.

STUDY GUIDE

REVIEW QUESTIONS

1. In standardized testing, test tasks are presented under standard conditions so that the student's performance can be compared to the performance of the _____ _____ .
2. Which of the following statements describe(s) an adequate testing environment?
   a. One of the student's parents or the student's teacher is present in the testing room.
   b. Chairs and a table are available for the student and the tester.
   c. All of the equipment and test materials needed for the session are placed on the test table ready for use.
   d. The temperature and ventilation in the room are comfortable for the student.
   e. The testing room is located near popular school activities such as music and physical education.
3. Which of the following is not good practice in introducing the student to the testing situation?
   a. Tests should be scheduled at the same time as the student's favorite classroom activities.
   b. Physical needs of the student should be attended to before testing begins.
   c. The student should be informed about the purpose of testing.
   d. The tester should explain to the student what will happen during the test, including the length of the session, types of test activities, and so forth.
4. Preparing a student psychologically for testing is called
   a. establishing the basal.
   b. establishing rapport.
   c. coaching.
   d. projective analysis.
5. Suppose a professional began test administration with item number 10 in an attempt to establish a basal of four consecutively numbered correct responses. If the student failed item 10, what test item should be administered next?
6. Match each term in Column A with the appropriate description from Column B.

Column A	Column B
a. Basal	___ Test questions used to teach students how to do test tasks
b. Coaching	___ The point in the test at which it can be assumed the student would receive full credit for all easier items
c. Demonstration items	___ The practice of helping a student arrive at the answer to a test question
d. Ceiling	___ The point at which it can be assumed the student would receive no credit for all the more difficult items

7. Give two reasons why it is important to observe the student's behavior during test administration.
8. Calculate the student's chronological age in these examples:

Student's Birth Date	Date of Testing	Chronological Age
a. 12-2-92	1-3-00	_____
b. 6-28-84	9-15-01	_____
c. 11-20-95	10-6-00	_____

9. Find the raw scores for each of the following tests. Each item is worth 1 point. The basal is three consecutive correct responses, and the ceiling is three consecutive incorrect responses.

Test A	Test B
1. _____	18. ___+___
2. _____	19. ___+___
3. ___+___	20. ___+___
4. ___+___	21. ___−___
5. ___+___	22. ___+___
6. ___−___	23. ___−___
7. ___+___	24. ___+___
8. ___−___	25. ___−___
9. ___−___	26. ___−___
10. ___−___	27. ___−___

Raw score _____   Raw score _____

10. Choose the statement that best explains the meaning of the score.
   a. When a student earns a percentile rank score of 54, this means that 54% of the test questions were answered correctly.
   b. An age equivalent score of 10-3 indicates that the student's raw score is equal to the average raw score of grade 10.3 students in the norm group.
   c. If test standard scores are distributed with a mean of 100 and a standard deviation of 15, a standard score of 85 indicates performance one standard deviation below the mean.
   d. If test standard scores are distributed with a mean of 50 and a standard deviation of 10, a standard score of 70 indicates performance two standard deviations below the mean.

11. A student received a standard score of 100 on a test in which the mean standard score is 100, the standard deviation is 15, and the scores are normally distributed. This score
   a. falls at the 50th percentile.
   b. is within the 5th stanine.
   c. indicates performance at the mean.
   d. All of the above statements are true.

12. Match the standard score with the appropriate score range. The standard scores are normally distributed with a mean of 100 and a standard deviation of 15.

Standard Score	Range of Performance
a. 117	_____ Above average performance
b. 83	_____ High average performance
c. 68	_____ Average performance
d. 135	_____ Low average performance
e. 105	_____ Below average performance

13. A student earned a standard score of 73 on a test with a standard error of measurement of 6. In what range of scores would the student's true score be expected to fall 68% of the time?

14. How are computers best used in assessment?
   a. administration of tests of intellectual performance
   b. conversion of raw scores to derived scores
   c. interpretation of results
   d. preparation of test reports

15. Testing procedures can be modified if the professional is interested in studying the student's performance under alternate administration conditions. One example is to extend or to remove the time limits for test tasks. Give four other examples.

ACTIVITIES

1. Select one of the individual achievement tests used in special education and examine its manual. See if these topics are discussed:
   a. setting up the testing environment
   b. introducing the student to the testing situation
   c. observing the student's test behavior
   d. training requirements for testers
2. Observe a professional administering a standardized test. Follow along in the test manual during administration.
3. Practice test administration and scoring with a peer, using a norm-referenced test approved by the course instructor.
4. Interview two or more professionals who administer educational tests. You might talk with a special educator, a school psychologist, and a speech-language pathologist. Ask each to describe the types of test scores he or she prefers and why.
5. Suggest ways to modify test administration procedures for students who
   a. work very slowly.
   b. have reading problems.
   c. have handwriting problems.
   d. have short attention spans.

DISCUSSION QUESTIONS

1. Why is it important that tests be administered only by trained professionals? Identify some errors that untrained persons might make when administering tests and scoring student responses.
2. Explain this statement: "Testing skills should be so well learned that they are automatic, so professionals can devote their attention to observation of the student's behavior."
3. Compare the advantages and disadvantages of percentile ranks and standard scores for reporting test results.
4. When test administration procedures are modified, the results are called alternate scores. Discuss the usefulness of these scores and the cautions that must be observed in their interpretation.
5. Describe how bias can intrude into assessment during test administration and scoring. Suggest strategies for preventing bias.

CHAPTER 5

INFORMAL ASSESSMENT

- Differences between Formal and Informal Assessment
- Types of Informal Techniques
- Observation, Work Sample Analysis, and Task Analysis
- Curriculum-Based Assessment Strategies
- Procedures Using Informants
- Interpreting Informal Assessment Results
- Avoiding Bias in Informal Assessment

Teachers use informal assessment techniques every day—when they observe the behavior of a student in the classroom, examine a student's paper and attempt to find a pattern of errors, or interview a student about the procedures he or she has used to solve a problem or answer a question. The major advantage of informal assessment techniques is their relevance to instruction. In fact, many of the informal assessment strategies used in special education can be viewed as curriculum-based measures. Informal techniques provide information about the student's current levels of performance, aid in the selection of instructional goals and objectives, point to the need for instructional modifications, document student progress, and suggest directions for further assessment. Whereas norm-referenced measures focus on the student's ability to function in a structured testing situation, informal measures more closely approximate typical classroom conditions.

Informal assessment is useful not only for the evaluation of student performance but also for the study of instructional settings and curricular tasks. Because it extends beyond the student to the characteristics of the task to be learned and the instructional environment, informal assessment allows a more ecological approach to the study of special needs.

This chapter describes the many different types of informal assessment tools available to teachers. The next chapter, Classroom Assessment Techniques, focuses on the use of informal procedures in instructional settings. Included in that chapter are discussions of some of the newer assessment approaches that combine two or more informal techniques. Examples are portfolio assessment, functional assessment, curriculum-based measurement, and action research.

DIFFERENCES BETWEEN FORMAL AND INFORMAL ASSESSMENT

Informal assessment tools help the professional gather information about the current status of the student, the task, or the setting. Tools are designed to describe current conditions, not to predict future performance. There are several important areas of difference between informal measures and formal measures such as norm-referenced tests.

The first is standard of reference. With norm-referenced tests, the student's performance is compared to that of a norm group. With informal measures, the student's performance is compared to specific instructional concerns such as the sequence of learning tasks within the curriculum of the school or the conduct standards of a particular classroom.

The second difference is technical adequacy. Most informal tools are not standardized, and few provide information about reliability and validity. If teachers design informal measures for use in their own classrooms, no information about psychometric quality is available unless it is gathered by teachers themselves. It is not that the quality of informal assessment is poor; rather, it is generally unknown.

Efficiency is the third area. Norm-referenced tests are usually efficient measures. When evaluating the efficiency of an informal assessment tool, the time and personnel requirements for its design, administration, scoring, and interpretation must all be taken into account. Designing, administering, and scoring an informal tool is a time-consuming process. However, administration procedures are often quite straightforward in comparison to those for norm-referenced tests. Paraprofessionals such as instructional aides can be trained to administer some of the easier informal measures. Despite this, the teacher must be involved in the critical steps of designing the measure and interpreting its results. Even in administration, some measures require the expertise of a professional familiar with the school curriculum and the expectations for performance within the classroom learning environment.

The fourth difference between informal and formal measures is specificity. Formal measures generally assess larger segments of the curriculum, and their coverage of these segments is selective rather than comprehensive. A norm-referenced test may include a broad range of items chosen to represent a general curriculum area, but each specific skill within that curriculum area is measured by only a few test items or none at all. In contrast, informal measures tend to focus on one or more subskills within a curriculum area in an attempt to assess these thoroughly. Their purpose is to gather sufficient information to allow teachers to monitor student progress or make instructional planning decisions.

TYPES OF INFORMAL TECHNIQUES

There are many types of informal assessment techniques, and it is useful to have some way of conceptualizing them. One important dimension is whether informal strategies introduce a test task into the assessment situation, that is, how obtrusive they are. With procedures such as observation, no test task is presented to the student; he or she is simply observed within the natural environment of the classroom or whatever setting is of interest. Informal inventories, classroom quizzes, and criterion-referenced tests, on the other hand, exemplify assessment procedures in which something is added to the environment; the tester introduces test tasks to the student in order to observe how these specific tasks are carried out.

A second dimension of importance is whether measures are direct or indirect. Direct measures attempt to answer an assessment question about a particular student or classroom condition by assessing that characteristic or condition. If the question concerns a student's ability to read a fourth grade science text, the student is asked to read the science text. Indirect measures rely upon some less direct source such as an informant. An indirect means of determining a student's ability to read a science text would be to interview the student's teacher.

The dimensions of directness and obtrusiveness can be used to sort informal assessment techniques into three classes: (a) observation, task

analysis, and other direct and unobtrusive procedures; (b) curriculum-based assessment techniques such as inventories and criterion-referenced tests that are direct but obtrusive; and (c) procedures using informants such as checklists and interviews that are indirect and obtrusive.

OBSERVATION, WORK SAMPLE ANALYSIS, AND TASK ANALYSIS

These are fundamental assessment strategies that are basic to all types of assessment; skill in their use is critical for any assessment professional. These techniques allow the direct examination of student behaviors, tasks, and settings without the introduction of test tasks. They are important tools for gathering assessment information in the classroom, where they also serve as instructional tools. In addition, they are often used in conjunction with other data-collection strategies. For example, observation of the student's test behavior is a critical part of norm-referenced testing. Observation and other direct, unobtrusive procedures can be adapted for use with individuals of any age, in any curriculum area, and in any instructional setting or assessment situation.

Observation

Teachers are continually watching and listening to their students. They may not call this procedure observation, but by taking note of what their students say and do, teachers are conducting simple observations. When a potential problem is discovered during casual observation, more systematic observational procedures can be begun. Although observational techniques are often associated with the study of classroom conduct problems, they are just as appropriate for the study of academic, social, self-help, and vocational skills. Because observation involves the examination of student behaviors within the context of the natural environment, it produces information that often cannot be obtained from any other type of assessment procedure.

Student Leticia   Date January 4, 2001
Observer Ms. Brown
Classroom Activity: Independent seatwork
Reason for Observation: Leticia seems to be out of her seat constantly when she should be at her seat
                         working on her worksheet.

Time	Event
11:00–11:02	Leticia comes in from the playground, goes directly to her desk, and sits
11:02–11:05	Leticia sits while teacher hands out and explains spelling worksheet
11:05–11:08	Leticia gets pencil from desk, reads worksheet
11:08–11:09	Leticia begins to write, breaks pencil
11:09–11:13	Leticia gets up, walks to pencil sharpener, sharpens pencil, returns to seat
11:13–11:18	Leticia writes on worksheet
11:18–11:20	Leticia drops pencil on floor, gets up, picks up pencil, returns to seat
11:20–11:25	Leticia writes on worksheet
11:25–11:27	Leticia gets up, places worksheet in folder on teacher's desk
11:27–11:28	Leticia returns to seat, puts pencil in desk, looks around room
11:28–11:30	Leticia gets up, walks to teacher's desk, asks teacher if she can get a drink of water, teacher tells Leticia to return to her seat
11:30	Leticia begins to return to seat, lunch bell rings

FIGURE 5–1
Continuous Observation

According to Borich (1999), the least structured type of observation is the narrative report. In narrative reporting, the observer simply describes events in writing. The description may be of one type of event or incident (anecdotal record) or of a sequence of events (ethnographic record). In anecdotal recording, the observer is interested in a specific type of event. For example, a teacher might keep written records of a student's outbursts in class. In ethnographic recording, the observer attempts to describe everything that is occurring. For instance, a teacher observing a lesson in a colleague's classroom would attempt to record not only the actions of the teacher but also those of individual students. Both types of narrative reporting are relatively easy to carry out. However, interpretation of results is difficult because descriptions are often subjective in nature.

Systematic observation techniques help the teacher in specifying, recording, and analyzing student behaviors. In the most basic type of systematic observation, the teacher observes and records all the behaviors a student exhibits during some set time period. In contrast to narrative reporting, the teacher is concerned with specific student behaviors, rather than more global events. This technique, called continuous recording or narrative recording (Cooper, 1981), provides preliminary information to help the teacher determine if there is a problem that requires further study. For example, Figure 5–1 presents the record of a continuous observation of Leticia's behavior. The teacher decided to conduct this observation because Leticia seemed to be out of her seat "constantly" during times when she was expected to work at her desk. However, in analyzing the results of the observation, Leticia left her seat only five times in the half-hour period, and all of her excursions had reasonable purposes.

Sequence analysis is a second observational technique that is useful for gaining an overall picture of a student's performance (Sulzer-Azaroff & Mayer, 1977). As with continuous

TABLE 5-1
Sequence Analysis

TIME	ANTECEDENT	BEHAVIOR	CONSEQUENCE
9:05	Teacher asks the class a question.	John raises hand.	Teacher calls on Bill.
9:07	Teacher asks question.	John yells answer.	Teacher reprimands John.
9:11	Teacher asks question and reminds students to raise hands.	John raises hand.	Teacher calls on John and compliments him for raising his hand.

Note: From *Teaching Special Students in General Education Classrooms* 5/e by Lewis/Doorlag, © 1999. Reprinted by permission of Prentice-Hall, Inc., Upper Saddle River, NJ.

recording, the teacher observes and records all the behaviors of the student within a specified time period. In addition, an attempt is made to record the events or actions preceding and following each behavior. Identification of the antecedents and consequences of a student's behaviors provides information about how events in the environment may influence the student's actions. Consider the sequence analysis of John's classroom behavior in Table 5–1. Few conclusions can be drawn if only the student's actions are considered. However, when antecedents and consequences are taken into account, a more complete picture of the instructional interaction emerges. John's hand-raising behavior appears to be influenced by the actions of the teacher.

Continuous recording and sequence analysis are most often used in the initial stages of assessment to determine if a student's behavior merits further study. They provide a global picture of the student's actions in relationship to situational variables and assist the teacher in selecting specific behaviors that require intervention. However, they are time-consuming procedures and are best considered as screening tools to identify specific student behaviors for further observation.

As soon as a particular behavior or set of behaviors has been selected for study, plans can be made for conducting an observation focusing on these specific behaviors. The teacher follows several steps.

Describe the Behavior to be Observed

First, the behavior or behaviors of interest are clearly and precisely described. This facilitates communication among persons conducting the observation and allows discussion of results with the student, parents, and concerned professionals.

To conduct an observation, the behaviors must be both observable and measurable. A behavior is considered observable if its performance can be detected by an outside observer; "understanding the reading assignment" is not an observable behavior but "writing answers to comprehension questions" is. Descriptions of observable behaviors usually contain an action verb. Verbs such as *write, point to, name,* and *throw* describe actions that an observer can see or hear; verbs such as *understand, know, appreciate,* and *perceive* do not.

Behaviors that have clearly definable beginnings and endings are discrete behaviors; examples are writing spelling words and reading a paragraph aloud. Discrete behaviors are measured by counting their frequency or timing their duration. Some behaviors are not discrete; for example, it is difficult to detect the precise starting and ending points of behaviors such as staying on task and swearing in the classroom. Nondiscrete behaviors are also measurable, because during any given time period an observer can determine whether a student is displaying the behavior.

Select a Measurement System

If the behavior of interest is a discrete behavior, it is possible to measure its frequency, its duration, or both. *Frequency* refers to the number of times a behavior occurs; for example, the teacher may be interested in the frequency with which Joe completes math assignments. *Duration* is a

Example 1: Event Recording
   Student: Susie
   Behavior: Throwing paper airplanes in math class
   Measurement System: Event recording (the number of times Susie throws paper airplanes in math class)
   When Measured: Math period (9:00–9:30 a.m.) on 5 consecutive school days

Day 1	Day 2	Day 3	Day 4	Day 5
I I I I	JHtt	I I I	I I I	I I I I
Total = 4	Total = 5	Total = 3	Total = 3	Total = 4

Grand total for 5 days = 19 times

Example 2: Duration Recording
   Student: Philip
   Behavior: Sleeping during class
   Measurement System: Duration recording (the number of minutes Philip sleeps in class)
   When Measured: Every occurrence during class time for 5 consecutive school days

Day 1	Day 2	Day 3	Day 4	Day 5
11:15 – 11:30 2:05 – 2:25	—	1:55 – 2:10	2:00 – 2:20	10:35 – 10:40
Total = 35	Total = 0	Total = 15	Total = 20	Total = 5

Grand total for 5 days = 75 minutes

FIGURE 5–2
Observing Discrete Behaviors: Event and Duration Recording

measure of the length of a behavior, that is, how long it lasts in terms of seconds, minutes, or hours. For instance, if punctuality is a concern, information can be collected on the number of minutes late Seng arrives to class each day. Or a parent may have identified a young child's tantruming behavior as a target for observation; for this behavior, it may be important to consider both duration and frequency.

The following measurement systems are used to collect data about discrete behaviors (Alberto & Troutman, 1990):

- *Event recording.* The frequency of the behavior is noted in event recording. The observer simply makes a notation each time the behavior of interest occurs. The first example in Figure 5–2 shows how the teacher tallied Susie's behavior of throwing paper airplanes in class.
- *Duration recording.* Here the observer records the time a behavior begins and the

time it ends to determine its length. The second example in Figure 5–2 is the teacher's daily record of the amount of time Philip spent sleeping in class.

Latency recording is another option. In this system, the observer determines the amount of time it takes a student to begin doing something. For example, the teacher might be interested in how long it takes Jennifer to begin reading her library book after she returns to the classroom from recess.

For nondiscrete behaviors such as working independently or talking with peers, the use of interval recording and time sampling is recommended (Alberto & Troutman, 1990; Cooper, Heron, & Heward, 1987). With these techniques, the observer determines whether a behavior occurs during a specified time period. The class day, period, or activity is broken down into short intervals of a few minutes or even a few seconds,

---

Momentary Time Sampling

Student: Fred

Behavior: Writing on assigned worksheets

Measurement System: Momentary time sampling (determination if the behavior is occurring at the end of the interval)

Length of Interval: 3 minutes

When Measured: Independent study time (10:30–11:00 a.m.)

Interval Ends		Interval Ends	
10:33	X	10:48	X
10:36	O	10:51	O
10:39	X	10:54	O
10:42	X	10:57	X
10:45	O	11:00	O

X = Fred was writing on a worksheet at the end of the interval.

O = Fred was not writing on a worksheet at the end of the interval.

Results: Fred wrote on assigned worksheets in 5 of the 10 time intervals sampled, or 50%.

FIGURE 5–3

Observing Nondiscrete Behaviors: Interval Recording

and a record of the presence or absence of the target behavior is kept for each interval. These techniques can also be used with discrete behaviors if a complete record of every occurrence is not necessary.

Several variations of interval recording and time sampling are available:

- *Whole-interval recording.* The student is observed for the entire interval, and the observer notes if the target behavior occurs continuously throughout the interval. Observation intervals are very brief, usually only a few seconds.
- *Partial-interval time recording.* The student is observed for the entire interval, but the observer notes only if the behavior occurred at least once during the interval. Again, time intervals are very brief.
- *Momentary time sampling.* The student is observed only at the end of each interval; at that time, the observer checks to see if the behavior is occurring. Intervals are usually longer— 3, 5, or even 15 minutes—making this a more convenient method for classroom teachers. However, it is less accurate than interval

recording techniques because much of the student's behavior goes unobserved.

Figure 5–3 provides an example of momentary time sampling. Note that the X indicates occurrence of the target behavior and the O, nonoccurrence. Results are expressed as the number or percentage of time intervals in which the behavior of interest was displayed.

Set up the Data-Collection System

The next step in planning an observation is to determine logistics. Questions to be answered include the following:

- When and where will the observation take place?
- How many observation periods will there be, and how frequently will these occur?
- Who will act as the observer?
- How will observational data be recorded?

Determining the time and place of the observation must take into account the nature of the behavior. With infrequent behaviors, it may be

TABLE 5-2
Classroom Observation Techniques for Teachers

It is not necessary to stop teaching to observe; in fact, it is almost impossible to teach without observing! Try the following suggestions for integrating observations into your classroom procedures:

1. Carry a small card such as an index card; on it list the names of one or two target students and the problem behaviors you wish to observe (e.g., hitting, being out-of-seat, talking to others). Place a tally mark on the card (and possibly the time of the behavior) each time the behavior occurs. Start this system with one or two students and gradually expand it as your skills improve.

2. Require students to record on their in-class work their starting and finishing time. This approach permits the calculation of rate as well as frequency and accuracy data. Students can also note the times they leave and return to their desks; then the total amount of time in-seat each day or each period can be calculated.

3. Carry a stopwatch to measure the duration of behaviors. For example, start the watch each time Maynard leaves his seat, and stop it when he returns. Continue this (without resetting the watch) and time each occurrence of the behavior. At the end of the observation period, note the total amount of time recorded.

4. To count behaviors without interfering with the operation of the class, use wrist counters (golf counters), supermarket counters, paper clips moved from one pocket to another, navy beans in a cup, and other inexpensive devices.

5. Have a seating chart in front of you as you talk to the class. Place a tally mark by a student's name for each target behavior, such as asking a question, talking out, or answering a question correctly.

6. Recruit volunteers to observe in the classroom. Older students, parents, senior citizens, college students, or other students in the class can be excellent observers. If the teacher has developed a method to record the data and clearly stated the behavior to be observed, a nonprofessional should be able to conduct the observation.

Note: From *Teaching Special Students in General Education Classrooms* 5/e by Lewis/Doorlag, © 1999. Reprinted by permission of Prentice-Hall, Inc., Upper Saddle River, NJ.

desirable to collect observational data for each occurrence. However, if the behavior occurs frequently, it is usually impractical to observe every instance. Instead, it makes sense to select those times and settings where the behavior is of greatest concern. For example, if Henry's rough play on the playground during recess is a possible problem, he should be observed on the playground at that time.

One observation is not sufficient. More than one observation should be planned, and these should take place over time. A common practice is to observe daily for a minimum of 5 days. Observation should continue until a complete picture of the behavior has emerged. For example, if a behavior occurs only 3 or 4 times daily from Monday through Thursday but 10 times on Friday, it is advisable to observe for at least another week to determine if frequency will level off or continue to increase. There are two exceptions to the rule of multiple observations. Only one observation is needed if the behavior of interest is one that is not present in the student's repertoire

(e.g., the student has not learned how to subtract) or if the behavior is one that endangers the student or others.

Data are usually collected by the professional who designs the observation system. If the teacher is the observer, there is less disruption in classroom routine and less danger that the presence of an outsider will cause students to act differently. Although it takes some advance planning, teachers can collect observational data while they are teaching. Several techniques for facilitating teacher observations are presented in Table 5–2. Classroom observations may also be conducted by other professionals, instructional aides, volunteers, or even students, if the behavior is clearly stated, procedures are well specified, and observers are adequately trained.

Results of observations should be recorded on paper during the observational period or immediately thereafter to ensure that data are not forgotten. Although tally sheets such as those shown in Figures 5–2 and 5–3 are the most usual way of recording data, there is no set format. However, record forms should be designed to allow easy entry of information and encourage accurate reporting. Some teachers carry observational record forms on clipboards, and others enter data on index cards or in small notebooks. There is no set method; teachers should experiment until they find a comfortable strategy. Another option for recording data is audio- or videotaping. Although an observer is still required to listen to or view tapes to summarize results, taping is permanent. If a behavior is missed or is difficult to interpret, the tape can be replayed for clarification.

Select a Data-Reporting System

Observational data can be reported in statements such as "Susie threw paper airplanes in math class 19 times in a 5-day period." However, the more usual practice is to present results in a visual format such as a graph or chart. Graphs communicate large amounts of information quickly and facilitate the detection of trends and patterns. The most typical procedure is to plot observation results on a line graph where the x axis, or abscissa, represents time and the y axis, or ordinate, represents the behavior.

The simplest way to present frequency data is to plot the observed number of occurrences of the target behavior. The y axis becomes a scale for the number of times the behavior is exhibited, and the x axis depicts the different observational sessions. This procedure makes sense, however, only if all observational sessions are of equal duration and if each offers the student the same opportunity to perform the target behavior. If observations vary in duration, then it is more appropriate to report rate data than frequency data. For example, if the teacher observed the student 10 minutes on Monday, 15 minutes on Tuesday, and 12 minutes on Wednesday, results could be compared across observational sessions by converting the number of occurrences of the behavior into the *number of occurrences per minute* (calculated by dividing the observed number of occurrences by the number of minutes in the observational session). If, on Monday, the behavior occurred 20 times during the 10-minute observation period, its rate of occurrence would be 2 times per minute. That rate could then be directly compared to the rate of oc-

currence on Tuesday (e.g., 1.3 times per minute), Wednesday, and so forth.

Likewise, if the behavior of interest is the number of times the student correctly answers questions in science class, the student may have the opportunity to respond to 15 questions one day but only 8 the next. In such situations, the number of occurrences of the target behavior should be converted into *percentage of occurrences*. This is calculated by dividing the observed number of occurrences by the number of opportunities for occurrence during the observational period; this quotient is then multiplied by 100. If, for example, the student answered 10 out of 15 questions correctly, the percentage correct would be 67%. That percentage could then be directly compared to percentages achieved at other times when the student was provided with a different number of opportunities.

With duration data, it is possible to plot the actual number of seconds, minutes, or hours that the behavior persisted. However, if observational sessions vary in length, duration data should be converted to percentage data to express the *percentage of time* in which the behavior occurred. This is accomplished by dividing the observed duration of the behavior by the total length of the observation period and then multiplying the quotient by 100. Figure 5–4 presents examples of some of the ways that frequency and duration data for discrete behaviors can be depicted by graphing.

Graphs can also present results of observations of nondiscrete behaviors. Whatever technique is used to record data—whole-interval recording, partial-interval recording, or momentary time sampling—results can be plotted as the number of intervals in which the behavior occurred. If there is variation across observation sessions in the total number of time intervals observed, frequency data should be converted to percentage data. For example, Sara may stare out of the window in 13 of the 24 time intervals sampled on Monday and in 32 of the 55 time intervals sampled on Tuesday. Comparison becomes possible when these results are stated in terms of percentages: Sara's target behavior occurred in 54% of the time intervals sampled on Monday and in 58% of the time intervals sampled on Tuesday.

Example 1: Event Recording, Graphing Actual Frequency of Occurrence

Target Behavior: Throwing paper airplanes in math class

When Measured: Math period (9:00–9:30 a.m.) on 5 consecutive school days

[Observational sessions are equal in duration and offer equal opportunity for the behavior to occur.]

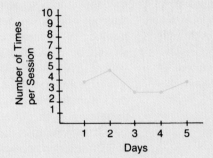

Example 2: Event Recording, Graphing Rate of Occurrence

Target Behavior: Talking out in class

When Measured: Independent work time for 5 consecutive school days

[Observational sessions offer equal opportunity for the behavior to occur but are of unequal duration.]

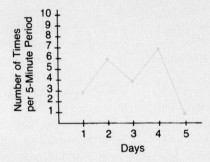

Example 3: Duration Recording, Graphing Percentage of Time

Target Behavior: Tantruming

When Measured: Grocery shopping for 5 consecutive shopping trips

[Observational sessions offer equal opportunity for the behavior to occur but are of unequal duration.]

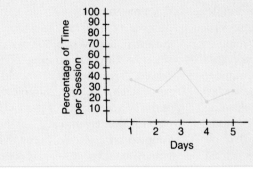

FIGURE 5-4
Reporting Observation Results for Discrete Behaviors

118

Carry Out the Observations

The final step is to actually carry out the planned observations. As this occurs, the observer should be alert to potential problem areas. Is the target behavior stated with sufficient precision? Is the measurement system appropriate for this behavior? Do data-collection procedures provide an adequate sampling of the student's typical responses? If two or more observers are involved in the data collection, interobserver reliability becomes an important concern. As Chapter 3 discussed, the percentage of agreement among observers is easily calculated. However, if percentage of agreement falls below 80%, interobserver reliability is in question. It may be necessary to describe the target behavior with more precision or provide observers with additional training.

Work Sample Analysis

Teachers also employ observation to study students' products. The teacher obtains a sample of student work—a written assignment, a test, an essay, an art project, or even a tape recording of oral reading responses or a classroom discussion—and analyzes it to determine areas of successful performance and areas in which the student may require assistance. Work sample analysis is most often used to assess academic skills, but it could be applied to any area in which a product results. This technique is a special type of observation, and it is sometimes referred to as permanent product analysis or outcome recording (Alberto & Troutman, 1990; Cooper, 1981).

Response Analysis

This technique considers both the correct and incorrect responses of the student. Like other types of observation, it involves the steps of describing the behavior, selecting a measurement system, and deciding upon a data-reporting system. In response analysis, the teacher is usually interested in these dimensions of human behavior: frequency, duration, rate, and percentage.

Figure 5–5 presents a work sample and several examples of the ways in which responses can be analyzed. Most typically, the teacher will select only one or two aspects of the student's behavior for study. The teacher is focusing on Louie's spelling in this response analysis. Although Louie's essay contains several errors, the response analysis shows that 78% of the words were spelled correctly.

Like other types of observation, response analysis should not be limited to a single sample of student behavior. Several work samples should be gathered over a period of time to determine the student's typical manner of responding. Results of response analyses can be graphed to facilitate interpretation.

Error Analysis

A second, more common approach to the study of student work samples is error analysis, which has a long history in special and remedial education. In the 1930s, Monroe (1932) suggested a procedure for the study of oral reading in which errors were categorized as additions, omissions, substitutions, repetitions, and so forth. Today, error analysis techniques are available for most subject areas.

The goal is identification of error patterns. The work sample is scored, all errors are noted, and then an attempt is made to sort the errors into meaningful categories. For example, on a math worksheet of 15 single-digit multiplication problems, Casey made six errors that fell into the following categories:

Error	Error Category
$8 \times 6 = 54$	8 fact/6 fact
$9 \times 7 = 64$	9 fact/7 fact
$9 \times 8 = 81$	9 fact/8 fact
$8 \times 7 = 48$	8 fact/7 fact
$8 \times 8 = 62$	8 fact
$9 \times 9 = 72$	9 fact

Results are then summarized to locate patterns of errors:

Error Category	Frequency of Occurrence
9 fact	3
8 fact	4
7 fact	2
6 fact	1

Task: Students are asked to write a short description of a favorite animal.

Transcription of Louie's essay:

My favorit animl is giraf. They got a long nek and spots. They eat lefs and trees and are very tall. They run fast in the jugle.

Time begun: 9:20 a.m.   Time finished: 9:35 a.m.

Response Analysis

Dimension	Analysis Results
Frequency	Number of words written = 27
	Number of words spelled correctly = 21
	Number of words spelled incorrectly = 6
Duration	Number of minutes required to write essay = 15

Rate

Rate of writing words

$$\frac{\text{Number of words written}}{\text{Number of minutes of writing}} = 1.8 \text{ words per minute}$$

Rate of spelling words correctly

$$\frac{\text{Number of words spelled correctly}}{\text{Number of minutes of writing}} = 1.4 \text{ words per minute}$$

Percentage

Percentage of words spelled correctly

$$\frac{\text{Number of words spelled correctly}}{\text{Number of words written}} \times 100 = 78\%$$

Percentage of words spelled incorrectly

$$\frac{\text{Number of words spelled incorrectly}}{\text{Number of words written}} \times 100 = 22\%$$

FIGURE 5–5

Response Analysis of a Student Work Sample

Casey has difficulty with some, but not all, multiplication facts. The problems that Casey missed required knowledge of the 6, 7, 8, and 9 facts. All errors took place in problems with some number multiplied by either 8 or 9. Because of this error pattern, the teacher's next move would be to assess Casey's knowledge of 8 and 9 multiplication facts with a criterion-referenced test or informal inventory.

The key to a successful error analysis is identification of one or more patterns of errors. However, not all error patterns are as easily detected as the one in the previous example. Sometimes a pattern does not emerge; the student may make several different types of errors, or mistakes may seem random. In many ways, error analysis is a subjective technique, relying upon judgments made by the teacher. He or she must decide which responses should be marked as errors, select the category system for classifying errors, and then determine if the student's mistakes fall into some sort of pattern. Also, there are no set criteria for judging the number or proportion of errors that constitute a possible problem. Thus, results of error analyses are best viewed as a guide for further assessment.

Task Analysis

Task analysis is an unobtrusive informal technique that focuses on curricular tasks rather than student performance. It is as much an instructional technique as an assessment strategy, and its purpose is to break down complex tasks into teachable subcomponents. Howell, Kaplan, and O'Connell (1979) define task analysis as "the process of isolating, sequencing, and describing all the essential components of a task" (p. 81). Cegelka (1995) adds that this process divides "a target behavior into a skill sequence that comprises its essential components or substeps" (p. 54).

The major role of task analysis in the instructional process is to assist in curricular design and specification of the instructional sequence. An instructional goal is selected and analyzed to determine the specific subskills that will support its accomplishment. Then the subskills or task subcomponents are arranged for instruction in an order that facilitates their acquisition. This is done in three steps:

1. Identify a specific instructional goal or objective.
2. Analyze the instructional objective into its essential component parts (i.e., the movements, actions, or responses that, when taken cumulatively, constitute the instructional objective).
3. Determine the entry level of the skill and specify the prerequisite skills (in other words, state at what point the particular skill sequence begins). (Berdine & Cegelka, 1980, p. 160)

There are several ways to approach the problem of analyzing a task into its subcomponents: analysis by temporal order, by developmental sequence, by difficulty level, and by structural task analysis. The method selected is determined to some extent by the nature of the task under consideration.

Analysis by Temporal Order

Some tasks follow a temporal order. In washing one's hands, the tap water must be turned on before hands can be rinsed. The teacher may choose to teach such tasks in the order they are performed or, in some cases, may proceed in a backward order by beginning with the last subtask in the sequence. This is called backward chaining; it is most useful when the task is difficult for the learner. By beginning at the end, backward chaining assures successful task completion in the early stages of learning.

Analysis by Developmental Sequence

Task subcomponents can also be ordered by developmental sequence. Affleck, Lowenbraun, and Archer (1980) explain a developmental sequence as "one in which a gradual progression of steps is built on previously acquired skills" (p. 87). One of the best examples is the traditional curriculum for the arithmetic operations of addition, subtraction, multiplication, and division. There is a definite hierarchy of subskills, and difficulty with a later skill may be due to failure to master an earlier, prerequisite skill.

Analysis by Difficulty Level

Some tasks have neither a definite temporal order nor a natural developmental sequence; however, they can be analyzed according to the ease with which their subcomponents can be acquired. A good example is the skill of writing letters in manuscript. This skill can be task analyzed by dividing lowercase letters into several clusters, beginning with the least difficult (Affleck et al., 1980, p. 90):

Straight line letters	lti
Straight line and slant letters	vxwyz
Circle and curve letters	ocs
Circle and line letters	abepgdq
Curve and line letters	jhmknfru

In assessment, task analysis serves a somewhat different purpose than served in instruction. It is used with tasks in which a student experiences difficulty. Troublesome tasks are analyzed, and the student's ability to perform each subtask or task subcomponent is assessed to locate the source of the difficulty. For example, if writing sentences with correct capitalization and punctuation appears to be a problem for Jorge, the teacher could task analyze this skill and then assess Jorge's ability to perform each step in the developmental sequence. A sample skill hierarchy for capitalization and punctuation appears in Table 5–3. To utilize this sequence for assessment, informal measures such as criterion-referenced tests are designed for each step of interest. With Jorge, the teacher could begin by assessing the skills listed for third graders, and

TABLE 5-3
Hierarchy for Capitalization and Punctuation Skills

Grade 1

Copies sentences correctly.
Capitalizes first word of a sentence.
Capitalizes first letter of a proper name.
Uses period at the end of a sentence.
Uses question mark after a written question.
Uses period after numbers in a list.

Grade 2

Capitalizes titles of compositions.
Capitalizes proper names used in written compositions.
Uses comma after salutation and after closing of a friendly letter.
Uses comma between day of the month and the year.
Uses comma between names of city and state.

Grade 3

Capitalizes the names of months, days, holidays; first word in a line of verse; titles of books, stories, poems; salutation and closing of letters and notes; and names of special places.
Begins to apply correct punctuation for abbreviations, initials, contractions, items in a list, quotations, questions, and exclamations.
Uses proper indentation for paragraphs.

Note: From *Teaching Students with Learning Problems* 5/e by Mercer/Mercer, © 1998. Reprinted by permission of Prentice-Hall, Inc., Upper Saddle River, NJ.

then work backward through the sequence to identify prerequisite skills not yet mastered. Instruction would then focus on mastery of these skills.

There are several strategies for conducting a task analysis in assessment. If the task in question is part of the standard curriculum, the teacher may have access to curriculum guides, scope and sequence charts, or published materials that describe the task's subcomponents. Otherwise, it is up to the teacher to determine the important task components. This is usually easiest for tasks with a definite temporal sequence. The teacher can perform the task and note each step that is taken. According to Berdine and Cegelka (1980), "To check the adequacy of the breakdown, the teacher should perform the task a second time following the steps outlined, adding or deleting steps as necessary" (p. 164).

It is also important to determine if the task can be performed in more than one acceptable sequence. For example, tying one's shoe is a task for which there are several successful sequences. Thus, the teacher should observe other adults and, if possible, students as they complete the task.

With tasks that do not follow a temporal order, subcomponents and their sequence must be determined by logic. One method is to list all the subtasks or subcomponents that appear to be involved in the task. These are then arranged in order, ranging from the least difficult to the most difficult, or by utility, ranging from the most necessary for task completion to the least necessary. Obviously, such a task analysis is somewhat subjective, and two teachers generating a subtask sequence for the same skill might disagree. However, flaws in the task analysis usually become apparent in the assessment phase. If the student can perform each subtask but not the task itself, it is likely that an important subtask has been omitted. If the student can perform what are considered to be difficult subcomponents but cannot perform easier ones, then the specified sequence is incorrect, at least for that student.

Structural Task Analysis

Another approach that may provide instructional information is an analysis of task demands

(McLoughlin & Kershman, 1978). Rather than specifying task subcomponents and sequence, the goal is to describe the task in terms of the demands placed upon the learner. This is sometimes called a *structural* task analysis, and it includes consideration of the following task characteristics:

- *Task directions.* The directions for completing the task may be presented verbally or in writing. They vary in number and can be either clear and concise or complex and confusing.
- *Presentation mode.* This refers to the way in which information necessary for task completion is provided to the learner; for example, the student may be required to listen to, read, or look at one or more sources of information.
- *Response mode.* This is the method used by the student in performing the task. The student may need to respond orally or make some sort of written response such as writing numbers, letters, words, sentences, or paragraphs.
- *Quantity requirements.* This task dimension is concerned with the number of responses the student must produce: the number of questions to answer, problems to solve, sentences to write, and so on.
- *Time requirements.* Some tasks are timed, and their successful completion depends on the speed of the learner.
- *Accuracy requirements.* These criteria specify the accuracy standards for successful task performance. For example, a teacher might require a minimum of 80% accuracy on in-class assignments.

Structural analysis of a classroom task helps identify specific instructional expectations. When these expectations are known, one can consider ways to modify the task demands to facilitate successful performance. In assessment, diagnostic probes are used to evaluate the effects of changing task demands systematically, and this strategy is described in the next section.

CURRICULUM-BASED ASSESSMENT STRATEGIES

Many types of informal assessments are curriculum-based. These measures and strategies assess school skills directly. Their content is determined by the standard school curriculum or the special course of study designed to meet the needs of a particular student with a disability. They are obtrusive because they require that a test task or a series of tasks be added to the instructional environment. However, curriculum-based techniques are used often in classrooms, and their results relate directly to instructional decision making.

Curriculum-based assessment can use any type of informal assessment strategy, even observation. However, the most common techniques are informal inventories, classroom quizzes, and criterion-referenced tests. The next sections describe these measures as well as diagnostic probes and diagnostic teaching. Other approaches, such as curriculum-based measurement (CBM) and portfolio assessment, are discussed in the next chapter.

Inventories and Classroom Quizzes

Informal inventories and quizzes assess a student's performance in a school skill area. Their standard of comparison is the curriculum. For example, the teacher may wonder about a new student's knowledge of geography or of punctuation and capitalization rules; another teacher might want to find out if the class has learned the American history material presented over the last few weeks. Inventories and quizzes answer these types of questions about present levels of functioning.

Inventories and quizzes are screening devices that assess selected portions of curricular areas; they are not intended to measure mastery of every fact, concept, and subskill in a particular domain. Because they assess only representative skills, they can sample a greater number of skill areas. For example, an arithmetic inventory might present some, but not all, addition fact problems, some subtraction facts, and some multiplication and division facts. The intent is to identify the general level of student functioning within the curricular area. However, more precise measures such as criterion-referenced tests are needed to find out about student performance in relation to all skills within this domain.

A major difference between informal inventories and classroom quizzes is the purpose for which they are used. Quizzes—or, as they are sometimes called, tests or examinations—typically assess whether students have acquired some body of knowledge or skills taught by the teacher. They are progress measures, and their results are used to evaluate the effects of teaching and learning. Inventories are more of a preteaching assessment tool. They are usually administered before instruction to determine where a need for instruction exists. Also, inventories generally cover a larger segment of the curriculum than covered by quizzes. A spelling inventory might contain selected words from several levels of difficulty (grade 1, grade 2, and so forth), whereas a classroom spelling quiz would include only those words for which instruction had been provided.

Informal Inventories

Inventories can be created by the teacher or purchased from test publishers. Inventories are commercially available for many subject areas, but the most common is the informal reading inventory. Teachers should understand the steps involved in designing an inventory so they can create such a measure if an appropriate one is not readily available. To design an informal inventory, the teacher should:

1. Determine the curriculum area in which the student is to be assessed.
2. Isolate a portion of the curriculum appropriate for the student's age, grade, and skill level.
3. Analyze the curriculum into testable and teachable segments. As in task analysis, the curriculum may be broken down into sequential steps, developmental steps, or difficulty levels.
4. Prepare test items for each segment of the curriculum, emphasizing the most important aspects of each segment.
5. If necessary, reduce the number of test items so the inventory is of manageable length.
6. Sequence the test items from easiest to most difficult or in random order if the student is expected to answer all items.

Figure 5–6 presents an example of such an informal inventory. The content area is handwriting, and it is designed for elementary grade students. The test items are representative of the content domain but include only selected subskills. In designing this inventory, the teacher analyzed the skill of handwriting into developmental steps: Students learn to print their name, then print the lowercase and capital letters, and so forth. Because students usually acquire these skills in this order, the test items are arranged in the developmental sequence to assure successful performance for students who have not yet mastered more advanced skills. However, test items are sometimes arranged in random order. If students are expected to answer all test items, random order reduces the possibility that clues from one item will help them answer others.

Because informal inventories do not typically include performance standards, students do not pass or fail these measures. Instead, the goal is to estimate the students' current levels of performance and identify areas in the curriculum requiring further assessment. Teachers should be cautious about basing instruction solely on the results of informal inventories. First, the quality of an inventory, like that of most informal measures, is usually unknown. With no information about reliability and validity, it is difficult to judge a measure's accuracy. However, Strickland and Turnbull (1990) maintain that informal inventories "can be constructed so that they exhibit both content and criterion validity" (p. 137). Second, because inventories do not usually contain standards for acceptable performance, the professional must decide how many errors constitute a potential skill weakness. If a student misses one or two items out of several of a particular type, is this a cause for concern? With informal inventories, the teacher is responsible for making that judgment.

If the teacher determines that inventory results indicate a potential problem area, the next step is to assess the skill area more closely. For example, if a student completes an addition skills inventory and performs successfully until encountering regrouping problems, the teacher should find out more about the student's skills in regrouping. The teacher could construct a criterion-referenced test to assess these skills and, if results indicated they were not yet mastered, begin instruction at this point in the curriculum.

Print your name on the line below.

Fill in the missing letters.

a cd fg ij l no qr tu w y

Print the uppercase (capital) letter that goes with each of the lowercase (small) letters below.

a A

b   f   d

g   r

Copy this sentence in your best printing.

Foxes and rabbits are quick, but turtles are slow.

Write your name in cursive on the line below.

Finish writing the cursive alphabet.

a b c

Write the following words in cursive.

dog____   like____   and____   the____

Write this sentence in your best cursive handwriting.

At the zoo you can see lions and tigers, elephants, bears, and monkeys.

FIGURE 5–6

Informal Inventory of Handwriting Skills

Note: From *Teaching Students in General Education Classrooms* 5/e by Lewis/Doorlag, © 1999. Reprinted by permission of Prentice-Hall, Inc., Upper Saddle River, NJ.

Classroom Quizzes

Classroom quizzes are usually designed by teachers, although sample quiz items may be available in teachers' manuals for textbooks or instructional materials. The first step in the development of a quiz is to identify the content of the instructional unit to be assessed. Because instruction has already taken place, instructional objectives should be available, and these are used to generate quiz items. If time constraints permit, each important objective should be represented by at least one quiz item.

The next step is to determine the type or types of items to be included in the quiz. Objective items are those for which the correct answer is readily identifiable (e.g., true-false and multiple-choice questions). Objective items are easily scored but time-consuming to construct. In contrast, more subjective items such as essay questions require less time to construct but are more difficult to score because the teacher must exercise judgment in evaluating student responses. In selecting the type of items to prepare, the teacher must also consider the nature of the subject matter to be assessed. Some curriculum areas, particularly those with a body of factual information, lend themselves well to measurement by objective questions. Other areas are better assessed with essays and other types of more subjective questions. The most common types of quiz items used by classroom teachers are:

- *True-false.* In this type of question, the student determines whether a statement is true or false.
- *Multiple-choice.* The student selects a word, phrase, or sentence that best completes a partial statement or answers a question.
- *Matching.* The student selects from one set of words, phrases, or sentences the one that best fits each of the words, phrases, or sentences in another set.
- *Completion.* The student finishes an incomplete sentence by furnishing a word or phrase.
- *Short answer.* The student provides a brief response such as a definition, a list of steps or examples, or a short description.
- *Problem.* The student solves some sort of mathematical problem.
- *Essay.* The student provides a prose response, usually of some length.

Airasian (1996) presents several rules for writing items for classroom quizzes:

1. Avoid wording and sentence structure that are ambiguous and confusing.
2. Use appropriate vocabulary.
3. Keep questions short and to the point.
4. Write items that have one correct answer.
5. Give information about the nature of the desired answer.
6. Do not provide clues to the correct answer. (pp. 104–112)

Although teachers should avoid embedding clues within questions, it is important that items are clear enough to give students direction for responding. This is particularly true for essay questions. Vague questions often result in vague, disorganized responses.

In designing quizzes for students with special needs, it is also important to consider academic skill demands. Students must be able to read quiz questions; a test is not an adequate measure of a curriculum area if a student fails because he or she could not decode the questions. For students with writing skill problems, objective items requiring a response of only one letter or number would be less difficult than, for example, an essay exam. Another concern is the physical appearance of the quiz. The print should be clear and readable, and pages should be uncluttered.

Classroom quizzes can be power tests or speed tests. With power tests, there are no time limits because the aim is to determine the extent of the student's knowledge in the curriculum area under assessment. In general, classroom quizzes should be power measures unless the instructional goal requires that students perform both accurately and quickly. However, with skill subjects, particularly basic academic skills, speed is often important.

The reliability of classroom quizzes can be determined by means of the Kuder-Richardson 21 formula, an estimate of inter-item consistency. The teacher needs to know three things to use this formula: K, the number of items in the test; $\overline{X}$, the mean of the scores; and σ^2, the variance of the scores (computed by squaring the standard deviation). These values are used in the following formula to yield r, the total test reliability:

$$r = \frac{K\sigma^2 - \overline{X}(K - \overline{X})}{\sigma^2(K - 1)}$$

It is also possible to gather information about characteristics of specific quiz items. One concern is the difficulty of the item, and this is determined by calculating the proportion of students who respond to the item correctly. To do this, simply divide the number of students with correct responses by the total number of students attempting the item. Brown (1981) recommends separating the class into two groups of students—those who score in the upper half on the quiz and those who score in the lower half—in order to use the following formula:

$$\text{Item difficulty} = \frac{\begin{array}{c}\text{Proportion} \\ \text{correct} \\ \text{(upper half)}\end{array} + \begin{array}{c}\text{Proportion} \\ \text{correct} \\ \text{(lower half)}\end{array}}{2}$$

The proportion correct for the upper half of the class is determined by dividing the number of upper-half students who answered the item correctly by the total number of students in the upper half; the proportion for the lower half is determined in the same way. This allows the teacher to compare the difficulty levels for these two segments of the class. Brown (1981) suggests that a difficulty level of .60 to .75 (60% to 75% of students responding correctly) is appropriate for most classroom exam items. However, Gallagher (1998) maintains that the acceptable item difficulty level (or item-achievement rank) should be set by the teacher based upon the nature of the assessment task and the expectations for student performance.

The discrimination index of a quiz item is a measure of how well the item differentiates between students who score well and those who do not. To determine the discrimination index, use this formula (Brown, 1981):

$$\begin{array}{c}\text{Item} \\ \text{discrimination}\end{array} = \begin{array}{c}\text{Proportion} \\ \text{correct} \\ \text{(upper half)}\end{array} - \begin{array}{c}\text{Proportion} \\ \text{correct} \\ \text{(lower half)}\end{array}$$

According to Gay (1985), when an item's discrimination index is greater than .30, that item is doing an adequate job of distinguishing between upper- and lower-half students. If the discrimina-

tion index is less than .30, the item should be reexamined and possibly rewritten. The index can be a negative number. For example, if 50% of the upper-half students and 80% of the lower-half students answer a quiz question correctly, the item's discrimination index would be −.30, a sign that the question is a misleading one. There are some situations in which a teacher would not want an item to discriminate. For example, the instructional goal might be that all students will tell time to the nearest minute with 100% accuracy.

Some objective items offer students a choice of responses. For instance, with multiple-choice questions, the student must select one response from the several possible answers presented. With this type of item, it is important to look at the wrong answers, sometimes called distractors. To conduct this type of analysis, the teacher records the number of students who select each of the possible responses. If a particular distractor is chosen by a large proportion of students, this may signal a poorly written item or an area of misunderstanding that merits further explanation or instruction.

Criterion-Referenced Tests

Like informal inventories and classroom quizzes, criterion-referenced tests (CRTs) compare a student's performance to the goals of the curriculum rather than to the performance of a norm group. However, CRTs typically sample more restricted curricular domains than sampled by inventories. An inventory might reveal a possible problem in decoding short vowels; a criterion-referenced test would identify the short vowels the student could read and those he or she could not. Another important feature of CRTs is their emphasis on mastery. These measures are scored as pass or fail: Either the student has mastered the skill under study or the student has not. This has direct implications for instruction; unmastered skills or their prerequisites may become the next curricular goal.

Placement tests are quite similar to criterion-referenced tests. Often furnished as part of an instructional material or textbook series, placement tests identify the point within the material where instruction should begin. Placement tests assess mastery of the content presented by the text or material. When the student achieves a specified level of accuracy, it is assumed that the content has been mastered. When he or she drops below this specified mastery level, the starting point for instruction is identified. Competency tests, too, are much like CRTs. A common school use of competency tests is to determine whether students have met state or district standards for high school graduation. Again, specific skills are assessed and performance is compared to a pre-specified level of mastery.

Criterion-referenced tests, placement tests, and competency tests are all commercially available. CRTs are easy to construct, and teachers may wish to design their own to match their instructional goals. Usually, however, teachers use the placement tests that accompany commercial materials, although it is certainly possible to adapt or even construct such measures. Because competency tests are used with large groups of students, perhaps even an entire school population, they are typically developed at the school or district level or purchased from a test publisher.

CRTs can be used to assess any behavior for which an instructional objective can be specified. They are easy to design, but their construction does require an investment of time and energy. The major steps are:

1. Decide what specific questions you want answered about a student's behavior. What ability (i.e., skill and knowledge) do you want to test?
2. Write a performance objective which describes how you are going to test the student. It should include (a) what the student must do (i.e., what behavior must be engaged in); (b) under what conditions the student will engage in this behavior; and (c) how well the student must perform in order to pass the test.
3. Use the performance objective to help you construct (i.e., write) your CRT. All of the necessary components of a CRT may be found in your performance objective. These components are (a) the directions for administration and scoring, (b) the criterion for passing the test, and (c) the materials and/or test items necessary. (Howell et al., 1979, pp. 96–97)

Questions about student performance can be generated from many sources. After observing a student in the classroom for a few days, the teacher can easily come up with several! Standardized test results may also suggest areas for further assessment. Other valuable sources are the results of informal measures such as inventories and work sample analyses.

Once an assessment question is specified, an instructional objective is selected. If the question concerns a standard area of the curriculum, it is likely that the appropriate instructional objective will be available in a curriculum guide or a similar source. If necessary, the teacher can construct the objective by specifying three things: the desired student behavior, stated in observable terms; the conditions under which the behavior should occur; and the criterion for acceptable performance of the behavior (Mager, 1975). Just as a target behavior must be pinpointed before it can be observed, the behavior to be assessed with a CRT must be clearly specified. For example, "knowing the alphabet" is too imprecise. It could be interpreted in many ways—reciting the alphabet, writing it in manuscript or cursive, saying the names or sounds of the letters, and so forth. If the teacher is interested in whether the student can recite the alphabet, the objective can begin as:

Say the names of the letters of the alphabet in order from memory.

The teacher then specifies the conditions under which the behavior should occur. What directions will the teacher provide? What materials will be available to the student? What constraints will be imposed upon performance? For the alphabet recitation example, the teacher decided to give one simple direction ("Say the alphabet"). No time constraints were imposed and no materials were necessary. The objective is:

When told by the teacher to "say the alphabet," the student will say the names of the letters of the alphabet in order from memory.

The last step is to set the criterion for acceptable performance. How well must the student perform to demonstrate mastery of the skill? Are any errors allowed? If so, how many or what percentage? Howell et al. (1979) suggest estab-

---

Criterion-Referenced Test

Task: Say the alphabet in order from memory.

Materials: Score sheet

Directions (to student): "Say the alphabet."

Directions (to tester): Record student responses verbatim. Do not allow the student to look at the score sheet.

Scoring: Count correct if the student says each of the 26 letters of the alphabet in the correct order. Count correct if letter names are intelligible even if not articulated perfectly. Count as incorrect if a letter name is omitted, added, or said out of order.

Criterion for Acceptable Performance: 100% accuracy

Score Sheet

Skill: Knowledge of the alphabet

Task: Say names of letters of the alphabet in order from memory

Student _____   Date _____

Age _____   Grade _____   Tester _____

Student responses (record verbatim):

_____

_____

_____

_____

FIGURE 5–7

Criterion-Referenced Test and Score Sheet

lishing criteria by means of "expert" populations. They recommend that the teacher identify individuals who possess the skill being assessed by the CRT, then administer the CRT to this group and use their minimum level of performance as the mastery standard. This may not be necessary with some skills if the teacher believes that the skill should be performed without errors. If this is the case in alphabet recitation, the objective becomes:

> *When told by the teacher to "say the alphabet," the student will say the names of the letters of the alphabet in order from memory with no errors.*

The criterion-referenced test in Figure 5–7 measures this instructional objective. The information at the beginning of the test is derived from the objective. The student behavior becomes the test task; the conditions under which the behavior is to be performed provide information about needed materials and directions, for both the student and the tester; and the objective's criterion

for acceptable performance becomes the criterion for passing the CRT. Additional scoring standards may also be necessary. In this case, the teacher decided to allow mispronunciations of letter names if they were intelligible. On the score sheet, the teacher records identifying information about the student and the test and then writes down the student's responses.

If a student passes a CRT, the teacher assumes that the student has mastered the objective, and assessment can progress to the next instructional step. If a student does not pass, the teacher moves backward through the curricular sequence and assesses a prerequisite skill. Instructional planning can begin once the skills the student has mastered are established.

However, the teacher must exercise some caution in interpreting results. First, CRTs tell only what a student can or cannot do; because they are not normed, they do not tell what a particular student is expected to do. If a student fails a CRT on shoe tying, the instructional implication appears to be to teach this skill. Although this skill would likely be appropriate for a young school-aged child, it would not be for a toddler. Other factors to be considered before translating CRT results into instructional action are the age of the student, the age-appropriateness of the skill, and the priority of the skill in relation to other possible instructional goals.

Another caveat common to all informal measures is the lack of information about reliability and validity. Teachers can improve the CRTs they construct by specifying standard procedures for test administration and scoring and by establishing mastery levels empirically rather than arbitrarily; procedures are also available for determining reliability and validity of CRTs (Howell et al., 1979).

Diagnostic Probes and Diagnostic Teaching

Diagnostic probes and diagnostic teaching involve the systematic manipulation of instructional conditions to determine the most appropriate strategy for teaching a particular skill to a student. The difference between these two procedures relates to the thoroughness with which they evaluate instructional alternatives. Diagnostic probes are typically brief, one-time measures of a single instructional option. Diagnostic teaching, on the other hand, takes place over an extended time period to investigate fully the differential effects of various instructional interventions.

Diagnostic Probes

Diagnostic probes are used to discover whether changing some aspect of a classroom task will have a positive effect upon student performance. For example, if the history teacher observes that a student is having difficulty with the daily quizzes on reading assignments, the teacher could design one or several diagnostic probes to investigate the relationship between the demands of the task and the student's ability to perform. The daily quiz could be modified in a number of ways, depending upon the type of difficulty the student is experiencing. For instance, if the student answers the first few questions but does not complete the quiz, the amount of time allowed

for this task could be increased or the number of questions reduced. Or if the student's writing skills appear to interfere with performance, the student could be permitted to respond orally or to tape-record answers.

The general procedures for the design of a diagnostic probe are:

1. The student's performance is assessed under the standard instructional condition.
2. Some aspect of the task or the instructional conditions that relate to the task is modified.
3. The student's performance is assessed under the modified condition and compared with previous performance.

This sequence of steps usually takes place within one instructional session. The teacher observes a possible performance problem and identifies a possible solution. Data are collected before the modification is made to establish the student's current performance level and again after the modification is in place. If necessary, a series of diagnostic probes are devised until the teacher has sufficient information to design a diagnostic teaching sequence.

The teacher can make several types of changes to improve student performance. Two major types of modifications relate to task characteristics and the instructional strategies used to teach the task. Structural task analysis is a useful way to analyze task characteristics. Among the factors to be considered are the difficulty level of the task; the conditions under which the student is expected to perform; the directions provided for task completion; presentation and response modes; and requirements for quantity, speed, and accuracy.

Table 5–4 summarizes several general methods of adapting instruction. Included are strategies for modifying the task itself and for changing the instructional conditions that relate to task performance. These suggestions are by no means exhaustive, but they do provide some direction for the development of diagnostic probes. Dimensions of instruction to consider are the methods used to present new information to students (lecture, discussion, demonstration, and so forth), the number and type of practice opportunities available, how feedback is provided, the

TABLE 5-4
Designing Diagnostic Probes

INSTRUCTIONAL DIMENSION	POSSIBLE MODIFICATIONS
Task Characteristics	
The difficulty level of the task	Divide the task into component subtasks for the student to perform separately; or, substitute an easier, prerequisite task
The conditions under which the task is performed	Alter the conditions by allowing the use of aids (e.g., calculators for mathematics tasks) or by providing cues and prompts
Task directions	Simplify and reduce the number of directions; provide oral as well as written directions
Presentation mode	Change the presentation mode to one that takes advantage of the student's strengths (e.g., change to oral presentation for students with reading problems); or, present information in more than one way
Response mode	Change the response mode to one that takes advantage of the student's strengths (e.g., change to oral responses for students with poor writing skills)
Quantity requirement	Reduce the number of required student responses
Speed requirement	Increase the amount of time allowed for task performance; or, remove time limits altogether
Accuracy requirement	Decrease the standards for successful task performance
Instructional Procedures	
Presentation of new information to students	Change the method of instruction to a more direct approach (e.g., use lecture or demonstration rather than discussion or discovery); or explain new information in several different ways; or, increase the number of times new information is presented
Practice opportunities for students	Increase the number of practice opportunities provided to students; improve the quantity and quality of feedback students receive during practice; alter the types of practice activities to relate more directly to target behaviors
Feedback to students on task performance	Give feedback more often; relate feedback not only to the accuracy of the response but also to the specific aspect of the task that the student performed correctly or incorrectly
Consequences to students for successful performance	Make the consequences for success more attractive
Learning materials	Revise or modify learning materials (e.g., textbooks, workbooks, worksheets) to a simpler level; or, substitute alternate materials
Pace of instruction	Slow the pace of instruction so less information is presented and practiced at one time
Providing students with alternate strategies for task performance	Change the way in which students approach the task by modifying current strategies; or, introduce new, more effective strategies

Note: From *Teaching Special Students in General Education Classrooms* 5/e by Lewis/Doorlag, © 1999. Reprinted by permission of Prentice-Hall, Inc., Upper Saddle River, NJ.

consequences for successful performance, the instructional materials, and the pace of instruction.

Another type of instructional change involves modifying the strategies that the student uses to approach the classroom task. It is the student's behavior that is altered, not a condition of instruction. The first step is observation of the student's interaction with the task. The methods the student employs in task performance are analyzed, and ineffective strategies are identified.

Then the teacher attempts to modify the student's strategy or substitute another, more effective strategy. For example, if a student's handwriting is poor and he or she grips the pencil awkwardly, the teacher may attempt to change the student's hand position. Or if a student studies new biology terms by staring at a page in the text, the teacher may demonstrate an alternative technique that requires active rehearsal.

Diagnostic probes are most useful for gathering preliminary information about the possible effectiveness of an instructional modification. Only in rare instances do probes yield sufficient information to justify making a change in the instructional environment. Probes provide hypotheses about modifications that may make a difference in student performance. These hypotheses can then be tested through diagnostic teaching.

Diagnostic Teaching

Diagnostic teaching systematically evaluates the relative effectiveness of two or more instructional techniques. It assists the teacher in deciding upon an instructional strategy for a particular student or group. The teacher carefully monitors student performance while presenting instruction first in one manner and then in another. Assessment data collected under each instructional condition are then compared to determine the more effective teaching technique.

For example, if Yvonne is having difficulty learning multiplication facts, the teacher might want to try some different types of practice activities for this skill. First, the teacher would identify the current instructional condition and assess the student's performance under this condition. In Yvonne's case, worksheets are the current practice activity; over a 1-week period, Yvonne has received scores ranging from 30% correct to 55% correct. Next, the teacher decides upon a new instructional strategy. This decision may be based on the results of a series of diagnostic probes. For multiplication facts, two alternatives to worksheets are flash card drills and computer-based drill and practice programs. These techniques allow practice of the skill while providing the learner with immediate feedback about the accuracy of her responses. The teacher then imple-

ments one of the new instructional approaches for a few days and continues to collect student performance data, usually on a daily basis.

The steps in diagnostic teaching are:

1. Identify the current instructional condition, the baseline condition.
2. Select or design an informal assessment tool to monitor student performance.
3. Assess the student's performance under the current instructional condition. Daily data collection for a 1-week period usually provides an adequate picture of current performance.
4. Select one or more new instructional strategies to evaluate.
5. Implement the first new instructional strategy for a brief period (e.g., one week). This is the first intervention phase.
6. Continue to regularly assess the student's performance.
7. Implement a second new instructional strategy, if desired.
8. Continue to regularly assess the student's performance.
9. Plot performance data for the baseline condition and the intervention phases on a graph. Compare performance across the conditions.

Only one thing at a time should be changed in diagnostic teaching. The baseline condition and the treatment phase should differ in only one important instructional variable. The instructional factor that produced the change in student behavior can then be identified. For instance, if the teacher changes the practice activity and sees an increase in student accuracy, the change in performance can be linked to the change in the practice activity. However, if several changes occur (e.g., a new practice activity is introduced, a peer tutor replaces the teacher, and the amount of instructional time is doubled), the teacher cannot attribute improved student performance to any single modification.

The graph in Figure 5–8 presents the results of the intervention with Yvonne, the girl having difficulty learning multiplication facts. Yvonne's teacher collected daily data on the percentage of questions Yvonne answered correctly. As can be seen from the graph, the new treatment—the flash card drill—appears to be a more effective instructional strategy than worksheet activities for Yvonne.

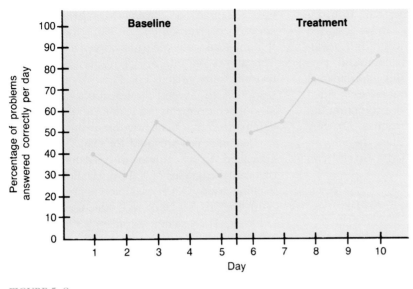

FIGURE 5-8
Diagnostic Teaching Results

Diagnostic teaching is actually classroom research. Because one student is studied, it is single-subject research. Diagnostic teaching can be approached in more than one way. The method just discussed is the simplest design: baseline followed by treatment (or AB). Although the AB design provides important information for classroom decision making, its major limitation is that some factor other than the treatment could be responsible for a change in student behavior. One way to overcome this limitation is by means of a reversal design: baseline followed by treatment, followed by a return to baseline conditions (ABA). Methods such as this are discussed in the next chapter in the section on action research. Also, Cooper et al. (1987) provide descriptions of available methodologies.

PROCEDURES USING INFORMANTS

Checklists, rating scales, questionnaires, and interviews are informal assessment procedures that make use of the expertise of an informant—a teacher, parent, employer, the student, or a peer. These measures are obtrusive and indirect; they access information about nonobservables such as values, beliefs, and opinions or past events. Informants are used in assessment for three purposes. First, they can provide a historical perspective. For example, the student's parents are likely the best source of information about acquisition of developmental milestones in the preschool years. Second, informants who have had extensive experience with the student can summarize their observations and offer opinions, judgments, and interpretations. A teacher, for instance, can provide information about the student's current levels of performance in each of the subject areas taught in the classroom. Third, informants can comment upon less observable concerns such as attitudes, values, and perceptions. Students can describe their attitudes toward school, for example.

However, there is always the danger of inaccuracy when information is gathered indirectly. Informants may not recall past events with clarity; their opinions may be based upon incomplete information. They may even report less than the truth. Information gathered from informants is subjective and should be interpreted as such. If this is kept in mind, informants can be a valuable addition to the assessment process. In fact, for some assessment questions, informants may be the only source of information available to the teacher.

The measures used to gather data from informants are very flexible. They can be designed to assess almost any domain: health and developmental history, educational background, current educational status, social and interpersonal skills, and attitudes toward school subjects. Such measures can be very structured, prompting the informant for every specific response. Or they can be quite open-ended, providing the informant with general questions that he or she can choose how to answer.

Checklists and Rating Scales

Checklists and rating scales are structured assessments. Specific questions are posed, and the informant selects a response rather than generating one. These measures are usually administered in written form to adult informants, although they can be presented orally to young children.

With checklists, the informant is provided with a list of descriptions, and the task is simply to check each description that applies to the student under assessment. The teacher, parent, or other informant reads each description, making a check beside each that is accurate. Checklists can be used for a variety of purposes, and Figure 5–9 presents two examples. The first is a curriculum checklist for teachers. The teacher considers each educational objective, then marks those attained by the student. The skills listed on this measure could be assessed directly if the teacher had insufficient information. In the second example, parents read descriptions of problem behaviors and circle those that apply to their child. Because this measure is written in less behavioral terms, it requires more interpretation. The parent must decide upon the meaning of statements such as "is very distracted" before determining if the description is accurate.

Rating scales require more from informants than a yes-no response. A description or statement is presented, and informants express their agreement with the description by selecting one of a series of ratings. Among the most common rating instruments are Likert-type scales (Likert, 1932), as noted in Chapter 3. The informant considers each statement, then chooses one of the specified responses: Strongly Agree, Agree, Neutral, Disagree, or Strongly Disagree. The responses to Likert-type scale items are often tied to numerical values (e.g., Strongly Disagree = 1). This allows the informant's responses to be statistically summarized. For example, if a teacher responds to several items about a student's school achievement, the teacher's ratings can be summarized by calculating the mean.

Rating scales are used for many purposes in education. A very common one is grading. The traditional letter grades of A, B, C, D, and F make up a rating scale. Other examples appear in Figure 5–10. The first is a Likert-type scale for rating pupil behavior. The teacher considers each skill (e.g., "Ability to follow directions") and rates the student's acquisition of the skill on a scale of 1 to 5. To facilitate the rating process, each possible choice is further described. A rating of 1 for following directions, for instance, means that the student is "Always confused; cannot or is unable to follow directions." The second rating scale is designed for students and assesses attitudes toward school.

Ranking is another strategy that can be used to question informants. In a ranking task, several alternatives are presented and the person must place them in order. For example, a student might be asked to rank several school activities by writing a number 1 by his or her favorite, a number 2 by the next favorite, and so forth. Ranking measures are sometimes valuable for obtaining information about preferences. However, they are less common than either checklists or rating scales, possibly because their results are somewhat more difficult to interpret.

Questionnaires and Interviews

Questionnaires are written measures designed to elicit information from informants. They can be very structured and contain questions similar to those found on checklists and rating scales. They may also contain other types of structured questions such as multiple-choice and true-false items. Less structured, open-ended questions can also be included. One example is the open-ended questionnaire that appeared in Figure 2–2 in Chapter 2. That measure was designed for use by general education teachers in referring a student for special education services.

Curriculum Checklist: Social Studies—Primary[a]

Understanding One's Community

_____ 1. States that people live together in families.
_____ 2. Tells that families live together in homes.
_____ 3. Gives the name of his community.
_____ 4. Tells his address.
_____ 5. States that all communities are not the same.
_____ 6. Tells the occupation of his parents.
_____ 7. Names some essential elements of a community such as homes, stores, and churches.
_____ 8. Tells the names of some community helpers such as the doctor, grocer, etc.

Parent Problem Behavior Checklist[b]

Directions: Read through the following list carefully and circle the number in front of each statement that describes a problem related to your child.

1. Lacks self confidence
2. Is hypersensitive—feelings easily hurt
3. Is frequently depressed—sad
4. Is easily flustered and confused
5. Is unsure
6. Is very distracted
7. Has short attention span and poor powers of concentration
8. Behavior not predictable—is sometimes good, sometimes bad
9. Exhibits poor muscular coordination—clumsy and awkward
10. Often has physical complaints: headaches, stomachaches, etc.
11. Is nervous and jittery—easily startled
12. Usually feels tired—drowsy
13. Is shy, bashful
14. Is attention-seeking, engages in "show-off" behavior
15. Quarrels and fights with other children

FIGURE 5-9

Examples of Checklists

Note: [a]From *Developing and Implementing Individualized Education Programs* (3rd ed.) (p. 480) by B. B. Strickland and A. P. Turnbull, 1990, New York: Merrill/Macmillan. Copyright 1990 by Macmillan Publishing Company. Reprinted by permission. [b]From "Parent Problem Behavior Checklist" by S. C. Larsen. Reprinted in *Educational Assessment of Learning Problems: Testing for Teaching* (p. 115) by G. Wallace and S. C. Larsen, 1978, Boston: Allyn & Bacon. Copyright 1978 by Allyn & Bacon. Reprinted by permission of Stephen C. Larsen.

Interviews are the oral equivalent of questionnaires. An interview might be more appropriate than a questionnaire in several situations: if there is a literacy barrier, if the informant needs help in feeling at ease before questioning begins, and if the task directions are complex and need explanation. In addition, an interviewer can guide the informant through the questioning, keep him or her on track, and probe for additional information when necessary.

Interviews are often used to gather information from parents, professionals, and students.

With students who have academic difficulties, interviews are usually preferable to questionnaires. Several questions can be used when interviewing students about their school performance:

- What are your best subjects in school? Why do you think you do your best in these subjects?
- What are your weakest subjects? What seems to cause the problems in these subjects?
- If you could change anything about your school day, what would it be? (Strickland & Turnbull, 1990, p. 265)

Pupil Behavior Rating Scale[a]

	1	2	3	4	5
Ability to Follow Directions	Always confused; cannot or is unable to follow directions	Usually follows simple oral directions but often needs individual help	Follows directions that are familiar and/or not complex	Remembers and follows extended directions	Unusually skillful in remembering and following directions
Comprehension of Class Discussion	Always inattentive and/or unable to follow and understand discussions	Listens but rarely comprehends well; mind often wanders from discussion	Listens and follows discussions according to age and grade	Understands well and benefits from discussions	Becomes involved and shows unusual understanding of material discussed
Ability to Retain Orally Given Information	Almost total lack of recall; poor memory	Retains simple ideas and procedures if repeated often	Average retention of materials; adequate memory for age and grade	Remembers procedures and information from various sources; good immediate and delayed recall	Superior memory for both details and content
Comprehension of Word Meanings	Extremely immature level of understanding	Fails to grasp simple word meanings; misunderstands words at grade level	Good grasp of grade level vocabulary for age and grade	Understands all grade level vocabulary as well as higher level word meanings	Superior understanding of vocabulary; understands many abstract words

Student Opinion Survey[b]

Directions: Read each statement carefully and indicate how much you agree or disagree with it by circling the appropriate letter(s) to the right.

Key:
SA—Strongly Agree
A—Agree
NS—Not Sure
D—Disagree
SD—Strongly Disagree

1. Science class is challenging.	SA	A	NS	D	SD
2. Reading is important.	SA	A	NS	D	SD
3. I like coming to school.	SA	A	NS	D	SD
4. I like doing science experiments.	SA	A	NS	D	SD
5. Homework is hard for me.	SA	A	NS	D	SD
6. Cheating is very bad.	SA	A	NS	D	SD
7. Learning about circles and triangles is useless.	SA	A	NS	D	SD
8. I do *not* like to work in small groups.	SA	A	NS	D	SD
9. Doing well in school is important.	SA	A	NS	D	SD
10. I believe that what I learn in school is important.	SA	A	NS	D	SD

FIGURE 5-10

Examples of Rating Scales

Note: [a]From *Learning Disabilities* (p. 21) by B. R. Gearheart, 1977, St. Louis: C. V. Mosby. Copyright 1977 The C. V. Mosby Company. Adapted from a project developed under Research Grant, USPHS Contract 108–65–42, Bureau of Neurological and Sensory Diseases. Reprinted by permission.
[b]From *Classroom Assessment* (p. 278) by J. H. McMillan, 1997, Boston: Allyn & Bacon. Copyright 1997 by Allyn & Bacon. Reprinted by permission.

Interviews, questionnaires, and other assessments that rely upon informants are indirect measures. The value of their results depends upon the informant's accuracy. Poor memory of past events, inadequate interpretation of current observations, faulty judgment, and lack of veracity can result in poor information. The teacher must be aware of these possibilities when interpreting reports of informants.

Clinical Interviews

Clinical interviews are a special type of assessment procedure. They are interviews in which the student acts as informant, and the interview questions are designed to identify the strategies the student uses when attempting to perform a task. For example, the teacher may be interested in learning more about how students go about solving mathematics problems, planning essays, or studying textbook chapters. Clinical interviews focus on the process the student follows in completing a task. The product is of secondary interest.

Some strategies are observable. Thus, when conducting a clinical interview, the professional carefully notes the student's behaviors. However, cognitive strategies cannot be observed, and the student's report becomes the basis of information about this aspect of task performance. The teacher takes note of what the student does and then asks the student to describe the thinking process that accompanies those actions.

Clinical interviews usually take place while the student is performing a task. For example, if the task is solving mathematics word problems, the student is supplied with several problems at an appropriate level of difficulty. Then, to find out about nonobservable strategies, the professional directs the student to "think out loud as you solve these problems." Then he or she watches, listens to the student's report, and asks questions to clarify meaning or to probe areas that were not discussed.

In some cases, interviews are conducted immediately after the student has finished the task. In the assessment of writing skills, for instance, it is not wise to interrupt the student in the act of composition. Instead, the interview takes place as soon as the student has finished writing. There should be no delay between the completion of the task and the start of the interview. Otherwise, the student may not be able to recall the exact series of steps taken in responding to the task.

Clinical interviewing is a sophisticated assessment technique. It requires expertise in the use of observation and interviewing techniques, knowledge of the curriculum area under assessment, and knowledge of the types of cognitive strategies that students are likely to employ in various types of tasks. The resulting data are subjective in that they are an informant's report of nonobservable behaviors. However, clinical interviews are the most direct means of gathering information about students' cognitive strategies and may provide important directions for the structuring of the teaching process.

INTERPRETING INFORMAL ASSESSMENT RESULTS

One of the hallmarks of informal assessment is its relevance to instruction. When informal procedures are designed by teachers to answer specific assessment questions about their students, results are immediately applicable to the solution of instructional problems. The data assist in the identification of areas for further assessment, in the description of the student's current classroom performance, and in the planning or modification of instructional strategies.

Despite the advantages of informal measures, there are also limitations that become apparent in the interpretation of assessment results. These concerns are summarized here.

Technical Adequacy

The greatest limitation of informal assessment tools is the lack of information about reliability and validity (Bennett, 1982). In many cases, the professional simply does not know whether a particular informal procedure is technically adequate. If technical data are not available for a measure, interpretation of its results must be approached with great caution.

All measurements contain error. With norm-referenced tests, the amount of error can be estimated using the standard error of measurement, and confidence intervals are constructed around observed scores to quantify the error factor. However, when there is insufficient psychometric information, the professional is left with the knowledge that assessment results are inaccurate, but the degree of inaccuracy is unknown.

The procedures for gathering information about the technical quality of some types of informal tools have been discussed throughout this chapter. For example, interrater reliability can be determined in observation, and there are techniques to study the reliability and other characteristics of criterion-referenced tests. Professionals should take advantage of any such available procedures.

At minimum, content validity should be evaluated. This type of validity relates to how well the tool fulfills the purpose of assessment by addressing the content of interest. Among the most important considerations are whether the assessment device includes a representative sample of the content domain and whether the assessment tasks are appropriate. If the student's problem is fighting on the playground, an observation conducted during shop class does not assess the domain of interest. If oral reading is the concern, the assessment task should be reading out loud, not matching words and pictures.

Selection of the Appropriate Tools for Assessment

The more direct the measure, the more useful the results. For example, if the student's handwriting skills are a concern, direct measures such as observation and work sample analysis provide instructionally relevant information. Reviewing the student's report card grades in handwriting is a less direct measure.

However, it is necessary to consider the purposes of assessment to determine whether a tool is appropriate. If the purpose is to find out if the student's handwriting skills are adequate for success in a general education classroom, interviewing the classroom teacher may be the most direct means of gathering the needed information.

Many informal assessment tools provide professionals with a wealth of information. However, the amount of data can become overwhelming and confuse, rather than facilitate, decision making. Assessment should be a carefully planned, systematic process. Once it has been learned that a student's spelling performance is satisfactory, it is not useful to continue gathering information about spelling. Only areas that represent educational needs should be assessed in depth. The more intensive informal procedures—criterion-referenced testing, diagnostic teaching, and clinical interviews—should be reserved for in-depth assessment.

Quality of the Sample of Behavior

All formal and informal measures rely upon behavior samples. It is impractical to observe all behaviors of a student or test skill in solving all the possible mathematics computation problems. As one author notes, "Objective based or not, most formal and informal tests provide only a 'snapshot' of the child's performance" (Bachor, 1979, p. 45). Thus, interpretation of assessment results must take into account the quality of the behavior sample. This holds true for all types of informal assessment tools, from observation and work sample analysis, to curriculum-based measures, to procedures that rely upon informants.

If the student's behavior is under assessment, that is the behavioral sample that is evaluated for representativeness. When persons other than the student contribute information, the representativeness of their behaviors must also be considered. The performance of teachers and parents, like that of students, can fluctuate over time.

Criteria for Evaluating Performance

One of the major difficulties in interpreting the results of many types of informal procedures is that there are no guidelines for determining whether a problem exists and, if one does, whether it is serious enough to warrant some kind of intervention. In most cases, it is left up to the professional to set the criteria. If an observation shows that the student talks out in English class once every 10 minutes on the average, the teacher must decide if this is a problem. Likewise, there are no set standards for evaluating the adequacy of a writing sample with 20% of the words misspelled.

Criterion-referenced tests do include performance criteria that are often based on professional judgment rather than empirical evidence. If a professional has set 80% accuracy as the standard for mastery on a CRT, other professionals may disagree and choose 70%, 90%, or even 100% as the criterion.

For the most part, informal procedures are designed to describe the behaviors that the student exhibits, the tasks he or she can complete, and the skills that are mastered and those that continue to require instruction. However, such procedures make no attempt to match the student's current performance with the performance appropriate for age, grade, and ability. For example, a CRT will reveal whether or not a student is able to multiply 3-digit by 3-digit numbers. Results will not show that this skill is not expected of first and second graders. Again, the professional must make this decision.

Translating Results into Instruction

If limitations are kept firmly in mind, professionals can draw and then act upon conclusions from informal data. Then assessment continues as information is collected to evaluate the effectiveness of instruction. By building ongoing assessment into the program, the teacher can monitor student progress and determine when instruction is working and when modifications are needed.

Bennett (1982) provides several suggestions for increasing the usefulness of informal data in planning the instructional program. These are:

1. Recognize that a variety of reasons may exist for a child's correct or incorrect performance on assessment tasks.
2. Try to determine reasons for correct and incorrect performance.
3. Try to determine the conditions under which the child performs the task best.
4. Use informal procedures as complements to formal procedures. (p. 339)

The third suggestion is important. The assessment process tends to focus on the student's problems. The information gathered describes inappropriate behaviors, unlearned skills, and unmastered tasks. But even more crucial is learning how to help the student succeed. A major purpose of assessment must be identification of the classroom conditions and instructional strategies that are likely to improve student performance.

Bennett's last suggestion also deserves comment. Informal assessment is best viewed as a complement to formal assessment. Neither type of procedure is best; both have their uses. Informal assessment is particularly valuable when it augments the results of standardized testing. For example, if a student's score on a formal reading test falls below the average range of performance for age peers, informal assessment can provide critical information about that student's reading performance. Among the possible informal strategies are observing the student during reading instruction, administering an informal reading inventory, analyzing correct and incorrect oral reading responses, interviewing the student to learn about attitudes toward reading and preferences in reading materials, designing a diagnostic teaching sequence, and conducting a clinical reading interview. Informal procedures can be a rich source of information for instruction. When coupled with formal tests, they complete the assessment picture.

AVOIDING BIAS IN INFORMAL ASSESSMENT

Unlike norm-referenced tests, informal measures have not been criticized as contributors to discriminatory assessment and placement practices. In fact, the opposite has occurred. Informal measures—criterion-referenced tests in particular—have been suggested as one possible solution to the problem of bias in assessment. Because CRTs compare performance to the goals of the local curriculum rather than to the performance of a norm group, it is assumed that the standard of comparison is fair. In addition, informal measures tend to assess skill areas in more depth than do norm-referenced tests, and thus they are more sensitive to small changes in pupil behavior.

However, teacher-constructed tests may also contain discriminatory language and content (Bailey & Harbin, 1980). If teachers are insensitive to and have insufficient information about the languages and cultures of their students, they may prepare biased measures. In constructing or selecting informal assessment tools, teachers should consider the same issues in nondiscriminatory assessment that they attend to when evaluating norm-referenced tests:

- Is the standard of comparison appropriate for the student in terms of race, ethnicity, culture, and gender?
- Are test items free from cultural bias?
- Is the language appropriate for the student?
- Does the measure bypass the limitations imposed by the disability?

Other considerations are the time, money, and personnel resources needed to implement a comprehensive criterion-referenced testing system (Duffey, Salvia, Tucker, & Ysseldyke, 1982), the narrow scope of such measures (Oakland, 1980), and the lack of information about their reliability and validity (Harris & Wolf, 1979).

Although informal measures may not replace norm-referenced tests as the instrument of choice for eligibility assessment, they do offer obvious advantages for classroom use. Teachers can design informal tools to answer specific assessment questions about a particular student. Results assist in making decisions about further assessment, current performance, and modification of instruction. Thus, results are instructionally relevant and directly applicable to classroom practice.

McCormack (1976) maintains that the assessment tools that best meet your needs are the ones you construct. Such measures must also be nonbiased to meet the needs of all students. According to Bailey and Harbin (1980), this can be done if:

1. The importance of the skills measured by the instrument and taught in the curriculum are agreed upon by culturally diverse groups within the school system.
2. Criterion-referenced items are constructed so as not to measure the skills of children from a particular cultural group unfairly.
3. Alternative instructional strategies are incorporated to meet the learning needs of individual children. (p. 593)

STUDY GUIDE

REVIEW QUESTIONS

1. Several of the purposes of assessment are listed below. Check each of the purposes that apply to informal procedures.
   _____ a. Provide direction for further assessment
   _____ b. Compare a student's performance to that of other students
   _____ c. Provide direction for planning or modifying instruction
   _____ d. Describe the student's current performance
2. Criterion-referenced tests, a curriculum-based assessment technique, are _____ (*direct* or *indirect*) _____ (*obtrusive* or *unobtrusive*) measures of student performance.
3. Decide whether each of these statements about observation is true or false.
   _____ a. Continuous observation, in which all the behaviors of the student are observed and recorded, is a preliminary technique used to identify possible problem behaviors.
   _____ b. In sequence analysis, the observer records the student's behavior and the events that precede and follow that behavior.
   _____ c. The first step in setting up an observation is to determine who will observe.
   _____ d. In duration recording, the observer counts the number of times the student displays the target behavior.
   _____ e. Graphs are used to report observational data.
4. In the least structured type of observation, called a(n) _____ report, the observer simply describes events in writing.

5. There are two ways in which work samples can be analyzed. In _____ analysis, the student's incorrect answers are studied. In _____ analysis, both correct and incorrect answers are considered.

6. Match the types of task analysis in Column A with the descriptions in Column B.

Column A	Column B
a. Temporal	_____ The characteristics of the task—directions; presentation and response modes; quantity, time, and accuracy requirements—are analyzed.
b. Developmental sequence	_____ Task subcomponents are identified, then put in order by ease of learning.
c. Difficulty	_____ The task is analyzed according to which behavior is performed first, which comes next, and so on.
d. Task structure	_____ Subtasks are arranged in a hierarchy according to which are typically learned or taught first, second, and so on.

7. The standard of comparison used to evaluate student performance on informal inventories, classroom quizzes, and criterion-referenced tests is the _____ , not the performance of other students.

8. Inventories and quizzes are screening devices that assess selected portions of curricular areas. (True or False)

9. Suppose a teacher wanted to design a criterion-referenced test to measure mastery of this objective:

   When given a worksheet with 20 2-digit plus 2-digit addition problems requiring regrouping, the student will write the correct answer to at least 15 of the problems within 5 minutes.

   a. What materials would be needed to administer the test?
   b. What instructions would the teacher give to the student?
   c. What would be the criterion for acceptable performance?

10. Find the false statement.
   a. Diagnostic probes and diagnostic teaching are both indirect, rather than direct, measures of student performance.
   b. Diagnostic probes and diagnostic teaching are instructional procedures as much as they are assessment procedures.
   c. With diagnostic probes, the teacher changes one element of the instructional situation to determine whether the student's performance will improve.
   d. Diagnostic teaching is a type of classroom research. The teacher observes the student's behavior under baseline conditions, then introduces an intervention and analyzes its effect on performance.

11. What are four informal assessment techniques used to gather data from informants?

12. On Likert-type scales, informants are asked to consider a statement, then indicate whether or not they _____ with the statement.

13. In a clinical interview, the professional observes the student perform a task and also asks the student to describe his or her thinking process. (True or False)

14. Interpretation of informal assessment results is difficult because
   a. results are relevant to classroom instruction.
   b. the technical quality of informal assessment tools is usually unknown.
   c. informal assessments generally do not offer standards for evaluating the acceptability of student performance.
   d. Answers b and c are correct.

15. Informal assessments designed by teachers may contain discriminatory language and content. (True or False)

ACTIVITIES

1. Obtain a copy of a published informal assessment device such as an informal inventory or a criterion-referenced test. Examine its manual. Does it describe the procedures used to develop the assessment device? Are reliability and validity discussed? Analyze the content validity of the measure.
2. Pick a specific behavior of a friend or classmate. Set up and carry out a plan for observing that behavior. If possible, enlist the aid of another observer and determine interobserver reliability.
3. Task analyze one of the following: writing a letter, making change, reading the want ads, baking a cake, or fixing a flat tire.
4. Write an instructional objective for one of the subtasks identified in Activity 3. Then develop a criterion-referenced test to measure mastery of the objective.
5. Visit a classroom and obtain several samples of student work. Do error analyses and then response analyses.
6. Prepare a questionnaire for use with elementary grade students to find out about their television viewing habits.

DISCUSSION QUESTIONS

1. Informal assessment techniques have many advantages, particularly in relation to classroom instruction, but they also have disadvantages. Discuss the pros and cons of informal assessment.
2. Compare and contrast direct and indirect informal procedures. Explain why direct measures of student performance are generally preferred.
3. Several informal techniques rely upon informants for the collection of assessment data. Discuss some of the cautions needed with informants.
4. Choose five informal techniques and describe how each could be used to monitor students' progress in instructional programs.
5. Bias can be found in informal assessments as well as in norm-referenced tests. Discuss some of the factors that teachers should keep in mind when attempting to design or select a nonbiased informal assessment tool.

CLASSROOM ASSESSMENT TECHNIQUES

Assessment is an integral part of the teaching process. Every day, teachers observe their students, evaluate the work that they do, and gauge their progress toward instructional goals. Classroom assessment serves two major purposes, and the first is ongoing evaluation of the instructional program. Teachers collect data about student performance to determine if interventions are successful. If they are not, changes are made. The intervention is modified or a new approach is introduced. The second purpose of classroom assessment is evaluation of the student's progress. This type of assessment provides information for regular reports to parents and for the IEP team to consider in its annual review of the student's instructional plan.

Informal assessment techniques are the tools of choice for classroom assessment. Strategies such as observation, error analysis, informal inventories, and classroom quizzes are used often to gather information about student performance. Other approaches that use a combination of informal techniques are also helpful. This chapter describes several of these approaches, including functional assessment, curriculum-based measurement, and portfolio assessment.

Formal testing is sometimes part of classroom assessment, particularly when students with disabilities spend all or part of the school day as members of general education classes. Students included in general education participate in "high-stakes" assessments, that is, the formal achievement tests administered to all students within a school, district, or state. The 1997 IDEA Amendments require that IEP teams determine whether accommodations are needed to enable students with disabilities to participate fully in the formal achievement measures administered to general education students. Because students also take part in routine classroom assessments alongside their typical peers, it may be necessary to develop similar accommodations for informal measures such as quizzes and tests.

TRENDS IN CLASSROOM ASSESSMENT

Two major influences have changed the direction of classroom assessment in general education in the past decade: alternative assessment and standards-based reform. Both are part of educational reform efforts designed to increase the quality of public education. In special education, the trends in classroom assessment are not as obvious. Informal assessment has always been preferred to formal tests in special education classrooms, and that has not changed. However, curriculum-based measures (including the portfolio assessment techniques of general education) have gained in popularity. There is new emphasis on combining informal approaches to gain a greater understanding of the reasons for students' behaviors. These general and special education trends are discussed in the sections that follow.

Alternative Assessment

Alternative assessment is a general education movement based, in part, upon dissatisfaction with the group-administered norm-referenced tests traditionally used by schools to measure student achievement. Standardized achievement tests have been criticized because of their lack of relevance to the instructional process, their failure to assess higher-order thinking skills, and the fragmented nature in which they assess important school skills (Popham, 1993; Schulz, 1992). Part of the problem is due to the format of these measures. When tests are administered to groups rather than to individuals, responses must be written; when large numbers of tests must be scored, multiple-choice responses are most efficient.

Another factor driving the alternative assessment movement relates to content; that is, what schools choose to measure to determine student progress. This concern is reflected in the many terms used to describe the movement: authentic assessment, direct assessment, outcome-based assessment, and performance assessment.

Worthen (1993) calls these approaches "alternative assessment" because:

> First, all are viewed as alternatives to traditional multiple-choice, standardized achievement tests; second, all refer to direct examination of student performance on significant tasks that are relevant to life outside of school. (p. 445)

Alternative assessment represents a dramatic shift not only in how assessment is conducted but also in what is assessed. First of all, in this model, assessment should center on tasks, not on the skills or subskills required for task completion. Thus, asking students to write a letter would be considered more appropriate than having them complete a worksheet on capitalization and punctuation skills. Second, assessment should address tasks that are important and authentic, rather than trivial and contrived. According to Willis (1990), assessment tasks should "resemble real tasks as closely as possible" (p. 4). Giving a speech is a real task; answering multiple-choice questions about giving speeches is not. Third, student performance should be assessed directly. Among the types of direct measures often advocated by proponents of alternative assessment are essays and other writing tasks, oral discourse, exhibitions (i.e., demonstrations or performances), experiments, and portfolios (Feuer & Fulton, 1993).

Another aspect of alternative assessment is its emphasis on thinking and problem-solving skills. Instead of merely coming up with a correct answer, students are expected to explain, demonstrate, or document the thinking processes they use. Students engage in authentic, contextualized tasks that emphasize the application of knowledge and skills, not the rote mastery of isolated facts (McMillan, 1997). Assessment also requires student participation. In portfolio assessment, for example, students are often responsible for collecting samples of their work and evaluating their own progress (Grady, 1992). Portfolio assessment, the most popular tool for alternative assessment at present, is discussed later in this chapter.

Alternative assessment, like any type of assessment, has its drawbacks (Madaus & Kellaghan, 1993; Maeroff, 1991). It is time-consuming and therefore expensive. Issues that have not yet been adequately addressed include the reliability and validity of alternative assessment tools and the criteria used to evaluate student performance. In many cases, performance standards tend to be subjective, rather than objective. Another concern is bias; as Worthen (1993) asks, "How can assessment bias that has plagued traditional tests be kept from operating in alternative assessments that allow more subjectivity?" (p. 448). In addition, students with disabilities may be at a disadvantage with some types of alternative assessment tasks. For example, students with poor writing skills will be penalized if they must demonstrate their understanding of concepts in science or social studies by producing a written report.

Standards-Based Reform

In contrast to the alternative assessment movement, standards-based reform focuses primarily on the content of assessment. In effect, standards set expectations for students. According to the National Research Council (1997):

> Standards-based reform includes content standards that specify what students should learn, performance standards that set the expectations for what students must know and do to demonstrate proficiency, and assessments that provide the accountability mechanism for monitoring whether these expectations have been met and by whom. (p. 3)

One important contributor to the standards movement is the Goals 2000: Educate America Act of 1994. As Table 6–1 shows, this law set forth eight major goals for the reform of education in the United States. Although these goals were too ambitious to be achieved by the start of the new century, they did direct the nation's attention toward the improvement of educational opportunities for all students.

Standards for student performance have been established in most school subjects. One of the first efforts was that of the National Council of Teachers of Mathematics (1989). Its *Curriculum and Evaluation Standards for School Mathematics,* which proposed standards for students in grades K–12, advocated a more conceptual approach to the

TABLE 6-1
National Education Goals

Goal 1: Ready to Learn
All children in America will start school ready to learn.

Goal 2: School Completion
The high school graduation rate will increase to at least 90 percent.

Goal 3: Student Achievement and Citizenship
American students will leave grades 4, 8, and 12 having demonstrated competency over challenging subject matter including English, mathematics, science, foreign languages, civics and government, economics, arts, history, and geography, and every school in America will ensure that all students learn to use their minds well, so they may be prepared for responsible citizenship, further learning, and productive employment in our modern economy.

Goal 4: Teacher Education and Professional Development
The Nation's teaching force will have access to programs for the continued improvement of their professional skills and the opportunity to acquire the knowledge and skills needed to instruct and prepare all American students for the next century.

Goal 5: Mathematics and Science
United States students will be first in the world in mathematics and science achievement.

Goal 6: Adult Literacy and Lifelong Learning
Every adult American will be literate and will possess the knowledge and skills necessary to compete in a global economy and exercise the rights and responsibilities of citizenship.

Goal 7: Safe and Disciplined, Alcohol- and Drug-Free Schools
Every school in America will be free of drugs, violence, and the unauthorized presence of firearms and alcohol, and will offer a disciplined environment conducive to learning.

Goal 8: Parental Participation
Every school will promote partnerships that will increase parental involvement and participation in promoting the social, emotional, and academic growth of children.

Note: From National Education Goals Panel, 1998, *National Education Goals*. Retrieved June 27, 1999 from the World Wide Web: http://negp.gov/webpg10.htm

teaching of mathematics (Bezuk & Cegelka, 1995). For example, the first standard for young students is entitled "Mathematics as Problem Solving":

> In grades K–4, the study of mathematics should emphasize problem solving so that students can—
> - use problem-solving approaches to investigate and understand mathematical content;
> - formulate problems from everyday and mathematical situations;
> - develop and apply strategies to solve a wide variety of problems;
> - verify and interpret results with respect to the original problem;
> - acquire confidence in using mathematics meaningfully. *(National Council of Teachers of Mathematics, 1989)*

At present, almost all states have adopted academic standards for their students, and most states have linked student assessment to those standards (American Federation of Teachers, 1998). Some states have also adopted accountability programs in which student achievement (or lack of it) results in consequences for schools or districts. Erickson, Ysseldyke, Thurlow, and Elliott (1998) describe several such measures, including funding increases for adequate or exemplary student gains; and probation, warnings, loss of accreditation, and takeover by state agencies for poor student performance.

Evaluation of students' achievement of statewide standards often utilizes both traditional and alternative assessment techniques. Although standardized tests may be used to gather information about competency in some subject areas, these are usually accompanied by more authentic measures such as student portfolios and performance-based assessments of task performance. In Kentucky, for example, students in grades 4 and 5, 7 and 8, and 11 and 12 are assessed in the following ways:

- Writing portfolios.
- On demand, open-response performance tasks in math, social studies, reading, science, practical living, arts, and humanities.
- More traditional, standardized achievement tests. (Kearns, Kleinert, Clayton, Burdge, & Williams, 1998, p. 16)

One of the major issues in standards-based reform is how best to include students with disabilities (Elliott, Kratochwill, & Schulte, 1998). Although these students often did not participate in state- and district-wide assessments in the past, the 1997 IDEA Amendments now mandate their inclusion. Some students will be able to participate in the assessments designed for their general education peers; others will require accommodations. Unfortunately, study of the effects of accommodations for students with disabilities is just beginning (National Research Council, 1997).

Issues and Trends in Special Education

Many of the current issues in special education classroom assessment relate to the new emphasis that the 1997 IDEA Amendments place upon access to general education. For the first time, federal law requires that IEP teams focus on the student's involvement with and progress in the general education curriculum. Also for the first time, IEP teams must determine how students will participate in general education assessments of academic achievement. With these changes, special educators face new challenges, including how best to evaluate students' progress in both special education and the general education classroom, how to grade students who are served by both general and special education, and how to design appropriate modifications to allow students with disabilities meaningful participation in general education assessments.

Special education assessment is also influenced by the trends in general education. Standards-based reform is important because standards apply to all students, including those with disabilities. In most states, measurement of academic progress is tied directly to standards, and students with disabilities now have the right to participate in that assessment process. Likewise, the alternative assessment movement has implications for special education. In alternative assessment, instead of answering multiple-choice questions on paper-and-pencil tests, students demonstrate proficiency by performing meaningful tasks selected for their authenticity. This type of assessment is routine for students with disabilities who are members of general education classrooms.

Trends in classroom assessment in special education reflect these influences to some degree. Perhaps the trend most related to general education practices is the increasing popularity of portfolio assessments. Portfolios often contain work done by the student in both general and special education, although it may be necessary to modify some of the requirements for general education assignments. For example, to demonstrate comprehension of a story, book, or play, a student may include a drawing or a videotape in the portfolio, rather than an essay or written report.

Other trends in special education classroom assessment are less related to general education. The three most prominent are functional assessment, curriculum-based measurement, and action research. All make use of informal assessment techniques to provide teachers with better information for instructional decisions. However, the approaches themselves are quite different. Functional assessment combines observation and interviewing in order to solve behavioral problems. It is a popular approach, often linked with the provision of positive behavior supports to students with classroom behavior problems. Curriculum-based measurement, in contrast, is concerned primarily with the assessment of academic skills. Brief probes of critical target behaviors are administered frequently and results are graphed to determine if progress is being made. The target behaviors assessed in this approach are predictors of academic achievement (e.g., the ability to read words quickly and accurately), not the authentic tasks favored in alternative assessment. The usefulness of curriculum-based measurement as a classroom assessment technique has been well documented in the research literature. The third approach, action research, is a variation of diagnostic teaching. The teacher acts as a researcher in an attempt to solve classroom problems. Baseline data are gathered, an intervention is introduced, and the effects of the intervention are evaluated. Unlike other types of research, the focus is on a local problem, and no attempt is made to generalize results to other settings or situations. These three techniques, along with portfolio assessment, are discussed in the sections that follow. The issues of managing student data, grading and report cards, and test accommodations are featured later in the chapter.

FUNCTIONAL ASSESSMENT

Functional assessment is an informal assessment technique designed to gather the information needed to plan positive behavioral interventions for students with challenging behaviors. According to the 1997 IDEA Amendments, when an IEP team plans a program for a student "whose behavior impedes his or her learning or that of others," that team must consider "if appropriate, strategies, including positive behavioral interventions, strategies, and supports to address that behavior" (*Federal Register,* 1999, §300.346(a)(2)(i)). In addition, a functional assessment must be conducted when students with IEPs are removed from a placement due to disciplinary reasons. The law states: "If the LEA [local education agency] did not conduct a functional behavioral assessment and implement a behavioral intervention plan for the child before the behavior that resulted in the removal . . . , the agency shall convene an IEP meeting to develop an assessment plan" (*Federal Register,* 1999, §300.520(b)(1)(i)).

The primary purpose of functional assessment (sometimes called *functional behavioral assessment*) is determination of the reason(s) for a student's inappropriate behaviors so that a suc-

cessful behavior change program can be implemented. Put simply, the goal is to understand the function of the inappropriate behavior for the student. To do this, it is necessary to understand the relationship between the student's behavior and environmental, social, cultural, and physiological factors. Quinn, Gable, Rutherford, Nelson, and Howell (1998) say that "functional behavior assessment looks beyond the overt topography of the behavior, and focuses, instead, upon identifying biological, social, affective, and environmental factors that initiate, sustain, or end the behavior in question" (p. 3). Sequence analysis, which was described in the last chapter, is a very simple kind of functional assessment because it attempts to determine relationships between behaviors and their antecedents and consequences (O'Neill et al., 1997).

Functional assessment makes use of a variety of informal assessment techniques. Two techniques are always included: direct observation of the student in order to fully describe the behavior in question, and interviews with persons knowledgeable about the student and the behavior. In some cases, other techniques are also used. Examples are record reviews (e.g., medical and educational histories), task and work sample analyses, and curriculum-based assessments such as informal inventories and skill probes.

O'Neill et al. (1997) identify five primary outcomes of the functional assessment process:

1. A clear *description of the problem behaviors,* including classes or sequences of behaviors that frequently occur together
2. Identification of the events, times, and situations that *predict* when the problem behaviors *will* and *will not* occur across the full range of typical daily routines
3. Identification of the *consequences that maintain the problem behaviors* (that is, what functions the behaviors appear to serve for the person)
4. Development of one or more *summary statements* or hypotheses that describe specific behaviors, a specific type of situation in which they occur, and the outcomes or reinforcers maintaining them in that situation
5. Collection of *direct observation data* that support the summary statements that have been developed (p. 3)

There are several approaches to functional analysis, and each identifies a somewhat different set of procedures (e.g., Fitzsimmons, 1998; LRE for LIFE Project, 1997; O'Neill et al., 1997; PACER Center, 1994; Quinn et al., 1998). However, all include these basic steps: (a) identification and description of the target behavior, (b) identification of factors that influence the behavior, (c) formulation and testing of a hypothesis to explain the behavior, and (d) development of a positive behavioral support plan.

Describing the Behavior

The first step is identification of the behavior of interest. As with any type of behavioral strategy, the behavior must be both observable and measurable. Its description must be precise. Quinn et al. (1998) give this example. "Trish hits other students during recess when she does not get her way" is an appropriate description because the behavior is easy to measure and record. A more global statement such as "Trish is aggressive" is not appropriate.

The next step is to gather observational data in order to fully describe the behavior. Depending upon the type of behavior under consideration, any of the observational strategies discussed in Chapter 5 can be used: narrative reporting, continuous recording, sequence analysis, event recording, duration recording, interval recording, or time sampling. O'Neill et al. (1997) recommend that data be collected for a minimum of 2 to 5 days using time sampling procedures. The LRE for LIFE Project (1997) suggests at least 3 days of observation. The student should be observed in a variety of settings to determine the conditions under which the behavior does and does not occur.

Identifying Factors that Influence the Behavior

The use of informants to learn about influences on the student's behavior is what sets functional assessment apart from standard behavioral observations. Although results of direct observations help to describe the behavior, rarely do they explain its causes. In order to arrive at hypotheses about possible causes, it is necessary to gather in-

formation from other sources. Those sources are the persons who know the student best: the student himself or herself and the student's teachers and others that work with him or her in the educational setting.

Interviews are typically used for data collection, although questionnaires may be appropriate in some situations. According to O'Neill et al. (1997), there are several topics to pursue in the interview. The informant should be asked to describe the behavior or behaviors of interest, including their frequency, duration, and intensity. The behavior should then be considered in relation to three factors: setting events, antecedents, and consequences. Setting events are events removed in time from the behavior that may affect its occurrence. O'Neill et al. identify seven important areas to consider: medications, medical or physical problems, sleep cycles, eating routines and diet, daily schedule, numbers of people, and staffing patterns and interactions. Antecedents are the events that immediately precede the behavior and may predict its occurrence. They include time of day, physical setting, people, and the activity in which the student is engaged (O'Neill et al.). Consequences or outcomes are what occur after the behavior.

Quinn et al. (1998) add that it is necessary to take into consideration the student's ability to perform the classroom task that appears to precipitate the problem behavior. There are two possibilities: a skill deficit (the student is unable to perform the task because he or she does not possess the necessary skills) or a performance deficit (the student has the needed skills but for some reason fails to perform). Quinn et al. offer these questions to guide the assessment team in its study of these factors:

Is the problem behavior linked to a skill deficit?
- Does the student understand the behavioral expectations for the situation?
- Does the student realize that he or she is engaging in unacceptable behavior, or has that behavior simply become a "habit"?
- Is it within the student's power to control the behavior, or does he or she need support?
- Does the student have the skills necessary to perform expected, new behaviors?

Does the student have the skill, but, for some reason, not the desire to modify his or her behavior?

- Is it possible that the student is uncertain about the appropriateness of the behavior (e.g., it is appropriate to clap loudly and yell during sporting events, yet these behaviors are often inappropriate when playing academic games in the classroom)?
- Does the student find any value in engaging in appropriate behavior?
- Is the behavior problem associated with certain social or environmental conditions?
  —Is the student attempting to avoid a "low-interest" or demanding task?
  —What current rules, routines, or expectations does the student consider irrelevant? (pp. 5–6)

Generating a Hypothesis

The goal of functional assessment is to gather sufficient information to be able to develop a hypothesis to explain the student's behavior. This hypothesis must take into account the behavior itself and the setting events, antecedents, and consequences that affect it. Determining the function or purpose of the behavior is part of this process. Lewis and Sugai (1999) state that:

> In general, children engage in problem behavior for one of two reasons: (a) to *get* something (e.g., adult or peer attention, access to a tangible object) or (b) to *avoid* something (e.g., difficult tasks, adult or peer attention). (p. 13)

O'Neill et al. (1997) suggest that the team conducting the functional assessment develop a summary statement or hypothesis describing the behavior and the factors influencing it. One of the examples they provide is:

> When Andrea begins to have difficulty with a reading or math assignment, she will put her head down, refuse to respond, and close her books to try to avoid having to complete the assignment. The likelihood of this pattern increases if Andrea has received teacher reprimands earlier in the day. (p. 17)

In this example, the problem behavior is Andrea's putting her head down, closing her books, and refusing to respond. The setting event, reprimands from the teacher, occurred earlier in the

school day. The immediate antecedent to the behavior is a difficult math or reading assignment. The consequence of her action is not having to complete the assignment. Thus, the function of Andrea's inappropriate behavior appears to be avoidance. Given this information, it appears likely that Andrea's problem behavior is a skill deficit, rather than a performance deficit.

Program Planning

The hypothesis about the reasons for the student's behavior can be verified through direct observation and/or by systematic manipulation of setting events, antecedents, and consequences. Once the assessment team is satisfied that it has sufficient data to support the hypothesis, the next step is development of an intervention plan.

Figure 6–1 presents an individual positive behavioral support plan for a third grader named Emily (Lewis & Sugai, 1999). The problem behaviors are described, along with the hypothesized functions of each. For example, the team believes that Emily interrupts academic instruction to gain the attention of the teacher and peers. Next, the team has identified replacement behaviors that will serve the same functions for Emily. For example, instead of blurting out answers during instruction, she will raise her hand before speaking. The plan includes objectives related to the replacement behaviors and a data collection system for monitoring Emily's progress. Finally, four types of intervention strategies are specified: the types of instruction Emily will receive, the antecedent strategies to be used during instruction, the consequent strategies for both the problem and replacement behaviors, and strategies for generalizing replacement behaviors to other situations.

CURRICULUM-BASED MEASUREMENT

Curriculum-based measurement (CBM), as its name implies, is a curriculum-based assessment strategy. Like informal inventories and classroom quizzes, CBM is a direct approach to the assessment of students' current skill levels in important school subjects. However, CBM differs from other

| Student | Emily | DOB | 7/25/88 | Grade | 3 |

Student _____Emily_____ DOB _7/25/88_ Grade _3_
Teacher _Mr. Leigh / Ms. Fernandez_ School _Twin Peeks Elem_
Plan case manager _____Mr. Sugai_____ Phone _555-5555_
IEP: Y N Plan start date _4/1/99_
Team will reconvene every __10__ days to monitor plan

Briefly describe the problem behavior(s)

Disrupts instruction during reading and math–blurts out answers, makes loud noises, makes jokes. Occurs 10-15 times per half hour class period.

Interrupts peer activities during centers and free time–grabs materials, calls peers names, physically places self at table. Occurs 80% of the time.

Briefly describe the function the problem behavior(s) serve the student (Testable Explanation)

During academic periods, Emily interrupts instruction to access teacher and peer attention.

During peer lead activities, Emily interrupts to access peer attention.

Briefly describe a desired replacement behavior(s) that will serve a similar function as the current problem behavior

Emily will raise her hand before speaking.
Emily will remain on-task 90% of the period.
Emily will talk only about task related topics.

Emily will ask peer permission prior to joining activities.
Emily will make neutral or positive comments toward peers.

Develop a behavioral objective incorporating the replacement behavior(s)

During academic periods, Emily will remain on-task 90% of intervals for 5 consecutive days.

During independent activities, Emily will make neutral or positive comments toward peers 80% of the opportunities for 5 consecutive days.

List/describe a data collection system to monitor replacement behavior and desired criteria

Academic periods-momentary time sampling, 1 minute intervals. On-task = listening to the teacher, comments relative to task, raise hand before speaking, working on assignments in 90% of the intervals.

Independent activities - event recording, record positive/neutral comments and negative comments. Positive/neutral comments in 80% of opportunities. Opportunities = neutral/positive + negative comments.

Outline the instructional strategies to teach the desired replacement behavior

Emily will receive social skill instruction outlining key "on-task" behaviors. Emily will also be taught to "self-manage" her on-task behavior.

Emily will receive social skill instruction focusing on appropriate peer initiations and interactions. Peer tutors will be recruited to assist in instruction.

Briefly describe the antecedent strategies that will accompany the above instructional strategies (e.g., pre-corrects, prompts, academic accommodations, schedule changes)

Pre-corrects will be used to prompt Emily on key social skills prior to academic and independent periods. Emily will be prompted to use her self management sheet prior to academic periods.

Peers will be prompted to follow class rules including ignoring students who do not comply with the rules.

Emily will receive a pre-correct prior to independent periods. Peer tutors will be prompted to assist Emily.

Outline the consequent strategies for the problem/replacement behavior (e.g. differential reinforcement, verbal praise, error correction statements)

During academic periods, the teacher will praise Emily approximately every 3-4 minutes if she is on-task. If Emily meets daily criteria on her self-management card, she can earn free-time minutes and select a peer to play with. If Emily is off-task, the teacher will provide specific verbal praise to a nearby compliant peer. If Emily continues to remain off-task, the teacher will use a simple redirective statement.

Peers who participated in the social skills training will provide verbal support to Emily if she successfully demonstrates the use of key social skills. If Emily meets her daily criteria, she can earn computer time and select a peer to work with. If Emily does not comply with the rules of the activity, the teacher will provide brief redirective statements.

Briefly describe what strategies will be used to promote generalized responding

The above strategies will be incorporated during all academic periods, including mainstream classes. "Peer tutors" will be used during other independent times (e.g., recess, cafeteria) once Emily meets criteria in the classroom.

Team Members and their responsibilities for implementation

Member	Responsibilities
Mr. Leigh	Instruction & Data Collection
Ms. Fernandez	Monitor self management in classroom
Ms. McCathren	Monitor program during lunch and recess
Ms. Garrison	Develop social skill lessons & self management plan

FIGURE 6-1
Sample Positive Behavior Support Plan

Note: From "Effective Behavior Support: A Systems Approach to Proactive Schoolwide Management" (p. 15) by T. J. Lewis and G. Sugai, 1999, *Focus on Exceptional Children 31*(6). Copyright 1999 by Love Publishing Company. Reprinted by permission.

TABLE 6–2

CBMs for Basic Skills

AREA	TESTING DURATION	DESCRIPTION AND TYPES OF SCORES DERIVED
Reading	1 minute	Students read passages orally, and the number of words read correctly and errors are counted.
Spelling	2 minutes	Students write words that are dictated orally, and the number of words spelled correctly and correct letter sequences are counted.
Mathematics Computation	2–5 minutes	Students write answers to computation problems, and the number of correct digits are counted.
Written Expression	3 minutes	After being given a story starter or topic sentence, students write a story. Number of words written, spelled correctly, and correct word sequences may be counted.

Note: From "Curriculum-Based Measurement and Problem-Solving Assessment: Basic Procedures and Outcomes" (p. 225) by M. R. Shinn and D. D. Hubbard, 1993, in E. L. Meyen, G. A. Vergason, and R. J. Whelan (Eds.), *Educating Students with Mild Disabilities,* Denver, CO: Love. Copyright 1993 by Love Publishing Company. Adapted by permission.

informal techniques because of the types of skills selected for assessment and the frequency with which assessment takes place.

In CBM, brief probes are used to collect samples of critical target behaviors such as reading words aloud, writing numbers, and writing words. For example, to assess oral reading proficiency, students read a passage aloud for 1 minute while the teacher tabulates the number of words read correctly. As Table 6–2 illustrates, the behavior samples are very brief (1 to 5 minutes) and assessment focuses on basic skills. Correct performance is the major concern; the processes underlying performance are not.

Probes are administered frequently (e.g., twice weekly), data are graphed, and the results are analyzed to determine whether the student's progress is adequate. For CBM to be effective, the behaviors of interest should be assessed directly, and measurement should be frequent so that needed instructional changes can be made quickly. A growing body of research in special education supports the usefulness of CBM for monitoring student progress and modifying instruction based on student performance (Deno, 1985; Deno & Fuchs, 1988; Deno, Marston, & Mirkin, 1982; Deno, Mirkin, & Chiang, 1982; Deno, Mirkin, Lowry, & Kuehnle, 1980; Fuchs, 1986; Fuchs, Deno, & Mirkin, 1984; Shinn & Hubbard, 1993).

Fuchs (1995) describes the process a teacher might use in designing CBM procedures to measure a student's progress toward mastery of third grade mathematics:

> He or she creates a pool of equivalent assessments, each of which samples the key problem types from the third grade curriculum. Each week, the student completes one or two assessments. Because each assessment is of equal difficulty and incorporates all of the important problem types to be learned over the year, the CBM data base produces a total score graphed over time to show progress over the year. (p. 1)

One of the most important aspects of CBM is the graphing of student performance data. A visual depiction of the student's progress helps teachers identify when changes need to be made to improve the rate of skill acquisition. Consider, for example, the three graphs in Figure 6–2. These graphs illustrate how CBM can assist in making decisions about instructional modifications (Hasbrouck, Woldbeck, Ihnot, & Parker, 1999). In each, the *y* axis is labeled *WCPM* for "words correct per minute." The numbers along the *x* axis are the weeks of the school year. Each dot is a data point: the student's score on one CBM probe. The dots are connected to show the student's progress throughout the year. The oblique line beginning at the first data point is the aimline. It represents the expected progress for the

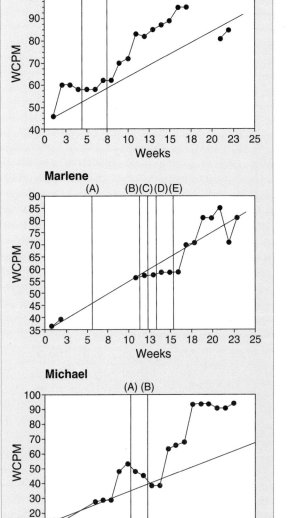

FIGURE 6-2

CBM Graphs

Note: From "One Teacher's Use of Curriculum-Based Measurement: A Changed Opinion" (pp. 123–124) by J. E. Hasbrouck, T. Woldbeck, C. Ihnot, and R. I. Parker, 1999, *Learning Disabilities Research & Practice, 14*(2). Copyright 1999 by Lawrence Erlbaum Associates, Inc. Reprinted by permission.

student. For example, in the first graph (Jeff), the expected rate of growth in WCPM is two words per week. When the student's performance is similar to that of the aimline, the intervention can be considered successful.

Another feature of CBM graphs is that they show the relationship between student performance and the interventions selected by the teacher. The letters at the top of the graphs (e.g., A, B) indicate an intervention change. In the first graph in Figure 6–2, Jeff made good progress at the start of the school year, then plateaued. His teacher moved him to a higher reading group (intervention A). When his performance did not change, the difficulty level of his reading materials was increased (intervention B). He then made excellent progress until weeks 18 to 20 when he was ill and absent from school; after his return, his progress continued. Marlene shows quite a different profile. At the start of the school year, there are several missing data points because of her frequent absences. The interventions introduced by her teacher (A, B, C, and D) were unsuccessful until the attendance problem was addressed (intervention E). At that point, Marlene began to make reading gains. In the third graph, Michael made such good progress at the start of the school year that his teacher moved him to a higher reading group (intervention A). His performance declined until he was moved back to his original group (intervention B), where his progress exceeded expectations.

Hasbrouck et al. (1999) recommend that teachers adopt CBM as a strategy for evaluating student progress and making decisions about the need for changes in instruction. According to these authors, CBM offers three major advantages:

> (a) immediate, accurate, and concrete positive feedback is provided to teachers, students, and parents when students are experiencing gains;
> (b) rapid identification of negative performance trends allows a teacher to quickly make responsive changes in students' programs; and
> (c) graphed results can be used to judge whether or not an intervention made in a student's program is having the desired effect, and respond accordingly. (p. 125)

CBM has also been suggested as a strategy for identifying students in need of support services such as special education (Deno, 1985; Marston & Magnusson, 1985; Peterson, Heistad, Peterson, & Reynolds, 1985). In this application, curriculum-based measures are administered to all students within a class, grade, or district, and local norms are constructed based upon their performance. For example, Peterson and others (1985) used a cutoff score at the 20th percentile on reading and math probes to discriminate between achievers and nonachievers. Marston and Magnusson (1985) maintain that curriculum-based measures are valid, sensitive to pupil growth, and cost-effective.

It is important to remember, however, that CBM is designed to assess only current school achievement. CBM does not address other important factors in eligibility decisions such as the presence of a disability and the role of factors such as the classroom learning environment in promoting (or failing to promote) student achievement. Unlike techniques such as functional assessment, CBM does not seek to identify the reasons for a student's lack of academic progress. It is a descriptive technique that provides information about student performance. From that information, teachers can determine if a problem exists; further assessment is needed to identify the cause of the problem and potential solutions.

ACTION RESEARCH

In action research, teachers seek answers to questions related to their professional practice. For example, a teacher may be interested in studying the effects of a new self-concept development program on the students he or she serves. Another might be interested in investigating the usefulness of a homework partnership program with parents. A special educator may want to study the ways in which computers assist students with writing problems. Questions such as these often arise in professional practice; action research is a systematic approach to their solution.

Unlike more formal research strategies, action research focuses on solutions to local problems. There is no attempt to generalize results to other students, teachers, or schools. As Hittleman and Simon (1997) comment, "action researchers seek answers to immediate questions

or problems" (p. 257). The problems addressed are practical problems, and there is no attempt to contribute to the development of educational theories (Gay, 1996).

According to Abdal-Haqq (1995), several terms in addition to "action research" have been used to describe systematic inquiry in the classroom: "practitioner research, teacher-as-scholar, practical inquiry, interactive research, classroom inquiry, and practice-centered inquiry" (p. 1). Likewise, authors suggest various definitions for the approach. For example, Johnson (1993) says that "action research is deliberate, solution-oriented investigation that is group or personally owned and conducted" (p. 1). In contrast, Borgia and Schuler (1996) define action research as "an approach to professional development and improved student learning in which teachers systematically reflect on their work and make changes in their practice" (p. 1).

There is agreement that action research is a systematic approach to inquiry based upon the scientific method. The process begins with a problem to solve or a question to answer. After carefully framing the purpose of the study, the teacher-researcher designs a research plan. He or she defines important variables, decides upon an intervention, selects a sample, chooses measurement tools, and outlines the procedures for the study. Data are collected on the variables of interest, either at the beginning and end of the study or throughout the implementation of the intervention. These data are then analyzed to provide answers to the question or problem under consideration.

This method of systematic inquiry is a familiar one to special educators because it is the foundation of many of the classroom assessment techniques used in special education. Diagnostic teaching, which was described in Chapter 5, is one example. It is a systematic approach to the investigation of the relative effectiveness of two or more instructional techniques. The teacher identifies a skill area of interest, collects baseline data on the student's performance under current instructional conditions, then introduces a new intervention. Data are collected to determine the effects of the intervention. If necessary, another intervention is introduced and its effects are evaluated. Other systematic inquiry methods include the two classroom assessment techniques described earlier in this chapter—functional assessment and CBM. Although CBM focuses on the measurement aspects of the research process, it is built upon a problem-solving model (Shinn & Hubbard, 1993). In this model, data are collected and graphed in order to determine the effectiveness of the instructional approach. In functional assessment, the research goal is somewhat different. Instead of evaluating an intervention, the purpose is determination of the function of inappropriate behaviors so that an effective behavioral support plan can be developed.

PORTFOLIO ASSESSMENT

Portfolio assessment is the most common type of alternative assessment used in classrooms today. Portfolios, as defined by Feuer and Fulton (1993), are "collections of a student's work assembled over time" (p. 478). According to Airasian (1996), their purpose is "to collect a series of pupil performances or products that show the pupil's accomplishments or improvement over time" (p. 162). Portfolios can be developed at any grade level for any subject area. Examples are writing, reading/language arts, mathematics, science, the arts, and career preparation programs, including teacher education (Martin, 1999; Wolf, 1991).

Portfolios are most valuable when they are systematically planned. Salend (1998) presents these guidelines:

1. Identify the goals of the portfolio
2. Determine the type of portfolio to be used
3. Establish procedures for organizing the portfolio
4. Choose a range of authentic classroom products that relate to the objectives of the portfolio
5. Record the significance of items included in students' portfolios
6. Review and evaluate portfolios periodically (pp. 37–40)

The goals for the portfolio should be consistent with the instructional goals for the student. For example, the portfolio for a student with IEP goals in reading, spelling, and written expression might emphasize accomplishments in the language arts. According to Salend (1998), the types of portfolios are (a) the showcase portfolio, containing examples of the student's best work, (b) the cumulative portfolio, documenting changes over time, (c) the goal-based portfolio, demonstrating progress toward specific goals such as those on the IEP, (d) the process portfolio, showing the steps the student follows in the development of products, and (e) the reflective portfolio, emphasizing the reflections of students, teachers, and parents on the learning process.

Once a framework is established, the teacher can plan the organization of the portfolio. There are a number of possibilities, including arranging the portfolio by instructional goal, by subject matter area (e.g., reading, mathematics), by themes, or in chronological order (Gelfer & Perkins, 1998). The next step is the selection of student work samples. Portfolios can contain almost anything that documents the student's progress such as "works in progress, samples of art work, math problems, collaborative projects, lists of books read, reports written, documentation of performances, quizzes, and any other useful examples of student work" (Grady, 1992, p. 23). Photos, audiotapes, videotapes, and other media can supplement print documents. Gelfer and Perkins (1998) also suggest including assessments such as teacher-made tests, curriculum-based assessments, and criterion-referenced tests. For example, in classrooms where CBM is used, the graphs showing the student's progress might become part of the portfolio.

The Vermont Portfolio Project has developed guidelines for writing and mathematics portfolios (Abruscato, 1993). The writing portfolio contains six samples of writing completed during the school year as well as the student's response to a "uniform writing assessment," a formal assignment given to all students within a grade level. The work samples are:

1. a table of contents;
2. a "best piece";
3. a letter;
4. a poem, short story, play, or personal narrative;
5. a personal response to a cultural, media, or sports exhibit or event or to a book, current issue, math problem, or scientific phenomenon;
6. one prose piece from any curriculum area other than English or language arts (for fourth-graders)

and three prose pieces from any curriculum area other than English or language arts (for eighth-graders); and

7. the piece produced in response to the uniform writing assessment, as well as related outlines, drafts, etc. (Abruscato, 1993, p. 475)

The mathematics portfolio contains five to seven best pieces, other work samples, and a letter to the portfolio evaluator.

In addition to student products, portfolios should contain information about the significance of the works included. When work samples are those selected by the student, that fact should be indicated in some way. For example, the student might write or tape-record a short explanation of why a particular piece was chosen. Grady (1992) suggests that student self-evaluations be incorporated into the portfolio. Student self-evaluations may take the form of an ongoing journal in which students reflect upon their progress, or written responses to specific questions from the teacher. Questionnaires completed by students and by parents can also be placed in the portfolio to provide information on topics such as students' preferred classroom activities and parents' reports of home study habits. Teachers, too, can make contributions to the portfolio. Among the possibilities are observations, progress notes, teacher comments about specific work samples, and records of student-teacher and parent-teacher conferences (Gelfer & Perkins, 1998; Grady, 1992; Pierce & O'Malley, 1992; Salend, 1998).

The final step is evaluation of the contents of the portfolio. Unlike work sample analysis, the goal is not the identification of error patterns or the number and types of correct and incorrect responses. Instead, the task is to determine whether students are able to demonstrate proficiency in the performance of significant, relevant tasks. To do this, standards or criteria must be established; the most common type is a rubric. Airasian (1996) defines scoring rubrics as "brief, written descriptions of different levels of pupil performance" (p. 154). The performance levels may be indicated by a numerical scale (e.g., 1 through 6) or by verbal labels. Examples of labels are *excellent, good, fair, poor; novice, intermedi-*

ate, advanced, superior; and *emerging, developing, achieving* (McMillan, 1997, p. 221). Each performance level is then linked to a description of student performance exemplary of that level.

For example, the Math Problem-Solving Portfolio Rating Form shown in Figure 6–3 begins with space for identifying information and several self-evaluation questions to be answered by the student. The next sections, to be completed by the teacher, are the rubrics. In each section, there are five performance levels, denoted by numerical ratings, and each is followed by a description of representative student performance at that level. For example, in the first section ("Quality of Reflection"), to perform at the highest level, the student must demonstrate excellent insight into his or her own problem-solving abilities. The teacher rates the student on each of the areas presented and then computes an average rating.

Portfolio assessment, like many other types of informal assessment, carries with it an element of subjectivity. In a sense, it is similar to gathering information from informants with tools such as rating scales and checklists: The teacher (or another judge) considers standards for performance, then rates student work samples in reference to those standards. However, the standards are not objective. They are holistic, qualitative descriptions that require the evaluator to exercise judgment. With an assessment strategy such as this, interrater reliability is a major concern (Oosterhof, 1994). Validity is another concern, particularly the predictive validity of portfolio assessment in relation to future success in school and adult pursuits. As is the case with other informal tools, however, information about the psychometric quality of portfolio assessment is seldom available.

Another potential disadvantage of portfolio assessment is the amount of time that is required, particularly for periodic evaluations (Oosterhof, 1994). Pierce and O'Malley (1992) present these suggestions for reducing time demands:

- Make the data collection part of daily instructional routines;
- Make students responsible for collecting information on a regular basis;
- Identify specific items that go into the portfolio and list them on a portfolio analysis form;

Math Problem-solving Portfolio Rating Form

Student's name: _____   *Check one:*
                                                        _____ Sample One
                                                        _____ Sample Two
                                                        _____ Final Sample

To Be Completed by Student:
1. Date submitted:
2. What does this problem say about you as a problem solver?

3. What do you like best about how you solved this problem?

4. How will you improve your problem solving skill on the next problem?

To Be Completed by Teacher *(circle the appropriate rating):*
1. Quality of Reflection

Rating	Description
5	Has excellent insight into his/her problem-solving abilities and clear ideas of how to get better.
4	Has good insight into his/her problem-solving abilities and some ideas of how to get better.
3	Reflects somewhat on problem-solving strengths and needs. Has some idea of how to improve as a problem-solver.
2	Seldom reflects on problem-solving strengths and needs. Has little idea of how to improve as a problem-solver.
1	Has no concept of him/herself as a problem-solver.

2. Mathematical Knowledge

5	Shows deep understanding of the problems, math concepts, and principles. Uses appropriate math terms, and all calculations are correct.
4	Shows good understanding of math problems, concepts, and principles. Uses appropriate math terms most of the time. Few computational errors.
3	Shows understanding of some of the problems, math concepts, and principles. Uses some terms incorrectly. Contains some computation errors.
2	Errors in the use of many problems. Many terms used incorrectly.
1	Major errors in problems. Shows no understanding of math problems, concepts, and principles.

FIGURE 6-3

Sample Rubric for Portfolio Evaluation—*continued*

Note: From *Authentic Assessment in the Classroom* by Tombari/Borich, © 1999. Reprinted by permission of Prentice-Hall, Inc., Upper Saddle River, NJ.

- Initially, use portfolios with only two or three students who need intensive monitoring;
- Use staggered data collection cycles where assessment data are collected from only a few students daily or weekly;
- Share responsibilities of data collection and interpretation with other school staff so that individual teachers do not become overwhelmed by the process; and

- Create common planning times for teachers and other staff involved in portfolio development. (p. 14)

MANAGING STUDENT DATA

No matter what techniques are used in classroom assessment, it is necessary to develop a system

3. Strategic Knowledge

Rating	Description
5	Identifies all the important elements of the problem. Reflects an appropriate and systematic strategy for solving the problem; gives clear evidence of a solution process.
4	Identifies most of the important elements of the problem. Reflects an appropriate and systematic strategy for solving the problem and gives clear evidence of a solution process most of the time.
3	Identifies some important elements of the problem. Gives some evidence of a strategy to solve the problems, but process is incomplete.
2	Identifies few important elements of the problem. Gives little evidence of a strategy to solve the problems, and the process is unknown.
1	Uses irrelevant outside information. Copies parts of the problem; no attempt at solution.

4. Communication

5	Gives a complete response with a clear, unambiguous explanation; includes diagrams and charts when they help clarify explanation; presents strong arguments that are logically developed.
4	Gives good response with fairly clear explanation, which includes some use of diagrams and charts; presents good arguments that are mostly but not always logically developed.
3	Explanations and descriptions of problem solution are somewhat clear but incomplete; makes some use of diagrams and examples to clarify points, but arguments are incomplete.
2	Explanations and descriptions of problem solution are weak; makes little, if any, use of diagrams and examples to clarify points; arguments are seriously flawed.
1	Ineffective communication; diagrams misrepresent the problem; arguments have no sound premise.

SUM OF RATINGS:_____
AVERAGE OF RATINGS: _____
Comments:

FIGURE 6-3
Sample Rubric for Portfolio Evaluation—*concluded*

for the management of student data. Not every piece of information can be saved, so decisions must be made about what types of information are most important. Then, that information must be organized in some way so that it can be retrieved when it is needed for making instructional decisions or reporting student progress.

Lewis and Doorlag (1999), in discussing the importance of systematic record-keeping procedures, say that "teachers should decide what data will be collected, how frequently, and

what methods will be used for recording" (p. 187). The first step is determining what areas are to be assessed as part of the instructional process, and the IEP provides guidance here. Assessment should focus on the student's progress toward his or her annual goals as well as any new areas of educational need that become apparent during the school year. The teacher then selects the methods to be used in classroom assessment. Again, the IEP provides guidance because it describes the strategies to be used by the educational team in monitoring the student's progress. However, in many cases, the assessment techniques listed on the IEP are quite general and the teacher must decide on specific strategies for data collection.

Any of the assessment procedures discussed in this or the previous chapter can be used to collect information in the classroom. The choice of a specific technique must be made based on the types of assessment questions the teacher is attempting to answer. For example, curriculum-based measurement provides precise information if the question concerns the rate of accurate performance in basic school skills such as reading words or solving computational problems. If the question concerns higher level skills and the student's ability to complete authentic tasks, portfolio assessment allows teachers to make judgments about changes in skill development over time.

The next concern is the frequency of assessment. At minimum, some evaluation of progress in important goal areas should take place at least once each week. In areas of particular concern (e.g., new problem behaviors), it may be necessary to gather data more frequently. Weekly assessment is usually not a time-consuming process. For example, depending upon the assessment question to be answered, teachers might evaluate student work samples, conduct a brief classroom observation, or administer a 1-minute probe as part of a curriculum-based measurement program. Of course, a more extensive evaluation of student performance is necessary when report cards are to be prepared or when the IEP is reviewed and revised.

After data have been collected, the teacher decides what types of records to maintain. In some cases such as portfolio assessment, the student's actual work samples will be preserved. In others, results of the assessment will be recorded on a graph, in a gradebook, or in some other form such as teacher notes. Whatever is saved must then be stored. There is no perfect storage system; teachers need to experiment to discover the one that works best for them. Some teachers use gradebooks; others use index cards, notebooks, or file folders to store assessment data; still others keep their records on a computer. Data may be organized by subject

area (reading, math, language arts, etc.) or by student; within these categories, information is usually arranged in chronological order. No matter what system is chosen, it should be one that allows easy retrieval of information. Assessment data are of no use if they cannot be located. The system should also include provisions for the storage of confidential information such as students' IEPs and test protocols and reports of eligibility assessments.

GRADING AND REPORT CARDS

Grades and report cards are part of the school experience for all students. Although grading procedures may be modified for students who receive special education services, the purposes remain the same. Based on a review of the literature, Bradley and Calvin (1998) identify six major purposes of grading:

- To measure progress toward the achievement of identified goals
- To assure that students have mastered specific content
- To identify certain students for special programs or courses
- To provide information for planning
- To motivate students to continue to perform well or to perform better
- To compare performance to that of other students (p. 25)

Airasian (1996) suggests that grades serve four purposes: informational, administrative, motivational, and guidance. In their administrative role, grades help educators make decisions about issues such as eligibility for graduation and promotion to the next grade.

There are several philosophical approaches to grading. Before grades can be assigned, teachers must identify the standard (or standards) of comparison they will use to evaluate a student's performance. In norm-referenced grading, a student is evaluated in relation to the performance of others; in criterion-referenced grading, grades are assigned in relation to preestablished performance standards (Airasian, 1996). Another option is what Christiansen and Vogel (1998) call the *self-referenced viewpoint:* Students are graded in relation to their own past performance. In other words, they are graded on the amount of progress they have achieved. Tombari and Borich (1999) sum up these and other choices by asking teachers to consider these possibilities:

> Should Marva's grade of 85 in eighth-grade science tell how much information she has acquired, how much she has learned relative to her classmates, how much effort she put into the class, her class attendance and punctuality, how much progress she made from the start of the term, how much she contributed to class discussions, her appreciation for science, or how well she got along with her peers and the teacher? (p. 209)

Federal law requires that parents of students with disabilities receive information about their child's progress toward IEP goals. Progress reports must be issued at least as frequently as the report cards designed for the parents of typical students. In many cases, students with disabilities participate in the general education curriculum and, as part of that experience, receive the same types of report cards as their peers without disabilities. When this occurs, it is necessary for general and special education teachers to collaborate in the grading process. Christiansen and Vogel (1998) present these guidelines for collaborating teachers:

1. Determine district, state, and federal policies and guidelines regarding grading.
2. Identify your own theoretical approaches to grading.
3. Identify your colleagues' theoretical approaches to grading.
4. Cooperatively determine the grading practices for individual students. (pp. 32–33)

Teachers should become aware of the policies that guide the grading process, then learn about each other's philosophical approach to grading. The next step is discussion of the specific procedures to use in assigning grades to individual students with disabilities.

Individualization is the key. Students with disabilities who are included in general education classrooms often require accommodations in instruction as well as assessment, and grading practices should reflect this. However, fairness is also important. Giving a student an *A* for completing half the work expected of others in the classroom seems unfair unless the criterion for successful performance is clearly stated. One approach is to develop differentiated standards for specific assignments. For example, the checklist in Figure 6–4 lists the number of points possible to earn for each component of the assignment —writing a business letter. In this case, the standards have been changed: The student was expected to include two support statements (rather than three) and spelling and sentence structure were not evaluated. The student received a grade of *A* because he earned 29 of 29 possible points; however, it is clear that this *A* is based on differentiated standards.

Report cards and/or progress reports for students with disabilities can also reflect differentiated grading procedures. As Figure 6–5 shows, there are several methods for reporting progress to parents. Some are adaptations of the standard report card (examples 1 and 2); others replace or supplement the standard report card with information about the student's progress toward or achievement of IEP goals and objectives (example 3). This last approach is likely to become more popular as districts implement federal special education requirements for keeping parents informed of their child's progress in school.

Bradley and Calvin (1998) present several suggestions to "level the playing field" in grading practices for students with disabilities. These suggestions include:

- Use points and percentages to grade differentiated assignments, rather than letter grades. For instance, if the length of an assignment is shortened, the student can be graded on the amount of work required and can earn 100% when points are converted into percentages (Polloway et al., 1994) . . .
- Match grading criteria for certain students with individualized education program (IEP) goals and objectives. Criteria for some may vary from the criteria for the majority of the class. For example, if you require students to respond in complete sentences, you may accept partial sentences from a student who is currently working on writing in complete sentences as an IEP goal, without taking off points or lowering the grade. You may want

Name Jonathan Smith		Date 1-2-98	
Checklist for the Business Letter			
Requirements (Components)	**possible points**	**points earned**	**Comments**
Heading	4	4	
Inside Address	4	4	
Greeting	2	2	
Spacing	3	3	
Body: 2,3 Support Statements	~~8~~ 6	6	2 required supports
Complete Sentences	~~10~~	/	Not graded. Need to work on punctuation. Capitals look good!
Correct Spelling	~~3~~	/	Not graded. Practice editing on computer.
Written in Pen	2	2	
Readable	5	5	
Closing	2	2	
Signature	1	1	
TOTAL	~~42~~ 29	29	

Grade A 100%

Attachments: _____rough copy_____

_____final copy_____

_____ _____
Student Signature Parent Signature

FIGURE 6–4

Differentiated Grading Standards for an Assignment

Note: From "Grading Modified Assignments: Equity or Compromise?" (p. 27) by D. F. Bradley and M. B. Calvin, 1998, *Teaching Exceptional Children, 31*(2). Copyright 1998 by The Council for Exceptional Children. Reprinted by permission.

to add a comment to the paper that encourages continued effort on that skill (Polloway et al., 1994) . . .

- Develop scoring rubrics that delineate the standards for grading and share them with students and parents when introducing assignments. It is appropriate to develop more than one scoring rubric for an assignment to differentiate (even for students without disabilities; Gersten et al., 1996; Wiggins, 1996).

- Use a variety of grading approaches to obtain grades. For example, include a grade for effort in your overall calculation, use portfolios of student work, include student self-assessment, and use student contracting to determine assignments and grading criteria (Bursuck et al., 1996; Friend & Bursuck, 1996).

- Avoid grading students strictly on effort or learning behaviors. All culminating grades should contain some type of academic component (Gersten et al., 1996). (pp. 28–29)

Report cards are a major way for teachers to inform parents of their children's progress in school. However, with students with special needs, grading performance in general education classes is often difficult. How should the teacher grade Judy, who is included in the fourth grade class but is successfully completing math assignments at the third grade level? Here are some alternatives:

1. State the student's current grade level in the academic subject, and grade the student's performance at that grade level.
   Judy, Grade 4
   Math grade level 3
   Math performance at Grade 3 level B

2. State the student's current grade level in the academic subject, and grade the student's work behaviors rather than skill performance.
   Judy, Grade 4
   Math grade level 3
   Works independently B
   Completes assignments B+
   Neatness B

3. State the student's IEP goals and objectives in the academic subject, and indicate which have been met and which still require work.
   Judy, Grade 4
   Goal: By the end of the school year, Judy will perform math computation problems at the 3.5 grade level. in progress
   Objectives:
   a. Judy will add and subtract two-digit numbers with regrouping with 90% accuracy. achieved
   b. Judy will write multiplication facts with 90% accuracy. achieved
   c. Judy will multiply two-digit numbers with regrouping with 90% accuracy. in progress
   d. Judy will write division facts with 90% accuracy. in progress

Other options include replacing traditional letter grades with simplified grading systems such as pass/fail or satisfactory/needs improvement (McLoughlin & Lewis, 1994). Teachers also can assign multiple grades in a subject area; for example, the student might earn one grade for reading achievement and another for effort in reading activities (Banbury, 1987).

FIGURE 6–5

Alternative Approaches to Report Cards
Note: From *Teaching Special Students in General Education Classrooms* 5/e by Lewis/Doorlag, © 1999. Reprinted by permission of Prentice-Hall, Inc., Upper Saddle River, NJ.

TEST ACCOMMODATIONS

Federal law requires IEP teams to determine what accommodations, if any, are needed by students with disabilities to allow their participation in the state-, district-, or schoolwide testing programs designed to assess the academic progress of all students. Most students with mild disabilities should be able to take part in these general education assessments, although many will require accommodations. For students with more severe disabilities who are unable to participate even with accommodations, the IEP team must develop alternate assessments. Salend (1998) suggests portfolio assessment be used as an alternate assessment; Ysseldyke and Olsen (1999) recommend a combination of approaches such as observations, interviews or surveys, record reviews, and performance-based tests.

Testing accommodations have been defined as "a change in the way that a test is administered or responded to by the person tested" (Elliott, Kratochwill, & Schulte, 1998). The testing modifications, discussed earlier in this book in the chapter on standardized tests (page 102–104), are examples of possible accommodations. It is important to recognize that accommodations can be used with assessment procedures other than norm-referenced tests. Students with disabilities who are members of general education classrooms often benefit when classroom assessment techniques are modified to accommodate their learning problems.

Like other aspects of the IEP, testing accommodations must be determined on an individual basis. There is no predetermined set of accommodations that fits with any particular disability label. The accommodations selected by the team must be listed on the IEP and, in one state, these modifications must be consistent with those used during instruction. According to Kearns et al. (1998), in Kentucky any accommodation "must be used as a regular part of instruction with that student" and "it cannot interfere with the test's purpose (e.g., a teacher could not read to a student the part of an assessment intended to measure silent reading comprehension)" (p. 17). The latter requirement is an attempt to preserve the validity of the test; a listening task is not a valid measure of reading skills.

Several authors have developed organizational frameworks that describe the range of possible test accommodations. One approach, the Assessment Accommodation Checklist (Elliott, Kratochwill, & Gilbertson, 1998), lists more than 70 accommodations within these eight domains:

- Motivation
- Assistance prior to administration of test
- Scheduling
- Setting
- Assessment directions
- Assistance during assessment
- Use of equipment or adaptive technology
- Changes in format (Elliott, Kratochwill, & Schulte, 1998, p. 11)

For example, scheduling modifications might include extending the time limits for a test or breaking administration into several short segments, rather than one long time period. Assistance during assessment could involve changing standard presentation and response modes. Instead of having to read test questions, the student might listen as they are read aloud by the teacher; instead of having to write a response, the student might dictate it.

Erickson and his colleagues (1998) present a simpler system. They divide testing accommodations into four types: timing, setting, presentation, and response. Timing accommodations are similar to the scheduling modifications described previously. Setting changes include administering the test in a different location or to a small rather than large group. Presentation accommodations involve changes such as reading the test aloud, providing test materials in an alternate format (e.g., large print, Braille, or audiotape), and repeating directions. In response accommodations, the student is permitted to answer test questions in an alternate manner such as by dictating or using a word processor.

States differ in the types of accommodations they allow for students with disabilities participating in mandated testing programs. According to a recent report (State-Wide Assessment Programs, 1998), half or more of the 50 states permitted these modifications:

- *Timing:* flexible scheduling, extra time, multiple/extra testing sessions
- *Setting:* small group administration, separate test session
- *Presentation:* large print, Braille or sign language, audiotaped instructions/questions

Modifications in response mode were less frequent. Twenty-one states allowed students to use word processors and 12 permitted audiotaped responses.

This situation is likely to change as state departments of education and local school districts begin to make serious attempts to implement the 1997 IDEA Amendments with their mandate for testing accommodations for students with disabilities. According to federal law, the IEP team makes decisions about accommodations and those decisions become part of the educational plan for each student with disabilities.

However, even in states where there are several testing accommodation options, all options are not used with equal frequency. Roszmann-Millican and Walker (1998), in a study of the accommodations used in Kentucky, found that the most common were readers for oral administration (30% of students) and paraphrasing or repeating directions (26%). Modifications of response mode were less common: scribes for dictation of responses (16%) and technology (11%).

When the IEP team is discussing possible test modifications, it is helpful to begin with an organizational framework such as one of those discussed here. Such frameworks describe the range of options available to the student so that potentially valuable accommodations are not overlooked. Also important to consider are the language and culture of the student. Culturally and linguistically diverse students with disabilities may require other types of accommodations such as translation of the test and modification of items that are culturally inappropriate (Valenzuela & Cervantes, 1998).

STUDY GUIDE

REVIEW QUESTIONS

1. Name two purposes of classroom assessment.
2. Which of the following statements about trends in general education assessment is/are true?
   _____ a. Norm-referenced standardized tests are the measure of choice in alternate assessment.
   _____ b. Standards-based reform is concerned with setting high academic standards for all students.
   _____ c. Assessment should address authentic tasks and higher level thinking skills.
   _____ d. All of the above are true.
3. Match the types of classroom assessments in Column A with the descriptions in Column B.

Column A	*Column B*
a. Functional assessment	_____ Student work is collected over time to assess growth.
b. Curriculum-based measurement	_____ The end result is development of a positive behavioral intervention plan.
c. Action research	_____ Teachers gather data to solve problems or answer questions about their professional practice.
d. Portfolio assessment	_____ Student performance is graphed in order to determine if instructional changes are needed.

4. Two types of data collection procedures are always used in functional assessment. Students are _____ and teachers are _____ .
5. The goal of functional assessment is to gather sufficient information to be able to develop a(n) _____ to explain the student's behavior.
6. Decide whether each of these statements about curriculum-based measurement is true or false.
   _____ a. Assessment takes place once or twice each month.
   _____ b. Students complete brief probes that are typically 5 to 6 minutes in length.
   _____ c. Basic skills such as reading words and writing numbers are assessed.
   _____ d. Results are converted to standard scores to allow monitoring of student progress.
7. Find the false statement about action research.
   a. It is based upon the scientific method.
   b. It is also called practitioner research.
   c. Its purpose is to contribute to the building of educational theories.
   d. Diagnostic teaching is an example of action research.
8. The scoring standards used in portfolio assessment are called _____ .

9. Which type of portfolio should be developed if the goal is to demonstrate student progress toward IEP goals and objectives?
   a. Showcase portfolio
   b. Cumulative portfolio
   c. Goal-based portfolio
   d. Process portfolio
10. Portfolio assessment is less subjective than other informal assessment techniques. (True or False)
11. In special education programs, some evaluation of student progress in important goal areas should take place at least once per
    a. day.
    b. week.
    c. month.
    d. semester.
12. In grading, teachers must identify the standard of comparison to be used. In _____-referenced grading, a student is evaluated in relation to preestablished performance standards.
13. The practice of modifying grading standards for students with special needs is called
    a. differentiated grading.
    b. standards assessment.
    c. self-referenced grading.
    d. testing accommodations.
14. Find the true statement:
    a. According to federal law, the standard academic assessments designed for general education students must also be administered to all students with disabilities.
    b. The most common type of testing accommodation is a change in the response mode the student uses to answer questions.
    c. Alternate assessments are typically used with students with mild disabilities; testing accommodations are used with students with more severe disabilities.
    d. The IEP team makes decisions about whether testing accommodations or alternate assessments are needed for students with disabilities.
15. Match the types of testing accommodations in Column A with the examples in Column B.

Column A	*Column B*
a. Timing	_____ The student types an essay using a word processor with a spelling checker.
b. Setting	_____ The teacher reads questions to the student.
c. Presentation	_____ The test is administered to a small group of students.
d. Response	_____ The student is allowed 2 hours, rather than 1, to complete the exam.
	_____ Math problems are written in large type with only a few problems to a page.
	_____ The student tape-records answers to test questions.

ACTIVITIES

1. Talk with two or more general educators about trends in assessment. What are their views of the alternative assessment movement? Standards-based reform? What are the effects of these trends on students with disabilities who are included in their classrooms?

2. Observe a student with classroom behavior problems. Describe the behavior(s), then develop a plan to conduct a functional assessment. Where would you begin? What steps would you take? What would you expect your final result to be?
3. Talk with a teacher who uses curriculum-based measurement to evaluate student progress. What skill areas are assessed? How often does data collection take place? What decision rules does the teacher use to determine when to change interventions?
4. Write a description of a portfolio you might develop to showcase your skills and abilities as a teacher. What would the portfolio include? How would it be organized?
5. Develop a plan for differential grading of a homework assignment. Describe the assignment, the standard grading criteria, and the modifications you would introduce. Include modifications for students who (a) work slowly, (b) have difficulty reading, and (c) have difficulty expressing themselves in writing.
6. Interview a special education teacher about testing accommodations. What types of accommodations are most common? What types does the teacher see as most effective?

DISCUSSION QUESTIONS

1. "Assessment is an integral part of the teaching process." Defend this statement using examples of classroom assessment techniques.
2. Describe the purposes of alternative assessment. How is portfolio assessment used to achieve these purposes? What are the weaknesses of portfolio assessment as a measurement tool? What are its advantages in relation to instruction?
3. Presume that you've been asked to participate in a debate about classroom assessment. You are an advocate for curriculum-based measurement; your opponent prefers approaches that emphasize higher-order thinking skills and the performance of authentic tasks. Prepare for the debate by identifying the strengths of your position and anticipating the arguments that your opponent will make.
4. One of the steps in functional assessment is identification of factors that influence the student's behavior. What types of factors should be considered? How would you go about determining if a particular factor actually does affect how the student behaves?
5. Differentiated grading standards and test accommodations help "level the playing field" for students with disabilities. How would you respond to a teacher who says that these practices are unfair?

PART III

ASSESSMENT OF GENERAL PERFORMANCE AREAS

CHAPTER 7

SCHOOL PERFORMANCE

School performance is usually equated with academic achievement. Parents and educators alike tend to view adequate performance in reading, language arts, mathematics, and other school subjects as the primary index of success in school. Although factors such as classroom behavior, study skills, and interpersonal skills may provide the foundation for successful achievement, school performance is evaluated in terms of classroom functioning, report card grades, and scores on achievement tests.

Students with special needs are characterized by school performance problems. They may have difficulty with one or two of the standard school subjects or be unable to cope with any of the demands of the general education curriculum. Poor school performance is one of the most common reasons why students are referred by teachers, parents, and others for special education assessment.

However, referral for special education assessment should not be the teacher's first response to a student's academic achievement problem. In fact, it should be one of the last steps. When an academic problem is identified, that should signal investigation of the student's current levels of proficiency *and* the instructional factors within the classroom. The teacher can implement one or a series of instructional modifications and gather data to determine if this change improves the student's performance.

In many school systems, teams of educators (sometimes called "child study committees") meet on a regular basis to help educators solve instructional problems. Teachers can use this resource as a prereferral strategy. The teacher describes the student's academic difficulties so the team can suggest ways to modify the classroom learning environment to improve the student's performance or to circumvent the academic skill problem. Or the team may recommend other resources such as remedial reading services or evaluation for the bilingual education program as alternatives to special education assessment.

Of course, special education is the appropriate option for some students. When this is the case, the teacher can assist by providing the assessment team with specific information about the student's current classroom performance. Among the types of information that the teacher can contribute are samples of the student's work, records of classroom activities and the student's success (or lack of success) in these activities, observational data, test scores, and data on the effects of instructional modifications.

When students are first referred for special education assessment, the team asks, *Is there a school performance problem?* Academic status is also a concern in planning the special education program, evaluating its effectiveness, and determining the continuing eligibility of students with disabilities for specialized services. School performance is generally assessed with measures of academic achievement, and the assessment team asks, *What is the student's current level of academic achievement? Are there apparent strengths and weaknesses in the various areas of school learning?*

At this level of questioning, the special education team is concerned with the student's overall academic performance. Once it has been established that a school skill problem exists, the team will do an in-depth examination of the student's performance in each pertinent area. Here, the focus is on assessment strategies that provide a global picture of the student's current achievement status. For example, consider the case of Joyce, a fourth grader who has difficulty coping with the demands of the general education classroom.

Joyce

Joyce is a new student in Mr. Harvey's fourth grade class. Her family recently moved to town from another state, and Joyce is having trouble adjusting to her new classroom. Mr. Harvey is concerned about Joyce. She is unable to read any of the fourth grade textbooks, her spelling and handwriting skills are poor, and she doesn't seem to like coming to school. Mr. Harvey has attempted to modify some aspects of the program for Joyce. She is currently working in a beginning third grade reading book and a second grade spelling book. However, although Joyce is making some progress, she remains far behind her classmates.

For these reasons, Mr. Harvey referred Joyce for special education assessment. The assessment team, including the resource teacher, Ms. Gale, decided that Joyce should be evaluated and secured permission from Joyce's parents. Joyce's mother and father share Mr. Harvey's concerns. They say that Joyce has always had a hard time with schoolwork but that this year seems even more difficult.

The team plans to begin its evaluation of Joyce by reviewing her school records and conducting interviews with her parents and her current classroom teacher. Then an individual achievement test that assesses several school subjects will be administered. The *Peabody Individual Achievement Test-Revised/Normative Update* was selected because it provides information about current skills in reading, mathematics, and spelling. As the IAP below shows, other tests or portions of tests may also be administered. The results of these assessments will help the team determine the severity of Joyce's school performance problem, a necessary step in deciding whether she is in need of special education services.

CONSIDERATIONS IN ASSESSMENT OF SCHOOL PERFORMANCE

In the assessment process, school performance is generally operationalized as academic achievement. In the elementary grades, the main concerns are the basic subjects of reading, spelling, handwriting, written expression, and mathematics. In the later elementary and secondary grades, the focus of the curriculum shifts to content area subjects such as science, history, and English and to vocational areas. However, basic school subjects such as reading and mathematics remain an important assessment consideration even during the high school years for lower performing students who have not yet mastered these skills.

Purposes

School performance is assessed for several reasons. It is a standard area of concern for classroom teachers, and school systems routinely evaluate the achievement status of their entire population. In special education, poor school performance is a necessary condition for the provision of

---

Individualized Assessment Plan

For:	*Joyce Dewey*	*4*	*10-0*	*12/1/00*	*Ms. Gale*
	Student's Name	Grade	Age	Date	Coordinator

Reason for Referral: Difficulty keeping up with fourth grade work in reading, spelling, and handwriting.

Assessment Question	Assessment Procedure	Person Responsible	Date/Time
What is the student's current level of academic achievement?	Interview with Mr. Harvey, Joyce's fourth grade teacher	Ms. Gale, Resource Teacher	12/6/00, 3:30 p.m.
	Review of Joyce's school records	Ms. Kellett, School Psychologist	12/5/00, 9 a.m.
	Interview with Joyce's parents	Ms. Kellett, School Psychologist	12/6/00, 7 p.m.
	Peabody Individual Achievement Test-Revised/ Normative Update	Ms. Gale, Resource Teacher	12/7/00, 9 a.m.
	Portions of other achievement tests, if necessary	Ms. Gale, Resource Teacher	to be determined

extraordinary instructional services. Once students begin to receive special education services, their progress in the acquisition of school skills becomes an important evaluation concern.

In seeking information about a student's school performance, the assessment team evaluates current academic achievement in relation to the demands of the general education curriculum. Results from achievement measures help the team discover whether the student has benefited from past instruction and has the necessary skills to learn successfully in the general education environment. If a school performance problem is identified, it may be determined that there is a mismatch between the needs of the student and the learning environment of the general education classroom. The team may then decide that the student requires special education services. Before eligibility for special education is determined, the relationship of the school performance problem to a disability must also be documented.

Academic achievement assessment may also contribute information to instructional decisions. Global measures of school learning are useful for identifying the major curriculum areas in which students may require special assistance. Such measures also contribute information about the effectiveness of special education programs by monitoring students' progress toward instructional goals. Of course, general measures of academic achievement can provide only preliminary information for instructional decisions. Their results must be supplemented with results from more specific tests and informal techniques to gain an accurate picture of students' strengths and weaknesses in various school subjects.

Issues and Trends

School performance and its assessment have raised many issues over past decades. Although most of these issues pertain to general education, they influence special education because most students with disabilities spend at least part of the school day in regular classrooms. One theme that has recurred time and time again is public concern over the quality of the American educational system. In the 1970s, this resulted in the back-to-basics movement and minimum competency test-

ing for grade advancement and high school graduation (Copperman, 1979; Gallup, 1978; Munday, 1979; Pipho, 1978). In the 1980s, the focus shifted to excellence in education, and several major commissions issued reports that criticized the state of public education and offered recommendations for improvement. Best known of the more than 25 reports is that of the National Commission on Excellence in Education (1983), which begins with these words:

> Our Nation is at risk. Our once unchallenged preeminence in commerce, industry, science, and technological innovation is being overtaken by competitors throughout the world . . . the educational foundations of our society are presently being eroded by a rising tide of mediocrity that threatens our very future as a Nation and a people. (p. 5)

Among the reforms called for in these reports was increased emphasis on content area curricula in the sciences, social studies, mathematics, English, foreign languages, and computer science. Longer school days and years, firmer discipline requirements, higher expectations and grading criteria, and improved preparation and remuneration of teachers were also stressed. States were quick to take action on these recommendations. For example, more than half of the states increased the number of academic units required for high school graduation (Bodner, Clark, & Mellard, 1987).

In 1990, then-President Bush and the nation's governors agreed upon six national education goals for the year 2000. These goals became the foundation for the Goals 2000: Educate America Act of 1994 passed during the Clinton administration. With agreement on national goals for public education came a call for national performance standards and a national achievement test to assess students' progress; both proposals continue to engender much debate.

School reform efforts continue today, and several important movements reflect fundamental changes in thinking about the purposes, conduct, and governance of education. The school restructuring movement signals a change in the overall governance structure, with decision-making powers moving to local schools to allow site-based management. In curriculum reform, there is movement away from instruction of isolated skills and toward a curriculum that integrates content in meaningful ways in order to emphasize higher-order thinking skills in place of rote memory. The accompanying trend in assessment is alternative assessment, with less reliance on multiple-choice tests and more on authentic tasks and meaningful performance standards; Chapter 6 described the alternative assessment movement and one of its most popular measurement strategies, portfolio assessment. Chapter 6 also discussed the standards-based reform movement, another important change in thinking about schooling in the United States. By the late 1990s, most states had adopted common academic standards for student performance and common measures for the assessment of student achievement of those standards.

It is important to note that the current reform efforts, like others before them, do not address the educational needs of students with disabilities directly. Although in some cases this population is incorporated in the reforms recommended for all students, in most cases accommodations for students with disabilities have not been considered until after the fact. This is particularly important when considered in light of trends in special education. In the 1980s, advocates made strong pleas for full-time placement of students with disabilities in general education classrooms (e.g., Stainback & Stainback, 1985, 1988, 1992; Stainback, Stainback, & Forest, 1989; Wang & Walberg, 1988; Will, 1986). Many special educators objected, warning that more than one placement option must be available if students' needs are to be addressed on an individualized basis (Fuchs & Fuchs, 1988, 1994; Hallahan, Keller, McKinney, Lloyd, & Bryan, 1988; Schumaker & Deshler, 1988). The result has been movement toward greater inclusion of students with disabilities, although other placement options remain available. For example, in school year 1995–96, approximately three-fourths of students with disabilities spent at least 40% of the school day in general education classrooms (U.S. Department of Education, 1998).

Current Practices

Assessment of academic achievement is a routine practice in general education today. Classroom teachers regularly assess pupil growth, and when students with disabilities are members of general education classrooms, they typically take part in these assessment activities. They may also participate in schoolwide testing programs, including the periodic administration of group achievement tests to monitor academic progress.

One problematic feature of general education assessment for students with learning problems is group test administration. Although group measures can provide some information, students with disabilities typically perform poorly on them. The 1997 IDEA Amendments require that testing accommodations be provided to students participating in state- or districtwide measures of academic achievement; however, the effects of these accommodations on students' performance are still under study. Because of this, individual tests of academic achievement are preferred for students with disabilities, particularly when information is being collected for decisions about eligibility for special education.

Individual administration allows the tester to direct the student's attention toward the test task, provide encouragement, and explain requirements. The student can be observed carefully to determine whether environmental factors influence performance. In addition, many individual tests attempt to separate out skills so that assessment of one does not require mastery of another. Thus, reading skills are not required except on measures of reading. The necessity for writing skills is also minimized, except when these are the subject of evaluation.

One of the first steps in special education assessment is the administration of an individual norm-referenced test of academic achievement. Tests that survey several areas of the curriculum, usually basic skill subjects, are most usual. Because the purpose at this point in the assessment process is to determine whether significant school performance problems exist, norm-referenced measures are appropriate. There has been much debate over the relative merits of norm-referenced versus criterion-referenced measures in achievement testing (Ebel, 1977; Perrone, 1977; Popham, 1978; Rudman, 1977), but norm-referenced tests remain the most common strategy for eligibility assessment. Norm-referenced measures provide the comparative information necessary for determining eligibility, and they are much more time-efficient. Criterion-referenced tests and other informal measures are typically used after eligibility has been established to provide more detailed descriptions of student performance in areas of educational need.

At present, the three major individual tests used to assess academic achievement in special education are the *Peabody Individual Achievement Test-Revised/Normative Update,* the *Wide Range Achievement Test-Revision 3,* and the achievement portion of the *Woodcock-Johnson Psycho-Educational Battery-Revised.* A newer measure, the *Wechsler Individual Achievement Test,* is also gaining popularity. These measures are described in later sections of this chapter, along with others such as the *Kaufman Test of Educational Achievement/Normative Update,* the *Diagnostic Achievement Battery* (2nd ed.), and the *Hammill Multiability Achievement Test.* In addition, two types of informal strategies are discussed later: criterion-referenced tests and curriculum-based measures. Although curriculum-based assessment relies on informal tools such as classroom quizzes, it has gained popularity as a method for determining whether students show school performance problems in the general education classroom.

SOURCES OF INFORMATION ABOUT SCHOOL PERFORMANCE

The assessment team can gather information about the student's school performance in several ways. In addition to individual tests of academic achievement, four major sources of information are school records, students themselves, teachers, and parents.

School Records

School records provide information about the student's past performance and educational history. Although current performance is the main concern, the team needs a picture of how the student has functioned in previous years and the type of services received. Records may also contain some current data, such as this year's report card grades.

School Grades. Both current and past report card grades and teachers' comments should be reviewed. Is the problem new, or does it reflect a continuing pattern of school performance difficulty? Do grades suggest academic achievement deficiencies in all areas or only in selected subjects?

Retentions. School records may show that a student has been retained or considered for retention. If retention was suggested, was poor academic achievement one of the major reasons? If the student was retained, what grade or grades were repeated? What were the effects of the grade repetition?

Special Services. Referral to special services may be part of a student's record. Has the student been recommended for remedial tutoring, bilingual evaluation, special education assessment, or other services? If so, what were the reasons for the referral, and what was its disposition? Did special services result in substantial improvement of school performance?

Attendance Record. Has the student been absent an excessive number of days in this school year or past years? What were the reasons for the attendance problem? Also consider the number of schools the student has attended. Was the student enrolled in several different schools over the past few years? If so, how similar were the academic curricula to the current course of study?

Group Achievement Test Results. With the cautions about group testing in mind, records should be examined to determine the student's scores on current and past group tests of academic achievement, measures of attainment of academic standards, and any other assessments relating to academic achievement. Are the student's scores indicative of a problem in school performance? Does he or she consistently score within the bottom one-third of age or grade peers in one or more academic areas? Are past and present results approximately the same, or is a problem just beginning to become apparent?

The Student

The assessment team can involve students in the evaluation process in several ways.

Individual Achievement Tests. One of the first steps after referral for special education services is participation in individual achievement tests. These measures provide an overview of the student's current standing in relation to other students in the major school subjects. In evaluating the results of these tests, the team considers both the student's behavior during the testing situation and the final scores.

Current Classroom Performance. School records and teachers provide some information about current classroom performance, but the student is the primary source. The team may want to observe the student in the classroom to see how he or she responds to instruction. Does the student participate by listening and watching, asking questions, and attempting to respond to the teacher's questions? What level of accuracy does the student achieve in classwork? In independent academic activities, is the student able to sustain attention, work without assistance, and achieve an acceptable level of accuracy? Samples of student work can also be analyzed.

Attitudes, Viewpoints, and Academic Goals. Interviews help determine students' perceptions of their own performance. Information can also be gathered with questionnaires, if the measures do not exceed the student's current reading and writing skills. Among the areas the team may wish to explore are the student's attitude toward school, favorite and most disliked school subjects, and perceptions of the reason for referral. In addition, students can report on their academic goals and perhaps their vocational aspirations. They may perceive a difficult subject as unimportant to their academic or vocational future and therefore expend little energy in attempting to master it.

Teachers

Teachers are an important source of information about current classroom functioning. Often the teacher initiates the referral for special education assessment after careful observation of the student's daily performance. Teachers should be consulted about several different aspects of school performance.

Reason for Referral. If the student's general education teacher was the source of the referral for special education assessment, the team should interview this teacher to find out more about the reasons for referral. Is the student able to meet regular classroom expectations for achievement in any subject areas? In what specific areas is the student experiencing difficulty? How does the student's performance compare with that of the rest of the class?

Past Classroom Performance. The student's former teachers may also be of assistance. They can describe classroom performance in past years, perhaps documenting a history of learning difficulties. Or they may be able to report about instructional strategies that proved successful.

Current Classroom Performance. Current teachers can provide up-to-date report card grades, results of classroom quizzes, and samples of assignments and other completed work. They can also report their daily observations of the student in the instructional environment. In addition, teachers can describe the academic level and quality of work the student is able to perform. Is the student using grade level materials? If so, is he or she able to master these? If the student is placed in more elementary materials, what is their level? Are they appropriate for current skills? Is the student attentive during instruction? Does he or she participate by asking and answering questions? Is the student able to work independently?

Instructional Modifications. Past and present teachers can provide information about the modification of instruction. If the student is unable to meet the classroom demands, what changes were made to increase the probability of success? What were the results of these changes? Does the student require more complete explanations of new concepts than required by most learners? Is it necessary to repeat and explain task instructions? Does the student need more opportunities for practice? Does allowing the student additional time increase accuracy? Or is it necessary to assign less or easier work?

Parents

Whereas teachers have the best opportunity for observing academic performance in the classroom, parents and other family members are best able to report about the use of academic skills at home and in the community.

Reason for Referral. If the student's parents initiated the referral for special education assessment, the team will want to find out why. Are the student's parents concerned about academic achievement? What led to this concern—poor grades, lack of skills or difficulty with academic tasks, discrepancies between siblings' performance?

Past Educational Performance. Parents can usually provide information about when their child first began showing signs of academic difficulties. Parents often become concerned about their child's school achievement long before the school takes official notice. Sometimes this is due to unrealistic expectations and aspirations for their child. Many times, however, parents make an accurate assessment because they know their child well and have ample opportunity to observe his or her performance.

Current Performance at Home and in the Community. Parents are the best source of information about how the student uses academic skills in the home and community. For example, parents can talk about how their child handles money, if and what he or she reads for pleasure, and how the child copes with composition tasks such as writing notes to family members. Parents can also report whether their child can tell time and make change, and whether he or she is able to read road signs, television schedules, and restaurant menus. Parents make a valuable contribution to the assessment team's study of school performance.

GROUP TESTS OF ACADEMIC ACHIEVEMENT

Group academic achievement tests are typically administered in general, not special, education. Their results help evaluate the performance of individuals and classes and determine the effectiveness of school programs. Many students with special needs take group tests along with their peers in the general education classroom.

Group tests of academic achievement usually contain several levels, so that one test series can be used from the earliest elementary grades through high school. The subject areas assessed are the basic skills of reading, mathematics, and language arts. Many tests also evaluate reference or study skills and content area subjects such as science and social studies. Because group administration procedures do not allow oral responses, assessment of reading is limited to silent reading skills. Handwriting, written expression, and written spelling are rarely included because test items tend to be multiple choice to facilitate scoring.

Students are usually furnished with test booklets that contain the items and directions. Directions are also orally presented to the group. Younger students may be allowed to record their answers directly in the test booklets, but older students use separate answer sheets. Some group measures provide practice tests that introduce students to the types of questions used and procedures for marking the answer sheet. Group tests can be scored by hand, and publishers may offer machine scoring services. With sophisticated computer-generated reports, results can be presented by class, grade, school, district, pupil, and test item.

Many types of scores are available for group measures. The most typical are grade equivalents, percentile ranks, and stanines. Many tests also link items to instructional objectives, so individual or class reports include a listing of mastered and unmastered skills.

Popular group tests of academic achievement include the *California Achievement Tests* (5th ed.) (1992), the *Comprehensive Tests of Basic Skills* (4th ed.) (1989, 1990), the *Iowa Tests of Basic Skills* (1996), the *Metropolitan Achievement Tests* (7th ed.) (Balow, Farr, & Hogan, 1992), and the *Stanford Achievement Tests* (9th ed.) (1996). These are traditional group tests in multiple-choice format, although some tests are beginning to include items that tap higher-order thinking skills. In addition, several publishers have introduced new group measures in free response format in response to the alternative assessment movement. Among these are portfolio assessment systems and performance-based measures in which students complete real tasks. One example is the *Riverside Performance Assessment Series* (1993), which includes measures of reading, writing, and mathematics.

The administration procedures used in group testing are not optimal for lower performing students for several reasons:

- Group tests require reading ability, even when assessing skills other than reading.
- Group tests are often timed.
- Students must write their answers, usually on a separate answer sheet.
- Group administration procedures assume that students can work independently, monitor their own behavior, and sustain attention to test tasks.

When interpreting results of group testing, it should be remembered that these measures tend to produce a low estimate of the performance of students with disabilities. In addition, very low test scores tend to be less reliable than scores within the average range.

However, group tests do have some uses in special education, particularly in the screening process. Results of the achievement tests administered at regular grade intervals should be reviewed carefully to identify students needing further assessment. Such tests can also provide information about the academic progress of students with disabilities in relation to their peers in the general education classroom.

INDIVIDUAL TESTS OF ACADEMIC ACHIEVEMENT

Individual achievement tests are preferred for assessment of school performance in special education. Like group measures, they are designed for a wide span of grades, usually kindergarten through grade 12. Instead of having separate versions for different grade levels, individual tests are usually limited to one version that includes a wide range of items arranged in order of difficulty.

As Table 7–1 shows, most individual achievement tests assess the basic skills of reading, mathematics, and spelling. Content subjects such as science and social studies are not included as often. Because these tests are individually administered, student responses can be written, oral, or even gestural. This allows the assessment of oral as well as silent reading, and

permits students with poor writing skills to bypass this difficulty when answering questions in other subject matter areas.

The following sections describe and critique several individual academic achievement tests used in special education. The *Peabody Individual Achievement Test-Revised/Normative Update* is discussed in the first section. Next are the *Wide Range Achievement Test-Revision 3,* the achievement portion of the *Woodcock-Johnson Psycho-Educational Battery-Revised,* and the *Wechsler Individual Achievement Test.*

PEABODY INDIVIDUAL ACHIEVEMENT TEST-REVISED/NORMATIVE UPDATE

The *Peabody Individual Achievement Test-Revised/Normative Update (PIAT-R/NU)* is a norm-referenced measure commonly used in special education for identifying academic deficiencies. This test was originally published in 1970 (Dunn & Markwardt) and revised in 1989 (Markwardt). A new version with updated norms appeared in 1998 (Markwardt). According to its manual, the *PIAT-R/NU* is "an individually administered achievement test providing wide-range screening in six content areas" (Markwardt, 1989, 1998, p. 1).

The *PIAT-R/NU* is made up of six subtests: General Information, Reading Recognition, Reading Comprehension, Mathematics, Spelling, and Written Expression. The most typical response format on the *PIAT-R/NU* is multiple-choice. The student is shown a test plate with four possible answers and asked to select the correct response.

- *General Information.* On this subtest, questions are read aloud by the tester. There are no visuals, and no choices are presented. The student listens to the question and responds orally. Test items sample several areas of knowledge, including science, social studies, fine arts, humanities, and recreation.
- *Reading Recognition.* The first 16 test items, in multiple-choice format, begin with simple matching questions. Students must select the letter or word identical to the stimulus, then progress to items that require students to locate words that begin with the same sound as

TABLE 7–1

Individual Tests of Academic Achievement

Name (Author)	Ages or Grades	SUBJECT AREAS ASSESSED				
		Reading	Math	Spelling	Written Language	Content Subjects
BRIGANCE ® Diagnostic Comprehensive Inventory of Basic Skills-Revised (Brigance, 1999)	Grades PreK–9, Ages 5-0 to 13-0	*	*	*	*	
Diagnostic Achievement Battery (2nd ed.) (Newcomer, 1990)	Ages 6-0 to 14-11	*	*	*	*	
Diagnostic Achievement Test for Adolescents (2nd ed.) (Newcomer & Bryant, 1993)	Ages 12-0 to 18-11	*	*	*	*	*
Hammill Multiability Achievement Test (Hammill, Hresko, Ammer, Cronin, & Quinby, 1998)	Ages 7-0 to 17-11	*	*	*		*
Kaufman Test of Educational Achievement/ Normative Update (Kaufman & Kaufman, 1998)	Ages 6-0 to 18-11	*	*	*		
Peabody Individual Achievement Test Revised/ Normative Update (Markwardt, 1998)	Ages 5-0 to 22-11, Grades K–12	*	*	*	*	*
Wechsler Individual Achievement Test (1992)	Ages 5-0 to 19-11	*	*	*	*	
Wide Range Achievement Test Revision 3 (Wilkinson, 1993)	Ages 5-0 to 74-11	*	*	*		
Woodcock-Johnson Psycho-Educational Battery-Revised (Woodcock & Johnson, 1989)	Ages 2 to 90+, Grades K–12 and college	*	*	*	*	*

that of a pictured object. Beginning with item 17, students are presented with words to read orally. Words are presented in isolation without context cues.

- *Reading Comprehension.* Students read a sentence silently and then select the picture that best depicts that sentence from a set of four pictures. The sentence may not be read more than once, and the student is not allowed to look at the sentence after the pictures have been exposed.

- *Mathematics.* On most items, the tester reads a question as the student views four possible responses. Test items begin with exercises that require matching of numerals and progress to areas such as numeration, basic operations, measurement, geometry, graphs and statistics, estimation, algebra, and advanced mathematics.

- *Spelling.* This subtest begins with multiple-choice items in which the student must discriminate the one response of four that is dif-

Peabody Individual Achievement Test-Revised/Normative Update (PIAT-R/NU)

F. C. Markwardt (1998)

Type: Norm-referenced test

Major Content Areas: General information, reading, mathematics, spelling, and written expression

Type of Administration: Individual

Administration Time: Approximately 1 hour

Age/Grade Levels: Grades K through 12, ages 5-0 to 22-11

Types of Scores: Grade and age equivalents, standard scores, percentile ranks, stanines; for the Written Expression subtest, grade-based stanines and developmental scaled scores

Computer Aids: *PIAT-R/NU ASSIST*

Typical Uses: A broad-based screening measure for the identification of strengths and weaknesses in academic achievement

Cautions: In administration, special rules apply concerning "false" basals and ceilings. Scoring is complicated by the need to use two sets of standard errors of measurement, one for raw scores and age/grade equivalents, another for standard scores. Results of the optional Written Expression subtest should be interpreted cautiously due to concerns about reliability. Information is needed about the *PIAT-R/NU*'s concurrent validity.

Publisher: American Guidance Service (www.agsnet.com)

ferent; more difficult items require students to select a letter that makes a particular sound. Beginning with item 16, the format of this subtest changes; the student is shown four ways of spelling a word and is asked to identify the correct spelling after hearing the word pronounced and read in a sentence.

- *Written Expression.* This optional subtest contains two levels. Level I is designed for students in kindergarten and grade 1, and Level II for grades 2 through 12. In Level I, students are asked to write their name, copy letters and words, and write letters, words, and sentences from dictation. In Level II, students are shown a stimulus picture and directed to write a story about that picture within a 20-minute time period. The tester can choose from two stimulus pictures, Prompt A and Prompt B.

Students must be able to attend to test tasks for several minutes at a time to participate in *PIAT-R/NU* administration. English-language skills are a

necessity for comprehension of directions and questions. However, the multiple-choice format used in several subtests reduces response requirements; students can answer either by pointing to the correct response, saying the answer, or saying the number of the answer. The student is required to speak only in General Information and later items of the Reading Recognition subtest. Writing is required only in the Written Expression subtest. Reading skills are not needed for the Mathematics and General Information subtests because the tester reads the questions to the student. Only the Written Expression subtest (Level II) is timed.

Technical Quality

The *PIAT-R/NU* was renormed in 1995–96 with 3,184 students in kindergarten through grade 12 and 245 young adults (ages 18–22). Approximately half of the students were males and half were females. Students were excluded if they were not proficient in English, but students in gifted and special education programs were included. The sample was selected to resemble the U.S. population as reflected in 1994 U.S. Census data. The final sample appears to resemble the nation as a whole in terms of geographic region, parental education level (an indicator of socioeconomic status), and race or ethnic group. Also, the sample appears to be representative of K–12 students who receive services in special and gifted education. For example, 5.9% of the sample was identified as learning disabled, similar to the 5.5% figure reported by the U.S. Department of Education (1995).

The *PIAT-R/NU* appears most appropriate for students in kindergarten through grade 12, although norms are also available for individuals ages 18 to 22. It is not appropriate for students who do not speak English. It is interesting to note that the 1995–96 renorming study revealed changes in academic performance since the 1986 norming of the *PIAT-R*. Markwardt (1998) reports:

> The average level of performance tends to have fallen at the earliest grades (grades 1 through 3) but has stayed the same or, in some cases, increased at the secondary level. . . . For below-average students, performance in the NU norm sample tends to be lower than in the original PIAT-R standardization sample. (p. 121)

Reliability and validity are also of concern in evaluating the technical quality of a norm-referenced test. However, the 1998 manual for the *PIAT-R/NU* does not provide new information; instead, it reports on the reliability and validity of the *PIAT-R* and its predecessor, the *PIAT*. On the *PIAT-R*, reliability was studied by several methods. For the five required *PIAT-R* subtests and the Total Test score, split-half and Kuder-Richardson reliability coefficients were above the suggested .80 minimum at all grade and age levels. Test-retest reliability was generally adequate for these subtests, although coefficients fell in the .70's for some subtests for grade 6/age 12 students.

Reliability was studied somewhat differently for the optional subtest, Written Expression. Level I of that subtest shows high interrater reliability (.90 for kindergarten and .95 for grade 1); however, internal consistency coefficients ranged from .60 to .69, and test-retest re-

liability was .56. On Level II of Written Expression, most internal consistency coefficients fell at .80 or above. In contrast, the median correlation coefficient for interrater reliability was .58 for Prompt A and .67 for Prompt B. In addition, the average degree of relationship between student performance on Prompt A and on Prompt B was .63, indicating less than satisfactory alternate-form reliability.

Concurrent validity of the *PIAT-R* was studied by assessing its relationship to the *Peabody Picture Vocabulary Test-Revised (PPVT-R)* (Dunn & Dunn, 1981), which the *PIAT-R/NU* manual describes as a measure of "verbal ability independent of reading ability or expressive language" (Markwardt, 1989, 1998, p. 66). The median correlation coefficient between *PPVT-R* results and results of individual *PIAT-R* subtests ranged from .50 to .72. Factor analysis was also used to investigate the *PIAT-R*'s validity. Three factors emerged, all of which appear to represent verbal skills. The first, described in the manual as "a general verbal-educational ability factor" (p. 72), includes the General Information, Mathematics, and Reading Comprehension subtests. The second factor includes Spelling and Reading Recognition and appears to relate more to verbal skills associated with symbol systems. The third factor is associated with the Reading Comprehension and Written Expression (Level II) subtests.

There is a need for more information about the relationship of the *PIAT-R/NU* to other tests of academic achievement. Although the 1995–96 renorming study included not only the *PIAT-R* but also three other achievement measures, the *PIAT-R/NU* manual does not discuss the relationships between results of these tests. The manual does provide summaries of more than 50 validity studies of the original *PIAT*. In general, the 1970 *PIAT* showed moderate correlations with individual measures such as the *Wide Range Achievement Test* (Jastak & Jastak, 1978), the *Woodcock-Johnson Psycho-Educational Battery* (Woodcock & Johnson, 1977), the *Woodcock Reading Mastery Tests* (Woodcock, 1973), and the *KeyMath Diagnostic Arithmetic Test* (Connolly, Nachtman, & Pritchett, 1971, 1976). However, all of these tests have undergone revisions.

Administration Considerations

According to the *PIAT-R/NU* manual, only "minimal" (p. 3) qualifications are required for test administration. Before results are used for educational decisions, however, the manual advises that testers study the administration and scoring procedures and practice test administration. Interpretation of test results requires additional expertise, particularly in the areas of measurement and curriculum.

The *PIAT-R/NU* is relatively easy to administer and score, and Parts II and III of the manual provide guidelines for these procedures. The testing materials include the manual, four administration booklets, and the Test Record in which the examiner records the student's responses and the student writes responses for the Written Expression subtest. The administration booklets are in easel format. The tester sits across the corner of the table from the student so that the tester can view both sides of the easel, as needed.

Subtests must be administered in a standard order, beginning with General Information, and the Test Record and test easels are arranged in that order. It is possible to omit a subtest, but the standard order must be maintained for the remaining subtests. The Reading Comprehension subtest is not administered to students who receive raw scores of less than 19 on the Reading Recognition subtest; when this occurs, the Reading Recognition raw score is also entered as the raw score for Reading Comprehension.

The *PIAT-R/NU* begins with standard introductory remarks that the tester reads to all students. Training exercises are available for all required subtests and for Level I of Written Expression. For the first subtest, General Information, the Test Record lists suggested starting places by grade level. According to the manual, the tester should adjust this starting place if there is reason to suspect that the student's achievement is either below or above that of typical grade peers. For the remaining required subtests, the suggested starting place is the raw score earned by the student on the previous subtest. Procedures for the Written Expression subtest are somewhat different. Level I is administered to

students showing less than grade 2 achievement in written expression skills, and Level II to those with grade 2 achievement or better; it is also possible to administer both levels.

There is no basal or ceiling on the Written Expression subtest; all items are administered on Level I, and Level II consists of only one task. On all other subtests, the basal is five consecutively numbered correct items, and the ceiling is five errors out of seven consecutively numbered items. The manual suggests that if the student misses the first item administered, the tester move backward five items in an attempt to locate the student's optimal performance range. It is possible on the *PIAT-R/NU* to encounter situations in which students appear to attain more than one basal or ceiling. For example, a student might answer items 5 to 9 correctly, miss item 10, then answer items 11 to 15 correctly. In this case, the lower-numbered items (5 to 9) are considered a "false basal"; the *higher-numbered* range of items (11 to 15) is considered the true basal, and failures below that basal are disregarded. Likewise, if two ceilings are established, that composed of *lower-numbered* items is considered the true ceiling; successes above that ceiling are disregarded.

Only Level II of the Written Expression subtest is timed. Students are allowed 20 minutes to write a story. However, the manual advises that students be encouraged to respond within 30 seconds to Mathematics items and within 15 seconds on other subtests.

The *PIAT-R/NU* Test Record is well designed. It states clearly the basal and ceiling rules and suggested starting points at the beginning of each subtest. The tester should circle the number of the first item administered and draw a bracket around the basal items and the ceiling items. As each item is administered, the student's response is recorded on the protocol and scored. On multiple-choice items, the number of the student's response is entered; on open-ended items, the tester records the student's actual response. Incorrect answers are indicated by a diagonal slash through the item number. Criteria for evaluating performance on the Written Expression subtest are presented in the manual and Test Record. For example, in Level II, the tester uses a 24-item rating scale to evaluate the story the student has written. The scoring guidelines should be carefully followed, and as a check for accuracy, the manual suggests that a second professional be asked to score students' stories.

Results and Interpretation

The *PIAT-R/NU* offers several types of total test and subtest scores. Both age and grade norms are available, and the tester must decide whether to compare the student's performance with that of age or grade peers. Grade norms are generally the most appropriate, and the *PIAT-R/NU* provides grade norms for fall, winter, and spring test administrations. However, if the student is placed in an ungraded or special class, the tester may choose to use age peers for comparison.

A variety of scores are available for the five required subtests, including grade or age equivalents, standard scores, and percentile ranks. Standard scores are distributed with a mean of 100 and a standard deviation of 15. Using the interpretation system suggested in Chapter 4, the range of average performance on the *PIAT-R/NU* is standard score 85 to 115. The manual provides guidelines for determining if differences between required subtests are statistically significant.

Confidence intervals can be constructed around each score. The Test Record provides standard error of measurement values for raw scores by grade and age levels and by confidence level (68%, 90%, and 95%). Somewhat different procedures are used for standard scores; the tester must refer to an appendix in the manual for the standard errors of measurement. Values are usually decimals, which are rounded to the nearest whole number. For numbers ending in .5, the number is rounded up if it is odd (e.g., 3.5) and down if it is even (e.g., 4.5). Standard scores are converted to percentile ranks by means of a table.

These types of results are not available for the Written Expression subtest. Raw scores on both Level I and Level II are converted to grade-based stanines. Stanines are a nine-point scale distributed with a mean of 5 and a standard deviation of approximately 2. On Level II, it is also possible to determine developmental scaled scores that allow comparison of a student's performance to that of all individuals within the stan-

dardization sample. These scores range from 1 to 15; the mean is 8 and the standard deviation is approximately 3. In addition to subtest scores, the tester can obtain a Total Reading Composite, Written Language Composite, and Total Test score. Total Reading includes both reading subtests, and the Total Test score is a composite of the five required subtests. The Written Language score combines the Spelling and Written Expression subtests. All global scores can be expressed as standard scores and percentile ranks.

PIAT-R/NU results can be plotted on two profiles: the Developmental Score Profile for age or grade equivalents, and the Standard Score Profile. General guidelines are provided on the Test Record for evaluating whether differences between scores indicate true differences in achievement; however, the manual should be consulted for specific criteria in determining whether differences are statistically significant.

Figure 7–1 presents sample *PIAT-R/NU* results for Joyce, the fourth grader with possible school performance problems. Note that grade norms were used to evaluate her performance and that a 68% confidence level was selected. The confidence interval for Joyce's Total Test performance is standard score 80 to 84. The chances that this range of scores includes Joyce's true score are about 68 out of 100. It can be concluded that, in overall academic achievement, Joyce is currently functioning within the low average range of performance when compared to grade peers. Inspection of the Standard Score Profile shows no overlap between some sets of scores (e.g., Mathematics and Spelling). By consulting the manual, it is possible to determine that a standard score difference of 26 between these two subtests (Mathematics standard score 95 − Spelling standard score 69) is statistically significant at the .01 level for students in grade 4. Likewise, according to the table in the manual, there is a significant difference at the .05 level between Joyce's performance in Mathematics and Reading Recognition but no significant difference between Mathematics and Reading Comprehension.

In evaluating *PIAT-R/NU* results, it is sometimes useful to analyze the student's responses to individual test items. For subtests with multiple-choice formats, this may not prove very informa-

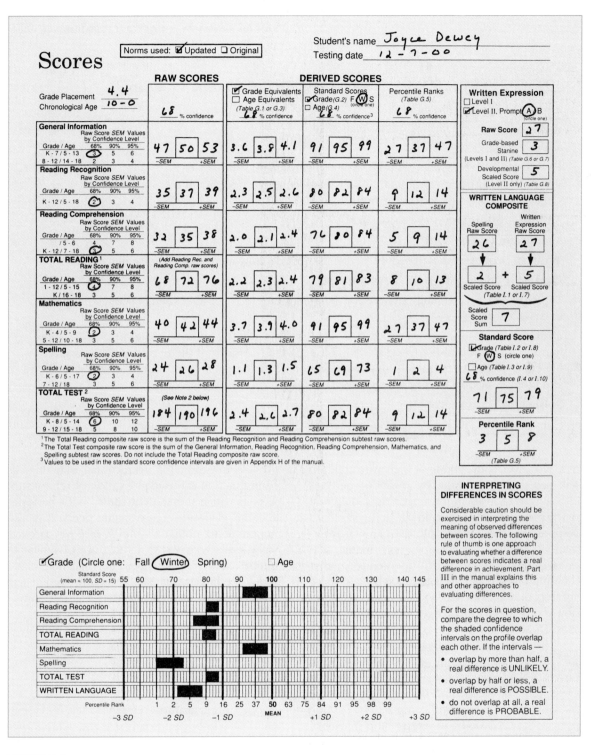

FIGURE 7–1

Sample Results from the *Peabody Individual Achievement Test-Revised/Normative Update*

Note: From Test Record, *Peabody Individual Achievement Test-Revised/Normative Update* by F. C. Markwardt Jr., 1998, Circle Pines, MN: American Guidance Service. Copyright 1998 by American Guidance Service, Inc. Reprinted by permission.

Wide Range Achievement Test-Revision 3 (WRAT3)

G. S. Wilkinson (1993)

Type: Norm-referenced test

Major Content Areas: Reading recognition, spelling, and arithmetic

Type of Administration: Primarily individual, although portions of the Spelling and Arithmetic subtests may be given to small groups

Administration Time: 15–30 minutes

Age/Grade Levels: Ages 5-0 to 74-11

Types of Scores: Standard scores, percentiles, grade equivalents, absolute scores

Computer Aids: WRAT3 Scoring Software

Typical Uses: A screening measure for the identification of possible strengths and weaknesses in basic school subjects

Cautions: Professionals should keep in mind that the WRAT3 is not intended to assess comprehension. Caution is also advised in determining which portions of the test are to be administered to a student. Further information is needed about the concurrent validity of the WRAT3 and other individual tests of achievement.

Publisher: Wide Range, Inc.

tive. However, some young or immature children will select their answers by position, perhaps choosing responses in the upper right quadrant of the page. The tester should check the student's response pattern for this. On the General Information, Reading Recognition, and Written Expression subtests, items are open-ended rather than multiple-choice. Response analysis of these subtests may provide clues to the student's storehouse of general knowledge, word attack strategies, and a variety of writing skills.

The *PIAT-R/NU* appears to be a useful tool for the assessment of school performance across a range of academic subjects. It includes measures of general knowledge and skills such as reading, mathematics, spelling, and composition. Caution is necessary, however, in interpreting results of the Written Expression subtest because its reliability is not well established. If information about writing skills is desired, the tester may choose to use this subtest as an informal measure. Like most other broad-based achievement measures that survey several academic subjects, the *PIAT-R/NU* does not produce results specific enough to

provide direction for instructional planning; its main function is the identification of school subjects in which the student shows poor performance in relation to age or grade peers. It is also important to note that the *PIAT-R/NU* assesses some skills with test tasks that are dissimilar to typical classroom activities. For instance, classroom spelling tasks usually require students to write spelling words, not select the correct spelling from several choices.

WIDE RANGE ACHIEVEMENT TEST-REVISION 3

Another popular norm-referenced test for assessment of school performance is the *Wide Range Achievement Test-Revision 3 (WRAT3)*. One of the oldest measures of academic achievement, the *WRAT* first appeared in the 1930s; the *WRAT3* is the sixth revision. According to the *WRAT3* manual, the purpose of this test is "to measure the codes which are needed to learn the basic skills of reading, spelling, and arithmetic"

(Wilkinson, 1993, p. 10). Although some portions of the *WRAT3* can be administered in group fashion, individual administration is preferred.

Two forms are available for the *WRAT3*—the Blue form and the Tan form. Each form contains three subtests.

- *Spelling.* Students write spelling words from dictation. The tester reads the word, then a sentence containing the word, and the student must write the word on the test form within a specified time period. A prespelling section is administered to young children (ages 5-0 to 7-11) and to older students who do not meet the specified criterion level on the dictation section of the subtest. In prespelling, students write (or print) their names and dictated letters. Prespelling activities are also timed.
- *Arithmetic.* Students write answers to arithmetic problems. They are given a page of computation problems and asked to solve as many as possible within 15 minutes. Items range from simple addition and other basic operations to computations involving fractions, decimals, and percentages. A prearithmetic section is administered to young children (ages 5-0 to 7-11) and to older students who fail to meet the specified criterion on the written section. In prearithmetic, students are timed, but responses are oral rather than written. Activities include counting objects, reading numbers, and answering oral addition and subtraction problems.
- *Reading.* On this subtest, students read lists of words aloud. Words are presented in isolation; each must be pronounced correctly within a specified time limit. A prereading section is administered to young children (ages 5-0 to 7-11) and to older students who fail to meet the specified criterion on the oral reading section. In the prereading section, the students name letters.

To participate in *WRAT3* administration, students must be able to attend to test tasks. Knowledge of English is a necessity, except for some portions of the written computation section of the Arithmetic subtest. Response requirements are demanding. Students must write their answers on two of the subtests and respond orally on the third. In addition, test activities are timed. Reading skills are necessary for the Reading subtest, oral reading of numerals is one of the prearithmetic tasks, and some of the written computation problems contain written directions.

Technical Quality

The *WRAT3* was standardized with a stratified national sample of 4,433 persons ranging in age from 5-0 to 74-11. The sample was selected to represent the national population in terms of gender, ethnicity, and socioeconomic status. According to the manual, "special education students were included in the sample as randomization would allow" (p. 27). Excluded were persons physically unable to respond to test items and those not proficient in English.

The *WRAT3* appears appropriate for a wide age span of individuals. Norms are based on a large sample representing the total U.S. population on several demographic variables. It is likely that students receiving special education services made up a portion of the sample, although their number and types of disabilities are unknown. The *WRAT3* is not appropriate for individuals who do not speak English.

Reliability of the *WRAT3* appears adequate. Internal consistency, alternate form, and test-retest reliability coefficients all fall within acceptable ranges. Item difficulty was studied using the Rasch model, and analysis results indicate that the items on each subject represent a range from very easy to difficult.

In evaluating the content validity of a test, it is necessary to consider that test's purpose. The purpose of the *WRAT3* is measurement of performance in the rote recall or code aspects of basic skills. The manual states that "the *WRAT3* was intentionally designed to eliminate, as totally as possible, the effects of comprehension" (p. 10). The test author appears to have attained this goal.

The *WRAT3* manual reports several types of validity studies. First, a relationship was found between age and performance on all three subtests; as age increased, scores improved. Second, study of the intercorrelations of the three subtests indicated a stronger relationship between the two language arts subtests (Reading and Spelling) than between either of these subtests and Arithmetic. The third set of investigations examined the concurrent validity of the *WRAT3* and measures of intellectual performance and academic achievement. Most pertinent are the relationships between this test and its predecessor, the *WRAT-R,* and other academic measures. Correlations between the two versions of the *WRAT* ranged from .79 to .99, a logical outcome because of the similarity of items in the two editions. Lower correlations were found when the *WRAT3* was studied in relation to group tests of academic achievement. For example, the correlations between scores on the *WRAT3* and *California Achievement Test* were .72 for reading, .77 for spelling, and .41 for math. Further information is needed on the concurrent validity of the *WRAT3* and the individual measures of achievement typically used in special education assessment.

The final validity study reported in the manual was a comparison of the *WRAT3* performance of four groups of children ages 8.5 to 12.5: those identified as "normal" (n = 111), learning disabled (n = 47), educably mentally handicapped (i.e., mildly retarded) (n = 24), and gifted (n = 40). Significant differences were found among groups. Results of a discriminant analysis indicated that the *WRAT3* successfully categorized 68% of these students. Least accurate was the categorization of normal students (56% accuracy).

Administration Considerations

Although formal training is not required to administer the *WRAT3,* the manual must be studied with care. Not all sections of the *WRAT-R* are given to all students. Each subtest at each level contains a skill section and a preskill section. The tester first determines whether to begin each subtest with the skill section or the preskill section. With younger children (ages 5-0 to 7-11), each subtest is started with the preskill section. With older students, testing begins with the skill section. However, if the student does not perform adequately on the skill section, the preskill section must then be administered.

WRAT3 subtests may be administered in any order, and it is not necessary to give all three.

WRAT3 subtests have no basals as the term is usually used, but the rules for administration of subtest preskill sections can be interpreted as rules for establishing basals. Ceilings of 10 consecutive errors are specified for the Spelling and Reading subtests. Arithmetic has a 15-minute time limit rather than a ceiling. All *WRAT3* tasks are timed. In Spelling, students are allowed 15 seconds to write a word, and in Reading, 10 seconds to read a word.

The *WRAT3* manual presents the instructions to be read to the student in red type, so they are easily located. It is somewhat difficult to locate other important information such as time limits, ceiling rules, and rules for preskill administration. However, the manual and test form remind the tester to follow the 5/10 rules for the Spelling and Reading subtests and the 5 rule/15-minute time limit for the Arithmetic subtest. The 5 rule states that older students should be given the preskill portion of the subtest if they fail to answer five items correctly in the skill portion. The 10 rule refers to the ceiling of 10 incorrect responses in a row.

The test form is used to record the student's responses. In some portions of the *WRAT3,* the tester is the recorder, and in others, such as Spelling, the student writes the answers. If handwriting is illegible, the tester should ask the student to read what he or she has written. The *WRAT3* manual recommends that testers record reading responses by circling the number of the item for words read correctly and marking a slash through the first letter of incorrect words. However, verbatim recording is necessary if the tester later wishes to analyze errors.

Calculation of raw scores on the *WRAT3* requires an alert tester. If preskill activities are not administered, the student receives full credit for these sections. This is equivalent to giving full credit for all items below the basal. The test form for the *WRAT3* alerts the tester by providing three boxes: one for the preskill raw score, the second for the skill raw score, and the third for the total raw score.

Results and Interpretation

The *WRAT3* offer several types of scores for each subtest but no total test or summary score. Only

WRAT3

WIDE RANGE ACHIEVEMENT TEST □ REVISION 3

NAME _David —_

DATE _11 / 17 / 00_   BIRTH DATE _6 / 3 / 86_   AGE _14-5_

SCHOOL _Ash middle School_   GRADE _8.3_

REFERRED BY _Ms. Coolidge, math_ EXAMINER _Mr. Blank_

BLUE TEST SCORES

	Raw Score	Std. Score	%ile Score	Grade Score	Absolute Score
READING	40	95	37	8	511
SPELLING	33	91	27	6	506
ARITHMETIC	29	75	5	4	497

Use only standard scores for comparisons

FIGURE 7-2

Sample *WRAT3* Results

Note: From the *Wide Range Achievement Test-Revision 3* by G. S. Wilkinson, 1993, Wilmington, DE: Wide Range, Inc. Copyright 1993 by Jastak Associates. Reprinted by permission.

age norms are available, extending from age 5 to age 75. The derived scores usually obtained from *WRAT3* raw scores are standard scores, percentile ranks, and grade equivalents. Absolute scores can also be obtained; according to the manual, these scores "give measurement of each variable across the whole continuum of that variable without regard to grade or age" (p. 33). Absolute scores are distributed on an interval scale with a mean of 500. Stanines, scaled scores, *T*-scores, and normal curve equivalents are also available.

Norms are provided for each of the two alternate forms and for a combination of the two. According to the manual, testers may wish to administer both forms because "this combined assessment will provide more opportunity for performance observation" (p. 9). It will also increase the reliability of results and enhance the precision with which grade scores can be reported. Grade scores on the norms tables for the Blue and Tan forms begin with K, proceed in yearly intervals (i.e., 1, 2) through grade 8, and end with HS and post-HS. Grade scores on norms tables for the combined version are much more precise decimal scores (e.g., 4.3, 6.2).

WRAT3 standard scores are distributed with a mean of 100 and a standard deviation of 15. It is expected that approximately 95% of the population will fall between standard score 70 and standard score 130. Thus, the range of average performance on the *WRAT3* is standard score 85 to 115. The *WRAT3* manual suggests a somewhat different classification system. Standard score ranges are 10 points, representing two-thirds of one standard deviation. For example, standard scores between 90 and 109 are considered Average.

The standard errors of measurement are reported in the *WRAT3* manual for each subtest in standard score units. Tables are provided so the tester can determine the exact standard error by the age of the person and subtest score received. The mean standard errors across all ages for the Blue and Tan forms respectively are: Reading, 4.5, 4.7; Spelling, 4.8, 4.9; Arithmetic, 5.7, 5.9.

Sample *WRAT3* results are shown in Figure 7–2 for a middle school student named David. David is currently in eighth grade and is having trouble in math. Only age norms are available on the *WRAT3,* so David's performance was compared to that of other students ages 14-0 to 14-11. David's *WRAT3* performance is reported in raw scores, standard scores, percentile ranks, grade equivalents, and absolute scores. Note that the grade scores for David are not expressed as decimals. *WRAT3* results can also be plotted on two types of profiles: a normal curve profile showing the relationship between standard scores and percentile ranks, and an absolute scale showing the relationship between selected subtest items, grade, and age.

Confidence intervals can be constructed around *WRAT3* standard scores. On the Arithmetic subtest, David earned a standard score of 75, and the standard error for this subtest at age 14 is 5.3 standard score points. If a 68% level of confidence is selected, the interval becomes standard scores 70 to 80. Thus, the chances that the range of standard scores from 70 to 80 includes David's true score are about 68 out of 100. These results indicate that David's performance on the *WRAT3* Arithmetic subtest falls in the low average range in comparison to age peers.

In evaluating a student's performance on the *WRAT3*, it may be useful to analyze specific responses. The *WRAT3* requires students to spell words in writing, write the answers to arithmetic computation problems, and read words orally. Answers may provide some information about how the student approaches these common school tasks. For example, the teacher may be able to compare the student's ability to spell phonetically regular and irregular words or to look at skills in pronouncing certain vowel and consonant sounds. Also, the Spelling and Arithmetic subtests provide samples of the student's handwriting that can be analyzed for legibility and error patterns.

However, in analyzing *WRAT3* scores and specific student responses, it is necessary to remain aware of the way in which this test assesses basic skills. In all subtests, only a small segment of the curriculum under study is sampled. On the Blue form of the Arithmetic subtest, for example, addition of whole numbers is represented by five problems, and subtraction of whole numbers by four. In Reading, only the skill of reading words in isolation is evaluated; the important skill of comprehension is not assessed. In fact, the Reading subtest might better be called "Reading Recognition" because of its failure to include anything but decoding tasks.

The *WRAT3* should not be used as the sole instrument for determining a student's current levels of academic achievement. It lacks coverage of some important skills, although the tasks it does contain resemble typical classroom activities. The reliability of the 1993 edition of the *WRAT* is adequate, but its relationship to other individual measures of academic achievement requires further study. In addition, results are neither specific nor comprehensive enough to assist in planning instructional programs.

WOODCOCK-JOHNSON PSYCHO-EDUCATIONAL BATTERY-REVISED, TESTS OF ACHIEVEMENT

The *Woodcock-Johnson Psycho-Educational Battery-Revised (Woodcock-Johnson-R)* is a norm-referenced measure made up of 35 subtests arranged in two main parts: the *Tests of Cognitive Ability* and the *Tests of Achievement*. Of concern here is the portion of the *Woodcock-Johnson-R* that focuses on academic achievement. However, one of the features of the *Woodcock-Johnson-R* is its capacity to assess both learning aptitude and academic performance within one assessment system. This feature is discussed in Chapter 9 in relation to discrepancy analysis and the identification of learning disabilities.

The *Woodcock-Johnson* was originally published in 1977. The revised 1989 version features several new subtests and a new organization of subtests into two levels: standard batteries and supplemental batteries. Standard batteries are administered first; then portions of the supplemental batteries are selected if further information is needed. In addition, two alternative forms of the *Tests of Achievement* are now available.

The *Woodcock-Johnson-R Tests of Achievement* are designed to provide information about four areas of the curriculum: reading, mathematics, written language, and knowledge. In both Form A and Form B, the standard achievement battery contains nine subtests, and the supple-

---

Woodcock-Johnson Psycho-Educational Battery-Revised (Woodcock-Johnson-R): Tests of Achievement

R. W. Woodcock & M. B. Johnson (1989)

Type: Norm-referenced test

Major Content Areas: Reading, mathematics, written language, and knowledge (science, social studies, and humanities)

Type of Administration: Individual

Administration Time: Approximately 1 hour for standard battery

Age/Grade Levels: Ages 2 to 90+; Grades K–12, college

Types of Scores: Grade and age equivalents, standard scores, percentile ranks, Relative Mastery Index (RMI) scores

Computer Aids: *Woodcock Scoring and Interpretive Program*

Typical Uses: A broad-based screening measure for the identification of strengths and weaknesses in academic achievement

Cautions: Some subtests are not administered if scores on other subtests fall below a specified level. Results are available for more than 30 subtests and skill areas, making hand scoring time-consuming and interpretation complicated. Test-retest reliability of the Writing Fluency subtest is not well established, and caution is needed in interpreting results of the Handwriting subtest due to low interrater reliability. No information is available regarding alternate form reliability.

Publisher: Riverside Publishing (www.riverpub.com)

---

mental battery contains five subtests. These measures are described in the next paragraphs by curriculum area. In each area, standard battery subtests are discussed first, then supplemental subtests.

Reading

- *Letter-Word Identification.* On the first test items, the student is shown a colored drawing and two or three small line drawings called rebuses; the student selects the rebus that depicts the colored drawing. Next, when shown a letter, the student must say its name. On more difficult items, the student is asked to pronounce real words.
- *Passage Comprehension.* Early items present several colored drawings and a phrase that describes one of the drawings; the student points to the drawing that corresponds to the phrase. Next, the student silently reads a passage of one or more sentences. In each passage is a blank space where one word has been omitted. The student's task is to say a word that correctly completes the sentence.
- *Word Attack* (Supplemental). The student is presented with nonsense words to read aloud. A pronunciation key is provided for the tester.
- *Reading Vocabulary* (Supplemental). The subtest is divided into two parts: Synonyms and Antonyms. The student reads a word aloud and then must supply either a word that means the same or one that has an opposite meaning.

Mathematics

- *Calculation.* The student is provided with pages that contain computation problems and writes the answer to each. Beginning items are simple number facts and basic operations. Also included are problems requiring manipulation of fractions and more advanced calculations using algebra, geometry, trigonometry, and calculus.

- *Applied Problems.* The student solves word problems. In the beginning items, the tester reads a question while the student looks at a drawing. On later items, the student is shown the word problem that the tester reads aloud. Answers are given orally on this subtest, but the student may use pencil and paper for computation.
- *Quantitative Concepts* (Supplemental). The student responds to oral questions concerning mathematics concepts. Items sample skills such as counting, understanding quantitative vocabulary, reading numerals, defining mathematical terms and symbols, and solving computational problems. Visuals accompany most test items.

Written Language

- *Dictation.* Items for young children include making marks, drawing lines, and writing individual letters. With older students, the test takes on a dictation format. Included are spelling items for which the tester dictates a word, capitalization items, and punctuation items for which the student writes the symbol for a punctuation mark. Usage items require knowledge of plural forms, comparatives, and superlatives.
- *Writing Samples.* This subtest is made up of a series of brief writing prompts to which the student responds. Early items only require one-word answers. On later items, students must write a complete sentence. Prompts vary in specificity and complexity. For example, in some items, the student must write a sentence describing a drawing; in others, a phrase must be expanded into a sentence or the student must write a sentence to complete a paragraph.
- *Proofing* (Supplemental). The student is shown a sentence or sentences with one error. After reading the passage silently, the student must locate the error and tell how to correct it. The tester may tell the student an occasional word but not an entire sentence. Like the Dictation subtest, this subtest contains items that assess punctuation and capitalization, spelling, and usage.
- *Writing Fluency* (Supplemental). Students are given 7 minutes to write sentences. Students

write to a series of prompts, each of which contains a drawing and three words. Sentences must describe the picture using the words provided.

Knowledge

- *Science.* The tester reads questions aloud, and the student replies orally. Drawings accompany some of the questions. Items sample general scientific knowledge, including aspects of biology, physics, and chemistry.
- *Social Studies.* Using the same format as the Science subtest, this measure assesses social sciences such as geography, political science, and economics.
- *Humanities.* Again, the same format is used to evaluate knowledge of art, music, and literature.

In addition to these subtests, it is also possible to obtain information about four other areas of Written Expression: Punctuation and Capitalization, Spelling, Usage, and Handwriting. This is accomplished through analysis of specific student responses on subtests such as Dictation and Proofing.

Three of the 14 achievement subtests on the *Woodcock-Johnson-R* are new to the 1989 edition: Writing Samples, Reading Vocabulary, and Writing Fluency. Also, Quantitative Concepts was recategorized as an achievement subtest; on the 1977 version of the *Woodcock-Johnson,* it was included as one of the tests of cognitive ability.

The relationships between *Woodcock-Johnson-R* achievement subtests are shown in Figure 7–3. Of the nine subtests in the standard battery, six are recommended for early childhood assessment. Within each academic area are two or more subskills that make up the broad skill. For example, reading is broken into Broad Reading, Basic Skills, and Comprehension. In selective testing, the two standard reading measures (Letter-Word Identification and Passage Comprehension) would be administered; then, if Basic Skills appeared to be a problem, the tester could choose to give the supplementary subtest Word Attack. Note that there are no supplementary subtests for the knowledge area.

Students must be able to attend to test tasks for several minutes at a time to participate in *Woodcock-Johnson-R* administration. English-language skills are a necessity (except for the Cal-

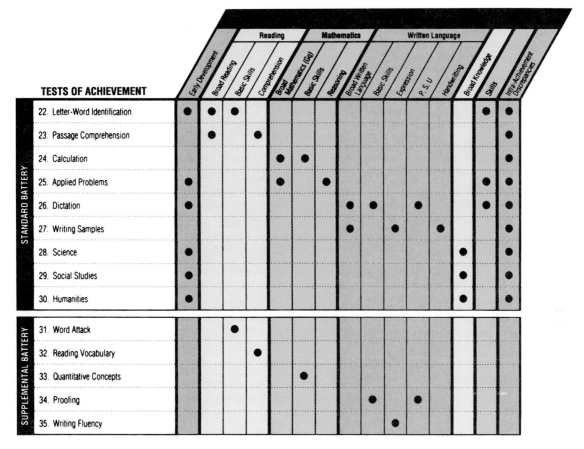

FIGURE 7-3

Selective Testing Table for the *Woodcock-Johnson-R Tests of Achievement*

Note: From *Woodcock-Johnson-Revised Tests of Achievement* by R. W. Woodcock and M. B. Johnson, 1989, Allen, TX: DLM Teaching Resources. Copyright 1989 by DLM Teaching Resources. Reprinted by permission.

culation subtest). However, a Spanish-language version of the *Woodcock-Johnson-R* battery, the *Batería Woodcock-Muñoz-Revisada* (Woodcock & Muñoz-Sandoval, 1996) is available.

Reading skills are required on the reading and written expression subtests. Students respond orally on 10 of the 14 subtests. Writing is required on Calculation and all written expression subtests except Proofing. The only subtest that is timed is Writing Fluency.

Technical Quality

The *Woodcock-Johnson-R* was standardized from 1986 to 1988 with a total of 6,359 subjects from more than 100 communities throughout the United States. The sample included preschool children ($n = 705$), students in grades K through 12 ($n = 3,245$), college students ($n = 916$), and adults not enrolled in secondary or postsecondary schools ($n = 1,493$). The sample was selected to resemble the national population on a range of variables such as geographic region, community size, sex, race, and Hispanic versus non-Hispanic origin; weighting procedures were used to assure that the sample distribution conformed to the population distribution on these variables.

Elementary and secondary grade students were randomly selected from the grade lists of general education classes. Students with severe disabilities were excluded unless they participated in mainstream classes. Also excluded were students with less than one year of experience in an English-speaking classroom environment.

The psychometric characteristics of the *Woodcock-Johnson-R* are reported in the *Woodcock-Johnson Technical Manual* (McGrew, Werder, & Woodcock, 1991). Several types of reliability were studied including split-half, test-retest, and interrater reliability; however, no information is provided on the alternate form reliability for the two forms of the *Tests of Achievement*. Internal consistency, as measured by the split-half method, appears adequate for all subtest and cluster scores on both Form A and Form B. The reliability of the timed Writing Fluency subtest was studied with test-retest rather than split-half methods. The median reliability coefficient for this subtest was .751 for Form A and .756 for Form B; on each form, coefficients fell below .80 for 14 of the 21 age groups studied. Test-retest reliability is adequate for standard battery subtest and cluster scores; no data are reported for supplementary battery subtests. Interrater reliability was studied for three of the achievement subtests: Writing Samples, Writing Fluency, and Handwriting. Coefficients fell at or above .80 for the writing subtests but ranged from .706 to .853 for Handwriting. Because of this, the manual recommends that two raters jointly score the handwriting measure.

Results of three studies of the *Woodcock-Johnson-R*'s concurrent validity with other measures of achievement are summarized in the technical manual. Across the three studies, moderate correlations were found between *Woodcock-Johnson-R* cluster scores and results of corresponding subtests on other measures. For example, correlations for the Broad Reading cluster were .883 with *PIAT-R* Total Reading and .573 to .865 with *WRAT-R* Reading. Those for the Broad Mathematics cluster were .688 with *PIAT-R* Mathematics and .641 to .705 with *WRAT-R* Arithmetic. Construct validity of the *Tests of Achievement* is supported by data showing systematic patterns of difference between samples of students identified as mentally retarded, learning disabled, normal, and gifted.

In general, the psychometric quality of the *Woodcock-Johnson-R* is quite high. However, results of the Writing Fluency and Handwriting subtests should be interpreted with caution due to

questions about reliability. Moreover, results of the two alternate forms of the test should not be considered equivalent until there are data to support this assumption.

Administration Considerations

The *Woodcock-Johnson-R* is designed for use by professionals trained in the administration and interpretation of individual tests. In learning this measure, testers should study the procedures for administration and scoring and should practice test administration under the supervision of an experienced examiner. Additional expertise is required for the interpretation of test results; professionals should be well grounded in measurement and curriculum and be thoroughly familiar with the range of scores available on the *Woodcock-Johnson-R*.

The achievement portion of the *Woodcock-Johnson-R* is quite easy to administer; instructions in the easel-style test notebooks are clear and complete. The first page of each subtest contains information on basal and ceiling rules and suggested starting points. Then each test page provides complete instructions for administration. What the tester should tell the student is highlighted in color. As needed, the tester is provided with a list of student responses that require questioning and the exact wording for queries. Test pages also provide pronunciation guides for difficult words.

The *Tests of Achievement* begin with standard introductory remarks that are read to all students. Then the tester selects the subtests to be administered. As Figure 7–3 illustrates, choices can be made from both the standard and the supplemental batteries based on the age of the student and the assessment questions under consideration.

Three of the standard battery subtests provide sample items. On the *Woodcock-Johnson-R,* recommended starting points are given by the student's estimated achievement level, not by actual grade placement. In some cases, starting points are based on performance on another subtest. For example, Writing Samples uses the student's raw score on Dictation to estimate the appropriate starting point; with students who earn raw scores of 7 or less on Dictation, Writing Samples is not administered and a score of 0 is assigned. Some of the supplementary subtests use similar rules, and testers must consider these carefully before selecting additional measures of deficit skill areas.

On most standard *Woodcock-Johnson-R* subtests, basals are established by success on six consecutively numbered items, and ceilings by six consecutive failures. On Writing Samples, there are no basals or ceilings as such; the range of items administered is determined by the student's Dictation raw score.

Rules for the supplemental subtests are somewhat more varied. The Word Attack subtest is always administered beginning with item 1. On Reading Vocabulary, the basal is four successes, and the ceiling four failures. Writing Fluency is a timed test; students begin with item 1 and continue writing for 7 minutes unless failure is obvious after the first 2 minutes of the test.

Testing on the *Woodcock-Johnson-R* proceeds in complete page units. Thus, if the student misses one of the first six items administered, the tester finishes giving the items on that test page before moving backward to the beginning of an earlier page. A similar procedure is used in establishing the ceiling.

During administration, the tester records the student's responses by writing a 1 for a correct answer and a 0 for an incorrect answer or no response. On the subtests in which the student writes on a separate answer sheet (Calculation, Dictation, Writing Samples, and Writing Fluency), the tester attempts to observe and score the student's responses as they are written. The test record form provides some space to record verbatim responses and notes about the student's test behavior.

Raw scores are calculated in the usual manner for *Woodcock-Johnson-R* achievement subtests. On the written expression subtests, scores can be determined for four additional skill areas. Student responses on the Dictation and Proofing subtests are analyzed to derive scores for Punctuation and Capitalization, Spelling, and Usage. A Handwriting score can be determined by analysis of the student's performance on Writing Samples. The manual provides specific scoring standards for Handwriting and for the Writing Samples and Writing Fluency subtests.

Proceeding from raw scores to final test results on the *Woodcock-Johnson-R* is a time-consuming process because of the number of scores this test produces. However, the test record form provides a shortcut for determining some types of scores. Next to the administration information for each subtest is a norms table that allows the tester to convert the student's raw score to an age and grade equivalent; a W score is also available, and its standard error of measurement is provided. These results can be plotted on an Age/Grade Profile, and the student's current age or grade can be compared with the W score confidence interval. However, the manual must be consulted to derive comparative scores such as percentile ranks and standard scores. The test-scoring program available from the publisher of the *Woodcock-Johnson-R* can greatly facilitate this process.

Results and Interpretation

Results of the *Woodcock-Johnson-R* academic tests can be reported by subtest, by academic areas (e.g., Broad Mathematics), and by subskills (e.g., Basic Mathematics and Mathematics Reasoning). More than 30 subtest and area results are produced, and each result can be expressed in a variety of scores: age equivalents, grade equivalents, standard scores, percentile ranks, and Relative Mastery Index (RMI) scores. Confidence intervals can be constructed around standard scores and percentile ranks. Standard scores are distributed with a mean of 100 and a standard deviation of 15. The *Woodcock-Johnson-R* features extended grade scores for individuals scoring below the average score obtained by kindergarten subjects or above the average score of grade 16.9 students. With extended grade scores, a superscript is added to the grade equivalent to denote percentile rank. Thus, grade K.0[10] would indicate performance at the 10th percentile of kindergarten students. Extended age scores are also available.

The RMI score contrasts the student's performance with that of others of the same grade placement or age. The RMI is stated as a fraction, the denominator of which is 90. The denominator indicates the percentage of mastery (90%) of average students. The numerator denotes the particular student's percentage of mastery. Thus,

---

Wechsler Individual Achievement Test (WIAT) (1992)

Type: Norm-referenced test

Major Content Areas: Reading, mathematics, spelling, written expression, listening comprehension, and oral expression

Type of Administration: Individual

Administration Time: 30–75 minutes (all subtests); 10–20 minutes (brief form)

Age/Grade Levels: Grades K through 12, ages 5-0 to 19-11

Types of Scores: Grade and age equivalents, standard scores, percentile ranks, stanines

Computer Aids: *Scoring Assistant for the Wechsler Scales* and *WISC-III Writer*

Typical Uses: A broad-based measure for identification of strengths and weaknesses in listening, speaking, and academic skills

Cautions: Special care is required when scoring the Reading Comprehension, Listening Comprehension, Oral Expression, and Written Expression subtests. Reliability falls below .80 for some subtests at some age/grade levels.

Publisher: Psychological Corporation (www.hbtpc.com)

---

an RMI of 25/90 indicates that when average students at the subject's age or grade level achieve 90% mastery, the subject would be expected to perform with 25% mastery.

Results of the *Woodcock-Johnson-R* can be plotted on a series of profiles to assist in interpretation. W scores are plotted in confidence intervals on the Age/Grade Profile to allow comparisons with the student's current age or grade. The Standard Score/Percentile Rank profile, also plotted in confidence intervals, compares student performance to that of age or grade peers in the norm group. Both types of profile are available for individual subtest scores and for broader area scores. In addition, procedures are available for comparing discrepancies in performance across achievement areas.

The *Woodcock-Johnson-R* appears to be a useful measure for the assessment of school performance across a wide range of academic areas and ages. However, as with similar broad-based assessment tools, its results are not specific enough to provide direction for instructional planning. Its purpose is the identification of skill areas in which students show poor performance

in relation to age or grade peers. One drawback of this test is the time required to score it, if other than age or grade scores are desired. Also, the interpretation process is complicated by the sheer number of scores and profiles produced.

WECHSLER INDIVIDUAL ACHIEVEMENT TEST

The *Wechsler Individual Achievement Test (WIAT)*, published in 1992, is an achievement measure designed to accompany the Wechsler tests of intellectual performance: the *Wechsler Preschool and Primary Scale of Intelligence-Revised* (Wechsler, 1989), the *Wechsler Intelligence Scale for Children-Third Edition* (Wechsler, 1991), and the *Wechsler Adult Intelligence Scale-Revised* (Wechsler, 1981). Its manual describes the *WIAT* as "a comprehensive individually administered battery for assessing the achievement of children who are in Grades K through 12" (p. 1). The *WIAT* can also be used as a screening instrument; in this application, only three of its subtests are administered.

The *WIAT* contains eight subtests. Two assess reading (Basic Reading, Reading Comprehension), two math (Numerical Operations, Mathematics Reasoning), two written language (Spelling, Written Expression), and two oral language (Listening Comprehension, Oral Expression). According to its manual, the *WIAT* is unique because it assesses all of the achievement areas included in the federal definition of learning disabilities: oral expression, listening comprehension, basic reading skills, reading comprehension, mathematics calculation, mathematics reasoning, and written expression. In addition, achievement results can be compared with results of one of the companion tests of intellectual performance to determine if a significant discrepancy exists; this feature is discussed in the next chapter and in Chapter 9 in relation to learning disabilities. The subtests of the *WIAT* are described in the following paragraphs.

- *Basic Reading.* In the first few items, the student looks at a drawing, then points to a word that labels the drawing, begins with the same sound, or ends with the same sound; the student chooses from four words. Later items require the student to read rows of words aloud.
- *Mathematics Reasoning.* In this subtest, the tester reads the items aloud; on most items, the student also sees the question or problem in sentence form. Drawings are included in some items, and the student is given paper and pencil for computations. Responses are oral. Items range from counting objects and simple addition to reading graphs and multistep problems involving fractions, volume, and area.
- *Spelling.* Here, the student writes letters and words to dictation. The student writes letters when given the letter name or the sound represented by a letter. On later items, the teacher reads a word aloud, then within the context of a sentence.
- *Reading Comprehension.* The student reads a short passage aloud or silently, then answers questions read aloud by the tester. The first few passages are illustrated with drawings.
- *Numerical Operations.* The student writes answers to mathematics computation problems in a separate Response Booklet. The first four

items are dictation; the tester reads the name of a number, and the student writes the numeral. Later problems range from one-digit addition and subtraction to operations with fractions, decimals, and algebraic equations.
- *Listening Comprehension.* This subtest begins with multiple-choice items; the tester reads a word and the student must point to one of four drawings that best depicts the word. In later items, the student looks at a drawing while the tester reads a story; the tester then asks a question about the story, and the student answers orally.
- *Oral Expression.* Here, the student must say the label of objects. As the student looks at a drawing of an object, the tester reads a definition aloud. Later items require the student to describe drawings, give directions, and explain how to perform tasks.
- *Written Expression.* The tester reads a description of a situation, and the student must write a response based on that situation within 15 minutes. The student writes in the separate Response Booklet.

Students must understand and speak English to participate in most *WIAT* subtests; five of the eight subtests require oral responses. Multiple-choice items are rare, and students respond by pointing only on the early items of two subtests: Basic Reading and Listening Comprehension. Writing is required on the two written language subtests as well as Numerical Operations; in addition, the student may use paper and pencil on the Mathematics Reasoning subtest. Reading skills are required only on the two reading subtests. The Written Expression subtest is timed; students are allowed 15 minutes to produce a writing sample.

Technical Quality

The *WIAT* was standardized with a sample of 4,252 children in grades K through 12 (ages 5 to 19). Both public and private school students were included, and approximately half of the students were male and half female. The sample was selected based on 1988 U.S. Census data, and the final sample appears to resemble the nation's population in terms of race/ethnicity, geographic region, and parents' educational levels (an index of socioeconomic status). According to the *WIAT* manual, students who did not understand or speak English were excluded; however, students with disabilities were included if they were "receiving mainstream special services in school settings" (p. 130). The *WIAT* manual reports that students with an identified learning disability, speech/language disorder, emotional disturbance, or physical disability made up 6% of the standardization sample; students identified as mildly mentally retarded or "borderline" accounted for another 1.4%.

The *WIAT* appears appropriate for kindergarten through grade 12 students who speak and understand English. Norms are based on a large national sample that represents the general U.S. population on several variables. In addition, the sample includes students with disabilities who receive at least a portion of their education in general education classrooms.

Three types of reliability were studied for the *WIAT*: internal consistency, test-retest, and interrater. Internal consistency was evaluated using the split-half method. Although split-half reliability is adequate across all grades and ages for composite scores, correlation coefficients dropped below the recommended minimum of .80 for some subtests. Most notable are the results for young students and those for students in several age/grade groups on the Numerical Operations, Listening Comprehension, and Written Expression subtests. For example, on Numerical Operations (fall administration), correlations ranged from .68 to .84 over all grades, with an average of .77; that average increased to .84 for spring administration. Reliability coefficients such as these cause the standard error of measurement to increase, thereby reducing the precision of test results.

Test-retest reliability is a concern for some *WIAT* subtests. The average correlation across grades was .76 for Listening Comprehension, .68 for Oral Expression, and .77 for Written Expression; that for the Language composite score was .78. In contrast, interrater reliability appears satisfactory for the four *WIAT* subtests in which scoring judgments are required; the only coefficient falling below .89 was that for Prompt 2 of the Written Expression subtest ($r = .79$).

The concurrent validity of the *WIAT* was studied by evaluating its relationship to other individual tests of achievement, group tests of achievement, school grades, and other measures. In general, results are quite positive. For example, *WIAT* results typically show correlations in the .70's and .80's with results of similar subtests of other individual tests. Correlations between the *WIAT* and *WRAT-R* range from .77 to .85; those between the *WIAT* and the *Woodcock-Johnson-R* range from .67 to .88. Relationships between *WIAT* results and school grades are also positive, although weaker. *WIAT* composite scores show correlations in the .40's for school grades in subjects such as reading, math, and spelling.

Administration Considerations

The *WIAT* manual says that professionals with "graduate-level training in the use of individually administered assessment instruments are qualified to administer the *WIAT* and interpret test results" (p. 6). Before using this test to gather data for educational decision making, however, the tester should practice both administration and scoring. Testers should pay special attention to the scoring guidelines provided for subtests in which judgment is required.

Although the scoring procedures require careful study, the *WIAT* is quite easy to administer. The testing materials include the manual, two stimulus books (in easel format), the Record Form (with a tear-out form for the student's responses on the Spelling subtest), and a separate Response Booklet for the Numerical Operations and Written Expression subtests. As with other tests using easels, the student and tester sit across the corner of a table from each other.

Subtests must be administered in the order they appear in the test easels and Record Form. It is possible to omit a subtest if the order is preserved. The Written Expression subtest is designed for students in grades 3 through 12; however, it may be omitted if the raw score on the Spelling subtest is 15 or lower. Reading Comprehension may be omitted if the raw score for Basic Reading is 8 or less. If the *WIAT* is used as a screening device, only three subtests are administered: Basic Reading, Mathematics Reasoning, and Spelling.

The tester begins each subtest by reading directions aloud to the student. The manual and Record Form list suggested starting points for each subtest based on the student's current grade placement. If there is indication that the student is performing below grade level, the starting point for the next lower grade can be used. On most subtests, the basal is five consecutively numbered correct responses. On Numerical Operations, problems are arranged in sets; if a student misses any problem in the first set administered, earlier sets are given until the student achieves a perfect score for a set. There are no basal rules for the last two subtests. All students begin Oral Expression with item 1 and there is only one test task on Written Expression.

Ceiling rules vary from subtest to subtest. The ceiling is six consecutive errors on Basic Reading and Spelling, five consecutive errors on Listening Comprehension, and four on Mathematics Reasoning and Reading Comprehension. Testing is discontinued on Numerical Operations when the student misses all of the problems within one set, and on Oral Expression when the student gives no answer for two consecutive items. Written Expression ends when the 15-minute time limit has elapsed.

The only timed subtest on the *WIAT* is Written Expression. However, time guidelines are provided for all subtests. For example, on Basic Reading, the student should require about 10 seconds to read each word. On the Listening Comprehension subtest, the tester reads a passage aloud to the student; that passage cannot be repeated. Two writing prompts are available for the Written Expression subtest, but only one is to be used during any one administration. The second prompt is provided for situations in which students are retested with the *WIAT*.

The *WIAT* Record Form is well designed, with ample room for recording students' responses. For each subtest, there are reminders of the time guidelines, basal (called the "reverse rule"), ceiling, and suggested starting points. On most subtests, the tester records a 1 if the item is correct and a 0 if it is incorrect. Scoring is straightforward on half of the subtests. However,

the four other subtests require that the tester use scoring criteria to rate students' responses. The manual (and stimulus books) provide guidelines for evaluating students' oral answers on Reading Comprehension, Listening Comprehension, and Oral Expression. Written Expression can be scored analytically or holistically; the procedures for each are described in the manual. In holistic scoring, the writing sample is rated on a scale of 1 to 6; this rating cannot be converted to derived scores such as standard scores. In analytic scoring, the writing sample is rated on six separate dimensions: ideas and development; organization, unity, and coherence; vocabulary; sentence structure and variety; grammar and usage; and capitalization and punctuation. The student receives a score of 1, 2, 3, or 4 on each dimension, and the scores are summed to yield the subtest raw score.

Results and Interpretation

The *WIAT* offers both age and grade norms. Grade norms are provided for fall, winter, and spring test administrations, but the manual cautions that age-based standard scores are required if the tester is interested in calculating aptitude-achievement discrepancies.

Subtest raw scores can be converted to a variety of derived scores including standard scores, percentile ranks, age and grade equivalents, and others. Standard scores are distributed with a mean of 100 and a standard deviation of 15. Confidence intervals can be constructed around standard scores; the tester can select either a 90% or a 95% confidence level.

The same types of scores are available for the *WIAT* composites. There are five composites: Reading, Mathematics, Language, Writing, and Total. The Reading composite raw score is computed by adding the raw scores of the two reading subtests: Basic Reading and Reading Comprehension. Likewise, the Mathematics composite is based on the two math subtests, the Language composite on the Listening Comprehension and Oral Expression subtests, and the Writing composite on Spelling and Written Expression. The Total composite reflects all eight subtests, except in the case of young children. In kindergarten, the Total composite includes the six subtests administered to this age group; in grades 1 and 2, it includes the seven subtests administered. The standard scores for *WIAT* composites are distributed with a mean of 100 and a standard deviation of 15. The first page of the *WIAT* record form, called the Summary, is detachable. On the front is space for identification information about the student and a table for recording the student's derived scores. The back contains a table used in analyzing ability-achievement discrepancies and a profile for plotting standard scores.

The Test Record is also designed to help professionals analyze the errors that students make. For example, on both math tests, there is a list of the skills assessed by each item. Checklists are provided on Basic Reading and Mathematics Reasoning to record the strategies used by the student when difficult words or problems were encountered. On spelling, the tester completes an error analysis grid to look for patterns in words with regular spellings, irregular words, and homophones. The *WIAT* manual discusses test items in terms of school curricula and suggests additional strategies for analysis of students' errors.

In summary, the *WIAT* appears to be a useful tool for assessing current school performance across a number of subject areas. These include reading (both decoding and comprehension), mathematics (both computation and problem solving), and written language (both spelling and composition). Unlike some measures, the *WIAT* does not assess science, social studies, or other content subjects. However, it does provide information about oral language, an area that is rarely assessed by individual achievement tests. Results of the *WIAT* are best used to identify school subjects in which the student shows poor performance in relation to age or grade peers.

OTHER INDIVIDUAL MEASURES OF ACADEMIC ACHIEVEMENT

Several other individual measures of academic achievement are available to the assessment team. One is the *Kaufman Test of Educational Achievement/Normative Update,* which is available in both brief and comprehensive forms. Another, the *Diagnostic Achievement Battery* (2nd

ed.), assesses spoken language as well as the basic school skills. The *Hammill Multiability Achievement Test,* a newer measure, assesses basic skills and general information. Also of interest are criterion-referenced tests of achievement, such as the *BRIGANCE*® *Diagnostic Comprehensive Inventory of Basic Skills-Revised,* although these are typically used in later stages of assessment to gather information for instructional planning.

Kaufman Test of Educational Achievement/Normative Update

The *Kaufman Test of Educational Achievement/ Normative Update (K-TEA/NU)* by Kaufman and Kaufman (1998) is an individual measure of academic performance for students ages 6-0 to 18-11 and grades 1 through 12. The Brief Form of the *K-TEA* takes 15 to 35 minutes to administer and includes three subtests: Mathematics, Reading, and Spelling. The Mathematics subtest contains written computation problems as well as application questions; the Reading subtest assesses both decoding and comprehension skills; and Spelling is a traditional dictation test. The reading comprehension task on the Brief *K-TEA/NU* is somewhat novel: the student reads a sentence, then follows the directions that the sentence provides (e.g., "Touch your right ear.").

The Comprehensive Form of this test requires about one hour to administer and offers five subtests:

- Mathematics Applications
- Reading Decoding
- Spelling
- Reading Comprehension
- Mathematics Computation

These subtests each contain a greater number of items than found in the Brief Form subtests. Also, the reading skills of decoding and comprehension are assessed in separate subtests, as are the mathematics skills of computation and applications.

The *K-TEA/NU* provides age and grade norms for fall and spring testing dates. Both forms offer standard scores and percentile ranks for each subtest and for a total test score called the Battery Composite. On the Comprehensive *K-TEA/NU,* two additional scores are available: Reading Composite and Mathematics Composite.

One feature of the *K-TEA/NU*'s scoring system is a systematic method for comparing results from subtest to subtest to determine whether significant differences exist. The tester computes the difference between the standard scores of two subtests, then consults a table to determine whether the observed difference is significant at the .05 level, significant at the .01 level, or not significant. If, for instance, a student's Mathematics score was found to be significantly different from his or her Spelling score at the .05 level, this would mean there was only a 5% chance that the observed difference was due to chance variation rather than being a true difference. The Comprehensive Form allows comparisons of global skills (e.g., Reading Composite versus Mathematics Composite) as well as within-skill comparisons (e.g., Reading Decoding versus Reading Comprehension).

Another important feature of the *K-TEA/NU* is the error analysis procedure offered on the Comprehensive Form. Every test item is keyed on the protocol to the specific skill category or the categories it assesses. For example, the Reading Decoding subtest has nine error categories, including prefixes and word beginnings, suffixes and word endings, and closed syllable (short) vowels. Reading Comprehension, in contrast, contains two types of questions: literal comprehension and inferential comprehension. Errors are noted by category and tabulated so that a student's performance can be compared to the average number of errors made by students in the same grade. These results are used to identify weak, average, and strong skill areas.

Diagnostic Achievement Battery (2nd ed.)

The *Diagnostic Achievement Battery* (2nd ed.) *(DAB-2)* by Newcomer (1990) is an individual achievement test for students ages 6-0 to 14-11. According to the manual, the *DAB-2* "can be used to assess children's abilities in listening, speaking, reading, writing, and mathematics" (p. 1). The test includes 12 subtests, although it is permissible to administer only a portion of these. Each subtest is designed to assess aspects of one area of achievement:

Achievement Area	*DAB-2 Subtest*
Listening	Story Comprehension
	Characteristics
Speaking	Synonyms
	Grammatic Completion
Reading	Alphabet/Word Knowledge
	Reading Comprehension
Writing	Punctuation
	Capitalization
	Spelling
	Written Composition
Math	Math Reasoning
	Math Calculation

Listening skills are assessed two ways. In the Story Comprehension subtest, the student listens to brief stories read by the tester and then answers questions about the stories. In the Characteristics subtest, the tester reads a statement ("All trees are oaks"), and the student must determine whether the statement is true or false. Speaking skills are also assessed two ways. The student must supply a synonym for the word presented by the tester in the Synonyms subtest. In Grammatic Completion, the tester reads unfinished sentences, and the student fills in the missing word. Among the grammatic forms assessed are plurals, possessives, and verb tenses.

Standard scores and percentile ranks are available for each *DAB-2* subtest. In addition, several composite scores can be determined. These include the Total Achievement Quotient, an index of overall test performance; quotients for each of the basic skill areas (listening, speaking, reading, writing, and mathematics); a Spoken Language Quotient (summarizing listening and speaking skills); and a Written Language Quotient (summarizing reading and writing skills).

Hammill Multiability Achievement Test

The *Hammill Multiability Achievement Test (HAMAT)* by Hammill, Hresko, Ammer, Cronin, and Quinby (1998) is an easy-to-use measure of basic academic skills. Designed for students ages 7-0 to 17-11, the *HAMAT* provides two alternate forms:

Form A and Form B. The *HAMAT* was developed in conjunction with a measure of intellectual performance, the *Hammill Multiability Intelligence Test (HAMIT)* (Hammill, Bryant, & Pearson, 1998).

Four subtests are included on the *HAMAT:*

- Reading
- Writing
- Arithmetic
- Facts

A novel task is used to assess reading skills. Students read brief passages and, in each passage, three sentences are incomplete. In place of one of the words in the original sentence is a bracket enclosing four words in bold type. The student must select the word that correctly completes the sentence. In the Writing subtest, the student writes sentences from dictation; spelling, capitalization, and punctuation must be correct for the student to receive credit. In Arithmetic, the student writes answers to computation problems and, in Facts, he or she answers questions related to school subjects such as science, social studies, and language arts.

Reading is required only on the Reading subtest. In Facts, the tester reads the questions to the student. The student writes sentences in Spelling, writes answers to computation problems in Arithmetic, and circles words in Reading. Subtests are not timed. The *HAMAT* can be administered in 30 minutes to 1 hour, depending upon the individual student.

Only age norms are available. Quotients (i.e., standard scores) are available for each subtest along with age equivalents, grade equivalents, and percentile ranks. A total test score, the General Achievement Quotient, is based upon performance on all subtests. Quotients are distributed with a mean of 100 and a standard deviation of 15. The *HAMAT* manual also provides tables for comparing differences between subtest scores (e.g., Reading versus Writing) and for comparing the total test score with results of measures of intellectual performance.

Criterion-Referenced Tests

The purpose of criterion-referenced tests is evaluation of student performance in relation to specific instructional objectives. Test items are tied to objectives, so results are immediately applicable to instructional planning. However, because criterion-referenced tests are designed to thoroughly assess mastery of specific skills and subskills, they typically take a long time to administer. The detailed information they provide, although very appropriate for instructional decisions, is not the type of information needed for eligibility decisions. Therefore, criterion-referenced measures are most often used in the later stages of assessment to pinpoint specific skills for instruction. But if criterion-referenced test results are available for a student referred for special education assessment, the team should consider these data in its study of the student's current levels of school performance.

Perhaps the most popular set of criterion-referenced tests is the Brigance series. Although they are called inventories, these measures are CRTs based upon instructional objectives. The series includes tests for early childhood, the elementary grades, and the secondary grades as well as a Spanish-language version for grades K through 8 and versions designed for students in secondary or postsecondary vocational programs.

The elementary version has recently been revised. Called the *BRIGANCE®* *Comprehensive Inventory of Basic Skills-Revised (CIB-R)* (Brigance, 1999), its tests are clustered into five major areas:

- Readiness
- Oral Language
- Reading
- Writing
- Mathematics

Overall, the *CIB-R* contains more than 150 separate criterion-referenced tests. As the test book states, the *CIB-R* "is much too extensive to administer in its entirety" (p. xii).

A feature of this new edition is that some tests have been standardized. The technical manual (Glascoe, 1999) or scoring software can be used to determine standard scores, percentile ranks, grade equivalents, and age equivalents for all Readiness tests (ages 5-0 to 6-6+) and 10 tests of academic skills (ages 6-0 to 13-0) tests in reading and math. Norms are available for ages 5-0 to 6-6+ (readiness) and 6-0 to 13-0 (reading and math).

CURRICULUM-BASED MEASUREMENT STRATEGIES

As Chapter 6 explained, curriculum-based measurement is a method of evaluating student performance using the school curriculum as the standard of comparison. It differs from formal tests because "the stimulus material that provides the occasion for student responses is the actual curriculum of the local school rather than a set of independent items or problems created by commercial test developers" (Deno & Fuchs, 1988, p. 483). According to Tucker (1985), "In curriculum-based assessment the essential measure of success in education is the student's *progress in the curriculum* of the local school" (p. 199).

Curriculum-based measurement is most useful for gathering information for instructional decisions. According to Blankenship (1985), there are three stages in the teaching process when curriculum-based measures provide important data: (a) at the planning stage before instruction begins, (b) immediately after instruction to determine whether mastery has occurred, and (c) periodically throughout the year to evaluate long-term retention. Curriculum-based measures have been shown to be valid, sensitive to pupil growth, and cost-effective (Marston & Magnusson, 1985).

It has also been suggested that curriculum-based measurement is a useful strategy in gathering information for decisions about pupil eligibility for services such as special education. Deno (1985) describes a simple procedure for peer referencing of curriculum-based measures. To obtain classroom or grade level "norms," the measure is administered to general education students; their average performance on the curricular task is then used as the standard for evaluating the performance of an individual student. In one example provided by Deno (1985), an individual sixth grader was reading from 30 to 55 words per minute, whereas the average rate for grade 6 students was 120 words per minute.

Curriculum-based measures do discriminate between successful members of general education classes and those with achievement problems. Marston and Magnusson (1985) compared general education, Title I, and special education students on the number of words read correctly;

general education students were superior to the other two groups. Peterson, Heistad, Peterson, and Reynolds (1985) used a cutoff score on reading and math curriculum-based measures to discriminate between achievers and nonachievers; 100% of the special education students studied fell below the 20th percentile cutoff on one or both measures, whereas 89% of general education students fell above the 20th percentile on both reading and math.

Results of curriculum-based measures can add to the data base that the assessment team assembles to determine whether a student shows poor school performance. Measures can be peer referenced with norms based on one classroom, a grade level within a school, or an entire district; or the assessment tool can stand by itself, with the curriculum as the standard of comparison. The resulting information is best used in eligibility decisions as an indicator of the magnitude of the school performance problem. In the prereferral stage, for example, curriculum-based measures can help teachers not only identify students who are not responding to instruction, but also evaluate the effects of instructional modifications introduced in the regular classroom.

However, curriculum-based measurement is most valuable as one source of information for planning and monitoring instruction. As Blankenship (1985) suggests, data from curriculum-based measures can be used in the IEP process to "(a) summarize a student's present levels of performance, (b) suggest appropriate goals and objectives, and (c) document pupil progress" (p. 238).

ANSWERING THE ASSESSMENT QUESTIONS

The assessment team gathers information about the student's academic achievement to determine current levels of school performance. One major concern in the assessment of any skill or ability is the technical adequacy of the measurement tool. Measures of academic achievement should be selected for use only after careful consideration of the evidence supporting their reliability and validity. Results should be interpreted with caution, with the measure's limitations kept firmly in mind.

Two other factors that are important in evaluating assessment results are the types of procedures used in data collection and the nature of the assessment tasks.

Types of Procedures

Many types of procedures are used to gather information about school performance: group and individual measures, norm-referenced and criterion-referenced tests, curriculum-based measures, school record reviews, observations, work sample analyses, questionnaires, and interviews of informants. Each of these methods is likely to produce somewhat different results, because each approaches the question of current school performance from a different perspective.

Group tests of academic achievement generally underestimate school performance abilities of students with academic difficulties. Group tests depend heavily upon reading skills and independent work skills—two areas in which lower-performing students tend not to excel. Individual measures tend to produce more accurate estimates of current performance and permit the sampling of a broader range of student skills. Therefore, they are preferred in special education.

Norm-referenced measures provide the most appropriate type of results for determining the existence and severity of a school performance problem. Although criterion-referenced measures are superior in describing specific instructional needs, norm-referenced test results tell where the student's performance falls in relation to other students. Such data are necessary for legal decisions such as eligibility for special education services.

Test results must be confirmed with information about how the student is coping with the demands of the current instructional environment. School records provide historical data and may contain current report card grades. School grades are one index of school performance, although they may be based upon subjective criteria and provide little information about a student's standing in relation to peers. Classroom observations and analyses of student work samples add de-

scriptive data about specific student actions and responses. If considered in relationship to the teacher's expectations and the standards for classroom performance, such data may corroborate school grades and test results. Curriculum-based measures also serve to document academic difficulties, particularly if their results reflect peer performance standards as well as curricular goals. Judgmental information is available from informants who are knowledgeable about the student's current school performance. Parents, teachers, and others have observed the student over long periods of time, forming opinions about the student's academic competence. The student can also provide information.

Nature of the Assessment Tasks

Assessment techniques differ in the ways they attempt to measure academic skills. There are obvious differences between group and individual administration, criterion-referenced standards and norm-referenced standards, and direct measures and techniques using informants. What may be less obvious are the variations among the individual norm-referenced tests commonly used to assess achievement.

Comprehensiveness. This concern relates to the number of academic skills assessed and the breadth of coverage within each skill area. For example, a test may say that it measures mathematics skills, but it may limit coverage to simple computation. Of the four major achievement tests described in this chapter, the *WRAT3* is clearly the least comprehensive.

All four measures assess reading recognition skills, math computation, and spelling. Reading comprehension, mathematical problem solving, and written expression are added by the *PIAT-R/NU,* the *Woodcock-Johnson-R,* and the *WIAT.* Only the *WIAT* includes measures of listening and speaking; only the *PIAT-R/NU* and the *Woodcock-Johnson-R* assess content area knowledge. All four tests require written responses, allowing analysis of the student's handwriting. Areas covered only by the *Woodcock-Johnson-R* are reading nonsense words and knowledge of word meanings, punctuation, capitalization, and English usage.

Test Tasks. The ways that skill areas are assessed differ from measure to measure. Task characteristics such as timing factors, type of question, presentation mode, and response mode may influence student performance. Also, some test tasks approximate typical classroom activities, whereas others do not.

The methods used by the *PIAT-R/NU,* the *WRAT3,* the *Woodcock-Johnson-R,* and the *WIAT* to assess reading recognition are very similar. The test task is oral reading of isolated words. However, test tasks for reading comprehension are quite different. The *Woodcock-Johnson-R* uses a cloze procedure; the student reads a passage with a word omitted and then attempts to supply the missing word. On the *PIAT-R/NU,* the student reads a passage and then selects the drawing that best illustrates the meaning of the sentence. Neither of these tasks resembles typical classroom reading comprehension activities. The task on the *WIAT* is much closer: the student reads a passage, then answers questions about it.

In Spelling, the *WRAT3,* the *WIAT,* and the *Woodcock-Johnson-R* Dictation subtest use a written test format. This task should be familiar to most students because it is routinely used in classroom assessment. On the *PIAT-R/NU,* spelling items are multiple choice and do not require writing. The student must differentiate between the correctly spelled word and three misspelled versions. This is a recognition task, whereas written spelling is a recall task. The Proofing subtest of the *Woodcock-Johnson-R* assesses the proofreading skills of error detection and correction, and is much more realistic than the *PIAT-R/NU* task.

Math computation is evaluated by written tests on the *WRAT3,* the *WIAT,* and the *Woodcock-Johnson-R* Calculation subtest. This format is often used in classroom practice activities and quizzes; most adults also solve computation problems with paper and pencil (or with calculators). The *PIAT-R/NU* again presents multiple-choice questions.

The *PIAT-R/NU,* the *WIAT,* and the *Woodcock-Johnson-R* assess composition skills. The writing task for older students on the *PIAT-/NU* is quite open-ended. Students must write a story that describes a stimulus picture. The *WIAT* uses a similar format. The *Woodcock-Johnson-R,* in contrast, provides a variety of prompts designed to elicit brief, one-sentence writing samples. On the Writing Samples subtest, students write sentences to describe a drawing, expand a phrase, or complete a paragraph. On the Writing Fluency subtest, students write sentences in response to prompts containing a drawing and three words.

Content area knowledge is assessed by the *PIAT-R/NU* and the *Woodcock-Johnson-R.* The *Woodcock-Johnson-R* contains three knowledge subtests, whereas the *PIAT-R/NU* combines all content area questions into one subtest, General Information. The test format is the same across the four subtests: The tester asks a question and the student answers orally.

An important difference between the *PIAT-R/NU* and the other tests is the *PIAT-R/NU*'s use of multiple-choice questions. This is both a strength and a limitation. Because the *PIAT-R/NU* bypasses writing skills on its Spelling and Mathematics subtests, it is a more appropriate measure of these subjects for students with severe writing disabilities or those with physical disabilities that impede writing. However, writing is integral to classroom spelling and mathematics tasks and to the use of these skills in adult life. Also, with multiple-choice questions, students are not asked to recall information, only to recognize it. If one of the concerns in assessment is classroom performance in either spelling or mathematics, measures requiring recall of information and written responses should be administered in place of or in addition to the *PIAT-R/NU.*

One of the major differences between the *WRAT3* and the other measures is its imposition of time limits. All test tasks on the *WRAT3* are timed. Speed requirements may penalize students who work accurately but slowly. However, classroom success usually depends on both speed and accuracy, particularly in the upper elementary grades and beyond.

Motivational Factors. In addition to comprehensiveness of content and the methods used to assess skills, tests may vary in their appeal to the student. For students with a history of school failure, tests that look like school tasks may seem demanding, difficult, or even forbidding. The

PIAT-R/NU, the *WIAT,* and the *Woodcock-John-son-R* appear less threatening than many, because they are in easel format and the test pages include drawings in addition to words and numbers. In contrast, the *WRAT3* test form gives every appearance of schoolwork. The first page contains three columns of blank lines to write spelling words, the middle pages are covered with math computation problems, and the last page is filled with rows of reading words. In addition, the *WRAT3* imposes stringent ceiling rules. For example, the student must misspell 10 words in a row before the Spelling subtest is discontinued. Prolonging a failure experience to this extent may affect the student's willingness to attempt other test tasks.

Documentation of School Performance

The assessment question that guides the team in its study of the student's academic functioning is this: *Is there a school performance problem?* The team determines the student's current levels of achievement in important school subjects and decides whether there are apparent strengths and weaknesses in the various areas of learning. To do this, the team gathers information from many different sources.

Usually the team will examine past records including group test data, interview the student's parents and teachers, observe and possibly interview the student, and administer an individual test of academic achievement. In some cases, a second individual test will be used to add to or help corroborate the results of the first. The team must also gather evidence that the student's academic difficulty is evident in the classroom, not just on standardized tests. Usually this is not an issue, because poor classroom performance is often the reason for the original referral. However, the team must try to explain any discrepancies between teacher reports and test results.

In its review of assessment results, the team attempts to describe the student's current levels of academic performance. At this point in the assessment process, these descriptions focus on the student's standing in relation to others. This type of interpretation was used to evaluate the assessment information gathered about Joyce, the

fourth grader introduced at the beginning of the chapter.

Joyce

Joyce has been referred for special education assessment by Mr. Harvey, her fourth grade teacher, because she is having difficulty with reading, spelling, and handwriting tasks. Her parents are also concerned, and they have given their permission for assessment.

The assessment team begins by reviewing Joyce's school records. She had taken a group achievement test in third grade at her previous school, and her reading and spelling scores fell between the 20th and 30th percentiles. Joyce's school grades have been average, and she has never been retained or referred for special services. She began kindergarten at her previous school, making this only the second school she has attended in 5 years.

Ms. Gale, the special education resource teacher, administers the *Peabody Individual Achievement Test-Revised/Normative Update* to Joyce. On the *PIAT-R/NU,* Joyce scores within the average range on General Information and Mathematics, the low average range in Reading Recognition and Reading Comprehension, and the below average to low average range in Spelling. Joyce's performance on Level II of the Written Expression subtest falls within the low average to average range (developmental scaled score 5); her printing was difficult to read and she made numerous spelling errors. Her overall performance in written language (Written Language Composite) falls within the low average range. (See Figure 7–1 for Joyce's *PIAT-R/NU* results.)

To confirm these test results, portions of the *Wechsler Individual Achievement Test* and the *Woodcock-Johnson Psycho-Educational Battery-Revised* are administered. Joyce's performance on the written spelling test of the *WIAT* also indicates achievement in the below average range. She printed the spelling words, and her letters were large, poorly spaced, and difficult to read. On the *Woodcock-Johnson-R,* Joyce scores within the low average range in Broad Reading. The reports of Joyce's teacher and parents agree with the team's test results. In the general education classroom, Joyce is placed in a beginning third grade reading book and a second grade spelling program. She is learning cursive writing but continues to print most of her assignments. At home, she likes to look at the pictures in her favorite storybooks but is unable to read most of the words. Last summer, when Joyce was on vacation, she wrote postcards to her friends, but her father helped her spell many of the words.

In its review of these results, the assessment team has concluded that Joyce is an average achiever in mathematics with probable school performance problems in reading, spelling, and handwriting. The team will continue assessment to determine whether Joyce's academic deficiencies are related to a disability.

STUDY GUIDE

REVIEW QUESTIONS

1. Read these statements and tell whether they are true or false.
   _____ a. The major concern in the assessment of school performance is academic achievement.
   _____ b. Students must show a school performance problem to be eligible for special education services.
   _____ c. When a general education teacher is concerned about a student's school performance, the teacher's first step is referral for special education assessment.
2. What are two reasons for assessing school performance?
3. Check *each* of the assessment devices and procedures that can be used to document school performance.
   _____ a. Classroom observations
   _____ b. Standardized tests
   _____ c. Personality measures
   _____ d. Group and individual achievement tests
   _____ e. Criterion-referenced measures
   _____ f. IQ tests
   _____ g. Interviews with parents, teachers, and students
   _____ h. Review of school records
4. Which of these statements is true?
   a. In the 1970s, public concern over the state of American education led to the back-to-basics movement.
   b. In the 1980s, the excellence in education movement stressed achievement in traditional content area subjects, not basic literacy skills.
   c. Current school improvement efforts involve school restructuring, standards-based reform, and alternative assessment.
   d. All of the above statements are true.
5. Find the best description of current practices in special education assessment of school performance.
   a. Only group tests are used.
   b. Only individually administered tests are used.
   c. Both group and individual measures are used, but individual tests are preferred.
   d. Both group and individual measures are used, but group tests are preferred.
6. What are two of the factors in group testing that may affect how well students with disabilities perform?

7. Match the assessment device or procedure in Column A with the description in Column B.

Column A	*Column B*
a. Review of school records	_____ The best source of information about the student's ability to use academic skills at home and in the community
b. Teacher interviews	_____ An individual achievement test for ages 5 through adult that assesses reading recognition, spelling, and arithmetic skills
c. Parent interviews	_____ A test system that includes measures of cognitive performance as well as academic achievement tests
d. *Peabody Individual Achievement Test-Revised/Normative Update*	_____ A standardized measure of reading, spelling, and mathematics with both a brief and a comprehensive form
e. *Wide Range Achievement Test-Revision 3*	_____ An individual measure that offers tests of reading comprehension, written expression, and general information
f. *Woodcock-Johnson Psycho-Educational Battery-Revised*	_____ The best source of data about the types of instructional modifications effective in improving classroom performance
g. *Wechsler Individual Achievement Test*	_____ A strategy for finding out about the student's past grades, attendance history, and other historical data
h. *Kaufman Test of Educational Achievement/Normative Update*	_____ An individual achievement test that includes measures of listening and speaking

8. Which score interpretation is *not* accurate?
   a. A standard score of 109 on the *PIAT-R/NU* indicates performance in the average range.
   b. A standard score of 89 on the *WIAT* indicates performance in the low average range.
   c. A standard score of 76 on the *WRAT3* indicates performance in the low average range.
   d. A standard score of 135 on the *Woodcock-Johnson-R* indicates performance in the above average range.

9. Tests with similar purposes such as the *PIAT-R/NU* and the *WRAT3* contain similar assessment tasks. (True or False)

10. If the special education assessment team finds that a student's current school achievement falls within the below average range of performance, which of the following conclusions can be drawn?
   a. The student is eligible for special education services.
   b. The student is not eligible for special education services.
   c. The student has school performance problems, and assessment should continue.
   d. The student has school performance problems that should be handled in the general education classroom.

ACTIVITIES

1. Review several group achievement tests. Compare the school subjects they assess, the time required for administration, and the scores.
2. Work with a peer to develop a parent checklist about children's use of academic skills at home and in the community.

3. Under the supervision of the course instructor, administer one of the individual achievement tests described in this chapter. Calculate all possible scores and analyze the results.
4. Design an interview procedure to determine students' perceptions about their school performance.
5. Visit the website of the publisher of the *PIAT-R/NU, Woodcock-Johnson-R,* or *WIAT*. What types of information does the publisher provide about the test? Are psychometric characteristics such as reliability and validity discussed?

DISCUSSION QUESTIONS

1. Debate the relative merits of group achievement tests and individually administered achievement tests for students with school performance problems.
2. Identify the subject matter areas usually assessed by individual achievement tests. Explain why these tests tend to include basic skills rather than content area subjects.
3. Compare and contrast the *PIAT-R/NU,* the *WRAT3,* the *WIAT,* and the *Woodcock-Johnson-R.* For what purposes and with what types of students are each of these measures best used?
4. Explain how informal assessment procedures such as record reviews and teacher and parent interviews help in answering questions about overall school performance.
5. Discuss the purposes of curriculum-based measurement and the best uses of this technique for eligibility and instructional decisions.

LEARNING APTITUDE

When students perform poorly in school, educators are interested in finding out why. One explanation for school performance problems is disabilities such as mental retardation, behavioral disorders, and learning disabilities. To determine whether a disability is influencing school learning, the assessment team begins to gather information about the student's current functioning in several major domains. One of these is general aptitude for learning.

General aptitude is important to consider in the assessment of students with poor school performance. Some students with disabilities show below average general aptitude and, as a consequence, below average school achievement. Others achieve poorly in school despite average potential for learning.

When students are referred for special education assessment, the team may begin by evaluating current school performance. If an achievement problem is documented, the team moves to a study of the student's cognitive and behavioral characteristics. The assessment question being addressed at such a point is this: *Is the school performance problem related to a disability?*

The team typically starts to investigate the possibility of a disability by evaluating general learning aptitude. The assessment of learning aptitude is traditionally associated with standardized measures of intellectual performance,

known also as intelligence (IQ) tests. However, general aptitude for learning can also be estimated by assessing adaptive behavior—the student's ability to adapt to and comply with environmental demands. Thus, the team is able to pose more specific questions: *What is the student's current level of intellectual performance? What is the student's current functioning level in adaptive behavior?*

At this level of questioning, the major goal is to obtain a global picture of the student's aptitude. In the process of investigation, however, the team may note indications of specific strengths and weaknesses. Consider the case of Joyce.

Joyce

Joyce, a student in Mr. Harvey's fourth grade class, has been referred for special education assessment. The team began by investigating Joyce's current school performance, and results of individual achievement tests suggested low to below average achievement in reading, spelling, and handwriting.

Next the team will assess Joyce's general aptitude for learning. Mental retardation is not suspected, because Joyce appears to be able to learn some types of material quite easily. For example, her mathematics performance is average for her age and grade.

Individualized Assessment Plan

For:	*Joyce Dewey*	*4*	*10-0*	*12/1/00*	*Ms. Gale*
	Student's Name	Grade	Age	Date	Coordinator

Reason for Referral: Difficulty keeping up with fourth grade work in reading, spelling, and handwriting.

Assessment Question	*Assessment Procedure*	*Person Responsible*	*Date/Time*
What is the student's current level of intellectual performance?	Interview with Mr. Harvey, Joyce's fourth grade teacher	Ms. Gale, Resource Teacher	12/6/00, 3:30 p.m.
	Review of Joyce's school records	Ms. Kellett, School Psychologist	12/5/00, 9 a.m.
	Wechsler Intelligence Scale for Children-Third Edition	Ms. Kellett, School Psychologist	12/12/00, 9 a.m.

Other disabilities remain a possibility, so the school psychologist will administer an individual test of intellectual performance, the *Wechsler Intelligence Scale for Children–Third Edition*. The results of this measure, along with the data gathered in reviews of school records and interviews with Joyce's classroom teacher, will assist the team in studying the relationship between poor school performance and possible disabilities.

CONSIDERATIONS IN ASSESSMENT OF LEARNING APTITUDE

Learning aptitude refers to an individual's capacity for altering behavior when presented with new information or experiences. Learning aptitude is required in many environments, and the classroom is only one example. Thus, general learning aptitude is assessed to gain a better understanding of the student's ability to cope with the demands of the instructional and other environments that require changes in behavior.

Purposes

General learning aptitude is a concern in the identification of several different disabilities. The disability most directly related to learning aptitude is mental retardation. It was defined in 1983 by the American Association on Mental Retardation as "significantly subaverage general intellectual functioning existing concurrently with deficits in adaptive behavior and manifested during the developmental period" (Grossman, 1983, p. 1). This definition—the one used in federal law—conceptualizes retardation as a developmental phenomenon that becomes apparent during childhood. It identifies two important indicators of mental retardation: below average intellectual performance and impaired adaptive behavior.

In 1992, the American Association on Mental Retardation revised its definition of mental retardation:

> *Mental retardation* refers to substantial limitations in present functioning. It is characterized

by significantly subaverage intellectual functioning, existing concurrently with related limitations in two or more of the following applicable adaptive skill areas: communication, self-care, home living, social skills, community use, self-direction, health and safety, functional academics, leisure, and work. Mental retardation manifests before age 18. (p. 1)

The major change in the definition was its requirement for limitations in at least two areas of adaptive skills.

Intelligence is a complex construct, and there have been many attempts to define it. According to Wechsler (1974), the author of several measures of intellectual functioning, intelligence is "the overall capacity of an individual to understand and cope with the world around him" (p. 5). In assessment, intellectual functioning is operationalized as performance on standardized tests of intelligence. Such measures claim to assess reasoning abilities, learning skills, and problem-solving abilities. However, most intelligence tests are essentially measures of verbal abilities and skills in dealing with numbers and other abstract symbols (Anastasi & Urbina, 1997). Because these skills and abilities are required in school learning, tests of intelligence are best viewed as measures of scholastic, not general, aptitude.

Adaptive skills are related to both personal independence and social responsibility (American Association on Mental Retardation, 1992). According to the 1983 AAMR definition, adaptive behavior is "the effectiveness or degree with which individuals meet the standards of personal independence and social responsibility expected for age and cultural group" (Grossman, 1983, p. 1). Expected adaptive behavior varies with the age of the individual. Preschool children are expected to learn to walk, talk, and interact with family members. School-aged children are expected to widen their circle of acquaintances and add academic skills to their repertoire. In addition, cultural and linguistic factors must be considered when assessing an individual's adaptive skills.

A student's adaptive behavior can be assessed by direct observation. Because this would be a time-consuming process, it is more usual to rely upon information provided by informants such as parents, teachers, and others who know the student well.

Both intelligence tests and measures of adaptive behavior seek to determine how well the student can adapt to and cope with environmental demands. However, these devices assess different environments. Tests of intellectual performance relate to the academic demands of school, whereas adaptive behavior measures look at performance in nonschool environments that require personal care, communication, social, civic, and vocational skills. By looking at both of these dimensions, it is possible to derive a more global picture of the student's current aptitude for learning.

In mental retardation, intellectual performance must be below average, *and* there must be two or more deficits in adaptive behavior. Poor scores on tests of intelligence are not sufficient evidence to support the identification of retardation. The individual must also be unable to meet age level expectations in important areas of adaptive behavior.

General learning aptitude is also a concern with other disabilities. In learning disabilities and behavioral disorders, the possibility of mental retardation must be ruled out. Thus, intelligence tests are used to gather evidence of average potential for learning. In addition, a major criterion for learning disabilities is a discrepancy between expected and actual achievement. Tests of intellectual performance provide the basis for predicting expected achievement. Assessment of adaptive behavior is less usual with learning disabilities and behavioral disorders, even though it can provide important information about the student's ability to cope with nonscholastic environments.

Issues and Trends

Intelligence testing has engendered more controversy than any other area in assessment. The issues raised by the intelligence testing debate concern the nature and definition of intelligence, the relative contributions of heredity and environment to intellectual performance, the usefulness and accuracy of IQ tests, and the appropriateness of these measures for members of diverse ethnic, cultural, and linguistic groups

(Ebel, 1977; Herrnstein, 1971; Holtzman & Wilkinson, 1991; Jones, 1988b; Perrone, 1977; Tyler, 1969; Valenzuela & Cervantes, 1998).

One factor underlying the controversies is a basic misunderstanding of the purpose of intelligence tests. Measurement of current intellectual performance has become confused with measurement of innate potential. Intelligence tests do not assess potential; they sample behaviors already learned in an attempt to predict future learning. They are built upon the premise that current performance is an indicator of future performance. Individuals who have learned from their environment and are able to perform certain tasks are assumed able to continue learning and achieving. Robinson and Robinson (1976) commented that intelligence tests "seem to measure with reasonable accuracy about half of what we need to know to predict how well individuals will do in school. This is, of course, what they were designed to do" (p. 22).

The use of intelligence tests in special education drew heated criticism in the 1970s, particularly in relation to the placement of culturally and linguistically diverse students. The major issue was the finding that special classes for students with mental retardation contained disproportionate numbers of students from diverse groups (Jones & Wilderson, 1976; Mercer, 1973). This overrepresentation was attributed to many factors, including reliance on only IQ scores for special education placement and the cultural loadings of intelligence measures.

In addition, the practice of administering English-language tests of intelligence to students whose primary language was not English resulted in lawsuits such as *Diana v. The State Board of Education* (1970, 1973) and *Guadalupe v. Tempe Elementary School District* (1972). Other litigation charged that intelligence tests were culturally biased and therefore discriminated against members of diverse groups (*Larry P. v. Riles,* 1972, 1979, 1984; *Parents in Action on Special Education v. Joseph P. Hannon,* 1980). The courts clearly supported the use of tests in the child's own language. However, test bias decisions have been contradictory. In the *Larry P.* case, it was ruled that intelligence tests are culturally biased and must not be used to assess African American students for possible placement in classes for students with mild mental retardation; in the *Parents in Action* case, the court held that intelligence tests are not racially or culturally biased.

In the mid-1970s, legislative action was taken in an attempt to address the concerns about intelligence testing held by professionals, parents of students identified as disabled, and others. The Education for All Handicapped Children Act of 1975 contained two major provisions to safeguard against testing abuses. The first was its adoption of the American Association on Mental Retardation definition of mental retardation. In this definition, mental retardation is identified by concurrent deficits in intellectual performance and adaptive behavior. Social adaptation has long been of interest to professionals in the field of mental retardation (Cegelka & Prehm, 1982). However, the need to consider nonscholastic performance was underscored by the findings of Mercer (1973) and others that some students who were labeled mentally retarded in school performed quite adequately at home and in their community.

The second major provision of federal law is a set of procedures for special education assessment. These procedures, described in detail in Chapter 3, require that testing be conducted in the language of the student, that measures be nondiscriminatory and validated for the purpose for which they are used, and that no single test score be the sole basis for determining special education placement.

Today, school systems and professional educators are aware of clear guidelines for the appropriate use of intelligence tests in special education assessment. That is not to say that procedures mandated by law are followed in all instances or that all questions about intelligence testing have been answered. Debate continues over measures of intellectual performance, their proper use, and social consequences (Bersoff, 1981; Carroll & Horn, 1981; Geisinger, 1992; Helms, 1992; Reschly, 1981; Scarr, 1981; Winzer & Mazurek, 1998).

The study of intelligence also continues. For example, Sternberg (1984b) has proposed a theory of intelligence with implications for the development of better, or at least more compre-

hensive, measures of intellectual performance. In Sternberg's theory, human intelligence is conceptualized in terms of the individual's mental mechanisms for processing information, the tasks or situations that involve the use of intelligence, and the sociocultural context in which the individual lives (Sternberg, Okagaki, & Jackson, 1990). Gardner (1987), in contrast, describes seven types of intelligence: linguistic, logical-mathematical, spatial, musical, bodily-kinesthetic, interpersonal, and intrapersonal. Such theories may revolutionize not only the way educators conceptualize intelligence but also the way they assess it.

Current Practices

Assessment of general learning aptitude takes place in both general and special education. In general education, school districts administer group intelligence tests to elementary grade populations, although this practice is far less common than group achievement testing. At the secondary level, measures such as the *Scholastic Aptitude Test* (n.d.) of the College Entrance Examination Board are used to predict success in higher education.

Group measures of general learning aptitude share the drawbacks of group achievement tests for lower performing students. In nationwide testing programs such as the *Scholastic Aptitude Test,* special administration procedures are available for students with disabilities. In general, however, individual tests are preferred because they provide a more accurate picture of current academic aptitude.

Individual tests of intellectual functioning are part of the assessment battery for most students under serious consideration for specialized services. Information about general learning aptitude is needed for initial decisions for many disabilities as well as for the periodic reevaluation of eligibility. As a rule, individual tests of intelligence are administered in educational settings only by school psychologists—specially trained and licensed professionals who perform this kind of assessment. However, some individual intelligence tests may be administered by any professional, without any formal training. This may bring about a major change in the way school assessment teams operate. If this occurs, it will be necessary to make sure that the professionals responsible for assessment of intellectual performance are adequately trained in the administration, scoring, and interpretation of these tests.

The first intelligence test was developed in 1905 in France by Alfred Binet and Theodore Simon. This measure, adapted for use in the United States and revised several times, is the *Stanford-Binet Intelligence Scale.* The individual measure most often used in schools today, the *Wechsler Intelligence Scale for Children-Third Edition,* is one of a family of intelligence tests developed by David Wechsler. The Wechsler scale, along with the *Tests of Cognitive Ability* of the *Woodcock-Johnson Psycho-Educational Battery-Revised,* are discussed in this chapter. Other measures of intellectual performance, such as the *Stanford-Binet Intelligence Scale: Fourth Edition* and the *Kaufman Assessment Battery for Children,* are also described.

Adaptive behavior is also of concern in the assessment of general learning aptitude, particularly when mental retardation is the disability under consideration. Most states include impaired adaptive behavior as one of the requirements for mental retardation (Bruininks, Thurlow, & Gilman, 1987; Patrick & Reschly, 1982). However, adaptive behavior is not routinely assessed in the identification of learning disabilities and behavioral disorders. This is unfortunate because many students with these mild disabilities experience difficulty in meeting expectations in nonscholastic environments as well as in the classroom.

Adaptive behavior is typically evaluated by interviewing parents, teachers, or others well acquainted with the student or by having them complete questionnaires. There has been interest in the assessment of adaptive behavior for several decades. In 1935, the first edition of the *Vineland Social Maturity Scale,* a parent interview form, was published by Doll; the latest edition appeared in 1984. This scale and others are discussed in a later section of this chapter. Featured in that section is the *AAMR Adaptive Behavior Scale-School* (2nd ed.).

SOURCES OF INFORMATION ABOUT LEARNING APTITUDE

There are several sources of information about learning aptitude in addition to formal measures. For example, the student's performance in actual learning situations at school or at home may provide clues about ability to acquire new skills and information. However, norm-referenced measures are usually the best source of comparative information about learning aptitude, at least for majority group students whose characteristics match those of the norm group. Informal measures are less useful in this area of assessment and are best used to verify and elaborate the results of formal measures.

School Records

School records contain information about the student's past performance. Unlike achievement, learning aptitude is a relatively stable characteristic, and past performance data may be worth considering.

Group Intelligence Test Results. Results of any current or past group tests of intellectual performance should be reviewed. Keeping in mind the limitations of group administration procedures for students with school performance problems, the team can evaluate test results to determine the student's standing in relation to age or grade peers.

Individual Intelligence Test Data. The student may have been referred for individual assessment in the past, and individual intelligence test data may be available. If the assessment took place within the recent past, results should be compared with current findings. If an individual intelligence test has been administered very recently (e.g., within the last year), the assessment team may decide that another administration is unnecessary.

Developmental and School Histories. School records may contain the student's developmental history, furnished by the student's parents, perhaps at the time of entry to school. Histories typically provide information about the student's early development and, therefore, are most useful in the lower elementary grades. Included may be the ages at which developmental milestones such as talking and walking were achieved, any birth or other medical problems, family history, and data about attendance in early education programs. Developmental histories may suggest delays in early development, a possible indication of depressed learning aptitude. Likewise, school histories may reveal information on retentions, past referrals, chronic problems in school learning, or teachers' comments about the student's general learning aptitude.

The Student

The student assists the study of learning aptitude by participating in test administration and, on occasion, performing nonschool tasks under observation. Students can also talk about how they perceive their own abilities as a learner.

Individual Tests of Intellectual Performance. The most usual way of gathering information about general learning aptitude is the administration of individual intelligence tests. During the hour or more of test administration, the tester observes the speed and accuracy with which the student completes each task. The tester also notes the way the student approaches each problem and plans and implements a strategy for a solution.

Current Adaptive Behavior. Adaptive behavior can be assessed by direct observation, especially if available informants are not able to provide important information. Students themselves may be used as informants. Older students may be able to report whether they can tell time, make change, or get along with peers. As with all informants, students' responses may not be accurate, particularly if the questions are unclear to them.

Teachers

Teachers observe the student in everyday learning situations and are important sources of information about aptitude.

Observed Learning Aptitude. Teachers can report about how a student learns new skills, information, and classroom routines and procedures. Does the student learn as quickly as class

peers? Is more practice needed or a greater number of explanations? How does the student go about learning, and what instructional strategies have proven successful in facilitating learning?

Current Adaptive Behavior in Nonscholastic School Activities. Teachers also observe their students participating in many activities that are unrelated to academic learning. For instance, they see students at play during recess and observe social interactions throughout the day. They may also see students in community settings on field trips. From this experience base, teachers can provide at least partial information about the student's current adaptive behavior.

Parents

Parents are the best source concerning the student's performance at home, in the neighborhood, and in the community. Their perspective is valuable because of the lifetime experience with their child in a wide range of activities and environments.

Developmental History. If school records do not contain the student's developmental history, parents can provide it. This information is most useful for younger elementary children; for older students, school histories are of interest.

Observed Learning Aptitude. Like teachers, parents have numerous opportunities to observe learning aptitude. Within their child's first few years of life, parents watch a great variety of learning experiences: the first step, the first words, the first friends, and the first moves toward independence as children begin to acquire skills in caring for themselves. Parents may be able to compare one child's rate of learning with siblings or age mates. They may also identify tasks the child learns easily and tasks he or she finds difficult.

Current Adaptive Behavior at Home and in the Community. Parents are the primary source of information about the student's nonschool adaptive behavior. Two methods that are used to gather these data are interviews and questionnaires. For example, the assessment team can interview the student's parents about the student's current interaction skills, personal hygiene, responsibility for household chores, handling of money, use of public transportation, and so forth.

GROUP TESTS OF INTELLECTUAL PERFORMANCE

Group intelligence tests are sometimes used in general education; their results may be available for students referred for special education assessment. Like all group-administered measures, their scores are likely to be low estimates of actual abilities of students with school performance problems. In particular, most group intelligence tests rely heavily upon reading skills. Poor scores on these measures may reflect poor reading ability as opposed to below average intellectual performance. Because of this and the other limitations, results of group intelligence tests should be used only as an indicator of the need for further assessment with individual tests.

Group tests of intellectual performance are typically designed with several levels, so one test series can be used for grades 1 through 12. The content of group tests varies somewhat, but most attempt to assess both verbal and quantitative reasoning skills. Some provide separate measures of verbal and nonverbal abilities, and some contain several subtests, each of which addresses a different cognitive skill. Most, however, produce total test scores that are similar to IQ scores that indicate overall cognitive functioning. Other summary scores such as percentile ranks and stanines for total test performance are usually also available.

As with group achievement tests, test items are typically in multiple-choice format. Directions are presented orally by the tester, and the student reads each question and responds in writing. Most tests are timed, and older students record their responses on separate answer sheets.

Many of the group tests available today are current editions of long-used measures. The *Otis-Lennon School Ability Test* (7th ed.) (Otis & Lennon, 1995), for example, is the modern version of the *Otis Group Intelligence Scale*, one of the earliest measures of its type developed in the United States. The *Otis-Lennon* is available in seven levels for students in kindergarten through grade 12. Its subtests assess verbal and nonverbal abilities; results include School Ability Index (SAI) scores, percentile ranks, and stanines for Verbal, Nonverbal, and total test performance. In contrast, the *Cognitive Abilities Tests* (2nd ed.) (Thorndike & Hagen, 1993) provide 10 levels for kindergarten through grade 12, and each level is arranged in three batteries: Verbal, Quantitative, and Nonverbal. Results include Standard Age Scores, percentile ranks, and stanines for each battery and for a total test composite. Designed for grades 2 through 12, the *Test of Cognitive Skills* (2nd ed.) (1992) assesses memory skills as well as verbal and nonverbal abilities.

Like group achievement measures, group intelligence measures are most useful in screening programs. When group measures are administered to large segments of the school population, results should be reviewed to identify students who need further assessment.

INDIVIDUAL TESTS OF INTELLECTUAL PERFORMANCE

Individual tests may be designed for a special age group, such as preschool children or students between the ages of 6 and 18, or may be appropriate for the entire age range from early childhood through adulthood. Unlike group tests, individual tests are usually available in only one version that is divided into sections by either subtests or age levels. Subtests contain items that attempt to assess the same skill or ability, and test items are arranged in order of difficulty. When tests are broken into age levels, each age level usually contains a variety of tasks that assess different skills and abilities.

Most individual tests of intellectual performance assess both verbal and nonverbal reasoning. Verbal skills may be emphasized, but nonverbal abilities are evaluated by means of figural or mathematical problem-solving tasks. Measures of memory are often included, as are visual-motor coordination tasks. Academic skill demands are deemphasized on individual intelligence tests. Reading is not required, and written responses are usually limited to drawing or writing numbers. Information is presented orally or with pictures or objects, and students answer orally or with some type of motoric response.

Several well-known individual tests of intellectual performance are listed in Table 8–1. Each is described in terms of age span and types of results. The next sections of this chapter discuss intelligence measures for school-aged children, beginning with the *Wechsler Intelligence Scale for Children-Third Edition.*

WECHSLER INTELLIGENCE SCALE FOR CHILDREN-THIRD EDITION*

The *Wechsler Intelligence Scale for Children-Third Edition (WISC-III)* (Wechsler, 1991) is the individual test most often used to assess general intellectual performance of school-aged individuals. It replaces the previous edition, the *Wechsler Intelligence Scale for Children-Revised (WISC-R)* (Wechsler, 1974), and it is one of a family of tests that spans all age levels. The *Wechsler Preschool and Primary Scale of Intelligence-Revised (WPPSI-R)* (Wechsler, 1989) is appropriate for children between the ages of 3-0 and 7-3, and the

Wechsler Adult Intelligence Scale-Third Edition (WAIS-III) (Wechsler, 1997) is used for persons between the ages of 16 and 89. A new measure, the *Wechsler Abbreviated Scale of Intelligence* (1999), provides a quick estimate of intellectual performance for ages 6 to 89. There is a version of the *WISC-R* that is adapted for children who are deaf (Anderson & Sisco, 1977), and there are two Spanish-language versions. The *Escala de Inteligencia Wechsler para Niños-Revisada* (1983) is designed for students from Chicano, Puerto Rican, and Cuban backgrounds; the *Escala de Inteligencia Wechsler para Niños-Revisada de Puerto Rico* (1993) was normed with Puerto Rican children. A Spanish version of the original *WAIS* (Green & Martinez, 1968) is also available.

The *WISC-III* assesses general intellectual functioning by sampling performance on many different types of activities. According to Wechsler (1974), intelligence is not a single trait but "a multidetermined and multifaceted entity" (p. 5). In special education assessment, the *WISC-III* is often used to gain an overall estimate of the student's current global intellectual performance. This measure may also provide information about strengths and weaknesses in specific areas of aptitude.

Weschsler Intelligence Scale for Children-Third Edition (WISC-III)

D. Wechsler (1991)

Type: Norm-referenced test

Major Content Areas: General verbal aptitude, general performance aptitude

Type of Administration: Individual

Administration Time: 30–70 minutes (regular battery)

Age/Grade Levels: Ages 6-0 to 16-11

Types of Scores: Three IQ scores (Verbal, Performance, and Full Scale), four Index scores (Verbal Comprehension, Perceptual Organization, Freedom from Distractibility, and Processing Speed), scaled scores for each subtest. Test-Age Equivalent scores by subtest.

Computer Aids: *Scoring Assistant for the Wechsler Scales and WISC-III Writer*

Typical Uses: A wide-range measure of general intellectual performance and specific cognitive abilities

Cautions: This test is not appropriate for students who do not understand and speak English.

Publisher: Psychological Corporation (www.hbtpc.com)

Wechsler Intelligence Scale for Children and *WISC-III* are registered trademarks of The Psychological Corporation.

TABLE 8-1
Individual Tests of Intellectual Performance

NAME (AUTHOR)	AGES	RESULTS
Columbia Mental Maturity Scale (Burgemeister, Blum, & Lorge, 1972)	3½ to 10	Age score, percentile rank, stanine, Maturity Index
Comprehensive Test of Nonverbal Intelligence (Hammill, Pearson, & Wiederholt, 1997)	6-0 to 89-11	IQ scores (Nonverbal, Pictorial Nonverbal, and Geometric Nonverbal); subtest standard scores, percentile ranks, and age equivalents
Das-Naglieri Cognitive Assessment System (Naglieri & Das, 1997)	5-0 to 17-11	Standard scores for Scales (Full, Planning, Attention, Simultaneous, and Successive); subtest scaled scores
Hammill Multiability Intelligence Test (Hammill, Bryant, & Pearson, 1998)	6-0 to 17-11	Standard scores and percentile ranks for Composites (General, Verbal, and Nonverbal Intelligence); subtest standard scores, percentile ranks, and age equivalents
Kaufman Adolescent & Adult Intelligence Test (Kaufman & Kaufman, 1993)	11 to 85+	IQ scores (Fluid, Crystallized, and Composite Intelligence), subtest scaled scores, and percentile ranks
Kaufman Assessment Battery for Children (Kaufman & Kaufman, 1983)	2-6 to 12-5	Global standard scores (Mental Processing Composite, Sequential Processing, Simultaneous Processing, and Nonverbal), subtest scaled score, and percentile ranks
Kaufman Brief Intelligence Test (Kaufman & Kaufman, 1990)	4 to 90	IQ Composite, subtest standard scores, and percentile ranks
Learning Potential Assessment Device (Feuerstein et al., 1979)	Children and youth	Clinical description of the student's cognitive modifiability
Leiter International Performance Scale-Revised (Roid & Miller, 1997)	2-0 to 20-11	IQ score; subtest standard scores, percentile ranks, and age equivalents
McCarthy Scales of Children's Abilities (McCarthy, 1972)	2½ to 8½	General Cognitive Index, MA, and scaled scores for five scales: Verbal, Perceptual-Performance, Quantitative, Memory, and Motor
Raven Progressive Matrices (Raven, 1938, 1947, 1962)	5 to adult	Percentile rank
Slossom Intelligence Scale-Revised (Nicholson & Hibpshman, 1990)	3-0 to adult	Mean Age Equivalent, Total Test Standard Score, percentile rank, stanine

TABLE 8-1
Individual Tests of Intellectual Performance—*Continued*

NAME (AUTHOR)	AGES	RESULTS
Stanford-Binet Intelligence Scale (4th ed.) (Thorndike, Hagen, & Sattler, 1986)	3-0 to adult	Composites for Verbal Reasoning, Abstract-Visual Reasoning, Quantitative Reasoning, Short-Term Memory, and total test; subtest standard scores
Swanson-Cognitive Processing Test (Swanson, 1996)	4-11 to 76	Standard scores for Composites (Semantic, Episodic, Total) and Components (Auditory, Visual, Prospective, Retrospective) for Initial, Gain, and Maintenance testing; subtest scale scores
System of Multicultural Pluralistic Assessment (Mercer & Lewis, 1977b)	5 to 11	School Functioning Level (*WISC-R* IQ scores) and Estimated Learning Potential (*WISC-R* results rescored using alternate norms)
Test of Nonverbal Intelligence (3rd ed.) (Brown, Sherbenou, & Johnsen, 1997)	6-0 to 89-11	*TONI-3* quotient, percentile rank
Universal Nonverbal Intelligence Test (Bracken & McCallum, 1998)	5-0 to 17-11	Quotient scores and percentile ranks for Full Scale, Memory, Reasoning, Symbolic, and Nonsymbolic; subtest scaled scores and age equivalents
Wechsler Abbreviated Scale of Intelligence (1999)	6 to 89	Verbal IQ, Performance IQ, and Full Scale IQ; subtest scaled scores
Wechsler Adult Intelligence Scale-Third Edition (Wechsler, 1997)	16 to 89	Verbal IQ, Performance IQ, and Full Scale IQ; factor-based index scores (Verbal Comprehension, Working Memory, Perceptual Organization, Processing Speed); subtest scaled scores
Wechsler Intelligence Scale for Children-Third Edition (Wechsler, 1991)	6-0 to 16-11	Verbal IQ, Performance IQ, and Full Scale IQ; factor-based index scores (Verbal Comprehension, Perceptual Organization, Freedom from Distractibility, Processing Speed); subtest scaled scores
Wechsler Preschool and Primary Scale of Intelligence-Revised (Wechsler, 1989)	3-0 to 7-3	Verbal IQ, Performance IQ, Full Scale IQ, and subtest scaled scores
Woodcock-Johnson Psycho-Educational Battery-Revised (Woodcock & Johnson, 1989)	2 to 90+	Age and grade equivalents, standard scores, percentile ranks, and Relative Mastery Index (RMI) scores for individual subtests; Broad Ability; cognitive factors (Long-Term Memory, Short-Term Memory, Processing Speed, Auditory Processing, Visual Processing, Comprehension-Knowledge, Fluid Reasoning); and several areas of scholastic aptitude

The *WISC-III* contains 13 subtests; 10 are required and 3 are supplementary. Only the required subtests are used to determine IQ scores. Subtests are classified as either Verbal or Performance, and these are alternated in administration.

Verbal scale subtests require students to listen to questions and answer orally. To preserve the confidentiality of the test items, the examples cited are similar, but not identical, to *WISC-III* tasks.

- *Information*. The student responds orally to general information questions such as "How many eyes do you have?" and "From what animal do we get hamburger?"
- *Similarities*. The student must describe how two things (pony and cow, or car and airplane) are alike.
- *Arithmetic*. The tester reads arithmetic problems to the student, and the student responds orally. All computations must be done mentally; paper and pencil are not furnished. Visuals are used with the first few test items. On the last six items, the student is given a word problem and told to read it aloud. The tester may read the problems if the student cannot.
- *Vocabulary*. The student must tell the meaning of words. The tester asks, "What is a ____?" or "What does ____ mean?"
- *Comprehension*. The student answers questions that require social reasoning, such as "What are some reasons why we need fire-fighters?"
- *Digit Span* (Supplementary). The tester reads a series of numbers to the student at the rate of one digit per second. On the first portion of the test, the student attempts to repeat the digits in the order read by the tester. On the second portion, digits are repeated backwards.

Performance subtests are visual-motor tasks. The student listens to oral directions, looks at stimulus materials, and responds motorically. Performance subtests are timed.

- *Picture Completion*. The student is shown a color drawing of an object or a scene that is missing some important part. The student must point to or say what is missing.
- *Coding*. In this paper-and-pencil task, the student is shown a code, such as one geometric design for each of the digits. Then rows of digits are presented, and the student must write in the correct geometric design for each digit. The code remains available to the student during the task.
- *Picture Arrangement*. Several cards with pictures are presented, and the student arranges these to tell a story.
- *Block Design*. The student is given several colored cubes or blocks and a picture of a design. The cubes must be arranged into an identical design.
- *Object Assembly*. Puzzle pieces must be arranged into the correct shape.
- *Symbol Search* (Supplementary). The student is shown a symbol and must determine if its match appears in a row of three symbols. Older students see two target symbols and must determine if either appears in a row of five symbols. Students respond by marking the "yes" or the "no" box.
- *Mazes* (Supplementary). This subtest is another paper-and-pencil task in which the student attempts to solve mazes.

The *WISC-III* is appropriate for students who can sustain attention for extended periods of time. This test is long and may be administered in more than one session. English-language competence is a necessity. Students must be able to understand test directions and questions and answer questions in English. Both oral and motor responses are required. No reading, handwriting, or spelling skills are needed, but mental arithmetic is assessed.

Technical Quality

The *WISC-III* was standardized on 2,200 students ages 6 through 16 in public and private schools. Equal numbers of males and females were included at each age level. The standardization sample was selected to resemble the United States as described in 1988 Census data. The variables used in the stratified sampling plan were race/ethnicity (Whites, Blacks, Hispanics, other), geographic region, and parent education; the final sample approximated the total population on these variables. In terms of race/ethnicity, the sample was made up of

70.1% students identified as White, 15.4% identified as Black, 11.0% identified as Hispanic, and 3.5% other (i.e., Native American, Eskimo, Aleut, Asian, and Pacific Islander).

According to the *WISC-III* manual, "Students receiving special services in school settings were not excluded" (p. 22). Students receiving Chapter 1 services and those with learning disabilities, speech/language disabilities, emotional disturbance, or physical disabilities accounted for 7% of the sample. Students unable to speak and understand English were excluded. Thus, the *WISC-III* standardization sample appears to represent the English-speaking portion of the U.S. school population.

The reliability of the *WISC-III* was studied by the split-half method for most subtests. Verbal, Performance, and Full Scale IQs have average reliabilities of .95, .91, and .96, respectively, across all ages; those for Index scores range from .85 to .94. Average reliability coefficients range from .77 to .87 for Verbal subtests and from .69 to .87 for Performance subtests. Test-retest reliability is adequate across ages for IQ and Index scores, and interrater reliability coefficients fell at or above .90. The concurrent validity of the *WISC-III* was studied with a number of tests, including the *WISC-R*. Correlations for these two versions of the *WISC* were .90 for Verbal IQ scores, .81 for Performance IQ, and .89 for Full Scale IQ. Differences between IQ scores were also identified; the *WISC-III* can be expected to produce Verbal IQ scores that are approximately 2 points lower than those on the *WISC-R*, Performance IQ scores approximately 7 points lower, and Full Scale IQs approximately 5 points lower. The *WISC-III* manual suggests that this occurs because the standardization sample of the *WISC-R* is outdated.

WISC-III Full Scale IQ scores show moderate correlations with group tests of ability such as the *Otis-Lennon School Ability Test* ($r = .73$), group achievement tests (.74), and school grades (.47). No information is provided in the manual regarding the relationship of the *WISC-III* to other commonly used individual tests of academic aptitude such as the *Woodcock-Johnson Psycho-Educational Battery-Revised* or the *Stanford-Binet Intelligence Scale* (4th ed.).

Validity was also investigated through factor analytic studies and studies with special groups (e.g., students with learning disabilities). Factor analyses support the *WISC-III* Verbal/Performance dichotomy as well as the recombination of subtests into Index scores. Results of research with special groups support the usefulness of the *WISC-III* for differential diagnosis.

Administration Considerations

According to the manual, *WISC-III* examiners "should have training and experience in the administration and interpretation of standardized, clinical instruments such as the *WISC-R* or other Wechsler intelligence scales" (p. 10). Licensed school psychologists are usually the only professionals permitted to administer individual intelligence tests like the *WISC-III* in school settings. Other professionals, however, should be knowledgeable about such tests, even if they are not responsible for their administration and scoring.

Results and Interpretation

The *WISC-III* provides global IQ scores, Index scores, and subtest scaled scores. Derived scores are determined by age norms; grade norms are not available.

The global scores available from the *WISC-III* are: Verbal IQ, based on performance on the five required Verbal subtests; Performance IQ, based on performance on the five required Performance subtests; and Full Scale IQ, based on performance on all 10 required subtests. These IQ scores are standard scores distributed normally with a mean of 100 and a standard deviation of 15. Average standard errors for IQ scores are low (Verbal IQ, 3.5 IQ points; Performance IQ, 4.5 IQ points; Full Scale IQ, 3.2 IQ points).

Four factor-based Index scores are produced on the *WISC-III*, and each is based upon a combination of subtests. The Verbal Comprehension factor reflects four Verbal Scale subtests: Information, Similarities, Vocabulary, and Comprehension. Perceptual Organization is made up of four Performance Scale subtests: Picture Completion, Picture Arrangement, Block Design, and Object Assembly. Freedom from Distractibility is composed of the Arithmetic and Digit Span subtests, and Perceptual Speed consists of the Coding and Symbol Search subtests. Like IQ scores, Index scores are distributed with a mean of 100 and a standard deviation of 15. Subtest scaled scores are standard scores distributed normally with a mean of 10 and a standard deviation of 3. Standard errors vary according to subtest. Average errors on Verbal subtests range from 1.1 to 1.5; those on Performance subtests range from 1.1 to 1.7. Subtest scaled scores, IQ scores, and Index scores are plotted on profiles that appear on the front of the record form.

The *WISC-III* manual provides tables for analyzing differences between various types of results. It is possible to determine whether differences between Verbal and Performance IQs (and between Index scores) are statistically significant and to find out how unusual a particular score discrepancy is. For example, across all ages, a difference of 11.3 IQ points between Verbal and Performance IQs is significant at the .05 level. However, a Verbal/Performance discrepancy of 11 points is seen in 40.5% of the standardization sample; in contrast, a VIQ/PIQ discrepancy of 22 points occurred in only 9.3% of the sample. Other possible analyses include comparing the score of one subtest with average subtest results, examining differences between individual subtests, and studying test scatter. Scatter is the amount of variation in the student's performance on various subtests; it is determined by subtracting the lowest subtest scaled score from the highest. When scatter is computed across all 10 subtests, a difference of 5 scaled score points is seen in 93% of the norm group; only 10% show scatter of 11 or more scaled score points.

IQ and scaled scores can be interpreted using the standard score range system suggested in Chapter 4. However, Wechsler provides a somewhat different system. IQ scores between 90 and 109 are considered Average, and this range incorporates approximately 50% of the population. IQs of 80 to 89 are rated as Low Average, 70 to 79 as Borderline, and 69 and below as Intellectually Deficient. Above the mean, IQs 110 to 119 are classified as High Average, 120 to 129 as Superior, and 130 and above as Very Superior.

Results of individual tests such as the *WISC-III* provide information about one criterion for

mental retardation—subaverage intellectual functioning. According to the American Association on Mental Retardation (1992), mental retardation is indicated when general intellectual functioning is significantly subaverage; that is:

> an IQ standard score of approximately 70 to 75 or below, based on assessment that includes one or more individually administered general intelligence tests developed for the purpose of assessing intellectual functioning. These data should be reviewed by a multidisciplinary team and validated with additional test scores or evaluative information. (p. 5)

This guideline takes two important factors into account: the standard error of measurement of IQ scores, and the clinical judgment of the assessment team. On the *WISC-III*, norms tables provide results at two confidence levels: 90% and 95%. At the 90% level, an IQ score of 70 would fall in the range 66 to 77, and an IQ of 72 would fall in the range 68 to 79. Determination of whether these scores indicate subaverage intellectual performance is left to the assessment team. Of course, the individual's adaptive behavior must also be evaluated.

Figure 8–1 presents *WISC-III* results for Joyce, the fourth grader described at the start of this chapter. Joyce was 10-0 at the time of testing, so her performance was compared to that of other 10-year-olds. Note how subtest, IQ, and Index scores are plotted on the *WISC-III* profile.

With the *WISC-III*, the examiner selects a confidence level (90% or 95%), then reports results in confidence intervals rather than as single scores. In writing the report on Joyce, the psychologist might say:

> On the *Wechsler Intelligence Scale for Children-Third Edition,* Joyce earned a Verbal IQ in the range 102 to 113, a Performance IQ in the range 88 to 101, and a Full Scale IQ in the range 96 to 106. The chances that these score ranges include Joyce's true scores are about 90 out of 100. The IQ results indicate that Joyce is currently functioning within the average range in verbal abilities, performance abilities, and general intellectual functioning.

In summary, the *WISC-III* appears to be an appropriate individual measure of general intellectual functioning. It is well standardized and

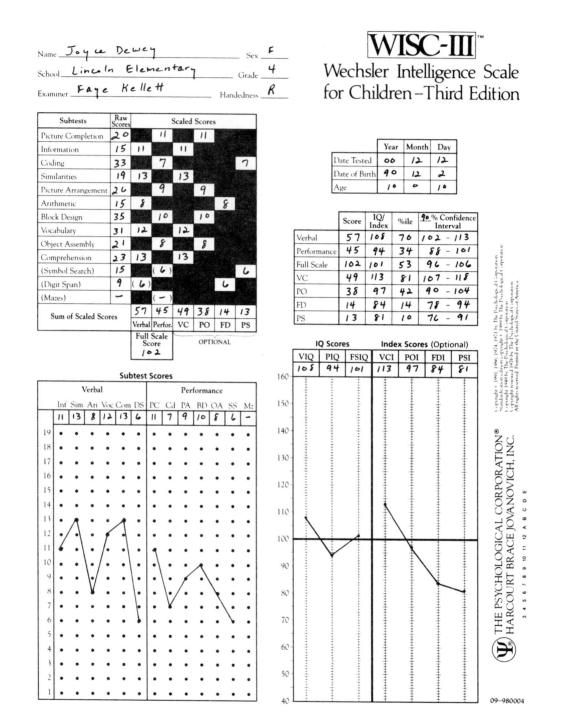

® THE PSYCHOLOGICAL CORPORATION®
Ⓨ® HARCOURT BRACE JOVANOVICH, INC.

3 4 5 6 7 8 9 10 11 12 A B C D E

09–980004

FIGURE 8–1

Sample *WISC-III* Results

Note: Reproduced from the *Wechsler Intelligence Scale for Children-Third Edition* by D. Wechsler. Copyright © 1991 by The Psychological Corporation, a Harcourt Assessment Company. Reproduced by permission. All rights reserved.

reliable, and the available validity data are adequate. The results of this measure provide information about general levels of intellectual performance as well as more specific mental abilities. The Wechsler tests have a long history, and they are well known and widely accepted in education. The *WISC-III* is likely the individual intelligence test most frequently used in schools today.

WOODCOCK-JOHNSON PSYCHO-EDUCATIONAL BATTERY-REVISED, TESTS OF COGNITIVE ABILITY

The *Woodcock-Johnson Psycho-Educational Battery-Revised* (*Woodcock-Johnson-R*) was introduced in Chapter 7, where part two of the battery, the *Tests of Achievement*, was discussed as a measure of school performance. The first part, the *Tests of Cognitive Ability*, is presented here.

The *Tests of Cognitive Ability* serve several purposes. First, they provide an estimate of overall intellectual functioning, similar to the Full Scale IQ of the *WISC-III*. Second, subtests are clustered into seven cognitive factors to allow description of more specific abilities. The factors, based on the Horn-Cattell theory of intellectual processing (Woodcock & Mather, 1989), are Long-Term Retrieval, Short-Term Memory, Processing Speed, Auditory Processing, Visual Processing, Comprehension-Knowledge, and Fluid Processing. Third, subtests are also arranged into aptitude clusters to allow prediction of academic achievement in reading, mathematics, written language, and knowledge. Fourth, the student's performance on the *Tests of Cognitive Ability* can

---

Woodcock-Johnson Psycho-Educational Battery-Revised
(Woodcock-Johnson-R): Tests of Cognitive Ability

R W. Woodcock & M. B. Johnson (1989)

Type: Norm-referenced test

Major Content Areas: Broad cognitive ability, seven cognitive factors, four types of scholastic aptitude

Type of Administration: Individual

Administration Time: Less than 1 hour for standard battery

Age/Grade Levels: Ages 2 to 90+; Grades K–12, college

Types of Scores: Grade and age equivalents, standard scores, percentile ranks, Relative Mastery Index (RMI) scores

Computer Aids: *Woodcock Scoring and Interpretative Program*

Typical Uses: A broad-based measure of general cognitive functioning, specific cognitive abilities, and academic aptitudes

Cautions: Administration rules vary from subtest to subtest. Results are available for more than 35 subtests and cognitive areas, making scoring time-consuming and interpretation complicated. Results should be interpreted cautiously due to concerns about test-retest reliability, possible differences between global scores on the *Woodcock-Johnson-R* and other tests of cognitive functioning, and the relatively low predictive power of the Written Language Aptitude score.

Publisher: Riverside Publishing (www.riverpub.com)

be compared with achievement scores from part one of the battery to contrast expected and actual achievement.

There are 21 cognitive ability tests arranged in two levels: the standard battery (7 subtests) and the supplemental battery (14 subtests). As with the *Woodcock-Johnson-R* achievement tests, the standard battery is administered first; then portions of the supplemental battery are selected if further information is needed. Alternate forms are not available for the *Tests of Cognitive Ability*.

The cognitive ability subtests are described in the next paragraphs by cognitive factor. Within each factor, standard battery subtests are discussed first, then supplemental subtests.

Long-Term Retrieval

- *Memory for Names*. The tester teaches the student the names of line drawings of space creatures. A page containing several drawings is exposed, and when the tester names a creature, the student must point to it. The tester corrects any errors made by the student.
- *Visual-Auditory Learning* (Supplemental). The tester teaches the student a series of visual symbols that stand for words. Then the student is asked to "read" sentences made up of the symbols. The tester corrects student errors or supplies a word if the student hesitates for more than 5 seconds.
- *Delayed Recall–Memory for Names* (Supplemental). This subtest is administered 1 to 8 days after Memory for Names is given. The task is the same except the tester does not teach the names of the space creatures, and errors are not corrected.
- *Delayed Recall–Visual-Auditory Learning* (Supplemental). This subtest is administered 1 to 8 days after Visual-Auditory Learning is given. The task is the same except the tester does not teach the labels for visual symbols, and errors are not corrected.

Short-Term Memory

- *Memory for Sentences*. The student listens to sentences read by the tester or presented by the Test Tape and attempts to repeat each sentence verbatim. Young children begin by repeating single words and short phrases.

- *Memory for Words* (Supplemental). The tester or Test Tape reads a series of unrelated words, and the student repeats the words in order.
- *Numbers Reversed* (Supplemental). The tester or Test Tape reads a series of digits at a rate of one digit per second; the student repeats the digits in backward order.

Processing Speed

- *Visual Matching*. On this paper-and-pencil task, the student is shown rows of numbers. The student must circle the two identical numbers in each row. Three minutes are allowed.
- *Cross Out* (Supplemental). This paper-and-pencil task requires the student to look at a row of 20 small drawings and cross out the 5 drawings identical to the first drawing in the row. Three minutes are allowed.

Auditory Processing

- *Incomplete Words*. The tester or Test Tape presents words with one or more phonemes missing (e.g., tele-ision for television); the student must pronounce the word.
- *Sound Blending* (Supplemental). The tester or Test Tape presents words broken into parts, and the student must say the word. On earlier items, words are broken into two parts; on more difficult items, each phoneme is pronounced.
- *Sound Patterns* (Supplemental). The Test Tape is used for all but the first few sample items. The student listens to pairs of sound sequences to tell if they are the same or different. Sound sequences may differ in an individual phoneme, in the order or speed with which sounds are presented, in tone or intonation, or in length of tones or pauses.

Visual Processing

- *Visual Closure*. The student must tell what a drawing or photograph depicts. Drawings are incomplete and/or partially obscured by superimposed lines; photos show objects from unusual perspectives.
- *Picture Recognition* (Supplemental). The student is shown a stimulus page with one or more drawings on it; after 5 seconds, a new page is revealed that contains some of the stimulus drawings and others that are

similar. The student must identify the stimulus drawings.

- *Spatial Relations* (Supplemental). A geometric figure divided into two or more pieces is presented. The student must select from a series of shapes those that, when combined, make the original figure.

Comprehension-Knowledge

- *Picture Vocabulary.* The student is shown a drawing and is asked to say what it is. In early items, the tester presents a set of drawings, names one, and directs the student to point to it.
- *Oral Vocabulary* (Supplemental). In the first part of this subtest, the tester reads a word, and the student must give its synonym. In the second part, the student provides an antonym for the word read by the tester. Test pages show the words that the tester reads.
- *Listening Comprehension* (Supplemental). The tester or Test Tape reads a sentence or paragraph with one word missing, and the student must supply that word.
- *Verbal Analogies* (Supplemental). The tester reads verbal analogies (e.g., "*Big* is to *little* as *up* is to . . ."), and the student completes them.

Fluid Reasoning

- *Analysis-Synthesis.* The student is shown a key that defines a relationship between colors. For example, red with green may equal black. With the key present, the student solves puzzles in which one or more colors have been omitted. Error responses are corrected. There is a 1-minute time limit for more difficult items.
- *Concept Formation* (Supplemental). The student is shown two sets of drawings, one set of which is inside boxes. The student must tell one or more concepts that differentiate the boxed drawings. Examples are color, size, shape, and number.
- *Spatial Relations* (Supplemental). This subtest assesses both Fluid Reasoning and Visual Processing; see the "Visual Processing" section for a description.
- *Verbal Analogies* (Supplemental). This subtest assesses both Fluid Reasoning and Comprehension-Knowledge; see the "Comprehension-Knowledge" section for a description.

Figure 8–2 shows the relationships among *Woodcock-Johnson-R* cognitive ability subtests. Of the seven subtests in the standard battery, five are recommended for early childhood assessment. All subtests in the standard battery are administered to derive a Broad Ability score. Subtests may be combined in a number of ways to obtain information about various cognitive factors and areas of scholastic aptitude. For example, the cluster score for the cognitive factor of Long-Term Retrieval is determined by performance on one standard battery subtest, Memory for Names, and one supplementary subtest, Visual-Auditory Learning. Two other supplementary subtests are available if further information is needed about this factor.

Students must be able to attend to test tasks for several minutes at a time to participate in *Woodcock-Johnson-R* administration. English-language skills are a necessity, except perhaps for Processing Speed subtests and some Visual Processing subtests. However, a Spanish-language version of the *Woodcock-Johnson-R* battery, the *Batería Woodcock-Muñoz-Revisada* (Woodcock & Muñoz-Sandoval, 1996), is available.

No reading is required. On the standard battery, the most typical response mode is oral. However, on Memory for Names, the student points to the answer, and Visual Matching is a paper-and-pencil task. The Processing Speed subtests are timed. The Test Tape is used to present items on all Short-Term Memory and Auditory Processing subtests and on one Comprehension-Knowledge subtest. With immature students and others who have difficulty with the Test Tape, the tester may read the items, except on the Sound Patterns subtest. The student must be able to discriminate colors on the Analysis-Synthesis subtest.

Technical Quality

As discussed in Chapter 7, the *Woodcock-Johnson-R* was standardized from 1986 to 1988 with more than 6,300 subjects ranging in age from 2-0 to 90+. Preschool children, K–12 students, college students, and adults were included. The K–12 group was drawn from general education classes, and students were excluded only if their sole placement was special education or if they had less than 1 year's experience in an English-language classroom.

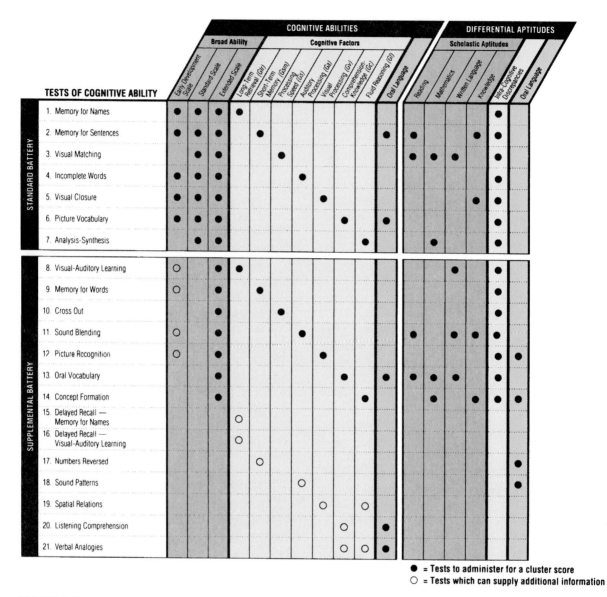

FIGURE 8-2

Selective Testing Table for the *Woodcock-Johnson-R Tests of Cognitive Ability*

Note: From *Woodcock-Johnson-Revised Tests of Cognitive Ability* by R. W. Woodcock and M. B. Johnson, 1989, Allen, TX: DLM Teaching Resources. Copyright 1989 by DLM Teaching Resources. Reprinted by permission.

Weighting procedures were used to assure that the entire standardization sample resembled the national population on variables such as geographic region, community size, sex, race, and Hispanic versus non-Hispanic ethnicity.

Information about the psychometric characteristics of the *Woodcock-Johnson-R* is found in the *Woodcock-Johnson Technical Manual* (McGrew, Werder, & Woodcock, 1991). Internal consistency, as measured by the split-half method, is reported for most subtests and all cluster scores; test-retest reliability replaces split-half for subtests with speed components (Visual Matching and Cross Out). Split-half reliability is adequate for most subtests and all clusters; two coefficients fall below .80: Incomplete Words (.787) and Visual Closure (.721). Test-retest reliability coefficients, corrected for age, are presented for 14 of the 21 cognitive subtests; of these, only 2 fall above .80. Of particular concern are Picture Recognition (.522), Incomplete Words (.631), Memory for Words (.646), Memory for Names (.672), and Visual Closure (.692). Test-retest reliability falls below .80 for four cognitive clusters: Long-Term Retrieval (.774), Short-Term Memory (.794), Auditory Processing (.763), and Visual Processing (.672). The test-retest reliability of the *Woodcock-Johnson-R* cognitive tests is not well established.

Results of studies of the *Woodcock-Johnson-R*'s concurrent validity with other measures of intellectual performance are presented in the *Technical Manual*. Findings indicate relationships in the mid-.60's to low .70's between the Broad Cognitive Ability (Standard) score of the *Woodcock-Johnson-R*, the *WISC-R* Full Scale IQ, and the *Stanford-Binet IV* Composite. Results from one study of grade 3 and 4 students ($n = 72$) show a pattern identified as a concern with the first edition of the *Woodcock-Johnson* (Reeve, Hall, & Zakreski, 1979): while the group's mean *Woodcock-Johnson-R* Broad Cognitive Ability (Standard) score was 103.6, means for total scores on the *Stanford-Binet IV* and the *WISC-R* were 112.7 and 114.9, respectively.

The relationship of *Woodcock-Johnson-R* Scholastic Aptitude scores to achievement results was examined as one method of studying predictive validity. In general, Scholastic Aptitude scores for Reading, Mathematics, Written Language, and Broad Knowledge show correlations in the .60's and .70's with their achievement cluster counterparts (e.g., *W-J-R* Broad Reading, Broad Mathematics). One exception is Written Language Aptitude; its correlation with the Broad Written Language achievement score fell to .586 at grade 3 and to .565 at grade 5. Correlations between Scholastic Aptitude scores and results from other achievement tests such as the *PIAT* and *WRAT-R* ranged from the .30's to the .60's.

Construct validity of the *Woodcock-Johnson-R* is supported by results of factor analyses and by data showing systematic patterns of difference between samples of students identified as gifted, "normal," learning disabled, and mentally retarded. However, the strongest predictors of group membership were *Woodcock-Johnson-R* achievement scores, not cognitive clusters.

Administration Considerations

The *Tests of Cognitive Ability* are more difficult to administer than the achievement portion of the *Woodcock-Johnson-R*. Consider the diversity of the seven subtests in the standard battery. Five subtests require that all students begin with item 1; basal rules on the other two subtests are either four or six consecutively numbered successes. Two subtests use cutoff scores in lieu of ceilings; on the other subtests, ceiling rules vary from four to eight consecutively numbered failures. One subtest, Visual Matching, is timed. Two use the Test Tape. On the two subtests that are controlled learning tasks (Memory for Names and Analysis-Synthesis), student errors are to be corrected by the tester.

The *Tests of Cognitive Ability* begin with standard introductory remarks that are read to all students. Then the tester selects the subtests to be administered. As Figure 8–2 illustrates, choices can be made from both the standard and the supplemental batteries based on the age of the student and the assessment questions under consideration. Suggested starting points are given by the student's estimated ability level, not by actual grade placement.

Raw scores are calculated in the usual manner. As with the achievement tests, the test record booklet provides tables for converting raw scores to age and grade equivalents. The tables for the subtests in which cutoff scores are used instead of ceilings (e.g., Memory for Names and Analysis-Synthesis) are a bit more complicated; norms are arranged by the number of items administered. As with the *Tests of Achievement*, the manual must be consulted to derive comparative scores such as percentile ranks and standard scores. This time-consuming process can be shortened substantially by using the *Woodcock Scoring and Interpretive Program.*

Results and Interpretation

The *Tests of Cognitive Ability* produce a great number of results. The Broad Ability Standard Scale summarizes performance on the standard battery. A Broad Ability Extended Scale is also available; it takes into account all standard battery subtests as well as seven of the supplementary subtests. Results can also be reported by subtest, by cognitive factor, and by areas of scholastic aptitude. More than 35 subtest and area results are produced, and each result can be expressed as an age and grade equivalent, a standard score, a percentile rank, and a Relative Mastery Index (RMI) score. Extended age and grade scores are provided, and standard scores are distributed with a mean of 100 and a standard deviation of 15.

Results of the *Woodcock-Johnson-R* can be plotted on a series of profiles to assist in interpretation. W scores are plotted in confidence intervals on the Age/Grade Profile to allow comparisons with the student's current age or grade. The Standard Score/Percentile Rank profile, also plotted in confidence intervals, compares student performance to that of age or grade peers in the norm group. Both types of profile are available for individual subtest scores and for broader area scores. In addition, procedures are provided for comparing discrepancies in performance across cognitive ability areas and between scholastic aptitudes and areas of achievement; these procedures are discussed in the next chapter.

The *Tests of Cognitive Ability* are an interesting set of measures that span a wide age range. The *Woodcock-Johnson-R* addresses a number of cognitive factors, and several of these factors are of particular interest in the assessment of learning disabilities. The drawbacks of this measure include its length (a total of 21 subtests), the time required for hand scoring if other than age or grade scores are needed, and the difficulties associated with interpreting the large number of scores and profiles produced.

OTHER INDIVIDUAL MEASURES OF INTELLECTUAL PERFORMANCE

The assessment team can choose from several other individual tests of intellectual performance. The *Kaufman Assessment Battery for Children,* like the *Woodcock-Johnson-R,* contains aptitude measures as well as measures of academic achievement. Also available are age scales such as the *Slosson Intelligence Scale-Revised* and the 1973 *Stanford-Binet Intelligence Scale,* in which test items are arranged by age levels rather than by subtest. The *Stanford-Binet Intelligence Scale: Fourth Edition,* the most recent version, represents a major revision of this classic test; it is no longer an age scale. Two newer measures are the *Hammill Multiability Intelligence Test,* a companion to the *Hammill Multiability Achievement Test* described in Chapter 7, and the *Das-Naglieri Cognitive Assessment System.* Nonverbal measures of intellectual performance are discussed in the section on approaches to nonbiased assessment.

Kaufman Assessment Battery for Children

The *K-ABC* (Kaufman & Kaufman, 1983) is an individual measure, designed to be administered by professionals such as school psychologists who are trained in individual intelligence testing. The battery is appropriate for children ages 2-6 to 12-5 and contains mental processing and achievement subtests. Among the global scores derived from the mental processing subtests is the Mental Processing Composite, an index of overall intellectual performance. Two other global scores are measures of more specific abilities—Sequential Processing and Simultaneous Processing. All global scores are distributed with a mean of 100 and a standard deviation of 15. According to the *K-ABC*'s Interpretive Manual, "sequential processing places a premium on the serial or temporal order of stimuli when solving problems; in contrast, simultaneous processing demands a gestalt-like, frequently spatial, integration of stimuli to solve problems with maximum efficiency" (p. 2). *K-ABC* subtests are:

Sequential Processing Subtests

> Hand Movements (ages 2-6 through 12-5)
>
> Number Recall (ages 2-6 through 12-5)
>
> Word Order (ages 4-0 through 12-5)

Simultaneous Processing Subtests

> Magic Window (ages 2-6 through 4-11)
>
> Face Recognition (ages 2-6 through 4-11)
>
> Gestalt Closure (ages 2-6 through 12-5)
>
> Triangles (ages 4-0 through 12-5)
>
> Matrix Analogies (ages 5-0 through 12-5)
>
> Spatial Analogies (ages 5-0 through 12-5)
>
> Photo Series (ages 6-0 through 12-5)

Achievement Subtests

> Expressive Vocabulary (ages 2-6 through 4-11)
>
> Faces and Places (ages 2-6 through 12-5)
>
> Arithmetic (ages 5-0 through 12-5)
>
> Riddles (ages 3-0 through 4-11)
>
> Reading/Decoding (ages 5-0 through 12-5)
>
> Reading/Understanding (ages 7-0 through 12-5)

The *K-ABC* manual contains instructional suggestions for teaching academic skills by using students' sequential or simultaneous processing strengths. Although remedial suggestions are based upon research results, further validation of this intervention approach is needed. Anastasi and Urbina (1997) caution that the simultaneous and sequential subtests on the *K-ABC* could also be interpreted as measures of verbal and nonverbal reasoning.

On the *K-ABC*, it is possible to make comparisons between processing scale scores, and between each of these and achievement. A supplementary scoring system (Kamphaus & Reynolds, 1987a, 1987b) allows computation of two additional aptitude scores (Verbal Intelligence Composite and General Intelligence Composite) and provides a system for determining whether global scores are significantly different. For example, it is possible to compare General Intelligence and Reading.

Also available on the *K-ABC* is a Nonverbal Scale composed of several mental processing subtests. On these subtests, directions can be given in pantomime, and only motor responses are required. The Nonverbal Scale is recommended for students with hearing impairments or speech and language disorders, and for those who do not speak English. For bilingual Hispanic students, the *K-ABC* manual provides information for Spanish-speaking examiners about giving test directions in Spanish and allowing Spanish responses.

The *K-ABC* appears to be a promising measure of intellectual performance with several interesting features, including a nonverbal scale and tests of two types of processing abilities. However, norms are available only up to age 12-5, its use is restricted to trained professionals such as school psychologists, and further validation of its remedial approach is needed. In addition, criticism has been leveled at the *K-ABC* in reference to its theoretical base (Sternberg, 1984a), its sequential-simultaneous factor structure (Strommen, 1988), and its relevance to instructional planning (Salvia & Hritcko, 1984).

Newer measures by the same authors are the *Kaufman Adolescent & Adult Intelligence Test (KAIT)* (1993) for ages 11 to 85+ and the *Kaufman Brief Intelligence Test (K-BIT)* (1990) for ages 4 to 90. Neither contains achievement measures. Both use a model of intelligence based on fluid and crystallized abilities rather than on sequential and simultaneous processing. Problem-solving tasks that assess crystallized abilities require the use of acquired knowledge; in contrast, new information must be processed to complete tasks that assess fluid abilities. The Core Battery of the *KAIT* is made up of six subtests: three on the crystallized scale and three on the fluid scale. The *K-BIT* contains two subtests: Vocabulary, a verbal measure of crystallized thinking, and Matrices, a nonverbal measure of fluid thinking.

Stanford-Binet Intelligence Scale: Fourth Edition

Unlike its predecessors, the 1986 edition of the *Stanford-Binet* (Thorndike, Hagen, & Sattler) is not an age scale. Although it retains many of the same types of items as found in earlier editions, this test is organized by subtests. This new edition represents several major changes: Items are arranged by skill areas rather than age; several scores are available, not just one global IQ score; and abilities other than verbal aptitude are emphasized. These changes make the *Stanford-Binet IV* much more similar to measures such as the *WISC-III* and the *Woodcock-Johnson-R.*

Designed for persons age 2 through adult, the *Stanford-Binet IV* contains 15 subtests that assess four areas of intellectual performance:

Verbal Reasoning

> Vocabulary
>
> Comprehension
>
> Absurdities
>
> Verbal Relations

Abstract/Visual Reasoning

> Pattern Analysis
>
> Copying
>
> Matrices
>
> Paper Folding and Cutting

Quantitative Reasoning

> Quantitative
>
> Number Series
>
> Equation Building

Short-Term Memory

> Bead Memory
>
> Memory for Sentences
>
> Memory for Digits
>
> Memory for Objects

According to the manual, Verbal Reasoning and Quantitative Reasoning subtests measure crystallized abilities, whereas Abstract/Visual Reasoning subtests assess fluid-analytic abilities. Experiences outside of school provide the knowledge base for fluid-analytic abilities, but schooling is the major influence on crystallized abilities. Thorndike and colleagues (1986) say that "the crystallized-abilities factor could also be called a scholastic- or academic-ability factor" (p. 4).

Results on the *Stanford-Binet IV* are normalized standard scores called Standard Age Scores (SAS), a term that is somewhat mislead-

ing. These are standard scores based on age norms, not age equivalents. Subtest Standard Age Scores are distributed with a mean of 50 and a standard deviation of 8. Subtest results can be combined into four area scores (Verbal Reasoning, Abstract/Visual Reasoning, Quantitative Reasoning, and Short-Term Memory) and an overall composite similar to a global IQ score. Area and total test Standard Age Scores have a mean of 100 and a standard deviation of 16.

Several important changes were made in the *Stanford-Binet* in its fourth revision. These changes may help to overcome some of the criticisms of previous editions, particularly concerns about overemphasis of verbal aptitude. As research accumulates on this measure, it will become possible to make comparisons between it and other tests such as the *WISC-III* and the *Woodcock-Johnson-R* that attempt to assess a variety of intellectual abilities.

Hammill Multiability Intelligence Test

The *Hammill Multiability Intelligence Test (HAMIT)* by Hammill, Bryant, and Pearson (1998) is a measure of intellectual performance developed in conjunction with the *Hammill Multiability Achievement Test (HAMAT).* The *HAMIT* is designed for students ages 6-0 to 17-11; only one form is available.

According to its manual, the *HAMIT* is a "special use version" (p. vii) of the *Detroit Tests of Learning Aptitude-4* (Hammill et al., 1998). The *DTLA-4* is discussed in the next chapter as a measure of specific learning abilities. Eight of the 10 *DTLA-4* subtests have been incorporated intact into the *HAMIT.* These subtests are:

Verbal Subtests

- Word Opposites
- Sentence Imitation
- Basic Information
- Word Sequences

Nonverbal Subtests

- Design Sequences
- Design Reproduction
- Symbolic Relations
- Story Sequences

HAMIT results include three composite quotients: General Intelligence (based on all subtests), Verbal Intelligence, and Nonverbal Intelligence. These scores are distributed with a mean of 100 and a standard deviation of 15. Subtest standard scores are distributed with a mean of 10 and a standard deviation of 3. The manual provides guidelines for determining whether significant discrepancies exist between *HAMIT* quotients and results of measures of academic achievement such as the *HAMAT, PIAT-R, WIAT, Woodcock-Johnson-R,* and *WRAT3.*

Das-Naglieri Cognitive Assessment System

The *Das-Naglieri Cognitive Assessment System (CAS)* by Naglieri and Das (1997) is based on the PASS theory of cognitive processing. PASS stands for Planning, Attention, Simultaneous, and Successive (i.e., sequential). The *CAS* is designed to assess these processes in students ages 5-0 to 17-11. The Basic Battery contains eight subtests, two measuring each of the four processes:

Planning

- Matching Numbers
- Planned Codes

Attention

- Expressive Attention
- Number Detection

Simultaneous

- Nonverbal Matrices
- Verbal-Spatial Relations

Successive

- Word Series
- Sentence Repetition

The Standard Battery contains 12 subtests—one additional subtest in each of the four PASS areas.

Results include standard scores for the Full Scale and each of the four PASS Scales. Subtest scaled scores are also available. The manual provides guidelines for determining whether discrepancies exist between results from the *CAS* and the *Woodcock-Johnson-R.*

NONVERBAL MEASURES AND OTHER APPROACHES TO NONBIASED ASSESSMENT

Concern about the potential bias of traditional measures of intellectual performance has led to the development of alternative strategies for the assessment of learning aptitude in culturally and linguistically diverse students. One early effort was the design of the *Culture Fair Intelligence Tests* (Cattell, 1950; Cattell & Cattell, 1960, 1963, 1977). These group-administered measures stress figural reasoning and deemphasize verbal skills and school learning. Another approach has been the nonstandard use of traditional measures such as IQ tests. Examples are the *System of Multicultural Pluralistic Assessment* and the *Learning Potential Assessment Device.* Most common today, however, are nonverbal tests of intellectual performance and measures in languages other than English. The next paragraphs describe some of the nonverbal tests available today as well as other approaches to nonbiased assessment. Measures in languages other than English are discussed in Chapter 14.

Nonverbal Measures of Intellectual Performance

Nonverbal measures of intelligence may be useful for students with hearing, speech, or language disorders, or for those whose language is not English. The Performance scale of the *WISC-III*, for example, deemphasizes verbal skills and is sometimes considered a nonverbal intelligence measure, even though directions are given verbally. Other well-known nonverbal tests include the *Raven Progressive Matrices*, the *Leiter International Performance Scale-Revised*, and the *Test of Nonverbal Intelligence* (3rd ed.).

Raven Progressive Matrices. The *Raven Progressive Matrices* are nonverbal tests in which the student is shown a design or matrix with a part missing. The student must then select, from several choices, the piece that best completes the matrix. This task requires figural reasoning and is the only task used on the three versions of the

Matrices. These are the *Standard Progressive Matrices* (Raven, 1938) for ages 6 to 18+, the *Coloured Progressive Matrices* (Raven, 1947) for ages 5 to 11 and adults with mental and physical impairments, and the *Advanced Progressive Matrices* (Raven, 1962) for age 12 through adults. These tests were originally standardized in England, but recent American norms are available from the tests' U.S. distributor, The Psychological Corporation. Portions of the manual were updated in 1988, 1994, and 1998.

Leiter International Performance Scale-Revised. The *Leiter-R* (Roid & Miller, 1997) is an update of the original nonverbal measure of intellectual performance published by Leiter in 1948. Like its predecessor, the *Leiter-R* is completely nonverbal. A typical test task requires the student to place response cards in the correct order based upon a stimulus design. The Visualization and Reasoning Battery of the *Leiter-R* contains 10 subtests; examples are Classification, Sequential Order, Matching, Figure-Ground, and Form Completion. New to the revised *Leiter* is the Attention and Memory Battery, which also provides 10 subtests. The *Leiter-R* is appropriate for ages 2-0 to 20-11. Results include an overall IQ score as well as subtest standard scores, percentile ranks, and age equivalents.

Test of Nonverbal Intelligence (3rd ed.). The *Test of Nonverbal Intelligence* (3rd ed.) *(TONI-3)* (Brown, Sherbenou, & Johnsen, 1997) is a much newer nonverbal measure. On this test, the examiner pantomimes instructions, and the subject responds by pointing to one of several possible answers. Test items assess problem solving with abstract, figural designs. The student is shown a set of figures with one or more figures missing. The individual must determine the rule or rules governing the set (e.g., matching, analogies, progressions) and then select the figure that best completes the set from several options.

The *TONI-3* offers two alternate forms. Results are reported as standard scores with a mean of 100 and a standard deviation of 15. The test was standardized on 3,451 persons, ages 6-0 to 89-11, and the standardization sample approximates the U.S. population in terms of race, ethnicity, geographic location, and urban-rural residence. Individuals with disabilities were included in the sample. Internal consistency, test-retest, and alternate forms reliability is adequate, and results of validity studies indicate that *TONI-3* results are related to results from other nonverbal measures of intelligence such as the Performance Scale of the *WISC-III* and *WAIS-R*. The *TONI-3* is a useful tool for the measurement of nonverbal problem-solving ability.

Other Approaches to Nonbiased Assessment

Traditional measures of intellectual performance such as the *WISC-R* and Raven's *Progressive Matrices* have been used in nontraditional ways in an attempt to improve assessment practices for culturally and linguistically diverse students. The two assessment systems described here represent interesting approaches to nonbiased assessment, although neither has gained widespread acceptance.

System of Multicultural Pluralistic Assessment. The *System of Multicultural Pluralistic Assessment (SOMPA)* (Mercer & Lewis, 1977b) is a battery of nine measures designed to provide information about the general learning aptitude of children ages 5 to 11 from diverse sociocultural backgrounds and white, African American, and Hispanic ethnic groups. The *SOMPA* assesses performance from three separate perspectives: Medical, Social System, and Pluralistic.

Medical measures evaluate the student's current health status to determine whether pathological conditions are interfering with physiological functioning. Social System measures determine whether the student is meeting performance expectations for school and social roles. Academic role performance is assessed with the *WISC-R*. Social role performance is assessed with the *Adaptive Behavior Inventory for Children (ABIC)* (Mercer & Lewis, 1977a), a parent interview form that elicits information about the student's ability to cope with nonacademic environments.

The pluralistic perspective of the *SOMPA* is concerned with whether the student is meeting performance expectations for age and sociocultural group. The Sociocultural Scales are used to assess the student's current environment. Included are questions about family size and structure, socioeconomic status, and urban acculturation. Then the *WISC-R* is rescored to compare the student with his or her sociocultural group rather than with standard norms. The new *WISC-R* scores are considered measures of Estimated Learning Potential.

The *SOMPA* has been heavily criticized for its lack of national norms (standardization took place in California only), its failure to include school performance tasks, its lack of validity data for the Estimated Learning Potential score, and its failure to provide guidelines for use of the battery in educational decisions (Clarizio, 1979; Goodman, 1979; Oakland, 1979). Salvia and Ysseldyke (1991) conclude that the *SOMPA*, at best, should be viewed as an experimental measure. Sattler (1988) is particularly critical of the Estimated Learning Potential (ELP) score. According to Sattler, *"There is no justification for using the ELP for any clinical or psychoeducational purpose"* (p. 354).

Learning Potential Assessment Device. The assessment system proposed by Feuerstein and colleagues (1979) is another nontraditional approach to evaluation of learning aptitude. According to Feuerstein, children learn through interactions with adults in mediated learning experiences. In these interactions, the adult "mediates" the world to the child "by framing, selecting, focusing, and feeding back environmental experiences" (p. 71). In Feuerstein's view, cultural deprivation results from inadequate mediated learning; culturally deprived children have not assimilated their own culture.

In the *Learning Potential Assessment Device (LPAD)*, the tester becomes a teacher and attempts to provide the student with mediated learning. To accomplish this, the *LPAD* is administered using a test-teach-test format. This device is actually a collection of measures, some adapted from experimental tasks, others from published instruments such as Raven's *Progressive Matrices*. The student first performs reasoning tasks without assistance from the examiner. The examiner then steps into the instructional role and attempts to provide the student with more sophisticated strategies for task solution.

Test tasks are then presented again without coaching. This approach is sometimes called *dynamic* or *interactive assessment*.

The aim is to assess the student's cognitive modifiability rather than current intellectual status. The examiner observes the student's performance and forms a judgment about deficient cognitive functions and the ability to learn. Test tasks are not normed and scores are not emphasized. Instead, the *LPAD* is intended for clinical use, and its results are primarily descriptive rather than quantitative.

This measure and the accompanying intervention program, Instrumental Enrichment (Feuerstein et al., 1980), are still under study (Feuerstein et al., 1981; Feuerstein, Miller, Rand, & Jensen, 1981; Frisby & Braden, 1992; Harth, 1982). Although the *LPAD* is an interesting system that attempts to address the central question of ability to learn, it is unlikely to be widely used in schools. It is a clinical measure tied to the expertise of the individual examiner, and produces results that appear less objective than those of traditional tests. For more information on the *LPAD* and similar approaches, see the Fall 1992 special issue of the *Journal of Special Education* on interactive assessment. Also of interest is the *Swanson-Cognitive Processing Test* (Swanson, 1996), a newer norm-referenced measure of intellectual performance that incorporates dynamic assessment techniques.

ADAPTIVE BEHAVIOR MEASURES

Adaptive behavior is usually not measured directly. Instead, the student's parents or teachers act as informants about the student's current nonacademic functioning. Interviews are typically used with parents, and written questionnaires with teachers.

There are several norm-referenced measures of adaptive behavior available today, as Table 8–2 illustrates. This table lists the names of the measures, the ages for which each is appropriate, the person or persons who act as informants, and the type of measure (e.g., interview). In the next section, the *AAMR Adaptive Behavior Scale-School* (2nd ed.) is described. Other measures are then discussed briefly.

TABLE 8-2

Measures of Adaptive Behavior

NAME (AUTHOR)	AGES	INFORMANT	TYPE OF MEASURE
AAMR Adaptive Behavior Scale-Residential and Community (2nd ed.) (Nihira, Leland & Lambert, 1993)	18 to 60+	Teacher or other professional	Questionnaire
		Parent	Interview
AAMR Adaptive Behavior Scale-School (2nd ed.) (Lambert, Nihira, & Leland, 1993)	3 to 21	Teacher	Questionnaire
		Parent	Interview
Adaptive Behavior Evaluation Scale-Revised (McCarney, 1995)	5 to 18	Teacher	Questionnaire
		Parent	
Adaptive Behavior Inventory (Brown & Leigh, 1986)	5-0 to 18-11	Teacher	Questionnaire
Adaptive Behavior Inventory for Children (Mercer & Lewis, 1977a)	5 to 11	Parent	Interview
Assessment of Adaptive Areas (Bryant, Taylor, & Rivera, 1996)	3 to 80 (persons with mental retardation), 3 to 18 (persons without mental retardation)	Results from the *AAMR Adaptive Behavior Scale* (2nd ed.)	Score conversion system
Checklist of Adaptive Living Skills (Morreau & Bruininks, 1991)	Infants to mature adults	Teacher	Questionnaire
Scales of Independent Behavior-Revised (Bruininks, Woodcock, Weatherman, & Hill, 1996)	Infants to 80+ years	Parent or teacher	Interview or questionnaire
Vineland Adaptive Behavior Scale (Sparrow, Balla, & Cicchetti, 1984)			
• Interview editions	• Birth to 18-11 and low-functioning adults	• Parent	• Interview
• Classroom edition	• 3 to 12-11	• Teacher	• Questionnaire
Weller-Strawser Scales of Adaptive Behavior for the Learning Disabled (Weller & Strawser, 1981)	Students identified as learning disabled	Teacher	Questionnaire

AAMR ADAPTIVE BEHAVIOR SCALE-SCHOOL (2ND ED.)

The *AAMR Adaptive Behavior Scale-School* (2nd ed.) *(ABS-S:2)* by Lambert, Nihira, and Leland (1993) is the most current edition of a series of adaptive behavior measures developed by the American Association on Mental Retardation (AAMR), formerly the American Association on Mental Deficiency (AAMD). A companion measure, the *AAMR Adaptive Behavior Scale-Residential and Community* (2nd ed.) (Nihira, Leland, & Lambert, 1993), is also available.

The *ABS-S:2* is an indirect measure of adaptive and maladaptive behaviors. Norms extend from age 3 to age 21 for individuals with mental retardation; those for students without retardation begin at age 3 but extend only to age 18. According to its manual, results of the *ABS-S:2* can be used to identify strengths and weaknesses in adaptive behavior, to determine if students show below average performance in this area, and to document student progress.

The *ABS-S:2* is a print questionnaire. It can be completed by professionals such as teachers, if they are sufficiently familiar with the student's skill levels. If they are not, the scale can be used as an interview; the professional asks the questions, and a parent or another person who knows the student well answers.

Part One of the *ABS-S:2* addresses adaptive behavior skills related to personal independence.

AAMR Adaptive Behavior Scale-School (2nd ed.) (ABS-S:2)

N. Lambert, K. Nihira, & H. Leland (1993)

Type: Norm-referenced questionnaire (or interview)

Major Content Areas: Adaptive and maladaptive behavior

Type of Administration: Print questionnaire or individual interview

Administration Time: Approximately 30 minutes

Age/Grade Levels: Ages 3 to 21 (students with mental retardation); ages 3 to 18 (students without mental retardation)

Types of Scores: Standard scores and percentile ranks for 16 domains and 5 factors; age equivalents for Part One domains and factors

Computer Aids: *ABS-S:2 Scoring Software and Report System*

Typical Uses: An indirect measure of several dimensions of adaptive and maladaptive behavior

Cautions: The classification system recommended in the manual for *ABS-S:2* scores is somewhat unusual

Publisher: PRO-ED (www.proedinc.com)

It includes nine domains: Independent Functioning (e.g., eating, toilet use, dressing), Physical Development, Economic Activity, Language Development, Numbers and Time, Prevocational/Vocational Activity, Self-Direction, Responsibility, and Socialization. Part Two is concerned with social behaviors, including those that can be classified as maladaptive. There are seven Part Two domains: Social Behavior, Conformity, Trustworthiness, Stereotyped and Hyperactive Behavior, Self-Abusive Behavior, Social Engagement, and Disturbing Interpersonal Behavior.

Technical Quality

The *ABS-S:2* was standardized with two groups: 2,074 students with mental retardation from 40 states, and 1,254 individuals without mental retardation from 44 states. Both samples appear to resemble the general school-aged population in race and geographic region; however, rural students are overrepresented. Eighty-seven percent of the students in the non-mental retardation sample were placed in general education classes. The sample of students with mental retardation includes individuals with IQ scores of less than 20 (12%), those with

IQ scores from 20 to 49 (48%), and those with IQ scores from 50 to 70 (40%). Fifty percent of these students were placed in self-contained special education classes; 68% lived at home.

The reliability of the *ABS-S:2* appears adequate. Average internal consistency correlation coefficients fall above .80 for all domain and factor scores for both norm groups. Interrater reliability also appears satisfactory. Validity was studied in a number of ways. Part One of the *ABS-S:2* shows moderate correlations with results of other measures of adaptive behavior. As would be expected, results of Part Two, the portion of the *ABS-S:2* that assesses maladaptive behavior, are not related to results of other adaptive behavior scales. Similar findings are reported for studies of the relationships between Parts One and Two of the *ABS-S:2* and tests of intellectual performance.

The technical quality of the *ABS-S:2* is much improved over that of the previous edition. The standardization samples have been broadened to include students from more than two states, the samples are described in detail, reliability is adequate, and there is information about the relationship of this scale to other measures of adaptive behavior.

Administration Considerations

Either professionals or paraprofessionals may complete the *ABS-S:2* as a questionnaire, but trained professionals are needed when the scale is used as an interview form with parents. The manual advises the use of an interpreter if the student's parents communicate in a language other than English.

Results and Interpretation

Raw scores for each of the 16 domains can be converted into percentile ranks and standard scores using either the mental retardation or the non-mental retardation norms. Domain standard scores are distributed with a mean of 10 and a standard deviation of 3. The standard score classification system recommended in the manual is somewhat unusual. Standard scores of 6 and 7 are described as "Below Average," those in the 4–5 range "Poor," and those from 1–3 "Very Poor." Age equivalent scores can be obtained for Part One domains only.

The *ABS-S:2* Profile/Summary Form is used to convert students' scores on individual items to factor scores. There are five factors—three derived from Part One items and two from Part Two items:

- The *Personal Self-Sufficiency* factor is composed of items from the Independent Functioning and Physical Development domains.
- The *Community Self-Sufficiency* factor is composed of items from the Independent Functioning, Economic Activity, Language Development, Numbers and Time, and Prevocational/Vocational Activity domains.
- The *Personal-Social Responsibility* factor is composed of items from the Prevocational/Vocational Activity, Self-Direction, Responsibility, and Socialization domains.
- The *Social Adjustment* factor is composed of items from the Social Behavior, Conformity, and Trustworthiness domains.
- The *Personal Adjustment* factor is composed of items from the Stereotyped and Hyperactive Behavior and Self-Abusive Behavior domains.

Raw factor scores are computed and converted to percentile ranks and quotients. Again, either the mental retardation or the non-mental retardation norms can be used. Quotients are standard scores distributed with a mean of 100 and a standard deviation of 15. The manual classifies quotients from 80 to 89 as "Below Average." Those from 70 to 79 are considered "Poor," and those below 70 "Very Poor." Age equivalent scores can be obtained for Part One factors only.

Assessment of Adaptive Areas (AAA) (Bryant, Taylor, & Rivera, 1996) is a system for converting results from the *ABS-S:2* to scores that are directly related to the adaptive skill areas named in the 1992 AAMR definition of mental retardation. Results from the *ABS-S:2* are transferred to the *AAA* record booklet so that raw scores can be determined for the 10 adaptive skill areas:

- Communication
- Self-Care
- Home-Living
- Social
- Community Use
- Self-Direction
- Health and Safety
- Functional Academics
- Leisure
- Work

Raw scores can then be converted to standard scores, percentile ranks, and age equivalents. Standard scores in the *AAA* are distributed with a mean of 10 and a standard deviation of 3. The *AAA* manual describes performance in the standard score 8–12 range as "Average."

The *ABS-S:2* appears to be a useful measure for the study of several dimensions of adaptive and maladaptive behaviors in school-aged students. In addition, this version of the scale shows many improvements over the previous version. However, results are best used to identify areas of need; further assessment will likely be necessary to plan instructional programs for individual students.

OTHER MEASURES OF ADAPTIVE BEHAVIOR

Several measures of adaptive behavior in addition to the *ABS-S:2* are available to professionals. These include the most recent update of the *Vineland Social Maturity Scale* (Doll, 1935,

1965), one of the earliest measures of adaptive behavior. This measure is described in the following sections along with the *Scales of Independent Behavior-Revised* (a companion to the *Woodcock-Johnson-R)*, the *Weller-Strawser Scales of Adaptive Behavior for the Learning Disabled,* and the *Adaptive Behavior Evaluation Scale-Revised.*

Vineland Adaptive Behavior Scales

The *Vineland Adaptive Behavior Scales* (Sparrow, Balla, & Cicchetti, 1984) are updates and revisions of Doll's *Vineland Social Maturity Scale.* Doll's instrument was a parent interview form, but the new *Vineland* contains three separate scales: two interview editions in survey or expanded form, and a classroom edition.

The interview editions are used by trained interviewers with parents or others who know the student well. The survey form includes fewer items than included in the expanded interview form and, consequently, requires less administration time. Interviews are conducted in a semistructured format; that is, the interviewer uses his or her own words to probe respondents about the student's current functioning. Interview items are not read. When the interviewer has gathered sufficient information about the student's participation in specific activities, he or she rates the student on the scale's items. Interview editions of the *Vineland* are designed for assessment of children from birth to age 18-11 and low-functioning adults. A Spanish version of the survey form is available.

The classroom edition is a print questionnaire completed by the student's teacher. It is appropriate for ages 3 to 12-11 and requires approximately 20 minutes. The classroom and interview editions assess four adaptive behavior domains and several subdomains:

- *Communication* domain. Includes the Receptive, Expressive, and Written subdomains.
- *Daily Living Skills* domain. Includes the Personal, Domestic, and Community subdomains.
- *Socialization* domain. Includes the Interpersonal Relationships, Play and Leisure Time, and Coping Skills subdomains.

- *Motor Skills* domain. Includes the Gross and Fine subdomains.

The Motor Skills domain is intended for children up to age 6, but it can be used with older persons with physical or other disabilities. The interview editions also contain *Maladaptive Behavior,* an optional domain for individuals age 5 and above.

The interview editions were standardized with a national sample of 3,000 persons, ages birth to 19, and a supplementary sample of 1,788 individuals with disabilities, including adults with mental retardation and children in residential facilities for individuals with emotional disturbance, visual impairments, and hearing impairments. For the classroom edition, the national standardization sample contained 2,925 students, ages 3 to 13. Each of the national samples was selected to represent the U.S. population as described in 1980 Census data. However, the classroom edition sample appears to differ from the national population on several variables. For instance, 7.2% of the sample represents rural communities, whereas 29% of the nation's population is classified as living in rural communities.

Standard scores are available for each of the adaptive behavior domains and for the Composite score, a summary of the four domains. Standard scores are distributed with a mean of 100 and a standard deviation of 15. Only Age Equivalent scores can be computed for subdomains. On the interview editions, students can be compared to both national norms and norms derived from the supplementary sample of persons with disabilities. Also, a standard score is available for the optional domain, Maladaptive Behavior.

The revised *Vineland* scales, particularly those designed for use with parents, appear to be useful instruments for the study of several areas of adaptive behavior. One limitation is the amount of training needed to properly administer the semistructured parent interview. The *Vineland* manuals restrict administration of the interview editions and scoring and interpretation of all editions to "a psychologist, social worker, or other professional with a graduate degree and specific training in individual assessment and test interpretation."

Scales of Independent Behavior-Revised

The *Scales of Independent Behavior-Revised (SIB-R)* (Bruininks, Woodcock, Weatherman, & Hill, 1996) are considered companion measures to the *Woodcock-Johnson Psycho-Educational Battery-Revised.* The *SIB-R* adds adaptive behavior and problem behavior to the domains of cognitive ability and achievement assessed in this multidimensional battery.

The *SIB-R* is a structured interview that is appropriate for gathering information about persons ranging in age from infancy through 80+ years. The respondent can be anyone who knows the child or adult well. The *SIB-R* can also be used as a checklist; for example, knowledgeable respondents can answer questions directly on the *SIB-R* form, rather than being interviewed.

The *SIB-R* is made up of four Adaptive Behavior clusters, each of which contains several subscales:

Motor Skills
> Gross-Motor Skills
>
> Fine-Motor Skills

Social Interaction and Communication Skills
> Social Interaction
>
> Language Comprehension
>
> Language Expression

Personal Living Skills
> Eating and Meal Preparation
>
> Toileting
>
> Dressing
>
> Personal Self-Care
>
> Domestic Skills

Community Living Skills
> Time and Punctuality
>
> Money and Value
>
> Work Skills
>
> Home/Community Orientation

These 14 subscales require 45 to 60 minutes to administer, and results are summarized by a Broad Independence (Full Scale) score. A Short

Form is also available, as well as an Early Development Form for children from birth to age 6 and students with severe disabilities.

An optional Problem Behavior Scale assesses eight areas of maladaptive behavior organized into three clusters:

Internalized Maladaptive Behavior
- Hurtful to Self
- Unusual or Repetitive Habits
- Withdrawal or Inattentive Behavior

Asocial Maladaptive Behavior
- Socially Offensive Behavior
- Uncooperative Behavior

Externalized Maladaptive Behavior
- Hurtful to Others
- Destructive to Property
- Disruptive Behavior

Norms are based on a national sample of more than 2,100 persons. A variety of scores are available, including age equivalents, percentile ranks, standard scores, Relative Mastery Indexes (RMIs), and Maladaptive Behavior Indexes (MBIs). In addition, an overall Support Score can be calculated. The Support Score, which takes into consideration both adaptive and maladaptive behaviors, indicates the intensity of support that will be required by the student. Because the *SIB-R* is part of the *Woodcock-Johnson-R* system, its results can be related directly to results of that battery's cognitive ability tests.

Weller-Strawser Scales of Adaptive Behavior for the Learning Disabled

Unlike most adaptive behavior measures, the *Weller-Strawser Scales of Adaptive Behavior* (Weller & Strawser, 1981) are designed for use with only one population: students already identified as learning disabled. The *Weller-Strawser* is a checklist that is completed by professionals after a period of observation of the student under study. Its purpose is not to determine eligibility for special services but rather to identify areas of need for instructional planning.

Weller and Strawser (1981) describe the four areas of adaptive behavior assessed by this instrument:

- *Social Coping.* "Assesses the manner in which the learning disabled student deals with environmental situations."

- *Relationships.* "Assesses how the learning disabled student relates to others."

- *Pragmatic Language.* "Assesses the learning disabled student's use of language in those social situations which are language based."

- *Production.* "Assesses *how* the learning disabled produces rather than *what* is produced." (pp. 11–12)

Both an Elementary and a Secondary scale are available, each containing 35 items. On each item, the teacher reads descriptions of appropriate and inappropriate behaviors and selects the one that best describes the student.

The two language subtests on the *Weller-Strawser* assess areas that are not usually included on measures of adaptive behavior. The Pragmatic Language subtest is concerned with areas such as ability to interpret gestures and facial expressions, the use of intuition and reasoning, and sense of humor. The Production subtest attempts to assess concentration, generalization of learning, organizational skills, and need for modification of instruction. Although these areas may be of concern with some students with learning disabilities, they are not usually considered dimensions of adaptive behavior.

One major limitation of this instrument is that it classifies student performance into only two categories: mild-moderate deficit or moderate-severe deficit. Even if a student's behavior is rated as appropriate on all items, results will indicate mild-moderate deficits in all areas. Another major concern is the lack of information about the standardization sample. Teachers of students with learning disabilities from urban and rural areas of six states rated the behavior of their students. The manual reports that "a total of 236 students between the ages of six and eighteen were selected by the teachers for inclusion in the rating. Of these 236 students, 154 were of elementary age and 82 were of secondary age" (p. 66). No other descriptive data about the standardization sample are provided.

Adaptive Behavior Evaluation Scale-Revised

The *Adaptive Behavior Evaluation Scale-Revised (ABES-R)* (McCarney, 1995) includes two versions: a School Version and a Home version. Both are questionnaires designed to be completed by persons who are familiar with the student who is being assessed.

The *ABES-R* assesses the 10 adaptive skill areas included in the 1992 AAMR definition of mental retardation (Communication, Self-Care, Home-Living, and so forth). Norms are available for ages 5 through 18, with separate norms for males and females. Results include standard scores and percentile ranks for each of the 10 subscales as well as a Total Scale Quotient. The test package includes the *Adaptive Behavior Intervention Manual-Revised* (McCarney, McCain, & Bauer, 1995), a collection of suggestions for objectives, goals, and interventions related to the areas assessed by the *ABES-R*.

The *ABES-R* was standardized with more than 7,000 students from 24 states. There appear to be differences between the standardization sample and the nation as a whole in terms of race (sample 84.0% White; nation 76.2%), urban-rural residence, and geographic region. The *ABES-R* has adequate test-retest, interrater, and internal consistency reliability. Its validity was studied in several ways, including its relationship to other measures of adaptive behavior. The *ABES-R* appears to be related to measures such as the Classroom Edition of the *Vineland Adaptive Behavior Scales* and the *Adaptive Behavior Inventory*.

ANSWERING THE ASSESSMENT QUESTIONS

The assessment team gathers information about intellectual performance and adaptive behavior to arrive at an estimate of the student's current learning aptitude. In evaluating assessment results, the team compares and contrasts the student's academic aptitude, which is measured by tests of intellectual performance, with current levels of functioning in nonacademic activities. The disability of mental retardation is indicated only when both intellectual performance and adaptive behavior are below average. In learning disabilities and behavioral disorders, intellectual performance must be within the average range, and adaptive behavior may be either adequate or below average.

Types of Procedures

Several types of assessment strategies are used to study learning aptitude: group tests of intellectual performance, individual intelligence tests, school records, parent interviews, questionnaires and checklists for teachers, and direct observation of students' adaptive behavior. Each of these methods is likely to produce somewhat different results.

Results from measures of intellectual performance are not expected to be equivalent to those from measures of adaptive behavior. These two strategies assess different skill domains, and although there is some relationship between academic aptitude and adaptive behavior (Harrison, 1987), students may perform poorly in one of these areas but adequately in the other.

Intellectual performance is assessed with group and individual tests, and parents and teachers may provide supplementary information about the student's aptitude for school learning. Individual tests are preferred over group measures. In special education assessment, there is no substitute for individually administered tests of intellectual performance. The information provided by parents and teachers is useful to corroborate test results; if major discrepancies occur, the team should continue its investigation, perhaps by administering a second individual test. Like group test results, the reports of parents and teachers should be considered preliminary data—less accurate than results of individual measures. As Robinson and Robinson (1976) observe, "There is little doubt that a much higher percentage of individuals were inappropriately labeled as mentally retarded, or, conversely, not retarded, when such labels depended completely on the subjective appraisal of teachers and physicians" (p. 23).

Adaptive behavior may be assessed directly through the presentation of test tasks or by observation, but usually informants are asked about the student's typical performance. Direct measurement can be very time-consuming; for a comprehensive assessment, the professional would have to observe and evaluate the student's behavior in a wide range of situations. The primary persons who serve as informants regarding adaptive behavior are parents and teachers. Because of their different perspectives, parents and teachers may provide different estimates of the student's current functioning (Harrison, 1987). Parents see their child in settings that impose quite different demands from those of the classroom. Also, parents and children share experiences over a number of years. Teachers, in contrast, see students in academic situations and nonscholastic school activities. They are usually acquainted with students for only one school year, but are able to evaluate the performance of a particular child in relation to the typical performance of agemates. Neither the parent's nor the teacher's perspective is the "right" one. Each is able to provide only part of the picture of adaptive behavior.

Another factor that influences adaptive behavior assessment is the method used to question informants. The typical strategies are face-to-face interviews and print questionnaires. Interviews allow personal contact, and the interviewer can explain the purpose of the assessment, answer any questions, and probe the informant's unclear responses. In addition, interviews do not require reading and writing skills. However, interviews take more time than do print methods, and respondents may be more willing to answer personal questions on paper. Interviews typically are used with parents, and print methods with teachers, but of course there are exceptions.

Nature of the Assessment Tasks

Assessment instruments differ in the ways they attempt to measure learning aptitude. Among the important differences are the comprehensiveness of measures and tasks that assess the domains of interest. In the evaluation of intellectual performance, most measures attempt to be comprehensive. Individual intelligence tests typically sample several types of reasoning skills, although some of the nonverbal tests restrict assessment to one type (e.g., figural reasoning or problem solving).

However, the comprehensiveness of a measure is influenced by the nature of its assessment tasks. For example, the *WISC-III*, the *Woodcock-Johnson-R*, and the *Stanford-Binet IV* are designed to evaluate several different reasoning skills. In contrast, tests such as the 1973 *Stanford-Binet* and the *Slosson Intelligence Scale-Revised* emphasize verbal tasks. At the opposite extreme, nonverbal tests like the *TONI-3* deemphasize verbal abilities and rely solely on performance tasks to evaluate intellectual performance.

Tests that differ on the nature of the tasks used to assess performance may produce quite different results. For example, if a student were to score notably higher on *WISC-III* performance subtests than on verbal subtests, results of nonverbal tests would probably produce higher estimates of current intellectual performance than results of tests emphasizing verbal abilities. This would not necessarily mean that either type of measure was inappropriate, only that each provided merely part of the picture.

The content across adaptive behavior measures is quite similar (Kamphaus, 1987). Most scales include items that assess self-help or daily living skills, socialization and interpersonal relations, and independent functioning in the home and community. Questions about communication skills, motor development, and sensory capabilities are also common. Some measures include additional areas. The *Vineland* Maladaptive Behavior domain and the Problem Behavior Scale on the *SIB-R* are examples. Although measures may be similar in content, they vary in the persons used as informants and the ways that information is collected. These differences may influence the estimated level of current adaptive behavior.

Documentation of Learning Aptitude

The broad assessment question that guides the team in its study of the student's learning aptitude is this: *Is the school performance problem related to a disability?* This question is multifaceted, and the team usually begins its investigation by gathering data about one major concern: general learning aptitude. Two specific assessment questions provide the structure for this part of the process: *What is the student's current level of intellectual performance? What is the student's current functioning level in adaptive behavior?*

Information is gathered from many sources. School records are reviewed for results of group tests of intellectual performance and data on the student's developmental and school history. Intellectual performance is assessed with individual norm-referenced tests, which are usually administered by school psychologists. To obtain information about adaptive behavior, teachers and parents may be interviewed or asked to complete questionnaires.

The team reviews assessment results and attempts to describe the student's current levels of learning aptitude. These descriptions are norm-referenced; they depict the student's standing in relation to peers. If current performance is within the below average range in both intellectual performance and adaptive behavior, the team may decide that the student meets eligibility criteria for mental retardation—provided, of course, that a school performance problem has been documented. If intellectual functioning is not below average, the student may still be eligible for special education services. In such a case, it would be necessary to satisfy eligibility criteria for either learning disabilities or behavioral disorders. For example, consider the results of the learning aptitude assessment for Joyce, the fourth grader with school performance problems.

Joyce

Results of individual achievement tests have confirmed that Joyce is experiencing difficulty in reading, spelling, and handwriting. Continuing the assessment, the team begins an investigation of general learning aptitude. No results of group intelligence tests are found in the school records, and the brief developmental history that Joyce's mother completed at the beginning of the school year does not suggest major developmental delays. Mr. Harvey, Joyce's teacher, reports that Joyce learns some skills quite easily, and Joyce's parents confirm this. Because of this, mental retardation is not suspected, and the team does not plan to assess adaptive behavior.

The school psychologist, Ms. Kellett, meets with Joyce and administers the *Wechsler Intelligence Scale for Children-Third Edition*. Joyce scores within the average range in verbal abilities, performance abilities, and general intellectual functioning. On the *WISC-III* factor-based Index scores, Joyce's performance falls within the average to high average range on Verbal Comprehension, the average range on Perceptual Organization, and the low average to average range on Freedom from Distractibility and Processing Speed. Joyce shows unusual discrepancies between Index scores. A difference of 29 points between Verbal Comprehension and Freedom from Distractibility occurred in only 3.5% of the standardization sample; a difference of 32 points between Verbal Comprehension and Processing Speed occurred in only 5.7% of the standardization sample. (See Figure 8–1 for Joyce's *WISC-III* results.)

The assessment team concludes that Joyce shows average intellectual performance with possible weaknesses in specific cognitive abilities. The team will continue assessment and explore the possibility of learning disabilities.

STUDY GUIDE

REVIEW QUESTIONS

1. What is learning aptitude?
2. Read these statements and tell whether they are true or false.

    _____ Learning aptitude is assessed by evaluating two dimensions of behavior: intellectual performance and adaptive behavior.

    _____ Adaptive behavior is operationalized as performance on standardized tests of intelligence.

    _____ Intelligence tests contain items that require reasoning, problem solving, and scholastic aptitude.

    _____ Measures of adaptive behavior assess competence in areas such as self-help, socialization, communication, and motor development.

3. Select the statement that best describes current practices in the assessment of learning aptitude.

    a. Learning aptitude is assessed only when the disability of mental retardation is suspected.

    b. All students referred for special education assessment are evaluated in terms of adaptive behavior.

    c. When students show below average performance on tests of intellectual performance, adaptive behavior is assessed.

    d. Group tests are preferred for the study of intellectual performance.

4. Many of the controversies related to special education assessment center on misuse of intelligence tests. List two safeguards of federal law that help prevent the inappropriate use of these measures.

5. Check *each* of the assessment devices and procedures that can be used to document learning aptitude.

    _____ a. Group intelligence tests

    _____ b. Measures of adaptive behavior

    _____ c. Norm-referenced achievement tests

    _____ d. Parent and teacher interviews

    _____ e. Early developmental history

    _____ f. Individual measures of intellectual performance

    _____ g. Criterion-referenced tests of reading and mathematics

    _____ h. Observation of the student's behavior in nonacademic settings

6. Match the test of intellectual performance in Column A with the description in Column B.

Column A

a. *Wechsler Intelligence Test for Children-Third Edition*

b. *Woodcock-Johnson Psycho-Educational Battery-Revised, Tests of Cognitive Ability*

c. *Kaufman Assessment Battery for Children*

d. *Stanford-Binet Intelligence Scale: Fourth Edition*

e. *Test of Nonverbal Intelligence* (3rd ed.)

Column B

___ A measure for school-aged children that provides scores for Sequential Processing and Simultaneous Processing

___ Includes a Verbal Scale and a Performance Scale and four factor-based Index scores

___ Results include scores for Verbal Reasoning, Abstract/Visual Reasoning, and Quantitative Reasoning

___ Provides estimates of Reading Aptitude, Mathematics Aptitude, and Written Language Aptitude

___ Test items assess one ability area: problem solving with abstract, figural designs

7. Decide whether these statements about measures of adaptive behavior are true or false.

_____ The *Adaptive Behavior Evaluation Scale-Revised* is an observation system for use in school and home settings.

_____ Two forms of the *AAMR Adaptive Behavior Scale* (2nd ed.) are available, one for use in school and the other for individuals in residential and community settings.

_____ The *Weller-Strawser* is designed for use with students identified as learning disabled.

_____ The *Vineland Social Maturity Scale* assesses four major adaptive behavior domains: Communication, Daily Living Skills, Socialization, and Motor Skills.

_____ The *Scales of Independent Behavior-Revised* is a companion measure to the *Wechsler Intelligence Scale for Children-III.*

8. Which statement best describes the assessment system used to evaluate intellectual functioning and other areas related to school performance?

a. The *Woodcock-Johnson Psycho-Educational Battery-Revised* provides tests of cognitive ability and academic achievement.

b. The *Kaufman Assessment Battery for Children* assesses mental processing, school achievement, and classroom behavior.

c. The *System for Multicultural Pluralistic Assessment* is a comprehensive battery for the assessment of medical status, academic achievement, sociocultural characteristics, adaptive behavior, and estimated learning potential.

d. The *Hammill Multiability* tests measure school achievement, intellectual performance, and adaptive behavior.

9. Match the range of performance in Column A with the assessment results in Column B.

Column A

a. Above average performance

b. High average performance

c. Average performance

d. Low average performance

e. Below average performance

Column B

___ *WISC-III* Verbal IQ 72

___ *WISC-III* subtest scaled score 12

___ Subtest Standard Age Score 50 on the *Stanford-Binet IV*

___ Total test score 140 on the *TONI-3*

___ Broad Ability standard score of 62 on the *Woodcock-Johnson-R* Tests of Cognitive Ability

10. Which type of measure is typically used in the assessment of intellectual performance?
    a. Norm-referenced tests
    b. Informal measures such as criterion-referenced tests
11. If the special education assessment team finds that a student performs in the below average range in academic achievement, intellectual performance, and adaptive behavior, which of the following conclusions can be drawn?
    a. The student is eligible for special education services because of learning disabilities.
    b. The student is eligible for special education services because of mental retardation.
    c. The student is eligible for special education services because of behavioral disorders.
    d. The student is not eligible for special education services.

ACTIVITIES

1. Observe a professional administering either the *Wechsler Intelligence Scale for Children-Third Edition* or the *Stanford-Binet Intelligence Scale: Fourth Edition.* Analyze the results.
2. Under the supervision of the course instructor, practice assessing adaptive behavior by either completing a teacher questionnaire or interviewing a parent.
3. Obtain one of the assessment systems described in this chapter (e.g., *Woodcock-Johnson-R, K-ABC).* Review its contents and the directions for administration.
4. Identify the main components of interactive (or dynamic) assessment. Then compare this approach to the informal assessment techniques of diagnostic teaching and clinical interviewing.
5. Interview members of school assessment teams to find out how adaptive behavior is assessed. What measures do they prefer? Is adaptive behavior included as part of the assessment plan for most students who are referred to special education?

DISCUSSION QUESTIONS

1. Explain why both intellectual performance and adaptive behavior are considered in the assessment of learning aptitude.
2. Discuss the reasons why learning aptitude is of interest for all special students, not just students with mental retardation.
3. In the assessment of learning aptitude, the special education team gathers data to help determine whether a school performance problem is related to a disability. Explain why norm-referenced measures are preferred.
4. Review the information presented in this chapter about the technical quality of measures of adaptive behavior. For what purposes and with what types of students is each of these measures best used?
5. There have been several attempts to develop nonbiased measures of intellectual performance. These include the *SOMPA,* the *Learning Potential Assessment Device,* and the tests that emphasize nonverbal abilities. Discuss the rationale behind each approach.

CHAPTER 9

SPECIFIC LEARNING ABILITIES AND STRATEGIES

- Considerations in Assessment of Specific Learning Abilities
- Sources of Information about Specific Learning Abilities
- Screening for Sensory Impairments
- Screening for Learning Disabilities
- Measures of Perceptual-Motor Skills and Other Specific Learning Abilities
- Test Batteries for Specific Ability Assessment
- Assessment of Learning Strategies
- Discrepancy Analysis
- Answering the Assessment Questions

Specific learning abilities and strategies are one of the assessment team's major concerns in considering a student's eligibility for special education services. Students may show school performance problems despite average intellectual performance; one reason for this may be deficits in specific learning abilities. Such students are usually identified as learning disabled. Individuals with other disabilities may also experience difficulty in certain learning abilities and strategies. For example, attentional problems are often associated with students identified as behavior disordered.

In planning a student's assessment, the special education team poses several questions about disabilities. The major concern is this: *Is the school performance problem related to a disability?* Assessment usually begins with study of the student's current school performance and general aptitude for learning. Then the team continues by investigating other domains, including specific learning abilities.

Vision and hearing are important considerations for all students, including those with possible deficits in specific learning abilities. Screening for vision and hearing problems is conducted in schools routinely. The results of screening procedures should be reviewed when students are referred for special education assessment. Although vision and hearing are not considered specific learning abilities, they are closely related. Thus, the assessment team asks, *What is the status of the student's sensory abilities?*

Assessment of specific learning abilities has traditionally emphasized discrete ability areas such as memory, visual perception, auditory discrimination, and so forth. Professionals are also becoming interested in the ways that students use their specific abilities in situations requiring learning, that is, in their learning strategies and study skills. These concerns lead the team to two assessment questions: *What is the student's current level of development in specific learning abilities? What is the student's current functioning level in strategies for learning and study skills?* In the assessment of learning disabilities, it is also necessary to determine whether there is a discrepancy between expected and actual school performance. Therefore, the team asks, *Is there a substantial discrepancy between the student's actual achievement and the achievement level expected for that student?*

At this stage in assessment, the team attempts to identify specific strengths and weaknesses in the student's repertoire of skills for school learning. Observations made in the evaluation of academic achievement, intellectual performance, and adaptive behavior may prove useful if they indicate potential difficulties in specific learning abilities and strategies. In the case of Joyce, for example, the team was interested in learning more about Joyce's specific abilities after observing her performance on the *WISC-III.*

Joyce

Joyce, a student in Mr. Harvey's fourth grade class, has been referred for special education assessment because of concerns about her current classroom functioning. Thus far in the assessment process, it has been established that Joyce has a school performance problem despite having average intellectual performance.

The team will next consider Joyce's specific learning abilities and strategies. The first areas of investigation will be vision and hearing; the team will consult school records to determine the results of the most recent screenings. On the *WISC-III,* Joyce showed low performance on measures of freedom from distractibility and processing speed. The team will investigate these possible problem areas further by observing Joyce's learning strategies in classroom tasks and by interviewing Joyce and her fourth grade teacher. For example, Ms. Gale, the special education resource teacher, will observe Joyce's techniques for learning new spelling words and then will interview Joyce about her choice of strategies. In addition, Ms. Gale will administer the *Detroit Tests of Learning Aptitude* (4th ed.), a norm-referenced test that assesses several specific learning abilities.

As a final step, if learning disabilities are suspected, the team will compare Joyce's current achievement levels with expected achievement to determine whether a substantial discrepancy can be documented.

CONSIDERATIONS IN ASSESSMENT OF SPECIFIC LEARNING ABILITIES

The term *specific learning abilities* refers to an individual's capacity to participate successfully in certain aspects of the learning task or in certain types of learning. Among the specific abilities that interest educators are attention, perception, memory, and the processes of receiving, associating, and expressing information. Specific abilities are more circumscribed than general learning aptitude; they usually do not affect all areas of learning. In young children, the development of specific abilities is often viewed as a precursor to the acquisition of academic skills. In this context, specific abilities may be regarded as readiness skills; this type of assessment is described in Chapter 16 on evaluation in the preschool years. Specific abilities are also a concern for older students who fail to acquire basic academic skills at the expected rate.

Learning strategies are a newer area of interest. Educators are concerned with the ways that individuals utilize specific learning abilities in situations that require the acquisition of new skills or information. Alley and Deshler (1979) define learning strategies as "techniques, principles, or rules that will facilitate the acquisition, manipulation, integration, storage, and retrieval of information across situations and settings" (p. 13). Lenz, Ellis, and Scanlon (1996) add that "an individual's approach to a task is called a strategy when it includes how a person thinks and acts when planning, executing, and evaluating performance on a task and its outcomes" (p. 5). Whereas assessment of specific abilities is essentially a static process, learning strategy assessment is dynamic. Its primary focus is the methods employed by the individual to interact with the demands of the learning task.

Purposes

Learning abilities and strategies are assessed to determine the student's strengths and weaknesses in various types and methods of learning.

Individualized Assessment Plan

For: *Joyce Dewey*   *4*   *10-0*   *12/1/00*   *Ms. Gale*
         Student's Name   Grade   Age   Date   Coordinator

Reason for Referral: Difficulty keeping up with fourth grade work in reading, spelling, and handwriting.

Assessment Question	Assessment Procedure	Person Responsible	Date/Time
What is the status of the student's sensory abilities?	Review of Joyce's school records for results of hearing and vision screens	Ms. Kellett, School Psychologist	12/5/00, 9 A.M.
What is the student's current level of development in specific learning abilities and strategies?	Classroom observation and interview	Ms. Gale, Resource Teacher	12/13/00, 9:30 A.M.
	Detroit Tests of Learning Aptitude (4th ed.)	Ms. Gale, Resource Teacher	To be determined
Is there a substantial discrepancy between actual and expected achievement?	Discrepancy analysis	All members of the assessment team	12/14/00, 3:30 P.M.

This information may help those who plan instructional interventions for any student, and it is also important in determining whether school performance problems are related to the condition of learning disabilities.

The disability of specific learning disabilities is defined by federal law as:

> . . . a disorder in one or more of the basic psychological processes involved in understanding or in using language, spoken or written, which may manifest itself in an imperfect ability to listen, think, speak, read, write, spell, or to do mathematical calculations. (*Federal Register,* 1999, §300.7(c)(10))

In this definition, the term *basic psychological processes* refers to learning abilities such as attention, perception, and memory. Learning disabilities are viewed as specific ability deficits that contribute to performance problems in basic school skills.

In determining whether students are eligible for special education services for learning disabilities, the assessment team typically evaluates current levels of development in specific abilities. However, federal guidelines specify three criteria for eligibility, none of which is directly concerned with specific learning abilities:

1. A severe discrepancy between achievement and intellectual ability must be documented. The discrepancy must occur between expected and actual achievement in at least one of the following skill areas: oral expression, listening comprehension, written expression, basic reading skill, reading comprehension, mathematics calculation, or mathematics reasoning.
2. The discrepancy must exist despite the provision of appropriate learning experiences. Underachievement cannot be due simply to lack of instruction.
3. The discrepancy cannot be the result of other disabilities or conditions or of environmental, cultural, or economic disadvantage.

Thus, assessment of specific learning abilities and strategies is only one part of the process of establishing eligibility for learning disabilities services.

This type of assessment is not limited to students with suspected learning disabilities. For students with disabilities in other areas, the assessment team may gather information about specific abilities and strategies in an attempt to better understand individual learning problems. Students with mental retardation and those with behavioral disorders may also show strengths in certain areas and weaknesses in others. Knowledge about study skills and learning strategies may provide the team with important data for planning the educational intervention program.

Issues and Trends

The study of specific abilities and strategies in the field of special education has focused on one population—students with learning disabilities. The issues and trends discussed here have resulted from learning disabilities research and practice but clearly have implications for the assessment of students with other types of disabilities.

There has been much debate in the learning disabilities literature about the definition of this condition, appropriate procedures for its assessment, and effective strategies for educational intervention (Lerner, 2000; Lewis, 1988). Much controversy has centered on the notion of specific learning abilities. In the early years of the field, special educators hypothesized that school achievement problems were related to deficits in specific learning abilities and that achievement could be improved by either remediating (remedying) the weakness or circumventing it by teaching through the student's strengths. For example, a student with poor reading skills might also score poorly on measures of visual perception. In the remediation of deficits approach, educational treatment focuses on improving the student's visual perception, in the hope that he or she would then become able to acquire skills in reading. In the utilization of strengths approach, the educational program in reading emphasizes auditory skills such as phonics and avoids visual skills such as sight word recognition. This second approach is also known as the preferred modality method because students are typically classified according to their strongest learning modality—visual, auditory, or kinesthetic.

Many of the pioneers in the learning disabilities field developed tests and other measures to detect specific deficits. For example, Frostig worked in the area of visual perception (Frostig & Horne, 1964; Frostig, Lefever, & Whittlesey, 1966), Kephart in perceptual-motor skills (Roach & Kephart, 1966), and Kirk in psycholinguistic processing (Kirk & Kirk, 1971; Kirk, McCarthy, & Kirk, 1968). Several of these measures were accompanied by instructional programs designed to remediate problem areas. The tests identified deficits; the companion educational programs provided activities to remediate the deficits.

In the 1970s, researchers began to study the effectiveness of these interventions. First to come under scrutiny were perceptual and perceptual-motor treatments (Coles, 1978; Hallahan & Cruickshank, 1973; Hammill & Larsen, 1974b; Larsen, Rogers, & Sowell, 1976), particularly tests and instructional programs that focused on visual perceptual deficits (Hammill, Goodman, & Wiederholt, 1974; Hammill & Wiederholt, 1972; Larsen & Hammill, 1975; Wiederholt & Hammill, 1971). In assessing the usefulness of perceptual-motor training programs, Hammill (1982) concluded that "the efficacy of providing such training to children has not been sufficiently demonstrated to warrant the expenditure of the school's funds or the teacher's time" (p. 408). The effectiveness of remediating deficit psycholinguistic abilities was also debated (Hammill & Larsen, 1974a; Kavale, 1981; Larsen, Parker, & Hammill, 1982; Minskoff, 1975; Newcomer & Hammill, 1975, 1976; Sowell, Parker, Poplin, & Larsen, 1979; Sternberg & Taylor, 1982; Torgesen, 1979).

In their critical appraisal of the deficit remediation approach, Arter and Jenkins (1979) reached the following conclusions:

> There have been many attempts to train specific abilities. Psycholinguistic, visual perceptual, auditory perceptual, and motor abilities have all been the focus of training. . . . Ability training succeeded about 24% of the time in well designed investigations. It is difficult to escape the conclusion that abilities measured in differential diagnosis are highly resistant to training by existing procedures.
>
> Given this, it would certainly be surprising to find that ability training improved academic performance. Indeed, the research shows that more often than not academic performance is not improved. (p. 547)

Similar conclusions have been reached in evaluations of the preferred modality approach (Larrivee, 1981; Meyers, 1980; Ringler & Smith, 1973; Tarver & Dawson, 1978; Waugh, 1973). As Larrivee concluded in her review of research on modality preferences and beginning reading instruction, "Differentiating instruction according to modality preference apparently does not facilitate learning to read" (p. 180).

In addition to the criticism of the instructional programs derived from specific ability tests, many of the instruments themselves have come under attack. The major charge has been lack of adequate technical quality (Arter & Jenkins, 1979; Coles, 1978; Salvia & Ysseldyke, 1998). Although several of the newer measures of specific abilities are technically adequate, many of the older tests fail to meet minimum reliability and validity requirements.

Despite the controversies surrounding evaluation and training of specific learning abilities, many special educators remain interested in their assessment. One indicator of this is the popularity of the learning styles approach to instruction (Carbo, 1982, 1984; Carbo, Dunn, & Dunn, 1986; Dunn, 1984, 1988; Dunn, Dunn, & Price, 1979), a strategy that includes assessment of students' perceptual preferences. Like its predecessor, the preferred modality method, the learning styles approach has been heavily criticized (e.g., Snider, 1992; Stahl, 1988). The reason for continued interest may be the apparently logical relationship between readiness skills, such as visual perception, and more advanced school skills, such as reading. Also, Lewis (1983) points out the intuitive appeal of some notions underlying the specific ability approach: "It makes sense that instructional procedures should take into account the strengths and weaknesses of the learner" (pp. 232–233). This concept is known as aptitude-treatment interaction (Cronbach & Snow, 1977). According to Lloyd (1984), an aptitude-treatment interaction occurs "when instruction differentiated on the basis of learner characteristics leads to greater achievement" (p. 8).

Another issue in specific ability assessment is definition of learning disabilities. Most of the traditional definitions emphasize perceptual and/or information-processing deficits, and the characteristics they describe are difficult to operationalize into assessment practices. A newer definition, proposed by the National Joint Committee on Learning Disabilities (1994), shifts focus away from specific abilities, instead emphasizing performance problems in basic school skills:

> *Learning disabilities* is a general term that refers to a heterogeneous group of disorders manifested by significant difficulties in the acquisition and use of listening, speaking, reading, writing, reasoning, or mathematical abilities. These disorders are intrinsic to the individual and presumed to be due to central nervous system dysfunction.

In contrast, the definition adopted by the Learning Disabilities Association (1986) stresses the long-term nature of the disability and its effects on both school and nonschool performance. Unfortunately, neither of these definitions translates directly into a plan for assessment.

One important trend is the movement toward consideration of learning strategies, in addition to or in place of specific learning abilities. Researchers have begun to identify characteristic strategies of students with learning disabilities, and evidence suggests that learning strategies are susceptible to training (Hallahan, 1980; Schumaker, Deshler, Alley, Warner, & Denton, 1982; Swanson, 1989, 1993; Wong, 1980). Swanson (1999), in a large-scale study of intervention research, concludes that strategy instruction is the one intervention approach that narrows the achievement gap between students with learning disabilities and their general education peers. Although results are promising, further study is critical. There is a particular need to develop reliable and valid measures of learning strategies and study skills appropriate for classroom use. If practitioners are to assess the learning strategies and study skills of students with school performance problems, they will require a set of technically adequate assessment tools.

Another important trend is the recent interest in phonological awareness and its relationship to the development of beginning reading skills (Lerner, 2000). According to a recent report of the National Research Council, phonological awareness can be defined as the "ability to attend to the sounds of language as distinct from its meaning"

(Snow, Burns, & Griffin, 1998, p. 52). There is evidence to suggest that deficits in phonological processing contribute to difficulty in the acquisition of decoding and spelling skills (e.g., Felton & Wood, 1989; Wagner & Torgesen, 1987). Like the early remediation of deficits approach in learning disabilities, interest in phonological awareness has led to the development of assessment devices and intervention programs. However, there appears to be research support for the usefulness of training phonological skills in young children (e.g., O'Connor, Jenkins, Leicester, & Slocum, 1993; Torgesen & Barker, 1995; Wagner, Torgesen, & Rashotte, 1993). Measures of phonological processing are discussed in Chapter 11, the chapter on reading assessment.

Current Practices

Specific learning abilities and strategies are a concern in both general and special education. In general education, young children in the early elementary grades often take part in group readiness testing. Readiness tests evaluate development in preacademic skills such as listening, memory, matching, letter recognition, and language. Results of such measures may be available for students with disabilities but, like all group test results, should be interpreted with caution. Sensory abilities are also of interest in general education, and most schools routinely screen students for possible hearing and vision impairments. These results are extremely important for students referred for special education assessment because undetected vision or hearing problems can contribute to difficulties in school performance.

In special education, the assessment team often decides to evaluate specific learning abilities, particularly if learning disabilities are suspected. The team may begin with a screening device such as the *Learning Disabilities Evaluation Scale* or the *Learning Disabilities Diagnostic Inventory*. The team may also use one or more of the many currently available individual tests. Some of these measures are designed to assess one ability area. Examples include the *Goldman-Fristoe-Woodcock Test of Auditory Discrimination* and the *Bruininks-Oseretsky Test of Motor*

Proficiency. Other measures, such as the *Detroit Tests of Learning Aptitude* (4th ed.), attempt to evaluate several different abilities.

Another tactic is administration of those portions of individual tests of intellectual performance that include measures of specific abilities. For instance, the team may be interested in the specific learning abilities assessed by the *Wechsler Intelligence Scale for Children-Third Edition* or the *Stanford-Binet Intelligence Scale: Fourth Edition.*

Great caution must be exercised in selecting tests or subtests to assure that reliable and valid measures are chosen. If no adequate formal measure can be found, the team may decide to use informal techniques. This is often the case in the assessment of learning strategies and study skills because few formal measures are available. Caution is needed here too. Validity and reliability are just as important in the selection of informal measures as they are in the selection of formal measures. If technical data are not available for an informal test or procedure, the team should make every effort to gather such data, or they should select another measure.

Another type of assessment that can be conducted by the special education team is discrepancy analysis. This occurs when information is needed about eligibility for learning disabilities services. Discrepancy analysis does not usually involve gathering new data. Results of current achievement tests are compared with results of current intellectual performance tests to determine whether important differences between actual and expected achievement exist.

SOURCES OF INFORMATION ABOUT SPECIFIC LEARNING ABILITIES

There are several sources of information about students' specific learning abilities, learning strategies, and study skills. School records, teachers, parents, and the students themselves are all able to make important contributions.

School Records

School records may provide some clues to a student's past or current levels of functioning. Of

particular importance are records of results of periodic vision and hearing screenings.

Readiness Test Results. Results of group tests of school readiness may be available for some students. Readiness measures are usually administered at the end of kindergarten or at the beginning of first grade, so results are most meaningful for first and second graders.

Results of Vision and Hearing Screening. The team should review the student's health record to determine the dates and results of vision and hearing screenings. If possible problems were indicated, the team should check to see if the student was referred for further assessment and what the results were. Were recommended treatments carried out? For example, if corrective lenses were prescribed, were eyeglasses or contact lenses purchased, and does the student wear them as directed? If there is no record of recent vision and hearing checks, the team should arrange for these as soon as possible.

Information about Aptitude-Achievement Discrepancies. There may be some information in the school records that points to discrepancies between the student's aptitude for learning and actual achievement. For example, past teachers may have commented about the student's failure to achieve to capacity. Or the school record may contain results of group achievement and intelligence tests administered earlier in the student's school career. Although these types of data are historical rather than current, they may indicate a continuing pattern of performance.

The Student

The student is an important participant both in the formal assessment of specific abilities and strategies and in informal assessment. Older students in particular can assist the team by describing their strategies for learning.

Individual Measures of Specific Learning Abilities. Students may participate in the administration of individual tests of specific abilities when technically adequate measures are available. Specific ability tests are often designed for elementary grade students. With older students, the team may administer pertinent subtests of individual tests of intellectual performance. During test administration, the student is carefully observed to determine the strategies he or she uses for task completion.

Current Learning Strategies and Study Skills. Informal techniques are typically used to evaluate these. Students can be observed in the classroom to determine what methods they use to learn new material. For example, an observer can record a student's behaviors during lectures, class discussions, or independent work periods. Interviewing is another technique. Students can be asked to describe the study methods they use in school and at home. They can also be interviewed while engaged in a learning task. In addition, samples of the student's work may provide clues about poor work habits or inefficient study strategies.

Teachers

Teachers have many opportunities to observe the specific learning abilities, strategies, and study skills of students in their classroom.

Current Abilities and Strategies for Learning. Teachers can describe how students go about learning new skills and information. In particular, teachers should be asked to discuss any learning problems that the student exhibits. For example, does the student have difficulty paying attention to relevant aspects of the task at hand? Is he or she unable to remember previously learned material? Teachers can also report about students' current study skills. Does the student listen to directions and ask questions when necessary? Is he or she able to follow directions?

Current Aptitude-Achievement Discrepancies. Teachers may be able to comment about the match between the achievement expected of a particular student and that student's current performance. For instance, a teacher may observe that a student appears to understand the course material in class discussions but performs poorly on written examinations. Such observations are important indicators of aptitude–achievement discrepancies.

Parents

Like teachers, parents have many opportunities to observe their child in learning situations. Parents also have information about their child's current health status and medical history in relation to vision and hearing problems.

History of Treatment for Vision and Hearing Problems. If school records do not contain information about the student's vision and hearing, parents may be able to supply this. If routine vision or hearing checks at school or by the family physician indicated possible problems, the student's parents can describe what treatments, if any, were recommended and carried out. If necessary, parents can refer school personnel to the appropriate medical professional for more information.

Home Observations of Current Learning Abilities and Strategies. Based upon observations of their child in many learning situations, parents can describe typical strategies for learning and recurrent problems. They may comment, for example, on their child's attention span, perseverance in problem solving, or ways of remembering things. Parents can also describe the study strategies used at home to complete class assignments.

SCREENING FOR SENSORY IMPAIRMENTS

A first priority in the assessment of any student referred for school performance problems is to determine his or her current status in vision and hearing. Undetected and untreated sensory impairments can interfere with school learning. Sensory acuity in hearing and vision is the concern in screening. Acuity refers to the ability of the sense organ to register stimuli. Sensory screening programs identify students in need of in-depth assessment. These persons are then referred to appropriate health professionals for a comprehensive examination.

Vision

Vision can be impaired in many ways. Students may have difficulty seeing objects at a distance. In this condition, known as nearsightedness or myopia, near vision is clearer than far vision. Far-sightedness, or hyperopia, is the opposite; vision is clearer for objects at a distance. A third type of disorder, astigmatism, is a condition in which vision is blurred or distorted. Myopia, hyperopia, and astigmatism are considered refractive disorders. They are very common among school-aged children but are usually correctable with eyeglasses or contact lenses (Caton, 1985). When a vision problem can be corrected, it is not considered a disability.

Other types of vision problems are muscle disorders, restricted peripheral vision, and impairments in color vision. Muscle disorders involve the external muscles that control eye movement. An example is strabismus, or "crossed eyes," in which a muscle imbalance prevents the eyes from focusing simultaneously on the same object. Peripheral, or "side," vision refers to the wideness of the visual field. If peripheral vision is severely impaired, the visual field is limited so the individual only sees objects directly in front of him or her; this condition is known as tunnel vision. Tunnel vision, if uncorrected, is considered a severe enough disability to be included as a type of legal blindness. Disorders can also occur in color vision, reducing the ability to distinguish between colors. Although color blindness is not considered a disability, it can have a deleterious effect on some aspects of school performance. Teachers must know when they have color-blind students so color-cued materials and other educational uses of color can be minimized.

The most usual method of screening for vision problems is the *Snellen Chart*. This chart, used with older children and adults, contains several different letters of the alphabet. The letters vary in size, with the largest placed at the top. The individual stands 20 feet away from the chart and attempts to read all of the letters, first covering one eye and then the other. A modified version of the chart is available for young children and those unable to read. It contains only the letter *E,* but that letter is rotated into four different positions (Figure 9–1). The person responds by telling or showing which way the letter is pointing.

The Snellen Chart measures far-distance vision, and results are expressed as a fraction. For instance, the fraction 20/20 indicates normal vi-

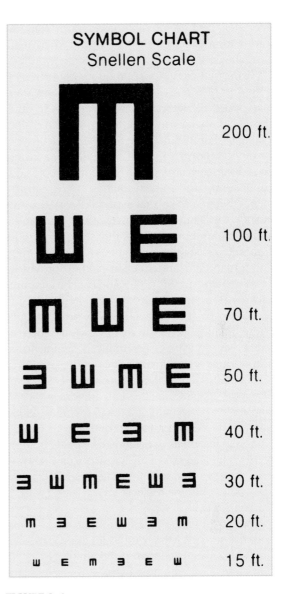

FIGURE 9–1
Snellen Chart
Note: National Society for the Prevention of Blindness. 79 Madison Avenue, New York, NY 10016.

sion. The numerator of the fraction stands for the distance the individual stands from the chart when reading the letters, and the denominator stands for the distance at which persons with normal vision are able to read the same letters. Thus, a person with 20/100 vision is able to read at 20 feet what a person with normal vision can read at 100 feet. Students are considered legally blind when visual acuity is 20/200 or less in the better eye after the best possible correction (National Information Center for Children and Youth with Disabilities, 1997).

Far-distance vision, although important, is only one of the areas in which visual disorders may occur. To detect possible problems in other aspects of visual acuity, different techniques are available. For instance, the Keystone Telebinocular device allows appraisal of far-distance vision, near-distance vision, depth perception, color discrimination, and other abilities. Other instruments that assess several aspects of visual acuity include the Titmus Vision Tester and the Bausch and Lomb Orthorater. Such devices offer a more comprehensive picture of the student's current vision than the standard chart method provides.

Teachers, other professionals, and parents can assist in the detection of potential vision problems by being aware of warning signs. These include physical manifestations such as red or watery eyes, a pronounced squint, irritation of the eyelids, irregularities of the pupils, or obvious muscle imbalances such as crossed eyes (National Society to Prevent Blindness, 1977; Smolensky, Bonvechio, Whitlock, & Girard, 1968). Among the behavioral symptoms are lack of attention to information presented visually, holding of reading materials very close to or far away from the eyes, and inability to see the chalkboard and other distant objects (Beverstock, 1991; Smolensky et al., 1968).

When potential vision problems are identified, the student is referred to an appropriate vision specialist, usually an ophthalmologist or an optometrist. Ophthalmologists are physicians who specialize in eye disorders. Not only do they conduct comprehensive vision examinations, they may also prescribe drugs or perform surgery. Optometrists conduct vision examinations and prescribe corrective lenses, but they are not physicians and do not provide medical or surgical treatment. A third professional, the optician, prepares corrective lenses according to the optometrist's or ophthalmologist's prescription.

Many visual impairments can be treated through medical intervention, surgery, and/or the relatively simple prescription of corrective lenses. If vision specialists recommend a treatment regimen, the school should be aware of what is oc-

curring and cooperate as necessary. For example, if eyeglasses are prescribed to correct poor near-distance vision, the classroom teacher can assist by making sure the student wears the glasses during reading and writing activities.

Hearing

The two primary types of hearing loss are conductive and sensorineural. With conductive losses, some obstruction or interference in the outer or middle ear blocks the transmission of sound. The inner ear is intact, but sound does not reach it. Among school-aged children, conductive losses are the most common type of hearing impairments (Frank, 1998). They may be caused by excessive buildup of wax in the auditory canal or collection of fluid in the middle ear (otitis media). Many conductive losses can be corrected by medical or surgical treatment (Moores & Moores, 1988). For example, fluid in the middle ear can be treated with a surgical procedure called a myringotomy, in which a small tube is placed in the eardrum to allow drainage (Frank, 1998). Hearing aids usually benefit individuals with conductive losses.

Sensorineural losses are caused by damage to the inner ear. Sound travels to the inner ear but is not transmitted to the brain. Sensorineural hearing losses are not as responsive to medical and surgical treatment as are conductive hearing losses (Heward, 1996), although hearing aids that amplify sounds may prove beneficial. Individuals can also show a mixed hearing loss—both a conductive and a sensorineural hearing loss.

Hearing screening, like vision screening, is routine in most schools today. However, teachers and parents should also be aware of some hearing loss symptoms, so that they can initiate hearing checks for students with possible problems. This is particularly important because some hearing losses are intermittent; a student with impaired hearing may be able to pass a routine screening (Frank, 1998). Some of the signs of hearing loss are physical problems associated with the ears, poor articulation of sounds and confusion of similar sounding words, turning of the head toward the source of sound, extreme watchfulness when people are speaking in an attempt to lip read, frequent requests to speakers for repetitions, speaking in a monotone, and speaking very quietly (Smolensky et al., 1968; Stephens, Blackhurst, & Magliocca, 1982).

The dimensions of sound that are important in the assessment of hearing are intensity and frequency. Intensity refers to the loudness of sound and is measured in units called decibels (dB). Zero decibels is the threshold of normal hearing. At a distance of 5 feet, a whisper registers 20 dB, conversational speech 40 to 65 dB, and a loud shout 85 dB (Green, 1981). The frequency of a sound refers to its pitch, whether it is high or low. For example, the keys on a piano are arranged by pitch, from low to high. Frequency is measured in hertz units (Hz), and the range of frequencies considered most important for hearing conversational speech is from 500 to 2000 Hz (Heward, 1996).

In school hearing screening programs, an instrument called a pure tone audiometer is used to produce sounds of different frequencies and intensities. Students are usually individually tested. The student wears earphones, listens for tones generated by the audiometer, then raises a hand or pushes a button when a tone is heard. In pure tone audiometric screening, or sweep testing, tones are generated at several frequencies, first for one ear, then for the other. If the student fails this screening procedure, it is typically repeated at a later date. The next step is a pure tone threshold test, which is usually administered by a trained professional such as an audiologist. In this procedure, sounds are presented at several frequencies, and the intensity is varied to determine the exact decibel level at which the student can detect the sound.

Figure 9–2 shows the record of a pure tone threshold test for a student with a mild hearing impairment. This graph is called an audiogram. The horizontal axis is marked off in frequency units, and the range of frequencies critical for

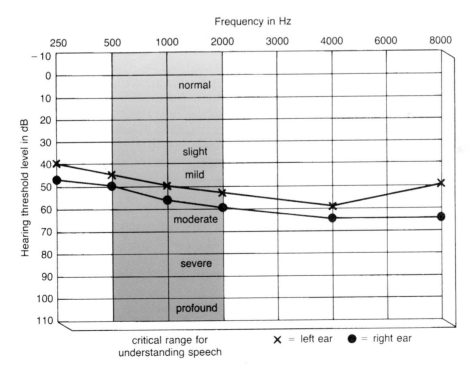

FIGURE 9–2

Sample Audiogram

Note: From *Exceptional Children* (5th ed.) (p. 354) by W. L. Heward, © 1996. Reprinted with permission of Prentice-Hall, Inc., Upper Saddle River, NJ.

speech is shaded. The vertical axis represents the hearing threshold level, the lowest intensity at which sound can be detected. For example, at 500 Hz, the student was able to hear sounds at 45 dB with the left ear (marked on the audiogram by an *x*) and sounds at 50 dB with the right ear (marked by a •). Persons with normal hearing would be able to detect sounds at intensities somewhere between 0 and 10 dB. If a person's threshold exceeds normal limits, a hearing loss is indicated. For example, if the threshold is 60 dB, a 60-dB loss is reported.

When possible hearing losses are identified, students are referred to hearing specialists. Otologists are physicians who specialize in disorders of the ear; they conduct comprehensive hearing examinations and provide medical and surgical treatments. Audiologists are not physicians, although they often work closely with otologists. The audiologist evaluates hearing and prescribes hearing aids for losses that cannot be corrected. Otologists and audiologists use several techniques in addition to pure tone audiometry to evaluate hearing. These include tympanometry (to detect problems with the eardrum and middle ear), speech audiometry (to determine the threshold levels for speech), and special assessment procedures for infants, young children, and other persons who are difficult to test (Frank, 1998; Green, 1981; Moores & Moores, 1988).

SCREENING FOR LEARNING DISABILITIES

School screening programs often attempt to identify students with possible problems in areas other than vision and hearing impairments. One example is learning disabilities, the most commonly identified disability in U.S. schools (U.S. Department of Education, 1998). Some districts develop their own screening measures to locate students in need of more in-depth assessment. Others use published measures such as the *Learning Disability Evaluation Scale-Renormed* (McCarney, 1996) and the *Learning Disabilities Diagnostic Inventory* (Hammill & Bryant, 1998).

The *Learning Disability Evaluation Scale-Renormed (LDES-R)* is a questionnaire designed

to be completed by teachers who are familiar with the student under consideration. Items contain a description of problem behaviors, and the teacher rates the frequency with which these behaviors occur ("rarely or never," "inconsistently," "all or most of the time"). Items are divided into seven subscales:

- Listening
- Thinking
- Speaking
- Reading
- Writing
- Spelling
- Mathematical Calculations

These possible problem areas correspond directly to the areas listed in the federal definition of learning disabilities. Embedded within the subscales are items that address attention, auditory discrimination, visual perception, fine-motor skills, information processing, and several types of memory.

The *LDES-R* was standardized with more than 6,000 students from 26 states. The sample appears to approximate the U.S. population as a whole, although White students are overrepresented, as are students from the North-Central portion of the country. Internal consistency, test-retest, and interrater reliabilities are adequate. Results of the *LDES-R* appear to be related to results of the *WISC-R* and measures of achievement such as the *PIAT*. In addition, the *LDES-R* appears to be able to discriminate students with learning disabilities and general education students.

Results of the *LDES-R* are reported by subscale and by total test. Separate norms are available for males and females ages 6 to 18. Subscale raw scores are converted to standard scores (mean = 10, SD = 3). The total test score is expressed as a Learning Quotient (mean = 100, SD = 15) and percentile rank. Accompanying the *LDES-R* are two books—one with suggested interventions for teachers (McCarney & Bauer, 1995) and the other with recommendations for parents (McCarney & Bauer, 1991).

The *Learning Disabilities Diagnostic Inventory (LDDI)* is a similar measure. This teacher questionnaire, designed for use with students ages 8-0 to 18-11, contains six scales:

- Listening
- Speaking
- Reading
- Writing
- Mathematics
- Reasoning

On each item, the teacher rates the frequency with which the student displays the problem behavior: "Frequently" (1, 2, or 3), "Sometimes" (4, 5, or 6), or "Rarely" (7, 8, or 9). Like the *LDES-R*, the *LDDI* contains items that are related to specific abilities, such as perception, motor skills, memory, and information processing.

In the standardization of the *LDDI*, 522 teachers rated 2,152 students with identified learning disabilities. Teachers were primarily special educators. Each scale was normed separately, using only those students with identified problems in the area being assessed. Reliability of the *LDDI* appears adequate. Validity was studied in a number of ways, including investigation of the profiles of three groups of students. Of the students with learning disabilities, 86% had *LDDI* profiles likely or possibly characteristic of learning disabilities. In contrast, 10% of achieving students and 30% of students with mental retardation had such profiles. These findings suggest that the *LDDI* correctly categorizes most, but not all, students.

Raw scores on the six scales are converted to stanines and percentile ranks. No total test score is available. Results are entered in a profile table (Figure 9–3), which classifies scores by their likelihood of indicating a processing disorder. For example, scales with scores that fall below stanine 6 are identified as "Likely." The examiner then completes the Diagnostic Conclusions section of the form. The final result is a statement about the student's likelihood of having a learning disability.

MEASURES OF PERCEPTUAL-MOTOR SKILLS AND OTHER SPECIFIC LEARNING ABILITIES

Traditional measures of specific learning abilities are concerned with factors such as attention, perception, and memory and with the information-processing abilities of reception, association, and expression. Specific abilities are difficult to delimit and define because they are based on inferences about mental processes. For instance, it is impossible to observe or measure directly how a person perceives incoming sensory information. It is possible only to study the person's overt responses or his or her report of the experience and then make inferences about what may have occurred during perception.

Perception can be defined as the psychological ability to process or use the information received through the senses. According to Lerner (2000), perception is "the intellect's ability to give meaning to sensory stimulation" (p. 265). Perception depends on the physiological ability of the sense organs to receive information. Visual and auditory acuity are of primary concern to educators, but there is also interest in information received through other senses, particularly tactile and kinesthetic input. Tactile information is received through the sense of touch, and kinesthetic information from the feelings of muscles and body movements.

Memory is the ability to recall previously learned information. The memory process can be described in many ways. For example, memory can be differentiated according to the period of time that has elapsed since original learning. Educators are usually most concerned with long-term memory ability, but information must pass through short-term memory before it is stored for long-term recall.

Attention is the process whereby an individual's awareness is directed toward some stimulus or set of stimuli. Kirk and Chalfant (1984) define attention as "the process of selectively bringing relevant stimuli into focus" (p. 77). Attention can be considered a prerequisite not only for other specific abilities such as memory and perception, but also for any type of learning activity. Although the importance of attention cannot be denied, it is very difficult to separate it from other factors.

Information processing refers to the set of abilities that govern the way people receive and respond to incoming information. The three major components of information processing are reception of information, association of incoming information with previously stored information,

Learning Disabilities Diagnostic Inventory

Section I. Identifying Information About the Student and Examiner

Student Name _Samuel Doe_

Female ☐ Male [X] Grade _4_

	Year	Month	Day
Date of Rating	1996	12	15
Date of Birth	1987	11	14
Age	9	1	1

City, State _Austin, Texas_

Examiner's Name _Dr. Pearson_

Examiner's Position _Diagnostician_

Section II. Record and Profile of Scores

Record of Scores

	Raw Score	%ile	Stanine			Raw Score	%ile	Stanine
1. Listening (LI)	94	84	7	4. Writing (WT)		51	47	5
2. Speaking (SP)	103	95	8	5. Mathematics (MT)		101	99	9
3. Reading (RD)	46	42	5	6. Reasoning (RE)		60	75	6

Profile of Scores

Stanine	LI	SP	RD	WT	MT	RE	Likelihood of an Intrinsic Processing Disorder
7, 8, 9	✔	✔	☐	☐	✔	☐	**Unlikely**
6			☐	☐	☐	✔	**Possibly**
1, 2, 3, 4, 5			✔	✔	☐	☐	**Likely**

Section III. Diagnostic Conclusions

The student is unlikely to have learning disabilities.
   This diagnostic conclusion is based on the fact that either all LDDI scores fall above 6 or all LDDI scores fall below 6.

✔**The student is likely to have learning disabilities.**
   This diagnostic conclusion is based on the fact that at least one LDDI score falls above 6 and at least one LDDI score falls below 6.
         Area(s) of LD (Check all that apply)
         Listening   ✔Writing
         Speaking   Mathematics
         ✔Reading   Reasoning

The student may have learning disabilities.
   This diagnostic conclusion is based on the fact that the profile is equivocal (i.e., neither of the previous conclusions was checked—see the LDDI manual for details).

FIGURE 9–3

Sample *Learning Disabilities Diagnostic Inventory* Results

Note: From *Learning Disabilities Diagnostic Inventory* (p. 22) by D. D. Hammill and B. R. Bryant, 1998, Austin, TX: PRO-ED. Copyright 1998 by PRO-ED. Reprinted by permission.

and expression. Information processes are also referred to as psychological processes. The term *psycholinguistic abilities* describes the psychological processing of linguistic information. Language disorders are often a concern in the assessment of information-processing abilities, as are disorders of thinking and reasoning. In fact, measures of information processing often share many characteristics of language and intellectual performance tests.

Table 9–1 presents a listing of measures of specific learning abilities, although the older ones are no longer widely used in educational assessment, particularly those related to perception. The next sections of this chapter briefly describe several tests of specific learning abilities. Discussion of the older measures is limited because of the technical problems of many of these instruments and because these measures represent a traditional, rather than a contemporary, approach to assessment of learning disabilities.

Tests of Perception

Measures of perceptual abilities usually focus on either auditory or visual perception, rather than on the perceptual process as a whole. Among the assessment concerns in visual perception are visual discrimination, figure-ground discrimination, spatial relationships, and form perception (Wallace & McLoughlin, 1979). Discrimination is the ability to detect likenesses and differences among stimuli, and figure-ground discrimination is the ability to differentiate relevant stimuli (the figure) from irrelevant stimuli (the background). Spatial relationships refer to perception of the relative positions of objects in space, and form perception is concerned with the size, shape, and position of visual stimuli. In auditory perception, auditory discrimination and auditory blending are of interest (Wallace & McLoughlin, 1979). Auditory blending is the ability to combine separate sounds into a whole.

Visual perception was considered one of the most important specific abilities in early assessment programs because of the hypothesized relationship between visual perception deficits and reading disorders. One of the best-known early measures is the *Developmental Test of Visual Per-*

ception (Frostig et al., 1966). This test is not commonly used in schools today because of its failure to separate motor skills from perceptual skills, the age and limited representativeness of its standardization sample, the low reliabilities of subtests, and the lack of adequate evidence of validity (Hammill & Wiederholt, 1972).

A new version of the *Developmental Test of Visual Perception* by Hammill, Pearson, and Voress was published in 1993. The *DTVP-2* overcomes the problems of the first edition by separating the assessment of visual perception and visual-motor skills and by meeting criteria for psychometric quality. It was standardized on 1,972 children from 12 states, and the standardization sample resembled the U.S. population in race, ethnicity, geographic region, urban-rural residence, and handedness. Internal consistency, test-retest, and interscorer reliability are adequate. The *DTVP-2* total test score (General Visual Perception) shows good agreement with results from other measures of visual perception and visual-motor skills such as the *Motor-Free Visual Perception Test* ($r = .78$) and the *Developmental Test of Visual-Motor Integration* (.87) and with Performance Scale IQs on the *WISC-R* (.87).

Designed for students ages 4-0 to 10-11, the *DTVP-2* contains eight subtests:

1. *Eye-Hand Coordination.* The student must draw a line from one drawing to another without leaving the path connecting the two drawings.
2. *Position in Space.* The student looks at a geometric figure, then selects the figure that is exactly like it from a set of possible responses.
3. *Copying.* The student draws a copy of a geometric design; the model is present while the student draws.
4. *Figure-Ground.* Here, the student is shown a set of geometric forms (e.g., circle, square, star) and must tell which of these forms appear in a drawing composed of several forms and perhaps a distracting background.
5. *Spatial Relations.* The stimulus is a grid with evenly spaced dots; some of the dots are connected by lines to form a pattern. The student

TABLE 9-1
Measures of Specific Learning Abilities

Name (Author)	Ages or Grades	SPECIFIC ABILITIES ASSESSED			
		Perception	Motor Skills	Memory and Attention	Information Processing
Auditory Discrimination Test (2nd ed.) (Reynolds, 1987; Wepman, 1975)	4 to 8-11	*			
Bender Gestalt Test for Young Children (Koppitz, 1963, 1975)	5 to 9		*		
Bruininks-Oseretsky Test of Motor Proficiency (Bruininks, 1978)	4-6 to 14-6		*		
Detroit Tests of Learning Aptitude (4th ed.) (Hammill, 1998)	6-0 to 17-11		*	*	*
Detroit Tests of Learning Aptitude-Adult (Hammill & Bryant, 1991a)	16-0 to 79-11		*	*	*
Detroit Tests of Learning Aptitude-Primary (2nd ed.) (Hammill & Bryant, 1991b)	3-0 to 9-11	*	*	*	*
Developmental Test of Visual Perception (2nd ed.) (Hammill, Pearson, & Voress, 1993)	4-0 to 10-11	*	*		
Developmental Test of Visual-Motor Integration (4th ed.) (Beery, 1997)	3-0 to 17-11	*	*		
Goldman-Fristoe-Woodcock Auditory Skills Test Battery (Goldman, Fristoe, & Woodcock, 1976)	3 to adult	*		*	
Goldman-Fristoe-Woodcock Test of Auditory Discrimination (Goldman, Fristoe, & Woodcock, 1970)	5-0 to adult	*			
Illinois Test of Psycholinguistic Abilities (Kirk, McCarthy, & Kirk, 1968)	2-4 to 10-3	*		*	*
Learning Disabilities Diagnostic Inventory (Hammill & Bryant, 1998)	8-0 to 18-11	*	*	*	*
Learning Disabilities Evaluation Scale-Renormed (McCarney, 1996)	6 to 18	*	*	*	*
Motor-Free Visual Perception Test-Revised (Colarusso & Hammill, 1995)	4-0 to 11-6	*			
Purdue Perceptual-Motor Survey (Roach & Kephart, 1966)	6 to 10		*		
Test of Gross Motor Development (Ulrich, 1985)	3 to 10		*		
Test of Memory and Learning (Reynolds & Bigler, 1994)	5-0 to 19-11			*	
Test of Visual-Motor Integration (Hammill, Pearson, & Voress, 1996)	4-0 to 17-11		*		
Wechsler Memory Scale-Third Edition (Wechsler, 1997)	16 to 89			*	

must reproduce the pattern on a second grid by connecting the appropriate dots.

6. *Visual Closure.* The student sees a complete figure. He or she must then select from a series of incomplete figures the one that, if completed, would match the stimulus.

7. *Visual-Motor Speed.* In this subtest, the task is to add special marks to some geometric shapes but not to others. The student sees a page of shapes and is given 1 minute to add marks to all the appropriate shapes.

8. *Form Constancy.* The student must find a stimulus shape in drawings in which it is a different size, a different color, in a different position, and/or shown against a distracting background.

Results of the *DTVP-2* include subtest standard scores (mean = 10, SD = 3) and three composite standard scores (mean = 100, SD = 15). The composites are General Visual Perception, which includes all subtests; Motor-Reduced Visual Perception, a composite of subtests that deemphasize motor skills (subtests 2, 4, 6, and 8); and Visual-Motor Integration, a composite of subtests in which students must respond motorically (subtests 1, 3, 5, and 7).

Another measure of several visual perception skills is the *Motor-Free Visual Perception Test-Revised (MVPT-R)* (Colarusso & Hammill, 1995). The *MVPT-R* manual describes this measure as "a test of visual perception which avoids any motor involvement . . . a quick, highly reliable, and valid measure of overall visual perceptual processing ability in children and adults" (p. 7). Like most perceptual measures, it offers norms only for elementary-aged children. Five different tasks are used to assess visual perception:

- *Figure-Ground.* The student must determine in which of four drawings a stimulus figure is embedded.
- *Spatial Relationships.* The student is shown a stimulus figure, then must determine which of four drawings contains it; in the drawings, the stimulus may be a different size, a different color, or in a different position.
- *Visual Memory.* The student views a stimulus figure for 5 seconds. The stimulus is removed, and the student must select a figure identical to it from four choices.

- *Visual Closure.* The student identifies which of four drawings, if completed, would be identical to a stimulus figure.
- *Visual Discrimination.* When shown four drawings, the student selects the one that is different from the other three.

Although the *MVPT-R* assesses several skills, only total test scores are available. These include a Perceptual Age score and a standard score called a Perceptual Quotient.

The technical quality of the *MVPT-R* is better than that of many tests of specific abilities published in the 1960s and 1970s. The standardization sample was composed of a group of 912 children without disabilities from two states. The sample included approximately equal numbers of males and females; Hispanic and "other" students were somewhat overrepresented and Black and white students underrepresented. However, test reliabilities appear adequate. In support of the validity of the original version of the *MVPT,* the test authors note that it "correlated higher with other measures of visual perception (median $r = 0.49$) than it did with tests of intelligence (median $r = 0.31$) and school performance (median $r = 0.38$)" (p. 24).

Auditory perception has also been a concern in special education assessment, particularly in relationship to speech and language problems. Measures that evaluate several auditory skills are available. For example, the *Goldman-Fristoe-Woodcock Auditory Skills Test Battery* (Goldman, Fristoe, & Woodcock, 1976) contains tests that assess aspects of auditory selective attention, discrimination, and memory, along with sound-symbol relationships. However, auditory discrimination has been the main focus in assessing auditory perceptual skills.

The *Goldman-Fristoe-Woodcock Test of Auditory Discrimination* (Goldman, Fristoe, & Woodcock, 1970) is an individual, norm-referenced test of discrimination under both quiet and noise conditions. It is designed for age 5-0 through adulthood. The individual looks at four line drawings, listens to a tape, and then selects the drawing that depicts the word read on the tape. The four drawings have names that are similar in sound (e.g., *wake, rake, lake,* and *make*). This test was standardized on a limited sample representing only three states, and small samples were used to study test-retest reliability and concurrent validity. More information is needed to substantiate the technical adequacy of this measure.

One of the best-known measures of perceptual ability is the *Auditory Discrimination Test* by J. M. Wepman (1975). In the late 1980s, this test was standardized on a national sample of more than 1,800 children ages 4 through 8 (Reynolds, 1987). According to the manual for the second edition, the Wepman test is "a brief, easy-to-administer procedure for the assessment of children's ability to discriminate between commonly used phonemes in the English language" (p. 1).

About 5 minutes are required for administration. Two alternate forms are provided, and the test task is the same on each: The tester reads a pair of words, and the student listens and tells whether the words are the same or different. Of the 40 word pairs read to the student, 30 differ in only one sound (e.g., *tub* versus *tug*), and 10 pairs contain identical words.

Standard scores are available on the Wepman test for the first time with the second edition. They are normalized *T*-scores with a mean of 50 and a standard deviation of 10. The student's raw score is converted to a standard score, a percentile rank, and a Qualitative Score, which describes current functioning level (i.e., very good development, above average ability, average ability, below average ability, or below the level of adequacy). The test-retest and alternate form reliability of the Wepman test appears satisfactory, and its validity is supported by moderate correlations with other measures of auditory discrimination.

The Wepman test has typically been used as a screening device to identify students with poor auditory discrimination skills. However, before using this measure, the student's ability to comprehend the concepts of *same* and *different* and sustain attention during test administration must be considered, along with the tester's ability to accurately pronounce the word pairs.

Tests of Motor Skills

Motor skills are required in many school endeavors. In the classroom, for example, handwriting is a very important mode of expression. The development of motor skills may be delayed in students with physical impairments such as cerebral palsy. Physicians have the major responsibility for treatment of physical impairments, but they are often assisted by physical therapists, occupational therapists, and adaptive physical education teachers.

Problems in motor skill development may also occur in students without obvious physical impairments. The two major areas of concern to educators are gross-motor development and fine-motor development. Gross-motor skills, such as running, jumping, and throwing, involve the large muscles of the body. In contrast, fine-motor skills involve the small muscles. Examples of school-related fine-motor tasks are cutting with scissors, tracing, copying, and writing. Many of these skills involve both fine-motor ability and visual perception; this combination is called eye-hand coordination. Other motor skills of interest are balance, rhythm, laterality, directionality, body image, and body awareness (Wallace & McLoughlin, 1979).

Some measures of motor development are comprehensive in an attempt to assess both gross- and fine-motor skills. An early example is the *Purdue Perceptual-Motor Survey* (Roach & Kephart, 1966). It evaluates five types of motor skills: Balance and Posture, Body Image and Differentiation, Perceptual-Motor Match, Ocular Control, and Form Perception. This measure is no longer widely used.

A more recent measure is the *Bruininks-Oseretsky Test of Motor Proficiency* (Bruininks, 1978), which is based on the *Lincoln-Oseretsky Motor Development Scale* (Sloan, 1954). The *Bruininks-Oseretsky* is an individual, norm-referenced test for students ages 4 to 14; it contains eight subtests:

Gross Motor Skills

Subtest 1: Running Speed and Agility

Subtest 2: Balance

Subtest 3: Bilateral Coordination

Subtest 4: Strength

Gross and Fine Motor Skills

Subtest 5: Upper-Limb Coordination

Fine Motor Skills

Subtest 6: Response Speed

Subtest 7: Visual-Motor Control

Subtest 8: Upper-Limb Speed and Dexterity

The *Bruininks-Oseretsky* produces two scores for each subtest: a standard score and an age equivalent. Composite scores are available for gross-motor performance, fine-motor performance, and total performance.

The *Bruininks-Oseretsky* is a well-constructed test that appears to be useful for the assessment of fine- and gross-motor functioning. It was standardized in 1977 on a sample of 765 students selected to resemble the U.S. population. Test-retest and interrater reliability are adequate, and content validity appears satisfactory.

A more recent measure, the *Test of Gross Motor Development (TGMD)* (Ulrich, 1985), assesses two areas of gross motor development in children ages 3 to 10: locomotor skills and object control skills. On the Locomotion subtest, students are asked to demonstrate skills such as running, hopping, leaping, and skipping. The Object Control subtest includes tasks such as striking a ball with a bat, bouncing a ball, and catching a ball. The test manual clearly describes the procedures for administration and the criteria for evaluating student performance. Results include subtest standard scores and percentiles and a global standard score, the Gross Motor Development Quotient.

The *TGMD* was standardized on 909 subjects from eight states. This sample resembled the U.S. population in terms of gender, race, and community size; the geographic distribution of the sample was somewhat different from that of the nation as a whole. The manual provides evidence to support the reliability of the *TGMD*, its content validity, and its ability to differentiate between children with and without disabilities. Information is also needed on the relationship of the *TGMD* to other measures of motor development.

Many of the instruments developed to assess motor skills are concerned with only one ability: the fine-motor skill of eye-hand coordination. This skill is emphasized because it is required in many educational activities, most notably handwriting. Among the measures designed to evalu-ate eye-hand coordination are the *Bender Visual-Motor Gestalt Test* (Bender, 1938) and its adaptation for young children (Koppitz, 1963, 1975), the Visual-Motor Integration subtests of the *Developmental Test of Visual Perception* (2nd ed.) (described earlier), the *Developmental Test of Visual-Motor Integration* (4th ed.) (Beery, 1997), and the *Test of Visual-Motor Integration* (Hammill, Pearson, & Voress, 1996). All of these tests require students to copy geometric designs. On the *Bender Gestalt Test for Young Children* (Koppitz, 1963, 1975), for instance, children ages 5 to 11 copy nine geometric designs. Although the *Bender Gestalt* has been recommended as an indicator of intellectual functioning level, minimal brain dysfunction, and emotional disturbance (Koppitz, 1975), it is best viewed simply as a test of eye-hand coordination.

The *Developmental Test of Visual-Motor Integration* (4th ed.) is a popular measure of eye-hand coordination that was first published in 1967. The fourth edition includes updated norms and two new supplemental subtests (in addition to Visual-Motor Integration): Visual Perception and Motor Coordination. The original measure, the Visual-Motor Integration subtest, is available in a full format (for ages 3 through adult) and a short format (for ages 3 through 7). The *VMI* may be administered individually or to groups; administration requires 15 minutes or less. Norms are provided for ages 3-0 through 17-11.

The fourth edition of the *VMI* was standardized with 2,614 children. The standardization sample appears representative of the nation as a whole in ethnicity, urban-rural residence, geographic region, and socioeconomic status. Reliability of the *VMI* is adequate, and results appear related to those of other measures of eye-hand coordination.

The Visual-Motor Integration subtest is to be administered first. It contains 24 geometric forms to be copied by the student (Figure 9–4). Testing continues until the student fails three consecutive forms. Although administration of this subtest is fairly easy, scoring can be quite complicated. Each item is scored pass or fail using the criteria and examples provided in the manual, and a protractor is needed to evaluate some forms. For example, to pass the form called Vertical-Horizontal Cross [+], the student's drawing must contain two

Form 13, Open Square and Circle

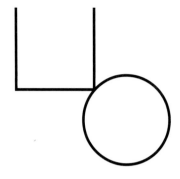

Form 18, Circle and Tilted Square

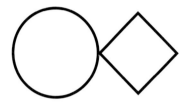

FIGURE 9-4

Sample Items from the *Developmental Test of Visual-Motor Integration* (4th ed.)

Note: From the *Developmental Test of Visual-Motor Integration* (4th ed.) by Keith Beery. Copyright 1997 by Keith Beery. Used by permission of Modern Curriculum Press, Inc.

lines that are fully intersecting *and* continuous, *and* at least one-half of each line must be within 20 degrees of its correct orientation.

On the Visual Perception subtest, the student looks at a stimulus design, then must find an identical design in an array of possible responses. On the Motor Coordination subtest, the student attempts to draw lines within the boundaries of a design. Global scores are available for each of the three subtests, and each can be expressed as a standard score, percentile rank, and age equivalent.

The *Test of Visual-Motor Integration (TVMI)* is a very similar measure. Designed for ages 4-0 to 17-11, it contains 30 forms for students to copy. Younger students complete items 1 to 18 and older students (ages 11 to 18) items 13 to 30. The *TVMI* may be administered to individuals or groups in 15 to 30 minutes. One difference between this measure and the *VMI* is that students may earn 0, 1, 2, or 3 points on each item, de-

pending upon the accuracy of their response. Results include a standard score, percentile rank, and age equivalent for total test performance.

Measures of Memory and Attention

Like perception, memory is often separated into two separate abilities on the basis of sensory input channel. Although the auditory-visual distinction may be of interest, memory can be described in several other important ways:

- *Type of information to be recalled.* In some memory tasks, the information to be stored for later retrieval is familiar and meaningful to the learner. This type of information is usually easier to recall than unfamiliar or nonmeaningful material.
- *Time since original learning.* Another variable is the amount of time that intervenes between original learning and recall. Short-term memory tasks require recall immediately after learning. Long-term memory tasks impose an interval of at least several seconds or minutes between learning and recall.
- *Type of memory.* This dimension distinguishes between the recognition of information learned previously and its recall. In recognition memory, the learner simply says whether or not information has been presented earlier. In recall memory, a more difficult task, the learner must reproduce the information.
- *Organization of recall.* In memory tasks, information can be retrieved in more than one way. Free recall is the retrieval of information in any order. In contrast, serial recall requires a fixed order. Serial recall is required in school tasks such as counting from 1 to 100 and reciting the alphabet in order. In paired-associate recall, the learner associates a response with a particular stimulus; when the stimulus is produced, the learner must recall the response. A common classroom task that requires paired-associate recall is saying letter names when written letters are presented.

Despite the many types of memory required in classroom learning, the majority of memory tests assess only short-term recall, usually in the serial mode. The most usual type of memory task on norm-referenced measures is short-term serial recall of nonmeaningful information. Auditory memory is often assessed with digit span tasks, in which students listen to and attempt to repeat series of numbers. Visual memory tasks are more varied; some use nonmeaningful shapes or isolated letters, and others employ pictures or photographs.

Most of the commonly used measures of memory are subtests from tests of intellectual performance or comprehensive specific ability batteries; several of these are described in Table 9–2. One notable exception is the *Test of Memory and Learning (TOMAL)* (Reynolds & Bigler, 1994). This comprehensive measure for students ages 5-0 through 19-11 contains 10 core and 4 supplementary subtests of memory functioning. Subtests are classified as verbal or nonverbal, and they assess a range of memory abilities including serial, free recall, and associative memory as well as both immediate and delayed recall. Results include an overall composite (Composite Memory Index) and these summary scores:

- Verbal Memory Index
- Nonverbal Memory Index
- Delayed Recall Index
- Sequential Recall Index
- Free Recall Index
- Associative Recall Index
- Learning Index
- Attention/Concentration Index

The *Wechsler Memory Scale-Third Edition* (Wechsler, 1997) is another useful instrument. However, it is designed for adolescents and adults with norms extending from ages 16 to 89.

Attention is another specific ability of interest in special education assessment. It is a difficult ability to measure because a learner's attention cannot be separated from the task. When persons attend, they attend *to* something, and that task or situation may influence how well attentional resources are deployed. Because of the inability to isolate attention from other factors, attention is often assessed informally through observation.

Before attending behavior can be observed, it must be operationally defined. For instance, paying attention to a workbook assignment might be defined by behaviors such as looking at the workbook page and writing answers to ques-

tions on the page. Of course, such observable behaviors are only indicators of the process of attention. Attention is inferred when the student engages in behaviors related to task completion.

Another source of information is the reports of teachers and parents. Persons who know the student well act as informants by participating in interviews and completing questionnaires and rating scales. This is the strategy most often used in assessment when attention deficit hyperactivity disorders (ADHD) are suspected. Chapter 10 discusses procedures for the assessment of attention deficits, hyperactivity, and impulsivity.

TEST BATTERIES FOR SPECIFIC ABILITY ASSESSMENT

Whereas some measures are designed to assess one particular learning ability, others attempt a more comprehensive evaluation. Such measures are made up of several subtests, each focusing on one or more specific abilities. Historically, the best-known measures of this type are the *Illinois Test of Psycholinguistic Abilities,* an information-processing test battery developed by Kirk, McCarthy, and Kirk (1968), and the *Detroit Tests of Learning Aptitude* (Baker & Leland, 1967). The 1968 edition of the *Illinois Test of Psycholinguistic Abilities* has not been revised. The newest version of the *Detroit Tests of Learning Aptitude* is described in the next section. This is followed by a discussion of the use of intelligence tests as measures of specific abilities.

Detroit Tests of Learning Aptitude (4th ed.)

The original version of this test was developed in the 1930s by Baker and Leland and then revised in 1967. In 1984, a new version was published by Hammill. The *Detroit Tests of Learning Aptitude* (2nd ed.) *(DTLA-2),* as this edition was called, was a complete revision and restandardization. The current edition is the *Detroit Tests of Learning Aptitude* (4th ed.), or *DTLA-4* (Hammill, 1998). Versions for young children (Hammill & Bryant, 1991b) and for adults (Hammill & Bryant, 1991a) are also available.

TABLE 9-2
Measures of Memory on Tests of Intellectual Performance

Type of Memory	Auditory or Visual	Meaningful or Nonmeaningful	Type of Information	Test	Subtest
Short-term recognition	Visual	Meaningful	People's faces	K-ABC	Face Recognition
Short-term serial recall	Auditory	Meaningful	Sentences	DTLA-4	Sentence Imitation
				S-B	Memory for Sentences
				W-J-R	Memory for Sentences
		Nonmeaningful	Isolated words	DTLA-4	Word Sequences
				K-ABC	Word Order
				W-J-R	Memory for Words
			Digits	K-ABC	Number Recall
				S-B	Memory for Digits
				WISC-III	Digit Span
				W-J-R	Numbers Reversed
	Visual	Nonmeaningful	Geometric forms	DTLA-4	Design Reproduction
			Hand movements	K-ABC	Hand Movements
			Letters	DTLA-4	Reversed Letters
			Position of stimuli	K-ABC	Spatial Memory
			Shapes, colors	K-ABC	Bead Memory
			Unrelated objects	DTLA-4	Design Sequences
				S-B	Memory for Objects
Long-term paired-associate recall	Visual and Auditory	Nonmeaningful	Words associated with shapes	W-J-R	Visual-Auditory Learning
				W-J-R	Delayed Recall–Visual-Auditory Learning
			Words associated with drawings	W-J-R	Memory for Names
				W-J-R	Delayed Recall—Memory for Names

Key to test names:

DTLA-4—Detroit Tests of Learning Aptitude-4 (Hammill, 1998)

K-ABC—Kaufman Assessment Battery for Children (Kaufman & Kaufman, 1983)

S-B—Stanford-Binet Intelligence Scale: Fourth Edition (Thorndike, Hagen, & Sattler, 1986)

WISC-III—Wechsler Intelligence Scale for Children-Third Edition (Wechsler, 1991)

W-J-R—Woodcock-Johnson Psycho-Educational Battery-Revised (Woodcock & Johnson, 1989)

The *DTLA-4* is an individual, norm-referenced test designed to assess a variety of specific cognitive abilities. It is appropriate for students ages 6-0 to 17-11, and it contains 10 subtests:

- *Word Opposites*. The tester says a word and the student must say a word that is opposite in meaning.
- *Design Sequences*. The student is shown a page with a series of designs. The page is removed and the student must reproduce the series using blocks. If an error is made, the tester shows the page again; no more than three trials are allowed.
- *Sentence Imitation*. The tester says a sentence and the student must repeat it verbatim.
- *Reversed Letters*. The tester says a series of letters at a rate of one per second; the student must write the letters in reverse order.
- *Story Construction*. The student is shown a picture and must make up a story about it.
- *Design Reproduction*. The student is shown a geometric design. After 5 seconds, the design is removed. After 5 more seconds, the student is asked to draw the design.
- *Basic Information*. The tester asks questions related to daily life, science, geography, and history, and the student responds orally.
- *Symbolic Relations*. The student is shown a page with several designs at the top. One design (or more) is missing. The student must find the design that completes the pattern in the choices at the bottom of the page.
- *Word Sequences*. The tester says a series of unrelated words and the student must repeat them in order.
- *Story Sequences*. The tester presents a set of pictures that tell a story and the student must put them in order. The student puts a chip with the number 1 on it on the first picture, a chip with a number 2 on the second, and so on.

The *DTLA-4* is quite similar to the previous version. Changes include the deletion of the Picture Fragments subtest, the revision of the Story Sequences subtest so that it is now untimed, and the use of color pictures for Story Sequences and Story Construction. Administration of the *DTLA-4* requires 50 minutes to 2 hours.

On the *DTLA-4*, standard scores and percentile ranks are computed for each subtest, and subtest results can be combined into several Composite scores. See Figure 9–5 for a sample *DTLA-4* protocol. Subtest standard scores are distributed with a mean of 10 and a standard deviation of 3; Composite scores are distributed with a mean of 100 and a standard deviation of 15. The General Mental Ability Composite is a total test score that reflects performance on all subtests; the Optimal Composite summarizes performance on the four subtests in which the student earned the highest scores. According to the *DTLA-4* manual, this score "represents the best estimate of mental ability when inhibiting factors are suppressed" (p. xii). Subtest results can also be combined into Domain Composites and Theoretical Composites.

The *DTLA-4* assesses three domains: Linguistic, Attentional, and Motoric. Two Composite scores are provided for each domain; one of these scores emphasizes the ability under consideration, and the other deemphasizes it. For example, in the Linguistic Domain, the Verbal Composite includes subtests that stress word knowledge and use, whereas subtests that contribute to the Nonverbal Composite deemphasize verbal abilities. In the Attentional Domain, subtests that require attention, concentration, and short-term memory make up the Attention-Enhanced Composite; subtests that stress long-term memory contribute to the Attention-Reduced Composite. Likewise, on the Motoric Domain, subtests with high motor skill demands are combined into the Motor-Enhanced Composite, and those that are relatively motor-free comprise the Motor-Reduced Composite. One of the purposes of the *DTLA-4* is "to determine strengths and weaknesses among developed mental abilities" (p. 24), and the Domain Composites provided by this measure facilitate this task.

Subtest results can also be combined into what the *DTLA-4* calls Theoretical Composites. Each of these sets of scores represents a different theory of intelligence. For example, the Wechsler Composites are called Verbal Scale and Performance Scale, reflecting the two major scales on Wechsler tests such as the *WISC-III*. In fact, the Wechsler Composites are identical to the *DTLA-4*'s Linguistic Domain Composite scores: Verbal and

DTLA–4

Detroit Tests of Learning Aptitude

Profile/Summary Form

Fourth Edition

Section I. Identifying Information

Name __Luis__   Female ☐ Male ☑ Grade __6__

	Year	Month	Day
Date Tested	97	11	16
Date of Birth	85	7	8
Age	12	4	8

School __Bedichek Middle__

Examiner's Name __Dr. Rivera__

Examiner's Title __Diagnostician__

Section II. Record of DTLA–4 Subtest Scores

Subtest	Raw Score	%ile	Standard Score	Age Equivalent	Rating
I. Word Opposites (WO)	33	37	9	11-3	Average
II. Design Sequences (DS)	122	37	9	11-3	Average
III. Sentence Imitation (SI)	15	37	9	11-3	Average
IV. Reversed Letters (RL)	38	75	12	16-9	Average
V. Story Construction (SC)	14	50	10	11-9	Average
VI. Design Reproduction (DR)	36	63	11	13-0	Average
VII. Basic Information (BI)	11	5	5	8-3	Poor
VIII. Symbolic Relations (SR)	15	16	7	8-6	Below Average
IX. Word Sequences (WS)	12	37	9	10-0	Average
X. Story Sequences (SS)	27	25	8	9-9	Average

Section III. Profile of DTLA–4 Subtest Scores

Standard Scores	Word Opposites	Design Sequences	Sentence Imitation	Reversed Letters	Story Construction	Design Reproduction	Basic Information	Symbolic Relations	Word Sequences	Story Sequences	Standard Scores
20	·	·	·	·	·	·	·	·	·	·	20
19	·	·	·	·	·	·	·	·	·	·	19
18	·	·	·	·	·	·	·	·	·	·	18
17	·	·	·	·	·	·	·	·	·	·	17
16	·	·	·	·	·	·	·	·	·	·	16
15	·	·	·	·	·	·	·	·	·	·	15
14	·	·	·	·	·	·	·	·	·	·	14
13	·	·	·	·	·	·	·	·	·	·	13
12	·	·	·	X	·	·	·	·	·	·	12
11	·	·	·	·	·	X	·	·	·	·	11
10	·	·	·	·	X	·	·	·	·	·	10
9	X	X	X	·	·	·	·	·	X	·	9
8	·	·	·	·	·	·	·	·	·	X	8
7	·	·	·	·	·	·	·	X	·	·	7
6	·	·	·	·	·	·	·	·	·	·	6
5	·	·	·	·	·	·	X	·	·	·	5
4	·	·	·	·	·	·	·	·	·	·	4
3	·	·	·	·	·	·	·	·	·	·	3
2	·	·	·	·	·	·	·	·	·	·	2
1	·	·	·	·	·	·	·	·	·	·	1

Additional copies of this form (#8564) may be purchased from PRO-ED, 8700 Shoal Creek Blvd., Austin, TX 78757-6897, 512/451-3246, Fax 512/451-8542

FIGURE 9-5

Sample *Detroit Tests of Learning Aptitude* (4th ed.) Results

Note: From *Detroit Tests of Learning Aptitude* (4th ed.) (pp. 64–65) by D. D. Hammill, 1998, Austin, TX: PRO-ED. Copyright 1998 by PRO-ED. Reprinted by permission.

Section IV. Workspace for Computing Composites

Global Composites	WO	DS	SI	RL	SC	DR	BI	SR	WS	SS	=	Sum of Std. Scores	Quotient	%ile
General Mental Ability	9	9	9	12	10	11	5	7	9	8	=	89	92	30
Optimal (select highest four scores)	9			12	10	11					=	42	103	58

DOMAIN COMPOSITES: WO DS SI RL SC DR BI SR WS SS

Linguistic

	WO	DS	SI	RL	SC	DR	BI	SR	WS	SS	=	Sum	Quotient	%ile
Verbal	9		9		10		5		9		=	42	89	23
Nonverbal		9		12		11		7		8	=	47	96	39

Attentional

	WO	DS	SI	RL	SC	DR	BI	SR	WS	SS	=	Sum	Quotient	%ile
Attention-Enhanced		9	9	12		11			9	8	=	58	98	45
Attention-Reduced	9				10		5	7			=	31	85	16

Motoric

	WO	DS	SI	RL	SC	DR	BI	SR	WS	SS	=	Sum	Quotient	%ile
Motor-Enhanced		9		12		11				8	=	40	100	50
Motor-Reduced	9		9		10		5	7	9		=	49	87	19

THEORETICAL COMPOSITES: WO DS SI RL SC DR BI SR WS SS

Cattell and Horn

	WO	DS	SI	RL	SC	DR	BI	SR	WS	SS	=	Sum	Quotient	%ile
Fluid Intelligence		9		12		11		7			=	39	98	45
Crystallized Intelligence	9		9		10		5		9	8	=	50	89	23

Das

	WO	DS	SI	RL	SC	DR	BI	SR	WS	SS	=	Sum	Quotient	%ile
Simultaneous Processing	9		9		10	11	5	7			=	51	90	25
Successive Processing		9		12					9	8	=	38	97	42

Jensen

	WO	DS	SI	RL	SC	DR	BI	SR	WS	SS	=	Sum	Quotient	%ile
Associative Level		9	9	12		11		9			=	50	100	50
Cognitive Level	9				10		5	7		8	=	39	85	16

Wechsler

	WO	DS	SI	RL	SC	DR	BI	SR	WS	SS	=	Sum	Quotient	%ile
Verbal Scale	9		9		10		5		9		=	42	89	23
Performance Scale		9		12		11		7		8	=	47	96	39

FIGURE 9–5
Continued

Nonverbal. Other Theoretical Composites are Cattell and Horn (Fluid and Crystallized Intelligence), Das (Simultaneous and Successive Processing), and Jensen (Associative and Cognitive Levels). According to the *DTLA-4* manual, the Cattell and Horn model separates intelligence into two sets of abilities: fluid intelligence, which emphasizes nonverbal, culture-free processes, and crystallized intelligence, which emphasizes skills acquired through direct instruction or from one's culture. In the Das model, simultaneous processing involves working with stimuli that are presented concurrently, while successive processing involves sequential stimuli. Jensen's model includes associative level thinking, in which there is a high correspondence between the forms of the stimulus and the required response, and cognitive level thinking, in which stimulus input must be transformed to produce a response.

The *DTLA-4* was renormed with 1,350 persons from 37 states. However, some members of the norm group were tested in 1989–90 as part of the development of the *DTLA-3* and others were tested in 1996–97. The sample included ages 6-0 to 17-11, and it appears to approximate the national population in race, ethnicity, urban-rural residence, geographic area, and family income. Students with disabilities made up 11% of the sample.

Internal consistency and test-retest reliability are adequate for *DTLA-4* Composite scores and for most subtests. Some subtests show reliability coefficients below .80, although all coefficients equal or exceed .70. For example, the subtest with the lowest average internal consistency (.79) is Story Construction; across ages, its reliability coefficients range from .73 to .85. Across ages, test-retest reliability coefficients fall below .70 for three subtests: Design Sequences (.71), Reversed Letters (.73), and Story Sequences (.76). However, reliability coefficients for all composite scores are .90 or above.

Validity was studied in a number of ways, including investigation of the relationship of the *DTLA-4* to other measures of intellectual performance. Note, however, that the concurrent validity studies reported in the manual refer to the third edition of the *DTLA;* the *DTLA-4* manual explains that the items on these two editions are virtually identical. The General Mental Ability Composite score on the *DTLA-3* shows good agreement with the Broad Cognitive Ability (Standard) score on the *Woodcock-Johnson-R* (r = .91) and the Mental Processing score of the *K-ABC* (r = .82). Other *DTLA-3* Composite scores show mixed results. For example, the *K-ABC* Sequential and Simultaneous Processing scores would be expected to be related to the *DTLA-3* Successive and Simultaneous Processing Composites. Although the two measures of sequential processing are related (r = .84), the Simultaneous Composite of the *DTLA-3* shows a stronger correlation with the *K-ABC* Sequential score (r = .80) than with the *K-ABC* Simultaneous score (r = .70).

Factor analytic studies with the *DTLA-4* provide partial confirmation. The manual states that "Because the DTLA-4 subtests were constructed to measure cognitive abilities, we expected they would load on a single factor" (p. 152). The first factor analysis identified one dominant factor, general mental ability. In the second analysis, two factors were identified: verbal and nonverbal ability. Confirmatory factor analyses supported the three domains on the *DTLA-4* (Linguistic, Attentional, and Motoric) and the four theoretical composites.

Other Versions of the DTLA. The *Detroit Tests of Learning Aptitude-Primary* (2nd ed.) *(DTLA-Primary:2)* is a downward extension of the *DTLA-4* for children ages 3-0 to 9-11. It employs many of the same kinds of test tasks and produces the same General Mental Ability and Domain Composites as the *DTLA-4*. There are three major differences between the tests. The *DTLA-Primary:2* is not organized by subtests; items of all types are merged into one sequence by difficulty level. Also, the *Primary:2* contains some tasks that are not found on the version for older students; examples are articulation, draw-a-person, motor directions, oral directions, picture identification, and visual discrimination. Third, the Theoretical Composites of the *DTLA-4* are not available on the *Primary:2*.

The *Detroit Tests of Learning Aptitude-Adult (DTLA-A)* is designed for persons ages 16-0 to 79-11. It contains 12 subtests, 9 of which are equivalent to subtests on the *DTLA-4*. The three subtests that are not found on the version for school-aged individuals are Mathematical Problems, Quantitative Relations, and Form Assembly. The *DTLA-A* provides the same types of results as the *DTLA-4:* subtest standard scores, General and Optimal Mental Ability Composites, Domain Composites (Linguistic, Attentional, and Motoric), and Theoretical Composites.

The *Hammill Multiability Intelligence Test (HAMIT)* by Hammill, Bryant, and Pearson (1998), which was described in the previous chapter, is a shorter version of the *DTLA-4*. It contains 8 subtests, rather than 10. The two subtests that were omitted are Reversed Letters and Story Construction. The *HAMIT* produces only three composite scores: General, Verbal, and Nonverbal Intelligence.

Intelligence Tests as Measures of Specific Cognitive Abilities

Results of tests of intellectual performance are sometimes used to provide information about students' specific learning abilities. When specific abilities are the focus of assessment, the scores of interest are individual subtest results and composite scores that result from combinations of subtests, not global IQ scores.

This practice began with the criticism leveled at early tests of specific abilities. Faced with a shortage of technically adequate specific ability tests, practitioners turned to well-respected instruments such as the Wechsler family of intelligence tests. Also, the norms of some specific ability measures do not extend into the middle and high school grades, limiting their usefulness to younger age ranges. Another impetus for this practice was the introduction of a new generation of intelligence tests designed to provide not only estimates of overall aptitude for learning, but also information about more specific cognitive abilities.

The individual intelligence test most often used as an information source about specific abilities is the *WISC-III,* the *Wechsler Intelligence Scale for Children-Third Edition* (Wechsler, 1991). *WISC-III* results are available for most students who are assessed for possible special education placement, and these results are examined to determine strengths and weaknesses in various cognitive abilities.

WISC-III analysis is often recommended as part of the process in the identification of learning disabilities. However, interpretation of *WISC-III* results can take many forms, from identification of the lowest subtest scores to a search for subtest scatter and Verbal-Performance discrepancies. Many of these procedures have been thoroughly studied with the *WISC-R,* and reviews of research (Kaufman, 1981; Kavale & Forness, 1984) are beginning to indicate a consensus on the utility of various approaches.

This body of research suggests that analysis of Verbal-Performance discrepancies and subtest scatter are not fruitful procedures for identification of learning disabilities. However, results may provide information about a student's relative strengths and weaknesses. Of particular interest are the subtests in which students with learning disabilities typically show their poorest performance: Arithmetic, Coding, Information, Digit Span, and Mazes. On the *WISC-III,* the Arithmetic and Digit Span subtests are combined in the Freedom from Distractibility Index, and the Perceptual Speed Index contains Coding and a new subtest, Symbol Search.

Table 9–3 presents several of the newer tests of intellectual performance and the cognitive abilities they measure. The *DTLA-4* is included because it can be classified as either a test of intellectual performance or a measure of specific learning abilities. As can be seen from this table, the *WISC-III* provides four factor-based Index scores in addition to Verbal and Performance IQs; the *Woodcock-Johnson Psycho-Educational Battery-Revised* (Woodcock & Johnson, 1989) assesses seven cognitive factors. The fourth edition of the *Stanford-Binet Intelligence Scale* (Thorndike, Hagen, & Sattler, 1986) provides information on short-term memory as well as verbal, quantitative, and abstract/visual reasoning. Both *Kaufman* scales offer measures of two types of processing: simultaneous and sequential on the *Kaufman Assessment Battery for Children* (Kaufman & Kaufman, 1983) and fluid and crystallized on the *Kaufman Adolescent & Adult Intelligence Test* (Kaufman & Kaufman, 1993).

The newer intelligence tests appear to be quite useful for the study of specific cognitive abilities. However, it is important to remember that there is not yet a rich research literature supporting these approaches. Thus, professionals should proceed with caution as they begin to use these new measures to assist in the study of specific learning abilities.

ASSESSMENT OF LEARNING STRATEGIES

In recent years, interest has shifted from the study of isolated specific abilities to consideration of learning strategies. Learning strategies are the methods that students employ when faced with a

TABLE 9–3
Specific Abilities Assessed by Tests of Intellectual Performance

TEST	SCORES REPRESENTING SPECIFIC ABILITIES
Wechsler Intelligence Scale for Children-Third Edition	Verbal Scale IQ Performance Scale IQ Verbal Comprehension Index Perceptual Organization Index Freedom from Distractibility Index Perceptual Speed Index
Woodcock-Johnson Psycho-Educational Battery-Revised	Long-Term Retrieval Short-Term Memory Processing Speed Auditory Processing Visual Processing Comprehension-Knowledge Fluid Reasoning
Stanford-Binet Intelligence Scale: Fourth Edition	Verbal Reasoning Abstract/Visual Reasoning Quantitative Reasoning Short-Term Memory
Kaufman Assessment Battery for Children	Sequential Processing Simultaneous Processing
Kaufman Adolescent & Adult Intelligence Test	Fluid Scale IQ Crystallized Scale IQ
Detroit Tests of Learning Aptitude (4th ed.)	Verbal Composite Nonverbal Composite Attention-Enhanced Composite Attention-Reduced Composite Motor-Enhanced Composite Motor-Reduced Composite Verbal Scale Performance Scale Fluid Intelligence Crystallized Intelligence Simultaneous Processing Successive Processing Associative Level Cognitive Level

learning task. This change is due in part to the criticism leveled against traditional specific ability assessments and treatment programs. It is also due to current research findings about the nature of learning disabilities.

Research Findings

Research results indicate that many students with learning disabilities are characterized by ineffi-cient and ineffective strategies for learning (Lewis, 1983). This finding has been reported in relation to the specific learning abilities of both attention and memory. Hallahan and Reeve (1980), in their summary of research on selective attention, conclude:

> . . . it appears that the most parsimonious expla-nation for the learning disabled child's tendency to have problems in attending to relevant cues

and ignoring irrelevant cues is his inability to bring to the task a specific learning strategy. (p. 156)

Research on memory supports this (Swanson & Cooney, 1996; Torgesen, 1980). Students with learning disabilities tend to recall less information than students without disabilities. They approach the learning task differently and are less likely to engage in active rehearsal during the study period. However, when students with learning disabilities are required to rehearse, their recall improves, sometimes to the level of typical students (Torgesen & Goldman, 1977). These findings led Torgesen (1977) to hypothesize that students with learning disabilities are passive learners. Swanson (1989) disagrees; in his review of research, he concludes that "a more accurate characterization of LD children is that they are *actively inefficient* learners" (p. 10).

Deshler and other researchers at the University of Kansas have carried out a series of studies on the learning characteristics of adolescents identified as learning disabled (e.g., Alley, Deshler, Clark, Schumaker, & Warner, 1983; Deshler, Schumaker, Alley, Warner, & Clark, 1982; Schumaker, Deshler, Alley, & Warner, 1983). Their results indicate that many adolescents with learning disabilities exhibit immature executive functioning; that is, these students are unable to create and apply an appropriate strategy to a novel problem (Schumaker et al., 1983). In addition, the study skills and strategies of secondary-aged students with learning disabilities are deficient. Among the areas of difficulty are note taking, attention to teachers' statements, listening comprehension, scanning of textbook passages, monitoring of writing errors, and test-taking skills (Deshler et al., 1982).

Although deficient learning strategies and study skills appear to characterize students with learning disabilities, these strategies may be susceptible to training (Lerner, 2000; Lewis, 1983). Torgesen's (1980) work in memory illustrates this point. Research at the University of Kansas on the efficacy of learning strategy interventions also supports the feasibility of training (Deshler et al., 1982). The Strategy Instruction Model (SIM) developed at the University of Kansas begins with assessment of the student's current strategies for

learning. New strategies are then taught, first in isolation, then with controlled academic materials, and finally with actual school texts and assignments (Deshler, Alley, Warner, and Schumaker, 1981). Three types of strategies are included in SIM: acquisition strategies, storage strategies, and strategies for the demonstration and expression of knowledge (Lenz et al., 1996).

Approaches to Assessment

Although progress has been made in the development of instructional models, the assessment of learning strategies has received little attention. According to Pressley, Borkowski, Forrest-Pressley, Gaskins, and Wile (1993), "No one has yet devised a formal assessment that captures the many dimensions of good information processing" (p. 361). However, these authors suggest that the *Surveys of Problem-Solving and Educational Skills* (Meltzer, 1987) is a promising measure. In practice, professionals tend to rely upon informal assessment tools to gather information about learning strategies. Specific ability tests do not provide sufficient information, because they measure abilities in isolation rather than in the context of actual learning tasks. More pertinent data are produced by observations, work sample analyses, student questionnaires and interviews, and teacher interviews.

Suggestions for the design of informal tools for the assessment of learning strategies are available in the study skills literature. However, study skills are not the same as learning strategies. The term *learning strategy* is usually reserved for the general cognitive strategies that students apply to tasks in which learning is expected: strategies for the deployment of attention, for the rehearsal of skills and information to be learned, for generating and evaluating solutions to problems, and so forth. In contrast, study skills are more closely tied to specific school tasks and often require at least rudimentary proficiency in reading and writing. Despite these differences, both learning strategies and study skills are concerned with the student's *use* of specific abilities. Evaluation of study habits can provide some insight into the ways the student interacts with the learning task.

According to Cohen and de Bettencourt (1983), students are responsible for five aspects of independent learning activities: following directions, approaching tasks, obtaining assistance, gaining feedback, and gaining reinforcement. These five components could form the basis for designing an observation of student study behavior.

Brown (1978) discusses study behaviors and suggests methods for informal assessment. First, the student's work habits should be observed within the context of the classroom. Among the factors to be considered are the frequency and duration of on-task and off-task behaviors; any classroom conditions or events that appear to distract the student; and variations in performance from one time or one subject matter area, or one teacher to another. A second assessment method is discussion with the student. Students can be asked to describe their usual methods of approaching and completing class assignments.

Students can be interviewed while they are working on a study task or just after they have completed it. This allows the interviewer to ask specific questions about a particular task. Students simply report their actions, rather than attempting to recall or make judgments about their typical behaviors. Some questions that could be asked in situations in which students are learning new information are:

• Think about things you just did in studying _____ . What did you do first?
• Did you begin by looking over the information to be learned?
• Did you try to organize the information in any way? If so, how did you organize it?
• Was there anything in the material that you didn't understand? If there was, how did you try to figure it out?
• In your studying, did you do anything to help you remember the information? What did you do? Did you look at it? Say it to yourself? Picture it in your mind? Take notes? Outline the information?
• Can you recall the information now? Do you think you'll be able to remember it tomorrow?
• Will you study this information again? If so, will you use the same study methods?

These questions attempt to elicit student comments about the use of strategies such as previewing, organizing, problem solving, and rehearsing. In light of the research findings about students' lack of active task participation, the questions about rehearsal techniques are of special interest. Some students may report using verbal rehearsal—the material to be learned is said aloud or subvocally. Others may talk about visual imagery—the construction of mental visual images—as a strategy for learning. Both verbal rehearsal and visual imagery have been found useful as mnemonic devices or memory aids for students with learning disabilities (Rose, Cundick, & Higbee, 1983). Students who report no rehearsal strategy or say they simply look at the material may be in need of strategy training.

The *Study Skills Counseling Evaluation (SSCE)* (Demos, 1976) is a published assessment device designed to "rapidly and objectively identify study weaknesses" (p. 1). It is a print questionnaire with norms for high school students, 2-year college students, and 4-year college students.

The *SSCE* contains 50 items that assess five study skill areas:

• Study-Time Distribution
• Study Conditions
• Taking Notes
• Preparing and Taking Examinations
• Other Habits and Attitudes

The student reads each statement (e.g., "I study in several short sessions") and then marks the best description of his or her current study habits: very often, often, sometimes, seldom, or very seldom. The *SSCE* total test raw score is converted to a percentile rank. In addition, the manual provides guidelines for rating performance in each of the study skill areas as Very Strong, Strong, Average, Weak, or Very Weak. These ratings can be plotted on a summary profile to provide a graphic representation of strengths and weaknesses.

The *SSCE* is a normed instrument, but very little information is provided in the manual about the standardization sample. Although this is a concern, the *SSCE* could be used as an informal device, or local norms could be developed. In interpreting results of this or other self-report measures, it must be remembered that not every student is able—or willing—to provide totally accurate information.

Most published study skills questionnaires are designed for high school and college students. The *Study Attitudes and Methods Survey* (Michael, Michael, & Zimmerman, 1985) includes the dimensions of academic interest and drive, study habits, and lack of study anxiety. An older measure, the *Survey of Study Habits and Attitudes* (Brown & Holtzman, 1967a, 1967b), extends down to grade 7 and is available in both English and Spanish. It evaluates study methods, motivation for studying, and attitudes toward scholastic activities.

Levine, Clarke, and Ferb (1981) report the results of a study in which students with learning disabilities, ages 9 and above, rated themselves on several dimensions of learning behavior. The instrument, the *Self-Administered Student Profile,* was made up of quotations gathered from children with learning disabilities. The items represented the categories of Memory, Selective Attention, Visual-Spatial Orientation, Gross Motor Function, Fine Motor Function, Sequential Organization, Language, Academic Performance, Social Interaction, and Overall Working Efficiency.

The most common problems identified by students in this study were in the areas of memory and selective attention. For example, 45% of the sample reported that, "A lot of times I do things too fast without thinking"; 36% said, "It's hard for me to keep my mind on work in school"; and 28% said, "I have trouble remembering things the teacher just said a little while ago." In general, there was good agreement between students' reports and those of their teachers, parents, and clinic staff.

Assessment of learning strategies is a relatively new endeavor in special education, and, at present, assessment teams rely primarily on informal techniques if there is interest in evaluating strategies for learning and study skills. The previous paragraphs have provided some suggestions about important factors to consider in designing student observations, interviews, and questionnaires. Upcoming chapters on the assessment of academic skills include additional recommendations for the study of learning strategies as they relate to reading, mathematics, and written language.

DISCREPANCY ANALYSIS

One of the major criteria for the identification of learning disabilities is a discrepancy between expected and actual performance. It is assumed that a learning disability will have a negative effect upon school functioning, so students will not achieve as well as would be expected from their general intellectual level. According to federal guidelines, for a student to qualify for learning disabilities services, the team must establish a severe discrepancy between ability and achievement in one or more of these subject matter areas: oral expression, listening comprehension, written expression, basic reading skill, reading comprehension, mathematics calculation, and mathematics reasoning.

The discrepancy notion appears clear and straightforward until it must be operationalized; then numerous questions arise. These include choice of measures of ability and achievement, and the setting of standards to determine how large the difference between scores must be to indicate a discrepancy and how large that discrepancy must be to be considered severe. The simplest of these decisions is the choice of measures. In practice, ability is assessed with tests of intellectual performance, and achievement with achievement tests. But even this choice is complicated by factors such as the range of scores available on many measures.

Traditional Methods of Discrepancy Analysis

Several methods have been suggested for discrepancy analysis, although none has escaped criticism. One traditional method used by practitioners is the years-below-grade-level procedure. In this procedure, the student's grade score on some measure of academic achievement is subtracted from current grade placement. A discrepancy is indicated when the student is found to be more than 2 years below grade level. For example, if a mid-year fourth grade student (grade placement = 4.5) earns a grade equivalent of 1.3 on a reading test, the student could be said to achieve 3.2 years below grade level, a difference considered indicative of a discrepancy. Although this method is easy to use, it is not an appropriate way to analyze discrepancies. It does not take differences in ability into account. It assumes average ability by making actual grade placement the standard of comparison.

Another major difficulty with this method is its use of grade scores. As Chapter 3 explained, grade equivalents are not equal-interval scores; thus, they may not legitimately be added or subtracted. Berk (1982) discusses some of the deficiencies of grade equivalent scores. These scores:

1. Invite seemingly simple but misleading interpretations
2. Assume that the rate of learning is constant throughout the school year . . .
3. Are derived primarily from interpolation and extrapolation rather than from real data
4. Are virtually meaningless in the upper grade-levels for subjects that are not taught at those levels
5. Do not comprise an equal-interval scale
6. Exaggerate the significance of small differences in performance
7. Vary markedly from test to test, from subtest to subtest within the same test battery, from grade to grade and from percentile to percentile. (p. 12)

Because of these deficiencies and its other limitations, the years-below-grade-level method is not recommended for discrepancy analysis.

A second traditional method makes use of expectancy formulas to estimate the student's expected level of achievement. For example, the expectancy formula of Harris (1970) is calculated by subtracting 5.0 years from the student's measured mental age (MA). Thus, a student of MA 9.0 would be expected to achieve at the 4.0 grade level. This expected grade level is then compared to the student's grade score on some test of achievement. The Bond and Tinker (1967) formula is similar, but IQ, rather than MA, is used as the aptitude measure. Several other expectancy formulas have also been proposed (Bureau of Education for the Handicapped, 1976; Monroe, 1932; Myklebust, 1968).

Expectancy formulas share one of the major limitations of the years-below-grade-level approach: Current achievement is expressed in grade equivalent scores. In addition, age equivalent scores such as mental ages are subject to the same deficiencies seen in grade equivalent scores. Another major criticism of expectancy formula methods is that they do not consider reliability. The reliability of each of the compared scores is of interest, as is the reliability of the obtained discrepancy score.

Standard Score Methods of Discrepancy Analysis

One way of overcoming the limitations of age and grade scores is to replace them with standard scores. Standard scores are interval data and may be manipulated arithmetically by addition or subtraction. Standard scores must be distributed with the same mean and standard deviation to compare them from one measure to another. Norm groups used to derive these standard scores must also be comparable.

The simplest method of discrepancy analysis using standard scores is to subtract one score from another. For example, if a student receives a standard score of 105 on an IQ test and a standard score of 82 on an achievement test, the difference between the two scores would be 23. This new score, 23, is called a difference score. In some locations, districts set guidelines for how large the difference score must be to indicate a severe discrepancy. For example, the guideline might be a difference score equal to 1 (or 1.5) standard deviations. If each of the tests being compared had standard score standard deviations of 15, the difference needed to indicate an important discrepancy would then be 15 (or 22.5) standard score points.

However, because this approach does not take into account the measurement error present in each of the two scores, Anastasi and Urbina (1997) suggest an alternative procedure. Instead of comparing scores directly, confidence intervals are constructed around each obtained score using each test's standard error of measurement. Then these score ranges are compared to determine whether there is an overlap. For example, using a 95% confidence interval, the IQ score range might be 99 to 111, and the achievement score range 72 to 92. If there is no overlap between the score ranges, it is likely there is a difference between the obtained ability and achievement scores.

To gain more precision, Anastasi and Urbina (1997) recommend calculation of the standard error of difference between scores. The standard error of difference is used to determine whether an observed difference occurred by chance or whether the difference is likely a true difference. It is computed with the formula

$$SE_{diff} = SD\sqrt{2 - r_1 - r_2}$$

where SE_{diff} is the standard error of the difference, SD is the standard deviation of the two tests, r_1 is the reliability coefficient for test 1, and r_2 is the reliability coefficient for test 2. For example, if the standard deviation of each test is 15, and the tests' reliabilities are .90 and .92, the standard error of the difference would be 6.36. To find out how large a difference is needed at various levels of confidence, the standard error of the difference is multiplied by:

1.64 to determine the difference likely to occur by chance 10% of the time;

1.96 to determine the difference likely to occur by chance 5% of the time; and

2.58 to determine the difference likely to occur by chance 1% of the time.

If the 5% (.05) level is selected, the standard error of the difference is multiplied by 1.96: 6.36 × 1.96 = 12.46. Thus, the difference between the two scores must be at least 12 to signify a real difference at the .05 level. That is, there is a 95% probability that a difference of 12 signifies a true difference and only a 5% probability that this difference is due to chance.

The standard error of difference method is not a perfect solution to the problem of score comparisons. If the tests being compared are related, the reliability of the difference score is affected. The higher the correlation between the tests, the lower the reliability of the difference score. Schulte and Borich (1984) provide procedures for computing the reliabilities of difference scores when the correlation between measures is known. Other factors that influence the accuracy of difference scores are regression effects and the lack of homogeneity among the standard errors of measurement within a particular test.

Many authors (Algozzine, Forgnone, Mercer, & Trifiletti, 1979; Cone & Wilson, 1981; Hanna, Dyck, & Holen, 1979; Reynolds, 1984, 1992; Salvia & Ysseldyke, 1998) have suggested additional methods of discrepancy analysis, most notably the regression approach. At present, however, there does not appear to be agreement about the most appropriate method, although criticism of expectancy formulas and the years-below-grade-level approach is consistent (Berk, 1982, 1984; Cone & Wilson, 1981; Sattler, 1988).

Several studies have compared the effects of using various discrepancy analysis procedures. For example, Forness, Sinclair, and Guthrie (1983) applied seven expectancy formulas and a "years-behind" method to the ability and achievement scores of 92 students. The eight methods of discrepancy analysis produced quite different results. The percentage of children identified as learning disabled by the different formulas ranged from a low of 10.9% to a high of 37.0%. Ysseldyke, Algozzine, and Epps (1983) reported similar findings. In addition, it appears that some general education students would be classified as learning disabled if ability-achievement discrepancy is the sole criterion.

Another concern is the willingness of teachers and other professionals to use the more elaborate discrepancy analysis procedures. These procedures require time-consuming computations that are considered difficult by many professionals. One alternative is to choose tests with built-in systems for discrepancy analysis.

Tests with Built-in Discrepancy Analysis Systems

Many unanswered questions about discrepancy analysis remain. Despite this, assessment teams must evaluate students for placement in programs for students with learning disabilities. One approach to the problem is use of some of the newer measures of ability and achievement that have built-in procedures for discrepancy analysis. Computer programs are available to assist with scoring and discrepancy analyses for many of these measures.

In some cases, one instrument includes measures of both intellectual performance and academic achievement. Examples include the *Woodcock-Johnson-R* and the *K-ABC*. In others, tests of aptitude and achievement are separate but linked though common standardization procedures. Companion tests include the *WISC-III* and *Wechsler Individual Achievement Test* (1992) and the two Hammill measures, the *Hammill Multiability Intelligence Test* and the *Hammill Multiability Achievement Test* (Hammill, Hresko, Ammer, Cronin, & Quinby, 1998). Occasionally, tests that are not part of a system will provide sufficient information for discrepancy analyses. One example is the *Woodcock Reading Mastery Tests-Revised/Normative Update* (Woodcock, 1998), which allows comparison of a student's reading performance with results of aptitude measures such as the *WISC-III*, the *Woodcock-Johnson-R*, and the *K-ABC*. However, not all tests offer systems for discrepancy analysis, and those that do often employ different methods.

Discrepancy Analysis on the Woodcock-Johnson-R.

The *Woodcock-Johnson-R* battery includes both tests of cognitive abilities and tests of school achievement. Among the many results that can be obtained are scores for three types of discrepancies: intra-cognitive, intra-achievement, and aptitude-achievement discrepancies. Intra-cognitive discrepancies compare results on the various cognitive factors formed as composite scores from results of cognitive subtests. Similarly, intra-achievement discrepancies compare results on composite achievement scores. Although these types of discrepancies provide information about a student's strengths and weaknesses in various cognitive and academic skills, they are typically not used as part of the process for identification of learning disabilities. However, Mather and Healey (1989) maintain that intra-cognitive discrepancies should be considered in identification because they provide valuable information about the nature of the learning disability.

On the *Woodcock-Johnson-R,* the system for analyzing aptitude-achievement discrepancies makes use of two types of scores: aptitude cluster scores and achievement cluster scores. However, for aptitude measures, professionals can choose between a global score (Broad Cognitive Ability) or the specific scholastic aptitude scores generated for reading, mathematics, and written language. The choice is an important one because the cognitive subtests that make up a specific scholastic aptitude cluster may be the ones in which an individual with learning disabilities does poorly. If this occurs, there may not be significant discrepancy between the student's lowered aptitude score and a low achievement score.

For example, the Reading Aptitude composite score is obtained from subtests designed to assess four cognitive factors:

- Test 2, Memory for Sentences—Short-Term Memory
- Test 3, Visual Matching—Processing Speed
- Test 11, Sound Blending—Auditory Processing
- Test 13, Oral Vocabulary—Comprehension-Knowledge

These factors represent areas in which students with learning disabilities often experience difficulty.

Another concern is the use of composite scores as measures of students' academic achievement. The Broad Reading cluster, for example, contains the two reading tests from the *Woodcock-Johnson-R* standard battery: Letter-Word Identification and Passage Comprehension. The two supplementary battery tests, Word Attack and Reading Vocabulary, are not included. When considering cluster scores, it is important also to examine the results of the subtests that make up the cluster. If the cluster contains two subtests, a student may do well on one and poorly on the other, ending up with an average score for the cluster. According to the Learning Disabilities Association's position paper on eligibility (1990), "The Specific Learning Disabilities condition selectively interferes with one's abilities; consequently, the **use of composite scores is inappropriate**" (p. 2a).

On the *Woodcock-Johnson-R,* aptitude-achievement discrepancies are analyzed by determining an expected standard score for achievement and comparing that score to the actual achievement score earned by the student. The expected standard score is the average achievement score of persons in the norm group who match the student being assessed on two variables: age (or grade) and score on the aptitude measure. The comparison yields two new scores: a discrepancy percentile rank and a standard deviation of the difference score. The discrepancy percentile rank provides information on the percentage of persons in the norm group (with the same age/grade and same aptitude score) who earned scores equal to or lower than that of the student being assessed. Thus, a discrepancy percentile rank of 30 indicates that 70% of the peer group earned scores higher than that of the student. The standard deviation of the difference score is expressed in standard error of estimate units. According to the test manual, this is the appropriate standard deviation statistic to use when eligibility criteria require "a difference equal to or greater than one and one-half times the standard deviation" (p. 95) or a similar standard. Standard deviation of the difference scores of -1.00 fall at about the 15th percentile; those of -1.50 fall at about the 6th percentile.

Analysis of Discrepancies on the Wechsler Tests. The manual for the *Wechsler Individual Achievement Test (WIAT)* provides procedures for analyzing discrepancies between performance on *WIAT* subtests and composites and results of Wechsler IQ tests for students ages 5-0 to 19-11. In this system, the Full Scale IQ score from the *WPPSI-R,* the *WISC-III,* or the *WAIS-R* is used as the index of ability. Formulas are included in the manual for professionals who wish to substitute a Wechsler Verbal or Performance IQ for the Full Scale score. The *WIAT* offers two types of discrepancy analysis: the simple-difference method and the predicted-achievement method. However, the manual recommends that the predicted-achievement method be used.

In the predicted-achievement method, the student's Full Scale IQ is used to determine predicted-achievement scores for each of the *WIAT* subtests and composite scores (i.e., Reading, Mathematics, Language, and Writing). Then the student's actual achievement scores are subtracted from the predicted-achievement scores to produce difference scores. Each difference score is examined to determine (a) if the difference is significant, and (b) the frequency with which differences of this magnitude occurred in the norming sample. Consider, for example, the case of Joyce.

Joyce

Joyce, the fourth grader referred for school performance problems, has been tested with the *WISC-III* and several measures of academic achievement, including the Spelling subtest from the *WIAT.* To determine whether Joyce's measured achievement is different from her current intellectual performance, the assessment team decides to conduct a discrepancy analysis.

The team chooses to use the predicted-achievement method recommended in the *WIAT* manual. In this method, the student's Full Scale IQ on the *WISC-III* is used to determine predicted-achievement scores. Joyce's Full Scale IQ score was 101; according to the *WIAT* manual, her predicted-achievement score for the Spelling subtest is 101. However, she earned a standard score of 72 on Spelling. Thus, the difference score is 29 (computed by subtracting 72 from 101).

The team consults the appropriate tables and finds that this difference is not only significant at the .01 level, but also rare. Less than 1% of the norming sample showed a discrepancy of this magnitude between expected and actual spelling achievement. Therefore, the team concludes that it is probable that Joyce's current performance in spelling is discrepant from her intellectual performance.

Recommended Procedures

In attempting to determine whether a discrepancy exists between expected and actual achievement, the assessment team should consider the following suggestions:

1. When comparing ability and achievement scores, use scores from valid and reliable tests with comparable norm groups.
2. When using tests with built-in discrepancy analysis systems, be aware of the way in which these systems go about comparing expected and actual achievement. In particular, consider which measure(s) of learning aptitude are used to determine the student's expected level of achievement. In addition, when aptitude or

achievement scores are composites, also consider the student's performance on the subtests or other components that make up the composite scores.

3. To compare results of tests that do not provide discrepancy analysis systems, follow these steps:

    a. Construct confidence intervals around each score and determine whether there is an overlap in score ranges.

    b. Compute the standard error of the difference to determine whether the observed difference is likely due to chance or to a true difference.

    c. If the degree of relationship between the ability and achievement tests is known, determine the reliability of the difference score.

4. Whatever method of discrepancy analysis is used, confirm that the discrepancy exists within the school environment. Substantiate that the student's actual classroom performance is below expectation levels.

5. Keep in mind that a discrepancy between ability and achievement is only one of the criteria for the identification of learning disabilities.

This last point is an important one. The Council for Learning Disabilities (1986) maintains that the high incidence rates in programs for students with learning disabilities are due to the inclusion of students whose low achievement or underachievement is caused by factors other than learning disabilities. The Learning Disabilities Association (1990) underscores this point with its assertion that "**Specific learning disabilities is not synonymous with underachievement**" (p. 2a).

ANSWERING THE ASSESSMENT QUESTIONS

The assessment team gathers several types of information to describe the student's current specific learning abilities and strategies. Visual and auditory acuity are checked to determine whether a sensory impairment is influencing school performance. In some cases, teachers will complete questionnaires designed to identify students at risk for learning disabilities. Specific abil-

ity tests may be administered if perceptual-motor skills, memory, or information-processing abilities are of interest. Results of tests of intellectual performance may also be considered, if they provide information about specific cognitive abilities. The team may use informal techniques such as observations, questionnaires, and interviews to learn more about learning strategies and study skills. If learning disabilities are suspected, the student's current scores on measures of ability and achievement will be compared to determine if there is a substantial discrepancy between expected and actual achievement.

Types of Procedures

A wide range of assessment techniques is used to study specific learning abilities, learning strategies, and study skills. Because these techniques provide information for several different assessment questions, they are not expected to produce equivalent results. For example, the evaluation of sensory acuity is a separate procedure from the evaluation of specific learning abilities. A student may perform adequately in both of these areas, in neither, or in only one.

Results of specific ability measures are not expected to be equivalent to the findings of informal evaluations of learning strategies and study skills. There are several reasons for this. First, students may perform differently in these two areas of functioning. An individual can show adequate specific abilities when these are assessed in isolation, but may have difficulty applying them in actual school learning tasks. A student also might compensate for poor specific abilities by developing appropriate learning strategies and study skills.

Second, the types of measures typically used in the evaluation of specific learning abilities are quite different from those used to assess learning strategies and study skills. Most specific ability measures are individual, norm-referenced tests. In contrast, learning strategies and study skills are usually assessed informally. Students are observed while they are engaged in learning activities or are questioned about study strategies through interviews or questionnaires. Such informal techniques do not produce comparative data. For example, if an observation reveals that a student attends to the teacher's lecture in 60% of the time intervals sampled, this may or may not indicate typical performance for the student's age and grade.

A third consideration is the directness of the measures. Specific ability tests and student observations are more direct methods of assessment than are interviews and questionnaires used to elicit students' descriptions of their typical learning strategies and study skills. Indirect measures that rely upon informants may produce less accurate results than direct assessment of the behaviors under consideration.

Technical quality is a fourth concern. Most specific ability measures are standardized tests, with information available concerning their standardization, reliability, and validity. Most informal learning strategy measures do not have such information. Yet norm-referenced tests are not always preferable to informal strategy assessments. Many of the older norm-referenced measures of specific learning abilities fail to meet minimum criteria for adequate reliability and validity and, thus, should not be used as tools in educational decision making. In many cases, informal measures are the only alternative to technically inadequate tests. Regardless, technical quality is still an important concern. The assessment team should attempt to identify informal techniques that are documented as both reliable and valid.

Nature of the Assessment Tasks

Assessment devices that appear to measure the same skill or ability may, in fact, be measuring quite different factors. This may occur because different test tasks are used for assessment. For example, evaluation of auditory discrimination is the purpose of both the *Goldman-Fristoe-Woodcock Test of Auditory Discrimination* and the Wepman *Auditory Discrimination Test* (2nd ed.), but these measures demand different skills. On the Wepman, the student simply listens to the tester read a pair of words. No visual stimuli are presented, and the test is administered in a quiet environment. The student responds by saying whether the words presented were the same or different. In contrast, the *Goldman-Fristoe-Woodcock* uses a taped presentation, and the student hears one

word. The student is also shown four pictures and must select the picture that represents the word read on the tape. This test includes two subtests: one in which the listening environment is quiet and the other in which a noisy environment is simulated.

Likewise, tests of visual perception may use dissimilar assessment tasks. For instance, the *Developmental Test of Visual Perception* (2nd ed.) requires students to draw, whereas the *Motor-Free Visual Perception Test-Revised* does not. Each of these two tests assesses several areas of visual perception, but only figure-ground perception, spatial relationships, and visual closure are common to both measures.

Several types of assessment tasks evaluate memory. Some emphasize the auditory presentation of information, others stress visual input. The required response mode may be verbal or motor. Most memory tasks assess short-term recall, but the type of information to be recalled varies widely: numbers, words, sentences, shapes, pictures of common objects, photographs of people's faces, and so on. The student may be required to recall in the exact order of presentation, in reverse order, or in no particular order. Because there are important differences between test tasks, it is certainly possible for a student to perform well on one type of memory task and poorly on another.

Documentation of Specific Learning Abilities and Strategies

Specific learning abilities and strategies are one major concern of the assessment team as they attempt to answer the question, *Is the school performance problem related to a disability?* The disability condition under consideration in this phase of the assessment process is learning disabilities. Four specific assessment questions are pertinent:

1. What is the status of the student's sensory abilities?
2. What is the student's current level of development in specific learning abilities?
3. What is the student's current functioning level in strategies for learning and study skills?
4. Is there a substantial discrepancy between the student's actual achievement and the expected achievement level?

The first question, relating to vision and hearing, is asked for all students referred for special education assessment. Although the other questions relate most directly to learning disabilities, they may also be of interest for students with other types of mild disabilities.

The assessment team gathers information from many sources to answer these questions. School records are reviewed for results of group measures of school readiness and vision and hearing screenings. Specific learning abilities are assessed with individual norm-referenced tests, including specific ability measures and tests of intellectual performance. To evaluate learning strategies and study skills, students are observed, or they may complete questionnaires or participate in interviews. Teachers and parents contribute by sharing observations of the student's specific abilities and strategies. When learning disabilities are considered a possibility, IQ and achievement data are compared using discrepancy analysis techniques.

Determination of eligibility for learning disabilities services rests upon discrepancy analysis. The team must demonstrate that there is a severe discrepancy between the student's expected achievement, based upon intellectual performance, and actual achievement. In addition, the assessment team is usually interested in identifying some reason for poor achievement, such as low or below-average performance in one or more specific abilities or evidence of ineffective learning strategies or study skills. According to federal guidelines, the team must also establish that underachievement is *not* primarily due to another disability; to lack of instruction; or to environmental, cultural, or economic disadvantages.

Joyce

At this point in Joyce's assessment, the team has substantiated the school performance problems noted by Mr. Harvey, Joyce's fourth grade teacher. It has also been established that Joyce's current intellectual performance is within the average range. The assessment team then moves on to an investigation of specific learning abilities and strategies.

School records are reviewed for the results of Joyce's most recent hearing and vision tests. Both vision and hearing were checked at the beginning of the year when Joyce entered the school district, and no problems were noted. According to Joyce's parents, she has never been treated for a vision or hearing impairment.

When Joyce was given the *WISC-III,* the assessment team noticed two possible areas of difficulty: the Freedom from Distractibility and Processing Speed factors. To learn more about Joyce's attention to tasks and memorization strategies, the resource teacher, Ms. Gale, observes Joyce as she studies her new spelling words for the week. No attentional problems are noted. Joyce starts the task immediately and appears to remain on task during the entire study period. However, because she writes slowly, she requires more time to complete the assignment than the other students in the class.

Joyce's assigned task is to study each word and then write it 10 times. Ms. Gale observes that Joyce begins by slowly writing her name on her paper. She then copies five new words from the book to the first line of her paper. Joyce's strategy for writing each word 10 times is this: To write the first word, *home,* she copies the *h* 10 times down her paper, then she copies the *o* 10 times, and so forth, until she has finished that word. She repeats this procedure with each of the new spelling words. After the observation, Ms. Gale talks with Joyce about her study tactics. Joyce says she has always written her spelling words that way because it is quicker. When asked what she did to try to remember how to spell the words, Joyce says she looked at their shapes.

Ms. Gale then interviews Joyce's teacher, Mr. Harvey, who reports that Joyce seems to remember some things, such as math facts, quite well but has difficulty with reading and spelling words. He also mentions that Joyce has problems remembering a series of oral directions. He often has to repeat instructions for her, especially if they contain several steps. Ms. Gale also questions Joyce's teacher about fine-motor skills.

According to Mr. Harvey, Joyce prints most of her assignments. Her printing is large, the spacing is poor, and many of the letters are difficult to read.

To gather more information about Joyce's memory and motor skills, Ms. Gale administers the *Detroit Tests of Learning Aptitude* (4th ed.). Joyce's overall General Mental Ability Composite on this measure is within the average range of performance. However, her scores fall within the low average range on the Attention-Enhanced and Motor-Enhanced Composites. She earned her lowest subtest score on Reversed Letters, a measure of short-term memory with a motor component. These test results are in agreement with the results of the informal assessments of specific learning abilities. In addition, because the *DTLA-4* is a norm-referenced measure, these results suggest that Joyce performs memory and motor tasks less well than the majority of her peers.

After reviewing these data, the assessment team decides to continue its investiga-tion of the possibility of learning disabilities by carrying out a discrepancy analysis. The team uses the predicted-achievement method to evaluate the observed difference between Joyce's performance on the *WISC-III* Full Scale, a measure of aptitude, and her performance on the *WIAT* Spelling subtest, a measure of achievement. From the analysis results, the team determines that the discrepancy between aptitude and spelling achievement is likely a true difference.

The team concludes there is evidence to suggest a discrepancy between ability and achievement. From the information gathered about specific abilities and strategies, it appears that Joyce's underachievement may be related to poor memory, inefficient memorization strategies, and a possible problem in fine-motor skills. Although learning disabilities seem highly probable, the team will continue its assessment by studying Joyce's classroom behavior and social-emotional status.

STUDY GUIDE

REVIEW QUESTIONS

1. Specific learning abilities and strategies are assessed for which of the following reasons?
   a. to assist in determining whether school performance problems are related to learning disabilities
   b. to aid in the planning of instructional interventions for any student
   c. to identify students with behavior disorders
   d. answers *a* and *b*
   e. all of the above
2. The specific learning abilities most often studied are memory, _____ , and _____ .
3. In the assessment of learning strategies, educators are concerned with the ways that students use specific learning abilities in situations that require the acquisition of new skills or information. (True or False)
4. According to federal law, which of the following are criteria for eligibility for learning disabilities services? Check all that apply.
   _____ a. A deficit in one or more specific learning abilities or strategies
   _____ b. Poor school performance
   _____ c. A severe discrepancy between achievement and intellectual ability
   _____ d. The discrepancy must exist despite the provision of appropriate learning experiences.
   _____ e. The discrepancy cannot be the result of other disabilities or conditions.

5. Read these statements and determine whether each is true or false.

_____ Most of the research on specific learning abilities comes from study of students with mental retardation.

_____ The traditional approach to assessment of specific learning abilities stresses identification of deficits in areas such as visual perception, auditory discrimination, and eye-hand coordination.

_____ Measures such as the *Woodcock-Johnson-R* and the *WISC-III* are often used to provide information about specific cognitive abilities.

_____ Learning strategies and study skills are a new area of interest in the study of learning disabilities, but as yet there are few measures available to assess them.

6. Check each of the assessment devices and procedures that can be used to gather information about specific learning abilities and strategies.

_____ a. Individual tests of intellectual performance

_____ b. Informal inventories and criterion-referenced tests

_____ c. Interviews with parents and teachers

_____ d. Measures of adaptive behavior

_____ e. Discrepancy analysis

_____ f. Behavior problem checklists

_____ g. Classroom observations

7. Complete this sentence. Vision and hearing screening . . .

a. should be conducted with all students, not only those referred for special education assessment.

b. is designed to identify students with possible problems in auditory or visual discrimination.

c. uses devices like the audiometer to identify vision problems and measures like the Snellen Chart to identify hearing problems.

d. produces results that allow teachers to prescribe remedial treatments.

8. Match the perceptual-motor measure in Column A with the description in Column B.

Column A	*Column B*
a. *Auditory Discrimination Test*	_____ A measure of eye-hand coordination in which students copy geometric designs
b. *Motor-Free Visual Perception Test-Revised*	_____ A test in which students listen to pairs of words and tell whether the words are the same or different
c. *Developmental Test of Visual Perception* (2nd ed.)	_____ Assesses visual perception by having students point to the correct answer
d. *Detroit Tests of Learning Aptitude* (4th ed.)	_____ Assesses abilities in the linguistic, attentional, and motoric domains
e. *Developmental Test of Visual-Motor Integration* (4th ed.)	_____ A measure of visual perception that provides scores for General Visual Perception, Motor-Reduced Visual Perception, and Visual-Motor Integration

9. Find the true statements about learning strategies.

a. Many students with learning disabilities show inefficient and ineffective strategies for learning.

b. Students with learning disabilities recall less information than typical students because they actively rehearse the material to be learned.

c. It is not possible to teach students new strategies for learning.

    d. There are few measures available for the assessment of learning strategies.

    e. Measures of study skills provide some information about the ways students go about learning tasks.

10. Complete this sentence. Discrepancy analysis . . .

    a. is used to determine whether there is a significant discrepancy between expected and actual achievement.

    b. is used to determine whether there is a significant discrepancy between general intellectual performance and performance on one or more measures of specific learning abilities.

    c. is best accomplished with expectancy formulas.

    d. is best accomplished by determining the difference between the student's current grade in school and grade scores on an achievement test.

11. If the special education team finds that a student with average intelligence performs in the low average or below average range in academic achievement, what conclusion can be drawn?

    a. The student may be eligible for special education services for students with mental retardation.

    b. The student may be eligible for special education services for students with learning disabilities.

    c. The student is not eligible for special education services.

    d. The student is eligible for special services in reading.

ACTIVITIES

1. Locate one of the specific ability tests described in this chapter. Examine its manual for information on standardization procedures, reliability, and validity.

2. Under the supervision of the course instructor, administer one of the specific ability tests described in this chapter. Calculate the scores and analyze the results.

3. Select a classroom learning task and analyze its components. Consider the specific learning abilities and strategies required by the task.

4. Design an interview procedure to determine the learning strategies that students use in school tasks such as answering reading comprehension questions or solving mathematics problems.

5. Talk with school personnel in your area to see how they go about assessing students with learning disabilities. Do they use tests of specific learning abilities and, if so, which ones? Results from tests of intellectual performance? Do they consider learning strategies and study skills? How do they assess these? Do they conduct discrepancy analyses? What methods are used?

DISCUSSION QUESTIONS

1. Describe how specific learning abilities and strategies can affect students' performance in school subjects such as reading, mathematics, handwriting, and composition.

2. Compare the relative merits of the learning strategies approach to the assessment of learning disabilities and the specific learning abilities approach.

3. Discuss the pros and cons of using IQ tests as measures of specific cognitive abilities. In your discussion, describe how tests such as the *WISC-III,* the *Woodcock-Johnson-R,* and the *Stanford-Binet IV* can be used for this purpose.

4. Explain the rationale for discrepancy analysis. Why are the years-below-grade-level and expectancy-formula methods not recommended? How do tests such as the *Woodcock-Johnson-R* and the *WIAT* go about discrepancy analysis?

CLASSROOM BEHAVIOR

- Considerations in Assessment of Classroom Behavior
- Sources of Information about Classroom Behavior
- Behavior Rating Scales and Checklists
- Direct Observation and Functional Assessment
- Attention Deficits and Hyperactivity
- Self-Concept and Peer Acceptance
- School Attitudes and Interests
- The Learning Environment
- Answering the Assessment Questions

Some students are referred for special education assessment because their school behavior is judged inappropriate. Such students may be disruptive in class, disturbing instruction. They may not pay attention and/or may show excessive activity. They may be disobedient, unresponsive, or even aggressive. They fail to meet the teacher's expectations for appropriate classroom conduct, and their behavior calls attention to itself. These students may be eligible for special education services if they meet criteria for the disability of behavioral disorders and if this disability adversely affects school performance. Of course, students with behavioral disorders are not the only ones who exhibit inappropriate classroom behaviors. School conduct problems may also be found in students with mild retardation, individuals with learning disabilities, and even students not identified as disabled.

Problem behaviors are the most obvious concern in assessment of classroom behavior, but there are several other important dimensions. These include the student's self-concept and self-esteem, how well the student is accepted by peers, and the student's interests and attitudes toward school. Also of interest are the characteristics of the classroom learning environment and its effects on the student's ability to behave appropriately. These dimensions of behavior are important considerations for all students referred for special education assessment.

Assessment of classroom behavior starts with a general question: *What is the student's current status in classroom behavior and in social-emotional development?* Answers to this question provide the team with an overall view of the student's current behavioral competence. More specific questions may be asked if preliminary data indicate a need. For example, if the student under study appears to exhibit inappropriate behaviors, the team may ask, *Is there evidence of a severe conduct problem?* and *What are the characteristics of the classroom learning environment?* The first question helps the team describe the student's current performance, and the second focuses attention on classroom factors that may influence behavior. If self-concept or peer interactions are of concern, the assessment question would be, *What is the student's current status in self-*

concept and acceptance by peers? To find out more about the student's perceptions of school and ways to motivate him or her, the team could ask, *What are the student's current interests and attitudes toward school and learning?* For some students, all of these questions are pertinent. With other students, the team may concentrate on one or two areas.

The results of the classroom behavior assessment assist the team in determining eligibility for special education services for individuals with behavioral disorders. Results also provide the basis for designing instructional programs to improve classroom behavior. Very specific information is needed for program design, so the assessment tools selected for the study of classroom behavior usually include informal techniques. Formal, norm-referenced measures may also be used, but informal assessment is stressed. In evaluating Joyce's classroom behavior, for example, the team relied heavily upon techniques such as interviews, observations, and inventories.

Joyce

The assessment team has almost finished its initial evaluation of Joyce, the fourth grader referred for academic skill problems. The team has established that Joyce has a school performance problem despite average intellectual performance, and her underachievement is probably due to a learning disability. Next, the team will consider Joyce's classroom behavior.

Although Joyce's teacher reported no classroom conduct problems, the team is interested in Joyce's relationships with her peers. To study this further, the team will observe Joyce interacting with her fourth grade classmates. The observer, Ms. Gale, will look at Joyce's peer interactions in the classroom and in at least one nonacademic setting such as the lunchroom or the playground. In the classroom observation, Ms. Gale will also take note of the characteristics of the learning environment and Joyce's interactions with her teacher.

The team is also interested in Joyce's self-concept and her attitudes toward school

Individualized Assessment Plan

For: *Joyce Dewey*   *4*   *10-0*   *12/1/00*   *Ms. Gale*
            Student's Name   Grade   Age   Date   Coordinator

Reason for Referral: Difficulty keeping up with fourth grade work in reading, spelling, and handwriting.

Assessment Question	Assessment Procedure	Person Responsible	Date/Time
What is the student's current status in self-concept and acceptance by peers?	Observation of peer interactions in the classroom and in nonacademic settings	Ms. Gale, Resource Teacher	1/3/01 1/4/01 1/5/01—Times vary
	Self-Esteem Index	Ms. Kellett, School Psychologist	1/9/01, 1:30 P.M.
What are the student's current interests and attitudes toward school and learning?	Informal interest inventory	Ms. Gale, Resource Teacher	1/9/01, 2 P.M.
What are the characteristics of the classroom learning environment?	Classroom observation	Ms. Gale, Resource Teacher	1/4/01 and 1/8/01

and learning. In a previous interview, Joyce's parents described her as a generally happy child who has many friends in her neighborhood. This year, however, they noticed that Joyce doesn't seem to like school as well as she used to. She's not interested in practicing her reading or other academic skills at home, and she sometimes talks about how different she feels from the other students in her class.

To assess Joyce's self-concept, the team will administer one of the self-concept measures designed for elementary grade students. At present, the team plans to evaluate Joyce's attitudes toward school informally. An informal interest inventory will be used to find out about Joyce's current preferences in school and leisure activities. If more information is needed, Ms. Gale will interview Joyce.

CONSIDERATIONS IN ASSESSMENT OF CLASSROOM BEHAVIOR

Classroom behavior is a broad term that encompasses a range of nonacademic school behaviors. Included are the student's conduct within the school setting, response to school rules, interpersonal relationships with teachers and other students, and self-concept and attitude toward school. A classroom behavior problem can interfere with academic performance; likewise, poor academic achievement can influence classroom conduct, precipitating inappropriate social behaviors.

Purposes

Classroom behavior and social-emotional development are assessed to gain information about a student's current ability to meet the nonacademic demands of the classroom and other learning environments. The student's classroom behavior is an important consideration when planning instructional programs. It is also of interest in the identification of mild disabilities, particularly behavioral disorders.

Students with behavioral disorders are characterized by the seriously inappropriate behaviors they exhibit over time. In federal law, this disability is called emotional disturbance:

> The term means a condition exhibiting one or more of the following characteristics over a long period of time and to a marked degree that adversely affects a child's educational performance.
>
> (A) An inability to learn which cannot be explained by intellectual, sensory, or health factors.
> (B) An inability to build or maintain satisfactory interpersonal relationships with peers and teachers.
> (C) Inappropriate types of behaviors or feelings under normal circumstances.
> (D) A general pervasive mood of unhappiness or depression.
> (E) A tendency to develop physical symptoms or fears associated with personal or school problems.
>
> The term includes schizophrenia. The term does not apply to children who are socially maladjusted, unless it is determined that they have an emotional disturbance. (*Federal Register,* 1999, §300.7(c)(4))

To meet eligibility criteria for the disability of serious emotional disturbance, students must show a behavior disorder that is both severe and persistent. In addition, the disorder must act as a negative influence upon school performance.

The definition lists several characteristics of behavior disorders; the student must display one or more of these. One possible disorder is an inability to learn. Students whose learning problems can be explained by other disabilities are excluded from consideration here. For example, if a student's difficulties in learning can be attributed to mental retardation, that student is not considered emotionally disturbed under the "inability to learn" criterion. Other characteristics listed as indicators of emotional disturbance are unsatisfactory interpersonal relationships, inappropriate behavior, depression and other mood

disorders, and fears and physical symptoms associated with school and personal problems.

In assessment, there are two major approaches to the identification of behavior disorders. In the first approach, teachers, instructional aides, parents, and others who are well acquainted with the student provide information about the student's current behavioral status. The purpose is to determine whether the student's behavior is perceived as inappropriate by important persons in the environment. Various assessment strategies are used to gather information from informants: rating scales, checklists, interviews, and questionnaires. Some of these provide norms in addition to eliciting informants' judgments. In the second approach, emphasis is on direct observation of the student and the environment in which the student is experiencing difficulty. According to Algozzine, Ruhl, and Ramsey (1991), assessment should "focus on observable behavior in the school setting and describe what students do versus what they think or feel" (p. 16).

Direct observation and the questioning of informants are not mutually exclusive. In fact, both are typically used. Teachers and parents point to the existence of a behavior problem, and direct observation allows intensive study of that problem.

Issues and Trends

Many of the issues related to assessment of classroom behavior are tied to issues within the field of behavioral disorders. One basic concern is what to call this disability. *Emotional disturbance* is the more traditional term and the one used in federal law. However, many educators prefer the term *behavioral disorders* because it emphasizes behaviors, and behaviors can be changed. The professional organization for educators of students with this disability is the Council for Children with Behavioral Disorders (a division of the Council for Exceptional Children), and the journal it publishes is called *Behavioral Disorders.* This organization has taken a strong stand on terminology and called for replacement of the term *emotionally disturbed* with the term *behaviorally disordered* (Huntze, 1985).

Differences in terminology are reflections of theoretical differences. There are several theoretical approaches to the study of behavioral disorders; in each, the disability is viewed in a somewhat different way. As Table 10–1 shows, each theoretical model has its own way of describing disordered behavior, goals for educational intervention, and methods of instruction. Each also approaches assessment differently. For example, the behavioral model holds that behavioral disorders are the result of learning; the student has learned inappropriate behaviors or failed to learn appropriate behaviors. Its focus is on the overt behaviors of the student. In contrast, the ecological approach emphasizes the student's interactions with the environment. Behavioral disorders are seen as problems in interaction, not as a dysfunction within the student. In assessment, both student and environmental characteristics are studied.

Another major issue is definition of the disability. As Shea (1978) observed, "There appear to be as many definitions of behavior-disordered children and youth as there are authors to write about them and purposes for writing them" (p. 5). Defining this disability is difficult for several reasons:

- Lack of an adequate definition of mental health and normal behavior
- Differences among conceptual models
- Difficulties in measuring emotions and behavior
- Relationships between ED/BD and other handicapping conditions
- Differences in the functions of socialization agents who categorize and serve children (Hallahan & Kauffman, 1991, p. 174)

Deciding if behaviors are inappropriate is a somewhat subjective process. The same behavior may be judged appropriate at one age but not at another. For example, ceaseless activity and exploration are expected of 2-year-olds, but not of sixth graders. Culture and gender influence behavioral expectations. What is viewed as normal play among boys may be labeled aggressive in girls. Because it is not possible to set up one standard for normal behavior, it is also difficult to state criteria for disordered behavior, except in very severe cases. Obviously, there would be little debate over the inappropriateness of behaviors such as assault or arson.

At present, school practices in the assessment and treatment of behavioral disorders appear to be influenced most by the behavioral model. In

this approach, applied behavioral analysis techniques are used to identify behaviors of interest, to observe and measure those behaviors, and then to change them through manipulation of environmental events (Alberto & Troutman, 1990; Cooper, Heron, & Heward, 1987). The ecological perspective has also gained support, at least in assessment (Swap, 1974; Thurman, 1977). For example, in the functional assessment approach, there is interest not only in the behavior of the student but also in the influences of the environment in which the student must function.

Current Practices

Classroom behavior is a concern of all teachers, and assessment of student behavior is a regular occurrence in both general and special education. At the classroom level, teachers typically rely on informal techniques such as observation to gather information about student behavior. When assessment is conducted to determine a student's eligibility for special programs, more formal instruments may be used.

In general, special education assessment begins with the questioning of informants. Most typically, informants are interviewed or asked to complete one of the many available behavioral rating scales or checklists. Many of the commonly used rating scales are formal, normed instruments. This chapter describes several of these rating scales, including the *Behavior Rating Profile* (2nd ed.), the *Behavior Evaluation Scale-2,* and the *Social Skills Rating System.*

Both formal and informal measures are available to study other aspects of student behavior such as attention disorders and hyperactivity, self-concept, and acceptance by peers. These too are described in this chapter. Formal measures are typically selected if the goal of assessment is to determine whether a problem exists. If the goal is to gather information for program planning, informal tools are preferred. Informal techniques are also used to investigate the student's interests and attitudes toward school as well as the classroom learning environment and its effects upon student behavior.

As Table 10–2 on page 292 shows, current practices in the educational assessment of behavior problems incorporate many types of formal

TABLE 10-1

Theories of Behavioral Disorders

	PSYCHOANALYTIC APPROACH	PSYCHOEDUCATIONAL APPROACH	HUMANISTIC APPROACH	ECOLOGICAL APPROACH	BEHAVIORAL APPROACH
The Problem	A pathological imbalance among the dynamic parts of the mind (id, superego, ego)	Involves both underlying psychiatric disorders and readily observable misbehavior and underachievement	Belief that the student is out of touch with his or her own feelings and can't find fulfillment in traditional educational settings	Belief that the student interacts poorly with the environment; student and environment affect each other reciprocally and negatively	Belief that the student has learned inappropriate responses and failed to learn appropriate ones
Purpose of Educational Practices	Use of psychoanalytic principles to help uncover underlying mental pathology	Concern for unconscious motivation/underlying conflicts and academic achievement/positive surface behavior	Emphasis on enhancing self-direction, self-evaluation, and emotional involvement in learning	Attempts to alter entire social system so it will support desirable behavior when intervention is withdrawn	Manipulates student's immediate environment and the consequences of behavior
Characteristics of Teaching Methods	Reliance on individual psychotherapy for student and parents; little emphasis on academic achievement; highly permissive atmosphere	Emphasis on meeting individual needs of the students; reliance on projects and creative arts	Use of nontraditional educational settings in which the teacher serves as resource and catalyst rather than as director of activities; nonauthoritarian, open, affective, personal atmosphere	Involves all aspects of a student's life, including classroom, family, neighborhood, and community, in teaching useful life and educational skills	Involves measurement of responses and subsequent analyses of behaviors to change them; emphasis on reward for appropriate behavior

Note. From David P. Hallahan & James M. Kauffman, *EXCEPTIONAL CHILDREN: Introduction to Special Education* (6th ed.), 1994, p. 229. Reprinted with permission of Allyn & Bacon.

TABLE 10-2

Formal Measures of Classroom Behavior and Related Concerns

NAME (AUTHORS)	AGES OR GRADES
Classroom Behavior and Social-Emotional Development	
BASC (Behavior Assessment System for Children) (Reynolds & Kamphaus, 1998)	Ages 2-6 to 18
Behavior Evaluation Scale-2 (McCarney & Leigh, 1990)	Grades K–12
Behavior Rating Profile (2nd ed.) (Brown & Hammill, 1990)	Grades 1–12 and ages 6-6 to 18-6
Behavioral and Emotional Rating Scale (Epstein & Sharma, 1998)	Ages 5-0 to 18-11
Burks' Behavior Rating Scales (Burks, 1977)	Grades 1–9
Child Behavior Checklist (Achenbach, 1991)	Ages 4 to 18
Comprehensive Behavior Rating Scale for Children (Neeper, Lahey, & Frick, 1990)	Ages 6 to 14
Devereux Behavior Rating Scales–School Form (Naglieri, LeBuffe, & Pfeiffer, 1993)	Ages 5 to 18
Emotional and Behavior Problem Scale (McCarney, 1989)	Ages 4-6 to 21
Mooney Problem Check Lists (Mooney & Gordon, 1950)	Grades 7–12 and college
Revised Behavior Problem Checklist (Quay & Peterson, 1987)	Grades K–8 regular class; grades K–12 special class
Scale for Assessing Emotional Disturbance (Epstein & Cullinan, 1998)	Ages 5 to 18
School Behavior Checklist (Miller, 1977)	Ages 4 to 13
School Social Skills Rating Scale (Brown, Black, & Downs, 1984)	School ages
Social Skills Rating System (Gresham & Elliott, 1990)	Ages 3-0 to 4-11 and grades K–12
Social-Emotional Dimension Scale (Hutton & Roberts, 1986)	Ages 5-6 to 18-5
Vineland Social-Emotional Early Childhood Scales (Sparrow, Balla, & Chicchetti, 1998)	Ages birth to 6
Walker Problem Behavior Identification Checklist, Revised (Walker, 1983)	Ages 2 to 5 and grades K–6
Attention Disorders and Hyperactivity	
Attention Deficit Disorders Evaluation Scale (2nd ed.) (McCarney, 1995a, 1995b)	Ages 3 to 18
Attention-Deficit/Hyperactivity Disorder Test (Gilliam, 1995)	Ages 3 to 23
BASC Monitor for ADD (Kamphaus & Reynolds, 1998)	Ages 4 to 18
Children's Attention and Adjustment Survey (Lambert, Hartsough, & Sandoval, 1990)	Grades K–5
Conners' Rating Scales-Revised (Conners, 1997)	Ages 3 to 17
Self-Concept	
Coopersmith Self-Esteem Inventories (Coopersmith, 1981)	Ages 8 to adult
Culture-Free Self-Esteem Inventories (2nd ed.) (Battle, 1992)	Grades 2–9 and ages 16 to 65
Multidimensional Self Concept Scale (Bracken, 1992)	Grades 5–12
Piers-Harris Children's Self Concept Scale (Piers & Harris, 1984)	Grades 4–12
Dimensions of Self-Concept (Michael, Smith, & Michael, 1984)	Grades 4–12 and college
Self-Esteem Index (Brown & Alexander, 1991)	Ages 8-0 to 18-11
Student Self-Concept Scale (Gresham, Elliott, & Evans-Fernandez, 1992)	Grades 3–12
Tennessee Self-Concept Scale (2nd ed.) (Fitts & Warren, 1996)	Ages 7 through adult
Peer Acceptance	
Behavior Rating Profile (2nd ed.) (Brown & Hammill, 1990)	Grades 1–12 and ages 6-6 to 18-6
Peer Attitudes toward the Handicapped Scale (Bagley & Greene, 1981)	Grades 4–8

measures. However, tests of personality are seldom included. Personality tests are indirect measures, not direct measures of behavior or even attitude or opinion surveys. For example, on projective tests, the student is presented with ambiguous stimuli, and then personality traits are inferred from the student's descriptions of these stimuli. One problem with such measures is their lack of technical adequacy (Salvia & Ysseldyke, 1991; Taylor, 2000). Another is their lack of educational relevance. Because of these limitations, personality measures are rarely used in schools today.

SOURCES OF INFORMATION ABOUT CLASSROOM BEHAVIOR

Several sources can contribute information about the student's current and past classroom behavior: school records, parents, teachers, and the student himself or herself. In addition, the student's peers may be questioned about their perceptions to determine how well the student is accepted by classmates.

School Records

School records may help the team gain a historical perspective of the student's classroom behavior problem. If the problem is long-standing, particular attention should be paid to the results of past interventions.

Discipline and Attendance Records. Educational records usually contain information about school disciplinary actions. For example, if the student has been sent to the principal or vice principal for breaking classroom or school rules, there will likely be a record of the incident and the disciplinary action that resulted. The team should examine these records to determine whether the student has a history of conduct problems. Also, attendance records should be reviewed for information about truancy, chronic tardiness, and excessive school absences. If the student has come into conflict with the law, school records may contain information about the charges and their disposition (probation, referrals for counseling or

other services, jail sentences, and so forth). In addition, the team should take special note of any information about reported incidents of child abuse, alcohol or substance abuse, or attempted suicide.

Observations of Former Teachers. The student's former teachers may have left some written records of their observations of the student's classroom behavior. The team should consider report cards from previous years, copies of letters from teachers to parents, and any past referrals for special education assessment.

Past Services. Also of interest are any services that the student received in relation to behavioral problems. For example, the student may have received school counseling services, or the school may have suggested counseling services to the student's family. If records are available, the team should attempt to determine the types of services provided and the effects of those services on the student's behavior.

The Student

The student assists in the assessment of classroom behavior by participating in observations and by answering questions about current behavior, attitudes, and perceptions.

Current Classroom Behavior. Direct observation of student behavior is one of the most valuable techniques for gathering data about classroom conduct. The student's role in this assessment technique is simply to behave as usual. This is facilitated if the observer takes care not to call attention to the observation process or to the particular student under study.

Current Attitudes and Perceptions. The student can also participate by acting as an informant about his or her own behavior and attitudes. For instance, some behavior rating scales are designed to be completed by students, allowing them to rate their own behaviors. In the assessment of self-concept, interests, and attitudes toward school, students are the primary source of information. They may complete interest inventories, talk about their attitudes about school and learning, or reply to questions on measures of self-concept.

Teachers

Teachers have the best opportunity of all professionals to observe and evaluate the student's day-to-day behavior in the classroom. Teachers are also an excellent source of information about the characteristics of the classroom learning environment.

Observations of Current Behavior. Behavioral rating scales and checklists are often used to gather information from teachers about student behavior. These measures allow teachers to share their observations of the student's typical behavior patterns and their judgments about the appropriateness of the student's classroom conduct. Interviews are also useful for eliciting teachers' opinions, particularly about environmental factors that may precipitate behavioral problems.

Characteristics of the Learning Environment. Teachers can provide firsthand information about the characteristics of their classroom. Among the major considerations are the teacher's rules for classroom conduct, strategies for rewarding appropriate behavior, and standard disciplinary techniques. Because there may be wide variations among the behavioral demands of different classrooms, it is important to consider the teacher's standards when interpreting his or her reports of problem behaviors.

Peers

Peers are usually not participants in special education assessment but, in the area of classroom behavior, they can contribute information about the student's social acceptance and interpersonal relationships.

Peer Acceptance and Interactions. Peers can be involved in the assessment process in two major ways. The first area of interest is the general attitudes of typical peers toward students with learning and behavior problems. These attitudes can be surveyed through interviews or with a questionnaire designed for this purpose. This provides information about peer attitudes toward students with disabilities in general. To find out about acceptance of a particular student, it is necessary to use sociometric techniques, another as-sessment strategy. These techniques sample students' opinions about the peers with whom they would like to work and play. The results provide a picture of the social interactions within a classroom, identifying students who are and are not accepted by their classmates.

Parents

Parents may be unfamiliar with classroom behavior, but they can discuss their child's behavior in the home and other nonschool settings.

Observations of Current Behavior. A student with classroom behavior problems may or may not act inappropriately at home. The same types of inappropriate behavior could occur both at school and at home, the student could show a different set of problem behaviors at home, or home behavior could be acceptable. Parents can discuss their observations of their child's typical conduct and any concerns they might have. They can describe what approaches they have used in trying to improve problem behaviors and the results of these efforts. If the problem is long-standing, parents may be able to share information about intervention programs in which the child and, perhaps, the family have participated.

Characteristics of the Home Environment. Because the rules for behavior at home may be quite different from school demands, parents should be asked to describe the behavioral expectations they hold for their child. Also of interest are their strategies for encouraging appropriate behavior and discouraging inappropriate behavior. What type of discipline system is used in the home? What consequences does the child face for breaking the rules? The child's parents can also provide information about family makeup. Are both parents present in the home? Does the child have brothers and sisters? Are there other individuals or family members living in the home as part of the family? In addition, the assessment team should be alert to any major changes or stresses within the family such as divorce, unemployment, or the protracted illness or death of a family member. Such changes affect family dynamics and may have an influence on the student's ability to behave appropriately in school.

Behavior Rating Profile (2nd ed.) (BRP-2)

L. L. Brown & D. D. Hammill (1990)

Type: Norm-referenced teacher rating scale, parent rating scale, student checklist, and sociogram

Major Content Areas: School behavior, home behavior, interpersonal relationships

Type of Administration: Individual for teachers, parents, and students; group for peers

Administration Time: 10–15 minutes for teachers, 20 minutes for parents, 15–30 minutes for students, 15 minutes for peers

Age/Grade Levels: Ages 6-6 to 18-6, grades 1–12

Types of Scores: Standard scores, percentile ranks

Computer Aids: N/A

Typical Uses: Identification of students with possible behavioral disorders who may be in need of further assessment

Cautions: On the *Student Rating Scales,* some students may require assistance in reading the checklist items.

Publisher: PRO-ED (www.proedinc.com)

BEHAVIOR RATING SCALES AND CHECKLISTS

A wide variety of rating scales and checklists are available for assessing classroom behavior. These measures vary in several ways: the age of the student to be rated, the person or persons used as informants, the types of behaviors included on the scale, and the scores produced. The following sections describe scales that focus on in-school behaviors.

Behavior Rating Profile (2nd ed.)

The *Behavior Rating Profile* (2nd ed.) (*BRP-2*) is an interesting norm-referenced measure because it attempts to provide a comprehensive picture of the student's current behavioral status. Information can be gathered from four types of informants—students themselves, teachers, parents, and peers—to assess the student's performance in the home, at school, and in interpersonal relationships.

The *BRP-2* is made up of four measures that correspond to the different types of informants. The self-rating scale, called the *Student Rating Scales,* is composed of 60 items. One-third of the items are concerned with school behaviors, one-third with home behaviors, and one-third with peer interactions. For instance, "I often break rules set by my parents" is a home item, whereas "I can't seem to concentrate in class" is a school item. The student reads each item and checks whether it is true or false. If necessary, the tester may read the questions aloud to the student and explain the meaning of unknown words.

The *Teacher Rating Scale* is made up of 30 descriptions of school behaviors. The teacher reads each item and determines whether the description is "very much like the student," "like the student," "not much like the student," or "not at all like the student." An example of an item on the teacher scale is "The student doesn't follow class rules." The manual recommends that the student be present in the classroom at least a month before teacher or peer ratings are taken.

The *Parent Rating Scale* is quite similar to the teacher scale, except that it contains descriptions of home behaviors (e.g., "My child is shy; clings to parents"). Each description is rated as "very much like my child," "like my child," "not much like my child," or "not at all like my child." The *Parent Rating Scale* can be completed by the child's mother or father (or other caregivers), or both parents can rate their child independently.

The peer portion of the *BRP-2* is not a rating scale. Instead, a sociometric technique is used, and the student's classmates are asked questions such as "Which of the students in your class would you most (least) like to . . . ?" Several sets of questions are available, each tapping a different aspect of interpersonal relationships. For example, students can name the peers they would most like to have as friends. According to the *BRP-2* manual, a minimum of 20 peers must participate for scoring to be accurate.

As Figure 10–1 illustrates, results from the *BRP-2* can be plotted on a profile. Standard scores are produced by each of the rating scales and the sociograms, and percentile ranks are also available. Standard scores are distributed with a mean of 10 and a standard deviation of 3; the range of average performance is standard score 7 through 13. Several scores are available from the *BRP-2,* depending upon which of the scales were administered. If the student under study completed the *Student Rating Scales,* three separate scores are reported: Home, School, and Peer. There is one score for each teacher who rated the student and one for each parent. Also, each sociometric question answered by the student's peers produces a score. Data can be gathered from all of these sources, or, depending upon the purposes of assessment, only one portion of the *BRP-2* can be selected for administration.

The *BRP-2* was standardized on approximately 2,500 general education students, 1,500 teachers, and 2,000 parents from 26 states. The internal consistency of the scales appears adequate, as does the test-retest reliability (with the exception of the *Student Rating Scales* for grades 1 and 2 students). The standard error of measurement is low. On the parent, teacher, and student scales, standard error ranges from .4 to 1.6 standard score points over all grade levels.

Concurrent validity was studied by examining the relationships between *BRP-2* scores and results from other rating scales. In general, *BRP-2* results were found to be consistent with those from other measures. The diagnostic validity of

the *BRP-2* was investigated by comparing the ratings of five groups of students, and different group profiles emerged. Normal students and those identified as gifted achieved higher scores than did students with disabilities. Among students with disabilities, the lowest scores were earned by students with mental retardation, followed by students identified as emotionally disturbed. The scores of students with learning disabilities fell between those of normal students and the scores of students with emotional disturbance.

The *BRP-2* appears to be a reliable and valid tool for gathering information from a range of informants about perceptions of a student's behavior in several different ecologies. It is one of the few instruments that allows students to rate themselves and that involves peers in the assessment process.

Other Measures That Use Informants

Two other measures of behavior of interest to educators are the *Behavior Evaluation Scale-2* (McCarney & Leigh, 1990) and the *Social Skills Rating System* (Gresham & Elliott, 1990).

Behavior Evaluation Scale-2. The *BES-2* is a potentially useful measure because it is linked to the federal definition of emotional disturbance. Appropriate for grades K through 12, this instrument contains 76 descriptions of student behaviors, and teachers rate each behavior according to the frequency with which it occurs. There are seven choices ranging from "never or not observed" to "continuously throughout the day."

The *BES-2* is designed to gather information about the five types of behavior disorders described in federal law. Each item on the scale relates to one of these disorders, and results are available for five subscales: Learning Problems, Interpersonal Difficulties, Inappropriate Behavior, Unhappiness/Depression, and Physical Symptoms/Fears. Subscale standard scores are distributed with a mean of 10 and a standard deviation of 3; an overall score called the Behavior Quotient is distributed with a mean of 100 and a standard deviation of 15. The *BES-2* manual recommends that teachers observe students for at least one month before completing the rating scale. The informant should be the teacher with primary instructional responsibility for the stu-

Behavior Rating Profile
Second Edition

PROFILE AND
RECORD FORM

Section I. Identifying Information

Student's Name **MICKEY R.**
Parents'/Guardians' Names **SARAH ; MICHEAL R.**
School **GOLDWYN MIDDLE SCHOOL** Grade **6**
Teacher's Name/Subject Taught **D. ROSE - HOMEROOM**
                    E. ARDENE - LANGUAGE ART
                    M. BLUNDEN - P.E.
Examiner's Name **B. HARTLEY**
Examiner's Title **DIAGNOSTICIAN**

	Year	Month
Date of BRP–2 Testing	**89**	**3**
Student's Date of Birth	**77**	**8**
Student's Age at Testing	**11**	**7**

Section II. Results of the BRP-2

	Raw Score	PR	SS	SEm
Student Rating Scales: Home	8	9	6	1
Student Rating Scales: School	7	9	6	1
Student Rating Scales: Peer	10	25	8	1
Teacher Rating Scale/Teacher #1	7	.4	2	1
Teacher Rating Scale/Teacher #2	7	.4	2	1
Teacher Rating Scale/Teacher #3	11	1	3	1
Parent Rating Scale/Mother	14	.1	1	1
Parent Rating Scale/Father	9	.1	1	1
Sociogram/Question #1	8	63	11	1
Sociogram/Question #2	10	63	11	1
Sociogram/Question #3	10	63	11	1

Section III. Results of Other Tests

Test Name	Date of Testing	Equivalent Quotient
1. IPC	3/89	89
2. DTLA-2	2/89	92
3. DAB TOTAL	2/89	80
4.		
5.		

Section IV. Profile of Scores

Standard Scores	STUDENT RATING SCALES Home	School	Peer	TEACHER RATING SCALE Teacher 1	Teacher 2	Teacher 3	PARENT RATING SCALE Mother	Father	Other	SOCIOGRAM Question 1	Question 2	Question 3	OTHER TESTS 1. IPC	2. DTLA-2	3. DAB	4.	5.	Quotient Scores
20	·	·	·	·	·	·	·	·	·	·	·	·	·	·	·	·	·	150
19	·	·	·	·	·	·	·	·	·	·	·	·	·	·	·	·	·	145
18	·	·	·	·	·	·	·	·	·	·	·	·	·	·	·	·	·	140
17	·	·	·	·	·	·	·	·	·	·	·	·	·	·	·	·	·	135
16	·	·	·	·	·	·	·	·	·	·	·	·	·	·	·	·	·	130
15	·	·	·	·	·	·	·	·	·	·	·	·	·	·	·	·	·	125
14	·	·	·	·	·	·	·	·	·	·	·	·	·	·	·	·	·	120
13	·	·	·	·	·	·	·	·	·	·	·	·	·	·	·	·	·	115
12	·	·	·	·	·	·	·	·	·	·	·	·	·	·	·	·	·	110
11	·	·	·	·	·	·	·	·	·	✗	✗	✗	·	·	·	·	·	105
10	·	·	·	·	·	·	·	·	·	·	·	·	·	·	·	·	·	100
9	·	·	·	·	·	·	·	·	·	·	·	·	·	✗	·	·	·	95
8	·	·	✗	·	·	·	·	·	·	·	·	·	✗	·	·	·	·	90
7	·	·	·	·	·	·	·	·	·	·	·	·	·	·	·	·	·	85
6	✗	✗	·	·	·	·	·	·	·	·	·	·	·	·	✗	·	·	80
5	·	·	·	·	·	·	·	·	·	·	·	·	·	·	·	·	·	75
4	·	·	·	·	·	·	·	·	·	·	·	·	·	·	·	·	·	70
3	·	·	·	·	·	✗	·	·	·	·	·	·	·	·	·	·	·	65
2	·	·	·	✗	✗	·	·	·	·	·	·	·	·	·	·	·	·	60
1	·	·	·	·	·	·	✗	✗	·	·	·	·	·	·	·	·	·	55

Standard Scores: Mean = 10. Standard Deviation = 3

FIGURE 10–1

Sample *Behavior Rating Profile* (2nd ed.) Results

Note: From *Behavior Rating Profile* (2nd ed.) (p. 27) by L. L. Brown and D. D. Hammill, 1990, Austin, TX: PRO-ED. Copyright 1990 by PRO-ED. Reprinted by permission.

Behavior Evaluation Scale-2 (BES-2)

S. B. McCarney & J. E. Leigh (1990)

Type: Norm-referenced teacher rating scale and optional observation system

Major Content Areas: The characteristics of serious emotional disturbance as identified in federal law (e.g., inability to learn, inability to build or maintain satisfactory interpersonal relationships)

Type of Administration: Individual

Administration Time: 15–20 minutes for rating scale

Age/Grade Levels: Grades K through 12

Types of Scores: Standard scores and percentiles for each subscale; overall quotient and percentile rank

Computer Aids: *BES-2 Quick Score Program*

Typical Uses: Identification of strengths and weaknesses in the behavioral domains described in federal law

Cautions: Students of color are underrepresented in the standardization sample.

Publisher: Hawthorne Educational Services

dent; with secondary students, more than one teacher should complete the scale. If more precise data are required for educational decision making, professionals can use the supplementary Data Collection Form, an observation system for collecting frequency data on each of the behaviors included in the scale.

The *BES-2* was standardized with 2,272 students from 31 states; students identified as disabled made up 12% of the sample. The standardization sample appears to represent the national population in geographic region, urban-rural residence, and parental education level. However, white students are overrepresented (89.5% versus 84.7% of the nation), as are students with Anglo-European ethnicity. Internal consistency and interrater reliabilities of the *BES-2* are adequate. Validity is supported by studies of the relationship of *BES-2* results, *BRP* results, and teacher ratings; in addition, the scale appears to differentiate between students with identified behavioral disorders and normally achieving students.

Social Skills Rating System. There are three levels of the *SSRS* to accommodate children from

age 3 through students in grade 12. The Preschool level (ages 3-0 to 4-11) includes a parent and a teacher rating scale. At the Elementary level (grades K through 6), there are three scales: one for parents, one for teachers, and a third for students in grades 3 through 6. The Secondary level (grades 7 through 12) provides rating scales for parents, teachers, and students.

On each of the instruments, the informant reads descriptions of behavior, then rates each according to the frequency with which it occurs ("never," "sometimes," or "very often"). On all scales except the elementary student scale, informants also identify the importance of each behavior ("not important," "important," "critical"). Informants should know the student well and be able to read at the grade 3 level. Instructions and items can be read aloud to students with reading problems.

There is some variation in the behaviors assessed by the various instruments. Parents are asked to consider two behavioral domains: social skills and problem behaviors. Teachers, in contrast, rate three: social skills, problem behaviors, and academic competence. Students rate them-

---

Social Skills Rating System (SSRS)

F. M. Gresham & S. N. Elliott (1990)

Type: Norm-referenced teacher rating scale, parent rating scale, and student rating scale

Major Content Areas: Social skills, problem behaviors, and academic competence

Type of Administration: Individual

Administration Time: 15–20 minutes for teachers and students, approximately 20 minutes for parents

Age/Grade Levels: Preschool (ages 3 to 5), Elementary (grades K–6), and Secondary (grades 7–12) forms for parents and teachers; Elementary (grades 3–6) and Secondary (grades 7–12) forms for students

Types of Scores: Standard scores, percentiles ranks for scales; for each subscale, classification of social skills and problem behaviors by frequency

Computer Aids: *AGS Computer Assist for SSRS*

Typical Uses: Identification of strengths and weaknesses in social skill development

Cautions: Grade 3 reading level is required; however, items can be read to students. The student standardization sample appears to differ from the national population in several ways, including underrepresentation of Hispanic students. Reliability falls below acceptable levels on some subscales; of particular concern is the test-retest reliability of the elementary grade student instrument.

Publisher: American Guidance Service (www.agsnet.com)

---

selves only on social skills. Results for each scale (Social Skills, Problem Behaviors, and Academic Competence) are expressed in standard scores (mean = 100, SD = 15) and percentile ranks. Separate results are obtained for each rater.

Two of the scales are divided into subscales so that professionals can compare the frequency with which different types of behaviors occur. The Social Skills subscales are Cooperation, Assertion, Responsibility, Empathy, and Self-Control. Subscales for Problem Behaviors are Externalizing, Internalizing, and Hyperactivity. Frequency of behavior is described as "more," "average," or "fewer." The manual defines "average" as "performance within one standard deviation above or below the standardization sample comparison group mean" (p. 49). With Social Skills, higher frequencies are desirable; with Problem Behaviors, lower frequencies are desirable. Results are entered for all raters on the Graphic Profile Summary so that comparisons can be made across subscales and across parent, teacher, and student informants.

An interesting feature of the *SSRS* is its attempt to link assessment with instruction. In fact, the summary protocol is called the Assessment-Intervention Record. In addition to considering scale and subscale results, the assessment team is directed to analyze responses to individual rating scale items to identify possible instructional targets. Four types of items are of interest: social skills strengths, social skills performance deficits, social skills acquisition deficits, and problem behaviors. In social skills, only those items identified by the rater as "important" or "critical" are considered. Strengths are behaviors that occur "very often." Performance deficits refer to behaviors that occur "sometimes," and acquisition deficits to those that "never" occur. With problem behaviors, those that occur "very often" are of interest.

The *SSRS* was standardized on approximately 4,000 students, 1,000 parents, and 300 teachers from 18 states. Students who spend at least 75% of their time in special education classes made up 17% of the sample (n = 219). Separate norms are available on the *SSRS* by age and by gender; separate norms for students with disabilities are provided on the elementary teacher scale. However, the student sample appears different from the national population in several respects. When compared to the nation as a whole, the student standardization sample contains more students with disabilities, fewer Hispanic students (6.1% versus 11.5% for the nation), fewer students from the Northeast and West, and fewer rural students.

Internal consistency and test-retest reliabilities are generally adequate for scale and subscale results on the teacher instruments. The parent and student instruments, however, show reliability coefficients below .80 on several subscales. Of particular concern is test-retest reliability for the elementary grade student instrument; the coefficient for the total scale is .68, and those for the subscales range from .52 to .66. The validity of the *SSRS* is supported by correlations between its results and those from other rating scales.

Comparison of Behavior Rating Scales and Checklists

The *BRP-2*, the *BES-2*, and the *SSRS* are but three of the many behavior rating scales and checklists available, as shown in Table 10–2. Most of these measures are designed for school-aged populations, particularly elementary grade students. Measures for preschool children are much rarer; among those available are the *Social Skills Rating System* and the *Vineland Social-Emotional Early Childhood Scales* (Sparrow, Balla, & Cicchetti, 1998).

Most behavior rating scales and checklists use teachers, or teachers and parents, as informants. The student and peers are involved less often. Exceptions are the *Behavior Rating Profile* (2nd ed.), which includes teachers, parents, students, and peers, and the *Social Skills Rating System,* which includes teachers, parents, and students. Another exception is *BASC (Behavior Assessment System for Children)* (Reynolds & Kamphaus, 1998), although its student scale is designed to assess personality traits rather than behavior.

Measures also vary on the types of behaviors they ask informants to consider and the theoretical frameworks used to interpret behavioral ratings. For example, the research instrument developed by Quay and Peterson (1987), the *Revised Behavior Problem Checklist,* classifies student behaviors according to six domains: Conduct Disorder, Socialized Aggression, Attention Problems-Immaturity, Anxiety-Withdrawal, Psychotic Behavior, and Motor Excess. Gresham (1982) reports that the *BPC* is the teacher rating scale with the strongest base of empirical support. The *Child Behavior Checklist* (Achenbach, 1991) organizes behaviors into internalizing (e.g., withdrawal), externalizing (e.g., aggression), and other (e.g., attention problems). The parent and teacher rating scales on the *BASC* address both externalizing and internalizing problems as well as school problems, other problems, and adaptive skills.

Some measures have as their purpose the assessment of personality rather than behavior disorders. For example, the *Burks' Behavior Rating Scales* (Burks, 1977) is "specifically designed to identify patterns of pathological behavior shown by children" (p. 5). This measure clusters items into 19 categories, such as Excessive Self-Blame, Excessive Anxiety, Poor Ego Strength, and Poor Reality Contact. At the other extreme are measures such as the *Behavior Rating Profile* (2nd ed.) and the *Behavior Evaluation Scale-2* that focus on observable behaviors.

A great many behavior rating scales and checklists are available to screen students with possible behavioral disorders, so it is necessary to select the most appropriate measure for the assessment task at hand. Psychometric quality, theoretical characteristics, the type of informants consulted, and the age and grade of the student must be considered. In addition, there may be considerable overlap among the factors measured by similar teacher scales; one teacher rating scale or checklist is usually sufficient. If adaptive behavior has been assessed, results should be reviewed, because adaptive behavior measures often include questions about student behavior, interpersonal relationships, and social-emotional development.

DIRECT OBSERVATION AND FUNCTIONAL ASSESSMENT

Behavior rating scales and checklists provide preliminary information about student conduct problems. Like teacher and parent interviews, they are screening techniques. Further study is needed for two reasons. First, rating scales, checklists, and interviews rely upon informants rather than direct evaluation of student behavior. Direct measures are needed to substantiate the existence of a behavioral problem. Second, the results of many screening measures are too general to assist in program planning.

Direct observation of student behavior is the recommended procedure for in-depth study of the possible problem behaviors identified by rating scales, checklists, and interviews. Observation is a versatile assessment technique that can be used to study any type of student behavior—appropriate or inappropriate, academic or social, at home or at school. In the assessment of school behavior problems, data are gathered about the frequency and/or duration of specific student behaviors within the classroom learning environment. The assessment team may decide to use direct observation to describe the student's behavior problems or as the basis for a functional assessment of those problems.

Direct Observation

The first step in planning an observation is to decide which behavior will be studied. It is possible to observe and record all of the behaviors that a student displays within a certain time period, but observations usually focus upon one or more specific behaviors. Results of rating scales, checklists, and teacher and parent interviews may suggest possible behaviors of concern. These sources are most useful for identifying possible inappropriate behaviors because they tend to focus on classroom conduct problems. In classroom observations, it is also important to consider the student's academic behaviors. Wallace and Kauffman (1986) have identified four significant classes of academic behavior: (a) accepting tasks provided by the teacher, (b) completing tasks within a reasonable amount of time,

(c) working neatly and accurately, and (d) participating in group activities.

The procedures for conducting behavioral observations were described in detail in Chapter 5, the chapter on informal assessment. The major steps are briefly reviewed here.

Describe the Behavior to Be Observed. Before a behavior can be observed, it must be described clearly and precisely. "The student is disruptive" is too general a statement; it must be translated into one or more precise descriptions. For example, a disruptive student might be described as one who talks or yells out during class without permission. Talking and yelling are behaviors that can be observed and counted, and as such they are suitable targets for observation.

Select a Measurement System. There are several systems available for the measurement of behaviors. Discrete behaviors can be measured by counting their frequency and/or by timing their duration. With nondiscrete behaviors such as talking with peers, interval recording or time sampling is used. The observation period is broken into several short time intervals, and the observer notes whether the behavior is or is not occurring at some point in each interval.

Set Up the Data-Collection System. There are several considerations in setting up the data-collection system: who will collect the data, when and where the observations will occur, how many observations will take place, and how data will be recorded. In general, observations should be scheduled at the time and location where the target behavior is most likely to occur. The student's teacher may collect observational data, or another member of the assessment team may act as observer. Several observations should be conducted; one observation is not sufficient to provide a picture of the student's typical pattern of behavior. If classroom conduct is the concern, the student should be observed daily for a minimum of 5 school days.

Select a Data-Reporting System. The results of observations are usually graphed. Graphs communicate large amounts of information quickly and allow identification of trends and patterns in behaviors. Graphs can be used to report any type

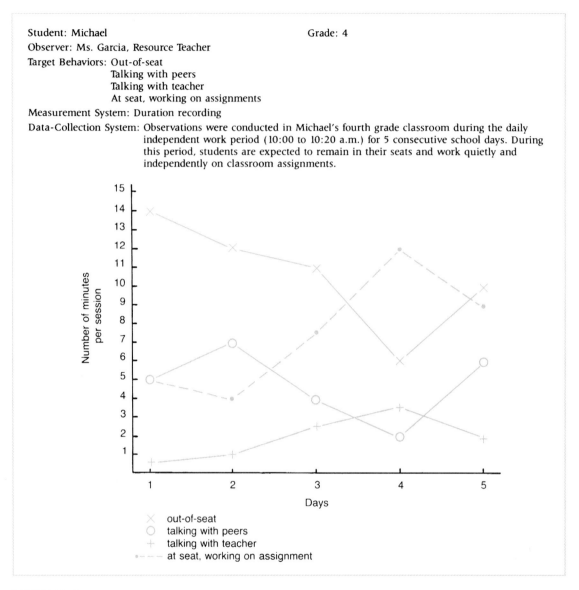

Student: Michael   Grade: 4
Observer: Ms. Garcia, Resource Teacher
Target Behaviors: Out-of-seat
                  Talking with peers
                  Talking with teacher
                  At seat, working on assignments
Measurement System: Duration recording
Data-Collection System: Observations were conducted in Michael's fourth grade classroom during the daily
                        independent work period (10:00 to 10:20 a.m.) for 5 consecutive school days. During
                        this period, students are expected to remain in their seats and work quietly and
                        independently on classroom assignments.

×   out-of-seat
○   talking with peers
+   talking with teacher
•----   at seat, working on assignment

FIGURE 10–2
Sample Graph of Observation Results

of observational data: frequency, rate, and percentage of occurrence; duration; percentage of time; and so forth. Examples of several types of graphs were provided in Chapter 5. A graph that reports the results of a series of observations of several behaviors is depicted in Figure 10–2. In this example, Michael was observed during the daily classroom work period to determine how long each day he sat at his seat and worked qui-

etly on his assignment without talking with others. Also of interest were three behaviors incompatible with quiet, independent, in-seat work: out-of-seat, talking with peers, and talking with the teacher.

Carry Out the Observations.   Observations are carried out, and then the final step—interpretation of results—takes place. Data are evaluated to determine whether or not a behavior problem exists, that is, whether or not intervention is needed. The process of making this decision is complex. Observations are informal techniques without norms or other guidelines to assist in evaluating whether a particular student's behavior is acceptable. There are no criteria that indicate how frequent or of what duration a behavior must be to warrant special attention. Thus, professionals must rely on their own best judgments when interpreting observation results.

Eaves (1982) has proposed a possible alternative. In Eaves's model, information is collected about student behavior in two ways: Rating scales are completed by important persons in the student's environment, and student behavior is directly observed. A major feature of this model is that local or regional norms are developed for specific student behaviors. Observation becomes a norm-referenced technique, and it is possible to determine how one student's behavior compares to that of age or grade peers. In an example provided by Eaves, a student showing disruptive behavior 24% of the time scores at the 98th percentile in disruptiveness. One who is noncompliant 1.8% of the time scores at the 99th percentile in noncompliance. Such a system would greatly facilitate the interpretation of observational data. However, as Eaves points out, this proposal is not yet a reality. Before such a system could be used, standardized observation schedules would have to be developed and normative data collected for different regions, age levels, and types of classrooms.

Functional Assessment

Functional assessment is an informal assessment technique that includes direct observation. However, its purpose is more than description of problem behaviors. Functional assessment is tied directly to program planning. It is designed to gather the information necessary to develop positive behavioral support plans to improve the classroom functioning of students with inappropriate behaviors.

The procedures for functional assessment were discussed in Chapter 6. The major steps are reviewed briefly here.

Describing the Behavior. The first step in functional assessment is to observe the behavior directly. To do this, the assessment team follows the procedures for observations, beginning with the development of a precise description of the behavior. As in any observation, data are collected over a period of time until a clear picture of the behavior emerges.

Identifying Factors that Influence the Behavior. The next step is to gather information about environmental factors that may be influencing the student's behavior. Informants such as the student and his or her teacher are interviewed about the problem behavior. Interview questions focus on the antecedents and consequences of the behavior as well as setting events (i.e., events that influence a behavior even though they occur at a different time). Examples of setting events are diet, medications, sleep patterns, and medical problems.

Generating a Hypothesis. Data collection continues until the assessment team has sufficient information to determine the reason for the behavior. In general, inappropriate behaviors serve one of two functions for students: They allow students to get something they want (e.g., attention) or avoid something they don't want (e.g., difficult academic tasks) (Lewis & Sugai, 1999). Once the function of the behavior is understood, the team can develop a summary statement or hypothesis describing the behavior and the factors influencing it.

Program Planning. After the hypothesis is verified, the team can begin to design the positive behavioral support plan for the student. This plan identifies replacement behaviors that serve the same function as the student's inappropriate behaviors. Those replacement behaviors then become the focus of instruction.

ATTENTION DEFICITS AND HYPERACTIVITY

In recent years, there has been increased interest in problem behaviors related to attention and activity level (Lerner & Lerner, 1991; Lerner & Lowenthal, 1993; Lerner, Lowenthal, & Lerner, 1995; Shaywitz & Shaywitz, 1992; Silver, 1992).

Attention deficits refer to difficulties in focusing and sustaining attention; hyperactivity is excessive activity. Both of these problem behaviors are difficult to define because they depend upon the age of the student and the situation in which the behavior is displayed. Two-year-olds are expected to be more active and have shorter attention spans than ten-year-olds; a higher level of activity is expected on the ball field than in the classroom.

Despite the inherent definitional problems, students with difficulties in these areas are often identified as having attention deficit disorder (ADD) or attention deficit hyperactivity disorder (ADHD). These disorders are quite common; the Council for Exceptional Children (1992) estimates that 3% to 5% of school-aged children have ADD. Although not considered a separate disability under federal laws, ADD and ADHD were added by the 1997 IDEA Amendments to the list of conditions covered under the category "other health impairment." The *Diagnostic and Statistical Manual of Mental Disorders* (4th ed.) (1994) of the American Psychiatric Association provides diagnostic criteria for attention and hyperactivity disorders. According to the *DSM-IV* criteria, the condition must exist for at least 6 months, begin before age 7, appear in more than one environment (e.g., home, school, workplace), and cause "clinically significant distress or impairment in social, academic, or occupational functioning" (p. 84). See Table 10–3 for more information about this definition.

It is important to keep in mind that several of the behaviors described in the *DSM-IV* definition may be caused by factors other than ADD or ADHD. For example, Ortiz (1991), cited by the Council for Exceptional Children (1992), warns that "as many as 10 out of 14 of the behaviors typically associated with ADD are typical of students who are acquiring a second language" (p. 11). Silver (1992) cautions that the label of ADHD should be applied only when behaviors of hyperactivity, distractibility, and/or impulsivity are both chronic and pervasive.

There are several measures available to assist professionals in the assessment of attention deficits and hyperactivity. Items related to attention and activity levels often appear on rating scales and checklists that survey a range of classroom behaviors. For example, hyperactivity is one of the subscales of Problem Behaviors on the *Social Skills Rating System* (Gresham & Elliott, 1990), and Motor Excess is one of five behavioral domains on the *Revised Behavior Problem Checklist* (Quay & Peterson, 1987). In contrast, measures such as the *Attention Deficit Disorders Evaluation Scale* (2nd ed.) (McCarney, 1995a, 1995b), the *Conners' Rating Scales-Revised* (Conners, 1997), and the *Children's Attention and Adjustment Survey* (Lambert, Hartsough, & Sandoval, 1990) are more limited in scope because their major purpose is study of attention deficits and hyperactivity.

The *Attention Deficit Disorders Evaluation Scale* (2nd ed.) is a rating scale designed for use with school-aged children and adolescents. Both a school and a home version are available, and each contains descriptions of behaviors that reflect inattention, impulsivity, and hyperactivity. These descriptions are designed to relate directly to the *DSM-IV* diagnostic criteria for ADHD. The informant rates each behavior according to the frequency with which it occurs. The scale includes five ratings: "does not engage in the behavior" (0), "one to several times per month" (1), "one to several times per week" (2), "one to several times per day" (3), and "one to several times per hour" (4). The *ADDES-2* manual contends that these quantifiers help make this scale less subjective than those found in other instruments.

Two types of results are produced by the *ADDES-2:* standard scores for the two subscales (Inattentive and Impulsive-Hyperactive) and a total scale percentile rank. Standard scores are distributed with a mean of 10 and a standard deviation of 3. It should be noted that separate norms are used for male and female students. Another feature of the *ADDES-2* is a *DSM-IV* worksheet that allows professionals to identify which characteristics from the definition were identified as problem areas by the teacher or parent rating the student. Also available are supplementary books with recommended instructional activities for teachers (McCarney, 1994) and parents (McCarney & Bauer, 1995).

The school version of the *ADDES-2* was standardized with approximately 5,800 students in 30 states. The standardization sample appears to represent the national population in race and urban-rural residence, although students from the north-central portion of the country are

TABLE 10-3
Definition of ADHD

The American Psychiatric Association (1994) identifies several characteristics related to attention deficit hyperactivity disorder. The first set of characteristics relates to inattention and the second to hyperactivity-impulsivity. Three classifications are possible: ADHD, Combined Type (if the individual meets criteria for both Inattention and Hyperactivity-Impulsivity); ADHD, Predominantly Inattentive Type (if the individual meets criteria for Inattention but not Hyperactivity-Impulsivity); and ADHD, Predominantly Hyperactive-Impulsive Type (if the individual meets criteria for Hyperactivity-Impulsivity but not Inattention).

Inattention

Six (or more) of the following symptoms of **inattention** have persisted for at least 6 months to a degree that is maladaptive and inconsistent with developmental level:

Inattention
(a) often fails to give close attention to details or makes careless mistakes in schoolwork, work, or other activities
(b) often has difficulty sustaining attention in tasks or play activities
(c) often does not seem to listen when spoken to directly
(d) often does not follow through on instructions and fails to finish schoolwork, chores, or duties in the workplace (not due to oppositional behavior or failure to understand instructions)
(e) often has difficulties organizing tasks and activities
(f) often avoids, dislikes or is reluctant to engage in tasks that require sustained mental effort (such as schoolwork or homework)
(g) often loses things necessary for tasks or activities (e.g., toys, school assignments, pencils, books, or tools)
(h) is often easily distracted by extraneous stimuli
(i) is often forgetful in daily activities

Hyperactivity-Impulsivity

Six (or more) of the following symptoms of **hyperactivity-impulsivity** have persisted for at least 6 months to a degree that is maladaptive and inconsistent with developmental level:

Hyperactivity
(a) often fidgets with hands or feet or squirms in seat
(b) often leaves seat in classroom or in other situations in which remaining seated is expected
(c) often runs about or climbs excessively in situations in which it is inappropriate (in adolescents or adults, may be limited to subjective feelings of restlessness)
(d) often has difficulty playing or engaging in leisure activities quietly
(e) is often "on the go" or often acts as if "driven by a motor"
(f) often talks excessively

Impulsivity
(g) often blurts out answers before questions have been completed
(h) often has difficulty waiting in turn
(i) often interrupts or intrudes on others (e.g., butts into conversations or games) (pp. 83–84).

Note: Reprinted with permission from the *Diagnostic and Statistical Manual of Mental Disorders, Fourth Edition.* Copyright 1994, American Psychiatric Association.

***Attention Deficit Disorders Evaluation Scale* (2nd ed.)**

(ADDES-2), Home Version* and *School Version

S. B. McCarney (1995a, 1995b)

Type: Norm-referenced teacher rating scale and parent rating scale

Major Content Areas: Inattention and impulsivity-hyperactivity

Type of Administration: Individual

Administration Time: 15–20 minutes (school version), 15 minutes (home version)

Age/Grade Levels: Ages 4 through 18 (school version), ages 3 through 18 (home version)

Types of Scores: Standard scores for two subscales; overall percentile rank

Computer Aids: *ADDES Quick Score*

Typical Uses: Identification of possible problems in attention and/or activity level

Cautions: The standardization sample for the school version shows some variation from the U.S. population in geographic distribution.

Publisher: Hawthorne Educational Services

overrepresented. Test-retest, internal consistency, and interrater reliability are adequate. The validity of the *ADDES* is supported by its relationship to other measures of ADHD and by its ability to differentiate between students with and without attention deficit hyperactivity disorder.

Perhaps the best-known measures of ADHD are the *Conners' Rating Scales-Revised,* a set of several tools for use by parents and teachers of students ages 3 to 17. Both a short and a long form are available for the parent and teacher scales; short and long adolescent self-report scales are available as well. Spanish-language versions of all scales can be purchased from the publisher.

Teachers and parents read descriptions of student behaviors and choose one of four ratings: "not true at all (never, seldom)" (0), "just a little true (occasionally)" (1), "pretty much true (often, quite a bit)" (2), or "very much true (very often, very frequent)" (3). The short form of the teacher scale contains 28 items, and the long form contains 59. The short form for parents contains 27 items, and the long form has 80.

The short-form rating scales produce three subscale scores (Oppositional, Cognitive Problems/Inattention, and Hyperactivity) and the

Conners' ADHD Index score. The long forms yield additional subscale scores (Anxious-Shy, Perfectionism, Social Problems, and, on the parent form only, Psychosomatic), the Conners' Global Index score, and the DSM-IV Symptom Subscales. The DSM-IV Symptom Subscales include rating scale items that assess Inattentive Symptoms and Hyperactive-Impulsive Symptoms. Raw scores are plotted on profiles where their equivalent *T*-scores can be determined. *T*-scores are distributed with a mean of 50 and a standard deviation of 10. On the *CRS-R,* higher scores are indicative of possible problem areas. Norms are available by age and gender; separate norms are provided for African American/Black students for the adolescent self-rating scales.

According to the manual, the *CRS-R* was standardized with "a large normative sample (8,000+)" (p. 2) from 45 U.S. states and 10 Canadian provinces. This sample included not only parents and teachers but also adolescents who completed self-ratings. All students were in general education; students in special education classes were excluded from the samples. The sample for each of the *CRS-R* measures is described in terms of the ages of students, their ethnicity, and median annual household income.

Conners' Rating Scales-Revised (CRS-R)

C. K. Conners (1997)

Type: Norm-referenced teacher rating scales, parent rating scales, and adolescent self-rating scales

Major Content Areas: Problem behaviors including inattention and hyperactivity

Type of Administration: Individual

Administration Time: 5–10 minutes (short form), 15–20 minutes (long form)

Age/Grade Levels: Ages 3 to 17

Types of Scores: *T*-scores for subscales

Computer Aids: *Conners' Rating Scales-Revised Computer Program*

Typical Uses: Identification of possible problems in attention and/or hyperactivity

Cautions: Results should be interpreted with caution because of concerns about reliability and validity. In addition, students in special education classes were excluded from the standardization samples for the parent and teacher rating scales, and students of color appear underrepresented.

Publisher: Multi-Health Systems Inc. (www.mhs.com)

Students of color, particularly those identified as African American/Black, appear to be underrepresented in the teacher and parent samples and overrepresented in the adolescent samples.

Internal consistency reliability of the *CRS-R* is adequate; however, test-retest reliability falls below .70 for several subscales of the long forms of the parent and teacher scales. No information is available concerning interrater reliability. In terms of validity, results from the long and short forms of *CRS-R* measures appear to be related. However, there is little agreement between parent and teacher ratings. For example, correlations between teacher and parent short-form results ranged from .25 to .49 for males and from .06 to .52 for females.

The *Children's Attention and Adjustment Survey* is a set of two rating scales designed for school and home use. Each form contains 31 descriptions of behaviors that informants rate as "not at all" characteristic of the student, "a little," "quite a bit," or "very much." Included are items that describe behaviors related to inattention, impulsivity, hyperactivity, and conduct problems (e.g., "Defiant," "Lies"). Scores are determined for each of these areas and, in addition, three composites. On the

school form, the ADD composite includes items from the Inattention and Impulsivity scales; the ADHD composite includes ADD and Hyperactivity items; and the *DSM III-R* ADHD composite is based on 7 of the 15 ADHD items.

Separate norms are provided for the home and school scales but not by age or by gender. Standard scores and percentile ranks can be determined for each scale and composite. Raw scores are plotted on a profile; scores that fall within the shaded area of the profile are considered "below the criteria for indicating a potential problem." It should be noted that high scores indicate potential problems, not low scores; also, criteria change from one scale to the next (and from one form of the scale to the other). For example, potential problems are indicated by a standard score of 111 on Inattention, 112 on Impulsivity on the school form, and 114 on the home rating of Impulsivity.

The *Children's Attention and Adjustment Survey* was standardized on approximately 4,000 elementary grade students from two counties in California. Internal consistency reliability of the scales is generally adequate. However, although

---

Children's Attention and Adjustment Survey, Home Form and School Form

N. Lambert, C. Hartsough, & J. Sandoval (1990)

Type: Norm-referenced teacher rating scale and parent rating scale

Major Content Areas: Inattention, impulsivity, hyperactivity, and conduct problems

Type of Administration: Individual

Administration Time: 2–5 minutes

Age/Grade Levels: Ages 5 through 13

Types of Scores: Standard scores and percentiles for each subscale

Computer Aids: N/A

Typical Uses: Identification of possible problems in attention, activity level, and/or conduct

Cautions: Results should be interpreted with caution because high (not low) scores indicate potential problems. Caution is also required because standardization took place in only one state, and further information is needed about test-retest reliability.

Publisher: American Guidance Service (www.agsnet.com)

---

the manual reports test-retest reliability coefficients, these are not meaningful because the two scale administrations took place 3 years apart. In terms of validity, the scales show low to moderate correlations with other parent and teacher rating instruments.

In conclusion, it is important to remember that measures that assess specific behaviors such as hyperactivity, impulsivity, and inattention play the same role in assessment as the more general behavior rating scales and checklists. They help identify possible areas of need that may warrant further evaluation. If further assessment is needed, direct observation is the recommended procedure.

SELF-CONCEPT AND PEER ACCEPTANCE

Students with school performance problems may have poor self-concepts, perceiving themselves as failures in academic pursuits. Students may also experience difficulty in their interactions with classmates. Their peers may fail to accept

them as friends or as regular members of the classroom social group. The next sections describe several of the measures available for exploring these areas.

Self-Concept

Both formal, norm-referenced measures and informal assessment devices are available for the study of self-concept and self-esteem. One popular norm-referenced measure is the *Piers-Harris Children's Self-Concept Scale*. It is a self-report form, and norms are available for grades 4 through 12. According to its manual, the *Piers-Harris* was designed primarily as a research instrument. However, it is often used in schools as a screening device to identify students who have possible self-concept problems.

The *Piers-Harris* is made up of 80 declarative statements such as "My classmates make fun of me," "I am smart," and "I give up easily." In the elementary grades, the tester reads the statements aloud to students. In middle and high school, students are expected to read the statements themselves. Items are written at a third grade reading

---

"The Way I Feel About Myself,"
The Piers-Harris Children's Self-Concept Scale

E. V. Piers & D. B. Harris (1984)

Type: Norm-referenced student checklist

Major Content Areas: Self-concept

Type of Administration: Group

Administration Time: 15–20 minutes

Age/Grade Levels: Grades 4 through 12

Types of Scores: Percentile ranks, stanines

Computer Aids: *PH CSCS Disk*

Typical Uses: Designed as a research tool; also used in the identification of students with possible needs in the area of self-concept development

Cautions: Best used as an informal measure unless local norms are developed.

Publisher: Western Psychological Services (www.wpspublish.com)

---

level, and both positive and negative statements are included. Students respond by circling "yes" if they feel the statement describes them or "no" if they feel the statement does not.

Raw scores on the *Piers-Harris* range from 0 to 80, with higher scores indicating more positive self-concepts. For students in grades 4 through 12, raw scores can be converted to percentile ranks and stanines. Six cluster scores can also be obtained, although these are raw scores. The clusters correspond to six dimensions of self-concept: Behavior, Intellectual and School Status, Physical Appearance and Attributes, Anxiety, Popularity, and Happiness and Satisfaction.

Although its manual was revised in 1984, the *Piers-Harris* was standardized in the 1960s. Piers and Harris (1969) recommend caution in the use of these norms because "they are based on data from one Pennsylvania school district and are therefore generalizable only to similar populations" (p. 13). Users of the test are encouraged to develop local norms, rather than rely upon the norms provided in the manual. The reliability of the *Piers-Harris* appears adequate, with 11 of the 16 reliability coefficients reported by Piers (1977) at the .80 level or above. With respect to validity,

correlations between the *Piers-Harris* and other measures of self-concept range from .40 to .85.

The *Coopersmith Self-Esteem Inventories* are another set of measures available for the assessment of self-concept. Three measures make up the set: the School Form, the Adult Form, and a teacher rating scale entitled *Behavioral Academic Self-Esteem* (Coopersmith & Gilberts, 1981). Of interest here is the School Form, the only one of the three measures that is normed.

The School Form of the *Coopersmith* contains 58 statements such as "I have a low opinion of myself" and, "I'm proud of my schoolwork." Both positive and negative statements are included. Students read each statement and then check whether the statement is "like me" or "unlike me." The tester is allowed to read the statements aloud if students have difficulty reading. If a short form of the measure is desired, only the first 25 items are administered. However, norms are not available for the short form.

Items on the *Coopersmith* school inventory are divided into four subscales: General Self, Social Self-Peers, Home-Parents, and School-Academics. Raw scores from each of the subscales are added together; the sum is then multiplied by 2 to produce

Coopersmith Self-Esteem Inventories

S. Coopersmith (1981)

Type: Norm-referenced student checklist (a teacher rating scale without norms and an adult form without norms are also available)

Major Content Areas: Self-esteem

Type of Administration: Group or individual

Administration Time: Approximately 10 minutes

Age/Grade Levels: School Form for students ages 8 to 15, Adult Form for ages 16 and up

Types of Scores: Percentile ranks for students in grades 4 through 8 (School Form); no norms available for the Adult Form or teacher rating scale

Computer Aids: N/A

Typical Uses: Identification of students with possible needs in the area of self-esteem

Cautions: Best used as informal devices unless local norms are developed.

Publisher: Consulting Psychologists Press (www.cpp-db.com)

the Total Self raw score. In addition, there is a Lie Scale that is used to evaluate the veracity of students' responses. Total Self scores can be converted to percentile ranks, but norms are not available for subscale scores or for the Lie Scale.

Norms for the *Coopersmith* School Form were developed by Kimball (1973) with a sample of approximately 7,600 public school students in grades 4 through 8. According to Coopersmith (1981), the standardization sample included "all socioeconomic ranges and Black and Spanish-surname students" (p. 17). No further description is offered. Coopersmith advises caution in the use of these norms and strongly recommends the development of local norms. The *Coopersmith*'s reliability appears adequate, and there is some support for its validity. The manual states that significant correlations have been found between the *Coopersmith* and other measures of self-esteem.

Like the *Piers-Harris,* the *Coopersmith* is best used as an informal device. If norms are desired, local norms should be developed. In addition, Coopersmith (1981) recommends supplementing the results of the student checklist with teacher ratings and observations.

In recent years, several new self-concept measures have been published, and most are

well standardized and show adequate reliability and validity. Unfortunately, however, not all measures meet minimum standards for psychometric quality. For example, the standardization samples for the *Culture-Free Self-Esteem Inventories* (2nd ed.) (Battle, 1992) are not well described. The manual states that the school form was "standardized on boys and girls in the United States and Canada in Grades 2 through 9" (p. 4); no other information is provided. In addition, although these measures are labeled "culture-free," the manual does not provide evidence to support this claim.

Instruments such as the *Multidimensional Self Concept Scale (MSCS)* (Bracken, 1992) and the *Self-Esteem Index (SEI)* (Brown & Alexander, 1991) are more promising. The *MSCS* is a self-report scale for students in grades 5 through 12. Students read 150 statements such as "I often feel dumb" and "I enjoy life," then rate each according to how well it applies to them ("Strongly agree," "Agree," "Disagree," "Strongly disagree"). Six areas of self-concept are addressed: social, competence, affect, academic, family, and physical. Standard scores and percentile ranks are available for each of these areas and for total test. The statements on the scale are written at the

---

Multidimensional Self Concept Scale (MSCS)

B. B. Bracken (1992)

Type: Norm-referenced student rating scale

Major Content Areas: Global self-concept; social, competence, affect, academic, family, and physical self-concept

Type of Administration: Individual (or group)

Administration Time: 20–30 minutes

Age/Grade Levels: Grades 5 through 12

Types of Scores: Standard scores and percentile ranks for total test and each subscale

Computer Aids: N/A

Typical Uses: Identification of strengths and weaknesses in several dimensions of self-concept

Cautions: Students of color are somewhat underrepresented in the standardization sample; students from southern states are overrepresented.

Publisher: PRO-ED (www.proedinc.com)

---

third grade level; the tester may read them aloud to the student, as needed, and explain the meanings of any unknown words.

The *MSCS* was standardized on approximately 2,500 students from nine states. African-American and Hispanic students are somewhat underrepresented in the sample; students from the northeastern portion of the country are underrepresented, and those from the South are overrepresented (52.5% versus 35% for the nation). Internal consistency reliability coefficients fall at or above .86 for both genders and all grade levels on all scales and total test. Test-retest reliability coefficients range from .73 to .90. *MSCS* total test results show strong correlations with total scores on the *Coopersmith Self-Esteem Inventory* ($r = .73$) and the *Piers-Harris Children's Self-Concept Scale* ($r = .85$).

The *Self-Esteem Index* is a self-report rating scale for students ages 8-0 to 18-11. It contains 80 statements that students rate as "always true," "usually true," "usually false," or "always false." Each statement contributes to one of four self-esteem scales: perception of familial acceptance, perception of academic competence, perception

of peer popularity, and perception of personal security. The *SEI* is designed for either group or individual administration. The examiner may provide students with assistance with word meanings, but the manual discourages oral administration.

Results include standard scores and percentile ranks for each of the four scales as well as a total test Self-Esteem Quotient. The *SEI* was standardized with 2,455 students from 19 states; students identified as seriously emotionally disturbed were excluded from the sample. The standardization sample appears to approximate the U.S. population in terms of geographic region, urban-rural residence, ethnicity, and race. Internal consistency reliability coefficients fall at or above .80 for ages 9 through 18; at age 8, four of the five reported coefficients fall in the .70s. No information is provided on test-retest reliability. *SEI* results show low to moderate correlations with teachers' ratings of student self-esteem (.21 to .43); however, much stronger correlations are reported between the *SEI*'s Self-Esteem Quotient and total test results of the *Piers-Harris* (.77) and the *Coopersmith* (.83).

Self-Esteem Index (SEI)

L. Brown & J. Alexander (1991)

Type: Norm-referenced student rating scale

Major Content Areas: Overall self-esteem; perceptions of familial acceptance, academic competence, peer popularity, and personal security

Type of Administration: Individual (or group)

Administration Time: Approximately 30 minutes

Age/Grade Levels: Ages 8-0 to 18-11

Types of Scores: Standard scores and percentile ranks for each of the four scales and for total test

Computer Aids: N/A

Typical Uses: Identification of strengths and weaknesses in several areas of self-esteem

Cautions: Some students may have difficulty reading the items on the *SEI*. No information is available on test-retest reliability.

Publisher: PRO-ED (www.proedinc.com)

Several informal student checklists are also available for the study of self-concept. Two examples appear in Figure 10–3. Students can also be interviewed about their perceptions of self-worth, or some types of observational data can be collected. For example, it is possible to count the number of negative statements a student makes about himself or herself and compare that total with the number of positive statements. Some students make frequent comments such as "I'm dumb" or "I can't do that," whereas others are much more positive in their self-appraisal.

Peer Acceptance

Attitude scales are used to evaluate general education students' perceptions of individuals with school performance problems. These scales provide information about peer attitudes toward students with disabilities in general. They do not assess how well peers accept a particular student.

One example of a general attitude scale is the *Peer Attitudes toward the Handicapped Scale (PATHS)* (Bagley & Greene, 1981). Although the *PATHS* is no longer in print, it provides a model for obtaining information about students' atti-

tudes toward others with disabilities. The *PATHS* consists of a series of paragraphs that describe students with disabilities and the problems they experience. Descriptions of pupils with physical, learning, and behavioral problems are included. For example, one description is:

> Stephen cannot follow directions, and his teacher must tell him at least three times what to do; even then, Stephen might still not know what to do. He is unable to do the classwork and is failing every subject.

Students read each description and then select the place where the student with disabilities should work: "Work with me in *My Group*," "Work in *Another Group* (with someone else)," "Work in *No Group* (with no other students)," "Work *Outside of Class* (in another class or room)," or "*Stay at Home* (and not come to school)."

To find out how a particular student is perceived by his or her classmates, sociometric techniques are used (Asher & Taylor, 1981). The most common technique is the nomination method. Students nominate the peers they would most or least like to associate with in some activity. Sev-

Adjective Check List

Directions: Put an X by each word that describes you.

_____ 1. smart	_____ 7. quarrelsome	_____ 13. bothersome
_____ 2. funny	_____ 8. fidgety	_____ 14. cranky
_____ 3. tired	_____ 9. energetic	_____ 15. eager
_____ 4. happy	_____ 10. friendly	_____ 16. honest
_____ 5. blue	_____ 11. shy	_____ 17. lazy
_____ 6. busy	_____ 12. sad	_____ 18. selfish

Behavioral Check List

Directions: Put an X by each description that fits you.

_____ 1. makes friends easily	_____ 6. seems to lack confidence
_____ 2. not as smart as most kids	_____ 7. is a good leader
_____ 3. likes to be alone	_____ 8. enjoys school
_____ 4. is fun to be with	_____ 9. feelings are easily hurt
_____ 5. laughs a lot	_____ 10. daydreams a lot

FIGURE 10-3

Sample Self-Concept Checklists for Students

Note: From *Teacher Diagnosis of Educational Difficulties* (p. 192) by R. M. Smith, 1969, New York: Merrill/Macmillan. Copyright 1969 by Macmillan Publishing Company. Reprinted by permission.

eral activities appropriate for the students' age are presented: playing a game, working on a class art project, attending a school assembly, and so forth. For example, students can be asked to respond to questions such as:

1. Name the students in this class you would most (least) like to play with during recess.
2. Name the students you would most (least) like to sit next to in class.
3. Name the students you would most (least) like to work with on a class assignment.

A measure of this kind is included in the *Behavior Rating Profile* (2nd ed.) (Brown & Hammill, 1990), described earlier in this chapter, and norms are provided for students in grades 1 through 12. Or sociometric data can be collected informally. Class results are then analyzed to determine how many positive and negative nominations each student received.

Rating scales can also be used to collect sociometric data. For instance, on the *Peer Acceptance Scale* (Bruininks, Rynders, & Gross, 1974), each student in the class rates every other student using the picture rating scale shown in Figure 10–4. The possible ratings are "Friend" (illustrated by two persons playing together), "All Right," and "Wouldn't

Like." An advantage of this procedure is that results are available for all members of the group, not just for those students nominated by their peers.

Sociometric instruments such as the ones just described can be used to determine how well individual students are accepted by their peers. However, student ratings of other students must remain confidential. Students should be encouraged not to share their responses with others (Lewis & Doorlag, 1999), and teachers

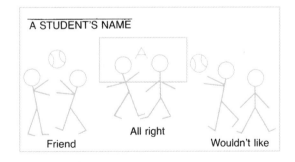

FIGURE 10-4

A Picture Rating Scale

Note: From the "Peer Acceptance Scale" by R. H. Bruininks, J. E. Rynders, and J. C. Cross, 1974, *American Journal of Mental Deficiency, 78,* pp. 377–83. Copyright 1974 by the American Association on Mental Deficiency. Reprinted by permission.

should not report results to students. Informing students that they are poorly accepted by their peers is likely to have a negative effect upon self-concept.

SCHOOL ATTITUDES AND INTERESTS

A student's interests and attitudes may be related to how well that student performs in school. Poor academic achievement, frustration in complying with classroom rules, and difficulty relating to teachers and peers do not lead to positive attitudes toward the school experience. Likewise, disinterest and negative attitudes can contribute to school performance problems. The relationships among interests, attitudes, and school behaviors are complex, usually making it impossible to determine which factors were causes and which were effects.

Attitudes toward School

Several measures are available for gathering information from students about their perceptions of the school experience. These measures assess students' attitudes toward various school subjects or their attitude toward specific classroom practices. In both of these important areas, the majority of assessment tools are informal and include interviews, questionnaires, and checklists.

A few formal measures have been developed to assess school attitudes. One example is the *Estes Attitude Scales (EAS)* (Estes, Estes, Richards, & Roettger, 1981), which is now out of print. The elementary version of the *EAS* contains three attitude scales: Mathematics, Reading, and Science. The tester reads statements such as "It is easy to get tired of math" and "Reading is fun for me" aloud to the students. Students respond by checking "I agree," "I don't know," or "I disagree."

The secondary version of the *EAS* assesses attitudes toward English and social studies in addition to math, reading, and science. Reading is required, but test items are written at a grade 6 reading level. Examples of secondary level items are "Work in English class helps students do better work in other classes" and "Much of what is taught in social studies is not important." Students respond to each statement by checking "I strongly agree," "I agree," "I cannot decide," "I disagree," or "I strongly disagree."

If comparative information is not needed, informal measures of attitudes toward school may suffice. Interviews or questionnaires could be used to elicit students' views about the school subjects they like most and least and those they perceive as most and least valuable.

Several informal devices are available for assessing students' perceptions of classroom practices. For example, Figure 10–5 presents an attitude survey appropriate for use with secondary students. This questionnaire contains items that pertain to school attitudes, self-concept, interactions with teachers, and peer relationships. Students are asked to decide whether things at school are better this year than last year. The student reads each item (e.g., "I get along better with the other students") and then selects a response: "much more," "more," "the same," "less," or "much less."

Another technique for gathering information about attitudes involves the use of incomplete sentences. For example, students could be asked to complete sentences such as the following:

- For me, school is _____ .
- Learning new things in school makes me feel _____ .
- When the teacher asks me to read out loud in class, I _____ .
- When I have math problems to solve, I _____ .
- In my opinion, writing a story or a composition is _____ .

Interests

Interests are assessed to learn more about students' likes and dislikes. Information about students' preferences among subjects may prove useful in academic counseling. Knowledge of preferred leisure activities may help teachers select rewards for classroom behavior management programs or choose high-interest instructional materials.

The simplest way to find out about interests is to ask students to describe their favorite activities—the things that they most enjoy doing. Kroth (1975) has developed an informal survey

---

Student Questionnaire

I'd like to know if things are different for you at school this year. I will read you a statement. Think about the sentence and then check one of the blanks on your paper (*much more, more, the same, less,* or *much less*).

1. I get along better with the other students.
2. Other children in the class tease me about my school work.
3. My teachers are more patient with me when I have problems in my work.
4. I like school more this year.
5. My school work seems easier.
6. My principal knows me better this year.
7. Other people understand my learning problems in school.
8. My guidance counselor has helped me understand my learning problems.
9. I have really improved my school work in the resource room.
10. My mother helps me more with my homework.
11. My father helps me more with my homework.
12. My parents are more patient with me with my school work.
13. My parents yell at me when I get poor grades.
14. My parents see my teacher more this year.
15. My parents are pleased with my homework.
16. The resource room has helped me do my school work better in all my classes.
17. I feel better about myself.
18. Learning is more fun.
19. I know that I'll continue to improve my school work even though I'll be slow in some subjects.
20. I have talked with my principal more this year.
21. Many of my classroom assignments are too hard for me to do.
22. I have problems learning things that other kids learn very easily.
23. If other children tease me about school, I can control myself because I understand myself better.
24. I know why it's important to do well in school.
25. I don't think I'm stupid.
26. I take pride in my accomplishments.
27. I learn more in the resource room than in my other classes.
28. I feel that I'll be successful some day.
29. When I do poorly in school, it depresses me.
30. I think my teachers understand me better.

FIGURE 10-5

Attitude Survey for Secondary Students

Note: From *The Resource Room: An Access to Excellence* (pp. 181–182) by M. F. Hawisher, 1975, Lancaster: South Carolina Region V Educational Services Center. Copyright 1975 by South Carolina Region V Educational Services Center. Reprinted by permission.

that is a series of open-ended questions about student preferences:

- The things I like to do after school are:
- If I had ten dollars I'd:
- My favorite TV programs are:
- My favorite game at school is:
- My best friends are:
- My favorite time of day is:
- My favorite toys are:
- My favorite record is:
- My favorite subject at school is:
- I like to read books about: (p. 18)

These questions could be used as the basis for an informal interest interview or questionnaire.

THE LEARNING ENVIRONMENT

The assessment techniques described so far have focused primarily on the student: problem behaviors (including attention deficits and hyperactivity), self-concept, acceptance by peers, interests, and attitudes toward school. Although this is a necessary part of the assessment process, it is also important to consider the characteristics of the classroom and the other environments where the student must function. In the ecological approach to assessment, both student and environmental characteristics are of interest.

Ecological assessment studies the match (or mismatch) between the behaviors of the student and the constraints imposed by the environment. Thurman (1977) has identified three factors to consider: (a) the student's deviant or nondeviant behavior, (b) the student's functional competence, and (c) the tolerance of the microecology (i.e., the classroom) for deviant and/or incompetent student behaviors. Environments with a high tolerance for differences accept greater ranges of student behaviors.

Smith, Neisworth, and Greer (1978) also recommend comprehensive assessment of the learning environment. In addition to evaluation of student performance, they identify four major environments for assessment: instructional (curriculum, methods, and materials), social, services within the school and classroom, and physical.

The next sections describe strategies for assessing school learning environments. Included are techniques for gathering information about the expectations teachers hold for behavior, the instructional demands placed upon the student in the classroom learning environment, interactions between students and teachers, and physical characteristics of the environment.

Observations, interviews, and other informal procedures are typically used to assess the classroom learning environment. One published system for this purpose is *The Instructional Environment Scale-II (TIES-II)* (Ysseldyke & Christenson, 1993). This system is made up of three components: a classroom observation, a structured student interview, and a structured teacher interview. When these data have been collected, the Instructional Rating Profile is completed. The Profile describes the learning environment in terms of 12 factors identified as critical for student learning. The factors are Instructional Match, Teacher Expectations, Classroom Environment, Instructional Presentation, Cognitive Emphasis, Motivational Strategies, Relevant Practice, Informed Feedback, Academic Engaged Time, Adaptive Instruction, Progress Evaluation, and Student Understanding. *TIES-II* is not a normed measure, but each of the factors is described in detail, and examples are provided of appropriate practices.

Behavioral Expectations

Teachers differ in the behavioral expectations they hold for students. The same student behav-ior may be considered appropriate by one teacher but inappropriate by another. Thus, consideration of the teacher's standards for classroom conduct is necessary in the investigation of student behavior problems. The most straightforward way of gathering this information is to interview the teacher. Classroom observations are another useful source of data.

One area of interest is classroom rules. In many classrooms, the rules for behavior are stated explicitly so students understand which behaviors are acceptable and which are not. Rules may even be posted on a bulletin board as a reminder to students. Affleck, Lowenbraun, and Archer (1980) recommend that classroom rules:

1. Be very few in number.
2. State what behavior is desired from the children (e.g., Complete your work. Stay at your desks. Work quietly.) rather than stating all of the behaviors you do not wish children to exhibit (e.g., Don't walk around the room. Don't hit others.).
3. Be simple and clearly stated.
4. Be guidelines that you, the teacher, can directly enforce. (pp. 35–36)

In some classrooms, the rules for conduct are not clearly spelled out. If students are confused about the rules for behavior, they may be unable to comply with those rules. To help students understand class rules, Clarizio and McCoy (1983) suggest "listing the rules on the board, having the student explain in his own words what the rules mean, minimizing distractions while giving directions, and keeping rules short" (p. 547).

The classroom behavior management system is closely related to the rules for conduct. This system may be a formal, explicit contingency management program or a less formal approach. Among the questions to consider in studying the classroom behavior management system are:

- Do students have a clear understanding of the expectations for classroom conduct? Are they aware of which behaviors are considered acceptable and which are considered unacceptable?
- Are students aware of the consequences of appropriate and inappropriate behavior?

- What happens in the classroom when students behave appropriately? Is appropriate behavior rewarded in some way?
- What types of rewards or reinforcers are provided? Are students rewarded with social reinforcers like teacher praise? Can they earn activity reinforcers such as free time in the media center or the opportunity to do a special art project? Are tangible rewards like stars, notes home to parents, or school supplies used for reinforcement? Are edible rewards provided?
- Is there a formal system for rewarding appropriate behavior? For example, do students earn points for good behavior and later trade their points for reinforcers? If a formal system is in place, does it include provisions for inappropriate behavior?
- What happens in the classroom when students behave inappropriately? Is inappropriate behavior ignored, or are there consequences?
- What are the consequences of inappropriate behavior? Does the teacher verbally rebuke the student? Does the student lose privileges or previously earned rewards? Is the student sent to the principal or kept in at recess or after school?
- Are consequences delivered consistently to all students at all times?
- How does the classroom behavior management system relate to the rules of the school and the school's behavior management system?

Instructional Demands

The instructional demands in the classroom learning environment can have an influence on student behavior. If students are faced with academic expectations that they are unable to fulfill, they may react by displaying inappropriate classroom behaviors. In assessing problem classroom behaviors, it is important to consider not only the behavior itself, but also the instructional events and conditions that precede it. Clarizio and McCoy (1983) suggest several questions to ask about the antecedents of problem behaviors:

- At what time of the class, day, week, or year does the problem occur?
- In what subject matter does the problem occur?

- What degree of accuracy is demanded for a given assignment?
- Who is present? What are they doing?
- Where is the child?
- By whom does the child sit when the student misbehaves?
- What is the size of the group when the student misbehaves?
- Is the student academically capable of completing assignments? (p. 549)

These questions relate to instructional antecedents, but the consequences of a problem behavior in terms of instruction are also important. What happens when a student behaves inappropriately? Do the academic demands change in some way?

The school curriculum has a major impact on the instructional conditions of the classroom because curriculum dictates what students are taught. The curriculum specifies not only the particular skills and information students should learn, but also the scope of these skills and the sequence of instruction.

Instructional materials, methods, and activities are used to implement the curriculum. Whereas curriculum is concerned with *what* is taught, instruction is concerned with *how* new skills and information are taught. Included under instructional considerations are learning materials such as texts and workbooks, specific learning activities such as classroom and homework assignments, and the instructional methods used by the teacher to present new information. In evaluating instructional materials, some major characteristics to consider are content, instructional procedures, opportunities for practice, initial and ongoing assessment, review activities, and motivational value.

Many of the factors considered in the evaluation of instructional materials are also pertinent to the evaluation of classroom learning activities. In addition, these questions may prove useful:

1. Do the learning activities match the instructional goals and objectives for the student?
2. Has the student mastered the prerequisite skills necessary for the learning activity?
3. Are the directions for the activity clear and comprehensible?

4. Does the activity present information in a way that is appropriate for the student? For example, if the task requires the student to read, is the level of the reading material appropriate for the student?

5. Are the types of responses required by the activity appropriate for the student?

6. Does the activity provide adequate opportunity for practice of newly learned skills and information?

7. Is there adequate feedback to students about the accuracy of their responses?

8. Is the activity motivating? Is some type of reinforcement provided for successfully completing the activity?

9. Is the classroom environment conducive to participation in and completion of the learning activity?

Popham and Baker (1970) provide additional questions that focus on the student's involvement with the learning task: Does the student know the point of the activity? Precisely what is expected? The value of the activity? Does the student have adequate practice to do the task well?

Also of interest are teachers' instructional strategies and the ways they attempt to modify instruction for students with learning problems. Lewis and Doorlag (1999) discuss four kinds of instructional adaptations teachers can make when students encounter problems with classroom learning tasks. The most drastic modification involves removing the task that students are experiencing difficulty with and substituting an alternative task. This adaptation should be considered a last resort. Table 10–4 shows several other changes that can be tried first, including modifying the learning materials and activities, changing the procedures used to teach new skills and information, and altering the requirements for successful task completion. The teacher can be observed or interviewed to determine what types of instructional modifications have been tried and the results. In addition, when the student, rather than the learning environment, is under assessment, this hierarchy for altering instructional procedures can form the basis of a series of diagnostic probes or diagnostic teaching sequences.

Putnam, Deshler, and Schumaker (1993) describe a system for analysis of the demands of the

---

TABLE 10–4
Ways of Adapting Instructional Activities

IF students experience difficulty in task performance, **TRY** these adaptations of . . .

Materials and activities:
1. Clarify task directions
2. Add prompts to the learning task
3. Teach to specific student errors

Teaching procedures:
4. Give additional presentation of skills and information
5. Provide additional guided practice
6. Make consequences for successful performance more attractive
7. Slow the pace of instruction

Task requirements:
8. Change the criteria for successful performance
9. Change task characteristics
10. Break each task into smaller subtasks

BEFORE selecting an alternative task.
IF NECESSARY, substitute a similar but easier task or a prerequisite task.

Note: From *Teaching Special Students in General Education Classrooms* (5th ed.) (p. 109) by Lewis/Doorlag, © 1999. Reprinted by permission of Prentice-Hall, Inc., Upper Saddle River, NJ.

---

instructional setting for students at the secondary level. Among the domains of interest are requirements for student assignments, tests, and class participation. A hierarchical approach is used. Each domain is analyzed to determine required performance areas. Then each performance area is analyzed to identify the elements that comprise it. For example, classroom tests require three performance areas: preparing for the test, answering test questions, and following directions. The demand elements involved in following test directions are readability, length, sentence structure, and clarity. Once instructional demands have been analyzed, it becomes possible to identify the learning strategies that students require to meet those demands.

Student-Teacher Interactions

Interactions between teacher and student are one of the key factors in the classroom learning environment. Teachers can influence student conduct and academic performance by how they react to students' appropriate and inappropriate behaviors. For example, if a student volunteers to answer questions in class but is repeatedly ignored by the teacher, the student may stop attempting to participate or may resort to inappropriate behavior to gain the teacher's attention.

Assessment of student-teacher interactions is best accomplished by observation. The assessment team can design its own observation system or adopt one of the many available systems and modify it, if necessary. For example, the *Brophy-Good Teacher-Child Dyadic Interaction System* (Brophy & Good, 1969) is designed to assess the verbal interactions between the teacher and each individual student in the classroom. For each interaction, information is gathered about the classroom activity, the initiator of the interaction, the nature of the interaction, the appropriateness of the student's response, and the type of feedback provided by the teacher. Chapman, Larsen, and Parker (1979) describe the five types of student-teacher interactions of interest in the *Brophy-Good* system:

> A *response opportunity* occurs when the child publicly attempts to answer a question or problem posed by the teacher. *Recitation* occurs when the child reads aloud, describes some experience, goes through the arithmetic tables, or makes some other extended oral presentation. A *procedural contact* refers to an interaction between the teacher and the child concerning supplies and equipment or to matters concerning the child's individual needs. A *work-related contact* is any interaction involving homework, seat work, or other written work assigned to the child. A *behavioral contact* occurs when the teacher disciplines the child or makes comments regarding his classroom behavior. (pp. 227–228) [italics added]

In this system, data are recorded on each interaction as it occurs, so that the sequence of events in classroom interactions can be analyzed.

The *Flanders' Interaction Analysis Categories* (Flanders, 1970) is another system for observing teacher-student interactions. This system targets three types of behavior for observation: teacher talk, pupil talk, and silence. These behaviors are further broken down into 10 categories used for coding. The observer uses the codes to record the type of interaction that occurs every 4 seconds for a short period of time each day over several days.

The *EBASS (EcoBehavioral Assessment System Software)* (Greenwood, Carta, Kamps, & Delquadri, 1997) is a computer-based classroom observation system developed at the Juniper Gardens Children's Project at the University of Kansas. This well-designed system includes three instruments, one of which is appropriate for both general and special education K–12 classrooms. That instrument, the *MS-CISSAR,* allows the observer to gather data about student, teacher, and ecological events. For example, three types of student events are observed: academic responses, competing responses, and task management (e.g., raising hand, manipulating materials). Teacher events include teacher definition (e.g., regular teacher, special educator, aide), teacher position, teacher behavior, teacher focus, and teacher approval. Among the events under study in the classroom ecology are setting (e.g., regular classroom, resource room), physical arrangement, activity, task, and instructional grouping. In using the *EBASS,* a trained observer enters data directly on a portable computer. That data can then be analyzed in several ways, including the percentage of occurrence of any specific type of event and analysis of the student's academic engagement over time.

Observation systems such as the *Brophy-Good, Flanders,* and *EBASS* may be modified as needed. Depending upon the purpose of the observation, it may become necessary to add or delete behavioral categories. The behaviors of interest in observation depend upon the particular situation: the grade level of the classroom, the specific classroom activities, the characteristics of the student and teacher, and the assessment questions under study. However, an unfavorable learning environment is indicated when observations show few interactions between students and teacher and few positive teacher responses to student behaviors.

Students may be able to contribute information about student-teacher interactions or at least their perceptions of those interactions. For example, the rating scales in Figure 10–6 are designed to probe students' opinions of the teacher's performance. Each contains several descriptions of teacher behavior in language tailored to the level of elementary or secondary students. Included on the scales are

Interaction Checklist (Elementary)

	Always 3	Seldom 2	Never 1
1. I can get extra help from the teacher when I need it.	☐	☐	☐
2. The teacher praises me when I do well.	☐	☐	☐
3. The teacher smiles when I do something well.	☐	☐	☐
4. The teacher listens attentively.	☐	☐	☐
5. The teacher accepts me as an individual.	☐	☐	☐
6. The teacher encourages me to try something new.	☐	☐	☐
7. The teacher respects the feelings of others.	☐	☐	☐
8. My work is usually good enough.	☐	☐	☐
9. I am called on when I raise my hand.	☐	☐	☐
10. The same students always get praised by the teacher.	☐	☐	☐
11. The teacher grades fairly.	☐	☐	☐
12. The teacher smiles and enjoys teaching.	☐	☐	☐
13. I have learned to do things from this teacher.	☐	☐	☐
14. When something is too hard, my teacher makes it easier for me.	☐	☐	☐
15. My teacher is polite and courteous.	☐	☐	☐
16. I like my teacher.	☐	☐	☐

Interaction Checklist (Secondary)

The teacher

	Always 5	Sometimes 4	Often 3	Seldom 2	Never 1
1. is genuinely interested in me	☐	☐	☐	☐	☐
2. respects the feelings of others	☐	☐	☐	☐	☐
3. grades fairly	☐	☐	☐	☐	☐
4. identifies what he or she considers important	☐	☐	☐	☐	☐
5. is enthusiastic about teaching	☐	☐	☐	☐	☐
6. smiles often and enjoys teaching	☐	☐	☐	☐	☐
7. helps me develop skills in understanding myself	☐	☐	☐	☐	☐
8. is honest and fair	☐	☐	☐	☐	☐
9. helps me develop skills in communicating	☐	☐	☐	☐	☐
10. encourages and provides time for individual help	☐	☐	☐	☐	☐
11. is pleasant and has a sense of humor	☐	☐	☐	☐	☐
12. has "pets" and spends most time with them	☐	☐	☐	☐	☐
13. encourages and provides time for questions and discussion	☐	☐	☐	☐	☐
14. respects my ideas and concerns	☐	☐	☐	☐	☐
15. helps me develop skills in making decisions	☐	☐	☐	☐	☐
16. helps me develop skills in using time wisely	☐	☐	☐	☐	☐

FIGURE 10–6

Student Rating Scales for Evaluating the Teacher's Performance

Note: From *The Exceptional Student in the Regular Classroom* (6th ed.) (pp. 133–134) by Gearhart/Weishahn, © 1996. Reprinted by permission of Prentice-Hall, Inc., Upper Saddle River, NJ.

items relating to the teacher's attention to individual differences and strategies for providing praise and encouragement.

The Physical Environment

Physical conditions can influence the effectiveness of the classroom learning environment. A noisy room, poorly arranged surroundings, and uncomfortable temperatures can impair both students' and teachers' ability to perform at their best. Reynolds and Birch (1977) have developed a system for evaluating the physical conditions of classrooms, including factors such as space and facility accommodations, teaching-learning settings, and instructional materials. Contrasting descriptions of poor and adequate physical environments are provided as guidelines. For example, the following characteristics indicate a learning environment with inadequate space and facility accommodations:

> (a) The classroom is essentially untreated for sound.
>
> (b) Access to the class involves difficult elevation and entry problems for students in wheelchairs.
>
> (c) There are no amplification devices.
>
> (d) There are no partitioned areas for small group work.
>
> (e) Movement to washrooms, lunchrooms, and other essential areas is difficult for the orthopedically or visually impaired students.
>
> (f) Space is very limited—thus inflexible.
>
> (g) Storage space is almost totally lacking in the classroom. (p. 134)

A more ideal classroom in terms of space and facilities has these features:

> The classroom is carpeted and/or otherwise treated effectively for sound control; access and entry present no problems for any student; storage, flexible partitioning possibilities, sound amplification, varied furniture, and like matters are provided adequately. (p. 134)

These and other descriptions can be used to rate the suitability of the physical conditions in classroom learning environments.

Whatever classroom space is available should be arranged carefully to facilitate instruc-tion. Lewis and Doorlag (1999) suggest several factors to consider:

1. *Sound.* Separate quiet areas from noisy areas.
2. *Convenience.* Store equipment, supplies, and materials near where they are used; locate instructional groups near the chalkboard.
3. *Student traffic patterns.* Make traffic patterns direct; discourage routes that lead to disruptions (e.g., students distracting others when turning in assignments or moving to new activities). Also, make sure that traffic areas are uncluttered and wide enough to accommodate the flow of student traffic, particularly during transitions from one activity to another (Stainback, Stainback & Froyen, 1987).
4. *Teacher mobility.* Use an open room arrangement so that the teacher can move quickly and easily to any location. This allows the teacher to "respond to student needs as well as to potential behavior problems" (Cegelka, 1995b, p. 139).
5. *Flexibility.* Ensure that all classroom activities can be accomplished; make areas multipurpose or use different arrangements for different tasks. Stainback, Stainback, and Slavin (1989) recommend classrooms with "areas that can be opened, closed, or screened off depending on the needs of students when working on different tasks" (p. 140).
6. *Density.* Arrange student seating so that personal space is preserved; avoid crowding. High density can reduce attentiveness and increase dissatisfaction and aggressiveness (Doyle, 1986; Zentall, 1983) (p. 179).

In arranging the classroom, there are a great many alternatives to the traditional configuration of straight rows of desks. Turnbull and Schulz (1979) recommend that classroom learning environments include such features as individual and group work areas, manipulative and listening centers, and rest and recreation areas. There are a number of options for arranging seating for classroom instruction: students can be seated at a table, on a rug, or on the floor; in chairs; or in more permanent arrangements such as groupings of desks and chairs.

Comprehensive checklists for evaluating the physical environment of the classroom and of the school have been developed by Smith, Neisworth, and Greer (1978). Among the areas of concern are the safety of the learning environment, its accessibility to students with physical impairments and other disabilities, and physical factors such as lighting, temperature, noise, and color. Some of the questions that relate to physical conditions in instructional settings include the following:

- Are related compatible activities arranged together and unrelated, incompatible activities separated within the classroom?
- Have an appropriate time and place been designated and assigned for all activities?
- Is there a variety of places where different sized groups can meet and work?
- Are there special places that individual children can go (a) for isolation, (b) for rest and quiet, (c) to let off steam, (d) to reward themselves, (e) for private instruction, (f) to work independently, (g) to be disciplined privately?
- Are the furnishings (desks, displays, etc.) moveable to provide a variety of groupings and areas within the room for different learning tasks?
- Can the teacher control visual distractions between groups of children (by separating groups, raising room dividers, etc.)?
- Are storage facilities accessible to the students for getting out and putting away materials which they are allowed access to? (pp. 151–152)

ANSWERING THE ASSESSMENT QUESTIONS

The assessment team can choose to gather several types of information in its study of the student's current classroom behavior. Behavior rating scales and checklists serve as screening measures to identify possible problem behaviors. If problems are indicated, assessment continues with in-depth study of the behaviors of interest by direct observation or functional assessment. The characteristics of the learning environment are also investigated to determine whether classroom factors are contributing to the student's behavioral difficulties. With some students, other dimensions of behavior may be assessment concerns—the student's self-concept, acceptance by peers, attitudes toward school, and current interests.

Types of Procedures

The assessment techniques used to study classroom behavior supply information for several dif-

ferent assessment questions; thus, they are not expected to produce equivalent results. Dimensions such as classroom behavior and self-concept are viewed as separate concerns, and results in one area are not expected to duplicate results in the other.

Assessment of classroom behavior relies heavily upon the information provided by informants. Teachers, parents, peers, and students themselves share their views through rating scales, checklists, interviews, and questionnaires. In interpreting these data, it is important to recognize that measures depending upon informants are indirect. Whenever possible, results of indirect measures should be confirmed with more direct techniques.

Another characteristic of the strategies used in the study of classroom behavior is that many are informal techniques. Some dimensions of classroom behavior do not lend themselves to norm-referenced assessment; an example is the study of environmental influences. Available norm-referenced tools tend to be either screening devices like behavior rating scales and checklists or measures of student characteristics such as self-concept. However, some of these normed instruments have been criticized because of poor or unsubstantiated technical quality.

Informal measures have both advantages and disadvantages. In general, informal tools are designed to provide instructional information, and their results are more detailed and specific than those from formal measures. If the purpose in assessment is to learn more about the student and the learning environment to devise an instructional program, informal techniques are preferred. However, a major disadvantage of informal measures is that their technical quality is typically unknown. They may be valid and reliable or technically inadequate. Therefore, results of informal measures must be interpreted with caution, particularly when used for decisions about program eligibility.

Nature of the Assessment Tasks

Assessment devices that appear to measure the same behavioral domains may, in fact, evaluate quite different dimensions. In selecting measures for the study of classroom behavior and interpreting their results, it is important to take into account how each measure goes about assessment.

Behavioral rating scales and checklists provide an excellent example of the range of variations that can occur among measures with similar purposes. For example, rating scales and checklists differ in the person or persons they select to act as informants; the identity of the informant is an important consideration in the selection of an assessment tool. Teachers and parents view students from different perspectives, and if classroom behavior is the major concern, teachers are likely the better source of information. The observations of parents may be different from those of teachers, and peers may disagree with both teachers and parents. If students are given the opportunity to rate themselves, their self-perceptions may provide another perspective that is different from the perceptions of others. One way to account for divergent views from various informants is to include them all in the assessment process.

Rating scales and checklists can also vary on several other dimensions. These include types of student behaviors that informants are asked to consider, the underlying theoretical frameworks that influence the selection of behaviors and the methods used to derive results, and the ways in which informants are required to respond. Because of these areas of possible difference, rating scales and checklists that appear similar may, in fact, measure quite different aspects of student behavior.

Other types of procedures also bear scrutiny. Observations of student behaviors are influenced by the way the behavior is defined, the measurement system selected, the times and places that observations occur, the number of times the student is observed, and so forth. Likewise, observations of student-teacher interactions are affected by the coding system used to categorize behaviors. On sociograms, the specific questions that students are asked may determine their willingness to accept or reject a particular peer. Important differences are also likely to be found

among measures of self-concept, attitude scales, and informal interest inventories.

Documentation of Classroom Behavior

Classroom behavior is one of the primary concerns of professionals on the assessment team as they attempt to answer the question, *Is the school performance problem related to a disability?* However, classroom behavior is an important consideration for all students referred for special education assessment, not only for those who qualify for services for behavioral disorders. The general question under study is, *What is the student's current status in classroom behavior and social-emotional development?* This question is pertinent for any student with a school performance problem because of the possible relationship between poor achievement and inappropriate school behavior.

More specific questions about classroom behavior include:

- Is there evidence of a severe conduct problem? Of an attention deficit or hyperactivity?
- What are the characteristics of the classroom learning environment?
- What is the student's current status in self-concept and acceptance by peers?
- What are the student's current interests and attitudes toward school and learning?

These specific questions may be germane for some students but not for others.

The assessment team gathers data from many sources to answer the questions about classroom behavior. School records are reviewed for information about disciplinary history and attendance. Current behavior is studied by administering norm-referenced rating scales and checklists to informants such as teachers and parents. If the results of these screening measures point to possible problems, classroom observations are conducted and information is gathered about the environment in which the student is expected to perform. With some students, other dimensions of classroom behavior are of interest, and the assessment team may investigate the student's self-concept, level of acceptance by peers, or current interests and attitudes toward school. In the study of classroom behavior, teachers, parents, the student, and even peers share their observations and perceptions of the student's ability to conform to the behavioral expectations of the classroom learning environment.

In analyzing the assessment results, the team's task is to describe the student's current behavioral status. This description is based to some extent on the norm-referenced data provided by behavior rating scales and checklists. However, many of the techniques used to study specific aspects of the student's behavior are informal strategies. Informal techniques are an excellent source of instructional information but do not provide comparative data. Thus, the team must proceed cautiously in interpreting the results and in drawing conclusions about performance deficiencies.

Determination of eligibility for programs for students with behavioral disorders rests upon documentation of a severe and persistent behavioral disability. The assessment team must demonstrate that a behavioral disorder exists, that it is neither a mild nor a transitory problem, and that the disorder exerts an adverse effect upon school performance. According to federal law, several types of disorders are possible: an inability to learn that is not explainable by other factors, unsatisfactory relationships with peers and teachers, inappropriate behaviors and feelings, a general mood of unhappiness or depression, and physical symptoms or fears developed in association with school or personal problems.

Classroom behavior is also an important concern for students who do not exhibit behavioral disorders. For instance, professionals may be interested in documenting behaviors related to ADHD such as inattention, distractibility, impulsivity, and hyperactivity. In addition, any student, with or without disabilities, can require educational intervention at some time during his or her school career because of a behavioral difficulty. Consider, for instance, the case of Joyce, the fourth grader with school performance problems.

Joyce

The assessment team continues its study of Joyce by investigating several aspects of classroom behavior. Conduct problems are not a concern—Joyce's teacher had reported earlier that Joyce was a well-behaved student. However, to learn more about Joyce's interactions with peers and her teacher, the team has decided to begin assessment by observing Joyce's interactions in the classroom and in nonacademic activities such as recess.

Ms. Gale, the resource teacher, conducts a series of observations over several days. One purpose of these observations is to determine how Joyce relates to her peers in the fourth grade classroom, and no problems are noted in this area. Joyce appears to have many friends among the boys and girls in her class. She interacts socially with the other students in the classroom, and at recess she is always included in one of the play groups.

The second purpose for observation is study of the classroom learning environment and Joyce's interactions with her teacher, Mr. Harvey. Although Joyce does not exhibit inappropriate classroom behavior, some areas of difficulty are identified. First, Joyce frequently asks the teacher to repeat or further explain the directions for academic tasks. This occurs at an average of three times per hour, a much higher rate than that of other students in the class. In addition, Joyce often requests help from the teacher when attempting to complete her classroom assignments. Again, her request rate is high in comparison to that of other students. Because of Joyce's requests for attention, Mr. Harvey interacts with her more frequently than he does with most other students. Despite this, Joyce often fails to complete her work on time. Seventy percent of her assignments are turned in either late or unfinished.

The *Self-Esteem Index* is administered to Joyce to learn more about her self-concept and self-perceptions. Items are read to Joyce because of her difficulties in reading. Test norms are not used, but Joyce's responses are tallied for the four types of questions included on the *SEI*. In only one area, perceptions of academic competence, do the majority of Joyce's responses indicate a negative self-concept.

Ms. Gale then interviews Joyce about her attitudes toward school. Joyce reports that she likes some parts of school, such as art and recess and sometimes math, but that she is "dumb" in reading and spelling. She says she might like to read stories and books if she knew how, but that reading is "very hard to do." Joyce completes an informal interest inventory with Ms. Gale's assistance. Joyce's least favorite school activities are reading, doing workbooks, and writing her spelling words. For leisure activities, she prefers playing with her friends and her new puppy. She says she does not read for pleasure, but she sometimes looks at magazines and books with pictures.

In reviewing these results, the assessment team concludes that Joyce's peer interactions are satisfactory and her classroom behavior is acceptable. However, the team notes that Joyce appears to have difficulty remembering and understanding the directions for classroom assignments. Joyce's difficulties may be due in part to problems in memory and in part to the difficulty level of her class-

room work. Thus, the team suggests that Joyce's classroom teacher provide her with less-difficult assignments in an attempt to decrease her need for assistance and increase her rate of completion. The team also determines that Joyce shows needs in the areas of self-concept and attitude toward school. These needs probably are related to her poor academic performance.

The team has now gathered sufficient information to make a decision about Joyce's eligibility for special education services. School performance problems in reading, spelling, and handwriting have been documented, and the disability of learning disabilities has been substantiated through discrepancy analysis and the identification of deficits in memory, memorization strategies, and fine motor coordination. Mental retardation, sensory impairments, and behavioral disorders have been ruled out as causes of Joyce's difficulties in academic achievement. Given these data, the team concludes that Joyce meets eligibility criteria for programs for students with learning disabilities. The next steps in assessment will focus on gathering data about Joyce's specific instructional needs to plan her individualized program.

STUDY GUIDE

REVIEW QUESTIONS

1. Assessment information about classroom behavior is used to make eligibility decisions and to plan classroom intervention programs. (True or False)
2. What are three areas of classroom behavior that may be assessed?
3. Which of the following statements is false?
   a. One of the disabilities included under the 1997 IDEA Amendments is emotional disturbance.
   b. In the field of emotional disturbance, there is a lack of consensus about both terminology and definition.
   c. There are several theoretical models of behavior disorders.
   d. School practices in the assessment and treatment of students with behavior problems are most influenced by the psychoanalytic model.

4. Check each of the assessment devices and procedures that can be used to gather information about classroom behavior.

_____ a. Behavior rating scales and checklists

_____ b. Individual tests of intellectual performance

_____ c. Self-concept measures and sociograms

_____ d. Observations of student behavior and student-teacher interactions

_____ e. Measures of reading, mathematics, and study skills

_____ f. Environmental checklists

_____ g. Test of memory, perception, and attention

5. Rating scales and checklists are used to obtain information about the student's behavior from informants such as _____ , _____ , and _____ .

6. Most of the behavior rating scales and checklists designed to identify students with conduct disorders are based upon the same set of problem behaviors. (True or False)

7. Match the assessment device or procedure in Column A with the description in Column B.

Column A	*Column B*
a. Behavioral observation	____ Teachers, parents, students themselves, and students' peers act as informants
b. *Social Skills Rating System*	____ A self-report scale for students that assesses self-perceptions
c. *Behavior Evaluation Scale-2*	____ Teachers and parents rate inattention, impulsivity, and hyperactivity
d. *Attention Deficit Disorders Evaluation Scale*	____ Its rating scales address problem behaviors, social skills, and academic competence
e. *Multidimensional Self Concept Scale*	____ Based on the federal definition of emotional disturbance
f. *Behavior Rating Profile* (2nd ed.)	____ A very flexible technique used to study a wide range of student and teacher behaviors

8. Conducting a classroom observation requires several steps. The first step is, *Describe the behavior to be observed.* What are the other four steps?

9. To find out about how a particular student is perceived by his or her classmates, _____ techniques can be used. For example, the teacher can ask each student to nominate the peers he or she would most like to play with during recess.

10. Find the true statement or statements.

a. Measures of personality are often used in the assessment of classroom behavior because they provide educationally relevant information.

b. In ecological assessment, the student is considered to be the source of the learning problem.

c. Among the concerns in the study of the student's learning environment are behavioral expectations, instructional demands, student-teacher interactions, and the physical environment of the classroom.

d. When assessing the instructional environment, consider the classroom curriculum and the instructional methods, materials, and learning activities used to teach that curriculum.

11. If the special education team finds that a student with average intelligence performs in the low average or below average range in academic achievement *and* in one or more areas of classroom behavior, what conclusion can be drawn?

a. The student may be eligible for special education services.

b. The student should receive counseling or psychotherapy services.

   c. The student is not eligible for special education services.

   d. The student should be returned to the general education classroom.

ACTIVITIES

1. Locate one of the measures of student behavior described in this chapter. Examine its manual for information on standardization procedures, reliability, and validity. Check the *Mental Measurements Yearbook* series for a review of the measure.

2. Administer a measure such as the *Behavior Rating Profile* (2nd ed.). Calculate the scores produced and analyze the results.

3. Construct a checklist for use by students to assess one of the following:

   a. Self-concept

   b. Attitude toward school

   c. Interactions with teachers

   d. Peer relationships

4. Design a questionnaire or an interview procedure for use with teachers to find out about the major instructional characteristics of the classroom learning environment.

5. Talk with school personnel in your area to see how they go about assessing students with behavioral disorders. Do they use behavior rating scales or checklists? If so, which ones? Is the student's classroom behavior observed as part of the assessment process? How does the assessment team go about gathering information from teachers and parents? Is the classroom learning environment considered as a possible contributor to the student's behavioral difficulties? How is the impact of the learning environment assessed?

DISCUSSION QUESTIONS

1. Describe how classroom behavior can affect students' performance in subjects such as reading, mathematics, handwriting, and composition.

2. One of the areas of debate in the field of behavioral disorders is definition of the condition. Identify the essential components of a definition of this disability, and for each component, prepare a list of relevant assessment procedures.

3. Two major approaches to the identification of behavioral disorders are direct observation of student behavior and reliance on the information provided by informants such as teachers and parents. Discuss the pros and cons of each approach, and tell why both are necessary for a balanced picture of the student's current behavioral status.

4. Explain the rationale for assessing the student's environment as a possible contributor to behavioral problems. Consider classroom instructional demands and the behavioral expectations that teachers hold for students.

PART IV

ASSESSMENT OF
ACADEMIC AREAS

READING

Teachers, parents, and the American citizenry place great value on literacy, and reading is considered to be the most important of the basic literacy skills. In the elementary grades, much of the curriculum focuses on skill acquisition in reading, and in the secondary grades, reading is a major vehicle for the presentation of information in content area subjects. In our society, people are expected to be proficient readers; illiteracy is a definite handicap.

Reading is often an area of difficulty for students with disabilities. Young students may not learn the basic skills of reading at the expected rate; they may fall far behind their classmates in their ability to decode and understand the written word. Older students who are even further behind in reading may lack the skills needed to use reading as a tool for learning other skills and subjects.

Once students are found eligible for special education services, the focus in assessment shifts to instructional planning. The question that guides this phase of assessment is, *What are the student's educational needs?* Because reading is often an area of need for students with mild disabilities, the assessment team may ask, *What is the student's current level of reading achievement? What are the student's strengths and weaknesses in the various skill areas of reading?*

At this level of questioning, the team is concerned more about the student's ability to perform important reading tasks than about how performance compares with that of other students. Although norm-referenced information can be useful in determining which reading skills are areas of need, criterion-referenced information and other types of informal data provide specific descriptions of the student's current status in skill development. Consider, for example, the assessment team's plans for evaluating the reading skills of Joyce. Joyce is the fourth grader described in the last few chapters who was recently found eligible for special education services for students with learning disabilities.

Joyce

Joyce's problem in reading is one of the reasons she was referred for special education assessment by Mr. Harvey, her fourth grade teacher. Joyce is unable to read any of the fourth grade texts in her classroom, and she is now working in a beginning third grade reading book. Results of individual achievement tests such as the *PIAT-R/NU* confirmed that Joyce's reading performance is below that expected for her age and grade. Joyce considers reading one of her least favorite of school subjects; she feels that she is "dumb" in reading.

The assessment team believes that instruction in reading will be an important part of Joyce's individual education program. Evaluation of Joyce's current reading skills will begin with administration of the *Woodcock Reading Mastery Tests-Revised/Normative Update,* a norm-referenced measure that evaluates several components of the reading process including sight word vocabulary, word attack skills, and passage comprehension. In addition, an informal reading inventory will be administered to gather information about Joyce's oral reading skills and her ability to derive meaning from the material she reads.

Then informal assessment strategies will be selected to further explore the particular reading skills that appear to be areas of weakness for Joyce. For example, if sight word vocabulary seems to be a need, the team could devise a criterion-referenced test to assess Joyce's mastery of standard lists of sight words for first, second, and third grade students. Or, if comprehension skills are a concern, the team could analyze the types of errors Joyce makes in her attempts to answer comprehension questions.

The results obtained from these assessments will be used to develop part of the individualized special education program for Joyce.

CONSIDERATIONS IN ASSESSMENT OF READING

Of all academic skills, reading is most often the subject of special education assessment. For many educators, reading is one of the most critical of all school subjects, particularly in the elementary cur-

---

Individualized Assessment Plan

For: *Joyce Dewey*   *4*   *10-0*   *12/1/00*   *Ms. Gale*
      Student's Name   Grade   Age   Date   Coordinator

Reason for Referral: Difficulty keeping up with fourth grade work in reading, spelling, and handwriting.

Assessment Question	Assessment Procedure	Person Responsible	Date/Time
What is the student's current level of reading achievement?	*Woodcock Reading Mastery Tests-Revised/Normative Update*	Ms. Gale, Resource Teacher	1/10/01, 10 A.M.
	Informal reading inventory such as the *Analytical Reading Inventory* (6th ed.)	Ms. Gale, Resource Teacher	1/11/01, 9 A.M.
What are the student's strengths and weaknesses in the various skill areas of reading?	Error analysis of oral reading responses on formal tests	Ms. Gale, Resource Teacher	1/11/01, 2 P.M.
	Additional informal strategies, selected on the basis of results of formal testing	Ms. Gale, Resource Teacher	To be determined

---

riculum that focuses on the acquisition of basic skills. In the secondary grades, students are expected to use their reading skills to gain information in subject areas such as English, history, and the sciences. Because many special students do not meet these expectations, reading is a major concern in special education assessment.

Purposes

Students' reading skills are assessed for several reasons. In determining eligibility for special education programs, overall school performance is investigated, and reading is an important component of school achievement. In addition, general education teachers monitor their students' progress in reading. Group achievement tests include subtests to evaluate reading skills, and reading proficiency is one of the minimum competencies assessed by many schools and districts for grade advancement and high school graduation.

In special education, reading skills are assessed not only for determining program eligibility, but also for planning instruction, and that is the focus of this chapter. Information from general achievement tests such as the *PIAT-R/NU*, the *WIAT*, or the *Woodcock-Johnson-R* is insufficient. It is necessary to gather additional data about the student's specific strengths and weaknesses to describe current levels of reading performance. It then becomes possible to project annual goals for the student and specify instructional objectives.

Reading assessment does not stop when the student's individualized educational program has been planned. Special educators begin to monitor the student's progress in acquiring targeted skills, and in ongoing assessment, data are gathered on a weekly or even a daily basis. Reading assessment continues throughout the student's special education program, if reading is a focus of specialized instruction. At least once a year, the educational plan is reviewed, and evaluation data are gathered to determine the student's current levels of reading achievement.

Skill Areas

Reading is a complex process involving many skills. There is continuing debate over the nature of the reading process, but most experts acknowledge that reading involves the recognition and decoding of printed text and the comprehension of that text as meaningful information. According to Schreiner (1983), "The act of reading consists of two separate but interrelated stages: (a) decoding or pronouncing the printed elements and (b) assigning some meaning to these same elements" (p. 71).

Three divergent models of proficient reading have been proposed (Chall & Stahl, 1982). These models differ in the amount of importance they attach to text and meaning, two aspects of the reading process. In the *bottom-up model,* it is hypothesized that proficient readers proceed from text to meaning; first, individual letters and words are perceived and decoded, and then comprehension of the text's meaning takes place. Reading is considered a text-driven or stimulus-driven activity; it depends on the reader's skill in lower-level processes such as word recognition. In contrast, the *top-down model* emphasizes what are considered the higher-level processes of comprehension. The skilled reader relies on prior knowledge and previous experience, questioning and hypothesis testing, and comprehension of the meaning of textual material rather than decoding of individual text elements. The third model is the *interactive model,* which emphasizes both text and meaning. In this model, reading is viewed as "an interactive process where the reader strategically shifts between the text and what he already knows to construct his response" (Walker, 1992, p. 7).

The debate over the relative importance of text versus meaning or decoding versus comprehension carries over into the classroom and the strategies selected for reading instruction. Traditional approaches to reading instruction tend to be skills-based (i.e., bottom-up). Beginning instruction focuses on the development of decoding skills; comprehension skills are not emphasized until learners have some facility with decoding. Examples are traditional basal reader programs, phonics-based approaches, linguistic methods, and programmed instruction.

A newer approach, whole language instruction, is based upon the top-down and interactive models of reading. Reading is not broken down into subskills such as decoding. In fact, reading is integrated with the other language arts (speaking, listening, and writing). Whole language is often described as a philosophy rather than an instructional approach (Westby, 1992); in this philosophy, "Language is a natural phenomenon and literacy is promoted through natural, purposeful language functions" (Lapp & Flood, 1992, p. 458). In the whole language classroom, language learning takes place in a social context in which students use language for real (i.e., authentic) purposes. Students read whole texts, not fragments, and those texts tend to be children's literature rather than stories constructed solely for inclusion in textbooks. Throughout, meaning and motivation are emphasized; the development of isolated skills is deemphasized. Despite the popularity of whole language, research results do not point to the superiority of this approach over basal reader programs (e.g., Stahl & Miller, 1989). In addition, authors such as Lerner, Cousin, and Richeck (1992) and Mather (1992) warn that students with mild disabilities will require supplementary skills instruction if they are to succeed in a whole language classroom.

In recent years, experts have come to recommend a combined approach to reading instruction, one that emphasizes the development of abilities not only in the decoding of print but also in the comprehension of textual meaning. The recent report of the National Research Council's Committee on the Prevention of Reading Difficulties in Young Children (Snow, Burns, & Griffin, 1998) describes the reading process in this way:

> Reading as a cognitive and psycholinguistic activity requires the use of form (the written code) to obtain meaning (the message to be understood), with the context of the reader's purpose (for learning, for enjoyment, for insight). (p. 33)

Another new direction is the interest in phonological processing and its relationship to the acquisition of beginning reading skills. Lerner (2000) describes the readiness skill of phonological awareness as "the ability to recognize that the words we hear are composed of individual sounds within the word" (p. 268). Because failure to develop phonological processing abilities can impede the acquisition of beginning reading skills, it is believed that young children with potential problems in this area should be identified so that they can receive appropriate training (Torgesen & Barker, 1995; Wagner & Torgesen, 1987). To this end, several measures of phonological processing skills have been developed in recent years.

In the assessment of reading itself (rather than reading readiness skills), traditional measures tend to be skills-based. They focus on the student's ability to decode text and respond to questions about the meaning of the text he or she has read. As Garner (1983) observed, these measures are product-oriented, and they are based on a bottom-up view of the reading act. Reading tests and inventories do not stress the interaction between the reader and the text. Thus, informal assessment strategies are needed to gather information about the student's background knowledge, language facility, knowledge of text structure, and the metacognitive strategies he or she chooses to use when interacting with text (Samuels, 1983).

Formal reading tests and inventories typically include measures of students' decoding and comprehension skills. Decoding skills are word recognition skills; decoding occurs when a student looks at a word, or the letters that make up the word, and then pronounces the word. Decoding can be accomplished in several ways. Words that are familiar to the student may be recognized by sight; such words are called sight words or sight vocabulary. When words are unfamiliar, the student may attempt to use phonic analysis. The student looks at each letter, or grapheme; recalls the sound, or phoneme, associated with the letter; and blends the sequence of sounds into a word. Another method of decoding unfamiliar words is structural analysis. In this method, words are broken into syllables to analyze prefixes, suffixes, root words, and endings. In the third approach to decoding, the context of the sentence or paragraph in which the unfamiliar word appears is the subject of analysis. The student uses the meaning of the passage and the grammatical structure of the text as aids in word recognition. Phonic, structural, and contextual analyses are not necessarily independent strategies; students can use one, two, or all three of these methods to decode an unfamiliar word.

Decoding skills are assessed in several ways by reading tests and inventories. One typical method is to present students with a list of words to read aloud. The task may be untimed to allow students the opportunity to use phonic and structural analysis skills. However, tasks are timed if the purpose is to assess sight vocabulary or if the speed of decoding is a concern. Lists of phonetically regular words or nonsense words may be used to evaluate the student's ability to apply phonic analysis skills. Nonsense words force students to analyze each word rather than relying upon sight recognition. Another common method of assessing decoding involves the reading of connected text rather than isolated words. Students are presented with sentences or paragraphs to read aloud. Passage reading provides students with the opportunity to use contextual analysis skills as well as other methods of decoding. Also, it becomes possible to observe the student's oral reading fluency and phrasing and his or her rate of reading connected text.

On traditional reading tests and inventories, comprehension skills are assessed by asking students questions about material they have just read. Students may read the text silently or orally, depending upon whether decoding skills are also under study. The text may be a sentence, a paragraph, or a series of paragraphs making up a story or essay. Comprehension questions may be multiple-choice or completion items, but most typically, the student provides oral responses to open-ended questions. Comprehension questions may probe the student's understanding of the literal meaning of the passage or require inferential thinking and critical analysis (Bartel, 1986b). For example, students may be asked to recall the details of the passage, remember a sequence of events, state the main ideas, explain the meaning of vocabulary words, make judgments, draw conclusions, or evaluate ideas or actions.

The ability to use reading skills in everyday situations is an area rarely included on measures of reading performance; informal techniques are needed to evaluate students' ability to apply their skills in decoding and comprehension to real reading tasks. Reading is a useful skill only when the student is able to read quickly and accurately enough to use it as a tool to gain new information. For example, in everyday life, readers apply their skills when they read signs, posters, letters, magazines and newspapers, television schedules, and the like. These important applications of reading should not be neglected in assessment.

Current Practices

In schools today, the assessment of reading achievement is common practice both in general and special education. Because of the high interest in reading and the complexity of this skill area, a great number and variety of measures and techniques are available to assess reading performance.

Academic achievement tests typically include one or more subtests designed to evaluate students' mastery of reading skills. This is true both for the group-administered achievement measures used in general education and for the individual tests preferred in special education. The school performance measures described in Chapter 7 each contain at least one reading achievement measure.

Norm-referenced reading tests are more directly related to instructional planning. Sometimes called diagnostic reading tests, these measures survey several subskills within the broad area of reading to identify specific strengths and weaknesses. Because these tests are norm-referenced, the information they provide is comparative.

There are a number of reading tests available, and these vary somewhat in the range of skills they assess. Some tests are designed for comprehensive assessment of the reading process and include measures of several of the important reading skills. One example is the *Woodcock Reading Mastery Tests-Revised/Normative Update*. Other measures concentrate on a particular component of reading. There are tests that assess only comprehension skills and others that assess only word recognition skills. On some measures, oral reading is the concern, whereas on others it is silent reading. The majority of reading tests are administered individually to allow testers the opportunity to observe students' performance.

Another type of measure often used in reading assessment is the informal reading inventory. Reading inventories are made up of graded word lists and graded reading selec-

tions. For instance, an inventory might contain a series of word lists and passages ranging from a primer reading level up to grade 8 reading level. Students begin by reading material at the lower grade levels; they continue reading until the material becomes too difficult to decode and/or to comprehend. These measures are grade-referenced, not norm-referenced. The standard of comparison is the grade level of the material the student is reading, not the performance of other students. There are several informal reading inventories available.

Inventories are only one type of informal strategy used in reading assessment. There are a great many informal assessment tools for reading, and these represent all of the standard types of measures and techniques. Among the most commonly used are criterion-referenced tests of specific reading objectives, error analysis of students' oral reading performance, teacher checklists, diagnostic teaching, and clinical reading interviews. Informal techniques are also used to investigate the classroom learning environment and its relationship to students' reading performance.

Table 11–1 provides a listing of several of the reading measures used in special education. Each is categorized by type—formal test, informal reading inventory, criterion-referenced test, or curriculum-based measure—and information is included about the grades or ages for which each measure is intended and whether administration is group or individual. In addition, the table notes if the measure is designed to assess decoding skills, comprehension skills, or both.

This chapter describes each of the major strategies used in schools today for the assessment of reading. Formal reading tests are discussed first, and the next sections introduce three of these. Included are a comprehensive measure of reading, the *Woodcock Reading Mastery Tests-Revised/Normative Update,* and two measures that each concentrate on one major reading skill, the *Gray Oral Reading Tests* (3rd ed.) and the *Test of Reading Comprehension* (3rd ed.). The following sections describe formal measures of phonological processing followed by informal reading inventories and other informal assessment strategies.

TABLE 11–1

Measures of Reading

NAME (AUTHOR)	AGES OR GRADES	TYPE OF MEASURE*	GROUP OR INDIVIDUAL	SKILL AREA(S) ASSESSED	
				DECODING	COMPREHENSION
Analytical Reading Inventory (6th ed.) (Woods & Moe, 1999)	Primer to grade 9 functioning level	IRI	Individual	X	X
BRIGANCE® Diagnostic Assessment of Basic Skills, Spanish Edition (Brigance, 1983)	Kindergarten to grade 8	CRT	Individual	X	X
BRIGANCE® Diagnostic Comprehensive Inventory of Basic Skills-Revised (Brigance, 1999)	Pre-kindergarten to grade 9	CRT	Individual	X	X
BRIGANCE® Diagnostic Inventory of Essential Skills (Brigance, 1981)	Grade 6 to adult education	CRT	Individual	X	X
Classroom Reading Inventory (8th ed.) (Silvaroli, 1997)	Preprimer to grade 8 functioning level	IRI	Individual	X	X
Diagnostic Reading Scales (Spache, 1981)	Grades 1–8 functioning level	NRT	Individual	X	X
Durrell Analysis of Reading Difficulty (3rd ed.) (Durrell & Catterson, 1980)	Grades 1–6	NRT	Individual	X	X
Ekwall/Shanker Reading Inventory (3rd ed.) (Ekwall & Shanker, 1993)	Preprimer to grade 9 functioning level	IRI	Individual	X	X
English-Español Reading Inventory for the Classroom (Flynt & Cooter, 1999)	Preprimer to grade 9 functioning level	IRI	Individual	X	X
Flynt-Cooter Reading Inventory for the Classroom (3rd ed.) (Flynt & Cooter, 1998)	Preprimer to grade 9 functioning level	IRI	Individual	X	X
Formal Reading Inventory (Wiederholt, 1986)	Ages 7–18	NRT	Individual	X	X
Gates-McKillop-Horowitz Reading Diagnostic Test (Gates, McKillop, & Horowitz, 1981)	Grades 1–6	NRT	Individual	X	X
Gilmore Oral Reading Test (Gilmore & Gilmore, 1968)	Grades 1–8	NRT	Individual	X	X
Gray Oral Reading Tests (3rd ed.) (Wiederholt & Bryant, 1992)	Ages 6–19	NRT	Individual	X	X
Gray Oral Reading Tests-Diagnostic (Bryant & Wiederholt, 1991)	Ages 6–13	NRT	Individual	X	X

(Continued)

TABLE 11-1
Measures of Reading—Continued

NAME (AUTHOR)	AGES OR GRADES	TYPE OF MEASURE*	GROUP OR INDIVIDUAL	SKILL AREA(S) ASSESSED	
				DECODING	COMPREHENSION
Hudson Education Skills Inventory (Hudson, Colson, Welch, Banikowski, & Mehring, 1989)	Grades K-12	CRT	Individual	X	X
Informal Reading Inventory (5th ed.) (Burns & Roe, 1999)	Preprimer to grade 12 functioning level	IRI	Individual	X	X
Monitoring Basic Skills Progress: Basic Reading (2nd ed.) (Fuchs, Hamlett, & Fuchs, 1997)	Grades 1-7	CBM	Individual	X	X
Reading Miscue Inventory (Goodman, Watson, & Burke, 1987)	Grades 1-8+ functioning level	IRI	Individual	X	X
Slosson Oral Reading Test-Revised (Slosson & Nicholson, 1990)	Preschool to adult	NRT	Individual	X	
Standardized Reading Inventory (2nd ed.) (Newcomer, 1999)	Ages 6-14	NRT	Individual	X	X
Stanford Diagnostic Reading Test, Fourth Edition (Karlsen & Gardner, 1995)	Grades 1.5-13	NRT	Group	X	X
Stieglitz Informal Reading Inventory (2nd ed.) (Stieglitz, 1997)	Preprimer to grade 9 functioning level	IRI	Individual	X	X
Test of Early Reading Ability (2nd ed.) (Reid, Hresko, & Hammill, 1989)	Ages 3-10	NRT	Individual	X	X
Test of Reading Comprehension (3rd ed.) (Brown, Hammill, & Wiederholt, 1995)	Ages 7-18	NRT	Individual	X	X
Test of Word Reading Efficiency (Torgesen, Wagner, & Rashotte, 1999)	Grades 1-12+; ages 6-25	NRT	Individual, small group	X	X
Woodcock Diagnostic Reading Battery (Woodcock, 1997)	Grades kindergarten-16.9; ages 4-90+	NRT	Individual	X	
Woodcock Reading Mastery Tests-Revised/Normative Update (Woodcock, 1998)	Grades kindergarten-16.9; ages 5-75+	NRT	Individual	X	X

*NRT stands for norm-referenced test, IRI for informal inventory, CRT for criterion-referenced test, and CBM for curriculum-based measure.

Woodcock Reading Mastery Tests-Revised/ Normative Update (WRMT-R/NU)

R. W. Woodcock (1998)

Type: Norm-referenced test

Major Content Areas: Reading readiness, basic reading skills (word identification and word attack), word and passage comprehension

Type of Administration: Individual

Administration Time: 30–45 minutes

Age/Grade Levels: Grades K through 16.9 (college senior), ages 5-0 through 75+

Types of Scores: Grade and age equivalents, percentile ranks, standard scores, and Relative Performance Index scores for subtests and clusters

Computer Aids: *WRMT-R/NU ASSIST*

Typical Uses: A broad-based reading test for the identification of strengths and weaknesses in reading skill development

Cautions: Care should be taken in the interpretation of results because of the unusual assessment tasks used to evaluate comprehension. More information is needed about the concurrent validity of the *WRMT-R/NU*. Hand-scoring the test is time-consuming if results such as standard score ranges are desired.

Publisher: American Guidance Service (www.agsnet.com)

WOODCOCK READING MASTERY TESTS-REVISED/NORMATIVE UPDATE

The *Woodcock Reading Mastery Tests-Revised/ Normative Update (WRMT-R/NU)* is a norm-referenced measure that is used to pinpoint students' strengths and weaknesses. The original version of this test was published in 1973, revised in 1987, and a new version with updated norms was published in 1998. According to its manual, the *WRMT-R/NU* is "suitable for a variety of applications in both educational and noneducational settings" (p. 10); its uses include clinical assessment and diagnosis, individual program planning, selection and placement, and research.

Two forms of the *WRMT-R/NU* are available: Form G and Form H. The forms are not identical. Form G, the complete battery, is made up of four tests of reading achievement and a readiness section; Form H contains only alternate forms of the reading achievement tests. The four subtests common to both forms are:

- *Word Identification.* Students are shown rows of individual words (e.g., *is, listen*), and they must pronounce each word within about 5 seconds.
- *Word Attack.* Nonsense words and syllables (e.g., *ift, lundy*) are presented instead of real words. The student reads each aloud.
- *Word Comprehension.* This subtest includes three parts. On Antonyms, the student reads a word aloud and supplies its opposite. On Synonyms, the student reads a word and supplies a word that means the same. On Analogies, the student reads a row of three words representing an incomplete analogy (e.g., *mother–big, baby–__*) and supplies the missing word.
- *Passage Comprehension.* This subtest uses a cloze procedure to assess comprehension skills.

The student is presented with a brief passage with one word omitted. The student reads the passage silently and then attempts to supply the missing word. Easier passages are accompanied by drawings.

Form G also contains three measures of reading readiness:

- *Visual-Auditory Learning.* This subtest, borrowed from the *Woodcock-Johnson Psycho-Educational Battery,* is a "miniature 'learning-to-read' task" (p. 4). The student is shown visual symbols that the tester labels. The student repeats the word associated with each symbol, then attempts to read sentences composed of the symbols.
- *Letter Identification.* Individual letters are arranged in rows, and the student must say the name (or sound) of each. Letters appear in upper- and lowercase, in manuscript and cursive, and in a variety of type styles.
- *Supplementary Letter Checklist.* This two-part checklist (Capital Letters and Lowercase Letters) is a supplementary informal measure that can be used to determine a student's ability to give either the names or the sounds of the letters. The only results are raw scores.

The *WRMT-R/NU* is designed for students from kindergarten through college, but young children and nonreaders may experience success only on the readiness subtests. English-language skills are particularly important for the Word Comprehension and Passage Comprehension subtests, in which students must supply missing words. Students respond orally on all *WRMT-R/NU* subtests; no writing is required.

Technical Quality

In 1995–96, the American Guidance Service renormed several of its tests including the *WRMT-R,* the *Peabody Individual Achievement Test-Revised* (discussed in Chapter 7), and the *KeyMath-Revised* (discussed in Chapter 12). In all cases, renorming was carried out with a sample of 3,184 students in kindergarten through grade 12 and 245 young adults (ages 18–22). Approximately half of the students were males and half were females. Students were excluded if they

were not proficient in English, but students in gifted and special education programs were included. The sample was selected to resemble the U.S. population as reflected in 1994 U.S. Census data. The final sample appears to resemble the nation as a whole in terms of geographic region, parental education level (an indicator of socioeconomic status), and race or ethnic group. Also, the sample appears representative of K–12 students who receive services in special and gifted education. For example, 5.9% of the sample was identified as learning disabled, similar to the 5.5% figure reported by the U.S. Department of Education (1995).

The *WRMT-R/NU* appears most appropriate for students in grades kindergarten through grade 12 and individuals aged 5 to 22. Norms for older persons (grades 13–16 and ages 23–75+) were not updated in the 1995–96 renorming. According to the *WRMT-R/NU* manual, reading performance among K–12 students in the United States has changed little since the test was last revised, except for one segment of the population:

> Overall, comparison of the NU and original WRMT-R norms indicates little change in the level of performance of students who are average to above average for their grade or age, but a decline in the performance of students who are below average. (p. 135)

In evaluating technical quality, it is also important to consider the reliability and validity of a test. However, the manual for the normative update only provides information about previous versions of the test—the 1987 *WRMT-R* and the 1973 *WRMT.* Split-half reliability of the *WRMT-R* is generally adequate. For subtest and cluster scores on Forms G and H, most reliability coefficients fell above .80. Low coefficients were found for grade 5 students on Letter Identification (.34) and the Readiness Cluster (.54); Passage Comprehension was somewhat low for both grade 5 (.73) and grade 11 (.68) students. Information is also needed on test-retest and alternate form reliability.

Concurrent validity of the *WRMT-R* was studied by examining its relationship to the reading tests of the *Woodcock-Johnson Psycho-*

Educational Battery. Correlations ranging from .85 to .91 were found between total reading scores on these two measures. The manual also presents data to support the relationship of the 1973 *WRMT* with measures such as the reading subtests on the *PIAT* and the *WRAT.* Clearly, further information is needed about the 1998 *WRMT-R/NU* and its relationship to newer measures such as the *PIAT-R/NU,* the *WRAT-3,* and the *Woodcock-Johnson-R.*

Administration Considerations

Although formal training is not required to administer the *WRMT-R/NU,* inexperienced testers should study the test manual, administer at least two practice tests, and be observed and evaluated by an experienced examiner. Practice activities for administration, scoring, and interpretation are provided in the *WRMT-R/NU* manual. The *WRMT-R/NU* is a relatively easy test to administer, although its scoring is somewhat complicated.

Test books are in easel format. Each subtest begins with a tabbed page that contains any special administration information, scoring directions, basal and ceiling rules, and suggested starting points. Starting points are based on the student's estimated reading grade level, not the current grade in school. However, all individuals begin the Visual-Auditory Learning and Word Attack subtests with item one. Sample items are provided for Word Attack, Word Comprehension, and Passage Comprehension.

The *WRMT-R/NU* is set up for administration by page units. The tester always begins with the first item on a test page and continues until the last item is administered. This procedure influences how basals and ceilings are established. On all subtests except Visual-Auditory Learning, the basal is six consecutive items passed, and the ceiling is six consecutive items failed. If it is necessary to move to easier items to establish a basal, the tester first finishes the page on which testing was begun, then moves backwards one page and begins with the first item. Likewise, in locating the ceiling, testing continues to the end of the page, even if the student has already made six consecutive errors. As stated on the Test Record,

the basal is "the first 6 consecutive correct responses that begin with the first item on an easel page," and the ceiling is "the last 6 consecutive failed responses that end with the last item on an easel page."

Test items are scored as they are administered, and on most subtests, correct responses are marked "1" and incorrect responses "0." The Test Record is well designed, and there is ample room to record students' error responses on all subtests. The procedures for the Visual-Auditory Learning subtest are somewhat different from those for the rest of the test. Students' errors are circled, and the numbers of errors are counted. Also, there is no basal or ceiling. Instead, at certain points in the subtest, the tester compares the cumulative number of errors to a cutoff criterion to determine whether to continue testing. For example, after Test Story 4, testing is stopped if the student has made 25 or more errors.

It is not necessary to administer all subtests of the *WRMT-R/NU;* the tester can select any portion of the battery that is of interest. The Word Attack subtest can be omitted (and a score of 0 recorded) if the student earns 0 or 1 on Word Identification. However, the tester may choose to administer Word Attack if there is reason to believe that the student will achieve success. Subtests may be administered in any order.

Results and Interpretation

The *WRMT-R/NU* offers a variety of scores. For each subtest, it is possible to obtain a grade equivalent, age equivalent, percentile rank, Relative Performance Index (RPI), and standard score. *WRMT-R/NU* grade and age scores are extended scales. At the upper and lower ends, percentile rank superscripts are added to make scores more precise. For example, a grade equivalent of K.0^{35} indicates performance at the 35th percentile for beginning kindergarten students. The Relative Performance Index (RPI) score is a ratio; for example, an RPI of 85/90 indicates that the student is expected to perform tasks at 85% mastery that average students of his or her age or grade would perform at 90%

mastery. Several other types of scores are available, including *T*-scores, stanines, normal curve equivalents, and standard scores with a mean of 100 and a standard deviation of 15. It is also possible to construct confidence intervals around scores so that RPI, percentile rank, and standard scores are expressed as ranges.

Subtest scores can be combined into cluster scores. The Readiness Cluster is made up of the two readiness subtests, the Basic Skills Cluster consists of the Word Identification and Word Attack subtests, and the Reading Comprehension Cluster of the two comprehension subtests. The Full Scale Total Reading Cluster is a global score for the four reading achievement tests; the Short Scale Total Reading Cluster includes only Word Identification and Passage Comprehension. The same types of scores that are available for subtests can be computed for clusters.

Figure 11–1 shows a sample Summary of Scores from the *WRMT-R/NU* Test Record. Form G was administered, although the readiness portion was omitted. The shaded area in each block of scores contains what the manual calls optional scores. It would be possible to compute only those in the unshaded area: the RPI and percentile rank. If standard score ranges are desired, however, computation is a lengthier process. The *WRMT-R/NU ASSIST* computer scoring program can be used to minimize scoring time.

The *WRMT-R/NU* offers several profiles that can be plotted to help with interpretation of test results. An Instructional Level Profile appears in Figure 11–2; the results shown are those of the sample case presented in the previous figure. Across the top of the profile is the grade equivalent scale, and the shaded portion of the graph for each subtest indicates the student's instructional range. The lower end corresponds to the student's easy reading level (the grade level at which the student's RPI would be 96/90). The upper end is the difficult reading level corresponding to an RPI of 75/90. The heavy vertical line marks the instructional reading level (RPI 90/90).

The tester can also plot the Percentile Rank Profile and three Diagnostic Profiles: readiness, basic skills, and comprehension. The Diagnostic Profiles show *WRMT-R/NU* results as well as results from the *Woodcock-Johnson Psycho-Educational Battery* (Woodcock & Johnson, 1977) and the *Goldman-Fristoe-Woodcock Auditory Skills Test Battery* (Goldman, Fristoe, & Woodcock, 1976). For example, on the comprehension profile, oral comprehension can be compared with reading comprehension.

Two additional procedures provide more information on specific reading skills. Decoding skills can be analyzed with the Word Attack Error Inventory. The inventory lists skills and sound categories, and items from the Word Attack subtest are linked to appropriate categories. The skill areas included are single consonants and digraphs, consonant blends, vowels, and multisyllabic words. If a student read *wab* as *wid* on the Word Attack subtest, two errors would be marked on the inventory: the short sound of the vowel *a,* and the consonant *b*. It is also possible to look at vocabulary skills as measured by the Word Comprehension subtest. Each item on that test is categorized by the type of vocabulary it assesses: general reading, science-mathematics, social studies, or humanities. The number correct in each category is counted, and the results are plotted on the Content Area portion of the Diagnostic Comprehension Profile.

A useful feature of the *WRMT-R/NU* is the procedure it offers for aptitude-achievement discrepancy analysis. Any subtest or cluster standard score from the *WRMT-R/NU* can serve as the achievement score. Among the tests that can provide the aptitude score are the *WISC-III,* the *K-ABC,* and the *Woodcock-Johnson-R.* The tester consults a table in the manual to determine the expected correlation between the two tests, then finds the expected achievement score in another table. If actual achievement is less than expected, the difference is computed, and another table is used to determine the percentage of the population showing the same or greater discrepancy.

The *WRMT-R/NU* produces many scores, and interpretation should focus on the results most pertinent to the assessment questions under investigation. Standard score ranges help the examiner determine the reading skills in which the student shows low or below average per-

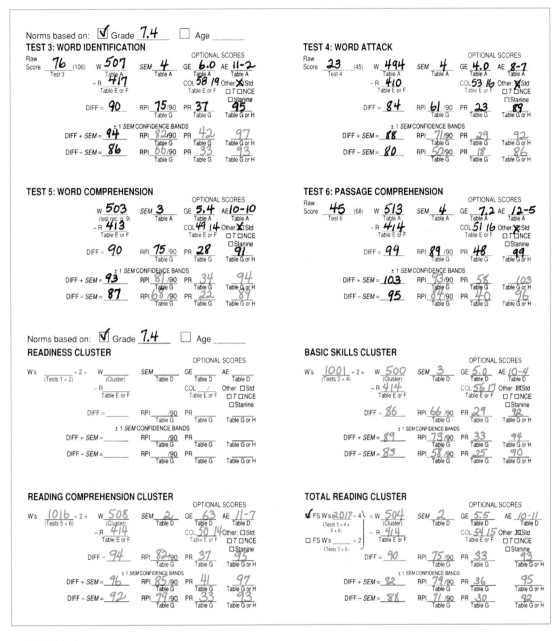

FIGURE 11–1

Sample Summary of Scores from the *Woodcock Reading Mastery Tests-Revised/Normative Update*

Note: From *Woodcock Reading Mastery Tests-Revised/Normative Update, Forms G and H, Examiner's Manual* (p. 47) by R. W. Woodcock, 1998, Circle Pines, MN: American Guidance Service. Copyright 1998 by American Guidance Service, Inc. Reprinted by permission.

formance in comparison to peers. The Relative Performance Index provides information about the student's expected mastery relative to grade peers; this score may be of interest when the assessment team is considering the advisability of including students with disabilities in general education classes for reading instruction. The instructional range may prove helpful in estimating the student's current instructional level on various reading tasks.

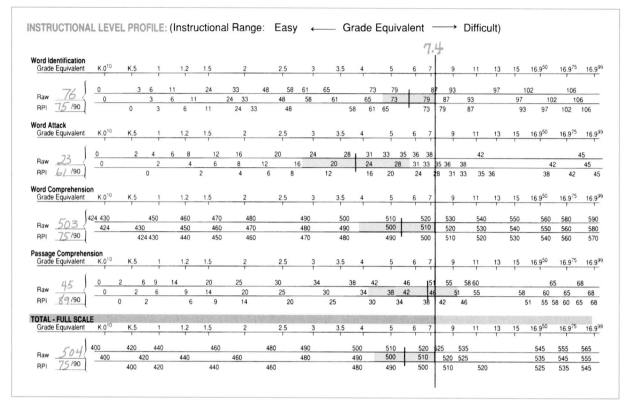

FIGURE 11-2

Sample Instructional Level Profile from the *Woodcock Reading Mastery Tests-Revised/Normative Update*

Note: From *Woodcock Reading Mastery Tests-Revised/Normative Update, Forms G and H, Examiner's Manual* (p. 48) by R. W. Woodcock, 1998, Circle Pines, MN: American Guidance Service. Copyright 1998 by American Guidance Service, Inc. Reprinted by permission.

It is also possible to compare performance in different reading skill areas. In the area of decoding, results of the Word Identification subtest, a measure of sight vocabulary, can be compared with results of the Word Attack subtest, a measure of phonic and structural analysis. Results of the two comprehension subtests can also be contrasted. However, these subtests are not traditional measures of comprehension skills. Word Comprehension, in addition to being a measure of vocabulary, also assesses reasoning ability in its analogies portion. Passage Comprehension employs a cloze procedure to evaluate students' understanding of the material they have read; this procedure is quite different from the comprehension tasks used in classroom reading instruction.

Further information about strengths and weaknesses can be gathered by analyzing students' responses to specific test items. The *WRMT-R/NU* provides systems for analysis of word attack errors, vocabulary knowledge, and skill in identification of upper- and lowercase letters. The tester might also want to consider the student's responses to items on the Word Identification subtest.

Results of the *WRMT-R/NU* help the professional determine the student's current levels of achievement in reading readiness, basic reading skills, and comprehension. These results are most useful for identifying areas of strengths and educational needs. They also provide valuable direction for further assessment. Informal strategies are used to further investigate weaknesses suggested by *WRMT-R/NU* results and to

---

Gray Oral Reading Tests (3rd ed.) *(GORT-3)*

J. L. Wiederholt & B. R. Bryant (1992)

Type: Norm-referenced test

Major Content Areas: Oral reading speed, accuracy, and comprehension

Type of Administration: Individual

Administration Time: 15–30 minutes

Age/Grade Levels: Ages 6-6 to 18-11

Types of Scores: Percentile ranks, standard scores, Oral Reading Quotient (ORQ)

Computer Aids: N/A

Typical Uses: Identification of strengths and weaknesses in oral reading skills

Cautions: The *GORT-3* is a measure of oral reading skills; some students show better comprehension when reading silently. Results should be interpreted with caution because of the need for further evidence of the validity of this test.

Publisher: PRO-ED (www.proedinc.com)

---

probe skills not assessed (e.g., oral reading of connected text).

GRAY ORAL READING TESTS (THIRD EDITION)

The *Gray Oral Reading Tests* (3rd ed.) *(GORT-3)* assess students' ability to read passages aloud quickly and accurately with adequate comprehension. The current version of this test is the second update of a popular measure developed by William S. Gray (1967). According to the manual, the *GORT-3* is designed to identify students with problems in reading, determine students' strengths and weaknesses, and document progress in reading.

Two alternate forms of the *GORT-3* are available: Forms A and B. Each contains 13 reading passages that increase in difficulty, and each passage is followed by five comprehension questions. The task remains the same throughout the test. The student reads the passage aloud as the tester records errors and times the student. Then the tester reads comprehension questions and four possible answers as the student follows along; the student selects the correct response (A,

B, C, or D). Several types of questions are asked, including those that assess literal, inferential, critical, and affective comprehension.

The *GORT-3* is designed for students ages 6-6 to 18-11, but beginning readers may experience difficulty because the first passages are written at a grade 1 (rather than a preprimer) readability level. English-language skills are a necessity for success on the *GORT-3*. Writing is not required; all student responses are oral.

Technical Quality

The *GORT-3* was standardized with 1,485 students from 18 states. The sample appears to approximate the national population in terms of sex, urban-rural residence, race, ethnicity, and geographic region. No information is provided on whether students with disabilities or non-English-speaking students were included as part of the norm group.

Internal consistency reliability is adequate for all scores on the *GORT-3*. Alternate form reliability is also acceptable for all scores except Comprehension ($r = .62$). Concurrent validity was studied by examining the relationship between *GORT-3* results and those from other measures of reading. In general, moderate correlations were found between the *GORT-3* Oral Reading Quotient and equivalent scores on the *Formal Reading Inventory,* the *Iowa Tests of Educational Development,* the *California Achievement Test,* and the *Diagnostic Achievement Battery* (2nd ed.); coefficients ranged from .40 to .74. Also, the *GORT-3* total test score appears related to teachers' ratings of students' reading skills (.63 to .74). However, more information is needed about the validity of this test, particularly its relationship to individual tests of reading commonly used in special education assessment.

Administration Considerations

Because there is only one type of task on the *GORT-3,* administration is straightforward. Suggested starting points are provided by grade level. For example, students in grades 3 and 4 should begin with Story 3. Testing begins with the suggested story and continues until two sets of basals and ceilings are reached: one set for the Comprehension Score and the other for the Passage Score. The Comprehension Score basal and ceiling are based upon the student's performance on the comprehension questions following each passage. In contrast, the Passage Score basal and ceiling are determined by considering the rate at which the student reads the passage and the number of oral reading errors he or she makes.

For each passage administered, the tester reads a sentence or two about the story as motivation, then tells the student to begin reading orally from the appropriate page in the Student Book. When the student has completed the passage, the tester turns to the page containing comprehension questions and reads these aloud as the student looks on. The tester records the student's responses.

When the student is reading orally, the tester must do two things: (a) record any errors the student makes, and (b) time how many seconds it takes the student to read each passage. Two systems are available for recording errors. In the first system, a slash mark (/) is used to denote deviations from the printed page. A slash is made on each word that is not read correctly and in the space between words when errors such as additions, repetitions, or self-corrections occur. Each word and space can account for only one error. Thus, if the student read "The big cat" as "The great

really big cat," only one error would be marked in the space between "The" and "big." If the student hesitates, the word is supplied by the tester and counted as an error. Students are allowed 10 seconds to sound out a word but only 5 seconds if there is no audible attempt to read the word.

The second recording system is used if the tester wants to analyze student errors. It combines slashes with verbatim recording. The manual contains guidelines for marking the Examiner Record Booklet. Tape-recording the student's oral reading for later analysis is allowed, although print deviations should be marked with a slash during test administration.

Results and Interpretation

Each passage on the *GORT-3* produces four raw scores. The Comprehension raw score is simply the number of comprehension questions answered correctly. The Rate raw score is based upon the time required by the student to read the passage; the Accuracy raw score reflects the number of times the student deviated from the text. Both Rate and Accuracy raw scores range from 1 to 5; they are determined from tables that accompany the passages. The Passage raw score is simply the sum of the Rate and Accuracy scores.

Total test Rate, Accuracy, Passage Score, and Comprehension Score results are then converted to percentile ranks and standard scores. Standard scores are distributed with a mean of 10 and a standard deviation of 3. Two summary scores are available that reflect overall test performance: a percentile rank score and the Oral Reading Quotient (ORQ), a standard score distributed with a mean of 100 and a standard deviation of 15. The standard error of measurement for the ORQ is 3 standard score points at all ages; those for the other four *GORT-3* scores are 1 standard score point.

An important feature of the *GORT-3* is the procedure it provides for analysis of student errors or miscues. A portion of the protocol is used to record each substitution error and categorize the way in which it was similar to the text word. This system is based on the work of the Goodmans (K. S. Goodman, 1969, 1976; Y. Goodman & Burke, 1972). Types of miscues include errors similar in meaning to the text word, errors simi-

Test of Reading Comprehension (3rd ed.) (TORC-3)

V. L. Brown, D. D. Hammill, & J. L. Wiederholt (1995)

Type: Norm-referenced test

Major Content Areas: Silent reading comprehension and vocabulary

Type of Administration: Individual or small group

Administration Time: 30 minutes to 1-1/2 hours

Age/Grade Levels: Age 7-0 to 17-11

Types of Scores: Percentile ranks, standard scores, Reading Comprehension Quotient (RCQ); age and grade equivalents

Computer Aids: N/A

Typical Uses: Identification of strengths and weaknesses in the development of comprehension skills and knowledge of word meanings

Cautions: The *TORC-3* is a measure of silent reading comprehension. To participate in *TORC-3* administration, students must be able to work independently. Testers should take care in scoring this measure; items on several subtests require two responses, and on the Sentence Sequencing subtest, responses can earn 0, 2, 3, 4, or 5 points.

Publisher: PRO-ED (www.proedinc.com)

lar in grammatical function, and errors with graphic/phonemic similarity. Self-corrections are also noted. The number and percentage of each type of miscue are then determined. For example, out of 10 miscues on a particular passage, 5 (or 50%) may have involved words with similar meanings, and 7 (or 70%) words with similar grammatical functions. The *GORT-3* protocol provides space for recording information about other types of miscues (omissions, additions, dialectical variations, and reversals) as well as observations of other reading behaviors.

The *GORT-3* is a useful measure for analyzing students' skills in oral reading. It is not as complete a measure as the *WRMT-R/NU,* but it assesses areas that the *WRMT-R/NU* does not, specifically oral reading of connected text and reading rate. However, the *GORT-3* may underestimate the comprehension skills of those students for whom silent reading improves understanding. Results of the *GORT-3* provide information about strengths and weaknesses related to oral reading, and they are best used to identify areas needing further assessment.

Also of interest is the *Gray Oral Reading Tests-Diagnostic* (Bryant & Wiederholt, 1991), an expanded version of the *GORT-3.* This set of measures assesses oral reading comprehension with passages similar to those on the *GORT-3* and also includes several subtests that evaluate students' decoding skills. These subtests are Decoding, Word Attack, Word Identification, Morphemic Analysis, Contextual Analysis, and Word Ordering.

TEST OF READING COMPREHENSION (THIRD EDITION)

The *Test of Reading Comprehension* (3rd ed.) *(TORC-3)* does not attempt to measure all aspects of the reading process. Instead, it emphasizes comprehension skills, silent reading, and knowledge of word meanings.

The *TORC-3* contains eight subtests. Instructions for each subtest are read to the student, and most subtests include one or two demonstration items. The student reads the test questions silently and then records responses on a separate answer sheet. No time limits are imposed.

It is not necessary to administer the entire battery. However, four subtests are used to determine the Reading Comprehension Quotient, an index of general reading comprehension ability. If this information is desired, the entire General Comprehension Core should be administered.

General Comprehension Core

- *General Vocabulary.* The student is presented with three stimulus words that are related in some way. He or she then considers four possible responses and chooses two that relate to the stimulus words. For example, if the stimulus words are *white, red,* and *green,* the possible responses might be:
  A. *blue*
  B. *sky*
  C. *yellow*
  D. *no*
  The student should select answers A and C.
- *Syntactic Similarities.* In this subtest, the student reads five sentences and chooses the two that are most similar in meaning. In the following example from the *TORC-3* manual, sentences A and D are most similar:
  A. Sam plays.
  B. Sam will not play.
  C. Sam played.
  D. Sam is playing.
  E. Sam is going to play.
- *Paragraph Reading.* Students read six one- or two-paragraph selections and answer five multiple-choice questions about each. The questions require students to select the best title for the passage, recall details, and make inferences and negative inferences. On the negative inference questions, students identify the sentence that does not go with the selection.
- *Sentence Sequencing.* Five sentences that make up a paragraph are listed in random order. The student's task is to determine the sequence in which the sentences should appear. The student responds by writing the letters that correspond to the sentences.

Diagnostic Supplements

- *Mathematics Vocabulary.* As in the first subtest, General Vocabulary, the student is shown three stimulus words that are related in some way. Four possible responses are presented, and the student selects the two that are related to the stimulus words. The vocabulary assessed on this subtest includes numerals, mathematical symbols, number words, and mathematical terms.
- *Social Studies Vocabulary.* The format for this subtest is the same as that for Mathematics Vocabulary, but the words are drawn from social studies.
- *Science Vocabulary.* The format remains the same, but the vocabulary words are drawn from science.
- *Reading the Directions of Schoolwork.* On this subtest, the student reads directions and then attempts to follow them. According to the *TORC-3* manual, "example commands are 'Write your name' and 'Circle the one that does not belong' " (p. 7).

The *TORC-3* is designed for students ages 7-0 to 17-11. The supplementary subtest, Reading the Directions of Schoolwork, is recommended for beginning and remedial readers; norms extend only through age 12-11. The manual points out that because the *TORC-3* requires only silent reading, it is appropriate for students who speak a dialect, those with articulation problems, and deaf students.

On the *TORC-3,* students must be able to work independently. Students answer all questions by writing. Proficiency in taking tests is expected, because students write their answers on a separate answer sheet. Six of the eight subtests are multiple-choice, and students respond by making an *X* on the letter of the correct answer or answers. On Sentence Sequencing, students write letters in blank spaces on the answer sheet. It is possible to allow students to write directly in their test booklets if the separate answer sheet causes difficulties. If students are unable to write, they can respond orally or point to the correct response. The answer sheet is not used for the Reading Directions subtest. Separate pages are provided so that students can draw lines and circles; make check marks; and write words, numbers, and sentences as directed after each question.

Technical Quality

The standardization sample for the third edition of the *TORC* consisted of 1,962 students from 19 states. The sample appears to approximate the national school-age population in terms of sex, urban-rural residence, geographic region, race, and ethnicity. Students with disabilities who were enrolled in general education classes were included; for example, students with learning disabilities make up 6% of the norm group.

Three types of reliability were studied in preparation of this edition of the *TORC*: internal consistency, test-retest, and interrator. All reliability coefficients are satisfactory. Six studies of concurrent validity are described in the manual, including one that used the third edition of the *TORC*. Results indicate a moderate relationship between *TORC* results and those of other measures of reading. For example, correlations between *TORC-3* General Comprehension Core subtest scores and the Broad Reading score from the *Woodcock-Johnson-R* range from .44 to .59. Evidence is also presented to support the *TORC*'s ability to differentiate between average readers and students with reading difficulties. However, additional information is needed about the *TORC-3*'s relationship to reading tests that are commonly used in special education assessment, particularly newer measures such as the *WRMT-R/NU*.

Administration Considerations

Administration of the *TORC-3* requires no special training. However, in learning to administer this test, the manual recommends that professionals should administer the test to at least three different individuals and be observed by someone who is experienced in test administration, scoring, and interpretation.

The *TORC-3* is quite easy to administer. The tester reads the instructions for the subtest to the student, administers available demonstration items, and then allows the student to work independently. Students begin each subtest with item 1 and continue until a ceiling is reached. For most subtests, the ceiling is three errors out of any five consecutive items. There is no ceiling on the Reading Directions subtest; students attempt all items. Testers should consult the manual for specific ceiling rules for the Paragraph Reading and Sentence Sequencing subtests.

Scoring the *TORC-3* is somewhat more difficult. For example, on the five subtests that require students to mark two responses, credit is given only if both responses are correct. Raw scores should be calculated carefully, particularly on Sentence Sequencing. On this subtest, students can earn 0, 2, 3, 4, or 5 points for each question, depending on the order in which they arrange the sentences to form a paragraph.

Results and Interpretation

The *TORC-3* provides standard scores and percentile ranks for each subtest. Subtest standard scores have a mean of 10 and a standard deviation of 3. The Reading Comprehension Quotient (RCQ) is a global score that is indicative of the student's overall skill level in reading comprehension. This score is based on the results of the General Comprehension Core subtests. The RCQ is a standard score distributed with a mean of 100 and a standard deviation of 15. The RCQ and subtest scores are plotted on the *TORC-3* profile, as Figure 11–3 illustrates. These results are for an 8-year-old student who shows low average performance on two *TORC-3* subtests: Mathematics Vocabulary and Science Vocabulary.

More important than classifying students' scores in *TORC-3* interpretation is the identification of strengths and weaknesses in reading comprehension. The general comprehension subtests provide information about the student's ability to comprehend silently read material. The diagnostic subtests assess performance of classroom-related comprehension tasks. Of particular interest with younger elementary students is skill in reading and following written directions. With older elementary students and those in middle and high school, content areas become important, particularly when students are included in general education classes for these subjects.

Section II. TORC-3 Subtest Results											

General Reading Comprehension Core

	RS	AE	GE	%ile	SS
General Vocabulary	15	10-0	5.0	75	12
Syntactic Similarities	4	8-6	3.4	37	9
Paragraph Reading	9	9-3	4.2	50	10
Sentence Sequencing	11	7-9	2.7	37	9
Total of Standard Scores					40
Reading Comprehension Quotient (RCQ)					100

Diagnostic Supplements

	RS	AE	GE	%ile	SS
Mathematics Vocabulary	3	<7-3	<2.2	9	6
Social Studies Vocabulary	5	7-3	2.2	16	7
Science Vocabulary	1	<7-3	<2.2	9	6
Reading the Directions of Schoolwork	22	9-9	4.7	75	12

Section III. TORC-3 Profile			

FIGURE 11–3

Sample *Test of Reading Comprehension* (3rd ed.) Profile

Note: From *Test of Reading Comprehension* (3rd ed.) (p. 24) by V. L. Brown, D. D. Hammill, & J. L. Wiederholt, 1995, Austin, TX: PRO-ED. Copyright 1995 by PRO-ED. Reprinted by permission.

TORC-3 results are helpful in determining the student's current levels of performance in several different comprehension skills. Informal techniques are then used to gather information about the specific skills that may require educational intervention. However, comprehension is related to the student's ability to recognize and pronounce words, and the *TORC-3* does not assess decoding skills or oral reading speed, as does the *GORT-3*. Also, it is not as complete a measure as the *WRMT-R/NU*. However, it addresses other important aspects of the reading process. Among the *TORC-3*'s features are the use of a standard classroom task to assess silent reading comprehension, the inclusion of a reading directions task for younger students, and the provision of standard score results for content area vocabulary subtests.

MEASURES OF PHONOLOGICAL PROCESSING

In the past decade, several measures of phonological processing have been developed to assess students' awareness of the sounds that make up spoken words and their ability to recognize similarities and differences among sounds. Some measures, such as the *Test of Phonological Awareness* (Torgesen & Bryant, 1994), are designed for young children. Others, such as the *Comprehensive Test of Phonological Processing* (Wagner, Torgesen, & Rashotte, 1999), are appropriate for both young children and older students in the elementary, middle, and high school grades.

The *Test of Phonological Awareness (TOPA)* contains two levels, one for kindergarten children (ages 5-0 through 6-11) and the other for early elementary grade students (ages 6-0 through 8-11). The *TOPA* can be administered individually or to groups and it requires approximately 15–20 minutes. On both levels, the examiner reads directions as children follow along in a student booklet. All directions require that children attend to a row of four drawings as the examiner says the name of the first drawing (the stimulus figure) and the names of three possible response drawings. Students must then mark the one drawing that is similar to or different from the stimulus figure in some way.

The tasks on the Kindergarten level of the *TOPA* require students to locate drawings that begin with the same sound as the stimulus figure or that begin with a different sound. For example, in the first demonstration item, the stimulus is a drawing of a bat and the three possible responses are drawings of a horn, bed, and cup; students are asked to mark the drawing that starts with the same sound as *bat*. On the Early Elementary level, students must identify drawings that end with the same sound as the stimulus figure or that end with a different sound. *TOPA* results include an overall standard score called a quotient (distributed with a mean of 100 and a standard deviation of 15) and a percentile rank score. Standard scores can be converted to stanines, if desired.

The *Comprehensive Test of Phonological Processing (CTOPP)* is designed for students ages 5-0 through 24-11. Two levels are available, one for ages 5 and 6 and the other for ages 7 and above. Both are based on a model of phonological processing that contains three types of abilities: phonological awareness, phonological memory (i.e., the temporary storage of phonological information), and rapid naming (i.e., the retrieval of phonological information from long-term memory).

The *CTOPP* for students ages 7 through 24 contains six Core subtests and six Supplemental subtests. Each phonological processing ability is assessed by two Core subtests; the Supplemental subtests provide additional information on phonological awareness and rapid naming, if desired. The Core subtests are:

Phonological Awareness

- *Elision.* Students repeat a word, then must say what remains when one or more sounds are deleted from the word.
- *Blending Words.* When students hear two or more sounds that make up a word, they must say the word.

Phonological Memory

- *Memory for Digits.* Students repeat numbers from memory; the digits are presented at the rate of 2 per second.
- *Nonword Repetition.* Students listen to nonsense words from 3 to 15 sounds long, then repeat them.

Rapid Naming

- *Rapid Digit Naming.* Students must say the name of random numbers on a page.
- *Rapid Letter Naming.* Students must say the name of random letters on a page.

Similar measures are included on the *CTOPP* for younger students.

Subtest raw scores can be converted to age and grade equivalents, percentile ranks, and standard scores (distributed with a mean of 10 and a standard deviation of 3). Composite scores are determined by combining subtest results. Three Composites are available on both levels: Phonological

Awareness, Phonological Memory, and Rapid Naming Composites. On the level for older students, it is also possible to calculate the Alternate Phonological Awareness and Alternate Rapid Naming Composites, if appropriate supplemental subtests were administered.

It is important to keep in mind that measures such as the *TOPA* and the *CTOPP* assess reading readiness skills, not reading itself. Although information about students' phonological processing abilities may be useful when considering various instructional approaches, it does not shed light on current reading performance. Measures such as the formal tests described in the last section and the informal reading inventories, to be discussed next, provide that type of information.

INFORMAL READING INVENTORIES

Standardized tests are but one of the many types of assessment tools available for the study of students' reading skills. Another popular kind of measure, particularly for classroom use, is the informal reading inventory (IRI). IRIs assess both decoding and comprehension skills. They are made up of graded word lists and reading selections that the student reads orally. The tester notes any decoding errors and records the student's answers to the comprehension questions accompanying each reading selection.

IRIs are grade-referenced measures; the word lists and passages are arranged in order of difficulty according to school grade levels. They are informal measures, and their purpose is to provide information about the student's reading skills in relation to the grade level system of the general school curriculum.

The results obtained from IRIs are grade level scores. Typically, informal inventories provide three reading levels: the Independent Level, the Instructional Level, and the Frustration Level. A student's Independent Level is the level of graded reading materials that can be read easily with a high degree of comprehension and few errors in decoding. At this level, the student reads independently, without instruction or assistance from the teacher. Reading materials at the student's Instructional Level are somewhat more difficult; this is the level appropriate for reading instruction. Materials at the Frustration Level are too difficult for the student; decoding errors are too frequent and comprehension too poor for instruction to occur. According to Kirk, Kliebhan, and Lerner (1978), the usual criteria for determining these three reading levels are:

- 98% to 100% word recognition accuracy and 90% to 100% accuracy in comprehension for the Independent Level;
- 95% word recognition accuracy and 75% accuracy in comprehension for the Instructional Level; and
- 90% or less word recognition accuracy and 50% or less accuracy in comprehension for the Frustration Level.

These standards have been criticized by some experts as being too stringent. For instance, Spache (1972) warned that "if the teacher employs an Informal Reading Inventory (IRI) for his estimate of instructional level, he may be expecting children to read with a very unrealistic degree of oral accuracy" (p. 25).

Figure 11–4 presents a sample preprimer reading passage from the *Informal Reading Inventory* (5th ed.) by Burns and Roe (1999). The tester introduces the task by reading a sentence that provides a purpose for reading. The student reads the selection orally and then responds to eight comprehension questions read by the tester. The number and percentage of word recognition and comprehension errors made by the student are recorded to determine whether the selection falls at the student's Independent, Instructional, or Frustration reading level.

Several published informal reading inventories are available for classroom use, or professionals can construct their own IRIs by selecting reading passages of various difficulty levels from a series of reading textbooks (Gillespie-Silver, 1979; Johnson, Kress, & Pikulski, 1987). Designing an IRI requires time and effort, but the advantage is that locally prepared inventories can reflect the reading series used in a particular school or district.

INTRODUCTORY STATEMENT: Read this story to find out what Joe wanted and if he got what he wanted.

Joe saw a goat.

The goat walked up to him.

Joe liked the goat.

He wanted the goat for a pet.

"Hello, Goat!" said Joe.

The goat put his head on Joe's hand.

"Good Goat," said Joe.

Joe ran to Dad.

"Dad! Dad!" he called.

"Look! Look!"

Joe's Dad saw the goat.

He did not like it.

"Can I keep the goat?" asked Joe.

"No! No! Not a goat!" said Dad.

"Why not?" asked Joe.

"Goats are not clean," said Dad.

Joe looked at the goat.

He looked at Dad.

Then he started to cry.

[*Note:* Do not count as a miscue mispronunciation of the name Joe. You may pronounce this word for the student if needed.]

COMPREHENSION QUESTIONS

_____ main idea
1. What is this story about?
(Joe finds a goat that he wants for a pet, or Dad won't let Joe have a goat for a pet.) [If a child just says "Joe and a goat" or "a goat," say "What about Joe and the goat?" or "What about the goat?"]

_____ sequence
2. What was the first thing that happened in the story? (Joe saw a goat.)

_____ detail
3. How did Joe feel about the goat he found? (He liked it.)

_____ sequence
4. What did the goat do after Joe saw him?
(Accept either "walked up to Joe" or "put his head on Joe's hand.")

_____ detail
5. Who did Joe call to see the goat? (Dad)

_____ detail
6. What did Joe's Dad think about the goat? (He didn't like it.)

_____ cause and effect/ detail
7. Why did Joe's Dad tell Joe that he could not keep the goat?
(because goats are not clean)

_____ inference
8. How did Joe feel when his Dad told him he couldn't keep the goat?
(sad; unhappy)

FIGURE 11–4

Sample Graded Passage from the *Informal Reading Inventory*

Note: From *Informal Reading Inventory* (5th ed.) (p. 92) by P. C. Burns and B. D. Roe, 1999, Boston: Houghton Mifflin. Copyright 1999 by Houghton Mifflin. Reprinted by permission.

Selecting an Informal Reading Inventory

All informal reading inventories share several general characteristics. Their major emphasis is oral reading, they use lists of words and reading passages to assess reading skill, and they take both decoding and comprehension into account when determining the student's Instructional Reading Level. However, there are some differences that should be evaluated when selecting an IRI for use in assessment. Among the factors to consider are the number of forms provided, whether measures of listening skill and silent reading are included, the number and grade levels of word lists and passages, the types of comprehension questions asked, and the availability of optional tests and other features.

The *Analytical Reading Inventory (ARI)* (6th ed.) by Woods and Moe (1999) is worthy of note for several reasons. First, it is one of the few inventories that provide a complete description of the procedures used in development and validation. Readability results are presented for each of the passages on the *ARI*, along with vocabulary diversity scores and information about average passage lengths.

Second, the *ARI* contains both narrative and expository passages carefully prepared to be "motivational and nonsexist in nature" (p. 230). In addition, the content of the graded selections is consistent across the three forms of the *ARI*. At the grade 6 level, for example, all passages describe African American inventors or scientists. Because the content of a passage affects its appeal to readers, consistency helps to ensure the equivalence of alternate forms.

Third, the *ARI* provides several types of comprehension questions ranging from those that require literal thinking about the passage to those in which the reader must make interpretations about the text. The four question types (in order, from most to least literal) are retells in fact, puts information together, connects author and reader, and evaluates and substantiates. At least one of each type of question accompanies each reading passage.

A fourth feature of the *ARI* is that it encourages both quantitative and qualitative analysis of decoding errors. Drawing from the work of the Goodmans and others (K. Goodman, 1973a; Y. Goodman & Burke, 1972), the authors of the *ARI* use the term *miscue* instead of *error.* Miscues are defined as deviations from the printed text. All readers make miscues, and miscues are not necessarily evidence of a problem in reading. For example, miscues such as the substitution of *the* for *a* do not change the meaning of the text and thus do not affect comprehension. On the *ARI*, miscues can be analyzed both quantitatively and qualitatively. Quantitative analysis involves following the traditional procedure of counting the different types of errors made by the student (e.g., omissions, insertions, substitutions). In qualitative analysis, the examiner notes each miscue, then determines how similar the miscue is to the original text. One important consideration is semantic similarity, that is, whether or not the miscue changes the meaning of the text. Figure 11–5 shows a sample passage from the *ARI* with miscues analyzed both quantitatively and qualitatively.

Most informal reading inventories are designed for elementary and middle school students. One exception is the *Informal Reading Inventory* (5th ed.) (Burns & Roe, 1999), which contains passages from preprimer to grade 12 level. Another noteworthy measure is the *English-Español Reading Inventory for the Classroom* (Flynt & Cooter, 1999). It provides narrative and expository passages from preprimer to grade 9 levels both in English and in Spanish.

Some IRIs include supplementary measures. For example, the *Ekwall/Shanker Reading Inventory* (3rd ed.) (Ekwall & Shanker, 1993) provides several strategies for the evaluation of reading and readiness skills. Among these are the Basic Sight Words test and the El Paso Phonics Survey. In addition, the graded word list on the Ekwall inventory is the San Diego Quick Assessment (LaPray & Ross, 1969), an informal measure often used to estimate word recognition skill level.

Two other measures are attempts to make reading inventories less informal. The *Standardized Reading Inventory* (2nd ed.) *(SRI-2)* (Newcomer, 1999) has set procedures for administration and scoring, and information is available about its reliability and validity. Although the first edition of the *SRI* was not normed, the *SRI-2* contains norms

Cueing Systems			
L I N E #	Miscue	Grapho-phonically Similar I M F (word level)	Syntactically Acceptable Unacceptable (sentence level)	Semantic Change in Meaning (CM) No Change in Meaning (NCM) (sentence level)

Prior Knowledge/Prediction

☐ Read the title and predict what the story is about. *About a road, it's got a lot of cars*

Q: What do you know about a busy road?

SR: *We live near a road that has a lot of cars.*

☐ Read the first two sentences and add more to your prediction.

The boy yells at his dog because he's going to get hit.

Q: What do you know about a dog getting hit on a road?

SR: *I had a dog that got hit when he ran across the road.*

Prior Knowledge

☑ a lot
☐ some
☐ none

L I N E #	Miscue	Grapho-phonically Similar I M F (word level)	Syntactically Acceptable Unacceptable (sentence level)	Semantic Change in Meaning (CM) No Change in Meaning (NCM) (sentence level)
5	*ready*	I	A	CM
6	*hold*		A	NCM
7	*The*	IM	U	CM
7	*street*	I	U	CM
8	*to*	IF	A	CM

Buzzy SC

	The Busy Road	O	I	S	A	Rp	Rv
1	"Look out, you'll get hit!" I/yelled as my dog ran across/the						
2	*Thad SC no SC* *nose* busy road./Thud was the/noise I heard, and then I saw my pup/						
3	*scar SC* lying in the street. "Oh, no!" I shouted. I felt scared inside. "Rex is						
4	my best friend!" I wanted to cry out. I knew that he was hurt, but						
5	*ready* he'd be all right/if I could get help fast. I knew I had to be brave.			/			
6	*str SC hold* "Mom! Dad!" I/yelled as I ran/straight home. I tried to fight			/			
7	*The st street* back the tears. They/started rolling down my face(anyway)as I	/		/ /			
8	*to* blasted through the door. "Rex has been hit, and he needs help/			/			
9	now!" I cried out. "Please hurry so we can save him!"						

TOTALS

Number of miscues ___6___   Number of self-corrections ___4___

Fluency: Does the reader . . .

☐ read smoothly?   ☐ word-by-word?   ☑ read words in meaningful phrases?

☑ use pitch, stress, and intonation to convey the meaning of a text?

☐ repeat words and phrases because he or she is monitoring the meaning (self-correcting)?

☑ repeat words and phrases because he or she is just trying to sound out the words?   *noise, started*

☑ use punctuation to divide the text into units of meaning?   *most times*

☐ ignore the punctuation?

Rating Scale

1 = clearly labored, disfluent reading/very slow pace   3 = poor phrasing/intonation/reasonable pace

2 = slow and choppy reading/slow pace   ④= fairly fluent reading/good pace

Summary

☑ Most, ☐ few, ☐ no   miscues were graphophonically similar to the word in the passage.

☑ Most, ☐ few, ☐ no   miscues were syntactically matched.

☐ Most, ☑ few, ☐ no   miscues maintained the author's meaning.

☑ The self-corrections demonstrate that the reader monitors the meaning.

Form C, Level 2

FIGURE 11–5

Sample Analysis of Miscues from the *Analytical Reading Inventory*

Note: From *Analytical Reading Inventory* by Woods/Moe, © 1995. Adapted by permission of Prentice-Hall, Inc., Upper Saddle River, NJ.

for students ages 6 to 14. Students read passages orally as the examiner records word recognition errors. Students then read the passage silently before answering comprehension questions. Scores are available for Passage Comprehension, Word Recognition Accuracy, and total test (Reading Quotient). An optional Vocabulary in Context subtest is also available. The *Formal Reading Inventory (FRI)* (Wiederholt, 1986) is a similar norm-referenced measure. The *FRI* is composed of a series of passages that students read silently and orally; standard score results are available for silent reading, and oral reading miscues can be analyzed informally.

OTHER INFORMAL STRATEGIES

Assessment for instructional planning in reading relies upon informal strategies, including the informal reading inventories described in the previous section. Here the focus is on other types of informal techniques: teacher checklists, error analysis, cloze and maze procedures, diagnostic teaching and clinical reading interviews, criterion-referenced tests, curriculum-based measurement, questionnaires and interviews, and portfolio assessment.

Teacher Checklists

Checklists are a quick and efficient means of gathering information from teachers and other professionals about their observations and perceptions of students' reading skills. The reading behaviors described on checklists can be of any kind: decoding, comprehension, oral reading, silent reading, or a combination. Most typically, checklists are designed to identify difficulties in reading or are curriculum checklists used to record and monitor reading skills development. An example of a reading difficulty checklist appears in Figure 11–6.

Error Analysis

One of the most frequently used techniques in the informal assessment of reading is error analysis. It is a traditional technique that dates back to the 1930s when Marion Monroe (1932) described common types of oral reading errors. Error analysis is a study of the mistakes that students make. Unlike the more general procedure—response analysis—it does not take into consideration both correct and incorrect responses. In reading assessment, incorrect responses provide information about how the student is processing the text and suggest directions for instructional interventions.

Error analysis is generally used to investigate decoding mistakes in oral reading. The first step in conducting an error analysis is to select material for the student to read. That material may be a word list or some sort of connected text. If the teacher is interested in the student's ability to read common words—words that appear with high frequency in reading books and other text materials—the teacher could select a list like that shown in Table 11–2. This high-frequency word list is Johnson's (1971) updated version of the *Dolch Basic Sight Word List* (Dolch, 1953). It includes 220 words commonly found in reading texts for the primary grades.

Lists of "survival" reading words are also available. These contain words believed to be necessary for minimal literacy in today's society. Included are words found on warning signs and notices (e.g., "Danger," "Keep Out," "Poison") and words used to provide information (e.g., "Rest Rooms," "This Way Out," "Restaurant") (Kaluger & Kolson, 1978).

If connected text is the concern, the teacher can choose from the passages provided on informal inventories and some standardized tests, a series of graded textbooks for reading instruction, or other materials such as content area textbooks or library books on topics of interest. A basal reading series is a good source of reading selections, particularly if the teacher is also interested in determining the student's instructional reading level. The teacher should gather several levels of graded readers so the student can begin reading at a level at which he or she can experience success.

The next step is to decide what types of responses will be considered errors and how these errors will be classified. In the reading of word lists, mispronunciations and nonpronunciations are typically viewed as errors. Mispronunciations occur when the student decodes a

	1st Check	2nd Check	3rd Check		
1				Word-by-word reading	Oral Reading
2				Incorrect phrasing	
3				Poor pronunciation	
4				Omissions	
5				Repetitions	
6				Inversions or reversals	
7				Insertions	
8				Substitutions	
9				Basic sight words not known	
10				Sight vocabulary not up to grade level	
11				Guesses at words	
12				Consonant sounds not known	
13				Vowel sounds not known	
14				Vowel pairs and/or consonant clusters not known (digraphs, diphthongs, blends)	
15				Lacks desirable structural analysis (Morphology)	
16				Unable to use context clues	
17				Contractions not known	
18				Comprehension inadequate	Oral Silent
19				Vocabulary inadequate	
20				Unaided recall scanty	Study Skills
21				Response poorly organized	
22				Unable to locate information	
23				Inability to skim	
24				Inability to adjust rate to difficulty of material	
25				Low rate of speed	
26				High rate at expense of accuracy	
27				Voicing-lip movement	Other Abilities
28				Lacks knowledge of the alphabet	
29				Written recall limited by spelling ability	
30				Undeveloped dictionary skills	

TEACHER
SCHOOL

NAME
GRADE

D—Difficulty recognized
P—Pupil progressing
N—No longer has difficulty

The items listed above represent the most common difficulties encountered by pupils in the reading program. Following each numbered item are spaces for notation of that specific difficulty. This may be done at intervals of several months. One might use a check to indicate difficulty recognized or the following letters to represent an even more accurate appraisal:

FIGURE 11–6

Reading Difficulty Checklist

Note: From *Locating and Correcting Reading Difficulties* (5th ed.) (p. 6) by E. E. Ekwall, 1989, New York: Merrill/Macmillan. Copyright 1989 by Macmillan Publishing Company. Reprinted by permission.

357

TABLE 11–2

High-Frequency Word List

PREPRIMER	PRIMER	FIRST	SECOND	THIRD
1. the	45. when	89. many	133. know	177. don't
2. of	46. who	90. before	134. while	178. does
3. and	47. will	91. must	135. last	179. got
4. to	48. more	92. through	136. might	180. united
5. a	49. no	93. back	137. us	181. left
6. in	50. if	94. years	138. great	182. number
7. that	51. out	95. where	139. old	183. course
8. is	52. so	96. much	140. year	184. war
9. was	53. said	97. your	141. off	185. until
10. he	54. what	98. may	142. come	186. always
11. for	55. up	99. well	143. since	187. away
12. it	56. its	100. down	144. against	188. something
13. with	57. about	101. should	145. go	189. fact
14. as	58. into	102. because	146. came	190. through
15. his	59. than	103. each	147. right	191. water
16. on	60. them	104. just	148. used	192. less
17. be	61. can	105. those	149. take	193. public
18. at	62. only	106. people	150. three	194. put
19. by	63. other	107. Mr.	151. states	195. thing
20. I	64. new	108. how	152. himself	196. almost
21. this	65. some	109. too	153. few	197. hand
22. had	66. could	110. little	154. house	198. enough
23. not	67. time	111. state	155. use	199. far
24. are	68. these	112. good	156. during	200. took
25. but	69. two	113. very	157. without	201. head
26. from	70. may	114. make	158. again	202. yet
27. or	71. then	115. would	159. place	203. government
28. have	72. do	116. still	160. American	204. system
29. an	73. first	117. own	161. around	205. better
30. they	74. any	118. see	162. however	206. set
31. which	75. my	119. men	163. home	207. told
32. one	76. now	120. work	164. small	208. nothing
33. you	77. such	121. long	165. found	209. night
34. were	78. like	122. get	166. Mrs.	210. end
35. her	79. our	123. here	167. thought	211. why
36. all	80. over	124. between	168. went	212. called
37. she	81. man	125. both	169. say	213. didn't
38. there	82. me	126. life	170. part	214. eyes
39. would	83. even	127. being	171. once	215. find
40. their	84. most	128. under	172. general	216. going
41. we	85. made	129. never	173. high	217. look
42. him	86. after	130. day	174. upon	218. asked
43. been	87. also	131. same	175. school	219. later
44. has	88. did	132. another	176. every	220. knew

Note: From "The Dolch List Reexamined" by D. D. Johnson, 1971, *The Reading Teacher, 24,* pp. 455–56. Copyright 1971 by the International Reading Association. Reprinted with permission of Dale D. Johnson and the International Reading Association.

word incorrectly; for example, he or she may read *who* when the text says *how*. Mispronunciation errors are often classified by the types of letter sounds in which the mistakes occur: consonant sounds, vowel sounds, blends (e.g., the first two letters in *tree* and *glass*), digraphs (e.g., the first two letters in *ship* and *chalk*), and diphthongs (e.g., the last two letters in *cow* and *toy*). Nonpronunciation occurs when the student fails to say a word. If word recognition speed is a major concern, the teacher can set a time limit for responding. For example, if 2 seconds are established as the time limit, correct responses produced after the 2-second time period would be scored as nonpronunciations.

Several types of errors can occur when students read connected text. Most systems of error analysis include at least four classes of errors:

- *Additions.* The reader adds words or parts of words to the printed text. For example, if the text is "the brown dog," the reader says, "the *big* brown dog."
- *Substitutions.* The reader mispronounces a word or parts of words; this type of error is also called a mispronunciation. For example, if the text is "the small house," the reader says, "the small *horse.*"
- *Omissions.* The reader fails to pronounce words or parts of words. This error occurs when readers skip words, when they hesitate in responding, or when they say they do not know a word and the teacher supplies it. For example, if the text is "the gnarled old tree," the reader might omit the word "gnarled" and read, "the old tree."
- *Reversals.* The reader changes the order of the words in a phrase or sentence or the order of sounds within a word. For example, if the text is "There were many seagulls," the reader says, " *Were there* many seagulls.*"

Repetitions are another type of reading behavior considered an error by some professionals. A repetition occurs when the reader repeats a word or a series of words. For example, if the text is "The man walked to the levee," the reader says, "The man walked to the *walked to the* levee." Other behaviors sometimes viewed as errors are disregard of punctuation and poor phrasing in oral reading. However, most educators

agree that if a student makes and then corrects an error, the error is not counted.

When collecting a reading sample for error analysis, two copies of the reading material are needed: one for the student to read and another for the teacher's use in recording the student's responses. A standard set of symbols is used for noting errors:

- The symbol $_\wedge$ indicates an *addition;* the $_\wedge$ is placed in the text where the word or word part has been added, and the addition is written above the text. For example, "The $^{big}_\wedge$brown dog."
- A *substitution* is marked by crossing out the mispronounced word and writing the substituted word above it. For example, "The small ~~house~~ ^{horse}."
- *Omissions* are shown by drawing a circle around the word, word part, or series of words the student left out. For example, "The(gnarled)old tree."
- The symbol $\sim$ indicates a *reversal* of words or parts of a word. For example, "There were| many seagulls."
- *Repetitions* are marked by drawing an arrow under the word or words repeated. For example, "The man walked to the levee."

The next step is analysis of the student's errors. In the traditional approach to analysis, the professional simply counts the number of errors that occurred in each class. However, it is also necessary to decide which errors are instructionally important for the student under study. Most educators would agree that substitutions and omissions have instructional relevance, but other types of errors may be of less concern. Errors such as the addition of an *-s* ending or an occasional repetition usually do not alter the sense of the passage.

An alternate method of error analysis takes into account the quality of the errors that readers make. In this qualitative analysis system, errors are called miscues (K. Goodman, 1973a, 1973b; Y. Goodman & Burke, 1972). According to Burke (1973), "Even proficient adult readers make miscues with some regularity" (p. 21). As noted earlier in this chapter, miscues are not necessarily cause for alarm. Efficient readers are still able to comprehend the meaning of text, because the types of errors they make tend to preserve meaning. Inefficient readers, in contrast, make errors that change the meaning of the text (Goodman, 1973b).

Figure 11–5 (p. 355) provides an example of qualitative analysis. Miscues are analyzed to determine whether they represent a change in meaning from the original text. For example, the substitution of *hold* for *fight* in "*fight back the tears*" is semantically correct and does not alter meaning. However, the substitution of *ready* for *right* in "*he'll be all right*" does change the sense of the passage.

The miscues that produce changes in meaning can be further analyzed. Burke (1973) suggests that the student's miscue and the original text be compared in three ways:

1. Graphic Similarity: How much do the two words *look* alike?
2. Sound Similarity: How much do the two words *sound* alike?
3. Grammatical Function: Is the grammatical function of the reader's word the same as the grammatical function of the text word? (p. 23)

These questions are drawn from the short form of the *Reading Miscue Inventory* (Goodman & Burke, 1972). The most acceptable miscue is semantically correct. Less acceptable are errors that are grammatically correct but semantically incorrect and errors that fit the graphic or phonic characteristics of the text but are semantically and grammatically incorrect.

Error analysis techniques can be used to study comprehension as well as decoding skills. One way to do this is to ask students comprehension questions after they have finished reading a passage. Or students can be asked to retell the story they have read or summarize the major points of an expository passage. In selecting reading materials for the assessment of comprehension, the type of material is an important consideration. Expository, narrative, and other types of texts such as poetry and plays are organized differently, and the reader's experience with the type of text may affect comprehension. According to Lapp and Flood (1992), comprehension is influenced "not only by linguistic cues and semantic content but also by the knowledge that we bring to a passage" (p. 120).

Several kinds of questions can be used to assess students' understanding of the meaning of a passage. To evaluate literal comprehension, the student can be asked to state the main idea of the passage, propose a title for the selection, recall details from the passage, remember a series of events or ideas, and explain the meaning of vocabulary words introduced in the reading selection. Inferential thinking is assessed by asking questions that force students to go beyond the information provided in the passage; students can be asked to draw conclusions, make predictions, evaluate ideas or actions, suggest alternative endings for a narrative, and so forth. In preparing comprehension questions to accompany a reading selection, professionals should ensure that the questions are text-dependent. Questions should be answerable only by students who have read the text.

Analysis of comprehension errors is conducted in the same way as analysis of decoding errors. A sample of the student's responses is gathered, and errors are noted and classified. Most typically, the classification system is based on the various types of comprehension questions: main idea, fact, sequence, vocabulary, inference, conclusion, and so forth. The number of errors in each category is totaled to help the professional identify the comprehension skills in which the student requires additional instruction.

The Cloze Procedure

The cloze procedure (Bormuth, 1968; Jongsma, 1971) is an informal technique for determining whether a particular textbook or other reading material is within a student's instructional reading level. To use the cloze procedure, the teacher selects a passage of approximately 250 words. The first and last sentences of the passage are left intact. In the rest of the passage, every fifth word is deleted and replaced with a blank. For example, the sentence "The little dog sat down beside the boy" would become "The little dog sat _____ beside the boy." The student reads the passage and attempts to fill in each of the blanks. If the student correctly supplies between 44% and 57% of the missing words, the passage is considered to be at the student's instructional level (Bormuth, 1968; Burron & Claybaugh, 1977).

This technique is also useful for assessing comprehension skills. By omitting every fifth (or seventh or *n*th word), the teacher forces the student to rely on the context clues within the passage to derive meaning. Figure 11–7 provides an example.

Two variations of the cloze procedure are the maze and the limited cloze (Baumann, 1988). The maze is essentially the same as the standard cloze except that students are presented with choices for each omitted word; this changes the task from completion to multiple-choice. In the limited cloze, the student may refer to a list of the omitted words arranged in random order. Baumann (1988) warns that "there is limited empirical evidence linking maze or limited cloze performance to other comprehension measures" (p. 178).

Diagnostic Teaching and Clinical Reading Interviews

In reading assessment, diagnostic teaching procedures are often based on the results of a clinical reading interview. Clinical reading interviews combine the techniques of observation, interviewing, and diagnostic probes. The professional observes the student who is engaged in some type of reading task, but assessment does not stop with observation. Students are questioned about their reading strategies, comprehension of the material, and background knowledge about passage content. In addition, the teacher can alter the nature of the reading task to determine how instructional adaptations will affect the student's reading performance. Consider the following example:

Theresa was referred to Mr. Considine, a Chapter 1 teacher, for help with her reading. Theresa was

---

Teacher reads these directions: Here is a story with some words left out. Each time a word is left out, it has been replaced with a line. When you come to a line, try to figure out what word should be in that blank. Ready—begin.

Jan has a cat.

The cat's <u>name</u> is Tab.

Tab does not <u>like</u> dogs.

One day <u>a</u> dog ran after Tab.

<u>Tab</u> ran up a tree.

The dog could not go <u>up</u> the tree.

Then <u>the</u> dog went away.

Grade one reading level

- -

Jan has a cat.

The cat's _____ is Tab.

Tab does not _____ dogs.

One day _____ dog ran after Tab.

_____ ran up a tree.

The dog could not go _____ the tree.

Then _____ dog went away.

FIGURE 11–7

The Cloze Procedure as a Measure of Comprehension Skills

Note: From *Locating and Correcting Reading Difficulties* (5th ed.) (p. 251) by E. E. Ekwall, 1989, New York: Merrill/Macmillan. Copyright 1989 by Macmillan Publishing Company. Reprinted by permission.

in the lowest group in a third-grade classroom and seemed to have great difficulty reading with comprehension.

Remembering a recent workshop for Chapter 1 teachers that he had attended, Mr. Considine reached for the easiest book in a set of graded readers instead of the diagnostic reading test he typically used. He asked Theresa to read for him from successively more difficult readers until she could proceed no further without his assistance. Then he began to prompt her, to read in unison with her, to read sentences before she read them, to read all of the words that surrounded an unfamiliar one to cue it, and to employ other techniques for helping Theresa read orally with good expression. He also asked her to dictate a story from her personal experience; then he printed the story and helped her to read it with good expression.

From all of the techniques Mr. Considine used he got a good diagnostic picture of Theresa's strengths and weaknesses in reading. In addition, and perhaps more important, he was able to identify some promising strategies for helping Theresa read with understanding. (Otto & Smith, 1983, pp. 24–25)

As this example illustrates, clinical reading interviews are dynamic procedures. The professional observes, questions, changes the reading task, and then observes and questions again. The goal of the process is to provide information about promising strategies for reading instruction.

Clinical interviews focus on the interaction between the reader and the text; they allow the professional to go beyond the product of the reading act to evaluate the process. There are many important factors to consider when exploring the reading process, including the student's background knowledge, familiarity with the structure of the text (e.g., narrative or expository), understanding of anaphoric terms, facility with language, and use of metacognitive strategies (Samuels, 1983).

For example, students may or may not have background knowledge about the content and structure of the passage. These factors are critical for comprehension; if the student is totally unfamiliar with the content being presented, compre-

hension will suffer despite adequate decoding skills.

Anaphoric terms are words that are used as substitutes for words or phrases that have already appeared in a text. In the text "The dog and cat ate their supper. They liked it." there are three anaphoric terms: *their* and *they,* referring to the dog and cat, and *it,* referring to the supper. Students who are unable to identify the referents of anaphoric terms will lose the meaning of the passage.

Metacognitive strategies are the methods that readers use to think about their interactions with the text. Effective readers think about both the content of the material and the reading process. According to Samuels (1983), the active reader asks such questions as:

- Why am I reading this?
- Do I want to read this for superficial overview or for detail?
- Do I know when there is a breakdown in comprehension?
- When there is a breakdown in understanding, what can I do to get back on the track again?
- What are the major and minor points of this text?
- Can I summarize or synthesize the major points made in this text? (pp. 6–7)

The professional can adapt these questions and use them to investigate the way the student interacts with text during a clinical reading interview.

In addition to asking questions, the professional can introduce diagnostic probes. For example, if decoding skills are a concern, the teacher can change the task by reading aloud with the student, pronouncing the difficult words for the student, or providing clues for the difficult words. Sometimes the teacher may wish to have the student read the entire passage alone, without assistance, and then intervene. If the teacher discovers that the student has difficulty with a particular set of decoding skills such as medial vowel sounds or word endings, those skills can be taught, and then the student can attempt the passage again with the teacher providing help as needed. Having the student do repeated readings of a passage is an excellent technique for evaluating his or her ability to learn and apply new skills.

What is learned about the student's skill levels and responsiveness to various types of instruction during the clinical reading interview is then used to design a diagnostic teaching sequence. Diagnostic teaching is a more structured process. Data are collected to describe the student's entry level skills; then an instructional intervention is begun and consistently continued over several days. The student's performance is monitored daily to determine whether the intervention is effective and should be included as part of the instructional program.

Criterion-Referenced Tests

Criterion-referenced tests assess the student's mastery of specific skills within the reading curriculum. They are based upon instructional objectives and, as Chapter 5 described, are quite easy to construct. For example, if mastery of high-frequency reading words is a goal of the instructional program, the teacher could use the word list presented in Table 11–2 as the basis of a criterion-referenced test. The objective for this test might be: *The student will read the high-frequency list aloud and pronounce at least 200 of the 220 words correctly.* The teacher would present each of the words to the student, keep track of errors, and then evaluate the student's performance to determine whether the objective had been achieved.

Several criterion-referenced tests of reading are commercially available, and professionals may select from these rather than constructing measures themselves. It is less time-consuming to use a criterion-referenced test that has already been prepared, but the time saved is wasted unless the measure adequately reflects the classroom curriculum. In evaluating criterion-referenced tests, professionals should carefully study the objectives upon which these measures are based to ensure that the skills included are important ones. Results of criterion-referenced tests should be relevant to the student's curriculum and immediately applicable to instruction.

The series of criterion-referenced tests by Brigance is one of the more popular sets of measures. This series includes the *BRIGANCE® Diagnostic Inventory of Early Development-Revised*

(1991) for children from birth through age 7, the *BRIGANCE® Diagnostic Comprehensive Inventory of Basic Skills-Revised (CIBS-R)* (1999) for pre-kindergarten through grade 9, and the *BRIGANCE® Diagnostic Inventory of Essential Skills* (1981) for grade 6 through adult education. A Spanish edition of the *Basic Skills* inventory (Brigance, 1983) is also available. Each of these measures contains several tests of reading; even the inventory for preschool children offers tests of readiness and basic reading skills.

The *CIBS-R* for elementary and middle school students assesses several types of reading skills: word recognition, grade placement, oral reading, reading comprehension, word analysis, and functional word recognition. Table 11–3 lists the names of the tests that assess these skill areas. Like all of the *BRIGANCE®* measures, the *CIBS-R* provides instructional objectives for each test. For example, the objective for the Basic Sight Vocabulary test is:

> By __(date)__, when shown a list of 400 basic sight vocabulary words, __(student's name)__ will correctly pronounce __(quantity)__ of the words.

Unlike the other *BRIGANCE®* measures, some of the tests on the *CIBS-R* have been normed and results can be expressed as standard scores, percentile ranks, and grade equivalents. In the area of reading, the normed tests are the Word Recognition Grade-Placement Test, Reading Vocabulary Comprehension Grade-Placement Test, and Word Analysis Survey. A computer program, the *CIBS-R Standardized Scoring Conversion Software,* is available to assist in the scoring process.

The *Essential Skills* measure is intended for older elementary and secondary grade students. It contains the same types of tests as those found in the *CIBS-R,* but skills are assessed at somewhat higher grade levels. For example, the reading comprehension portion of *Essential Skills* extends through the grade 11 level. Other features of both of these measures are the tests that assess functional skills such as reading direction words, warning and safety signs, and informational signs.

Many other criterion-referenced tests attempt to provide comprehensive coverage of the read-

TABLE 11-3
Reading Tests on the *BRIGANCE® Diagnostic Comprehensive Inventory of Basic Skills-Revised*

Word Recognition Grade Placement

Word Recognition Grade-Placement Test

Oral Reading

Reads Orally at Preprimer or Primer Level
Reads Orally at Lower First-Grade or Upper
First-Grade Level
Reads Orally at Lower Second-Grade or Upper
Second-Grade Level
Reads Orally at Lower Third-Grade or Upper
Third-Grade Level
Reads Orally at Fourth-Grade or Fifth-Grade Level
Reads Orally at Sixth-Grade or Seventh-Grade Level
Reads Orally at Eighth-Grade or Ninth-Grade Level

Reading Comprehension

Reading Vocabulary Comprehension Grade-
Placement Test
Comprehends Passages at Primer Level
Comprehends Passages at Lower First-Grade Level
Comprehends Passages at Upper First-Grade Level
Comprehends Passages at Lower Second-Grade
Level
Comprehends Passages at Upper Second-Grade
Level
Comprehends Passages at Lower Third-Grade Level
Comprehends Passages at Upper Third-Grade Level
Comprehends Passages at Fourth-Grade Level
Comprehends Passages at Fifth-Grade Level
Comprehends Passages at Sixth-Grade Level
Comprehends Passages at Seventh-Grade Level
Comprehends Passages at Eighth-Grade Level
Comprehends Passages at Ninth-Grade Level

Word Analysis

Word Analysis Survey
Auditory Discrimination
Identifies Initial Consonants in Spoken Word
Substitutes Initial-Consonant Sounds
Substitutes Short-Vowel Sounds
Substitutes Long-Vowel Sounds
Substitutes Final-Consonant Sounds
Substitutes Initial-Blend and Initial-Digraph Sounds

Word Analysis *continued*

Reads Words with Common Endings
Reads Words with Vowel Digraphs and Diphthongs
Reads Words with Phonetic Irregularities
Reads Suffixes
Reads Prefixes
Divides Words into Syllables

Supplemental and Related Lists/Skill Sequences:
States Word Having Same Initial Sound
States Word Having Same Short-Vowel Sound
States Word Having Same Long-Vowel Sound
States Word Having Same Final-Consonant
Sound
States Word Having Same Initial Blend or
Digraph Sound
Vowel Digraphs and Diphthongs
Phonetic Irregularities
Common Rules for Phonetic Irregularities
Suffixes
Prefixes
Comprehends Meanings of Prefixes

Functional Word Recognition

Basic Sight Vocabulary
Direction Words
Number Words
Warning and Safety Signs
Informational Signs
Warning Labels
Food Labels

Supplemental and Related Lists/Skill Sequences:
Contractions
Abbreviations
Direction Words for Writing Activities
Direction Words for Speaking Activities
Direction Words for Study Activities
Direction Words for Physical Activities
Warning and Safety Signs
Informational Signs
Warning Labels
Labels on Packaged Foods

Note: From *BRIGANCE® Diagnostic Comprehensive Inventory of Basic Skills-Revised* by A. H. Brigance, 1999, N. Billerica, MA: Curriculum Associates, Inc. Copyright 1999 by Curriculum Associates, Inc. Adapted by permission.

ing skill area. For example, the *Hudson Education Skills Inventory* (Hudson, Colson, Welch, Banikowski, & Mehring, 1989) provides criterion-referenced measures of reading readiness, sight vocabulary, phonic analysis, structural analysis, and comprehension skills for kindergarten through grade 12. In using a criterion-referenced instrument such as this, the professional selects and administers only those tests that address the skills of interest for the particular student.

Curriculum-Based Measurement

Curriculum-based measurement (CBM) techniques can be used to evaluate oral reading fluency, that is, the rate at which students are able to accurately decode words in oral reading tasks. This type of assessment is considered curriculum-based because the reading materials are randomly selected from those to be taught during the school year. Tindal and Marston (1990) provide specific instructions for conducting a curriculum-based reading assessment. Two copies of a reading passage or word list are prepared; the teacher's copy should have numbers at the side of the text indicating the cumulative word count. The student reads aloud for 1 minute and the teacher records errors. To begin, the teacher gives these directions:

> When I say "start," begin reading at the top of this page. If you wait on a word too long, I'll tell you the word. If you come to a word you cannot read, just say "pass" and go on to the next word. Do not attempt to read as fast as you can. This is not a speed reading test. Read at a comfortable rate. At the end of one minute, I'll say "stop." (Tindal & Marston, 1990, p. 148)

Substitutions, omissions, and reversals are counted as errors; words are pronounced by the teacher (and counted as errors) when the student hesitates for 3 seconds. Additions and self-corrections are not counted as errors; more than one mispronunciation of the same proper noun is considered only one error.

The teacher scores the CBM by determining the number of words read correctly during the 1-minute time period. Results are typically graphed so that the student's progress can be monitored over time. On the graph, the aim line represents the instructional goal for the student; the trend line is a record of actual progress.

It is also possible to develop local norms for curriculum-based measures such as the reading fluency task just described (Howell, Fox, & Morehead, 1993; Tindal & Marston, 1990). By transforming an informal procedure into a norm-referenced one, it becomes possible to compare one student's rate to that of typical students in the same classroom or grade level in order to determine if a school performance problem exists. Shinn (1988) describes procedures for norms development.

Monitoring Basic Skills Progress (MBSP) (2nd ed.) (Fuchs, Hamlett, & Fuchs, 1997) is a commercially available curriculum-based measure that is administered by computer. One of its four parts is Basic Reading. On this test, the student is presented with a 400-word reading passage with every seventh word omitted. Students read silently and, when they come to a missing word, they click on the blank to see three possible responses. Students continue reading until the passage is completed or 2.5 minutes elapse, whichever comes first. Passages are available for grades 1 through 7 and each is a complete story.

As soon as a student has completed a passage, the program automatically computes and displays the student's current score as well as his or her progress over time. The score is the number of correct words. In addition, the program stores student data so that it can be accessed later by the teacher. These data are presented on a graph, as Figure 11–8 illustrates, along with the goal line (G) (i.e., aim line) and the trend line (T). In the first example in Figure 11–8, the program reports that a teaching change is needed because the student is not making appropriate progress; in the second example, a teaching change is needed because the student's rate of progress is faster than expected.

Questionnaires and Interviews

Questionnaires and interviews are used in reading assessment to gather information about students' views and opinions: their attitudes toward reading, perceptions of the reading process, opinions of their own reading abilities, likes and dislikes in reading materials, and so on. Interviews are preferred for younger students and those with poor reading skills; print questionnaires are reserved for more mature students who are able to read with comprehension and answer in writing.

Example 1

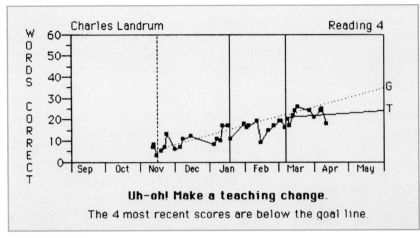

Example 2

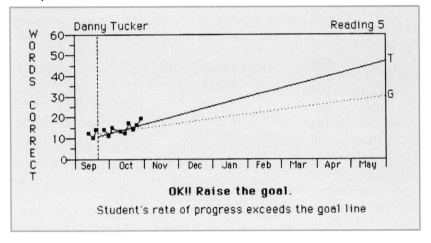

FIGURE 11-8

Results from *Monitoring Basic Skills Progress: Basic Reading* (2nd ed.)

Note: From *Monitoring Basic Skills Progress: Basic Reading* (2nd ed.) (p. 8, 10) by L. S. Fuchs, C. L. Hamlett, and D. Fuchs, 1997, Austin, TX: PRO-ED. Copyright 1990 by PRO-ED. Reprinted by permission.

Students can be interviewed to find out their attitudes toward reading and preferences in reading materials. The teacher could ask questions such as:

- Is reading one of your better subjects in school?
- What types of reading activities are the easiest for you? Which are the hardest?
- If you could read a story about anything in the world, what would the story be about?
- What magazines do you read or look at?
- Do you ever read the newspaper? If so, what parts of the paper do you read?

- Would you rather read true stories or stories that the author makes up?
- What are your hobbies? Have you ever read a book, a story, or a magazine article about one of your favorite activities?
- What was the last thing you read for fun? When did you read it? What did you enjoy about it?

The questionnaire in Figure 11–9 is designed for secondary grade students, but some of the questions could be adapted for interviews with

A. Strategies of effective reading
1. Which one of the following statements best describes what you do when you can't seem to understand what you're reading?
   a. I re-read.
   b. I stop reading and do something else for awhile.
   c. I keep reading to the end.
   d. I ask someone else to read it and explain it to me.
   e. I try to find something easier to read.
2. Which one of the following is most descriptive of your rate of reading?
   a. I read everything at about the same speed.
   b. I adjust my rate according to the difficulty of the reading materials.
   c. I adjust my rate according to my interest in the reading materials.
   d. I adjust my reading rate according to my purpose for reading.
3. When I want to get an idea of what a book is about, I
   a. read the book from beginning to end
   b. look for the author's name
   c. consult the book's index
   d. consult the book's table of contents
   e. ask the librarian or my teacher

B. General attitude toward reading
1. Choose one of the following that best describes your attitude toward reading:
   a. I like to read almost anything.
   b. I like to read, but only what interests me.
   c. I do some reading, but I don't really like it.
   d. I don't like to read at all.
2. If I had to learn about the writing of the Declaration of Independence, I would rather
   a. have my teacher tell us about it
   b. see a movie or TV program about it
   c. read about it
3. How many books have you read during the past month that weren't assigned in school?
   a. None
   b. One
   c. Two
   d. Three or more

C. Self-evaluation
1. With which one of the following do you have the most trouble in reading?
   a. Understanding the meaning of difficult words

b. Remembering what I read
   c. Understanding the main ideas
   d. Reading fast enough
2. In which of the following school subjects do you find the reading most difficult?
   a. Science
   b. Social Studies
   c. Mathematics
   d. English
3. Do you think you need extra help in reading?
   a. Yes
   b. No

D. Work-study skills and library habits
1. Did you go to the library to find reading materials during the past month?
   a. Not at all
   b. Once or twice
   c. Three or more times
2. Which of the following have you used most often to find a book in the library?
   a. The card catalog
   b. Browsing
   c. Asking someone
3. Choose one of the following to describe why you usually go to a library (school or community library):
   a. To study or read on my own
   b. To look up information for homework assignments
   c. To take books out to read for fun
   d. I hardly ever go to the library

E. Reading interests
This is best tested by a format that allows the student to rate his interests from high to low:
Directions: For each of the types of reading matter listed below, choose the rating that best describes your interest in it.
   Ratings: a. high interest
   b. medium interest
   c. low interest—read only if assigned
   d. no interest at all—dislike
1. A short story or novel
2. An article that tells how to make or repair something
3. Newspapers and magazines
4. An article or book about something I have a special interest in (such as sports, clothes, music)
5. An article, story, or book about a person I admire

FIGURE 11–9

Reading Questionnaire for Older Students

Note: Reproduced from *Iowa Silent Reading Tests* by R. Farr (Ed.) by permission. Copyright © 1973 by Harcourt Brace Jovanovich, Inc. All rights reserved.

younger readers. The purpose of this measure is to elicit information from students about their attitudes toward reading, their study skills and work habits, and their reading interests. In addition, students are asked to describe the strategies they use when reading and to evaluate their own reading performance.

Portfolio Assessment

Reading is usually one of the areas represented in language arts portfolios. Separate portfolios for reading are not common. First of all, the act of reading typically does not result in a permanent product. Second, teachers using the whole language approach tend to integrate the language arts so that reading and writing activities overlap. For example, students might keep written logs or journals to record their reactions to the books and stories they read.

Lapp and Flood (1992) suggest several types of information that can be placed in students' portfolios to document progress in reading. Possibilities include:

- Results of standardized tests and informal assessments,
- Student self-assessments,
- Samples of the types of materials read throughout the year as part of classroom instruction, and
- Information about participation in a voluntary leisure reading program (e.g., number of books read each month).

The *Language Arts Assessment Portfolio (LAAP)* (Karlsen, 1992) is a published system for portfolio assessment of reading, writing, listening, and speaking for students in grades 1, 2, and 3. The *LAAP* is not a collection of tests; instead, classroom language arts materials and activities are used to evaluate student performance. The system includes two evaluation booklets: one for the teacher and one for the student. In the area of reading, the teacher's booklet contains rating scales and checklists to document student progress and identify problems in oral and silent reading. The student self-evaluation booklet is used for self-ratings and to record reactions to stories and books read. The *LAAP* also provides blackline masters for a Student Interest Survey and Reading Log.

WITHIN THE CONTEXT OF THE CLASSROOM

The assessment procedures described so far have been student-centered measures designed to evaluate the student's current levels of performance in important reading skills. In this section, the emphasis shifts to assessment tools and techniques for studying the classroom learning environment and its influence on the student's reading abilities.

The Instructional Environment

In the elementary grades, assessment of the instructional environment must take into account the reading curriculum and the instructional methods and materials used to implement that curriculum. The most common elementary reading program centers on either a basal reading series, children's literature, or a combination of the two. Some of the newer basals reflect this approach by including selections from children's literature. A basal series is a set of graded reading textbooks that span a number of grade levels, usually from the beginning reading levels (preprimer and primer) through the end of grade 6 or grade 8. Assessment of the instructional factors that influence younger students begins with a study of the classroom reading program:

1. What is the major component of the classroom reading program? A basal reading textbook? Children's literature? Another approach?
2. Does the basal reading series used in the classroom stress text, meaning, or the interaction between text and meaning? If the reading program is not based on a basal series, what is the major component?
3. Do the reading materials build on the students' language and background experiences, or do they present unfamiliar content?
4. How many levels of the basal or other reading materials are in use? Is there a range of books to accommodate the range of student skills? Or if a third grade classroom is under study, are only grade 3 reading books available?
5. What types of materials are used to supplement instruction? Workbooks? Worksheets? Computer-based instructional programs? Reading games? Leisure reading books?
6. What types of reading skills are stressed in classroom instruction? Decoding? Comprehension? Oral reading? Silent reading?
7. Are decoding skills taught? If so, which are emphasized? Sight vocabulary? Phonic analysis? Structural analysis? Contextual analysis? A combination?
8. Is the reading curriculum organized so the sequence of instruction is logical and the instructional steps are of appropriate size?
9. Is reading instruction based on ongoing as-

sessment? How often are performance data collected for monitoring students' progress? What strategies are used to determine the starting points for students entering the program?

10. How are students grouped for reading instruction? Does the entire class receive instruction at one time? Is the class divided into large groups of 10 to 15 students each? Smaller groups of 5 to 8 students? How much individualization takes place in each group?

11. What instructional techniques does the teacher use to present new skills and information? Lecture? Discussion? Demonstration and modeling?

12. In what types of learning activities do students participate? Oral reading? Silent reading? Completing workbook pages or worksheets? Writing book reports?

13. How is supervised practice incorporated into the reading program? On the average, how many minutes per day do students spend practicing their reading skills?

14. What changes, if any, have been made in the standard reading program to accommodate the needs of special learners such as the student under assessment?

The nature of the materials that students are required to read is an important factor both for beginning readers and for secondary students expected to use reading as a tool for learning in other subject areas. Among the critical characteristics of reading materials are the topic of the text, the style in which the text is written, format, and readability (Samuels, 1983).

The topic of the text has a direct effect on the reader's ability to read with comprehension; more familiar topics are more easily understood. The clarity of the author's writing style also affects text comprehensibility. Passages that contain too many anaphoric terms, those with poor transitions from event to event or idea to idea, and those containing long sentences with too much information are difficult to comprehend. In addition, if there is a mismatch between the information presented in the text and the background knowledge of the reader, the author may fail to communicate with the intended audience. Format also plays a role in text comprehensibility. Reading materials should be printed clearly, and the text should be organized to facilitate reading and review. In evaluating the format of textbooks, professionals should check to see if chapters are structured with design features such as headings, subheadings, abstracts, summaries, and review questions.

The readability of a passage is influenced by its content, vocabulary, and organization, and by the structure of its sentences. However, most of the readability formulas available for measuring reading levels take only one or perhaps two of these factors into account. For example, Fry's (1968) readability graph, presented in Figure 11–10, uses sentence length and the number of syllables per word to estimate readability. The professional selects three 100-word passages from a book or article, counts the number of sentences and syllables in each passage, and then uses the graph to determine readability; readability estimates are stated in terms of grade level.

Readability formulas and graphs can help the professional evaluate reading materials and match the difficulty levels of materials to students' skill levels. This is particularly important with content area textbooks. Science, social studies, and other content subject texts are graded, but their grade levels refer to the difficulty of the subject matter, not to reading difficulty. Thus, a grade 9 science book is likely to contain grade 9 science material, but it may or may not be written at a grade 9 reading level. Readability graphs and formulas can also be used to determine the approximate reading levels of other types of materials, such as library books, short stories, passages in reference books, and magazine or newspaper articles. The Fry (1968) graph is a relatively quick and easy method for estimating readability. It can be used for materials that range from grade 1 to college level, and extensions are available for preprimer and primer materials (Maginnis, 1969) and for materials at college and graduate school levels (Fry, 1977).

The Interpersonal Environment

The major factors that relate to reading within the interpersonal environment of the classroom are the interactions between students and teachers

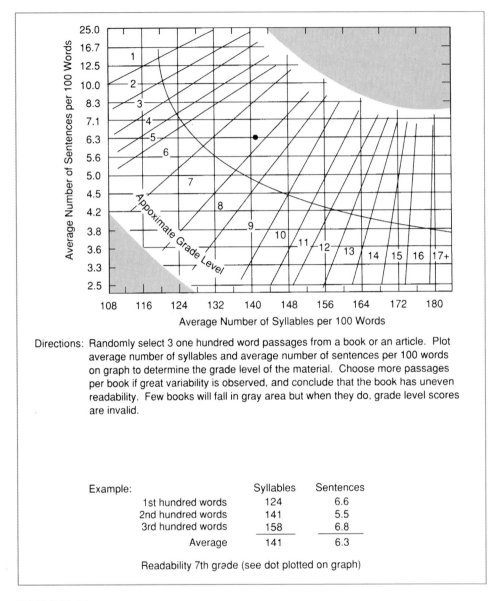

Directions: Randomly select 3 one hundred word passages from a book or an article. Plot
average number of syllables and average number of sentences per 100 words
on graph to determine the grade level of the material. Choose more passages
per book if great variability is observed, and conclude that the book has uneven
readability. Few books will fall in gray area but when they do, grade level scores
are invalid.

Example:	Syllables	Sentences
1st hundred words	124	6.6
2nd hundred words	141	5.5
3rd hundred words	158	6.8
Average	141	6.3

Readability 7th grade (see dot plotted on graph)

FIGURE 11-10

Fry Readability Graph

Note: From "A Readability Formula That Saves Time," by E. Fry, April 1968, *Journal of Reading, 11,*
pp. 513–516.

and the social relationships among students. The most effective way of assessing these interpersonal dimensions is observation. Classroom observations that are scheduled when students are engaged in reading activities can provide answers to the following questions:

- What occurs when a student makes an error in oral reading? Does the teacher correct the student? Ignore the error? Ask another student to assist?

- How does the student react to the teacher's corrections?

- What do other students do when a peer makes oral reading errors? Do they laugh, tease, or ridicule the student?
- Are poor readers accepted by others in the classroom? Do they participate with their peers in social and free-time activities?
- What happens when a student reads correctly? Does the teacher confirm the correct responses? Praise the student? Provide a tangible reward or token?
- Are students able to work independently on silent reading assignments and on workbook and other writing activities? Or do certain students require frequent assistance from the teacher?

Another factor to consider when evaluating student-teacher interactions is the amount of time teachers spend teaching reading and students spend practicing reading skills. Studies of programs for students with mild disabilities indicate that students are actively engaged in reading for only a few minutes each day (Leinhardt, Zigmond, & Cooley, 1981; Thurlow, Graden, Greener, & Ysseldyke, 1983; Zigmond, Vallecorsa, & Leinhardt, 1980). The amount of time that students and teachers spend in instructional interactions is likely to have a direct effect on the amount of progress that students make in their attempts to develop reading skills.

The Physical Environment

The physical environment of the classroom can also affect students' reading performance. Environmental factors such as lighting, temperature, and ventilation influence the students' and the teacher's comfort levels and can either facilitate or hinder the teaching-learning process. In addition, the physical arrangement of the classroom is an important consideration, particularly in relation to seating configurations and allocation of classroom space.

Some of the questions that can be asked about the classroom's physical environment and its impact on reading instruction are:

1. What seating arrangements are used for reading instruction? Are students seated so they can easily see and hear the teacher?

2. Is the lighting in the classroom adequate for reading?
3. Is classroom space structured so areas for noisier activities are separated from the areas for quieter activities like reading?
4. How are students' seats arranged for independent work? Are students' desks or tables positioned so students do not distract one another?
5. Are there any quiet work areas or "offices" within the classroom where students can go to escape from distractions?
6. Is there a variety of reading materials in the classroom for student use? Do the materials cover a wide range of topics, interest levels, and reading levels? Are the materials accessible to students?
7. Is a computer available in the classroom for students to practice reading skills? Are students trained in the operation of computer equipment? Do students have access to a variety of educationally sound software programs in reading?
8. What types of reading materials are available in the school library or media center? Are these materials accessible to students?

ANSWERING THE ASSESSMENT QUESTIONS

The major purpose of reading assessment is description of students' current levels of educational performance. There are many assessment tools designed for this purpose. They represent numerous types of techniques: diagnostic reading tests, informal reading inventories, error analysis procedures, clinical reading interviews, diagnostic teaching, cloze and maze procedures, criterion-referenced tests, curriculum-based measures, teacher checklists, interviews, observation, portfolios, and other informal strategies. Because of the great number and diversity of assessment tools for reading, it is particularly important that the assessment process be carefully planned. Assessment begins with comprehensive measures that sample several reading skills. When potential problem areas are identified, these areas are assessed further, usually with informal measures and techniques.

Nature of the Assessment Tools

Tools for reading assessment vary in the range of reading skills they assess. Comprehensive measures such as the *Woodcock Reading Mastery Tests-Revised/Normative Update* attempt to evaluate a wide range of reading skills, whereas an instrument such as the *Test of Reading Comprehension* (3rd ed.) focuses on a narrower set of skills. However, most measures today are comprehensive, and they assess both decoding and comprehension skills. Table 11–1 illustrated this point. Of the 28 reading measures described, only 4 assess either decoding or comprehension, but not both.

Assessment tools can also vary in depth of skill coverage. Standardized tests typically sample several skills and levels but provide only a few representative test items in each area. For example, a subtest on phonic analysis may devote only two or three test items to the skill of decoding consonant-vowel-consonant words. Informal measures, particularly criterion-referenced tests, allow study of specific skills in much greater depth.

Measures of reading may also differ by the types of reading tasks that students are required to perform. Table 11–4 describes several of the more common measures of decoding and comprehension and the ways these measures go about assessment. In the area of decoding, all of the measures except the *GORT-3* require students to read lists of words aloud. However, measures differ on the number of words on each list, the actual words included, and whether time limits are imposed.

In the area of comprehension, assessment tasks are much more varied. The *GORT-3* and the *Analytical Reading Inventory* (6th ed.) use the standard tasks of reading graded passages and answering comprehension questions based on the content of the passages. However, questions are open-ended on the *ARI* but multiple-choice on the *GORT-3*. The task on the *TORC-3* is somewhat different; students read standard types of passages, then read the multiple-choice comprehension questions themselves, rather than listening to the tester read them. The *WRMT-R/NU* uses

a cloze procedure to assess comprehension; no questions are asked. The student reads passages silently and then attempts to supply the word missing in each.

Oral reading is required on the comprehension tasks on the *GORT-3* and the *ARI;* the *WRMT-R/NU* and the *TORC-3* employ silent reading tasks. Students respond orally on each of the measures except the *TORC-3*. The *TORC-3* and the *GORT-3* use multiple-choice comprehension questions; the *WRMT-R/NU*, a completion task; and the *ARI*, open-ended questions.

Clearly, there are important differences among measures of reading in the ways they assess decoding and comprehension skills. These differences must be considered in selecting the tools for reading assessment and in interpreting the results of the assessment.

The Relationship of Reading to Other Areas of Performance

When the assessment team begins to evaluate and interpret its results, one of the major tasks is the study of the relationships among areas of performance. Academic skills such as reading may influence or be influenced by several other areas.

A student's general aptitude for learning can have an effect on the ease and speed with which reading skills are acquired. In general, students with lower than average general intelligence are expected to progress at a somewhat slower rate than students of average intellectual ability. There have been several attempts to quantify the relationship between IQ and reading, and reading expectancy formulas have resulted (Bond & Tinker, 1967; Harris, 1970; Myklebust, 1968). These formulas use the student's current intellectual performance and sometimes other factors, such as age or years in school, to predict an expected reading level.

Expectancy formulas have several limitations, most notably their reliance on age and grade scores, and their use is not recommended. Instead, the standard score procedures described in Chapter 9 are preferred for comparing and contrasting IQ test results and results from measures of reading. Measures such as the *WRMT-R/NU*, the *Wechsler Individual Achieve-*

TABLE 11-4

Assessment Tasks Used to Evaluate Reading Skills

READING SKILL	MEASURE	SUBTEST	PRESENTATION MODE	RESPONSE MODE
Decoding	*Gray Oral Reading Tests* (3rd ed.)	(entire test)	Look at a series of graded passages.	Read each passage aloud as quickly and accurately as possible.
	Analytical Reading Inventory (6th ed.)	Word Lists	Look at lists of isolated words.	Read each word aloud.
	Woodcock Reading Mastery Tests-Revised/Normative Update	Word Attack	Look at lists of nonsense words and syllables.	Read each word or syllable aloud.
	Woodcock Reading Mastery Tests-Revised/Normative Update	Word Identification	Look at lists of isolated words.	Reach each word aloud within 5 seconds.
Comprehension	*Gray Oral Reading Tests* (3rd ed.)	(entire test)	Look at a series of graded passages; listen to multiple-choice comprehension questions read aloud by the tester.	Read the passages orally; answer the comprehension questions by saying the letter of the correct answer.
	Analytical Reading Inventory (6th ed.)	Graded Passages	Look at a series of graded passages; listen to questions read aloud by the tester.	Make predictions about each passage; read each passage orally; retell each passage and, if necessary, answer comprehension questions.
	Test of Reading Comprehension (3rd ed.)	Paragraph Reading	Look at paragraphs, then read multiple-choice comprehension questions.	Silently read each paragraph and the comprehension questions that accompany it; mark answers on the separate answer sheet.
	Woodcock Reading Mastery Tests-Revised/Normative Update	Passage Comprehension	Look at a passage with one word missing.	Read the passage silently and say the missing word.

ment Test, and the *Woodcock-Johnson Psycho-Educational Battery-Revised* provide procedures for the analysis of aptitude-achievement discrepancies.

Like general learning aptitude, specific learning abilities and strategies can influence the student's success in the acquisition and application of reading skills. Problems in attention, memory, or other areas such as phonological awareness can hinder skill development, particularly the acquisition of basic decoding skills. Inefficient learning strategies can interfere when students attempt to read with comprehension. In the secondary grades, poor learning strategies may combine with poor reading skills to prevent students from successfully using reading as a study technique.

Classroom behavior may be related to reading performance. Inappropriate classroom conduct can impede classroom learning, including acquisition and application of reading skills. Poor achievement can also affect a student's behavior. Difficulty in reading can result in lowered self-concept and negative attitudes toward school and learning. Achievement problems can even influence peer relationships and the student's conduct in social and instructional situations.

Reading pervades the school curriculum. It has a direct impact on several other areas of school performance, particularly language arts subjects. Writing skills such as spelling and composition are directly affected by delayed development in reading. In written language, the expressive skill of writing is built upon the receptive skill of reading. Likewise, the development of beginning reading skills is influenced by the student's oral language proficiency.

Reading can also affect the student's ability to perform successfully in mathematics and other subjects. Although arithmetic computation usually does not require reading skills, other mathematics tasks do. Students are often asked to read explanations in mathematics textbooks, to read the directions for mathematics worksheets or workbook pages, and to read word problems.

Reading is almost a necessity for content area subjects such as science, history, English, and social studies. Even in the elementary grades, students may be expected to use reading to acquire content area information. At the secondary level, reading assignments are routine. Students are expected to learn by reading textbooks and other materials. Students can bypass their poor reading skills by using aids such as taped versions of textbooks, but students with disabilities who are included in general education classrooms will still be expected to achieve at least a minimal level of reading proficiency.

In addition, there are very real reading demands in the adult world. Reading is a necessity for most occupations, and the average adult is constantly faced with text to read: street and traffic signs, signs on buildings and restroom doors, commercial ads, want ads, newspapers, magazines, television schedules, job application forms, postcards and letters, grocery labels, labels on cosmetics and medications, menus, and the like.

The ability to read and comprehend everyday reading materials such as these is an important concern for all students, particularly older students with special instructional needs.

Documentation of Reading Performance

The general question that guides the assessment team in its study of reading skills is, *What are the student's educational needs?* The purpose of this phase of assessment is to describe precisely the student's current skill levels; these data then serve as the basis for planning the student's educational program. The first question that the team attempts to answer is, *What is the student's current level of reading achievement?* Then additional information is gathered about areas in which the student appears to be experiencing difficulty. The result is a description of the student's current performance in reading that is specific enough to answer the question, *What are the student's strengths and weaknesses in the various skill areas of reading?*

Data are gathered from many sources using many types of assessment tools. The team usually begins by reviewing school records, results of individual achievement tests, interviews with parents and teachers, and classroom observations to plan the reading assessment. Next, a diagnostic reading test may be administered to survey the student's skills in several areas of reading. Test results are used to identify potential problem areas, and these skills and subskills are further assessed with informal measures and techniques.

There are many alternatives for reading assessment—tests, inventories, error analysis procedures, and clinical reading interviews, among others—and the assessment team must choose its tools carefully to avoid duplication and ensure that assessment is as efficient as possible. As a general rule, the more specific measures and techniques such as criterion-referenced tests and clinical reading interviews are reserved for in-depth analysis of potential weaknesses.

Answering the assessment questions about reading is one step toward planning the student's Individualized Education Program. For example, Joyce, the fourth grader, was referred for problems in reading.

Joyce

Joyce is unable to read any of the grade 4 textbooks in her classroom. She is now working in a beginning third grade reading book with some success. Previous assessment with the *PIAT-R/NU* and interviews with Mr. Harvey, Joyce's teacher, confirm that Joyce's current reading performance is below that expected for her age and grade.

The assessment team begins its study of Joyce's reading skills by administering Form H of the *Woodcock Reading Mastery Tests-Revised/Normative Update*. Joyce earns these scores:

Subtest	Standard Score Range
Word Identification	72–75
Word Attack	79–86
Word Comprehension	83–90
Passage Comprehension	79–85
Cluster	
Basic Skills	74–77
Reading Comprehension	81–82
Full Scale Total Reading	77–80

Joyce's overall performance on the *WRMT-/NU* falls within the low average range. Her comprehension skills appear stronger than her decoding skills. Joyce shows low average performance on the Word Identification subtest, a measure of sight vocabulary, and low average to average performance on the Word Attack subtest, a measure of skill in phonic analysis of unknown words.

Next, the *Analytical Reading Inventory* (6th ed.) is administered to gain more information about Joyce's oral reading abilities. According to this inventory, Joyce's Independent Reading Level is grade 1, her Instructional Level is grade 2, and her Frustration Level is grade 3. On the reading passages, Joyce makes very few comprehension errors until she reaches frustration level.

Joyce's oral reading responses on the *WRMT-R/NU* and the *ARI* are analyzed to identify patterns of errors. Joyce can recognize only a few words by sight. When she does not recognize a word, she attempts to decode it by sounding it out and by using available context clues. However, Joyce shows weak phonic analysis skills, and the majority of her decoding errors are substitutions that involve mispronunciation of vowel sounds. In reading connected text, Joyce appears to look at the initial consonant of the word and then guess from context. Most of her substitutions make sense in context and begin with the correct initial consonant sound.

A series of criterion-referenced tests are used for further analysis of Joyce's decoding skills. On the *BRIGANCE® Diagnostic Comprehensive Inventory of Basic Skills-Revised,* Joyce shows strengths in knowledge of consonant sounds, short-vowel sounds, and consonant blends. However, results indicate that Joyce has not yet mastered long-vowel sounds, consonant digraphs, and diphthongs. The updated version of the Dolch high-frequency word list (Table 11–2) is used to assess Joyce's sight word vocabulary. Of the 220 words, Joyce is able to recognize 97; most of her errors occur in the second and third grade lists.

After careful analysis of these results, the assessment team is ready to describe Joyce's current levels of reading performance. Their conclusions are as follows:

- Joyce's current instructional reading level is grade 2, as measured by the *Analytical Reading Inventory*. At this level, Joyce comprehends well but requires assistance in decoding.
- In general, Joyce's comprehension skills are more advanced than her decoding skills. She uses context to help her decode unknown words.
- Joyce can recognize most preprimer and primer sight words. She has not yet mastered grades 1, 2, and 3 sight words.
- Joyce knows the sounds of consonants and consonant blends and the short sounds of vowels. She has not yet mastered long-vowel sounds, consonant digraphs, and diphthongs.

REVIEW QUESTIONS

1. Which of the following is the major reason for assessing reading skills?
   a. To determine whether the student has a disability
   b. To gather information about specific learning abilities
   c. To aid in planning the instructional program
   d. To evaluate the effectiveness of instructional practices in the general education classroom

2. The two skill areas of primary concern in the assessment of reading are decoding and _____ . In addition, there is growing interest in the _____ between the reader and the text he or she is reading.

3. Decoding can be accomplished in many ways. Check each of the strategies available to readers for decoding *unfamiliar* words:
   _____ a. Sight recognition
   _____ b. Structural analysis
   _____ c. Phonic analysis
   _____ d. Readability analysis
   _____ e. Contextual analysis

4. In schools today, reading is assessed by
   a. group and individual measures.
   b. norm-referenced and criterion-referenced tests.
   c. informal inventories and clinical interviews.
   d. answers *a* and *c*
   e. answers *b* and *d*

5. Diagnostic reading tests usually assess a wide range of reading skills rather than one single area. (True or False)

6. Match the assessment device or procedure in Column A with the description in Column B.

Column A	*Column B*
a. *Woodcock Reading Mastery Tests-Revised/Normative Update*	____ Assesses only silent reading skills
b. *Test of Reading Comprehension* (3rd ed.)	____ A test that considers both speed and accuracy in decoding
c. *Analytical Reading Inventory* (6th ed.)	____ An informal reading inventory for persons reading between the primer and grade 9 levels
d. *Gray Oral Reading Tests* (3rd ed.)	____ A computer-based measure that uses a modified cloze procedure
e. *Monitoring Basic Skills Progress: Basic Reading* (2nd ed.)	____ Includes readiness measures such as Visual-Auditory Learning and Letter Identification

7. Which of these statements about reading measures are true and which are false?
   a. Decoding skills are assessed on the *Woodcook Reading Mastery Tests-Revised/Normative Update* and the *Gray Oral Reading Tests* (3rd ed.).
   b. Most reading measures include a test of structural analysis skills.

c. Informal inventories evaluate both decoding and comprehension skills.

d. The *Test of Reading Comprehension* (3rd ed.) uses oral reading to assess comprehension skills.

8. Match the description with the assessment results.

a. An area of strength

____ Reading Comprehension Quotient 110 on the *Test of Reading Comprehension*

b. A possible area of educational need

____ Grade 1.6 Instructional Level on an informal reading inventory for a grade 4 student

____ RPI score of 50/90 on one subtest of the *WRMT-R/NU*

____ Scaled score 4 on the Paragraph Reading subtest of the *TORC-3*

9. The results of informal reading inventories are estimates of three reading levels: the _____ level, the _____ level, and the _____ level.

10. Find the true statements about informal assessment of reading.

a. On curriculum-based measures of reading fluency, students read classroom materials aloud for 1 minute.

b. In reading assessment, response analysis is used to identify the miscues that students make in decoding and comprehension.

c. Having students read high-frequency word lists is one way of assessing comprehension of connected text.

d. With the cloze procedure, the student reads a selection from which words have been omitted and attempts to fill in the missing words.

e. Clinical reading interviews are one way of studying how the student interacts with the text.

f. An example of a criterion-referenced test that includes reading skills is the *BRIGANCE® Diagnostic Comprehensive Inventory of Basic Skills-Revised.*

11. Check each type of response that is commonly considered to be a decoding error on informal reading inventories and oral reading tests.

_____ a. Omissions

_____ b. Substitutions

_____ c. Disregard of punctuation

_____ d. Listening comprehension

_____ e. Inference and main idea

_____ f. Additions

12. What three aspects of classroom environments should be evaluated when students experience difficulty in reading?

13. Poor reading skills would likely have the most effect on which school subject?

a. Mathematics

b. Spelling

c. Speaking and listening skills

d. Physical education

14. If the special education team finds that a student shows poor performance in reading comprehension, what conclusion can be drawn?

a. The student is eligible for special education services for students with mental retardation.

b. The special education program should focus on improving decoding skills.

c. The student does not qualify for special education services.

d. A possible IEP goal would be improving reading comprehension.

ACTIVITIES

1. Interview elementary and secondary teachers about their perceptions of the importance of reading skills. Ask them to identify activities in their classrooms in which students with poor reading skills would have difficulty. Are there major differences between the viewpoints of elementary and secondary educators?
2. Locate several group achievement tests and examine how each assesses reading. Are all of the major skills covered?
3. Under the supervision of the course instructor, administer one of the reading tests discussed in this chapter. Calculate all possible scores and analyze the results to determine strengths and weaknesses.
4. Under the supervision of the course instructor, administer relevant portions of one of the criterion-referenced tests of reading discussed in this chapter. Prepare a report that includes recommendations for instructional objectives.
5. Do a work sample analysis of a student's oral reading performance. Identify and analyze all errors according to a system presented in this chapter.
6. Observe in a classroom and note the important features of the instructional, interpersonal, and physical environments that may influence reading performance.

DISCUSSION QUESTIONS

1. Reading is the primary literacy skill, and literacy is highly valued in today's society. Discuss some barriers to adult success that face persons who read poorly.
2. Describe how reading skills can affect how well a student is able to perform in school subjects such as mathematics, composition, and content areas.
3. Compare and contrast the use of formal and informal assessment tools in the study of reading. For what purposes are formal tools most appropriate? Informal tools? Consider, for example, the differences between a diagnostic reading test and a curriculum-based measure.
4. Explain the rationale for assessing the instructional environment of the classroom as a possible contributor to reading problems. Then describe some of the ways that classroom demands can be altered so students with difficulty in reading can participate in learning activities successfully.

MATHEMATICS

Mathematics, like reading, is one of the basic school subjects. Young students are expected to acquire the vocabulary of mathematics; learn to count, recognize, and write numerals and mathematical symbols; understand quantitative terminology; and begin to solve quantitative problems. Arithmetic operations are also a part of the elementary school curriculum; students learn to manipulate quantities with the computational processes of addition, subtraction, multiplication, and division. Mathematics learning continues in the secondary grades, where students are required to apply their knowledge of mathematics in solving quantitative problems. Some secondary students also expand their repertoire of skills by studying algebra, geometry, trigonometry, and perhaps even calculus.

Many students with special needs encounter difficulty in their attempts to learn the basic skills of mathematics and in their efforts to apply these skills in mathematical problem solving. Although mathematics does not pervade the school curriculum in the same way that reading does, quantitative thinking is a necessity in the adult world. Mathematics-based tasks such as handling money, telling time, and measuring are a common part of daily life, as are problem-solving situations such as comparative shopping. Poor skill development in mathematics is a cause for concern, particularly when planning the educational program for students with special needs.

Math skills are assessed in order to gather information for instructional planning. The general question that the assessment team seeks to answer is, *What are the student's educational needs?* Two specific questions are asked: *What is the student's current level of mathematics achievement? What are the student's strengths and weaknesses in the various skill areas of mathematics?*

The major concern is description of the student's current levels of performance. Informal measures and techniques are preferred because they provide specific information about the student's status in skill development. Results of norm-referenced tests may help professionals differentiate educational needs from skills in which the student shows adequate progress.

Assessment for program planning is a selective process that concentrates on the skills and subskills that have been identified as possible problems. If a student's progress in an academic subject such as reading or mathematics is satisfactory, that subject will not be part of the student's special educational program and, thus, in-depth assessment is not necessary. For example, Joyce, the fourth grader whose assessment was described in previous chapters, is successful in mathematics. Therefore, the assessment team will not gather additional data about Joyce's mathematics abilities. In place of Joyce, consider the needs of another student, David. David is an eighth grader whose primary area of difficulty is mathematics.

David

David has been referred for special education assessment by his eighth grade math teacher, Ms. Coolidge. David's math grades were poor in seventh grade, and this year he is failing. In the classroom, he is not able to cope with eighth grade math tasks and instead is reviewing basic number facts and operations. The results of individual achievement tests such as the *WRAT-3* and the *Woodcock-Johnson-R* confirm that David's math performance is below that expected for his age and grade.

The assessment team has determined that David is eligible for special education services, and it is anticipated that specialized instruction in mathematics will be an important part of David's individualized program. To begin the study of David's math performance, the *KeyMath Revised/Normative Update* will be administered. This measure assesses a wide variety of skills, and results will help the team determine the directions for further assessment.

As appropriate, informal measures and techniques will be used to explore the particular skills that appear to be areas of weakness for David. For example, if problem solving seems to need strengthening, the team may conduct a clinical math interview, observing and talking with David as he verbalizes his steps in solving a quantitative problem. Or if David's knowledge of number facts is a concern, the team may devise or select an informal inventory, criterion-referenced test, or curriculum-based measure to evaluate his command of specific addition, subtraction, multiplication, or division facts. David's individualized program in mathematics will be based upon the results of these assessments.

CONSIDERATIONS IN ASSESSMENT OF MATHEMATICS

Students' mathematics and arithmetic skills are often the subject of special education assessment. One of the primary aims of the elementary school curriculum is the development of proficiency in mathematical thinking and computation, and elementary mathematics skills become the foundation for secondary grade mathematics. When students fail to meet the expectations of the general education curriculum in the acquisition and application of mathematics skills, mathematics becomes a major assessment concern.

Purposes

In general education, teachers routinely monitor their students' progress in mathematics, and it is one of the school skills evaluated by the group achievement tests that are administered at regular intervals throughout the grades. In addition, mathematics proficiency is a competency area that is assessed by many schools and districts for grade advancement and high school graduation.

In special education, mathematics skills are investigated at the start of assessment to determine the student's eligibility for special education services. When mathematics is identified as an area of need for a particular student, assessment continues in order to gather the detailed information necessary for program planning. Precise information about the student's current status in mathematics is the basis for establishing the instructional goals of the Individualized Education Program.

Individualized Assessment Plan

For:	*David Burke*	*8*	*13-7*	*11/10/00*	*Mr. Block*
	Student's Name	Grade	Age	Date	Coordinator

Reason for Referral: David is failing grade 8 math; he is working on basic number facts and operations rather than grade level material.

Assessment Question	Assessment Procedure	Person Responsible	Date/Time
What is the student's current level of mathematics achievement?	*KeyMath Revised/Normative Update*	Mr. Block, Resource Teacher	11/16/00, 9:40 A.M.
	Error analysis of current math homework assignments and quizzes	Mr. Block, Resource Teacher, and Ms. Coolidge, Grade 8 Math Teacher	11/14/00, 3 P.M.
What are the student's strengths and weaknesses in the various skill areas of mathematics?	Error analysis of David's responses on the *KeyMath-R/NU*	Mr. Block, Resource Teacher	11/16/00, 2 P.M.
	Additional tests and/or informal assessments, as indicated by the results of formal testing	Mr. Block, Resource Teacher	To be determined

Assessment continues throughout the student's special education program. The cycle of gathering data about current skills, planning instructional interventions, and monitoring the success of those interventions is repeated for as long as the student needs specially designed mathematics instruction.

Skill Areas

Mathematics is a complex body of knowledge, but its skill hierarchy is developmental. Mathematical thinking begins in the preschool years when children acquire the rudiments of a quantitative vocabulary and start to learn counting and other fundamental skills. The written language of mathematics, made up of numerals and symbols, is built upon this conceptual framework. Young students learn to read and write numerals and mathematical symbols and to manipulate quantities through computation. Mathematical problem solving is also introduced to young students as they are developing facility with computational operations.

The developmental nature of mathematics is apparent in the school curriculum. Skills are built one upon the other, and there is a set order for the acquisition of new learning. For example, the general mathematics skills taught in the elementary grades are prerequisite to the higher mathematics of the secondary grades and college.

It is important to distinguish between *mathematics,* the general field of study, and one of its components, *arithmetic.* Reid and Hresko (1981) provide these definitions:

> Mathematics refers to the study or development of relationships, regularities, structures, or organizational schemata dealing with space, time, weight, mass, volume, geometry, and number.
>
> Arithmetic refers to the computational methods used when working with numbers. (p. 292)

Arithmetic is a computational skill. It is concerned with the operations of addition, subtraction, multiplication, and division, and the algorithms involved in these operations. Algorithms are step-by-step procedures for solving computational problems (Ashlock, 1998).

Mathematics is much broader in scope than arithmetic. Although it includes computation, it also encompasses mathematical readiness, number systems and numeration, quantitative prob-

lem solving, geometry, measurement, the applications of time and money, and higher mathematics such as algebra and calculus. Skill in computation should not be equated with mathematics proficiency.

In the 1960s, the "new math" curriculum dominated mathematics instruction with its emphasis on exploration, discovery, and conceptual understanding. The back-to-basics movement of the 1970s changed the instructional focus to the development of basic skills. In the next decade, groups such as the National Council of Teachers of Mathematics (1980) called for educators to give problem-solving skills the highest priority in mathematics instruction.

In its landmark book, *Curriculum and Evaluation Standards for School Mathematics,* the National Council of Teachers of Mathematics (1989) called for a reform in mathematics instruction similar in scope to the whole language movement in reading, writing, and other language arts. The NCTM proposed five general mathematics goals for all students:

1. that they learn to value mathematics,
2. that they become confident in their ability to do mathematics,
3. that they become mathematical problem solvers,
4. that they learn to communicate mathematically, and
5. that they learn to reason mathematically. (p. 5)

Accompanying these goals were recommendations for changes in the ways in which mathematics is taught. Students should be actively involved in authentic problem-solving activities, even at the earliest grade levels. For example, the *Standards* indicate that in kindergarten through grade 4, teachers should decrease reliance on memorization and worksheets and emphasize problem-solving approaches. Students should use manipulatives, calculators, and computers; they should engage in cooperative learning and write and talk about mathematics.

As yet, these reforms have had little effect on practices in special education assessment. Traditional measures tend to focus on computational skills, problem solving, and the more common applications such as geometry and measurement. Computational skills are typically evaluated with paper-and-pencil tasks. The student is presented with written problems that require addition, subtraction, multiplication, or division of whole numbers, fractions, or decimals:

$$\begin{array}{r} 5 \\ + 4 \\ \hline \end{array} \qquad \begin{array}{r} 26 \\ - 19 \\ \hline \end{array} \qquad \begin{array}{r} 639 \\ \times 748 \\ \hline \end{array}$$

$$4.2\overline{)509.3} \qquad \frac{3}{16} + \frac{5}{32} =$$

The student then attempts to solve the problems, often within a specified time limit. On most tests, students are allowed to use pencil and paper for calculation; however, some measures require mental computation. To solve computational problems, the student must read and understand numerals and symbols. Math facts must be recalled from memory or calculated. Then the student must select and correctly apply the appropriate algorithm when solving the problem.

Mathematical problem solving is often assessed by means of story problems that present a quantitative problem in a prose format. Within the story is the problem situation, the numerical data the student must manipulate, and information about the type of manipulation necessary. For example, the problem might state:

> George had five apples. He gave two apples to Susan. How many apples did George have left?

The student must read or listen to the story, identify the problem and the pertinent data for its solution, select the appropriate operation and algorithm, and perform the computation correctly. On some tests, students are required to read the story problems themselves; this is not the best method of assessment for students with poor reading skills. As with computational tests, some measures of problem solving allow the use of paper and pencil, whereas others require mental computation.

In some ways, the distinction between computation and problem solving in mathematics is analogous to that between decoding and comprehension in reading. Just as comprehension relies on decoding, mathematical problem solving relies on arithmetic computation.

As in reading, traditional measures of mathematics performance are product-oriented, not process-oriented. To investigate the interactions between the student and the mathematical "text," it is necessary to use informal strategies. Error analysis procedures provide some information about the student's strategies; clinical math interviews are useful when investigating the student's methods of interacting with story problems.

Mathematics measures often attempt to assess application skills as well as computation and problem solving. Most typically, the applications involve the everyday uses of geometry, time, money, and measurement. Application skills are based on mathematics fundamentals, but because they incorporate new subject matter, they extend beyond simple calculation. For example, to apply mathematics skills to money, the student must learn new symbols such as $ and ¢, new terms such as *penny* and *nickel,* and new facts and equivalencies such as *1 nickel = 5 pennies.* Application skills are an important part of mathematics competency because they represent the most typical ways that the average adult uses mathematics in daily life and the world of work.

Current Practices

Assessment of mathematics achievement is common practice today in both general and special education. Next to reading, mathematics is probably the most frequently assessed school skill. Mathematics assessment is a standard part of the elementary school curriculum, and both group and individual tests of academic achievement include measures of mathematics proficiency.

The assessment tools listed in Table 12–1 are more directly related to instructional planning in special education. Included are standardized tests of mathematics performance, informal inventories, and criterion-referenced tests. Fewer measures are available for the assessment of mathematics than for assessment of reading.

Most standardized tests of mathematics are survey instruments. They assess a wide range of skills within the broad area of mathematics in an attempt to identify the student's strengths and weaknesses. An example is the *KeyMath Revised/ Normative Update.* The original version of this measure, the *KeyMath Diagnostic Arithmetic Test* (Connolly, Nachtman, & Pritchett, 1971, 1976) was consistently identified as one of the most often used tests in special education assessment (Mardell-Czudnowski, 1980; Thurlow

TABLE 12-1
Measures of Mathematics Performance

NAME (AUTHOR)	AGES OR GRADES	TYPE OF MEASURE*	GROUP OR INDIVIDUAL
BRIGANCE® Diagnostic Assessment of Basic Skills, Spanish Edition (Brigance, 1983)	Kindergarten to grade 8	CRT	Individual
BRIGANCE® Diagnostic Comprehensive Inventory of Basic Skills-Revised (Brigance, 1999)	Pre-kindergarten to grade 9	CRT	Individual
BRIGANCE® Diagnostic Inventory of Essential Skills (Brigance, 1981)	Grade 6 to adult education	CRT	Individual
Diagnostic Test of Arithmetic Strategies (Ginsburg & Matthews, 1984)	Grades 1–6	II	Individual
Hudson Education Skills Inventory (Hudson, Colson, Welch, Banikowski, & Mehring, 1989)	Grades K–12	CRT	Individual
KeyMath Revised/Normative Update (Connolly, 1998)	Grades K–9; ages 5-0 to 22-11	NRT	Individual
Monitoring Basic Skills Progress: Basic Math Computation (2nd ed.) (Fuchs, Hamlett, & Fuchs, 1998)	Grades 1–6	CBM	Individual
Monitoring Basic Skills Progress: Basic Math Concepts and Applications (Fuchs, Hamlett, & Fuchs, 1999)	Grades 2–6	CBM	Individual
Stanford Diagnostic Mathematics Test, Fourth Edition (1995)	Grades 1.5–12.9	NRT	Group
Test of Early Mathematics Ability (2nd ed.) (Ginsburg & Baroody, 1990)	Ages 3–9	NRT	Individual
Test of Mathematical Abilities (2nd ed.) (Brown, Cronin, & McEntire, 1994)	Ages 8-0 to 8-11	NRT	Group or Individual

*NRT stands for norm-referenced test, II for informal inventory, CRT for criterion-referenced test, and CBM for curriculum-based measure.

& Ysseldyke, 1979), perhaps because there were few alternatives for the assessment of mathematics skills. At present, however, there are several standardized instruments available, including the *Stanford Diagnostic Mathematics Test* (4th ed.) and the *Test of Mathematical Abilities* (2nd ed.).

In addition, there is a rich array of informal assessment strategies for the study of mathematics performance. These include all of the standard types of informal techniques, but among the most common are informal inventories, criterion-referenced tests of specific skills, error analysis procedures, curriculum-based measures, and clinical math interviews. As Table 12–1 shows, many of the criterion-referenced tests described as informal measures of reading assess mathematics skills as well.

This chapter describes each of the major strategies used in schools today for mathematics assessment. The *KeyMath Revised/Normative Update* is discussed first. Then other formal measures of mathematics performance are described. Later sections of the chapter present information about informal measures and techniques.

KEYMATH REVISED/NORMATIVE UPDATE

The *KeyMath Revised/Normative Update (KeyMath-R/NU)* is an individually administered test designed to "provide a comprehensive assessment of a student's understanding and application of important mathematics concepts and skills"

> ## KeyMath Revised/Normative Update (KeyMath-R/NU)
>
> A. J. Connolly (1998)
>
> **Type:** Norm-referenced and domain-referenced test
>
> **Major Content Areas:** Basic concepts, operations, and applications in mathematics
>
> **Type of Administration:** Individual
>
> **Administration Time:** 30–50 minutes
>
> **Age/Grade Levels:** Grades K through 9; ages 5-0 through 22-11
>
> **Types of Scores:** Standard score and percentile ranks for subtests, area scores, and total test; optional age and grade equivalents for area scores and total test
>
> **Computer Aids:** *KeyMath-R/NU ASSIST*
>
> **Typical Uses:** A broad-based mathematics test for the identification of strengths and weaknesses in mathematics skill development
>
> **Cautions:** Reliability of the *KeyMath-R/NU* is best for total test and area scores; further information is needed about concurrent validity. In administration, the Numeration Basal Item determines starting points for later subtests. Scoring is straightforward, but hand-scoring can be time-consuming if all types of results are desired.
>
> **Publisher:** American Guidance Service (www.agsnet.com)

(Connolly, 1998, p. 1). It is a norm-referenced test that also offers some of the features of criterion-referenced assessment. Test items are linked to skill domains and instructional objectives.

There are two forms of the *KeyMath-R.* Each contains 13 subtests that are organized into three major areas of mathematics. According to the manual, "Basic Concepts represent foundation knowledge; Operations represent computational skills; and Applications represent the use of knowledge and computational skills" (p. 8).

Basic Concepts Subtests

- *Numeration.* Items on this subtest are designed to evaluate the student's understanding of the number system. Among the skills assessed are counting, reading numbers, sequencing numbers, place value, and rounding.
- *Rational Numbers.* This subtest is concerned with the student's ability to identify, order, and compare fractions, decimal numbers, and percentages.

- *Geometry.* Included here are questions about spatial relations, likenesses and differences, pattern development, two- and three-dimensional shapes, and coordinate geometry.

Operations Subtests

- *Addition.* On the first few problems of this subtest, the student looks at a drawing, listens to problems read by the tester, and responds orally. On later items, the format changes to a paper-and-pencil task; the student is given a page of problems and asked to write the answers. Included are problems requiring addition of multidigit numbers (with and without regrouping), fractions, decimals, and mixed numbers.
- *Subtraction.* The tasks on this subtest are the same as on Addition, but the computations involve subtraction of multidigit numbers (with and without regrouping), fractions, decimals, and mixed numbers.
- *Multiplication.* Again, the same test tasks are used, but the problems require multiplication

of whole numbers, fractions, decimals, and mixed numbers.

- *Division.* The test tasks remain the same, but the student must solve problems involving division of whole numbers, fractions, decimals, and mixed numbers.

- *Mental Computation.* Paper and pencil are not allowed on this subtest. The tester reads a computation problem or a series of problems at the rate of one computation per second; problems cannot be repeated, and the student must respond orally within approximately 15 seconds. On other questions, the student looks at a problem as the tester reads it aloud; again, the student must answer within 15 seconds.

Applications Subtests

- *Measurement.* In this subtest, the student answers questions relating to common units of measurement (both standard and metric) and the use of measurement tools such as rulers and thermometers.

- *Time and Money.* Items evaluate the student's ability to complete tasks such as telling time, reading calendars, sequencing chronological events, identifying and counting coins and currency, and making change.

- *Estimation.* Here, the student solves problems by estimating the answer. Most items have a range of acceptable responses. Included are problems involving whole numbers, fractions, and units of measurement.

- *Interpreting Data.* This subtest assesses the student's ability to read and interpret graphs, charts, and tables. Simple problems involving probability and statistics are also included.

- *Problem Solving.* Both routine and nonroutine problems appear on this subtest. Routine problems provide direct cues to the correct operational procedures; nonroutine problems require the student to identify pertinent information, disregard extraneous information, and determine whether all needed information is available. The student must solve both types of problems and describe strategies for attacking nonroutine problems.

The *KeyMath-R/NU* is designed for students from kindergarten through grade 9 and ages 5-0 through 22-11. Reading skills are not needed, be-

cause the tester reads all questions and problems to the student. However, English-language skills are a necessity, particularly for subtests such as Problem Solving. On most *KeyMath-R/NU* subtests, students respond orally, but writing is required on four of the Operations subtests. All subtests except Mental Computation are untimed.

Technical Quality

In 1995–96, the American Guidance Service renormed several of its tests including the *Key-Math-R,* the *Peabody Individual Achievement Test-Revised* (see Chapter 7), and the *WRMT-R* (see Chapter 11). In all cases, renorming was carried out with a sample of 3,184 students in kindergarten through grade 12 and 245 young adults (ages 18–22). The standardization sample appears to represent the U.S. population as reflected in 1994 U.S. Census data. For more information, refer to the description of the *WRMT-R's* technical quality in Chapter 11.

The *KeyMath-R/NU* appears most appropriate for students in grades kindergarten through grade 9. Age norms extend from 5-0 to 22-11, if there is interest in assessment of the basic mathematics skills of older individuals. According to the *KeyMath-R/NU* manual, mathematics performance among K–9 students in the United States has changed since the test was last revised:

> To a moderate degree in the Basic Concepts Area and more dramatically in the Applications Area, above-average students are performing better now than a decade ago and below-average students are performing worse . . . [In the Operations Area] average performance has declined at most grade levels . . . (p. 114)

In evaluating technical quality, it is also important to consider the reliability and validity of a test. However, the manual for the normative update only provides information about previous versions of the test, the 1988 *KeyMath-R* and the 1976 *KeyMath.* Total test and area scores on the *KeyMath-R* show adequate split-half and alternate form reliability. However, several individual subtests do not meet minimum criteria. Alternate form reliability coefficients for grade-based scores fall below .80 for all 13 subtests; reliabilities are in the .70s for six subtests and in the .60s or .50s for the rest. Split-half reliability is lowest for grade-based scores earned by students in kindergarten and grades 1 and 2; in these grades, more than half the reliability coefficients fall below .70.

Concurrent validity of the *KeyMath-R* was studied by examining its relationship to the original *KeyMath* and to mathematics subtests on the *Comprehensive Tests of Basic Skills* and the *Iowa Tests of Basic Skills*. Total test scores of the two versions of the *KeyMath* are strongly related (.90); total mathematics subtest results from the group achievement tests show moderate correlations (.66 to .76) with *KeyMath-R* results. Further information is needed about the relationship of the *KeyMath-R/NU* to other individual tests of mathematics performance and to the individual measures of general achievement (e.g., the *PIAT-R/NU*) commonly used in special education.

Administration Considerations

No special training is required to administer the *KeyMath-R/NU*. According to the manual, this test can be administered by "regular and special education teachers, classroom aides and other paraprofessionals, as well as counselors, school psychologists, and others with special psychometric training" (p. 11). Test interpretation, however, is best accomplished by professionals with training in psychometrics and experience in teaching mathematics.

There are consistent basal and ceiling rules for all *KeyMath-R/NU* subtests. Basals are established by three consecutive correct responses, and ceilings by three consecutive errors. *KeyMath-R/NU* subtests must be administered in order. The test record provides a starting point for the first subtest, Numeration; students in kindergarten and grade 1 begin with item 1, those in grades 2 and 3 begin with item 6, and so forth. Starting points for the rest of the test are determined by the student's performance on Numeration. The basal is established and the "Numeration Basal Item" identified; this is the *first* item in the string of three consecutive responses needed for the basal. For example, if the basal was established with successes on items 12, 13, and 14, the Numeration Basal Item would be item 12. This number is then used to locate the appropri-

ate starting item for later subtests. The test record form indicates, for instance, that students earning a Numeration Basal of 0 to 17 should begin the Rational Numbers subtest with item 1.

Test books are in easel format. On the examiner's side are the directions and questions to be read to the student, the correct answers, and any special scoring instructions. On some items, the tester must point to information on the student's side of the easel. On most *KeyMath-R/NU* subtests, there are no time limits, and testers can repeat items for students as needed. However, on the Mental Computation subtest, items can be read only once, and students have approximately 15 seconds to respond. Written computation is required on the four basic operation subtests; the test record form contains the problems with ample space for computation.

On the *KeyMath-R/NU*, test items are scored as they are administered. Correct responses are marked "1" and incorrect responses "0." As Figure 12–1 shows, each item is keyed to a domain. On the Numeration subtest, the first domain is "Numbers 0–9," and it is evaluated in items 1 through 6. The tester records the student's performance (0 or 1) in the space provided for each item so that domain scores can be obtained. A line is drawn above the easiest item passed and below the most difficult item administered. All domains contain six items. Raw scores for domains are determined by counting the number of successes and the items assumed correct below the basal. The subtest's ceiling item is noted, and the total raw score for the subtest is computed by adding the domain scores.

Results and Interpretation

The *KeyMath-R/NU* offers a variety of scores. Norms are available by age and grade; grade norms are provided for fall and spring testing dates. Subtest results are expressed as percentile ranks and scaled scores (standard scores with a mean of 10 and a standard deviation of 3). Additional scores are available for the three areas (Basic Concepts, Operations, and Applications) and for the Total Test: percentile ranks, standard scores with a mean of 100 and a standard deviation of 15, and optional scores such as age and grade equivalents, normal curve equivalents, and stanines.

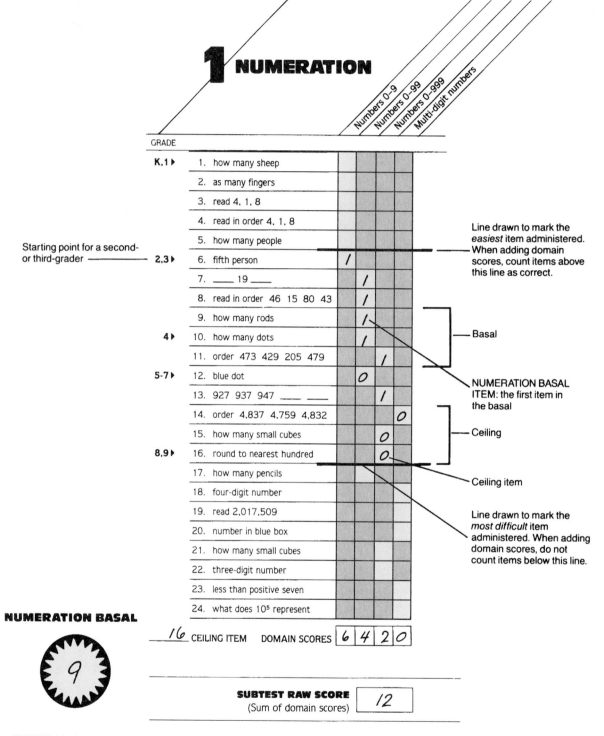

FIGURE 12-1

Sample Subtest Scoring on the *KeyMath Revised/Normative Update*

Note: From *KeyMath Revised/Normative Update, Forms A and B, Examiner's Manual* (p. 14) by A. J. Connolly, 1998, Circle Pines, MN: American Guidance Service. Copyright 1998 by American Guidance Service, Inc. Reprinted by permission.

Results can be plotted on a Score Profile. The tester chooses a confidence level (68% or 90%) and consults a table to determine the values needed to construct intervals around observed scores. Standard scores are plotted for Total Test and area results and scaled scores for subtests. It is also possible to compare the student's performance on the three areas assessed by the *KeyMath-R/NU*. The tester computes the observed difference between area standard scores and consults a table to determine whether these differences are significant at the .01 level, significant at the .05 level, or not significant.

Figure 12–2 presents the Score Profile and Area Comparisons for David, the eighth grader introduced at the start of this chapter. Form A was administered, and fall grade norms were used. The *KeyMath-R/NU* manual recommends selecting a 90% confidence level for profiling Total Test and area standard scores and a 68% confidence level for subtest scaled scores. David's overall mathematics performance fell within the low average range. The Basic Concepts area score was indicative of low average to average performance, and it was significantly higher than both Operations and Applications area scores. David had particular difficulty with the skills assessed on the Multiplication, Division, and Problem Solving subtests.

The *KeyMath-R/NU* provides procedures for analysis of students' performance by domain and by individual test item. As Figure 12–1 showed, each item is keyed to a specific domain. For example, there are three domains within the Division subtest: models and basic facts, algorithms to divide whole numbers, and dividing rational numbers. The Summary of Domain Performance, a table that appears on the test record, is used to evaluate the student's status in each domain. The student's domain scores are listed, and a table in the manual is checked to determine average domain scores for the student's grade. Then the student's performance in each domain is rated as Weak, Average, or Strong. On the Division subtest, David showed Average skill in models and basic facts but Weak performance in the other two domains.

Test items on the *KeyMath-R/NU* are also linked to specific objectives. For example, the objective for one of the Division items that David missed is "The student can divide a three-digit number when regrouping is required." This feature can be very helpful in preliminary planning of instruction if the objectives are addressed in the student's school mathematics program. Further assessment would be necessary, however, because *KeyMath-R/NU* objectives are evaluated by only one or two test items. Professionals can devise measures themselves or select a published material such as *KeyMath Teach and Practice* (Connolly, 1985).

KeyMath-R/NU results help evaluators to determine the student's current achievement in basic mathematics concepts, computational operations, and applications such as problem solving, estimation, time, money, and measurement. The *KeyMath-R/NU* is most useful as a screening device to identify possible strengths and weaknesses. Although further information must be gathered about each potential area of educational need, the *KeyMath-R/NU*'s organization of mathematics skills into domains and objectives facilitates this process. Results can be linked to specific skills and subskills, thereby proving helpful in the selection or design of appropriate informal tools for in-depth assessment.

OTHER FORMAL MEASURES

There are several other formal measures of mathematics skills in addition to the *KeyMath-R/NU,* and three of these are described in the next sections. Included are the *Stanford Diagnostic Mathematics Test* (4th ed.), a set of group-administered survey tests designed for grade 1 through high school; the *Test of Mathematical Abilities* (2nd ed.), an instrument that assesses mathematical aptitudes and students' attitudes toward math; and the *Diagnostic Test of Arithmetic Strategies,* a formal measure of the strategies that students use to solve computation problems.

Stanford Diagnostic Mathematics Test (4th ed.) (SDMT)

The *SDMT* is a norm-referenced test of several types of mathematics skills. Designed for group use, its major purpose is identification of areas of educational need.

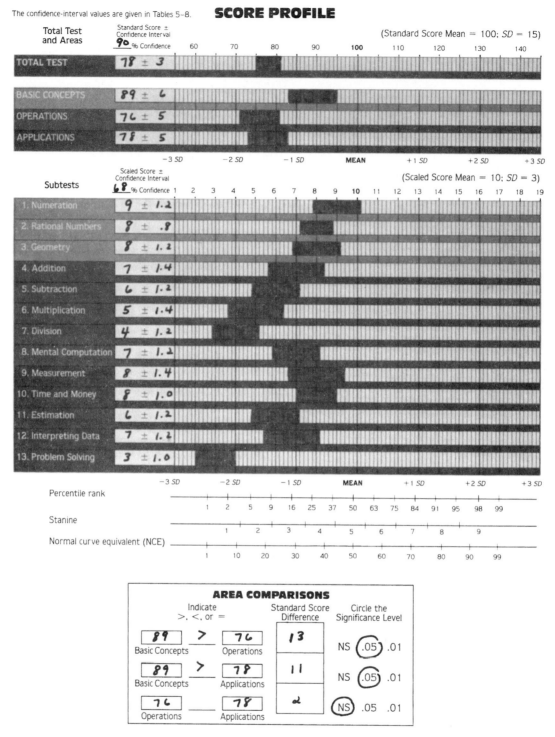

FIGURE 12-2

Sample Score Profile and Area Comparisons from the *KeyMath-R/NU*

Note: From *KeyMath Revised/Normative Update Individual Test Record, Form A* by A. J. Connolly, 1998, Circle Pines, MN: American Guidance Service. Copyright 1998 by American Guidance Service, Inc. Reprinted by permission.

Stanford Diagnostic Mathematics Test, Fourth Edition (SDMT)

(1995)

Type: Norm-referenced test

Major Content Areas: Concepts and applications, computation

Type of Administration: Group

Administration Time: Approximately 1.5 hours

Age/Grade Levels: Red Level, Grades 1.5 to 2.5; Orange Level, Grades 2.5 to 3.5; Green Level, Grades 3.5 to 4.5; Purple Level, Grades 4.5 to 6.5; Brown Level, Grades 6.5 to 8.9; Blue Level, Grades 9.0 to 12.9

Types of Scores: Percentile ranks, stanines, scaled scores, grade equivalents, Progress Indicators

Computer Aids: Scoring services available from publisher

Typical Uses: A broad-based test for the identification of strengths and weaknesses in mathematics skill development

Cautions: The *SDMT* is designed for group administration. Some questions are multiple-choice, some portions of the test are timed, and older students record their responses on a separate answer sheet. If students experience difficulty with group administration, the *SDMT* can be administered individually as long as the tester adheres to standard administration practices.

Publisher: Harcourt Brace Educational Measurement (www.hbem.com)

Six levels of the *SDMT* are available to meet the needs of students in grades 1 through high school, and there is some overlap between levels to accommodate students with problems in mathematics. For example, both the Green and Purple Levels provide norms for fourth graders, but the Green Level is more appropriate for low achievers because its content is based on the skills taught in the early elementary grades. To facilitate retesting, parallel forms are available for the upper three levels.

Each level contains two separate tests: a multiple-choice test and a free-response test. The free-response format is available so that teachers can analyze how students go about solving mathematical problems. Each multiple-choice and free-response test is divided into two subtests: Concepts and Applications, and Computation. Several concept and skill domains are assessed by each of these subtests, although content varies somewhat from level to level:

Concepts and Applications

- Numeration
- Patterns and Functions
- Probability and Statistics
- Graphs and Tables
- Problem Solving
- Geometry and Measurement

Computation

- Addition of Whole Numbers
- Subtraction of Whole Numbers
- Multiplication of Whole Numbers
- Division of Whole Numbers
- Operations with Fractions and Mixed Numbers
- Operations with Decimals and Percents
- Equations

It is possible to administer one or both subtests of the multiple-choice and free-response measures. To avoid tiring the students, it is suggested that only one subtest be given per day.

The *SDMT* is designed for group administration, and it is quite easy to administer. There are no basals or ceilings, and all responses are recorded by the student. The tester simply reads the specified directions to the student and times some of the tests. The *SDMT* can be hand-scored by the tester or sent to a commercial service for scoring.

To participate, students must be able to listen and attend to test directions and work independently. On the upper levels, students mark their responses on separate answer sheets. Several of the tests are timed. On the lower levels, reading skills are not required because the tester reads the word problems aloud. On the upper levels, students may request assistance in reading the questions.

Several types of scores are available for each *SDMT* subtest, including percentile ranks, scaled scores, stanines, and grade equivalents. Progress Indicator scores are also available. These scores provide information about how well the student is progressing in each of the concept and skill domains assessed by the *SDMT*. The student's raw score on each domain is compared to a cutoff score that indicates mastery of skills in that domain. If the student's score equals or exceeds the criterion, the Progress Indicator (PI) is +, meaning adequate progress. If the student's score falls below the criterion, the PI is −. The *SDMT* calls the Progress Indicator a criterion-referenced score because its reference point is the test's content, not test norms.

Although the *SDMT* is a group test, it can be administered individually as long as standard testing procedures are followed. Its advantages include norms that extend through grade 12, so it can be used with older high school students. In addition, it offers precise descriptions of the skills it assesses and provides information about skill mastery through the Progress Indicators. Like other diagnostic tests, however, the *SDMT* is best used as a broad-based survey of several areas of mathematics proficiency.

Test of Mathematical Abilities (2nd ed.) (TOMA-2)

The *TOMA-2* is an interesting test because it attempts to extend mathematics assessment be-

yond the traditional skills of computation and problem solving. According to the *TOMA-2* manual, other important factors are the "attitudes students might have toward mathematics, understanding the language of mathematics as represented by vocabulary used in teaching and learning, and familiarity with general mathematical information found in everyday life" (p. 1).

The *TOMA-2* contains five subtests:

- *Vocabulary.* Students are presented with 25 mathematical terms. They read the words and then write a brief definition of the term as it is used in a mathematical sense.
- *Computation.* Twenty-five computational problems appear on a page in the test booklet. These problems sample the basic operations as well as manipulation of fractions, decimals, money, percentages, and other types of mathematical expressions. Students write their responses directly in the test booklet.
- *General Information.* The tester reads questions to the student such as "How many pennies are there in a dime?" The student replies orally or writes answers in the test record book.
- *Story Problems.* The student reads brief story problems. Work space is provided for calculation, and the student writes the solution in this space and circles it.
- *Attitude toward Math (Supplemental).* The tester reads aloud statements such as "Math is easy for me." Students listen and then check one of these responses: Yes, definitely; Closer to Yes; Closer to No; No, definitely. This subtest is an adaptation of the mathematics portion of the *Estes Attitude Scales* (Estes, Estes, Richards, & Roettger, 1981), which is described in Chapter 10.

Both reading and writing are required on the *TOMA-2*, and students with skill problems in these areas may have difficulty with some subtests. However, test tasks are not timed. Students must read sentences on the Story Problems subtest. On the Vocabulary subtest, students must read terms and write definitions, although spelling, punctuation, and capitalization errors are not penalized. Clearly, English-language facility is a prerequisite for participation in the *TOMA-2*. If group administration procedures are used, then

Test of Mathematical Abilities (2nd ed.) (TOMA-2)

V. L. Brown, M. E. Cronin, & E. McEntire (1994)

Type: Norm-referenced test

Major Content Areas: Vocabulary, computation, general information, story problems, and attitude toward math

Type of Administration: Individual or group

Administration Time: 1–2 hours

Age/Grade Levels: Ages 8-0 through 18-11

Types of Scores: Scaled scores, percentile ranks, Math Quotient

Computer Aids: N/A

Typical Uses: Evaluation of attitudes toward mathematics and identification of strengths and weaknesses in mathematics skill development

Cautions: Students need both reading and writing skills to complete test tasks on the *TOMA-2*. Professionals should take extra care when evaluating students' responses to the open-ended questions on the Vocabulary and General Information subtests. Further information is needed about concurrent validity in relation to other measures of mathematics performance.

Publisher: PRO-ED (www.proedinc.com)

students must also be able to attend to test directions and work independently in a group.

The *TOMA-2* was standardized on approximately 2,000 students ages 8-0 to 18-11 from 26 states. The sample appears to resemble the national population in terms of gender, race, ethnicity, geographic region, and disability status. Internal consistency and test-retest reliability of the *TOMA-2* appear adequate. The concurrent validity of the original *TOMA* was studied in relation to the *KeyMath* and math subtests from the *PIAT* and *WRAT* with a small sample of students with learning disabilities ($n = 38$). Moderate correlations (.34 to .45) were found. In a more recent study using the *TOMA-2* and a larger sample ($n = 290$), a correlation of .61 was found between the *TOMA-2*'s Math Quotient score and the mathematics total score of the *SRA Achievement Series*. Further study is needed of the *TOMA-2*'s relationship to current versions of the individual tests of mathematics performance that are typically used in special education.

Formal training in assessment is recommended for testers who wish to administer the *TOMA-2*. The subtests should be presented in order. Students begin with item 1 on all subtests. On the Attitude toward Math subtest, students answer all items. On the other subtests, the ceiling is defined as three consecutive incorrect responses. When subtests are administered to groups, students are directed to complete as many items as they can; the tester then applies the ceiling rules when scoring the test.

Care must be taken in grading students' responses. In particular, the Vocabulary and General Information subtests require the tester to exercise judgment in determining whether responses are correct or incorrect. The manual provides scoring standards to assist in evaluating students' responses on these two subtests.

Scaled scores and percentile ranks are available for each *TOMA-2* subtest. The scaled scores are distributed with a mean of 10 and a standard deviation of 3. A total test score, the Math Quotient, is derived by combining results of the four required subtests; it is distributed with a mean of 100 and a standard deviation of 15. The standard error of measurement for the *TOMA-2* subtests ranges from .6 to 1.6 scaled score points, depending on the subtest and the age of the student. The standard error of the Math Quotient score ranges from 2.1 to 3.7. Results of the *TOMA-2* are plotted on a profile, as Figure 12–3 illustrates. These are the scores of a 10-year-old girl who shows average performance in all areas. Her lowest score was on Computation, where she earned a scaled score of 8.

The *TOMA-2* is a norm-referenced mathematics test that surveys several areas of performance. It assesses traditional mathematics skills and also offers measures of attitudes toward mathematics, mathematics vocabulary, and general mathematics information. As with other survey tests, the results of the *TOMA-2* are used to direct further assessment.

Diagnostic Test of Arithmetic Strategies (DTAS)

The *DTAS* is an older measure but one that is unique because it assesses the strategies students use in solving arithmetic computation problems. Although not norm-referenced, it is a formal assessment device with standard procedures for administration and scoring. Its scope is quite limited in comparison to tests like the *KeyMath-R/NU, SDMT,* and *TOMA-2*. Its purpose is the in-depth assessment of one important component of mathematical ability—arithmetic computation.

The *DTAS* contains four subtests: Addition, Subtraction, Multiplication, and Division. Their focus is not the answers that students give to computation problems. Instead, they are designed to elicit information about the ways students go about solving computation problems. To accomplish this, each subtest is divided into four sections.

Section 1: Setting Up the Problem. The tester reads problems to the student, who writes down each problem; the student is not required to solve the problems. For example, the tester might say, "Write down twenty-four plus eighteen." The student's responses are checked for several types of errors. Errors in writing numerals occur when the student writes 7 as Γ. Errors in writing numbers occur when numbers are written as they sound

---

Diagnostic Test of Arithmetic Strategies (DTAS)

H. P. Ginsburg & S. C. Mathews (1984)

Type: Diagnostic inventory with standard administration and scoring procedures

Major Content Areas: Setting up problems, number facts, written calculation, and informal skills

Type of Administration: Individual

Administration time: 20 minutes per subtest

Age/Grade Levels: Students in the elementary grades

Types of Scores: Norm-referenced scores are not available; results are the number and types of errors made by the student

Computer Aids: N/A

Typical Uses: Identification of successful and unsuccessful strategies for addition, subtraction, multiplication, and division

Cautions: The *DTAS* provide descriptive results rather than norm-referenced scores.

Publisher: PRO-ED (www.proedinc.com)

Section II. Record of TOMA-2 Scores

Subtest	Raw Score	%ile	Standard Score	Sum of Std. Scores	Descriptive Rating	Age Equivalent	Grade Equivalent
Vocabulary (VO)	3	50	10		Average	10-0	4.2
Computation (CO)	10	25	8	38	Average	8-6	2.7
General Information (GI)	17	63	11		Average	11-6	5.8
Story Problems (SP)	7	37	9		Average	9-6	3.7
Attitude Toward Math (AT)	38	16	7		Average		

Math Quotient = **97**

Section III. Profile of Test Scores

Subtest Scores | **Composite Score** | **Other Test Scores**

Subtest Scores columns: Vocabulary (VO), Computation (CO), General Information (GI), Story Problems (SP), Attitude Toward Math (AT)

Composite Score: TOMA-2 Math Quotient (MQ)

Other Test Scores: 1, 2, 3, 4, 5, 6, 7

Std. Scores	Std. Scores	Quotients	Quotients
20	20	150	150
19	19	145	145
18	18	140	140
17	17	135	135
16	16	130	130
15	15	125	125
14	14	120	120
13	13	115	115
12	12	110	110
11	11	105	105
10	10	100	100
9	9	95	95
8	8	90	90
7	7	85	85
6	6	80	80
5	5	75	75
4	4	70	70
3	3	65	65
2	2	60	60
1	1	55	55

Plotted values: Vocabulary (VO) = 10, Computation (CO) = 8, General Information (GI) = 11, Story Problems (SP) = 9, Attitude Toward Math (AT) = 11; TOMA-2 Math Quotient (MQ) ≈ 97.

FIGURE 12-3

Sample Results of the *Test of Mathematical Abilities* (2nd ed.)

Note: From *Test of Mathematical Abilities* (2nd ed.) (p. 16) by V. L. Brown, M. E. Cronin, and E. McEntire, 1994, Austin, TX: PRO-ED. Copyright 1994, by PRO-ED. Reprinted by permission.

(e.g., 204 for twenty-four) or when numbers are reversed. In addition, subtraction, and multiplication, alignment is incorrect if the student aligns numbers to the left rather than to the right. Sloppy alignment is also considered an error.

Section 2: Number Facts. Students are shown a simple facts problem and told to say the answer that comes into their head. The tester records how long it takes the student to respond and whether or not the response is correct. The skill under assessment is the student's ability to recall number facts quickly, accurately, and automatically. The tester observes the student and notes whether the student attempts to solve the problems by counting fingers, using whispered counting, or counting aloud.

Section 3: Written Calculation. The student is presented with 12 computation problems of increasing difficulty. He or she is directed to read each problem out loud, show all work on the answer sheet, and is told, "Tell me out loud what you are doing." The tester then analyzes several aspects of the student's work. To illustrate this, Figure 12–4 presents the scoring sheet for the Written Calculation section of the Addition subtest. The results are those of a 6-year-old second grader described in the *DTAS* manual.

First the professional determines whether the student's answer is correct or incorrect. Then the student's method of solving the problem is considered to see if the student used the standard school method or an informal one. The standard school method for addition involves beginning with the "ones" column and carrying when necessary. Informal methods are nonstandard procedures. For example, the student may begin with the larger number and count upwards; or a problem such as 42 + 54 might be simplified into two problems, 40 + 50 and 2 + 4. Second, the tester looks for any number fact errors that may have occurred. "Bugs" are another concern. Also called defective algorithms (Ashlock, 1998), bugs are systematic but inappropriate procedures for problem solving. The *DTAS* scoring sheet lists several possible types of bugs. For instance, the student might approach an addition problem as if it were a multiplication problem. Or the student might follow the rule that "0 makes 0." With this

bug, the sum of 15 + 20 would be calculated as 30, because 0 plus any number is 0. "Slips" are another error category in Written Calculation. According to the *DTAS* manual, slips are "relatively minor execution errors, and do not seem to result from basic faults in understanding or serious defects in the calculational procedure" (p. 4). Examples of slips in addition are skipping numbers and adding the same number twice.

Section 4: Informal Skills. Here the tester reads computation problems and the student must solve them mentally. For example, the tester might ask, "How much is twenty-seven and fourteen?" The purpose of this activity is to require the student to go beyond the standard school methods of problem solving. The student is presented with nontraditional problems (nontraditional because they require mental computation), and informal problem-solving procedures are observed. The tester then records which strategy the student employs. For example, on the Addition subtest, the tester notes whether the student used counting, simplification, imaginary column addition, or some other informal strategy. If the student fails to use an informal procedure, the tester prompts the student by suggesting a strategy.

According to the manual, the *DTAS* is appropriate for students "who are experiencing difficulty with addition, subtraction, multiplication, or division (roughly in grades 1–6)" (p. 9). Students must possess sufficient English-language skills to understand test directions and respond to questions. No reading skills are required, and students do not need to write letters or words. However, they are expected to write computation problems and solutions. None of the subtests are timed, but students are urged to work quickly on the Number Facts task. At first, students may be somewhat reluctant to explain how they are solving the problems on Written Calculation, but most will cooperate when encouraged by the tester.

Special training is not needed to administer the *DTAS*, but professionals should study the manual carefully and administer several practice tests. Subtests can be administered in any order, and it is not necessary to administer all subtests

---

SECTION IIB: WRITTEN CALCULATION

	Problems											
	5	6	7	8	9	10	11	12	13	14	15	16
1. Answer												
Correct (circle)	㊴	㉗	㊻	㉒	126	135	42	64	643	730	36	36
Incorrect (write in)	—	—	—	—	*136*	*145*	*312*	*514*	*533*	*620*	*30*	*38*
2. Standard school method	✓	✓	✓	✓	✓	✓	—	—	—	—	—	—
3. Informal method	—	—	—	—	—	—	—	—	—	—	—	—
4. Number fact error	—	—	—	—	✓	✓	—	—	—	—	—	—
5. Bugs												
A. Addition like multiplication	—	—										
B. Zero makes zero			—	—								
C. Add from left to right					—	—						
D. No carry: All digits on bottom							✓	✓	—	—		
E. No carry: Vanishing digit							—	—	✓	✓		
F. Carries wrong digit							—	—				
G. Wrong operation	—	—	—	—	—	—	—	—	—	—	—	—
H. Add individual digits	—	—	—	—	—	—	—	—	—	—	—	—
I. Other	—	—	—	—	—	—	—	—	—	—	—	—
6. Slips												
A. Skips numbers	—	—	—	—	—	—	—	—	—	—	✓	—
B. Adds twice	—	—	—	—	—	—	—	—	—	—	—	✓
C. Other	—	—	—	—	—	—	—	—	—	—	—	—

Notes: *Debbie started out by doing the standard school method on problems 5-8 which do not involve carrying. When carrying was introduced, she obviously did not know how to deal with it and either put all digits on the bottom or ignored the numbers to be carried. On the last two problems, she was sloppy, making two slips.*

FIGURE 12–4

Sample Results of the *Diagnostic Test of Arithmetic Strategies*

Note: From *Diagnostic Test of Arithmetic Strategies* (p. 34) by H. P. Ginsburg and S. C. Mathews, 1984, Austin, TX: PRO-ED. Copyright 1984 by PRO-ED. Reprinted by permission.

to any one student. The manual advises that a student be given only one of the four subtests during any one testing session. There are no basals and ceilings because students are encouraged to attempt all of the test items.

Scoring the *DTAS* requires more expertise than that required for many measures. The tester must evaluate the accuracy of the stu-

dent's responses and also describe the methods the student used to arrive at these responses. The manual provides guidelines for scoring each subtest, standards for scoring, and examples. Testers should take advantage of these resources.

The *DTAS* does not produce norm-referenced results. Instead, the results are descriptive. For each basic operation, it is possible to identify the strategies the student uses and the types of errors that occur consistently. For example, the results that appeared in Figure 12–4 indicate that the student experiences difficulty with carrying. When faced with addition problems that require carrying (or regrouping), the student relies upon two types of bugs. She fails to carry and writes all digits:

$$\begin{array}{r} 15 \\ + \ 29 \\ \hline 314 \end{array}$$

or she fails to carry but writes only the ones digit:

$$\begin{array}{r} 345 \\ + \ 296 \\ \hline 531 \end{array}$$

Descriptive results have direct implications for instruction, if the skill in question is an area of educational need for the student. Because the *DTAS* is not normed, it is impossible to compare the student's performance with age or grade peers. For example, the student may be progressing satisfactorily but simply not have reached the point in the mathematics curriculum where regrouping skills are taught. However, if the skill deficiency is perceived as a problem, *DTAS* results may be used to plan a course of instructional action. The manual provides suggestions for remedial activities.

CURRICULUM-BASED MEASURES: MONITORING BASIC SKILLS PROGRESS

Monitoring Basic Skills Progress (MBSP) is a collection of commercially available curriculum-based measures that include computer components. Two of its four parts assess mathematics skills: Basic Math Computation (2nd ed.) (Fuchs, Hamlett, & Fuchs, 1998) and Basic Math Concepts and Applications (Fuchs, Hamlett, & Fuchs, 1999). The Computation portion of *MBSP* is designed for students in grades 1 through 6 and the Concepts and Applications portion for those in grades 2 through 6.

Unlike the Basic Reading measure of *MBSP*, the math portions are not administered by computer. Instead, students take timed, paper-and-pencil math tests and then enter their answers into a computer program. The program scores the test and provides students and teachers with detailed feedback on performance.

Each of the *MBSP* math measures includes a student disk, teacher disk, and a book of tests designed to be copied by the teacher. There are 30 tests at each grade level, and all tests at one grade level contain the same types of items. There are 25 items on the Computation tests and 18 to 25 items on the Concepts and Applications tests. The *MBSP* manuals recommend that tests be given once a week to general education students and twice a week to students in special education. Tests must be timed by the teacher. Time limits for the Computation measures range from 2 to 6 minutes, depending upon grade level. Those for the Concepts and Applications measures range from 6 to 8 minutes.

The skills assessed by Basic Math Computation are the basic operations: addition, subtraction, multiplication, and division of whole numbers, fractions, and decimals. The Concepts and Applications measures, in contrast, assess a number of different skills, appropriate to the curricular changes from grade 2 to grade 6. Examples are counting, number concepts, numeration, measurement, charts and graphs, money, fractions, decimals, percentages, applied computation, word problems, geometry, ratios and probability, and variables. One important feature of both of these measures is the Skill Profile, a visual depiction of the skills the student has and has not mastered. Figure 12–5 provides an example. The graph at the top of the figure shows Brian's progress to date. Underneath the graph is the Skills Profile. In the second half of the figure is the Skills Profile Key. Using this Key, it can be seen that Brian has made good progress in the first goal, Adding. His performance has improved from "Cool" to "Warm" to "Very Warm" and is now "Hot," indicating skill mastery.

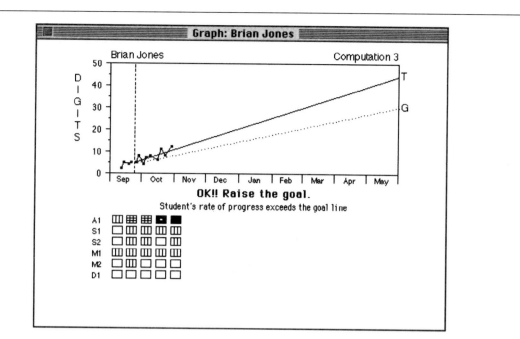

SKILLS PROFILE KEY - Grade 3

Abbreviations		Examples		
A1	Adding	35 +96	682 +645	375 + 87
S1	Subtracting with regrouping	43 - 26	437 - 85	
S2	Subtracting with regrouping using 0	406 - 398	500 - 367	
M1	Multiplying basic facts	3 × 5	9 × 6	
M2	Multiplying	57 × 3		
D1	Dividing basic facts	3⟌6	8⟌56	

Box Key

■ **Hot.** You've got it!

▣ **Very warm.** Almost have it.

▦ **Warm.** Starting to get it.

▥ **Cool.** Trying these.

□ **Cold.** Not tried.

FIGURE 12–5

Sample Results from *Monitoring Basic Skills Progress: Basic Math Computation* (2nd ed.)

Note: From *Monitoring Basic Skills Progress: Basic Math Computation* (2nd ed.) (pp. 7, 74) by L. S. Fuchs, C. L. Hamlett, and D. Fuchs, 1998, Austin, TX: PRO-ED. Copyright 1998 by PRO-ED. Reprinted by permission.

OTHER INFORMAL ASSESSMENT PROCEDURES

Assessment for instructional planning relies upon several informal measures and techniques in addition to curriculum-based measurement. Among the most common are teacher checklists, informal inventories, error analysis, diagnostic teaching and clinical math interviews, criterion-referenced tests, questionnaires and interviews, and portfolio assessment.

Teacher Checklists

Checklists are a quick and efficient method for gathering information from teachers and other professionals about their observations of students' performance in mathematics. Some checklists are designed so they are general in nature, surveying a wide range of mathematics content. Others are quite specific, focusing on a particular set of skills.

One major use of checklists is to document and monitor students' acquisition of mathematics skills. Curriculum checklists, such as the one shown in Figure 12–6, serve this purpose. This checklist

FIGURE 12–6
Curriculum Checklist for Mathematics Application Skills

1. Measurement—time/calendar

Early Childhood Education

_____ a. Can show time to the hour.

_____ b. Can read time to the hour.

_____ c. Can show time to the minute.

_____ d. Can identify time to the minute, by stating "so many minutes after the hour."

_____ e. Can tell time by fractions: _____ half hour, _____ quarter hour.

_____ f. Can count by 5-minute intervals.

_____ g. States there are 60 minutes in an hour, _____ 30 minutes in half-hour, _____ 12 hours in half-day, _____ distinguishes a.m. and p.m.

_____ h. Can read so many minutes before the next hour.

_____ i. States the number of days in a week, _____ months in a year.

_____ j. Tells names of days in a week.

_____ k. Can read names of days, _____ months.

_____ l. Uses the calendar to interpret date.

_____ m. Tells his or her birthday by _____ month, _____ day, _____ year.

Middle School Education

_____ n. Interprets written notation of time, e.g., 3:00, 3:01, 3:30, 3:45, etc.

_____ o. Writes time shown on a clock face.

_____ p. States number of seconds in a minute.

_____ q. Sets an alarm clock.

_____ r. Constructs time schedules, such as for homework or TV.

_____ s. Uses time schedules—bus, train, plane, subway.

_____ t. Reads public transportation schedules.

_____ u. Explains Daylight Saving Time.

FIGURE 12-6
Continued

High School Education

_____ v. Can use a time clock.

_____ w. Can explain meaning of *time and a half, double time.*

_____ x. Is on time for school, work.

_____ y. Explains and identifies different time zones in the world and can compute equivalent time across zones.

_____ z. Uses time in relationship to _____ speed, _____ distance, _____ cooking.

2. Measurement—clothing size

_____ a. Can interpret sizes of _____ clothes, _____ shoes, _____ underwear.

3. Measurement—temperature

_____ a. Can read and interpret temperature on a thermometer.

_____ b. Can use temperature in cooking.

4. Metric Measure

_____ a. Can relate metric measures to decimal notation.

_____ b. Can use metric measures in cooking; weights.

_____ c. Can convert values from one measure to another—metric to nonmetric, metric to metric, nonmetric to nonmetric (inches to feet, gallon to quarts).

_____ d. Tells approximate distance between locations in either kilometers or miles.

_____ e. Uses measures in basic shop work.

_____ f. Uses legend on map to estimate kilometers or miles.

_____ g. Tells how to use an odometer; a speedometer.

5. Economics

_____ a. States the approximate money value of objects, such as soda pop, crayons, movie ticket, postage stamps.

_____ b. Recognizes paper money to $20.00.

_____ c. Makes change up to $25.00.

_____ d. Writes all money amounts in decimal form.

_____ e. Uses ads in newspapers, on radio, TV, and on store front windows to compare prices of food, clothing, etc.

_____ f. Keeps daily record of expenditures.

_____ g. Can check sales tax on purchases computing percent.

_____ h. Computes hourly wage.

_____ i. Displays understanding of state and federal taxes.

_____ j. Displays understanding of social security tax and purpose of tax.

_____ k. Can estimate living expenses, such as rent, utilities.

_____ l. Can estimate cost of various licenses—auto, driver's, business.

_____ m. States basic bank interactions and their purpose: checking account, savings account, loan, interest on savings accounts, interest on loans.

_____ n. Can interpret bank statement.

_____ o. Can keep checking account balanced.

_____ p. States pros and cons of installment buying.

Note: From *Teaching Mathematics to Children with Special Needs* (pp. 252–253) by F. K. Reisman and S. H. Kauffman, 1980, New York: Merrill/Macmillan. Copyright 1980 by Macmillan Publishing Company. Reprinted by permission.

addresses application skills such as telling time, using a calendar, reading a thermometer, and applying consumer economics. This checklist could be completed during assessment and then updated as the student learns new skills.

Informal Inventories

Informal inventories survey a variety of skills to determine where the student's strengths and weaknesses lie. For example, an informal inventory that assesses arithmetic computation skills appears in Figure 12–7. This inventory contains problems that require the basic operations of addition, subtraction, multiplication, and division. However, the inventory provides only one or two items, at most, to evaluate a particular skill such as addition of two-digit numbers with regrouping. If results point to a possible skill deficiency, it is necessary to collect further data with more precise measures such as criterion-referenced tests.

Inventories are quite easy to construct, and professionals can design their own to assess whatever skill areas are of interest. For instance, if the teacher is curious about a student's understanding of place value concepts, he or she could devise a set of questions to probe this area of mathematics. The teacher might include activities such as the following:

> The number 48 is the same as 4 tens and 8 ones. Tell how many tens and ones make up these numbers.
>
> $15 = \underline{\hspace{1cm}}$ tens + $\underline{\hspace{1cm}}$ ones
>
> $36 = \underline{\hspace{1cm}}$ tens + $\underline{\hspace{1cm}}$ ones
>
> $72 = \underline{\hspace{1cm}}$ tens + $\underline{\hspace{1cm}}$ ones

Or if the teacher is interested in the student's ability to tell time, the teacher could prepare a set of drawings of clock faces, each showing a different time. One set might assess telling time to the hour (e.g., 4:00), another telling time to the half hour (e.g., 7:30), and so forth. The teacher should also consider including clocks with digital displays (e.g., 8:42 or 4:23:15).

Mathematics skills are usually assessed with paper-and-pencil tasks, but there are many other alternatives. If the teacher wants to learn more about the student's knowledge of basic math facts, problems could be presented orally, on paper, on the chalkboard, with flashcards, in horizontal notation (2 + 3 =) or vertical notation, and so forth. Students could respond orally instead of writing their answers and, if speed is a concern, the inventory can be timed.

Error Analysis

Mathematics is one of the school subjects best suited for error analysis because students respond in writing on most tasks, thereby producing a permanent record of their work. Also, there is usually only one correct answer to mathematical problems and questions, and scoring is unambiguous. Error analysis is a traditional technique in mathematics assessment; it dates back to the 1920s when professionals began to study the types of errors that characterize written computation (Brueckner, 1930; Buswell & John, 1925; Osborn, 1925).

Today, the most common use of error analysis in mathematics is assessment of computation skills. Cox (1975) differentiates between systematic computation errors and errors that are random or careless mistakes. With systematic errors, students are consistent in their use of an incorrect number fact, operation, or algorithm. Roberts (1968) studied the written computation of elementary grade students and identified four error types:

1. *Incorrect operation*. The student selects the incorrect operation. For example, if the problem requires subtraction, the student adds.
2. *Incorrect number fact*. The number fact recalled by the student is inaccurate. For example, the student recalls the product of 6 × 9 as 52.
3. *Incorrect algorithm*. The procedures used by the student to solve the problem are inappropriate. The student may skip a step, apply the correct steps in the wrong sequence, or use an inaccurate method. For example, in the subtraction problem 24 − 18, the student may begin by subtracting 4 from 8, using the algorithm "subtract the smaller number from the larger."
4. *Random error*. The student's response is incorrect and apparently random. For example, the student writes 100 as the answer to 42 × 6.

Addition

6	3	4	10	8	11
+2	+5	+0	+ 5	+3	+ 4

17	33	67	12	42	523
+ 5	+15	+71	+ 9	+ 9	+162

692
+349

Subtraction

6	3	4	17	98	47
−4	−3	−0	− 3	− 4	−32

10	14	27	7 − 5 = _____
− 3	− 6	−24	

17 − 12 = _____   18 − 9 = _____

176	253	462
− 36	− 89	−321

Multiplication

3	2	2	6	33	22	3
×2	×2	×8	×0	× 1	× 4	×22

232	204	8 × 6 = _____	7 × 7 = _____
× 3	× 2		

1403	105	2675	1760	22	17
× 2	× 3	× 3	× 5	×33	×12

46	60	328	6023
×32	×16	× 21	× 34

Division

3)3   2)4   3)963   6)18   5)155   2)1864

3)10   4)1208   7)56714   7)1500   22)484

36)864   15)3666

FIGURE 12–7

Informal Inventory of Computation Skills

Note: From *Clinical Teaching* (2nd ed.) (pp. 249–250) by R. M. Smith, 1974, New York: McGraw-Hill. Copyright 1974 by McGraw-Hill Company. Reprinted by permission.

According to Roberts, the most frequent type of error among students with achievement problems is the random error. For other students, incorrect algorithms are most common.

The first step in conducting an error analysis is to gather a sample of the student's work. The professional could administer an informal mathematics inventory or a computation subtest from a formal test. Or samples of recent classroom work could be obtained from the student's teacher; these might be homework assignments, worksheets, workbook pages, or classroom tests or quizzes.

The math sample is then graded to identify the errors that the student has made. In most cases, scoring is a straightforward process. However, difficulties may arise when a student's handwriting is hard to read. If an answer is illegible, the professional should ask the student for help in deciphering it. By using this procedure, the teacher can evaluate the student's math skills separately from his or her writing skills.

Next, the student's errors are categorized by type. Random errors, incorrect operations, inaccurate number facts, and defective algorithms are the usual categories. The professional may also want to consider two other types of errors assessed by the *Diagnostic Test of Arithmetic Strategies:* slips (careless, nonsystematic errors) and mistakes in setting up the problem.

Sometimes the answer to a computational problem is wrong for more than one reason. For instance, the student may recall a number fact inaccurately *and* employ an inappropriate operation or algorithm. In the following problem, the student used addition rather than subtraction and also recalled one addition fact incorrectly:

$$\begin{array}{r} 1 \\ 36 \\ -18 \\ \hline 55 \end{array}$$

Another concern is whether errors are systematic. If the student correctly adds $8 + 4$ in four problems but not in the fifth, the error is probably a slip rather than a number facts problem. A response analysis of the student's work, in which both correct and incorrect answers are analyzed, can provide this kind of information. One error

on one problem does not constitute an error pattern. The errors most relevant to instructional planning occur consistently over several problems and frequently over time.

Error analysis can also be used with mathematical problem-solving tasks such as story problems. Goodstein (1981) suggests that students' word problem errors be analyzed by following these steps:

1. Check to determine the magnitude of the discrepancy between the incorrect and correct response. Small discrepancies for large numbers will often indicate carelessness in the computational aspect of the task.
2. Check to determine if the magnitude of the response indicates selection of the proper operation. . . .
3. Check to determine if the response could have been the combination of other numerical data in the problem. (Obviously, this step is only used when extraneous information is present.) (pp. 42–43)

Cawley, Miller, and School (1987) report that secondary grade students with learning disabilities find indirect problems and those with extraneous information particularly difficult. Indirect problems, like the nonroutine problems on the *KeyMath-R/NU,* do not provide direct cues to the correct operation. If it appears that the student has chosen the incorrect operation or the wrong numerical data for computation, the next step would be to conduct a clinical interview to determine how the student goes about solving story problems.

Clinical Math Interviews and Diagnostic Probes

Whereas error analysis techniques focus on students' written products, clinical interviews elicit information about the procedures that students use to arrive at those products. Clinical interviews are the most appropriate technique for process analysis.

In conducting a clinical interview, the professional combines several informal techniques. The student is observed going about the mathematics task, and the professional takes note of any behaviors of interest. For example, on a computation task, the student may attempt to solve problems by counting fingers or by making hatchmarks on the paper. The student is interviewed to find out about the cognitive strategies he or she used to accomplish the task. Diagnostic probes are introduced to determine whether alternative strategies will improve the student's performance.

According to Cawley (1978), clinical math interviews are conducted *after* students have completed some mathematics task. The student's paper is scored, and then "The student is asked to verbalize the procedure that he or she used to do both the correct and incorrect problems" (p. 224). However, Bartel (1986a) recommends that the interview take place *while* students are engaged in the mathematics activity. Bartel suggests these guidelines for math interviews:

1. One problem area should be considered at a time.
2. The easiest problem should be presented first.
3. A written record or tape should be made of the interview.
4. The student should simultaneously solve the problem in written form and "explain" what he or she is doing orally.
5. The student must be left free to solve the problem in his or her own way without a hint that he or she is doing something wrong.
6. The student should not be hurried. (p. 200)

Neither approach is the perfect solution (Ashlock, 1998). When interviews are conducted during the activity, the process of thinking out loud may influence the way the student approaches the problem. When interviews take place after the work has been completed, the student may be unable to recall all of the steps that were followed or the reasoning that prompted those steps. To compensate for the shortcomings of these methods, Ashlock advises using both. Thus, the professional could interview the student after he or she has completed one set of tasks and then conduct a second interview as the student attempts another set of tasks.

One use of clinical interviews is the study of computational processes. In the classroom, teachers can present the student with arithmetic problems and then listen to the student's explanation of the strategies selected for problem solving. Mercer and Mercer (1998) provide an example:

The teacher gave Mary three multiplication problems and said, "Please do these problems and tell me how you figure out the answer." Mary solved the problems in this way:

$$
\begin{array}{ccc}
2 & 4 & 3 \\
27 & 36 & 44 \\
\times\,4 & \times\,7 & \times\,8 \\
\hline
168 & 492 & 562
\end{array}
$$

For the first problem, Mary explained, "7 times 4 equals 28. So I put my 8 here and carry the 2. 2 plus 2 equals 4, and 4 times 4 equals 16. So I put 16 here." Her explanations for the other two problems followed the same logic.

By listening to Mary and watching her solve the problems, the teacher quickly determined Mary's error pattern: She adds the number associated with the crutch (the number carried to the tens column) *before* multiplying the tens digit. (pp. 460–461)

Clinical interviews can also provide information about how students solve story problems. The solution involves several steps, and interviews are the best means for studying the student's skill in selecting and carrying out the appropriate procedures. According to Goodstein (1981), students must follow a four-step process in solving story problems:

1. Identification of the required arithmetic operation
2. Identification of the relevant set(s) of information
3. Appropriate and accurate display of the computation (this step is often unnecessary for simple computations and would be replaced by "accurate entry of the computational factors" if a calculator were to be used)
4. Accurate performance of the indicated computation (this step would automatically follow successful completion of steps 1–3, if a calculator were used) (p. 34)

To accomplish these steps, students must first read and comprehend the story problem. For many students with special needs, poor reading skills interfere with their ability to take this important first step. Next, the student must be familiar with the meanings of the quantitative terms that appear in the problem and the relationship between these terms and arithmetic operations. For example, when the problem asks, "How many are there *altogether*?" the addition operation is usually implied. When the student has identified the appropriate operation, the problem must be studied carefully to locate the values to add, subtract, multiply, or divide. To do this, relevant information must be recognized and irrelevant data discarded. For instance, if the problem says, "John has 3 kittens, Mary has 2 cats, and Marisol has 5 puppies," Marisol's pets are irrelevant if the student must determine "How many cats and kittens are there altogether?"

The professional can learn a great deal about the student's problem-solving skills by incorporating diagnostic probes into the clinical math interview. To do this, the student is given several story problems to solve and is instructed to "think out loud" throughout the entire process. When a problem area becomes apparent, the professional intervenes and provides a cue or an alternate strategy for accomplishing the task. Table 12–2 presents several diagnostic probes for use with story problems. For example, if the teacher suspects that poor reading skills are affecting the student's performance, the teacher can read the problem aloud to the student. If the student is then able to solve the problem successfully, reading becomes the instructional concern rather than mathematical problem-solving skills.

TABLE 12-2
Diagnostic Probes for the Study of Problem-Solving Skills

SUSPECTED AREA OF DIFFICULTY	SUGGESTED INTERVENTION
Decoding the words in the story problem	Read the story problem aloud to the student, and see if he or she can then solve the problem correctly.
Understanding the meaning of the situation described in the story problem	Ask the student to draw a picture that illustrates the problem.
	Provide the student with a picture illustrating the problem.
Selecting the appropriate operation (addition, subtraction, multiplication, or division)	Ask the student to explain the meaning of key quantitative terms that appear in the problem (e.g., "How many apples are there *altogether*?" or "How many children were *left*?").
	Tell the student which operation to use and see if he or she can then solve the problem correctly
Identifying the relevant and irrelevant information in the problem	If the problem requires knowledge of conceptual categories (e.g., dogs and cats are animals, but a doll is a toy), assess the student's understanding of the categories.
	Tell the student that the problem contains extra information, and ask him or her to try and find it.
Writing down the computational problem	Have the student dictate the problem while the professional writes it down.
Remembering number facts	Provide the student with manipulatives such as sticks or beans to use in figuring out the number facts that are needed.
	Provide the student with a calculator, and see if he or she can then solve the problem correctly.
Selecting the appropriate computational algorithm	If the student's algorithm is inaccurate, teach the student the appropriate procedure.
	Provide the student with a calculator, and see if he or she can then solve the problem correctly.

Criterion-Referenced Tests

Criterion-referenced tests are used to assess mastery of specific mathematics skills. For example, if the results of an informal math inventory or standardized test point to possible weaknesses in a particular set of skills, the professional can select or design a criterion-referenced test to evaluate the student's ability to perform those skills.

Professionals can prepare their own criterion-referenced measures based on the goals and objectives of the local curriculum, or they can select from commercially available tests. For example, mathematics skills are assessed by both the *BRIGANCE® Diagnostic Comprehensive Inventory of Basic Skills-Revised (CIBS-R)* (1999) for pre-kindergarten through grade 9 and the *BRIGANCE® Diagnostic Inventory of Essential Skills* (1981) for grade 6 through adult education. A Spanish edition of the *Basic Skills* inventory (Brigance, 1983) is also available.

The *CIBS-R* includes several math readiness measures for younger students (e.g., counting, recognition of numerals, number comprehension). Measures for older students are organized into 10 sections: Numbers, Number Facts, Computation of Whole Numbers, Percents, Time, Money, Fractions and Mixed Numbers, Decimals, U.S. Customary Measurement and Geometry, and Metrics. Norm-referenced scores are available for two Grade-Placement Tests in math on the *CIBS-R:* Computational Skills and Problem-Solving.

The *Essential Skills* measure stresses vocational as well as school skills and offers several tests of vocationally related mathematics abilities. For instance, there are 11 tests of Money and Finance, each of which is directed toward a real-world application of mathematics such as reading price signs and making change.

Questionnaires and Interviews

In mathematics assessment, questionnaires and interviews are used to gather information about students' viewpoints: their attitudes toward mathematics, perceptions of computation and the problem-solving process, opinions of their own abilities in the skill area of mathematics,

and so forth. Interviews are preferred for younger students and those with poor reading skills. Questionnaires are used only with students who can cope with reading and writing requirements.

Mercer and Mercer (1998) recommend sentence completion tasks for assessing students' attitudes toward arithmetic. In this procedure, the teacher reads an incomplete sentence to the student, who fills in the missing part. Examples of possible sentences are:

1. Math is very . . .
2. My best subject is . . .
3. During math I feel . . . (p. 461)

Interviews can also be used to find out about students' attitudes toward mathematics and perceptions of its usefulness in everyday life. For example, young students could be asked these open-ended questions:

- Is math one of your better subjects in school?
- What types of math activities are the easiest for you? Which are the hardest?
- Do you like to work addition problems? Subtraction problems? Multiplication? Division? Why or why not?
- Do you like to try to solve story problems? Why or why not?
- Most people use math skills every day. Can you name three things that people do with numbers?
- When was the last time you went to the store to buy something? How did you find out how much it cost? Did you pay for it? If you did, how did you figure out whether the salesperson gave you back the right change?
- Can you tell time? How do you do it?
- Suppose you wanted to find out how much you weigh. How would you do it? How could you find out how tall you are?
- Have you ever used a calculator to add or subtract numbers, or to multiply and divide? Is using a calculator easier than doing it in your head? Why or why not?

Several of these questions could be adapted into a questionnaire for older students by changing some of the terminology and substituting age-appropriate examples of everyday math activities.

Portfolio Assessment

In mathematics, as in language arts, students select several examples of their best work for inclusion in a portfolio. Those work samples might be classroom quizzes or assignments, group or individual projects, written math reports or math logs, or artwork related to mathematics. In the Vermont Portfolio Project, students must include five to seven "best pieces" of their mathematical work, other work samples, and a letter to the person who will evaluate their portfolio (Abruscato, 1993). Among the best pieces should be at least one investigation, one application, one puzzle, and no more than two group projects.

Mathematics portfolios can also contain results of standardized tests and informal assessments, student self-assessments, and student interest surveys and questionnaires. For instance, teachers might include checklists of student progress, graphs of results from curriculum-based math measures, and records of clinical math interviews.

WITHIN THE CONTEXT OF THE CLASSROOM

Up to this point, discussion has focused on assessment tools for gathering information about the student's performance. Here the emphasis shifts to procedures and techniques for studying the classroom learning environment and its influence on the student's mathematics abilities.

The Instructional Environment

Assessment of the instructional environment must take into account the mathematics curriculum and the instructional methods and materials used to implement that curriculum. In the elementary grades, basal textbook series are often the foundation of the mathematics program. Basal series vary in their approach to the teaching of mathematics, but most emphasize both computation and problem-solving skills.

The questions that follow provide a framework for studying the classroom mathematics program:

1. Which basal mathematics series is used in the classroom?
2. Is more than one level of the mathematics series in use in the classroom?
3. What instructional materials supplement the mathematics textbooks? Are manipulatives provided as computational aids? Are calculators available? Computer programs?
4. What types of mathematics skills are stressed in classroom instruction? Computation? Problem solving? Mathematics applications such as time, money, and measurement?
5. Is the mathematics curriculum organized so development of new skills is based on the mastery of prerequisite skills? Are the instructional steps of appropriate size?
6. Is instruction based upon ongoing assessment? How often are performance data collected for monitoring students' progress? What procedures are used to determine the starting points for students entering the mathematics program?
7. How are students grouped for mathematics instruction? How much individualization takes place in each group?
8. What instructional techniques does the teacher use to present new skills and information? Lecture? Demonstration? Discussion? Exploration? Cooperative learning?
9. In what types of learning activities do students participate? Do all mathematics activities involve paper-and-pencil tasks, or do students sometimes have the opportunity to respond orally?
10. How is supervised practice incorporated into the mathematics program? On the average, how many minutes per day do students spend practicing their mathematics skills?
11. What changes, if any, have been made in the standard mathematics program to accommodate the needs of special learners such as the student under assessment?

Wiederholt, Hammill, and Brown (1978) suggest that it is also important to consider the teacher's attitudes, capabilities, and expectations in relation to mathematics instruction.

One major concern is the focus of the mathematics curriculum. The back-to-basics movement is still a powerful force in shaping instructional programs in mathematics, despite the recent emphasis on the teaching of problem solving. Basic skills programs tend to emphasize drill and practice as a means to achieving computational proficiency.

Also of importance are the academic skill demands placed on the student in mathematics activities. Reading is a part of many mathematics tasks, particularly in the upper elementary and secondary grades. Poor reading skills can interfere with the student's ability to read mathematics textbooks, the directions on math worksheets, story problems, and so forth. If reading is a concern, the reading level of the mathematics textbook or other material should be determined using the procedures described in Chapter 11. If the material is too difficult for the student's current skills, the text could be rewritten at an easier reading level or a more suitable text substituted.

Many mathematics activities also require writing skills. Students are expected to write the answers to computational problems, and students must sometimes copy questions or problems onto their papers from the chalkboard or from their textbooks. Such tasks may interfere with the mathematics performance of students with handwriting difficulties. Students who write slowly may be unable to finish their work. If the student's writing is difficult to read, both the student and the teacher may be unable to decipher it.

It is also useful to look at other characteristics of mathematics tasks: the number of questions or problems students are expected to complete, the requirements for speed, and the expectations for accuracy. Sometimes students have the necessary skills to succeed with mathematics assignments, but they fail because they cannot meet performance criteria. They may work the first few problems correctly and then become discouraged by the number of problems left to complete. Or they may work too slowly to finish within the required time period. It may be that classroom standards are unduly stringent and some adjustment can be made. For example, the teacher might be willing to allow more time for each assignment or reduce the number of problems that students are expected to complete.

The Interpersonal Environment

Social relationships among students are an important component of the classroom's interpersonal environment. Students with achievement problems are often not well-accepted by their peers, but difficulties in mathematics seem to be better tolerated than difficulties in reading. Perhaps this is because, in mathematics, students make most of their responses privately, and peers are less aware of other students' performances. Another possible explanation relates to students' experiences with mathematics. All students make computational errors at one time or another, and this experience with failure may make achieving students more tolerant of those with persistent problems with mathematics. It is also possible that students value reading more highly than mathematics or that they perceive mathematics as the more difficult subject. Whatever the reason, mathematics skill deficiencies appear to be less socially debilitating than reading problems.

Interactions between students and teachers are also part of the interpersonal environment. In mathematics instruction, one of the primary ways the teacher communicates with students is by grading their math papers. There are several methods of grading, and some are more likely than others to encourage students in their efforts to learn mathematics skills. For example, for students with achievement problems, it is probably better to mark the correct responses rather than the errors. Such a paper is much less threatening than one covered with red checkmarks and a message such as "F—Try harder."

These questions should be considered when evaluating student-teacher interactions:

- In grading students' math papers, how does the teacher respond to errors? Does the teacher identify an incorrect response as an error? Correct it? Ignore the error?
- If the situation is a public one (e.g., students are solving problems at the board), what occurs when a student makes an error? Does the teacher use the same correction procedures as he or she uses in private interactions?
- How does the student react to the teacher's corrections? Is there a difference when the student is corrected in front of peers?

- What do other students do when a peer makes an error?
- What occurs when the student makes a correct response? Does the teacher confirm the response? Praise the student? Provide a tangible reward or token?
- Are students able to work independently on mathematics activities? Do certain students require frequent assistance from the teacher?

The Physical Environment

The physical environment of the classroom can also affect students' mathematics performance. The environment should be physically comfortable with lighting, temperature, and ventilation at appropriate levels, and classroom space should be arranged to facilitate mathematics instruction. In assessing the classroom's physical characteristics, some of the questions that can be asked are the following:

1. Are all students seated so they can easily see and hear the teacher? Can they see the chalkboard, if necessary?
2. Is the lighting in the classroom adequate?
3. Is the classroom space structured so that areas for noisier activities are separated from areas for quieter activities?
4. How are the students' seats arranged for independent work? Are students' desks or tables positioned so that students do not distract each other?
5. Are there any quiet work areas or "offices" within the classroom where students can go to escape from distractions?
6. Does the classroom offer a variety of mathematics learning materials, or are textbooks the only resource? If other materials are available, do they cover a wide range of skill levels? Are they accessible to students?
7. In elementary classrooms, is there a learning center for mathematics? If so, what materials and activities does it contain? Are manipulative materials such as computational aids available for student use?
8. Are calculators available to students? Are they accessible at all times, or are they reserved for special activities?
9. Is a computer available in the classroom for students to practice mathematics skills? Do

students have access to a variety of educationally sound software programs in the area of mathematics?

ANSWERING THE ASSESSMENT QUESTIONS

Mathematics skills are assessed in order to describe the student's current levels of educational performance. A wide variety of assessment tools is available for this purpose, including both formal and informal measures and techniques.

Nature of the Assessment Tools

Measures of mathematics performance vary in the range of skills they assess. Some are quite comprehensive, whereas others are more limited. Three of the formal tests described in this chapter—the *KeyMath Revised/Normative Update,* the *Stanford Diagnostic Mathematics Test* (4th ed.), and the *Test of Mathematical Abilities* (2nd ed.)—are considered wide-range measures because they assess a variety of skills. However, each covers a somewhat different set of skill areas. For example, the *KeyMath-R/NU* and the *SDMT* include computation, problem-solving, and mathematics applications. The *TOMA-2* does not assess mathematics applications, but does evaluate areas that the *KeyMath-R/NU* and the *SDMT* do not.

The criterion-referenced tests by Brigance are somewhat more restricted in range because they assess only application and computational skills. The *Diagnostic Test of Arithmetic Strategies,* a measure that assesses only computational skills, is even narrower in scope. However, the *DTAS* also provides error analysis procedures for studying students' mistakes in computation.

Another area of difference is the thoroughness with which skills are assessed. Comprehensive tests such as the *KeyMath-R/NU* and the *SDMT* sample several skills and skill levels but provide only a few representative test items in each area. For example, on the *KeyMath-R,* three test items are used to evaluate the student's skill in addition of fractions. Informal measures evaluate skills in much greater depth. On the *BRIGANCE® CIBS-R,* for example, an entire subtest is devoted to addition of fractions and mixed numbers.

Measures can also differ in the types of assessment tasks used to evaluate skill development. For instance, there are many differences between the *KeyMath-R/NU* and the *SDMT,* even though they both assess the same general skill areas. The *SDMT* requires written responses, whereas students usually answer orally on the *KeyMath-R/NU.* Many *SDMT* questions are multiple-choice, and several subtests are timed. The *KeyMath-R/NU* imposes time limits on only one subtest, and most test questions are open-ended.

Mathematics measures are most similar in the assessment tasks they use to evaluate students' computational skills. Typically, paper-and-pencil tasks are used; students read the problem and then write the answer. There are fewer similarities in the ways that problem-solving skills are assessed, as Table 12–3 illustrates. Although story problems are the basic tasks for evaluating problem solving on the *KeyMath-R/NU,* the *SDMT,* and

the *TOMA-2,* task characteristics differ from measure to measure. Such differences can affect the student's ability to respond to test tasks. Task characteristics are important considerations in selecting the tools for assessment and in interpreting assessment results.

The Relationship of Mathematics to Other Areas of Performance

When assessment is complete, the special education team begins to interpret the results and study the relationships between areas of performance. Academic skills such as mathematics may influence or be influenced by several other areas.

General learning aptitude is a consideration in the acquisition of any skill, and the student's progress in mathematics should be evaluated in relation to estimated intellectual potential. In general, students with lower than average general intelligence are expected to progress at a somewhat slower rate than students of average intellectual ability. However, IQ may be a better

TABLE 12–3

Assessment Tasks Used to Evaluate Mathematical Problem Solving

MEASURE	SUBTEST	PRESENTATION MODE	RESPONSE MODE
KeyMath Revised/Normative Update	Problem Solving	Listen to word problems read aloud by the tester; look at a test page with drawings and/or statements related to the problem.	Compute mentally and say the answer.
		Listen to nonroutine word problems read aloud by the tester; look at a test page with drawings and/or statements related to the problem.	Tell how to solve the problem or identify extraneous or missing information.
Stanford Diagnostic Mathematics Test, Fourth Edition	Concepts and Applications	Read brief story problems and a series of possible responses.	Write computations on scratch paper, as needed; select a response; mark the letter of the response on the appropriate space on the separate answer sheet; or, on the first three levels, mark the response in the test booklet.
Test of Mathematical Abilities (2nd ed.)	Story Problems	Read brief story problems.	Write computations in the workspace on the test page; write and circle the answer on the test page.

predictor of mathematical problem-solving ability than of rote computational skills. As with reading, expectancy formulas are not the best means of estimating the student's expected level of achievement. Standard score procedures are preferred. For example, if the student's current scores on a measure of intellectual performance fall within the average range, that student would be expected to show average achievement in mathematics.

Specific learning abilities and strategies also play a role in the student's ability to acquire and apply mathematics skills. Difficulties in attention, memory, or other areas such as visual and auditory perception can hinder skill development, particularly the acquisition of mathematics readiness skills and computational proficiency. Inefficient learning strategies may interfere with the student's practice of mathematics skills, resulting in further underachievement. In the secondary grades, poor learning strategies may combine with poor mathematics skills to prevent students from applying mathematics in other subject areas.

Classroom behavior may be related to mathematics performance. Inappropriate conduct in the classroom can impede academic learning. Likewise, poor achievement can affect a student's behavior. For example, a student who is unable to cope with a classroom mathematics assignment may react by causing a disturbance. Poor achievement can also influence the student's self-concept, his or her relationships with peers, and the attitudes the student holds toward both school and mathematics.

The student's skills in mathematics may have an impact on other areas of school performance. Basic mathematics competencies are needed in any classroom. To locate page 42 in a spelling book, the student must be able to count and read numerals. Teachers' directions often include quantitative terminology such as *first, last, next,* and *greater than.* In art class, the student may need to measure the dimensions of a canvas; in physical education, students may be asked to "count off by 2s."

In the secondary grades, students are expected to use mathematics in several school subjects. Proficiency in mathematics is often a requirement in the sciences. Even in social studies, students must be able to read and interpret graphs and tables. Mathematics is necessary in almost all vocational subjects, and measurement skills are particularly important. Measurement is needed for cooking, sewing, carpentry, mechanics, agriculture, and many other vocational areas. Skills in handling money and telling time are also important, not only in vocational preparation classes, but also in daily life. Students who have not learned to tell time or deal with simple money exchanges will face real barriers in their attempts to deal with the demands of adult life.

Achievement problems in other curriculum areas can interfere with the acquisition of mathematics skills. Oral language is the foundation for all school learning, and students with language problems may have difficulty acquiring and using the quantitative vocabulary of mathematics. Reading is needed for many mathematics tasks and is a critical component of the process of solving story problems. Difficulties with handwriting can be a real liability. In beginning math instruction, students must learn how to read and write numerals and mathematical symbols, and writing continues to be a necessary part of math activities throughout the school years.

Documentation of Mathematics Performance

The general assessment question that guides the special education team in its investigation of mathematics is, *What are the student's educational needs?* In this phase of assessment, the goal is to obtain sufficient data to describe the student's current levels of educational performance. The team begins by asking, *What is the student's current level of mathematics achievement?* A wide range of mathematics skills is surveyed, and then additional information is gathered about the areas in which the student appears to experience difficulty. This results in a specific description of the student's current skills, and the assessment team is able to answer the question, *What are the student's strengths and weaknesses in the various skill areas of mathematics?*

In mathematics assessment, data are gathered from many sources using many types of assessment tools. Usually, the team begins by reviewing school records, the results of individual achievement tests, and the data collected in interviews with parents and teachers and in classroom observations. Next, a test that evaluates a range of mathematics skills is administered to identify possible problem areas. Informal measures and techniques are then used to learn more about potential weaknesses. For example, the team may administer a series of criterion-referenced tests to assess specific computational skills. Or a clinical math interview may be conducted to learn more about the student's problem-solving strategies.

There are many types of tools available for mathematics assessment. The assessment team should select its tools with care so duplication is avoided and the assessment process is as efficient as possible. In general, the more specific procedures such as clinical interviews and criterion-referenced tests should be reserved for in-depth assessment of potential problem areas.

By answering the assessment questions about mathematics, the team moves closer to planning the student's Individualized Education Program. Current levels of educational performance in mathematics are documented and the areas of educational need in mathematics are identified. For instance, David was referred for assessment because of his difficulties with mathematics.

David

David is failing eighth grade mathematics. In math class, he is working on basic number facts and operations because he lacks the skills to participate in any of the regular eighth grade activities. Special education assessment has begun, and results of the *WRAT-3* and the *Woodcock-Johnson-R* have confirmed that David's current performance in mathematics is far below that expected for his age and grade.

To gather more information about David's skills across several areas of mathematics, Mr. Block, the special education resource teacher, administers the *KeyMath Revised/Normative Update* (see Figure 12–2). David's total test performance is within the standard score range of 75 to 81, which indicates overall low average performance. His Operations and Applications skills are significantly lower than his Basic Concepts skills. David shows

relative strengths in Numeration, Rational Numbers, Geometry, Measurement, and Time and Money. The areas in which David earns his lowest scores are Problem Solving, Division, and Multiplication. Based on these results, the team decides to concentrate its efforts on assessing David's problem-solving and computation skills.

Next, portions of the *BRIGANCE® Diagnostic Comprehensive Inventory of Basic Skills-Revised* are administered to pinpoint David's computational difficulties. David shows mastery of addition and subtraction number facts but is less successful with multiplication and division facts; the majority of David's errors occur on problems involving multiples of 6, 7, 8, and 9. In basic operations with whole numbers, David consistently has difficulty with problems that require regrouping. In addition and multiplication, he often fails to carry and instead writes the entire number as part of the answer. When multiplying two multidigit numbers, David uses the same strategy, and he does not cross-multiply; for example,

$$
\begin{array}{r}
25 \\
\times\ 34 \\
\hline
620
\end{array}
$$

In this problem, David multiplies 4×5 and writes the answer as 20. He then moves to the tens column and multiplies 3×2. In subtraction, he sometimes subtracts the smaller number from the larger, disregarding which is the minuend and which is the subtrahend. In division, he refuses to attempt problems that require regrouping, saying, "I can't do ones like this."

To assess David's skills in solving story problems, the team asks Ms. Coolidge, David's math teacher, to provide several samples of David's work. All of the papers provided to the assessment team had been graded *F*. However, most of David's errors were due to his failure to attempt all problems. On one assignment, for example, David solved the first two problems correctly and made a minor computational error on the third; he did not attempt the remaining seven problems, so his score on this paper was 20%.

The team uses clinical interviewing techniques to explore David's problem-solving skills. He is given 10 story problems and instructed to "think out loud" when solving them. He reads the problems accurately and is able to explain what operations are required. With simpler problems, David can identify the numbers to be used in computation and write the computational problem correctly. However, David's strategy is to include all of the numbers that the problem provides. With more difficult problems that contain extraneous information, this strategy is not successful. David also has difficulty carrying out the calculations. He works slowly, sometimes making hatchmarks on his paper to help him figure out number facts, and 7 of his 10 solutions are incorrect. David says that he likes "the thinking part of these problems, but not the math part."

After a careful analysis of these results, the assessment team is ready to describe David's current levels of mathematics performance. Their conclusions are as follows:

- At present, David's overall level of achievement in mathematics is within the low average range of performance, as measured by the *KeyMath Revised/Normative Update*. His greatest areas of weakness are mathematics operations and applications.

- David shows adequate knowledge of addition and subtraction facts. He has not yet mastered multiplication and division facts and has particular difficulty with multiples of 6, 7, 8, and 9. David has some knowledge of regrouping procedures but fails to use them consistently. In addition and multiplication, David does not always carry, and in subtraction, he sometimes subtracts the smaller number from the larger. David does not appear to know how to solve division problems that require regrouping or how to cross-multiply in multidigit multiplication.

- David receives failing grades on story problem assignments because he completes only a few problems.

- David is able to determine how to solve simple story problems, but many of his answers are incorrect because of computational errors.

STUDY GUIDE

REVIEW QUESTIONS

1. Mathematics performance is assessed to gain information about the student's educational needs and strengths and weaknesses in specific mathematics skills. (True or False)
2. Three major skill areas are considered in the assessment of mathematics: computation, _____ , and the _____ of mathematics skills to daily life situations.
3. In current school practices, mathematics is assessed by
   a. both formal and informal measures.
   b. individual and group tests.
   c. error analyses, informal inventories, and clinical math interviews.
   d. curriculum-based measures.
   e. all of the above .
4. Which is the most frequently used comprehensive measure of mathematics skills for students in the elementary grades?
   a. *KeyMath Revised/Normative Update*
   b. *Stanford Diagnostic Mathematics Test*
   c. *Test of Mathematical Abilities*
   d. *Diagnostic Test of Arithmetic Strategies*
   e. none of the above

5. The *BRIGANCE*® *Diagnostic Comprehensive Inventory of Basic Skills-Revised* is both norm-referenced and criterion-referenced. (True or False)

6. Match the assessment device or procedure in Column A with the description in Column B. (The answers in Column A may be used more than once.)

Column A	*Column B*
a. *KeyMath-R/NU*	___ A group test for students in grades 1 through 12
b. *Test of Mathematical Abilities* (2nd ed.)	___ Used to identify the strategies students use for addition, subtraction, multiplication, and division
c. *Diagnostic Test of Arithmetic Strategies*	___ Assesses Basic Concepts, Operations, and Applications with 13 subtests
d. *Stanford Diagnostic Mathematics Test*	___ Assesses Concepts and Applications as well as Computation
	___ An individual test with items referenced to skill domains and objectives
	___ Includes a measure of attitude toward mathematics and a test of mathematics vocabulary

7. Write the letter *S* before each test result that indicates an area of strength; write the letter *N* if results point to a possible area of educational need.
   _____ a. Stanine 1 Total score on the *Stanford Diagnostic Mathematics Test*
   _____ b. *KeyMath-R/NU* Geometry subtest scaled score of 11
   _____ c. *SDMT* Progress Indicator of + on the Addition Facts subtest
   _____ d. Math Quotient 75 on the *Test of Mathematical Abilities*
   _____ e. Scaled score 13 on a *TOMA-2* subtest

8. Students may arrive at incorrect answers to mathematics computation problems if they use correct facts but inappropriate _____.

9. One feature of the academic achievement tests by Brigance is that they include instructional objectives. (True or False)

10. Find the true statements.
    a. Many mathematics tests assess both computation and problem-solving skills.
    b. Mathematics measures may evaluate application skills such as time, money, and measurement.
    c. The difference between informal mathematics inventories and criterion-referenced tests is that inventories tend to measure skill domains thoroughly, rather than assessing only a few representative skills.
    d. The four most common types of computation errors are incorrect operations, incorrect number facts, incorrect algorithms, and random errors.
    e. Clinical math interviews are used to determine how well students perform when they are provided with computational aids such as calculators.

11. In assessing mathematics performance within the context of the classroom, it should be determined whether the curriculum stresses _____ or _____ skills.

12. Motor skills are necessary for what mathematics task?

13. If a student shows average intellectual performance, in what standard score range would you expect mathematics scores to fall?
    a. Less than standard score 70
    b. Standard score 70 to 84
    c. Standard score 85 to 115
    d. Standard score 116 to 130
    e. Greater than standard score 130

14. If the special education team finds that a student shows poor performance in mathematics computation, what conclusion can be drawn?
    a. The special education program should focus on improving problem-solving skills.
    b. The special education program should emphasize the use of computational skills in problems concerning time, money, and measurement.
    c. A possible educational goal would be to increase accuracy in addition, subtraction, multiplication, and division.
    d. The student should remain in the general education classroom and be provided with a calculator.

ACTIVITIES

1. Interview two special educators—one who serves elementary grade students and the other who serves students in middle or high school. Ask each to describe the mathematics skills they consider most important and to explain how they assess mathematics performance. Are there any differences in the skill areas they assess? For example, are application skills more of a concern to the secondary teacher?
2. Locate several group achievement tests and examine how each assesses mathematics. Are all the major skills covered?
3. Under the supervision of the course instructor, administer one of the mathematics measures discussed in this chapter. Calculate all possible scores and analyze the results to determine strengths and weaknesses.
4. Obtain a set of word problems that are appropriate for adult learners. Use these to conduct a clinical math interview with one of your peers. Then reverse roles so your peer becomes the interviewer and you act as the student. Compare the findings from the two interviews. Did you approach the problems in different ways and use different strategies for the solution?
5. Do a work sample analysis of a student's mathematics paper. Identify and analyze all errors according to one of the systems presented in this chapter.
6. Devise a set of diagnostic probes to investigate the reasons for failure on computational problems. Use the problem-solving probes in Table 12–2 as a guide.

DISCUSSION QUESTIONS

1. Mathematics plays an important role in daily activities. Discuss some of the ways that adults use mathematics at home and in the workplace.
2. Explain why mathematics is considered one of the basic school skills.
3. Discuss this statement: In some ways, the distinction between computation and problem solving in mathematics is analogous to the distinction between decoding and comprehension in reading.
4. Compare and contrast the three individual tests of mathematics performance described in detail in this chapter—the *KeyMath Revised/Normative Update,* the *Test of Mathematical Abilities* (2nd ed.), and the *Diagnostic Test of Arithmetic Strategies.* Include in your discussion a comparison of the content assessed by each measure and a description of the population for which each is appropriate. Conclude by presenting your recommendations regarding the best use of each test.
5. Describe the current reform movement in mathematics instruction; then discuss how mathematics assessment might change in response to this movement. For example, what types of assessment techniques could be used to evaluate students' participation in authentic mathematics tasks?

CHAPTER 13

WRITTEN LANGUAGE

- Considerations in Assessment of Written Language
- Strategies for Assessing Spelling
- Strategies for Assessing Handwriting
- Strategies for Assessing Composition
- Within the Context of the Classroom
- Answering the Assessment Questions

Written language is a basic method of communication in today's society. Adults are expected to be literate, and literacy includes not only the ability to read, but also the ability to write. As part of the routine of daily life, adults write shopping lists, business letters, e-mail messages, and notes to friends. They complete job applications, fill out tax forms, and write checks. Writing skills are a requirement for most occupations, and some jobs demand a high degree of proficiency in written language.

Writing is also an important skill during the school years, and its acquisition is stressed in the elementary grades. In the upper elementary grades and in middle and high school, students are expected to be able to express their thoughts in writing. This poses grave difficulties for individuals with poor written expression skills, and many students with special needs fall within this group.

In special education assessment, students' written language skills are studied to gather information for instructional planning. The broad question that guides this portion of the assessment process is, *What are the student's educational needs?* When written language is the concern, this general question is refined into two specific questions: *What is the student's current level of achievement in written language? What are the student's strengths and weaknesses in the various skill areas of written language?*

At this point in assessment, the major goal is description of the student's current status in important areas of the written language curriculum: spelling, handwriting, and composition. Consider how both formal and informal assessment strategies are part of the plan for learning more about the written expression skills of Joyce, the fourth grader whose assessment we have been following in the past few chapters.

Joyce

The team is now gathering data to assist in planning Joyce's Individualized Education Program. From the reports of Joyce's fourth grade teacher and from the results of individual achievement tests, the team is quite certain that Joyce could benefit from specially designed instruction in at least two areas of written language: spelling and handwriting.

In spelling, Joyce showed below average performance on both the *PIAT-R/NU* and the *WIAT,* and she is working in a grade 2 spelling book in her fourth grade classroom. To learn more about Joyce's spelling skills, the team will administer the *Test of Written Spelling-4,* a measure that assesses the student's ability to spell phonetically regular and irregular words. Then informal techniques will be used to explore the particular spelling skills that appear to be areas of weakness for Joyce. For example, if regular words appear to be a problem, the team may administer an informal inventory or criterion-referenced test that probes the student's ability to write the letters that correspond to various letter sounds.

Handwriting may also be an area of need for Joyce. In the school that Joyce attended last year, cursive writing was not introduced in the third grade, so Joyce entered fourth grade at a disadvantage. Mr. Harvey, her fourth grade teacher, has begun to teach Joyce cursive writing, but she continues to print the majority of her assignments. Despite 3 years of instruction, Joyce's printing is not good. To gather more information about handwriting, the assessment team will observe Joyce as she writes and will collect several samples of her printing and cursive writing. The observational data and writing samples will be carefully analyzed to detect any pattern of errors.

As yet, the assessment team has no information about Joyce's composition skills. Joyce's ability to write sentences, themes, essays, stories, and the like was not mentioned by Mr. Harvey when he referred Joyce for assessment, so the team will begin by interviewing Mr. Harvey. Then a broad range measure such as the *Test of Written Language-3* will be administered to help the team pinpoint Joyce's strengths and weaknesses in various composition skills. As necessary, informal procedures will be used to gather further information about specific areas of educational need.

Joyce's individualized program in written language will be based on the results of these assessments.

CONSIDERATIONS IN ASSESSMENT OF WRITTEN LANGUAGE

Written language skills are critical for successful school performance. Students with poor written language are at a decided disadvantage in attempting to meet the academic demands of the general education curriculum. Because many students with mild disabilities experience difficulty in this area, written language is often one of the areas of focus in special education assessment.

Purposes

Written language skills are assessed for many different reasons. Writing is considered an important part of the general education curriculum; teachers routinely monitor their students' progress in the acquisition of spelling, handwriting, and composition skills. Spelling and some aspects of composition are often included among the skills assessed by group achievement tests, and proficiency in written language is frequently one of the competency areas evaluated for grade advancement and high school graduation.

In special education, written language skills may be investigated at the start of assessment to determine the student's eligibility for special education services. In many cases, however, assessment is limited to only one aspect of written language—spelling—because that is the language skill emphasized on the traditional individual tests of achievement used in special education. Further investigation is needed if there is reason to believe that other aspects of written language may be areas of educational need.

Several measures of written language are currently available to assist the assessment team in identifying academic skill deficiencies. Norm-referenced tests help to pinpoint specific areas of difficulty, and informal techniques and procedures are then used to gather the detailed information needed for planning the educational program. The student's current levels of performance are described and specific strengths and weaknesses are noted in preparation for the establishment of

---

Individualized Assessment Plan

For:	Joyce Dewey	4	10-0	12/1/00	Ms. Gale
	Student's Name	Grade	Age	Date	Coordinator

Reason for Referral: Difficulty keeping up with fourth grade work in reading, spelling, and handwriting.

Assessment Question	Assessment Procedure	Person Responsible	Date/Time
What is the student's current level of achievement in written language?	Test of Written Language-3	Ms. Gale, Resource Teacher	1/12/01, 9 A.M.
What are the student's strengths and weaknesses in the various skill areas of written language?	Test of Written Spelling-4	Ms. Gale, Resource Teacher	1/12/01, 1 P.M.
	Observation and work sample analysis of handwriting	Ms. Gale, Resource Teacher	1/08/01, morning
	Additional informal strategies, as needed	Ms. Gale, Resource Teacher, and other team members, as needed	to be determined

the instructional goals and objectives of the individualized program plan.

Assessment continues when special education services begin, but it changes somewhat in character. The purpose becomes continuous monitoring of the student's educational progress. On an ongoing basis, special educators monitor the student's acquisition of targeted skills, and at least once each year, the educational plan is reviewed and modified as necessary.

Skill Areas

When considering the complex of skills and processes that contribute to proficiency in written language, it is important to understand the relationship between writing and other dimensions of language. Language is a communication system characterized by the use of symbols for the transmission of information. Language can be either spoken or written, and in both oral and written language there is an expressive and a receptive mode. In the expressive mode, the speaker or writer attempts to communicate ideas; in the receptive mode, the listener or reader attempts to comprehend the ideas expressed by the speaker or writer.

In the developmental sequence, oral language generally precedes written language. Most children begin to understand and use speech for communication within the first 3 years of life. Reading and writing skills come later, usually after children have completed some formal schooling. It also appears that receptive language skills emerge first: Young children learn to listen, then to speak; school-aged children learn to read, then to write.

In this developmental perspective, writing is the last skill to be acquired, and to some extent, it is dependent on the other language skills that underlie it. Poor oral language can inhibit the development of written language, just as lack of proficiency in reading can interfere with the acquisition of writing skills. However, students need not wait until they are proficient readers to begin writing; these skills can be developed simultaneously (Wells, 1981). As Westby (1992) points out, in the whole language approach to instruction, the language arts are viewed as inter-

dependent rather than separate skills that develop sequentially.

Writing is quite different from speech. Speech is essentially a social act (Litowitz, 1981). Both the sender and the receiver of the communication are present and are able to interact if a breakdown in communication occurs. Writing is a solitary act, and the writer is unable to exchange messages with the reader. In oral communication, information is transmitted in many ways, not only through spoken words. The facial expressions, gestures, posture, and body language of the participants all contribute to communication, as do the speaker's tone of voice and the loudness and speed with which the message is delivered. These methods of transmitting information are not available to the writer; the written symbols must stand alone.

In writing, the sender of the message must first conceptualize its content and then record the message so it is available and comprehensible to the receiver. To do this, the writer must have some skill in handwriting (or typing or keyboarding) and in spelling. In recording the message, the writer uses a pencil or pen (or a typewriter or computer keyboard) to form the smallest elements of written language, the individual letters, or graphemes. Letters are then combined into words, and the conventions of spelling determine how these letters are sequenced. As words are arranged into sentences, other conventions must be observed, including the rules for sentence formation, written syntax, and English usage. In addition, the writer must attend to the mechanical aspects of writing, factors that are not concerns in oral language: capitalization, punctuation, paragraphing, page format, and so forth.

In Smith's (1982) view, the act of writing imposes two distinct roles on the writer: author and secretary. The author's task is to generate ideas and compose the content of the writing. The secretary transcribes what the author composes. The secretary is concerned with the form of the writing and so attends to spelling, handwriting, capitalization, punctuation, and the like. Smith's analogy of the thinker and the scribe is a useful way of conceptualizing the writing process. It points up the range of skills required in writing

(Nodine, 1983) and provides a framework for thinking about those skills.

Writing is a process that involves (or should involve) several steps (Graves, 1985), and each step places different demands on the writer. Polloway and Payne (1993) identify three stages of writing: prewriting, writing, and postwriting. In the prewriting stage, the author is the dominant participant. Influenced by past input, motivation, and the purpose for writing, the author plans the content. The writing stage requires both author and secretary. As the author composes, the secretary performs the physical act of writing with attention to legibility, spelling accuracy, and other print conventions. The postwriting stage is the evaluation stage. While the secretary checks the accuracy of the mechanical aspects of the product, the author reviews the content: organization and sequence, logic and clarity, and the style in which it is written.

Mercer (1997) divides the writing process into five stages. In the first, Prewriting, the student selects a topic, considers the purpose for writing and the audience, selects a format (e.g., story, essay, poem), and gathers and organizes ideas for writing. The second stage, Drafting, involves writing a first draft; here, the student pays most attention to content, not the mechanical aspects of writing. In stage three, Revising, the student reviews what he or she has written, asks other students for feedback, and revises the content of the composition. The fourth stage, Editing, involves correction of errors in spelling, capitalization, punctuation, and other mechanics. As needed, the student may confer with the teacher during the editing stage. In the last stage, Publishing, the student reads his or her work to an audience or publishes it as a classroom book or newspaper or magazine article.

Teaching students how to write clearly and cogently is a major goal of American education. Together with reading and mathematics, writing is considered one of the basic school skills. Despite this, past classroom practices often assigned writing only a minor role in the curriculum (Graves, 1978; Isaacson, 1988). This led Freedman (1982) to call writing "the neglected basic skill" (p. 34). Another concern was that when writing instruction did occur, it was directed more toward improving the performance of the writer-as-secretary than that of the writer-as-author. Writing instruction tended to emphasize mechanical aspects such as handwriting, spelling, and usage (Alexander, 1983).

In the past few years, important changes have occurred in the ways that the teaching of writing is conceptualized (Moran, 1988; Nodine, 1983). One new direction is increased emphasis on writing as a thinking process and the stages that make up that process. Another is the whole language approach to integrated language arts instruction. According to Lerner, Cousin, and Richeck (1992), "Writing takes on a new role in whole language instruction and is just as important as reading" (p. 227). In addition, writing is currently viewed as an appropriate means of expression in all areas of curriculum, including mathematics.

Assessment practices are also undergoing changes, but there is still heavy emphasis on the more mechanical aspects of writing (Freedman, 1982; Moran, 1988). Poplin (1983) says, "Today most of our assessment devices tap very little of what is considered meaningful writing behavior" (p. 69). Instead, most measures concentrate on the secretarial dimensions of writing, perhaps because these dimensions are less difficult to assess.

Traditional measures of writing skills tend to focus on the skills of spelling, handwriting, and composition. Spelling is usually assessed with a paper-and-pencil task. The tester reads a word to the student, the word is read again in the context of a phrase or sentence, and the student responds by writing the word. Students can also be asked to spell orally, or spelling tasks can be designed in multiple-choice format. Multiple-choice tests usually present the student with several words, and the student selects the one that is correctly or incorrectly spelled.

Handwriting is generally assessed informally by comparing a sample of the student's writing with a set of performance criteria. An existing sample of the student's handwriting can be evaluated, or a new sample can be elicited. Depending upon the age and skill level of the student, the sample may be written in manuscript (printing) or cursive handwriting.

Composition can be defined as the process by which a writer creates a written product. On measures of composition skills, students are typically presented with a writing task; the sample that the student produces is then subjected to analysis. Several aspects of the sample can be evaluated: content, vocabulary, organization, logic, writing style, productivity, creativity, and the more mechanical dimensions such as handwriting and spelling.

Traditional measures of composition are concerned with the product of writing, not the process. Their purpose is the evaluation of the student's responses, not the interaction between the student and the task throughout the series of stages involved in writing. To gather information about the process of writing and how the student approaches and completes the task of composition, informal assessment strategies are a necessity.

Another area that traditional measures often neglect is the ability to apply composition skills in daily life tasks. Writing is a common part of daily living. Students should be competent in performing tasks such as writing notes, friendly letters, memoranda, and shopping lists; completing job applications and tax forms; and the like.

Current Practices

Writing assessment receives less attention than either reading or mathematics assessment. There are fewer measures of writing skills available, and those that exist tend to emphasize the more mechanical aspects of the process. Although most survey tests of academic achievement contain some measure of written language, the skills most often assessed are spelling, usage, and grammar. However, newer tests such as the *Peabody Individual Achievement Test-Revised/Normative Update* (Markwardt, 1998), the *Woodcock-Johnson Psycho-Educational Battery-Revised* (Woodcock & Johnson, 1989), and the *Wechsler Individual Achievement Test* (1992) do include measures of composition, as Chapter 7 described.

More directly related to instructional planning for students with disabilities are the assessment tools listed in Table 13–1. These include not only standardized tests but also criterion-referenced tests and other types of informal measures. The number of written language measures has increased dramatically in the past few years.

Some of the measures that are currently available are survey instruments. They are designed to assess a range of skills in order to identify the student's strengths and weaknesses. For instance, the *Test of Written Language-3* (Hammill & Larsen, 1996) assesses not only spelling and grammar, but also composition. Other measures concentrate on one specific skill area. The *Test of Written Spelling-4* (Larsen, Hammill, & Moats, 1999), for example, is limited to the investigation of spelling ability.

Informal strategies are a necessity in the assessment of writing skills because of the limited number of formal tools and the narrowness of their scope. Among the informal techniques most often used in writing assessment are observation, informal inventories, criterion-referenced tests, clinical interviews, work sample analysis procedures, and portfolio assessment. Informal strategies provide information not only about the student, but also about the characteristics of the classroom learning environment.

This chapter is organized around three major skill areas in written language assessment: spelling, handwriting, and composition. Spelling is the first topic of discussion, and the section that follows describes the major formal and informal assessment strategies available for the study of special students' spelling skills. Techniques for assessing handwriting are described next, followed by procedures for evaluating proficiency in composition.

STRATEGIES FOR ASSESSING SPELLING

Spelling is an academic skill that is usually included on the individual achievement tests used in special education assessment to establish the presence of a school performance problem. However, it is important to recognize that broad range achievement tests assess spelling skills in different ways. Many, like the *Wide Range Achievement Test-3* (Wilkinson, 1993), use recall tasks in which the student is required to remember and then write the correct spelling of words. Others, like the *Peabody Individual Achievement Test-Revised/Normative Update* (Markwardt, 1998), employ recognition tasks in which the

TABLE 13-1
Measures of Written Language

Name (Author)	Ages or Grades	Type of Measure*	Group or Individual	SKILL AREA(S) ASSESSED		
				Spelling	Handwriting	Composition
BRIGANCE® Diagnostic Comprehensive Inventory of Basic Skills-Revised (Brigance, 1999)	Pre-kindergarten to grade 9	CRT	Varies	X	X	X
BRIGANCE® Diagnostic Inventory of Early Development-Revised (Brigance, 1991)	Birth to age 6	CRT	Individual		X	
BRIGANCE® Diagnostic Inventory of Essential Skills (Brigance, 1981)	Grade 6 to adult education	CRT	Varies	X	X	X
Checklist of Written Expression (Poteet, 1980)	All	C	Individual	X	X	X
Denver Handwriting Analysis (Anderson, 1983)	Grades 3–8	II	Group or Individual		X	
Diagnostic Achievement Test in Spelling (Wittenberg, 1980)	Grades 2–10	NRT	Group	X		
Diagnostic Evaluation of Writing Skills (Weiner, 1980)	All	E	Individual	X	X	X
Diagnostic Spelling Test (Kottmeyer, 1970)	Grades 2–6	II	Group	X		
Hudson Education Skills Inventory (Hudson, Colson, Welch, Banikowski, & Mehring, 1989)	Grades K–12	CRT	Individual	X	X	X
Mather-Woodcock Group Writing Tests (Mather & Woodcock, 1997)	Grades 2–16	NRT	Group	X		X
Oral and Written Language Scales (Carrow-Woolfolk, 1996)	Ages 5 to 21	NRT	Small Group or Individual	X		X
Picture Story Language Test (Myklebust, 1965)	Ages 7 to 17	NRT	Group or Individual			X
Spellmaster Assessment and Teaching System (Greenbaum, 1987)	Kindergarten to grade 10	II	Group	X		
Test of Adolescent and Adult Language-3 (Hammill, Brown, Larsen, & Wiederholt, 1994)	Ages 12-0 to 24-11	NRT	Group			X
Test of Early Written Language-2 (Hresko, Herron, & Peak, 1996)	Ages 3-0 to 10-11	NRT	Individual	X	X	X
Test of Legible Handwriting (Larsen & Hammill, 1989)	Ages 7-0 to 18-6; grades 2 to 12	NRT	Group or Individual		X	
Test of Written Expression (McGhee, Bryant, Larsen, & Rivera, 1995)	Ages 6-6 to 14-11	NRT	Group or Individual	X		X
Test of Written Language-3 (Hammill & Larsen, 1996)	Ages 7-0 to 17-11	NRT	Group or Individual	X		X
Test of Written Spelling-4 (Larsen, Hammill, & Moats, 1999)	Ages 6-0 to 18-11	NRT	Group or Individual	X		
Woodcock Language Proficiency Battery-Revised (Woodcock, 1991)	Ages 3 to 80+	NRT	Individual	X		X
Zaner-Bloser Evaluation Scales (n.d.)	Grades 1 to 6	R	Group		X	

*NRT stands for norm-referenced test, *II* for informal inventory, *CRT* for criterion-referenced test, *C* for checklist, *E* for error analysis procedure, and *R* for rating scale.

student must identify the correctly spelled word. Recognition tasks are essentially proofreading and are related to the editing stage of the writing process; recall tasks are related more to the writing stage. The *Woodcock-Johnson Psycho-Education Battery-Revised* (Woodcock & Johnson, 1989) offers measures of both types of spelling skills in its Dictation and Proofing subtests.

Broad range achievement tests do not provide sufficient information for planning instructional programs in spelling. Thus, when a problem in spelling is indicated, further assessment must take place. The assessment team can select a norm-referenced test of spelling such as the *Test of Written Spelling-4*. In addition, a variety of informal techniques and procedures can be used to learn more about students' current spelling skills.

Test of Written Spelling-4

The *Test of Written Spelling-4 (TWS-4)* is a norm-referenced measure designed for students ages 6-0 to 18-11. The format of this test was changed in this edition. In the previous version, the *TWS* contained two subtests: Predictable Words, a test of skill in spelling words that conform to the rules of phonics (e.g., *bed, him)*, and Unpredictable Words, a measure of skill in spelling ir-regular words (e.g., *people, knew)*. In the fourth edition, the manual says that "because respected professionals questioned the value of having two subtests . . . , this practice has been abandoned" (p. viii).

Two forms of the *TWS-4* are available, Form A and Form B. Both are standard dictation tests. The tester reads a word to the student, reads the word in a sentence, and then reads the word again. The student responds by writing the word on the test answer sheet; no time limits are imposed. Each form contains 50 words (a compilation of words from the Predictable and Unpredictable subtests of earlier editions), and the manual provides suggested starting points by grade level. Testing begins at the starting point and continues until a ceiling of five consecutive errors is reached; at that point, it may be necessary to administer items below the starting point to establish a basal of five consecutive correct responses. Guidelines for group administration of the *TWS-4* are also available in the manual.

The *TWS* was not renormed in the preparation of the fourth edition. Instead, normative data were obtained from the norm groups used in the second and third editions. These groups included approximately 5,000 students from 23 states. According to the *TWS-4* manual, the sample ap-

---

Test of Written Spelling-4 (TWS-4)

S. C. Larsen, D. D. Hammill, & L. C. Moats (1999)

Type: Norm-referenced test

Major Content Areas: Spelling

Type of Administration: Individual or group

Administration Time: 15–25 minutes

Age/Grade Levels: Ages 6-0 to 18-11

Types of Scores: Standard score, percentile rank, age and grade equivalents

Computer Aids: N/A

Typical Uses: Evaluation of students' spelling skills

Cautions: It is not known whether students with disabilities were included in the norm group. Information is needed about the relationship of the *TWS-4* to other individual tests of achievement used in special education assessment.

Publisher: PRO-ED (www.proedinc.com)

proximates the 1997 U.S. school-age population in gender, urban-rural residence, race, geographic region, and ethnicity. No information is provided about the inclusion of students with disabilities in the norm groups.

The reliability of the *TWS-4* is satisfactory. Coefficients for internal consistency, alternative form, test-retest, and interrater reliability exceed .80. The manual presents evidence of moderate relationships between the *TWS-4* and results of group achievement tests and between the *TWS-4* and teachers' ratings of students' spelling skills. However, information is needed about the relationship of the *TWS-4* to the individual measures of achievement typically used in special education.

Only total test results are available on the *TWS-4*. Those can be expressed as a standard score, percentile rank, age equivalent ("Spelling Age"), and grade equivalent. The standard errors of measurement for *TWS-4* standard scores appear in the manual; they range from 3 to 5 standard score points, depending on the form of the test and the student's age.

Informal Techniques

Among the informal strategies that can provide information about spelling are work sample analysis, informal inventories, criterion-referenced tests, observation, and clinical interviews.

Work Sample Analysis. Spelling, like all written language skills, is well suited to work sample analysis because a permanent product is produced. Within every classroom, there are many types of spelling samples available for analysis: students' essays, book reports, test papers (including spelling tests), daily homework assignments, workbooks, and so forth. Error analysis procedures can be used to evaluate the spelling samples of older students who have achieved some proficiency. However, with younger students and others who are only beginning to acquire spelling skills, response analysis is the preferred technique.

Poplin (1983) points out that learning to spell is a developmental process, and young children go through a number of stages as they begin to acquire written language skills. Writing begins in the preschool years as young children observe and begin to imitate the act of writing. They practice with paper and pencil by drawing and scribbling and ask adults to write words for them so they can attempt to copy them. Soon children begin to write words and phrases on their own, using invented spellings. According to Poplin, spelling skills emerge in the following sequence:

a. Only 1–2 consonants represent words or phrases.
b. Most consonant sounds in words or phrases are represented, few or no vowels.
c. Tense (long) vowels emerge without their silent counterparts; lax (short) vowels are missing.
d. Lax vowels are represented by phonologically nearest tense vowel.
e. Most consonants are present and correct—except possibly double consonants, consonant blends, consonant digraphs, final consonant blends, those associated with morphological endings (e.g., *ing, ed, er, tion* and *sion*).
f. Rules are overapplied to regular words (e.g., *goed*).
g. Correct forms appear in a majority of instances. (p. 71) [italics added]

These stages provide a framework for the work sample analysis of the spelling of beginning writers.

When students' skills mature to the extent that many of their written words are spelled correctly, error analysis becomes an appropriate procedure. Several systems for categorizing spelling errors have been devised. Edgington (1968), for example, includes additions, omissions, reversals, and phonetic spelling of nonphonetic words as errors.

The *Spellmaster Assessment and Teaching System* (Greenbaum, 1987) contains a series of inventories to assess students' skill in spelling regular words, irregular words, and homophones. There are eight levels of the Regular Word Test, corresponding roughly to grades kindergarten to 10, and the score sheet for each level is designed for analysis of the student's responses. A portion of a sample score sheet is shown in Figure 13–1. Across the top are the spelling skills that are assessed on this level: beginning consonants, beginning blends, short vowels, and so on. The first spelling word, *lap,*

FIGURE 13–1

Spellmaster Error Analysis Score Sheet

Note: From *Spellmaster Assessment and Teaching System* by C. R. Greenbaum, 1987, Austin, TX: PRO-ED. Copyright 1987 by C. R. Greenbaum. Reprinted by permission of author.

SPELLMASTER

REGULAR WORD TEST 1

Name:

Grade: Date:

Number Right: _____

	Beginning Consonants	Beginning Blends	Short vowels a	e	i	o	u	Ending Consonants	Ending Blends	Additions	Omissions
1	l		a					p			
2	r						u	g			
3	h				i			d			
4		fl				o		p			
5	v			e				t			
6	y		a					m			
7	g				i				ft		
8		dr					u	m			
9	v		a					n			
10	f					o			nd		

is divided into three parts, and each letter appears under the appropriate heading. The tester circles the letter or letters where substitution errors occur; additions and omissions can also be noted on the score sheet. When all of the student's responses have been analyzed, a count is made of the number of errors in each category.

Others have suggested a simpler way to conceptualize errors in spelling: phonetic and nonphonetic misspellings (Howell & Kaplan, 1980; Mann, Suiter, & McClung, 1979). Phonetic mis-

spellings take place when the student attempts, unsuccessfully, to use the rules of phonics to spell a word. Either the student applies the rules incorrectly, or the word does not adhere to those rules. For instance, a student might write *kat* instead of *cat.*

Nonphonetic spellings, in contrast, do not appear to be based on the application of phonics rules. Some nonphonetic spellings are close approximations of the correct sequence of letters. For example, the student may recall most of the appropriate letters correctly but forget one or two, add an extraneous letter, or jumble the sequence somewhat (e.g., *lenht* for *length*). In some cases, nonphonetic spellings bear little or no resemblance to the word in question (e.g., *ob* for *house*). Such attempts are usually considered random spellings.

Informal Inventories. Teachers may find it useful to design an informal inventory to learn more about students' current levels of performance. One strategy involves selecting representative words from the basal spelling series used in the school or classroom. A short list of words from the first grade spelling textbook is assembled, a list from the second grade text, and so on, depending upon the skill level of the student. Then the teacher dictates the lists to the student and asks him or her to write each word. Results provide a rough estimate of the student's status in relation to the skill demands of the classroom spelling program.

Another strategy is to design an inventory around specific spelling skills. Mercer and Mercer (1998) provide an example designed to assess grades 2 and 3 spelling skills; it appears in Table 13–2. This is a diagnostic test, because each item is intended to measure one particular aspect of spelling. Thus, skill in writing the letters that correspond to the short vowel sounds is assessed by the first five items. By evaluating the student's performance in terms of the specific spelling skills assessed, the teacher can determine which areas may be in need of further assessment with criterion-referenced tests and other procedures.

Criterion-referenced Tests. These measures can help professionals identify which spelling skills have been mastered and which remain in need of instruction. Teachers can prepare their own criterion-referenced tests to measure progress toward curriculum objectives. For example, if spelling common words is an educational goal, the teacher could use the word list that appears in Figure 13–2 to construct a CRT. This list contains 250 words arranged in order of difficulty; each of the words included on the list is commonly found in children's writings. Criterion-referenced tests could also be de-

signed to assess students' mastery of words that are often misspelled (spelling demons) or to evaluate progress in the classroom spelling program.

There are also several published CRTs that offer tests of spelling. One example is the collection of tests by Brigance (1981, 1991, 1999). The test for elementary students, the *BRIGANCE® Diagnostic Comprehensive Inventory of Basic Skills-Revised* (Brigance, 1999), features a Spelling Grade-Placement Test and measures of skill in spelling initial consonants, initial blends and digraphs, suffixes, and prefixes. These measures are also available on the secondary level test, the *BRIGANCE® Diagnostic Inventory of Essential Skills* (Brigance, 1981), along with tests entitled Number Words, Days of the Week, and Months of the Year.

Observation. Observations can help determine how the student approaches the task of spelling. The observation should be scheduled during a time when the student will be writing an essay or engaging in any other type of activity that requires spelling. The observer must be quite near the student to see exactly how the student proceeds. Of special interest are any strategies the student employs when he or she is unsure of the spelling of a word.

In the elementary grades where spelling is taught directly, students can also be observed as they attempt to learn new spelling words. The observer should watch for the ways that the student attacks or fails to attack the memorization task. Does the student open the spelling book and simply stare at the words? Or is there some indication that the student is actively rehearsing the new words? For example, does he or she write the words? Say the letters of each word aloud or subvocally? Look at a word, cover it, and then attempt to write it?

Clinical Interviews. Clinical interviews can take place while students are writing, but there is danger of interrupting the students' thought processes and distracting them from the task at hand. Because of this, it is probably best to simply observe until students have finished writing. Then they can be questioned about the ways they coped with the spelling demands of the writing

TABLE 13–2
Diagnostic Spelling Test

SPELLING WORDS	SPELLING OBJECTIVES	SPELLING WORDS USED IN SENTENCES
1. man 2. pit 3. dug 4. web 5. dot	short vowels and selected consonants	The *man* is big. The *pit* in the fruit was hard. We *dug* a hole. She saw the spider's *web*. Don't forget to *dot* the i.
6. mask 7. drum	words beginning and/or ending with consonant blends	On Halloween the child wore a *mask*. He beat the *drum* in the parade.
8. line 9. cake	consonant-vowel-consonant-silent *e*	Get in *line* for lunch. We had a birthday *cake*.
10. coat 11. rain	two vowels together	Put on your winter *coat*. Take an umbrella in the *rain*.
12. ice 13. large	variant consonant sounds for *c* and *g*	*Ice* is frozen water. This is a *large* room.
14. mouth 15. town 16. boy	words containing vowel diphthongs	Open your *mouth* to brush your teeth. We went to *town* to shop. The *boy* and girl went to school.
17. bikes 18. glasses	plurals	The children got new *bikes* for their birthdays. Get some *glasses* for the drinks.
19. happy 20. monkey	short *i* sounds of *y*	John is very *happy* now. We saw a *monkey* at the zoo.
21. war 22. dirt	words with *r*-controlled vowels	Bombs were used in the *war*. The pigs were in the *dirt*.
23. foot 24. moon	two sounds of *oo*	Put the shoe on your *foot*. Three men walked on the *moon*.
25. light 26. knife	words with silent letters	Turn on the *light* so we can see. Get a fork and *knife*.
27. pill	final consonant doubled	The doctor gave me a *pill*.
28. bat 29. batter	consonant-vowel-consonant pattern in which final consonant is doubled before adding ending	The baseball player got a new *bat*. The *batter* hit a home run.
30. didn't 31. isn't	contractions	They *didn't* want to come. It *isn't* raining today.
32. take 33. taking	final *e* is dropped before adding suffix	Please *take* off your coat. He is *taking* me to the show.
34. any 35. could	nonphonetic spellings	I did not have *any* lunch. Maybe you *could* go on a trip.
36. ate 37. eight 38. blue 39. blew	homonyms	Mary *ate* breakfast at home. There are *eight* children in the family. The sky is *blue*. The wind *blew* away the hat.
40. baseball	compound words	They played *baseball* outside.

Note: From *Teaching Students with Learning Problems* 5th ed., by Mercer/Mercer, © 1998. Reprinted by permission of Prentice-Hall, Inc., Upper Saddle River, NJ.

THE STEP SYSTEM
Sequential Tasks for Educational Planning

CAJON VALLEY UNION SCHOOL DISTRICT
Special Education Department

Most appropriate for CA	8–3	4–6	7–9	10–12	13+
Reg. Class			x	x	x
Lang. Hdcp.			x	x	x
Comm. Hdcp.			x	x	x
Phys. Hdcp.		x	x	x	x
Sev. Hdcp.					

#7509

title: SPELLING: 250 MOST OFTEN USED WORDS

type: Curriculum Milestones

instructions

Student _____

1.0 Spells a, an, am, as, at, be, by, do, go, he.

2.0 Spells I, if, in, is, it, me, my, no, of, on.

3.0 Spells or, so, to, up, us, we, all, and, any, are.

4.0 Spells bed, big, boy, but, can, car, day, did, dog, eat.

5.0 Spells few, for, fun, get, got, had, has, her, him, his.

6.0 Spells how, let, man, may, men, new, not, now, off, old.

7.0 Spells one, our, out, put, ran, saw, say, see, she, tell.

8.0 Spells the, too, two, use, was, way, who, you, also, cold.

9.0 Spells away, back, best, book, boys, been, came, city, come, days.

10.0 Spells dear, don't, door, down, each, ever, find, fire, five, four.

11.0 Spells from, gave, girl, give, good, have, hard, help, here, home.

12.0 Spells hope, into, just, keep, kind, know, last, left, like, live.

13.0 Spells long, look, made, make, many, more, most, much, must, name.

14.0 Spells next, nice, once, only, over, play, read, room, said, side.

15.0 Spells snow, some, soon, stay, still, s,ure, take, than, that, them.

16.0 Spells then, they, this, time, told, took, town, tree, used, very.

17.0 Spells want, week, well, went, were, what, when, will, with, work.

18.0 Spells year, your, about, after, again, along, asked, comes, could, every.

19.0 Spells found, girls, going, great, happy, heard, house, large, lived, money.

20.0 Spells never, night, other, place, ready, right, small, their, there, these.

21.0 Spells thing, think, three, today, until, water, where, which, while, white.

22.0 Spells would, write, years, always, around, before, better, called, coming, didn't.

23.0 Spells enough, father, first, friend, letter, little, looked, mother, people, pretty.

24.0 Spells school, should, summer, things, wanted, winter, another, because, brother, country.

25.0 Spells getting, morning, started, teacher, thought, through, beautiful, children, Christmas, something.

DEVELOPED BY: Marie J. Griffith

DATE DEVELOPED: 1/2/79
Suggested Criterion: 80% Mastery

FIGURE 13-2
High Frequency Spelling Words

Note: Reprinted with permission of the Special Education Department of the Cajon Valley Union School District, El Cajon, California; STEP #7509 was developed by Marie J. Griffith.

429

task. Some of the questions that can be asked are as follows:

- When you're writing a sentence or a paragraph and you write down a word, how do you tell if you've spelled the word correctly?
- When you're not sure how to spell a word, what do you do?
  Do you guess at the spelling?
  Try to sound the word out?
  Write two or three possible spellings and then pick the one you think is right?
  Ask the teacher or a friend how to spell the word?
  Look the word up in a dictionary?
  Choose another word, one that you can spell?
- After you've finished writing, do you read and check what you've written?
- In checking your writing, what do you do if you find a word that you think may be spelled incorrectly?

Students can then be asked to look over the writing they have just completed and mark any words that they think might be incorrectly spelled. This provides some information about proofreading skills and the student's ability to spot errors in spelling.

STRATEGIES FOR ASSESSING HANDWRITING

Informal strategies such as rating scales, observation, error analysis, inventories, and criterion-referenced tests are used to assess the student's current proficiency in handwriting. A norm-referenced measure, the *Test of Legible Handwriting* (Larsen & Hammill, 1989), is also available. With younger children, manuscript handwriting (i.e., printing) is the concern. With older students, cursive handwriting is analyzed.

Rating Scales

Rating scales provide a method for judging whether a student's handwriting is poor enough to be considered an area of educational need. However, rating scales rely on the judgment of the professional who evaluates the student's

handwriting sample and, thus, their results can be somewhat subjective. Ratings can be made more objective if professionals are furnished with standards for judging students' handwriting, such as those with the *Zaner-Bloser Evaluation Scales*.

The *Zaner-Bloser Evaluation Scales* (n.d.) provide teachers with a standard method of collecting and rating handwriting samples. A separate scale is available for each grade from 1 through 6; manuscript writing is evaluated on the scales for grades 1 and 2, and cursive writing on the scales for grades 3 through 6. A cursive scale for grade 2 is also available. Each scale contains a handwriting selection for the students to copy.

Five factors are considered in judging handwriting skill: shape, slant, spacing, size, and smoothness. To help the teacher evaluate these factors, the *Zaner-Bloser* provides examples of Excellent, Good, Average, Fair, and Poor handwriting at each of the grade levels. Figure 13–3 shows two examples from the Grade 3 Scale—Average and Poor.

The teacher rates the student's handwriting in relation to the five factors listed in the figure. Each is judged as either Satisfactory or Needs Improvement. If all of the five factors are judged satisfactory, the student's handwriting is considered Excellent. If four of the five factors are judged satisfactory, the sample is considered Good. Three satisfactory areas result in a rating of Average, two satisfactory areas in a rating of Fair, and one satisfactory area in a rating of Poor.

The *Zaner-Bloser Evaluation Scales* are most useful for providing an estimate of the overall quality of the student's handwriting. However, in interpreting results, it is necessary to remember that these scales are not designed to assess a typical sample of the student's handwriting. Instead, the student copies a selection, first practicing it and then attempting to write it in his or her best handwriting. Having the opportunity to practice may result in an improvement from the student's usual performance. On the other hand, fatigue may interfere with the second attempt. It is also important to note that the *Zaner-Bloser* is untimed. The quality of the student's handwriting may change dramatically when speed becomes a necessity.

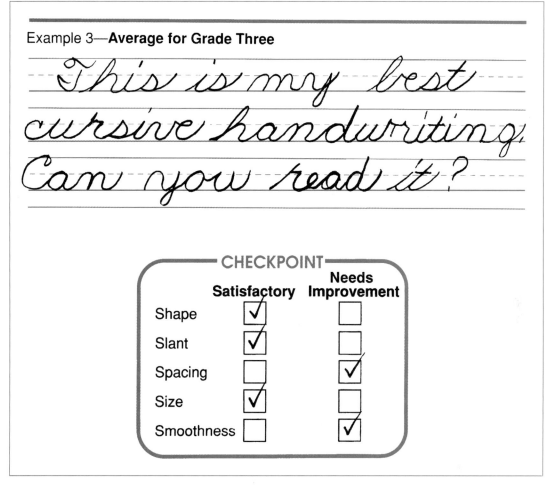

FIGURE 13-3
Writing Sample from the *Zaner-Bloser Evaluation Scales,* Grade 3
Note: From *Zaner-Bloser Evaluation Scales,* n.d. Reproduced with permission from Zaner-Bloser, Inc.

Observation and Error Analysis

Both observations and error analyses can provide information about how students approach handwriting. A student can be observed during an activity that requires writing, and then error analysis procedures can be applied to the writing sample that the student produces. In implementing these informal assessment techniques, it is important to consider not only the legibility of the student's writing, but also speed. A student must be able to write quickly if handwriting is to become a useful tool for communication.

Speed can be studied in several ways. For example, the teacher can ask the student to copy a passage of 100 words (or some other known length) and time how long it takes the student to complete this task. Or the teacher can time the student during a writing activity and then count the number of letters or words the student produced. These data can then be transformed into a rate measure, such as the average number of letters the student writes per minute.

In classroom observations of handwriting performance, the professional should take note of several student behaviors:

- How is the student seated? Are the desk and chair of appropriate size? Is the student sitting

FIGURE 13-3
Writing Sample from the *Zaner-Bloser Evaluation Scales,* Grade 3—(*Continued*)

upright with both feet on the floor under the desk?

- In what position is the student's paper? Is he or she holding it so it will not slip?
- How does the student hold the writing implement? Does the student grip the pen or pencil too tightly?
- Is the student writing with a pen or a pencil? Is it an appropriate size?
- On what type of paper is the student writing? What size is it? Is it lined? Are there guidelines between the lines? Are there margins?
- Does the student write with the right or left hand?

- When the student writes, does he or she move the entire hand smoothly across the page or move just the fingers in an attempt to draw each letter?
- Does the student press down when writing? Does he or she exert a great deal of pressure on the paper? If writing with a pencil, does the student break pencil points frequently?
- How often does the student erase or cross out mistakes?

When students are copying from the board or from a text or worksheet on the desk, they may make errors because they are unable to see the model clearly. If this occurs, it is important to determine if vision problems are a factor.

Any writing sample produced by the student can be used for error analysis, and daily classroom assignments are likely to provide the most typical sample of a student's handwriting. However, if written assignments require spelling and other language skills, poor handwriting may be the result of an attempt to compensate for poor skills in other areas. For instance, if a student is unsure whether to write *receive* or *recieve,* he or she may write the letters indistinctly, placing the dot for the *i* in the center between the two letters. Because such tactics interfere with the evaluation of handwriting, the teacher may wish to consider obtaining at least one writing sample in which the student copies the material.

Several systems of categorizing handwriting errors have been proposed. For example, Wiederholt, Hammill, and Brown (1978) suggest that the teacher examine the following features of students' manuscript writing:

1. Position of hand, arm, body, and/or paper
2. Size of letters: too small, large, etc.
3. Proportion of one letter or word to another
4. Quality of the pencil line: too heavy, light, variable, etc.
5. Slant: too much or irregular
6. Letter formation: poor circles or straight lines, lines disconnected, etc.
7. Letter alignment: off the line, etc.
8. Spacing: letters or words crowded or too scattered
9. Speed: too fast or too slow (p. 183)

Howell and Kaplan (1980) add that in analyzing cursive handwriting, teachers should take note of alignment, letter size, spacing, letter form, and spatial orientation.

Inventories and Criterion-Referenced Tests

Teachers can design informal inventories to gain general information about students' handwriting abilities. An inventory assessing both manuscript and cursive writing skills appeared in Chapter 5 on informal assessment. That chapter also presented a task analysis of the lowercase manuscript alphabet (Affleck, Lowenbraun, &

Archer, 1980) in which letters were divided into several clusters based on difficulty (e.g., straight line letters, straight line and slant letters, and so forth). That analysis and one of cursive letters by Graham and Miller (1980) provide a framework for developing informal inventories of basic handwriting skills. According to Graham and Miller, the cursive alphabet can be divided into the following clusters based on how the letters are formed:

Lowercase Letters	*Uppercase Letters*
i, u, w, t, r, s	C, A, E
n, m, v, x	N, M, P, R, B, D, U, V, W,
e, l, b, h, k, f	K, H, X
c, a, g, d, q	T, F, Q, Z, L
o, p, j	S, G
y, z	O, I, J, Y

The *Denver Handwriting Analysis* (Anderson, 1983) is a published inventory that assesses several cursive writing skills. It is designed for students in grades 3 to 8, but it can be used with other ages if cursive handwriting is a concern. The skills sampled include near-point and far-point copying, writing the cursive alphabet from memory, and writing the cursive equivalent of manuscript letters.

Criterion-referenced tests can also provide information about students' current handwriting skills. For example, the measures by Brigance (1981, 1991, 1999) offer several tests of handwriting. Manuscript writing is assessed on the *BRIGANCE® Diagnostic Inventory of Early Development-Revised* and the *BRIGANCE® Diagnostic Comprehensive Inventory of Basic Skills-Revised,* and cursive writing is assessed on the basic skills measure as well as the *BRIGANCE® Diagnostic Inventory of Essential Skills.* In addition, the essential skills battery includes measures of daily life handwriting tasks such as Addresses Envelope, Letter Writing, and Simple Application for Employment.

Test of Legible Handwriting (TOLH)

The *Test of Legible Handwriting (TOLH)* is a norm-referenced measure for students ages 7-0 to

18-6. It is an interesting test because the evaluation criteria it provides can be used to judge several types of handwriting samples. Possibilities include classroom work samples already produced by students and the story students write as part of the *Test of Written Language*. The *TOLH* also provides prompts for eliciting handwriting samples: picture prompts for story writing, and verbal prompts for writing a biographical sketch and a letter. The picture prompts are the same as those used in the *Test of Written Language*. After the tester reads directions for the writing task, students are allowed 15 minutes to produce a sample.

Handwriting is scored holistically on the *TOLH*. The major criterion is legibility, and the tester makes a judgment by comparing the student's handwriting to models in the manual's scoring guides. Three scoring guides are available, one for manuscript writing, one for right slant or perpendicular cursive writing, and one for left slant cursive handwriting. The manuscript guide is shown in Figure 13–4. For example, if the student's sample is comparable to the first model, a raw score of 8 would be assigned. If it is more legible, the raw score would be 9; if its legibility falls between the first and second models, the raw score would be 7. The *TOLH* includes

several handwriting samples for use by testers to practice scoring.

The raw score for each handwriting sample is converted to a standard score and percentile rank. Standard scores are distributed with a mean of 10 and a standard deviation of 3. When standard scores are available for at least two handwriting samples, a Legibility Quotient can be determined. The LQ is a standard score with a mean of 100 and a standard deviation of 15. In addition to rating each sample holistically, testers can also complete the Analysis of Handwriting Errors checklist on the back of the *TOLH* Profile/Record Form. Two checklists are available, one for cursive and one for manuscript, and each addresses letter formation (capital and lowercase), spatial relationships, and handwriting rate.

The *TOLH* was standardized in 1987 as part of the norming study for the second edition of the *Test of Written Language*. The *TOLH* standardization sample of 1,723 students from 19 states appears to approximate the national population in sex, urban-rural residence, race, and geographic region. Internal consistency, interscorer reliability, and test-retest reliability are all adequate. Interscorer reliability is particularly important with the *TOLH* because of its use of holistic scoring. A coefficient of .95 was reported in the manual for

---

Test of Legible Handwriting (TOLH)

S. C. Larsen & D. D. Hammill (1989)

Type: Norm-referenced test

Major Content Areas: Manuscript or cursive handwriting

Type of Administration: Individual or group

Administration Time: 20 minutes

Age/Grade Levels: Ages 7-0 to 18-6, grades 2 through 12

Types of Scores: Standard scores and percentiles for each writing sample; overall Legibility Quotient

Computer Aids: N/A

Typical Uses: Evaluation of students' ability to write legibly

Cautions: More information is needed about interrater reliability.

Publisher: PRO-ED (www.proedinc.com)

FIGURE 13-4

Manuscript Scoring Guide from the *Test of Legible Handwriting*

Note: From *Test of Legible Handwriting* (p. 10) by S. C. Larsen and D. D. Hammill, 1989, Austin, TX: PRO-ED. Copyright 1989 by PRO-ED. Reprinted by permission.

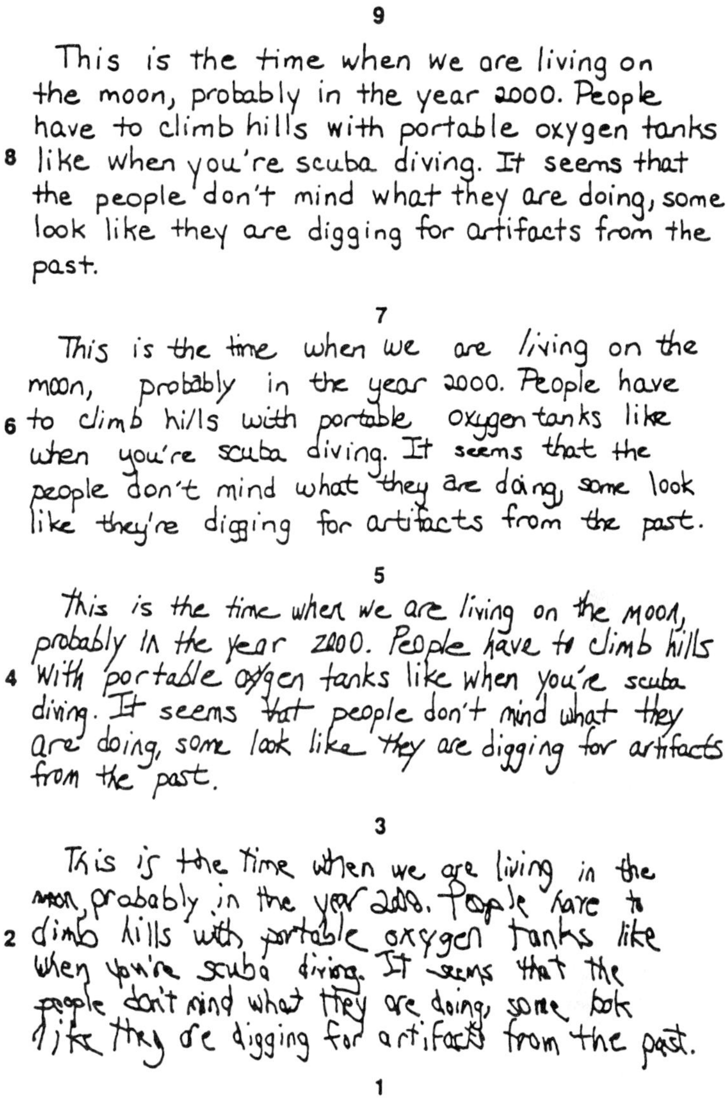

9

This is the time when we are living on the moon, probably in the year 2000. People have to climb hills with portable oxygen tanks like when you're scuba diving. It seems that the people don't mind what they are doing, some look like they are digging for artifacts from the past.

8

7

This is the time when we are living on the moon, probably in the year 2000. People have to climb hills with portable oxygen tanks like when you're scuba diving. It seems that the people don't mind what they are doing, some look like they're digging for artifacts from the past.

6

5

This is the time when we are living on the moon, probably in the year 2000. People have to climb hills with portable oxygen tanks like when you're scuba diving. It seems that people don't mind what they are doing, some look like they are digging for artifacts from the past.

4

3

This is the time when we are living in the moon, probably in the year 2000. People have to climb hills with portable oxygen tanks like when you're scuba diving. It seems that the people don't mind what they are doing, some look like they are digging for artifacts from the past.

2

1

this type of reliability; however, the study included only two raters. The validity of the *TOLH* is supported by a strong correlation between *TOLH* results and teachers' independent ratings of handwriting samples ($r = .92$).

The *TOLH* is "the first nationally standardized measure of handwriting readability" (Bailet, 1991, p. 178). As such, it is an important addition to the collection of measures available to professionals who are interested in the assessment of handwriting. Although more evidence supporting its interrater reliability is needed, the preliminary data reported in the *TOLH* manual are encouraging.

STRATEGIES FOR ASSESSING COMPOSITION

A student's ability to plan, write, and revise a piece of original writing can be assessed formally with the aid of standardized tests or informally with techniques such as rating scales, work sample analysis, criterion-referenced tests, observation, clinical interviews, and portfolios. Most of these assessment strategies focus on the written product the student creates. Only the informal procedures of observation and clinical interviewing allow the professional to assess the process the student engages in to produce a sample of writing.

The primary concern in the assessment of composition skills is the content of the student's writing, not its form. Areas of interest include the organization of the writing, the vocabulary used to express ideas, the style in which the composition is written, and the originality of the ideas expressed. However, the mechanical aspects of writing also play a role, albeit a secondary one, because a composition's intelligibility can be impaired by mechanical errors. Thus, some measures of composition take into account areas such as syntax, usage, capitalization, punctuation, and even spelling and handwriting.

The sections that follow introduce a wide range of strategies for the assessment of compo-

sition skills. First to be discussed is the *Test of Written Language-3,* a formal measure that evaluates several of the important skills in writing. Next, other formal tests are introduced, and finally, a variety of informal techniques are described. Because few formal tests are available, informal strategies play a major role in the assessment of composition skills.

Test of Written Language-3

According to its manual, the *Test of Written Language-3 (TOWL-3)* is designed to accomplish several purposes:

(a) Identify students who perform significantly more poorly than their peers in writing and who as a result need special help;
(b) Determine a student's particular strengths and weaknesses in various writing abilities;
(c) Document a student's progress in a special writing program; and
(d) Conduct research in writing. (Hammill & Larsen, 1996, p. 6)

Test of Written Language-3 (TOWL-3)

D. D. Hammill & S. C. Larsen (1996)

Type: Norm-referenced test

Major Content Areas: Conventional, linguistic, and conceptual components of written language

Type of Administration: Individual or group

Administration Time: 1-1/2 hours

Age/Grade Levels: Ages 7-0 to 17-11

Types of Scores: Subtest standard scores, percentile ranks, and age and grade equivalents; composite standard scores called quotients for Contrived Writing, Spontaneous Writing, and Overall Writing

Computer Aids: *PRO-SCORE System*

Typical Uses: Identification of strengths and weaknesses in several of the written language skills involved in composition

Cautions: Both reading and writing are required; students cannot be given reading assistance. The tester must be thoroughly familiar with the scoring standards for evaluating both the writing sample and subtest responses. More information is needed about the relationship of the *TOWL-3* to other academic achievement measures.

Publisher: PRO-ED (www.proedinc.com)

The third edition of this test offers two forms. Each form assesses three components of language: (a) the conventions or the rules for punctuation, capitalization, and spelling; (b) the linguistic component, which is concerned with written grammar and vocabulary; and (c) the conceptual component, which relates to the ability to produce written products that are logical, coherent, and sequenced. Writing is elicited through both contrived and spontaneous formats. Spontaneous writing is assessed by means of a writing sample that the student produces. The student is shown a picture (see Figure 13–5 for the stimulus picture from Form A) and directed to write an original story about it. Contrived formats are artificial ways of eliciting written language responses, and they typically focus on one discrete element of language such as written grammar or spelling. Contrived methods include such devices as dictation spelling tests, proofreading tasks, and multiple-choice items.

There are eight subtests on the *TOWL-3*. The student begins the test with the spontaneous writing task: writing a story in 15 minutes. The five contrived format subtests are then administered. After the test is completed, the tester scores the student's story to obtain results for the three spontaneous writing subtests.

Contrived Format Subtests

- *Vocabulary.* A list of words appears in the Student Response Booklet. The student reads each word, then writes a meaningful sentence that includes the word.
- *Spelling.* The tester dictates sentences, and the student writes them with attention to spelling (and to capitalization and punctuation). In scoring this subtest, only spelling errors are noted.

FIGURE 13–5

Stimulus Picture from the *Test of Written Language-3, Form A*

Note: From *Test of Written Language-3, Form A, Student Response Booklet* by D. D. Hammill and S. C. Larsen, 1996, Austin, TX: PRO-ED. Copyright 1996 by PRO-ED. Reprinted by permission.

- *Style.* The sentences written on the Spelling subtest are evaluated for capitalization and punctuation errors.
- *Logical Sentences.* The student reads sentences that contain errors in logic (e.g., "Sally is as sweet as salt") and must rewrite each sentence so that it makes sense.
- *Sentence Combining.* The student reads two sentences and must write one new sentence that combines the original sentences. For example, the sentences "Tom is big" and "Tom is a man" could be combined into "Tom is a big man."

Spontaneous Format Subtests

- *Contextual Conventions.* The student's writing sample is evaluated and points are assigned for demonstration of specific capitalization and punctuation rules and for correct spelling. For example, one point is earned if all sentences begin with capital letters.
- *Contextual Language.* The writing sample is evaluated in relation to sentence structure, grammar, and vocabulary. For example, students earn one point if the sample contains no sentence fragments.
- *Story Construction.* The content of the student's writing sample is evaluated in terms of its plot, sequence, characters, theme, and so on. For example, two points are earned if the story has an interesting beginning and one point if its beginning is "weak, ordinary."

The *TOWL-3* requires that students have both reading and writing skills. On several subtests, the student must read the words or sentences that prompt the writing task. If group administration procedures are used, students must listen and attend to test instructions as the tester reads them, then work independently. All tasks are untimed, except the 15-minute writing sample.

The *TOWL-3* was standardized in 1995 with 2,217 students from 23 states. The final sample approximates the national population in gender, urban-rural residence, race, geographic region, ethnicity, family income, and educational attainment of parents. Students with disabilities were included if they attended general education classes. Eleven percent of the sample was students with disabilities, with those with learning disabilities being the most common.

The reliability of *TOWL-3* global scores is well established. Internal consistency, alternate form, test-retest, and interscorer reliability coefficients all exceed .80 for the three composite scores. Subtest reliabilities are somewhat lower, as would be expected, although all are satisfactory. The lowest coefficients are found on the Contextual Conventions subtest: internal consistency, .70; alternate form, .71; and test-retest, .75.

The concurrent validity of the *TOWL-3* was studied by examining its relationship to a teacher rating scale called the *Comprehensive Scales of Student Abilities* (*CSSA*) (Hammill & Hresko, 1994). Moderate correlations were found between *TOWL-3* results and results of the Writing, Reading, Math, and General Facts Scales of the *CSSA*. In a study of students with disabilities, both those with learning disabilities ($n = 133$) and those with speech impairments ($n = 85$) showed poor writing performance on the *TOWL-3* in comparison with the norm group. Although these studies provide support for the validity of the *TOWL-3,* more information is needed about the relationship of this measure to other individual tests of academic achievement, particularly those that assess writing skills.

According to the manual, formal training in assessment is needed to administer and interpret results of the *TOWL-3*. In addition, testers should be "proficient in and knowledgeable about the rules that govern English language usage" (p. 9). Administration rules are straightforward. All students begin with the writing sample. Contrived subtests are then administered, and all students begin with item one. There is no basal, and testing continues until a ceiling of three consecutive errors is reached. The manual also provides guidelines for group administration of *TOWL-3* subtests.

All of the student's answers are written in the Student Response Booklet. During administration, the tester must observe what the student is writing in order to determine ceilings on the contrived subtests. The manual explains the rules for scoring and lists acceptable answers; the tester should study the scoring standards carefully. Each item is either correct (marked as "1") or incorrect ("0").

After testing, the writing sample is scored; the manual estimates that this will take around 15 minutes. Scoring standards have been simplified from those used in the second edition of the *TOWL*. However, it remains important for examiners to study the scoring standards for each subtest carefully. Items on the spontaneous subtests vary in value. Some are worth either zero or one point. Others range in point value from zero to two or three. The manual provides example writing samples that novice testers can use for scoring practice.

TOWL-3 results include four types of scores for each subtest: percentile ranks, standard scores (mean = 10, standard deviation = 3), age equivalents, and grade equivalents. Three composite scores are also available: the Contrived Writing Quotient, the Spontaneous Writing Quotient, and the Overall Writing Quotient. Quotients are standard scores with a mean of 100 and a standard deviation of 15. Standard errors of measurement are 2 standard score points for the Contextual Conventions subtest, 1 standard score point for all other subtests, 3 for the Contrived and Overall Writing Quotients, and 5 for the Spontaneous Writing Quotient.

Results can be plotted on a profile form; Figure 13–6 shows the profile for a 14-year-old student described in the *TOWL-3* manual. This student's overall test performance is within the low average range (standard score 70). However, he shows strengths in Contextual Conventions, Contextual Language, and Story Construction, all of which fall within the average range of performance.

The *TOWL-3* is a useful test because it includes methods for evaluation of several important components of written language. To do this, the *TOWL-3* departs from the typical format of standardized tests. While remaining within a norm-referenced framework, it incorporates one of the most valuable informal strategies for studying composition—the writing sample. Results are best used to identify strengths and weaknesses and to provide direction for further assessment.

Other Formal Measures

The *Test of Written Language-3* is only one of the formal measures that address comprehension skills. The *Picture Story Language Test* (Myklebust, 1965) is one of the earliest measures, and is rarely used today. More recent measures include broad-based tests that assess a range of oral and written language skills and tests that focus only on written language. Broad-based tests include the *Test of Adolescent and Adult Language-3* (Hammill, Brown, Larsen, & Wiederholt, 1994), the *Oral and Written Language Scales* (Carrow-Woolfolk, 1996), and the *Woodcock Language Proficiency Battery-Revised* (Woodcock, 1991). Examples of measures that assess only writing skills are the *Mather-Woodcock Group Writing Tests* (Mather & Woodcock, 1997) and the *Test of Written Expression* (McGhee, Bryant, Larsen, & Rivera, 1995).

Test of Adolescent and Adult Language-3. The *TOAL-3* is a norm-referenced measure developed for use with students ages 12-0 to 24-11. It assesses a wide range of language skills: listening, speaking, reading, and writing. The test is designed so professionals can view the student's current language skills in several different ways. For example, spoken language performance can be compared to written language performance, receptive language can be contrasted with expressive language, and vocabulary skills can be compared to grammar skills.

The *TOAL-3* contains two subtests that assess written language:

- *Writing/Vocabulary.* The student is given a word and asked to write a meaningful sentence that includes the word.
- *Writing/Grammar.* Two sentences are presented. The student must write a new sentence that combines the meaning of the original sentences.

These test tasks are the same as those used for two of the *TOWL-3's* contrived writing subtests—Vocabulary and Sentence Combining.

Subtest results are expressed as percentile ranks and standard scores. The student's performance on Writing/Vocabulary and Writing/Grammar is summarized by the Writing Quotient, a standard score with a mean of 100 and a standard deviation of 15. The *TOAL-3* manual provides guidelines for determining whether composite scores are significantly different. For example, there must be at least a 10-point discrepancy between the *TOAL-3*

TOWL-3

Test of Written Language
Third Edition

Form A ☑   Form B ☐

PROFILE/STORY SCORING FORM

Section I. Identifying Information			
Name _Floyd_	Male ✔	Female ___	
	Year	Month	Day
Date Tested	95	9	25
Date of Birth	81	3	4
Age	14	6	21
School _Harris_		Grade _8th_	
Examiner's Name _M. Cronin_			
Examiner's Title _Educ. Diagnostician_			

Section II. Record of Subtest Scores

Subtest	Raw Score	%ile	Std. Score
1. Vocabulary (VO)	8	5	5
2. Spelling (SP)	3	2	4
3. Style (ST)	4	2	4
4. Logical Sentences (LS)	7	2	4
5. Sentence Combining (SC)	5	9	6
6. Contextual Conventions (CC)	6	25	8
7. Contextual Language (CL)	11	16	7
8. Story Construction (StC)	7	25	8

Section III. Record of Other Test Scores

Name	Date	Std. Score	TOWL-3 Equiv.
1. SIT-2	8-95	86	86
2. TONI-2	6-95	94	94
3. Reading CTBS	6-95	3	85
4. Language CTBS	6-95	2	77
5. Math CTBS	6-95	4	92
6.			
7.			
8.			

Section IV. Computation of Composite Scores

TOWL-3 Composites	Standard Scores								Sum of Std. Scores	Quotients
	VO	SP	ST	LS	SC	CC	CL	StC		
Contrived Writing	5	4	4	4	6				= 23	(63)
Spontaneous Writing						8	7	8	= 23	(85)
Overall Writing	5	4	4	4	6	8	7	8	= 46	(70)

FIGURE 13-6

Sample Results of the *Test of Written Language-3*

Note: From *Test of Written Language-3* (p. 32) by D. D. Hammill and S. C. Larsen, 1996, Austin, TX: PRO-ED. Copyright 1996 by PRO-ED. Reprinted by permission.

Writing and Reading Quotients to consider these results different at the .05 confidence level.

The *TOAL-3* is one of the few tests of language designed specifically for older students. It is a survey of several important language skills, and its format encourages the comparison of performance across different dimensions of lan-guage. However, students write only sentences, not passages of connected text. Results of the *TOAL-3* are most useful for identification of broad areas of educational need. As with most norm-referenced measures, further assessment is necessary before instructional planning can begin.

Oral and Written Language Scales. This measure is composed of three scales: two that assess oral language (Listening Comprehension and Oral Expression) and one that assesses written language (Written Expression). The Written Expression Scale is designed for students ages 5 through 21. Items related to three skill areas are included: Conventions (e.g., letter formation, spelling, punctuation and capitalization), Linguistics (e.g., verb forms, sentences), and Content (e.g., coherence, supporting ideas). On all items, the tester reads directions and the student answers by writing in the Response Booklet. Items for young students require writing first and last names, writing letters, and copying words and sentences; questions for older students require the composition of sentences and short paragraphs. This measure can be administered individually or to small groups of students.

Although this scale assesses several different written language skills, only total scale scores are available. The Written Expression Scale raw score can be converted to an age- or grade-based standard score (distributed with a mean of 100 and standard deviation of 15), percentile rank, age equivalent, and grade equivalent. Results on the Written Expression Scale can be compared with those on the two oral language scales and with an overall score called the Language Composite. Like other broad-based measures, the Written Expression Scale helps to identify areas of need. However, the information it provides is not specific enough for planning the instructional program.

Woodcock Language Proficiency Battery-Revised. This measure is a shortened version of the *Woodcock-Johnson Psycho-Educational Battery-Revised* (Woodcock & Johnson, 1989). The *Language Proficiency Battery* is composed of 13 subtests that assess oral language, reading, and written language. Four written language subtests are included: Dictation, Proofing, Writing Samples, and Writing Fluency.

The Dictation and Proofing subtests evaluate the student's knowledge of the rules of punctuation, capitalization, spelling, and usage. On the Dictation subtest, the student writes the letter, word, or punctuation mark the tester dictates. On the Proofing subtest, the student reads a passage with an error and must identify and tell how to correct the error. These measures provide some information about the student's skill in dealing with the more mechanical aspects of written language. If the student's test performance indicates possible special needs in these areas, assessment should continue with criterion-referenced tests or other informal procedures.

The Writing Samples and Writing Fluency subtests move beyond the conventions of written language to assess content. However, on both of these subtests, students only write sentences; they are not required to produce a lengthy writing sample. On the Writing Samples subtest, the student responds to a prompt (e.g., write a sentence to describe a picture or complete a paragraph). On the timed Writing Fluency subtest, students write a sentence that describes a picture and incorporates three stimulus words. Other assessment procedures should be used if information is needed about the student's ability to plan, write, and revise longer texts such as compositions, essays, and stories.

Mather-Woodcock Group Writing Tests. Like the *Woodcock Language Proficiency Battery-Revised,* the *Group Writing Tests (GWT)* are an adaptation of the *Woodcock-Johnson Psycho-Educational Battery-Revised.* According to the *GWT* manual, "although the *Group Writing Tests* are similar in format to the tests in the *WJ-R,* all items for the *GWT* are new" (p. 1). Unlike the *Woodcock-Johnson-R,* the *GWT* is designed for group administration. Three levels are available: Basic (grades 2 to 3), Intermediate (grades 4 to 7), and Advanced (grades 8 to 16 and adults). Each level contains four subtests: Dictation Spelling, Editing, Writing Samples, and Writing Fluency. The Editing subtest is equivalent to the Proofing subtest in the *Language Proficiency Battery;* Dictation Spelling is similar to Dictation, except that only spelling skills are assessed. The other two subtests, Writing Samples and Writing Fluency, are identical in format to their counterparts on the *Language Proficiency Battery.* The *GWT* also includes a rating scale, the Writing Evaluation Scale, which can be used to evaluate samples of the student's writing such as classroom assignments, stories, or essays.

When the *GWT* is handscored, it is possible only to determine age and grade equivalents for each of the subtests. To obtain other subtest scores and composite scores, it is necessary to purchase the computer program from the publisher—the *Scoring and Reporting Program for the Group Writing Tests.* That program produces standard scores, percentile ranks, and grade or age equivalents for each of the four subtests and three composite scores. The composites are Basic Writing Skills (composed of the spelling and editing subtests), Expressive Writing Ability (composed of the writing fluency and writing samples subtests), and Total Writing.

Test of Written Expression. The *TOWE* is a two-part test for ages 6-6 to 14-11. The two parts are considered contrived and spontaneous evaluations of writing. According to the manual, the part called Items is a contrived evaluation with short-answer questions that assess "a broad array of writing skills (i.e., ideation, vocabulary, grammar, capitalization, punctuation, and spelling)" (p. 5). The second part, Essay, is a spontaneous evaluation similar to the writing sample portion of the *TOWL-3.* However, on the *TOWE,* the student writes a story after the tester reads a story starter; there is no visual stimulus.

TOWE results include standard scores, percentile ranks, and grade equivalents for the two parts, Items and Essay. A total test score is not available. The *TOWE* Record Form contains an optional error analysis grid if the tester is interested in looking for patterns of errors among the different types of skills assessed by the Items portion of the test. Like most norm-referenced measures of writing skills, the *TOWE* helps to identify areas of need. Further assessment with informal techniques is necessary for planning the instructional program.

Informal Techniques

Writing skills are often evaluated with informal techniques rather than formal, norm-referenced tests. Results of informal measures and techniques are used to describe current skill levels, particularly in areas for which no test results are available. They are invaluable for providing direction for instructional planning.

Rating Scales and Checklists. There are several ways to analyze students' writing samples, and one common approach is the use of a rating scale or checklist. For example, Figure 13–7 contains an expressive writing rating scale prepared by Affleck, Lowenbraun, and Archer (1980). The teacher selects one or, preferably, several samples of the student's writing and then analyzes content, vocabulary, sentences, paragraphs, mechanics, handwriting, and spelling. To direct the teacher's examination of these skill areas, the scale provides specific questions such as, "Do the sentences in the paragraph relate to one topic?"

Poteet's (1980) *Checklist of Written Expression* covers four major concerns in writing: penmanship, spelling, grammar, and ideation. Composition skills are included in the section on ideation, which appears in Figure 13–8. When using the checklist, the teacher considers several aspects of the student's writing sample: type of writing, level of abstraction (or substance), productivity, comprehensibility, and relationship to the reality of the writing task. The last section in the checklist, Style, is divided into three subsections: sentence sense, tone, and word choice.

Checklists and rating scales typically assess skill development by breaking the broad skill of composition down into more specific subskill areas. Holistic evaluation is another approach to the assessment of writing. This method, as its name implies, considers the writing sample as a whole, not in relation to individual elements (Moran, 1988). Errors or particular features of the writing are not counted. Instead, holistic scoring emphasizes the content of writing. Bailet (1991) says that "its purpose is to avoid analyzing a composition in terms of mechanistic features and to examine instead the composition's overall effectiveness in conveying ideas" (p. 167). According to Graham (1982), "The examiner reads the student's essay to obtain a general impression of its quality. . . . With this approach, the paper is to be read rapidly, and a score assigned on the basis of the examiner's instantaneous judgment" (p. 11). Dagenais and Beadle (1984) suggest that training is needed before professionals can conduct holistic evaluations.

Writing Sample Analysis. In addition to checklists and rating scales, work sample analysis techniques can be used to study students' writing

Child_____ Type of writing analyzed_____

Rating scale:
	1 poor	2 adequate	3 excellent

CONTENT

1 2 3   A. Does the writing clearly communicate an idea or ideas to the reader?
1 2 3   B. Is the content adequately developed?
1 2 3   C. Is the content interesting to the potential reader?

VOCABULARY

1 2 3   A. Does the writer select appropriate words to communicate his/her ideas?
1 2 3   B. Does the writer use precise/vivid vocabulary?
1 2 3   C. Does the writer effectively use verbs, nouns, adjectives and adverbs?
1 2 3   D. Does the vocabulary meet acceptable standards for written English (e.g., "isn't" vs. "ain't")?

SENTENCES

1 2 3   A. Are the sentences complete (subject and predicate)?
1 2 3   B. Are run-on sentences avoided?
1 2 3   C. Are exceptionally complex sentences avoided?
1 2 3   D. Are the sentences grammatically correct (e.g., word order, subject-verb agreement)?

PARAGRAPHS

1 2 3   A. Do the sentences in the paragraph relate to one topic?
1 2 3   B. Are the sentences organized to reflect the relationships between ideas within the paragraph?
1 2 3   C. Does the paragraph include a topical, introductory or transition sentence?

MECHANICS

1 2 3   A. Are the paragraphs indented?
1 2 3   B. Are correct margins used?
1 2 3   C. Are capitals used at the beginning of sentences?
1 2 3   D. Are additional capitals used as necessary in the written sample?
1 2 3   E. Is correct end of sentence punctuation used?
1 2 3   F. Is additional punctuation used as necessary in the written sample?

HANDWRITING

1 2 3   A. Is the handwriting legible?
1 2 3   B. Is the handwriting neat?

SPELLING

1 2 3   A. Does the writer correctly spell high frequency, irregular words?
1 2 3   B. Does the writer correctly spell phonetic words?

Note. Using these guidelines, the teacher can carefully examine a child's written work and pinpoint instructional needs. For example, it might be determined that the child needs instruction on writing complete sentences, using correct punctuation or proofing for spelling errors. Evaluation of more than one sample would increase the accuracy of these conclusions.

FIGURE 13-7

Expressive Writing Rating Scale

Note: From *Teaching the Mildly Handicapped in the Regular Classroom* (2nd ed.) (pp. 72–73) by J. Q. Affleck, S. Lowenbraun, and A. Archer, 1980, New York: Merrill/Macmillan. Copyright 1980 by Macmillan Publishing Company. Reprinted by permission.

IV. IDEATION
   A. Type of Writing
      1. Story _____ 2. Poem _____ 3. Letter _____ 4. Report _____ 5. Review _____
   B. Substance
      1. Naming _____ 2. Description _____ 3. Plot _____ 4. Issue _____
   C. Productivity
      1. Number of words written _____ 2. Acceptable number _____ 3. Too few _____
   D. Comprehensibility
      Easy to understand _____ Difficult to understand _____ Cannot understand _____
                                         _____ perseveration of words _____ illogical
                                         _____ perseveration of ideas _____ disorganized
   E. Reality
      _____ Accurate perception of stimulus or task
      _____ Inaccurate perception of stimulus or task
   F. Style
      1. Sentence Sense
         a. Completeness   Tallies:
            (1) complete sentences _____
            (2) run-on sentences _____
            (3) sentence fragments _____
         b. Structure
            (1) simple _____
            (2) compound _____
            (3) complex _____
            (4) compound/complex _____
         c. Types
            (1) declarative _____
            (2) interrogative _____
            (3) imperative _____
            (4) exclamatory _____
      2. Tone
         a. intimate _____ b. friendly _____ c. impersonal _____
      3. Word Choice (N = none, F = few, S = some, M = many)
         a. Formality
               formal _____ informal _____ colloquial _____
         b. Complexity
               simple _____ multisyllable _____ contractions _____
         c. Descriptiveness
               vague _____ vivid _____ figures·of speech _____
         d. Appropriateness
               inexact words _____ superfluous/repetitions _____ omissions _____

FIGURE 13–8

Checklist of Composition Skills

Note: From "Informal Assessment of Written Expression" by J. A. Poteet, 1980, *Learning Disability Quarterly, 3*(4), p. 92. Copyright 1980 by Council for Learning Disabilities. Reprinted by permission.

samples. Error analysis is most valuable for identifying possible areas of need in the mechanics of writing: spelling, handwriting, punctuation, capitalization, and so on. Response analysis, which takes into account both errors and correct responses, is the more useful technique for the evaluation of composition skills.

The *Diagnostic Evaluation of Writing Skills* (*DEWS*) (Weiner, 1980), is an error analysis pro-cedure that focuses attention on six aspects of written language:

- Graphic (visual features)
- Orthographic (spelling)
- Phonologic (sound components)
- Syntactic (grammatical)
- Semantic (meaning)
- Self-Monitoring Skills

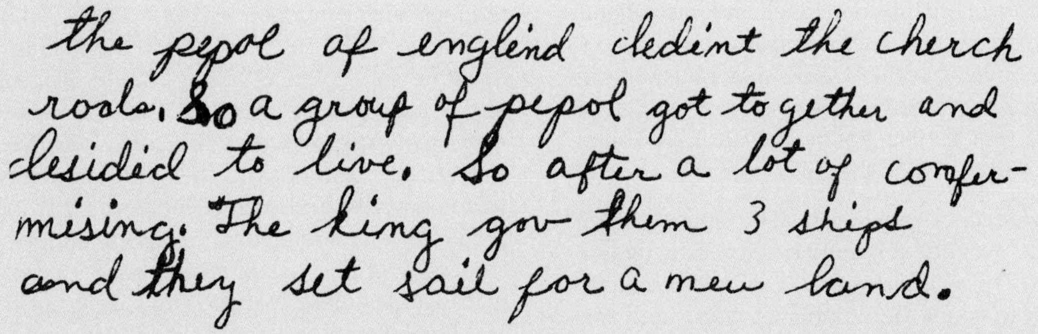

> *the pepol of englind dedint the cherch rools. So a group of pepol got to gether and desided to live. So after a lot of confermising. The king gov them 3 ships and they set sail for a mew land.*

TRANSCRIPTION OF THE ENTIRE ESSAY
the pepol of englind didint the cherch rools. So a group of pepol got to gether and desidid to live. So after a lot of comfermising. The king gov them 3 ships and they set sail for a mew land. they sailed a long ways for a to long tine. then they saw it land it was North amareca. they landid on plymouth rock. ther they started to beld the ferst coliny. the firs winter wase the hardes a lot of pepol dide from being sick. After the winter was over the ingin's becom frinds with them and to them how to hunt and grow food.

ENTIRE ESSAY AS READ BY THE STUDENT
The people of England didn't like the church rules. So a group of people got together and decided to leave. So after a lot of compromising the King gave them three ships and they set sail for a new land. They sailed a long ways for a long time. Then they saw it. Land! It was North America. They landed on Plymouth Rock. Then they started to build the first colony. The first winter was the hardest and a lot of people died from being sick. After the winter was over the Indians became friendly with them and taught them how to hunt and grow food.

FIGURE 13–9
Student Writing Sample

In the use of this procedure, students are asked to write an autobiography; approximately 30 minutes are allowed for writing and 15 minutes for revision. The writing sample is then studied to identify errors that may indicate a need for instruction. In the meaningful language category, the professional looks for errors in flexible vocabulary, coherence, logical sequencing, transitions, distinction between major and minor points, inferential thinking, and idiomatic and figurative language.

Content, organization, and vocabulary are among the critical factors that should be taken into account in the evaluation of composition skills (Wallace, Larsen, & Elksnin, 1992). As an ex-

ample, consider the writing sample that appears in Figure 13–9. This essay was written by a 17-year-old student in grade 11 in response to an assignment in history class to describe the pilgrims' journey to the New World. The first few sentences of the essay are presented in the student's own handwriting, followed by a verbatim transcription of the entire essay. Last is a record of the essay as read aloud by the student; note that, in reading the essay, the student filled in missing words and corrected many punctuation errors. An error analysis of this writing sample would document the extent of the student's difficulties with handwriting, spelling, capitalization, punctuation, and usage. However, a response analysis would reveal that the essay is meaningful, its content is expressed in an organized manner, and the student's word choice is accurate, if immature.

A number of other factors may be taken into account when analyzing students' writing (Polloway & Smith, 1982; Polloway, Patton, & Cohen, 1983). These include the following:

- *Productivity,* sometimes called fluency, refers to the quantity of writing produced by the student. The simplest way to evaluate productivity is to count the number of words and sentences in the writing sample and then determine the number of words per sentence. In general, longer sentences indicate a more mature writing style.
- *Sentences* can be analyzed according to their structure (simple, compound, complex, run-on, or fragment) and their type (declarative, interrogative, imperative, and exclamatory) (Polloway & Smith, 1982). Complete sentences are preferred to run-on sentences or sentence fragments, and compound and complex sentences are considered more advanced forms of expression than are simple sentences. In relation to sentence type, diversity is desirable when appropriate to content.
- *Vocabulary,* or the words selected by the student for inclusion in the writing sample, is another important consideration. The type-token ratio is a measure of the diversity of the vocabulary used by the writer. This ratio is determined by dividing the number of unique words in the writing sample by the total number of words in the sample. Polloway and Smith (1982) say that "a ratio of 1.0 would therefore indicate no redundancy while a ratio of .5 would suggest frequent repetition" (p. 344). In general, diversity of vocabulary is viewed as an indicator of mature writing.

Criterion-referenced Tests. Criterion-referenced tests are a flexible type of assessment tool that can be used to measure a variety of different composition skills. For example, the teacher could develop CRTs to assess a student's ability to write complete sentences, an organized paragraph containing both a topic sentence and several supporting sentences, or a brief story describing interactions between characters.

Published criterion-referenced tests such as the measures by Brigance (1981, 1999) also offer assistance in the study of composition skills. For example, a Sentence-Writing Grade Placement test is provided by the *BRIGANCE®* *Diagnostic Comprehensive Inventory of Basic Skills-Revised* (1999). This test assesses the student's ability to write complete and correct sentences that incorporate several stimulus words. For example, the student might be asked to compose a sentence that includes these words: *circus, escaped, after,* and *elephant.*

Criterion-referenced tests of practical writing skills appear on some of the Brigance measures. For example, the *BRIGANCE®* *Diagnostic Inventory of Essential Skills* (1981) provides measures of daily life writing skills. Included are tests that assess skill in completing several common types of applications—employment, Social Security number, credit card, and driver's permit—as well as common forms such as income tax returns and forms for unemployment compensation.

Another criterion-referenced measure, the *Hudson Education Skills Inventory* (Hudson et al., 1989), contains an array of composition measures that may be useful in classroom planning. Among the skills assessed are capitalization, punctuation, grammar, vocabulary, sentences, and paragraphs.

Observation and Clinical Interviews. Even though writing is essentially a private act, aspects of the writing process can be studied by observation. With classroom writing tasks, for example, it is possible to observe some of the actions the student takes in the three major steps of writing: preparing to write, writing, and reviewing and revising what has been written.

When a writing task is assigned, some students appear to engage in a planning process, whereas others begin to write immediately. Such observable behaviors are open to the scrutiny of the professional. For instance, the teacher could observe how much time is spent in the prewriting and postwriting stages as well as in the actual act of writing.

Table 13–3 lists the three major stages of writing and the typical behaviors expected of skilled and unskilled writers at each stage. For example, in the planning stage, skilled writers may discuss the assigned topic, spend time thinking about what to write, and make notes or draw diagrams. The descriptions in this table could be converted into an observation checklist or a set of questions for a student interview.

However, it is important to recognize that the writing process is not always made up of separate and distinct stages. As Graham (1982) observes, people approach writing in different ways. One person might write down thoughts as fast as they occur and then revise them later. Another might write and rewrite the first sentence until it is satisfactory and then proceed to the second sentence. Still another might carefully outline the story or essay and then write and edit it. A writer can also combine these strategies or switch from one to another during the act of writing.

Clinical interviews provide a method for gathering information about the nonobservable aspects of writing and the ways that the student interacts with the writing task. Interviews can be conducted before the student begins to write or after writing is completed (or both). However, while the student is writing, the professional

should simply observe and not interrupt the student's thoughts with questions.

Among the dimensions of writing that can be explored in clinical interviews are the student's perceptions of the purposes for writing and the audience for which the writing is intended. Martin (1983) summarizes these dimensions with the questions, "What is the writing for?" and "Who is it for?" According to Martin, the function (or purpose) of expressive writing can be viewed as a continuum, with transactional writing at one end and poetic writing at the other:

> Transactional writing, often called "expository," is concerned with some direct result or transaction like giving information, presenting an argument or a literary judgment, or writing reports, essays, or notes. It is the language of science, commerce, and technology and it is taken for granted that the writer can be challenged for truthfulness. . . .
>
> Poetic writing on the other hand is without any such *direct* practical purpose, and includes stories, poems, and plays. It is taken for granted that true or false is not a relevant question at the literal level. . . . (p. 3)

TABLE 13-3
The Stages of Writing for Skilled and Unskilled Writers

STAGE	UNSKILLED WRITER	SKILLED WRITER
Planning	Does not participate in prewriting discussions.	Explores and discusses topic.
	Spends little time thinking about topic before beginning composition.	Spends time considering what will be written and how it will be expressed.
	Makes no plans or notes.	Jots notes; draws diagrams or pictures.
Transcribing	Writes informally in imitation of speech.	Writes in style learned from models of composition.
	Is preoccupied with technical matters of spelling and punctuation.	Keeps audience in mind while writing.
	Stops only briefly and infrequently.	Stops frequently to reread. Takes long thought pauses.
Revising	Does not review or rewrite.	Reviews frequently.
	Looks only for surface errors (spelling, punctuation).	Makes content revisions, as well as spelling and punctuation corrections.
	Rewrites only to make a neat copy in ink.	Keeps audience in mind while rewriting.

Note: From "Effective Instruction in Written Language" (p. 291) by S. L. Isaacson, 1988, in *Effective Instructional Strategies for Exceptional Children* by E. L. Meyen, G. A. Vergason, and R. J. Whelan (Eds.), Denver: Love. Copyright 1988 by Love Publishing Company. Reprinted by permission.

Phelps-Gunn and Phelps-Terasaki (1982) suggest that these purposes are related to the different modes of discourse—narration, description, exposition, and argument—that writers select to communicate their ideas to readers.

In school writing tasks, there are several different audiences: peers; the teacher, viewed as a trusted adult; the teacher, in the role of critic and dispenser of grades; the student himself or herself (as in writing a journal, class notes, and memoranda); or the general public (Martin, 1983). How students perceive the audience and the function of writing can influence how they approach the writing task. To find out about these and other dimensions of writing, the professional can ask these questions before the student begins to write:

- You're going to be writing something in a few minutes. Tell me about the assignment. What are you expected to do?
- Who will you be writing to? With whom will you try to communicate? Your teacher? A friend? Yourself? If you'll be writing to your teacher, do you expect the teacher to give you a grade—or to read what you have written and then help you make it better?
- What purpose will you try to accomplish in writing? Will you try to tell an exciting story? Give the reader information? Present an argument?
- What will you do before you begin writing? Will you think about what you're going to write? Make notes? Prepare an outline?

The interview can be continued after the student has completed the writing task:

- You've finished your essay (or paragraph, story, book report, etc.). Tell me about what you've written.
- When you finished, did you read over what you had written? Did you make any changes? What did you change?
- While you were writing, what did you think about? Did you consider . . .
  The ideas you were writing about?
  What should come first, second, and so on?
  Choosing the exact words to express your meaning?

Spelling the words correctly, using correct punctuation, and following all the other rules for correct English?
- Do you think that you've accomplished your purpose in writing? Why or why not? If not, what do you need to change?
- You said that you would be writing to your teacher (or friend, self, etc.). Is your writing appropriate for that person? For example, is the vocabulary suitable? The tone? If not, what do you need to change?

Portfolio Assessment. Writing samples are the most common type of student work found in language arts portfolios. The "best pieces" that students select for their portfolios often represent a range of literary accomplishments: stories, poems, essays, reports, journals, plays, autobiographies, newspaper articles, movie and book reviews, student-authored books, and so on. In some cases, all drafts of a composition are included to document the process by which the final product was created. Self-evaluations and peer evaluations may also accompany some of the writing samples.

Teachers can contribute their evaluations of student work as well as results of formal and informal assessments. For example, with the *Language Arts Assessment Portfolio* (Karlsen, 1992), teachers rate the student's process of writing as well as the final product. Among the process concerns are the student's ability to engage in each of the stages of writing, his or her awareness of audience, and his or her independent editing skills. The teacher can also complete a spelling error analysis and rating scales on the mechanics of punctuation and capitalization. Students use the *LAAP* Self-Evaluation Booklets to describe what they have written and to rate themselves on writing process and product.

WITHIN THE CONTEXT OF THE CLASSROOM

Students and their written products have been the focus of discussion up to this point in the chapter. Now the emphasis shifts to study of the classroom learning environment and its influence on students' spelling, handwriting, and composition skills.

The Instructional Environment

Assessment of the influence of the instructional environment on students' written language must take into account the classroom curriculum and the instructional methods and materials used to implement that curriculum. However, investigating the written language program may be a bit more difficult than studying classroom practices in reading and mathematics. In the elementary grades, written language can be divided into several subjects, each of which is taught directly but separately from the others: spelling, handwriting, and English (or language). There may be separate textbooks for each of these subjects, with composition subsumed under the subject of language or English. In contrast, teachers who use the whole language approach may integrate writing into several areas of the curriculum, rather than teach it as one or more separate subjects. In the secondary grades, writing skills become part of the English curriculum, although students are expected to communicate in writing in all classes.

The amount of time devoted to instruction and the types of skills emphasized are two fundamental concerns in the evaluation of any instructional environment. These concerns are particularly important in written language instruction. Teachers who were studied in the 1980s did not allocate a great deal of instructional time to teaching writing skills (e.g., Alexander, 1983; Freedman, 1982; Leinhardt, Zigmond, & Cooley, 1981) and, when classroom time was spent on written language, the more mechanical aspects of writing such as spelling and handwriting were emphasized rather than composition. These problems should be less of a concern today because of the curricular changes brought about by whole language, integrated language arts, and the process approach to teaching writing. However, not all classrooms have implemented these changes. Thus, one of the first steps in assessing the learning environment should be a study of the classroom schedule and how that schedule is implemented.

The following questions provide a framework for evaluating the classroom program for teaching written language skills:

1. Are spelling skills included within the written language curriculum? If so, what does the curriculum stress—regular words, irregular words, spelling rules, or a combination?
2. Are handwriting skills included? If so, is manuscript or cursive writing taught? Does the curriculum emphasize accuracy in letter formation? Speed? Legibility?
3. Are composition skills included? Are they taught as part of the language arts or English program? Or is there a separate program for teaching composition? If so, what are its major components?
4. Where do skills such as capitalization and punctuation fit? Are they taught in conjunction with composition or as a separate skill area?
5. What textbook series are used in the classroom to teach written language skills? Is there a text for spelling? Handwriting? Language? English?
6. Are multiple levels of each of the written language textbooks in use in the classroom?
7. What instructional materials supplement the textbooks in the basal series? Are there word processing programs for the computer?
8. What types of writing skills are stressed in classroom instruction? Writing mechanics? Composition and the use of writing as a means of communication?
9. Is any attempt made to integrate the teaching of composition with instruction in spelling, handwriting, and usage? If so, how is this accomplished?
10. Is the written language curriculum organized so the sequence of instruction is logical?
11. Is instruction based on ongoing assessment?
12. How are students grouped for instruction? How much individualization takes place in each group?
13. What instructional techniques does the teacher use to present new skills and information? Lecture? Demonstration? Discussion? Exploration and discovery? Cooperative learning?

14. In what types of learning activities do students participate? In spelling and handwriting, do they complete workbook pages or worksheets? Do they copy each spelling word several times as a strategy for learning? In handwriting, do students practice writing letters, words, and symbols by copying from a model? What types of composition activities are available? Do students keep a journal? Write paragraphs? Stories? Letters? Poems? Book reports? Is expository or creative writing emphasized?

15. How is supervised practice incorporated into the written language program? On the average, how many minutes per day do students spend practicing their spelling skills? Handwriting skills? Composition skills?

16. What changes, if any, have been made in the standard program to accommodate the needs of special students such as the one under assessment?

Graham (1982) and Graham and Miller (1979, 1980) have summarized the research on effective methods for the teaching of spelling, handwriting, and composition in order to offer specific recommendations for classroom practice. These recommendations could serve as a set of standards for the evaluation of classroom practices.

According to Graham and Miller (1979), "The single most important factor in learning to spell is the student correcting his or her own spelling test under the teacher's direction" (p. 10). Some of the other research-based practices these authors advocate are:

• The presentation of spelling words in lists or columns to focus the student's attention on each word;

• Use of the test-study-test method in which students study only the words that they are unable to spell (in preference to the study-test method in which all words are studied); and

• The allocation of 60 to 75 minutes per week for spelling instruction.

Graham and Miller also describe instructional procedures not supported by research. These in-

clude the assumption that "writing words several times ensures spelling retention" (p. 10).

Some of the recommendations that Graham and Miller (1980) offer for an effective program in handwriting instruction are:

• Handwriting instruction is direct and not incidental.

• Handwriting is taught in short daily learning periods during which desirable habits are established.

• Skills in handwriting are overlearned in isolation and then applied in meaningful context assignments.

• Teachers stress the importance of handwriting and do not accept, condone, or encourage slovenly work.

• Although students do develop personal idiosyncrasies, the teacher helps them maintain a consistent, legible handwriting style throughout the grades. (pp. 5–6)

In relation to the teaching of composition skills, Graham (1982) suggests:

1. Students should be exposed to a broad range of writing tasks.

2. Strategies for reducing the number of cognitive demands inherent in the act of writing should be an integral part of a remedial composition program.

3. Writing error should not be overemphasized.

4. The composition program should be both pleasant and encouraging.

5. The composition program should be planned, monitored, and evaluated on the basis of assessment information. (pp. 6–9)

It is also important to consider the performance demands imposed on students in writing tasks. These include expectations for quantity (i.e., the number of words, sentences, or paragraphs expected), the requirements for speed, and the expectations for accuracy. Performance demands become a concern whenever writing activities are a part of instruction: writing a composition in English class, copying mathematics problems from the board, writing answers to questions on a history test, writing entries in a science lab notebook, and so on.

Classroom standards should be considered in relation to the student under assessment. Standards may be unrealistically high for this student, and some adjustment can be made to better the student's chances for success. For example, the teacher may be willing to allow the student more time for composition activities or reduce the amount of writing required. If handwriting is an area of difficulty, the teacher may permit the student to type, tape record, or dictate assignments to a peer.

The Interpersonal Environment

The major factors within the interpersonal environment that are of concern in assessment are social relationships among students and student-teacher interactions. Often, students with achievement problems are not well accepted by their peers. This can occur when students experience difficulty with written language, particularly when their attempts to communicate in writing are open to view by their peers. In most classrooms, students have many opportunities to see and read what other students write. For instance, it is routine practice to ask students to write on the board and to collect their themes, stories, essays, and the like, placing them on public display on classroom bulletin boards.

In written language instruction, most teacher-student interactions center on the student's written product. The student writes in an attempt to communicate, and the teacher reads and then grades the communication. There are several methods of grading, and some are more likely than others to encourage students in their efforts to learn writing skills. Covering a student's paper with red ink by marking every error may only discourage the student from further attempts. For students with an achievement problem in some aspect of written expression, it is better to emphasize what they have done correctly by drawing attention to their correct responses rather than errors. Graham (1982) says, "Only the most frequent and flagrant errors that appear in a child's writing should be treated" (p. 9). It is also possible to assign more than one grade to a paper. For example, the teacher might give one grade for spelling, handwriting, and other form considerations and another for the content.

These questions are of interest when evaluating interactions between students and teachers in written language instruction:

- In private student-teacher interactions (e.g., when the teacher communicates with students by grading their papers), how does the teacher respond to an error? Does the teacher identify the response as an error? Correct it? Ignore the error?
- If the writing situation is a public one (e.g., students are writing on the board), what occurs when a student makes an error? Does the teacher use the same correction procedures in public and private interactions?
- How does the student react to the teacher's corrections? Is there a difference when the student is corrected in front of peers?
- What do other students do when a peer makes errors in writing?
- What happens when a student makes a correct writing response? Does the teacher confirm the response? Praise the student? Provide a tangible reward or token?
- Are students able to work independently on writing activities? Do certain students require frequent assistance from the teacher?

The Physical Environment

The physical environment of the classroom is an important consideration in written language instruction. General environmental factors such as lighting, temperature, and ventilation can affect the physical comfort of teachers and students, thereby influencing the teaching-learning process. In addition, the seating arrangements for students and the writing tools provided can have an impact on their ability to perform, particularly in relation to handwriting. In assessing the classroom's physical environment, some of the major questions to consider are:

1. Are appropriate chairs provided for students? Can each student sit comfortably with hips touching the back of the chair and both feet resting on the floor (Graham & Miller, 1980)?
2. Are student desks (or other types of writing surfaces such as tables) an appropriate height for writing?
3. What types of writing implements are available in the classroom? Is there a selection of different types?

4. Are writing implements selected to meet the needs of individual students? For example, some students find primary-sized pencils easier to grip.

5. What types of paper are available in the classroom? Is there a selection of different types? For example, for younger students and those with severe handwriting problems, is there a supply of primary paper with guidelines between each pair of widely spaced lines?

6. Is the lighting in the classroom adequate for writing?

7. What seating arrangements are used for instruction in written language?

8. How are students seated for independent work?

9. Is the classroom space organized so areas for noisier activities are separated from areas for quieter activities such as writing?

10. Are there any quiet areas within the classroom where students can escape from distractions?

11. Does the classroom offer a variety of learning materials, or are textbooks the only resource? For example, are there computers and printers available in the classroom?

ANSWERING THE ASSESSMENT QUESTIONS

The major purpose of assessing written language is to describe the student's current levels of educational performance in this important school skill. A number of different types of assessment tools are available for this purpose.

Nature of the Assessment Tools

The tools available for the study of written language vary in several ways. One important dimension is the range of skills they are designed to assess. Some measures are comprehensive and evaluate a number of the major skill areas of written language. Others are more limited in scope. For example, handwriting is the sole concern of the *Test of Legible Handwriting,* and the *Test of Written Spelling-4* concentrates on spelling.

Of the assessment tools listed in Table 13–1, six could be considered comprehensive measures. Of these, all are informal measures, except the *Test of Early Written Language-2.* If norm-referenced information is needed for decisions about the severity of students' skill deficits, relatively few formal tests are available. The most comprehensive are measures such as the *Test of Written Language-3* and *Mather-Woodcock Group Writing Tests,* although they do not assess handwriting performance.

Assessment tools can also vary in the depth with which skills are assessed. In general, informal measures are likely to provide the most thorough coverage of individual skills. For example, the *BRIGANCE® Diagnostic Comprehensive Inventory of Basic Skills-Revised* offers several tests of spelling, and each considers a specific skill in depth: spelling initial consonants, suffixes, prefixes, and so forth.

Another way that assessment tools may differ is the types of tasks used to evaluate skill development. For example, as Table 13–4 shows, there are three basic strategies for the study of spelling: dictation tests, analysis of students' writing samples, and error detection tasks. Error detection, the least frequently used assessment strategy, is essentially a proofreading task. It is important to remember that detecting spelling errors is not the same skill as recalling correct spellings from memory. If both skills are of interest, both should be assessed.

A variety of assessment tasks are used to evaluate handwriting skills. The major strategies are based on analysis of a sample of the student's handwriting, but they differ in the way the writing sample is obtained. On copying tests, students are provided with a model and are directed to copy that model in their best handwriting. In contrast, classroom writing samples tend to represent the student's typical handwriting. Samples elicited on a test likely fall somewhere in between students' best and typical handwriting. A comparison of the handwriting samples that the student produces under divergent conditions can provide useful assessment information.

Composition skills are assessed in many ways, and writing samples are one common assessment task. However, the samples vary considerably in

TABLE 13-4   Assessment Tasks Used to Evaluate Written Language Skills

WRITTEN LANGUAGE SKILL	ASSESSMENT TASK	PRESENTATION MODE	RESPONSE MODE	EXAMPLES OF MEASURES USING THIS TYPE OF TASK
Spelling	Dictation test	Listen to a word (or a word and a sentence containing the word) read by the tester.	Write the word.	*Test of Written Spelling-4, Kottmeyer's Diagnostic Spelling Test*
		Listen to a sentence read by the tester.	Write the sentence.	Spelling subtest of the *Test of Written Language-3*
	Analysis of a classroom writing sample	An existing sample of the student's writing is analyzed.	—	*Checklist of Written Expression, Diagnostic Evaluation of Writing Skills*
	Error detection	Read a sentence that contains an error.	Identify the error and correct it.	Proofing subtest of the *Woodcock Language Proficiency Battery-Revised*
Handwriting	Copying test	Look at a sentence or paragraph written in legible handwriting.	Copy the model.	*Zaner-Bloser Evaluation Scales, Denver Handwriting Analysis*
	Analysis of a classroom writing sample	An existing sample of the student's writing is analyzed.	—	*Checklist of Written Expression, Diagnostic Evaluation of Writing Skills, Test of Legible Handwriting*
	Elicitation of a writing sample	Look at a picture.	Write a story about the picture.	*Test of Legible Handwriting*
		Listen to a prompt.	Write an autobiography or a letter in response to the prompt.	*Test of Legible Handwriting*
Composition	Elicitation of a writing sample	Look at a picture.	Write a story about the picture.	*Test of Written Language-3, Picture Story Language Test*
		Listen to a prompt.	Write a letter in response to the prompt.	Written Expression subtest of *Wechsler Individual Achievement Test,* Essay portion of *Test of Written Expression*
	Sentence writing	Read a word.	Write a sentence containing the word.	Vocabulary subtest of *Test of Written Language-3,* Writing/Vocabulary subtest of *Test of Adolescent and Adult Language-3*
		Read a sentence with a logical error in it.	Rewrite the sentence and correct the error.	Logical Sentences subtest of *Test of Written Language-3*
		Read a prompt.	Write a sentence in response to the prompt.	Writing Samples subtest of the *Woodcock Language Proficiency Battery-Revised* and of the *Mather-Woodcock Group Writing Tests*
		Look at a picture; read three words.	Write a sentence that describes the picture including the three words.	Writing Fluency subtest of the *Woodcock Language Proficiency Battery-Revised* and of the *Mather-Woodcock Group Writing Tests*
	Sentence combining	Read two sentences.	Write a new sentence that combines the meanings of the original sentences.	Sentence Combining subtest of *Test of Written Language-3,* Writing/Grammar subtest of *Test of Adolescent and Adult Language-3*

453

length, ranging from one sentence to a complete composition. On tests, students are directed to write a story about a standard stimulus such as one picture or a series of pictures. This technique is somewhat different from the collection of classroom writing samples. Because the task is standard for all students, norms can be developed for evaluating various aspects of written language performance. On the *Test of Written Language-3,* for example, the content of the writing sample is evaluated, vocabulary and sentence structure are assessed, and adherence to capitalization and punctuation rules is noted.

The Relationship of Written Language to Other Areas of Performance

A student's general aptitude for learning can affect the ease and speed with which academic skills are acquired. Hence, the student's current status in written language should be evaluated in relation to estimated intellectual performance. In general, students with lower than average general intelligence are expected to progress at a somewhat slower rate than students of average intellectual ability. The Verbal IQ is likely the best measure for estimating a student's potential for learning spelling and composition skills. In contrast, the Performance IQ may provide a better estimate of handwriting ability because of the motor components of this skill.

Specific learning abilities and strategies can influence the student's success in the acquisition and use of written language skills. Difficulties in attention, memory, or other areas such as visual perception and auditory discrimination can impede skill development, particularly the acquisition of basic spelling and handwriting skills. Fine-motor skills and eye-hand coordination are important considerations in relation to handwriting, the motor component of written language. Also, inefficient learning strategies can interfere with the student's attempts to learn new skills and apply already learned skills to the process of planning, writing, and revising a written product.

Classroom behavior may be related to written language performance. Inappropriate classroom conduct can impede any type of learning, including the acquisition of spelling, handwriting, and composition skills. Likewise, poor achievement can affect a student's behavior. Classroom writing activities often require that students work independently, and when written language is an area of difficulty, students may be unable to comply. The result may be disruptive behavior, frequent bids for the teacher's attention, and/or withdrawal from the academic situation.

In addition, achievement problems in other school skill areas can interfere with the acquisition of written language skills. In this regard, oral language and reading skills are the major concerns. Difficulties in the comprehension or expression of oral language can have a major impact on the student's ability to express thoughts in writing. Likewise, a lack of reading proficiency may inhibit the development of writing skills. Generally, students first learn to read words, then learn to write and spell them. Also, reading exposes students to the formal conventions of written language—sentences, paragraphs, capitalization, punctuation, and the like—and to the structural, syntactical, and vocabulary differences between written and oral language.

Just as other school skills can affect written language, writing skills influence the student's chances for success in other academic areas. Beginning in the early elementary grades, writing is a primary way that students demonstrate what they have learned. As the student proceeds through the various levels of education—from the primary grades to the intermediate grades to middle school and so on—an increasing proportion of school tasks require writing.

Writing, like reading, is a skill that pervades the entire curriculum. Students with poor spelling, handwriting, and composition skills will have difficulty not only when these skills are taught directly, but also when writing proficiency is a requirement in other curriculum areas. Almost all school subjects involve some degree of writing. Students who write very slowly will have difficulty completing their assignments on time. Those who write illegibly may fail an exam or assignment even though their responses are correct. Poor spelling and syntax may lower students' grades, even in subjects like history or biology.

Writing skills are also necessary for adult life. Adults use writing as a memory aid when they make note of a telephone number, write down an address, or make out a shopping list. People also write to communicate with others; they write postcards and e-mail messages to friends, fill out mail order forms, and compose business letters. Job applications are another feature of adult life, as are the forms that must be completed for a Social Security number, a driver's license, income taxes, and so on. In addition, some degree of writing proficiency is required in most occupations. In the assessment of written language, it is important to consider the student's ability to cope with adult writing tasks, as well as the degree of success in meeting classroom writing requirements.

Documentation of Written Language Performance

What are the student's educational needs? is the general assessment question that guides the special education team in its study of written language. The goal in this phase of assessment is to gather sufficient information for a precise description of the student's current levels of educational performance. The first question the team attempts to respond to is, *What is the student's current level of achievement in written language?* Additional data are then gathered about the writing skills that are possible areas of educational need. The result, a description of the student's current status in relation to written language, allows the team to answer this question: *What are the student's strengths and weaknesses in the various skill areas of written language?*

Answers to the assessment questions about written language make up one part of the database used to plan the student's Individualized Education Program. Results of formal tests and informal procedures document the student's current levels of performance in written language. From this information, the team identifies the areas of educational need that may become the priorities for special instruction. For example, consider the case of Joyce, the fourth grader with problems in spelling and handwriting.

Joyce

At this point in assessment, the team has some information about Joyce's current skills in spelling and handwriting. In both areas, Joyce's performance appears to be below average, and in her fourth grade classroom, she is working in a second grade spelling book and just beginning to learn cursive writing. However, little information is available about Joyce's composition skills. Mr. Harvey, Joyce's teacher, did not discuss composition when he made the referral, so the team decides to begin its in-depth study of written language by talking with him. In this interview, Mr. Harvey reports that Joyce writes quite slowly, her handwriting is difficult to read, and her spelling is poor. Despite this, Joyce seems to have good ideas. Although her compositions are short and hard to read because of her difficulties with handwriting and spelling, she is able to express her thoughts in writing.

The team administers the *Test of Written Language-3* to learn more about Joyce's composition skills, and these results are obtained:

Subtests	Standard Scores
Vocabulary	7
Spelling	6
Style	5
Logical Sentences	7
Sentence Combining	7
Contextual Conventions	6
Contextual Language	8
Story Construction	8
Composites	
Contrived Writing	75
Spontaneous Writing	83
Overall Writing	77

Joyce's overall performance on the *TOWL-3* indicates low average achievement in written language skills. However, on the writing sample, she shows strengths in Contextual Language and Story Construction.

Spelling, Style, and Contextual Conventions are areas of weakness. On the contrived subtests, Joyce asked for assistance in reading several of the words and sentences.

To investigate Joyce's difficulties with spelling, the *Test of Written Spelling-4* is given. Joyce's performance on this measure is consistent with her scores on the spelling subtests of the *PIAT-R/NU* and the *WIAT*. She earns an overall standard score of 69, indicating below average performance in spelling.

Ms. Gale, the special education resource teacher, administers an informal spelling inventory (see Table 13–2) to determine Joyce's pattern of errors with regular words. On this measure, Joyce is able to spell the short sounds of vowels and words that follow the consonant-vowel-consonant-*e* pattern (e.g., *line* and *cake*). In the 15 words that she attempts, she makes no errors with consonants. However, she is unable to spell words with two vowels together (e.g., *coat*), with *ow-ou* spellings of the *ou* sound, long and short *oo*, and final *y* as short *i*. Joyce is then asked to write the spellings of a portion of words in a high-frequency word list (see Figure 13–2). She spells the first two groups of 10 words correctly but then begins to experience difficulty. For example, she spells *any* as *ene* and *eat* as *et*.

Handwriting is the next area of study. Samples of Joyce's manuscript and cursive writing are obtained from Mr. Harvey and analyzed for possible error patterns. In manuscript, Joyce's letters are large, poorly spaced, and often difficult to read. As the following sample shows, she seems to have special difficulty writing circular letters like *a, o,* and *e:*

My name is Joyce.

Joyce has just begun to learn cursive writing. She is able to write all of the lower-case letters and has started to learn capitals. Her cursive writing is also large, but the spacing between letters and words is adequate. Letter formation is satisfactory, but she has not yet learned how to join some letters together with others:

my name is joyce.

A classroom observation is conducted when Joyce is participating in a writing activity. Joyce writes in manuscript to copy a paragraph from the board. Her chair and desk are of appropriate size, her posture is adequate, and she holds her paper and pencil correctly. However, she writes with a standard pencil on lined paper with narrow spaces and no guidelines. In forming letters, she makes one line, lifts her pencil from the paper, repositions the pencil, then writes a second line. For example, in writing an uppercase *M,* she makes four separate lines, lifting her pencil each time. This strategy, along with her frequent erasures, affects her writing speed.

After a thorough analysis of these results, the assessment team is prepared to describe Joyce's current levels of written language performance. They have reached these conclusions:

- At present, Joyce is functioning within the low average range in composition skills, as measured by the *Test of Written Language-3.*
- Joyce's spelling skills are quite deficient. On the *Test of Written Spelling-4,* she showed below average performance in overall spelling.
- Joyce's knowledge of regular spellings is limited to consonant and short vowel sounds and words that follow the consonant-vowel-consonant-*e* pattern. She is able to spell only a very few irregular words.
- On most classroom assignments, Joyce writes in manuscript. Her manuscript writing is large, poorly spaced, and difficult to read because of poor formation of some letters (e.g., *a, e,* and *o*). A larger pencil and paper with guidelines between widely spaced lines might help improve her legibility.

- Joyce's manuscript writing is slow because she lifts her pencil after each stroke and erases frequently.
- In cursive, Joyce's spacing and letter formation are adequate, and her writing is legible. She needs to learn the uppercase cursive alphabet and procedures for joining letters together.

STUDY GUIDE

REVIEW QUESTIONS

1. The major purpose for the assessment of written language skills is _____ .
2. What three skill areas are most often considered in the assessment of written language?
3. Find the true and false statements.
   a. In the developmental sequence, oral language generally precedes written language.
   b. Reading is an expressive language skill, whereas writing is a receptive language skill.
   c. Writing is often assessed by multiple-choice exams.
   d. One strategy frequently used to assess written expression is to obtain a writing sample.
   e. The most commonly assessed skill area in written language is composition.
4. Are traditional measures of written language more concerned with the process of writing, or with the product?
5. Match the assessment device or procedure in Column A with the description in Column B.

Column A	*Column B*
a. *Test of Written Language-3*	___ A standardized test that assesses the student's skills in spelling
b. *Test of Written Expression*	___ Assesses four aspects of written language including Dictation and Proofing
c. *Zaner-Bloser Evaluation Scales*	___ A rating scale for the evaluation of handwriting skills
d. *Test of Adolescent and Adult Language-3*	___ A writing sample is used to obtain scores for the Contextual Conventions and Contextual Vocabulary subtests
e. *Test of Written Spelling-4*	___ Includes tests of written vocabulary and grammar as well as tests of listening, speaking, and reading
f. *Woodcock Language Proficiency Battery-Revised*	___ Contains two parts, Items and Essay

6. Find the test results that indicate possible areas of educational need.
   a. Basic Writing Composite 74 on the *Mather-Woodcock Group Writing Tests*
   b. Overall Written Language Quotient 86 on the *Test of Written Language-3*
   c. Standard score 92 on one of the composite scores from the *Test of Adolescent and Adult Language-3*
   d. Total test standard score of 117 for a grade 4 student on the *Test of Written Spelling-4*
7. There are several systems for the analysis of spelling errors, but the simplest recognizes only two types of errors. Name the two types of misspellings.

8. Check each of the areas that should be considered in the evaluation of handwriting skills.

   _____ a. Letter formation

   _____ b. Spelling

   _____ c. Alignment and proportion

   _____ d. Size of letters and spacing

   _____ e. Punctuation and capitalization

   _____ f. Speed

9. On the *Test of Written Language-3,* a writing sample is elicited by asking students to _____ .

10. Writing samples can be analyzed for spelling, handwriting, grammar, punctuation and capitalization, and content and organization. (True or False)

11. Two fundamental concerns in the evaluation of the instructional environment of the classroom are the amount of _____ devoted to instruction and the types of _____ that are emphasized.

12. If a student shows high average intellectual performance, in what standard score range would you expect the student to perform in written language?

    a. Less than standard score 70

    b. Standard score 70 to 84

    c. Standard score 85 to 115

    d. Standard score 116 to 130

    e. Greater than standard score 130

13. If the special education team finds that a student shows poor performance in one aspect of written language, what conclusion can be drawn?

    a. If the problem is in spelling, it is likely that the student's handwriting is also poor.

    b. A problem in one area usually means that the student will show poor performance in all dimensions of written language.

    c. The student can perform poorly in one aspect of written language while showing adequate performance in other aspects.

    d. Written language skill is related to reading competence; if a student writes poorly, he or she also reads poorly.

ACTIVITIES

1. Write an Individualized Assessment Plan for an elementary grade student who has been referred because of problems in written language. Then tell how you would modify that plan for a secondary grade student with the same referral information.

2. Analyze the content of the individual achievement tests described in Chapter 7. Do these measures include tests of written language? If so, what writing skills are emphasized?

3. Under the supervision of the course instructor, administer one of the measures discussed in this chapter. Calculate all possible scores and analyze the results to determine strengths and weaknesses.

4. Obtain a writing sample from a student receiving special education services. Analyze that sample in terms of spelling, handwriting, form (written syntax, capitalization and punctuation, and so on), and content and organization. When you have completed your analysis, rate the adequacy of the sample using a scale such as that in Figure 13–7. Compare your ratings with those of another professional.

5. Devise a criterion-referenced test to assess some aspect of written expression. Be sure to base your CRT on an instructional objective that clearly specifies the student behavior of interest, the conditions under which that behavior should occur, and the criteria for acceptable performance.

DISCUSSION QUESTIONS

1. Writing, like reading and mathematics, is considered a basic school skill. Discuss the importance of written expression in the school curriculum and in adult life.
2. The teaching of writing has changed in the recent past due to influences such as the whole language movement and the process approach to writing. Describe the changes that have occurred and the implications of these changes for assessment of writing skills in general education classrooms.
3. In most classrooms, writing is a way for students to demonstrate what they have learned. Discuss how writing requirements can affect student performance in other school subjects. Consider teachers' expectations for quantity, speed, and accuracy in your answer.
4. At present, there are several individual tests to choose from when assessing composition skills. Using Table 13–4 as a guide, describe the major instruments and their strengths and weaknesses. Conclude by presenting your recommendations regarding the best use of each test.

CHAPTER 14

ORAL LANGUAGE AND BILINGUAL ASSESSMENT

- Considerations in Assessment of Oral Language
- Comprehensive Measures of Oral Language
- Strategies for Assessing Articulation
- Strategies for Assessing Morphology and Syntax
- Strategies for Assessing Semantics and Pragmatics
- Assessing Students Who Speak Nonstandard English
- Assessing Students Who Speak Languages Other Than English
- Within the Context of the Classroom
- Answering the Assessment Questions

Oral language is the most basic communication skill. One person talks, another listens, and information is transmitted. This communication process begins in infancy when babies first learn to attend to the sound of their parents' voices. By the time most children enter school, they are experienced oral communicators, able to understand the messages spoken by others and to express their own thoughts in speech. Oral language is the foundation for school learning. In the first few years of school, most new information is presented orally; students learn by listening and demonstrate what they have learned by speaking. As students progress through the grades, reading and writing skills take on increased importance, but oral language remains a basic means of communication between teacher and student. It is also the fundamental communication process for daily life. In most communication situations at home, at work, and at play, people exchange information by talking.

For many students with special needs, oral language is an area of concern. Students with disabilities may have difficulty understanding the language of others, expressing themselves in speech, or in both comprehension and production of oral language. Language is also a concern with students who speak nonstandard English or languages other than English. If standard English is the only language of communication in the classroom, linguistically diverse students may face real barriers in their attempts to understand and participate in instructional activities.

The purpose of oral language assessment is to gather information for instructional planning. The general question that guides this phase of assessment is, *What are the student's educational needs?* When oral language is the skill area under study, two specific questions are asked: *What is the student's current level of development in oral language?* and *What are the student's strengths and weaknesses in the various skill areas of oral language?* These questions apply to both linguistically diverse students and those whose only language is standard English. The goal in this phase of the assessment process is description of the student's current levels of educational performance.

Assessment for instructional planning is a selective process. If the student is making satisfactory progress in oral language or another skill area, the student's special education program will probably not address this skill and, thus, extensive assessment is unnecessary. However, it is often the case that the assessment team has little information about a student's current status in oral language. Before this or any other skill can be ruled out as an area of educational need, it is necessary to gather data to document the student's current performance. For example, consider Joyce, the fourth grader with achievement problems in the written language skills of reading, spelling, and handwriting.

Joyce

The assessment team has almost completed its evaluation of Joyce. Results suggest a discrepancy between Joyce's expected school performance and her actual achievement, and three major areas of educational need have been identified: reading, spelling, and handwriting.

To date, oral language has not been a concern in assessment. The original referral from Mr. Harvey, Joyce's classroom teacher, did not mention oral language, and Joyce's parents did not include listening and speaking skills among the areas that they perceived as possible problems. In its study of Joyce's performance in other areas, the team has not noticed any severe problems in oral communication, although classroom observation results indicate that Joyce has difficulty following oral directions. This difficulty probably is related to Joyce's poor performance on memory tasks, but it could also be influenced by problems in the comprehension of oral language.

To find out more about Joyce's proficiency in oral language, the team will administer the intermediate level of the *Test of Language Development-3,* a comprehensive measure of several areas of language functioning. If results of this test suggest that one or more components of oral language are possible areas of educational need, the

Individualized Assessment Plan

For: *Joyce Dewey*   *4*   *10-0*   *12/1/00*   *Ms. Gale*
            Student's Name   Grade   Age   Date   Coordinator

Reason for Referral: Difficulty keeping up with fourth grade work in reading, spelling, and handwriting.

Assessment Question	*Assessment Procedure*	*Person Responsible*	*Date/Time*
What is the student's current level of development in oral language?	*Test of Language Development-3, Intermediate*	Mr. Bell, Speech-Language Pathologist	1/16/01, 10 A.M.
What are the student's strengths and weaknesses in the various skill areas of oral language?	Additional tests and/or informal assessments, as necessary	Mr. Bell, Speech-Language Pathologist, and other team members, as needed	To be determined

assessment team will continue its investigation. Depending on the language skill to be assessed, the team may decide to administer another norm-referenced test, collect a language sample, conduct an observation, or use some other type of informal assessment strategy.

CONSIDERATIONS IN ASSESSMENT OF ORAL LANGUAGE

Students' oral language skills are the subject of study in general, special, and bilingual education. This skill area, more than many others, illustrates the multidisciplinary nature of the assessment process. Regular, special, and bilingual teachers are interested in promoting the language development of their students. They gather assessment data to measure students' progress. Speech-language pathologists serve students with severe oral communication disorders; their role in assessment is the administration of specialized measures to identify and describe disorders of speech and language. Bilingual educators are concerned with the communication skills of stu-

dents who are English language learners. They contribute by providing information about the student's competency in the first language and by reporting on progress in the acquisition of English-language skills.

Purposes

In general education, teachers monitor oral language skills to determine pupil progress and evaluate the effectiveness of the instructional program. However, after the early elementary grades, oral language is not usually taught as a separate school subject. Also, oral communication is not assessed by the group achievement tests that are used to measure students' school performance (although listening skills may be). This lack of attention to oral language reflects the assumption that students learn to listen and speak during the preschool years. Once in school, students are expected to be oral communicators, so the curriculum focuses on the acquisition of higher-level academic skills such as reading, writing, and mathematics.

When students have difficulty with oral communication in the general education classroom, they may be referred for special education assessment and/or bilingual assessment. The purpose of bilingual assessment, like that of special education assessment, is to determine whether the student is eligible for special services and, if so, what services are needed. If the student is identified as limited in English proficiency (LEP), special services may be offered. Among the services available in some school districts are bilingual education programs in which instruction takes place both in English and in the students' language, and ESL or ESOL programs in which English is taught as a second language. (*ESL* stands for English as a second language; *ESOL* means English for speakers of other languages.)

In special education assessment, oral language is usually a concern of the assessment team as it begins to gather data for planning the student's Individualized Education Program. Many students with mild disabilities have special instructional needs in oral language. In particular, students with mild retardation may show an overall delay in the acquisition of listening and speaking skills, and students with learning disabilities in written language may have equivalent needs in oral language. In addition, there is a large group of students for whom oral language is the primary disability area. This disability is called a communication disorder.

When oral language is identified as an area of educational need for a particular student, assessment is continued to gather the detailed information necessary for program planning. This occurs for all students with language needs, whatever the disability of the student or the language the student speaks. The goal at this point in assessment is description of the student's current performance so an appropriate educational program can be designed. Once that program is implemented, the cycle of gathering data about current skills, planning instructional interventions, and evaluating the success of those interventions is repeated for as long as the student remains in need of specially designed instruction.

Skill Areas

Language is a symbol system used for communication, and speech is one medium used to express language. Like written language, oral language can be receptive or expressive, depending on the person's role in the communication process. In oral language, speech is the expressive component, and listening is the receptive component. Polloway and Smith (1982) suggest that just as language is a vehicle for communication, it is also a vehicle for thought. In this view, thinking is conceptualized as a type of communication process in which inner language plays a major role.

There are many ways that language can be described, and the reception-expression dimension is only one. Another useful system is that proposed by Bloom and Lahey (1978). They suggest that language is composed of three interacting dimensions: form, content, and use. Language competence is the integration of these three dimensions of language.

Wiig and Semel's (1984) model of language includes similar components, as Figure 14–1 illustrates. In this model, four dimensions of language are described: language as sound sequences, language as a structured rule system (form), language as a meaning system (content), and language in communicative context (use).

The form of language is determined by the rules used to combine speech sounds into meaning units and meaning units into communications. Three aspects of language are involved: phonology, morphology, and syntax. Phonology is concerned with the smallest units of oral language, the speech sounds (phonemes). Expressive phonology is called articulation. Receptive phonology, the ability to recognize and comprehend phonemes, is auditory discrimination. The next level of language is morphology. A morpheme is the smallest meaningful unit of language. A morpheme may be a word such as *flower* or a meaningful part of a word such as the *-ing* in *growing*. Syntax refers to the grammatical rules for combining morphemes into comprehensible utterances. Like phonology, morphology and syntax have receptive and expressive components. For example, expressive syntax refers to the ability to produce grammatically acceptable speech.

For communication to occur, language must have meaning as well as form, and language meaning is called semantics. Semantics is concerned with the meaning of individual words and

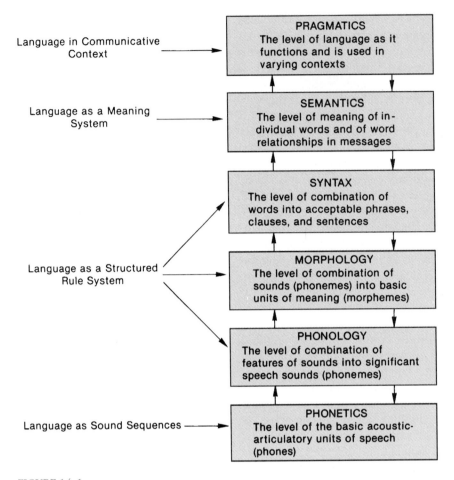

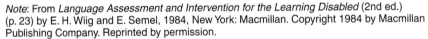

FIGURE 14-1

Dimensions of Oral Language

Note: From *Language Assessment and Intervention for the Learning Disabled* (2nd ed.)
(p. 23) by E. H. Wiig and E. Semel, 1984, New York: Macmillan. Copyright 1984 by Macmillan
Publishing Company. Reprinted by permission.

with the meaning that is produced by combinations of words. Receptive semantics is language comprehension, and expressive semantics is the production of meaningful discourse.

Pragmatics, or language use, is concerned with the speaker's purposes for communication and the ways that language is used to carry out those intents. Adults are able to analyze the social contexts in which communications occur and alter their language accordingly. They are influenced by the setting of the communication, the characteristics of the participants, the topic of conversation, and the goals and objectives of

each participant (Wiig & Semel, 1984). For example, if the communicative intent is to announce that dinner is ready, the language used to convey that message to one's family is likely to be different from that used with dinner guests.

Thus, oral language involves both reception and expression of communications, and those communications can be analyzed according to the dimensions of phonology, morphology, syntax, semantics, and pragmatics. In addition, oral communication is influenced by other aspects of the speech act (e.g., intonation, pitch, loudness, and stress) and by the nonverbal communications that accompany speech (e.g., facial expressions, body language, gestures). Children and adolescents can experience difficulty with any one or several of these dimensions.

In assessment, measures of oral language focus on the comprehension and production of language form and content. Pragmatics is a relatively new area of study and, thus, fewer measures have been developed for its assessment. In addition, traditional language measures are designed to evaluate students' products, not the process by which those products are created. When information is needed about a student's ability to use language in a variety of communicative contexts or about the cognitive processes that interact with language comprehension and production, informal measures are often the major type of assessment strategy available.

Many measures of oral language are designed for young children (preschoolers and children in the first few grades of school) because of the rapid rate at which language skills develop during this age period. Most measures are administered individually, a necessity when oral responses are required. Because language competence is such a complex skill area, many types of assessment tasks are used to evaluate students' oral language abilities.

Expressive phonology—the articulation of speech sounds—is assessed by eliciting samples of the student's speech. Auditory discrimination (receptive phonology) is measured by listening tasks. Tests of auditory discrimination were discussed in Chapter 9, the chapter on specific learning abilities and strategies, and thus will not be covered here.

Like articulation, expressive morphology and syntax are assessed by eliciting samples of the student's speech. With these skills, however, the concern is the structural adequacy of the utterance, not its phonological characteristics. Receptive skills are measured in a variety of ways, but one common technique involves having the student select a picture that illustrates a sentence read by the tester. For example, if the sentence is "The girl is talking to her mother," one picture might show a girl talking to her mother, another the mother talking while her daughter listens, and so forth.

The meaning component of language—semantics—is the subject of assessment not only on measures of oral language but also on many tests of intellectual performance. Most often, expressive skills are the concern, and a typical test task is word definition. Recognition tasks are used to assess receptive skills. With this type of task, the student listens to a word and selects from several drawings or photos the one that best represents the word's meaning.

Similar techniques are used to assess students' proficiency in languages other than English, and the same language dimensions are of interest. In bilingual assessment, the language that the child speaks upon entry to school is called the first language (L1), or the home or native language. The second language that the child learns is usually English and is called L2. The purpose of language assessment for bilingual learners is to determine the extent of their language proficiency in both languages so learning needs can be identified. The language in which the student is most proficient is called the dominant, or primary, language. Also of interest, particularly with older students, is language preference. The language in which a speaker is most proficient may not be the language in which he or she prefers to converse.

Whatever languages the student speaks, the ability to use oral language in everyday communication situations should not be neglected in assessment. Pragmatics is one facet of the application of language skills and is a necessary assessment concern. It is also important to evaluate the student's ability to deal with the form and meaning of language in everyday interactions. Tests measure language competence, but language performance is another matter. Although a student may define a word correctly on a test, he or she does not necessarily use the word correctly in discourse or, indeed, ever use the word in communication situations.

Current Practices

Assessment of oral language skills is not as common a practice as assessment of academic skills such as reading and mathematics. The group achievement and competency tests that are used in general education focus on written, not oral, language, and even individual tests of academic achievement rarely include listening and speaking skills. Two notable exceptions are the *Wechsler Individual Achievement Test* (1992) and the *Diagnostic Achievement Battery* (2nd ed.) (Newcomer, 1990).

Although oral language is not typically assessed by tests of academic achievement, it is often included on other types of measures. Tests of intellectual performance (unless they are designed as nonverbal measures) usually assess language skills in some way. For example, half of the subtests on the *Wechsler Intelligence Scale for Children-Third Edition* (Wechsler, 1991) are considered verbal subtests, and a Verbal Reasoning composite score is one of the results of the *Stanford-Binet Intelligence Scale-Fourth Edition* (Thorndike, Hagen, & Sattler, 1986). In addition, oral language skills are frequently one of the performance domains assessed by measures of adaptive behavior. Some of the instruments used to assess specific learning abilities also evaluate oral language.

Measures designed specifically for the study of oral language skills are more directly related to instructional planning. Several of these assessment tools are listed in Table 14–1. These measures are divided into five categories according to the skills they assess. First are survey measures (instruments that assess more than one aspect of oral language), which are followed by measures of phonology, measures of morphology and syntax, measures of semantics, and measures of pragmatics.

As Table 14–1 illustrates, there are a great many tools for the assessment of oral language, and these tools vary in the skill areas they address. Some measures are comprehensive, whereas others are limited to one domain. With the exception of pragmatics, each dimension of language is represented by a number of measures. For the most part, oral language assessments are designed for children in the elementary grades. However, some currently available measures extend oral language assessment into the secondary grades and even adulthood.

Informal techniques also play a role in oral language assessment. All of the standard types of informal devices and procedures are available, but the most common are criterion-referenced testing, informal inventories, language sample analysis, and checklists and rating scales.

This chapter describes many of the major strategies that are used in schools today for oral language assessment. Comprehensive measures of oral language are discussed first. These are followed by sections on measures of phonology, morphology and syntax, and semantics and pragmatics. In each section, formal and informal strategies are described briefly because of the number of devices and techniques available. Techniques for the assessment of linguistically diverse students are discussed later in the chapter.

COMPREHENSIVE MEASURES OF ORAL LANGUAGE

Of the oral language measures available today, several are designed to assess a wide range of language skills. Two versions of the *Test of Language Development-3* are described here: the primary level for young children and the intermediate level for students in the later elementary grades. Also discussed are the *Oral and Written Language Scales* (Carrow-Woolfolk, 1996), the *Woodcock Language Proficiency Battery-Revised* (Woodcock, 1991), and the *Test of Adolescent and Adult Language-3* (Hammill, Brown, Larsen, & Wiederholt, 1994).

Test of Language Development-3, Primary

The *TOLD-3 Primary* is an individual test of oral language for preschool and early elementary grade children. There are six core and three supplementary subtests on the *TOLD-3 Primary*. The *TOLD-3 Primary* assesses listening, organizing, and speaking skills in relation to phonology, syntax, and semantics. However, core subtests address only syntax and semantics. The *TOLD-3 Primary* subtests are:

Core Subtests

- *Picture Vocabulary* (Receptive Semantics). The tester reads a word, and the child points to the picture that best represents the word. The child chooses from four pictures.

TABLE 14–1
Measures of Oral Language

NAME (AUTHOR)	AGES OR GRADES	GROUP OR INDIVIDUAL	SKILL AREA(S) ASSESSED	
			RECEPTION	EXPRESSION
Survey Measures				
Bankson Language Test (2nd ed.) (Bankson, 1990)	Ages 3-0 to 6-11	Individual		X
BRIGANCE® Diagnostic Comprehensive Inventory of Basic Skills-Revised (Brigance, 1999)	Pre-kindergarten to grade 9	Individual	X	X
BRIGANCE® Diagnostic Inventory of Early Development-Revised (Brigance, 1991)	Birth to age 6	Individual	X	X
Clinical Evaluation of Language Fundamentals-Third Edition (Semel, Wiig, & Secord, 1995)	Ages 6 through 21	Individual	X	X
Oral and Written Language Scales (Carrow-Woolfolk, 1996)	Ages 3 to 21	Individual	X	X
Test of Adolescent and Adult Language-3 (Hammill, Brown, Larsen, & Wiederholt, 1994)	Ages 12-0 to 24-11	Varies by subtest	X	X
Test of Early Language Development (3rd ed.) (Hresko, Reid, & Hammill, 1999)	Ages 2-0 through 7-11	Individual	X	X
Test of Language Development-3, Intermediate (Hammill & Newcomer, 1997)	Ages 8-0 to 12-11	Individual	X	X
Test of Language Development-3, Primary (Newcomer & Hammill, 1997)	Ages 4-0 to 8-11	Individual	X	X
Utah Test of Language Development (3rd ed.) (Mecham, 1989)	Ages 3-0 to 9-11	Individual	X	X
Woodcock Language Proficiency Battery-Revised (Woodcock, 1991)	Ages 3 to 80+	Individual	X	X
Phonology				
Arizona Articulation Proficiency Scale (2nd ed.) (Fudala & Reynolds, 1986)	Ages 1-6 to 13-11	Individual		X
Auditory Discrimination Test (Reynolds, 1987; Wepman, 1975)	Ages 4 to 8-11	Individual	X	
Goldman-Fristoe Test of Articulation (Goldman & Fristoe, 1986)	Ages 2 to 16+	Individual		X
Goldman-Fristoe-Woodcock Test of Auditory Discrimination (Goldman, Fristoe, & Woodcock, 1970)	Ages 4 to 70+	Individual	X	
Photo Articulation Test (3rd ed.) (Lippke, Dickey, Selmar, & Soder, 1997)	Ages 3-0 to 8-11	Individual		X

Continued

467

TABLE 14–1
Measures of Oral Language—(*Continued*)

NAME (AUTHOR)	AGES OR GRADES	GROUP OR INDIVIDUAL	SKILL AREA(S) ASSESSED	
			RECEPTION	EXPRESSION
Morphology and Syntax				
Carrow Elicited Language Inventory (Carrow-Woolfolk, 1974)	Ages 3-0 to 7-11	Individual		X
Developmental Sentence Analysis (Lee, 1974)	Ages 2-0 to 7-11	Individual		X
Language Sampling, Analysis, and Training (3rd ed.) (Tyack & Venable, 1999)	Young children	Individual		X
Northwestern Syntax Screening Test (Lee, 1971)	Ages 3-11 to 7-1	Individual	X	X
Test for Auditory Comprehension of Language (3rd ed.) (Carrow-Woolfolk, 1999)	Ages 3-0 to 9-11	Individual	X	
Semantics				
Assessment of Children's Language Comprehension (Foster, Giddan, & Stark, 1983)	Ages 3 to 7	Individual	X	
Boehm Test of Basic Concepts–Preschool Edition (Boehm, 1986a)	Ages 3 to 5	Individual	X	
Boehm Test of Basic Concepts–Revised (Boehm, 1986b)	Grades K–2	Group	X	
Comprehensive Receptive and Expressive Vocabulary Test (Wallace & Hammill, 1994)	Ages 4-0 to 17-11	Individual	X	X
Expressive One-Word Picture Vocabulary Test-2000 Edition (Brownell, 2000a)	Ages 2 through 18	Individual		X
Expressive Vocabulary Test (Williams, 1997)	Ages 2-6 to 90+	Individual		X
Peabody Picture Vocabulary Test, Third Edition (Dunn & Dunn, 1997)	Ages 2-6 to 90+	Individual	X	
Receptive One-Word Picture Vocabulary Test-2000 Edition (Brownell, 2000b)	Ages 2 through 18	Individual	X	
Pragmatics				
Let's Talk Inventory for Children (Bray & Wiig, 1987)	Ages 4 to 8	Individual	X	X
Test of Pragmatic Language (Phelps-Terasaki & Phelps-Gunn, 1992)	Ages 5-0 to 13-11	Individual		X
Test of Pragmatic Skills (rev. ed.) (Shulman, 1986)	Ages 3-0 to 8-11	Individual		X

- *Relational Vocabulary* (Organizational Semantics). The tester reads two words and the child must tell how they are alike.
- *Oral Vocabulary* (Expressive Semantics). The tester reads a word and asks the child to define it orally.

- *Grammatic Understanding* (Receptive Syntax). The tester reads a sentence, and the child must choose the picture that best illustrates the meaning of the sentence. The three pictures presented to the child represent syntactically similar sentences. As the *TOLD-3 Primary*

Test of Language Development-3 (TOLD-3), Primary and Intermediate

P. L. Newcomer and D. D. Hammill (1997); D. D. Hammill and P. L. Newcomer (1997)

Type: Norm-referenced test

Major Content Areas: Primary: receptive, organizational, and expressive skills in phonology, syntax, and semantics; Intermediate: receptive and expressive syntax and semantics

Type of Administration: Individual

Administration Time: Primary: 30–60 minutes; Intermediate: 1 hour

Age/Grade Levels: Primary: ages 4-0 to 8-11; Intermediate: ages 8-0 to 12-11

Types of Scores: Percentile ranks, standard scores, and age equivalents for subtests; composite standard scores (quotients)

Computer Aids: *TOLD-P:3 PRO-SCORE System, TOLD-I:3 PRO-SCORE System*

Typical Uses: A broad-based test for the identification of strengths and weaknesses in oral language development

Cautions: The phonology subtests on the *TOLD-3, Primary* are most useful for children under age 7.

Publisher: PRO-ED (www.proedinc.com)

---

manual explains, "In response to the stimulus sentence 'He had ridden,' the child must select the picture that most closely depicts the sentence from among pictures of a man mounting a horse, a man riding a horse, and a man walking away from a horse" (p. 9).

- *Sentence Imitation* (Organizational Syntax). On this subtest, the tester reads a sentence, and the child must repeat it verbatim. This test task is based on the assumption stated in the manual that "it is easier for children to repeat or imitate grammatic forms that are part of their linguistic repertoires than it is to repeat those that are unfamiliar to them" (p. 9).
- *Grammatic Completion* (Expressive Syntax). The tester reads an unfinished sentence, and the child must supply the missing word. For example, the child might be asked to finish this sentence: "Cats are small, but birds are even _____ ." Included are items that assess plurals, possessives, verb tenses, and comparative and superlative adjectives.

Supplemental Subtests

- *Word Discrimination* (Receptive Phonology). The tester reads two words, and the child must say whether the words are the same or different. Different word pairs differ in only one phoneme.
- *Phonemic Analysis* (Organizational Phonology). The tester reads a word, then asks the child to repeat the word with one syllable deleted.
- *Word Articulation* (Expressive Phonology). Here the tester shows the child a picture and reads a sentence that describes it. The child is asked to name the picture. If he or she fails to respond correctly, the tester says the word and asks the child to repeat it (e.g., "That's a dog. Say *dog*."). The purpose is to assess articulation, not vocabulary.

According to the *TOLD-3 Primary* manual, the phonology subtests are most useful for children under the age of 7. However, norms are available for older children.

To participate in *TOLD-3 Primary* administration, children must understand and speak English and be able to respond to oral questions. The subtests are not timed, and reading and writing skills are not required. This test is quite easy to administer and score. All subtests begin with item 1, and the ceiling for all of the core subtests is five consecutive incorrect responses. There are no ceilings on the supplemental subtests; all items are administered. It is not necessary to administer all subtests. For example, the tester can select only those subtests that assess a specific language ability such as syntax or semantics. However, if all subtests are administered, the three supplementary subtests should be given at a different time from the six core subtests to reduce student fatigue.

The *TOLD-3 Primary* was standardized in 1996 with 1,000 children from 23 states. This sample appears to approximate the national population in geographic region, gender, race, urban-rural residence, ethnicity, family income, and educational attainment of parents. No information is provided about the home language of students in the sample. Students with disabilities made up 11% of the sample; most common were those with speech-language disorders and those with learning disabilities.

The internal consistency, test-retest, and interrater reliabilities of the *TOLD-3 Primary* are adequate. The manual reports several investigations that support the concurrent validity of the previous edition of *TOLD Primary* with other tests of oral language and with vocabulary measures from tests of intellectual performance. Moderate to high correlations were found between the current edition of the *TOLD Primary* and the *Bankson Language Test* (2nd ed.) (Bankson, 1990).

Percentile rank, standard scores, and age equivalents are available for each subtest. Subtest standard scores are distributed with a mean of 10 and a standard deviation of 3. Six composite scores called quotients are also available: Spoken Language Quotient (a summary of performance on all subtests), Semantics Quotient, Syntax Quotient, and Listening, Organizing, and Speaking Quotients. No composite score is provided for the phonology subtests. Quotients are standard scores (mean = 100, standard deviation = 15). Standard errors of measurement range from 1 to 2 standard score points for *TOLD-3 Primary* subtests and from 3 to 5 standard score points for composite quotients.

TOLD-3 Primary results are plotted on a profile, as Figure 14–2 illustrates. The profile on the left shows the child's quotient scores, and subtest scores are plotted on the other profile. In this example, the child's performance falls within the low average range in overall spoken language, listening skills, speaking skills, and semantics.

The *TOLD-3 Primary* is a useful measure for investigating the oral language skills of young children because it assesses several dimensions of language ability. It is best used at the start of language assessment to identify areas in which the child is proficient and areas that require further evaluation.

Test of Language Development-3, Intermediate

The intermediate level of the *TOLD-3* is designed for older elementary grade students. Like the primary version, it offers measures of receptive and expressive syntax and semantics. However, organizing skills are not assessed and measures of phonology are not included.

Six subtests make up the *TOLD-3 Intermediate:*

- *Sentence Combining* (Expressive Syntax). The tester reads two or more simple sentences, and the student must combine these into one new sentence. As the *TOLD-3 Intermediate* manual explains, "The sentences 'I like milk. I like cookies,' may be combined into 'I like milk and cookies' " (p. 7).
- *Picture Vocabulary* (Receptive Semantics). The tester reads a two-word phrase and shows the student a Picture Card with six photos. The student must point to the photo that the phrase describes best.
- *Word Ordering* (Expressive Syntax). The tester reads several (three to seven) words in random order, and the student must put the words in order to form a sentence. For example, the words *dog, the, big, is* would be reordered to construct the sentence, "The dog is big."

TOLD–P:3

Profile/Examiner Record Booklet

Test of Language Development–Primary **Third Edition**

Section I. Identifying Information

Name __Lee__   Female ☐ Male ☒   School __Highland Park Elem.__   Grade __K__

	Year	Month
Date Tested	96	11
Date of Birth	91	5
Age	5	6

Examiner's Name __W. Feng__

Examiner's Title __Speech Pathologist__

Section II. Record of Scores

Subtests

Core	Raw Score	Age Equiv.	%ile	Std. Score
I. Picture Vocabulary (PV)	7	3-3	9	6
II. Relational Vocabulary (RV)	5	3-9	9	6
III. Oral Vocabulary (OV)	2	3-9	9	6
IV. Grammatic Understanding (GU)	13	4-9	25	8
V. Sentence Imitation (SI)	9	5-0	37	9
VI. Grammatic Completion (GC)	6	4-6	25	8

Supplemental	Raw Score	Age Equiv.	%ile	Std. Score
VII. Word Discrimination (WD)	14	5-3	37	9
VIII. Phonemic Analysis (PA)	7	5-0	25	8
IX. Word Articulation (WA)	17	5-3	37	9

Composites

	PV	RV	OV	GU	SI	GC	Sums of SS	Quotients
Spoken Language (SLQ)	6	6	6	8	9	8	43	80
Listening (LiQ)	6			8			14	82
Organizing (OrQ)		6			9		15	85
Speaking (SpQ)			6			8	14	82
Semantics (SeQ)	6	6	6				18	74
Syntax (SyQ)				8	9	8	25	89

Other Test Data

Name	Date	Std. Score	TOLD-P:3 Equiv.
1. CTONI	9/96	85	85
2.			

Section III. Profile of Scores

Quotients	General Intelligence/Aptitude CTONI	Spoken Language (SLQ)	Quotients	Listening (LiQ)	Organizing (OrQ)	Speaking (SpQ)	Semantics (SeQ)	Syntax (SyQ)	Standard Scores	Picture Vocabulary	Relational Vocabulary	Oral Vocabulary	Grammatic Understanding	Sentence Imitation	Grammatic Completion	Word Discrimination	Phonemic Analysis	Word Articulation	Standard Scores
150			150						20										20
145			145						19										19
140			140						18										18
135			135						17										17
130			130						16										16
125			125						15										15
120			120						14										14
115			115						13										13
110			110						12										12
105			105						11										11
100			100						10										10
95			95						9										9
90			90						8										8
85	X		85						7										7
80		X	80						6										6
75			75						5										5
70			70						4										4
65			65						3										3
60			60						2										2
55			55						1										1

FIGURE 14–2

Sample Results for the *Test of Language Development-3, Primary*

Note: From *Test of Language Development-3, Primary* (p. 32) by P. L. Newcomer and D. D. Hammill, 1997, Austin, TX: PRO-ED. Copyright 1997 by PRO-ED. Reprinted by permission.

- *Generals* (Expressive Semantics). The tester reads three words, and the student must tell how the words are alike. The manual provides this example: "If the examiner were to say, 'Venus, Mars, and Pluto,' the child might say, 'They are all gods,' 'They are all mythical characters,' or 'They are all planets' " (p. 8).
- *Grammatic Comprehension* (Receptive Syntax). The student listens to the tester read sentences, some of which contain syntax errors. The student tells whether the sentence is correct or incorrect, but he or she is not required to provide corrections for errors. Included are items that contain errors in noun-verb agreement, plurals, pronouns, negatives, comparative and superlative adjectives, and adverbs.
- *Malapropisms* (Receptive Semantics). Malapropisms are words that are used in place of similar-sounding words, thereby altering the meaning of the sentence. In this subtest, the tester reads sentences containing malapropisms, and the student must say the word needed to replace the malapropism. The manual says, "For example, upon hearing, 'John took a phonograph of his family,' the child must provide the word *photograph*" (p. 8).

The *TOLD-3 Intermediate* is somewhat more difficult to administer than the primary version of the test. Subtests must be administered in order. Although all students start each subtest with item 1, ceiling rules vary from subtest to subtest. On Grammatic Comprehension, a ceiling is reached when the student makes three errors in any five consecutive items. On Picture Vocabulary, the student begins with item 1 on each Picture Card. Testing continues on each Picture Card until there are two errors in a row; the tester then moves to the next Picture Card until all nine are administered. On the four other subtests, the ceiling is straightforward: two incorrect responses in a row.

The *TOLD-3 Intermediate* was standardized in 1996 with 779 students from 23 states. The final sample appears to approximate the national population in geographic region, gender, race, urban-rural residence, family income, and educational attainment of parents. Native American students are somewhat overrepresented and African American students are somewhat underrepresented. Approximately 10% of the sample is students with disabilities, with those with learning disabilities and speech-language disorders most common.

The internal consistency, test-retest, and interrater reliabilities of the *TOLD-3 Intermediate* are adequate. The *TOLD-3* manual reports two studies of validity showing relationships between this test and other measures. Moderate correlations were found between the *TOLD-3 Intermediate* and a test of academic achievement; moderate to high correlations were reported between the *TOLD-3* and the *Test of Adolescent and Adult Language* (3rd ed.) (Hammill et al., 1994). It would also be helpful to have information about the relationship of the *TOLD-3 Intermediate* and other tests of oral language performance.

Subtest scores on the *TOLD-3 Intermediate* are age equivalents, percentile ranks, and standard scores. Five composite quotients are derived from subtest results: Spoken Language Quotient (an overall test score), Listening Quotient, Speaking Quotient, Semantics Quotient, and Syntax Quotient. The standard errors of measurement are 1 standard score point for subtest scores and 3 to 4 standard score points for composites.

The *TOLD-3 Intermediate* is a useful measure of oral language for older elementary grade students. Like the primary *TOLD-3,* it is best used at the start of assessment to identify the student's strengths and weaknesses in listening and speaking skills. Its results are not sufficiently specific to direct instructional planning.

Other Comprehensive Measures

In addition to the *TOLD-3,* several other comprehensive language measures are worthy of note. Those discussed in the next paragraphs attempt to broaden the scope of assessment by including not only oral, but also written, language skills.

Oral and Written Language Scales (OWLS). The *OWLS* (Carrow-Woolfolk, 1996) is composed of one written language and two oral language scales. The Written Expression Scale was described in Chapter 13. Of interest here are the two oral scales, Listening Comprehension and Oral Expression, which are designed for ages 3 through 21. On the Listening Comprehension Scale, the tester reads an item and the student responds by selecting one of four drawings. For example, the student may need to find the drawing of the doll or that of the smallest ball. On Oral Expression, the tester reads an item as the student looks at a drawing or drawings; the student must respond orally. For example, when the tester points to the drawings and says, "Here the boy is walking and here he is _____ ," the student may need to say "running."

The oral language scales of the *OWLS* measure the student's ability to understand and use individual words, grammatical forms, and meaningful language. According to Carrow-Woolfolk (1996), these scales assess the lexical, syntactic, pragmatic, and supralinguistic categories of oral language. The supralinguistic category refers to language tasks such as "comprehension of figurative language and humor; derivation of meaning from context, logic, and inference; and other higher-order thinking skills" (p. 21).

Despite the fact that many different abilities are included on the oral language scales of *OWLS,* only total scale scores are available. Raw scores for both the Listening Comprehension and Oral Expression Scales can be converted to a standard score (distributed with a mean of 100 and standard deviation of 15), percentile rank, and test-age equivalent. It is also possible to obtain an overall Oral Composite and, if the Written Expression Scale is administered, a total test score called the Language Composite. The oral language scales of the *OWLS,* like other broad-based measures, help to identify areas of need in oral language. However, further assessment is required in order to plan the instructional program.

Woodcock Language Proficiency Battery-Revised.
This measure by Woodcock (1991) is a shortened version of the *Woodcock-Johnson Psycho-Educational Battery-Revised* (Woodcock & Johnson, 1989). It contains five oral language subtests:

- *Memory for Sentences.* The student listens to a word, short phrase, or sentence, then attempts to repeat it verbatim.
- *Picture Vocabulary.* The student looks at a drawing and says what it is.

- *Oral Vocabulary.* The student listens to a word, then says its synonym or antonym.
- *Listening Comprehension.* The student listens to a sentence or paragraph with one word missing and tries to supply the missing word.
- *Verbal Analogies.* The tester reads verbal analogies (e.g., "Big is to little as up is to . . ."), and the student completes them.

These subtests do not represent a wide range of oral language skills; most are measures of receptive or expressive semantics. If the student's test performance indicates some difficulty in these areas, assessment would continue with additional formal tests or informal procedures.

Test of Adolescent and Adult Language-3 (TOAL-3).
The *TOAL-3* (Hammill et al., 1994) is a norm-referenced measure designed for students ages 12-0 to 24-11. It requires 1 to 3 hours to administer, but most subtests can be administered to groups. Two subtests assess listening skills and two evaluate speaking:

- *Listening/Vocabulary.* The student looks at four pictures in the booklet while the tester reads a word. The student chooses the two pictures that relate to the word.
- *Listening/Grammar.* The tester reads three sentences. The student selects the two sentences that are most similar in meaning.
- *Speaking/Vocabulary.* The tester reads a word. The student is asked to produce a meaningful oral sentence that incorporates the word. (This subtest must be administered individually.)
- *Speaking/Grammar.* The student listens to a sentence read by the tester and attempts to repeat the sentence verbatim. (This subtest must be administered individually.)

These subtests assess two dimensions of receptive and expressive language: semantics and syntax.

The *TOAL-3* is constructed so that professionals can compare a student's language skills in several ways. Subtest results are expressed as standard scores, and combinations of subtests produce a variety of language quotients. An overall test score, the General Language Quotient, is available along with quotients for these areas: Listening, Speaking, Reading, Writing, Spoken Language, Written Language, Vocabulary, Grammar,

Receptive Language, and Expressive Language. Thus, listening skills can be contrasted with speaking skills, and spoken language performance can be compared with written language performance. Subtest and composite results are plotted on profiles to facilitate comparisons, and the manual provides guidelines for determining whether differences are statistically significant.

STRATEGIES FOR ASSESSING ARTICULATION

Articulation refers to the production of speech sounds or phonemes. There are 44 speech sounds in the English language (Polloway & Smith, 1982). Twenty-five are consonantal sounds such as the initial phonemes in *mother* and *baby*. Consonantal sounds are produced by movements of the articulators (tongue, lips, teeth, palate, and so forth). There are also 19 vocalic sounds (e.g., the initial phonemes in *at* and *open*); when these are produced, the air passes through the mouth without obstruction. Table 14–2 presents the phonemes in the English language and examples of words containing these sounds.

Some experts separate vocalic sounds into two categories: vowels and diphthongs. Diphthongs are made up of a combination of two vowel sounds. Examples are the medial phonemes in each of these words: *paid, time, couch,* and *boil* (Culatta & Culatta, 1985).

In the assessment of articulation, a sample of the child's speech is gathered, and the speech sounds that are produced are evaluated in terms of accuracy and intelligibility. One way to gather a speech sample is simply to record the spontaneous utterances of the child. However, this is not efficient because it may take the child some time to produce all of the speech sounds. Standardized measures of articulation use other strategies, and one of the most common is to present pictures or other stimuli to elicit the production of specific phonemes. For example, the *Photo Articulation Test* (3rd ed.) (Lippke et al., 1997) contains 72 color photographs of objects. In naming these objects, the child produces all of the consonant, vowel, and diphthong sounds.

TABLE 14–2
Phonemes of the English Language

I. CONSONANTAL (25)		II. VOCALIC (19)	
/b/	ball	/ă/	cat
/ch/	chip	/ā/	cake
/d/	dog	/â/	air
/f/	farm	/ä/	art
/g/	goat	/ĕ/	leg
/h/	home	/ē/	meal
/j/	jump	/ĭ/	pin
/k/	kite	/ī/	ice
/l/	lamp	/ŏ/	log
/m/	moon	/ō/	road
/n/	nut	/ô/	stork, ball
/ng/	song	/oi/	boy
/p/	pig	/oo/	book
/r/	rug	/ōō/	moon
/s/	sun	/ou/	cow
/sh/	ship	/ū/	cube
/t/	top	/ŭ/	duck
/th/	thumb	/û/	fur, fern
/th/	that	/ə/	sofa, circus
/v/	vine		
/w/	witch		
/wh/	white		
/y/	yo-yo		
/z/	zipper		
/zh/	pleasure		

Note: From *Teaching Language Arts to Exceptional Learners* by E. A. Polloway and J. E. Smith, 1982, Denver: Love. Copyright 1982 by Love Publishing Company. Reprinted by permission.

The *Goldman-Fristoe Test of Articulation* (Goldman & Fristoe, 1986) employs three strategies for eliciting speech sounds. The Sounds-in-Words subtest is a picture-naming task; the student is shown pictures of familiar objects and is asked to name or answer questions about them. The Sounds-in-Sentences subtest is more unusual. It contains two stories that are accompanied by action pictures. The stories include words that have the speech sounds with which children most often have difficulty. The tester reads a story and then asks the student to retell it. The third subtest, Stimulability, is administered last. On this measure, the tester attempts to stimulate the student to produce phonemes that were misarticulated earlier in the test. The student is directed to watch and listen as the tester pronounces the target sound in a syllable, within a word, and in the context of a sentence.

Norm-referenced tests of articulation are usually administered by specially trained professionals such as speech-language pathologists. However, other professionals can collect preliminary data on students' articulation skills with informal procedures. The most common method is observation and analysis of the student's spontaneous speech. Also, any of the strategies used by formal measures can be adapted for informal assessment. For example, the student can be asked to name pictures or objects selected to represent the speech sounds.

Figure 14-3 provides a checklist in which speech sounds are listed in the order that they are typically acquired. The teacher can use this checklist to record observation results or the findings from other informal assessments.

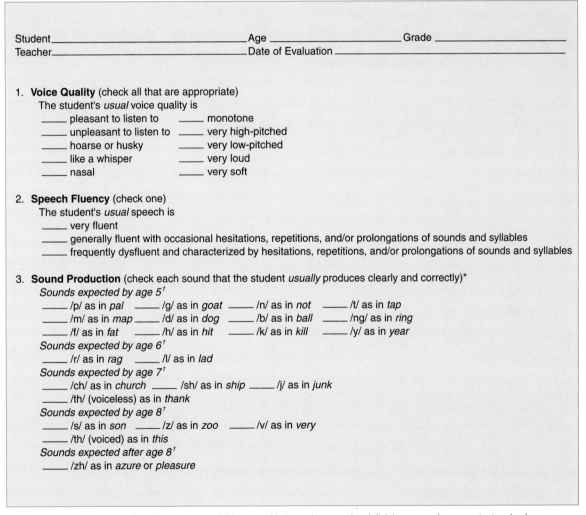

Student_____ Age _____ Grade _____
Teacher_____ Date of Evaluation _____

1. **Voice Quality** (check all that are appropriate)
   The student's *usual* voice quality is
   _____ pleasant to listen to   _____ monotone
   _____ unpleasant to listen to   _____ very high-pitched
   _____ hoarse or husky   _____ very low-pitched
   _____ like a whisper   _____ very loud
   _____ nasal   _____ very soft

2. **Speech Fluency** (check one)
   The student's *usual* speech is
   _____ very fluent
   _____ generally fluent with occasional hesitations, repetitions, and/or prolongations of sounds and syllables
   _____ frequently dysfluent and characterized by hesitations, repetitions, and/or prolongations of sounds and syllables

3. **Sound Production** (check each sound that the student *usually* produces clearly and correctly)*
   Sounds expected by age 5†
   _____ /p/ as in *pal*   _____ /g/ as in *goat* _____ /n/ as in *not*   _____ /t/ as in *tap*
   _____ /m/ as in *map*   _____ /d/ as in *dog*   _____ /b/ as in *ball* _____ /ng/ as in *ring*
   _____ /f/ as in *fat*   _____ /h/ as in *hit*   _____ /k/ as in *kill* _____ /y/ as in *year*
   Sounds expected by age 6†
   _____ /r/ as in *rag*   _____ /l/ as in *lad*
   Sounds expected by age 7†
   _____ /ch/ as in *church* _____ /sh/ as in *ship* _____ /j/ as in *junk*
   _____ /th/ (voiceless) as in *thank*
   Sounds expected by age 8†
   _____ /s/ as in *son*   _____ /z/ as in *zoo*   _____ /v/ as in *very*
   _____ /th/ (voiced) as in *this*
   Sounds expected after age 8†
   _____ /zh/ as in *azure* or *pleasure*

* Only consonant sounds are listed because most children are able to produce vowel and diphthong sounds upon entry to school.
† Age norms derived from Sander (1972).

FIGURE 14-3

Speech Checklist

Note: From *Teaching Special Students in General Education Classrooms* 5/e by Lewis/Doorlag, © 1999. Reprinted by permission of Prentice-Hall, Inc., Upper Saddle River, NJ.

STRATEGIES FOR ASSESSING MORPHOLOGY AND SYNTAX

Morphology and syntax, like phonology, are dimensions of language that relate to form. Morphology is concerned with the smallest meaningful units of language—morphemes—and how these are combined into words. Syntax is the relationship of words in phrases and sentences. Several formal measures of morphology and syntax are available for young children; in normal development, most of the formal features of language are learned during the preschool and early school years. The paragraphs that follow discuss formal measures of morphology and syntax as well as techniques for the analysis of language samples.

Formal Measures

Northwestern Syntax Screening Test (NSST). The *NSST* (Lee, 1971) is designed to identify problems in either receptive or expressive syntax. Syntax, as defined by this test, includes morphology. It is an individual test that is appropriate for young children ages 3-0 to 7-4. Two subtests are included—Receptive and Expressive. On the Receptive subtest, the student is shown a page containing four line drawings. The tester reads a sentence, and the student must select the drawing that represents its meaning. Two sentences are read for each page of four drawings, and the sentences vary in only one grammatical element. For example, the first sentence might be "The dog is *in front of* the couch" and the second "The dog is *on top of* the couch."

On the Expressive subtest, the student looks at two drawings while the tester reads a sentence describing each. Then, for each drawing, the tester asks, "Now, what's this picture?" The student is expected to recall the sentences read by the tester. Again, the sentence pairs differ in only one grammatical element (verb tense, preposition, singular or plural verb, etc.).

Percentile rank scores are available for each subtest. According to the manual, scores at the second to third percentile are considered below average, and children earning such scores "are almost certain to be in need of interventional language teaching" (p. 9).

The *NSST* is a screening test and, thus, its purpose is to identify children in need of further assessment. However, it is best used as an informal measure because of lack of information about technical quality. The manual does not discuss reliability and validity. In addition, the sample used to standardize this measure is inadequate. Only 344 children were included, half of whom were between the ages of 5-0 and 5-11. The children represented only seven schools from "middle-income and upper-middle-income communities" (p. 7).

Test for Auditory Comprehension of Language (3rd ed.) (TACL-3). The purpose of the *TACL-3* (Carrow-Woolfolk, 1999) is assessment of receptive vocabulary and syntax. It is an individual test for ages 3-0 through 9-11, and three subtests are included: Vocabulary, Grammatical Morphemes, and Elaborated Phrases and Sentences. The test format is similar to other measures of receptive language. A page with three full-color drawings is shown to the student, and the student must select the drawing that best represents the meaning of the word or sentence read by the tester.

The *TACL-3* was standardized with a national sample of over 1,000 students selected to represent the U.S. population in terms of gender, race, ethnicity, geographic region, and disability. Several types of scores are available, including standard scores, percentile ranks, and age equivalents.

Carrow Elicited Language Inventory (CELI). The *CELI,* also by Carrow-Woolfolk (1974), is a measure of expressive morphology and syntax for children ages 3-0 to 7-11. It is an individual test with one type of task: the tester reads and the child repeats a sentence. The imitation task was selected because research findings indicate a relationship between the form of children's spontaneous speech and the form of sentences they can imitate.

The 52 sentences on the *CELI* were constructed to assess several different grammatical categories and features: articles, adjectives, nouns, noun plurals, pronouns, verbs, negatives, contractions, adverbs, prepositions, demonstratives, and conjunctions. Percentile ranks are provided for the total test score as well as for each grammatical class. In addition, the student's errors are analyzed by type (substitution, omission, addition, transposition, reversal) and a percentile rank score is determined for each type. A Verb Protocol is available for in-depth analysis of the child's mastery of verb forms. Scoring the *CELI* is time-consuming.

A small, restricted sample from only one city was used to standardize the *CELI*. Standardization took place in 1973 in Houston, Texas, and the sample contained 475 white children "from middle socioeconomic level homes" (p. 8). Reliability and validity were investigated, but the study samples included only 20 to 25 children. For these reasons, the *CELI* is best used as an informal measure of expressive syntax and morphology.

Analysis of Language Samples

Language samples are another method for the assessment of expressive syntax and morphology. A sample of the child's language is elicited, tape recorded, and transcribed. The transcription is then analyzed using one of the methods described in the following paragraphs.

Mean Length of Utterance. The simplest way of analyzing a child's language sample is to compute the mean length of utterance (MLU). A sample of 50 consecutive utterances, at minimum, is needed for this procedure. The professional counts the number of morphemes that the child produced and divides this total by the number of utterances. MLU, according to Wiig and Semel (1984), "correlates positively (.80) with psychological scale values of degree of language development" (p. 370).

Brown (1973) developed a set of procedures for calculating MLU that has been adopted by most language development researchers (Bartel & Bryen, 1982). In Brown's system, analysis begins with the second page of the transcription of the child's language sample. The first 100 utterances are counted, although 50 are sufficient for a preliminary estimate. Inflections such as the possessive *s* and the regular past tense *d* are counted as separate morphemes. Repetitions are not counted; nor are fillers such as "um" and "oh." Compound words are counted as one morpheme, as are diminutives (e.g., *kitty)* and catenatives (e.g., *gonna, wanna).*

According to Brown, these procedures are reasonable only for language samples with mean lengths of utterance up to approximately 4.0. Thus, this technique is most useful for young children and children with serious language disorders.

Developmental Sentence Analysis. Developmental Sentence Analysis (Lee, 1974) is another technique. This is a norm-referenced procedure designed for children ages 2-0 to 6-11. In an interview situation, a clinician elicits a sample of the child's language using stimulus materials such as toys or pictures. The sample is transcribed and analyzed to determine what proportion of the child's utterances are complete sentences. In this system, a complete sentence is defined as a noun and verb in subject-predicate relationship. Thus, "doggie bark" is considered a complete sentence.

Fifty complete, consecutive sentences are needed to use the Developmental Sentence Scoring system. First, each word is categorized by its grammatical type. Lee states that the categories of grammatical forms included are those "showing the most significant developmental progression in children's language" (p. 136). These are:

1. Indefinite pronoun or noun modifier
2. Personal pronoun
3. Main verb
4. Secondary verb
5. Negative
6. Conjunction
7. Interrogative reversal in questions
8. *Wh*-question

A chart is then consulted to assign a point value to each word. Words representing higher developmental status receive higher point values. For example, among personal pronouns, first- and second-person pronouns such as *I* and *you* receive 1 point, third person pronouns such as *he* and *she* receive 2 points, and plurals such as *we* receive 3 points. Point values range from 1 to 8.

The total number of points assigned to words in the sample of sentences is determined and then divided by the number of sentences (50) to produce the Developmental Sentence Score (DSS). This score can be expressed as a percentile rank. A chart is provided for determining where the score falls in relation to the 10th, 25th, 50th, 75th, and 90th percentiles for each 6-month age group between ages 2-0 and 6-6. The norms for this procedure were derived using a sample of 200 children. Thus, there were only 20 boys and 20 girls at each age level. The children were from middle-class, monolingual homes in four states. Split-half reliability was reported as .73 over all ages, but coefficients fell in the .50's for children aged 2, 3, and 4. No information is provided about concurrent validity.

Because norms are based on a limited sample, reliability is low for very young children, and validity is not established, this technique is best viewed as an informal assessment strategy.

Language Sampling, Analysis, and Training (3rd ed.) (LSAT-3).

The *LSAT-3* (Tyack & Venable, 1999) is a similar approach to the analysis of children's expressive oral language. A sample of at least 100 sentences is elicited from the child and then transcribed. The number of words and the number of morphemes are counted for each sentence in order to determine the word-morpheme index. Then the child's utterances are analyzed according to several types of syntactical constructions: noun phrases, verb phrases, simple sentences, complex sentences, and questions and negatives. The results provide detailed information about the oral language needs of the child in relation to expressive morphology and syntax.

STRATEGIES FOR ASSESSING SEMANTICS AND PRAGMATICS

Semantics is concerned with the meaning of language. A variety of tests and other procedures are available to assess students' comprehension of language content and production of meaningful discourse. In contrast, pragmatics is concerned with language use or, in the words of Wiig and Semel (1984), language in a communicative context. Meaning is one aspect of pragmatics, but the major focus is the speaker's intent and the way that language is used to fulfill that intent.

Assessment of Language Meaning

Formal measures are available to assess both receptive and expressive semantics skills. The most typical test format for receptive measures is a picture-identification task. The tester reads a word or a sentence, and the student selects from several pictures the one that best illustrates the meaning of the word or sentence. The best-known measure of receptive semantics is the *Peabody Picture Vocabulary Test, Third Edition* (Dunn & Dunn, 1997), which is described in the next sections along with the *Expressive Vocabulary Test* (Williams, 1997) and the *Comprehensive Receptive and Expressive Vocabulary Test* (Wallace & Hammill, 1994). Strategies for informal assessment are also discussed.

Peabody Picture Vocabulary Test, Third Edition (PPVT-III).

The *PPVT-III* is an individual test of receptive vocabulary designed for ages 2-6 through 90+. Two forms of the test are available, and administration typically requires less than 15 minutes. The test task remains the same throughout the *PPVT-III*. The student is shown a page containing four line drawings. The tester reads a word, and the student points to or says the number of the drawing that represents that word.

The *PPVT-III* includes four training items; Figure 14–4 shows the stimulus pictures for one of these items. In presenting this item, the tester says, "Put your finger on *ball.*" Once the tester is sure that the student understands the test task, these directions can be varied; for example, the manual recommends substitutions such as "Show me _____" or "What number is _____ ?" The *PPVT-III* contains 204 test items arranged in 17 sets of 12 each. The tester consults the protocol for a suggested starting point, then begins administration with the first item in the suggested set. The entire set is administered. A basal set is achieved when the student makes no more than one error in the 12-item set. The ceiling set is reached when there are eight or more errors in the 12-item set.

The *PPVT-III* is not divided into subtests, and only age norms are available. One result is obtained: an index of total test performance. Several types of scores are used to report that result: standard score, percentile rank, stanine, and age equivalent. The student's score is plotted on a

FIGURE 14-4

Sample Training Item from the *Peabody Picture Vocabulary Test-III*

Note: From *Peabody Picture Vocabulary Test, Third Edition* by L. M. Dunn and L. M. Dunn, 1997, Circle Pines, MN: American Guidance Service. Copyright 1997 by Lloyd M. Dunn, Leota M. Dunn, and Douglas M. Dunn. Reprinted by permission.

profile on the record form, and a confidence interval is constructed around the score.

The 1997 edition of the *Peabody Picture Vocabulary Test* was standardized with 2,000 students ages 2 to 19 and 725 adults. The sample appears to resemble the U.S. population in terms of geographic region, educational level (for students, that of their parents), and race or ethnic group. Students with disabilities are included in the norm group in approximately the same proportion as in the total school population; gifted students are somewhat underrepresented. The *PPVT-III* manual notes that its sample "did not include persons who showed evidence of uncorrected vision or hearing loss, or who had limited proficiency in English" (p. 4). Reliability of the *PPVT-III* appears adequate. In relation to validity, the manual provides evidence that results of the *PPVT-III* are related to those of oral language measures and tests of intellectual performance.

The *PPVT-III* is a quick, easy-to-administer measure of receptive vocabulary. However, its manual contends that it is both an achievement test and a scholastic aptitude test. It is considered a test of achievement because it measures acquisition of English vocabulary, and an aptitude test because it assesses verbal skills, one of the components of many tests of intelligence. In the manual for the second edition of the *PPVT,* Dunn and Dunn (1981) observed, "It is *not,* however, a comprehensive test of general intelligence" (p. 2). In the current manual, these authors suggest that the *PPVT-III* is a **"screening test of intellectual functioning"** (p. 54). The *PPVT-III* is best used as a screening tool to measure one of the many dimensions of oral language development, receptive vocabulary.

Expressive Vocabulary Test (EVT). The *EVT* is an individual test of expressive vocabulary for ages 2-6 through 90+. Like the *PPVT-III,* it measures only one aspect of oral language. However, the *EVT* is composed of two types of test tasks, rather than one: labeling and synonyms. In the labeling items, students must look at a picture and tell what they see; only one-word responses are acceptable. In the synonym items, the tester reads a word and the student must say a word that means the same.

On the *EVT,* children younger than age 5 begin in the labeling portion of the test—items 1–38. Individuals age 5 and above begin the *EVT* in the synonym section—items 39–190—although it may be necessary to administer labeling items to obtain a basal. A basal is five correct responses in a row and a ceiling is five incorrect responses in a row. As on the *PPVT-III,* one overall result is obtained. *EVT* total test performance can be expressed as a standard score, percentile rank, stanine, and age equivalent. Results can also be plotted on a profile and compared with those of the *PPVT-III,* if there is interest in contrasting the student's receptive and expressive language skills.

Comprehensive Receptive and Expressive Vocabulary Test (CREVT). The *CREVT* is an interesting measure for two reasons. First, it is one of the few tests that assesses both receptive and expressive semantics. Second, it is available in two formats: the standard format (Wallace & Hammill, 1994) and a computerized format (Wallace & Hammill, 1997).

The *CREVT* is designed for students ages 4-0 to 17-11. It contains two subtests: Receptive Vocabulary and Expressive Vocabulary. On Receptive Vocabulary, the student looks at a set of six color photographs and points to the one that best depicts the word spoken by the examiner. On Expressive Vocabulary, the examiner says a word and the student must tell what it means. On the computer-assisted version of the *CREVT,* the student responds to receptive items directly on the computer. However, the examiner must score the student's responses to expressive items, then enter those scores into the computer program.

Results are available on the *CREVT* for Receptive Vocabulary, Expressive Vocabulary, and General Vocabulary (a total test score). These results include standard scores, percentile ranks, and age equivalents. Scores are calculated automatically on the computerized version of the *CREVT* and a detailed report can be printed.

Informal Assessment Strategies. It is also possible to use informal procedures to evaluate a student's ability to comprehend and produce meaningful language. Any of the tasks used on formal tests could be adapted for this purpose. For example, if receptive vocabulary is the area of interest, the teacher can present a set of pictures or objects, name one, and direct the child to point to it. Or the child can be asked to demonstrate the meaning of action words ("Show me *jump*") or prepositions ("Put the apple in *front* of the doll"). If expressive semantics is the concern, the student can be asked to label pictures or objects, define words, use words in sentences, provide synonyms or antonyms, describe objects or events, or tell a story.

Figure 14–5 presents a checklist for recording information about vocabulary development. It lists 38 types of vocabulary—body parts, clothing, classroom objects, and so forth—and two of the major language dimensions: identification (reception) and production. In using this form, it would be helpful to generate lists of words for each vocabulary type. These lists would vary from child to child due to differences in age, gender, interests, and environments. Once this checklist is expanded, it could form the basis for a series of observations of the student's language behavior. It could also provide the professional with a structure for designing a set of informal inventories to learn more about the student's receptive and expressive vocabulary.

Assessment of Language Use

Pragmatics refers to the way that language is used for communication in different situations. As language skills develop, children learn to modify their choice of words and grammatical structures according to the message they intend to convey and the situation in which the communication takes place. The context of the speech act is an important variable that is determined by several factors:

1. The social setting and occasion of the interaction
2. The location of the interaction
3. The characteristics of the participants (gender, race, ethnicity, etc.) in the interaction
4. The topic and purpose of the interaction
5. The spatial deployment of the participants (face-to-face, at a distance, nonvisible) in the interaction
6. The role or intent of the speaker (Wiig & Semel, 1984, p. 57)

The speaker's intent influences the content and form of language and the way the message is delivered. There are several different purposes of communication, and one system for categorizing these has been proposed by Wells (1973). According to Wiig and Semel (1984), this system includes five distinct language uses:

- *Ritualizing*. The ritualized use of language in social situations, as in greetings, farewells, introductions, turn taking, responses to requests, and so forth.
- *Informing*. The use of language to give or request information.
- *Controlling*. The use of language to control or influence the actions of the listener.
- *Feeling*. The use of language to express feelings or to respond to feelings or attitudes expressed by others.
- *Imagining*. The use of language to create an imaginary situation, as in storytelling, role playing, speculation, or the creation of fantasies.

By the end of the elementary grades, students are expected to comprehend the different functions of language and use language appropriately to accomplish each of these purposes (Wiig & Semel, 1984). As with other dimensions of language, competence in pragmatics develops over time. Findings from research by Wiig (1982b) and others suggest that children around the age of 6 communicate from a self-oriented perspective. However, by age 12, students adapt to the listener's needs. They are able to alter expectations, negotiate, state reasons and justifications, and communicate bad news so that its impact is softened.

Let's Talk Inventory for Children. The *Let's Talk Inventory for Children* (Bray & Wiig, 1987) is one of the few formal tools available for the assessment of pragmatic competence. It is an individual measure for ages 4 to 8. The assessment task is interesting. The student is shown a picture that illustrates a communication situation. Some pictures show peer interactions, others show interactions between a child and adult. A short narrative is read to the student describing the situation and the intent of the speaker. The student's task

Basic Vocabulary/Semantics	Identifies				Produces		
	Identifies persons, things or events labeled	Comprehends words in sentences in familiar contexts	Comprehends words in sentences in unfamiliar contexts	Labels persons, things or events	Uses words in sentences in familiar contexts	Uses words in sentences in unfamiliar contexts	
1. Body Parts							
2. Clothing							
3. Classroom Objects							
4. Action Verbs							
5. Verb Tasks							
6. Animals and Insects							
7. Outdoor Words							
8. Family Members							
9. Home Objects							
10. Meals							
11. Food and Drink							
12. Colors							
13. Adverbs							
14. Occupations							
15. Community							
16. Grooming Objects							
17. Vehicles							
18. Money							
19. Gender							
20. School							
21. Playthings							
22. Containers							
23. Days of the Week							
24. Months							
25. Emotions							
26. Numbers							
27. Celebrations and Holidays							
28. Spatial Concepts							
29. Quantitative Concepts							
30. Temporal Concepts							
31. Shapes							
32. Greetings and Polite Terms							
33. Opposites							
34. Materials							
35. Music							
36. Tools							
37. Categories							
38. Verbs of the Senses							

FIGURE 14-5

Vocabulary Checklist

Note: From "Language" (p. 24) by T. Serpiglia in *Diagnosing Basic Skills* by K. W. Howell and J. S. Kaplan, 1980, New York: Merrill/Macmillan. Copyright 1980 by Macmillan Publishing Company. Reprinted by permission.

is to formulate a speech act that is appropriate to the context, the audience, and the stated communicative intent.

Items are available to assess four of the major functions of language: ritualizing, informing, controlling, and feeling. The imagining function is not assessed, but the format of the test is role playing, a communication strategy that requires use of the imagining function. Items are also provided to assess receptive pragmatics, if the student experiences difficulty with the expressive tasks.

***Test of Pragmatic Skills* (rev. ed.).** Shulman's (1986) *Test of Pragmatic Skills* (rev. ed.) is designed for students ages 3 to 8. The test tasks are four guided play interactions in which the tester follows a script to elicit responses from the child. For example, in the first interaction, the student and tester use puppets to converse about favorite television shows. The test probes 10 types of communicative intents: requesting information, requesting action, rejection/denial, naming/labeling, answering/responding, informing, reasoning, summoning/calling, greeting, and closing conversation.

Test of Pragmatic Language. This measure by Phelps-Terasaki and Phelps-Gunn (1992) provides norms for students ages 5-0 to 13-11. It is designed to assess several aspects of pragmatic language including the effects of context variables (setting, event, and audience) and message variables (topic and purpose). The communication purposes included in the model underlying the *TOPL* are requesting, informing, regulating, expressing, ritualizing, and organizing.

The test tasks are designed to elicit language from the student; expressive skills are emphasized. On most items, the tester shows the student a picture and then asks a question about the communication situation it depicts. Although the *TOPL* samples several types of pragmatic language skills, the only results it provides are an overall standard score and percentile rank.

Informal Assessment Strategies. Informal strategies can also be used to investigate pragmatic performance. Mercer and Mercer (1998) suggest that

a spontaneous sample of the student's speech can be analyzed to determine the types of language functions the student uses. Videotaping is the best way to record the language sample, because it allows the professional to study the situation in which the communication occurred. If this is not possible, the student can be audiotaped while an observer records the events that occur before and after each speech act. The professional evaluates each utterance in relation to the events that preceded and followed it and then assigns the utterance to a function category.

There are several other strategies for informal assessment of pragmatic competence. Students can be observed as they engage in conversational interactions with peers and adults, or the teacher can set up a role-playing situation to evaluate specific types of communications. For example, if observations reveal that a student rarely uses language for the ritualizing function, the student could be asked to participate in role plays such as meeting a friend on the way to school, leaving a party, and so on. Receptive skills can be probed with videotapes or pictures that present conversational interactions. For example, if the controlling function of language is of interest, the teacher could show a picture of two children, one of whom is playing with a toy truck. The student would then be asked to select the more appropriate request: "Give me that truck!" or "May I please play with the truck a little while?"

Figure 14–6 presents a checklist (Wiig, 1982b) designed to record the pragmatics performance of preadolescents and adolescents. It covers four language functions, and several language behaviors are listed for each of the functions. For example, behaviors such as "Introduces him/herself appropriately" are included under the ritualizing function. The student is rated according to how often he or she engages in each language behavior. In addition, the professional can record the quality of the speech acts observed: informal, formal, direct, or indirect. This checklist is used to record results of observations and can also serve as a guide for planning further assessment of expressive pragmatics.

COMMUNICATION ACTS	RATINGS					QUALITY
	Never	Seldom	Sometimes	Often	Always	

COMMUNICATION ACTS	Never	Seldom	Sometimes	Often	Always	QUALITY
Ritualizing						
1. Greets others appropriately	1	2	3	4	5	
2. Introduces him/herself appropriately	1	2	3	4	5	
3. Introduces people to each other appropriately	1	2	3	4	5	
4. Greets others appropriately when telephoning	1	2	3	4	5	
5. Introduces him/herself appropriately when telephoning	1	2	3	4	5	
6. Asks for persons appropriately when telephoning	1	2	3	4	5	
7. Says farewell appropriately	1	2	3	4	5	
8. Asks others to repeat appropriately	1	2	3	4	5	
9. Gives name (first and last) on request	1	2	3	4	5	
10. Gives address (number, street, town, etc.) on request	1	2	3	4	5	
11. Gives telephone number on request	1	2	3	4	5	
Informing						
1. Asks others appropriately for name	1	2	3	4	5	
2. Asks others appropriately for address	1	2	3	4	5	
3. Asks others appropriately for telephone number	1	2	3	4	5	
4. Asks others appropriately for the location of belongings and necessities	1	2	3	4	5	
5. Asks others appropriately for the location of events	1	2	3	4	5	
6. Responds appropriately to requests for the location of events	1	2	3	4	5	
7. Asks others appropriately for the time of events	1	2	3	4	5	
8. Responds appropriately to requests for the time of events	1	2	3	4	5	
9. Asks others appropriately for preferences or wants	1	2	3	4	5	
10. Responds appropriately to requests for preferences or wants	1	2	3	4	5	
11. Tells others realistically about abilities	1	2	3	4	5	
12. Tells realistically about the levels of various abilities	1	2	3	4	5	
13. Asks appropriately for information by telephone	1	2	3	4	5	
14. Asks appropriately for permission to leave messages	1	2	3	4	5	
15. Tells appropriately who a message is for	1	2	3	4	5	
16. Leaves appropriately expressed messages	1	2	3	4	5	

Name _____ Birth Date _____ Sex _____
Address _____
Classroom _____ Teacher _____ Date _____
Other Information _____

FIGURE 14-6

Communication Skills Checklist

Note: From *Let's Talk: Developing Prosocial Communication Skills* (pp.23–25) by E. H. Wiig, 1982. Reprinted by permission of author.

COMMUNICATION ACTS	RATINGS					QUALITY
	Never	Seldom	Sometimes	Often	Always	

Controlling

	Never	Seldom	Sometimes	Often	Always
1. Suggests places for meetings appropriately	1	2	3	4	5
2. Suggests names for meetings appropriately	1	2	3	4	5
3. Asks appropriately for permission	1	2	3	4	5
4. Asks appropriately for reasons	1	2	3	4	5
5. Tells reasons appropriately	1	2	3	4	5
6. Asks appropriately for favors	1	2	3	4	5
7. Responds appropriately to request for favors:					
a. Accepts and carries out	1	2	3	4	5
b. Evades or delays	1	2	3	4	5
c. Rejects	1	2	3	4	5
8. Offers assistance appropriately	1	2	3	4	5
9. Makes complaints appropriately	1	2	3	4	5
10. Responds to complaints appropriately					
a. Accepts blame and suggests action	1	2	3	4	5
b. Evades or refers	1	2	3	4	5
c. Rejects blame	1	2	3	4	5
11. Asks for intentions appropriately	1	2	3	4	5
12. Responds appropriately to requests for intentions	1	2	3	4	5
13. Asks to discontinue actions appropriately	1	2	3	4	5
14. Asks appropriately for terms of contract:					
a. Pay	1	2	3	4	5
b. Work hours	1	2	3	4	5
c. Vacations, etc.	1	2	3	4	5
d. Other	1	2	3	4	5
15. Asks appropriately for changes in contractual terms:					
a. Pay	1	2	3	4	5
b. Work hours	1	2	3	4	5
c. Vacations, etc.	1	2	3	4	5
d. Other	1	2	3	4	5

Feelings

	Never	Seldom	Sometimes	Often	Always
1. Expresses appreciation appropriately	1	2	3	4	5
2. Apologizes appropriately	1	2	3	4	5
3. Expresses agreement appropriately	1	2	3	4	5
4. Expresses disagreement appropriately	1	2	3	4	5
5. Expresses support appropriately	1	2	3	4	5
6. Compliments appropriately	1	2	3	4	5
7. Expresses affection appropriately	1	2	3	4	5
8. Expresses positive feelings and attitudes appropriately	1	2	3	4	5
9. Expresses negative feelings and attitudes appropriately	1	2	3	4	5

ASSESSING STUDENTS WHO SPEAK NONSTANDARD ENGLISH

Not all persons who speak English pronounce the speech sounds in the same way; nor do they use the same syntax, morphology, and vocabulary. The variations that occur within languages are called dialects, and there are many dialects of English. For example, the English spoken in Great Britain is not the same as that spoken in America or in Australia. Within the United States, there are regional variations. Words are pronounced differently in Maine, New York, and Louisiana, and variations occur in grammatical structure and word meaning. In addition, some American English dialects are related to population characteristics rather than to geographic region. Examples are Black English and the English spoken by some persons whose first language is Spanish.

Many variations of English are spoken in the United States, and standard American English is only one. Standard American English is also referred to as Mainstream American English (Willis, 1998). Other dialects should be considered different from, but not inferior to, standard English. This is the issue of language difference versus language deficit (Polloway & Smith, 1982; Winzer & Mazurek, 1998). The deficit position holds that any dialect other than standard English is a restricted code and therefore represents a deficit; it is substandard, rather than nonstandard, English. The difference position, based primarily on studies of Black English, maintains that nonstandard English is a complete linguistic system, different from, but not inferior to, the standard dialect. Most educators today support the difference position. As Taylor (1990) comments, "No dialect is intrinsically a better way of speaking the language than any other dialect" (p. 131).

The language that a child or adult uses for communication is influenced by several factors. Wiig and Semel (1984) suggest that the major influences include:

- First language community and culture
- Race and ethnicity
- Geographic region
- Social class, education, and occupation
- Age
- Gender
- Peer group association and identification
- Situation-context (pp. 54–57)

The last factor, situation-context, refers to the setting in which a particular communication takes place. Speakers alter their language to fit the communicative context. This is called style or code switching, and bidialectical speakers are able to change from one dialect to another depending upon the situation, setting, and audience of the communication. For example, a person who speaks nonstandard English in one context (e.g., a conversation with a close friend) may speak standard English in another (e.g., a job interview) (Cohen & Plaskon, 1980).

In discussing the possible goals of language instruction for nonstandard English speakers, Cohen and Plaskon review three alternatives: eradication of the nonstandard dialect, complete acceptance of the nonstandard dialect, and bidialectalism. Of these options, the last is most commonly accepted. Teaching students to speak standard English while maintaining their competence in the original dialect allows them to meet linguistic demands in a variety of communication settings.

Dialectical Differences

Dialects differ along the major dimensions of language: phonology, morphology, syntax, semantics, and pragmatics. However, the areas of dialectical difference that have been studied most extensively are phonological differences and variations in morphology and syntax.

Black English is a dialect spoken by African Americans in large urban centers (Polloway & Smith, 1982). There are two recognized variations of Black English: standard Black English, used by educated African Americans for interpersonal communications; and Black English vernacular, or Ebonics, spoken primarily by working-class people (Taylor, 1990; Wiig & Semel, 1984). Although there are systematic differences between Black English and standard English, Wiig and Semel point out that "the overwhelming majority of utterances in Black English conform with the linguistic rules of Standard English" (p. 55).

Pronunciation of speech sounds is one area of difference. Engquist (1974) describes the most common phonological variations in Black English:

1. Softening of the *r* sound (e.g., sister/sistah, poor/po', Carter/Cahtuh).
2. Lessening of the *l* sound (e.g., help/hep, all/awe, tool/too).
3. Weakening of final consonants in clusters (e.g., past/pass, hold/hol, bent/ben).
4. Specific sound substitutions (e.g., *f* for *th,* as in mouth/mouf; *d* for *th,* as in this/dis; *i* for *e,* as in pen/pin; *ah* for *i,* as in I/ah). (as cited in Polloway & Smith, 1982, pp. 72–73)

Some phonological characteristics of Black English have morphological consequences. According to Bartel, Grill, and Bryen (1973), the most common morphological variations involve omissions of the final sounds of words. Final sounds are omitted in verbs (present, past, and future tenses), possessives, and plurals. For instance, when final /t/ and /d/ sounds are omitted, past tense verbs sound like present tense verbs ("pass" for "passed") (Cohen & Plaskon, 1980). When the final /l/ sound is omitted, future tense sounds like present ("she" for "she'll"). When the final /s/ or /z/ sound is omitted, singular verbs sound like plural verbs ("hit" for "hits"), and plural nouns sound like singular nouns ("cent" for "cents").

In Black English, variations occur in all parts of speech, but most often in verbs. Use of the verb *to be* in Black English is quite different from standard English. For example, the copula may be omitted (e.g., "He tired") or *be* used in place of other verb forms (e.g., "They always *be* messing around") (Ruddell, 1974).

Dialectical differences also occur in English speakers whose first language is Spanish. English is influenced by the first language, and several phonological, morphological, and syntactical variations result. The speech sounds in Spanish are not the same as those in English. Spanish has 18 consonant and 5 vowel sounds; English has 24 consonant and 12 to 14 vowel sounds (Merino, 1992). For example, Spanish does not have the vowel sounds in *pig, fat,* or *sun* (Wiig, 1982a). Thus, when Spanish-speakers learn English, they substitute phonemes they can pronounce for those not in their speech sound repertoire. For example, "chip" is pronounced "cheap," and "vat" is pronounced "bat" (Taylor, 1990).

Similarly, the morphology, syntax, and semantics of the Spanish language may interfere with English expression. A word or phrase in one language may convey an entirely different meaning when translated into another. Condon, Peters, and Sueiro-Ross (1979) cite these examples from Lado (1968):

- The Spanish compliment "Qué grueso estás," which is translated literally as "how fat you are," becomes an insult in English.
- The use of the name "Jesús" for a boy is quite common in Hispanic society, but not in the Anglo-Saxon community, where it is regarded as inappropriate, if not sacrilegious.
- To be "informal" in Spanish is "to be neglectful," but to be so in English simply conveys the notion of "casual" behavior. (Condon, Peters, & Sueiro-Ross, 1979, p. 82)

Word order and vocabulary differences between the two languages may also have an influence. For example, a student whose first language is Spanish might say, "The car red is mine" (rather than "The red car is mine") or "I have thirst" (rather than "I am thirsty") (Wiig, 1982a). Descriptions of some of the syntactical variations of Spanish-influenced English are provided in Table 14–3. Information is available about the characteristics of other, less common dialectical variations of English. Interested readers should refer to Wiig and Semel (1984) for descriptions of Appalachian English and the Southern White dialect, to Adler and Birdsong (1983) for the phonological characteristics of Mountain English, and to Cheng (1987) for a discussion of the influences of the Asian languages on English.

Assessment Strategies

Dialect must be considered in the assessment of oral language. A dialect is not a language disorder, but it can be mistaken for one if the professional conducting the assessment does not recognize its influence on receptive and expressive language. Terrell and Terrell (1983) discuss three types of errors that can occur if the role of dialect is not well understood. First, professionals can assume that all students from diverse groups are

TABLE 14-3
Syntactical Characteristics of Spanish-Influenced English

FEATURES	ENVIRONMENTS	EXAMPLES
Forms of *to be*	Absent in present progressive	He getting hungry (He is getting hungry)
Pronouns	Absent as subjects of sentences when subject obvious from preceding sentence	Carol left yesterday. I think is coming back tomorrow (Carol left yesterday. I think she is coming back tomorrow)
Third person (*-s*)	Absent in third person verb agreements	He talk fast (He talks fast)
Past (*-ed*)	Absent in past tense inflections	He walk fast yesterday (He walked fast yesterday)
Go with *to*	Future markings	He go to see the game tomorrow (He is going to see the game tomorrow)
No or *don't*	Imperatives	No do that (Don't do that)
The for possessive pronoun	With body parts	I hurt the finger (I hurt my finger)
Present tense markings	Progressive environments	I think he come soon (I think he is coming soon)
Locative adverbs	Placed near verb	I think he putting down the rifle (I think he is putting the rifle down)

Note: From "Language and Communication Differences" (p. 146) by O. L. Taylor, in *Human Communication Disorders* (3rd ed.) by G. H. Shames and E. H. Wiig (Eds.), 1990, New York: Merrill/Macmillan. Copyright 1990 by Macmillan Publishing Company. Reprinted by permission.

normal dialect speakers and thus fail to assess their language competence. Second, if students are assessed, professionals can overcompensate for dialect and assume that true disorders are dialectical characteristics. Third, professionals can undercompensate for dialect and mistake dialectical differences for language disorders.

Dialect is a concern in the assessment of skills other than oral language. Adler and Birdsong (1983), in their discussion of bias in standardized testing, point out the effects of dialect on students' performance on measures of auditory discrimination. For example, on the *Auditory Discrimination Test* by Wepman (1975), Adler and Birdsong identify six pairs of words that may sound alike to children who speak dialects (e.g., "tub/tug" and "pen/pin"). This is a serious problem. On the second edition of the *Auditory Discrimination Test* (Reynolds, 1987), a 7-year-old making six errors scores at the 16th percentile.

Dialectical differences also affect performance of academic skills. Variations in the pro-

nunciation of phonemes may result in what appear to be decoding errors in reading. Written language may be affected, too. If students spell words as they pronounce them, their spelling will not conform to standard English expectations. Likewise, dialectical variations in morphology, syntax, and semantics can result in compositions that contain nonstandard English sentences and paragraphs.

Unfortunately, there are no widely accepted standardized techniques for the assessment of language competence in students who speak dialects. Terrell and Terrell (1983) observe that "the development of dialect-sensitive or culture-fair language tests has not kept pace with the development of testing materials designed to assess the speech and language of standard-English speakers" (p. 3). This presents a major obstacle to the responsible professional. Whether a student speaks a dialect must be established in assessment. It cannot be assumed because of some ethnic, cultural, or social characteristic.

One strategy for the assessment of speakers of dialects is to rely on informal procedures. Leonard and Weiss (1983) recommend the collection of spontaneous speech samples in naturalistic settings; these samples are analyzed for instances of dialectical usage. However, in some cases, dialectical variations are similar to the speech produced by young, normally developing children and older children with language disorders. For example, both these children and persons who speak Black English may omit -s endings on possessives and plurals. Thus, it is most productive to concentrate on dialectical variations that are different from the variations that occur in normal development.

Sentence repetition is another useful informal technique (Adler & Birdsong, 1983). Sentence repetition tasks are based on the assumption that when children are asked to repeat a sentence, they will reconstruct the sentence and say it in their own dialect. Adler and Birdsong (1983) also suggest strategies for determining whether a particular utterance is nonstandard (dialectical) or substandard (an error). One approach is to interview other children who speak the dialect. If a significant number of children (e.g., 50%) use the linguistic pattern, it can be assumed to be part of the dialect.

Once the characteristics of the student's dialectical language have been established, it is possible to begin selecting tools for assessment. This process must take into account the possibility of bias. Taylor and Payne (1983) suggest that the language characteristics of individual test items be analyzed. Such an analysis would take into account the language characteristics of each test item, in relation to Standard English and the dialect of the student. In many cases, items will be answered in one way if the rules of standard English are followed and in another way (that would be scored as incorrect) if the rules of the nonstandard dialect are followed.

When tests contain such items, professionals face a limited number of options. The best solution is to eliminate the test from the battery and substitute another, more appropriate test. If a better measure is not available, the test can still be eliminated and informal procedures used in its place. Sometimes, however, comparative data are needed and informal procedures will not suffice. In such cases, there are two legitimate courses of action. First, the test can be renormed with members of the student's language group (Adler & Birdsong, 1983; Taylor & Payne, 1983). This is an expensive and impractical option unless a large number of students need revised norms. The second approach is to administer the test in the standard fashion and report two types of results: the student's score in relation to test norms and the expectations for standard English, and an alternate score in which dialectical responses (if correct according to the rules of the dialect) are scored as correct. Like all alternate scores, these must be interpreted with caution. However, by using this technique, the characteristics of the student's language are considered rather than ignored, and the student is not penalized for language differences. In addition, some information is produced about the student's relative proficiency in standard English and the dialect.

ASSESSING STUDENTS WHO SPEAK LANGUAGES OTHER THAN ENGLISH

The number of persons in the United States who speak languages other than English at home exceeds 30 million (Schmidt, 1992). The number of school-aged children with limited proficiency in the English language is also increasing (Winzer & Mazurek, 1998). In fact, the growth rate for this group is more rapid than that of the general school population (Baca & Almanza, 1991). The great majority of these students speak Spanish as their first language; Gollnick and Chinn (1991) report that "the U.S. Hispanic population (not including Puerto Rico) surpassed the 20-million mark in 1989" (p. 1). Among the other languages represented are Chinese, Filipino, French, German, Greek, Italian, Navajo, Polish, Portuguese, and Vietnamese.

Assessment of students who speak languages other than English has two purposes. The first is determination of the student's language proficiency, both in the first language (L1) and in English, the language of the school. With most students, English is the second language (L2), although English can be the third or even fourth language of the child. Assessment of language proficiency provides professionals with information about the student's relative competence in each language, so that the language or languages of assessment can be determined. Once this decision is made, assessment continues to explore the need for educational intervention.

With this population, intervention can take several forms, and one of the most common is bilingual education. Bilingual education programs are designed primarily for students with limited English proficiency (LEP), that is, for those who are English language learners. Bergin (1980) describes the major components of bilingual instructional programs:

- Native language instruction
- English as a second language (ESL)
- Cultural heritage
- Content area instruction (p. 21)

Several different models are used in the United States to deliver bilingual education (Baca, 1998; Gollnick & Chinn, 1990). In transitional models, first language instruction is provided only as a transition to English; when English skills have been developed, English becomes the language of instruction. Full bilingual models, in contrast, attempt to develop competency in both languages. Instruction takes place in the first language and in English for all school subjects throughout the program.

The development and maintenance of both languages has several advantages. Bilingualism itself is an advantage. The ability to communicate in more than one language is a strength that the regular curriculum of secondary schools attempts to impart to monolingual students via foreign language instruction. In addition, Cummins (1981, 1983) suggests that first and second language academic skills are interdependent. This is the theory of common underlying proficiency. Although the surface features of the first and second languages may differ, the cognitive and academic skills learned in one language will transfer to another language. Cummins (1983) explains this concept in relation to a Spanish-English bilingual program:

> Spanish instruction which develops first-language reading skills for Spanish-speaking students is not just developing *Spanish* skills, but also a deeper conceptual and linguistic proficiency which is strongly related to the development of *English* literacy and general academic skills. (p. 376)

When students are identified as both limited in English proficiency *and* disabled, decisions about appropriate services become more complex. In some cases, the student will receive both bilingual and special education services. In other cases, a bilingual special education program may be available. There are a number of ways that special and bilingual services can be combined: bilingual education with support from special education, special education with bilingual support services, special education with a bilingual teacher, and special education with a bilingual aide, volunteer, or peer tutor (Plata, 1982; Yates & Ortiz, 1998).

Language Proficiency

Payan (1989) defines language proficiency as:

> the degree to which the student exhibits control over the use of language, including the measurement of *expressive* and *receptive* language skills in the areas of phonology, syntax, vocabulary, and semantics and including the area of pragmatics or language use within various domains or social circumstances. (p. 127)

Proficiency in one language is judged independently from proficiency in other languages. It is possible for students to show proficiency in both the first language (L1) and English (L2), in L1 but not in L2, or in L2 but not in L1. Language proficiency is not a simple, unitary skill. According to Cummins (1981), there are two major dimensions of language proficiency. Basic interpersonal communication skills (BICS) are the spoken skills of the language community and are acquired by almost all community members. Cognitive/academic language proficiency (CALP), in contrast, is the set of language skills needed to function in the academic environment of school.

In second language learning, proficiency in basic interpersonal communication is acquired much more quickly than is cognitive/academic proficiency (Cummins, 1982). In face-to-face interpersonal communications, a variety of extralingual supports are available to assist communication: intonation, facial expression, loudness of voice, gestures, body language, and so forth. The communication is context-embedded. In the classroom, there are fewer extralingual cues, making the communication situation more context-reduced.

These differences have important implications for assessment. Evidence of competence in basic communication skills does not guarantee that the student will also speak and understand the language necessary for classroom communications. Mercer (1983) contends that "a thorough linguistic assessment of the bilingual student requires assessment of basic interpersonal communication skills in *both* languages and cognitive/academic skills in *both* languages" (p. 49).

Current practices in the assessment of language proficiency include two major steps. The home language is determined through a language background questionnaire or interview, and the student's skills are assessed with one of the available language proficiency measures (Gonzalez, Brusca-Vega, & Yawkey, 1997). The language background questionnaire or interview is used to gather information from the child's parents about which language or languages are spoken in the home. If a language other than English is spoken, this alerts the school that the student *may* also speak this language. As Payan (1989) comments, "The types of questions commonly presented in language background questionnaires will not directly identify the language the child commands readily but will describe the child's linguistic environment, the amount of language input received, and impressions of the child's communicative abilities" (p. 132).

To determine the child's language proficiency, it is necessary to assess the child. There are several measures available for this purpose, as Table 14–4 illustrates. However, with few exceptions, these measures are designed for students whose first language is Spanish. Although Spanish-speakers are the largest language minority group in the United States, many professionals are also interested in assessing the language proficiency of students who speak languages other than Spanish. As Lynch and Lewis (1987) observed, a major problem in assessment is "the lack of appropriate measures in many of the languages spoken by students in schools today; particular difficulties arise with the Pan-Asian group" (p. 404).

Cheng (1987) presents several informal tools for assessing the oral language skills of Asian students. In addition, she lists a number of language proficiency tests appropriate for this population that are available from school districts and other noncommercial sources. Roussel (1991) also provides information on language assessment tools for speakers of languages other than English; Langdon (1992) describes measures of language proficiency for speakers of Spanish.

Most of the instruments for assessing language proficiency in Spanish and English are designed to determine the student's dominant language. The dominant language (also called the primary language) is the language in which the student is most proficient. A more complex method of categorizing language proficiency was recommended in the *Lau Remedies* (Office for Civil Rights, 1975). The *Lau Remedies* were proposed by a federal task force established in response to the landmark *Lau v. Nichols* case (1974). The issue in this class-action suit was denial of equal educational opportunity to non-English-speaking students by providing instruction only in English. The *Lau Remedies* recognize five categories of language proficiency, and Cegelka (1988) describes these as follows:

1. Monolingual speaker of a language other than English; speaks this language exclusively.
2. Predominantly speaks the language other than English, although some English is spoken.
3. Bilingual, speaks both English and primary language with equal ease.
4. Predominantly speaks English, although not exclusively.
5. Monolingual speaker of English; speaks this language exclusively. (p. 555)

One issue in the use of tests that assess languages other than English is who will administer them. According to Juárez (1983), native-English-speakers should administer English versions of tests, and native-minority-language

TABLE 14-4
Measures of Language Proficiency

NAME (AUTHOR)	AGES OR GRADES	LANGUAGE(S)	ORAL LANGUAGE SKILLS ASSESSED
Basic Inventory of Natural Language (Herbert, 1996)	Grades Pre-K to adult	Spanish, English, and 30 other languages	A language sample is scored for fluency, complexity, and average sentence length.
Ber-Sil Elementary and Secondary Spanish Tests (Beringer, 1984, 1987)	Ages 5 to 12 and 13 to 17	Spanish, Tagalog, Ilokano; Elementary also available in Cantonese, Mandarin, Korean, Persian	Receptive vocabulary
Bilingual Syntax Measure I and II (Burt, Dulay, & Hernández-Chávez, 1978)	Grades Pre-K to 12	Spanish, English	Expressive syntax
Bilingual Verbal Ability Tests (Muñoz-Sandoval, Cummins, Alvarado, & Ruef, 1998)	Ages 5-0 to adult	Spanish, English, and 15 other languages	Receptive and expressive vocabulary
Dos Amigos Verbal Language Scales, 1996 Edition (Critchlow, 1996)	Ages 5 to 13	Spanish, English	Expressive vocabulary
Language Assessment Scales-Oral (Duncan & DeAvila, 1990)	Grades 1 to 12	Spanish, English	Phonemic, lexical, syntactical, and pragmatic aspects of language
Prueba de Desarrollo Inicial de Lenguaje (Hresko, Reid, & Hammill, 1982)	Ages 3 to 7	Spanish	Receptive and expressive syntax and semantics
Woodcock-Muñoz Language Survey, English and Spanish Forms (Woodcock & Muñoz-Sandoval, 1993)	Ages 4-0 to adult	Spanish, English	Receptive and expressive semantics

speakers should administer minority-language versions. Bilingual professionals are able to fill both roles, provided, of course, they have adequate training in test administration. Some measures attempt to minimize the need for minority-language proficiency by the tester by using audiotapes to present test items. This practice may help standardize administration procedures, but it does not eliminate the need for a tester who can speak the student's own language, understand the student's communications, and record responses to test items.

Another issue relates to the equivalency of language proficiency measures. Wald (1982) reports the results of a study that compared these three measures: the *Basic Inventory of Natural*

Language (BINL), the *Bilingual Syntax Measure (BSM),* and the *Language Assessment Scales (LAS).* Minimal correlations were found among the measures, and each identified a different portion of the population as limited in English proficiency (LEP). With the *BINL,* 73% of the students participating in the study were identified as LEP. Fewer were identified by the *LAS* (30%), and the smallest percentage by the *BSM* (19%).

Juárez (1983) contends that "informal measures tend to be more accurate predictors of communicative competence than formal tests" (p. 60). Generally, informal techniques are the only alternative if pragmatics is the concern. In addition, for many languages, informal assessment may be the only approach available if there is interest in evaluating both basic interpersonal communication skills and cognitive/academic language proficiency. Among the available informal strategies are observation of the student in communication situations, collection and analysis of samples of the student's natural language, and administration of informal inventories and criterion-referenced tests to evaluate specific receptive and expressive language skills.

Special Education Assessment for Bilingual Students

When students who speak languages other than English are referred for special education assessment, a first step is the study of language proficiency. If one language is clearly dominant, then special education assessment will take place in that language. For example, if the student speaks only Spanish, Spanish-language assessment tools should be selected.

When students show some proficiency in both English and their first language, then the decision about the language of assessment is not as straightforward. In general, the best course of action in this situation is to assess in both languages. Baca and Cervantes (1989) explain:

> Overall, it would be in the student's best interest to have as much data as possible regarding functioning in both languages in order to determine strengths and weaknesses, as well as to aid in the development of prescriptive measures for remediation. (p. 171)

The language of assessment is not the only consideration. The history of special education has been marked by controversy over the assessment of students from diverse groups and the disproportionate placement of such students in special education classes for individuals with mental retardation. Although concerns about testing abuses and inappropriate placement abated somewhat with the passage of PL 94-142 with its guarantees of due process and requirements for nondiscriminatory assessment, the issues continue to command attention today. As Gonzalez et al. (1997) report, in today's schools culturally and linguistically diverse students "are likely to be either overidentified,

underidentified, or misidentified as having disabilities" (p. 7).

In response to these problems, the National Academy of Sciences Panel on Selection and Placement of Students in Programs for the Mentally Retarded was formed. The report of that panel, *Placing Children in Special Education: A Strategy for Equity* (Heller, Holtzman, & Messick, 1982), addresses both assessment and instruction, and a two-phase comprehensive assessment process is recommended for eligibility decisions.

The first phase in assessment should be study of the student's learning environment and investigation of the nature and quality of general education classroom instruction. In Messick's (1984) words:

> Only after deficiencies in the learning environment have been ruled out, by documenting that the child fails to learn under reasonable alternative instructional approaches, should the child be exposed to the risks of stigma and misclassification inherent in referral and individual assessment. (p. 5)

Four types of information are gathered during the first phase of the comprehensive assessment process:

1. Evidence that the school is using programs and curricula shown to be effective not just for students in general but for the various ethnic, linguistic, and socioeconomic groups actually served by the school in question.
2. Evidence that the students in question have been adequately exposed to the curriculum by virtue of not having missed many lessons due to absence or disciplinary exclusions from class, and that the teacher has implemented the curriculum effectively (e.g., evidence that the teacher makes effective use of the flexibility afforded by the curriculum in choosing instructional strategies and materials, that the child receives appropriate direction, feedback, and reinforcement, that other children in the class are performing acceptably, etc.).
3. Evidence that the child has not learned what was taught.
4. Evidence that systematic efforts were, or are being, made to identify the learning difficulty and to take corrective instructional action, such as introducing remedial approaches, changing the

curriculum materials, or trying a new teacher. (Messick, 1984, p. 5)

The second phase of assessment is undertaken only if it is established that an achievement problem exists despite the provision of appropriate instruction in the regular classroom.

Current thinking in the field of bilingual special education endorses and extends this approach. As Baca and Almanza (1991) explain, the first concern is prevention of disabilities. In their view, prevention is:

> a way of empowering students from language minority backgrounds early in their lives so that they do not develop disabilities as a result of poor or inappropriate instruction or the lack of a culturally and linguistically responsive learning environment. (p. 21)

Second, prereferral services should be part of the school's response to academic learning problems. Only when appropriate instructional interventions have not proved successful should a student be referred for special education assessment. Ortiz and Garcia (1988) agree. In their eight-step model, when students experience academic difficulties, systematic efforts are made to "identify the source of the difficulty and take corrective action" (p. 10). Among the areas to consider are the characteristics of the teacher, the student's exposure to the curriculum, student characteristics, instructional approaches, and the methods used to monitor student progress.

With students who speak languages other than English, special education assessment is conducted in the language or languages in which students are most proficient. Several measures are available in a variety of skill areas for Spanish-speaking students, as Table 14–5 shows. As with language proficiency tests, Spanish is the language most often represented on minority-language versions of special education assessment devices. Most of the measures listed in Table 14–5 have English-language counterparts that have been discussed earlier.

Obviously, the methods used to develop Spanish-language tests affect both technical adequacy and educational usefulness. Payan (1989) warns that minority-language tests should not be direct translations of English-language tests. Literal translation may not take into account the subtle differences between languages and cultures, so items on the minority-language version of the test become either more difficult or easier than their English-language counterparts.

The characteristics of the standardization sample are a critical concern in selection of minority-language tests. Tests based on English-language measures may not have been renormed with minority-language speakers. If that is the case, professionals are forced to develop local norms or use the test as an informal measure; norms developed with English speakers are inappropriate for non-English-speaking students. If norms are available, the characteristics of the standardization sample must be carefully evaluated. As with English, there are many dialects of Spanish and of other languages. Lynch and Lewis (1987) caution that "Spanish-language tests prepared for use in Mexico may not be appropriate for Cuban refugees in urban areas of Florida or for Mexican-American students in the rural southwest" (p. 404).

The selection of appropriate tools for assessment becomes even more difficult when students speak languages other than Spanish. Often, no technically adequate measures are available in the student's language. When this occurs, professionals could choose not to assess the student or assess with English-language measures. However, neither of these tactics is acceptable. Failure to assess may result in inappropriate placement of the student in special education or retention in general education. Testing non-English speakers with English-language tests is clearly discriminatory.

More acceptable options include the use of interpreters to assist in administration of English-language measures and the development of informal measures in the student's language. Interpreters are not a perfect solution, although in many cases they may be the only alternative if the language of the student is not a common one. Plata (1982) describes several pitfalls in the use of interpreters for test administration:

(a) On-the-spot translation is very difficult, especially when the interpreter does not know the technical language found in test items.

(b) Many words lose their meaning in the translation process.

TABLE 14-5

Assessment Devices for Spanish-Speaking Students

ASSESSMENT AREA	NAME (AUTHOR)	ENGLISH-LANGUAGE COUNTERPART
Academic Achievement	*Aprenda: La prueba de logros en español, Segunda edición* (1997)	Coordinated with *Stanford Achievement Test Series*
	Batería Woodcock-Muñoz-Revisada (Woodcock & Muñoz-Sandoval, 1996)	*Woodcock-Johnson Psycho-Educational Battery-Revised* (Woodcock & Johnson, 1989)
	BRIGANCE® Diagnostic Inventory of Basic Skills, Spanish Edition (Brigance, 1983)	*BRIGANCE® Diagnostic Comprehensive Inventory of Basic Skills-Revised* (Brigance, 1999)
	Prueba de Lectura & Lenguaje Escrito (Test of Reading and Writing) (Hammill, Larsen, Wiederholt, & Fountain-Chambers, 1982)	None
	Spanish Assessment of Basic Education (2nd ed.) (1991)	Linked to *Comprehensive Tests of Basic Skills*
	TerraNova SUPERA (1997)	Linked to *TerraNova* assessment series
	Woodcock-Muñoz Language Survey, Spanish Form (Woodcock & Muñoz-Sandoval, 1993)	*Woodcock-Muñoz Language Survey, English Form* (Woodcock & Muñoz-Sandoval, 1993)
Intellectual Performance	*Batería Woodcock-Muñoz-Revisada* (Woodcock & Muñoz-Sandoval, 1996)	*Woodcock-Johnson Psycho-Educational Battery-Revised* (Woodcock & Johnson, 1989)
	Escala de Inteligencia Wechsler para Niños-Revisada (1983)	*Wechsler Intelligence Scale for Children-Revised* (Wechsler, 1974)
	Escala de Inteligencia Wechsler para Niños-Revisada de Puerto Rico (1993)	*Wechsler Intelligence Scale for Children-Revised* (Wechsler, 1974)
Adaptive Behavior	*Adaptive Behavior Inventory for Children* (Mercer & Lewis, 1977a)	Both English-language and Spanish-language versions are included.
	Scales of Independent Behavior (Bruininks, Woodcock, Weatherman, & Hill, 1984)	A Spanish version offers a Spanish-language test book and an English-language manual and response booklets.
	Vineland Adaptive Behavior Scales (Sparrow, Balla, & Cicchetti, 1984)	A Spanish-language version of the Survey Form for the Interview Edition is available.
Specific Learning Abilities	*Batería Woodcock-Muñoz-Revisada* (Woodcock & Muñoz-Sandoval, 1996)	*Woodcock-Johnson Psycho-Educational Battery-Revised* (Woodcock & Johnson, 1989)
	Prueba Illinois de Habilidades Psicolingüísticas (von Isser & Kirk, 1980)	*Illinois Test of Psycholinguistic Abilities* (rev. ed.) (Kirk, McCarthy, & Kirk, 1968)
	Survey of Study Habits and Attitudes, Spanish Edition (Brown & Holtzman, 1967b)	*Survey of Study Habits and Attitudes* (Brown & Holtzman, 1967a)
Classroom Behavior	*Perfil de Evaluación de Comportamiento* (Brown & Hammill, 1982)	*Behavior Rating Profile* (Brown & Hammill, 1983)
Oral Language*	*Prueba Boehm de Conceptos Básicos-Edición Revisada* (Boehm, 1987)	*Boehm Test of Basic Concepts-Revised* (Boehm, 1986b)
	Prueba de Desarrollo Inicial de Lenguaje (Hresko, Reid, & Hammill, 1982)	*Test of Early Language Development* (3rd ed.) (Hresko, Reid, & Hammill, 1999)
	Screening Test of Spanish Grammar (Toronto, 1973)	*Northwestern Syntax Screening Test* (Lee, 1971)
	Test de Vocabulario en Imágenes Peabody (Dunn, Lugo, Padillo, & Dunn, 1986)	*Peabody Picture Vocabulary Test-Third Edition* (Dunn & Dunn, 1997)
	Woodcock-Muñoz Language Survey, Spanish Form (Woodcock & Muñoz-Sandoval, 1993)	*Woodcock-Muñoz Language Survey, English Form* (Woodcock & Muñoz-Sandoval, 1993)

*See also the measures of language proficiency described in Table 14–4.

(c) The interpreter may not know all the possible terms or dialects applied to a word or concept, especially if the child being tested is from a different geographic region than that of the interpreter.

(d) There may be hostile feelings toward the examiner on the part of an interpreter who feels that he or she is "being used" to "cover up" inadequacies of the examiner or if the interpreter perceives the remuneration to be minimal for doing the work of a highly paid professional. (p. 4)

However, Plata concedes that "using interpreters to try to compromise the effect of the examinee's language on test results is better than no attempt at all" (p. 4). When English-language tests are administered via an interpreter, test norms no longer apply. Results should be viewed as alternate scores, or more realistically, the test should be treated as an informal measure.

The other strategy available to professionals is development of informal measures in the language of the student. As with norm-referenced tests, these should not be direct translations of English-language measures. The design of informal inventories, criterion-referenced tests, and other informal instruments requires proficiency in the child's language. If this is not available among the professional staff of the school or district, translators become necessary for the development of the assessments, and interpreters for their administration. Again, this is not a perfect solution to the problem, but it is sometimes a workable alternative for students who speak uncommon minority languages.

WITHIN THE CONTEXT OF THE CLASSROOM

The classroom learning environment is an important concern in the assessment of oral language skills, both for special students with educational needs in the area of oral language and for those who speak nonstandard English dialects or languages other than English. So far, discussion has focused on assessment strategies for gathering information about the student's performance. The emphasis now shifts to procedures and techniques for studying the classroom learning environment and its influence on the student's oral language skills.

The Instructional Environment

Oral language is usually not taught as a separate subject in general education classrooms, except in the early elementary grades. However, oral language demands pervade the entire curriculum. Students are expected to listen to and understand the teacher and others in the classroom. They are also expected to be fluent in the language of the classroom and to be able oral communicators.

One aspect of the learning environment is the communication skill of the teacher. This is important both in the early elementary grades, where most of the instructional content is delivered orally, and in the secondary grades, where teachers rely heavily on lecture as a method for the presentation of new information. Factors to consider are as follows:

- When oral directions are given, does the teacher prepare the students for what is to come?
- Does the teacher make sure that the purposes for listening are clear to each student?
- Is the teacher usually talking, or does the teacher listen to students as speakers? (Russell & Russell, 1959)

Other dimensions of teacher behavior that may influence students' ability to listen effectively are described by Alley and Deshler (1979):

1. *Nonlinguistic communication.* Does the teacher make effective use of gestures, eye contact, pauses?
2. *Preorganizers.* Does the teacher present an overview that stresses the major points of the material to be covered?
3. *Organization.* Does the teacher present information in a logical, organized fashion?
4. *Pace.* Does the teacher present the information at varied paces—slowing down for important points and repeating them for emphasis?
5. *Examples.* Does the teacher use examples to illustrate points and give concrete examples of abstract information? (p. 289)

Another area of interest is the number and types of oral responses required of students in the classroom learning environment. In the early years of elementary school, speaking is a primary way that students respond to classroom activities. They read aloud, answer questions orally, and participate in group discussions. In middle and high school, teachers continue to expect students to communicate orally. In a study by Knowlton and Schlick, reported in Schumaker and Deshler (1984), secondary teachers considered communication skills important and identified specific skills such as "speaking clearly, making oral reports, participating in discussions, and explaining reasons for one's actions" (p. 25).

The teacher's instructional response to students with language differences or disorders should also be considered in assessment. In correcting student errors, does the teacher stress language form (i.e., articulation and grammar) or meaning and usage? What changes, if any, have been made in the standard instructional program to accommodate the needs of learners such as the student under assessment? Are listening tasks restructured for students with difficulty in receptive language? Are speaking tasks modified in any way for students with problems in language production?

Polloway and Smith (1982) provide specific suggestions for the instruction of students with special language needs, particularly those who speak nonstandard English or languages other than English. These include the following:

- Avoid negative statements about the child's language, exercising particular caution in front of large groups. Rather than saying, "I don't understand you" or "You are not saying that right" several times, the teacher should use a statement such as, "Could you say that in a different way to help me understand?"
- Reinforce oral and written language production. A first goal in working with language-different students is to maintain and subsequently increase the language output. Reinforcing desired production will insure that this goal is reached.
- Set aside at least a short period during the day to stress language development.
- Involve persons from the linguistically different community in the total school program as much as

possible so that these persons, as well as "native" speakers, can share language experiences.
- As the teacher, you should model standard English usage. For example, when a student says, "Dese car look good," you could say, "Yes, these cars do look good." (pp. 83–84)

The Interpersonal Environment

The interpersonal environment of the classroom is an important area of concern in the study of oral language performance because communication is a social event. At least two persons must participate: a speaker who transmits information and a listener who acts as the recipient.

In assessing the interpersonal dimension, it is necessary to determine whether students have opportunities to practice oral language skills as part of classroom activities. Some of the questions that can be asked are:

- Is the teacher the primary speaker in the classroom? That is, are students expected to act as listeners rather than speakers? How many opportunities per day, on the average, do students have to respond orally in class? What types of responses are most typical—yes and no answers, short responses of a few words, several sentences?
- Are there opportunities for students and the teacher to communicate in large group settings?
- Do students speak with the teacher individually or in small group settings?
- Are students allowed or encouraged to communicate with each other?
- Are there opportunities for students to communicate in structured situations such as small group discussions, cooperative learning groups, role playing activities, class meetings, debates, panel discussions, and the like?

It is also important to evaluate the instructional interactions when classroom activities require oral communication. For example, when students make errors in speaking, how does the teacher respond? Is the error identified? Does the teacher correct it?

The Physical Environment

The way the physical environment of the classroom is arranged influences students' opportunities for interaction and the practice of oral communication skills. Cohen and Plaskon (1980) describe two classroom seating arrangements, one that inhibits student interaction and another that encourages communication among students. In the traditional classroom environment, students are seated at desks arranged in rows, so each student is isolated from all but a few peers. As Figure 14–7 shows, the modified classroom environment represents a more ideal arrangement because "there will be multiple opportunities for children to engage in conversation, discussion, and problem solving with each other" (Cohen & Plaskon, p. 22). In addition, the teacher will be able to interact with individual students as needed without calling attention to any particular student.

The physical environment can also affect listening skills. Soundproofing or carpeting decreases the overall noise level of the room. The areas of the classroom used for listening and independent study should be separated from the areas where less quiet activities take place. Some classrooms have listening centers where one or several students can listen to tapes or records through earphones. These centers can be used to provide instruction in listening skills and for free-time activities such as listening to music or stories.

ANSWERING THE ASSESSMENT QUESTIONS

The purpose of the study of oral language is to describe the student's current levels of performance in this important area of functioning. There are a great many assessment strategies available for this purpose. Many are norm-referenced tests, whereas others are informal measures such as language samples and informal inventories. These tools aid the assessment team in gathering information about the student's current status in oral language development.

Nature of the Assessment Tools

Measures of oral language vary along several dimensions, one of the most obvious being the language they assess. The most common language is, of course, English. However, several tests evaluate students' skills in Spanish, and some assess both English- and Spanish-language proficiency.

FIGURE 14–7

Classroom Seating Arrangements

Note: Adapted with permission of Merrill, an imprint of Macmillan Publishing Company, from *Language Arts for the Mildly Handicapped* (pp. 201, 203) by S. B. Cohen and S. P. Plaskon. Copyright © 1980 Merrill Publishing Company, Columbus, Ohio.

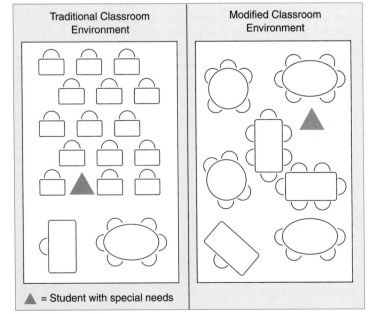

Formal tests of proficiency in other languages are less common, although informal measures may be available.

Language measures also vary in the range of skills they assess. Some measures attempt to be comprehensive, whereas others concentrate on one or perhaps two of the major dimensions of language. Several current test batteries include measures of phonology, morphology, syntax, and semantics. However, measures are not truly comprehensive unless they include the newest area of language study—pragmatics.

Oral language is a complex skill made up of many subskills. Because of this, some measures attend to only one specific area of functioning. Examples include measures of articulation, those that assess morphology and syntax, and vocabulary tests. Some tests are so specific that they address an area as restricted as expressive syntax or receptive semantics.

Measures also differ in depth of skill coverage. Thus, norm-referenced tests tend to sample several skills and/or several skill levels, but only a few representative test items are provided in each area. Most informal measures are designed to evaluate skills in much greater depth. An example is language sample analysis, in which every utterance is recorded, transcribed, and analyzed. A wealth of information concerning the student's productivity, the semantic aspects of the communication, and the specific morphological and syntactical characteristics of the student's language is the result.

Measures use different assessment tasks to evaluate similar oral language skills. For example, the student's command of morphology and syntax is assessed by tasks such as sentence repetition, sentence combination, and identification of pictures that best represent the meaning of sentences. Clearly, differences among test tasks must be considered in the selection of the tools for assessment and in the interpretation of results.

The Relationship of Oral Language to Other Areas of Performance

When assessment is complete, the special education team begins to interpret the results and study the relationships between and among areas of performance. General learning aptitude is one area of interest. Because general aptitude can influence the rate and success with which skills are acquired, the student's progress in oral language should be evaluated in relation to the estimated level of intellectual functioning. Verbal IQ scores are most appropriate for this purpose. However, the relationship between language and intelligence is reciprocal. Just as intelligence can affect language development, students' language skills can affect performance on measures of intellectual performance. This is a particular concern with students whose language is dissimilar from the formal standard English used on IQ tests.

Specific learning abilities also play a role in the student's ability to acquire and use oral language skills. Difficulties in attention and memory can hinder language development, as can poor auditory discrimination. Again, the relationship is reciprocal. Language is an integral part of learning strategies such as verbal rehearsal, and students use language to regulate their own learning behavior and focus attention.

Classroom behavior may be influenced by language development. Students with poor receptive language skills may appear inattentive, fail to follow directions, or seem to ignore the teacher. Students with poor expressive skills may be reluctant to speak in class, especially in situations in which peers can take notice of their errors or the differences between their language and standard English. Such students may refuse to answer questions and participate in class discussions; they may engage in disruptive behavior to draw attention away from their difficulties with language. Also, self-concept and attitude toward school are likely to be affected.

Oral language skills have an impact on other areas of school performance. All school subjects require listening and speaking skills, at least to some extent. In classrooms at all grade levels, from preschool through college, students are expected to learn by listening. The demands for speaking skills are almost as great. No matter what subject or what grade level, the teacher will ask questions and expect students to respond orally. Students who enter school with delays in receptive or expressive language development are likely to experience difficulty in the acquisition of reading, mathematics, and written language skills as well as content area subjects.

Oral language also pervades daily life. At home and at work, people communicate with each other through speech. They talk face-to-face and on the telephone to family members, friends, neighbors, and acquaintances; they talk to facilitate vocational pursuits and to accomplish routine tasks such as shopping. Students with severe language disorders may require training to succeed at the oral communication tasks that make up much of the fabric of daily life.

Documentation of Oral Language Performance

The general question that guides the assessment team in its study of student performance is, *What are the student's educational needs?* Two specific questions are asked in relation to the student's oral communication skills: *What is the student's current level of development in oral language? What are the student's strengths and weaknesses in the various skill areas of oral language?*

Many types of data are gathered to answer these questions. The team may begin by reviewing school records and the information collected in classroom observations and interviews with teachers and parents. Formal tests may then be administered to evaluate the student's oral language performance in relation to that of age or grade peers. Informal assessment strategies such as language sampling, informal inventories, and criterion-referenced tests may also play a role by describing the specific skill areas in which the student shows educational needs.

As with other areas of assessment, the team should select its tools with care so that duplication is avoided and the assessment process is as efficient as possible. This is an important concern in the study of oral language skills because of the great number of available formal measures. In addition, the more specific procedures such as language sampling should be reserved for in-depth assessment of potential problem areas.

By answering the assessment questions about oral language, the team moves closer to planning the student's individualized education program. In the case of Joyce, assessment results indicated that oral language was not a skill area requiring special instruction.

Joyce

The assessment team has identified Joyce as learning disabled, and to date three areas of academic underachievement have been documented. Although Joyce's oral language skills appear adequate, she has difficulty following oral directions in the classroom, a problem that may relate to receptive language. Thus, the team decides to investigate language development by administering the intermediate level of the *Test of Language Development-3*. Joyce's scores on all subtests of the *TOLD-3* fall within the average range of performance. To corroborate these results and gather further information about Joyce's difficulty with oral directions, the assessment team develops an informal inventory to assess comprehension of typical classroom directions. For example, the first direction is "Write your name on the upper left-hand corner of the paper." Joyce follows single directions without difficulty. However, when directions are combined into a series (e.g., "Next to number 3 on your paper, write your last name and draw a circle around it"), Joyce is unable to comply. These results substantiate the team's belief that Joyce's failure to follow classroom directions is related to memory, not to receptive language.

The special education team has completed its evaluation of Joyce and the learning environment of her fourth grade classroom. Results indicate that Joyce is in need of specialized instruction in reading, spelling, and handwriting. Next, Joyce's parents will meet with members of the school staff to plan the individualized educational program.

STUDY GUIDE

REVIEW QUESTIONS

1. Oral language skills are assessed to
   a. determine whether students are eligible for special education services from a speech-language pathologist.
   b. identify educational needs in the area of speech and language.
   c. find out if students are in need of bilingual education services.
   d. all of the above
   e. answers a and b
2. What five dimensions of oral language are of interest in special education assessment?
3. Which of the following statements are true and which are false?
   a. In the developmental sequence, receptive language generally precedes expressive language.
   b. Listening is an expressive language skill, whereas speaking is a receptive language skill.
   c. Another term for receptive phonology is auditory discrimination.
   d. Articulation is the production of morphemes, the smallest meaningful units of language.
   e. Pragmatics refers to the use of language in communicative contexts.
4. Most measures of oral language assess language form, content, and use. (True or False)
5. Students who speak a nonstandard version of English are said to speak a(n) _____ of English.
6. Match the assessment device or procedure in Column A with the description in Column B.

Column A	*Column B*
a. *Test of Language Development-3, Primary*	____ Assesses expressive phonology
b. *Comprehensive Receptive and Expressive Vocabulary Test*	____ Used to evaluate receptive and expressive phonology, syntax, and semantics in pre-school and early elementary grade children
c. *Test of Adolescent and Adult Language-3*	____ In oral language, produces three scores: Listening Comprehension, Oral Expression, and Oral Composite
d. *Goldman-Fristoe Test of Articulation*	____ There are two versions of this test, one of which is computerized
e. *Oral and Written Language Scales*	____ Contains four oral language subtests: Listening Vocabulary and Grammar, and Speaking Vocabulary and Grammar

7. Which measure would you select if you wished to assess both receptive and expressive syntax?
   a. *Northwestern Syntax Screening Test*
   b. *Test for Auditory Comprehension of Language* (3rd ed.)
   c. *Carrow Elicited Language Inventory*
   d. Language sampling
8. Which measure would you choose to assess pragmatics?
   a. *Peabody Picture Vocabulary Test, Third Edition*
   b. *Boehm Test of Basic Concepts-Revised*
   c. *Let's Talk Inventory for Children*
   d. *Test of Language Development-3, Intermediate*

9. There are many ways to analyze samples of students' oral language. In most systems, the words uttered by the student are analyzed according to their morphological and syntactical characteristics. However, the simplest method is calculation of the mean _____ of _____ , an indicator of overall language development.

10. Nonstandard forms of English such as Black English and Spanish-influenced English are considered language deficits, not language differences. (True or False)

11. With students who speak languages other than English,
    a. the first step in assessment is determination of the student's language proficiency in the first language and in English.
    b. special education assessment takes place in the student's primary language, whenever feasible.
    c. bilingual education services may be provided as well as special education services.
    d. all of the above

12. Oral language development is most related to _____ aptitude.

13. If a student shows low average intellectual performance, in what standard score range would you expect that student to perform in oral language?
    a. Less than standard score 70
    b. Standard score 70 to 84
    c. Standard score 85 to 115
    d. Standard score 116 to 130
    e. Greater than standard score 130

14. Poor oral language skill development may affect
    a. reading.
    b. composition.
    c. mathematics.
    d. classroom behavior.
    e. interactions with peers and teachers.
    f. all of the above.

15. If the special education team finds that an English-speaking student shows poor performance in oral language, what conclusion can be drawn?
    a. The student may be eligible for bilingual education services.
    b. The student requires individualized instruction in reading, writing, listening, and speaking.
    c. Special education services should be provided in the area of oral language, if the student meets eligibility criteria for one of the disabilities.
    d. The student will require an interpreter for all assessments.

ACTIVITIES

1. Write an Individualized Assessment Plan for an elementary grade student who has been referred because of problems in oral language. In writing the plan, attempt to include measures of all major dimensions of language: phonology, morphology, syntax, semantics, and pragmatics.

2. Under the supervision of the course instructor, administer one of the oral language survey measures discussed in this chapter. Calculate all possible scores and analyze the results to determine strengths and weaknesses.

3. Obtain a language sample from a student receiving special education services. Analyze that sample using a method described in this chapter.

4. Devise an interview form for use with parents of young school-aged children to find out about the language environment of the home.
5. Observe in a classroom and note the important features of the instructional, interpersonal, and physical environments that may influence oral language performance.

DISCUSSION QUESTIONS

1. Oral language is the communication mode most often used in everyday discourse among adults. Why then is oral language not included among the basic school skills?
2. Pragmatics is the newest area of language study. Explain what is meant by pragmatics, and tell how this dimension of language can be assessed.
3. Explain why it is necessary to consider the oral language of students who speak nonstandard English when assessing intellectual performance, reading, written language, and other school subjects.
4. The primary language of the student should be the language in which the special education assessment is conducted. However, technically adequate assessment tools are not always available in the student's language. Discuss the alternatives open to the assessment team when this occurs. Include in your discussion the advantages and disadvantages of each alternative.

PART V

SPECIAL CONSIDERATIONS

All students are part of a larger context of family and community, and parents and other family members are important partners in their children's education. When children and adolescents have learning problems, parents and family members are even more essential. They play vital roles in accurately assessing learning needs, planning effective programs, and monitoring the success of those programs. The importance of parents has been recognized in special education law since the passage of PL 94-142 in 1975, and the commitment to parental involvement continues to be a strong component of the 1997 amendments of IDEA.

For most students, parents are the primary adults in their lives. Increasingly, however, other relatives have responsibility for parenting. U.S. Census Bureau figures, as reported by the Children's Defense Fund (1999), indicate that in 1998, 5.4 million children lived in homes headed by a relative. Of those, 2.13 million (39%) lived with relatives *without a parent present*. In the years between 1990 and 1998, the percentage of children living with relatives without a parent present grew by 52%. In those same years, children living with at least one grandparent without a parent present increased by 52%—the fastest growing proportion of children living with a relative (Children's Defense Fund). As kinship care increases and the definition of family changes to include a variety of parental relationships, the importance of extending parent involvement to include other family members is clear. Therefore, this chapter focuses on parent *and* family involvement in assessment and planning for students with learning difficulties. Legal regulations determine who is invited to participate in assessments, and who can attend IEP meetings and make and formalize decisions related to a student's assessment, program, and placement; but teachers and administrators can create a climate in which parents feel comfortable including other members of the family who are important to them and to their son or daughter. This chapter also emphasizes a model of parent/family-professional collaboration that is based on

respect, differentiated roles, and mutual problem-solving. In this model, the ultimate goal is parent and family empowerment—empowerment that will provide students with learning difficulties optimal educational support and advocacy (Dunst, Trivette, & Deal, 1988; Epstein, 1990; Kroth & Edge, 1997).

PARENT-PROFESSIONAL COLLABORATION IN ASSESSMENT

Benefits of Parent-Professional Collaboration

Parent-professional collaboration is a model that is useful in all aspects of general and special education. In assessing students with learning difficulties, working with parents or other family members as partners can be invaluable (Berdine & Cegelka, 1995; Correa, 1991; Turnbull & Turnbull, 1990; Walker & Singer, 1993). Parents know more about their own sons and daughters than does anyone else, and they will be the constant in their son's and daughter's lives (Cutler, 1993). When children are younger, parents can provide information about development, preferences for various activities, and strategies for keeping the child on task. In the elementary and middle school years, they can provide teachers with information about their son's or daughter's performance outside of school in applied academic skills such as telling time; reading signs, books, newspapers, or magazines; using money to make purchases; understanding the rules of games; the amount of time required to complete homework; and general knowledge. They can also provide information about their child's social interactions, motivation, memory, and activity level. Parents often provide valuable insights into their son's or daughter's self concept—information that can be used to help teachers understand students' with learning disabilities motivation to use instructional strategies (Meltzer & Reid, 1994). As students enter high school and young adulthood, parents contribute additional information about applied academic skills, work experience, motivation, interpersonal relationships, and post-school goals and aspirations.

In addition to the information that parents and family members can provide that contributes to assessment and program planning, parents can become part of the data-gathering process. Parents can "take data" in a variety of situations to help teachers determine whether students are generalizing school skills into other settings. Parents can also gauge the validity of test scores by watching their son's or daughter's performance or seeing the profile of results. For example, they may be able to tell the teacher that their child knows the answer to items that she or he failed in a test situation, or they may be surprised at seeing a higher level of performance than they see at home.

Finally, families have the right to be involved in the assessment process. Since the inception of PL 94-142 in 1975, rights that mandate parent involvement in the assessment have existed in the following areas: "(1) notice of referral, (b) permission to test, (c) information concerning assessment results, (d) participation in IEP development, (e) permission for placement in special education programs, (f) review of the IEP at least annually, and (g) rights to an appeal process regarding the decisions made" (McLoughlin & Lewis, 1994, p. 484). In addition, the right to a nonbiased assessment—one that does not discriminate on the basis of language, race, culture, gender, socioeconomic status, religion, or other child and family characteristics—is also guaranteed in special education legislation. Parental rights related to assessment were strengthened in the 1997 Amendments to IDEA to include: (1) *informed* parental consent prior to assessment *or reevaluation;* (2) right to seek an independent educational evaluation; and (3) inclusion of parent input in determining eligibility for special education. Parents' legal rights are clearly stipulated; but more importantly, these rights represent recommended practice. When parents and professionals work collaboratively from identification and referral to assessment, eligibility determination, intervention, and progress monitoring, students receive better services.

Parent and Professional Roles in Assessment

In any partnership or collaboration, it is important to understand each participant's role and expectations. Understanding the different ways in which parents and teachers contribute to the assessment process and the expectations that each may have is a first step. Correa (1991) describes the roles that parents and professionals play in special education. For parents, these roles include: "providing information, reinforcing school programs at home, asserting and advocating for quality services, and understanding the professionals' role" (p. 262). Professionals also have roles that have expanded in recent years. According to Correa, these include: "providing information on student progress, results of diagnostic evaluations, and upcoming school events . . . parent training and advocacy, interpreting medical reports, being an active listener, and working with culturally diverse students and their families" (p. 252). In assessment, parent and professional roles are parallel, with each partner's role supporting and enriching the other. Both parents and professionals can (1) participate in identification and referral for assessment; (2) gather assessment information about the student; (3) ensure that cultural, linguistic, and sociocultural diversity are taken into account in assessment, interpretation of findings, and program development; (4) discuss and interpret findings and results; (5) develop and implement interventions; and (6) monitor student progress. Table 15–1 illustrates ways in which parent and professional roles are overlapping and complementary and the contributions that each can make to the assessment process.

However, parental involvement should not be judged normatively. Parents' degree of involvement varies depending upon their comfort with schools and professionals; life situation; cultural, linguistic, and economic background; beliefs about and expectations of professionals; and the extent to which professionals create a collaborative climate. Although the majority of parents are involved daily in their children's lives and informal education, they may not be comfortable assuming all of the roles that are suggested in Table 15–1.

TABLE 15-1
Roles of Parents and Professionals in the Assessment Process

1. Participate in identification and referral for assessment.	**Parents:** Bring concerns to professionals; describe concerns; keep records that support concerns; make formal referral; agree to assessment; talk with son or daughter about the assessment process.
	Professionals: Bring concerns to parents; describe concerns; keep records that support concerns; talk with family about referral; explain referral, identification, and assessment process and procedures to parents in clear, jargon-free language; assist parents with procedures required for informed consent; talk with student about assessment process and procedures.
2. Gather assessment information about the student.	**Parents:** Provide relevant developmental, health, and behavioral history; describe current concerns; discuss relevant family information such as cultural identity, home language, expectations for son or daughter; provide data from daily perspective about the concerns being assessed.
	Professionals: Select appropriate assessment strategies and instruments; describe instruments, strategies, and criteria for selection to parents; solicit parents' data on the concerns being assessed; conduct assessment.
3. Ensure that cultural, linguistic, and sociocultural diversity are taken into account in assessment, interpretation of findings, and program development.	**Parents:** Share cultural, linguistic, and sociocultural information that may influence assessment outcomes and interpretation of assessment results.
	Professionals: Talk with parents and family members about the importance of cultural, linguistic, and sociocultural issues in understanding their son's or daughter's needs; select assessment instruments and strategies that are nonbiased; provide support and information consistent with cultural and personal preferences throughout the assessment process; ensure that interpreters are available to families who are more comfortable communicating in a language in which professionals are not fluent; maintain confidentiality.
4. Discuss and interpret findings and results.	**Parents:** Talk with professionals about the findings; provide interpretations based on daily life with your son or daughter; ask questions; seek clarifications.
	Professionals: Explain assessment findings clearly without jargon; seek parental and family input on interpretations; determine validity of findings from parents' point of view.
5. Develop and implement interventions.	**Parents:** Reinforce learning informally at home; participate with professionals when possible on carryover of specific interventions such as behavior management; talk with son or daughter openly and positively about interventions; stay informed about son's or daughter's program and services; advocate for quality in all aspects of the program.
	Professionals: Design instructional and behavioral plans; solicit parents input on plans and strategies; implement plans.
6. Monitor student progress.	**Parents:** Observe son or daughter at home and in other nonschool settings; describe changes (or lack of change) to professionals; talk with son or daughter about his or her progress.
	Professionals: Collect data on effectiveness of the interventions; share data with parents; seek parental suggestions for modifying interventions.

STRATEGIES FOR DEVELOPING PARENT-PROFESSIONAL PARTNERSHIPS IN THE ASSESSMENT PROCESS

General Strategies

The range and variations among family constellations, circumstances, resources, and preferences is staggering. Just as student differences require individualization, so, too, do strategies for encouraging parents and family members to become partners in the assessment process. There is no recipe. However, there are some general strategies that professionals can employ to increase the likelihood that families will enter into partnerships.

Creating a Family-Friendly Environment. No one wants to go where he or she is not wanted. If parents feel unwanted, disrespected, or dismissed in school settings or by school personnel, they will minimize contact. An initial step in creating a family-friendly environment is to ensure that the school, its faculty, staff, and policies are welcoming to parents and families. If the school itself is unfriendly toward parents, it is unlikely that they will feel comfortable enough to engage in a partnership around assessment. Welcoming strategies are endless and can be tailored to the specific demographics of each school, but the following provide examples:

- Clearly marked entrances and signage so that families know how to approach the school building and don't feel lost when they enter the campus.
- Immediately acknowledging parents' presence and indicating that someone will help them—even in the busiest office.
- Signage in, personnel who speak, and written materials in the languages that predominate in the neighborhood.
- Events or approaches that incorporate community needs or ways of doing things; e.g., a room where family members can drop in and have tea, a web page about the school that includes information on referral and assessment, or after-school programs.

Communicating Positively. No one wants to get bad news, but some parents of students with learning difficulties receive little else when they interact with professionals (Lynch & Stein, 1987). Although there will always be times when negative information about behavior, performance, or progress must be shared, change the ratio to ensure that parents hear more positives than negatives from the school. If parents are assured that not every interaction is going to be negative, they are more likely to risk participating in the assessment process. Incorporate the following when communicating with families:

- Call or send a note to parents when their son or daughter does something well or has a good day.
- Provide frequent, positive communication with parents in their preferred language.
- Communicate negatives factually; enlist parents in problem solving; and avoid assigning blame.
- Invite communication through class newsletters and an open-door policy.

Providing Information and Support. All tasks are easier when we know what is expected. Most parents aren't teachers, and they may have little knowledge of or experience with assessment policies, procedures, and practices. Encourage involvement and participation by providing information in laypersons' language and encouraging families to contribute their knowledge and expertise in ways that are realistic and comfortable for them:

- Provide information about assessment in approachable formats such as frequently asked questions (FAQs) and videotaped demonstrations.
- With parental permission, enlist veteran parents to share their experiences and serve as mentors or guides during the assessment process.
- Provide families with easy ways to give input such as sharing their child's strengths and needs with you over a cup of coffee, making a list of their child's strengths, completing behavioral checklists, or charting the number of words that the child requests help with when reading a story.
- Use the input that families provide, and make it clear that it is useful and valued.

These general strategies provide the threshold that allows parents and other family members to enter into collaborative partnerships. Each can be tailored to the particular family, situation, and professional involved.

Strategies that Support Students and Families from Diverse Cultural and Linguistic Backgrounds and Families Unfamiliar with Assessment Practices

Nonbiased assessment is one of the cornerstones of IDEA and best practice. Therefore, assessment strategies, instruments, practices, and procedures must be examined for their appropriateness and validity across cultures, languages, and life experiences. For example, a low score on a test of English reading comprehension for a monolingual, Spanish-speaking, 10-year-old whose family recently moved to the United States from Mexico cannot be considered valid. Although the previous example seems obvious in the extreme, bias is often more subtle. The results of an assessment conducted in English with a high school student who recently arrived from Russia and seems to have fluent English may be biased and inaccurate. Although the student may comfortably engage in everyday conversation in English, he may not have the language proficiency to respond to academic material. The difference in language mastery that supports basic interpersonal skills (BICS) versus the mastery that is described as cognitive academic language proficiency (CALP) dramatically influences assessment outcomes (Cummins, 1981). Likewise, a child who has been taught to be cooperative, not competitive, may not raise her hand to respond even when she knows the correct answer or she may try not to excel and call attention to herself in class.

Parents who do not speak the language of the school, who are unfamiliar with schooling in the United States or schooling in general, or who come from groups that have not been welcomed in America's schools, may find it particularly difficult to be active participants in assessment. Rather than interpreting their reluctance as lack of involvement, professionals have an obligation to reach out to find ways to make participation a possibility (Lynch & Stein, 1987). An initial step in reaching out is the examination of one's own attitudes, beliefs, and behaviors—developing an awareness of one's own habits, customs, and stereotypes that are culturally based (Harry, 1992a: Lynch, 1998). The majority of professionals put high value on education, and the demographics of teachers and other professionals suggest that their life experiences may have been different from those of the families that they work with and the students that they teach. Given the description of students and teachers in today's schools, poverty, racial discrimination, and recent immigration are more common for students and families than for teachers and other professionals (National Center for Educational Statistics, 1997). Thus, professionals may need to develop new strategies for interacting with and learning from parents who differ from themselves on many dimensions.

Although examples of diversity that relate to cultural and linguistic differences between parents and professionals are most often selected, there are other differences that may bias assessment results and/or make it difficult for parents to participate. For example, the results of a test of general information may be accurate, but they may be completely unrelated to the *ability* of a middle school student whose family is homeless. Tests in basic skill areas may be equally accurate but nonpredictive for this student. Without experience in using money or reading, test performance will not be optimal. Likewise, parents facing crises in the most basic areas of survival such as adequate housing, food, health care, and ability to earn a living cannot be expected to participate actively in assessment without considerable support.

Culture, language, and life circumstances influence family-professional partnerships in the assessment process. In discussing these issues in relation to the assessment of young children, Lynch and Hanson (1996) describe several issues that are equally applicable to collaborating with families of students with learning difficulties from a wide range of diverse backgrounds. These issues are briefly described and discussed in the paragraphs that follow.

The Expert Model. Partnering with families who view professionals as "experts" presents challenges when establishing a collaborative relationship. When parents consider disagreement, questioning, and speaking out to be rude or disrespectful or feel that their own life experience gives them little to say to a professional, it can be difficult to engage them as active participants. To mediate this barrier, professionals may want to use a bilingual/bicultural/sociocultural mediator who can talk with parents about family concerns and, with parental permission, share this information with professionals on the assessment team. Written checklists or questionnaires in the family's preferred language may provide another alternative to the barrier of professional as expert. However, written materials may create other difficulties such as inappropriate reading levels, nonexistent or inadequate translations, or formats that are unfamiliar to some families. Sometimes a conversation, free of jargon, that encourages parents to talk about their son's or daughter's strengths and needs as well as their own concerns can be the most effective way to approach families who view professionals as experts.

Instruments and Strategies. A primary consideration in selecting instruments and strategies is the availability of the instrument in the student's primary language. This is not only critical to achieving a nonbiased assessment, but is also critical to gathering accurate information. Assuming that parents share their child's primary language, it also enables them to understand what is being asked if they are observing the assessment or talking with professionals about the results. If an appropriate instrument is available in the child's primary language, finding an assessor who is fluent in the language or an interpreter who can assist is the next step. Use of a nonfluent assessor or someone who is fluent but not trained in assessment or the instrument being used leads to inaccurate findings and loss of parental confidence in the assessment process.

Another important issue related to selecting appropriate instruments and strategies is their face validity or the assessor's ability to explain why various items are included. For example, the ability to remember a sequence of numbers forward and backward measures concentration and short-term memory, skills that are extremely important to learning letter-sound relationships, solving mathematical problems, and completing a task in sequential order. However, to a family member without training in assessment or much knowledge of the underlying skills needed for

school success, remembering a series of numbers may seem meaningless. Explaining what is being measured and why it is important provides a bridge that enables parents to participate.

Sharing Information. Sharing information clearly and caringly about assessment processes, procedures, and results is part of the larger issue of communication discussed later in this chapter. However, its importance cannot be overemphasized. For most of us, any sort of assessment—a physical exam, a test in a university class, or weighing in after a month of dieting—produces anxiety. For families of children with learning difficulties, the anxiety may be increased. Therefore, giving information clearly and sensitively is critical. The meaning of disability varies from person to person and family to family (Hanson & Lynch, 1992; Kroth & Edge, 1997). Learning for the first time that one's son or daughter has a disability may have different meanings across cultures as well (Harry, 1992b). For example, if boys are more prized by the culture than girls, learning that a son has a learning difficulty may be more difficult for the family to accept. Or, if academic achievement is a lower priority for a family than getting along well with others, learning that a child has learning problems may be somewhat easier to accept than learning that the child has a behavior disorder. Regardless of what professionals expect the family's reaction to be, communicating caringly is essential.

Clarity of communication is also critical. In an ethnographic study that involved low-income Puerto Rican families in the United States, Harry (1992b) described the difficulties that arise when differences in family and professional language interfere with shared meaning. Some Puerto Rican families interpreted "mental retardation" to mean "crazy" (loco), and this interpretation of their child's problem had no validity for them. Others could not understand how an assessment could determine that their son or daughter had mental retardation when the child was learning to speak English—a skill that they did not possess. Being clear about the meaning of words that are used in assessment and helping families incorporate the meaning into their own context is one of the most important ways in which professionals can support families to become partners.

COMMUNICATING WITH PARENTS AND FAMILIES

In addition to the general strategies described in the previous section, there are additional qualities, characteristics, and communication strategies that have been linked to effective interactions with parents and other family members. Although communicating effectively with families has become a central part of service delivery for professionals who work with young children (see Chapter 16), its importance has not been stressed equally at other age levels. This section reviews communication strategies in relation to working with families of students with learning difficulties.

Qualities of Effective Communicators

Beckman, Frank, and Newcomb (1996) discuss three qualities that professionals can bring to their interactions with parents that lay the groundwork for effective communication: respect, nonjudgmental attitude, and empathy. This is not surprising. If one reflects on the characteristics of good friends and confidants, it is likely that these three qualities are present. For families of students with disabilities, respect is critical—respect for their knowledge, opinions, points of view, concerns, advocacy, and sometimes withdrawal from professional contacts and requests. Differences between parental and professional views of the student's behavior, performance, and potential often occur. This, too, is not surprising. The differences inherent in school and home environments and value systems often produce differences in perspectives (Kroth & Edge, 1997). However, respect, even in disagreement, is foundational to effective communication.

Maintaining a nonjudgmental attitude is another quality of an effective communicator (Beckman et al., 1996). When parents trust professionals to listen without criticizing, they are more likely to share information, ask questions, or seek help with problems that they are experiencing. Parenting is a complex job filled with moment-to-moment decision making, and some parenting decisions are better than others. Parents can't always help with their son's or daughter's homework or implement the carefully de-signed behavioral support plan that has been developed at school. Freedom to discuss what they can and cannot do without being made to feel inadequate or incompetent is important to most people. As stated by Paul, Beckman, and Smith (1993), "professionals must recognize that families may have different values, and attempt to affirm the parent's value system" (p. 84).

Empathy is the third characteristic that Beckman et al. (1996) consider foundational to building effective parent-professional partnerships. Empathy is the ability to identify with another's feelings and to see the world from his or her perspective (Turnbull & Turnbull, 1990). This does not mean that the professional responds with, "I know just how you feel" when a family shares its concerns. No one can know how another individual feels, but it is possible to acknowledge another's feelings and provide emotional and cognitive support.

Communication Skills

There are numerous discussions of communication skills in the special education literature (e.g., Beckman, 1996; Kroth & Edge, 1997; Morsink, Thomas, & Correa, 1991; Paul & Simeonsson, 1993; Seligman, 1983; Turnbull & Turnbull, 1990). Each of these discussions describes skills that facilitate effective communication and provides tips to help professionals improve their interactions with families. The skills outlined in the paragraphs that follow are those discussed by Turnbull and Turnbull.

Listening is one of the most important components of communicating. According to Kroth and Edge (1997), "skilled listeners work diligently to understand the messages, and when they become confused, they seek to eliminate the confusion by seeking clarification" (p. 84). When building and maintaining family-professional partnerships, listening to parents and families is an essential skill. Listening is not a passive role in which the words of another sweep over the listener with little impact. Instead, listening is active and requires the listener's full attention and engagement to the speaker's content and feeling. Listening is one way to show respect, to learn, and to help parents engage in problem solving as they present information. Good listeners are comfortable with and allow silences to occur. They use their face and posture to demonstrate their attentiveness, and they focus on what is being said rather than on what they are going to say. Finally, good listeners respond to content and feeling by acknowledging that they have understood both.

Verbal communication skills are also important in parent-professional interactions. Turnbull and Turnbull (1990) discuss the following types of verbal responses: ". . . furthering responses, paraphrasing, response to affect, questioning, and summarization" (p. 164). Furthering responses are techniques used to encourage others to continue to speak or elaborate. Saying "uh-huh" and reiterating what has been said in the language of the family are "furthering" strategies (Turnbull & Turnbull). Paraphrasing is a restatement of what has been said using one's own words. It can be used to clarify, to ensure that the message has been clearly understood, and to demonstrate interest and attention to parents' comments.

Responding to affect requires that professionals understand parents' feelings when they provide information. Whether the feeling is one of joy, triumph, sadness, or anger, the professional responds by verbalizing the feelings accurately and with the same degree of intensity as the feeling was expressed (Turnbull & Turnbull, 1990). For example, a parent's comment such as the following, "It's *really* difficult for Nathan now that his little sister is reading better than he is" might be responded to in this way, "You're feeling sad and concerned about Nathan as he falls behind his sister in reading." Or, the following joyful comment from a parent, "It was the first time she had ever brought a paper home and felt proud enough of it to put it on the refrigerator" might elicit this response, "It sounds as if you are thrilled and relieved about her accomplishment."

Questioning and summarizing are also cited as valuable communication techniques (Turnbull & Turnbull, 1990). Open-ended questions elicit more information and enable parents to respond in ways that are most comfortable for them. Close-ended questions typically produce limited responses, do not encourage elaboration, and

may sound more like police questioning than collaboration. For example, "Tell me the kinds of things Jason does when he works with you at your store" is likely to provide much richer information than asking "Does Jason use the cash register at your store?"

Summarizing provides a way to ensure that parents' primary points have been heard accurately. Summarizing may occur to aid in problem solving, to bring closure to one part of the interview, or to conclude the meeting. All of these techniques support positive parent-professional communication and encourage family-professional collaboration.

INTERVIEWING AND CONFERENCING WITH PARENTS AND FAMILIES

Every interaction with parents—written or spoken, on the phone or in person, one-to-one or through an interpreter—is an opportunity to support family-professional collaboration. However, interviewing families and conferencing with them provide extended opportunities to develop or maintain a positive partnership. Interviews are typically conducted to gather information. Conferences are usually held to share information, discuss the assessment and develop the IEP, or discuss progress. Because many of the principles of effective collaboration are similar for interviewing and conferencing, both are discussed in the sections that follow.

Although family interviews are used extensively in gathering information about very young children to develop Individualized Family Service Plans for students with severe disabilities, they are used less frequently in the field of mild disabilities. Keogh (1999) argues for the value of including information about family structure, climate, and *especially* daily routines as a way of extending assessment to capture information that may improve professionals' ability to design optimal interventions. The following section suggests strategies for conducting family interviews or conferencing with families. Family interviews are also discussed in Chapter 16, Early Childhood Assessment.

Preparing for the Interview or Conference

Inviting families to participate in an interview or conference is the first step. Contact can be made by note, telephone, or e-mail—whatever approach is likely to be the most effective. The way in which the request for an interview is presented is important, especially if families have not been invited to participate in the assessment process in recent years. Professionals should communicate that parental input is an important and valued part of assessment. An informal conversation with parents about their son's or daughter's strengths and needs–as well as the parents' goals, expectations, and preferences–would be helpful. If there are specific issues or types of information that the team would like to have addressed, it may be helpful to let parents know in the initial contact so that they can formulate their thoughts prior to the interview.

Communicating the purpose of a conference is equally important. Some families may perceive an invitation to a conference or IEP meeting as intimidating. If they are unfamiliar with professionals, schooling, or the special education processes and procedures, the conference may be viewed with anxiety. Parents whose previous contacts with teachers and schools have been negative may assume that this meeting, too, will be filled with bad news. Being clear about the goals of the conference—to discuss assessment results, to work together to develop the best educational program, or to consider the types of support services—can relieve anxiety. Parents who have already participated in an interview, contributed information, and become better acquainted with the professionals, procedures, and process can also feel more positive about meeting with the teacher or the IEP team.

Determining whether any special accommodations, such as an interpreter for the deaf or an interpreter/translator in another language, are needed for parents' participation is another part of planning. Finding a mutually convenient time and place for the interview or conference is the next step. Conferences are usually conducted at school to make it easier to share work samples or involve other team members. Interviews can be conducted in the home, at school, or someplace in the neighborhood that is comfortable and provides adequate privacy for parents to share information confidentially.

Interviews in the home can be especially helpful. Seeing the student's surroundings, meeting other family members, and having the student see the teacher at his or her home can support the home-school alliance. Interviews in the home are more time consuming, but the time is usually well spent. When considering an interview in the home, several factors are important: (1) the family's comfort and willingness, (2) appropriateness based upon the student's age, and (3) safety. Families vary in their willingness to invite "outsiders" into their home. Many will be pleased or even honored to have their son's or daughter's teacher visit; others will find it intrusive. Only families can make that decision, so providing choices for the interview location is important. Although it is not uncommon for teachers of young children to conduct home visits, it becomes less common as students get older. For a teacher of a middle or high school student to come to the student's home may cause the student to be embarrassed or teased by peers. Whenever a visit to a student's home is likely to cause discomfort for the family or student, it is not appropriate. Finally, the professional's safety is another factor that should be considered. Some neighborhoods are not safe for the families who live there; they may be particularly unwelcoming to strangers.

If *arranging for an interpreter* is necessary, ensure that someone who is trained in interpreting and is fluent in the family's language and dialect is available. Working through interpreters requires preparation. The nature and content of the interview or conference should be shared with interpreters prior to the meeting. A glossary of specific terms or words that will be used should be provided so that the interpreter can determine the best way to present the underlying concept when direct translation would be inaccurate or inappropriate. Giving the interpreter and family an opportunity to talk prior to the interview can also be an important strategy. It provides family members with a contact in their own language and allows them to ask questions about the process. It enables each to become comfortable with the other's way of speaking, pacing, and vocabulary so that the time available for the interview can be optimized. For more information on working through interpreters, see Langdon, Siegel, Halog, and Sánchez-Boyce (1994) and Lynch (1998).

Formulating questions or strategies for presenting information is an important part of the planning process. In an interview, open-ended approaches are often preferable (e.g., Keogh, 1999; Kroth & Edge, 1997; Wayman, Lynch, & Hanson, 1990). However, an outline of what is to be covered is an important aid as professionals become comfortable with interviewing families. In some instances, having families tell their story may be an appropriate way to initiate the interview (Keogh); in others, general questions about the family's observations of the child's behavior, interests, or skills may provide the best approach. In both of these examples, the interviewer can follow up on parents' responses and focus on areas of particular concern or importance. Sometimes the interviewer may want specific information that can be elicited by questions like the following: "When you take Caleb to a restaurant, how does he behave?" "You mentioned that Luz enjoys going to the mall with her friends. Does she make purchases independently or does she need help?" "What does Martin do from the time he gets home from school to the time he goes to bed?" General suggestions for planning and conducting interviews follow; for more specific guidelines, refer to Molyneaux and Lane (1982; 1990) or Kroth and Edge (1997).

Planning for a conference is also important. Conferences are often structured to allow professionals to present information without seeking information from parents, and without allowing time for discussion or opportunities for joint problem solving. Conferences should be structured thoughtfully to supply information in clear, jargon-free, family-friendly language *and* to engage parents in discussion and dialogue about the information.

Conducting Interviews and Conferences

The *opening* of an interview or conference provides an opportunity to establish rapport and reduce each participant's anxiety. It is also the time for introductions of those present and clarification of the purpose and goals of the meeting. The amount of time allotted for this portion can only be judged by the family's preferences and the amount of time available. Some families expect and need an extended warm-up time; others want to minimize the "small talk" and "get down to business." Family preferences may be a matter of comfort, the amount of time available, or of cultural style and expectations. As professionals become more experienced in working with families, judging when to go slowly or when to move on becomes easier.

Conferences, especially those that involve several team members, are often time limited. When this is the case, it is helpful for the teacher to talk or meet with parents prior to an official meeting so that parents can talk with others, process information, and formulate questions. When a meeting must be concluded at a specific time, it is important that all parties are aware of the time limitation. That allows the most important issues to be addressed. Decision making should occur only after families have had an opportunity to review the information, ask questions, and seek clarification.

Because most interviewers need to take notes, the opening of an interview is also the time to explain why notes are necessary and to request the family's permission. This author has found it helpful to keep the notepad in full view and to go over the notes at the end of the interview so that families know what has been written. Another strategy to ensure that families do not feel threatened by notetaking is to use carbonless copy paper and leave a set of the notes with the family at the end of the interview. Novice interviewers often express a desire to audiotape interviews. Although an audiotape can be helpful in reconstructing what was said, it requires additional time to replay and/or transcribe. Therefore, it is recommended that audiotaping be done only when an exact transcription is needed.

Notes in conferences may be more or less formal. In a parent-teacher conference, teachers may want to jot down notes. In that case, the strategies mentioned in the previous paragraph are equally applicable. In a more formal conference or IEP meeting with several participants, a designated recorder is typically responsible for completing district forms. These, too, should be discussed and shared with the family and not finalized until they have had the opportunity to review them.

The *interview or conference* with families should be nonthreatening in content and approach. In interviews, families can be encouraged to tell their story and describe their son's or daughter's strengths and needs, or asked to respond to specific questions related to providing an appropriate educational program. Questions about motivation, interest, and self-concept as well as learning, performance, goals, and aspirations may be included in this portion of the interview. The interviewer can follow up on parents' responses as needed or use parents' comments as prompts to pursue more specific information.

In conferences, parents may be asked their opinions, experiences, and observations related to the material being presented. They should also be asked what questions and concerns they would like to discuss. Setting an informal agenda at the beginning of the conference enables each participant to be heard.

All people respond to reinforcement, and many of us respond to social approval. Although the interviewer should show interest in parents' comments, it is important not to inadvertently provide reinforcement for certain types of content. For example, if the interviewer nods, smiles, and says "that's interesting" every time parents mention something related to their child's social skills, parents are likely to try to provide more information in that area and omit other areas of importance. If parents stray from the topic or avoid certain areas, it is appropriate to gently redirect them to the issue. The same strategies can be used to ensure that conferences are focused.

Interviews should not be one-way with only professionals posing questions. Families should also have opportunities to ask questions, request information, and seek the interviewer's opinion. One of the goals of family-professional collaboration is the give and take between parents and professionals. An interview that models this is consistent with the collaborative model being promoted. The same is true for conferences.

If the interview or conference is being conducted through an interpreter, several additional issues need to be considered. A relaxed style that allows for comfortable pacing is an important element. Pausing to allow time for translation and recognizing that not as much can be covered in translated interactions are also important. Instead of speaking to the translator, the professional should speak to the parents and respond to them as their words are being translated.

In *closing* the interview or conference, the professional may want to summarize what has been addressed and share notes that were taken. It is also the time to ask if parents or other family members have "anything else" that they want to ask or share. In addition to expressing appreciation for their time and willingness to participate, professionals should give parents a clear statement of the next steps in the assessment or implementation process as well as the accompanying timelines. In an assessment, a schematic diagram that includes steps in the process and projected timelines for each step may be helpful.

Interpreting, Reporting, and Using Information from Interviews and Conferences

Interpreting information shared by families can be simple or complex. In educational situations, interpretation is typically straightforward, relying on the facts and perceptions voiced by parents. The goal of interpretation is to extrapolate the information that provides insight and knowledge about the student's behavior, skills, motivation, and so forth so that it can be used to optimize the educational program. A search for underlying meaning, family dynamics, or pathology is not a goal of this sort of interviewing. Rather, it is important to learn about things such as the parents' objection to a job training experience that would place their daughter in a business downtown or their son's sudden interest in writing and spelling now that he is communicating with friends by e-mail.

Reporting interview information is typically done in a summary of the interview. Although background information that parents feel is important to understanding their son or daughter is included, the focus is on information that is relevant to educational planning. For family-professional collaboration to become a reality, parents must feel safe that the information they share will be used appropriately, and with confidentiality carefully maintained.

Information that parents discuss in conferences is usually not reported formally. Instead, it is incorporated into the program planning and implementation by the teacher or other relevant professional.

Incorporating information in planning and placement is the ultimate goal of the interview process. Learning that Carmen is a baseball fan and that math activities centered around batting averages, box scores, and lifetime scoring records are motivating to her can be used to design instruction that is engaging and relevant. Realizing that Jorge likes to read along with taped versions of adventure stories may provide an adaptation that will support his literacy skills. Knowing that Jake is a computer whiz may provide avenues for improving his self-concept and increasing opportunities for him to engage in higher-order thinking skills.

There are many common strategies in interviewing and conferencing with parents and families. Although strategies and approaches will be tailored to fit each parent and professional, the underlying qualities of effective communicators—respect, nonjudgmental attitude, and empathy—are foundational to effective interviewing and conferencing as well as to developing and maintaining parent-professional partnerships.

CONCLUSION

Working with parents and other family members in the assessment process brings critical information to educational planning and decision making, and the collaborative process strengthens the home-school alliance. Family perspectives help teachers target educational objectives, set priorities, and monitor the effectiveness of instructional strategies. Professional knowledge and expertise helps parents understand their son's or daughter's learning difficulties, find ways to support instruction in daily routines, and partner with professionals in evaluating outcomes.

STUDY GUIDE

REVIEW QUESTIONS

1. List three reasons why parents are important contributors to the assessment process.
2. Why does this chapter include family members other than parents as contributors to the assessment process?
3. What model does this chapter emphasize?
4. List at least three roles that parents and professionals can share in the assessment process.
5. Nonbiased assessment refers only to bias based on linguistic differences. (True or False)
6. Match the examples to the communication qualities each represents. Qualities can be used more than once.

Column A	Column B
a. Respect	___ Incorporates time for parents' questions and concerns
b. Nonjudgmental attitude	___ Expresses sadness when parent cries
c. Empathy	___ Listens without change of tone or expression when family describes a serious behavioral concern
	___ Addresses family by title and name

7. Paraphrasing is often used to clarify, to ensure that information was heard and interpreted accurately, and to show interest and attention. (True or False)
8. Furthering responses refers to the professional adding information from his or her experience to the parents' comments. (True or False)
9. Interviewing families in their homes is always an appropriate way to gather assessment information about a student. (True or False)
10. Match the following questions by type.

Column A	*Column B*
a. Open-ended	___ How often does Mark go the library with you?
b. Close-ended	___ Can Paula follow directions when she and her brother play board games?
	___ What happens when other children in the neighborhood refuse to play with Jennifer?
	___ What are Kevin's plans after he graduates?
	___ About how long does it take for Candace to finish her homework?

ACTIVITIES

1. Develop a brief set of interview questions that might be asked about any student. Interview one of your friends or classmates about his or her son or daughter, applying the communication strategies described in the chapter.
2. Brainstorm a list of things that parents could tell you about their son or daughter that would help you plan a better educational program for him or her.
3. Select a quality of an effective communicator and use it throughout the day. As you interact with friends, family members, classmates, and others, use the strategy. Be prepared to discuss your experiences, successes, failures, and what you learned from the experience.
4. Talk with someone who has served as an interpreter and someone who has participated in a situation in which interpretation was necessary. Ask them to describe their experience and what could have been done to improve it.

DISCUSSION QUESTIONS

1. Some teachers of students with learning difficulties are reluctant to involve parents and other family members in the assessment process. Why do you think this is the case?
2. Recall a situation in which you were being interviewed. Describe the specific positive and negative aspects of the experience and determine how your own experience could be applied to interviewing families.
3. What sort of information can parents provide that would help professionals address academic problems?

CHAPTER 16

EARLY CHILDHOOD ASSESSMENT

by Laura J. Hall

- Considerations in the Assessment of Young Children
- Screening
- Curriculum-Based and Criterion-Referenced Assessment
- Ecological Assessment, Observation, and Play-Based Assessment
- Norm-Referenced and Dynamic Assessment
- School Readiness
- Program Plans, Goals, and Objectives

An understanding of early childhood assessment is not only a necessity for special educators working with young children. It is important for all educators to have knowledge about the philosophy, methods, instruments, and focus of early childhood assessment. This information is important for special education teachers in elementary schools so that they have an awareness of the differences between the approaches and assessment techniques used by early childhood assessors compared with those used once families enter the school system. Teachers who have this understanding can be extremely helpful to families as they make the transition from preschool to elementary school services. Parents who have had experiences with early childhood assessment teams may expect similar attitudes and services once their child is enrolled in the school system. If teachers are aware of this expectation, they can serve as an effective communicator and true liaison with the family.

Knowledgeable special education teachers can also speak about the similarities and differences in assessment instruments used in early intervention compared with the school system to assist with keeping families informed. For example, they may be able to tell a parent that an assessment used in elementary school uses the same format as one used during early childhood. A broad understanding of the issues in assessment across all of the age ranges can only serve to make a teacher the most effective.

Parents, physicians, child-care providers, teachers, and others may notice a lag or unusual quality about a young child's development in one or more areas such as language, motor, or play skills. When children are in preschool, readiness for traditional schooling also becomes an important issue. Parents and others may indicate their concerns about their children's development and school readiness by comments such as, "Jai often wakes up at night, does not play with toys for as long as the other children his age, and his teacher claims that he does not complete tasks that require sustained attention" or "Carla was premature, remains small for her age, and cries easily, especially when requested to follow directions."

When children are younger than school age, the assessment question is not whether they have a specific disability such as a learning disability, mental retardation, or emotional disturbance. Diagnostic queries are frequently avoided for very young children. Assessment questions are focused on any apparent developmental delays or the "risk" for delays of the child so that suitable supports and interventions can be arranged in consultation with the family. Timmy, described in the following case study, is an example of a child who may have delays in one or more areas.

Timmy

Timmy is an attractive 2½-year-old who enjoys watching videos and playing outside on the slide, swings, and jungle-gym. He has a lovely laugh that is particularly strong when his Dad picks him up and holds him high in the air. Timmy's mother and day-care provider, Mrs. Jackson, both have some concerns about Timmy's development, especially in the area of speech and language.

Although Timmy uses some words, he typically communicates what he wants by grabbing objects or displaying a tantrum. Perhaps due to his lack of language skills, he avoids playing with other children, including his 4-year-old sister. He will play with his toy cars for hours, but if his sister tries to join him, he will turn away from her. Timmy's mother really wants her two children to play well together.

CONSIDERATIONS IN THE ASSESSMENT OF YOUNG CHILDREN

The most important consideration in the assessment of young children is the interrelationship between the child and his or her family. In fact, current philosophy guiding best practice indicates that questions about individual children are addressed through a focus of working with the family. Child assessment and family assessment are not considered two distinct areas, but since child issues and family issues are intertwined, together they form the focus of all assessment efforts. This family-centered approach (Dunst, Trivette, & Deal, 1988) to assessment and early intervention is recommended by the parents, teachers, and higher education personnel that comprise the Division of Early Childhood of the Council for Exceptional Children (McLean & Odom, 1996).

It is important for the assessor to be aware of the fact that the relationship with the family begins with the initial interaction. The tone of voice, language used, and expectations implied reveal a great deal about how the assessment will proceed. Contrast the following two introductory comments made to Timmy's parent:

a. Hi, Mrs. Brookes, I am Dr. Jones and I am a special educator from *Early Start* and I am calling to arrange a time when I can conduct an assessment on Timmy. I understand that he has been having some difficulties with language, so the speech therapist and I would like to conduct a few well-established assessments to determine the degree of his problem.

b. Hi, Mrs. Brookes, my name is Mary Jones and I am a special educator working with *Early Start*. I understand that you called about Timmy because you and his day-care provider, Mrs. Jackson, had some concerns about Timmy's language. Is this a good time to talk? I was wondering if I could assist by obtaining additional information about Timmy's language, and I am interested to know what type of information would be most useful for you and Mrs. Jackson.

Once family priorities are established prior to assessment, the context for the assessment is an issue for consideration. Current legislation requires that any form of early childhood intervention, including assessment, be conducted in the least restrictive and most "natural" environments. This may mean that assessments are conducted with parents in a comfortable environment for them, such as in their home, regardless of the form of assessment used.

Neisworth and Bagnato (1996) describe four recommended standards for making assessment choices that were devised through their synthe-

sis of assessment theory, models, and practices. These standards are briefly summarized as follows: (1) Assessment must be useful for early intervention and education (Treatment Utility) or must guide practice that contributes to beneficial outcomes. For example, assessment results that assist Timmy's parents and day-care provider to know what to teach in order to improve Timmy's use of language would be useful. Labeling his language difficulty alone may not be useful. (2) Assessment must be judged as valuable and acceptable (Social Validity). Assessor "b" in the previous example, who asked Timmy's mother and day-care provider what is important information for them, is more likely to conduct an assessment that is socially valid and valuable to the family. (3) Assessment must be based on a wide foundation of information (Convergent Assessment), underlines the importance of using multiple assessments and obtaining information from diverse sources. Timmy may use language differently in day-care, at home, with peers, with his parents, when upset, when most relaxed, etc. In order to obtain a good or valid understanding of Timmy's language usage, several people using various methods would need to contribute information. (4) Assessment-based decisions must be reached through team member consensus (Consensual Validity). A team approach to assessment, with family members as essential team members, that includes collaborative decision making is highly recommended (McLean & Odom, 1996).

Legislation

Federal legislation has had an impact on who is assessed, by whom, and where assessments take place. In 1975, PL 94-142 mandated a free, appropriate education in the least restrictive environment for all school-aged children with disabilities. It also gave parents the right to full involvement in decisions that related to classification and educational placement for their children. One section of the legislation offered small incentive grants to encourage states to develop programs for children ages 3 to 5 with disabilities. In 1985, 24 states had mandates for serving children younger than age 5 with disabilities, with the majority aimed at children ages 3 to 5 (Rossetti, 1990).

In 1986, PL 99-457 (Education of the Handicapped Act Amendments) was passed and required all states to provide services for all 3-to 5-year-old children with disabilities by the 1990–1991 school year. A section of this legislation—Title 1, Handicapped Infants and Toddlers—established a new discretionary program designed for infants and toddlers and their families. In addition to providing infants and young children with services, the family's needs were to be addressed in an Individualized Family Service Plan.

The Individuals with Disabilities Education Act Amendments (IDEA) of 1997 and regulations of 1999 contributed to the mandates for the assessment of and services for young children with disabilities by requiring the development and provision of services for young children birth through age 2 with developmental delays or "at risk" of experiencing a substantial developmental delay (Part C). This legislation emphasizes that parents play a critical role in protecting the rights of their children with delays and in any decisions made regarding their child. Parental consent is required prior to conducting any evaluation or re-evaluation of a child. Part C of the 1997 Amendments states that early intervention services for infants and toddlers birth through age 2 are to be delivered in "natural environments." Education in the least restrictive environment and involvement with typical peers is also strengthened in all Individualized Educational Plans with the added requirement that there is an explanation regarding the extent to which children will *not* be involved with peers without disabilities, followed by a rationale for this practice. Accountability systems and outcome measures or benchmarks and goals are also emphasized in this legislation.

Legislation requires that an Individualized Family Service Plan (IFSP) be devised for all recipients of early intervention services (birth through age 2). The components of the IFSP must include the following to comply with the law:

- A statement of the infant's or toddler's present levels of physical (including hearing, vision, and health status), cognitive, communication,

social or emotional, and adaptive development, based on acceptable, objective criteria.

- A statement of the family's resources, priorities, and concerns relating to enhancing the family's capacity to meet the developmental needs of its infant or toddler with a disability.
- A statement of the major outcomes expected to be achieved for the infant or toddler and family, and the criteria, procedures, and time lines to be used to track progress and to determine whether modifications or revisions of the goals or services are necessary.
- A statement of specific early intervention services necessary to meet the needs of the infant or toddler and the family and of the necessary frequency, intensity, and method of delivering services.
- A statement of the natural environments in which early intervention services shall be appropriately provided.
- The projected dates for initiation of services and the anticipated duration of such services.
- The name of the service coordinator, who is a member of the profession most immediately relevant to the infant's, toddler's, or family's needs, or who is otherwise qualified to carry out all the applicable duties, and who will be responsible for the implementation of the plan and for coordination with other people and agencies.
- The steps to be taken to support transition of the toddler with a disability to services provided by public school districts.

The legal requirements for the Individualized Educational Plan for preschool-aged children ages 3 through 5 are the same as those for older students. The stated requirements for Part B of the IDEA clearly include children ages 3 through 21 with disabilities.

Purposes

The reasons for early childhood assessment overlap with those described in Chapter 1 and include screening, eligibility, planning goals and objectives, monitoring progress, and program evaluation. The importance of early screening for possible developmental delays is well accepted. An in-depth assessment is conducted as a follow-up to a screening to determine the nature of any difficulties and to identify the appropriate services and sources of support to address them (Scandall, 1997a). Skills in one domain, such as language or motor, do not develop in isolation and difficulties in one area can affect the others. For example, a child with language or motor delays may not play or interact with peers in the same way as do typically developing children. Screening for and addressing delays when a child is very young may prevent greater delays in multiple areas in the future.

Assessment to determine service eligibility is an issue for early childhood as well as for school-aged children. Children birth through 2 years of age are eligible for services (a) if they are experiencing developmental delays in one or more of the areas of cognitive, physical, communication, social or emotional, and adaptive development; or (b) if they have a diagnosed physical or mental condition that has a high probability of resulting in developmental delay; or are at risk for developmental delays (at the State's discretion). Definitions of risk and delay, and the recommended assessment methods and instruments to determine risk and delay, vary across and within states of the United States (Widerstrom, 1997).

Children ages 3 through 5 are eligible for special education services if they have an identified disability such as mental retardation, speech or language impairment, or learning disability, or, at the discretion of the State, are experiencing developmental delays as defined by the State. Eligibility for services specific to a particular domain (i.e., speech) or disability requiring a particular pattern of delays (i.e., in communication and play), such as those that identify autism, may require an assessment that confirms these delays or disabilities.

Assessment data are used for planning any intervention or objectives included as part of Individualized Family Service Plans (IFSPs) used in infant and toddler programs and Individualized Education Plans (IEPs), which are written when the child is in preschool. In addition to a focus on the child's delays, the assessment for the IFSP addresses the resources and sources of support available to the family and in the community, as well as the priorities for the family. Bennett,

Lingerfelt, and Nelson (1990) recommend that early interventionists aim to include the following four strategies when planning goals and objectives with the family: specification and prioritization of family needs and aspirations; utilization of existing family strengths and capabilities; identification of sources of support and resources for meeting needs and achieving aspirations; and the creation of opportunities for the development of additional skills and competencies.

As the young child nears age 3, and again at elementary school age, it is critical to guarantee the continuation of vital support services during these transition phases. "Effective procedures for transitions reduce stress and help children, families, and professionals to bridge the differences between programs" (Rosenkoetter, Hains, & Fowler, 1994, p. 3). Parents report not knowing what will happen to their child once the child enters kindergarten as a disempowering experience (Macvean, 1999). Information from current assessments may facilitate the exchange of information between early childhood agencies and the educational system.

The final two reasons for assessment—program monitoring and evaluation—are also purposes for assessment in early childhood (Sandall, 1997a). Any goals agreed upon on the IFSP/IEP are evaluated and changed as needed. Early childhood services are increasingly required to demonstrate the benefits of their programs, and accountability of services is an integral aspect of any reputable early intervention service. Furthermore, obtaining comprehensive research evidence of the factors that result in beneficial outcomes of early intervention is recommended so that program personnel can place their resources to maximize gains (Bryant & Maxwell, 1997).

Areas Assessed

Consistent with the philosophy of viewing child development within the context of the family system, a complete assessment addresses family strengths and needs in addition to child strengths and delays. An effective family assessment should "cover important family domains, incorporate multiple sources and measures, recognize the importance of family values and traditions, determine family priorities for goals and services, vary according to program type and demands, and evaluate family outcomes on a regular basis" (Bailey & Simeonsson, 1988a, p. 9). In addition, discussion of critical events and potential stressors for families as well as family needs and sources of support available (Trivette, Dunst, & Deal, 1997) are important components of an assessment.

Assessment of young children also encompasses all of the main areas of development. Physical factors (hearing, vision, neurological status, etc.) figure prominently in any assessment and children typically obtain a medical examination from a physician to determine if any delays are a result of a primarily physical anomaly. Concept formation and other cognitive functions like attention and problem solving also are usually evaluated.

Another broad area that is assessed is language and communication skills, including both receptive and expressive use of vocabulary and pragmatics. Due to the key role of language in thinking, comprehension, and the formation of social relationships, speech and language are a frequent focus of early childhood assessment. Gross- and fine-motor skill delays would affect exploration and play and, therefore, motor skills are another key area of assessment. Social-emotional development is assessed in the context of both the home and the play group or school setting. Self-help and adaptive skills are important area addressed by assessment teams. Assessment that is useful will focus on what the child can do given any identified delays in order to determine the effect of any problems. If the child can function well during daily activities, including self-help activities, then it would be concluded that the effects of an identified delay were minimal.

When the child reaches ages 4 and 5, school readiness becomes a focus of evaluation and may include early reading, mathematics, and writing skills. Goal 1 of the National Educational Goals is *All children in America will start school ready to learn* (National Education Goals Panel, 1998). Oral language and motor development continue to be major elements in assessment. The importance of social behavior expands to include typical classroom demands and expectations of teachers. School attitude and work habits, including the child's ability to follow directions and attend to tasks, are also evaluated during this period.

Issues

There is an emphasis in current legislation to provide services in natural environments, which are defined as those that are natural or normal for the child's age peers without disabilities or delays, such as within community agencies, organizations, or homes. In these environments, children with delays or disabilities have an opportunity to interact and play with their typically developing peers. Providing services in natural environments can result in families building relationships within their community that may result in increased sources of support. Identifying and creating service opportunities in natural environments promote a focus on child and family strengths. Services that are not conducted in natural environments require justification. It is the challenge for early intervention service providers to assure quality service that addresses identified benchmarks and objectives in natural environments.

Since it is highly recommended that assessment is linked to practice (Neisworth & Bagnato, 1996) or linked to curriculum (Bagnato, Neisworth, & Munson, 1997; Puckett & Black, 2000), then it would be important for the assessor to be aware of and to influence the curriculum that will be used during early intervention services. "A curriculum is an organized set of activities and experiences designed to achieve particular developmental or learning objectives" (Hanson & Lynch, 1989, p. 158). Ideally, any initial assessment would be instrumental in the design of the individualized curriculum. The objectives for any group of young children would be incorporated into or serve as the framework for the activities and experiences designed by early intervention personnel. Progress with objectives would be monitored on an ongoing basis during these activities (Bagnato et al.). Assessment would be an integral component of service delivery rather than an event that occurs prior to, or periodically during, an early intervention or preschool program.

Although conventional, norm-referenced measures are not recommended due to their lack of articulation with the commonly used, functional curriculum (Bagnato et al., 1997; Puckett & Black, 2000), these measures are still used. Pressures on assessors of young children to support eligibility decisions based on comparisons with chronologically aged peers and to demonstrate child progress with reliable and valid instruments are two reasons why the use of such measures continues. Proponents of alternative assessment measures argue that young children in this age range are highly individualistic in the progression through developmental stages because of a variety of factors including the home and community environment.

Thus, there is considerable demand for ecological assessments. The child's development must be considered in light of the family and cultural context as well as other environmental factors. Ecological assessments require observations within a setting such as the home, and preferably multiple settings, so that the environmental effects on participants can be determined (Pellegrini, 1996). Typically observations begin with a narrative description of what is occurring within the setting followed by some more systematic collection of information. The design, arrangement, and implementation of ecological assessments require skill, experience, and time.

"Choices of assessment materials and methods in early intervention are expanding" (Neisworth & Bagnato, 1996, p. 25). Choosing the team members, choosing the times and places for assessment, and choosing when and how to interact with all team members, especially the child's family, are some of the choices made by assessors working with young children and their families. Each of these choices requires consideration of the issues that make up the choices, and effective assessors must continually balance these issues. Some of the issues that require this balancing act for the assessment team are listed in Table 16-1.

Current Practices

In 1991, the Division of Early Childhood (DEC) established a Task Force on Recommended Practices in early intervention/early childhood special education. One of the major content areas, or strands, was assessment. A group of representatives worked together to identify a list of standards that were rated and validated by 500 individuals, including DEC members, family members, and higher education personnel. Table 16-2 lists these recommended practices for determining eligibility, program placement, program planning, and monitoring.

TABLE 16-1
The Balancing Act of an Early Childhood Assessor

BALANCING:	WITH:
Collecting sufficient information	Intrusion in the family
Using a team for multiple perspectives	Intrusion in the family
Selecting and using ecologically valid assessments	Time and cost
Seeking multiple and diverse opinions	Interpretation of assessment information that is integrated and coherent
Developing an early intervention program in a natural environment with developmentally appropriate activities	Developing program evaluation that is ongoing, authentic, and addresses issues of efficacy of early intervention
Embedding educational goals in enjoyable activities with peers	Collecting ongoing, relevant data on individual child progress with established goals
Providing information to others to maximize outcomes	Maintaining confidentiality

TABLE 16–2
DEC Recommended Practices

- Professionals gather information from multiple sources (e.g., families, other professionals, paraprofessionals, and previous service providers) and use multiple measures (e.g., norm-referenced, interviews, etc).
- Professionals gather information on multiple occasions.
- Team members discuss qualitative and quantitative information and negotiate consensus in a collaborative decision-making process.
- Team members select assessment instruments and procedures that have been field tested with children similar to those assessed for the purposes intended.
- Assessment approaches and instruments are culturally appropriate and nonbiased.
- Professionals employ individualized, developmentally compatible assessment procedures and materials that capitalize on children's interests, interactions, and communication styles.
- Materials and procedures, or their adaptations, accommodate the child's sensory and response capabilities.
- Professionals assess strengths as well as problems across developmental or functional areas.
- Measures and procedures facilitate education and treatment (i.e., intervention or curriculum objectives) rather than only diagnosis and classification.
- Measures are sensitive to child and family change.
- Professionals assess not only skills acquisition but also fluency, generalization, and quality of progress.
- Professionals maintain confidentiality and discretion when sharing information.
- Curriculum-based assessment procedures are the foundation or "mutual language" for team assessment.

Note: From "DEC Recommended Practices" (pp. 379–380), in S. L. Odom & M. E. McLean (Eds.), *Early Intervention/Early Childhood Special Education: Recommended Practices.* Austin, TX: PRO-ED. Copyright 1996 by PRO-ED. Reprinted by permission.

Curriculum-based assessment procedures are those that obtain data on child competencies by evaluating the child's skills as they are displayed while interacting with the materials and peers that are found within the curriculum used in early childhood programs. This form of assessment is classified as an informal assessment approach due to the fact that the behaviors observed, the questions asked by the assessor, and the tasks that create the assessment may vary across children and are usually not standardized. Experts in the area of early childhood assessment argue that by using curriculum-based assessment techniques, the assessor obtains an "authentic" picture of the child's competencies in comparison to inauthentic assessment techniques, which include contrived tasks with unfamiliar materials administered in an unfamiliar setting (Bagnato et al., 1997). The use of curriculum-based assessment techniques is one of the hallmarks of current practices in early childhood special education.

Natural physical and social environments are the recommended settings for obtaining information from assessment procedures. Using the child's own toys, common household items, common toys within the preschool setting, and toys with adaptive qualities helps to create an assessment that captures the child's strengths (Bagnato et al., 1997). Complete reliance on formally administered tests or parent and teacher interviews may provide a partial or biased perspective of abilities or disabilities.

The formation of an assessment team that includes family members as equal contributors is required by legislation and recommended practice (McLean & Odom, 1996). It is recognized that no single agency or professional discipline can meet the diverse, individual, and often complex needs of young children with delays or disabilities and their families (Sandall, 1997b). Although the multiple perspectives of team members can be obtained using several models, one in which there is high collaboration in the planning, collection, and evaluation of assessment information across team members is highly recommended. The transdisciplinary model meets this criterion with the benefit of team members with various areas of expertise (e.g., speech therapist, early childhood educator, parent) who learn from each other as they share the skills and information from their discipline (Sandall).

Along with a growing understanding of the ways in which culture influences our style and interpretation of interactions, priorities, and customs, early interventionists are required to be aware of their own culture (Lynch, 1998) as well as the culture of the families with whom they work. "Culture is not a rigidly prescribed set of behaviors or characteristics, but rather a framework through which actions are filtered or checked as individuals go about daily life" (Hanson, 1998, p. 4). Although it is important to have a broad understanding of the typical beliefs, values, and practices of the families that comprise the communities where the early interventionist works, it is also important to remain sensitive to the uniqueness of each family. "The goal of cultural learning is insight, not stereotype" (Lynch, p. 67). Cultural understanding enhances the assessor's ability to choose the most appropriate assessment methods and tools and to interact with the family in an effective manner.

SCREENING

In the first stage of the assessment process, the assessment question asked is: *Is there an indication of possible developmental delay(s) that warrant further assessment?* A screening is a brief assessment aimed at identifying those infants/children who may be demonstrating developmental delays due to differences as compared with standard expectations for children of the same age range and cultural background (Bondurant-Utz & Luciano, 1994). Due to the understanding that early intervention can prevent the occurrence of more severe delays and difficulties for the child and family if delays are detected and addressed, an effort is made to find children with developmental delays or those at risk for delays. Strategies for finding and screening young children vary, and may include public education about the importance of early intervention in order to build community awareness; establishing a formal network of informed agencies that serves as a referral system; disseminating information about the screening

system and the number of families served as a means of maintaining local publicity and contacts; and canvassing the community for children in the designated age range to identify those who need screening by means of local announcements of screening events or through a systematic survey (Peterson, 1987).

The *Ages and Stages Questionnaires* (Squires, Potter, & Bricker, 1999), is an example of a screening instrument. This instrument is a set of developmental surveys that are completed by parents periodically when their child is between 4 and 54 months of age. Each of the questionnaires, which are available in English and Spanish, contain 30 developmental items divided into five areas: communication, gross motor, fine motor, problem-solving, and personal-social. Scoring can take as little as 1 minute and can be completed by paraprofessional or clerical staff under the guidance of a professional (Squires et al., 1999). The validity of the questionnaires has been obtained using standardized assessments with an overall agreement of .83, and test-retest reliability for 175 parents is reported to exceed .90. The accompanying guide includes a section on cultural and language adaptations. The major advantages of this instrument are that it assists parents in monitoring their own child's development and assures they have a critical role in any assessment of their child.

Screening instruments used by professionals who are trained to implement them are typically divided into domains or areas that are evaluated. The *Denver Developmental Screening Test (Denver II)* (Frankenburg et al., 1990) was designed to screen developmental delays in children from birth through age 6 in the areas of personal, social, fine motor-adaptive, language, and gross motor. Children from the Denver area, including those with typically Anglo, African-American, and Spanish surnames, were used as the comparison group. No children with disabilities were used in the comparison sample. Although it is the best known screening instrument, it significantly under-identifies children (Bondurant-Utz & Luciano, 1994).

The *Developmental Observation Checklist System (DOCS)* (Hresko, Miguel, Sherbenou, & Burton, 1994) is a screening tool that is comprised of three interrelated components: child development, child behavior, and the family's coping ability and stress. This multidimensional approach can be used with families who have children between the ages of birth and 6 years whose dominant language is English. The developmental checklist focuses on language, social, motor, and cognitive skills using functional activities. Parents rate their child's behavior as well as their own stress and support. The three components of the *DOCS* take approximately 30 minutes to complete (Hresko et al.).

Screening instruments are also used if developmental delays appear to indicate a specific disability. For example, the *Autism Screening Instrument for Educational Planning* (Krug, Arick, & Almond, 1993) uses multiple measures to determine if the child has a pattern of skills and behaviors that are similar to those of individuals diagnosed with autism. According to the American Psychiatric Association (1994), these would include qualitative impairments in the areas of social interaction and communication as well as restricted, repetitive, and stereotyped patterns of behavior, interests, and activities. The complete package includes an autism behavior checklist; an educational assessment that addresses the five areas of staying seated, receptive language, expressive language, body concept, and speech imitation; an interactive assessment that measures social responses and responses to requests; and an analysis of a sample of vocal behavior from the child.

Screening procedures may also identify preschool-age children who are considered gifted and talented. The field of gifted education has emphasized the benefits of early intervention (Stile, 1996). Enriched preschool programs provide opportunities for these young children to demonstrate their strengths and an environment where their high potential can be nurtured (Kitano, 1990). The same recommendations of multiple measures and multiple approaches to more in-depth assessment following screening are relevant for young children who are gifted and talented (Stile, 1996).

Regardless of the screening procedures selected, it is important for assessors to assure that those who administer screening instruments are well qualified and experienced in performing screening tasks, that multiple forms of assessments are used, especially those that obtain input from parents, and that more in-depth assessments and, most importantly, follow-up services, are available (Bondurant-Utz & Luciano, 1994).

CURRICULUM-BASED AND CRITERION-REFERENCED ASSESSMENT

Another important assessment question to consider in the early childhood years is: *Are young children able to perform the developmental skills needed in order to communicate, play, and adapt to their daily routine successfully?* This question can be addressed using curriculum-based assessment (CBA) by evaluating the young child's performance of the goals and objectives that are part of, or embedded in, the early intervention or preschool program and home routine. The foundation of curriculum-based assessment is the developmental or hierarchical sequence of competencies that enables teams of parents and professionals to establish current functional levels (Neisworth & Bagnato, 1996). Curriculum-based assessments can be conducted in natural settings and during structured and unstructured activities (Neisworth & Bagnato).

Bagnato et al. (1997) have published a description, or "snapshot," and review of curriculum-based assessment instruments in their book, *Linking Assessment and Early Intervention*. This book serves as an excellent guide for the selection of assessment measures. Each of the assessment instruments reviewed was rated on a scale of 1.0 (negligible) to 3.0 (exemplary) on the six dimensions outlined in Table 16–3. Several of these measures are described in the following paragraphs, beginning with those that received the highest rating, or 3.0, in all six dimensions.

The *Hawaii Early Learning Profile (HELP)* received a score of 3.0 in all six dimensions for both the *Birth to 3* (Parks, Furono, O'Reilly, Inatsuka, Hoska, & Zeisloft-Falbey, 1994) and the *Preschooler* (ages 3–6) (Vort Corporation, 1995) versions. The assessment is made by observing the child's activity under ongoing or arranged circumstances as well as through parent interviews (Bagnato et al., 1997). The *HELP* is organized into strands that identify a range of skills

TABLE 16-3
Standards for Desirable Early Childhood Assessments

STANDARD	LINK DIMENSION
Authenticity	• Bases assessments on sequential authentic goals contained within a curriculum's developmental hierarchy or task analysis • Taps natural developmental competencies • Emphasizes areas of strength rather than areas of concern • Relies on child's actual performance, work samples, and videotaped records • Requires use of developmentally appropriate and familiar toys and materials or necessary adaptive toys • Promotes natural circumstances for assessments • Converts contrived test items into authentic tasks • Balances quantitative and qualitative performance information
Convergence	• Accepts/incorporates multiple data sources, including curriculum-compatible and authentic information • Focuses on assessment in natural contexts • Relies on play-style stagings of assessments to complement natural displays of behavior • Ensures broader coverage of the child and family's developmental ecology • Promotes inter- or transdisciplinary modes of teamwork • Is family centered in outlook process
Collaboration	• Relies on family as the primary source of authentic child performance data • Supports consensus decision making and use of collaborative problem solving and judgments as the most valid assessment process • Fosters in situ cross-talking and consensus decisions among parents and professionals about the child's capabilities, needs, and family priorities
Equity	• Adapts tasks to accommodate child's functional limitations • Emphasizes criteria task/competencies demonstrated by the child irrespective of functional limitation • Uses test-teach-test approach to identify primary response mode and to generalize its use by the child with various materials, activities, and settings • Conducts assessments via a natural test-teach-test framework that blends testing and teaching • Seeks to uncover and foster the child's learning-to-learn skills and abilities
Sensitivity	• Uses sequential curricular goals and graduated metrics to monitor small increments of individual progress • Links authentic assessment tasks to authentic curriculum goals and authentic curriculum goals to authentic interventions • Underscores activity-based interventions in natural home and preschool settings and using natural activities • Links to real-life IEP/IFSP goals
Congruence	• Accomplishes major purposes and missions of early childhood and special education • Uses developmentally appropriate styles of assessment that emphasize play, natural observations, and parent reports • Contains tasks and procedures that allow flexible accommodations for young children with wide individual differences, in particular developmental delays and disabilities • Encompasses content and procedures that have field-derived social and treatment validities to support their suitability for use with young children, particularly those with special needs

Note: From Bagnato, S. J., Neisworth, J. T., & Munson, S. M. (1997). *Linking Assessment and Early Intervention: An Authentic Curriculum-based Approach* (p. 73). Baltimore: Paul H. Brookes. Reprinted by permission.

within a dimension of competence (such as cognitive and regulatory/sensory organization). A full description of the following areas appears under each item: a complete definition of the item, the assessment materials needed, assessment procedures in easily replicable detail, adaptations that could be made to elicit the skill, instructional materials, and instructional activities that can be used to teach the item. Figure 16–1 shows a sample item—*kicks a stationary ball using a 2-step start*—listed under the gross-motor domain in the preschool assessment and curriculum guide. The interrelationship among assessment, curriculum, and intervention is clear from this example.

Also receiving a rating of 3.0 for each criterion established in Table 16–3 are the four volumes of the *Assessment, Evaluation, and Programming System (AEPS) for Infants and Children*. Volume 1 contains the measurement system for birth to age 3 (Bricker, 1993) and Volume 2 is the companion volume, containing a corresponding curriculum for the same ages (Cripe, Slentz & Bricker, 1993). Volumes 3 and 4 include the measurement (Bricker & Pretti-Frontczak, 1996) and curriculum (Bricker & Waddell, 1996) content for ages 3 to 6.

Assessment and curriculum items are organized by six key domains: social, social-communication, fine motor, gross motor, adaptive, and cognitive. The assessment tool is flexible enough to be used with children with motor and sensory impairments (Bagnato et al., 1997). In addition to the clear interface between measurement and curriculum and the detailed descriptions of the directions and materials needed for each item, this curriculum-based system has a number of other noteworthy features. There is a goal and objective written for each item and the objective contains a criterion for success. Suggestions for environmental arrangements to maximize skills are included and the importance of the skill for each item in the curriculum is also described. Figure 16-2 is an example of an item, *correctly activates simple toy,* found in the cognitive domain. Bagnato et al. state that "there appears to be no instrument better than AEPS for providing precise yet family-friendly assessment for early intervention" (1997, p. 95).

Another highly rated (Bagnato et al., 1997) and widely used set of curriculum-based measures is *The Carolina Curriculum for Infants and Tod-*

dlers with Special Needs (Johnson-Martin, Jens, Attermeier, & Hacker, 1991) and *The Carolina Curriculum for Preschoolers with Special Needs* (Johnson-Martin, Attermeier, & Hacker, 1990). Child behaviors, organized into five developmental domains, are listed along with a situation to elicit activities or a description of a position or activity in which the skills are likely to be observed. A recording sheet includes a column alongside each item to record the date when the skill is mastered. The curriculum includes activities that facilitate the development and learning of skills, and includes suggestions for group activities (Johnson-Martin, Attermeier, & Hacker).

Curriculum-Compatible and Criterion-Referenced Measures

Criterion-referenced tests (CRTs) measure a child's performance or mastery of a skill or sequence of skills (Bondurant-Utz & Luciano, 1994). The focus on mastery or achievement of the criterion-referenced assessments used in early childhood is on developmental sequences and milestones. Since early childhood services and programs include activities that are designed to promote skills based on young children's typical developmental patterns, the criteria included in CRTs are often consistent with, or "compatible" with, the curriculum in these early childhood programs. Bagnato et al. (1997) describe curriculum-compatible assessment instruments as those that are not part of a specific curriculum but are useful for instructional planning and ongoing assessment. Due to the fact that curriculum-compatible assessments include items that are listed in hierarchies or sequences, it is easy to develop objectives to address the domains assessed as the basis for the curriculum.

The *BRIGANCE*® *Diagnostic Inventory of Early Development-Revised* (Brigance, 1991) is an example of a frequently used criterion-referenced and curriculum-compatible measure. The instrument focuses on developmental skills divided into 11 domains and can be used for infants and children with a developmental age up to 7 years. The measure is appropriate for children with mild to moderate delays or disabilities. Figure 16–3 is a sample item, *prespeech gestures,* from the speech and language skills area. Assessors could use the *BRIGANCE*® along with other forms of

3.159 Kicks a stationary ball using a 2-step start

Strand: 3-7A **Age:** 38-48m 3.2-4y

Definition

Place a stationary ball (soccer, rubber) on a flat surface at least 5 feet away from the child. The child will kick the ball, using a two-step start, any distance or any direction.

Assessment Materials

A 10-inch ball (soccer, rubber, plastic or utility), masking tape.

Assessment Procedures

Level One:

1. Place a 2-foot piece of tape on the ground or floor and set the ball about 3 feet in front of the tape. Note: The placement of the ball should allow the child to use a two-step start from the tape.
2. Ask the child to watch closely as you demonstrate standing on the line, taking two steps and kicking the ball.
3. It is important not to count out loud as you take the steps.
4. How you kick the ball is important, not where you kick it.
5. Ask the child to stand on the tape, and place the ball at the appropriate distance in front of her.
6. Say, "Kick the ball."
7. Allow her two tries.
8. Observe her as she kicks the ball, watching for: (1) the two-step approach, (2) whether she firmly places one foot near the ball and puts her other leg in a straight line behind it, (3) whether her arms are in opposition to her legs (left foot planted and right arm forward in front of body, right foot straight in a kicking position and left arm behind the body); (4) that her kicking leg moves forward, kicks the ball, and the kicking leg follows through.
9. If the child demonstrates a problem in the basic kick, by pushing the ball instead of kicking it, bending her knees before straightening her leg for the kick, if her arms are inactive and not in opposition to her leg movement, if she loses balance after the kicking motion, or if she appears to be clumsy and out of synchronization, direct assistance is recommended. The following are some suggestions: (1) Increase the size of the ball; (2) Walk her through the movements of approaching the kick, kicking the ball, and the follow through; (3) Tell the child the steps to take, for example, "Stand, Ready, Step, Step and Hold, Foot Back, Swing Forward, Kick Ball"; (4) Place footprints on the floor that are color-coded, left foot, right foot, and ask the child to follow the path before she kicks the ball; (5) Physically assist her by pointing to which leg or foot she should move and which arm to swing in opposition.
10. After you have provided assistance and allowed her to practice, repeat the assessment above.

Level Two:

11. Observe the child as she kicks a ball during playtime or a physical exercise period.

Adaptations

Some children lack the ability to integrate a visual stimulus with a motor action. A child must convert one type of information (visual—the stationary ball) to another type of information (motor—kick the ball). If the child's sensory system (converting one type of information to another) is delayed, she may exhibit difficulty responding with a motor action based on a visual stimuli. Often such a child reacts only to one process and finds visual-motor integration difficult. To assist a child with her kicking skills, the following is recommended: (1) Use a large, soft, easy-to-kick, textured ball; (2) Remind her to get ready to kick the ball; (3) Walk her through the kicking motion; (4) Provide physical assistance to her as she tries to kick the stationary ball.

Instructional Materials

A 10-inch ball (soccer, rubber, plastic), a goal post (can be set up by putting two chairs back-to-back to represent the uprights of a miniature goal post; the space between the backs of the two chairs should be about 30 inches). Masking tape.

Instructional Activities

1. Place the miniature goal posts 6 feet in front of the ball. Attach a short strip of tape to the ground for a starting line where the child will stand. Place the ball at least two steps in front of the starting line.
2. Ask the child to stand on the starting line.
3. Tell her to kick the ball and to try to make it go through the posts.
4. She may use her right or left foot.
5. Give her one point if she kicks the ball through the posts.
6. Allow her to continue in an effort to improve her total points.

FIGURE 16-1

Sample Item from the *Help for Preschoolers Assessment & Curriculum Guide*

Note: From *HELP for Preschoolers Assessment & Curriculum Guide* (pp. 229–230) by Vort Corporation, 1995, Palo Alto, CA: Vort Corporation. Copyright 1995 by Vort Corporation. Reprinted by permission.

Objective 1.1 Correctly activates simple toy

DEVELOPMENTAL PROGRAMMING STEPS

☑ The objective above is the most basic step for the skill to be taught. Most children will benefit from the activities outlined here that emphasize this skill. For children who need more instruction, consider designing programming steps from the *environmental arrangements* suggestions or from the *instructional sequence* outlined.

IMPORTANCE OF SKILL

This skill represents the child's ability to produce actions that take into account the specific properties of the object. The child differentiates actions that activate specific objects from those that merely produce interesting results. Therefore, the child begins to identify the items that easily produce specific actions (e.g., balls roll and bounce, rattles shake).

PRECEDING OBJECTIVE

Cog C:1.2   Acts on mechanical and/or simple toy in some way

CONCURRENT OBJECTIVES

FM A:2.2 Holds an object in each hand	Cog D:1.1 Imitates motor action that is commonly used
FM B:3.1 Uses either hand to activate objects	Cog G:1.3 Uses simple motor actions on different objects
GM A:3.5 Bears weight on one hand and/or arm while reaching with opposite hand	SC A:1.1 Turns and looks toward object and person speaking
	SC A:3.1 Engages in vocal exchanges by cooing
GM B:1.4 Sits balanced without support	Soc A:2.2 Responds to familiar adult's social behavior
GM D:4.4 Rolls ball at target	Soc C:1.5 Entertains self by playing appropriately with toys

TEACHING SUGGESTIONS

Activity-Based

- Provide the child with a variety of objects and toys that are activated directly by a simple action (e.g., shaking, banging, hitting, rolling, squeezing).
- Select toys that produce effects that are interesting to the child.
- Offer toys that are activated by different actions. For example, rattles and bells are activated by shaking; larger objects, such as a roly-poly toy, are activated by a push with the arm and hand; and squeeze-toys are activated by squeezing.
- Make sure the child has time to thoroughly explore and exercise a number of actions (e.g., mouthing, shaking, banging) on an object before you expect correct activation.
- Introduce objects within an interactive, turn-taking game and demonstrate the toys' correct use.

Environmental Arrangements

- Use toys that continue a movement after an initial activation (e.g., rocking horse, wobbly toy, wind chimes, toy with pendulum). Use toys that produce a sound (e.g., bell, drum) or a visual effect (e.g., a transparent rattle full of beads).
- Join in the child's play with the toy. Demonstrate the correct use of a toy the child is already using or manipulating. Encourage the child to incorporate new movements into play if he or she is holding a rattle with moving parts (demonstrate how to make other parts move).

Instructional Sequence

- Model or have a peer model activating a toy and then hand it to the child. If necessary, give specific instructions (e.g., say, "Shake the bells," "Kick the ball").
- If the child does not use a simple toy correctly, provide verbal directions to encourage the child and to focus the child's attention (e.g., say, "Look at this," "Something funny is going to happen").
- Physically assist the child to activate simple toys.

TEACHING CONSIDERATIONS

1. Adapt your choice of a toy to the sensory impairment of the child (e.g., use a wobbly toy that a child with a motor impairment can activate with a light touch, or use a noise-producing toy for a child with a visual impairment).
2. If the child has a severe visual impairment, allow tactile exploration of the toy before expecting the child to activate it. Provide verbal cues and describe the toy as the child touches it.
3. Consult a qualified specialist for further techniques for the child with a visual, hearing, or motor impairment.
4. Consider safety with all objects that the child handles. Never leave the child unattended with potentially hazardous objects.

FIGURE 16-2

Sample Item from the *Assessment, Evaluation, and Program Systems (AEPS) for Infants and Children*

Note: From *Assessment, Evaluation, and Programming System for Infants and Children: Vol. 2 AEPS Curriculum for Birth to Three Years* (pp. 275–276) by J. Cripe, K. Slentz, and D. Bricker, 1993, Baltimore: Brookes. Copyright 1993 by Brookes. Reprinted by permission.

Prespeech Gestures

Skill: Exhibits prespeech gestures.

Developmental Record Book: Page 10.

Comprehensive Skill Sequence: Page 120.

Class Record Book: Page 12.

Assessment Methods: Interviewing the parent(s). Observing the child performing the skill, formally or informally.

Material: An environment that is natural for the child.

Discontinue: After failure on two consecutive skills.

Time: Your discretion.

Accuracy: Give credit for each positive answer to the criterion question (*CQ*).

Note: Observe the Child at One Month of Age: By one month of age, there is usually observable evidence that the child
- enjoys the warmth and sensations of a bath.
- enjoys the snugness of being wrapped and securely held.
- reacts positively to being comforted and having needs met.
- reacts negatively to discomfort and denial.

References: The following references were used to sequence the prespeech gestures skills and behaviors and to validate the developmental ages. (See **Bibliography,** pages 255–256.)

2:239, 250	26:51
4:118–120	30:199
11:72	35:4–5
12:140, 166	41:238
13:280	47:2
15:216	48:431
20:161–163	49:329–332
23:265	53:24, 201
24:143–146, 154	

◆ ◆ ◆
Objectives

By _____(date)_____ , when provided with the appropriate stimuli, _____(child's name)_____ will (list as appropriate)
1. smile.
2. smile when talked to.
3. laugh aloud.
4. raise arms when parent says *Come here* or *Up* while reaching toward child.
5. shake head for no.
6. wave "bye-bye."
7. show affection.
8. nod head for yes.
9. gesture to make wishes known.
10. point to something he/she wants another to see.
11. combine gestures and utterances to make wishes known.

◆ ◆ ◆
Directions

See pages 94–95 for the goals and methods for this assessment and how the criterion questions (*CQs*) listed after each skill may be used for assessing the skill.

0 1 1. Smiles.
   CQ: **Does _____ smile?**

2. Smiles when talked to.
   CQ: **Does _____ have a spontaneous social smile? Does he/she smile when talked to?**

3. Laughs aloud.
   CQ: **Does _____ laugh aloud?**

0 4 4. Raises arms when parent says *Come here* or *Up* while reaching toward child.
   CQ: **Does _____ raise his/her arms when a parent says *Come here* or *Up* and reaches toward him/her?**

0 10 5. Shakes head for no.
   CQ: **Does _____ shake his/her head from one side to the other for no, indicating understanding of a simple question for which the answer is no?**

6. Waves "bye-bye."
   CQ: **Does _____ wave "bye-bye" at the appropriate time with apparent understanding?**

7. Shows affection.
   CQ: **Does _____ show affection to others by giving them a kiss, a hug, or a pat?**

8. Nods head for yes.
   CQ: **Does _____ nod his/her head up and down for yes, indicating understanding of a simple question for which the answer is yes?**

1 0 9. Gestures to make wishes known.
   CQ: **Does _____ use gestures such as reaching, pointing, or motioning to make his/her wishes known?**

1 3 10. Points to something he/she wants another to see.
   CQ: **Does _____ point to something he/she wants another person to see?**

11. Combines gestures and utterances to make wishes known. 1 6
   CQ: **Does _____ use gestures and sounds or utterances to make wishes known?**

FIGURE 16-3

Sample Item from the *BRIGANCE® Diagnostic Inventory of Early Development-Revised*

Note: From *BRIGANCE® Diagnostic Inventory of Early Development-Revised* (p. 99–100) by A. H. Brigance, 1991, North Billerica, MA: Curriculum Associates. Copyright 1991 by Curriculum Associates. Reprinted by permission.

assessment as part of the multiple measures recommended for best practice.

The *Pediatric Evaluation of Disability Inventory (PEDI)* is an example of a curriculum-compatible instrument that is designed for children with various sensory, motor, and neurological delays (Haley, Coster, Ludlow, Haltiwanger, & Andrellos, 1992). This instrument contains three measurement scales—caregiver assistance, functional skills, and modifications, for use with children age 6 months to 7 years. Content domains include categories such as self-protection, getting in and out of the car, eating, and floor locomotion.

ECOLOGICAL ASSESSMENT, OBSERVATION, AND PLAY-BASED ASSESSMENT

Another important assessment question is: *Given a particular context (home, an activity, an adult), which skills does the child display?* Keen observational skills are critical for the assessor who is guided by current legislation and philosophy that emphasizes conducting assessments in natural environments using familiar contexts and materials. To comply with best practice recommendations, the assessor must obtain information about the child's developmental skills by observing the child interacting with and within the context of familiar settings. The format and focus of the observation will vary depending upon the priorities and questions from the family and other assessment team members. The better the assessment team is at selecting methods that will result in the desired information, the more valid will be the assessment. If the assessors have a variety of skills in observational, ecological, and play-based methods to draw upon, the more likely the assessment will be conducted in an effective and valid manner.

Ecological Assessment

An ecological approach to assessment helps the team to understand the range of responses that a child and family may exhibit under a variety of conditions (Bondurant-Utz & Luciano, 1994). The assessment team that uses the ecological approach focuses on understanding the interrelationship between the child and family and the family and its environment (Bronfenbrenner, 1979) and uses this information to determine intervention and support strategies. The goal of the observer who is using the ecological approach is to identify patterns and sequences of behaviors given a specific context (Bondurant-Utz & Luciano). The techniques selected and used should take into account the culture, socioeconomic status, and value system of the child and family (Bailey & Wolery, 1989).

Assessment instruments and interview guides have been developed in order to obtain an understanding of the family factors that influence the developmental outcomes for the child with disabilities or delays, or the child who is at risk for delays. Examples of some of these assessment tools will now be described. It is important to note that when the term "family" is used, the broad definition of parents and family as described in Chapter 15, and the cultural considerations in determining family membership, should be applied when using the family assessments.

Family Interviews and Rating Scales. Although family assessment utilizes many methods, the family interview is particularly useful for gathering data about family characteristics, family strengths and priorities, and family perceptions of situations, events, goals, and services (Bailey & Simeonsson, 1988b). A structured interview is better than paper-and-pencil tests because the interviewer can monitor whether he or she is being intrusive, language and questions can be changed to meet a family's values and culture, a family can more easily screen its responses, and there is more flexibility (Hanson & Lynch, 1989). The communication skills described in Chapter 15 would be necessary to conduct a sensitive and informative interview. Good listening skills are very important, as are the abilities to maintain neutrality and listen and respond in a manner that is nonjudgmental. Parents and other family members must be regarded as equals; that is, their perceptions must be regarded as having equal value to those of other assessment team members. Finally, competence, openness, and a genuine desire to help the family are essential. Table 16–4 contains a description of five phases in a family-focused interview (Bailey & Simeonsson, 1988a). Notice the emphasis on obtaining the family's perspective of any issues and of establishing family priorities.

TABLE 16-4
Phases of a Family-Focused Interview

INTERVIEW PHASE	PURPOSE
1. Preliminary Identify high-priority needs Identify difficulties in parent-child interaction Specify child characteristics that have potential family impact Note upcoming critical events	Prepare for interview by summarizing assessment data
2. Introduction Explain purpose of the interview Confirm time allotted and format Disucss confidentiality Structure physical environment (if possible)	Reduce parents' anxiety and create appropriate listening environment
3. Inventory Make opening statement Allow parents to do most of the talking	Validate and elaborate information from assessment Identify additional areas of family needs, strengths, and resources
4. Summary, priority, and goal setting Make summarizing statements Explore family's priorities Set goals collaboratively	Clarify consensus and disagreement between parents Agree on definition of family needs Establish priorities and set goals
5. Closure Express recognition and appreciation of parents' contribution Ask if family members have additional concerns or thoughts about interview	Recognize parents' efforts Allow concerns about interview to emerge

Note: From *Family Assessment in Early Intervention* (p. 194) by D. B. Bailey & R. J. Simeonsson, 1988a, New York: Merrill/Macmillan. Copyright 1988 by Macmillan Publishing Company Reprinted by permission.

In addition to the general topics addressed in a family interview, information about a specific area such as child development or parent-child interaction may be obtained using a parent report survey, questionnaire, or behavior scale. The *Vineland Adaptive Behavior Scale* is used to obtain parents' opinions on the skills of their child in the domains of communication, daily living skills, socialization, and motor skills (Sparrow, Balla, & Cicchetti, 1984). This scale can be used to discuss children from birth through adulthood and provides information about the developmental skills and adaptive behavior that is viewed by family members. Figure 16–4 displays a sample score summary and profile for the Interview Edition Survey Form.

An adaptive behavior scale is one of the measures recommended for determining difficulties related to attention deficits or hyperactivity (Barkley, 1998). Another measure used to assess difficulties with attention that is completed by parents is a re-

port measure specifically designed to address behavioral issues. Parents complete the *Home Situations Questionnaire (HSQ)* by rating the occurrence and severity of their child's behavior across 16 different home and public situations such as "when asked to do chores" or "when you are visiting someone's home" (Barkley, 1987).

Stress, Coping, Strengths, and Needs. If the family and assessors would like information about parental stress in addition to information obtained during a family interview, then the *Parenting-Stress Index (PSI)* (Abidin, 1983) may facilitate discussion and augmentation of family support. This 101-item questionnaire requires parents to rate their agreement or satisfaction with statements on a scale of 1 (strongly disagree) to 5 (strongly agree). Responses to items in parent and child domains are compared to normative samples. The parent domains include depression, attachment, restriction of role, competence, social isolation, relationship

Vineland Adaptive Behavior Scales: INTERVIEW EDITION Survey Form

Individual's name _Sally_   Chronological age _13-5-7_

Date of interview _5-10-84_   Supplementary norm group (if applicable) _____

Before beginning the score summary, read Chapter 5 in the manual.

SCORE SUMMARY

SUBDOMAIN		Raw Score	Standard Score X=100, SD=15 Tables B.1 and B.2	Band of Error 90 % Confidence Table B.3	National %ile Rank Table B.4	Stanine Table B.4	Supplementary Norm Group %ile Rank Table B.5	Adaptive Level Tables B.6 and B.8	Supplementary Norm Group Adaptive Level Tables B.7 and B.9	Age Equivalent Tables B.10 and B.11
	Receptive	26						Adeg		7-10
	Expressive	60						Mod Lo		8-9
	Written	40						Adeg		13-6
COMMUNICATION DOMAIN SUM		126	96	± 11	39	5		Adeg		12-6
	Personal	77						Adeg		13-6
	Domestic	34						Adeg		16-0
	Community	45						Adeg		12-6
DAILY LIVING SKILLS DOMAIN SUM		156	99	± 8	47	5		Adeg		13-6
	Interpersonal Relationships	45						Adeg		9-8
	Play and Leisure Time	26						Lo		6-8
	Coping Skills	31						Adeg		12-0
SOCIALIZATION DOMAIN SUM		102	78	± 11	7	2		Mod Lo		9-6
(For ages to 5-11-30)	Gross									
	Fine									
MOTOR SKILLS DOMAIN SUM				±						
	SUM OF DOMAIN STANDARD SCORES		273							
ADAPTIVE BEHAVIOR COMPOSITE			88	± 7	21	3		Adeg		11-10

SCORE PROFILE

(See Chapter 5 in the manual to graph scores.)

	Standard Score ± Band of Error
COMMUNICATION DOMAIN	96 ± 11
DAILY LIVING SKILLS DOMAIN	99 ± 8
SOCIALIZATION DOMAIN	78 ± 11
MOTOR SKILLS DOMAIN	±
ADAPTIVE BEHAVIOR COMPOSITE	88 ± 7

Standard Score: 20 30 40 50 60 70 80 90 100 110 120 130 140 150 160

percentile rank: 1 2 5 9 16 25 37 50 63 75 84 91 95 98 99

-5SD -4SD -3SD -2SD -1SD MEAN +1SD +2SD +3SD +4SD

OPTIONAL **MALADAPTIVE BEHAVIOR DOMAIN** (Administer for ages 5-0-0 and older)		Raw Score	Maladaptive Level: Table B.12	Supplementary Norm Group Maladaptive Level: Table B.13
	Part 1	7	Intermediate	
	Parts 1 and 2			

FIGURE 16-4

Sample Summary and Profile from *Vineland Adaptive Behavior Scales*

Note: From *Vineland Adaptive Behavior Scales, Interview Edition, Survey Form Manual* (p. 127) by S. S. Sparrow, D. A. Balla, & D. V. Cicchetti, 1984, Circle Pines, MN: American Guidance Service. Copyright 1984 by American Guidance Service. Reprinted by permission.

with spouse, and health. The child domains include adaptability, acceptability, demandingness, mood, distractibility, and reinforcement of parents.

It is important to consider critical events, because families of infants and children with disabilities and delays may experience added stress from both normal life events and events that, by their nature, are stressful. The diagnosis of a child's disability, the lack of developmental milestones, efforts in obtaining services, transitions such as preschool to elementary school programs, and medical crises, can pose particular challenges for these families (Bailey & Simeonsson, 1988a). It is important that assessors are

aware of whether such events are occurring in the families with whom they are working.

Family members may report that they are having difficulty coping with the situation of caring for a child with a delay or disability. Exploring this issue through discussion with an open and sensitive early interventionist may be the most effective response to such a comment. If the results from a coping scale would enhance this discussion, then a measure such as the *Ways of Coping Inventory* (Folkman, Lazarus, Dunkel-Shetter, DeLorgis, & Gruen, 1986) could be used.

Support from family, friends (informal), and agency personnel (formal) is often needed to address stress and enhance coping. Inventories and surveys have been designed to assist early interventionists in assessing the needs of families for resources, including sources of support. The *Family Needs Survey* (Bailey & Simeonsson, 1988b) and the *Family Needs Scale* (Dunst, Cooper, Weeldreyer, Snyder, & Chase, 1988) were developed for use as an initial step in identifying and addressing the needs of families. A factor analysis on the *Family Needs Scale* resulted in the following factors for the 41 items of the scale: basic resources, specialized child care, personal and family growth items, financial and medical resources, child education, meal preparation, future child care, financial budgeting, and household support. The *Family Strengths Profile* (Trivette, Dunst, & Deal, 1988) is a complementary instrument used to record the family's current resources and strengths (such as commitment, sense of purpose, problem-solving, positivism, and flexibility).

Once needs and strengths are identified, the family's preferences for how needs are addressed should be determined. An instrument that may facilitate this discussion is the *Family Information Preference Inventory* (Turnbull & Turnbull, 1990), which has 37 items arranged across five areas: teaching the child at home, advocacy and working with professionals, planning for the future, helping the family relax and enjoy life more, and finding and using more support. Regardless of which surveys and inventories are used, it is the early childhood assessment team, together with the family, that works to devise an individualized plan to address issues and concerns.

Direct Observation

One means of determining patterns of behavior is through direct or systematic observation. For example, the assessment team might want to observe Timmy's use of language during meal times at home. The question from the team would be formulated as follows:

Given a familiar and comfortable environment (at home during meals with family) what vocalizations, words, and gestures are used by Timmy?

This question can be addressed through a variety of observational methods from which the team would need to choose.

Observers could use a developmental checklist with predetermined and defined communication and language skills; the item is checked when it is observed during the meal. A narrative recording could be used when observers attempt to write down the language as it is occurring within the context (Pellegrini, 1996). If the team has a well-defined question such as Timmy's use of incomplete sentences or misuse of pronouns, then the systematic observation of these behaviors could be obtained using event recording or a time-sampling method. These observational methods would enable the assessor to either count the number of times the behavior has occurred (event recording) or estimate the occurrence of the behavior (time-sampling) given the context (see Alberto & Troutman, 1999, for a more complete description of these observational techniques). The team could also use the same method across several settings and compare Timmy's language among different contexts. In addition, the team could identify the factors in the environment that facilitated Timmy's best performance or helped Timmy to use his best language skills. This information would be very helpful for determining any educational strategies.

If family members agree that the information is important, the assessor may choose to include a measure of parent-child observation. Depending upon the purpose of the observation, the assessor may select a predesigned inventory, scale, or coding system. Careful consideration of the purpose of the instrument should be made when deciding about whether to use a predesigned observational tool or to create one designed for the specific purposes of the assessment (Pellegrini, 1996).

Parents' use of effective instructional techniques can be assessed by using the *Teaching Skills Inventory* (Rosenberg, Robinson, & Beckman, 1984), which rates variables such as clarity of instruction, effectiveness of prompts, and modifications of tasks from videotaped interactions. Current emphasis is on incorporating any teaching into the family routine or already occurring activities.

Many of the available observation instruments were designed to be used during play interactions. Examples include the *Parent/Caregiver Involvement Scale* (Farran, Kasari, Comfort, & Jay, 1986), which measures adult involvement across 11 behaviors such as verbal responsiveness and control;

the *Social Interaction Assessment/Intervention* (McCollum & Stayton, 1985), which scores turn-taking, imitation, etc. from videotaped play interactions; and the *ECO* (MacDonald & Gillette, 1989), which addresses turn-taking, communication, and conversational pragmatics through the use of a rating scale and interview. Early childhood assessors can consider how any of these observational instruments could be used in conjunction with a play-based assessment.

Play-Based Assessment

When observational methods are used in the context of play, they are referred to as play-based assessments. The behaviors that the assessment team may be interested in could be play behaviors and skills. For example, if the assessment team is concerned about the characteristics of autism, then observing the child at play and evaluating play skills would be very important since unusual play skills or the lack of play skills is one of the defining characteristics of this disability. Table 16–5 provides a list of questions that can be addressed about the quality of play using systematic observation (Sattler, 1988).

Play also can be used as the context for assessing one or more domains in addition to play skills. Play is one of the main contexts for young

TABLE 16-5
Possible Observation Areas to Assess Children's Play

Entrance into the play room
- Does the child go into the playroom easily?
- Does the child ask to hold the mother's or interviewer's hand on the way?
- Does the child approach the toys, or does he or she cling to the mother?

Initiation of play activities
- Is the child a quick or slow starter?
- Does the child require help in getting started?
- Does the child need encouragement and approval?
- Is the child able to direct his or her own play?
- Does the child require active and steady guidance?
- Does the child show initiative, resourcefulness, or curiosity?
- Is the child impulsive?
- Does the child initiate many activities but seldom complete them, or does he or she maintain interest in a single activity?

Energy expended in plan
- Does the child work at a fairly even pace, or does he or she use much energy in manipulating the play materials, making body movements, and making verbalizations?
- Does the child seem to pursue an activity to the point of tiring himself or herself?
- Does the child start to work slowly and then gain momentum until the actions are energetic, or does he or she gradually lose momentum?
- Does the child seem listless, lethargic, lacking in vitality?

Manipulative actions in play
- Is the child free or tense in handling the play materials?
- Are movements large and sweeping or small and precise?
- Are movements smooth?
- Are play materials used in conventional or unconventional ways?

Tempo of play
- Does the child play rapidly or with deliberation?
- Is the pace of play hurried or leisurely?
- Does the pace of play vary with different activities or is it always about the same?

Body movements in play
- Does the child's body seem tense or relaxed?
- Are the child's movements constricted or free?
- Are the child's movements uncertain, jerky, or poorly coordinated?
- Are movements of hands and arms free, incorporating the whole body rhythmically, or are movements rigid, with only parts of the body being used?
- Does the child use the right hand, the left hand, or both hands?

Verbalizations
- Does the child sing, hum, use nonsense phrases, or use adult phrases as he or she plays?
- Does the child giggle appropriately?
- What is the general tone of the child's voice tones (for example, loud, shrill, excitable, soft, aggressive, tense, enthusiastic, or matter-of-fact)?
- What does the child say?
- What is the purpose of the child's verbalizations, judging from the intonation?

Tone of Play
- What is the general tone of the child's play (for example, angry, satisfied, hostile, impatient)?
- Does the child throw, tear, or destroy play materials?
- Is the child protective of play materials?
- If aggression is present, does it have a goal or is it random?
- Does aggression increase, causing the play to get out of hand and posing a threat of damage to the playroom or interviewer?

Integration of play
- Is the play goal-directed or fragmentary?
- Does the play become more integrated over time?
- Does the play have form, or is it haphazard?
- Is the child's attention sustained or fleeting?
- Is the child easily distracted?
- Are there any peculiar elements to the play?

Creativity of play
- Is the play imaginative or stereotyped?
- Does the child use simple objects for play, or are special toys needed?
- Does the play show elements or improvisation or constriction?

Products of play
- What play materials are preferred?
- What objects are constructed or designs completed during play?
- Do the products have a recognizable form?
- How does the child achieve form?
- Does the child show interest in the product?
- Does the child tell a story about the product?
- Does the child show the interviewer and/or parent the product?
- Does the child want to save the product?
- Does the child want to give the product to someone?
- Does the child use the product for protective or aggressive purposes?
- Is the child overly concerned with neatness, alignment, or balance of the play materials?

Age appropriateness of play
- Is the play age-appropriate?
- Are there changes in the quality of the play?

Attitude toward adults reflected in play
- Does the child comply with adult request or do what he or she thinks adults expect of him or her?
- Does the child imitate adult manners accurately?
- Does the child protect himself or herself from adults?
- Does the child attempt to obtain tender responses from adults?
- Does the child follow his or her own ideas independently of adults?

Note: From *Assessment of Children* (3rd ed.) (pp. 418–419) by J. M. Sattler, 1988, San Diego, CA: Author. Copyright 1988 by Jerome M. Sattler, Publisher. Reprinted by permission from the publisher and author.

children and is an activity that is frequently engaged in at home and in toddler programs and preschools. Therefore, it is an ideal "natural" environment in which to conduct an assessment. Using play as a means of assessing cognitive development can be considered as an alternative approach to standardized or norm-referenced assessments (Bondurant-Utz & Luciano, 1994). The assessor can observe the child organize materials, interact with playmates, and interact with toys in both structured and unstructured play situations as a means of determining strengths and weaknesses in the area of cognitive development.

If screening determines that further assessment is necessary to provide information about the quality and degree of Timmy's delays, and Timmy's family agrees to further assessment, then arranging a play environment would be an appropriate context for such an evaluation. Since Timmy likes cars, it would be good to include tracks and tunnels to be used by Timmy and to see if he will pretend that the car is on the track. It would be helpful to have peers playing nearby to see if Timmy will engage in parallel play with the cars and if he notices the other children nearby.

The assessment of all major domains through structured and free-play situations is the approach used by Linder (1993). This Transdisciplinary Play-based Assessment (TPBA) approach uses a transdisciplinary team who designs, observes, and evaluates the skills of a young child who is interacting with the team, family, and materials in the context of play. Linder (1993) writes that play opportunities and experiences influence cognitive understanding, emotional development, social skills, language usage, and physical and motor development and therefore is an important context for the evaluation of all of these skills. This ecological approach can be individualized to address the questions of the assessment team. The general structure and approximate time needed for each phase of a TPBA play session is outlined in Table 16–6. The challenges for assessors who use this approach are the organization of the team, the time it takes to plan the individualized activities that elicit the priority behaviors, conducting the assessment over multiple periods of time and contexts, and the development of a coherent plan as a consequence of the assessment (see Table 16–1).

TABLE 16-6
Transdisciplinary Play-Based Assessment Session

			TIME ALLOTTED
Phase I	Unstructured facilitation		20–25 minutes
Phase II	Structured facilitation		10–15 minutes
Phase III	Child–child interaction		5–10 minutes
Phase IV	Parent–child interaction		
	A. Unstructured		5 minutes
	B. Separation		
	C. Structured		5 minutes
Phase V	Motor play		
	A. Unstructured		5–10 minutes
	B. Structured		5–10 minutes
Phase VI	Snack		5–10 minutes
		Total Time	60–90 minutes

Note: From Transdisciplinary Play-Based Assessment: A Functional Approach to Working with Young Children (p. 43) by T. W. Linder, 1990, Baltimore: Brookes. Copyright 1990 by Brookes. Reprinted by permission.

NORM-REFERENCED AND DYNAMIC ASSESSMENT

Sometimes the assessment team is interested in answering this question: *How do the child's skills compare with those of other children his or her age?* Norm-referenced tests use standardized procedures and materials to present selected tasks to elicit specific skills (Bondurant-Utz & Luciano, 1994). Performance is evaluated to a set criterion that is compared to a reference group. The primary purpose of norm-referenced assessments is to measure a child's performance level in relation to other children. Norm-referenced tests can provide information about delays in development compared with typically developing peers, which is why they are used for eligibility purposes. If states define delay by a comparison with typical development using standard deviations, or percentages such as 25% delay, or by months of delay, then comparisons with norms from reference groups from standardized assessment instruments are supported.

Norm-referenced tests are commonly administered by psychologists who receive specific training in the design, administration, and scoring of these instruments. For example, the *Bayley Scales of Infant Development-Second Edition* (Bayley, 1993) is a three-part evaluation of a child from birth through age 30 months, consisting of a Mental Scale (memory, learning, sensory-perception), a Motor Scale (fine and gross motor), and Behavior Rating Scale (attention, interests, emotions, etc.). Infants are observed while doing tasks and parents report about performance or assist the child to complete the task successfully. The *Battelle Developmental Inventory* (Newborg, Stock, Wnek, Guidubaldi, & Svinicki, 1988) can be used with infants and young children from birth through age 8. Five domains—personal-social, adaptive, motor, communication, and cognitive—contain 341 developmental skills with suggestions for adaptations for specific sensorimotor disabilities. An accompanying curriculum is in development for use with this curriculum-compatible assessment (Bagnato et al., 1997). Additional norm-referenced tests that can be used to measure intellectual performance with preschool-aged children were described in Chapter 7.

Dynamic assessment is a method that is considered an extension of existing, normed, static tests (Lidz & Thomas, 1987). The components of a dynamic assessment are to test, teach, and retest. The aim is to determine which strategies, if any, assist the learner to be successful with test items. A dynamic assessment measure designed for use with preschool children, the *Preschool Learning Assessment Device (PLAD)* was created as an extension of the norm-referenced *Kaufman Assessment Battery for Children (K-ABC)* (Kaufman & Kaufman, 1983). In the *PLAD,* two subtests of the *K-ABC*—triangles and matrices—are administered, first in the standardized fashion and then with pre-identified mediation strategies (Lidz & Thomas). For example, strategies used if errors are made when the child is asked to draw a picture of a child include modeling, using puzzles to describe body parts, helping the child to verbalize what the task is, asking the child how she or he plans to proceed, and encouraging additions and alternatives. Following the mediated activities, the item is repeated or the child is asked once again to draw a picture. Dynamic assessment methods help with the identification of child strengths and provide information on the processes the child uses to respond to test items. The original dynamic assessment, the *Learning Potential Assessment Device (LPAD),* was discussed in Chapter 7.

SCHOOL READINESS

In readiness assessment, the question of interest is: *Does the child have the preacademic and behavioral skills that would facilitate learning in elementary school classrooms?* The *BRIGANCE® K & 1 Screen-Revised* (Brigance, 1987) for kindergarten and first grade is a brief survey of critical developmental skills in the domains of general knowledge and comprehension (e.g., color recognition), speech and language (e.g., syntax and fluency), gross motor (e.g., hopping), fine motor, (e.g., draw a person), mathematics, (e.g., numerals in sequence), readiness (e.g., recites alphabet), basic reading skills (e.g., auditory discrimination), and manuscript writing (e.g., prints personal data). The *BRIGANCE*® also contains a supplementary Teacher Rating Form and a Parent Rating Form with items similar to the screening items.

The *Developmental Indicators for the Assessment of Learning-Revised (Dial-R)* (Mardell-Czudnowski & Goldenberg, 1990) is a 25- to 30-minute mass screening procedure for children aged 2 to 6 years. Children move through various stations for testing and observation. *DIAL-R* consists of 24 items spread equally over three areas (gross and fine motor, concepts, and communication) that reflect actual expected classroom behaviors. Behavioral observations are made on a checklist after each administration for such behaviors as clumsiness and hyperactivity. A parent information form is also completed. Another screening tool designed with a focus on classroom performance and behavior, the *Academic Performance Rating Scale* (DuPaul, Rapport, & Perriello, 1990), is recommended by Russell Barkley (1990), an expert in the area of attention deficit disorder. This scale was developed to provide a means of screening for school functioning quickly. It is a teacher rating scale of academic productivity and accuracy in major subject areas with norms based on a sample of children from central Massachusetts.

Assessments have been designed to determine skills in specific academic areas such as reading and math. The *Test of Early Reading Ability* (2nd ed.) *(TERA-2)* (Reid, Hresko, & Hammill, 1989) and the *Test of Early Mathematics Ability* (2nd ed.) *(TEMA-2)* (Ginsburg & Baroody, 1990) are two screening instruments that can be administered to preschoolers. The *TERA-2* requires children to listen, express themselves orally, and point to responses of print, pictures, and numerals. The *TEMA-2* contains 35 informal problems (counting and calculation) and 30 formal problems (number facts, base-ten concepts) to which children must respond verbally and nonverbally by writing numerical answers. Both of these norm-referenced instruments are reported to identify children who are significantly different from their preschool-aged peers in the early development of these skills.

The *Peabody Picture Vocabulary Test Third Edition (PPVT-III)* (Dunn & Dunn, 1997) can be used with children from age 21 months to determine receptive vocabulary abilities. The child responds to questions from the administrator by pointing to one of an array of four possible pictorial selections. The *Test of Early Language Development* (3rd ed.) *(TELD-3)* (Hresko, Reid, & Hammill, 1999) assesses receptive and expressive grammatical forms and content of language for children from age 3. The *Test of Early Written Language* (2nd ed.) *(TEWL-2)* (Hresko, Herron, & Peak, 1996) is designed to be used with children ages 3 through 10 to evaluate basic and contextual writing skills, including the identification of writing materials and letters and the child's ability to draw and understand signs and words.

McCormick and Kawate (1982) had kindergarten teachers rate a list of survival skills. Those recommended as "very important" or "absolutely essential" included independent task work (i.e., stays on task without extra teacher attention); group attending/participation (i.e., focuses visual attention on speaker(s), shifting focus appropriately); following class routine; appropriate classroom behavior (i.e., waits appropriately); self-care; direction following; social/play skills (i.e., maintains play with peers for an appropriate length of time); and functional communication (i.e., states needs). The authors recommend that preschool assessment include these skills.

PROGRAM PLANS, GOALS, AND OBJECTIVES

The important next step in assessment is development of the intervention plan. The team focuses on this question: *How will early intervention personnel assist young children and their families to maximize strengths and develop new skills?*

Individualized Family Service Plans

Families of a child aged birth through age 2 who receive services must have an Individualized

Family Service Plan. "In order to develop a meaningful and useful IFSP, the process must be one that encourages and respects families, responds to their priorities and concerns, and builds on their strengths" (Sandall, 1997c, p. 241). Discussing family strengths during an initial interview sets a positive tone and facilitates family participation (Bondurant-Utz & Luciano, 1994). A contributing factor of a family's strength is the resources available. Resources and sources of support can be described in four categories (Trivette et al., 1997): (1) personal and social network members that include those individuals to whom a family can turn to seek advice, assistance, and nurturance, such as partners, friends, and neighbors; (2) associational groups such as church and outdoor groups, fitness clubs, and charities, etc.; (3) community programs and professionals that include agencies that provide services, including schools; and (4) specialized professional services such as special education and early intervention programs.

Given the resources available to the family, the assessment team identifies target outcomes. Outcomes specify what is to occur and what is expected as a result of these actions (Sandall, 1997c). Outcomes should be written in easily understood terms so that everyone on the assessment team will be able to know if the outcome has been reached. The criteria and time lines for meeting the goal or outcome should be identified with particular attention to how family members define success in meeting the specific goals. A sample page from an IFSP (Bennett et al., 1990), which includes benchmarks and objectives fabricated for Timmy and his family, is found in Figure 16–5. Note that the goals are written to strengthen family and child performance with services delivered at home and in center-based and community-based programs.

Timmy

The opportunity for Timmy to practice his language and communication skills and his ability to interact and play with his sister are the priorities for the Brookes family. Through multiple assessments (family interview, observation, play-based, and curriculum-based)

it was determined that Timmy has a developmental delay in the area of language. He is also delayed in his play skills compared with other children his age. Timmy is eligible for early intervention services, and during the IFSP process it was agreed upon that the focus of the efforts by all team members would be in the area of language. His communication, language, and play skills would receive ongoing monitoring so that a change in emphasis could be arranged at any time. All team members are hoping that with a focus on speech and language now, and when Timmy is in preschool, that he may be ready for kindergarten with his peers.

When the child reaches age 3, the family begins to receive services from the Department of Education, which requires an Individualized Educational Plan rather than the IFSP. This plan also includes goals and objectives as a means of evaluating progress with identified outcomes.

Program Monitoring and Ongoing Assessment

Although benchmarks, goals, and outcomes are required to be reviewed at least every 6 (IFSP) or 12 (IEP) months, an accountable early intervention service would plan to evaluate whether or not services were addressing goals on a much more frequent basis. Several challenges to obtaining ongoing assessment must be addressed. Curriculum-based assessments are recommended (Bagnato et al., 1997) because the transition from establishing areas of delay to defining the curriculum for addressing the delay with an accompanying measure of change is comparatively smooth. If measures that do not have an accompanying curriculum are used, such as norm-referenced instruments, then service providers must develop the curriculum based on results of these measures along with creating a monitoring system.

Service delivery in natural environments creates an opportunity for group activities of children with and without disabilities or delays. Early childhood interventionists need to assure that goals are being addressed in these heterogeneous groups as well as monitoring progress with the

Name ___Timmy Brookes___ **Date** ___OPD.0___ **Family's Name** ___Brookes___ **IFSP#** _1_ **FIPP Staff Member** ___Jan Lee___

Date / #	NEED/PROJECT OUTCOME STATEMENT	SOURCE OF SUPPORT/ RESOURCE	COURSE OF ACTION	FAMILY'S EVALUATION Date	FAMILY'S EVALUATION Rating
3-16 / 1	Family has requested a workable transportation plan to meet all preferred appointments.	Jan will provide support and information. Grandparents, neighbors, and colleagues have volunteered some rides to specific appointments.	Jan will provide information on transportation funded by Early Start and on public transportation. Parents will talk with grandparents and colleagues about car pooling possibilities.	3-16-2000 5-24-2000	3 7
3-16 / 2	The Brookes family would like "to see Timmy talk more," and the team will focus on getting Timmy to state, "I want" consistently to request desired items, objects, or events.	Sam (Early Start speech therapist) will work with Timmy weekly on this goal. Parents will communicate with Sam and provide consistent approach at home.	Timmy will attend Early Start's toddler program once a week for speech and language service.	3-16-2000 5-24-2000	3 5
3-16 / 3	Timmy will increase his vocabulary words to 25 words.	Parents, grandparents, neighbors, sister, Early Start staff and Mrs. Jackson (day-care provider) will all focus on teaching Timmy the identified vocabulary words.	Sam will establish a list of target words with parents and notify other Early Start staff and Mrs. Jackson.	3-16-2000 5-24-2000	3 3
3-16 / 4	Mrs. Brookes would like Timmy and his sister to share toys during parallel play activities at least once a day.	Early Start Service Coordinator will suggest strategies. Mrs. Jackson will arrange activities during day-care.	Service coordinator will meet with parents and Mrs. Jackson to share strategies to promote play between Timmy and his sister. Preferred activities for both children will be identified.	3-16-2000 5-24-2000	4 6

Family's Evaluations

1...Situation changed, no longer a need
2...Situation unchanged, still a need, goal, or project
3...Implementation begun, still a need, goal, or project
4...Outcome partially attained or accomplished
5...Outcome accomplished or attained, but not to the family's satisfaction
6...Outcome mostly accomplished or attained to the family's satisfaction
7...Outcome completely accomplished or attained to the family's satisfaction

FIGURE 16-5
Portion of the IFSP for Timmy

goals. Carrying pencil and paper to these activities may be cumbersome. Recalling observations made at the end of the day may be inaccurate, and the use of videotape to record activities for review later is time-consuming and costly. With consideration of these challenges, a method for monitoring progress with identified outcomes is extremely important. Most young children with disabilities and delays and their families cannot wait 6 months to find out that an activity or method of service delivery was ineffective. Serial or ongoing assessment must be incorporated into the design of the service. The frequency of monitoring would depend on the importance of the goal, the degree to which progress is being made, and the demands on the caregivers (Wolery, 1996).

Activity-based interventions in which clearly defined goals are embedded in enjoyable activities (Bricker & Cripe, 1992) facilitate ongoing assessment. Incorporating goals into the family routine or in fun activities is an important component of service delivery. Observing the effect of these events on outcomes and recording these observations facilitates communication with other service delivery and assessment team members, and provides important information for future reference.

Program Evaluation

Outcome evaluations for individual programs and for the early intervention field have become increasingly in demand. Funding sources, as well as participating families, want to know if programs have been able to minimize or prevent developmental problems from occurring for children at risk (Guralnick, 1997). Two meta-analyses support the effectiveness of early intervention programs (Casto & Mastropieri, 1986; Shonkoff & Hauser-Cram, 1987). However, Guralnick writes that a major task for future research is to identify those specific program features (curriculum, intensity of service, role of parent involvement) that are associated with optimal outcomes for children and families. Regardless of the positive outcomes for the field in general, the evaluation of the effectiveness for specific programs also remains a key challenge.

Recommended practice for program evaluation from the Division of Early Childhood of the Council for Exceptional Children (Snyder & Sheehan, 1996) includes the following four attributes: utility, feasibility, propriety, and technical adequacy. Evaluation practices are considered useful if they support the abilities of early intervention stakeholders in a credible, informative, and timely manner. When designing program evaluation methods, the constraints of resources, time, and the political context need to be considered. The ethical and constitutional rights of participants in program evaluation need to be taken into account in evaluation design, as well as the use of technical methods that are valid, reliable, accurate, fair, and replicable. "Program evaluators in early intervention and early childhood special education, whether an individual classroom teacher addressing an isolated question or an external evaluation team examining a comprehensive service delivery system must negotiate and compromise in order to generate the most technically sound and useful information" (Snyder & Sheehan, p. 377). Accepting this challenge of continuing to improve the quality of services to best meet the priorities and needs of families who have young children with delays and disabilities through ongoing assessment is the responsibility of all early childhood special educators.

STUDY GUIDE

REVIEW QUESTIONS

1. The most important consideration in the assessment of young children is the interrelationship between the _____ and the _____ .
2. Where are early intervention services to be delivered according to Part C of the Individuals with Disabilities Education Act?

3. Assessment to determine service eligibility is not an issue for young children birth through age 2. True or false?

4. Which of the following developmental areas is/are typically assessed for possible delays?
   a. Physical factors (e.g., hearing, vision, neurological status)
   b. Cognitive development
   c. Language and communication skills
   d. Gross- and fine-motor development
   e. All of the above

5. Curriculum-based assessment
   a. is recommended as a best practice in early childhood assessment.
   b. allows comparison of one child's performance to that of others his or her age.
   c. allows the assessor to obtain an authentic picture of the child's competencies
   d. answers a and b
   e.   answers a and c

6. Parents serve as equal partners with professionals on early childhood assessment teams. True or false?

7. A(n) _____ is a brief assessment aimed at identifying those infants/children who may be demonstrating developmental delays.

8. Which of the following is *not* a curriculum-based assessment?
   a. *Denver Developmental Screening Test*
   b. *Hawaii Early Learning Profile*
   c. *AEPS for Infants and Children*
   d. none of the above; all are curriculum-based assessments

9. Match the assessment question in Column A with the assessment device or procedure in Column B.

Column A	*Column B*
a. Is there an indication of possible developmental delays that warrant further assessment?	___ Curriculum-based assessments
	___ Measures such as the *Test of Early Reading Ability*
b. Are young children able to perform the developmental skills needed in order to communicate, play, and adapt to the daily routine?	___ Screening measures such as the *Ages and Stages Questionnaires*
c. Given a particular context, which skills does the child display?	___ Ecological assessment, direct observation, and play-based assessment
d. How do the child's skills compare with those of others his or her age?	___ Norm-referenced measures such as the *Bayley Scales of Infant Development*
e. Does the child have the pre-academic and behavioral skills needed in elementary school classrooms?	

10. Which of the following assessments encourage parental input?
    a. *Vineland Adaptive Behavior Scale*
    b. *Bayley Scales of Infant Development*
    c. Transdisciplinary Play-Based Assessment
    d. *Test of Early Written Language*
    e. *Hawaii Early Learning Profile*

11. For what do the letters IFSP stand?

ACTIVITIES

1. Find out what agencies in your community assess infants and young children. What procedures do they use?
2. Select one observational method and observe a young child during play for 15 minutes. What skills do you observe? Is there any evidence of delays?
3. Describe how you would embed a child's individualized objectives in a typical preschool activity (such as circle time).
4. Observe a person who is assessing a young child using a structured assessment procedure. What are the noticeable differences from assessing older children?
5. Observe a family interview. How did the interviewer structure the questions and modify them as needed? Did the interviewer focus on family strengths?

DISCUSSION QUESTIONS

1. Some families may look to you for guidance in the selection of priorities for themselves and their young child. How can you support these families while encouraging them to identify their strengths, needs, and priorities?
2. Using multiple measures to obtain assessment information is supported in policy and practice. How will you determine which measures to use with which family?
3. Special educators frequently state that they do not have time for program evaluation assessment. Discuss why it is important for special educators of young children to be involved in program evaluation and describe the link between ongoing assessment and program evaluation.

CHAPTER 17

ASSESSMENT FOR TRANSITION PLANNING

by Jeanne B. Repetto

- Considerations in the Assessment of Adolescents and Young Adults
- Strategies for Transition Assessment
- Providing Transition Services
- Assessment for College and Other Postsecondary Settings

When adolescents and young adults with mild disabilities are assessed, questions about future adult roles and needed transition services invariably arise. To address these questions, the assessment team must consider the transition process and the types of services and supports students will require to successfully move from the K–12 educational system to the adult world.

Transition assessment is an individualized, ongoing process that assists students to identify their interests, preferences, strengths, and abilities in relationship to the preparation for adult roles including employment, postsecondary education, independent living, community involvement, and social/personal relationships (Sitlington, Neubert, Begun, Lombard, & Leconte, 1996). The general assessment question to be answered for adolescents and young adults with disabilities is: *What are the student's transition-related interests, preferences, strengths, and abilities?* Although students' school learning needs must be clarified for instructional purposes, transition service needs must also be addressed directly in a systematic fashion.

Phillip

Phillip is a 16-year-old ninth grader who has been identified as mildly retarded. At his last 3-year evaluation, Phillip performed in the below average range on measures of general intelligence, adaptive behavior, and academic achievement. His main instructional needs are in reading, mathematics, and written language; he also has poor fine-motor coordination. Phillip has difficulty with remembering, sequencing, and organizing his thoughts, as well as in making decisions. His parents and teachers agree that his program should stress functional skills for post-school community adjustment, including vocational guidance and education.

As part of the assessment for this year's IEP review, several measures will be administered to gain more information about Phillip's transition needs. These measures will evaluate his interest, awareness, and knowledge of occupations; his aptitudes for certain jobs; and his community adjustment.

CONSIDERATIONS IN THE ASSESSMENT OF ADOLESCENTS AND YOUNG ADULTS

Appropriate transition assessment and services are essential to meet the needs of students with disabilities. Recent follow-up studies of individuals with mild disabilities indicate that, compared to nondisabled peers, they experience (a) higher unemployment and/or underemployment, (b) higher work dissatisfaction, (c) less participation in community and leisure activities, (d) higher dependency on family and friends, and (e) higher rates of academic failure in postsecondary education (Lichtenstein, 1993; Sitlington, Frank, & Carson, 1992; Wagner, Blackorby, Cameto, Hebbeler, & Newman, 1993).

The *Seventeenth Annual Report to Congress on the Implementation of the Individuals with Disabilities Education Act (IDEA)* (U.S. Department of Education, 1995) reported on the relationship of secondary school experiences to early post-school outcomes for individuals with disabilities. Data collected in 1993 indicated that 28% of students with learning disabilities and 48% of youth with emotional disabilities exited school prior to graduation or completion of a vocational program. These early school leavers were less likely to enroll in post-secondary vocational or academic education. Further, they experienced difficulty obtaining and retaining jobs. On a more positive note, the report suggests that successful experiences in the secondary grades positively impact the post-school adjustment of these students (deFur, 1999).

Transition services that include an individualized outcome-oriented program for students with disabilities will provide them with this needed success while they are in school. Three major components of transition planning include (Brolin, 1995; Clark & Kolstoe, 1995; Repetto & Webb, 1999; Sarkees-Wircenski & Scott, 1995):

- General and continuing education,
- Career development, and
- Specific vocational programming.

The first component consists of general knowledge, basic academic skills, aesthetic preparation, physical education, and so forth.

Career development, the second component, is defined by the National Occupational

Information Coordination Committee (1994) as "the lifelong process through which individuals come to understand themselves as they relate to the world of work and their role in it" (p. 3). Work in this context includes all life roles (i.e., family member, employee, student, friend). These roles change as one progresses through life, causing one to be in a state of continued growth and progress. Clark and Kolstoe (1995) describe this progression with these words: "One's career is one's progress, or transition, through life as a family member, citizen, and worker" (p. 31). Thus, career development is a lifelong process that involves a broad array of experiences ranging from the awareness level to the self-actualization level.

Specific vocational programming, the third element in transition planning, is an important aspect of the schooling of students with mild disabilities (Brolin, 1995; Cobb & Neubert, 1999; Sarkees-Wircenski & Scott, 1995). Such training cannot be left to chance after students leave school. There is much to be said for demonstrating early that students can learn to have saleable skills. Such a vocational emphasis in the curriculum often makes schooling more meaningful. Students with vocational skills are in a more competitive position relative to untrained peers, have had a chance to demonstrate their potential, and can eliminate unrealistic occupational goals.

Legal Mandates for Transition Assessment, Planning, and Services

PL 101-476, the Individuals with Disabilities Education Act (IDEA) (1990), and PL 105-17, the IDEA Amendments of 1997, mandate transition planning for persons with disabilities. Students with disabilities are to be invited to IEP meetings when transition services are discussed. According to federal law, transition services are a coordinated set of activities for a student with a disability that:

(1) is designed within an outcome-oriented process, that promotes movement from school to post-school activities, including postsecondary education, vocational training, integrated employment (including supported employment), continuing and adult education, adult services, independent living, or community participation;

(2) is based on the individual student's needs, taking into account the student's preferences and interests; and

(3) includes

(i) instruction;

(ii) related services;

(iii) community experiences;

(iv) the development of employment and other post-school adult living objectives; and

(v) if appropriate, acquisition of daily living skills and functional vocational evaluation. (*Federal Register,* 1999, §300.29(a))

The 1997 IDEA Amendments require that transition planning begin early in the student's secondary career:

(1) for each student with a disability beginning at age 14 (or younger, if determined appropriate by the IEP team), and updated annually, a statement of the transition service needs of the student under the applicable components of the student's IEP that focuses on the student's courses of study (such as participation in advanced-placement courses or a vocational education program); and

(2) for each student beginning at age 16 (or younger, if determined appropriate by the IEP team), a statement of needed transition services for the student, including, if appropriate, a statement of the interagency responsibilities or any needed linkages. (*Federal Register,* 1999, §300.347(b))

PL 105-332, the Vocational and Technical Education Act of 1998, mandates that "the state plan must include a description of strategies for special populations, including how they will be provided with equal assess to activities, will not be discriminated against, will be provided with programs designed to enable special populations to meet or exceed state adjusted levels of performance, and prepare special populations for further learning and for high skill, high wage careers" (Kochhar, 1998, p. 14). Of particular significance here is that an assessment of the student's interests, abilities, and special needs with respect to successfully completing the vocational education program is not mandated, but is rather left to local districts and states to show how this need is met through local and state plans.

The Americans with Disabilities Act (ADA) of 1990 gives civil rights protections to individuals with disabilities similar to those provided to individuals on the basis of race, sex, national origin, and religion. It guarantees equal opportunity for individuals with disabilities in employment, public accommodations, transportation, state and local government services, and telecommunication. Employers cannot discriminate against persons with disabilities in hiring and promotion, cannot inquire about an applicant's disability or subject the applicant to a test to screen out persons with disabilities, and must provide reasonable accommodation such as job restructuring or adaptive equipment. Other pieces of legislation that safeguard the civil rights of persons with disabilities are Sections 503 and 504 of PL 93-112, the Rehabilitation Act Amendments of 1973. Section 503 regulates the hiring, training, advancement, and retention of qualified workers with disabilities by employers under contract with the federal government for more than $2,500. Section 504 guarantees accessibility to programs, a public education, and the elimination of discriminatory admission procedures, testing, and interviews.

Additional pieces of legislation that support transition planning and assessment are the Rehabilitation Act Amendments of 1992, the Job Training Partnership Act (JTPA) Amendments of 1992, and the School-to-Work Opportunities Act (STOWA) of 1994. STOWA is notable because of its focus on all adolescents, not only students with disabilities, having transition planning and assessment.

The assessments and evaluations that are necessary to provide appropriate transition services require a cooperative team effort. General and special educators and the other core assessment team members call upon vocational educators and rehabilitation counselors for assistance. Together they gather the necessary data. Whereas some of the assessment measures described in this chapter may be given by any team member, others require specialists. Their expertise is especially important for interpretation of results.

Assessment Models

Transition assessment is the foundation for transition planning and services provision. Informa-

tion gathered through ongoing transition assessment can help students establish post-school goals and determine the types of support necessary to assist them in obtaining their goals in educational, vocational, and community settings. In order to establish the needs, preferences, and interests of students with mild disabilities for transition planning and to design such IEPs, a complete and appropriate assessment is necessary. The types of information generally required in a transition assessment are degree of awareness and knowledge of careers and the world of work, general aptitude and work/study habits, interests, skills for specific occupations, and level of community adjustment. The assessment team must also gather data concerning the student's medical, academic, personal-social, and learning strategy needs required for educational placement; the age-appropriate formal tests and informal procedures described in earlier chapters are used for this purpose. All of the information is combined to provide a clear profile of strengths and weaknesses and a base for developing a comprehensive and coordinated transition program.

Many of the components of transition assessment can be collected through a good vocational assessment, which has been characterized as the beginning point of transition planning and services (Leconte, 1999). Vocational assessment is an ongoing process of identifying individual student characteristics, strengths and weaknesses, and interests, as well as education, training, and placement needs. These provide the information to begin planning an individual's career pathway. Because not all students require a full vocational assessment, the process can be conceptualized in levels (Illinois State Board of Education, 1987; Sarkees-Wircenski & Scott, 1995).

Level I, Screening. This level is performed with all students with disabilities and involves reviewing and integrating all preexisting student information into a student profile. Because students must be thoroughly assessed for academic programming, these data are readily available. Also, student interests are identified, and the perceptions of teachers, parents, and the students themselves are gathered. Of particular interest is assessment of motor and perceptual skills and work-related behaviors, motivation, and attitudes. For most students, this level of assessment should be adequate for assignment to appropriate vocational programs. Existing school personnel should be able to perform this level of assessment.

Level I information can be gathered from a number of sources (Illinois State Board of Education, 1987; Leconte, 1999; Sarkees-Wircenski & Scott, 1995). These include:

- Cumulative data review,
- Attendance records,
- School academic transcripts,
- Medical records,
- Career interest testing,
- Aptitude and ability testing,
- Student, parent, and teacher interviews,
- Informal teacher assessment,
- Student observation, and
- Interests inventories.

Level II, Exploration. This level involves collecting information about learning styles, values, career maturity, and job readiness. Specific formal and informal tests may be used, as well as work sample and work evaluation systems. The latter compensate for difficulties that students have with the paper-and-pencil tests and general ability/aptitude screening instruments frequently used in Level I assessment. Trained personnel are necessary at this level; for example, vocational assessment specialists are needed for administering work samples and other work evaluation systems.

Level II information is available from the following sources (Illinois State Board of Education, 1987; Leconte, 1999; Sarkees-Wircenski & Scott, 1995):

- Career maturity ratings,
- Job readiness,
- Work samples,
- Work-related behaviors/employability skills, and
- Learning style inventories.

Level III, Vocational Evaluation. This level is appropriate when more information is needed

regarding a student's cognitive ability, physical abilities and limitations, and/or social-emotional behaviors. Actual placement in a job or training program may be less threatening than other procedures and is necessary to gather the kind of information needed. Functional living skills are a particular focus. The assessment may be conducted outside the school by trained specialists utilizing simulated or actual contract work.

Sources for Level II information include the following (Illinois State Board of Education, 1987; Leconte, 1999; Sarkees-Wircenski, & Scott, 1995):

- Simulated job station,
- Functional living skills,
- Production work, hands-on activities,
- Situational assessment, and
- Contracted work.

The Vocational Evaluation and Work Adjustment Association (VEWAA, 1975) developed the hierarchy of levels to represent a building-block approach to services. The information gathered is meant to be cumulative and provide the foundation for the next level of assessment. Further, the number of students receiving the services can be configured as an inverted pyramid, with the most students receiving Level I services and only a few students receiving the Level III evaluation.

Another approach to conceptualizing vocational assessment is represented by the *McCarron-Dial Evaluation System* (McCarron & Dial, 1986), which measures five factors using the following procedures:

1. Verbal-cognitive: The *Wechsler Adult Intelligence Scale-Revised* (Wechsler, 1981) or the *Stanford-Binet Intelligence Scale* (Terman & Merrill, 1973; Thorndike, Hagen, & Sattler, 1986) and the *Peabody Picture Vocabulary Test-Revised* (Dunn & Dunn, 1981)
2. Sensory: *Bender Visual Motor Gestalt Test* (Bender, 1938) and the *Haptic Visual Discrimination Test* (McCarron & Dial, 1976)
3. Motor: *McCarron Assessment of Neuromuscular Development* (McCarron, 1976, 1982)
4. Emotional: *Observational Emotional Inventory* (McCarron & Dial, 1976, 1986)
5. Integration-coping: *Dial Behavior Rating Scale* (McCarron & Dial, 1973)

An individual's strengths and weaknesses in these areas are organized in a standardized individual evaluation profile. The data are used to develop the vocational training and transitional components of an individual plan.

As with the academic skills discussed in previous chapters, the types of information gathered depend on the assessment questions being asked. The first, *What is the student's level of awareness and knowledge about occupations?*, identifies the student's general background, experience, use of terminology, and so on, in choosing a career or a job. Second, *What are the general aptitudes and work or study habits?*, addresses a broad range of vocational, cognitive, and behavioral prerequisites. Third, the student's responses to an array of career and vocational options are addressed in this question: *What are the student's career or vocational interests?* Finally, we ask, *What are the skills for specific work?* to determine current skill

levels for entry-level jobs. These assessment questions occur throughout the process and lead to the development of a vocational profile that is used in program planning; they also dictate the types of assessment strategies to be used.

Assessment for transition planning takes the information gathered through vocational assessment and incorporates it into a broader transition assessment process, as illustrated in Figure 17–1. According to the Division on Career Development and Transition (Sitlington et al., 1996), the transition assessment process has three major components:

1. *Student assessment.* Student strengths, interests, preferences, and needs are identified. Information is gathered through the use of various evaluation and assessment techniques.
2. *Evaluation of environments.* Potential living, work, and educational settings are analyzed

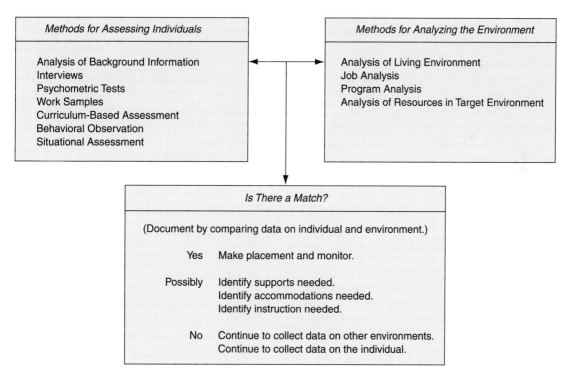

FIGURE 17-1

The Transition Assessment Process

Note: From *Assess for Success: Handbook on Transition Assessment* (p. 99) by P. L. Sitlington, D. A. Neubert, W. Begun, R. Lombard, & P. J. Leconte, 1996, Reston, VA: The Council for Exceptional Children. Copyright 1996 by The Council for Exceptional Children. Reprinted by permission.

to determine environmental demands and supports. Information is gathered through a living environment analysis, a job analysis, and a program analysis. Program analysis, for example, determines if needed supports/accommodations are available at the university where a student with learning disabilities is planning to attend.

3. *Determining a match.* The student's strengths, interests, preferences, and needs are compared with his or her potential living, work, and educational demands and supports. This comparison assists students in setting their post-school goals and in planning for needed transition services (e.g., instructional services to prepare for these goals).

The following are additional assessment questions to be addressed in the transition assessment process. They supplement the questions related to vocational planning described previously.

- Does the student want or need postssecondary education? If so, is he or she able to advocate for himself or herself to obtain needed accommodations and supports?
- What leisure/community activities does the student enjoy? Is the student able to access these activities? Does he or she need accommodations to participate in these activities?
- Is the student able to be a self-advocate in various situations?
- Is the student able to set up and maintain a household? If not, what supports or instruction are needed?

Issues in Transition Assessment

Legislative mandates for transition services impact special education assessment and service delivery. Transition planning for all students age 14 or older with a disability must be based on the student's transition needs, preferences, and interests. School districts must provide transition assessment to determine these needs, preferences, and interests. This is an enormous task. It requires the reconceptualization of the IEP process and the provision of transition assessment for a large number of students. In spite of current efforts to comply with the mandate, many districts lag behind (Clark, 1998).

Students with disabilities are often excluded from basic vocational assessment activities (Leconte, 1999). Reasons for this exclusion include (a) the greater challenges and needs of students with disabilities, (b) the inadequacy of resources, and (c) the inadequacy of personnel to address this need. The technical quality of current assessment procedures is also an issue, and untrained personnel often administer and interpret important tests. Another concern is the rapidly changing nature of jobs and life tasks due to technological advances. For example, as shopping on the Internet becomes more commonplace, the ability to read text on the computer screen takes on additional importance.

The range of laws crossing over several disciplines that support transition planning has paved the way for interdisciplinary collaboration in assessment for transition planning (Leconte, 1999). This collaboration has helped to diminish past territorial issues among special education, vocational education, and rehabilitation counseling that affected students' access to appropriate assessments and programs. Special educators, vocational evaluators, and vocational rehabilitation counselors now work together to provide vocational assessment to students with disabilities. However, limited resources and lack of interagency agreements may negatively impact this collaboration.

Another issue for students with mild disabilities who want career or vocational guidance and preparation may be created by their cognitive, academic, or behavioral problems. These characteristics often prevent entry into programs because students lack prerequisite grades, fail exams, or are judged unfit. These students may also want to continue their education after high school but find their aspirations basically limited by the vocational preparatory perspective. This "either/or" mentality governs much career counseling of these students and fails to reflect possible accommodations in testing and college entrance requirements.

It is important to recognize that students' preparation for post-school life is not only focused on getting a job. Students may want to go to school, get married, and participate in leisure and recreational activities. As we have discussed, the evaluation and preparation for these aspects of their lives are necessary and should be conceptualized as part of and incorporated into comprehensive transition assessment programs.

Collecting Assessment Information

The answers to transition assessment questions require considerable information not only about careers and occupations but also about the students. The assessment techniques currently employed are therefore often multidimensional. There are a variety of assessment techniques available, some applicable for gathering many kinds of data and others only useful in specific cases (Clark, 1998; Sitlington et al., 1996).

Cumulative Data Review. One vital aspect of transition assessment is examination of attendance records, grades, test scores, and available special education assessments of intellectual, academic, and behavioral areas. The information provides a context in which transition needs can be understood and appropriate services chosen. Also, knowledge of a student's task-approach preferences, motivation, and academic abilities shapes how vocational instruction will be delivered.

Medical Examination. Students should have a physical as a preliminary measure. Such data may be available in school records, or a physical examination may need to be arranged. Factors that might complicate training and job placement can be compensated for or avoided. Corrective measures, as in the case of vision losses, or rehabilitation may be necessary.

Student, Parent, and Teacher Interviews. Students should be asked about interests and leisure-time activities, the types of work they have done at home, and the part-time and summer jobs they have held. Also, their knowledge about and aspirations for jobs and community life could be tapped informally.

It is important to establish parents' aspirations for their children's future employment, schooling, and community life because these shape students' perceptions. Parents also can provide their view of their children's strengths and weaknesses and describe their perceptions of appropriate vocations and professions for their children.

Teachers have a good deal of information about the cognitive and affective skills of students. Their experience with the work-related behaviors of students, such as attention and task completion, is a valuable resource. They have knowledge about how students like to approach and complete tasks. Teachers also can describe instructional approaches that are successful for particular students.

Students, teachers, and parents can provide data about social skill development that is essential to vocational placement and job maintenance. It is important to know how students adapt to school, home, and other settings and how well they interact with peers and authority figures. A comparison of perspectives may reveal the need for socialization training in certain settings or with certain target groups.

Follow-up studies of school leavers can yield useful information about the relevance and quality of secondary school preparation in this area (Peterson, 1988). Responses to written surveys, phone interviews, and face-to-face contacts can confirm or dispute the usefulness of the program. Employers and co-workers, parents and other family members, and the individuals themselves can be called on to profile their job ability and satisfaction, as well as to evaluate the preparation program and current support system.

Interest Inventories. Students are asked about occupational and professional preferences through informal and formal ways. Some students can clearly state their likes and dislikes in terms of future work. In other cases, observation of hobbies and leisure-time activities provides useful information. In inventories and surveys, students choose among different types of activities and indicate the one they like the most.

Vocational Aptitude/Ability Testing. General aptitude and ability tests are available to assess broad and multiple competencies for certain types of work. Also, there are specific aptitude tests for particular job skills such as fine- and gross-motor dexterity, use of tools, and speed and accuracy of motor and perceptual-motor performance. Although the results of these types of tests may suggest some aptitude or readiness for certain types of training or work, actual success or failure may be affected by many other factors (Wimmer, 1982). These tests may also present the opportunity to observe students' communication skills, physical endurance, work habits and attitudes, ability to follow directions, and tolerance for stress.

Job Readiness. This assessment concerns job-seeking skills such as interviewing skills. Job-keeping skills such as punctuality and response to supervision are also important to assess. This analysis can be conducted through a variety of means, including observation, testing, and interviews with teachers and parents.

Community Environment Analysis. This assessment concerns the future living environment of students. It focuses on the demands of both the home and community environments. The identification of the skills needed to locate an apartment is an example.

Job Analysis. This procedure is a task analysis of the specific skills required by a job and is often a prerequisite for other assessments. The *Dictionary of Occupational Titles (DOT)* (U.S. Department of Labor, 1977, 1982, 1986, 1991) provides skill descriptions of jobs that can assist in beginning a job analysis. The *DOT* can also be found on the Occupational Information Network (O*Net) at www.doleta.gov/programs/onet. However, on-site analysis is imperative. For that purpose, observations and interviews should be used to gather information to complete the following five basic steps of conducting a job analysis (McDonnell, Wilcox, & Hardman, 1991):

1. Identify the basic observable and measurable task necessary to complete a job.
2. Identify the environmental cues that prompt the completion of the job.
3. Identify the average time per task that makes up the job or number of products required to complete the job.
4. Identify the quality control for each job task.
5. Identify the exceptions to the normal routine.

Postsecondary Education Environment Analysis. This concerns the identification of the courses, program, and/or total postsecondary educational environment. Information gathered might include course load, course requirements, available academic and financial supports, etc.

Commercial Work Sample Systems. There are a number of commercially available work sample systems. They vary in the types of tasks required of the students and in their resemblance to actual jobs or components of jobs (Clark & Kolstoe, 1995). Some systems assess student performance on actual features of a job, such as sorting mail. Others assess skills on generic tasks common to a number of jobs, such as independent problem solving. The results indicate specific skill development in those tasks as well as allow for generalizations to similar jobs. Although expensive, these assessment systems do provide comprehensive efforts to establish a clear profile of student entry skills.

Locally Developed Work Samples and Simulations. To reflect job placements in a particular locale, work samples can also be developed and standardized locally. They are simulated representations of work tasks or activities that may or may not represent an actual job or part of a job (Clark & Kolstoe, 1995). Such procedures not only reveal student competence on specific work tasks, but also provide information about work habits, stamina, and social skills. Students have the opportunity for hands-on exposure to job requirements before actually entering the market. Work samples may be a full-scale replica of a local job or a representation of one common job component in a variety of local jobs (e.g., using a cash register).

Behavioral Analysis. This approach permits a systematic and functional analysis of the students' actual job performance and is similar to diagnostic teaching, which was described in Chapter 5. It involves specifying the work behavior being observed, describing the environmental work conditions, establishing the student's initial level of performance, initiating the job training program or actual job, and continuing observations during the program to establish improved skill competence. A variety of elements can be changed, and the student's performance can be observed: environmental conditions (e.g., noise level, number of people in the work area), instructional methods (e.g., verbal directions, computer), types of reinforcement (e.g., praise, tangibles), and schedule of reinforcement (e.g., immediate, daily). Such information can be used in improving both training and on-the-job performance.

Curriculum-Based Assessment. This assessment is related to the student's needs in the school curriculum. Beyond the academic evaluation mentioned in previous chapters, this assessment concerns determining the student's level of transition and community adjustment.

Situational Assessment. Students are also observed regularly by supervisory staff in performing training or actual work activities. This on-site assessment is quantified, or at least structured, on rating forms that cover areas of supervisor interest. Unforeseen strengths and weaknesses that go unnoticed in more artificial training activities often become apparent in such situations. Although this form of assessment is intentionally flexible and broad-based to permit inclusion of a variety of topics, ratings and other comments should be as objective as possible.

The typical transition programs for which these assessments qualify students are usually school- or employer-based (Cegelka, 1985). The school-based approach has the greatest impact on education and is directed toward adult occupational adjustment. This model has three stages: (a) career awareness, during which young students are introduced to the values and types of work; (b) career orientation and exploration, during which they learn about job options and jobs of interest; and (c) career preparation, during which they acquire the technical prerequisites for occupations or college.

Another popular model provides for career or vocational experiences outside the school. Experience-based career education programs draw on academic, general, and vocational curricula. They make use of banks, factories, and other settings by arranging for a series of supervised placements of 2 or more weeks for students.

In the case of students with mild disabilities, an infused approach in a school situation is highly likely; that is, the career education and other cur-

ricula are integrated. Therefore, the scope of an assessment must encompass both academic and vocational concerns, as in Phillip's case.

Phillip

The team has developed the Individualized Assessment Plan for Phillip. The IAP lists several assessment questions related to planning the transition program for Phillip. The questions center around four areas: Phillip's knowledge of various careers, his interests in different occupations, his specific work skills, and his abilities in transition and community adjustment. Members of the team will interview Phillip and administer an interest inventory and work sample evaluations. In addition, Phillip, his parents, and his teacher will each complete portions of the *Transition Planning Inventory,* a set of measures designed to coordinate the planning process.

STRATEGIES FOR TRANSITION ASSESSMENT

The five main assessment questions asked in regard to transition needs of students with mild disabilities are:

- *What is the student's level of awareness and knowledge of occupations?*
- *What are the student's general aptitudes and work or study habits?*
- *What are the student's career or vocational interests?*
- *What is the student's level of performance in specific work skills?*
- *What are the student's abilities in the areas of transition and community adjustment?*

A variety of standardized procedures are available to assess different aspects of transition preparation. Table 17–1 provides a list of commercially available tests and assessment procedures related to transition. The next sections of this chapter describe examples of some of the major types of assessments.

TABLE 17–1
Commercially Available Tests and Assessment Procedures

	Employment	Further Education/ Training	Leisure Activities	Daily Living	Community Participation	Health	Self-Determination	Communication	Interpersonal Relationships
Achievement									
Adult Basic Learning Examination		X						X	
Brigance Inventory of Essential Skills		X						X	
Iowa Test of Basic Skills		X						X	
Peabody Individual Achievement Test		X						X	
Woodcock-Johnson Psycho-Educational Battery		X						X	
Adaptive Behavior									
AAMR Adaptive Behavior Scales	X			X	X			X	X
Adaptive Behavior Inventory	X	X		X	X			X	X
Normative Adaptive Behavior Checklist	X		X	X	X			X	X
Scales of Independent Behavior	X		X	X	X			X	X
Vineland Adaptive Behavior Scale	X			X	X			X	X
Street Survival Skills Questionnaire				X	X	X			
Aptitude									
APTICOM Program	X	X							
Armed Services Vocational Aptitude Battery	X	X							
Differential Aptitude Test	X	X							
General Aptitude Test Battery (GATB)	X	X							
JEVS Work Sample System	X								
McCarron-Dial Evaluation System	X								
MESA	X								
Micro-TOWER System	X								
Occupational Aptitude and Interest Scale-2	X	X							
Talent Assessment Program	X								
TOWER System	X								
Communication									
Communicative Abilities in Daily Living								X	
Woodcock Reading Mastery Test								X	
Individual Reading Placement Inventory								X	
Test of Written Language								X	
Functional Capacity									
Functional Assessment Profile	X			X			X	X	X
General Health Questionnaire						X			
Life Functioning Index	X	X		X				X	
Personal Capacities Questionnaire	X			X			X	X	X
Independent Living Behavior Checklist				X	X				
Learning Styles									
Learning Style Inventory	X							X	
Learning Styles and Strategies	X							X	
Manual Dexterity									
Crawford Small Parts Dexterity Test	X								
Minnesota Rate of Manipulation Test	X								
Pennsylvania BiManual Work Sample	X								
Purdue Pegboard	X								

Occupational Interest	Employment	Further Education/Training	Leisure Activities	Daily Living	Community Participation	Health	Self-Determination	Communication	Interpersonal Relationships
California Occupational Preference Survey	X								
Career Assessment Inventory	X								
Career Decision Maker	X								
Career Maturity Inventory	X								
Edwards Personal Preference Schedule	X								
Minnesota Importance Questionnaire	X								
Occupational Aptitude and Interest Scale	X								
Pictorial California Occupational Preference Survey	X								
Reading-Free Interest Inventory	X								
Self-Directed Search	X								
Strong-Campbell Interest Inventory	X								
USES Interest Check List	X								
USES Interest Inventory	X								
Wisconsin Career Information System	X								
Personality/Social Skills									
Adult Personality Inventory									X
Analysis of Coping Style									X
Basic Personality Inventory									X
California Personality Inventory									X
Clinical Analysis Questionnaire									X
Differential Personality Questionnaire									X
Katz Adjustment Scale									X
Parent Adolescent Communication Scale									X
Personality Factor Questionnaire									X
Psychological Screening Inventory									X
Rosenberg Self-Esteem Scale									X
Tennessee Self-Concept Scale									X
Work Personality Profile	X								X
Work Values Inventory	X								X
Prevocational/Employability									
Brigance Employability Skills Inventory	X								
Job Readiness Scale	X								
Preliminary Diagnostic Questionnaire	X								
Social and Prevocational Information Battery	X			X	X	X			
Vocational Diagnosis and Assessment of Residual Employability	X								
Vocational Behavior Checklist	X								
Transition/Community Adjustment									
Brigance Life Skills Inventory				X	X	X		X	
Enderle-Severson Transition Scale	X	X	X	X	X				X
LCCE Knowledge and Performance Battery	X		X	X	X	X			X
Social and Prevocational Information Battery	X			X	X	X			
Tests for Everyday Living	X			X	X	X			
Transition Behavior Scale	X			X	X				X
Transition Planning Inventory	X	X	X	X	X	X	X	X	X
Quality of Life Questionnaire							X		X
Quality of Student Life Questionnaire							X		X

Note: From "Transition Planning Assessment for Secondary-Level Students with Learning Disabilities" by G. M. Clark, 1996, *Journal of Learning Disabilities, 29*(1), pp. 76–92. Copyright 1996 by PRO-ED Inc. Reprinted with permission.

What Is the Student's Level of Awareness and Knowledge of Occupations?

An essential aspect of career and vocational assessment is establishing the level of awareness and knowledge that students have about careers and jobs. Among the many procedures available is the *Social and Prevocational Information Battery-Revised* (Halpern & Irvin, 1986). Additionally, competency and criterion-referenced testing and job analysis are useful, as well as a consideration of the relationship among student performances.

The *Social and Prevocational Information Battery-Revised (SPIB-R)* is a set of nine tests directly related to the long-range goals of work study or experience programs in secondary schools. They are as follows:

SPIB-R Tests	*Long-Range Goals*
Job Search Skills	Employability
Job-Related Behavior	
Banking	Economics
Budgeting	Self-Sufficiency
Purchasing	
Home Management	Family Living
Physical Health Care	
Hygiene and Grooming	Personal Habits
Functional Signs	Communication

The tests are presented orally; reading is not required.

The *SPIB-R* was standardized on over 900 junior and senior high school students with mental retardation in Oregon who were mostly Caucasian. Conversion tables for each test and the total test are available for comparing a student's performance to the percentage correct and percentiles of the reference group, at either the junior or senior high level. A typical interpretation is:

> *A junior high school student who achieved a raw score of 26 on the Banking Test correctly answered 84% of the items and scored better than approximately 93% of the students in the reference group.*

The *BRIGANCE® Diagnostic Inventory of Essential Skills* (Brigance, 1981) contains aspects of career and vocational assessment to determine a person's level of awareness and knowledge about occupations, as well as to answer other assessment questions concerning reading and understanding employment vocabulary, abbreviations, and ads. The subtests can be used to gather baseline data and later evaluation information, and they can also be related to other assessment systems or school district competency lists. Kokaska and Brolin (1985, Appendix, pp. 403–409) provide a chart that connects vocational and other skills in this *BRIGANCE® Inventory* with the career education competencies just described.

Another form of assessment is job analysis, a systematic way of observing jobs to determine what the worker does, how and why he or she does it, and the skill involved in performance. During field trips, students can be encouraged to complete a form containing such considerations as a brief description of the work, the skills required for the job (academics, physical demands, etc.), work conditions (noise, heating, lighting, ventilation, etc.), training required, salary and hours, and good and poor features of the job. The information can be reviewed and discussed later with the student in probing realistic knowledge and interests. If students are suitably interested, the jobs can be broken down by task analysis.

Additionally, the assessment team must consider the results of examination of work awareness and knowledge in connection with the students' opportunities for experience, cultural and linguistic background, and other factors. Their cognitive, academic, or behavioral disabilities may restrict their ability to notice and examine vocational options. Some students may be slower than their peers in acquiring interest and knowledge in this area.

What Are the Student's General Aptitudes and Work or Study Habits?

The assessment of aptitudes can be a complex task. Intellectual, academic, and linguistic abilities are generally included in this area. Most vocational aptitude surveys attempt to assess these types of abilities: numerical, spatial, form perception, clerical perception (e.g., proofreading words and numbers), motor coordination, finger dexterity, manual dexterity, eye-hand-foot coordination, and color discrimination. Many questions have been raised not only about the definition and measurement of vocational aptitudes, but also about the relevance of tasks used in tests and their relationship to actual jobs.

Aptitudes are measured in a variety of ways. For example, the *General Aptitude Test Battery (GATB)* (U.S. Employment Services, 1982a), contains 12 subtests written at sixth grade reading level. The *Nonreading Aptitude Test Battery (NATB)* (U.S. Employment Services, 1982b) is a nonreading version of the *GATB* that measures the same aptitude areas; however, it includes no arithmetic problems and vocabulary items are presented orally. The work samples discussed later in this chapter also probe such aptitudes. The following paragraphs describe the *APTICOM*® *Occupational Aptitude Test Battery* (Jewish Employment & Vocational Service, 1985), the *Occupational Aptitude Survey and Interest Schedule* (2nd ed.) *(OASIS-2)* (Parker, 1991), measures of manual dexterity, and informal procedures.

The *Occupational Aptitude Test Battery* is a portion of the *APTICOM*® system, which also assesses interests and academically related skills. It is a norm-referenced survey of general learning, verbal, numerical, spatial, form perception, clerical perception, motor coordination, and finger and manual dexterity aptitudes. It is a group or individually administered test, and requires 60 to 90 minutes along with the other portions. The *Occupational Aptitude Test Battery* is appropriate for secondary students and adults. Eleven tests measure aptitudes derived by the Department of Labor and related to occupational success.

The *Occupational Aptitude Survey and Interest Schedule* (2nd ed.) *(OASIS-2)* is composed of the *Aptitude Survey-2* and the *Interest Schedule-2,* each of which is norm-referenced for students in grades 8 through 12. The *Aptitude Survey-2* contains five subtests representing six different vocational aptitudes:

Subtest	Aptitude Areas
Vocabulary and Computation	General Ability
Vocabulary	Verbal Aptitude
Computation	Numerical Aptitude
Spatial Relations	Spatial Aptitude
Word Comparison	Perceptual Aptitude
Making Marks	Manual Dexterity

The *Interest Schedule-2* is composed of 240 statements across 12 interest areas: artistic, scientific, nature, protective, mechanical, industrial, business detail, selling, accommodating, humanitarian, leading-influencing, and physical performing. Students mark whether they like, dislike, or are neutral about each interest item.

Figure 17–2 presents a sample *Aptitude Survey* profile for an eleventh grader. Percentile ranks and stanines are available for each of the six aptitude factors. This student's scores all equal or exceed the 50th percentile or stanine 5. She has notable strengths in General Ability, Verbal Aptitude, Numerical Aptitude, and Perceptual Aptitude. These scores suggest that she has the aptitude for many professions, including physician, engineer, and scientist.

Manual dexterity tests can be used to gather information about students' aptitude for the many occupations that require fine-motor dexterity and eye-hand coordination. Manual dexterity tests generally require the placement and/or joining of small screws, bolts and nuts, and similar objects. Tool usage may also be needed. These tests may serve to establish entry level dexterity skills, help students identify realistic jobs, and provide motivation to acquire needed skills (Brolin, 1995).

Examples are:

- *Crawford Small Parts Dexterity Test* (Crawford & Crawford, 1956). Students use tweezers to pick up a pin, place it in a hole on a board, and put a collar over it. After all 36 pins and collars are in place, 30 screws are placed through a plate with a screwdriver.
- *Purdue Pegboard* (Purdue Research Foundation, 1968). Students place pins in holes with the right, left, and both hands. They also assemble pins, collars, and washers on a board in a minute's time.
- *Pennsylvania BiManual Work Sample* (Roberts, 1945). Students assemble and disassemble 105 nuts and bolts and place them in holes on a board.
- *Talent Assessment Program* (Talent Assessment Inc., 1972, 1980, 1985, 1988). Students perform 10 work samples requiring gross and fine finger and manual dexterity, visual and tactile discrimination, and retention of details.

Name: **SMITH**   **KATY**
       LAST   FIRST

Date of Birth: Mo: **Nov** Day: **24** Yr: **1973**

Today's Date: Mo: **APR** Day: **1** Yr: **1991**

Sex: M _____   F **X**   Grade: **11**

School **MADISON HIGH SCHOOL**

City: **MADISON**   State: **TX.**

Occupational Aptitude Survey and
Interest Schedule, Second Edition,
by Randall M. Parker

STUDENT PROFILE

SECTION I — RECORD OF SCORES

SUBTEST	RAW SCORE	APTITUDE FACTOR	PERCENTILE	STANINE
Vocabulary + Computation	61	General Ability	99	9
Vocabulary	35	Verbal Aptitude	97	9
Computation	26	Numerical Aptitude	97	9
Spatial Relations	12	Spatial Aptitude	75	6
Word Comparison	37	Perceptual Aptitude	90	8
Making Marks	62	Manual Dexterity	50	5

SECTION II — PROFILE OF SCORES
OASIS APTITUDE FACTORS

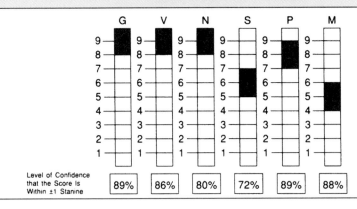

FIGURE 17–2

OASIS-2 Aptitude Survey

Note: From *OASIS-2 Aptitude Survey* by R. M. Parker, 1991, Austin, TX: PRO-ED. Copyright 1991 by R. M. Parker. Reprinted with permission.

These dexterity measures can be very frustrating for students with fine-motor coordination problems and a desire to do these or related kinds of jobs. In such cases, the assessment team may use results to direct instruction in these areas and also to explore alternative ways for students to perform similar tasks with automated or other forms of assistance. Professionals must avoid using performance on such measures as a general predictor of vocational ability.

The *BRIGANCE® Employability Skills Inventory* (Brigance, 1995a) is an informal measure designed to assess basic skills and employability skills needed to gain and maintain employment. Use of the inventory helps to pinpoint known skills and skills that need to be learned in the areas of career awareness and understanding, job-seeking and knowledge, reading skills, speaking and listening skills, pre-employment writing, and math skills and concepts. Students are rated in the areas of self-concept and attitudes, responsibility and self-discipline, motor coordination and job requirements, thinking skills/abilities and job requirements, job interview preparation, job interview skills, and work experience. The inventory is appropriate for use with secondary students with disabilities.

Other sources can also contribute information about aptitudes and work or study skills. Assessment data concerning intelligence, adaptive behavior, academics, communication skills, and so forth, can supplement any information gathered by these procedures. Interviews of the students, parents, and teachers can document work experience, current demonstration of required aptitudes, and motivation to work.

Appropriate work or study habits are very important. In addition to broad technical entry skills for work, work and study habits are critical for success on the job and in postsecondary training settings. Direct questioning of students, parents, and teachers or observations will reveal their presence. Some interview concepts taken from the Attitude Rating Scale of the *BRIGANCE® Diagnostic Inventory of Essential Skills* (Brigance, 1981) are:

- Applies himself or herself when given a task
- Is receptive to direction and suggestions
- Accepts criticism without pouting or getting angry (p. 256)

This *BRIGANCE® Inventory* also contains other rating scales in the areas of responsibility, self-discipline, and personality.

What Are the Student's Career or Vocational Interests?

Student interests and preferences must be taken into consideration in developing the transition plan. However, assessing interests is not easy. Many well-known and commonly used interest inventories have proven to be unsatisfactory for persons with disabilities because of requirements for verbal abilities and broad work experience (Brolin, 1995). In addition, some persons with disabilities have erroneous perceptions about jobs and low expectations for themselves. The *Reading-Free Vocational Interest Inventory-Revised* (Becker, 1988) and the *Wide Range Interest-Opinion Test (WRIOT)* (Jastak & Jastak, 1979) are representative of interest surveys that use pictures, rather than text, to determine students' views. In addition, there is a potential assessment role for needs assessment, interviews, criterion-referenced tests, and other informal approaches.

The *Reading-Free Vocational Interest Inventory-Revised (R-FVII-R)* is a picture interest inventory designed to measure vocational interests of students with mental retardation and learning disabilities. It consists of 55 sets of three pictures; in each set, the student chooses the most appealing picture in terms of the work represented. Figure 17–3 provides an example; the student has circled the picture of a person raking leaves as the job he or she would most like to do. There is no reading or writing involved on the *R-FVII-R*. The tester reads the directions and also checks that students are marking the form correctly when working in a group.

Results can be used for vocational planning and placement. Percentile ranks are derived for 11 interest areas, and areas of high and low interest are identified. In the example in Figure 17–4, Tom shows high interest in three areas: Clerical, Patient Care, and Personal Service.

The *Wide Range Interest-Opinion Test (WRIOT)* surveys 18 vocational interest areas (e.g., sales, social service, and mechanics) and 8 personal attitudes (e.g., sedentariness, risk, and ambition). It contains 450 pictures arranged in

FIGURE 17-3

Sample Item from the *Reading-Free Vocational Interest Inventory-Revised*

Note: From *Reading-Free Vocational Interest Inventory-Revised* (p. 1) by R. L. Becker, 1981, Columbus, OH: Elbern Publications. Copyright 1981, 1988 by Elbern Publications. Reprinted with permission.

150 combinations of 3. Students examine each set of three pictures and mark the letter on an answer sheet that corresponds with the most attractive and least appealing ones. Directions are read to students, and they do not need to read or write.

The two types of *WRIOT* results—vocational areas and personal attitudes—are interpreted separately. The largest positive interest areas, the largest negative interest areas, and those falling in the median or average range are analyzed. A sample interpretation is:

> *Mike has particularly strong interests in physical science, mathematics, mechanics, machine operation, protective services, and social science. He seems very positive in his attitudes and is highly motivated to do well.*

In addition to examining students' interests, it may be necessary to perform needs assessments among faculty, parents, and the community. Also, during the implementation of the plan and afterwards, assessment of the needs and priorities of involved groups can suggest much needed improvements. Questions such as *Is inclusion in general education an effective way to provide career education to these students?* and *Is career education intended for students who are not able to succeed in an academic program?* can be posed to school personnel to determine their orientation to ca-

reer education for students with disabilities (Brolin, Cegelka, Jackson, & Wrobel, 1978). Depending on the audience, questionnaires or interviews can be used to assess priorities and reactions.

Also, the work community needs to be surveyed to establish current perceptions of students with disabilities, availability of jobs, and accommodations that need to be and can be made for students. For students who are interested in occupations requiring advanced training or with aspirations for higher education, technical schools and colleges need to be surveyed. These data should be combined with student interests to aid in realistic planning.

All too often students are simply not asked about their career and vocational aspirations, impressions, and interests. The tests and complex measurement systems structure the assessment process so that they may not get an opportunity to express themselves comfortably. Therefore, interviewing students is highly recommended. Interviews are also useful vehicles for contacting the families of clients, who influence their career and vocational aims. Parents and other family members shape a person's interests and aspirations by their own type of employment and experience, opinions about careers and work, and so forth. Such information may help to explain student entry behavior and alert educators to environmental factors

INDIVIDUAL PROFILE SHEET

Last Name ___Wilson___ First ___Tom___ Date ___8-29-?___

Grade ___9___ Age: ___15___ yrs. ___2___ mos. Date of Birth ___6-29-66___

School ___C.C.S.___ City ___Columbus___ State ___Ohio___

Male Norm Used ___EMR, 13-15___ Female Norm Used _____

Key Letter	Raw Score	T Score	Percentile	Stanine	Interest Area	Symbol	Interest High	Interest Low
A	1	31	3	1	Automotive	Auto		✓
B	4	31	3	1	Building Trades	B Tr		✓
C	11	66	95	8	Clerical	Cl	✓	
D	1	34	5	2	Animal Care	An Cr		✓
E	2	40	15	3	Food Service	F S		✓
F	10	66	95	8	Patient Care	P Cr	✓	
G	3	40	15	3	Horticulture	Hort		✓
H	7	43	25	4	Housekeeping	Hsk		
I	16	71	98	9	Personal Service	P Sv	✓	
J	5	55	70	6	Laundry Service	Ly		
K	5	49	45	5	Materials Handling	M Hg		

FIGURE 17-4

Reading-Free Vocational Interest Inventory-Revised Profile

Note: From *Reading-Free Vocational Interest Inventory-Revised* (p. 18) by R. L. Becker, 1988, Columbus, OH: Elbern Publications. Copyright 1988 by Elbern Publications. Reprinted with permission.

567

that might influence student performance and motivation.

Criterion-referenced tests such as the *BRIGANCE® Diagnostic Inventory of Essential Skills* (Brigance, 1981) can also be used to assess student occupational interests, especially Job Interest and Aptitudes. Among the items are "Do you prefer to work alone or with others?", "Would you prefer to work with people or to work with objects?", and "Would you prefer a job which requires a lot of training to develop skills or one that requires little training?" (p. 259).

What Is the Student's Level of Performance in Specific Work Skills?

Work samples are designed to assess students' skills and attitudes on tasks that are similar to those they are apt to perform in actual work situations. Samples offer an opportunity to observe work habits and assess levels of interest.

The commercially designed work samples are related to the specific jobs or job families described in the *Dictionary of Occupational Titles (DOT)* (U.S. Department of Labor, 1977, 1982, 1986, 1991). In selecting a work sample, it is important to consider whether the system takes into account academic, verbal, and experiential limitations; allows for more than one trial, repetition of instructions, and checks for comprehension; and has appropriate content and predictive validity and norms for persons with disabilities (Brolin, 1982). The *Wide Range Employability Sample Test (WREST)* (Jastak & Jastak, 1980) and the *Singer Vocational Evaluation System (VES)* (Singer Company Career Systems, 1982) are two examples. Additional assessment possibilities are the design of one's own work samples, the use of simulations, and other informal techniques. It is particularly important to draw on the experience of local employers, work supervisors, and co-workers to validate job descriptors.

The *Wide Range Employability Sample Test (WREST)* evaluates productivity and technical work skills through 10 concrete tasks. These tasks are folding, stapling, packaging, measuring, stringing, gluing, collating, color matching, pattern matching, and assembling. Students perform these eye-hand coordination tasks after demonstrations and practice trials. One- and two-step

instructions are involved. The test requires minimal math skills and no reading. The practice trials are not timed, but the tests are. However, the worker can complete the task even if the designated time is up. Suggestions for modifications for specific disabilities are given in the manual. Norms are provided for three groups: general population, sheltered workshop, and industrial sample.

Three total scores can be obtained: production quality (error total), production quantity (time total), and technical productivity rating (average of the two). Also, workers are observed and rated for behavior and attitudes. Observations focus on 10 areas: Appearance, Attendance, Punctuality, Perseverance, Organization of Work, Relations with Co-Workers, Relations with Supervisor, Flexibility, Safety Practices, and Conformity to Rules.

Phillip

On the *WREST,* Phillip showed good performance in production quality but average to poor performance in production quantity. He experienced some difficulty with finger dexterity and spatial abilities but demonstrated better coordination, color discrimination, manual dexterity, and ability to follow oral instructions and demonstrations.

The *Singer Vocational Evaluation System (VES)* is a set of 27 work samples that provide information for vocational training and placement. Some skill areas covered are drafting, electric wiring, plumbing and pipe fitting, refrigeration and air conditioning, sales processing, masonry, sheet metal, cooking and baking, engine service, medical services, cosmetology, data calculation and recording, filing, shipping and receiving, packaging and materials handling, electronics assembly, office services, and basic laboratory analysis. The *VES* was designed to provide simulated, hands-on experience in selected occupations specifically for populations with special needs, that is, individuals with social and educational disadvantages, mild retardation, and physical disabilities. The presentation is audiovisual, removing many demands for reading.

The *VES* work samples are set up at stations, which include a filmstrip and audiotape. After a brief orientation, students rate their interest in the job represented by the work sample. Instructions and stop-go points are recorded on the tape. There are also prescribed checkpoints where evaluators determine the accuracy of student work and reinstruct or repeat the instructions if necessary. Evaluators observe students while they do the tasks and, at the end of the activity, the students rate their interest in the job a second time, as well as their performance. The evaluator also rates the performance and discusses the ratings with the student. Work samples may be used again with the same students to measure learning.

Phillip

Phillip was able to complete all of the *VES* cooking and baking, small engine, and bench assembly samples, as long as the evaluator was nearby to intervene in difficult situations and provide encouragement. Phillip recognized some tools at each of the work stations. Difficulties with finger dexterity and spatial abilities persisted on the bench assembly and small engine tasks. He expressed preference for the Cooking Sample above all others, stating that he did not mind the clean-up because he does that at home. Phillip does not seem very ambitious or self-disciplined.

Sometimes it is more appropriate to develop a work or job sample for assessment purposes than to use a commercially prepared one. Professionals may want to capture the key aspects of local work conditions, fill a gap in available work samples, or follow up on a job interest expressed by one or more students. According to Brolin (1982), the major types of work samples are:

1. Indigenous work sample, representing the major elements of a local job
2. Job sample, replicating an actual industrial job
3. Cluster trait work sample, developed for a group of worker traits related to a series of jobs
4. Simulated work sample, replicating one segment of related work factors and tools of an industrial job

5. Single-trait work sample, evaluating one isolated characteristic that may be related to one specific job

The use of such samples accommodates typical problems of persons with disabilities (test anxiety, language problems, attention deficits, and so forth), provides a chance to see a person demonstrate potential and interest, and thus develops a realistic basis for planning.

To develop a work sample, a series of activities is necessary (Brolin, 1982). First, local jobs should be catalogued by types of business, perhaps using the *DOT* guidelines. Also, more specific job reviews can be performed to identify particular information such as salaries and benefits, equipment and machines used, physical demands, and so forth. Second, it is necessary to decide what work samples should be developed, based on current job availability, time expenditure and expense in development, training for the job possibilities in that area, and long-range usefulness of samples.

Third, each job is carefully analyzed in terms of needed preparation, required licenses, and available supervision, in addition to *DOT* standardized concerns. A methods analysis about real and potential problem areas leads to improved work samples.

Fourth, construction of a mock-up work sample follows, with special attention given to the needs of the persons with disabilities using it. Fifth, the sample should be normed on a large enough representative group, because use of industrial norms is usually inappropriate.

Sixth, work samples are described in appropriate detail to permit standardized administration and easy understanding. Brolin (1982) considers the following elements essential: *DOT* Code, related jobs, prerequisites, workplace diagram and materials list, instructions for the evaluator, instructions for the evaluees, scoring procedures, interpretation, and special considerations. Seventh, work samples should be validated in a variety of ways, particularly by following up with former users. Giving students the opportunity to do the job in an actual industry is an important step in work sample design.

Another useful procedure to assess student aptitudes, skills, and interests in certain careers/jobs is to provide simulated settings. Some schools have set up student-run minibusinesses, such as stores to sell school supplies or food. Even having students perform a classroom project in an industrial fashion (e.g., using an assembly line) can prove useful by acquainting them with work basics and by providing a basis for discussion. Schloss, Smith, Hoover, and Wolford (1987) describe an assessment model that integrates many of these informal assessment approaches to assess not only competencies for specific work but also the individual's flexibility and coping skills.

There are a variety of formal measures available to accommodate the psychological, academic, and behavioral limitations of persons with mild disabilities. It is also important to note the many informal assessment techniques, such as student interviews and/or questionnaires, built into published or teacher-made work samples and simulations. Behavioral observations are a critical aspect of this kind of assessment to measure student work habits, interpersonal skills, and work-related behaviors. Of particular interest is how diagnostic teaching techniques are employed at regular intervals to help students analyze their performance, ask questions, and get necessary assistance. These techniques permit task modifications to enhance performance. Appropriate individual plans can then be devised based on defined interests, demonstrated work competency, and observed job performance variables.

What Are the Student's Abilities in the Areas of Transition and Community Adjustment?

An essential aspect of addressing student needs is determining abilities and interests in domains that are specific to transition planning, These domains include independent living skills, life skills, self-determination, postsecondary education and employment, and personal-social skills (Brolin, 1995; Clark, 1998). Table 17–2 provides a listing of several standardized transition-referenced assessments. These include the *Transition Planning Inventory (TPI)* (Clark & Patton, 1997), the *Life Centered Career Education (LCCE) Competency Assessment Knowledge Batteries* (Brolin, 1992b), and the *BRIGANCE® Life Skills Inventory* (Brigance, 1995b). Another measure of interest is

the *Self-Determination Knowledge Scale (SDKS)* (Hoffman, Field, & Sawilowsky, 1996).

The *Transition Planning Inventory (TPI)* provides school personnel with a method to comply with federal transition mandates and assist students in their transition planning. The *TPI* is comprised of: a student form (see Figure 17–5), a home form, a school-based personnel form, and a profile and further assessment recommendation form. These parts are completed independently by the student, parents/guardians, and school professional.

Forty-six transition planning statements are organized into the following areas: employment, further education/training, daily living, leisure activities, community participation, health, self-determination, communication, and interpersonal relationships. Each rater determines the student's level of functioning in these planning areas. In addition, the home form requests preferences and interests that are likely in post-school settings. Ratings and information are compiled on the Profile and Further Assessment Recommendation Form, which gives a visual display of data and is useful in developing the transition IEP. For example, see Figure 17–6 for a portion of the *TPI* Profile for Mike, a 15-year-old tenth grader who is recovering from a head injury.

The Life Centered Career Education (LCCE) Competency Assessment Knowledge Batteries is a curriculum-based assessment instrument. This instrument assesses the career education knowledge and skills of students with disabilities in grades 7 through 12. The battery is a standardized, criterion-referenced set of 200 multiple-choice questions spread across the three domains of the LCCE model: awareness, exploration, and occupational and guidance. This assessment is designed to be used with the *Life Centered Career Education (LCCE) Competency Assessment Performance Batteries* (Brolin, 1992c) as part of the *LCCE* curriculum program (Brolin, 1992a).

The *BRIGANCE® Life Skills Inventory* (Brigance, 1995b) evaluates basic skills and life skills in the context of real-world situations. This criterion-referenced inventory assesses students' listening, speaking, reading, writing, comprehending, and computing skills. There are nine sections assessed: speaking and listening skills, money and finance, functional writing skills, food, words on common signs and warning labels, clothing, telephone

TABLE 17-2

Assessment Instruments for Transition Planning

INSTRUMENT	TARGET GROUP	FEATURES
Social and Prevocational Information Battery–Revised (Halpern et al., 1986)	Adolescents and adults with mild mental retardation or low-functioning students with learning disabilities; designed primarily for juniors and seniors in high school.	1. Subscales include Banking, Budgeting and Purchasing Skills, Job Skills and Job-Related Behavior, Home Management, Health Care, Hygiene and Grooming, and Ability to Read Functional Words. 2. Orally administered except for items on functional signs. 3. True-false item format. 4. 277 items across seven subtests. 5. 20 to 30 minutes administration time per subtest.
Tests for Everyday Living (Halpern et al., 1979)	All junior high students and average- to low-functioning high school students in remedial programs, including those labeled as having learning disabilities or learning handicaps.	1. Subtests include Purchasing Habits, Banking, Budgeting, Health Care, Home Management, Job Search Skills, and Job-Related Behavior. 2. Orally administered except where reading skills are critical to an item. 3. 245 items across seven subtests. 4. Diagnostic at the subtest level. 5. 20 to 30 minutes administration time per subtest.
Work Adjustment Scale (McCarney, 1991) [Revised/shortened version of *Transition Behavior Scale* (McCarney, 1989)]	Any disability group; individuals with mild to severe levels of disability.	1. Subscales include Work Related, Interpersonal Relations, and Social/Community Expectations. 2. Ratings are completed by at least three persons, including teachers and employers. 3. Items are rated on a 3-point scale. 4. Estimated completion time is 15 minutes. 5. Scores in percentile ranks based on a national standardization sample.
Responsibility and Independence Scale for Adolescents (Salvia, Neisworth, & Schmidt, 1990)	Higher functioning students with mild educational disabilities, students at risk, or juvenile offenders; appropriate for students 12-0 through 19-11 years of age.	1. Subscales include Domestic Skills, Money Management, Citizenship, Personal Planning, Transportation Skills, Career Development, Self-Management, Social Maturity, and Social Communication. 2. Administration time is 30 to 45 minutes. 3. Scale scores and percentile ranks used for norm indicators.
Quality of Life Questionnaire (Schalock & Keith, 1995)	Individuals with mild to severe cognitive disabilities, ages 18 and older.	1. Subscales include Satisfaction, Competence/Productivity, Empowerment/Independence, and Social Belonging/Community Integration. 2. Administered in interview format for persons who have communication skills, two independent ratings for those who do not have communication skills. 3. Items are rated on a 3-point scale. 4. Administration time is estimated at 20 minutes. 5. Scores in percentile ranks are based on standardization sample.

Continued

TABLE 17-2

Assessment Instruments for Transition Planning—*Continued*

INSTRUMENT	TARGET GROUP	FEATURES
Quality of Student Life Questionnaire (Keith & Schalock, 1995)	All disability groups, ages 14–25; individuals with mild through severe levels of disability.	1. Subscales include Satisfaction, Well-Being, Social Belonging, and Empowerment/Control. 2. Adminstered in interview format for most persons; alternative formats include a written format or obtaining independent ratings and averaging. 3. Items are rated on a 3-point scale. 4. Administration time is estimated at 15 minutes. 5. Scores in percentile ranks are based on secondary and postsecondary standardization sample.
Transition Competence Battery for Deaf Adolescents and Adults (Reiman & Bullis, 1993)	Deaf adolescents and adults who communicate manually; ages approximately 14–25.	1. Subtests include Job Seeking Skills for Employment, Work Adjustment Skills for Employment, Job Related Social/Interpersonal Skills, Money Management Skills for Independent Living, Health and Home Skills for Independent Living, and Community Awareness Skills for Independent Living. 2. Average readability level for battery is 4.17. 3. Administered individually or in small groups in approximately 4 hours. 4. Multiple-choice format. 5. Items presented via a signed (Pidgin Signed English) videodisk presentation in combination with a simply worded, illustrated test booklet. 6. 243 items across the six subtests.
BRIGANCE® Employability Skills Inventory (Brigance, 1995a)	High-functioning adolescents and adults with mild disabilities.	1. Subscales include Career Awareness and Understanding, Job Seeking and Knowledge, Reading Skills, Speaking and Listening Skills, Preemployment Writing, and Math Skills and Concepts. 2. Optional supplemental assessment through rating scales on self-concept attitudes, responsibility and self-discipline, motor coordination and job requirements, thinking skills/abilities and job requirements, job-interview preparation, job-interview skills, and work experience. 3. Approximately 1,400 items across six subtests. 4. Requires reading or listening comprehension of high school level material.

Continued

TABLE 17-2

Assessment Instruments for Transition Planning—*Continued*

INSTRUMENT	*TARGET GROUP*	*FEATURES*
BRIGANCE® Life Skills Inventory (Brigance, 1995b)	All disability populations, high school ages and adults; mild cognitive disabilities, with reading grade levels 2–8.	1. Subscales include Speaking and Listening, Functional Writing, Words on Common Signs and Warning Labels, Telephone Skills, Money and Finance, Food, Clothing, Health, Travel and Transportation. 2. Administered individually or in groups; oral or written. 3. Supplemental rating scales in the areas of speaking skills, listening skills, health practices and attitudes, self-concept, and auto safety. 4. Learner Record Book to show inventory performance and instructional objectives generated from results.
Transition Planning Inventory (Clark & Patton, 1997)	All disability populations, ages 14–25; mild through severe levels of disability.	1. Transition planning areas for rating include Employment, Further Education/Training, Daily Living, Leisure Activities, Community Participation, Health, Self-Determination, Communication, and Personal Relationships. 2. 6-point rating scale completed independently by student, parent/guardian, and a school representative. 3. Three administration formats: self-administration, guided administration, and oral administration. 4. 46 inventory items plus 15 open-ended items on the student form (optional on parent form) related to preferences and interests. 5. Profile and Further Assessment Recommendations Form provides a visual comparison of the three ratings and a means of specifying further assessments needed. 6. A Planning Notes Form is provided to assist an IEP team to move from assessment results to individualized planning. 7. Administration and Resource Guide provides case studies illustrating the interpretation and use of the inventory for IEP planning, and an extensive list of more than 600 transition goals across the nine planning areas and 46 items.
Life-Centered Career Education (LCCE) Competency Assessment Knowledge Batteries (Brolin, 1992b)	Mild cognitive abilities; moderate to severe learning disabilities; mild to moderate behavioral disorders; Grades 7–12.	1. Curriculum-based assessment related to LCCE curriculum. 2. 200 multiple-choice items covering 20 of 22 LCCE competencies. 3. Standardized on national sample. 4. Estimated administration time is 1 to 2 hours.

Note: From *Assessment for Transition* (pp. 33–35) by G. M. Clark, 1998, Austin, TX: PRO-ED. Copyright 1998 by PRO-ED. Reprinted with permission.

TPI

Transition Planning Inventory Student Form

Section I. Student Information

Name _____

Date _____

Birth Date _____

School _____

Parent's/Guardian's Name _____

Section II. Likely Postschool Setting(s)

Directions: Fill in based on what you think will happen after high school.

EMPLOYMENT/FURTHER EDUCATION OR TRAINING

☐ work/full-time

☐ work/part-time

☐ vocational training

☐ college/university

☐ other _____

LIVING ARRANGEMENT

☐ live by myself

☐ live with my parents or other relatives

☐ live with others who are not related to me (without adult supervision)

☐ live with others who are not related to me (with adult supervision)

☐ other _____

Section III. Planning Area Inventory

Directions: Rate yourself based on what you think is your *current* level of competence using a scale of 0 to 5 to indicate your level of agreement with each statement. For example, if you strongly disagree with the statement, circle "0." If you strongly agree with the statement, circle "5."

If you do not think planning is necessary because a statement does not fit you, circle "NA" (for "not appropriate"). If the statement fits you, but you do not know your level of competence, circle "DK" (for "don't know").

Planning Areas	Not Appropriate	Strongly Disagree 0	1	2	3	4	Strongly Agree 5	Don't Know
EMPLOYMENT								
1. I know about jobs I am interested in and what they require.	NA	0	1	2	3	4	5	DK
2. I can choose a job that fits my interests and abilities.	NA	0	1	2	3	4	5	DK
3. I know how to get a job.	NA	0	1	2	3	4	5	DK
4. I have the work habits and attitudes for keeping a job and being promoted—with or without special help.	NA	0	1	2	3	4	5	DK
5. I have the knowledge and skills needed for a specific job—with or without special help.	NA	0	1	2	3	4	5	DK

FIGURE 17–5

Transition Planning Inventory, Student Form

Note: From *Transition Planning Inventory, Student Form* (p. 1) by G. M. Clark & J. R. Patton, 1997, Austin, TX: PRO-ED. Copyright 1997 by PRO-ED, Inc. Reprinted with permission.

Planning Areas	School Rating (Strongly Disagree → Strongly Agree)	Home Rating (Strongly Disagree → Strongly Agree)	Student Rating (Strongly Disagree → Strongly Agree)	Knowledge/Skills Goals	Linkage Goals
Section V. Profile					
EMPLOYMENT					
1. knows job requirements and demands	NA 0 1 (2) 3 4 5 DK	NA 0 1 2 (3) 4 5 DK	NA 0 1 2 3 (4) 5 DK	✓	
2. makes informed choices	NA 0 (1) 2 3 4 5 DK	NA 0 1 2 (3) 4 5 DK	NA 0 1 2 3 (4) 5 DK		
3. knows how to get a job	NA 0 (1) 2 3 4 5 DK	NA 0 1 2 (3) 4 5 DK	NA 0 1 2 3 4 (5) DK		
4. demonstrates general job skills and work attitude	NA 0 1 (2) 3 4 5 DK	NA 0 1 2 (3) 4 5 DK	NA 0 1 2 3 4 (5) DK	✓	
5. has specific job skills	NA 0 (1) 2 3 4 5 DK	NA 0 1 2 (3) 4 5 DK	NA 0 1 2 3 (4) 5 DK		✓
FURTHER EDUCATION/TRAINING					
6. knows how to gain entry into community employment training	NA 0 (1) 2 3 4 5 DK	NA 0 1 (2) 3 4 5 DK	NA 0 1 2 (3) 4 5 DK		
7. knows how to gain entry into GED program	NA 0 (1) 2 3 4 5 DK	NA 0 1 (2) 3 4 5 DK	NA 0 1 2 (3) 4 5 DK		
8. knows how to gain entry into vocational/technical school	NA 0 (1) 2 3 4 5 DK	NA 0 1 (2) 3 4 5 DK	NA 0 1 2 (3) 4 5 DK		
9. knows how to gain entry into college or university	NA 0 (1) 2 3 4 5 DK	NA 0 1 (2) 3 4 5 DK	NA 0 1 2 3 4 5 (DK)		✓
10. can succeed in a postsecondary program	NA (0) 1 2 3 4 5 DK	NA 0 (1) 2 3 4 5 DK	NA 0 1 2 3 4 5 (DK)		
DAILY LIVING					
11. maintains personal grooming and hygiene	NA 0 1 2 (3) 4 5 DK	NA 0 1 2 3 (4) 5 DK	NA 0 1 2 3 (4) 5 DK		
12. knows how to locate place to live	NA 0 1 (2) 3 4 5 DK	NA 0 1 2 3 (4) 5 DK	NA 0 1 2 (3) 4 5 DK		
13. knows how to set up living arrangement	NA 0 1 (2) 3 4 5 DK	NA 0 1 2 3 (4) 5 DK	NA 0 1 2 (3) 4 5 DK		
14. performs everyday household tasks	NA 0 1 2 (3) 4 5 DK	NA 0 1 2 3 4 (5) DK	NA 0 1 2 3 (4) 5 DK		
15. manages own money	NA 0 1 2 (3) 4 5 DK	NA 0 1 2 3 4 (5) DK	NA 0 1 2 3 (4) 5 DK		
16. uses local transportation systems	NA 0 1 2 (3) 4 5 DK	NA 0 1 2 3 4 (5) DK	NA 0 1 2 3 (4) 5 DK		
LEISURE ACTIVITIES					
17. performs indoor activities	NA 0 1 2 (3) 4 5 DK	NA 0 1 (2) 3 4 5 DK	NA 0 1 2 3 (4) 5 DK	✓	
18. performs outdoor activities	NA 0 1 2 (3) 4 5 DK	NA 0 (1) 2 3 4 5 DK	NA 0 1 2 (3) 4 5 DK	✓	
19. uses settings that offer entertainment	NA 0 1 2 (3) 4 5 DK	NA 0 1 (2) 3 4 5 DK	NA 0 1 2 (3) 4 5 DK	✓	
COMMUNITY PARTICIPATION					
20. knows basic legal rights	NA 0 1 (2) 3 4 5 DK	NA 0 1 (2) 3 4 5 DK	NA 0 1 2 3 (4) 5 DK	✓	
21. participates as an active citizen	NA 0 1 (2) 3 4 5 DK	NA 0 1 (2) 3 4 5 DK	NA 0 1 2 3 4 (5) DK	✓	
22. makes legal decisions	NA (0) 1 2 3 4 5 DK	NA (0) 1 2 3 4 5 DK	NA 0 1 2 3 (4) 5 DK	✓	
23. locates community services and resources	NA 0 (1) 2 3 4 5 DK	NA 0 1 (2) 3 4 5 DK	NA 0 1 2 3 (4) 5 DK	✓	
24. uses services and resources successfully	NA 0 (1) 2 3 4 5 DK	NA 0 (1) 2 3 4 5 DK	NA 0 1 2 3 (4) 5 DK	✓	
25. knows how to obtain financial assistance	NA 0 1 (2) 3 4 5 DK	NA (0) 1 2 3 4 5 DK	NA 0 1 2 3 (4) 5 DK	✓	

FIGURE 17–6

Sample *TPI Profile*

Note: From *Transition Planning Inventory* (p. 55) by G. M. Clark & J. R. Patton, 1997, Austin, TX: PRO-ED. Copyright 1997 by PRO-ED, Inc. Reprinted with permission.

skills, health, and travel and transportation. It is recommended for use with students with disabilities.

The *Self-Determination Knowledge Scale (SDKS)* is a curriculum-based measure to be used as the pretest and posttest for *Steps to Self-Determination: A Curriculum to Help Adolescents Learn to Achieve their Goals* (Field & Hoffman, 1996). The instrument assesses students' cognitive knowledge of self-determination in relationship to the skills taught in the curriculum. It has a reading level of approximately fifth grade.

PROVIDING TRANSITION SERVICES

Design of an appropriate secondary and postsecondary transition program should be based on the completion of the necessary levels of assessment and the answers to the main assessment questions about transition needs. Information about career and vocational knowledge, aptitude, study and social skills, interests, and technical skills is combined with transition and community adjustment information and needs are identified. Also, students' limitations in cognitive, academic, and behavioral areas must be taken into account when designing the IEP and transition program. Many of the procedures just described facilitate this program development by providing profiles of strengths and weaknesses and organizing the information into a comprehensive overview. For example, the *McCarron-Dial Evaluation System* (McCarron & Dial, 1986) organizes data from the instruments used to assess its various dimensions into an individual plan that integrates vocational considerations with content areas.

IEP Design

In the case of Phillip, as with many students with mild disabilities, vocational education is integrated with instruction in basic skills and content areas, such as social studies and science. Phillip lacks knowledge of the world of work and must familiarize himself with occupational possibilities. Past experience, observations of his behavior on the *WREST* and *VES,* and his responses to items on the *BRIGANCE® Diagnostic Inventory of Essential Skills* also indicate the need for developing appropriate work habits.

Phillip's secondary-level instruction in reading, mathematics, and spelling must be done in the context of his overall needs. Phillip's IEP goals address highly functional skills such as reading directions and using technical vocabulary. In language arts, for example, Phillip is learning to read bus schedules, complete a job application, compose a resume, and communicate on the telephone. Quantitative skills are practiced in reference to money use and management. Compensatory skill development is stressed, such as using a calculator for computation.

Phillip's IEP includes goals to develop his fine-motor skills to improve manual dexterity for possible future employment in food preparation or serving, gardening, and similar occupations. Also, Phillip requires assistance in analyzing work options and deciding on the more suitable ones. He must also continue to develop social skills and work habits (such as asking for assistance) that are useful in a work situation. Like so many students, he needs to mature socially and emotionally to be better prepared to work under supervision, with co-workers, and alone. He must develop a better style of communication, learn how to take feedback and criticism, and prepare to engage in the daily give-and-take of the workplace.

Phillip

With suitable progress, Phillip should be in a better position to benefit from specific vocational preparation. The next school year will be devoted to establishing prerequisite academic skills, work habits and attitudes, and manual dexterity, as well as providing Phillip with work experience in a part-time school or community job. His current program will place him with his typical peers most of the school day—good preparation for future employment in the mainstream.

Home and Community

Transition assessment and programming must take into account the school, home, and community of the students. Cognitive, academic, and/or behavioral deficits of students with mild disabilities dictate special considerations in preparing for careers or vocations. In assessment, it is necessary to make accommodations for limitations in reading, writing, motor, attention, and other skills. Accurate information can often be gathered only by individualized procedures or other special assessment conditions.

Transition programs must also be coordinated with other services for students with disabilities. Integration of services and inclusion are the keynotes of an appropriate program for students with mild disabilities. The collaboration of general and special education teachers, vocational educators, agency personnel, students, families, and others is essential.

The homes and families of students with mild disabilities are also factors in providing appropriate services. Parents and other family members serve as models for career and vocational aspirations. From them come awareness and knowledge about work, as well as encouragement for developing appropriate occupational attitudes and habits. The student with mild disabilities may be reflecting parental work attitudes and interests on an inventory. Families may or may not have the resources to help their children seek work; finding paid employment for persons with disabilities is often the result of assistance from families and friends (Hasazi, Gordon, & Roe, 1985). The cultural values of the family need to be considered when directing a student toward certain occupations if family support is needed.

The community is another important consideration in evaluating transition needs and conceptualizing student programs. Assessment personnel must have an excellent grasp of the local job market and the conditions of other environments in which students wish to function. A receptive and flexible employment environment is essential for successful preparatory programs because it not only guarantees opportunities for practicing saleable skills, but also holds the promise of continued employment.

Knowing what the community needs both now and in the future is important information to combine with the current performance and potential profiles of secondary students. Job analyses are therefore a critical tool for special educators and vocational teachers. Professionals must also monitor available positions and work to maintain good communication between the schools and the community. Of particular usefulness is the analysis of the occupational site's capability and willingness to make accommodations for students with disabilities like Phillip.

Appropriate services in the area of career preparation must not focus only on career and vocational education. These must be combined with support for students' transition along two additional dimensions of community adjustment—the home and neighborhood environment, and the social and interpersonal network (Halpern, 1985; Sitlington et al., 1996). Students like Phillip require a broader preparation for their movement into the adult community. They must learn how to live fully in their homes and neighborhoods and learn how to benefit from available services and recreational opportunities. Also, they need to be able to engage in daily communications, family life, friendships, and other social-emotional mainstays. Success in one area such as employment or social relationships does not mean success in the others (Halpern, 1985). Problems such as inability to maintain a happy home life may have a detrimental effect on a person's overall adjustment, even if he or she is gainfully employed.

It is also important to avoid restrictive projections by limiting occupational and environmental preparations of students with disabilities. They may wish to go to trade school or college and accept such challenges in spite of past and current difficulties. They should be taught the skills appropriate for those situations and given strategies to obtain the assistance they need.

ASSESSMENT FOR COLLEGE AND OTHER POSTSECONDARY SETTINGS

It is reasonable to expect that more and more students who have mild disabilities will aspire to technical training and 2- and 4-year college studies. Technical colleges and institutions of higher learning are finding these students already enrolled or seeking admission. The number of university freshmen claiming to have learning disabilities is increasing, as are the requests for special testing arrangements (Vogel, 1985). Ten percent of all postsecondary students are identified as having a disability in recent federal data (Gajar, 1998). In fact, an increasing number of students with learning disabilities are pursuing not only undergraduate, but graduate and professional degrees (Henderson, 1995). Another indication of this increase is the 90% rise in the number of universities who are providing support services to students with disabilities (Brinkerhoff, Shaw, & McGuire, 1993; Yost, Shaw, Cullen, McGuire, & Bigaj, 1994).

The main legal imperatives requiring colleges to offer support services are Section 504 of the Rehabilitation Act of 1973, as it applies to postsecondary educational programs that receive federal monies (Vogel, 1982), and the ADA of 1990. Accurate identification and assessment procedures pose a particular challenge because the definitions of disabilities such as learning disabilities are vague and are not consistently used by colleges and universities. Although many students are aware of their disabilities before leaving high school, others do not realize they have a learning disability until they are in college. After being diagnosed, it becomes the responsibility of postsecondary students to disclose their disability and the extent to which it may affect their academic success (Lynch & Gussel, 1996). These students become eligible for support services on the basis of appropriate documentation, and with the right accommodations they can experience success in college (Brackett & McPhearson, 1996; Larson & Aase, 1997).

Table 17–3 outlines possible admission requirements for students with mild disabilities

TABLE 17-3
Postsecondary Education and Training Options

DIMENSION

Option	Admission Requirements	Emphasis	General Information	Outcome
Colleges, Universities	*Regular* High school diploma or GED SAT or ACT GPA and/or class rank *Special or Provisional* SAT/ACT may be waived or lower scores accepted Other factors (e.g., potential, goals) considered Remedial or study skills classes may be required *Cooperative (special program within college)* Joint decision between college and special program Must disclose disability Some require ACT/SAT Some require high school diploma/GED	4-year program Extensive selection of majors (>400) Sample a variety of courses during first 2 years Select major in last 2 years Some colleges specialize (music, design, technology)	Tuition varies greatly State-supported generally less costly Financial aid usually available Several sources of help available (counseling, peer tutoring, learning labs, math centers)	Bachelor of Science Degree, Bachelor of Arts Degree
Community and Junior Colleges, Public, 2-Year	Usually open admission 18 years or older Most require high school diploma or GED for credit courses	2-year program Liberal arts subjects Training in specific occupations (hotel management, auto mechanics, marketing, dental hygiene) Many also have remedial or developmental courses for upgrading basic academic skills Provides student with opportunity to try out college by taking one or two courses	Available in or near most cities Less expensive than 4-year programs Committed to serving educational and training needs of local communities Provides opportunity to build a better academic record that can be transferred to a 4-year program Provides opportunity to upgrade academic and job skills and work toward improved employment opportunities or a career change	Associates of Arts Degree, Certificate in Specific Occupations
Junior Colleges, Private, 2-Year	High school diploma or GED Usually an entrance exam (SAT or ACT)	General course of study Prepares students to transfer to a 4-year liberal arts institution	Most are small, residential schools Small class sizes	Associates of Arts Degree

DIMENSION

Option	Admission Requirements	Emphasis	General Information	Outcome
	Usually request GPA and/or class rank Experience and personal qualities usually considered	Opportunities to improve reading, writing, and math skills Opportunities to train for a new career	Individualized attention	
Vocational Education Schools, Public and Private, 2 Years or Less	Usually open admission Some require high school diploma or GED Some require SAT, ACT, or admission tests	*Community Junior Colleges* Occupational training and liberal arts training can be combined *2-Year Technical Institutes/Colleges* Degree programs in skill areas needed to enter and advance in specific occupational fields Academic course usually related to occupational areas *Area Vocational Centers or Single-Specialty Public Vocational and Technical Schools* Available in a few areas Offer training in a single-specialty skill (e.g., aviation, truck driving, barbering) *Private* Trade, technical, or business schools Offers training in a variety of occupational skills Practical training in fields requiring 2 years or less	Great variability in patterns of service due to the state laws that govern (e.g., some states may offer vocational education through the community college system, whereas others might offer through technical institutes) Also great variability in state requirements for licenses to practice trades and courses of study to complete programs	Associates of Arts, Certificate

*Adapted from *Unlocking Potential: College and Other Choices for Learning Disabled People. A Step-by-Step Guide* (pp. 46–47, 53–56, 81), by B. Scheiber & J. Talpers, 1987, Bethesda, MD: Adler & Adler.

Note: From *Transition from School to Young Adulthood* (pp. 41–43) by J. Patton and C. Dunn, 1998, Austin, TX: PRO-ED. Copyright 1998 by PRO-ED. Reprinted with permission.

who seek technical and advanced education (Patton & Dunn, 1998; Scheiber & Talpers, 1987; Vogel, 1987). Some schools have open admissions, and students with special needs are automatically accepted. Other students meet the minimal entrance requirements just as typical students do; that is, they provide evidence of acceptable high school grades, performance on college admission tests like the SATs or ACTs, and so forth. Still others request modifications of test administration procedures because of their learning disabilities, such as taking the tests untimed or having a reader or scribe. Other suggested modifications to evaluation procedures include providing essay exams instead of objective exams (or vice versa), allowing an exam to be taken in a separate room with a proctor, allowing alternate methods of demonstrating mastery of course objectives, allowing the use of computer exams and scoring sheets, and permitting the use of references and calculators (Gajar, Goodman, & McAfee, 1993; Vogel & Sattler, 1981).

There is no consistently used battery of tests for students with disabilities on campuses and universities. However, the two most frequently mentioned are the *Wechsler Adult Intelligence Scale-Third Edition* (Wechsler, 1997) and the *Woodcock-Johnson Psycho-Educational Battery-Revised* (Woodcock & Johnson, 1989).

Informal assessment techniques also figure prominently in postsecondary assessment, including observation and interviews. Vogel (1987) suggests:

- Ask students about the nature of their learning disability, things that were easy and hard to learn, their best and worst subjects, reasons for seeking more education and in what areas, their occupational plans.
- Ask institutions about the number of students with special needs on campus, the services available, preparation of advisors and instructors for accommodating students, the willingness of faculty to provide support.
- Ask faculty about their willingness to work with students with special needs, instructional style and individualization, and nature and flexibility of evaluation strategies.

Areas that should frequently be the object for assessment are students' study habits (note taking, organization, time management, test taking); listening and comprehension skills for following class lectures and oral expression for participating in class activities; vocabulary, grammar, and production necessary for written expression; and the social and interpersonal skills needed for interaction with teachers and peers (Vogel, 1987).

Much can be accomplished with students like Joyce, whose learning disabilities were described in Chapters 7 through 14, long before they apply to or appear on a college campus. An appropriate transition assessment would establish Joyce's knowledge of and interest in possible fields of study. Many of the academic skills and learning strategies that are the subject of middle and high school assessment are applicable to the college setting and, when taught, provide an important foundation. Transitional plans for Joyce must prepare her for the college environment so that she can explain her needs well to instructors, seek out available services, use strategies independently to compensate for her disabilities, and cope with the increased demands for organizational, interpersonal, and other skills.

Of no less significance is a student's ability to engage in recreational and leisure-time activities. Researchers (Brolin, 1995; Clark & Kolstoe, 1995; White et al., 1983) indicate that students with learning disabilities as well as others need to be well prepared to use their free time and participate in life in their communities. Also, the personal-social goals in the IEP should be extended to anticipate the transition to adult relationships, marriage, and childrearing.

Full community adjustment is based on adequate preparation in all of these areas (Brolin, 1995; Clark & Kolstoe, 1995; Halpern, 1985). This perspective is very similar to the one used for Brolin's career education competency curriculum described earlier. Students such as Phillip and Joyce require a transition plan conceptualized as part of their total preparation for and movement to the adult world.

STUDY GUIDE

REVIEW QUESTIONS

1. Transition assessment is ongoing throughout an adolescent's and young adult's school career. (True or False)
2. Transition and vocational education are synonymous. (True or False)
3. Other than PL 105-17, no other federal laws regulate transition assessment and planning for persons with disabilities. (True or False)
4. Three major components of transition planning are: _____ , _____ , and _____ .
5. Technological advances may make some vocational assessments unrepresentative of the work situation. (True or False)
6. The *DOT* is the _____ .
7. A simulation of an activity in the work world is a(n) _____ .
8. All students with disabilities need a Level III vocational evaluation. (True or False)
9. Through transition _____ , students can identify their interests, preferences, strengths, and abilities in relationship to their preparation for future adult roles.
10. The response mode on the *Reading-Free Vocational Interest Inventory-Revised* is
    a. answering questions orally.
    b. writing sentences.
    c. marking pictures.
    d. all of the above
11. Commercially available instruments should be the sole method of gathering data for transition planning. (True or False)
12. Two commercial work sample analysis systems are _____ and _____ .
13. Reading is required on the *WREST*. (True or False)
14. Transition assessment and planning must take into account the school, home, and community of the student. (True or False)
15. There is a consistently used standardized test battery for students with disabilities entering college. (True or False)

ACTIVITIES

1. Visit your local school district's transition program. Describe and critique its assessment system.
2. Administer a vocational interest inventory to a student. What did you learn? What more do you need to know in order to give suitable guidance?
3. Using the directions in this chapter and the *DOT,* analyze a job in your community.
4. Interview a special educator, vocational education teacher, and rehabilitation counselor about their mutual roles in transition assessment.
5. Interview a high school student with a disability about his or her career plans. Are the plans reflected in current assessment instruments and transition programs?

DISCUSSION QUESTIONS

1. Read the article by Sitlington, Frank, and Carson (1992) mentioned in this chapter. Discuss the implications for transition assessment.
2. Discuss ways to assess a college environment for meeting the needs of a student with learning disabilities who wants higher education.
3. Sitlington, Neubert, Begun, Lombard, and Leconte (1996) and others in the field of transition worry that an emphasis on only the work skills of students is short-sighted. Discuss a more comprehensive assessment for transition planning.

Answers to Review Questions

Chapter 1

1. Special education assessment is the systematic process of gathering educationally relevant information to make legal and instructional decisions about the provision of special services.
2. disabilities
3. True
4. False
5. identification, determination of eligibility, program planning, monitoring of student progress, program evaluation
6. a. informal, b. informal, c. formal, d. informal, e. formal, f. informal
7. False
8. b, c, d, c, a, b
9. False
10. f, e, b, a, c, d
11. True
12. d, a and b, d, e, b, c, d, c
13. 14
14. consultation to general educator, special materials, modification of tests, in-class instruction by special educator
15. False

Chapter 2

1. legal, instructional
2. instructional, legal
3. 5, 6, 1, 9, 3, 7, 4, 2 10, 8
4. Individualized Assessment Plan
5. educational, disability
6. True, True, False, True, True, False
7. Due process
8. True
9. conferences with students and parents, review of educational records, changes in the classroom environment, instructional modifications, changes in behavior management

10. False
11. False
12. True
13. c, e, a, b, a, b, d
14. c
15. b

Chapter 3

1. False, True, True, False
2. educational
3. c
4. b
5. age, grade, and gender of norm group members; selection method; representativeness; size; recency
6. e
7. d, b, a, c, e
8. standard error of measurement
9. True, False, True, True
10. high, low
11. c
12. b
13. 85
14. False, False, False, False
15. informal

Chapter 4

1. norm group
2. b, d
3. a
4. b
5. item 9
6. c, a, b, d
7. Any two of the following: to determine whether the student is comfortable during test administration, gather information about how the student approaches a work situation, determine the student's response style and work style, collect data on the student's

583

attitudes and perceptions, look for warning signs of disabilities
8. a. 7-1, b. 17-3, c. 4-11
9. Test *A* 6, Test *B* 22
10. c
11. d
12. d, a, e, b, c
13. 67 to 79
14. b
15. any four of the following: paraphrase test instructions, provide a demonstration, change the presentation mode, change the response mode, allow the student to use aids, provide prompts, give feedback, offer positive reinforcement, change the physical location of the test, change the tester

Chapter 5

1. a, c, d
2. direct, obtrusive
3. a. True, b. True, c. False, d. False, e. True
4. narrative
5. error, response
6. d, c, a, b
7. curriculum
8. True
9. a. worksheet with 20 2-digit plus 2-digit addition problems requiring regrouping, b. "Write the answers to these problems. You have five minutes.", c. at least 15 of the 20 problems must be correct
10. a
11. rating scales, checklists, questionnaires, interviews
12. agree
13. True
14. d
15. True

Chapter 6

1. ongoing evaluation of the instructional program, evaluation of student progress
2. b, c
3. d, a, c, b
4. observed, interviewed
5. hypothesis
6. a. False, b. False, c. True, d. False
7. c

8. rubrics
9. c
10. False
11. b
12. criterion
13. a
14. d
15. d, c, b, a, c, d

Chapter 7

1. a. True, b. True, c. False
2. Any two of the following: to determine if there is a problem in academic achievement, to identify areas of educational need, to assess academic progress
3. a, b, d, e, g, h
4. d
5. c
6. Any two of the following: time limits, reading skills are required, students respond in writing, instructions are presented orally, independent work skills are assumed
7. c, e, f, h, d, b, a, g
8. b
9. False
10. c

Chapter 8

1. Learning aptitude refers to an individual's capacity for altering his or her behavior when presented with new information or experiences.
2. True, False, True, True
3. c
4. Any two of the following: tests must be nondiscriminatory, tests must be administered in the language of the student, tests must be validated for the purpose for which they are used, tests must be administered by trained professionals, no one test score may be the sole basis for determining educational placement
5. a, b, d, e, f, h
6. c, a, d, b, e
7. False, True, True, True, False
8. a
9. d, c, c, a, e
10. a
11. b

Chapter 9
1. d
2. perception, attention
3. True
4. b, c, d, e
5. False, True, True, True
6. a, c, e, g
7. a
8. e, a, b, d, c
9. a, d, e
10. a
11. b

Chapter 10
1. True
2. Any three of the following: conduct problems, attention and activity levels, self-concept, acceptance by peers, interests and attitudes toward school and learning, influence of the classroom learning environment
3. d
4. a, c, d, f
5. teachers, parents, peers
6. False
7. f, e, d, b, c, a
8. (2) select a measurement system, (3) set up the data-collection system, (4) select a data-reporting system, (5) carry out the observations
9. sociometric
10. c, d
11. a

Chapter 11
1. c
2. comprehension, interaction
3. b, c, e
4. e
5. True
6. b, d, c, e, a
7. True, False, True, False
8. a, b, b, b
9. independent, instructional, frustration
10. a, d, e, f
11. a, b, f
12. instructional, interpersonal, physical
13. b
14. d

Chapter 12
1. True
2. problem solving, application
3. e
4. a
5. True
6. d, c, a, d, a, b
7. N, S, S, N, S
8. algorithms
9. True
10. a, b, d
11. computation, problem solving
12. writing numerals
13. c
14. c

Chapter 13
1. to gather information for planning the instructional program
2. spelling, handwriting, and composition
3. True, False, False, True, False
4. the product
5. e, f, c, a, d, b
6. a
7. phonetic, nonphonetic
8. a, c, d, f
9. write a story about a picture
10. True
11. time, skills
12. d
13. c

Chapter 14
1. d
2. phonology, morphology, syntax, semantics, pragmatics
3. True, False, True, False, True
4. False
5. dialect
6. d, a, e, b, c
7. a
8. c
9. length, utterance
10. False
11. d
12. verbal
13. b
14. f
15. c

Chapter 15

1. (i) Parental input is required by law. (ii) Parents know more about their own children than anyone else. (iii) Parents are the constant in students' lives.
2. (i) An increasing number of children live in families that do not have a parent present. *or* (ii) Students can only be considered within the context of their family, and family often refers to more than the student's parents.
3. Family-professional or parent-professional collaboration
4. (i) Participate in identification and referral for assessment. (ii) Gather assessment information. (iii) Ensure that cultural, linguistic, and sociocultural diversity are taken into account. (iv) Discuss and interpret findings and results. (v) Develop and implement interventions. (vi) Monitor student progress.
5. False
6. a, c, b, a
7. True
8. False
9. False
10. b, b, a, a, b

Chapter 16

1. child, family
2. natural environment
3. True
4. e
5. e
6. True
7. screening
8. a
9. b, e, a, c, d
10. a, b, c, e
11. Individualized Family Service Plan

Chapter 17

1. True
2. False
3. False
4. General and continuing education, career development, and specific vocational programming.
5. True
6. *Dictionary of Occupational Titles*
7. work sample
8. False
9. assessment
10. a
11. False
12. Any two of the following: *Wide Range Employability Sample Test (WREST), Singer Vocational Evaluation System (VES),* or others mentioned in chapter
13. False
14. True
15. False

GLOSSARY

Accommodations   With tests, any changes in the ways in which a test is administered and/or scored.

Action research   An investigation in which an educator seeks the solution to a local problem.

Acuity   The physiological ability to receive sensory information.

Adaptive behavior   The ability to cope with the demands of the environment; includes self-help, communication, and social skills.

Advocacy   Clear expression of support for the rights of persons with disabilities and their families.

Age score   Also called *age equivalent;* a score that translates test performance into an estimated age; reported in years and months.

Algorithm   A procedure used to perform a mathematical operation.

Alternate score   A score resulting from the administration of standardized tests under altered conditions.

Anecdotal records   Written notes kept by teachers on a daily basis about student performance and needed modifications of instructional programs.

Application skills   The ability to use reading, mathematics, and other academic skills in real-life situations.

Articulation   The production of the speech sounds or phonemes.

Assessment   The systematic process of gathering educationally relevant information in order to make legal and instructional decisions about the provision of special services to students with disabilities.

Assistive technology   Any technology, including computers, designed specifically to enhance the performance of individuals with disabilities.

Attention   The selective narrowing or focusing on the relevant stimuli in a situation; a prerequisite for perception, memory, and all types of learning activities.

Attention deficit hyperactivity disorder (ADHD)   A term used in psychiatric classification systems to describe individuals with poor attention, impulsivity, and sometimes hyperactivity.

Basal   In test administration, the point at which it can be assumed that the student would receive full credit for all easier test items.

Bilingual education   The provision of special services to students whose primary language is not English; may include instruction in the primary language, training in English language skills, and development of multicultural awareness.

Ceiling   In test administration, the point at which it can be assumed that the student would receive no credit for all more difficult test items.

Checklist   An informal assessment device that allows an informant to quickly scan a list of descriptions and check those that apply to the student in question.

Chronological age   The number of years and months since birth.

Classroom quiz   An informal assessment tool, usually designed by teachers, to assess students' classroom learning.

Clinical interview   Asking a student questions about the strategies used to perform a task as it is performed or immediately afterwards.

Cloze procedure   A technique for assessing reading skills in which words are omitted from a text and the student is asked to fill in the missing words.

Coaching   In test administration, the practice of helping the student arrive at answers.

Composition   Also called *written expression;* the subskill of written language in which writers produce connected text.

Comprehension skills   In reading, the ability to understand what is read; may be assessed via oral or silent reading.

Computation skills   In mathematics, the arithmetic operations of addition, subtraction, multiplication, and division as applied to whole numbers, fractions, and decimals.

Computer-assisted testing   Assessment in which a computer administers a test and/or scores it.

Conferences   Formal meetings at which professionals and parents of students with disabilities discuss assessment results, eligibility, placement, program design, and other matters.

Confidence interval   A range of scores in which it is likely that the student's true score will fall; constructed by means of the standard error of measurement.

Continuous recording   An observational technique in which all of the student's behaviors are studied.

Correlation   A descriptive statistic that expresses the degree of relationship between two sets of scores.

Criterion-referenced test   An informal assessment device that assesses skill mastery; compares the student's performance to curricular standards.

Curriculum-based assessment   Any informal assessment technique or procedure that evaluates the student's performance in relation to the standard school curriculum.

Curriculum-based measurement   A type of curriculum-based assessment characterized by frequent and direct measurement of critical school behaviors; often includes 1-minute timed samples of reading, math, and writing skills.

Decoding   The process by which readers analyze a word in order to pronounce it; includes sight recognition, phonic analysis, structural analysis, and contextual analysis.

Demonstration   In test administration, tasks similar to test items that are used to teach test procedures to the student.

Diagnosis   The process of establishing the cause or causes of an illness or condition and prescribing appropriate treatment.

Diagnostic probe   An informal technique in which a test task or instructional condition is altered in order to observe if a change in the student's performance results.

Diagnostic teaching   An informal assessment strategy in which two or more instructional conditions are compared to determine which is most effective.

Dialect   An alternate form of a language that differs in some way from the standard form.

Discrepancy analysis   The procedure in which scores are compared to determine whether they are significantly different; most often used to compare expected and actual achievement in the identification of learning disabilities.

Due process   Procedural safeguards established to insure the rights of students with disabilities and their parents.

Duration recording   An observational technique in which the length (or duration) of the target behavior is noted.

Dynamic assessment   Also called *interactive assessment;* assessment using the test-teach-test format.

Ecological approach   An approach to assessment that focuses on the student's interaction with the environment rather than on the deficits of the student.

Error analysis   A type of work sample analysis in which the incorrect responses of the student are described and categorized.

Event recording   An observational technique in which the frequency of the target behavior is noted.

Expressive language   The production of language for communication; for example, speaking and writing.

Family-centered approach   Approach to assessment and intervention in which both child and family issues are considered.

Fine motor skills   In motor development, the use of the small muscles of the body, especially in eye-hand coordination tasks.

First language   The language learned first by an individual; also called *home language or native language.*

Formal assessment   Assessment procedures that contain specific rules for administration, scoring, and interpretation; generally norm-referenced and/or standardized.

Formative evaluation   Ongoing evaluation; results are used for program modification.

Functional assessment   Also called *functional behavioral assessment;* a systematic procedure in which observational data are collected to determine the reasons for inappropriate behavior so that a behavior change program can be designed.

Grade score   Also called *grade equivalent;* a score that translates test performance into an estimated grade; expressed in grades and tenths of grades.

Gross motor skills   In motor development, the use of the large muscles of the body.

Group test   A test administered to more than one student at the same time.

Hyperactivity   Excessive activity.

IDEA   The Individuals with Disabilities Education Act and its amendments.

Inclusion   Integration of students with disabilities physically, academically, and socially with age peers.

Individual test   A test administered to one student at a time.

Individualized Assessment Plan (IAP)   A plan in which the steps and procedures of the assessment are organized according to the reasons for the assessment.

Individualized Education Program (IEP)   A written educational plan developed for each school-aged student eligible for special education.

Individualized Family Service Plan (IFSP)   A written plan that describes the needs of infants and toddlers and their families and specifies the goals to be achieved and services they will receive to achieve those goals.

Informal assessment   Assessment procedures without rigid administration, scoring, and interpretation rules; includes criterion-referenced tests, task analysis, inventories, and so forth.

Informal Reading Inventory (IRI)   An informal assessment device that measures both word recognition and comprehension skills; scores include Instructional, Independent, and Frustration reading levels.

Intelligence   The ability of an individual to understand and cope with the environment; generally assessed with intelligence or "IQ" tests that are measures of academic aptitude.

Interindividual assessment   Assessment that compares the performance of the student to the performance of others.

Interval   The scale of measurement characterized by equal intervals between points in the scale.

Interview   An informal assessment procedure in which the tester questions an informant.

Intraindividual assessment   Assessment that compares a student's performance on various measures to one another; results in a statement of "relative" strengths and weaknesses.

Inventory   An informal assessment device that samples the student's ability to perform selected skills within a curricular sequence.

IQ   Intelligence quotient; a standard score yielded by measures of intellectual performance.

Job analysis   A task analysis of the specific skills required by a job.

Language proficiency   The degree to which an individual is skilled in a language; when students speak languages other than English, proficiency is assessed to determine the primary language.

Language sample   A sample of oral language used for analysis.

Latency   In test administration, the amount of time between presentation of the test question and the student's response.

Learning aptitude   The capacity for altering one's behavior when presented with new information; the ability to learn; generally measured by tests of intellectual performance and adaptive behavior.

Learning environment   The instructional, interpersonal, and physical characteristics of the classroom which may influence student performance.

Learning strategies   Methods used by individuals in their interactions with learning tasks.

Least restrictive environment   According to federal special education laws, the educational placement for students with disabilities that is as close to the general education classroom as feasible.

MA   Mental age; a score yielded by some measures of intellectual performance.

Mainstreaming   See *inclusion.*

Mean   The arithmetic average; a measure of central tendency.

Median   The middle score in a distribution of scores; a measure of central tendency.

Memory   The ability to retrieve previously learned information.

Mild disabilities   The disabilities of mild mental retardation, learning disabilities, and emotional disturbance (behavioral disorders); considered mild in relation to more severe disabilities.

Miscue   A decoding error in reading.

Mode   The most common score; a measure of central tendency.

Morphology   The study of morphemes, or the smallest meaningful units of language.

Motor skills   Skills using the small and large muscles of the body; includes fine and gross motor skills.

Natural environment   The environment expected to include individuals without disabilities who are peers of individuals with disabilities.

Nominal   The scale of measurement in which data are sorted into categories.

Nondiscriminatory assessment   Assessment that does not penalize students for their gender, native language, race, ethnicity, culture, or disability.

Norm-referenced test   A test that compares a student's performance to that of the students in the norm group.

Normal curve equivalent   A normalized standard score with a mean of 50 and a standard deviation of 20.06; has the same range and midpoint as percentile rank scores but is an equal interval scale.

Observation   An informal assessment technique that involves specifying, counting, and recording student behaviors.

Oral language   The reception and expression of the pragmatic, semantic, syntactical, morphological, and phonological aspects of language; involves listening and speaking.

Ordinal   The scale of measurement in which data are arranged in rank order.

Percentile rank   A score that translates student test performance into the percentage of the norm group that performed as well as or poorer than the student on the same test.

Perception   The psychological ability to process or use information received through the sense organs.

Phonological processing   Awareness of the sounds that make up words and the ability to recognize likenesses and differences among sounds.

Phonology   Study of phonemes or speech sounds, the smallest units of oral language.

Play-based assessment   A technique used in early childhood assessment in which young children are observed within the context of play.

Portfolio assessment   The analysis of student work samples, self-evaluations, and other materials assembled in portfolios to document student progress over time.

Pragmatics   Study of the use of language for communication.

Prereferral strategies   Modifications of the general education program to promote student success and prevent referral to special education.

Primary language   The language in which an individual is most proficient; also called *dominant language.*

Problem-solving skills   In mathematics, the use of computational skills to solve a problem; usually assessed via word problems.

Profile   A graph upon which scores are plotted.

Protocol   The test form or student answer booklet.

Public Law 94-142   The Education for All Handicapped Children Act of 1975; mandates free, appropriate, public education for all students with disabilities.

Questionnaire   An informal assessment device in which the informant reads questions and writes the answers.

Range   A descriptive statistic that expresses the spread of a distribution.

Rating scale   An informal assessment device in which the informant judges or rates the performance of the student.

Ratio   The scale of measurement characterized by equal intervals between points in the scale and a true zero.

Raw score   The first test score calculated; usually indicates the number of correct responses plus the number of items assumed correct.

Readability   A measure of the ease with which a text can be read; usually expressed as a grade level.

Receptive language   The processing of language, as in listening and reading.

Related services   Special services that students with disabilities may need to benefit from special education; includes transportation, speech pathology and audiology, and counseling.

Reliability Refers to a test's consistency; types of reliability include test-retest, alternate form, split-half, and interrater.

Response analysis A type of work sample analysis in which both errors and correct responses are considered.

Semantics The aspect of language that deals with meaning, concepts, and vocabulary.

Sequence analysis An observational technique in which the antecedents and consequences of the student's behaviors are studied.

Service delivery models A continuum of special education arrangements through which students with disabilities receive services.

Sociometric technique An assessment procedure used to determine how students perceive their peers.

Special education Specially designed instruction to meet the unique needs of students with disabilities.

Specific learning abilities Readiness skills such as attention, perception, and memory.

Standard deviation A descriptive statistic that expresses the amount of variability within a set of scores.

Standard error of difference between scores A statistic used to estimate whether an observed difference between scores is a true difference.

Standard error of measurement A statistic that estimates the amount of measurement error in a score.

Standard score A derived score with a set mean and standard deviation; examples are IQ scores, scaled scores, and T-scores.

Standardization sample The group used to establish scores on norm-referenced tests.

Standardized test A test in which the administration, scoring, and interpretation procedures are standard or set; usually norm-referenced.

Stanine A derived score equivalent to a range of standard scores; stanines divide the distribution into nine ranges.

Structural task analysis A type of task analysis in which the performance demands of the task (e.g., speed and accuracy requirements) are studied.

Summative evaluation Evaluation done at the end of a program to determine its effectiveness.

Supplementary aids and services Supports provided to students with disabilities to allow them to participate in the general education program.

Surrogate parent A person assigned by the state to represent a person with a disability if the parents cannot be identified, if the parents are unknown, or if the person is a ward of the state.

Syntax The grammatical structure of language.

Task analysis An informal assessment technique in which a task is broken into its essential components or subtasks.

Team approach An approach to assessment that requires the active involvement of professionals from many fields, parents, perhaps the person with a disability, and other interested parties.

Test A sample of student behavior collected under standard conditions.

Test-scoring programs Software programs used on computers to assist in scoring tests.

Tester One who administers and scores tests.

Time-sample recording An observational technique in which it is noted whether the target behavior occurs at some time within a specified time interval; used with nondiscrete behaviors.

Transition The movement from one environment or service system to another; for example, the movement from school-based special education services to postsecondary education or vocational training options.

Validity The degree to which a test measures what it purports to measure; types of validity include content, criterion-referenced (predictive and concurrent), and construct.

Work sample analysis An informal assessment technique in which samples of student work are studied.

Work sample A permanent product produced by the student (e.g., a homework assignment, test paper, or composition).

Writing Expressive written language; includes spelling, handwriting, usage, and composition.

Writing sample A sample of the written language produced by the student that is used for analysis.

Written language Includes the receptive skill, reading, and the expressive skill, writing.

REFERENCES

Abdal-Haqq, I. (1995). *ERIC as a resource for the teacher researcher* (ERIC Digest). Retrieved July 10, 1999 from the World Wide Web: http://www.ed.gov/databases/ERIC_Digests/ed381530.html

Abidin, R. R. (1983). *Parenting-stress index.* Charlottesville, VA: Pediatric Psychology Press.

Abruscato, J. (1993). Early results and tentative implications from the Vermont Portfolio Project. *Phi Delta Kappan, 74,* 474–477.

Achenbach, T. M. (1991). *Manual for the child behavior checklist/4–18.* Burlington, VT: University of Vermont Department of Psychiatry.

Adler, S., & Birdsong, S. (1983). Reliability and validity of standardized testing tools used with poor children. *Topics in Language Disorders, 3*(3), 76–87.

Affleck, J. Q., Lowenbraun, S., & Archer, A. (1980). *Teaching the mildly handicapped in the regular classroom* (2nd ed.). New York: Merrill/Macmillan.

Airasian, P. W. (1996). *Assessment in the classroom.* New York: McGraw-Hill.

Alberto, P. A., & Troutman, A. C. (1990). *Applied behavior analysis for teachers* (3rd ed.). New York: Merrill/Macmillan.

Alberto, P. A., & Troutman, A. C. (1999). *Applied behavior analysis for teachers* (5th ed.). Englewood Cliffs, NJ: Prentice-Hall.

Alexander, N. (1983). A primer for developing a writing curriculum. *Topics in Learning & Learning Disabilities, 3*(3), 55–62.

Algozzine, R., Forgnone, C., Mercer, C., & Trifiletti, J. (1979). Toward defining discrepancies for specific learning disabilities: An analysis and alternatives. *Learning Disability Quarterly, 2*(4), 25–31.

Algozzine, R., Ruhl, K., & Ramsey, R. (1991). *Behaviorally disordered? Assessment for identification and instruction.* Reston, VA: The Council for Exceptional Children.

Alley, G., & Deshler, D. (1979). *Teaching the learning disabled adolescent.* Denver, CO: Love.

Alley, G., & Foster, C. (1978). Nondiscriminatory testing of minority and exceptional children. *Focus on Exceptional Children, 9,* 1–14.

Alley, G. R., Deshler, D. D., Clark, F. L., Schumaker, J. B., & Warner, M. M. (1983). Learning disabilities in adolescent and adult populations: Research implications (part II). *Focus on Exceptional Children, 15*(9), 1–14.

American Association on Mental Retardation. (1992). *Mental retardation: Definition, classification, and systems of supports* (9th ed.).Washington, DC: Author.

American Educational Research Association, American Psychological Association, & National Council on Measurement in Education. (1985). *Standards for educational and psychological testing.* Washington, DC: American Psychological Association.

American Federation of Teachers. (1996). *Making standards matter 1996* [WWW document]. URL http://www.aft.org//research/ reports/standard/ index.htm#Table.

American Federation of Teachers. (1998). *Making standards matter 1998: Executive summary.* Washington, DC: Author. Retrieved June 27, 1999 from the World Wide Web: http://www.aft.org/k12/standards98/index.htm

American Psychiatric Association. (1994). *Diagnostic and statistical manual of mental disorders, Fourth Edition.* Washington, DC: Author.

American Psychological Association. (1986). *Guidelines for computer-based tests and interpretations.* Washington, DC: Author.

Anastasi, A. (1988). *Psychological testing* (6th ed.). New York: Macmillan.

Anastasi, A., & Urbina, S. (1997). *Psychological testing* (7th ed.). Upper Saddle River, NJ: Prentice-Hall.

Anderson, P. L. (1983). *Denver handwriting analysis.* Novato, CA: Academic Therapy Publications.

Anderson, R. J., & Sisco, F. H. (1977). *Standardization of the WISC-R performance scale for deaf children.* Washington, DC: Gallaudet College, Office of Demographic Studies.

Aprenda: La prueba de logros en español, Segunda edición. (1997). San Antonio, TX: Harcourt Brace Educational Measurement.

Arter, J. A., & Jenkins, J. R. (1979). Differential diagnostic-prescriptive teaching: A critical appraisal. *Review of Educational Research, 49,* 517–555.

Artiles, A. J., & Trent, S. C. (1994). Overrepresentation of minority students in special education: A continuing debate. *Journal of Special Education, 27,* 410–437.

Ary, D., Jacobs, L. C., & Razavieh, A. (1990). *Introduction to research in education* (4th ed.). Fort Worth, TX: Harcourt Brace Jovanovich.

Asher, S. R., & Taylor, A. R. (1981). Social outcomes of mainstreaming: Sociometric assessment and beyond. *Exceptional Education Quarterly, 1,* 13–30.

Ashlock, R. B. (1998). *Error patterns in computation* (7th ed.). Upper Saddle River, NJ: Merrill/Prentice-Hall.

Baca, L. (1998). Bilingualism and bilingual education. In L. M. Baca & H. T. Cervantes (Eds.), *The bilingual special education interface* (3rd ed.) (pp. 26–45). Upper Saddle River, NJ: Merrill/Prentice-Hall.

Baca, L. M., & Almanza, E. (1991). *Language minority students with disabilities.* Reston, VA: Council for Exceptional Children.

Baca, L. M., & Cervantes, H. T. (1989). Assessment procedures for the exceptional child. In L. M. Baca & H. T. Cervantes (Eds.), *The bilingual special education interface* (2nd

ed.) (pp. 153–181). New York: Merrill/Macmillan.

Bachor, D. G. (1979). Using work samples as diagnostic information. *Learning Disability Quarterly, 2*(2), 45–52.

Bagley, M. T., & Greene, J. F. (1981). *Peer attitudes toward the handicapped scale.* Austin, TX: PRO-ED.

Bagnato, S. J., Neisworth, J. T., & Munson, S. M. (1997). *Linking assessment and early intervention: An authentic curriculum-based approach.* Baltimore: Brookes.

Bailet, L. L. (1991). Written language test reviews. In A. M. Bain, L. L. Bailet, & L. C. Moats (Eds.), *Written language disorders* (pp. 165–187). Austin, TX: PRO-ED.

Bailey, D. B. & Wolery, M. (1989). *Assessing infants and preschoolers with handicaps.* Columbus OH: Charles E. Merrill.

Bailey, D. B., & Harbin, G. L. (1980). Nondiscriminatory evaluation. *Exceptional Children, 46,* 590–596.

Bailey, D. B., & Simeonsson, R. J. (1988a). *Family assessment in early intervention.* New York: Merrill/Macmillan.

Bailey, D. B., & Simeonsson, R. J. (1988b). Home-based early intervention. In S. L. Odom & M. B. Karnes (Eds.), *Early intervention for infants and children with handicaps: An empirical base* (pp. 199–215). Baltimore: Brookes.

Baker, H. J., & Leland, B. (1967). *Detroit tests of learning aptitude* (rev. ed.). Indianapolis, IN: Bobbs-Merrill.

Balow, I. H., Farr, R. C., & Hogan, T. P. (1992). *Metropolitan achievement tests* (7th ed.). San Antonio, TX: Harcourt Educational Measurement.

Banbury, M. (1987). Testing and grading mainstreamed students in regular education subjects. In A. Rotatori, M. Banbury, & R. A. Fox (Eds.), *Issues in special education* (pp. 177–186). Mountain View, CA: Mayfield.

Bankson, N. W. (1990). *Bankson language test* (2nd ed.). Austin, TX: PRO-ED.

Barkley, R. A. (1987). *Defiant children: A clinician's manual for parent training.* New York: Guilford Press.

Barkley, R. A. (1990). *Attention-deficit hyperactivity disorder: A handbook for diagnosis and treatment.* New York: The Guilford Press.

Barkley, R. A. (1998). *Attention-deficit hyperactivity disorder: A handbook for diagnosis and treatment.* (2nd ed.) New York: The Guilford Press.

Bartel, N. R. (1986a). Problems in mathematics achievement. In D. D. Hammill & N. R. Bartel (Eds.), *Teaching students with learning and behavior problems* (4th ed.) (pp. 178–223). Austin, TX: PRO-ED.

Bartel, N. R. (1986b). Teaching students who have reading problems. In D. D. Hammill & N. R. Bartel (Eds.), *Teaching students with learning and behavior problems* (4th ed.) (pp. 23–89). Austin, TX: PRO-ED.

Bartel, N. R., & Bryen, D. N. (1982). Problems in language development. In D. D. Hammill & N. R. Bartel (Eds.), *Teaching children with learning and behavior problems* (3rd ed.) (pp. 283–376). Boston: Allyn & Bacon.

Bartel, N. R., Grill, J. J., & Bryen, D. N. (1973). Language characteristics of black children: Implications for assessment. *Journal of School Psychology, 11,* 351–364.

Battle, J. (1992). *Culture-free self-esteem inventories* (2nd ed.). Austin, TX: PRO-ED.

Baumann, J. F. (1988). *Reading assessment.* New York: Merrill/Macmillan.

Bayley, N. (1993). *Bayley scales of infant development–Second edition (BSID-II).* New York: Psychological Corp.

Becker, R. L. (1981, 1988). *Reading-free vocational interest inventory–Revised.* Columbus, OH: Elbern.

Beckman, P. (Ed.). (1996). *Strategies for working with families of young children with disabilities.* Baltimore: Brookes.

Beckman, P. J., Frank, N., & Newcomb, S. (1996). Qualities and skills for communicating with families. In P. J. Beckman (Ed.), *Strategies for working with families of young children with disabilities* (pp. 31–46). Baltimore: Brookes.

Beery, K. E. (1997). *Developmental test of visual-motor integration* (4th ed.). Parsippany, NJ: Modern Curriculum Press.

Bender, L. (1938). A visual motor gestalt test and its clinical use. *The American Orthopsychiatric Association Research Monographs, 3.*

Bennett, R. L. (1982). Cautions for the use of informal measures in the assessment of exceptional children. *Journal of Learning Disabilities, 15,* 337–339.

Bennett, T., Lingerfelt, B. V., & Nelson, D. E. (1990). *Developing individualized family support plans: A training manual.* Cambridge, MA: Brookline Books.

Berdine, W. H., & Cegelka, P. T. (1980). *Teaching the trainable retarded.* New York: Merrill/Macmillan.

Berdine, W. H., & Cegelka, P. T. (1995). Collaborative consultation: A key to effective educational delivery. In P. T. Cegelka & W. H. Berdine, *Effective instruction for students with learning difficulties* (pp. 19–46). Boston: Allyn & Bacon.

Bergin, V. (1980). *Special education needs in bilingual programs.* Rosslyn, VA: National Clearinghouse for Bilingual Education.

Beringer, M. L. (1984). *Ber-Sil secondary Spanish test.* Rancho Palos Verdes, CA: Ber-Sil.

Beringer, M. L. (1987). *Ber-Sil elementary Spanish test.* Rancho Palos Verdes, CA: Ber-Sil.

Berk, R. A. (1982). Effectiveness of discrepancy score methods for screening children with learning disabilities. *Learning Disabilities, 1*(2), 11–24.

Berk, R. A. (1984). An evaluation of procedures for computing an ability-achievement discrepancy score. *Journal of Learning Disabilities, 17,* 262–266.

Bersoff, D. N. (1981). Testing and the law. *American Psychologist, 36,* 1047–1056.

Beverstock, C. (1991). *Your child's vision is important.* Newark, DE: International Reading Association.

Bezuk, N. S., & Cegelka, P. T. (1995). Effective mathematics instruction for all students. In P. T. Cegelka & W. H. Berdine (Eds.), *Effective instruction for students with learning difficulties* (pp. 345–383). Boston: Allyn & Bacon.

Binet, A., & Simon, Th. (1905). Méthodes nouvelles pour le diagnostic du niveau intellectuel des anormaux. *L'Année Psychologique, 11,* 191–255.

Blankenship, C. S. (1985). Using curriculum-based assessment data to make instructional decisions. *Exceptional Children, 52,* 233–238.

Bloom, L., & Lahey, M. (1978). *Language development and language disorders.* New York: Wiley.

Bodner, J. R., Clark, G. M., & Mellard, D. F. (1987). *State graduation policies and program practices related to high school special education programs: A national study.* Lawrence, KS: University of Kansas.

Boehm, A. E. (1986a). *Boehm test of basic concepts—Preschool version.* San Antonio, TX: Psychological Corporation.

Boehm, A. E. (1986b). *Boehm test of basic concepts–Revised.* San Antonio, TX: Psychological Corporation.

Boehm, A. E. (1987). *Prueba Boehm de conceptos básicos–edición revisada.* San Antonio, TX: Psychological Corporation.

Bond, G. L., & Tinker, M. A. (1967). *Reading difficulties: Their diagnosis and correction* (2nd ed.). New York: Appleton-Century-Crofts.

Bondurant-Utz, J. A., & Luciano, L. B. (1994). *A practical guide to infant and preschool assessment in special education.* Boston: Allyn & Bacon.

Borgia, E. T., & Schuler, D. (1996). *Action research in early childhood education* (ERIC Digest). Retrieved July 10, 1999 from the World Wide Web: http://www.ed.gov/databases/ERIC_Digests/ed401047.html

Borich, G. D. (1999). *Observation skills for effective teaching* (3rd ed.). Upper Saddle River, NJ: Merrill/Prentice-Hall.

Bormuth, J. R. (1968). The cloze readability procedure. *Elementary English, 45,* 429–436.

Bracken, B. A. (1992). *Multidimensional self concept scale.* Austin, TX: PRO-ED.

Bracken, B. A., & McCallum, R. S. (1998). *Universal nonverbal intelligence test.* Itasca, IL: Riverside.

Brackett, J., & McPhearson, A. (1996). Learning disabilities diagnosis in postsecondary students: A comparison of discrepancy-based

diagnosis models. In N. Gregg, C. How, & A. Gay (Eds.), *Adults with learning disabilities: Theoretical and practical perspectives* (pp. 68–84). New York: Guildford Press.

Bradley, D. F., & Calvin, M. B. (1998). Grading modified assignments: Equity or compromise? *Teaching Exceptional Children, 31*(2), 24–29.

Bray, C. M., & Wiig, E. H. (1987). *Let's talk inventory for children.* San Antonio, TX: Psychological Corporation.

Bricker, D. (1993). *Assessment, evaluation, and programming system for infants and children: Vol. 1 AEPS measurement for birth to three years.* Baltimore: Brookes.

Bricker, D. & Cripe, J. J. W. (1992). *An activity-based approach to early intervention.* Baltimore: Brookes.

Bricker, D., & Pretti-Frontczak, K. (1996). *Assessment, evaluation, and programming system for infants and children: Vol. 3 AEPS measurement for three to six years.* Baltimore: Brookes.

Bricker, D., & Waddell, M. (1996). *Assessment, evaluation, and programming system for infants and children: Vol. 4 AEPS curriculum for three to six years.* Baltimore: Brookes.

Brigance, A. H. (1981). *BRIGANCE® diagnostic inventory of essential skills.* North Billerica, MA: Curriculum Associates.

Brigance, A. H. (1983). *BRIGANCE® diagnostic inventory of basic skills, Spanish edition.* North Billerica, MA: Curriculum Associates.

Brigance, A. H. (1987). *BRIGANCE® K & 1 screen–Revised.* North Billerica, MA: Curriculum Associates.

Brigance, A. H. (1991). *BRIGANCE® diagnostic inventory of early development–Revised.* North Billerica, MA: Curriculum Associates.

Brigance, A. H. (1995a). *BRIGANCE® employability skills inventory.* North Billerica, MA: Curriculum Associates.

Brigance, A. H. (1995b). *BRIGANCE® life skills inventory.* North Billerica, MA: Curriculum Associates.

Brigance, A. H. (1999). *BRIGANCE® diagnostic comprehensive inventory of basic skills–Revised.* North Billerica, MA: Curriculum Associates.

Brinkerhoff, L. C., Shaw, S. E., & McGuire, J. M. (1993). *Promoting postsecondary education for students with learning disabilities: A handbook for practitioners*. Austin, TX: PRO-ED.

Brolin, D. (1992a). *Life-centered career education (LCCE) curriculum program*. Reston, VA: The Council for Exceptional Children.

Brolin, D. (1992b). *Life-centered career education (LCCE) competency assessment knowledge batteries*. Reston, VA: The Council for Exceptional Children.

Brolin, D. (1992c). *Life-centered career education (LCCE) competency assessment performance batteries*. Reston, VA: The Council for Exceptional Children.

Brolin, D. (1995). *Career education: A functional life skills approach* (3rd ed.). Englewoods Cliffs, NJ: Prentice-Hall.

Brolin, D. E. (1982). *Vocational preparation of persons with handicaps* (2nd ed.). New York: Merrill/Macmillan.

Brolin, D. E., Cegelka, P., Jackson, S., & Wrobel, C. (1978). *Official policy of The Council for Exceptional Children as legislated by the 1978 CEC Delegate Assembly*. Reston, VA: Council for Exceptional Children.

Bronfenbrenner, U. (1979). *The ecology of human development*. Cambridge, MA: Harvard University Press.

Brophy, J., & Good, T. (1969). *Teacher-child dyadic interaction: A manual for coding classroom behavior* (Report Series No. 127). Austin, TX: Research & Development Center for Teacher Education, University of Texas.

Brown, F. G. (1981). *Measuring classroom achievement*. New York: Holt, Rinehart & Winston.

Brown, L., & Alexander, J. (1991). *Self-esteem index*. Austin, TX: PRO-ED.

Brown, L., & Hammill, D. D. (1990). *Behavior rating profile*. (2nd ed.). Austin, TX: PRO-ED.

Brown, L., & Leigh, J. E. (1986). *Adaptive behavior inventory*. Austin, TX: PRO-ED.

Brown, L., Sherbenou, R. J., & Johnsen, S. K. (1997). *Test of nonverbal intelligence* (3rd ed.). Austin, TX: PRO-ED.

Brown, L. J., Black, D. D., & Downs, J. C. (1984). *School social skills rating scale*. East Aurora, NY: Slosson Educational Publications.

Brown, L. L., & Hammill, D. D. (1982). *Perfil de evaluación del comportamiento*. Austin, TX: PRO-ED.

Brown, L. L., & Hammill, D. D. (1983). *Behavior rating profile*. Austin, TX: PRO-ED.

Brown, R. (1973). A *first language: The early stages*. Cambridge, MA: Harvard University Press.

Brown, V. L. (1978). Independent study behaviors: A framework for curriculum development. *Learning Disability Quarterly, 1*(2), 78–84.

Brown, V. L., Cronin, M. E., & McEntire, E. (1994). *Test of mathematical abilities* (2nd ed.). Austin, TX: PRO-ED.

Brown, V. L., Hammill, D. D., & Wiederholt, J. L. (1995). *Test of reading comprehension* (3rd ed.). Austin, TX: PRO-ED.

Brown, W. F., & Holtzman, W. H. (1967a). *Survey of study habits and attitudes*. San Antonio, TX: Psychological Corporation.

Brown, W. F., & Holtzman, W. H. (1967b). *Survey of study habits and attitudes, Spanish edition*. San Antonio, TX: Psychological Corporation.

Brownell, R. (Ed.). (2000a). *Expressive one-word picture vocabulary test–2000 edition*. Novato, CA: Academic Therapy Publications.

Brownell, R. (Ed.). (2000b). *Receptive one-word picture vocabulary test–2000 edition*. Novato, CA: Academic Therapy Publications.

Brueckner, L. J. (1930). *Diagnostic and remedial teaching in arithmetic*. Philadelphia, PA: Winston.

Bruininks, R. H. (1978). *Bruininks-Oseretsky test of motor proficiency*. Circle Pines, MN: American Guidance Service.

Bruininks, R. H., Rynders, J. E., & Gross, J. C. (1974). Social acceptance of mildly retarded pupils in resource rooms and regular classes. *American Journal of Mental Deficiency, 78*, 377–383.

Bruininks, R. H., Thurlow, M., & Gilman, C. J. (1987). Adaptive behavior and mental retardation. *Journal of Special Education, 21*, 69–88.

Bruininks, R. H., Woodcock, R. W., Weatherman, R. F., & Hill, B. K. (1984). *Scales of independent behavior.* Chicago: Riverside.

Bruininks, R. H., Woodcock, R. W., Weatherman, R. F., & Hill, B. K. (1996). *Scales of independent behavior–Revised.* Itasca, IL: Riverside.

Bryant, B. R., & Wiederholt, J. L. (1991). *Gray oral reading test-Diagnostic.* Austin, TX: PRO-ED.

Bryant, B. R., Taylor, R. L., Rivera, D. P. (1996). *Assessment of adaptive areas.* Austin, TX: PRO-ED.

Bryant, D., & Maxwell, K. (1997). The effectiveness in early intervention for disadvantaged children. In M. J. Guralnick (Ed.), *The effectiveness of early intervention* (pp. 23–46). Baltimore: Brookes.

Bureau of Education for the Handicapped. (1976, November 29). *Federal Register, 41*(230), 54207.

Burgemeister, B. B., Blum, L. H., & Lorge, I. (1972). *Columbia mental maturity scale* (3rd ed.). San Antonio, TX: Psychological Corporation.

Burke, C. (1973). Preparing elementary teachers to teach reading. In K. S. Goodman (Ed.), *Miscue analysis: Application to reading instruction* (pp. 15–29). Urbana, IL: ERIC Clearinghouse on Reading & Communication Skills.

Burks, H. F. (1977). *Burks' behavior rating scales.* Los Angeles: Western Psychological Services.

Burns, P. C., & Roe, B. D. (1999). *Informal reading inventory* (5th ed.). Boston: Houghton Mifflin.

Burron, A., & Claybaugh, A. L. (1977). *Basic concepts in reading instruction* (2nd ed.). New York: Merrill/Macmillan.

Burt, M. K., Dulay, H. C., & Hernández-Chávez, E. H. (1978). *Bilingual syntax measure I and II.* San Antonio, TX: Psychological Corporation.

Buswell, G. T., & John, L. (1925). *Fundamental processes in arithmetic.* Indianapolis, IN: Bobbs-Merrill.

California achievement tests (5th edition). (1992). Monterey, CA: CTB/McGraw-Hill.

Carbo, M. (1982). *The reading style inventory.* Roslyn Heights, NY: Learning Research Associates.

Carbo, M. (1984). Research in learning style and reading: Implications for instruction. *Theory into Practice, 23*(1), 72–76.

Carbo, M., Dunn, R., & Dunn, K. (1986). *Teaching students to read through their individual learning styles.* Englewood Cliffs, NJ: Prentice-Hall.

Carroll, J. B., & Horn, J. L. (1981). On the scientific basis of ability testing. *American Psychologist, 36,* 1012–1020.

Carrow-Woolfolk, E. (1974). *Carrow elicited language inventory.* Chicago: Riverside.

Carrow-Woolfolk, E. (1996). *Oral and written language scales.* Circle Pines, MN: American Guidance Service.

Carrow-Woolfolk, E. (1999). *Test for auditory comprehension of language* (3rd ed.). Austin, TX: PRO-ED.

Casto, G., & Mastropieri, M. A. (1986). The efficacy of early intervention programs: A meta-analysis. *Exceptional Children, 52,* 417–424.

Caton, H. R. (1985). Visual impairments. In W. H. Berdine & A. E. Blackhurst (Eds.), *An introduction to special education* (2nd ed.) (pp. 235–280). Boston: Little, Brown.

Cattell, R. B. (1950). *Culture fair intelligence test: Scale 1.* Champaign, IL: Institute for Personality and Ability Testing.

Cattell, R. B., & Cattell, A. K. S. (1960). *Culture fair intelligence test: Scale 2.* Champaign, IL: Institute for Personality and Ability Testing.

Cattell, R. B., & Cattell, A. K. S. (1963). *Culture fair intelligence test: Scale 3.* Champaign, IL: Institute for Personality and Ability Testing.

Cattell, R. B., & Cattell, A. K. S. (1977). *The culture fair intelligence tests* (rev.). Champaign, IL: Institute for Personality and Ability Testing.

Cawley, J. F. (1978). An instructional design in mathematics. In L. Mann, L. Goodman, & L. L. Wiederholt (Eds.), *Teaching the learning-disabled adolescent* (pp. 201–234). Boston: Houghton Mifflin.

Cawley, J. F., Miller, J. H., & School, B. A. (1987). A brief inquiry of arithmetic word-problem-solving among learning disabled secondary students. *Learning Disabilities Focus, 2*(2), 87–93.

Cegelka, P. T. (1985). Career and vocational education. In W. Berdine & A. E. Blackhurst (Eds.), *An introduction to special education* (2nd ed.) (pp. 573–617). Boston: Little, Brown.

Cegelka, P. T. (1988). Multicultural considerations. In E. W. Lynch & R. B. Lewis (Eds.), *Exceptional children and adults* (pp. 545–587). Glenview, IL: Scott, Foresman.

Cegelka, P. T. (1995). An overview of effective education for students with learning problems. In P. T. Cegelka & W. H. Berdine (Eds.), *Effective instruction for students with learning difficulties* (pp. 1–17). Boston: Allyn & Bacon.

Cegelka, P. T. (1995). Identifying and measuring behavior. In P. T. Cegelka & W. H. Berdine (Eds.), *Effective instruction for students with learning difficulties* (pp. 47–79). Boston: Allyn & Bacon.

Cegelka, P. T., & Prehm, H. J. (1982). The concept of mental retardation. In P. T. Cegelka & H. J. Prehm (Eds.), *Mental retardation* (pp. 3–20). New York: Merrill/Macmillan.

Chall, J. S., & Stahl, S. A. (1982). Reading. In H. E. Mitzel (Ed.), *Encyclopedia of educational research* (5th ed.) (pp. 1535–1559). New York: Free Press.

Chapman, R. N., Larsen, S. C., & Parker, R. M. (1979). Interactions for first-grade teachers with learning disordered children. *Journal of Learning Disabilities, 12,* 225–230.

Cheng, L. L. (1987). *Assessing Asian language performance: Guidelines for evaluating limited-English-proficient students.* Rockville, MD: Aspen.

Children's Defense Fund. (1998). *The state of America's children yearbook 1999.* Washington, DC: Author.

Christiansen, J., & Vogel, J. R. (1998). A decision model for grading students with disabilities. *Teaching Exceptional Children, 31*(2), 30–36.

Clarizio, H. F. (1979). In defense of the IQ test. *School Psychology Digest, 8,* 79–88.

Clarizio, H. F., & McCoy, G. F. (1983). *Behavior disorders in children* (3rd ed.). New York: Harper & Row.

Clark, G. M. (1998). *Assessment for transition planning.* Austin, TX: PRO-ED.

Clark, G. M., & Kolstoe, O. P. (1995). *Career development and transition education for adolescents with disabilities.* Boston: Allyn & Bacon.

Clark, G. M., & Patton, J. R. (1997). *Transition planning inventory.* Austin, TX: PRO-ED.

Cobb, R. B., & Neubert, D. A. (1999). *Vocational education: Emerging vocationalism.* In F. R. Rusch & J. G. Chadsey (Eds.), *Beyond high school: Transition from school to work* (pp. 101–126). Boston: Wadsworth.

Cohen, S. B., & de Bettencourt, L. (1983). Teaching children to be independent learners: A step-by-step strategy. *Focus on Exceptional Children, 16*(3), 1–12.

Cohen, S. D., & Plaskon, S. P. (1980). *Language arts for the mildly handicapped.* New York: Merrill/Macmillan.

Colarusso, R. P., & Hammill, D. D. (1995). *Motor-free visual perception test–Revised.* Novato, CA: Academic Therapy.

Coles, G. S. (1978). The learning disabilities test battery: Empirical and social issues. *Harvard Educational Review, 18,* 313–340.

Comprehensive tests of basic skills (4th ed.). (1989, 1990). Monterey, CA: CTB/McGraw-Hill.

Condon, E. C., Peters, J. Y., & Sueiro-Ross, C. (1979). *Special education and the Hispanic child: Cultural perspectives.* Philadelphia: Teacher Corps Mid-Atlantic Network, Temple University.

Cone, T. E., & Wilson, L. R. (1981). Quantifying a severe discrepancy: A critical analysis. *Learning Disability Quarterly, 4,* 359–371.

Conners, C. K. (1997). *Conners' rating scales-Revised.* North Tonawanda, NY: Multi-Health Systems.

Connolly, A. J. (1985). *KeyMath teach and practice.* Circle Pines, MN: American Guidance Service.

Connolly, A. J. (1998). *KeyMath revised/Normative update.* Circle Pines, MN: American Guidance Service.

Connolly, A. J., Nachtman, W., & Pritchett, E. M. (1971, 1976). *KeyMath diagnostic arithmetic test.* Circle Pines, MN: American Guidance Service.

Cooper, J. O. (1981). *Measuring behavior* (2nd ed.). New York: Merrill/Macmillan.

Cooper, J. O., Heron, T. E., & Heward, W. L. (1987). *Applied behavior analysis.* New York: Merrill/Macmillan.

Coopersmith, S. (1981). *Coopersmith self-esteem inventories.* Palo Alto, CA: Consulting Psychologists Press.

Coopersmith, S., & Gilberts, R. (1981). *Behavioral academic self-esteem, A rating scale.* Palo Alto, CA: Consulting Psychologists Press.

Copperman, P. (1979). The achievement decline of the 1970s. *Phi Delta Kappan, 60,* 736–739.

Correa, V. I. (1991). Family-based applications. In C. V. Morsink, C. C. Thomas, & V. I. Correa, *Interactive teaming: Consultation and collaboration in special programs* (pp. 247–274). New York: Merrill.

Council for Exceptional Children. (1992). *Children with ADD: A shared responsibility.* Reston, VA: Author.

Council for Learning Disabilities. (1986). *Inclusion of nonhandicapped low achievers and underachievers in learning disability programs. A position paper of the Council for Learning Disabilities.* Overland Park, KS: Author.

Cox, L. S. (1975). Diagnosing and remediating systematic errors in addition and subtraction computations. *The Arithmetic Teacher, 22,* 151–157.

Crawford, J. E., & Crawford, D. M. (1956). *Crawford small parts dexterity test.* San Antonio, TX: Psychological Corporation.

Cripe, J., Slentz, K., & Bricker, D. (1993). *Assessment, evaluation, and programming system for infants and children: Vol. 2 AEPS curriculum for birth to three years.* Baltimore: Brookes.

Critchlow, D. C. (1996). *Dos amigos verbal language scales, 1996 edition.* Novato, CA: Academic Therapy.

Cronbach, L. J., & Snow, R. E. (1977). *Aptitudes and instructional methods.* New York: Irvington.

Culatta, R., & Culatta, B. K. (1985). Communication disorders. In W. H. Berdine and A. E. Blackhurst (Eds.), *An introduction to special education* (2nd ed.) (pp. 145–181). Boston: Little, Brown.

Cummins, J. (1981). The role of primary language development in promoting educational success for language minority students. In California State Department of Education, *Schooling and language minority students: A theoretical framework* (pp. 3–49). Los Angeles: Evaluation, Dissemination & Assessment Center.

Cummins, J. (1982, February). Tests, achievement, and bilingual students. *Focus* (National Clearinghouse for Bilingual Education), *9,* 1–8.

Cummins, J. (1983). Bilingualism and special education: Program and pedagogical issues. *Learning Disability Quarterly, 6,* 373–386.

Cutler, B. C. (1993). *You, your child, and "special" education: A guide to making the system work.* Baltimore: Brookes.

Dagenais, D. J., & Beadle, K. R. (1984). Written language: When and where to begin. *Topics in Language Disorders, 4*(2), 59–85.

Davis, W. A., & Shepard, L. A. (1983). Specialists' use of tests and clinical judgment in the diagnosis of learning disabilities. *Learning Disability Quarterly, 6,* 128–138.

deFur, S. H. (1999). Special education, transition, and school-based services: Are they meant for each other? In S. H. deFur & J. R. Patton (Eds.), *Transition and school-based services: Interdisciplinary perspectives for enhancing the transition process* (pp. 15–50). Austin, TX: PRO-ED.

Demos, G. (1976). *The study skills counseling examination.* Los Angeles: Western Psychological Services.

Deno, S. L. (1985). Curriculum-based measurement: The emerging alternative. *Exceptional Children, 52,* 219–232.

Deno, S. L., & Fuchs, L. S. (1988). Developing curriculum-based measurement systems for data-based special education problem solving. In E. L. Meyen, G. A. Vergason, & R. J. Whelan (Eds.), *Effective instructional strategies for exceptional children* (pp. 481–504). Denver, CO: Love.

Deno, S. L., Marston, D., & Mirkin, P. K. (1982). Valid measurement procedures for continuous evaluation of written expression. *Exceptional Children, 48,* 368–371.

Deno, S. L., Mirkin, P. K., & Chiang, B. (1982). Identifying valid measures of reading. *Exceptional Children, 49,* 36–45.

Deno, S. L., Mirkin, P. K., Lowry, L., & Kuehnle, K. (1980). *Relationships among simple measures of written expression and performance on standardized achievement tests* (Research Report No. 22). Minneapolis, MN: University of Minnesota Institute for Learning Disabilities. (ERIC Document Reproduction Service No. ED 197 508).

Deshler, D. D., Alley, G. R., Warner, M. M., & Schumaker, J. B. (1981). Instructional practices for promoting skill acquisition and generalization in severely learning disabled adolescents. *Learning Disability Quarterly, 4,* 415–422.

Deshler, D. D., Schumaker, J. B., Alley, G. R., Warner, M. M., & Clark, F. L. (1982). Learning disabilities in adolescent and young adult populations: Research implications. *Focus on Exceptional Children, 15*(1), 1–12.

Diana v. State Board of Education. Civ. No. C-70 37 RFP (N.D. Cal. 1970, 1973).

Dolch, E. W. (1953). *The Dolch basic sight word list.* Champaign, IL: Garrard.

Doll, E. A. (1935). A genetic scale of social maturity. *The American Journal of Orthopsychiatry, 5,* 180–188.

Doll, E. A. (1965). *Vineland social maturity scale* (rev. ed.). Circle Pines, MN: American Guidance Service.

Duffey, J. B., Salvia, J., Tucker, J., & Ysseldyke, J. (1982). Nonbiased assessment: A need for operationalism. *Exceptional Children, 47,* 427–434.

Duncan, S. E., & DeAvila, E. A. (1990). *Language assessment scales-oral.* Monterey, CA: CTB Macmillan/McGraw-Hill.

Dunn, L. M. (1968). Special education for the mildly retarded—Is much of it justifiable? *Exceptional Children, 35,* 5–22.

Dunn, L. M., & Dunn, L. M. (1981). *Peabody picture vocabulary test–Revised.* Circle Pines, MN: American Guidance Service.

Dunn, L. M., & Dunn, L. M. (1997). *Peabody picture vocabulary test (Third Edition).* Circle Pines, MN: American Guidance Service.

Dunn, L. M., & Markwardt, F. C. (1970). *Peabody individual achievement test.* Circle Pines, MN: American Guidance Service.

Dunn, L. M., Lugo, D. E., Padilla, E. R., & Dunn, L. M. (1986). *Test de vocabulario en imágenes Peabody.* Circle Pines, MN: American Guidance Service.

Dunn, R. (1984). Learning style: State of the science. *Theory into Practice, 23*(1), 10–18.

Dunn, R. (1988). Teaching students through their perceptual strengths or preferences. *Journal of Reading, 31,* 304–309.

Dunn, R., Dunn, K., & Price, G. E. (1979). *Learning style inventory.* Lawrence, KS: Price Systems.

Dunst, C. J., Cooper, C. S., Weeldreyer, J. C., Snyder, K. D., & Chase, J. H. (1988). Family needs scale. In C. J. Dunst, C. M. Trivette, & A. G. Deal (Eds.), *Enabling and empowering families: Principles and guidelines for practice.* (pp. 149–151). Cambridge, MA: Brookline Books.

Dunst, C. J., Trivette, C. M., & Deal, A. G. (1988). *Enabling and empowering families: Principles and guidelines for practice.* Cambridge, MA: Brookline Books.

DuPaul, G. J., Rapport, M., & Perriello, L. M. (1990). *Teacher ratings of academic performance: The development of the Academic Performance Rating Scale.* Unpublished manuscript, University of Massachusetts Medical Center, Worcester, MA.

Durrell, D. D., & Catterson, J. J. (1980). *Durrell analysis of reading difficulty* (3rd ed.). San Antonio, TX: Psychological Corporation.

Eaves, R. C. (1982). A proposal for the diagnosis of emotional disturbance. *Journal of Special Education, 16,* 463–476.

Ebel, R. L. (1977). *The uses of standardized testing.* Bloomington, IN: Phi Delta Kappa Educational Foundation.

Edgington, R. (1968). But he spelled it right this morning. In J. I. Arena (Ed.), *Building spelling skills in dyslexic children* (pp. 23–26). San Rafael, CA: Academic Therapy Publications.

Ekwall, E. E., & Shanker, J. L. (1993). *Ekwall/Shanker reading inventory* (3rd ed.). Boston: Allyn & Bacon.

Elliott, S. N., Kratochwill, T. R., & Gilbertson, A. (1998). *The assessment accommodation checklist.* Monterey, CA: CTB/McGraw-Hill.

Elliott, S. N., Kratochwill, T. R., & Schulte, A. G. (1998). The assessment accommodation checklist. *Teaching Exceptional Children, 31*(2), 10–14.

Engquist, G. (1974). *Black dialect: Deficient or different?* Unpublished manuscript, University of Virginia.

Epstein, J. L. (1990). School and family connections: Theory, research, and implications for integrating sociologies of education and family. In D. G. Unger & M. B. Sussman (Eds.), *Families in community settings: Interdisciplinary perspectives* (pp. 99–124). New York: Haworth.

Epstein, M. H., & Cullinan, D. (1998). *Scale for assessing emotional disturbance.* Austin, TX: PRO-ED.

Epstein, M. H., & Sharma, J. M. (1998). *Behavior and emotional rating scale.* Austin, TX: PRO-ED.

Erickson, R., Ysseldyke, J., Thurlow, M., & Elliott, J. (1998). Inclusive assessments and accountability systems. *Teaching Exceptional Children, 31*(2), 4–9.

Escala de inteligencia Wechsler para niños–Revisada. (1983). San Antonio, TX: Psychological Corporation.

Escala de inteligencia Wechsler para niños–Revisada de Puerto Rico. (1993). San Antonio, TX: Psychological Corporation.

Estes, T. H., Estes, J. J., Richards, H. C., & Roettger, D. (1981). *Estes attitude scales.* Austin, TX: PRO-ED.

Farran, D., Kasari, C., Comfort, M., & Jay, S. (1986). *Parent/caregiver involvement scale.* Greensboro: University of North Carolina, Continuing Education.

Federal Register. (1999, March 12). Washington, DC: U.S. Government Printing Office.

Felton, R. H., & Wood, F. B. (1989). Cognitive deficits in reading disability and attention deficit disorder. *Journal of Learning Disabilities, 22,* 3–13, 22.

Feuer, M. J., & Fulton, K. (1993). The many faces of performance assessment. *Phi Delta Kappan, 74,* 478.

Feuerstein, R., in collaboration with Rand, Y., & Hoffman, M. D. (1979). *The dynamic assessment of retarded performers.* Baltimore, MD: University Park Press.

Feuerstein, R., in collaboration with Rand, Y., Hoffman, M. D., & Miller, R. (1980). *Instrumental enrichment.* Baltimore, MD: University Park Press.

Feuerstein, R., Miller, R., Hoffman, M. D., Rand, Y., Mintzker, Y., & Jensen, M. R. (1981). Cognitive modifiability in adolescence: Cognitive structure and the effects of intervention. *Journal of Special Education, 15,* 269–287.

Feuerstein, R., Miller, R., Rand, Y., & Jensen, M. R. (1981). Can evolving techniques better measure cognitive change? *Journal of Special Education, 15,* 201–219.

Field, S., & Hoffman, A. (1996). *Steps to self-determination: A curriculum to help adolescents learn to achieve their goals* (Instructor's Guide). Austin, TX: PRO-ED.

Fitts, W. H., & Warren, W. L. (1996). *Tennessee self-concept scale* (2nd ed.). Los Angeles: Western Psychological Services.

Fitzsimmons, M. K. (1998). *Functional behavior assessment and behavior intervention plans* (ERIC EC Digest #E571). Reston, VA: ERIC Clearinghouse on Disabilities and Gifted Education. Retrieved July 4, 1999 from the World Wide Web: http://www.ericec.org/digests/e571.htm

Flanders, N. (1970). *Analyzing teacher behavior.* Menlo Park, CA: Addison-Wesley.

Flynt, E. S., & Cooter, R. B. (1998). *Flynt-Cooter reading inventory for the classroom* (3rd ed.). Upper Saddle River, NJ: Merrill/Prentice-Hall.

Flynt, E. S., & Cooter, R. B. (1999). *English-español reading inventory for the classroom.* Upper Saddle River, NJ: Merrill/Prentice-Hall.

Folkman, S., Lazarus, R. S., Dunkel-Shetter, C., DeLorgis, A., & Gruen, R. J. (1986). The dynamics of a stressful encounter: Cognitive appraisal, coping and encounter outcomes. *Journal of Personality and Social Psychology, 50,* 992–1003.

Forness, S. R., Sinclair, E., & Guthrie, D. (1983). Learning disability discrepancy formulas: Their use in actual practice. *Learning Disability Quarterly, 6,* 107–114.

Foster, R., Giddan, J. J., & Stark, J. (1983). *Assessment of children's language comprehension.* Austin, TX: PRO-ED.

Frank, T. (1998). Hearing difficulties. In J. Salvia & J. E. Ysseldyke, *Assessment* (7th ed.) (pp. 409–430). Boston: Houghton Mifflin.

Frankenburg, W. K., Dodds, J., Archer, P., Bresnick, B., Mashka, P., Edelman, N., & Shapiro, H. (1990). *Denver developmental screening test (Denver II).* Denver, CO: Denver Developmental Materials, Inc.

Freedman, S. W. (1982). Language assessment and writing disorders. *Topics in Language Disorders, 2*(4), 34–44.

Frisby, C. L., & Braden, J. P. (1992). Feuerstein's dynamic assessment approach: A semantic, logical, and empirical critique. *Journal of Special Education, 26,* 281–301.

Frostig, M., & Horne, D. (1964). *The Frostig program for the development of visual perception.* Chicago: Follett.

Frostig, M., Lefever, W., & Whittlesey, J. R. B. (1966). *Developmental test of visual perception* (rev.). Palo Alto, CA: Consulting Psychologists Press.

Fry, E. (1968). A readability formula that saves time. *Journal of Reading, 11,* 513–516, 575–577.

Fry, E. (1977). Fry's readability graph: Clarifications, validity, and extension to level 17. *Journal of Reading, 21,* 242–252.

Fuchs, D. S., & Fuchs, L. S. (1988). Evaluation of the Adaptive Learning Environment Model. *Exceptional Children, 55,* 115–127.

Fuchs, D. S., & Fuchs, L. S. (1994). Inclusive schools movement and the radicalization of special education reform. *Exceptional Children, 60,* 294–309.

Fuchs, D. S., Fuchs, L. S., Benowitz, S., & Barringer, K. (1987). Norm-referenced tests: Are they valid for use with handicapped students? *Exceptional Children, 54,* 263–271.

Fuchs, L. S. (1986). Monitoring progress among mildly handicapped pupils: Review of current practice and research. *Remedial and Special Education, 7*(5), 5–12.

Fuchs, L. S. (1995). *Connecting performance assessment to instruction: A comparison of behavioral assessment, mastery learning, curriculum-based measurement, and performance assessment* (ERIC Digest E 530). Reston, VA: ERIC Clearinghouse on Disabilities and Gifted Education.

Fuchs, L. S., Deno, S. L., & Mirkin, P. K. (1984). The effects of frequent curriculum-based measurement and evaluation on pedagogy, student achievement, and student awareness of learning. *American Educational Research Journal, 21,* 449–460.

Fuchs, L. S., Hamlett, C. L., & Fuchs, D. (1997). *Monitoring basic skills progress: Basic reading* (2nd ed.). Austin, TX: PRO-ED.

Fuchs, L. S., Hamlett, C. L., & Fuchs, D. (1998). *Monitoring basic skills progress: Basic math computation* (2nd ed.). Austin, TX: PRO-ED.

Fuchs, L. S., Hamlett, C. L., & Fuchs, D. (1999). *Monitoring basic skills progress: Basic math concepts and applications.* Austin, TX: PRO-ED.

Fudala, J. B., & Reynolds, W. M. (1986). *Arizona articulation proficiency scale* (2nd ed.). Los Angeles: Western Psychological Services.

Gajar, A. (1998). Postsecondary education. In F. R. Rusch & J. G. Chadsey (Eds.), *Beyond high school: Transition from school to work* (pp. 383–405). Boston: Wadsworth.

Gajar, A., Goodman, L., & McAfee J. (1993). *Secondary schools and beyond: Transition of individuals with mild disabilities.* New York: Merrill.

Gallagher, J. D. (1998). *Classroom assessment for teachers.* Upper Saddle River, NJ: Merrill/Prentice-Hall.

Gallup, G. H. (1978). The 10th annual Gallup poll of the public's attitudes toward public schools. *Phi Delta Kappan, 60,* 33–45.

Gardner, H. (1987). Beyond the IQ: Education and human development. *Harvard Educational Review, 57,* 187–193.

Garner, R. (1983). Correct the imbalance: Diagnosis of strategic behaviors in reading. *Topics in Learning & Learning Disabilities, 2*(4), 12–19.

Gates, A. I., McKillop, A. S., & Horowitz, E. C. (1981). *Gates-McKillop-Horowitz reading diagnostic tests* (2nd ed.). New York: Teachers College Press.

Gay, L. R. (1985). *Educational evaluation and measurement* (2nd ed.). New York: Merrill/Macmillan.

Gay, L. R. (1996). *Educational research* (5th ed.). Upper Saddle River, NJ: Merrill/Prentice-Hall.

Geisinger, K. F. (Ed.). (1992). *Psychological testing of Hispanics*. Washington, DC: American Psychological Association.

Gelfer, J. I., & Perkins, P. G. (1998). Portfolios: Focus on young children. *Teaching Exceptional Children, 31*(2), 44–47.

Gillespie-Silver, P. (1979). *Teaching reading to children with special needs*. New York: Merrill/Macmillan.

Gilliam, J. E. (1995). *Attention-deficit/hyperactivity disorder test*. Austin, TX: PRO-ED.

Gilmore, J. V., & Gilmore, E. C. (1968). *Gilmore oral reading test*. San Antonio, TX: Psychological Corporation.

Ginsburg, H. P., & Baroody, A. J. (1990). *The test of early mathematic ability* (2nd ed.). Austin, TX: PRO-ED.

Ginsburg, H. P., & Mathews, S. C. (1984). *Diagnostic test of arithmetic strategies*. Austin, TX: PRO-ED.

Glascoe, F. P. (1999). *CIBS-R standardization and validation manual*. North Billerica, MA: Curriculum Associates.

Goldman, R. M., & Fristoe, M. (1986). *Goldman-Fristoe test of articulation*. Circle Pines, MN: American Guidance Service.

Goldman, R. M., Fristoe, M., & Woodcock, R. W. (1970). *Goldman-Fristoe-Woodcock test of auditory discrimination*. Circle Pines, MN: American Guidance Service.

Goldman, R. M., Fristoe, M., & Woodcock, R. W. (1976). *Goldman-Fristoe-Woodcock auditory skills test battery*. Circle Pines, MN: American Guidance Service.

Gollnick, D. M., & Chinn, P. C. (1990). *Multicultural education in a pluralistic society* (3rd ed.). New York: Merrill/Macmillan.

Gollnick, D. M., & Chinn, P. C. (1991). *Multicultural education for exceptional children*. ERIC Digest. Reston, VA: Council for Exceptional Children.

Gonzales, E. (1982). Issues in assessment of minorities. In H. L. Swanson & B. L. Watson (Eds.), *Educational and psychological assessment of exceptional children* (pp. 375–389). St. Louis, MO: Mosby.

Gonzalez, V., Brusca-Vega, R., & Yawkey, T. (1997). *Assessment and instruction of culturally and linguistically diverse students with or at-risk of learning problems*. Boston: Allyn & Bacon.

Goodman, J. F. (1979). Is tissue the issue? A critique of SOMPA's models and tests. *School Psychology Digest, 8,* 47–62.

Goodman, K. S. (1969). Analysis of oral reading miscues: Applied psycholinguistics. *Reading Research Quarterly, 5,* 9–30.

Goodman, K. S. (1973b). Miscues: Windows on the reading process. In K. S. Goodman (Ed.), *Miscue analysis: Application to reading instruction* (pp. 1–14). Urbana, IL: ERIC Clearinghouse on Reading & Communication Skills.

Goodman, K. S. (Ed.). (1973a). *Miscue analysis: Application to reading instruction*. Urbana, IL: ERIC Clearinghouse on Reading and Communication Skills.

Goodman, K. S. (1976). Behind the eye: What happens in reading. In H. Singer & R. B. Ruddell (Eds.), *Theoretical models and processes in reading*. Newark, DE: International Reading Association.

Goodman, Y., & Burke, C. (1972). *Reading miscue inventory*. New York: Macmillan.

Goodman, Y., Watson, D. J., & Burke, C. L. (1987). *Reading miscue inventory: Alternative procedures*. Katonah, NY: Richard C. Owen.

Goodstein, H. A. (1981). Are the errors we see true errors? Error analysis in verbal problem solving. *Topics in Learning and Learning Disabilities, 1*(3), 31–45.

Grady, E. (1992). *The portfolio approach to assessment*. Bloomington, IN: Phi Delta Kappa Educational Foundation.

Graham, S. (1982). Composition research and practice: A unified approach. *Focus on Exceptional Children, 14*(8), 1–16.

Graham, S., & Miller, L. (1979). Spelling research and practice: A unified approach. *Focus on Exceptional Children, 12*(2), 1–16.

Graham, S., & Miller, L. (1980). Handwriting research and practice: A unified approach. *Focus on Exceptional Children, 13*(2), 1–16.

Graves, D. (1978). *Balancing the basics: Let them write.* New York: Ford Foundation.

Graves, D. H. (1985). All children can write. *Learning Disabilities Focus, 1*(1), 36–43.

Gray, W. S. (1967). *Gray oral reading tests.* Austin, TX: PRO-ED.

Green, R. F., & Martinez, J. N. (Trans.). (1968). *Escala de inteligencia Wechsler para adultos.* San Antonio, TX: Psychological Corporation.

Green, W. W. (1981). Hearing disorders. In A. E. Blackhurst & W. H. Berdine (Eds.), *Introduction to special education* (pp. 154–205). Boston: Little, Brown.

Greenbaum, C. R. (1987). *Spellmaster assessment and teaching system.* Austin, TX: PRO-ED.

Greenwood, C. R., Carta, J. J., Kamps, D., & Delquadri, J. (1997). *Ecobehavioral assessment systems software (EBASS), practitioner's manual* (version 3.0). Kansas City, KS: Juniper Gardens Children's Project, University of Kansas.

Gresham, F. M. (1982). A model for the behavioral assessment of behavior disorders in children: Measurement considerations and practical application. *Journal of School Psychology, 20,* 131–144.

Gresham, F. M., & Elliott, S. N. (1990). *Social skills rating system.* Circle Pines, MN: American Guidance Service.

Gresham, F. M., Elliott, S. N., & Evans-Fernandez, S. (1992). *Student self-concept scale.* Circle Pines, MN: American Guidance Service.

Grossman, H. J. (Ed.). (1983). *Classification in mental retardation* (1983 rev.).Washington, DC: American Association on Mental Deficiency.

Guadalupe v. Tempe Elementary School District. Civ. Act. No. 71-435 (D. Ariz. 1972).

Guralnick, M. J. (1997). Second-generation research in the field of early intervention. In M. J. Guralnick (Ed.), *The effectiveness of early intervention* (pp. 3–20). Baltimore: Brookes.

Haley, S. M., Coster, W. J., Ludlow, L. H., Haltiwanger, J. T., & Andrellos, P. J. (1992). *Pediatric evaluation of disability inventory.* Boston, MA: PEDI Research Group.

Hallahan, D. P. (Ed.). (1980). Teaching exceptional children to use cognitive strategies [Entire issue]. *Exceptional Education Quarterly, 1*(1).

Hallahan, D. P., & Cruickshank, W. M. (1973). *Psychoeducational foundations of learning disabilities.* Englewood Cliffs, NJ: Prentice-Hall.

Hallahan, D. P., & Kauffman, J. M. (1991). *Exceptional children* (5th ed.). Englewood Cliffs, NJ: Prentice-Hall.

Hallahan, D. P., & Reeve, R. E. (1980). Selective attention and distractibility. In B. K. Keogh (Ed.), *Advances in special education* (Vol. 1, pp. 141–181). Greenwich, CT: J.A.I.

Hallahan, D. P., Keller, C. E., McKinney, J. D., Lloyd, J. W., & Bryan, T. (1988). Examining the research base of the Regular Education Initiative: Efficacy studies and the Adaptive Learning Environments model. *Journal of Learning Disabilities, 21,* 29–35, 55.

Halpern, A. S. (1985). Transition: A look at the foundations. *Exceptional Children, 51,* 479–486.

Halpern, A. S., & Irvin, L. K. (1986). *Social and prevocational information battery–Revised.* Monterey, CA: CTB Macmillan/McGraw-Hill.

Hammill, D. D. (1982). Assessing and training perceptual-motor skills. In D. D. Hammill & N. R. Bartel (Eds.), *Teaching children with learning and behavior problems* (3rd ed.) (pp. 379–408). Boston: Allyn & Bacon.

Hammill, D. D. (1984). *Detroit tests of learning aptitude* (2nd ed.). Austin, TX: PRO-ED.

Hammill, D. D. (1998). *Detroit tests of learning aptitude* (4th ed.). Austin, TX: PRO-ED.

Hammill, D. D., & Bryant, B. R. (1991a). *Detroit tests of learning aptitude–Adult.* Austin, TX: PRO-ED.

Hammill, D. D., & Bryant, B. R. (1991b). *Detroit tests of learning aptitude–Primary* (2nd ed.). Austin, TX: PRO-ED.

Hammill, D. D., & Bryant, B. R. (1998). *Learning disabilities diagnostic inventory.* Austin, TX: PRO-ED.

Hammill, D. D., & Hresko, W. P. (1994). *Comprehensive scales of student abilities.* Austin, TX: PRO-ED.

Hammill, D. D., & Larsen, S. C. (1974a). The effectiveness of psycholinguistic training. *Exceptional Children, 41,* 5–15.

Hammill, D. D., & Larsen, S. C. (1974b). The relationship of selected auditory perceptual skills and reading ability. *Journal of Learning Disabilities, 7,* 429–435.

Hammill, D. D., & Larsen, S. C. (1996). *Test of written language* (3rd ed.). Austin, TX: PRO-ED.

Hammill, D. D., & Newcomer, P. L. (1997). *Test of language development-3, Intermediate.* Austin, TX: PRO-ED.

Hammill, D. D., & Wiederholt, J. L. (1972). Review of the Frostig Visual Perception Test and the related training program. In L. Mann & D. Sabatino (Eds.), *The first review of special education, Volume I* (pp. 33–48). Philadelphia, PA: Journal of Special Education Press.

Hammill, D. D., Brown, V. L., Larsen, S. C., & Wiederholt, J. L. (1994). *Test of adolescent and adult language* (3rd ed.). Austin, TX: PRO-ED.

Hammill, D. D., Bryant, B., & Pearson, N. (1998). *Hammill multiability intelligence test.* Austin, TX: PRO-ED.

Hammill, D. D., Goodman, L., & Wiederholt, J. L. (1974). Visual-motor processes: What successes have we had in training them? *The Reading Teacher, 27,* 469–478.

Hammill, D. D., Hresko, W. P., Ammer, J. J., Cronin, M. E., & Quinby, S. S. (1998). *Hammill multiability achievement test.* Austin, TX: PRO-ED.

Hammill, D. D., Larsen, S. C., Wiederholt, J. L., & Fountain-Chambers, J. (1982). *Prueba de lectura y lenguaje escrito.* Austin, TX: PRO-ED.

Hammill, D. D., Pearson, N. A., & Voress, J. K. (1993). *Developmental test of visual perception* (2nd ed.). Austin, TX: PRO-ED.

Hammill, D. D., Pearson, N. A., & Voress, J. K. (1996). *Test of visual-motor integration.* Austin, TX: PRO-ED.

Hammill, D. D., Pearson, N. A., & Wiederholt, J. L. (1997). *Comprehensive test of nonverbal intelligence.* Austin, TX: PRO-ED.

Hanna, G. S., Dyck, N. J., & Holen, M. C. (1979). Objective analysis of achievement-aptitude discrepancies in LD classification. *Learning Disability Quarterly, 2*(4), 32–38.

Hanson, M. J. (1998). Ethnic, cultural, and language diversity in intervention settings. In E. W. Lynch & M. J. Hanson (Eds.), *Developing cross-cultural competence: A guide for working with children and their families* (pp. 3–22). Baltimore: Brookes.

Hanson, M. J., & Lynch, E. W. (1989). *Early intervention: Implementing child and family services for infants and toddlers who are at-risk or disabled.* Austin, Texas: PRO-ED.

Hanson, M. J., & Lynch, E. W. (1992). Family diversity: Implications for policy and practice. *Topics in Early Childhood Special Education, 12,* 283–306.

Harris, A. (1970). *How to increase reading ability* (5th ed.). New York: McKay.

Harris, L. P., & Wolf, S. R. (1979). Validity and reliability of criterion-referenced measures: Issues and procedures for special educators. *Learning Disability Quarterly, 2*(2), 84–88.

Harrison, P. L. (1987). Research with adaptive behavior scales. *Journal of Special Education, 21,* 37–68.

Harry, B. (1992a). An ethnographic study of cross-cultural communication with Puerto Rican-American families in the special education system. *American Educational Research Journal, 29,* 471–494.

Harry, B. (1992b). Developing cultural self-awareness: The first step in values clarification for early interventionists. *Topics in Early Childhood Special Education, 12,* 333–350.

Harth, R. (1982). The Feuerstein perspective on the modification of cognitive performance. *Focus on Exceptional Children, 15*(3), 1–12.

Hasazi, S. B., Gordon, L. R., & Roe, C. A. (1985). Factors associated with the employment status of handicapped youth exiting high school from 1979 to 1983. *Exceptional Children, 51,* 455–469.

Hasbrouck, J. E., Woldbeck, T., Ihnot, C., & Parker, R. I. (1999). One teacher's use of curriculum-based measurement: A changed opinion. *Learning Disabilities Research & Practice, 14*(2), 118–126.

Heller, K. A., Holtzman, W. H., & Messick, S. (Eds.). (1982). *Placing children in special education: A strategy for equity.* Washington, DC: National Academy Press.

Helms, J. E. (1992). Why is there no study of cultural equivalence in standardized cognitive ability testing? *American Psychologist, 47,* 1083–1101.

Henderson, C. (1995). The American freshman: National norms. *College freshmen with disabilities; A statistical profile.* Washington, DC: Health Resource Center, American Council on Education, U.S. Department of Education.

Herbert, C. H. (1996). *Basic inventory of natural language.* San Bernardino, CA: CHECpoint Systems.

Herrnstein, R. (1971). I.Q. *Atlantic Monthly, 228,* 43–64.

Heward, W. L. (1996). *Exceptional children* (5th ed.). Englewood Cliffs; NJ: Merrill/Prentice-Hall.

Hittleman, D. R., & Simon, A. J. (1997). *Interpreting educational research* (2nd ed.). Upper Saddle River, NJ: Merrill/Prentice-Hall.

Hoffman, A., Field, S., & Sawilowsky, S. (1996). *The self-determination knowledge scale* (Forms A & B). Austin, TX: PRO-ED.

Holtzman, W. H., Jr., & Wilkinson, C. Y. (1991). Assessment of cognitive ability. In E. V. Hamayan & J. S. Damico (Eds.), *Limiting bias in the assessment of bilingual students* (pp. 247–280). Austin, TX: PRO-ED.

Howell, K. W., & Kaplan, J. S. (1980). *Diagnosing basic skills.* New York: Merrill/Macmillan.

Howell, K. W., Fox, S. L., & Morehead, M. K. (1993). *Curriculum-based evaluation* (2nd ed.). Pacific Grove, CA: Brooks/Cole.

Howell, K. W., Kaplan, J. S., & O'Connell, C. Y. (1979). *Evaluating exceptional children.* New York: Merrill/Macmillan.

Hresko, W. P., Herron, S. R., & Peak, P. K. (1996). *Test of early written language* (2nd ed.). Austin, TX: PRO-ED.

Hresko, W. P., Herron, W. P., & Peak, P. K. (1996). *Test of early written language* (2nd ed.). Austin, TX: PRO-ED.

Hresko, W. P., Miguel, S. A., Sherbenou, R. J., & Burton, S. D. (1994). *Developmental obser-*
vation checklist system: Examiner's manual. Austin, TX: PRO-ED.

Hresko, W. P., Reid, D. K., & Hammill, D. D. (1982). *Prueba de desarrollo inicial de lenguaje.* Austin, TX: PRO-ED.

Hresko, W. P., Reid, D. K., & Hammill, D. D. (1999). *Test of early language development* (3rd ed.). Austin, TX: PRO-ED.

Hudson, F. G., Colson, S. E., Welch, D. L. H., Banikowski, A. K., & Mehring, T. A. (1989). *Hudson education skills inventory.* Austin, TX: PRO-ED.

Huntze, S. L. (1985). A position paper of The Council for Children with Behavioral Disorders. *Behavioral Disorders, 3,* 167–174.

Hutton, J. B., & Roberts, T. G. (1986). *Social-emotional dimension scale.* Austin, TX: PRO-ED.

Illinois State Board of Education. (1987). *Vocational assessment of secondary special needs students.* Springfield, IL: Illinois State Board of Education.

Impara, J. C., & Plake, B. S. (Eds.). (1998). *The thirteenth mental measurements yearbook.* Lincoln, NE: Buros Institute of Mental Measurements.

International Reading Association. (1981). *Resolution on misuse of grade equivalents.* Newark, DE: Author.

Iowa tests of basic skills. (1996). Itasca, IL: Riverside.

Isaacson, S. L. (1988). Effective instruction in written language. In E. L. Meyen, G. A. Vergason, & R. J. Whelan (Eds.), *Effective instructional strategies for exceptional children* (pp. 288–306). Denver: Love.

Jastak, J. F., & Jastak, S. R. (1978). *Wide range achievement test* (1978 rev. ed.). Wilmington, DE: Jastak Associates.

Jastak, J. F., & Jastak, S. R. (1979). *Wide range interest-opinion test.* Wilmington, DE: Jastak Associates.

Jastak, J. F., & Jastak, S. R. (1980). *Wide range employability sample test.* Wilmington, DE: Jastak Associates.

Jewish Employment and Vocational Service. (1985). *APTICOM® occupational aptitude test battery.* Philadelphia: Vocational Research Institute.

Johnson, B. (1993). *Teacher-as-researcher* (ERIC Digest). Retrieved July 10, 1999 from the World Wide Web: http://www.ed.gov/databases/ERIC_Digests/ed355205.html

Johnson, D. D. (1971). The Dolch list reexamined. *The Reading Teacher, 24,* 455–456.

Johnson, M. S., Kress, R. A., & Pikulski, J. J. (1987). *Informal reading inventories* (2nd ed.). Newark, DE: International Reading Association.

Johnson-Martin, N. M., Attermeier, S. M., & Hacker, B. J. (1990). *The Carolina curriculum for preschoolers with special needs.* Baltimore: Brookes.

Johnson-Martin, N. M., Jens, K. G., Attermeier, S. M., & Hacker, B. J. (1991). *The Carolina curriculum for infants and toddlers with special needs.* Baltimore: Brookes.

Jones, R. L. (Ed.). (1988). *Psychoeducational assessment of minority group children, A casebook.* Berkeley, CA: Cobb & Henry.

Jones, R. L., & Wilderson, R. B. (1976). Mainstreaming and the minority child: An overview of issues and a perspective. In R. L. Jones (Ed.), *Mainstreaming and the minority child* (pp. 1–13). Reston, VA: Council for Exceptional Children.

Jongsma, E. (1971). *The cloze procedure as teaching technique.* Newark, DE: International Reading Association.

Juárez, M. (1983). Assessment and treatment of minority-language-handicapped children: The role of the monolingual speech-language pathologist. *Topics in Language Disorders, 3*(3), 57–66.

Kaluger, G., & Kolson, C. J. (1978). *Reading and learning disabilities* (2nd ed.). New York: Merrill/Macmillan.

Kamphaus, R. W. (1987). Conceptual and psychometric issues in the assessment of adaptive behavior. *Journal of Special Education, 21,* 27–35.

Kamphaus, R. W., & Reynolds, C. R. (1987a). *Clinical and research applications of the K-ABC.* Circle Pines, MN: American Guidance Service.

Kamphaus, R. W., & Reynolds, C. R. (1987b). *Kamphaus/Reynolds K-ABC analysis form.* Circle Pines, MN: American Guidance Service.

Kamphaus, R. W., & Reynolds, C. R. (1998). *BASC monitor for ADHD.* Circle Pines, MN: American Guidance Service.

Karlsen, B. (1992). *Language arts assessment profile.* Circle Pines, MN: American Guidance Service.

Karlsen, B., & Gardner, E. F. (1995). *Stanford diagnostic reading test, Fourth edition.* San Antonio, TX: Harcourt Brace Educational Measurement.

Kaufman, A. S. (1981). The WISC-R and learning disabilities assessment: State of the art. *Journal of Learning Disabilities, 14,* 520–526.

Kaufman, A. S., & Kaufman, N. L. (1983). *Kaufman assessment battery for children.* Circle Pines, MN: American Guidance Service.

Kaufman, A. S., & Kaufman, N. L. (1990). *Kaufman brief intelligence test.* Circle Pines, MN: American Guidance Service.

Kaufman, A. S., & Kaufman, N. L. (1993). *Kaufman adolescent & adult intelligence test.* Circle Pines, MN: American Guidance Service.

Kaufman, A. S., & Kaufman, N. L. (1998). *Kaufman test of educational achievement/Normative update.* Circle Pines, MN: American Guidance Service.

Kavale, K. (1981). Functions of the Illinois Test of Psycholinguistic Abilities (ITPA): Are they trainable? *Exceptional Children, 47,* 496–510.

Kavale, K. A., & Forness, S. R. (1984). A meta-analysis of the validity of Wechsler scale profiles and recategorizations: Patterns or parodies? *Learning Disability Quarterly, 7,* 136–156.

Kearns, J. F., Kleinert, H. L., Clayton, J., Burdge, M., & Williams, R. (1998). Principal supports for inclusive assessment. *Teaching Exceptional Children, 31*(2), 16–23.

Keogh, B. (1999). Revisiting families of children with learning disabilities. *Learning Disabilities, 9*(3), 81–85.

Kessen, W. (1965). *The child.* New York: Wiley.

Kimball, O. M. (1973). Development of norms for the *Coopersmith Self-Esteem Inventory:* Grades four through eight. (Doctoral dissertation, Northern Illinois University, 1972).

Dissertation Abstracts International, 34, 1131–1132.

Kirk, S. A., & Chalfant, J. C. (1984). *Academic and developmental learning disabilities.* Denver, CO: Love.

Kirk, S. A., & Kirk, W. D. (1971). *Psycholinguistic learning disabilities: Diagnosis and remediation.* Urbana: University of Illinois Press.

Kirk, S. A., Kliebhan, J. M., & Lerner, J. W. (1978). *Teaching reading to slow and disabled readers.* Boston: Houghton Mifflin.

Kirk, S. A., McCarthy, J. J., & Kirk, W. D. (1968). *Illinois test of psycholinguistic abilities* (rev. ed.). Urbana: University of Illinois Press.

Kitano, M. K. (1990). A developmental model for identifying and serving young gifted children. *Early Childhood Development and Care, 63,* 19–31.

Kochhar, C. (1998). Analysis of the special populations provisions in the 1998 Carl D. Perkins Vocational Technical Education Act Amendments. *The Journal for Vocational Special Needs Education, 21* (1), 3–20.

Kokaska, C. J., & Brolin, D. E. (1985). *Career education for handicapped individuals* (2nd ed.). New York: Merrill/Macmillan.

Koppitz, E. M. (1963). *The Bender gestalt test for young children.* New York: Grune & Stratton.

Koppitz, E. M. (1975). *The Bender gestalt test for young children, Volume II: Research and application, 1963–1973.* New York: Grune & Stratton.

Kottmeyer, W. (1970). *Teacher's guide for remedial reading.* New York: McGraw-Hill.

Kroth, R. L. (1975). *Communicating with parents of exceptional children.* Denver, CO: Love.

Kroth, R. L., & Edge, D. (1997). *Strategies for communicating with parents and families of exceptional children* (3rd ed.). Denver, CO: Love.

Krug, D. A., Arick, J. R., & Almond, P. J. (1993). *Autism screening instrument for educational planning.* Austin, TX: PRO-ED.

Lambert, N. M. (1981). Psychological evidence in *Larry P. v. Wilson Riles:* An evaluation by a witness for the defense. *American Psychologist, 36,* 937–952.

Lambert, N., Hartsough, C., & Sandoval, J. (1990). *Children's attention and adjustment survey.* Circle Pines, MN: American Guidance Service.

Lambert, N., Nihira, K., & Leland, H. (1993). *AAMR adaptive behavior scale-School* (2nd ed.). Austin, TX: PRO-ED.

Langdon, H. W. (1992). Speech and language assessment of LEP/bilingual Hispanic students. In H. W. Langdon & L. L. Cheng (Eds.), *Hispanic children and adults with communication disorders* (pp. 201–271). Gaithersburg, MD: Aspen.

Langdon, H. W., Siegel, V., Halog, L., & Sánchez-Boyce, M. (1994). *The interpreter translator process in the educational setting.* Rohnert Park, CA: Resources in Special Education, Sonoma State University.

Laosa, L. M. (1977). Nonbiased assessment of children's abilities: Historical antecedents and current issues. In T. Oakland (Ed.), *Psychological and educational assessment of minority children* (pp. 1–20). New York: Brunner/Mazel.

Lapp, D., & Flood, J. (1992). *Teaching reading to every child* (3rd ed.). New York: Macmillan.

LaPray, M., & Ross, R. (1969). The graded word list: Quick gauge of reading ability. *Journal of Reading, 12,* 305–307.

Larrivee, B. (1981). Modality preference as a model for differentiating beginning reading instruction: A review of the issues. *Learning Disability Quarterly, 4,* 180–188.

Larry P. v. Riles. C-71-2270-RFP (N.D. Cal. 1972), 495 F. Supp. 96 (N.D. Cal. 1979) Aff'r (9th Cir. 1984), 1983–84 EHLR DEC. 555:304.

Larsen, S. C., & Hammill, D. D. (1975). Relationship of selected visual perceptual abilities to school learning. *Journal of Special Education, 9,* 282–291.

Larsen, S. C., & Hammill, D. D. (1989). *Test of legible handwriting.* Austin, TX: PRO-ED.

Larsen, S. C., Hammill, D. D., & Moats, L. C. (1999). *Test of written spelling* (4th ed.). Austin, TX: PRO-ED.

Larsen, S. C., Parker, R. R., & Hammill, D. D. (1982). Effectiveness of psycholinguistic training: A response to Kavale. *Exceptional Children, 49,* 60–66.

Larsen, S. C., Rogers, D., & Sowell, V. (1976). The use of selected perceptual tests in differentiating between normal and learning disabled children. *Journal of Learning Disabilities, 9,* 85–90.

Larson, N., & Aase, S. (1997). *From screening to accommodation: Providing services to adults with learning disabilities.* Columbus, OH: AHEAD.

Lau v. Nichols. (1974). 414 U.S. 562–572.

Learning Disabilities Association. (1986). *ACLD description: Specific learning disabilities. A position paper of the Learning Disabilities Association (formerly the Association for Children with Learning Disabilities).* Pittsburgh, PA: Author.

Learning Disabilities Association. (1990). *Eligibility for services for persons with specific learning disabilities. A position paper of the Learning Disabilities Association.* Pittsburgh, PA: Author.

Leconte, P. J. (1999). Vocational evaluation. In S. H. deFur & J. R. Patton (Eds.), *Transition and school-based services: Interdisciplinary perspectives for enhancing the transition process* (pp. 387–417). Austin, TX: PRO-ED.

Lee, L. L. (1971). *Northwestern syntax screening test.* Evanston, IL: Northwestern University Press.

Lee, L. L. (1974). *Developmental sentence analysis.* Evanston, IL: Northwestern University Press.

Leinhardt, G., Zigmond, N., & Cooley, W. (1981). Reading instruction and its effects. *American Educational Research Journal, 18,* 343–361.

Leiter, R. G. (1948). *Leiter international performance scale.* Chicago: Stoelting.

Lenz, B. K., Ellis, E. S., & Scanlon, D. (1996). *Teaching learning strategies to adolescents and adults with learning disabilities.* Austin, TX: PRO-ED.

Leonard, L. B., & Weiss, A. L. (1983). Application of nonstandardized assessment procedures to diverse linguistic populations. *Topics in Language Disorders, 3*(3), 35–45.

Lerner, J. (2000). *Learning disabilities* (8th ed.). Boston: Houghton Mifflin.

Lerner, J. W., & Lerner, S. R. (1991). Attention deficit disorder: Issues and questions. *Focus on Exceptional Children, 24,* 1–17.

Lerner, J. W., & Lowenthal, B. (1993). Attention deficit disorders: New responsibilities for the special educator. *Learning Disabilities, 4*(1), 1–8.

Lerner, J. W., Cousin, P. T., & Richeck, M. (1992). Critical issues in learning disabilities: Whole language learning. *Learning Disabilities Research & Practice, 7,* 226–230.

Lerner, J. W., Lowenthal, B., & Lerner, S. R. (1995). *Attention deficit disorders.* Pacific Grove, CA: Brooks/Cole.

Levine, M. D., Clarke, S., & Ferb, T. (1981). The child as a diagnostic participant: Helping students describe their learning disorders. *Journal of Learning Disabilities, 14,* 527–530.

Lewis, R. (1983). Learning disabilities and reading: Instructional recommendations from current research. *Exceptional Children, 50,* 230–240.

Lewis, R. B. (1988). Learning disabilities. In E. W. Lynch & R. B. Lewis (Eds.), *Exceptional children and adults* (pp. 352–406). Glenview, IL: Scott, Foresman.

Lewis, R. B., & Doorlag, D. H. (1999). *Teaching special students in general education classrooms* (5th ed.). Upper Saddle River, NJ: Merrill/Prentice-Hall.

Lewis, T. J., & Sugai, G. (1999). Effective behavior support: A systems approach to proactive schoolwide management. *Focus on Exceptional Children, 31*(6), 1–24.

Lichtenstein, S. (1993). Transition from school to adulthood: Case studies of adults with learning disabilities who dropped out of school. *Exceptional Children, 59,* 336–347.

Lidz, C. S., & Thomas, C. (1987). The preschool learning assessment device: Extension of a static approach. In C. S. Lidz (Ed.), *Dynamic assessment: An interactional approach to evaluating learning potential* (pp. 288–326). New York: The Guilford Press.

Likert, R. (1932). A technique for the measurement of attitudes. *Archives of Psychology,* No. 140.

Linder, T. W. (1990). *Transdisciplinary play-based assessment: A functional approach to working with young children*. Baltimore: Brookes.

Lippke, B. A., Dickey, S. E., Selmar, J. W., & Soder, A. L. (1997). *Photo articulation test* (3rd ed.). Austin, TX: PRO-ED.

Litowitz, B. E. (1981). Developmental issues in written language. *Topics in Language Disorders, 1*(2), 73–89.

Lloyd, J. W. (1984). How shall we individualize instruction—Or should we? *Remedial and Special Education, 5*(1), 7–15.

LRE for LIFE Project. (1997). *Suggested guidelines for implementing positive behavior support strategies.* Knoxville, TN: Author. Retrieved July 4, 1999 from the World Wide Web: http://web.ce.utk.edu/lre/full/sugguide.htm

Lynch, E. W. (1998). Developing cross-cultural competence. In E. W. Lynch & M. J. Hanson (Eds.), *Developing cross-cultural competence: A guide to working with children and their families* (2nd ed.) (pp. 47–89). Baltimore: Brookes.

Lynch, E. W., & Hanson, M. J. (1996). Ensuring cultural competence in assessment. In M. McLean, D. B. Bailey, & M. Wolery (Eds.), *Assessing infants and preschoolers with special needs* (pp. 69–95). Englewood Cliffs, NJ: Merrill.

Lynch, E. W., & Lewis, R. B. (1987). Multicultural considerations. In K. A. Kavale, S. R. Forness, & M. Bender (Eds.), *Handbook of learning disabilities, Volume I, Dimensions and diagnosis* (pp. 399–416). Boston: College-Hill.

Lynch, E. W., & Stein, R. C. (1987). Parent participation by ethnicity: A comparison of Hispanic, Black, and Anglo families. *Exceptional Children, 54,* 105–111.

Lynch, R. T., & Gussel, L. (1996, March/April). Disclosure and self-advocacy regarding disability-related needs: Strategies to maximize integration in postsecondary education. *Journal of Counseling and Development, 74,* 352–357.

MacDonald, J., & Gillette, Y. (1989). *ECO: A partnership program.* Chicago: Riverside Publishing.

Macmillan, D. L., & Reschly, D. J. (1998). Overrepresentation of minority students: The case for greater specificity or reconsideration of the variables examined. *Journal of Special Education, 32,* 15–24.

Macvean, M. (1999, November). *Parental empowerment.* Paper presented at the 6th National Conference for the Donald Beasley Institute, Inc., Dunedin, New Zealand.

Madaus, G. F., & Kellaghan, T. (1993). The British experience with "authentic" testing. *Phi Delta Kappan, 74,* 458–469.

Maddox, T. (Ed.). (1997). *Tests: A comprehensive reference for assessments in psychology, education, and business.* Austin, TX: PRO-ED.

Maeroff, G. I. (1991). Assessing alternative assessment. *Phi Delta Kappan, 73,* 272–281.

Mager, R. F. (1975). *Preparing instructional objectives* (2nd ed.). Belmont, CA: Fearon.

Maginnis, G. (1969). The readability graph and informal reading inventories. *The Reading Teacher, 22,* 534–538.

Mann, P. H., Suiter, P. A., & McClung, R. M. (1979). *Handbook in diagnostic-prescriptive teaching* (2nd ed.). Boston: Allyn & Bacon.

Mardell-Czudnowski, C. D. (1980). The four Ws of current testing practices: Who; what; why; and to whom–An exploratory survey. *Learning Disability Quarterly, 3*(1), 73–83.

Mardell-Czudnowski, C., & Goldenberg, D. (1990). *Developmental indicators for the assessment of learning–Revised.* Edison, NJ: Childcraft.

Markwardt, F. C. (1989). *Peabody individual achievement test–Revised.* Circle Pines, MN: American Guidance Service.

Markwardt, F. C. (1998). *Peabody individual achievement test–Revised/normative update.* Circle Pines, MN: American Guidance Service.

Marston, D., & Magnusson, D. (1985). Implementing curriculum-based measurement in special and regular education settings. *Exceptional Children, 52,* 266–276.

Martin, D. B. (1999). *The portfolio planner.* Upper Saddle River, NJ: Merrill/Prentice-Hall.

Martin, N. (1983). Genuine communications. *Topics in Learning & Learning Disabilities, 3*(3), 1–11.

Mather, N. (1992). Whole language reading instruction for students with learning disabilities: Caught in the cross fire. *Learning Disabilities Research & Practice, 7,* 87–95.

Mather, N., & Healey, W. C. (1989). Deposing aptitude-achievement discrepancy as the imperial criterion for learning disabilities. *Learning Disabilities, 1*(2), 40–48.

Mather, N., & Woodcock, R. W. (1997). *Mather-Woodcock group writing tests.* Itasca, IL: Riverside.

McCarney, S. B. (1989). *Emotional and behavior problem scale.* Columbia, MO: Hawthorne Educational Services.

McCarney, S. B. (1994). *The attention deficit disorders intervention manual* (2nd ed.). Columbia, MO: Hawthorne Educational Services.

McCarney, S. B. (1995). *Adaptive behavior evaluation scale-Revised.* Columbia, MO: Hawthorne.

McCarney, S. B. (1995a). *Attention deficit disorders evaluation scale, Home version* (2nd ed.). Columbia, MO: Hawthorne Educational Services.

McCarney, S. B. (1995b). *Attention deficit disorders evaluation scale, School version* (2nd ed.). Columbia, MO: Hawthorne Educational Services.

McCarney, S. B. (1996). *The learning disability evaluation scale–Renormed.* Columbia, MO: Hawthorne Educational Services.

McCarney, S. B., & Bauer, A. M. (1991). *The parent's guide to learning disabilities.* Columbia, MO: Hawthorne Educational Services.

McCarney, S. B., & Bauer, A. M. (1995). *The learning disability intervention manual* (rev. ed.). Columbia, MO: Hawthorne Educational Services.

McCarney, S. B., & Bauer, A. M. (1995). *The parent's guide to attention deficit disorders* (2nd ed.). Columbia, MO: Hawthorne Educational Services.

McCarney, S. B., & Leigh, J. E. (1990). *Behavior evaluation scale-2.* Columbia, MO: Hawthorne Educational Services.

McCarney, S. B., McCain, B. R., & Bauer, A. M. (1995). *Adaptive behavior intervention manual-Revised.* Columbia, MO: Hawthorne.

McCarron, L. (1976, 1982). *McCarron assessment of neuromuscular development.* Dallas, TX: McCarron-Dial Systems.

McCarron, L., & Dial, J. (1973). *Dial behavior rating scale.* Dallas, TX: McCarron-Dial Systems.

McCarron, L., & Dial, J. (1976). *Haptic visual discrimination test.* Dallas, TX: McCarron-Dial Systems.

McCarron, L., & Dial, J. (1976, 1986). *Observational emotional inventory.* Dallas, TX: McCarron-Dial Systems.

McCarron, L., & Dial, J. (1986). *McCarron-Dial evaluation system manual.* Dallas, TX: McCarron-Dial Systems.

McCarthy, D. (1972). *McCarthy scales of children's abilities.* San Antonio, TX: Psychological Corporation.

McCollum, J., & Stayton, V. (1985). Infant/parent interaction: Studies and intervention guidelines based on the SIAI model. *Journal of the Division of Early Childhood, 9*(2), 125–135.

McCormack, J. E., Jr. (1976). The assessment tool that meets your needs: The one you construct. *Teaching Exceptional Children, 8,* 106–109.

McCormick, L., & Kawate, J. (1982). Kindergarten survival skills: New directions for preschool special education. *Education and Training of the Mentally Retarded, 17,* 247–252.

McDonnell, J., Wilcox, B., & Hardman, M. (1991). *Secondary programs for students with developmental disabilities.* Boston: Allyn & Bacon.

McGhee, R., Bryant, B. R., Larsen, S. C., & Rivera, D. M. (1995). *Test of written expression.* Austin, TX: PRO-ED.

McGrew, K. S., Werder, J. K., & Woodcock, R. W. (1991). *Woodcock-Johnson technical manual.* Chicago, IL: Riverside.

McLean, M. E., & Odom, S. L. (1996). Establishing recommended practices in early intervention/early childhood special education. In S. L. Odom & M. E. McLean (Eds.), *Early intervention/early childhood special education: Recommended practices* (pp. 1–22). Austin, TX: PRO-ED.

McLoughlin, J. A. (1985). Training educational diagnosticians. *Diagnostique, 10* (1–4), 176–196.

McLoughlin, J. A., & Kershman, S. (1978). Including the handicap. *Behavioral Disorders, 4,* 31–35.

McLoughlin, J. A., & Lewis, R. B. (1994). *Assessing special students* (4th ed.). New York: Merrill/Macmillan.

McMillan, J. H. (1997). *Classroom assessment.* Boston: Allyn & Bacon.

Mecham, M. J. (1989). *Utah test of language development* (3rd ed.). Austin, TX: PRO-ED.

Meltzer, L., & Reid, D. K. (1994). New directions in the assessment of students with special needs: The shift toward a constructivist perspective. *The Journal of Special Education, 28,* 338–355.

Meltzer, L. J. (1987). *Surveys of problem-solving & educational skills.* Cambridge, MA: Educators Publishing Service.

Mercer, C. D. (1997). *Students with learning disabilities* (5th ed.). Upper Saddle River, NJ: Merrill/Prentice-Hall.

Mercer, C. D., & Mercer, A. R. (1998). *Teaching students with learning problems* (5th ed.). Upper Saddle River, NJ: Merrill/Prentice-Hall.

Mercer, J. R. (1973). *Labeling the mentally retarded.* Berkeley, CA: University of California Press.

Mercer, J. R. (1983). Issues in the diagnosis of language disorders in students whose primary language is not English. *Topics in Language Disorders, 3*(3), 46–56.

Mercer, J. R., & Lewis, J. F. (1977a). *Adaptive behavior inventory for children.* San Antonio, TX: Psychological Corporation.

Mercer, J. R., & Lewis, J. F. (1977b). *System of multicultural pluralistic assessment.* San Antonio, TX: Psychological Corporation.

Merino, B. J. (1992). Acquisition of syntactic and phonological features in Spanish. In H. W. Langdon & L. L. Cheng (Eds.), *Hispanic children and adults with communication disorders* (pp. 57–98). Gaithersburg, MD: Aspen.

Messick, S. (1984). Assessment in context: Appraising student performance in relation to instruction quality. *Educational Researcher, 13*(3), 3–8.

Meyers, M. J. (1980). The significance of learning modalities, modes of instruction, and verbal feedback for learning to recognize written words. *Learning Disability Quarterly, 3*(3), 62–69.

Michael, W. B., Michael, J. J., & Zimmerman, W. S. (1985). *Study attitudes and methods survey.* San Diego, CA: EdITS.

Michael, W. B., Smith, R. A., & Michael, J. J. (1984). *Dimensions of self-concept.* San Diego, CA: EdITS.

Miller, L. C. (1977). *School behavior checklist.* Los Angeles: Western Psychological Services.

Minskoff, E. H. (1975). Research on psycholinguistic training: Critique and guidelines. *Exceptional Children, 42,* 136–144.

Molyneaux, D., & Lane, V. W. (1982). *Effective interviewing: Techniques and analysis.* Boston: Allyn & Bacon.

Molyneaux, D., & Lane, V. W. (1990). *Successful interactive skills for speech-language pathologists and audiologists.* Frederick, MD: Aspen.

Monroe, M. (1932). *Children who cannot read.* Chicago: University of Chicago Press.

Mooney, R. L., & Gordon, L. V. (1950). *The Mooney problem check lists* (rev. ed.). San Antonio, TX: Psychological Corporation.

Moores, D. F., & Moores, J. M. (1988). Hearing disorders. In E. W. Lynch & R. B. Lewis (Eds.), *Exceptional children and adults* (pp. 276–317). Glenview, IL: Scott, Foresman.

Moran, M. R. (1988). Options for written language assessment. In E. L. Meyen, G. A. Vergason, & R. J. Whelan (Eds.), *Effective instructional strategies for exceptional children* (pp. 465–480). Denver: Love.

Morreau, L. E., & Bruininks, R. H. (1991). *Checklist of adaptive living skills.* Chicago: Riverside.

Morsink, C. V., Thomas, C. C., & Correa, V. I. (1991). *Interactive teaming: Consultation and collaboration in special programs.* New York: Merrill.

Muñoz-Sandoval, A. F., Cummins, J., Alvarado, C. G., & Ruef, M. L. (1998). *Bilingual verbal ability tests.* Itasca, IL: Riverside.

Munday, L. A. (1979). Changing test scores, especially since 1970. *Phi Delta Kappan, 60,* 496–499.

Myklebust, H. R. (1965). *Development and disorders of written language. Volume one: Picture story language test.* New York: Grune & Stratton.

Myklebust, H. R. (1968). Learning disabilities: Definition and overview. In H. R. Myklebust (Ed.), *Progress in learning disabilities* (Vol. I) (pp. 1–15). New York: Grune & Stratton.

Naglieri, J. A., & Das, J. P. (1997). *Das-Naglieri cognitive assessment system*. Itasca, IL: Riverside.

Naglieri, J. A., LeBuffe, P. A., & Pfeiffer, S. I. (1993). *Devereux behavior rating scales-School form*. San Antonio, TX: Psychological Corporation.

National Center for Educational Statistics. (1997). *Mini-digest of education statistics 1997*. Washington, DC: U.S. Department of Education, Office of Educational Research and Improvement.

National Commission on Excellence in Education. (1983). *A nation at risk: The imperative for educational reform*. Washington, DC: U.S. Government Printing Office.

National Council of Teachers of Mathematics. (1980). *An agenda for action: Recommendations for school mathematics in the 1980's*. Reston, VA: Author.

National Council of Teachers of Mathematics. (1989). *Curriculum and evaluation standards for school mathematics*. Reston, VA: Author.

National Education Goals Panel. (1998). *National education goals*. Retrieved June 27, 1999 from the World Wide Web: http://negp.gov/webpg10.htm

National Information Center for Children and Youth with Disabilities. (1997). *General information about visual impairments: Fact sheet number 13*. Washington, DC: Author.

National Joint Committee on Learning Disabilities. (1994). *Collective perspectives on issues affecting learning disabilities*. Austin, TX: PRO-ED.

National Occupational Information Coordinating Committee. (1994). *Program guide: Planning to meet career development needs, school-to-work transition programs*. Washington, DC: Author.

National Research Council. (1997). *Executive summary: Educating one & all, students with disabilities and standards-based reform*. Washington, DC: National Academy Press.

National Society to Prevent Blindness. (1977). *Signs of possible eye trouble in children* (Pub. G-112). New York: Author.

Neeper, R., Lahey, B. B., & Frick, P. J. (1990). *Comprehensive behavior rating scale for children*. San Antonio, TX: Psychological Corporation.

Neisworth, J. T., & Bagnato, S. J. (1996). Assessment for early intervention: Emerging themes and practices. In S. L. Odom & M. E. McLean (Eds.), *Early intervention/early childhood special education: Recommended practices* (pp. 23–57). Austin, TX: PRO-ED.

Newborg, J., Stock, J. R., Wnek, J., Guidubaldi, J., & Svinicki, J. S. (1988). *Battelle developmental inventory (BDI)*. Chicago: Riverside Publishing Co.

Newcomer, P. L. (1990). *Diagnostic achievement battery* (2nd ed.). Austin, TX: PRO-ED.

Newcomer, P. L. (1999). *Standardized reading inventory* (2nd ed.). Austin, TX: PRO-ED.

Newcomer, P. L., & Bryant, B. R. (1993). *Diagnostic achievement test for adolescents* (2nd ed.). Austin, TX: PRO-ED.

Newcomer, P. L., & Hammill, D. D. (1975). ITPA and academic achievement: A survey. *The Reading Teacher, 28,* 731–741.

Newcomer, P. L., & Hammill, D. D. (1976). *Psycholinguistics in the schools*. New York: Merrill/Macmillan.

Newcomer, P. L., & Hammill, D. D. (1997). *Test of language development-3, Primary*. Austin, TX: PRO-ED.

Nicholson, C. L., & Hibpshman, T. L. (1990). *Slosson intelligence test, SIT-R, for children and adults* (1991 ed.). East Aurora, NY: Slosson Educational Publications.

Nihira, K., Leland, H., & Lambert, N. (1993). *AAMR adaptive behavior scale-Residential and community* (2nd ed.). Austin, TX: PRO-ED.

Nodine, B. F. (1983). Foreword: Process not product. *Topics in Learning & Learning Disabilities, 3*(3), ix–xii.

Oakland, T. (1979). Research on the *Adaptive Behavior Inventory for Children* and the Estimated Learning Potential. *School Psychology Digest, 8,* 63–70.

Oakland, T. (1980). Nonbiased assessment of minority group children. *Exceptional Education Quarterly, 1*(3), 31–46.

Oakland, T., & Laosa, L. M. (1977). Professional, legislative, and judicial influences on psychoeducational assessment practices in schools. In T. Oakland (Ed.), *Psychological and educational assessment of minority children* (pp. 21–51). New York: Brunner/Mazel.

O'Connor, R. E., Jenkins, J. R., Leicester, N., & Slocum, T. A. (1993). Teaching phonological awareness to young children with learning disabilities. *Exceptional Children, 59,* 532–546.

Office for Civil Rights. (1975). *Task force findings specifying remedies for eliminating past education practices ruled unlawful under Lau vs. Nichols.* Washington, DC: Author.

O'Neill, R. E., Horner, R. H., Albin, R. W., Sprague, J. R., Storey, K., & Newton, J. S. (1997). *Functional assessment and program development for problem behavior* (2nd ed.). Pacific Grove, CA: Brooks/Cole.

Oosterhof, A. (1994). *Classroom applications of educational measurement* (2nd ed.). New York: Merrill/Macmillan.

Ortiz, A. A. (1991, November). Testimony before the CEC Task Force on Children with Attention Deficit Disorders, New Orleans, LA.

Ortiz, A. A., & Garcia, S. B. (1988). A prereferral process for preventing inappropriate referrals of Hispanic students to special education. In A. A. Ortiz & B. A. Ramirez (Eds.)., *Schools and the culturally diverse exceptional student: Promising practices and future directions* (pp. 6–18). Reston, VA: Council for Exceptional Children.

Osborn, W. J. (1925). Ten reasons why pupils fail in mathematics. *The Mathematics Teacher, 18,* 234–238.

Otis, A. S., & Lennon, R. T. (1995). *Otis-Lennon school ability test* (7th ed.). San Antonio, TX: Psychological Corporation.

Otto, W., & Smith, R. J. (1983). Skill-centered and meaning-centered conceptions of remedial reading instruction: Striking a balance. *Topics in Learning and Learning Disabilities, 2*(4), 20–26.

PACER Center. (1994). *What is functional assessment?* Minneapolis, MN: Author. Retrieved July 4, 1999 from the World Wide Web: http://www.pacer.org.parent/function.htm

Parents in Action on Special Education v. Joseph P. Hannon. No. 74 C 3586 (N.D. Ill. 1980).

Parker, R. (1991). *Occupational aptitude survey and interest schedule—The aptitude survey* (2nd ed.). Austin, TX: PRO-ED.

Parks, S., Furono, S., O'Reilly, K., Inatsuka, T., Hoska, C. M., & Zeisloft-Falbey, B. (1994). *Hawaii early learning profile: HELP (Birth to 3).* Palo Alto, CA: VORT Corporation.

Patrick, J. L., & Reschly, D. J. (1982). Relationship of state educational criteria and demographic variables to school-system prevalence of mental retardation. *American Journal of Mental Deficiency, 86,* 351–360.

Patton, J., & Dunn, C. (1998). *Transition from school to young adulthood.* Austin, TX: PRO-ED.

Patton, J. M. (1998). The disproportionate representation of African Americans in special education: Looking behind the curtain for understanding and solutions. *Journal of Special Education, 32,* 25–31.

Paul, J. L., & Simeonsson, R. J. (1993). *Children with special needs: Family, culture, and society* (2nd ed.). Fort Worth, TX: Harcourt Brace Jovanovich.

Paul, J. L., Beckman, P., & Smith, R. L. (1993). Parent and sibling perspectives. In J. L. Paul & R. J. Simeonsson, *Children with special needs: Family, culture, and society* (2nd ed.), (pp. 77–96). Fort Worth, TX: Harcourt Brace Jovanovich.

Payan, R. M. (1989). Language assessment for the bilingual exceptional child. In L. M. Baca & H. T. Cervantes (Eds.), *The bilingual special education interface* (2nd ed.) (pp. 125–152). New York: Merrill/Macmillan.

Pellegrini, A. D. (1996). *Observing children in their natural worlds: A methodological primer.* Mahwah, NJ: Lawrence Erlbaum Associates.

Perrone, V. (1977). *The abuses of standardized testing.* Bloomington, IN: Phi Delta Kappa Educational Foundation.

Peterson, J., Heistad, D., Peterson, D., & Reynolds, M. (1985). Montevideo individualized prescriptive instructional management system. *Exceptional Children, 52,* 239–243.

Peterson, M. (1988). *Vocational assessment of special students for vocational education: A state-of-the-art review.* Columbus, OH: National Center for Research in Vocational Education, The Ohio State University.

Peterson, N. (1987). *Early intervention for handicapped and at-risk children: An introduction to early childhood special education.* Denver: Love.

Phelps-Gunn, T., & Phelps-Terasaki, D. (1982). *Written language instruction.* Rockville, MD: Aspen Systems.

Phelps-Terasaki, D., & Phelps-Gunn, T. (1992). *Test of pragmatic language.* Austin, TX: PRO-ED.

Pierce, L. V., & O'Malley, J. M. (1992, Spring). *Performance and portfolio assessment for language minority students* (NCBE Program Information Guide Series, No. 9). Retrieved July 1, 1999 from the World Wide Web: http://www.ncbe.gwu.edu/ncbepubs/pigs/pig9.htm

Piers, E. V. (1977). *The Piers-Harris children's self-concept scale* (Research monograph no. 1). Los Angeles: Western Psychological Services.

Piers, E. V., & Harris, D. B. (1969). *The Piers-Harris children's self-concept scale.* Los Angeles: Western Psychological Services.

Piers, E. V., & Harris, D. B. (1984). *The Piers-Harris children's self-concept scale: Revised manual.* Los Angeles: Western Psychological Services.

Pipho, C. (1978). Minimum competency testing in 1978: A look at state standards. *Phi Delta Kappan, 59,* 585–588.

Plata, M. (1982). *Assessment, placement, and programming of bilingual exceptional pupils: A practical approach.* Reston, VA: ERIC Clearinghouse on Handicapped & Gifted Children, Council for Exceptional Children.

Polloway, E. A., & Payne, J. S. (1993). *Strategies for teaching learners with special needs* (5th ed.). New York: Merrill/Macmillan.

Polloway, E. A., & Smith, J. E. (1982). *Teaching language skills to exceptional learners.* Denver: Love.

Polloway, E. A., Patton, J. R., & Cohen, S. B. (1983). Written language for mildly handicapped children. In E. L. Meyen, G. A. Vergason, & R. L. Whelan (Eds.), *Promising practices for exceptional children: Curriculum implications* (pp. 285–320). Denver: Love.

Popham, W. J. (1978). The case for criterion-referenced measurements. *Educational Researcher, 7,* 6–10.

Popham, W. J. (1993). Circumventing the high costs of authentic assessment. *Phi Delta Kappan, 74,* 470–473.

Popham, W. J., & Baker, E. L. (1970). *Systematic instruction.* Englewood Cliffs, NJ: Prentice-Hall.

Poplin, M. S. (1983). Assessing developmental writing abilities. *Topics in Learning and Learning Disabilities, 3*(3), 63–75.

Poteet, J. A. (1980). Informal assessment of written expression. *Learning Disability Quarterly, 3*(4), 88–98.

Pressley, M., Borkowski, J. G., Forrest-Pressley, D., Gaskins, I. W., & Wile, D. (1993). Closing thoughts on strategy instruction for individuals: The good information-processing perspective. In L. J. Meltzer (Ed.), *Strategy assessment and instruction for students with learning disabilities* (pp. 355–377). Austin, TX: PRO-ED.

Puckett, M. B., & Black, J. K. (2000). *Authentic assessment of the young child.* Columbus, OH: Merrill.

Purdue Research Foundation. (1968). *Purdue pegboard.* Chicago: Science Research Associates.

Putnam, M. L., Deshler, D. D., & Schumaker, J. B. (1993). The investigation of setting demands: A missing link in learning strategy instruction. In L. J. Meltzer (Ed.), *Strategy assessment and instruction for students with learning disabilities* (pp. 325–353). Austin, TX: PRO-ED.

Quay, H. C., & Peterson, D. R. (1983, 1987). *Revised behavior problem checklist.* Coral Gables, FL: University of Miami.

Quinn, M. M., Gable, R. A., Rutherford, R. B., Nelson, C. M., & Howell, K. (1998).

Addressing student problem behavior: An IEP team's introduction to functional behavioral assessment and behavior intervention plans (2nd ed.). Washington, DC: Center for Effective Collaboration and Practice. Retrieved July 5, 1999 from the World Wide Web: http://www.air-dc.org/cecp/resources/problembehavior/main.htm

Raven, J. C. (1938). *Standard progressive matrices*. London: H. K. Lewis. [American distributor: Psychological Corporation]

Raven, J. C. (1947). *Coloured progressive matrices*. London: H. K. Lewis. [American distributor: Psychological Corporation]

Raven, J. C. (1962). *Advanced progressive matrices*. London: H. K. Lewis. [American distributor: Psychological Corporation]

Reeve, R. E., Hall, R. J., & Zakreski, R. S. (1979). The *Woodcock-Johnson Tests of Cognitive Ability:* Concurrent validity with the *WISC-R. Learning Disability Quarterly, 2*(2), 63–69.

Reid, D. K., & Hresko, W. P. (1981). *A cognitive approach to learning disabilities.* New York: McGraw-Hill.

Reid, D. K., Hresko, W., & Hammill, D. D. (1989). *Test of early reading ability* (2nd ed.). Austin, TX: PRO-ED.

Repetto, J. B., & Webb, K. W. (1999). A model for guiding the transition process. In S. H. deFur & J. R. Patton (Eds.), *Transition and school-based services: Interdisciplinary perspectives for enhancing the transition process* (pp. 421–442). Austin, TX: PRO-ED.

Reschly, D. J. (1981). Psychological testing in educational classification and placement. *American Psychologist, 36,* 1094–1102.

Reynolds, C. R. (1984). Critical measurement issues in learning disabilities. *Journal of Special Education, 18,* 451–476.

Reynolds, C. R. (1992). Two key concepts in the diagnosis of learning disabilities and the habilitation of learning. *Learning Disability Quarterly, 15,* 2–12.

Reynolds, C. R., & Bigler, E. D. (1994). *Test of memory and learning.* Austin, TX: PRO-ED.

Reynolds, C. R., & Kamphaus, R. W. (1998). *BASC: Behavior assessment system for children.* Circle Pines, MN: American Guidance Service.

Reynolds, M. C., & Birch, J. W. (1977). *Teaching exceptional children in all America's schools.* Reston, VA: Council for Exceptional Children.

Reynolds, W. M. (1987). *Wepman's auditory discrimination test manual* (2nd ed.). Los Angeles: Western Psychological Services.

Ringler, L. H., & Smith, I. (1973). Learning modality and word recognition of first grade children. *Journal of Learning Disabilities, 6,* 307–312.

Riverside performance assessment series. (1993). Itasca, IL: Riverside.

Roach, E. G., & Kephart, N. D. (1966). *The Purdue perceptual-motor survey.* New York: Merrill/Macmillan.

Roberts, G. H. (1968). The failure strategies of third grade arithmetic pupils. *The Arithmetic Teacher, 15,* 442–446.

Roberts, J. R. (1945). *Pennsylvania bimanual work sample.* Circle Pines, MN: American Guidance Service.

Robinson, N. M., & Robinson, H. B. (1976). *The mentally retarded child* (2nd ed.). New York: McGraw-Hill.

Roid, G., & Miller, L. (1997). *Leiter international performance scale-Revised.* Chicago: Stoelting.

Rose, M. D., Cundick, B. P., & Higbee, K. L. (1983). Verbal rehearsal and visual imagery: Mnemonic aids for learning disabled children. *Journal of Learning Disabilities, 16,* 352–354.

Rosenberg, S., Robinson, C., & Beckman, P. (1984). Teaching skills inventory: A measure of parent performance. *Journal of the Division of Early Childhood, 8*(2), 107–113.

Rosenkoetter, S. E., Hains, A. H., & Fowler, S. A. (1994). *Bridging early services for children with special needs and their families: A practical guide for transition planning.* Baltimore: Brookes.

Rossetti, L. M. (1990). *Infant-toddler assessment: An interdisciplinary approach.* Boston: College Hill Publication.

Roszmann-Millican, M., & Walker, S. (1998, November). *Accommodating students with learning disabilities in statewide performance assessments.* Paper presented at the annual meeting of Council for Learning Disabilities, Albuquerque, NM.

Roussel, N. (1991). Annotated bibliography of communicative ability tests. In E. V. Hamayan & J. S. Damico (Eds.), *Limiting bias in the assessment of bilingual students* (pp. 320–343). Austin, TX: PRO-ED.

Ruddell, R. B. (1974). *Reading language instruction: Innovative practices.* Englewood Cliffs, NJ: Prentice-Hall.

Rudman, H. C. (1977). The standardized test flap. *Phi Delta Kappan, 59,* 178–185.

Russell, D. H., & Russell, E. F. (1959). *Listening aids through the grades.* New York: Bureau of Publications, Teachers College, Columbia University.

Salend, S. J. (1998). Using portfolios to assess student performance. *Teaching Exceptional Children, 31*(2), 36–43.

Salvia, J., & Hritcko, T. (1984). The *K-ABC* and ability training. *Journal of Special Education, 18,* 345–356.

Salvia, J., & Ysseldyke, J. E. (1991). *Assessment* (5th ed.). Boston: Houghton Mifflin.

Salvia, J., & Ysseldyke, J. E. (1998). *Assessment* (7th ed.). Boston: Houghton Mifflin.

Samuda, R. (1975). *Psychological testing of American minorities.* New York: Dodd, Mead.

Samuels, S. J. (1983). Diagnosing reading problems. *Topics in Learning and Learning Disabilities, 2*(4), 1–11.

Sandall, S. R. (1997a). Developmental assessment in early intervention. In A. H. Widerstrom, B. A. Mowder, & S. R. Sandall (Eds.), *Infant development and risk: An introduction* (pp. 211–235). Baltimore: Brookes.

Sandall, S. R. (1997b). The family service team. In A. H. Widerstrom, B. A. Mowder, & S. R. Sandall (Eds.), *Infant development and risk: An introduction* (pp. 155–173). Baltimore: Brookes.

Sandall, S. R. (1997c). The Individualized Family Service Plan. In A. H. Widerstrom, B. A. Mowder, & S. R. Sandall (Eds.), *Infant development and risk: An introduction* (pp. 237–245). Baltimore: Brookes.

Sarkees-Wircenski, M., & Scott, J. (1995). *Vocational special needs.* Homewood, IL: American Technical Publishers, Inc.

Sattler, J. M. (1988). *Assessment of children* (3rd ed.). San Diego, CA: Author.

Scarr, S. (1981). Testing *for* children: Assessment and the many determinants of intellectual competence. *American Psychologist, 36,* 1159–1166.

Scheiber, B., & Talpers, J. (1987). *Unlocking potential: College and other choices for learning disabled people. A step-by-step guide.* Bethesda, MD: Adler & Adler.

Schloss, P. J., Smith, M., Hoover, T., & Wolford, J. (1987). Dynamic criterion-referenced vocational assessment: An alternative strategy for handicapped youth. *Diagnostique, 12,* 74–86.

Schmidt, P. (1992). Census data find more are falling behind in school. *Education Week, 11*(38), 1, 9.

Scholastic aptitude test. (n.d.). Princeton, NJ: Educational Testing Services. (new edition each year)

Schreiner, R. (1983). Principles of diagnosis of reading difficulties. *Topics in Learning and Learning Disabilities, 2*(4), 70–85.

Schulte, A., & Borich, G. D. (1984). Considerations in the use of difference scores to identify learning-disabled children. *Journal of School Psychology, 22,* 381–390.

Schulz, E. (1992, September). Enemy of innovation. *Teacher Magazine,* pp. 28–31.

Schumaker, J. B., & Deshler, D. D. (1984). Setting demand variables: A major factor in program planning for the LD adolescent. *Topics in Language Disorders, 4*(2), 22–40.

Schumaker, J. B., & Deshler, D. D. (1988). Implementing the Regular Education Initiative in secondary schools: A different ball game. *Journal of Learning Disabilities, 21,* 36–42.

Schumaker, J. B., Deshler, D. D., Alley, G. R., & Warner, M. M. (1983). Toward the development of an intervention model for learning disabled adolescents: The University of Kansas Institute. *Exceptional Education Quarterly, 4*(1), 45–74.

Schumaker, J. B., Deshler, D. D., Alley, G. R., Warner, M. M., & Denton, P. H. (1982). Multipass: A learning strategy for improving reading comprehension. *Learning Disability Quarterly, 5,* 295–304.

Seligman, M. (Ed.). (1983). *The family with a handicapped child: Understanding and treatment.* New York: Grune & Stratton.

Semel, E., Wiig, E. H., & Secord, W. A. (1995). *Clinical evaluation of language fundamentals–Third edition*. San Antonio, TX: Psychological Corporation.

Shaywitz, S. E., & Shaywitz, B. A. (Eds.). (1992). *Attention deficit disorder comes of age*. Austin, TX: PRO-ED.

Shea, T. M. (1978). *Teaching children and youth with behavior disorders*. St. Louis: Mosby.

Shinn, M. R. (1988). Development of curriculum-based local norms for use in special education decision-making. *School Psychology Review, 17*(1), 61–80.

Shinn, M. R., & Hubbard, D. D. (1993). Curriculum-based measurement and problem-solving assessment: Basic procedures and outcomes. In E. L. Meyen, G. A. Vergason, & R. J. Whelan (Eds.), *Educating students with mild disabilities* (pp. 221–253). Denver, CO: Love.

Shonkoff, J. P., & Hauser-Cram, P. (1987). Early intervention for disabled infants and their families: A quantitative analysis. *Pediatrics, 80,* 650–658.

Shulman, B. B. (1986). *Test of pragmatic skills* (rev. ed.). Tucson, AZ: Communication Skill Builders.

Silvaroli, N. J. (1997). *Classroom reading inventory* (8th ed.). Boston: McGraw-Hill.

Silver, L. B. (1992). *Attention-deficit hyperactivity disorder*. Washington, DC: American Psychiatric Press.

Singer Company Career Systems. (1982). *Singer vocational evaluation system*. Rochester, NY: Singer.

Sitlington, P. L., Frank, A. R., & Carson, R. (1992). Adult adjustment among high school graduates with mild disabilities. *Exceptional Children, 59,* 221–233.

Sitlington, P. L., Neubert, D. A., Begun, W., Lombard, R. C., & Leconte, P. J. (1996). *Assess for success: Handbook on transition assessment*. Reston, VA: The Council for Exceptional Children.

Sloan, W. (1954). *Lincoln-Oseretsky motor development scale*. Chicago: Stoelting.

Slosson, R. L., & Nicholson, C. L. (1990). *Slosson oral reading test—Revised*. East Aurora, NY: Slosson Educational Publications.

Smith, F. (1982). *Writing and the writer.* New York: Holt, Rinehart, & Winston.

Smith, R. M., Neisworth, J. T., & Greer, J. B. (1978). *Evaluating educational environments*. New York: Merrill/Macmillan.

Smolensky, J., Bonvechio, L. R., Whitlock, R. E., & Girard, M. A. (1968). *School health problems*. Palo Alto, CA: Fearon.

Snider, V. E. (1992). Learning styles and learning to read: A critique. *Remedial and Special Education, 13*(1), 6–18.

Snow, C. E., Burns, S., & Griffin, P. (Eds.). (1998). *Preventing reading difficulties in young children*. Washington, DC: National Academic Press.

Snyder, S., & Sheehan, R. (1996). Program evaluation. In S. L. Odom & M. E. McLean (Eds.), *Early intervention/early childhood special education: Recommended practices* (pp. 359–378). Austin, TX: PRO-ED.

Sowell, V., Parker, R., Poplin, M., & Larsen, J. (1979). The effects of psycholinguistic training on improving psycholinguistic skills. *Learning Disability Quarterly, 2*(3), 69–77.

Spache, G. D. (1972). *Diagnostic reading scales*. Monterey, CA: CTB Macmillan/McGraw-Hill.

Spache, G. D. (1981). *Diagnostic reading scales* (rev. ed.). Monterey, CA: CTB Macmillan/McGraw-Hill.

Spanish assessment of basic education (2nd ed.). (1991). Monterey, CA: CTB Macmillan/McGraw-Hill.

Sparrow, S. S., Balla, D. A., & Cicchetti, D. V. (1984). *Vineland adaptive behavior scales*. Circle Pines, MN: American Guidance Service.

Sparrow, S. S., Balla, D. A., & Cicchetti, D. V. (1998). *Vineland social-emotional early childhood scales*. Circle Pines, MN: American Guidance Service.

Squires, J., Potter, L., & Bricker, D. (1999). *The ASQ user's guide for the Ages and Stages Questionnaires: A parent completed, child-monitoring system*. Baltimore: Brookes.

Stahl, S. (1988). Is there evidence to support matching reading styles and initial reading methods? *Phi Delta Kappan, 70,* 317–322.

Stahl, S. A., & Miller, P. D. (1989). Whole language and language experience approaches for beginning reading: A quantitative research synthesis. *Review of Educational Research, 59,* 87–116.

Stainback, S., & Stainback, W. (Eds.). (1985). *Integrating students with severe handicaps into regular schools.* Reston, VA: Council for Exceptional Children.

Stainback, S., & Stainback, W. (1988). Educating students with severe disabilities. *Teaching Exceptional Children, 21*(1), 16–19.

Stainback, S., & Stainback, W. (1992). *Curriculum considerations in inclusive classrooms.* Baltimore, MD: Brookes.

Stainback, S., Stainback, W., & Forest, M. (Eds.). (1989). *Educating all students in the mainstream of regular education.* Baltimore, MD: Paul H. Brookes.

Stanford achievement tests (9th ed.). (1996). San Antonio, TX: Harcourt Educational Measurement.

Stanford diagnostic mathematics test, Fourth edition. (1995). San Antonio, TX: Harcourt Brace Educational Measurement.

State-wide assessment programs. (1998, Spring). *Research Connections in Special Education* (No. 2). Reston, VA: ERIC/OSEP Special Project, ERIC Clearinghouse on Disabilities and Gifted Education, Council for Exceptional Children.

Stephens, T. M., Blackhurst, A., & Magliocca, L. (1982). *Teaching mainstreamed students.* New York: Wiley.

Sternberg, L., & Taylor, R. L. (1982). The insignificance of psycholinguistic training: A reply to Kavale. *Exceptional Children, 49,* 254–256.

Sternberg, R. J. (1984a). The *Kaufman Assessment Battery for Children:* An information-processing analysis and critique. *Journal of Special Education, 18,* 269–279.

Sternberg, R. J. (1984b). What should intelligence tests test? Implications of a triarchic theory of intelligence for intelligence testing. *Educational Researcher, 13*(1), 5–15.

Sternberg, R. J., Okagaki, L., & Jackson, A. S. (1990). Practical intelligence for success in school. *Educational Leadership, 48,* 35–39.

Stieglitz, E. L. (1997). *Stieglitz informal reading inventory* (2nd ed.). Boston: Allyn & Bacon.

Stile, S. W. (1996). Early childhood education of children who are gifted. In S. L. Odom & M. E. McLean (Eds.), *Early intervention/early childhood special education: Recommended practices* (pp. 309–328). Austin, TX: PRO-ED.

Strickland, B. B., & Turnbull, A. P. (1990). *Developing and implementing individualized education programs* (3rd ed.). New York: Merrill/Macmillan.

Strommen, E. (1988). Confirmatory factor analysis of the *Kaufman Assessment Battery for Children:* A reevaluation. *Journal of School Psychology, 26,* 13–23.

Sulzer-Azaroff, B., & Mayer, G. R. (1977). *Applying behavior-analysis procedures with children and youth.* New York: Holt, Rinehart & Winston.

Swanson, H. L. (1989). Strategy instruction: Overview of principles and procedures for effective use. *Learning Disabilities Quarterly, 12,* 3–14.

Swanson, H. L. (1993). Principles and procedures in strategy use. In L. J. Meltzer (Ed.), *Strategy assessment and instruction for students with learning disabilities* (pp. 61–92). Austin, TX: PRO-ED.

Swanson, H. L. (1996). *Swanson-cognitive processing test.* Austin, TX: PRO-ED.

Swanson, H. L. (1999). *Interventions for students with learning disabilities.* New York: Guilford Press.

Swanson, H. L., & Cooney, J. B. (1996). Learning disabilities and memory. In D. K. Reid, W. P. Hresko, & H. L. Swanson (Eds.), *Cognitive approaches to learning disabilities* (3rd ed.) (pp. 287–314). Austin, TX: PRO-ED.

Swap, S. M. (1974). Disturbing classroom behaviors: A developmental and ecological view. *Exceptional Children, 41,* 163–172.

Talent Assessment Inc. (1972, 1980, 1985, 1988). *Talent assessment program.* Jacksonville, FL: Author.

Tarver, S. G., & Dawson, M. M. (1978). Modality preference and the teaching of reading: A review. *Journal of Learning Disabilities, 11,* 5–17.

Taylor, O. L. (1990). Language and communication differences. In G. H. Shames & E. H.

Wiig (Eds.), *Human communication disorders* (3rd ed.) (pp. 126–158). New York: Merrill/Macmillan.

Taylor, O. L., & Payne, K. T. (1983). Culturally valid testing: A proactive approach. *Topics in Language Disorders, 3*(3), 8–20.

Taylor, R. L. (2000). *Assessment of exceptional students* (5th ed.). Boston: Allyn & Bacon.

Terman, L. M., & Merrill, M. A. (1937). *Measuring intelligence.* Boston: Houghton Mifflin.

Terman, L. M., & Merrill, M. A. (1973). *Stanford-Binet intelligence scale, Form L-M, 1972 edition.* Chicago: Riverside.

TerraNova SUPERA. (1997). Monterey, CA: CTB/McGraw-Hill.

Terrell, S. L., & Terrell, F. (1983). Distinguishing linguistic differences from disorders: The past, present, and future of nonbiased assessment. *Topics in Language Disorders, 3*(3), 1–7.

Test of cognitive skills (2nd ed.). (1992). Monterey, CA: CTB Macmillan/McGraw-Hill.

Thorndike, R. L., & Hagen, E. P. (1993). *Cognitive abilities test* (2nd ed.). Chicago: Riverside.

Thorndike, R. L., Hagen, E., & Sattler, J. (1986). *Stanford-Binet intelligence scale: Fourth edition.* Chicago: Riverside.

Thurlow, M. L., & Ysseldyke, J. E. (1979). Current assessment and decision-making practices in model programs for the learning disabled. *Learning Disability Quarterly, 2,* 15–24.

Thurlow, M. L., Graden, J., Greener, J., & Ysseldyke, J. E. (1983). LD and non-LD students' opportunities to learn. *Learning Disability Quarterly, 6,* 172–183.

Thurman, S. K. (1977). Congruence of behavioral ecologies: A model for special education programming. *Journal of Special Education, 11,* 329–334.

Tindal, G. A., & Marston, D. B. (1990). *Classroom-based assessment.* New York: Merrill/Macmillan.

Tombari, M., & Borich, G. (1999). *Authentic assessment in the classroom.* Upper Saddle River, NJ: Merrill/Prentice-Hall.

Torgesen, J. K. (1977). The role of nonspecific factors in the task performance of learning disabled children: A theoretical assessment. *Journal of Learning Disabilities, 10,* 5–17.

Torgesen, J. K. (1979). What shall we do with psychological processes? *Journal of Learning Disabilities, 12,* 514–521.

Torgesen, J. K. (1980). Conceptual and educational implications of the use of efficient task strategies by learning disabled children. *Journal of Learning Disabilities, 13,* 364–371.

Torgesen, J. K., & Barker, T. A. (1995). Computers as aids in the prevention and remediation of reading disabilities. *Learning Disability Quarterly, 18,* 76–87.

Torgesen, J. K., & Bryant, B. R. (1994). *Test of phonological awareness.* Austin, TX: PRO-ED.

Torgesen, J. K., & Goldman, T. (1977). Rehearsal and short-term memory in reading disabled children. *Child Development, 48,* 56–61.

Torgesen, J. K., Wagner, R. K., & Rashotte, C. A. (1999). *Test of word reading efficiency.* Austin, TX: PRO-ED.

Toronto, A. S. (1973). *Screening test of Spanish grammar.* Evanston, IL: Northwestern University Press.

Trivette, C. M., Dunst, C. J., & Deal, A. G. (1988). Family strengths profile. In C. J. Dunst, C. M. Trivette, & A. G. Deal (Eds.), *Enabling and empowering families: Principles and guidelines for practice.* Cambridge, MA: Brookline Books.

Trivette, C. M., Dunst, C. J., & Deal, A. G. (1997). Resource-based approach to early intervention. In S. K. Thurman, J. R. Cornwell, & S. R. Gottwald (Eds.) *Contexts of early intervention: Systems and settings* (pp. 73–92). Baltimore: Brookes.

Tucker, J. A. (1985). Curriculum-based assessment: An introduction. *Exceptional Children, 52,* 199–204.

Turnbull, A. P., & Schulz, J. B. (1979). *Mainstreaming handicapped students.* Boston: Allyn & Bacon.

Turnbull, A. P., & Turnbull, H. R. (1990). *Families, professionals, and exceptionality* (2nd ed.). New York: Merrill/Macmillan.

Turnbull, A. P., Strickland, B. B., & Brantley, J. C. (1982). *Developing and implementing individualized education programs* (2nd ed.). New York: Merrill/Macmillan.

Turnbull, R., & Cilley, M. (1999). *Explanations and implications of the 1997 Amendments to IDEA*. Upper Saddle River, NJ: Merrill/Prentice-Hall.

Tyack, D., & Venable, G. P. (1999). *Language sampling, analysis, and training* (3rd ed.). Austin, TX: PRO-ED.

Tyler, L. E. (Ed.). (1969). *Intelligence: Some recurring issues*. New York: Van Nostrand-Reinhold.

U.S. Department of Education. (1991, September 16). *Memorandum: Clarification of policy to address the needs of children with attention deficit disorders within general and/or special education*. Washington, DC: Office of Special Education and Rehabilitative Services.

U.S. Department of Education. (1995). *Seventeenth annual report to Congress on the implementation of The Individuals with Disabilities Education Act*. Washington, DC: Author.

U.S. Department of Education. (1998). *Twentieth annual report to Congress on the implementation of The Individuals with Disabilities Education Act*. Washington, DC: Author.

U.S. Department of Labor. (1977, 1982, 1986, 1991). *Dictionary of occupational titles* (4th ed.). Washington, DC: U.S. Government Printing Office.

U.S. Employment Services. (1982a). *General aptitude test battery (GATB)*. Washington, DC: U.S. Government Printing Office.

U.S. Employment Services. (1982b). *Nonreading aptitude test battery (NATB)*. Washington, DC: U.S. Government Printing Office.

Ulrich, D. A. (1985). *Test of gross motor development*. Austin, TX: PRO-ED.

Valenzuela, J. S. de, & Cervantes, H. T. (1998). Procedures and techniques for assessing the bilingual exceptional children. In L. M. Baca & H. T. Cervantes (Eds.), *The bilingual special education interface* (pp. 168–187). Upper Saddle River, NJ: Merrill/Prentice-Hall.

Vocational Evaluation and Work Adjustment Association. (1975). *Vocational evaluation project: Final report*. Menomonie, WI: Materials Development Center, University of Wisconsin-Stout.

Vogel, S. A. (1982). On developing LD college programs. *Journal of Learning Disabilities, 15,* 518–528.

Vogel, S. A. (1985). Comments on "Are commonly used predictors of college success applicable to the learning disabled?" *Thalamus, 5,* 62–74.

Vogel, S. A. (1987). Issues and concerns in LD college programming. In D. Johnson & J. Blalock (Eds.), *Adults with learning disabilities* (pp. 239–276). Orlando, FL: Grune & Stratton.

Vogel, S. A., & Sattler, J. (1981). *The college student with learning disability: A handbook for university admissions officers, faculty, and administration*. Illinois Council for Learning Disabilities.

von Isser, A., & Kirk, W. (1980). *Prueba Illinois de habilidades psicolingüísticas*. Tucson: University of Arizona.

VORT Corporation. (1995). *HELP for preschoolers assessment & curriculum guide*. Palo Alto, CA: Author.

Wagner, M., Blackorby, J., Cameto, R., Hebbeler, K., & Newman, L. (1993). *The transition experiences of young people with disabilities: A summary of findings from the National Longitudinal Transition Study of Special Education Students*. Menlo Park, CA: SRI International.

Wagner, R. K., & Torgesen, J. K. (1987). The nature of phonological processing and its causal role in the acquisition of reading skills. *Psychological Bulletin, 101,* 192–212.

Wagner, R. K., Torgesen, J. K., & Rashotte, C. (1993). *The efficacy of phonological awareness training for early reading achievement: A meta-analysis*. Unpublished manuscript, Florida State University.

Wagner, R. K., Torgesen, R. K., & Rashotte, C. A. (1999). *Comprehensive test of phonological processing*. Austin, TX: PRO-ED.

Wald, B. (1982). On assessing the oral language ability of limited-English-proficient students: The linguistic bases of the noncomparability of different language proficiency assessment measures. In S. S. Seidner (Ed.), *Issues of language assessment* (pp. 117–124). Illinois State Board of Education.

Walker, B., & Singer, G. H. S. (1993). Improving collaborative communication between professionals and parents. In G. H. S. Singer & L. Powers (Eds.), *Families, disability, and empowerment: Active coping skills and strategies for family intervention* (pp. 285–315). Baltimore: Brookes.

Walker, B. J. (1992). *Diagnostic teaching of reading* (2nd ed.). New York: Merrill/Macmillan.

Walker, H. M. (1983). *Walker problem behavior identification checklist* (rev.). Los Angeles: Western Psychological Services.

Wallace, G., & Hammill, D. D. (1994). *Comprehensive receptive and expressive vocabulary test.* Austin, TX: PRO-ED.

Wallace, G., & Hammill, D. D. (1997). *Comprehensive receptive and expressive vocabulary test-Computer administered.* Austin, TX: PRO-ED.

Wallace, G., & Kauffman, J. M. (1986). *Teaching students with learning and behavior problems* (3rd ed.). New York: Merrill/Macmillan.

Wallace, G., & McLoughlin, J. (1979). *Learning disabilities: Concepts and characteristics* (2nd ed.). New York: Merrill/Macmillan.

Wallace, G., Larsen, S. C., & Elksnin, L. K. (1992). *Educational assessment of learning problems* (2nd ed.), Boston: Allyn & Bacon.

Wang, M. C., & Walberg, H. J. (1988). Four fallacies of segregationism. *Exceptional Children, 55,* 128–137.

Waugh, R. P. (1973). Relationship between modality preference and performance. *Exceptional Children, 6,* 465–469.

Wayman, K. I., Lynch, E. W., & Hanson, M. J. (1990). Home-based early intervention services: Cultural sensitivity in a family systems approach. *Topics in Early Childhood Special Education, 10,* 56–75.

Wechsler abbreviated scale of intelligence. (1999). San Antonio, TX: Psychological Corporation.

Wechsler, D. (1974). *Wechsler intelligence scale for children–Revised.* San Antonio, TX: Psychological Corporation.

Wechsler, D. (1981). *Wechsler adult intelligence scale–Revised.* San Antonio, TX: Psychological Corporation.

Wechsler, D. (1989). *Wechsler preschool and primary scale of intelligence–Revised.* San Antonio, TX: Psychological Corporation.

Wechsler, D. (1991). *Wechsler intelligence scale for children–Third edition.* San Antonio, TX: Psychological Corporation.

Wechsler, D. (1997). *Wechsler adult intelligence scale–Third Edition.* San Antonio, TX: Psychological Corporation.

Wechsler, D. (1997). *Wechsler memory scale–Third edition.* San Antonio, TX: Psychological Corporation.

Wechsler individual achievement test. (1992). San Antonio, TX: Psychological Corporation.

Weiner, E. S. (1980). Diagnostic evaluation of writing skills. *Journal of Learning Disabilities, 13,* 43–53.

Weller, C., & Strawser, S. (1981). *Weller-Strawser scales of adaptive behavior for the learning disabled.* Novato, CA: Academic Therapy Publications.

Wells, C. G. (1981). *Learning through interactions: The study of language development.* Cambridge, England: Cambridge University Press.

Wells, G. (1973). *Coding manual of the description of child speech.* Bristol, England: University of Bristol School of Education.

Wepman, J. M. (1975). *Auditory discrimination test* (rev. 1973). Palm Springs, CA: Research Associates.

Westby, C. E. (1992). Whole language and learners with mild handicaps. *Focus on Exceptional Children, 24*(8), 1–16.

White, W. J., Deshler, D. D., Schumaker, J. B., Warner, M. M., Alley, G. R., & Clark, F. C. (1983). The effects of learning disabilities on post-school adjustment. *Journal of Rehabilitation, 49,* 46–50.

Widerstrom, A. H. (1997). Newborns and infants at risk for or with disabilities. In A. H. Widerstrom, B. A. Mowder, & S. R. Sandall (Eds.), *Infant development and risk: An introduction* (pp. 3–19). Baltimore: Brookes.

Wiederholt, J. L. (1986). *Formal reading inventory.* Austin, TX: PRO-ED.

Wiederholt, J. L., & Bryant, B. R. (1992). *Gray oral reading test* (3rd ed.). Austin, TX: PRO-ED.

Wiederholt, J. L., & Hammill, D. D. (1971). Use of the Frostig-Horne perception program in the urban school. *Psychology in the Schools, 8,* 268–274.

Wiederholt, J. L., Hammill, D. D., & Brown, V. (1978). *The resource teacher: A guide to effective practices.* Boston: Allyn & Bacon.

Wiig, E. H. (1982a). Communication disorders. In N. G. Haring (Ed.), *Exceptional children and youth* (3rd ed.) (pp. 81–109). New York: Merrill/Macmillan.

Wiig, E. H. (1982b). *Let's talk: Developing prosocial communication skill.* San Antonio, TX: Psychological Corporation.

Wiig, E. H., & Semel, E. (1984). *Language assessment and intervention for the learning disabled* (2nd ed.). New York: Merrill/Macmillan.

Wilkinson, G. S. (1993). *Wide range achievement test–Revision 3.* Wilmington, DE: Wide Range, Inc.

Will, M. C. (1986). Educating children with learning problems: A shared responsibility. *Exceptional Children, 52,* 411–415.

Williams, K. T. (1997). *Expressive vocabulary test.* Circle Pines, MN: American Guidance.

Williams, R. L. (1972). *The BITCH test (Black intelligence test of cultural homogeneity).* St. Louis, MO: Williams & Associates.

Williams, R. L. (1974). Black pride, academic relevance, and individual achievement. In R. W. Tyler & R. M. Wolf (Eds.), *Crucial issues in testing* (pp. 13–20). Berkeley, CA: McCutchan.

Willis, S. (1990). Transforming the test. *ASCD Update, 32*(7), 3–6.

Willis, W. (1998). Families with African American roots. In E. W. Lynch & M. J. Hanson (Eds.), *Developing cross-cultural competence* (2nd ed.) (pp. 165–207). Baltimore: Brookes.

Wimmer, D. (1982). Career education. In E. Meyen (Ed.), *Exceptional children in today's schools* (pp. 151–184). Denver: Love.

Winzer, M. A., & Mazurek, K. (1998). *Special education in multicultural contexts.* Upper Saddle River, NJ: Merrill/Prentice-Hall.

Wittenberg, W. (1980). *Diagnostic achievement test in spelling.* Baldwin, NY: Barnell Loft.

Wolery, M. (1996). Monitoring child progress. In M. McLean, D. B. Bailey, Jr., & M. Wolery (Eds.), *Assessing infants and preschoolers with needs* (pp. 519–560). Englewood Cliffs, NJ: Prentice-Hall.

Wolf, K. P. (1991). Teaching portfolios: Focus for new clearinghouse and network. *Portfolio News, 3*(1), 7, 22.

Wong, B. Y. L. (1980). Activating the inactive learner: Use of questions/prompts to enhance comprehension and retention of implied information in learning disabled children. *Learning Disability Quarterly, 3*(1), 29–37.

Woodcock, R. W. (1973). *Woodcock reading mastery tests.* Circle Pines, MN: American Guidance Service.

Woodcock, R. W. (1991). *Woodcock language proficiency battery-Revised.* Chicago: Riverside.

Woodcock, R. W. (1997). *Woodcock diagnostic reading battery.* Itasca, IL: Riverside.

Woodcock, R. W. (1998). *Woodcock reading mastery tests–Revised/Normative Update.* Circle Pines, MN: American Guidance Service.

Woodcock, R. W., & Johnson, M. B. (1977). *Woodcock-Johnson psycho-educational battery.* Chicago, IL: Riverside.

Woodcock, R. W., & Johnson, M. B. (1989). *Woodcock-Johnson psycho-educational battery–Revised.* Chicago, IL: Riverside.

Woodcock, R. W., & Mather, N. (1989). WJ-R tests of cognitive ability-Standard and supplemental batteries: Examiner's manual. In R. W. Woodcock & M. B. Johnson, *Woodcock-Johnson psycho-educational battery–Revised.* Chicago: Riverside.

Woodcock, R. W., & Muñoz-Sandoval, A. (1993). *Woodcock-Muñoz language survey, English and Spanish forms.* Chicago: Riverside.

Woodcock, R. W., & Muñoz-Sandoval, A. F. (1996). *Batería Woodcock-Muñoz–Revisada.* Itasca, IL: Riverside.

Woods, M. L., & Moe, A. J. (1999). *Analytical reading inventory* (6th ed). Upper Saddle River, NJ: Merrill/Prentice-Hall.

Worthen, B. R. (1993). Critical issues that will determine the future of alternative assessment. *Phi Delta Kappan, 74,* 444–454.

Yates, J. R., & Ortiz, A. A. (1998). Developing Individualized Education Programs for exceptional language minority students. In L. M. Baca & H. T. Cervantes (Eds.), *The bilingual special education interface* (3rd ed.) (pp. 188–212). Upper Saddle River, NJ: Merrill/Prentice-Hall.

Yoshida, R. K. (1984). Planning for change in pupil evaluation practices. In C. A. Maher, R. J. Illback, & J. E. Zins (Eds.), *Organizational psychology in the schools* (pp. 262–282). Springfield, IL: Thomas.

Yost, D. S., Shaw, S. E., Cullen, J., McGuire, J. M., & Bigaj, S. (1994). Practices and attitudes of postsecondary LD services providers in North America. *Journal of Learning Disabilities, 27* (10), 631–640.

Ysseldyke, J., & Christenson, S. (1993). *The instructional environment system-II.* Longmont, CO: Sopris West.

Ysseldyke, J., & Olsen, K. (1999). Putting alternate assessments into practice: What to measure and possible sources of data. *Exceptional Children, 65,*175–185.

Ysseldyke, J. E., Algozzine, B., Regan, R. R., Potter, M., Richey, L., & Thurlow, M.

(1980). *Psychoeducational assessment and decision-making: A computer-simulated investigation* (Research Report No. 32). Minneapolis: University of Minnesota Institute for Research on Learning Disabilities.

Ysseldyke, J., Algozzine, B., & Epps, S. (1983). A logical and empirical analysis of current practice in classifying students as handicapped. *Exceptional Children, 50,* 160–166.

Ysseldyke, J. E., Algozzine, B., Regan, R., & McGue, M. (1981). The influence of test scores and naturally occurring pupil characteristics on psychoeducational decision making with children. *Journal of School Psychology, 19,* 167–177.

Ysseldyke, J. E., Thurlow, M., Graden, J., Wesson, C., Algozzine, B., & Deno, S. (1983). Generalizations from five years of research on assessment and decision-making: The University of Minnesota Institute. *Exceptional Educational Quarterly, 4,* 75–95.

Zaner-Bloser evaluation scales. (n.d.). Columbus, OH: Zaner-Bloser.

Zigmond, N., Vallecorsa, A., & Leinhardt, G. (1980). Reading instruction for students with learning disabilities. *Topics in Language Disorders, 1*(1), 89–98.

TEST INDEX

625

AUTHOR INDEX

SUBJECT INDEX